ISBN 978-0-666-84482-8
PIBN 10768435

VOL. XXIII. NO. 1.   SUPPLEMENT TO   JANUARY 1, 1916.

HORTICULTURE

INDEX TO VOLUME XXII

Illustrated articles are marked with *

Vol. XXII
No. 1
JULY 3
1915

HORTICULTURE

J. M. Lupton
President-elect American Seed Trade Association.

Published Every Saturday at 147 Summer Street, Boston, Mass.
Subscription, $1.00

In writing to Advertisers kindly mention Horticulture

LIST OF ADVERTISERS

FOR BUYERS' DIRECTORY AND READY REFERENCE GUIDE
SEE PAGES 20, 21, 22, 23

NOTES ON CULTURE OF FLORISTS' STOCK

CONDUCTED BY

John J. M. Farrell

Questions by our readers in line with any of the topics presented on this page will be cordially received and promptly answered by Mr. Farrell. Such communications should invariably be addressed to the office of HORTICULTURE.
"If vain our toil, we ought to blame the culture, not the soil."—*Pope.*

Asters

It is unwise to figure on sufficient rainy spells at this season of the year and much safer in this case to rely on the hose for aster success than on the heavens until the first center bud appears, however, not much watering will be necessary and should not be applied unless the first part of the season proves uncommonly dry. But as soon as the buds begin to form and right along through the entire picking season great quantities of water are needed for the bringing forth of large and perfectly formed flowers, such as alone will make the growing of asters profitable. Where the field is a large one this could not be done anyway. The best plan then to follow is to water one part or section of the field one day, another the next day and so on, until at the end of four or five days the entire field has been gone over, when, should the weather continue dry, the process should be repeated.

Callas

Callas that have bloomed or been growing all winter should have a rest during the summer, which allows them to recuperate up new vigor for another season's flowering. They will ripen up better when placed in a warm sunny position until they need to be shaken out again the last of July or the first half of August when they can be potted up. Calla tubers are so inexpensive that it hardly pays to raise one's own stock, but if a quantity of the smaller offsets are planted out in rich ground they will increase in size surprisingly and can be potted up early in September, if carefully lifted, so as to keep the roots intact. Well watered and stood for a few days in partial shade they will grow right ahead and soon fill the pots with roots, or they can be planted in 3-inch pots and later shifted into 5-inch and plunged out of doors and they will make strong plants by end of September.

Chrysanthemums

Those who grow chrysanthemums in the house from first to last can give them better attention at all times. Do not neglect giving them a good syringing early every morning, which will allow the foliage time to dry out nicely before night-fall, but during dark or cloudy weather keep the plants as dry as possible. It should always be remembered that these plants will never stand humid or stagnant atmosphere. So first of all see that they have plenty of fresh air. During the hot weather, damping down will be necessary two or three times a day on the walks or paths. Go over the beds every day and water the dry places. Do not let the plants get overrun with fly before using effective means to keep them under control.

Adiantums

Now is the time to make new beds of adiantum for future cutting. No asparagus, no matter how soft and feathery will ever take the place of adiantum and every retail grower who can provide a house in which he can maintain a temperature not less than 60 degrees during zero weather, should devote some bench room to its culture. Stocks out of 2½ inch pots is all right but better and quicker results will be obtained by making use of larger plants. The present is as good a time as any to prepare for planting out, and even if you should not get as large and as fine fronds as your wholesaler supplies, you will appreciate having a good number of plants to cut from next winter. The adiantum like most members of the fern family, flourishes in mellow loam. This with a fair amount of well-rotted cow manure and a little sharp sand will do nicely. Provide good drainage and allow about one foot of space between the plants.

Pansies

To have pansies for winter flowering now is the time to make a sowing. Sow broadcast in a cold frame where the soil has been worked and raked until it is fine and mellow. Sow not too thickly, cover with fine soil and press firmly all over with a board, then water gently with a fine hose. Keep shaded until they begin to come up. When seedlings have made growth so they can be nicely handled they can be transplanted into other frames. The soil should be made rich and quite a bit of leaf mold mixed in. They can be planted from 6 to 8 inches apart each way. The pansy is quick to germinate and during the few days intervening between sowing seed and the little plants showing through the ground keep the beds constantly moist. Evening and morning watering may not be enough. Water ten times if necessary and never let the surface of the bed become parched.

Solanums

In order to have these in good sized plants by the fall they will want constant attention. Where they are planted out go over the ground every week and hoe and cultivate them. Keep the plants pinched back regularly so they will form bushy plants. Those that are grown under pot culture will want shifts from time to time.

Next Week:—Carnations; Calceolarias; Easter Lilies; Mignonette; Orchids; Repairing Boilers and Piping.

HORTICULTURE

VOL. XXII   JULY 3, 1915   NO. 1

PUBLISHED WEEKLY BY

HORTICULTURE PUBLISHING CO.

147 Summer Street, Boston, Mass.

Telephone, Oxford 292.

WM. J. STEWART, Editor and Manager.

Entered as second-class matter December 8, 1904, at the Post Office at Boston, Mass., under the Act of Congress of March 3, 1879.

CONTENTS

The record of six months

Our readers will kindly take notice of the index to the contents of Vol. XXI, which accompanies this number of HORTICULTURE. One would scarcely realize from a perusal of the issues as they appear from week to week the vast amount of useful horticultural literature that has been thus assembled during the short space of six months, and all delivered at your address every week for the sum of fifty cents. Surely no valid complaint can be made that the horticultural press does not give the subscriber his full money's worth. We are aware, of course, that there are journals which give greater bulk than HORTICULTURE but in the words of one of our friends, "they are not HORTICULTURE and cannot take its place." HORTICULTURE's contents have a distinctive permanent quality and it is not without a certain grateful pride that we send forth this tabulated summary of our work for the first half of the year 1915.

The test of fitness

Secretary Saunders' recommendation to the American Peony Society that it discountenance the placing on the market of any new variety of peony until it has proven its superiority to varieties already disseminated will meet with universal approval. The only possible dissenter to the carrying out of this principle might be the man with a pet production which to his magnified vision will loom up with an effulgence invisible to anyone else. For peonies, sweet peas, carnations, roses, chrysanthemums, dahlias or any other genus of flowers which is being developed by the hybridist, the fond worker who can see only the virtues and none of the defects in his "creations" will continue to be the big stumbling block but the time has come when each and all must submit to the cold-blooded scrutiny of the special society judges and without the sanction of such one's pets are not likely to travel very far from their birthplace.

For greater efficiency

A strong note in the Nurserymen's Convention at Detroit last week, as indicated by the reports which have reached us, was the need of "a better national association." It is a more hopeful sign in the case of an individual or an organization that dereliction or other imperfection be acknowledged from within rather than charged from without. We make no indictment against the nurserymen's organization when we say that this point was well taken. There is no association with which we have to do that could not materially raise its standard of efficiency and be made far more useful than at present. It only requires that this fact be felt and confessed and that the upbuilding and improvement be seriously taken in hand forthwith. If we were disposed to pick a flaw in the body above mentioned we might say that a little less conservatism and a more enterprising attitude towards the new and improved garden material continually being brought to light by hybridists and collectors would undoubtedly be welcomed by the garden loving public of this country.

Lively times ahead

The coming fall promises to be one of the liveliest, if not the very liveliest, thus far in the matter of flower shows. Apart from the usual multitude of annual fall exhibitions by local societies we now find four very ambitious projects in the field for this year, all aiming to be more or less national in scope, namely, in Cleveland, Rochester, Chicago and San Francisco. All these are scheduled for October and early November except Rochester, which is a September proposition. All hope to attract trade exhibitors from far and near and it certainly will keep any exhibitor of trade stock hustling to cover all the ground that it will be to his direct interest to reach. To the S. A. F. is due the credit for having innitiated these trade enterprises and proved their value commercially to both those who want to sell and those who wish to buy, and particularly for having made the discovery of the value of the trade annex in a public flower show as a revenue producer and assistant annihilator of that dread bugbear known as a deficit. But our country is growing very rapidly horticulturally as well as otherwise and any trade dealer who seeks to maintain a position of national prominence will have to dig down deeper and deeper into his pockets and draw more heavily on his resources of energy and enterprise as the years pass. To trade paper advertising and the trade exhibitions must he resort and that liberally if he expects to hold his main line of trenches.

AMERICAN SWEET PEA SOCIETY.

The sweet pea exhibition held in the Palace of Horticulture, Panama-Pacific International Exposition, June 11-13, under the auspices of the American Sweet Pea Society and under the management of F. G. Cuthbertson was a wonderful show and pronounced success. On Friday, the Exposition officials recognized the occasion and designated the day as "Sweet Pea Day," sending Commissioner Chas. Vogelsang, who, in a neat speech presented the president with a bronze plaque in commemoration of the event. They also furnished a brass band of forty pieces. Papers were read by F. G. Cuthbertson and Mrs. Scannavina, president of the State Floral Society.

The show was extremely popular and thousands of people visited it, packing the aisles from morning until ten o'clock at night on each of the three days. A more successful show has never been held in California. Nothing but sweet peas were shown. The management had to change the date hurriedly twice on account of the weather, and it says a good deal for the enthusiasm of the California growers that such a show was attained. The vestibule of the Palace of Horticulture was filled to overflowing with magnificent sweet pea blossoms. Perhaps the greatest feature of the show were the floral designs which reflected great credit on the local florists.

During the afternoon Commissioner Vorlesang, representing the President of the Exposition, presented Lester L. Morse, as president of the American Sweet Pea Society, with a bronze plaque. President Morse replied and expressed his pleasure at being able to hold such an exhibition at the Panama-Pacific International Exposition.

The judges for the gardeners' and amateur classes were Fred H. Howard, of Howard & Smith, Nurseryman, Los Angeles; Emory E. Smith, of Emery & Smith, San Francisco; John McLaren, superintendent of parks, San Francisco. The decorative classes were judged by G. A. Dennison, Chief of Horticulture. During the afternoon the show was thronged with visitors, and from all accounts, the California Sweet Pea Show has come to stay.

Following are the prizes awarded:

Championship of California: This was won by David Bassett, gardener for Louis Stern, Menlo Park, Cal., with well grown examples of Elfrida Pearson, Illuminator, Margaret Atlee, King Edward Spencer, New Margaret Madison, Nubian, King White and Mrs. Cuthbertson. Second prize went to Mrs. R. Greig, Berkeley, Cal. Third to Mrs. R. P. Reed, San Francisco. The competition in this class was very keen and the judges were given considerable work to arrive at their decision. This was the "star" class of the exhibition.

The Burpee first prize for twelve varieties of Spencers went to Emile Ralston, San Jose, Cal.

Peter Henderson prizes for six vases Spencers: 1st, E. A. Richards, Berkeley, Cal., with the varieties Mrs. Cuthbertson, New Margaret Madison, King White, Nubian, Margaret Atlee and King Edward Spencer; 2nd, S. M. Spaulding, Menlo Park, Cal.; 3rd, Joe Penicke, Stamford University, Cal.

American Sweet Pea Society prizes for vase of lavender Spencers: 1st, S. M. Spaulding with Asta Ohn; 2nd, Roy L. Donley, Berkeley, Cal.

Waldo Rohnert prizes for Pink Spencers: 1st, David Bassett with Elfrida Pearson; 2nd, Mrs. T. Sachau, San Leandro, Cal., with New Miriam Beaver.

Waldo Rohnert prizes for white Spencers: 1st, Roy L. Donley with King White; 2nd, Emile Ralston.

C. C. Morse & Co. prizes for Grandifloras: 1st, John Smith, Berkeley, Cal.; 2nd, E. F. Delger, Menlo Park, Cal.

Braslan Seed Growers Co. cup for twelve Spencers: 1st, David Bassett. Rosabelle and Mrs. C. W. Breadmore were especially fine in this class.

American Sweet Pea Society silver medal for six vases Spencers: 1st, Roy L. Donley with Margaret Madison, Elfrida Pearson, Sunproof Crimson, Illuminator, King White and Margaret Atlee; 2nd, Mrs. Annie Jennings, Menlo Park, Cal.

Best vase of Red Spencers: Mrs. T. Sachau, San Leandro, with King Edward Spencer.

Best Vase of Pink Spencer: John Smith, Berkeley, Cal., with Mrs. Hugh Dickson.

Best Vase of Cream Spencer: Mrs. T. Sachau with Margaret Atlee.

Best Vase of Spencers in the exhibition: John Smith.

Most gracefully arranged vase of sweet peas, mixed colors, Miss Evelyn McLean, San Francisco, with a dainty combination of New Margaret Madison and New Miriam Beaver. The competition in this class was very keen and the exhibits attracted a great deal of attention during the afternoon.

For the President's silver cup there were four entries. Prize was awarded to the Francis Floral Co., San Francisco, for a jewelled bridal parasol design. The design stood ten feet high and each section of the parasol was a different color of Spencer sweet peas. The other designs were as follows: Pelicano, Rossi & Co., "Liberty Bell," standing about 5 feet 6 inches high and worked in White Spencer, Helen Lewis, King Edward Spencer and Constance Oliver. Frank R. Clark of the Blossom Shop, "Tower of Jewels." Mrs. R. E. Darbee, "Horn of Plenty."

In the class open to seed growers and seedsmen, C. C. Morse & Co. put up a magnificent collection, covering 200 sq. ft. and representing 200 varieties of Spencers. The exhibition was the best ever seen on the coast and perhaps the finest ever put up in America.

New Miriam Beaver occupied the center and showed off to splendid advantage against the black velvet background. Countess Spencer and Margaret Atlee made the two corner posts for the exhibit. The new variety, Scintillator, a cream ground Aurora, aroused great interest. The jury recommended that an award of merit be given to this variety. To add interest to their exhibit, Messers. Morse & Co., showed a small vase of the original blue and purple sweet pea, then to represent a stage ahead a vase of Grandifloras and a vase of giant Spencers, having stems twenty-five inches long and large, beautiful blossoms. This exhibit was awarded the gold medal of the British National Sweet Pea Society and was recommended by the jury of awards for a medal of honor from the P. P. I. E.

W. Atlee Burpee & Co. of Philadelphia, Pa., were awarded the silver medal presented by the British National Sweet Pea Society for their splendid display, covering 100 sq. ft., nicely set up by Mr. Ellings, of the Lynch Nursery Company, Menlo Park. The center portion of the exhibit was entirely given over to Burpee & Company's novelty "Fiery Cross." The jury of the Panama-Pacific International Exposition recommended that a gold medal be awarded to Messrs. Burpee & Co., for their exhibit. The collection included about fifty of Burpee & Company's leading novelties and especially fine vases of Margaret Atlee, Thomas Stevenson, Helen Grosvenor, King Manuel, Stirling Stent and King

C. C. Morse & Co.'s Exhibit at the Sweet Pea Exhibition, Palace of Horticulture, P. P. I. E., June 11, 1915.

Edward Spencer. Messrs. Burpee & Co. are to be congratulated on the spirit they showed in arranging for this exhibition at so great a distance from Philadelphia. An award of merit was voted for 'Fiery Cross.'

The L. D. Waller Seed Co. of Guadalupe, Cal., put up a very fine exhibit. In spite of the long distance which the flowers had to travel, they arrived in fine condition. The silver gilt medal was well deserved.

Waldo Rohnert exhibited a collection of fifty varieties, standard sorts.

Ant. C. Zvolanek, Lompoc, Cal., showed a collection of early flowering Spencers and general Spencers, gathered from his exhibit in the gardens of the Panama-Pacific International Exposition. The varieties of winter flowering Spencers were very attractive.

Newport Show Postponed.

Owing to reports from different sections of the lateness of the season for sweet peas, we have decided to postpone the exhibition at Newport until July 15th and 16th. The final schedule is now ready for distribution.
                    HARRY A. BUNYARD, Secretary.

AMERICAN ASSOCIATION OF NURSERYMEN.

The 40th Annual Meeting of this Association which was held at the Hotel Cadillac, Detroit, on June 23, 24 and 25, was very successful in attendance, business and recreation. Mayor Marx voiced a cordial welcome when President Chase called the opening session to order, J. Pitkin of Newark, N. J. responding. Among the in-

formal proceedings were a trip through the parks on Wednesday and an entertainment at Lake St. Clair on Friday.

The report of Secretary Hall, which follows, shows the progress of the organization during the past year.

Annual Report of Secretary John Hall.

Your Secretary is pleased to report a more prompt response from members to the exhortation contained in the announcement of this convention, and to state further that the registration in the badge book for 1915 is the largest ever published with the exception of the years 1906 and 1913; also the amount of cash turned over to the treasurer is the largest during the same period with the exception of 1913. Four hundred and twenty-six names appear in the badge book for this year, and a leaf insert containing others received too late for publication, has been printed for use of members, thus bringing the total membership on the 15th day of June to 435. $3,130 were sent to the treasurer up to June 3.

The income from memberships and badge book for the past ten years are as follows:

1906	$2,014.29
1907	2,967.50
1908	2,883.60
1909	2,786.30
1910	2,340.00
1911	2,771.85
1912	747.70
1913	.314.15
1914	077.15
1915	$3,130.90

The record of deaths during the past year is quite lengthy:

1914—Aug. 26. Hiram T. Jones. Elizabeth, N. J.; Sept. 3, Leigh Overman. Spokane, Wash.; Sept. 8. Peter Boblender. Tippe-

canoe City, O.; Sept. 20, Albert Van Balen, of Felix & Dykhuis, Boskoop, Holland; Dec. 14, Joseph G. Harrison, Berlin, Md.; Dec. 17, Mrs. Jessie F. Moss, Huntsville, Ala.

1915—Feb. 16, George C. Seager, Rochester, N. Y.; Feb. 21, H. Frank Darrow, New York, N. Y.; March 14, Franz Meredith, Koleen, Ind.; March 22, Howard E. Merrell, Geneva, N. Y.; May 4, Eugene Willett, North Collins, N. Y.; June 3, Henry J. Weber, Nursery, Mo. We mention also the following: Mrs. V. A. Vanicek, Newport, R. I.; Mrs. D. S. Lake, Shenandoah, Iowa; Mrs. Charles Ilgenfritz, Monroe, Mich.

The financial statement of the secretary is thus:

RECEIPTS

June 16, 1914. Balance in bank....	$81.15
March 16, 1915. Membership and accounts due	241.25
June 2, 1915. Membership and badge book advertisements......	2,808.50

Totals	$3,130.90
Disbursements	$3,130.90

A personal reference in closing: We desire to make reference to the conference between the Executive Committee and ourself following last year's meeting, when the matter of appointment of secretary was left to those gentlemen. The consideration shown me and the kindly treatment accorded, prompt me to desire to express my appreciation and thanks, resulting in my continuation in office for the year. We have endeavored to perform the duties of the position faithfully, and if it is the pleasure of the Association to continue the relationship we promise fidelity to the best interests of the organization.

Many valuable papers were read on topics of vital interest to the nursery trade. Optimism was the key-note throughout.

Officers were elected as follows: President, E. S. Welch, Shenandoah,

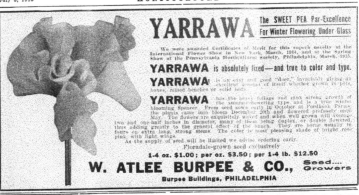
Ia.; vice-president, John Watson, Newark, N. Y.; secretary, John Hall, Rochester, N. Y.; treasurer, Peter Youngers, Geneva, Neb. Milwaukee, Wis., was chosen as the meeting place for 1916.

ROCHESTER PLANS BIG FLOWER SHOW

Rochester, N. Y., is arranging for a big flower show from August 30 to September 11. It is to be held under the auspices of the Rochester Exposition, declared to be the biggest municipal exposition in the United States, now in its eighth year and attended annually by upward of 250,000 people. This is the first year of the flower show, and if it meets with the same success as have the other departments of the exposition, the Rochester Flower Show will soon be recognized as a national event.

The exposition includes many of the best features to be found at big state fairs and is attended by people from all over the country. Co-operating with the management of the exposition is a committee of five members of the Rochester Florists' Association, which has an enviable record for the artistic nature of its flower shows. The members of the committee are George B. Hart, chairman, who is the president of the local Florists' Association; Charles H. Vick, of James Vick's Sons; Harry E. Bates, of Lord & Burnham Co.; Fernando J. Keller, of J. B. Keller's Sons, and A. H. Salter, of Salter Brothers. Until last year, Mr. Vick was superintendent of the flower show at the New York State Fair at Syracuse and is well known to growers and florists everywhere. This year he is devoting his entire energy to the Rochester Flower Show.

It is the hope of the committee to make Rochester the meeting place for the grower and the florist, the seedsman and the importer. As an inducement for the big growers and seedsmen to exhibit their plants, flowers and other products at Rochester, the committee makes the very attractive proposition of free space for all exhibitors. There is to be absolutely no charge of any kind for space or entry fees.

One of the best buildings at Exposition Park, which is owned by the municipality, has been assigned to the flower show. It contains upward of 20,000 square feet of unobstructed floor space, with high skylight roof, well equipped with water and sewer outlets; in fact, having been constructed specially for exhibition purposes. It is provided with every convenience, and those who go to Rochester will undoubtedly find it to be the most ideally adapted hall for a flower show that they have yet encountered.

Not only does the committee purpose to exert every effort to have the biggest growers in the country make exhibits, but they also intend to see that the retail florists and others interested in the trade go to Rochester. It is believed that the Rochester show will furnish a splendid opportunity for business, bringing the growers and retailers together to get acquainted.

The city of Rochester has a population of 250,000, with another three-quarters of a million within a radius of fifty miles. With this immense population and with the personal invitations to be sent out to the florists of all the eastern states, there will undoubtedly be a big attendance. Not only the interests which appeal to the growers directly, but also to their families, will be an extra inducement to visit the Rochester show. The Exposition's motto is "entertaining, educational and inspirational." Its Horse Show is second to none in the country. The best known stables in the country exhibit their blue-ribbon horses. The Art Loan Exhibit brings together oil paintings and water colors by the famous artists of America. The display of fruits and vegetables is unrivalled in this country. The central location of the city, with its numerous railroads, affords excellent facilities for easy access; its excellent park system, its beautiful drives, its fine residential sections, with their lawns, shrubbery and planting, will attract growers both private and commercial, as well as the trade in general.

HONOR FOR A ROSE LOVER.

The gold medal of the Massachusetts Horticultural Society has been bestowed upon Miss Sarah B. Fay, of Woods Hole, Mass., by vote of the garden committee in recognition of her devotion to the rose. The committee visited Miss Fay's rose garden on Thursday, June 24, and found an unprecedented display of H. P. and H. T., and other June roses, probably the most extensive collection of established plants in this country, comprising many thousands of specimens in many hundred varieties. There is also a superb collection of rambler roses, but these were not in bloom at the time of the committee's visit. The estate has been under the care of M. H. Walsh for many years, and while the cultural success is, of course, due to him, yet his achievement is owing to Miss Fay's support and encouragement and would not have been possible were it not for her devotion to the rose, and so the highest award in the Society's power was most worthily bestowed.

BOTANICAL GARDEN AT FREDERICK, MD.

Frank C. Hargett, has been named superintendent of the Educational and Botanical gardens of Frederick, Md. Besides being in charge of the gardens Mr. Hargett will conduct experiment work with valuable plants and flowers in Frederick. Observations and returns from these experiments will be filed with the United States Department of Agriculture. Plants and flowers from all sections of the world will be placed in this garden by the governmental authorities for experimental purposes.

The board of trustees of this new institution are William F. Gude, Washington; Richard Vincent, Jr., White Marsh, Md., George W. Hess, superintendent of the United States Botanical Gardens, and Mayor Lewis H. Fraley, of Frederick, Md.

SEED TRADE

AMERICAN SEED TRADE ASSOCI-ATION.

The thirty-third annual convention of the American Seed Trade Association held in San Francisco the week of June 21st was largely and enthusiastically attended. The party of eastern delegates, about. sixty, arrived Saturday night after a pleasant side entertainment in Southern California. where they were met by President L. L. Morse of this city. Monday evening a reception was held for the delegates at the home of Mr. and Mrs. Morse with about 95 present. The convention was called to order Tuesday morning at the Palace of Horticulture on the exposition grounds. The officers made their reports, new members were proposed, and Prof. H. E. Van Norman, Dean of the California State Farm School at Davis, Cal., read a paper on "The Value of Technical Training for the Seedsman."

Wednesday morning a bronze medal was presented the association on behalf of the Exposition, and short responses were made by President Morse and First Vice-President Lupton on behalf of the eastern delegates. At Wednesday's business session, the following new members were admitted: C. E. DePuy Co., Pontiac, Mich.; Pacific Seed Co., Caldwell, Ida.; Valley Seed Co., Sacramento, Cal.; Vogeler Seed and Produce Co., Salt Lake City, Utah; Waldo Bohnert. Gilroy, Cal. Papers were read as scheduled. "Horticulture in the Hawaiian Islands," by Prof. John N. Gilmore, Agricultural College. University of California; "Seed-Growing in the Northwest," by E. C. Johnson of the Portland Seed Co., Portland, Ore.; "Flower Seeds in California," by L. C. Routzahn of Arroyo Grande. Cal.; and a paper by Mark L. Germain of Los Angeles, Cal.

The annual banquet on Wednesday evening was a very enjoyable affair. It was held at the club rooms of the San Francisco Commercial Club in the Merchants Exchange building, and the place was beautifully decorated for the occasion. Watson S. Woodruff made an ideal toastmaster, amusing the 125 diners between courses in original manner. The typical Californian menu was appreciated by all. Contemporaneous talks were given by L. L. Morse, F. W. Bolgiano, E. L. Page, K. B. White. S. F. Leonard, M. L. Germain, L. C. Routzahn, L. S. Payn, J. Charles McCullough. W. C. Langbridge, R. Simmers, F. Leckenby, E. O. Pieper. In appreciation of his services as president, L. L. Morse was presented with a handsome watch.

The final business session was held on Thursday morning. Officers were elected as follows: President, J. M. Lupton, Mattituck, L. I., N. Y.; first vice-president, Kirby B. White, De-

troit, Mich.; second vice-president, F. W. Bolgiano, Washington, D. C.; secretary-treasurer, C. E. Kendel, Cleveland, O.; assistant secretary, S. F. Willard, Jr., Cleveland. O. Executive committee, L. L. Morse, C. C. Massie, H. Simmers, J. Chas. McCullough, Watson S. Woodruff. Membership committee, Albert McCullough, Ben P. Cornell and R. G. Hastings. Cincinnati was recommended as the next meeting place. The meeting came to an end with the seating of President Lupton.

Friday morning the party started on a two-day tour of inspection of the extensive seed farms in San Benito and Santa Clara counties. Various forms of entertainment were enjoyed on the trip, notable among which was a barbecue at San Juan, Friday noon, under the supervision of Waldo Rohnert.

CATALOGUES RECEIVED.

McFarland Publicity System. Harrisburg, Pa.—A handsomely printed and embellished trade booklet under the title of "Publicity that Spurs Business."

The Advance Co., Richmond, Ind.—New Catalogue U. Ventilating Apparatus and Greenhouse Fittings. Well printed and illustrated on heavy coated paper and containing eight more pages than its predecessors, this catalogue, giving net prices on all the various devices and fittings offered by this company, will be found very beneficial as a ready reference at all times by the greenhouse florist trade. A handy index to the contents is given.

Ant. C. Zvolanek, Lompoc, Cal.—List of Winter Orchid and other Sweet Peas. Useful booklet for everyone interested in advanced sweet pea culture. The list of novelties for 1915 is very appetizing. Mr. Zvolanek has also published an instructive 50-page handbook on Commercial Sweet Pea Culture in Greenhouse and Outdoors. It gives the life history of the Winter Flowering Sweet Pea with full directions for culture; also tells how to

pick. keep and ship the blooms. The price of this manual is 50 cents.

The value of imports of horticultural material to the port of New York for the week ending June 19, is given as follows: Sulphate of potash, $100,-180; fertilizer, $6.056; clover seed, $14,011; grass seed, $8,788; trees and plants, $2,702.

Of Interest to Retail Florists

NEW FLOWER STORES.

Vancouver, B. C.—J. M. Hazlewood, 477 Kingsway.

Milwaukee, Wis.—Ella Voelzke, 3802 Lisbon avenue.

Raleigh, N. C.—J. L. O'Quinn & Co., 126 W. Martin street.

Chicago, Ill.—Miss Ida Masilowth, 1116 S. Halsted street.

BUSINESS TROUBLES

New York, N. Y.—Theodore E. Hahn, florist, 2574 Broadway, liabilities, $2,466.

Kansas City, Mo.—Linwood Florist, 31st and Park avenue, Jas. S. Pepper, proprietor, in bankruptcy.

NEWS NOTES

New Castle, N. H.—Wm. Lefebre of Swarthmore, Pa., has leased the greenhouses of C. W. Eaton.

Reading, Pa.—The business of E. H. Beers & Co. has been taken over by the Rosedale Floral Company.

San Francisco, Cal.—G. H. Evans, proprietor of the Jordan Park Floral Company has sold his business to F. E. Stratton.

Superior, Wis.—Wm. Berg has purchased the interest of his partner, G. Tjensvold, in the Superior Floral Company, and will continue the business.

Springfield, N. J.—A heavy explosion in an adjoining quarry broke a great many panes of glass in the range of the Springfield Floral Company.

Brooklyn, N. Y.—The Court Square Flower Company at 11 Court Square suffered a loss of $300 on Friday morning, June 25, when a fire started in the store from an unknown cause.

Wilson Station, Ct.—On June 28th, the greenhouses and barn of Anders Christensen, market gardener, were damaged by fire to the extent of $10,000. The cause of the fire is unknown, and the loss is only partially covered by insurance.

Fall River, Mass.—In the District Court, June 23, in the case of George L. Freeman vs. Carrillo & Baldwin, orchid importers, the judge gave the decision to the defendants. The case grew out of a contract made by Carrillo and Freeman in Bogota, Colombia, in 1906.

Marion, Mass.—Colonel H. E. Converse, winner of many prizes in the flower shows, and his wife and party were thrown from the Converse automobile in Canton and badly bruised. They collided with an auto truck. The truck was overturned and the driver badly injured. The Converse machine caught fire and was destroyed.

FRANK L. GRAY.

ST. LOUIS MEETINGS FOR JULY.

The Retail Florists' Association will meet on Monday evening, July 19th, at the Mission Inn Garden, at Grand and Magnolia avenues. Secretary Fred C. Weber, Jr., says that six new members have made application for membership.

The Florist Club will hold its regular monthly meeting, Thursday, July 8th. Secretary Beneke has prepared nine questions for discussion and these, with the nomination of officers, will feature this meeting which is called for 2 P. M.

The Ladies' Florists' Home Circle will hold their monthly gathering on Wednesday afternoon, July 14th, at the home of Mrs. John Steidel in Olivette, Mo. Weather permitting, the meeting will be held on the lawn in the front of the house.

The County Growers' Association will meet Wednesday night, July 7th, at Eleven Mile House. The closing of the wholesale house from Saturday noon until Monday will come up for discussion. Secretary Deutchmann has sent special notices to all members and a large attendance is expected.

CLEVELAND FLOWER SHOW.

We have received an excellent diagram and floor plan of the Coliseum in which the proposed Cleveland Flower Show will be held on November 10th to 14th. Spaces are shown in various sizes, with prices for use of same for trade exhibits. Assignments will be made in rotation as received, subject to the approval of the exhibitor. Copies have been sent to all live manufacturers and dealers. Anyone who has not received a copy can obtain same by addressing Cleveland Flower Show, 356 Leader Building, Cleveland, Ohio.

PERSONAL.

Sam Murray of Kansas City and Arnold Ringier of Chicago have been desporting at Excelsior Springs, Mo.

A postal card from Yokohama, Japan, tells of the arrival of Harry Bayersdorfer on June 15, after a pleasant voyage.

Charles Evans, salesman for Johnston, the florist, Providence, R. I., and Miss Bertha Tuszard, of Olneyville, were married June 21.

George Woodward, employed by L. C. Holton, florist, Bennington, Vt., underwent an operation on his eyes in New York last week, and there is a decided improvement.

Richard Rothe has left the employ of Henry A. Dreer to devote his full time and energies to the development of his own place The Glenside Hardy Flower Gardens in Glenside, Pa. Mr. Rothe is going to specialize in hardy perennials and designing and laying out of herbacous gardens.

NEWS ITEMS FROM EVERYWHERE

BOSTON.

Thomas F. Galvin is in New York this week.

N. F. McCarthy & Co.'s plant auction sales closed for the season last Friday. The spring sales have been above the average in attendance and prices obtained.

N. F. McCarthy informs us that owing to dissatisfaction with the work of Eber Holmes at Montrose Greenhouses, Mr. Holmes is no longer in his employ.

P. Welch is probably the only wholesaler offering a daily supply of that finest of summer roses, President Carnot. They are coming in abundantly at present and are superb.

Morris August, florist at Dudley street elevated station, and Miss Matilda Levy, were married on Sunday, June 27. They are now on their honeymoon at Atlantic City.

Tom. Benwell the popular salesman for A. H. Hews Company of North Cambridge will celebrate, next September, the fiftieth anniversary of his connection with this long established pottery concern.

A. S. Burns, Jr., of Spring Valley, N. Y., accompanied by Thos. Tracey, Ed. Tracey and Fred. Henkes of Albany were in Boston on Monday, on their way home from a trip to the White Mountains and Old Orchard Beach in Mr. Burns' auto.

An informal meeting to discuss the Hoffman failure was held at the Flower Market, on Monday, by some of the heaviest creditors. The plan of the receiver to sell the business is not looked upon with favor and will be blocked if sufficient opposition can be assembled.

Penn the Florist had three electric truck loads of flowers for the Lowell wedding at Mattapoiset. Stopping for gasoline on the way the decorators were surprised to find how well known this house had become throughout the country districts even, through Penn's liberal newspaper advertising policy.

Sweet sultan, larkspurs, gypsophila and water lilies are favorite window decorative material at the present time. The water lilies are seen in many varieties and are the central feature in many window displays. Galvin is using Cyperus alternifolius in association with them, with excellent effect.

A fire, which started from some unknown cause in the shed in the rear of the building at 647 Warren street, Roxbury, occupied by William C. Bowditch, a florist, did considerable damage Wednesday afternoon when it spread through the entire block between 645 and 663 Warren street, scorching the rear of the buildings.

R. and J. Farquhar & Co., are so well pleased with the range of pit houses erected at their Dedham nurseries last year that they have started to add six more of similar style, 12 by 110 feet,

each, for young plant stock. They are also building another light storage house 5 by 200, with a 12 ft. lean-to on each side.

CHICAGO.

Mr. and Mrs. Simpson, 3656 Ogden avenue, will motor to Rockford, Ill., for a Fourth of July visit with relatives.

Mr. and Mrs. Chas. L. Washburn celebrated the third anniversary of their marriage with a dinner party at the Hinsdale Country Club, June 29th.

Mr. and Mrs. Frank Oechslin leave early in July for a tour of the West with the Panama Exposition as the objective point.

John Poehlmann, Jr., is now regularly installed as assistant in the wholesale store of Poehlmann Bros. at 35 E. Randolph.

Vacations are beginning at Zech & Mann's, the first to enjoy an outing being the youngest employee of that firm, Gale Fanning, who goes to Jacksonville, Ill.

The committee of arrangements for the Chicago Florists' Club picnic have named July 23rd as the day for the event. St. Paul's Park, at Morton Grove has been secured.

News of the death of Louis Dreher in Denver, Colorado, was heard with regret by those who knew him. It is stated by August Poehlmann, whose foreman he was 22 years ago, that Mr. Dreher was the first man in the west who knew how to grow roses successfully on a large commercial place. He brought to them the system of feeding roses which has been employed there ever since. He spent his last five years in Denver, being in the employ of C. T. Maier and Emil Glauber, until his last illness.

New York.—Charles E. Applegate, retail florist, of Brooklyn, is looking for jewels said to be worth $2,000 which disappeared from the pocket of a coat while the suit was being rehabilitated at a tailor's shop.

PHILADELPHIA.

Commodore Westcott's family are sojourning at Wildwood on a brief vacation.

The S. S. Pennock-Meehan Co. announce that after July 1 store closes at 5 p. m. Saturdays at 1 p. m. July 5 all day.

Samuel S. Pennock accompanied by his oldest son Charles spent a few days at Cornell and vicinity recently. They took in the rose show there—among other interesting things—and returned home on the 26th.

Pennock Bros. executed an important order for Thousand Islands this week. The week previous Battles had the Duke wedding near New York. These are just straws giving a slight indication that Philadelphia is on the map and that her flower trade is more than local.

The florists are still busy explaining how they lost that ball game to the seedsmen at the recent club picnic. "Bum umpiring," "ringers," "hard luck," etc., but none of them will admit that the seedsmen had the better team. Maybe another game would clear the air.

Michell's will have another big gathering of the clans similar to that of two years ago at Andalusia. The date is set for August 28th. Particulars later. Nearly 1000 attended the last lawn and inspection party. It will be a holiday for the whole store and nursery employees as well as for their friends and invited guests.

I once heard our esteemed editor accused by one of his censorious friends of being "young in years but old in crime." After reading his charming account of the Westcott celebration at Waretown on the 18th, I think this should now be amended to elderly in years but young and lovely in spirit. His "fine Italian hand" has lost none of its cunning.

John Habermehl is the proud possessor of a diamond scarf pin presented to him by Miss Marie Louise Wanamaker, granddaughter of Hon. John Wanamaker, "to remind him of her wedding day"—which took place at St. Mark's Church on the 28th. Mr. Habermehl did the church decoration and also that for the reception later (114 tables) at the Wanamaker country residence at Jenkintown.

View on Base Ball Field During the Game at Outing of Florists' Club of Philadelphia.

H. A. Dreer, Inc., has arranged with the Bureau of City Real Estate, Philadelphia, to improve one of the large plots in front of Convention Hall; and now a force of workmen are preparing the ground and making attractive flower beds. These will be cared for during the summer and fall, and it is Dreer's intention to make a suitable display on this plot during the National Flower Show, which will be held in Convention Hall next march. This, of course, is in addition to the display which it is their intention to make in the building during the flower show.

WASHINGTON, D. C.

Adolph E. Gude, Jr., son of Adolphus Gude, has gone to Lompoc, Cal., where he will spend his summer vacation on the sweet pea range of A. C. Zvolanek. Ernest Gude, son of William F. Gude, is a member of a surveying party now in Ohio.

Two beds, each about 30 x 100 feet are being placed on the west slope of the Capitol grounds, being a part of the floral scheme incident to the coming encampment of the Grand Army in September. The beds represent the Grand Army badges and are made up in the colors of that organization.

A new greenhouse is to replace the old one now on the reservation of the Marine Corps, Comptroller of the Treasury Downey having ruled that current appropriations are now available' to cover the cost which will amount to between $250 and $300. It is to be used for housing the plants used on the reservation and parade grounds.

George W. Hess will soon go to New York City preparatory to sailing for New Orleans, La., to become the guest of Senator Broussard. Mr. Hess, who is the superintendent of the United States Botanic Gardens, expects to be gone a month or more and while in the South will look about with a view to obtaining specimens of southern plants not now represented in the collection at the Garden.

SAN FRANCISCO.

C. W. Ward is down from his nursery at Eureka, Cal., on a combined business and pleasure trip.

J. Edw. Johnson, superintendent of the Pikes Peak Floral Co., Colorado Springs, Colo., is visiting the exposition.

Assistant Manager Elder of the Lord & Burnham Co., arrived a few days ago, accompanied by Mrs. Elder, to attend the Panama-Pacific exposition.

J. W. Walters, well-known florist of Los Angeles, Cal., stopped over here a few days ago on his return from Honolulu, where he had been on a pleasure trip.

Joseph's establishment on Grant avenue was closed two days following the death of Mrs. B. M. Joseph, wife of the proprietor, on June 21 after an extended illness. Mr. Joseph has the sympathy of the trade in his bereavement.

The California Railroad Commission has granted the Sloan Seed Co. of Palo Alto authority to issue its common stock to Frank C. Sloan in exchange for his going business and to sell its preferred stock, 2500 shares of the par value of $10 each, at par.

PITTSBURGH.

Earl Tipton, of the A. W. Smith Company, will leave next Monday to spend the summer at the nursery farm near Canfield, Ohio.

Dr. Otto C. Jennings, Curator of the Herbarium of Carnegie Institute Museum, and Mrs. Jennings, have left for a four months' botanizing trip on the Pacific coast, from Seattle to San Diego.

Last Friday Edward L. McGrath, manager of the Blind Floral Company, was unfortunate in having his home damaged by lightning, amounting to approximately $150. His company is replacing the benches throughout the greenhouses at West View.

NEW CORPORATIONS.

Louisville, Ky.—Goodloe Seed Company, capital stock, $50,000.

Palo Alto, Cal.—Sloan Seed Company. Incorporators: F. C., J. E. and D. L. Sloan.

Floral Park, N. Y.—John Lewis Childs, Inc., seed and flower business, capital stock, $400,000. Incorporators, J. L., Mary C. and Vernon G. Childs.

New Rochelle, N. Y.—Siebrecht & Son, Rose Hill Nursery, capital stock $10,000. Incorporators: Isabel S. Munroe, Emma S. and Henry A. Siebrecht, New Rochelle.

New York, N. Y.—A. L. Young & Co., florists, capital stock, $25,000. Incorporators, A. L. Young, Hermanu Scommodau, New York, Fred Lightfoot, Rutherford, N. J.

PUBLICATION RECEIVED.

The Pioneer Boys of the Yellowstone, by Harrison Adams. Just as the schools close and the boys are free to indulge their craving for adventure and woods-craft topics comes this entertaining story which takes up the characters exploited in the Pioneer Boys of Missouri and continues the tale of their fortunes and adventures along their pathway toward the far-distant Pacific. No more absorbing vacation book is offered for the young lads and it should have a big sale, as do all the books published by the Page Company of Boston. 346 pages. 6 full page illustrations. Price $1.25.

ST. LOUIS NOTES.

Henry G. Berning and Miss Emma Bruenig were married on Tuesday, June 29th. Miss Bruenig is a sister of the late Mrs. Berning who died several months ago. This marriage was a promise to Mrs. Berning before she died. They left for a six weeks' trip East.

The W. S. Wells Floral Co. doing business for the past two years at Chontran and Sarah streets has closed up shop. Mr. Wells has accepted a position as keeper of the grounds at the Washington University. Mr. Wells is vice-president of the St. Louis Florist Club.

Flower Market Reports

BOSTON Last week's record was a bright one, considering the season, and stock found a fair market as a rule. This week the summer dullness has settled down with crushing weight and with a suddenness unprecedented and unlooked for. There is "nothing doing" for the time being and it is fortunate that the receipts are being reduced from day to day in the wholesale establishments. Peonies are finished and the rose and carnation growers are sending in much reduced quantities. Carnations, however, are in immovable surplus and the quality is not any too good. Sweet peas are very fine. So are cattleyas, but they are plentiful and nobody seems to want them, which is unfortunate and much to be regretted from many viewpoints. The quality of the roses coming in is excellent and the rose seems to have at least as good an outlook for the next few weeks as any other item on the list.

BUFFALO Quite a satisfactory week's business was had the previous week. Weddings, school commencements, etc., greatly helped to swell the week's receipts. The supply and quality of flowers was good considering the severe hot weather the growers had to contend with. In the rose line My Maryland was the leader and Shawyer second and at times not enough of the choice stock could be had. Killarney is running small and of poor color. Red Killarney is fair; Sunburst, Taft and Ward excellent, and sales on all roses has been exceptionally good. Friday and Saturday saw a good cleaning up of carnations, although prices were not high. Lilies are over abundant. Some choice indoor America gladioli are excellent; lily of the valley and lots of outdoor and indoor sweet peas have had a fair sale.

CHICAGO Last week closed with a little spurt of business. Buyers were out in force, keen to see bargains, and a lot of stock moved out of the wholesalers' way. Prices varied greatly, but the average was low, the wholesalers recognizing the fact that summer is here and the retailer is taking chances on selling again. The quality all around is all that can be desired. No extreme heat has reduced the vitality of stock and a fair amount of sunshine has kept color good. Peonies might be said to be all cut now, the few that straggle in being poor, and cold storage stock is showing up very satisfactorily, evidently not having been damaged to any extent by the frost. Prices hold up the best on peonies, American Beauties are of extra good quality and the long ones are in excess of the short lengths. Of carnations and roses in general there is any amount and the price depends upon the quantity you want and how good a talker you are. The miscellaneous stock is so large at present that some consider it a detriment to the market.

CINCINNATI The market is going through the usually quiet spell for early summer. The call for stock is very weak and unsteady, while the supply, on the other hand, is large and comprises heavy offerings of all seasonable flowers, most of them of general high quality.

NEW YORK Business has practically shut down with the regular retail trade of the city and what sales are made are mainly to the small traders, at prices fixed to fit the emergency and the persuasive powers of the buyer. The situation is less embarrassing than last week—not because sales are more active but on account of the very material shortening up of supplies, as is usual at this date. It will require a considerable reduction in the cuts, however, before the proper balance between supply and demand will be reestablished.

PHILADELPHIA There was a more cheerful atmosphere in the wholesale cut flower centers here when your correspondent made his weekly Monday visits on the 28th. The oversupply of the previous two weeks was not so pronounced and the depressing fog was largely dissipated. Of course, this is not saying much, as business is slow, taking it all round. But the season is advancing and the Fourth is almost upon us, so a great deal can not reasonably be expected in the way of flower business. High grade roses were not nearly so plentiful, the bulk of the stock being short and under standard. Carnations are getting smaller, the supply less, and the shipping quality of the stock is not very good. Cattleyas have been in increased supply and prices have fallen considerably. Lily of the valley sells well—better than usual for the season; there seem to have been more indoor weddings in late June this year, which called for lots of this item. A marked improvement is reported in the lily situation. The glut is over and prices back again to nearly normal. Long-

(Continued on page 19)

ASTERS

For the first cuts of Asters the quality is unusually good—all colors, pinks, whites and purples, in any quantity.

Special	$3.00 per 100
Fancy	2.00 " "
First (short stems)	1.00 " "
GLADIOLI	$4.00 per 100
America	6.00 " "
VALLEY, Special	$4.00 per 100
Extra	3.00 " "
CATTLEYAS	$5.00 per dozen
WHITE ORCHIDS	.50 per flower
MIXED ORCHIDS (in limited supply)	$5.00 and $10.00 boxes

S. S. PENNOCK-MEEHAN CO.

The Wholesale Florists of Philadelphia

NEW YORK, 117 W. 28th St.
PHILADELPHIA, 1608-1620 Ludlow St.
BALTIMORE, Franklin and St. Paul Sts.
WASHINGTON, 1216 H St., N. W.

WHOLESALE FLOWER MARKETS — TRADE PRICES—Per 100 TO DEALERS ONLY

	BOSTON July 1		ST. LOUIS June 28		PHILA. June 28	
Roses						
Am. Beauty, Special	10.00 to	16.00	20.00 to	30.00	20.00 to	25.00
" " Fancy and Extra	6.00 to	8.00	12.00 to	15.00	12.50 to	15.00
" " No. 1	3.00 to	5.00	5.00 to	8.00	6.00 to	10.00
Killarney, Richmond, Extra	2.00 to	4.00	3.00 to	5.00	3.00 to	6.00
" " Ordinary	.50 to	1.00	2.00 to	3.00	1.00 to	2.00
Hillingdon, Ward, Sunburst, Extra	2.00 to	4.00	5.00 to	8.00	3.00 to	6.00
" " Ordinary	.50 to	1.00	3.00 to	4.00	1.00 to	2.00
Arenberg, Radiance, Taft, Extra	2.00 to	4.00	...... to		3.00 to	5.00
" " Ordinary	.50 to	1.00	...... to		1.00 to	2.00
Russell, Hadley, Ophelia, Mock	2.00 to	8.00	5.00 to	6.00	7.50 to	15.00
Carnations, Fancy	.75 to	1.00	2.00 to	3.00	1.00 to	3.00
Ordinary	.35 to	.50	.75 to	1.00	.50 to	1.00
Cattleyas	10.00 to	20.00	35.00 to	40.00	20.00 to	40.00
Dendrobium formosum	...... to		40.00 to	50.00	40.00 to	50.00
Lilies, Longiflorum	8.00 to	4.00	4.00 to	5.00	10.00 to	12.00
Rubrum	...... to	3.00	...... to		...... to	
Lily of the Valley	2.00 to	3.00	3.00 to	4.00	2.00 to	4.00
Daisies	.50 to	1.00	.30 to	.50	.50 to	.75
Stocks	1.00 to	1.50	4.00 to	5.00	1.00 to	2.00
Snapdragon	2.00 to	4.00	2.00 to	4.00	1.00 to	2.00
Gladioli	1.00 to	3.00	3.00 to	4.00	3.00 to	6.00
Sweet Peas	.15 to	.75	.25 to	.50	.25 to	.75
Gardenias	10.00 to	12.00	1.00 to	2.00	...... to	
Adiantum	.50 to	1.00	1.00 to	1.25	.75 to	1.00
Smilax	10.00 to	12.00	10.00 to	15.00	...... to	20.00
Asparagus Plumosus, Strings (100)	25.00 to	50.00	35.00 to	50.00	...... to	50.00
" " & Spren. (100 Bchs.)	25.00 to	35.00	15.00 to	20.00	20.00 to	50.00

Flower Market Reports

(Continued from page 17)

stemmed gladioli are a strong feature of the market both in quantity and quality and they go well. The same may be said of the large flowering delphiniums, although we cannot expect these to remain with us much longer.

PITTSBURGH With the exception of the inevitable funeral work, which, from the florists' point of view is "remarkably good," the season is over, the harvest practically ended. Outdoor larkspur, coreopsis, foxglove and delphinium are at their best but it is the sweet peas that are taking better than anything else and meeting a ready sale at fair prices. Gladioli are also in demand but the prices are pathetically low. Carnations are still fairly good, but with the exception of ramblers, which are fine, but without sale, the roses show the effect of the warm weather. American Beauties are all off.

SAN FRANCISCO June business among the retailers was a little above the average of former years owing to the many Exposition functions in addition to the usual work for school exercises, weddings, etc. Stock continues plentiful and most lines show excellent quality. The offerings of gladioli are very heavy, but they manage to clean up at low prices. Good carnations are rather scarce. Dahlias are more abundant, especially Delice, which show good quality and meet with much favor. A few yellow callas are offered and are easily disposed of at higher prices than can be obtained for white. Unusually fine supplies of Lilium giganteum for this time of the year are coming in from down the peninsula. The market is well supplied with good roses and the short-stemmed specimens are almost in excessive supply. Some nice Irish Elegance is appearing and the limited supply is readily absorbed. Cecile Brunner still gives good satisfaction both in quantity and quality. Taft sells well, and Sunburst is popular. Greens are plentiful.

ST. LOUIS. The market continues in an over crowded condition which promises to last for some time. There are plenty of fine roses and carnations, with prices exceedingly low. Sweet peas and gladioli are giving the wholesaler some trouble now as the glut is on since the outdoor gladioli came in. The growers are complaining of too much rain which has caused outdoor stock to suffer much of late.

WASHINGTON Last week was a very quiet one. There is far more stock coming in than the market can possibly absorb and more than half of it is finding its way to the trash piles. There are plenty of good quality flowers, although the locally grown roses and carnations are not much as to size. These are easily supplanted by those from the northern ranges where the retailer or the customer is willing to pay a slightly advanced price. There are more than enough gardenias to fill all demand. There

is also a plentiful supply of orchids which, with lily of the valley, are the only flowers which seem to hold a price. In most of the other varieties the customer's own price is seldom if ever refused, the dealers being only too glad to find a purchaser for the stock.

VISITORS' REGISTER.

Denver, Colo.—Henry Penn and wife, Boston.

New York—R. Vincent, Jr., White Marsh, Md.; Thomas F. Galvin, Boston.

Philadelphia—James Brown, Coatesville, Pa.; Stephen Mortensen, Southampton, Pa.; Walter Heck, Reading, Pa.

Washington—D. T. Connor, representing Lord & Burnham Co., and I. Rosnosky, representing H. F. Michell, both of Philadelphia.

San Francisco—Howard Earl, representing W. Atlee Burpee; W. C. Laughridge and Mrs. Langhridge, Albany, N. Y.; Frank C. Woodruff, Orange, N. J.

Boston—J. J. Lane, Garden City, N. Y.; Franklin D. Hartshorn and Mrs. Hartshorn, Augusta, Me.; Leonard Barron, Garden City, N. Y.; Mr. Hurst, Little Rock, Ark.

Detroit, Mich.—Winfried Roelker, New York; Jas. McHutchison, New York; C. R. Burr, Manchester, Conn.; W. A. Harrison, York, Neb.; C. B. Knickman, New York; W. H. Wyman, No. Abington, Mass.

Cincinnati—Mr. and Mrs. C. J. Ohmer and son of West Palm Beach, Fla.; Miss Margaret Weiland, Evanston, Ill.; Dr. H. Dux, Jacksonville, Fla.; S. A. Gregg, Charleston, W. Va.; Mr. Gutmann, Atlanta, Ga.

Chicago—George Stiles, Oklahoma City, Okla.; E. H. Trader, Uniontown, Pa.; Mrs. Joseph Laho, Joliet, Ill.; J. Furrow and A. Furrow, Guthrie, Okla.; W. G. Miller, Peru, Ind.; Harry Balsley, Detroit, Mich.; Mr. Meier of Meier, Schroeder Co., Green Bay, Wis.

NEW YORK QUOTATIONS PER 100. To Dealers Only

MISCELLANEOUS	Last Half of Week ending June 26 1915		First Half of Week beginning June 28 1915	
Cattleyas	10.00	to 30.00	10.00	to 30.00
Lilies, Longiflorum	1.00	to 3.00	2.00	to 4.00
" Rubrum	1.00	to 2.00	1.00	to 2.00
Lily of the Valley	.75	to 2.00	1.00	to 2.00
Daisies	......	to 1.00	......	to 1.00
Stocks	......	to 1.00	......	to 1.00
Snapdragon	.50	to 1.00	.50	to 1.00
Gladioli	1.00	to 3.00	1.00	to 3.00
Peonies	.75	to 1.50	1.00	to 3.00
Sweet Peas	.05	to .75	.05	to .75
Corn Flower	......	to 2.00	......	to 1.00
Gardenias	8.00	to 12.00	8.00	to 12.00
Adiantum	.50	to .75	.50	to .75
Smilax	8.00	to 15.00	8.00	to 15.00
Asparagus Plumosus, strings (per 100)	15.00	to 35.00	15.00	to 35.00
& Spren (100 bunches)	10.00	to 20.00	10.00	to 20.00

TEXAS STATE FLORISTS' ASSOCIATION.

The enclosed report from the different cities gives an idea of what we are expecting at Ft. Worth. These reports are just from the larger towns—to say nothing of the towns where there are only two or three florists. The outlook is certainly bright for a record breaking attendance.

R. C. KERR, Pres.

Houston, Texas.—After a canvass of the florists of Houston, I find that all but two will be in attendance at Ft. Worth.—Paul M. Carroll.

San Antonio, Texas.—I have talked to the florists of San Antonio. They are all enthusiastic about the Ft. Worth convention—90 per cent. of them will be on hand.—F. C. Suchy.

Austin, Texas.—I phoned all the florists of Austin; every one to a single man says he is planning to go to the convention.—Chas. Alb, Jr.

Waco, Texas.—I hope there will be no big business in Waco during convention week, for every florist, and most of the employees, are planning big on the convention.—T. J. Wolfe.

Sherman, Texas.—Sherman florists and nurserymen will be at the convention with bells on.—A. F. Kochle.

Galveston, Tex.—Galveston florists are going to lock up shops July 6th and 7th, for they certainly expect to attend the Ft. Worth convention.—Mrs. M. A. Hansen.

Alvin, Tex.—Alvin is a small town, but believe me, we will make a large showing at the Ft. Worth convention. I think every florist is going.—Mrs. J. W. Carlisle.

Corsicana, Tex.—The florists of Corsicana are anticipating a fine time at Ft. Worth.—Wm. Clowe.

Denison, Tex.—Denison florists will be in Ft. Worth during the convention.—Miss Allie Isttd.

Dallas, Tex.—The Dallas Florists' Club will go to the convention in a special interurban car. I know of no one who expects to stay at home. I will bring four employees besides myself.—Otto Lange.

El Paso, Tex.—It is a long jump from El Paso to Ft. Worth, but we feel the trip and expense worth while. Count on a good delegation from El Paso.—Patten Floral Co.

Ft. Worth, Tex.—Everything is in readiness for the convention. I have had notice of shipments of many exhibits. Convention Hall is in shape and ready for staging. The Florists' Club has completed all details. The Chamber of Commerce and merchants of the city are going to cooperate to the fullest extent. Everything looks bright for a grand time.—W. J. Baker.

Buyer's Directory and Ready Reference Guide

Advertisements under this head, one cent a word.   Initials count as words.

Display advertisers in this issue are also listed under this classification without charge. Reference to List of Advertisers will indicate the respective pages.

Buyers failing to find what they want in this list will confer a favor by writing us and we will try to put them in communication with reliable dealers.

For List of Advertisers See Page 3

LILY OF THE VALLEY—Continued
Loechner & Co., New York City.
Lily of the Valley Pips.
For page see List of Advertisers.

LIQUID PUTTY MACHINE
Metropolitan Material Co., Brooklyn, N. Y.
For page see List of Advertisers.

MASTICA
F. O. Pierce Co., New York City.
For page see List of Advertisers.

NATIONAL NURSERYMAN
National Nurseryman Publishing Co., Inc.,
Rochester, N. Y.
For page see List of Advertisers.

NIKOTEEN
Nicotine Mfg. Co., St. Louis, Mo.
For page see List of Advertisers.

NIKOTIANA
Aphine Mfg. Co., Madison, N. J.
For page see List of Advertisers.

NURSERY STOCK
P. Ouwerkerk, Weehawken Heights, N. J.
For page see List of Advertisers.

W. & T. Smith Co., Geneva, N. Y.
For page see List of Advertisers.

Bay State Nurseries, North Abington, Mass.
Hardy, Northern Grown Stock.
For page see List of Advertisers.

Bobbink & Atkins, Rutherford, N. J.
For page see List of Advertisers.

Framingham Nurseries, Framingham, Mass.
For page see List of Advertisers.

August Rolker & Sons, New York City.
For page see List of Advertisers.

NUT GROWING.
The Nut-Grower, Waycross, Ga.
For page see List of Advertisers.

ONION SETS
Schilder Bros., Chillicothe, O.
Onion Seed—Onion Sets.
For page see List of Advertisers.

ORCHID FLOWERS
Jas. McManus, New York, N. Y.
For page see List of Advertisers.

ORCHID PLANTS
Julius Roehrs Co., Rutherford, N. J.
For page see List of Advertisers.

Lager & Hurrell, Summit, N. J.
For page see List of Advertisers.

PALMS, ETC.
Robert Craig Co., Philadelphia, Pa.
For page see List of Advertisers.

August Rolker & Sons, New York City.
For page see List of Advertisers.

A. Leuthy & Co., Roslindale, Boston, Mass.
For page see List of Advertisers.

PANDANUS VEITCHI
Julius Roehrs Co., Rutherford, N. J.
For page see List of Advertisers.

PAINT AND PUTTY.
Hammond's Paint & Slug Shot Works,
Beacon, N. Y.
Hammond's Greenhouse White Paint and
Twemlow's Old English Putty.

PEONIES
Peonies. The world's greatest collection.
1200 sorts. Send for list. C. BETSCHER,
Canal Dover, O.

PECKY CYPRESS BENCHES
A. T. Stearns Lumber Co., Boston, Mass.

PIPE AND FITTINGS
Kroeschell Bros. Co., Chicago.
For page see List of Advertisers.

King Construction Company,
N. Tonawanda, N. Y.
Shelf Brackets and Pipe Hangers.
For page see List of Advertisers.

PLANT AND BULB IMPORTS
Chas. Schwake & Co., New York City.
For page see List of Advertisers.

August Rolker & Sons, New York City.
For page see List of Advertisers.

PLANT TRELLISES AND STAKES
Seele's Tieless Plant Stakes and Trellises. H. D. SEELE & SONS, Elkhart, Ind.

PLANT TUBS
H. A. Dreer, Philadelphia, Pa.
"Riverton Special."

POINSETTIAS.
A. Henderson & Co., Chicago, Ill.
For page see List of Advertisers.

POINSETTIAS—10,000 TRUE TYPE XMAS
RED.
Shipped in 2½ in. paper pots at $5.00 per
100; $50.00 per 1,000. MIAMI FLORAL CO.,
Dayton, Ohio.

RAFFIA
McHutchison & Co., New York, N. Y.
For page see List of Advertisers.

RHODODENDRONS
P. Ouwerkerk, Hoboken, N. J.
For page see List of Advertisers.

Framingham Nurseries, Framingham, Mass.
For page see List of Advertisers.

RIBBONS AND CHIFFONS
S. S. Pennock-Meehan Co., Philadelphia, Pa.
For page see List of Advertisers.

ROSES
Poehlmann Bros. Co., Morton Grove, Ill.
For page see List of Advertisers.

P. Ouwerkerk, Hoboken, N. J.
For page see List of Advertisers.

Robert Craig Co., Philadelphia, Pa.
For page see List of Advertisers.

W. & T. Smith Co., Geneva, N. Y.
American Grown Roses.
For page see List of Advertisers.

Bay State Nurseries, North Abington, Mass.
For page see List of Advertisers.

August Rolker & Sons, New York City.
For page see List of Advertisers.

Framingham Nurseries, Framingham, Mass.
For page see List of Advertisers.

A. N. Pierson, Inc., Cromwell, Conn.
For page see List of Advertisers.

F. R. Pierson Co., Tarrytown, N. Y.
Winter Flower Roses.
For page see List of Advertisers.

Wood Bros., Fishkill, N. Y.
For page see List of Advertisers.

THE CONARD & JONES COMPANY,
Rose Specialists.
West Grove, Pa. Send for offers.

SEASONABLE PLANT STOCK
R. Vincent, Jr. & Sons Co., White Marsh
Md.
For page see List of Advertisers.

SEED GROWERS
California Seed Growers' Association.
San Jose, Cal.
For page see List of Advertisers.

SEEDS
Carter's Tested Seeds,
Seeds with a Pedigree.
Boston, Mass., and London, England.
For page see List of Advertisers.

SEEDS—Continued
Schilder Bros., Chillicothe, O.
Onion Seed—Onion Sets.
For page see List of Advertisers.

Joseph Breck & Sons, Boston, Mass.
For page see List of Advertisers.

Kelway & Son,
Langport, Somerset, England.
Kelway's Celebrated English Strain Garden
Seeds.
For page see List of Advertisers.

J. Bolgiano & Son, Baltimore, Md.
For page see List of Advertisers.

A. T. Boddington, New York City.
For page see List of Advertisers.

Chas. Schwake & Co., New York City.
For page see List of Advertisers.

Michell's Seed House, Philadelphia, Pa.
New Crop Pansy Seeds.
For page see List of Advertisers.

W. Atlee Burpee & Co., Philadelphia, Pa.
For page see List of Advertisers.

R. & J. Farquhar & Co., Boston, Mass.
For page see List of Advertisers.

J. M. Thorburn & Co., New York City.
Seeds for Present Sowing.
For page see List of Advertisers.

S. Bryson Ayres Co., Independence, Mo.
Sweet Peas.
For page see List of Advertisers.

Loechner & Co., New York City.
For page see List of Advertisers.

Ant. C. Zvolanek, Lompoc, Cal.
Winter Flowering Sweet Pea Seed.
For page see List of Advertisers.

John H. Allan Seed Co., Sheboygan, Wis.
Choice Varieties Pea and Bean Seeds.
For page see List of Advertisers.

S. S. Skidelsky & Co., Philadelphia, Pa.
For page see List of Advertisers.

W. E. Marshall & Co., New York City.
Seeds, Plants and Bulbs.
For page see List of Advertisers.

August Rolker & Sons, New York City.
For page see List of Advertisers.

Burnett Bros., 98 Chambers St., New York.
For page see List of Advertisers.

Fottler, Fiske, Rawson Co., Boston, Mass.
Aster Seed.

SKINNER IRRIGATION SYSTEM
Geo. N. Barrie, Brookline, Mass.
For page see List of Advertisers.

SPHAGNUM MOSS
Sphagnum Moss—10-bbl. bales, $1.90;
5-bbl. bale, 90c.; Laurel, 90c. bag. Get
prices on large lots. JOS. H. PAUL, P. O.
156, Manahawkin, N. J.

Live Sphagnum moss, orchid peat and
orchid baskets always on hand. LAGER
& HURRELL, Summit, N. J.

Sphagnum Moss—Clean, dry, 85c. per
5-bbl. bale; 10 bales, $8.00. Cash, please.
GEORGE THOREN, Mayetta, N. J.

STOVE PLANTS
Orchids—Largest stock in the country—
Stove plants and Crotons, finest collection.
JULIUS ROEHRS CO., Rutherford, N. J.

SWEET PEA SEED
W. Atlee Burpee & Co., Philadelphia, Pa.
Winter Flowering Sweet Pea Yarrawa.
For page see List of Advertisers.

Ant. C. Zvolanek, Lompoc, Calif.
Gold Medal of Honor. Winter Orchid Sweet
Peas.
For page see List of Advertisers.

S. Bryson Ayres Co.,
Sunnyslope, Independence, Mo.
For page see List of Advertisers.

For List of Advertisers See Page 3

New Offers In This Issue

In writing to Advertisers kindly mention Horticulture

Clubs and Societies

NEW BEDFORD HORTICULTURAL SOCIETY.

A well patronized rose show under the auspices of the New Bedford Horticultural Society was held in the Free Public Library Building on June 25.

The growing interest in these shows is shown not only in the increasing numbers who visit them, but in the many amateurs who exhibit or who desire to do so. Indeed, there were so many entries at this particular show that the committee had to refuse almost half of them.

The most conspicuously beautiful display was that of Galen N. Stone, mgr. Arthur Griffin. His Canterbury bells won a special award of merit. His flowers were so cleverly arranged that each one showed to the best advantage, and that in itself is an art not always displayed by some of the finest growers. Many hybrid roses and hybrid perpetuals, teas and hybrid teas were displayed and the general exhibition of outdoor perennials which were unusually fine. The judges were C. W. Young and James Garthley.

Special recognitions were as follows: Tripp cup to Miss Alice Stackpole. Awards of merit to W. K. Smith for tuberous begonias, Alice Stackpole for Austrian copper rose, L. J. Hathaway, Jr., for sweet williams, Mrs. E. C. Jones for sweet peas, Joseph Figneiredo for roses, H. A. Jahn for larkspur, A. J. Fish for climbing roses, Galen Stone for gaillardias, Canterbury bell, larkspurs, F. H. Taber for rose J. B. Clark, Mrs. Horatio Hathaway, gard. Dennis Shea, for cut flowers, and H. E. Converse, supt. D. F. Roy, for general exhibit. First class certificate to C. W. Young for new hybrid strawberry (Marshall × Big Ben). The regular prizes were won by H. E. Converse, A. Nolet, Margaret Anthony, J. C. Forbes, F. G. Tripp, Alice Stackpole and W. F. Turner.

AMERICAN DAHLIA SOCIETY.

The executive board of the American Dahlia Society, consisting of the president and others, met at the secretary's office, New York, on Saturday morning, June 26. Many new members were reported and finances are in good condition. Pres. Vincent produced a tentative schedule of premiums which was adopted with some few amendments as far as it was possible to go, as many of the parties offering prizes had not stated the amount and others are to be heard from. The advisability of issuing some sort of publication or treatise on the list of varieties, their growing, etc., as soon as practicable was discussed, also the question of trial grounds in different sections of the country.

In the discussion regarding the Fall Show strong objection was raised to having it at the Bronx, the committee as a whole deciding to request the Council of the Horticultural Society of New York to obtain the use of the Museum of Natural Science for the Dahlia Society. An offer was also received from the Pennsylvania Horticultural Society offering their hall, etc., in Philadelphia for the show.

An adjourned meeting was held in the afternoon at the Bronx Botanical Garden, jointly with the Council of the Horticultural Society. The undesirability of the Bronx was talked over both in regard to getting the exhibits there, and the doubtful outlook for getting a justifiable attendance. The Council agreed to try to obtain the Museum location and the result

will be known within a few days. The date selected for the show is September 23-24-25.

As there had been some complaint of the distribution of circulars and business advertising during some shows, the Dahlia Committee pledged themselves not to allow this to be done by any firm exhibiting. The Council agreed to donate $100 towards premiums.

CONNECTICUT HORTICULTURAL SOCIETY.

At the meeting on June 25 President Mason had on exhibition a very fine collection of roses, comprising 45 varieties. President Mason is much pleased with the growth made by Nova Zembla which in his opinion is equal to Margaret Dickson and Karl Druschki. President Mason was awarded a first class diploma, and H. L. Ritson received honorable mention.

Alfred Dixon, W. W. Hunt and Mrs. William H. Palmer have been appointed a committee to draw up resolutions regarding the death of the late James J. Goodwin, a life member. The June Flower Show cleared about $80, all expenses paid. The next meeting will be held in September.

ALFRED DIXON, Sec'y.

NEW YORK FLORISTS' CLUB.

President Harry A. Bunyard has appointed the following nominating committee to select candidates for office, 1916:

Nominating Committee.—Joseph A. Manda, chairman; John Donaldson, Walter F. Sheridan, Frank H. Traendly, Charles H. Totty, Charles B. Weathered, Charles Weber.

JOHN YOUNG, Sec'y.

SOCIETY OF AMERICAN FLORISTS AND ORNAMENTAL HORTICULTURISTS

Department of Plant Registration.

Frank D. Pelicano, 119 Gutenberg St., San Francisco, Cal., submits for registration the following new violets:

"Anne Evans"; a sport from "Swanley White" with flowers very much larger. Color, porcelain blue tinted with lavender, about the shade of a Czar Peter hyacinth. Plant strong and healthy, making quantities of fine foliage.

"Quaker Lady"; a seedling from a cross between Single White and California. Flowers single and about the same size as "Giant Violet." A strong healthy grower. Color lavender shaded with delft blue, a shade darker than the "Palma" violet.

Any person objecting to the registration or to the use of the proposed name, is requested to communicate with the Secretary at once. Failing to receive objection to the registration, the same will be made three weeks from this date.

JOHN YOUNG, Sec'y.

June 22, 1915.

CLUB AND SOCIETY NOTES.

The Horticultural Society of New York had an attractive free exhibition of seasonable flowers at the Bronx Botanical Garden on June 26 and 27.

The monthly meeting of the Florists' and Gardeners' Club of Rhode Island was held at 96 Westminster street, Providence, on Monday evening, June 28.

The Cincinnati Florists Society members will be the guests of Max Rudolph at his home on July 12th, when the annual meeting of the society will be held.

The annual rose show of the Worcester County Horticultural Society was held in Horticultural Hall, Worcester, Mass., on June 24. Roses, herbaceous perennial flowers, strawberries, cherries and early vegetables were shown in profusion.

A large delegation of members of the National Association of Gardeners expects to attend the annual Sweet Pea Show of the American Sweet Pea Society to be held on July 15 and 16 at Newport, R. I. Those going by way of New York will leave on the Fall River line of steamers on Wednesday afternoon at five o'clock from Pier 14, foot of Fulton street, North River. As this is the vacation season and passenger traffic is heavy, it is suggested that staterooms be secured in advance. Advices from Boston say that a big delegation from the New England city will also journey to Newport to attend the Show.

M. C. EBEL, Secretary.

The New Hampshire Horticultural Society held its annual summer meeting at the State College, Durham, more than 200 attending.

President E. T. Fairchild addressed the gathering. After the inspection of the college the visitors were taken in automobiles to the experimental orchard, where Prof. J. M. Gourley explained the work the college is doing there. Lunch was served on the lawn in front of the Agricultural building. There were addresses by Wilfrid Wheeler, secretary of the Massachusetts State Board of Agriculture, and William N. Craig of Brookline, Mass. Miss Sarah L. Bates assisted by Miss Mary Sanborn, gave a demonstration of canning.

GREENHOUSES BUILDING OR CONTEMPLATED.

Canton, S. D.—R. R. Hartvic, one house.

Salisbury, Md.—Geo. H. Benedict. house 60 x 150.

Lewiston, Me.—Ernest Saunders, one 425 ft. house.

Grand Rapids, Mich.—Eli Cross, two 300 ft. rose houses.

Woodside, N. Y.—Otto Muller, three houses each 25 x 100.

New Haven, Ct.—John Peterson, South End, one house.

W. Hoboken, N. J.—Wm. Gullicksen, 4th street, three houses.

Clinton, Ill.—S. Grimsley, South Monroe street, house 50 x 125.

Houston, Tex.—Mrs. Cotney, Washington avenue, house 32 x 100.

Moorhead, Minn.—J. W. Briggs, Front and 8th streets, one house.

Milton, Mass.—I. Tucker Burr, conservatory. Lord & Burnham Boston

Dallas, Tex.—Sarver Floral Co., house 20 x 165; Reed Floral Company, house 20 x 100.

Concord, Mass.—Samuel Lufkin, iron frame house 32 x 225. Lord & Burnham Boston office.

HAIL STORM IN NEW ENGLAND

A fierce thunder storm accompanied by a heavy fall of hail stones swept over a section of Massachusetts and Rhode Island on Saturday, June 26, doing great damage to garden crops and trees, killing chickens and smashing greenhouse glass on all sides. Among the latter were the greenhouses of Brown and A. J. Boothman, North Adams, Mass.; Samuel Kinder & Bro., Frederick A. Geisler, Starr L. Booth, Col. S. P. Colt, LeBaron Bradford, William L. McKee, Robert A. Black and the Kingsthorpe Greenhouses all of Bristol, R. I. Other localities in southeastern Massachusetts and Rhode Island were hit but details are missing.

HORTICULTURE

Window Display of Flower Baskets

In the New Store of Samuel Murray, Kansas City, Mo.

Published Every Saturday at 147 Summer Street, Boston, Mass.
Subscription, $1.00

LIST OF ADVERTISERS

FOR BUYERS' DIRECTORY AND READY REFERENCE GUIDE
SEE PAGES 52, 53, 54, 55

NOTES ON CULTURE OF FLORISTS' STOCK

CONDUCTED BY

John J. M. Farrell

Questions by our readers in line with any of the topics presented on this page will be cordially received and promptly answered by Mr. Farrell. Such communications should invariably be addressed to the office of HORTICULTURE.
"If vain our toil, we ought to blame the culture, not the soil."—*Pope.*

Carnations

Most carnation growers are now busy planting. Some may have planted a house or two earlier but this is the beginning of the real housing period. As soon as the benches are emptied clean them and give a good coating of whitewash. After applying the whitewash fill the benches at once. Do not leave them exposed to the sun and air for a week or two if you want them to last. Give the plants six inches of rich soil. I cannot see where anything is gained by planting carnations in three or four inches of soil. See that the plants are not set too deep. Deep planting is the cause of a great deal of stem rot. Water at the base of each plant and give frequent sprayings until the plants take hold. Keep the soil moist on top by heavy sprayings but continue to water at the base of the plants for a few weeks to prevent the soil becoming sour, and to encourage root action.

Calceolarias

Calceolaria hybrida makes a very imposing plant when grown right. The seed can be sown from now up to the first week in August for next season's trade. Get a very sandy mixture of soil and some clean leaf mold. Give the pans a good watering so as to have them wet through then scatter the seeds thinly over the surface. Press the seed gently into the soil with brick or piece of board. They require no covering of soil. Lay a pane of glass over the pans and place in a frame where the shade should be heavy at first and towards fall it should become lighter. Avoid extremes either way in watering as these young plants are very susceptible to damp. The loss through damping off is lessened by timely shifting from box to box. When they have made from four to six leaves they should be potted into small pots still using a light sandy mixture. They should have a fine syringing overhead several times a day in bright hot weather.

Easter Lilies

Much of the plant growers attention now centers in the stock to be had in readiness for next Easter. Without question lilies hold the foremost place. Get good strong bulbs which are the best in the end. For winter flowering the bulbs should be potted and started just as soon as they can be procured. There is a good demand for lilies all through the winter and a few dozens a week are acceptable to every country florist who has design orders to fill. The bulbs generally used for early

forcing will do well in five-inch pots singly, or larger ones to a six-inch pot. Use good fibrous loam and some well rotted cow manure. The potting soil should be rich but without green manure. In potting the tops of the bulb ought to be just level with the surface of the soil.

Mignonette

Those who want to cut good mignonette should not delay in sowing the seed. One very successful grower of mignonette sows the seed in three-inch pots, a few seeds in three little groups in each pot. It is safer, however, to sow a pinch of seed on the bench or bed where they are to remain and flower. One foot of space each way is not too much room to give the plants. As is well known the mignonette is a difficult plant to transplant and if the soil drops off the roots the little plants are a long time in making a start. A dozen plants may come up where you sowed your pinch of seed and will not harm anything till the little seedlings are an inch high; then you must pull up all but the strongest plant. The chief enemy of the young mignonette is the larva of the sulphur-colored cabbage butterfly which lays its eggs in August and September. As soon as you see that the butterfly is abroad spray the plants lightly and then dust them with powdered helle-bore.

Cypripediums

Cypripediums are now in active growth and as the roots fill the pots and pans nicely a little weak liquid manure once a week should be applied. Avoid the use of all chemicals. A little later as the roots become more matted the strength can be slightly increased. Ventilate freely on every favorable opportunity. Keep the plants free from thrips by sponging occasionally with a weak solution of tobacco water and give light fumigating once or twice every fortnight to keep off the pests. Watch the plants so they do not suffer for water but do not keep them wet all the time as the compost will become sour. A moist atmosphere during all seasons is essential to their well being. In wet weather admit air freely, otherwise the fleshy leaves are very liable to rot or become spotted.

Repairing Boilers and Piping

Now is the time to look over the boilers and piping and do whatever repairing is needed. The season of cold weather may seem far off but it will slip around before we know it. With leaky boilers or pipes it will be impossible to keep up the right temperature.

Next Week:—Chrysanthemums; Lorraine Begonias; Rambler Roses; Pruning Flowering Shrubs; Starting Freesias; Perennial Lupines and Larkspurs.

HORTICULTURE

VOL. XXII   JULY 10, 1915   NO. 2

PUBLISHED WEEKLY BY
HORTICULTURE PUBLISHING CO.
147 Summer Street, Boston, Mass.

Telephone, Oxford 292.
WM. J. STEWART, Editor and Manager.

SUBSCRIPTION RATES:

One Year, in advance, $1.00; To Foreign Countries, $2.00; To Canada, $1.50.

ADVERTISING RATES:

Per inch, 30 inches to page......................... $1.00
Discounts on Contracts for consecutive insertions, as follows:
One month (4 times), 5 per cent.; three months (13 times), 10 per cent.; six months (26 times), 20 per cent.; one year (52 times), 30 per cent.
Page and half page space, special rates on application.

Entered as second-class matter December 8, 1904, at the Post Office at Boston, Mass., under the Act of Congress of March 3, 1879.

CONTENTS

The welcome rain

This section of the country has good reason to be thankful for the copious rains of the past few days. The deficient rainfall of the winter and spring, following two years of light precipitation had given much concern and another dry month would have been a costly experience. As a result of the recent downpours the country has taken on a rare beauty. Trees, lawns and gardens are dressed in fresh vivid green, such as is seldom seen in July and the summer visitor this year will find Boston and all the country around more charming than ever. A heavy cut of hay and other field crops seem now assured. The money value of the rain, so much needed, far outweighed the disappointment of the holiday interruption.

An interesting paper

We commend to the attention of our readers and advise a careful perusal of the address of R. C. Kerr, as president of the Texas State Florists' Association. It is a well-considered and very earnest presentation of the various phases and needs of commercial floriculture as it exists today, not alone in Texas, but in practically every section of the country. Mr. Kerr's advice then, can be read with profit by all, wherever located, who have the welfare of their business at heart. To one suggestion only would we take exception —that of an all-South association. In our humble opinion the establishing of sectional divisions other than state organizations, except as integral parts of the national society, would be a step in the wrong direction, tending to weaken the latter in the supremacy which is its strongest asset.

Will it work?

The nurserymen have taken a radical step in the new form of constitution and by-laws which they have adopted. The result of the working out of these important changes in the government of the Association will be watched with interest by other organizations of like character. The work which must be undertaken by any national society worthy of the name becomes each year more and more serious and costly and how to get the needed money for such legitimate purposes without unfavorably affecting the membership is a problem. The proposition to gather and compile yearly statistics of available stock in the hands of member growers with a view to an elimination of surplus nursery products and a better adjustment and balance of supply and demand suggests some far-reaching possibilities but, obviously, the project must have the co-operation and support of a large majority of the nursery concerns in order to be effective.

Summer trade prospects

Visiting Newport and other places of summer resort we find every available living space taken up for the season. Whatever money is spent by Americans for summer recreation this year will be spent in their own country but just how much that fact will benefit the flower and plant business remains to be seen. It is an open secret that economy has been an influential factor with the annual summer sojournings of many American families in Europe and it is not expected that these people will do much in the way of lavish spending at home this season. In Newport nothing sensational in floral decoration is anticipated by the florists. Small affairs will be the rule but should there be an abundance of such, as is hoped, they will yield more profit and general satisfaction than are usually derived from more pretentious undertakings. Altogether the outlook is not bad and it is greatly to be desired that the realization may far exceed the most sanguine forecast. The horticultural industries are certainly all in need of a good boost.

Selaginellas

The genus *Selaginella*, often known to gardeners as *Lycopodium*, to which it is closely allied, is a very extensive one containing as it does over three hundred species. Many of these are important garden plants; several species being especially valuable for carpeting the surface of the soil where large plants, such as palms, are planted out, or for growing under the benches, thus providing a beautiful mat of green. Others are well adapted for growing as specimen plants in pots, pans, or hanging baskets. Their range is very extensive some of them being hardy, but the majority require greenhouse conditions and as by far the largest number of them are found in the tropics, the warm house is the place where they are most in evidence.

The Selaginellas are of fairly easy culture, requiring to be grown under moderately moist conditions in a light, rich soil, preferably containing a proportion of peat. In general those that are suitable for growing in pans require to be propagated afresh every year if the best results are to be obtained. The cuttings, which should be two or three inches in length, may be taken in February or March, inserted in the pans in which they are to remain, and kept close and shaded until they are rooted. In making up a hanging basket of Selaginella it is better to start the cuttings in a pan and obtain strong plants before transferring them to the basket. The kinds that are suitable for carpeting will usually take care of themselves once they are established, but it may be necessary at intervals to replant if they show signs of becoming brown and worn out.

The following are amongst the best of the garden Selaginellas.

S. uncinata. This plant is usually known in the trade as *S. caesia;* it is perhaps the best of them all for a basket plant. The long graceful shoots are produced in great abundance and the coloring of the leaves is of the most exquisite character, changing from a metallic bluish green to a beautiful copper color. It may be grown under either cool or warm house treatment, but it does best under tropical conditions. The photograph shows a plant growing in the Brooklyn Botanic Garden in a 12 inch basket; it is over 3 feet in length and almost 2 feet in diameter.

S. Kraussiana is another species suitable for baskets, although this does not produce shoots anywhere near the length of the preceding. It is of rather compact growth and is of a beautiful dark green color. This is the plant so valuable and so often used for carpeting under benches. It does well under cool house conditions.

S. Martensii and its varieties are all good carpeting plants for the cool house. It is a vigorous grower, rapidly covering the positions assigned to it. A variety having silvery variegation is particularly worth growing.

S. cuspidata is a tropical species of tufted habit. The leaves are pale green in color, the lower ones having silvery edges. This also is an excellent carpeting plant.

S. Emmeliana is a tropical species of more or less upright habit with feathery fern like growths which are very graceful. Unfortunately it is somewhat slow growing, but the appearance of a well grown pan amply compensates for the extra care necessary to obtain good specimens. The variety, known as *S. Emmeliana aurea.* having leaves of a golden yellow, is a desirable variety.

S. caulescens known in the trade as *S. amoena* is another species having erect stems, which are from 6 to 12 inches long. The coloring is bright green and the

SELAGINELLA UNCINATA, SYN. S. CAESIA.

plant is distinctly fern like. It should be grown under stove conditions.

S. grandis is perhaps the finest of the erect growing Selaginellas. It produces stems, which under good conditions attain a height of 2 feet, covered with bright green leaves. To have this plant to best advantage it is necessary to grow it in a wardian case in a tropical house, covering the surface with living sphagnum.

S. Wildenovii, which often goes under the trade name of *S. caesia arborea*, is a climbing species of great merit. If planted out in a warm house and given liberal treatment it will often make stems of 20 feet or more in length. The leaves of this species have the metallic sheen which is so attractive, varying in color from bluish green to copper.

S. lepidophylla is the well known "Resurrection Plant" often obtainable in a dry state in stores that specialize in novelties. It is not of particularly handsome appearance, but is worth growing as a curiosity.

This does not by any means exhaust the list of Selaginellas which are valuable for greenhouse decoration. There are many other species and varieties of merit, and it is to be hoped that in the future greater interest will be taken in this genus of elegant and attractive plants.

Montague Free

Brooklyn Botanic Garden.

CLUBS AND SOCIETIES

AMERICAN ASSOCIATION OF NURSERYMEN.

The new constitution adopted by the American Association of Nurserymen at its Convention in Detroit provides for two classes of members, viz.: Active or voting members, who shall be actively engaged in the nursery business; Associate, or non-voting members, embracing horticultural implement makers, dealers in supplies, and those in the allied trades.

The annual membership fee for active members will be $5 with additional dues based on the amount of annual business done by each. For instance, $10,000 to $20,000, the minimum, would pay $5 additional, while the maximum of $100,000 or over would pay $50 additional dues.

Members in 1915 will constitute the membership of the association upon payment of the fees as per new schedule, and thereafter all applicants shall be elected by the association by a majority vote; or, where applications for membership are made at a time other than at the annual meeting, the executive committee may, upon a majority vote, elect such applicants.

All exhibitors of products on manufactured goods must be members of the association, and the charge for exhibitors will be determined by the executive committee.

Perhaps one of the most important provisions in the by-laws is number five, a portion of which reads:

"If, in their (the Executive Committee) judgment, it is deemed advisable, they may cause to be gathered and compiled once a year, statistics showing the available stock in the hands of member growers, and shall use every means at their command to bring the buyer and seller together upon fair and reasonable terms. It shall be within the province of the executive committee, after carefully considering the matter of supply and demand, to make such recommendations to members of the association as, in their minds, seem wise, just and desirable, looking to the stimulation of trade and the elimination of surplus nursery products."

Further, it is provided that if such statistics and recommendations are prepared the executive committee shall cause to be printed in convenient form said statistics and recommendations, copy of which shall be furnished to every member of the association.

Another important item of business transacted was the passage of a resolution looking to the establishment of a court of arbitration before which may be brought questions in dispute between members, in connection with shipments of stock purchased, such as complaints regarding size and shape of stock, etc., and the reductions claimed for such things, etc.

In the list of new officers as published last week, the following were omitted:

Executive Committee—One year: J. B. Pilkington, Portland, Ore.; Lloyd C. Stark, Louisiana, Mo. Two years: J. H. Dayton, Painesville, O.; Henry B. Chase, Chase, Ala. Three years: J. T. Mayhew, Waxahachie, Texas; T. J. Smith, Geneva, N. Y.

The permanent time for holding the annual meeting is fixed for the third Wednesday in June in each year.

Under the new constitution the secretary is "chosen by the executive committee, and shall hold office subject to the approval of said executive committee." John Hall, Rochester, N. Y., was chosen by this committee to succeed himself.

WAKING THEM UP.

The St. Louis Florist Club's secretary has sent to each member the following very pointed and impressive communication:

Who's Who in the Florist Club and Why?

Who is to Blame?

These question require a genius to proclaim.

WHY don't more of our members attend the Florist Club meetings?

WHY can't you be present at this week's meeting on Thursday afternoon, July 8th, at 2 o'clock, and help us in nominating a good and efficient set of officers for the coming year?

WHY is it that the same 25 or 30 regulars are always present at our meetings?

WHY don't the other 75 per cent. come and enjoy our interesting meetings?

WHY can't they come and assist the officers who are trying to hold up our reputation as being the best and largest attended Florist Club in the country?

WHY can't they as well as others arrange their business affairs so as to spend a few hours each month with friends in the trade?

WHY have we existed 29 years when others have failed?

WHY not let us count on you to attend this meeting and help us answer the above questions?

WHY not confer this one special favor on the officials and other members, and be present?

Respectfully,

J. J. BENEKE,　　　JULES BOURDET,
Secretary.　　　　　President.

GARDENERS' AND FLORISTS' CLUB OF BOSTON.

Field Day at Newport, R. I.

CHANGE OF DATE—IMPORTANT NOTICE

After notices for the Field Day at Newport, R. I., for July 8 had been mailed, word was received that the Secretary of the American Sweet Pen Society had changed the date of the exhibition to July 15 and 16. It has therefore been decided to postpone the field day until Thursday, July 15, 1915, leaving the South Station at 8.43 A. M. A number of members have written or telephoned their intentions to go on the original date, July 8. We hope all such will be able to go on July 15. There will be a drive through Newport, stopping at leading estates; a shore dinner is also being arranged for. A large attendance is certain. Write at once to the Secretary if you will go, and don't forget the ladies.

H. H. BARTSCH, Pres.
W. N. CRAIG, Sec'y.

MINNESOTA HORTICULTURAL SOCIETY.

It was richly worth a trip of nearly 500 miles to visit the summer meeting of this society, held on June 12. I have attended many gatherings of this nature, but never saw anything to compare with this. The exhibition of peonies and perennials was magnificent. One man had 175 kinds of peonies alone, comprising the latest introductions from the best propagators of Europe. The Brand Nursery Co. had the finest exhibition of native born ever shown. Some were of immense size and of marvelous beauty. One variety they had sold close for $5 per root. The American Peony Society was put far back in the shade by this exhibit. The large building of the Agricultural College was completely filled, besides crowding the stairways and anterooms. Nowhere on earth have I seen anything to compare with the peonies raised in the region of the twin cities.

An immense crowd were gathered; the day was perfect. A picnic dinner was held on the beautiful grounds. After that came speeches, short and sharp. Mr. Brand told how to raise peonies from seed. The writer spoke of the iris as the flower of the future —the family in bloom more than two months; the ease of propagating new varieties and their marvelous adaptation to the semi-arid regions, where other flowers cannot grow. He spoke of their fragrance and alluring loveliness and their use as a flower for Decoration Day, when the varieties of the red, white and blue made suitable bouquets for soldier's graves.

The show of columbines, coreopsis, delphiniums, oriental poppies, pyrethrums and Shasta daisies was very fine. Altogether it was a very pleasant and notable gathering comprising an immense crowd, from the twin cities and the surrounding country. The flower growers of this section have spared no pains to get the very best and they have succeeded grandly. The rich soil and congenial climate are favorable to the highest development of perennials.

C. S. HARRISON.

York, Pa.

AMERICAN DAHLIA SOCIETY.

President Vincent announces the pleasing fact that the Horticultural Society of New York has been able to make arrangements with the authorities of the American Museum of Natural History for the installation of the exhibition of the American Dahlia Society at the Museum on September 24, 25 and 26. The Council of the Horticultural Society has passed a resolution appropriating the sum of $100 for premiums to be offered at the Dahlia Show. James Stuart, chairman of the exhibition committee of the Horticultural Society, has called a meeting for July 14, when the details of the schedule will be considered.

TEXAS STATE FLORISTS' ASSO-CIATION.

This youngest and liveliest of the State Florists' organizations has been holding a meeting at Fort Worth this week as indicated in our advance notices in recent issues. Next week we shall be able to give an account of the proceedings. For the present our readers will find in the address of President Kerr plenty to interest and perhaps a new light on the present condition and promise for the future of floriculture in a section of the country hitherto in semi-obscurity.

PRESIDENT KERR'S ADDRESS.

Ladies and Gentlemen, Members of the Texas State Florists' Associa-tion.—Ever since you paid me the great honor of electing me to the highest office within your gift, I have anticipated this hour, not so much to harvest the honors and privileges ex-tended to your presiding officer as for the opportunity to express to you my deep felt gratitude and apprecia-tion of your kindness and good will toward me.

Our First Year's Work.

The twelve months past since we last met have been busy ones for those entrusted with the affairs of our organization. Your standing commit-tee have also been faithful to their trusts and duties, as their reports will reveal to you. We have pro-gressed and increased our influence to such a degree that a review of the year's proceedings might well be de-voted to laudations rather than to suggestions or criticisms.

It is certainly gratifying to note the widespread interest in our or-ganization the first year. When we consider the comparatively short time the Texas State Florists' Association has been in existence, it is remark-able what an immense growth it has made and what a power for good it has become. The large gathering here today is self-evident testimony of the fact that the florists of Texas are awake to the importance of organiza-tion. Organizing as we have done has not come voluntarily, but the ne-cessity of the times demand that we must pull together if we expect the accomplished results. One of our most valuable assets is to get to-gether and get acquainted. How many florists have you met at our two conventions, that you had heard of, or done business with, but had never seen until met in the conven-tion hall? This alone is worth our time and expense of this organization. Let us keep up this good work and enthusiasm.

Texas to the Front as a Flower Market.

This organization is only one year old, and in that short time we have done wonders toward making this a better flower market. There were more flowers shipped to the outside market this year than the past five years combined. We have grown more and bought less this year than any one year previous, and at the same time business has been normal —which goes to show what real good can be accomplished by real co-oper-ation.

The picture which appears herewith is reproduced from a photograph sent to us by Edmund Lawrence, gardener to Mrs. A. V. Schlaet, Westport, Conn. Concerning this beautiful Wisteria, Mr. Lawrence writes as follows:

Please find enclosed a photograph of a Wisteria chinensis in my Italian garden which is one of the many climbers around the 150 ft. pergola, forming a semicircle. This plant had 649 perfect clusters measuring from 17 to 29 inches in length. The photo-graph does not show all of the blooms, there being a large number over the top of the pergola. Gardeners say they have not seen anything like it around this locality. My culture, is to cut the tap root at the right time and to prune top growth severely in growing season.

That Experimental Range of Glass for Commercial Cut Flowers.

Prof. Kyle will tell us today what the possibilities are for this experi-mental station. I believe that it is the consensus of opinion that the florists of Texas are entitled to some means of carrying on practical ex-periments with commercial cut flow-ers.

The great amount of money spent each year for flowers is amazing, and to think that about 90 per cent of this is going out of the state is cer-tainly something that needs remedy. Every florist in the state of Texas should be vitally interested in this movement and avail himself of every opportunity to help the good work along. I believe our best means of securing this experimental range will be through the Horticultural Depart-ment at College Station—this being centrally located. I would like to see a good strong committee appointed to work on this matter and keep ham-mering away until we accomplish what we want.

The Annual Flower Show

We consider our first annual flower show a grand success. It demon-strated to us that this is the best means of educating the public in the proper use of flowers, also for creat-ing a greater demand. It is also a great education for the florists. Every designer and grower produces the best that he has—and then as the saying is, "No man knows it all." Then in this way good ideas are both scat-tered and gathered and taken home and put into practical use. I believe that the members will all agree that this is really the most important work of our association. I sincerely trust that the committee appointed for the ensuing year will work vigorously to see that this year's show will be larger and even better than last year's.

The Southern Trade Paper.

Every florist in the South should rally to the support of the "Southern Florist." This is our official organ and should be the means of communi-cating and carrying on our work. It is filling a long felt want. I want to state here that we could not be with-out the other trade papers, as they cover a field that we cannot cover, and the "Southern Florist" is not con-sidered a competitor by the other papers. Every florist should contrib-ute articles, also send in all news items from their respective towns. Practically every florist in Texas is a subscriber, and we have a wide cir-culation throughout the South. If you are interested in the welfare of the Southern florists, you will rally to the support of this organ. But, being a subscriber is not all; we need mate-rial to keep the South posted.

It is not my intention to criticise the other papers, but up to the last few months how many articles per-taining to Southern Florists, or South-ern Floral Culture, have you noted in these papers—and why? It is not because they are not interested in us, for they are; vitally interested in every section of the United States; but the real reason is that they are experiencing the same trouble we are having right now, and that is in get-ting the florists of the Southern cities to report and co-operate. They stand ready at all times to publish the news and any other articles submitted to them. We believe we have solved a problem by establishing a trade paper in our midst. Let every florist in the South realize that this medium is their paper and is working for their interest, and go home determined to take more interest in the future welfare of an organ that is working for their good. Let me pause here long enough to say—that this organization, nor any of its members (except Mr. Tackett), is not financially interested in this paper. It is only our moral support that we pledge.

The Florist Business on a Higher Plane.

The florist business as a general rule is considered about a third-class business, and about three cases out of four it is true. This is our own fault. We fail to conduct our business in a way that makes an impression on the business world. We are too busy outdoing the work that a $2.00 man can do, instead of work at the desk figuring profits and loss, store management, keeping a large and seasonable stock, discounting our bills, stimulating a demand for flowers, etc. It is my frank opinion that if the florists will use their heads more and muscles less, their greenhouses will show a gain instead of a loss. It is high time we are waking up to these things, and I believe this organization will bring about an improved condition.

Our Local Clubs.

When we first began on organization work, the plan was to organize clubs in each city and centralize these with the state organization as a central body. While the local clubs have not been as active as they should, the reports show that we have accomplished a great deal. We should realize the importance of the local clubs and stir up more interest and enthusiasm the coming year.

Remember the local clubs are no place to get together to discuss prices or control trade; nor is it the place to settle personal grievances. The florists should come together at the local clubs to work along lines to stimulate a greater demand for flowers and plants—such as pretty yard contests, co-operative advertising, stirring up interest in civic beautification, etc. The clubs that are working along these lines are accomplishing results. If your local club is lifeless, diagnose the case and see if the above mentioned does not apply.

Membership.

Every florist in the state of Texas should belong to this state organization. If you are not a member you are the loser. Cast your lot with the organization that is going to be the making of the florist business of Texas. In one short year we have made wonderful progress, but we need all of you, and you need us. If you have not taken out your membership —do so today before leaving the hall.

Affiliation with the S. A. F.

One of the most important matters for this organization to consider at this time is the best means of working with the S. A. F.—the parent body of all floricultural bodies of the United States. We are all vitally interested in the welfare of that organization, and we should take some steps toward stimulating more interest among the florists in the state of Texas. If it is possible, I would like to see our dues raised so as to include the S. A. F. membership. If we have one hundred such members, we are entitled to a member on the Board of Directors. Let us show the florists of the United States that we mean business; that when we start to do a thing we do it right. If it is not possible to include S. A. F. membership in our dues, then do the next best thing. But we must wake up to the importance of the co-operative organization. Remember, there is good to be derived for you personally.

Trade Exhibits.

It is certainly gratifying to note the very excellent display we have for our second convention. It shows that the wholesale concerns over the country realize that Texas is a great market; and are interested in us, and are willing to contribute toward helping to make this convention a success. I believe every member should show his appreciation by reciprocating when in need along these lines. Always keep your eyes on the concerns that show a tendency to help our organization— we can help them in return. I ask that a vote of thanks be extended to every concern who has contributed to this convention in the way of exhibits.

The Possibilities of an All-Southern Organization.

Before my trip to attend the meeting of the Board of Directors of the S. A. F. at Chicago, March 1, past—I made a pretty thorough canvass of the South, to sound out the florists on the advisability of an all-Southern organization. The florists throughout the South are in favor of such an organization as soon as business conditions are improved. I believe that in the course of a few years the time will be ripe. When we strike we want to make sure of success—just as our Texas organization has done. Until that time we await developments.

Conclusion.

However, I am not here to take up too much time. I think, perhaps, I have talked already as long as I should. I am not sure but what I am in the position of the fellow of whom I heard this story: "Bill had been courting Sally for some time. One evening under the influence of the moonlight, during a stroll in the park, Bill proposed to Sally, and she accepted him. They walked on for some time, nothing further being said on the part of either one; and Sally becoming a little alarmed said, 'Bill, why don't you talk some more?' Bill said, 'Well, Sally, I've been thinking maybe I talked too much already!'"

Now, let me thank you as a club, and individually, for your staunch allegiance to me as your president. When the great roll call comes and the hearts of all are known, you will find your names standing out as immortals on my heart. No vocabulary at my command can fully express to you my appreciation of your faith in me, and I want you to know that all you may credit me with doing has been done through your understanding and belief in me. No matter what may come between you and me in the future, you must know that your friendship, your organization of this club, and your spontaneous unanimous election of me as your president will be as a beacon light to me through all the years to come.

AMERICAN SWEET PEA SOCIETY.

The final schedule and program of the Seventh Annual Exhibition and Convention of the American Sweet Pea Society has been sent out by Secretary H. A. Bunyard, and copies of same may be had on application to Mr. Bunyard at 40 West 28th street, New York. As previously announced, the show will be held under the auspices of the Newport Horticultural Society and the Newport Garden Association at the Casino, Newport, R. I., on Thursday and Friday, July 15 and 16. Alexander McLellan is manager for the exhibition and the list of judges contains the names of twenty-four of the representative gardeners and florists of New York, New Jersey and New England States.

Section A contains thirteen special prizes for private gardeners; Section B ten for private gardeners and amateurs; Section C four for amateurs; Section D five society prizes for retail florists; Section E Mrs. Auchincloss' prizes for school children; Section F includes eight open and miscellaneous classes for medals and other trophies; Section G contains thirty-five special prizes offered by the Garden Association, Horticultural Society, Garden Club and others.

The program for the meeting of the American Sweet Pea Society is as follows:

FIRST DAY.

Thursday, July 15, 1915—3 P. M.

Address of welcome by Dr. Roderick Terry, President of the Newport Garden Association, and William MacKay, President of the Newport Horticultural Society.
President Morse's Address.
Secretary's Report.
Prof. A. C. Beal's report on Our Trial Grounds at Cornell University.
Treasurer's Report.
Nomination of officers for 1915-1916.
Invitation for the next meeting place.
Lecture: The Sweet Pea—By J. Harrison Dick, New York.
Election of officers.
Vote on the next meeting place.
Addresses and discussions.
Question box.

SECOND DAY.

Friday, July 16, 1915—2 P. M.

Unfinished business.
Lecture: "Sweet Peas for Amateurs"—By Geo. W. Kerr, Doylestown, Pa.

OYSTER BAY HORTICULTURAL SOCIETY.

The monthly meeting of the Oyster Bay (N. Y.), Horticultural Society was held on Wednesday, June 23rd. Fifty-eight vases of flowers, five dishes of vegetables, three dishes of fruit were on the exhibition tables. The judges reported as follows: Society's prize for roses, Jas. Duckham; peas, Frank Petroccia; strawberries, Arthur Patten. Howard C. Smith prize for sweet peas, 1st, Jas. Duthie; 2nd, Jas. Duckham. James Duthie prize for sweet peas, 1st, Frank Kyle; 2nd, C. E. Moyses. Honorable mention for climbing roses by John Sorosick, orchids by Jno. Ingram, iris, by John Ingram, and delphinium by Frank Kyle.

H. Gibson made a very interesting report on the visit of a delegation of gardeners, from Oyster Bay, to the Ward estate at New Rochelle. Mr. Woolson and Mr. Duthie gave humorous talks. It was decided to hold the annual outing in August. notice of time and place to appear in notice of next meeting.

CLEVELAND FLORISTS' CLUB.

Secretary Frank A. Friedley has sent out the following notice to the club members:

July meeting of the Florists' Club postponed from Monday, July 5th, to Monday, July 12th. Full announcement of the Annual Picnic will be made at that time.

Remember at the last meeting of the Club it was decided that all who participate in the Ball Game must be members of the Club. Foot races and all other sports open to all.

This letter is being mailed to all florists in Cleveland. If you are not now a member of the Cleveland Florists' Club you owe it to yourself and your business to join. We now have 133 live, active members. The dues are $1.00 per quarter. Send in your name and belong to the livest, most up-to-the-minute Florists' Club in the country.

We expect during the next few months to receive lots of advertising and publicity for our Big Flower Show through the trade papers:
The American Florist.
The Florists' Exchange.
The Florists' Review.
Horticulture.

Each of the above are $1.00 per year. The more we support them, the more they will advertise and support us. Perhaps you have had in mind to subscribe to another trade paper but always put it off. DO IT NOW! Send direct to the paper or papers you want or mark the ones you want on this list, return to the secretary with a one dollar bill for each paper and he will gladly get the paper for you. Boss, get a trade paper for some of your employees. It will pay you to do it. This is not an advertising scheme of the above papers. They know nothing of it. The Florists' Club wants each of these papers to have more subscribers in this vicinity than they have at present. Send your dollar NOW.

Thanks, Mr. Secretary.

NEW BEDFORD HORTICULTURAL SOCIETY.

That the annual rose show of the New Bedford Horticultural Society was a great success is beyond dispute. While this was primarily a rose show many vases of perennials enlivened the tables. The magnificent and imposing hybrid perpetuals were, for the most part, conspicuous by their absence, yet the dainty beauty of the hybrid teas and climbers, in varied array, made one forget their more stately brothers, and many were the demands upon the committee for advice in selection.

Among the features of the exhibit were the grand display of perennials from the Galen Stone place, the beautiful collection of teas and hybrid teas, most tastefully arranged, from the Converse estate, a fine display of Silver Moon and Dr. Van Fleet by A. J. Fish, a specimen specimen of Frau Karl Druschki by Mrs. Horatio Hathaway, a vase of Silver Moon, Dr. Van Fleet and Ruby Queen which won first prize for the best vase, basket or other display, and a perfectly superb specimen of the hybrid tea rose, Mabel Drew, winner of 1st for best specimen of rose introduced in this country since 1911.

Miss Alice Stackpole's exhibit which covered one entire table had many fine blooms tastefully arranged.

W. F. Turner.

LADIES SOCIETY OF AMERICAN FLORISTS.

Will correspondents of florists' papers, please omit using above society name in relation to private or local clubs. There is only one Ladies' S. A. F. As yet no member in California has been authorized to transact any business for this Society.

Mrs. Chas H. Maynard, Sec'y.

To Incorporate Boddington Business.

At a meeting of the creditors of A. T. Boddington, held July 1st, it was unanimously resolved to incorporate. The statement of the business transacted during the past four months was sufficiently favorable to warrant these gentlemen in making The Arthur T. Boddington Company, Inc., a permanency under this new title. This incorporation will be without prejudice to the claims of the creditors. In fact it was adopted for the purpose of safeguarding their interests.

The value of imports of horticultural merchandise into New York for the week ending June 26, is given as follows: Sulphate of potash, $12,500; nitrate of soda, $50,320; clover seed, $22,223; grass seed, $14,853; trees and plants, $676.

A CORRECTION.

Referring to our notes on the Sweet Pea exhibition held in San Francisco recently A. C. Zvolanek writes as follows:

It is correct that I have received the gold medal of honor, awarded to my winter-flowering orchid sweet peas which are planted and grown on the Exposition Garden, prior to the A. S. P. Show, by the superior jury of the Panama-Pacific Exposition and not, as you state from the A. S. P. Society. My sweet pea exhibit with the A. S. P. Show was non-competitive.

VISITORS' REGISTER.

Cincinnati—Mr. and Mrs. Carl Baum, Knoxville, Tenn.

Philadelphia—John J. Perry, manager for Pennock-Meehan Co., Baltimore, Md.

San Francisco—Howard M. Earl, Philadelphia, Pa.; Malcolm MacRorie, South Orange, N. J.

Cleveland—H. C. Geiger of the Florex Gardens, North Wales, Pa.; J. Muller, representing Julius Roehrs Co., Rutherford, N. J.

Washington—I. Rosnosky, representing H. F. Michell Co., Phila.; H. J. Ware, of Maltus & Ware, New York, N. Y.; Morris M. Cohen, of New York.

Boston—David Fairchild, Dept. of Agriculture, Washington, D. C.; H. Huebner, Groton, Mass.; J. J. Lane, representing Doubleday Page & Co., New York City.

Chicago—C. B. Knickman, repre-

senting McHutchison & Co., New York; Mrs. W. S. Evans of the La Salle Flower Shop, La Salle, Ill.; J. R. Cowgill, Canton, Ohio; Fred Marquard, Valparaiso, Ind.; Murray Sands, Jackson, Tenn.; Frank A. Volz of Joseph Volz & Son, Cincinnati, O.; W. J. Becker, Logansport, Ind.; H. Mauchett, Sioux City, Ia.

PERSONAL.

Louis Wax, of the Flower Shop Greenhouses, North Attleboro, Mass., and Miss Bertha Jordan of Philadelphia, were married last week.

M. H. Norton, Boston's veteran florist, celebrated his birthday anniversary on July 8. Looking hearty and fit he might lop ten years off his admitted age and never be suspected.

James Ritchie and Miss Viola Hathaway were married in St. George's Church, Newport, R. I., on Wednesday evening, June 30. Mr. Ritchie is the younger son of Mr. and Mrs. Stewart Ritchie and has been engaged for years with his father and brother, in the florist business.

NEWS NOTES.

Minneapolis, Minn.—Mr. Wast has purchased W. C. Drake's greenhouses at 3004 Fourth avenue.

Callicoon, N. Y.—The nursery business of Chas. G. Curtis, of Callicoon, N. Y., will, dating from July 1, be known as the Chas. G. Curtis Company. Mr. Curtis has for the past 14 years conducted a very successful business in collecting and growing native plants and trees, making a specialty of Rhododendron maximum. The business has been increasing very rapidly for several years past. The

new member of the firm is Miss Elizabeth Metzger, of Callicoon, N. Y. Miss Metzger is thoroughly acquainted with the business, she having been in Mr. Curtis' office for several years. The purpose of the new company is to enlarge the business. As soon as completed, the new company will occupy a large building now being erected, with yard and packing shed. The capital of the company is $10,000.

Of Interest to Retail Florists

HOW TO TREAT YOUR COMPETITORS.

Houston, Texas, has in her midst a florist who is "the very pink of courtesy", judging from the following contribution turned in by H. H. Kuhlmann, Jr., for the edification of the Texas State Florists at their convention in Houston.

Mr. President and Gentlemen:

"We all know that competition is success to all business, no matter what kind it is, so the policy that I find best is this:—forget that you have a competitor, forget that he exists. Don't go around and talk about him as you will be the one to suffer in the long run. If at any time you have anything to say about him speak good and forget his faults.

If at any time your customer comes in and you are out of the article she desires don't tell her that there is not any more in town; tell her that he has it and let her go to your competitor and she will come to you next time. When you meet him in company treat him as one of your best friends. If he insists on being treated in any other way, well just take him to your club and buy him a good drink and cigars."

We do not recall having ever met Mr. Kuhlmann, but we can imagine that he is such a man as Byron had in mind when he wrote

"Tho' modest, on his unembarrass'd brow Nature had written—'Gentleman.'"

BETWEEN NEW YORK AND BOSTON.

Many of our readers will no doubt have occasion to make the trip between New York and Boston this summer. To all who have not already given it a trial we would say most emphatically "All-the-Way-by-Water" is the ideal way. The great express passenger steamships, the white fliers Massachusetts and Bunker Hill, leave Pier 18, foot of Murray street, New York, every day, Sundays included, at 5 P. M. From Boston they leave India Wharf every evening at the same hour. Due at either destination at 8 A. M. This is a delightful experience, a sail through the entire length of Long Island Sound and the open Atlantic from Vineyard Sound around Cape Cod and up Massachusetts Bay. There is no comfort or luxury of travel that the Eastern Steamship Company does not provide for its patrons on this trip and its popularity is so pronounced that it becomes very essential to engage state room accommodations a few days in advance to make sure of same. Orlando H. Taylor, formerly Passenger Agent of the Fall River Line during the days of the greatest popularity of that route, is Passenger Traffic Manager of the outside line and counts among the New York and Boston florists many of his staunchest friends.

Sterling, Ill.—Robert Lundstrom has purchased the Sterling Flower Shop, formerly conducted by Harry Bent.

Exhibit of Products of the Yokohama Nursery Co.

FALL FLOWER SHOW.
Panama-Pacific International Exposition, October 21-26

The flowers, which have contributed so largely to the great beauty and wonder of the Panama-Pacific International Exposition will have another festival of their own this fall, supplementing the several shows that have proven so attractive during the life of the Exposition. The Fall Flower Show is scheduled to last from October 21 to October 26, and will take place at the Palace of Horticulture in the Exposition Grounds under the auspices of the Pacific Coast Horticultural Society in conjunction with the Department of Horticulture, P. P. I. E.

The Prizes

Special prizes for chrysanthemums in a contest open to all will include the Chrysanthemum Society of America's silver cup, Hitchings & Co.'s silver cup, The Wells-Totty prizes, the Henry A. Dreer prize, the A. N. Pierson Inc. prize, the Elmer D. Smith & Co. prize, the National Association of Gardeners' prize, the H. F. Michell Co.'s prize, the H. W. Buckbee silver cup and the Society of American Florists' and Ornamental Horticulturists' medals.

In Class A competition there will be 24 medals and money. Class B will be open to non-commercial growers only. Class C will be devoted to chrysanthemum plants; prizes, a silver cup, a medal or a money prize. Class D, cut flowers, will include displays of roses, carnations, lilies of the valley, lilies, herbaceous perennials, annuals, dahlias and begonias. Class E will be devoted to orchids, palms, stove and greenhouse plants, ferns, hanging baskets and miniature gardens. Class F, for non-commercial growers, will be devoted to orchids. Class C, vegetables. Class H, special features such as contests, table decorations, baskets of flowering and foliage plants and flowers; original floral design, corsage, bridal and bridesmaid's bouquet, artistic basket of cut flowers.

Those in charge of the show will be H. Plath, manager; John R. Fotheringham, assistant manager; T. Taylor, secretary. The exhibition committee includes Daniel McRorie, T. Taylor, F. Pelicano, E. James, Angelo J. Rossi, D.

Raymond, W. A. Houghof, Donald McLaren, Wm. Kettlewell, Wm. Munroe, John R. Fotheringham, P. Ellings and M. Poss. For full particulars and application blanks write H. Plath, 210 Lawrence Avenue, San Francisco.

ALL UP FOR CLEVELAND NEXT NOVEMBER.

The floor plan of The Cleveland Flower Show indicating the space set aside for trade exhibits in the big Flower Show, November 10-14, 1915, has just been mailed to prospective exhibitors and a copy forwarded to this office. The plan is a very simple one and no doubt will develop into a well arranged show, both for the trade exhibitors and the growers who participate in the competitive class of floral exhibits. The space is all on one floor and there are no balconies, with the result that every location is a good one and prices are figured to include the sign for the exhibitor, his partition railings and general decorations above the space.

This will be a good opportunity for firms desiring to come before private and commercial growers of northern Ohio and Southern Michigan as well as throughout the East. We see no reason why the Cleveland Show will not come up to the expectations of the live Cleveland organizations that are backing it.

The show committee of the Cleveland Florists' Club has been conducting a lively campaign with a result that we understand their guarantee fund is over-subscribed about $1,500. They raised $7,500 although they only set out to secure $6,000. The Cleveland Florists are plainly working together in backing a movement that is for the good of all and we wish them success. The total guarantee fund is $12,000 and it is entirely subscribed, or rather oversubscribed, as the Ohio

Horticultural Society has already put up half of that amount, $6,000. The Cleveland Florists' Club and the Cleveland Garden Club are co-operating in forwarding this enterprise which will be held in conjunction with the annual meeting and exhibition of the Chrysanthemum Society of America. George Bate is chairman of the publicity committee, 356 Leader Building, Cleveland, O.

BOSTON TO SAN FRANCISCO.

President Patrick Welch and Mrs. Welch together with as many of the New England people as choose to accompany them to San Francisco and return, starting from Boston on Aug. 4, at 10 A. M. and arriving back in Boston on September 2, visiting the many points of interest on the transcontinental routes going and coming and in various parts of California. Mr. Welch will be pleased to communicate full information as to details to any one requesting same. The cost of transportation for the round trip will be $104.20; lower berth Boston to San Francisco, and Los Angeles back to Boston $37.

BOSTON SWEET PEA EXHIBITION.

The annual Sweet Pea Exhibition of the Massachusetts Horticultural Society will be held at Horticultural Hall, Boston, on Saturday and Sunday, July 10 and 11. In addition to sweet peas there will be displays of other seasonable flowers, as well as of fruits and vegetables. There will be also collections of native wild flowers.

The exhibition is free and will be open Saturday from 12 to 6 and Sunday from 2 to 6 o'clock.

       Wm. P. Rich, Secretary.

C₀ny at the Panama-Pacific International Exposition.

TWO REPRESENTATIVE CARNA-TION GROWERS.

Frank P. Putnam of North Tewksbury, Mass., is one of the carnation growers who believe in early planting. His plants are all in the benches already, 26,000 of them all told, in two big houses. He keeps his young stock in pots from April till middle of June, when he throws out all his old plants and starts anew. He is very enthusiastic over Matchless of which he has two 200 ft. benches and this variety looks ideal with him. Gloriosa, Beacon, White Wonder and Pink Delight constitute the bulk of the other varieties he grows. Mr. Putnam is fond of the single early chrysanthemum of which he grows about seventy-five varieties, many of them of his own production. It may be recalled that he made a sensational exhibit of these at the Boston show last fall. A fine crop of tomatoes occupies part of one large house for the time being. These will be thrown out August 1.

At Billerica we find in Gustav Thommen, who manages the Backer place, a staunch advocate of the other method of carnation growing. Mr. Thommen says he sees nothing to gain by very early planting. His young stock is out in the field and sturdy stock it surely is. The science and practice of plant feeding is one of Mr. Thommen's hobbies and he has got it down to perfection. No finer houses of carnations could be seen anywhere at any time of the year than are in evidence at this place now in mid-July. The market price of carnations is away down, but at the lowest figure quotable there's a little fortune in sight in the myriads of tall-stemmed, sturdy blooms that here greet the eye and charm the heart of the admirer of fine carnations. It would indeed take an iron nerved man to tear up and throw away such stock.

HOW TO GROW CARNATIONS IN SOUTHEAST TEXAS.

A Paper read by Elizabeth O. Weissinger before the Texas State Florists' Association.

Carnation culture is a comprehensive subject—bounded by an infinite diversity of opinion. But, seven years ago when we took our courage in both hands, lacking capital and experience, and handicapped by "skirts," the ultimatum had gone forth that carnations could not be successfully or profitably grown in Southeast Texas. Nothing daunted, we built a house especially for carnations, 150x28x16, running north and south with roof and side ventilation; raised benches five feet wide, steam heated. We get field-grown plants from Oklahoma—hence we do not have to worry about our stock, and always get the best.

This season we planted white, light pink and rose Enchantress, also Herald. For our compost we use three or four parts good maiden loam to one of well decomposed stable fertilizer, which has been prepared at least three months in advance, before putting in benches which have been thoroughly scrubbed and whitewashed. We order plants for September delivery and plant directly to benches, twelve inches apart, and give a good watering to settle the soil about the roots.

We find many details about carnation growing that require constant attention and unremitting care. Spraying is most important during the warm days we have in the early fall. By this means the temperature can be reduced to a moist growing atmosphere. We frequently spray the under part of the foliage where the red spider makes its appearance, and always spray quickly.

We give our plants strong wire support, and though they may wilt a little during the day, as long as they are erect and crisp each morning, we do not worry over losing them. The way the soil is handled has a great deal to do with what you get out of it. Judicious use of fertilizer and lime, with constant forking to keep in good mechanical condition, and the "seeing eye" that appraises instantly of lurking danger.

The Beaumont Floral Co., owned and managed by women, represents faithful toil and the achievement possible to even unskilled women in "the man-made world."

"Who digs a well or plants a seed, a sacred pact he keeps with sun and sod; with these he helps refresh and feed the world, and enters partnership with God."

A QUESTION OF JUDGING.

Editor HORTICULTURE:

At the Pennsylvania Horticultural Society's recent meeting a premium was offered for "The Best Display of Hardy Perennials 12 distinct species (not varieties)." The winning exhibit was made up of twelve vases, among which were one vase of Dianthus barbatus and one of Dianthus Caryophyllus.

The question I want to ask through the columns of your valuable paper is—should the two varieties of Dianthus have disqualified this exhibit? In this same exhibit Centaurea Cyanus was shown. Do you consider that a perennial?

Yours Truly,
WM. ROBERTSON.

Jenkintown, Pa.

Dianthus barbatus and D. Caryophyllus are both perennials and distinct species, hence both are eligible in the class referred to. Centaurea cyanus is an annual and its presence as one of twelve perennials would be cause for disqualification.—Ed.

NEWS ITEMS FROM EVERYWHERE

CHICAGO.

The annual meeting of the stockholders of the Chicago Flower Growers' Association took place July 7.

If there are any number of florists going to the convention this year, they are very loth to make that fact known.

Miss C. Paradise, for many years bookkeeper for A. L. Vaughan Co., is spending two weeks at her old home in Michigan.

The failure of Paul Palos of Little Rock, Arkansas, has caused some stir in the wholesale market where his name is found on the books of several firms. He has written his creditors here that everything outstanding will be paid.

No one seems able to understand the ups and downs of flowers in public favor. Last year the colored nymphæas were among the most popular flowers, while this year they are meeting with slow sale. Quite possibly they may regain their prestige later in the season when anything suggestive of water will naturally find more favor.

At Wietor Bros., the carnation space will be reduced five houses to make room for more roses next year. The summer schedule of shipments went into effect at this house today and all stock will arrive in one lot. N. Wietor is rejoicing in the fact that his small son who has been ill with scarlet fever is now home from the hospital, and gaining strength daily.

Hoerber Bros. have given up the growing of carnations and their range of 200,000 square feet of glass, at Des Plaines, Ill., now houses only roses. Among the stock will be 10,000 Mrs. Russell plants to supply that rose to meet the popular demand. Hoosier Beauty and Ophelia will also be planted largely and there will be a good supply of Mrs. Ward. The abandoning of carnations by growers seems to be gaining ground and marks a change in the commercial lip of the "divine flowers."

Aloise Frey, remembered by his many friends as a former superintendent of Lincoln Park, is now making a success of his favorite work of adding improved varieties of flowers to the market supply. Just now his antirrhinums are among the finest offered here. They are cut from seedlings of his own hybridizing. His love of experimenting with new plants does not limit his success in other lines, as his carnations are just now bringing the highest prices in the salesroom of one of the largest houses in this market.

Chas. McKellar finds but little difference in the amount of business done in June as compared with that of former years. His reports of the Panama Exposition, which he visited in March, are of particular interest to his friends in the trade at this time, as they are now trying to decide the question of going to the convention. Mr. McKellar is enthusiastic in his descriptions of the trip and advises everyone to go who possibly can. He was greatly pleased with the horticultural part of the exhibit and had a good word for the hearty welcome Vice-President McRorie would be sure to extend to Chicago florists.

Sweet peas, two bunches for five cents, carnations two dozen for fifteen cents and roses seven cents a dozen, offered on State St. being a hard problem to the retail florist this summer. Some of the stuff is not worth even the price asked, but again stock is sold that is as good as the retail florist can buy. That he cannot use the amount that a large department store can handle is his misfortune and neither can he afford to sell at the small profit made by them, but the retail florist must live and keep up store expenses during the summer months. It has never been quite so hard for the retailer as it is just now for the buyers of the big stores are trying to outdo each other in sensational offerings.

WASHINGTON, D. C.

Mrs. J. A. Phillips, who operates the Flower Shop, at 14th and Harvard Sts., stands a good chance of visiting the Panama-Pacific Exposition at the expense of the management of a motion picture theatre. The company offers the trip to the lady selected by its patrons as being the most popular in the neighborhood and the energetic work of her friends in obtaining votes has placed her already second on the list of contestants.

Washington florists will participate in two outings during the month, the first of these being one given under the auspices of the Florists' Club at Great Falls, Va., on July 21, the second one being a week later at Chesapeake Beach, given by Kalllipolis Grotto. This latter is to be a triple affair as the florists of Baltimore are also to be invited and a large gathering from that city is expected. Edward S. Schmid and Fred H. Kramer are planning an unusual number of stunts. An effort is to be made to match the florists of the two cities in a baseball game.

A sentence of five years in the penitentiary was last week imposed upon Felipe Guasp, a former employee of the Leo Niessen Company, who was arrested and pleaded guilty to the charge of forgery, but because he has a wife and three small children, upon his promise to keep out of trouble in the future, he was placed on probation. Guasp, after being discharged, had sent a telegram to the Philadelphia office of the firm ordering a large amount of stock. A slip-up in the wording led to the discovery that it was fraudulent and suspicion was fastened on Guasp who was then arrested.

Spokane, Wash.

—Preparations are in progress for a fall flower show to be held the first week in September under the auspices of the Spokane Horticultural Society. Arrangements have been made for the use of the Armory for the show, and much interest is being shown in the event.

PITTSBURGH.

Mr. and Mrs. Karl Klinke, the former secretary of the McCallum Company, will leave next Monday to spend two weeks at Burleigh Falls, Ontario.

Murray McGrew, of G. P. Weaklin & Company, and family expects to leave next Saturday for a visit on the shore of Lake Erie in Northern Ohio.

To conform to the raising of downtown Penn avenue, the floor of Mrs. E. A. Williams' store is being likewise raised two feet. This will preclude the trouble of former years in case of a twenty-five foot flood stage.

J. W. Rhea, credit man for the E. C. Ludwig Company, will leave on Monday next to represent his firm at a business convention in Wheeling, W. Va. Louis R. Biehl, of the same company, and family will leave next Saturday for a two weeks' vacation at Niagara Falls and Canada.

The Japanese Flower Shop show window has been transformed into a charming summer scene through the introduction of an aquatic pool designed by the owner, Ray J. Daschbach. Nymphaeas and other water plants, live ducks and a rocky waterfall add to the picturesque effect.

To the A. W. Smith Company has been awarded the contract for the landscape work for the Schenley High School to begin in August. F. Russell Bower, the assistant landscape architect for the Smiths, is spending most of the summer in Ithaca, New York. Miss Elizabeth Boyd, and Miss Beckert of the store force are enjoying their vacations at home.

The marriage of Miss Loretta Grau, and Gilbert Ludwig, of the Ludwig Floral Company, was an informal home ceremony of last Thursday evening at the home of the bride's mother. The young couple left for a short Eastern trip. The bridegroom is the son of Mr. and Mrs. Julius W. Ludwig and the secretary of the firm, while the bride was for some time associated with the business office.

The family of William A. Clark of the Pittsburgh Cut Flower Company, have gone to their cottage on Lake Chautauqua, where they will be joined later by Mr. Clark. William Usinger and Joseph Gotti, employees of the Pittsburgh Cut Flower Company, left last Saturday night for a fortnight's tour of the Great Lakes, Cleveland, Sandusky and Detroit. William Colligan, will go to Mackinac, Michigan, early in August for his vacation.

In a recent statement, Dr. William M. Davidson, superintendent of schools, said that the school gardens introduced in the curriculum of the public schools on April 1st, 1914, to instruct and develop interest on the part of children in nature study work, had proved most satisfactory, both with regard to the instruction of the children and the garden products. John L. Randall is director of the School Garden and Nature Study Department.

AN UNIQUE AND ELEGANT FLOWER STORE.

View in the New Flower Store of Samuel Murray, Kansas City, Mo.

In the accompanying picture and in the one which appears as cover illustration for this issue we present views of the new flower store of Samuel Murray, Kansas City. Mr. Murray is known as one of the most progressive florists of this country and also a well-skilled plantsman. His success is due, first, to his industry, foresight and winning personality and secondly, to the skill and devotion of his assistants in the store and greenhouse. Miss Mary Hayden has been with him for sixteen years and Miss Elizabeth Hayden for nine years, and Mr. Murray generously credits these young ladies with the lion's share in the prestige which has come to the business as one of Kansas City's foremost commercial institutions. William Sharpe has been in charge of the greenhouses for the past 25 years, he and Mr. Murray having worked together in Peter Henderson's 30 years ago.

The new store depicted in our illustrations is one of the finest devoted to flower selling in this country. The lower walls are of rough yellow brick and the upper walls of weather beaten stone with full joints. The window is of dark olive green tile and "decorates" beautifully.

At the opening of the new place on June 2 a large number of floral and other tributes testified to the esteem in which Sam Murray is held by his fellow florists and employees. There was a resplendent bird cage with occupant, from the Misses Hayden; a gold horseshoe from Arnold Ringier; a magnificent bunch of American Beauties from George M. Kellogg Co.; a basket of roses from Arthur Newell; a basket of Killarney roses from T. J. Noll & Co.; one of lilies from

H. Kusick & Co.; horseshoe of American Beauties from W. J. Barnes & Sons; and two beautiful specimens of the new golden Sanseveria from R. S. Brown.

HORTICULTURE extends to Sam and his loyal retinue cordial good wishes for many years of prosperity and continued happiness in their new home.

BALTIMORE.

The gardeners of Baltimore have been given an additional week of opportunities to consult the three experts from the Maryland Agricultural College on their garden problems. The continued requests for advice caused them to decide to devote an extra week to this city, making their headquarters at City Hall. Prof. Anspon declared that he has seen no army worms in this city, and no evidence of any. A report of the arrival of these pests caused an examination of a large lawn which they were supposed to have attacked but none were found.

Members of the Gardeners' and Florists' Club of Baltimore will make a tour by automobile of all of the city's parks on Monday afternoon, July 12. An invitation has been extended to Mayor Preston and members of the Park Board to accompany the florists. Resolutions were adopted extending thanks to Mayor Preston for having the specialists from the Maryland Agricultural College come and assist in ridding Baltimore gardens of insect pests and diseases, and otherwise aiding in the culture of plants and flowers.

CINCINNATI.

The Cincinnati Florists' Society's annual meeting will be held on Monday, July 12, at Max Rudolph's. The annual election of officers will take place.

The annual outing of the Society will be held at Coney Island on Wednesday, July 21. Tickets may be had at any of the wholesale houses.

The Cincinnati Cut Flower Exchange were the first in the market with asters, this summer. They were from Chas. F. Hoffmeister's place at Fort Thomas, Ky.

WHOLESALE FLOWER MARKETS — TRADE PRICES—Per 100 TO DEALERS ONLY

Roses	CINCINNATI July 5		CHICAGO July 5		BUFFALO July 5		PITTSBURG July 5	
Am. Beauty, Special	..... to	25.00	15.00 to	30.00	20.00 to	25.00	15.00 to	20.00
" " Fancy and Extra	15.00 to	20.00	10.00 to	15.00	12.00 to	15.00	10.00 to	12.00
" " No. 1	6.00 to	10.00	3.00 to	10.00	6.00 to	10.00	6.00 to	8.00
Killarney, Richmond, Extra	4.00 to	6.00	4.00 to	5.00	5.00 to	7.00	6.00 to	8.00
" " Ordinary	2.00 to	3.00	2.00 to	3.00	2.00 to	4.00	4.00 to	4.00
Hillingdon, Ward, Sunburst, Extra	4.00 to	6.00	4.00 to	6.00	6.00 to	9.00	6.00 to	8.00
" " Ordinary	2.00 to	3.00	2.00 to	3.00	2.00 to	6.00	2.00 to	4.00
Arenberg, Radiance, Tah, Extra	4.00 to	6.00	..... to	......	6.00 to	8.00	6.00 to	8.00
" " Ordinary	2.00 to	4.00	..... to	......	2.00 to	6.00	2.00 to	4.00
Russell, Hadley, Ophelia, Mock	2.00 to	8.00	3.00 to	12.00	2.00 to	10.00	..... to	......
Carnations, Fancy	..... to	2.00	1.50 to	2.00	1.00 to	2.00	1.50 to	2.00
" Ordinary	..... to	1.00	.50 to	1.00	.75 to	1.00	..... to	1.00
Cattleyas	..... to	50.00	20.00 to	45.00	25.00 to	50.00	30.00 to	50.00
Dendrobium formosun	..... to	......	..... to	......	..... to	......	..... to	......
Lilies, Longiflorum	6.00 to	10.00	6.00 to	8.00	6.00 to	8.00	6.00 to	8.00
" Rubrum	4.00 to	8.00	..... to	......	3.00 to	5.00	..... to	......
Lily of the Valley	..... to	4.00	2.00 to	4.00	..... to	4.00	4.00 to	4.00
Daisies	.50 to	1.00	.25 to	.50	.50 to	1.00	1.00 to	2.00
Stocks	..... to	......	2.00 to	3.00	2.00 to	3.00	..... to	......
Snapdragon	2.00 to	4.00	2.00 to	3.00	3.00 to	5.00	..... to	......
Gladioli	3.00 to	6.00	2.00 to	6.00	4.00 to	5.00	2.00 to	6.00
Peonies	3.00 to	4.00	3.00 to	4.00	..... to	......	2.00 to	4.00
Sweet Peas	.35 to	.75	.25 to	.50	.15 to	.25	.10 to	.75
Gardenias	..... to	......	15.00 to	20.00	20.00 to	25.00	..... to	......
Adiantum	..... to	1.00	1.00 to	1.25	1.00 to	1.25	1.00 to	1.25
Smilax	..... to	12.50	10.00 to	12.00	..... to	15.00	10.00 to	15.00
Asparagus Plumosus, Strings (100)	..... to	50.00	40.00 to	50.00	40.00 to	50.00	35.00 to	50.00
" & Spren. (100 bchs.)	..... to	25.00	25.00 to	35.00	..... to	35.00	35.00 to	35.00

Flower Market Reports

BOSTON The usual stagnation of business activity customary to the fourth of July week as the dead centre between the past and the new season is the condition which all have to face this week. As to which particular flower gets hit the hardest at this inevitable juncture, years vary. This year it is the carnation which suffers worst, and this is all the more to be regretted because the quality of the flowers offered is so very good. However, there is a bit of light ahead for the summer resort florists are beginning to show up and a few orders have been placed already. So all eyes are turned toward the rising sun of the new day and, however disappointing the one just gone may have been, yet we realize it might have been worse. Look forward now, not back.

BUFFALO The market was rather dull the past week, summer conditions prevailing. There are any amount of roses, carnations, lilies, peas and sales have to be forced. Floral work has been very light and weddings being about over therefore very little business is coming to the wholesalers.

CHICAGO Real summer to a florist begins July 1st. This year is no exception. All the ear marks are to be seen except in the stock which is fresh and good. Customers were few after the two holidays, July 4th and 5th, and the cut of the two days was brought into a market almost devoid of buyers. The first days of the month had seen stock clean up fairly well though prices were made very low on large lots rather than consign them to the barrels, but after the 5th, business lagged sadly. The stock sold to the big department stores for their special sales, though it cleared the path of the wholesaler, curtailed the opportunity of the retailer to move even the scant amount his summer trade usually calls for. Peonies are still left in quantities in storage and the daily sales are not heavy, still few are lost. Carnations are remarkable for their substance and stiff stems and look more like the product of May than July. Roses are of every length and the stock is considered very good indeed for the season. Garden flowers are very much in evidence.

CINCINNATI Business taken as a whole is rather quiet. Some of the lines and the better grades of stock move fairly well but the market is not at all active. The offerings in the new roses are large and good. The supply of lilies is so large that the market is overloaded with them. Gladioli are in a good supply and sell fairly well. The first of the early asters came in the early part of this week. Other offerings include auratum and rubrum lilies, Water lilies, carnations, snapdragons and hardy hydrangea.

CLEVELAND Business this past week has been fair. Outside flowers arriving in large quantities. Peonies are about done and are now being used from storage and some of the florists claim they are not coming in very good shape. From all reports, there have been more peonies put in cold storage than ever before. A remarkable fact is the presence of peonies, gladioli, asters and dahlias on the market in quantities at the same time. Short Beauties and white roses have been less than the demand at times. Carnation plants suffered considerable from rains early in the season, but are coming along all right now.

NEW YORK As might be expected, the past week has been the dead low tide of the flower business in this city. There is no call for anything and nothing of a business nature to cause the faintest ripple on the apathy which has settled down over the wholesale district. Receipts of stock are much lighter as it does not pay to transport goods to a market which is not a market and so the labor of the wholesale people is materially lightened. No complaint can be found with the average quality of the material received, which is much better than we have been accustomed to see at this date. There is an abundance of really nice stock from which to fill orders if orders would only materialize. The situation is no different otherwise from other years. An upward movement may soon be looked for and even if slight it will be heartily welcomed.

Killarney, Richmond and Mrs.

PITTSBURGH Aaron Ward roses and Harrisii lilies are almost as of good quality as in winter, although naturally selling at low prices in order to meet the business demands. Other stocks are shortening up, but what is coming in is good. Carnations are still coming in fairly well and there are lots of outdoor sweet peas. The fine quality of this late stock is accounted for in the unusually cool, rainy weather, which, however, unfortunately promises anything but well for corn and grain.

(Continued on page 51)

WHOLESALE FLOWER MARKETS — TRADE PRICES—Per 100 TO DEALERS ONLY

	BOSTON July 5	ST. LOUIS July 4	PHILA. July 5
Roses			
Am. Beauty, Special	10.00 to 16.00	20.00 to 30.00	20.00 to 25.00
" " Fancy and Extras	6.00 to 8.00	10.00 to 15.00	12.50 to 15.00
" " No. 1	2.00 to 4.00	5.00 to 8.00	6.00 to 10.00
Killarney, Richmond, Extra	2.00 to 4.00	5.00 to 5.00	3.00 to 6.00
" " Ordinary	.50 to 1.00	2.00 to 3.00	1.00 to 3.00
Hillingdon, Ward, Sunburst, Extra	2.00 to 4.00	5.00 to 6.00	3.00 to 6.00
" " Ordinary	.50 to 1.00	3.00 to 4.00	1.00 to 2.00
Arenberg, Radiance, Taft, Extra	2.00 to 4.00	.... to	3.00 to 5.00
" " Ordinary	.50 to 1.00	.... to	1.00 to 2.00
Russell, Hadley, Ophelia, Mock	2.00 to 8.00	5.00 to 6.00	2.00 to 15.00
Carnations, Fancy	1.00 to 1.50	2.00 to 3.00	3.00 to 3.00
" Ordinary	.35 to .50	.75 to 1.00	.50 to 1.00
Cattleyas	10.00 to 15.00	40.00 to 40.00	20.00 to 40.00
Dendrobium formosum	.... to	40.00 to 50.00	40.00 to 50.00
Lilies, Longiflorum	8.00 to 4.00	4.00 to 5.00	10.00 to 12.00
Rubrum	.... to	.... to	.... to ....
Lily of the Valley	2.00 to 3.00	3.00 to 4.00	3.00 to 4.00
Daisies	.50 to 1.00	.30 to .50	.50 to .75
Stocks	1.00 to 1.50	4.00 to 5.00	1.00 to 2.00
Snapdragon	2.00 to 4.00	2.00 to 4.00	1.00 to 2.00
Gladioli	1.00 to 3.00	3.00 to 4.00	3.00 to 6.00
Peonies	.... to	.... to	.... to ....
Sweet Peas	.15 to .75	.25 to .50	.25 to .75
Gardenias	10.00 to 12.00	10.00 to 12.00	.... to ....
Adiantum	.50 to 1.00	1.00 to 1.75	.75 to 1.00
Smilax	10.00 to 12.00	20.00 to 25.00	.... to 20.00
Asparagus Plumosus, Strings (100)	25.00 to 50.00	35.00 to 50.00	.... to 50.00
& Spren. (100 Bchs.)	25.00 to 35.00	15.00 to 20.00	20.00 to 50.00

Flower Market Reports

(Continued from page 40)

SAN FRANCISCO The nearest approach to an over-supply of flowers experienced in the local market in several months was felt the past week, and the situation was due more to increased product than to decreased demand. There was plenty of stock showing excellent quality; much ordinary stock, and a good many supplies below standard in quality, which made it difficult to maintain prices on medium stock, and next to impossible to clean up inferior offerings even at extremely low prices. Counter trade seems to be keeping up better than usual for this time of year. Carnations and sweet peas are both plentiful and cheap, and show a wide range in quality. Some very fine dahlias are appearing. The supply of gladioli continues to increase, much of the stock being rather ordinary. Hydrangeas are offered freely with a good demand. Among the new outdoor stock coming in late, in June was some very nice godetia and cockcombs, which were readily absorbed. The cut of roses is as large as it was, and the shipping demand keeps up well. Mildew is causing some trouble, but complaints are not very serious. The market is well supplied with orchids.

ST. LOUIS The remarkably cool weather has caused the stock coming to this market to be of the best quality and the consignments are very large every day. Roses and carnations are looking well but the big cuts can hardly be disposed of unless at very cheap prices which have prevailed in this market all the past week. The great gluts in this market at present are in sweet peas and gladioli. These are very heavy each day. Outdoor stock of these in all varieties is coming in by the thousands and is hard to dispose of at any price. Other outdoor flowers have little if any sale. Everything is cheap and business is dull.

WASHINGTON Stock is very plentiful and for the most part good but even the best moves but very slowly. It is the usual early July dullness. Outdoor sweet peas are replacing the greenhouse stock which is fast disappearing. A nice lot of Sylvia, Charles Bruton and Delice were brought in last week to open the dahlia season and these moved fairly well because of being newcomers. A few asters were also shown but these were not wanted. There has been an oversupply of Hydrangea arborescens which does not find the ready sale of a few years ago when their production was confined to a few growers. The season is about over for yellow daisies yet some are still to be had. Lilies are good, but they are in little demand. Gladioli are holding their own. There are plenty of good cattleyas but the demand is fluctuating. Out-of-town business continues good and daily shipments are made to all southern points.

Detroit, Mich.—The Schroeter-Stahelin Company have dissolved partnership and the business will be hereafter conducted in the name of Hugo Schroeter.

NEWPORT, R. I.

What Robert Burns had to say about the miscarriage of "the best laid plans of mice and men" would apply very aptly to the experiences of the sweet pea growers in Newport. Just as the plants had reached that stage where a resplendent crop of exhibition flowers seemed assured there came a week of fog—fog of the typical Newport brand, that "one could cut with a knife"—and when it was over every bud was gone on most varieties. We visited Wm. Robertson, William Gray, James Bond, J. Urquhart, William Mackaye and other bright stars of the horticultural firmament and all had the same hard experience. The consequent postponement of the big show may, however, prove advantageous for the Lenox and Bar Harbor growers, whose crop is naturally later than that of Newport, a fact which their Newport rivals generously comment upon with magnanimous satisfaction. We hope that everything will now conspire to produce a record exhibition, but skillful and clever as the gardeners are they all have to submit to that final dictator—the weather. The rose garden in the Gov. Beekman place under the care of John Urquhart was a sight, however, which more than atoned for the denuded sweet peas. At this place we saw something of a novelty, gardenias thriving and blooming luxuriantly in cold frames.

The Newport retail florists—T. J. Gibson, Leikens, Bunyard, Gibson Bros., Armstrong, Wadley & Smythe and Schults—all except the first-named ranged along Bellevue avenue—are looking wistfully ahead to the coming two months, hoping for a prosperous season and a share of that money which in ordinary times would presumably be squandered in Europe, but not daring to make any rosy predictions. What beautiful roses they produce in that moist Newport climate! We saw some garden-grown Brunners in Gibson's that would charm the heart of the most exacting rose lover. Just now the delphiniums, Spanish irises, foxgloves and calceolarias are the main decorative features of the avenue show windows. Glorious beyond words was the Bunyard display of golden iris flanked by great vases of blue larkspur and indeed, the displays by all the above mentioned places were most attractive and artistic.

SAN FRANCISCO NOTES

F. C. Jaeger, of the Fairmont Floral Co., is spending a vacation in the southern part of the state.

Mrs. Yoch, landscape architect, of Los Angeles, Cal., is in San Francisco to study the landscaping of the Exposition.

Daniel MacRorie, of the MacRorie-McLaren Co., is entertaining his father, Malcome MacRorie, of New Jersey, who is here to attend the Exposition.

Mrs. Steele, of Steele's Pansy Gardens, Portland, Ore., is visiting the Exposition, the pansy beds of which are of particular interest to her as the plants were supplied by her firm.

At the next meeting of the local horticultural society the question of a florists' picnic this month or next will come up for discussion. The subject has been agitated in the trade and sentiment seems to favor an outing.

A new flower shop is being opened at 1846 Fillmore street under the name of the Motroni Art Floral Co. Mr. Motroni has just returned from Sacramento, Cal., where he has been since disposing of his business at Fillmore and Washington streets some months ago. He is having his new place nicely fitted up.

In anticipation of an increased demand for chrysanthemums on account of the Exposition, growers supplying this market have planted a larger acreage than in former years. The United Flower & Supply Co. expects to handle the output of between twenty-five and thirty acres, which is nearly twice the amount planted by the same growers last season. An early cut is in sight as buds are appearing three weeks ahead of the normal development.

NEW YORK QUOTATIONS PER 100.　To Dealers Only

MISCELLANEOUS	Last Half of Week ending July 3 1915	First Half of Week beginning July 5 1915
Cattleyas	8.00 to 25.00	8.00 to 20.00
Lilies, Longiflorum	1.00 to 3.00	1.00 to 3.00
Rubrum	1.00 to 2.00	1.00 to 2.00
Lily of the Valley	.75 to 2.00	1.00 to 2.00
Daisies	.50 to 1.00	.50 to 1.00
Stocks	..... to 1.00	..... to 1.00
Snapdragon	.50 to 1.00	.50 to 1.00
Gladioli	1.00 to 4.00	1.00 to 4.00
Peonies	.75 to 1.50	1.00 to 2.00
Sweet Peas	.25 to .75	.25 to .75
Corn Flower	..... to 1.00	..... to 1.00
Gardenias	8.00 to 12.00	8.00 to 12.00
Adiantum	.50 to .75	.50 to .75
Smilax	6.00 to 15.00	6.00 to 15.00
Asparagus Plumosus, sprigs (per 100)	15.00 to 35.00	15.00 to 35.00
" & Spren (100 bunches)	10.00 to 20.00	10.00 to 20.00

Buyer's Directory and Ready Reference Guide

Advertisements under this head, one cent a word.　Initials count as words.

Display advertisers in this issue are also listed under this classification without charge. Reference to List of Advertisers will indicate the respective pages.

Buyers failing to find what they want in this list will confer a favor by writing us and we will try to put them in communication with reliable dealers.

ACCOUNTANT

R. J. Dysart, 40 State St., Boston.
For page see List of Advertisers.

APHINE

Aphine Mfg. Co., Madison, N. J.
For page see List of Advertisers.

APHIS PUNK

Nicotine Mfg. Co., St. Louis, Mo.
For page see List of Advertisers.

ARAUCARIAS

Godfrey Aschmann, Philadelphia, Pa.

ASPARAGUS

Asparagus Plumosus—2¼-in., extra strong, $3.00 per 100; $22.50 per 1000. Seedlings, from greenhouse-grown seed, ready July 1st, $1.00 per 100; $5.00 per 1000. COLLINGDALE GREENHOUSES, Collingdale, Pa.

ASPARAGUS PLUMOSUS NANUS.

5,000 strong 3 and 4 in. pots ready for benching. 4 in. pots at $8.00 per 100, $75.00 per 1,000; 3 in. pots at $5.00 per 100, $50.00 per 1,000; 2¼ in. pots at $3.00 per 100, $22.50 per 1,000. MIAMI FLORAL CO., Dayton, Ohio.

ASPARAGUS SPRENGERI.

8,000 good 3 and 4 in. plants ready for benching. 4 in. pots at $8.00 per 100, $75.00 per 1,000; 3 in. pots at $5.00 per 100, $50.00 per 1,000; 2¼ in. pots at $3.00 per 100, $22.50 per 1,000. MIAMI FLORAL CO., Dayton, Ohio.

AUCTION SALES

Elliott Auction Co., New York City.
For page see List of Advertisers.

AZALEAS

P. Ouwerkerk, Hoboken, N. J.
For page see List of Advertisers.

BAY TREES

August Rolker & Sons, New York.
For page see List of Advertisers.

BAY TREES—Standard and Pyramids. All sizes. Price List on demand. JULIUS ROEHRS CO., Rutherford, N. J.

BEDDING PLANTS

A N. Pierson, Inc., Cromwell, Conn.
For page see List of Advertisers.

R. Vincent, Jr. & Sons Co., White Marsh, Md.
For page see List of Advertisers.

Wood Bros., Fishkill, N. Y.
For page see List of Advertisers.

BEGONIAS

Julius Roehrs Company, Rutherford, N. J.
For page see List of Advertisers.

Thomas Roland, Nahant, Mass.
For page see List of Advertisers.

A. M. Davenport, Watertown, Mass.
For page see List of Advertisers.

Begonia Lorraine, $12.00 per 100, $110.00 per 1,000; Begonia Glory of Cincinnati, $15.00 per 100, $140.00 per 1,000. JULIUS ROEHRS CO., Rutherford, N. J.

BOILERS

Kroeschell Bros. Co., Chicago.
For page see List of Advertisers.

King Construction Co., North Tonawanda, N. Y.
"King Ideal" Boiler.
For page see List of Advertisers.

Lord & Burnham Co., New York City.

Hitchings & Co., New York City.
For page see List of Advertisers.

BOXES—CUT FLOWER FOLDING

Edwards Folding Box Co., Philadelphia.
For page see List of Advertisers.

Folding cut flower boxes, the best made. Write for list. HOLTON & HUNKEL CO., Milwaukee, Wis.

BOX TREES

BOX TREES—Standards, Pyramids and Bush. In various sizes. Price List on demand. JULIUS ROEHRS CO., Rutherford, N. J.

BULBS AND TUBERS

J. M. Thorburn & Co., New York City.
For page see List of Advertisers.

Ralph M. Ward & Co., New York City.
Lily Bulbs.
For page see List of Advertisers.

John Lewis Childs, Flowerfield, L. I., N. Y.
For page see List of Advertisers.

August Rolker & Sons, New York City.
Holland and Japan Bulbs.
For page see List of Advertisers.

R. & J. Farquhar & Co., Boston, Mass.
For page see List of Advertisers.

S. S. Skidelsky & Co., Philadelphia, Pa.
For page see List of Advertisers.

Chas. Schwake & Co., New York City.
Horticultural Importers and Exporters.
For page see List of Advertisers.

A. Henderson & Co., Chicago, Ill.
For page see List of Advertisers.

Burnett Bros., 98 Chambers St., New York.
For page see List of Advertisers.

Henry F. Michell Co., Philadelphia, Pa.
For page see List of Advertisers.

Roman J. Irwin, New York City.
Hardy Lilies.
For page see List of Advertisers.

Fottler, Fiske, Rawson Co., Boston, Mass.
Summer Flowering Bulbs.
For page see List of Advertisers.

GREAT REDUCTION IN PRICES Of HOLLAND BULBS of all kinds. Send for Price List. THOMAS COGGER, 229 Laurel St., Melrose, Mass.

C. KEUR & SONS, HILLEGOM, Holland. Bulbs of all descriptions. Write for prices. NEW YORK Branch, 8-10 Bridge St.

CAMELLIAS

Julius Roehrs Co., Rutherford, N. J.
For page see List of Advertisers.

CANNAS

R. Vincent, Jr. & Sons Co., White Marsh, Md.
For page see List of Advertisers.

Wood Bros., Fishkill, N. Y.

Canna Specialists.
Send for Canna book.
THE CONARD & JONES COMPANY,
West Grove, Pa.

CARNATIONS.

F. Dorner & Sons Co., Lafayette, Ind.
For page see List of Advertisers.

Wood Bros., Fishkill, N. Y.
For page see List of Advertisers.

Leo Niessen Co., Philadelphia, Pa.
Field Grown Carnation Plants.
For page see List of Advertisers.

CARNATIONS—Continued

250,000 Field-Grown Carnation Plants. Grown in Soil Especially Suited for Carnations.
Quality Guaranteed to Please You.
July and Later Delivery.
Order Early.

PINK—	100	1000
Mrs. C. Edward Akehurst	$12.00	$100.00
Pink Sensation	12.00	100.00
Good Cheer	12.00	100.00
Alice	12.00	100.00
Enchantress Supreme	8.00	70.00
Peerless Pink	8.00	70.00
Gorgeous	8.50	70.00
Pink Delight	7.50	65.00
Philadelphia	8.00	70.00
Gloriosa	7.00	60.00
Mrs. C. W. Ward	7.00	55.00
Northport	7.00	55.00
Enchantress	7.00	55.00
Rose-pink Enchantress	7.50	60.00
Dorothy Gordon	7.00	55.00
Rosette	7.50	60.00
Winona	7.00	55.00
Winsor	7.00	55.00
VARIEGATED—		
Benora	8.00	70.00
RED—		
Champion	8.00	75.00
Princess Dagmar	8.00	70.00
Beacon	7.50	60.00
Comfort	6.00	45.00
The Herald	8.00	75.00
Pocahontas	8.00	70.00
St. Nicholas	8.00	70.00
Harlowarden	7.00	55.00
Victory	7.00	55.00
Eureka	7.00	55.00
Bonfire	7.50	65.00
WHITE—		
Matchless	8.00	70.00
White Wonder	7.50	60.00
White Enchantress	7.00	55.00
White Perfection	7.00	55.00
Alma Ward	7.00	55.00
YELLOW—		
Yellow Prince	8.00	70.00
Yellowstone	8.00	70.00

Write for complete price list of bedding and greenhouse plants.
S. S. PENNOCK-MEEHAN CO.,
1608-1620 Ludlow St.,　Philadelphia, Pa.

CARNATION STAPLES

Split carnations quickly, easily and cheaply mended. Pillsbury's Carnation Staple, 1000 for 35c.; 3000 for $1.00 post paid. I. L. PILLSBURY, Galesburg, Ill.

Superne Carnation Staples, for repairing split carnations, 35c. per 1000; 3000 for $1.00. F. W. WAITE, 85 Belmont Ave., Springfield, Mass.

CHRYSANTHEMUMS

Poehlmann Bros. Co., Morton Grove, Ill.
For page see List of Advertisers.

Wood Bros., Fishkill, N. Y.
Chrysanthemums Rooted Cuttings.
For page see List of Advertisers.

Chas. H. Totty, Madison, N. J.
For page see List of Advertisers.

R. Vincent, Jr., & Sons Co., White Marsh, Md.
Pompon Chrysanthemums.
For page see List of Advertisers.

Major Bonnaffon, Pacific Supreme, Alice Byron, Golden Glow, Chrysolora, rooted cuttings. $15.00 per 1,000; out of 2-in. pots, $20.00 per 1,000. SHEPARD'S GARDEN CARNATION CO., Lowell, Mass.

THE BEST 1915 NOVELTIES.
The Cream of 1914 Introductions.
The most popular Commercial and Exhibition kinds; also complete line of Pompons, Singles and Anemones. Trade list on application. ELMER D. SMITH & CO., Adrian, Mich.

For List of Advertisers See Page 31

In writing to Advertisers kindly mention Horticulture

For List of Advertisers See Page 31

SWEET PEA SEED

W. Atlee Burpee & Co., Philadelphia, Pa.
Winter Flowering Sweet Pea Yarrawa.

Ant. C. Zvolanek, Lompoc, Calif.
Gold Medal of Honor Winter Orchid Sweet
Peas.
For page see List of Advertisers.

S. Bryson Ayres Co.,
Sunnyslope, Independence, Mo.
For page see List of Advertisers.

THE ANGLE LAMP

Globe Gas Light Co., Boston, Mass.

VEGETABLE PLANTS

Celery plants, Golden Self blanching
(French Strain), Giant Pascal, White
Plume and Winter Queen, fine plants,
ready for field, $2.00 per 1000; $1.50 in
10,000 lots cash. BRILL CELERY GAR-
DENS, Kalamazoo, Mich.

CELERY PLANTS.

White Plume, Boston Market, Giant Pascal, Golden Self-blanching, $3.00 per 1000.
BRECK-ROBINSON NURSERY CO., Lexington, Mass.

VENTILATING APPARATUS

The Advance Co., Richmond, Ind.
For page see List of Advertisers.

The John A. Evans Co., Richmond, Ind.
For page see List of Advertisers.

VERMICIDES

Aphine Mfg. Co., Madison, N. J.
For page see List of Advertisers.

VINCAS

F. R. Pierson Co., Tarrytown, N. Y.
For page see List of Advertisers.

WEED DESTROYER

Pino-Lyptol Chemical Co., New York City.
For page see List of Advertisers.

WIRED TOOTHPICKS

W. J. Cowee, Berlin, N. Y.
For page see List of Advertisers.

WIREWORK

Reed & Keller, New York City.
For page see List of Advertisers.

WILLIAM E. HEILSCHER'S WIRE
WORKS, 264 Randolph St., Detroit, Mich.

WHOLESALE FLORISTS

Albany, N. Y.

Albany Cut Flower Exchange, Albany, N. Y.
For page see List of Advertisers.

Baltimore

The S. S. Pennock-Meehan Co., Franklin
and St. Paul Sts.
For page see List of Advertisers.

Boston

N. F. McCarthy & Co., 112 Arch St. and
31 Otis St.
For page see List of Advertisers.

Welch Bros. Co., 226 Devonshire St.
For page see List of Advertisers.

Patrick Welch, 262 Devonshire St., Boston,
Mass.
For page see List of Advertisers.

Brooklyn

Wm. H. Kuebler, 28 Willoughby St.
For page see List of Advertisers.

Buffalo, N. Y.

William F. Kasting Co., 383-87 Ellicott St.
For page see List of Advertisers.

Chicago

Poehlmann Bros. Co., Morton Grove, Ill.
For page see List of Advertisers.

Cincinnati

C. E. Critchell, 34-36 Third Ave., East.
For page see List of Advertisers.

WHOLESALE FLORISTS—Continued

Detroit

Michigan Cut Flower Exchange, 38 and 46
Broadway.
For page see List of Advertisers.

New York

H. E. Froment, 148 W. 28th St.
For page see List of Advertisers.

James McManus, 105 W. 28th St.
For page see List of Advertisers.

W. F. Sheridan, 133 W. 28th St.
For page see List of Advertisers.

P. J. Smith, 131 West 28th St., N. Y.
For page see List of Advertisers.

Moore, Hentz & Nash, 55 and 57 W. 26th St.
For page see List of Advertisers.

Charles Millang, 55 and 57 West 26th St.
For page see List of Advertisers.

W. P. Ford, New York
For page see List of Advertisers.

The S. S. Pennock-Meehan Co., 117 West
28th St.
For page see List of Advertisers.

Traendly & Schenck, 436 6th Ave., between
26th and 27th Sts.
For page see List of Advertisers.

Badgley, Riedel & Meyer, Inc., New York.
For page see List of Advertisers.

Woodrow & Marketos, 37 & 39 West 28th St.
For page see List of Advertisers.

George C. Siebrecht, 109 W. 28th St.
For page see List of Advertisers.

John Young & Co., 53 West 28th St.
For page see List of Advertisers.

M. C. Ford, 121 West 28th St.
For page see List of Advertisers.

Guttman & Reynor, Inc., 101 W. 28th St.,
New York.
For page see List of Advertisers.

Philadelphia

Leo, Niessen Co., 12th and Race Sts.
For page see List of Advertisers.

Edward Reid, 1619-21 Ranstead St.
For page see List of Advertisers.

The S. S. Pennock-Meehan Co., 1608-20
Ludlow St.
For page see List of Advertisers.

Stuart H. Miller, 1617 Ranstead St.
For page see List of Advertisers.

Richmond, Ind.

E. G. Hill Co.
For page see List of Advertisers.

Rochester, N. Y.

George B. Hart, 24 Stone St.
For page see List of Advertisers.

Washington

The S. S. Pennock-Meehan Co., 1216 H St.,
N. W.
For page see List of Advertisers.

THE NUT-GROWER

The unique monthly publication which furnishes reliable
and interesting up-to-date information regarding the value
of pecans and other edible nuts
and how to grow them for profit.

Subscription, $1.00 per year

Sample Copy Free

THE NUT-GROWER
WAYCROSS, GA.

In writing to Advertisers kindly mention Horticulture

Coming Events

SHOWS.

Newport, R. I., July 8-9.—Annual show and meeting of American Sweet Pea Society, in connection with Newport Garden Assoc. and Newport Hort. Soc.

Boston, Mass., July 10-11.—Sweet Pea exhibition of the Massachusetts Horticultural Society, Horticultural Hall.

Greenwich, Conn.. July 18-19.—Westchester and Fairfield Horticultural Society, summer show.

Winnetka, Ill., July 22.—Summer exhibition of Lake Shore Hort. Society.

Lenox, Mass.. July 27-28.—Summer exhibition of Lenox Horticultural Society.

Newport. R. I., Aug. 12, 13, 14.—Mid-summer exhibition of Newport Garden Club and Newport Horticultural Society.

Cleveland, O.. Aug. 13-14.—Gladiolus Society of Ohio exhibition.

Newport, R. I.. Aug. 18-19.—Fifth annual exhibition of the American Gladiolus Society.

Atlantic City, N. J., Aug. 26-29.—American Gladiolus Society exhibition.

Lewiston, Me., Aug. 27-28.—Fall exhibition in Lewiston City Hall of Lewiston and Auburn Gardeners' Union. Chas. S. Allen, President, Auburn, Me.; Mrs. Geo. A. Whitney, Secretary, 161 Winter St., Auburn, Me. Meetings first Friday in each month.

Rochester, N. Y., Aug. 30 to Sept. 11.—Rochester Exposition and Flower Show.

Hartford, Conn., Sept. 22-23.—Annual Dahlia exhibition of the Connecticut Horticultural Society, Unity Hall, Pratt St. Alfred Dixon, Sec.. Wethersfield.

Orange, N. J., Oct. 4.—Tenth Annual Dahlia, Fruit, Gladioli and Vegetable Show of N. J. Floricultural Society. Geo. W. Strange, Sec., 84 Jackson St.

Oyster Bay, L. I., N. Y., Oct. 5-6.—Dahlia Show of the Oyster Bay Hort. Society. Chrysanthemum Show, Nov. 2. Andrew R. Kennedy, Westbury, L. I., secretary.

Glen Cove, L. I., Oct. 7.—Dahlia Show of Nassau Co. Hort. Soc. Fall Show of Nassau Co. Hort. Soc., Oct. 28 and 29.

Poughkeepsie, N. Y., Oct. 28-29.—Annual flower show of Duchess County Horticultural Society. N. Harold Cottam, Sec., Wappingers Falls.

New York, N. Y., Nov. 3, 4, 5.—Annual Chrysanthemum Show of the American Institute, Engineering Societies Building.

Tarrytown, N. Y., Nov. 3-4-5.—Chrysanthemum Show in the Music Hall.

New York, N. Y., Nov. 4-7.—Annual Autumn exhibition of Hort. Soc. of New York, Museum of Natural History.

Chicago, Ill., Nov. 9-11.—Fall Flower Show of the Chicago Florists' Club and Horticultural Society of Chicago, to be held in the Coliseum.

Cleveland, O., Nov. 10-14.—Annual show and meeting of Chrysanthemum Society of America. In conjunction with the Cleveland Flower Show. Chas. W. Johnson, Sec., 2226 Fairfax Ave., Morgan Park, Ill.

**Cleveland, O., Nov. 10-14. — Cleveland Flower Show. The only show of national scope in the United States this fall. F. A. Friedley, Sec.. 356 Leader Building.

MEETINGS.

Dobbs Ferry, N. Y., July 10.—Dobbs Ferry Horticultural Society, Odd Fellows' Hall. B. Harms, Sec.

New York. N. Y., July 10.—Horticultural Society of New York at American Museum of Natural History. Geo. V. Nash, Sec., N. Y. Botanical Garden, Bronx Park, New York.

Newark, N. J., July 11.—Wein, Obst A Gartenbau Verein. 15 Newark St. Peter Caille, Sec., 111 Avon Ave.

New Orleans, La., July 11.—Gardeners' Mutual Protective Association, 114 Exchange Alley. John Parr, Sec., 4539 North Rampart St.

Rochester, N. Y., July 12.—Rochester Florists' Association, 95 Main St., East. H. B. Stringer, Sec., 47 Stone St.

Baltimore, Md., July 12.—Gardeners' and Florists' Club of Baltimore, Florists' Exchange Hall. St. Paul and Franklin Sts. Noah F. Flitton, Sec. Gwynn Falls Park, Sta. F., Baltimore.

Cincinnati, O., July 12.—Cincinnati Florists' Society, Jabez Elliott Flower Market. Alex. Ostendarp, Sec.

Cleveland, O., July 13.—Cleveland Florists' Club, Hotel Hollenden, Club Room B. Frank Friedley, Sec.

Holyoke, Mass., July 13.—Holyoke and Northampton Florists' and Gardeners' Club, at O. D. Allyn's houses.

Newport, R. I., July 13.—Newport Horticultural Society, Music Hall. Wm. Gray, Sec., Bellevue Ave., Newport.

Chicago, Ill., July 14.—Gardeners' and Florists' Union No. 10615, 232 North Clark St. Louis Heldtman, Sec., 3610 N. Richmond St.

New York, N. Y., July 14.—Annual Outing of the New York Florists' Club at Witzel's Point View Grove.

New Orleans, La.. July 15.—New Orleans Horticultural Society, Association of Commerce Bldg. C. R. Panter, Sec., 2320 Calhoun St., New Orleans.

Toronto, Ont., July 20.—Gardeners' and Florists' of Ontario, St. George's Hall, Elm St. Geo. Douglass, Sec., 159 Merton St., Toronto.

Newark, N. J., July 20.—Essex County Florists' Club, Krueger Auditorium, 25 Belmont Ave. John Crossley, Sec., 37 Belleville Ave.

San Francisco, Cal., July 26-30.—California Fruit Growers' Convention, Stanford University, Palo Alto.

San Francisco, Cal., Aug. 12-14.—Pacific Coast and California Asso. of Nurserymen.

San Francisco, Cal., August 12-14.—California Ass'n of Nurserymen. Henry W. Kruckeberg, Sec.-Treas., 237 Franklin St., Los Angeles.

San Francisco, Cal.. Aug. 17-19.—Society of American Florists and Ornamental Horticulturists.

San Francisco, Cal., August 17-19.—American Rose Society, Auditorium, San Francisco. Benjamin Hammond, Sec., Beacon, N. Y.

San Francisco, Cal., August 17-19.—National Ass'n of Gardeners, Auditorium, San Francisco. M. C. Ebel, Sec., Madison, N. J.

San Francisco. Cal., Aug. 18.—American Association of Park Superintendents.

San Francisco, Cal., August 18-20.—American Ass'n of Park Superintendents, Auditorium, San Francisco. Roland W. Cotterill, Sec.-Treas., Seattle, Wash.

Twin Cities, St. Paul, Minn., Aug. 24-28.—Annual convention of the Association of American Cemetery Superintendents, Minneapolis and St. Paul. Secretary, Vellett Lawson, Jr., Supt. of Elm Root Cemetery, River Grove, Ill.

San Francisco, Cal., August 23-25.—American Pomological Society, Berkeley, Cal. R. R. Lake, Sec., 2033 Park Rd., N. W., Washington, D. C.

San Francisco, Cal.. Sept. 3-5.—American Pomological Society.

Hartford, Conn.. Sept. 10.—Regular meeting Conn. Horticultural Society, County Bldg., Trumbull St. Alfred Dixon, Sec., Wethersfield.

CLEVELAND NOTES.

Ed. George of Storrs & Harrison Co., Painesville, and Guy Bate, Cleveland Cut Flower Co., Newton Falls, O., were in town Thursday to attend a meeting of the premiums committee of the Cleveland Flower Show.

Al. Barber of Jones-Russell Co. is off on a fishing trip with Geo. Bate of the Cleveland Cut Flower Co., to the Portage Lakes. As they are both well known as professional fishermen, each having a record a little better than the other, their report of the "actual happenings" of the trip, promises to be interesting.

The Cleveland Florists' Club meeting date has been changed from July 5th to the 12th on account of the holiday celebrations. An interesting subject for discussion will be the plans for the annual picnic of the club to be held later in the month. Some important plans for the Cleveland Flower Show will also come up at this meeting.

H. B.

CARNATION SUPPORTS.

It is now full time to stock up on carnation supports. There are many kinds, some better than others. The several devices made by the Carnation Support Co. of Connersville, Ind., are popular and substantial. Better throw out those old twisted tangles that have done duty for so many successive seasons and treat your carnations to a new, clean set throughout, and you will be proud of your house every time you have a visitor.

MORTGAGES RECORDED.

Warwick, R. I.—Maplehurst Greenhouses, Inc., to Marguerite S. Cannon. lot and improvements, corner Hope and Longmeadow avenues, $5,000. Maplehurst Greenhouses, Inc., to Helen A. Sturdy, lot and improvements, northwest corner Hope and Longmeadow avenues, $5,000.

NEW CORPORATIONS.

Rochester, N. Y.—Home Planters' Supply Co., horticultural products; capital stock, $35,000. Incorporators, M. Edith Ricker, Frank L. Pearce and Reuben D. Luetchford.

Secretary E. K. Thomas, Kingston, R. I. has arranged for an excursion of the members of the Rhode Island Horticultural Society and friends to Newport on the occasion of the Sweet Pea Exhibition. Mt. Hope steamer leaves Dyer street wharf. Providence, at 9.20 A. M., Thursday, July 15.

Obituary

William A. White.

William A. White, formerly engaged in the florist business in Boston, died at his home in Milford, Mass., on July 1. He was in his 71st year.

Mrs. Katherine Wattenscheidt.

Suddenly on the 28th at Atlantic City, N. J., Katherine Wattenscheidt, nee Garrett. Mrs. Wattenscheidt was a daughter of Mrs. M. A. Garrett who conducts a flower store at 2636 Germantown Ave., Philadelphia. She was actively associated with her mother in running the business and was well known in the trade.

Edward McGrath.

Mr. McGrath conducted a flower store at 2307 Ridge avenue, Philadelphia, for the past dozen years and was a well known man and well thought of in the trade. He had been in failing health for about a year until the end came June 30. Interment was at Cathedral Cemetery. A widow and one son survive.

J. E. Felthousen.

J. E. Felthousen, for over forty years in the greenhouse business, died at his home in Schenectady, N. Y. on June 18, aged 70 years. Bedding

Second Hand Greenhouse Material

FOR SALE

VENTILATORS AND FIXTURES.
Glass 9x12, 16x24, 14x24.

ROSEMERE CONSERVATORIES
Centre St., DORCHESTER, MASS.

---

plants were Mr. Felthousen's specialty. He was industrious, upright and held in high esteem in his native town of Schenectady and by the florists of the country with whom he had dealings.

GREENHOUSES BUILDING OR CONTEMPLATED.

Richmond, Va.—Ira L. Anderson, one house.

Plymouth, Pa.—Wm. G. Neilson, house, 35 x 100.

Ridgewood, N. J.—A. Thurston's Sons, one house.

Oskaloosa, Ia.—T. A. Greeve, Moninger house, 30 x 80.

Washington, D. C.—Marine Corps Reservation, one house.

Tewksbury, Mass.—J. K. Chandler & Sons, house 42 x 250 ft.

Toledo, O. — Wisner, the Florist, Delaware street, rebuilding.

Sterling, Ill.—Clarence Peckham, Erie Greenhouses, house, 25 x 130.

Oak Park, Ill.—A. H. Schneider, four Moninger houses, each 34 x 150.

Springfield, Mass.—Benjamin F. James, 661 White street, additions.

Scranton, Pa.—Poinsard Bros remodelling; Thos. J. Arner, additions.

Columbus, O.—Munk Floral Co., King and Queen avenues, house 22x175.

PATENTS GRANTED.

1,142,869. Hand Weeder. Salvador Alunan, Jaro, Philippine Islands.

1,142,991. Plant Shield. Louis F. Suddick, De Sota, Mo.

Vol. XXII
No. 3
JULY 17
1915

HORTICULTURE

Echinops Ritro

Published Every Saturday at 147 Summer Street, Boston, Mass.
Subscription, $1.00

LIST OF ADVERTISERS

FOR BUYERS' DIRECTORY AND READY REFERENCE GUIDE
SEE PAGES 84, 85, 86, 87

NOTES ON CULTURE OF FLORISTS' STOCK

CONDUCTED BY

John J. M. Farrell

Questions by our readers in line with any of the topics presented on this page will be cordially received and promptly answered by Mr. Farrell. Such communications should invariably be addressed to the office of HORTICULTURE.
"If vain our toil, we ought to blame the culture, not the soil."—*Pope.*

Chrysanthemums

Plants set in the benches in May will have made a foot or so of growth and will produce a bud some time in July. This is called a "break." Very early planted stock may produce a first bud in June and a second one in July which is obviously too early to retain so that advice to take first or second crowns is not very explicit. All buds produced in August are crown buds and a crown bud, by the way, is always distinguished by the shoots that appear around it and which soon grow up and take all the strength away from the bud if they are not removed. The terminal bud, which does not appear till September or later, always has a cluster of smaller buds around it in place of the small shoots, and this bud being produced some four weeks later than the crown bud will not produce so large a flower or so deep a flower because it has had another growth to mature while the crown bud has been putting that same strength to producing petals in the future flower.

Lorraine Begonias

Don't overlook keeping the flowers and buds removed. Growth is what you want now and not flowers. If the plants are free from green fly, as good a way as any to keep them so is to apply weekly a light spraying of a nicotine solution. Examine the stock carefully and if at all potbound don't wait for a time to shift but do not shift unless you are positive that the plants are in need of it. The main thing is to use a porous soil. We are making use of loam and leaf mold mixed with about one-fifth of well rotted cow manure for the present shifting and this with plenty of drainage in the pots seems to suit the plants nicely. Shade just enough to keep the foliage from burning. Avoid careless watering.

Rambler Roses

Pot culture during summer is the best method for plants to be forced during the winter. Failures in forcing are usually traceable to neglect during summer.

Pot grown ramblers will now have made canes of considerable length. Do not allow these to lie over on the ground but tie them up securely. Only in this way can they be well ripened. This is particularly necessary with Dorothy Perkins and other pink varieties which are somewhat prostrate in their natural habit. Reduce the number of shoots to four or five on each plant. If the pot ramblers are still indoors get them outside at once. Plunge them to their brims. Use the hose freely and there is little likelihood of red spider getting a foothold.

Pruning Flowering Shrubs

The time to prune flowering shrubs with the exception of hydrangeas and one or two other unimportant species is just after the flowering period. All the spring bloomers flower from the shoots made the previous season while the late summer and autumn flowering sorts require new young shoots for blooming. The pruning of the first named consists of cutting out much of the older shoots but not all, which will cause fresh growth for the next year's blooming.

Start Freesia Bulbs

Freesia bulbs that were forced last year and had good attention in the way of drying off will make fine bulbs to plant now. To get freesias in flower by Christmas or the New Year plant them right away in flats or pans. Place them two or three inches apart each way in good new soil well drained. Fibrous loam three parts. cow manure and leaf mold one part each will suit nicely. Place them in a cool place or cellar until they begin to show through when they should be brought out to full light. Water moderately until the foliage is well developed.

Perennial Lupines and Larkspurs

Seeds of these stately and gorgeous perennials should be sown now without delay. Sow in a cold frame. Give them some shade and they will germinate much better. When large enough they can be transplanted into other frames where they will make fine growth by late fall.

Next week—Bulb Compost; Eucharis amazonica; Gardenias; Orchids; Poinsettias; Starting Hollyhocks.

RESTING GRAFTED ROSES.

Editor HORTICULTURE.

Kindly advise me through the HORTICULTURE how far to cut back grafted roses for a rest, that were planted out in greenhouse last July, and how long should I rest them to get the best results this winter.   N. H. C.

New York.

Generally speaking, any of the forcing roses now in commerce should be cut back to about 12 inches when being made ready to start up after a rest, the length of time that they have been dried off governing somewhat this point. Some growers prefer to dry off the Teas and Hybrid Teas for approximately two weeks, getting the soil thoroughly dried out and hardening the wood well, being careful, of course, not to allow the wood to shrivel. Such a long period of drying will permit of cutting back low, say 10 to 12 inches.

Another system of handling carried-over roses and one which is meeting with a great deal of favor is that of simply withholding the water gradually and bringing the wood on the plants to a firm state, then cutting the plants back to 15 or 18 inches and starting right on again without the long period of rest. About a week is all that is necessary.

From the writer's observation this has given most excellent results and is worthy of a trial. Less time is lost during the resting period and wherever this has been tried the plants have started along quickly and made as strong a growth as could ever be expected from the former method.
      R.

SOWING MIGNONETTE.

I note in your last issue that Mr. Farrell in his notes advises sowing mignonette, for winter blooming, at once. It is just one month too early for New Jersey; to get the best results I find the middle of August the best, as early sowing is inclined to make it weak.   H. A. M.

New Jersey.

HORTICULTURE

VOL. XXII   JULY 17, 1915   NO. 3

PUBLISHED WEEKLY BY
HORTICULTURE PUBLISHING CO.
147 Summer Street, Boston, Mass.
Telephone, Oxford 292.
WM. J. STEWART, Editor and Manager.

Entered as second-class matter December 8, 1904, at the Post Office
at Boston, Mass., under the Act of Congress of March 3, 1879.

CONTENTS

A dilemma The great flood of roses and other flowers which has recently overwhelmed all
the big flower markets from the Atlantic
to the Mississippi river has given the flower trade a
difficult situation to solve. Each community has gone
about it in its own way as usual, but everywhere the
question of price has been lost entirely in the great
proposition of how to distribute the huge accumulations
without allowing them to reach the waste barrels. Naturally, at such a time the retail florist finds much to ex-
asperate and incite him to vengeance. In the curbstone
fakir the push-cart pedler and the department store

bargain counter he sees only a menace and a nuisance.
But, after all, when we read of the throngs of people
standing in a line reaching half way across a big department store in Chicago, eager to take advantage of
a sale of roses advertised at seven cents a dozen, a new
train of thought is set in motion and we find ourselves
wondering whether this bit of enterprise really did any
injury to the business of the legitimate retail florist or
whether he would have profited in the least if all that
surplus which was unloaded at a few dollars a thousand
had been thrown into the dump instead.

The Dutch bulb outlook It is in the air that we are in for a
season of low prices on Dutch bulbs.
This is in accord with our prediction last
January when, basing our convictions on
the views expressed by parties well-in-
formed on the situation in Holland, we said that in all
probability the better classes of Dutch bulbs would be
offered this season at prices which had appertained to
the more ordinary kinds heretofore. We now understand that the Dutch bulb-growers' union has decided
to cut hyacinth prices about one-half. Whether this
will induce the more general purchasing and planting
of these bulbs by the general public remains to be seen,
but, at least, it should. The worst feature of such a
situation, which is admittedly caused by accumulations
resulting from the lack of European demand, is the
demoralization attendant upon the unloading on the
American market of large consignments to be sold for
whatever they will bring. We had a taste of that last
year and the large seed houses, which are the heaviest
buyers of these goods, knowing what is likely to happen,
can hardly be expected to take any great chances now,
much as they might wish to help their Holland friends
in their pitiable dilemma. As to the tulips, while no
serious break in prices is looked for, yet a much better
grade for the same price seems probable. Darwins have
taken such a jump in demand that we shall have to pay
full rates, undoubtedly, for the genuine article.

"A condition not a theory" We are pleased to be able to tell our
readers that Mr. Ruzicka will from now
on resume his regular weekly articles
on rose culture under glass. In the
very practical chapter which he contributes this week,
referring to the marketing of roses at the present time,
it will be noted that he says, "Cut roses that arrive in
the crowded markets now must be strictly first class or
the price that they will bring will not be a profitable
one for the grower." This statement would hold true
as applied to almost any season of the year under the
present advanced skill in rose culture, of which Mr.
Ruzicka himself is recognized as a conspicuous exponent. Defective roses of any variety are not wanted in
any of the wholesale markets even for the cheap trade.
"Strictly first class" does not necessarily mean special
or exhibition grade, however, nor does it demand stems
of extraordinary length but it does mean straight stems,
clean glossy foliage, and buds well formed and even
colored—all cut at the right stage of development and
without a blemish. Anything else is held in contempt,
even by the street fakirs, no matter in what grade it
may pass muster by reason of length of stem. The
rose grower who would make a success of it today must
give it his individual attention, likewise must the rose
seller stick close to his job. On being asked why he
did not invest in a range of rose houses, Patrick Welch,
Boston's pioneer wholesale dealer sagely replied, "I turn
them into money; that's enough for any man to try
to do."

ROSE GROWING UNDER GLASS

CONDUCTED BY

Arthur C. Ruzicka

Questions by our readers in line with any of the topics presented on this page will be cordially received and promptly answered by Mr. Ruzicka. Such communications should invariably be addressed to the office of HORTICULTURE.

Late Planting

With low prices all through the spring months many of the larger growers held on to their stock a little longer, thus making up the shrinkage in returns. Many smaller growers did the same, and the result is that there are a great number of greenhouses that have not yet been planted. This work should now be pushed along, for we have every promise of a wet, dark fall, as there has been no dry weather this summer so far. Our section at least has had more rain than needed. If the planting is put off much longer, and a dark fall should follow, the plants will not have a show to become established before winter comes along, and the result will be poor stock, and plenty of worry for the grower. Where old plants are to be run over, or planted again, this should especially be attended to at once, as these are likely to suffer more than the young plants. In the rush of work, however, do not neglect to clean out the benches well, and see that they are properly whitewashed with a little copper sulphate added to the lime. This will kill all the fungus spores that it touches, and will help do away with the many diseases that the rose is subject to. Clean out underneath the benches, making sure that all the old soil is removed and wheeled out of the house. When through planting, it is well to clean out once more, and then scatter a little fresh slacked dry lime under the benches. This will make a large number of insects seek healthier climate, if it does not kill them at once.

Mildew

Do not make the mistake so often made by growers, and let all your fires out too soon. The weather so far has been remarkably cool, and there were only a few nights that the houses did not need any heat. A little steam to take the chill off in the early morning when the temperature outside drops away down, will go a great way to prevent mildew. The houses should not be allowed to go below 64 deg. F. at any time now, as the warm days run the temperature in the daytime away up. If the houses are allowed to drop as low as 54 the difference between the day and night air is too great. The little coal and the little extra attention that the houses will need when steam is kept on will be well paid for in the long run. Cut roses that arrive in the crowded markets now must be strictly first class or the price that they will bring will not be a profitable one for the grower. Keep the fires on until they are not needed. Then paint a little sulphur on the pipes here and there, about every ten feet on one steam pipe, for every twenty feet of width. Thus a house forty feet wide will get two painted pipes, where one twenty feet wide will only get one. Should mildew appear here and there in spite of all precautions and care, dust a little sulphur over it at once, or spray with Fungine. Do not let it spread, but check it at once.

Icing the Shipping Boxes

This will not be necessary where the icebox can be kept cool enough, but where natural ice is used to keep the box cool, it is bound to run a shade warmer than is best, and it will be necessary to ice the stock as it is shipped to the market. In doing this make sure that the ice is placed so that none of the buds will come in contact with it, as it will take the color out of them where it does touch. Beauties are the easiest to handle, as they are mostly long stemmed, and the ice can be put at the bottom of the boxes where there is no danger of its coming into contact with the buds.

Lining Boxes

It does not pay to use too little paper in the boxes during the hot weather, for the roses inside are bound to suffer. We put paper in the boxes in winter to keep the roses warm, and in the summer we ought to use it to keep the roses cool. Paper is a very poor conductor of heat, and several sheets in the boxes will keep the sun's hot rays out as much as it will keep Jack Frost out in the winter. Use at least four thicknesses and where ice is used, use six.

Fumigation

Do not neglect this in the least. This applies especially to the young newly planted houses, which should be kept clear of all insects at all costs. With the cool nights it is a very simple matter. Make sure that the houses are below 72 when you fumigate. The plants must not be dry either, for they are liable to burn. In using stems, make sure that they do not burn with a flame, as that would make hot smoke, which would be very apt to be injurious to the plants. Arrange so, if possible, that the plants will be syringed the next day. This will do away with a great many more insects. Never use tobacco stems in old houses where roses are still cut for the market. The blooms would likely be ruined, and will have an awful odor for a time to say the least. If the weather is too warm to fumigate, spray with any of the insecticides advertised in Horticulture. We prefer to fumigate, as some men cannot be trusted to mix insecticides for spraying just so, and the result would be that they would either be too strong, or else so weak as to be worthless.

CLUBS AND SOCIETIES

TEXAS STATE FLORISTS' ASSOCIATION.

That the convention held in Fort Worth last week was a great success from every standpoint was attested by everyone who attended. By the hour of opening Tuesday morning most of the visitors had arrived. The Convention Hall had been placed in readiness by the local entertainment committee and those who had brought exhibits had everything in place. The meeting was called to order at 10 A. M. by Vice-President W. J. Baker. Geo. B. Gay, superintendent of Parks of Fort Worth, represented the mayor in welcoming the convention to Fort Worth, and the visitors were welcomed on behalf of the Fort Worth florists by L. J. Tackett. H. B. Beck, of Austin, responded to the addresses of welcome. Following these addresses and the reading of the communication from Mr. Patrick Welch, President of the Society of American Florists, Mr. Baker introduced the President Mr. R. C. Kerr, in the following language:

"It is my duty as chairman to introduce our president, a man we all know and love, the man, but for whom there would not have been any Texas Association, a man who has done more for this association than all of us—Mr. Kerr, who will now take the chair." After President Kerr had resumed the chair and delivered his address as published in our issue of last week, the regular program was taken up and several very valuable speeches were delivered.

It was very gratifying to all Texas florists who attended to have present quite a number of out-of-the-state florists and supply houses and from the way the exhibits brought by these gentlemen were visited and looked over it was very evident that these were not only appreciated but were very profitable to all in attendance. The firms represented by exhibits were: A. L. Randall Co., Chicago, Ill.; J. A. Peterson & Sons, Cincinnati, Ohio; H. Bayersdorfer & Co., Philadelphia, Pa.; The Sefton Mfg. Co., Chicago, Ill.; Weatherford Pottery Co., Weatherford, Texas; Paducah Pottery Co., Paducah, Ky.; Talbot Mfg. Co., Fort Worth, Texas; Foley Greenhouse Mfg. Co., Chicago, Ill.; Bassett & Washburn, Chicago, Ill.; Burlington Willow Ware Mfg. Co., Burlington, Iowa; Poehlmann Bros. Co., Chicago, Ill.; H. J. Condron, Dickinson, Texas; Bud & Farley, Denison, Texas; Hans Schroeder, Temple, Texas; E. E. Stone, Dickinson, Texas.

Before adjournment of the first morning session each one present was called upon to rise and introduce himself, giving his address and the nature of his business. Each of the firms represented by exhibits were also called upon to come forward and state the name of the firm they represented and to make any other remarks that they chose to make. This privilege was very highly appreciated by these gentlemen. The first morning session continued until one o'clock, at which time adjournment was had and the ladies proceeded to the Westbrook Hotel, where a well attended reception was given them by the local

ladies' committee. At three o'clock the entire delegation was carried on an automobile ride over the city and to the greenhouses of J. E. McAdams, Geo. Kennedy, L. Cowell, W. B. Green, Baker Bros., Co., and Drumm Seed & Floral Co. Refreshments were served by J. E. McAdams, Drumm Seed & Floral Co., and Baker Bros. Co. The visitors were entertained for the evening at Byars Opera House.

At the Wednesday morning session the appointing of committee, hearing of reports and election of officers were the principal business transacted. Reports from representatives of different florists' clubs in Texas showing that some very excellent work is being done were made.

T. J. Wolfe of the Flower Show Committee reported the results of the show in Houston last fall. This re-

R. C. KERR
Re-elected President Texas State Florists' Association.

port showed receipts amounting to $1,217.78, and expenditures amounting to $1,251.90. This report shows a deficit of $34.12, but, Mr. Wolfe stated that there was considerable expense that had to be incurred for this first show that would not be necessary any more. All paraphernalia used in the flower show is being preserved and of course, will not have to be purchased for the next. It was decided to have another flower show this year, and Houston was selected as the place.

Dallas was selected as the next meeting place for the association in 1916. The election of officers resulted as follows: R. C. Kerr, president, Houston; Henry Greve, vice-president, Dallas; L. J. Tackett, secretary-treasurer, Fort Worth; Louis Ceasche, press representative, Dallas; Fritz Hensell, educational director, College Station, Texas. Directors for three years, H. Kaden, Gainesville, F. C. Suchy, San Antonio, A. B. Brown, Dallas.

There was much valuable instructions on different subjects of very great importance during these sessions and much good will certainly be the result.

One of the most important incidents was the appearance of Mr. Ed. L. Ayers, Chief Inspector of Washington Nursery of the Texas State Department of Agriculture, who discussed the workings of the Nursery and Orchards law and the importance of properly enforcing this law. Mr. Ayers assured the members that he wished to co-operate with them and to assist them in every way that he could, and assist in eradicating any trouble that they may have with their plants at any time. After Mr. Ayer's address there was quite a bit of discussion of the workings of the Inspection law and it was decided to make an effort to have the law amended so that it may be more beneficial to the florists. There was a legislative committee appointed to look after this question and the following gentlemen were named on this committee: Edward Hall, chairman, Austin; Mr. E. W. Judge, Bird Forest, and E. E. Stone, Dickinson.

At three o'clock the convention adjourned and proceeded to Forest Park where a baseball game between the local florists and the visiting florists was played, the result being 6 to 3 in favor of the visitors. This ball game was very much enjoyed by reason of the fact that the players were all florists. Lineups were as follows: Visiting Team.—Phil Foley, capt.; Bird Forest, catcher; J. A. Peterson, 1st b.; Corley, 2d b.; R. C. Kerr, pitcher; Alf, Sr., s. s.; Frank McCabe, 3rd b.; Gorey, l. f.; Gordon, c. f.; Prueer, r. f. Home Team.—R. Dunn, catcher; J. E. McAdams, pitcher; W. J. Baker, 1st b.; Byers, 2d b.; Bale, 3d b.; C. Brazier, c. f.; L. Cunningham, l. f.; Papworth, r. f.

Philip Foley, of Chicago threw the first two balls. R. C. Kerr pitched for the visiting florists and displayed much skill in this particular game.

Immediately following the ball game the barbecue was had and every one did justice to the meal. This concluded the program for the convention and everyone went away expressing themselves as having enjoyed their visit to Ft. Worth very much. We are quite sure that we express the sentiments of all Ft. Worth florists when we state that we are very glad to have had the craft in Ft. Worth and hope that it will not be many years until Ft. Worth will be again selected as the place for holding the convention.

Address of Patrick Welch, President S. A. F., to the Texas State Florists' Association.

Gentlemen of the Convention:

I sincerely regret that I am unable to fulfil the promise which I made to your honorable president some time ago to be present and address you on the question of the greatest importance to all state and national horticultural and floricultural societies—that is, affiliation with the Society of American Florists and Ornamental Horticulturists. I believe thoroughly in local organizations in our profession, but my experience of 30 years of membership in the Society of American Florists and Ornamental Horticulturists convinces me that membership in these local organizations should also be supplemented by membership in the national organization. The state organization is limited in the scope of its usefulness, and at best can only accomplish limited results. The Massachusetts Horticultural Society, one of the oldest societies in our country, having been founded in 1829, has greatly encouraged and developed floriculture and horticulture in New England, and its example has been followed by many organizations all over the country, and yet many of its leading members are members of our national organization, and are continually testifying to the benefits derived from the national society. Our society with its national charter, its membership coming from nearly every state and territory of this great United States, knowing the advantages and realizing the deficiencies of their respective state organizations, makes a mighty gathering, whose interests and influence reflect the impressions of our profession all over the country. The objects of the Society of American Florists and Ornamental Horticulturists are "to advance the love of floriculture and horticulture in America; to promote and encourage the development of their industries; to classify their products; to hold meetings and exhibitions; and to co-operate with National and State governments and horticultural bodies in disseminating horticultural knowledge.

Membership. All persons interested in horticulture, professionally or amateur, and manufacturers of and dealers in horticultural supplies are eligible to membership individually, and on payment of $5, other things being satisfactory, may be admitted to membership. The annual dues thereafter are $3 a year, and any annual member in good standing may become a life member on the payment of $25 and be exempt from all future assessments."

This society has handled questions of tariff, transportation, shipments, nation-wide publicity for our business, national flower shows, and other questions, to the advantage of all, during recent years especially, and will continue to do so more effectively in the future. The society feels, however, that every florist and horticulturist should obtain membership, and we therefore solicit the aid, assistance and co-operation of this Texas State Florists' Association and of other organizations. In order to encourage membership in our national organization, and at the same time to insure representation on our national board of directors, it is now one of our by-laws that whenever one hundred members of any society have become members of our organization its president shall have a seat in our board of directors—thus, we feel, assuring co-operation.

The dangers to co-operation come from within, and not from without, and the co-operation movement is no weaker nor stronger than the intelligent determination of those who engage in it, therefore let us have in the national organization your assistance in bringing it about. As John Stewart Mills has said, "All advantages that a man may possess arise from the power of acting in combination with his fellows, and of accomplishing by the united effort of members what could not be accomplished by the individual effort of individuals."

I believe that you will carry home from this convention a practical conception of the difficulties which beset our business, and the reward that

awaits its solution, and I feel that we in the National Society can help in this solution. I extend to every member of the Texas State Florists' Association a most sincere invitation to enroll as a member of the Society of American Florists and Ornamental Horticulturists. We look to the great state of Texas to send us some of its giant intellect to help in this society, and I feel that we will not be disappointed. On behalf of the national organization I want to extend to you their greeting and wishes for a most happy and prosperous year.

AMERICAN ASSOCIATION OF PARK SUPERINTENDENTS.

The American Association of Park Superintendents extend an invitation to members of the allied Horticultural Societies to join their special-car parties for the Pacific Coast Tour.

Reservations may be made through the committee or Thos. Cook & Son, 245 Broadway, New York City, who will also supply all information concerning details.

The train will follow an itinerary covering the most interesting routes of travel during the early autumn season. Leaving New York on Saturday, August 7th and eastern cities, and going westward via Chicago, Minneapolis, Glacier National Park, the Puget Sound Region, and the famous "Shasta" route, San Francisco will be reached at 6.50 P. M. on Monday, August 16th.

After attending the respective conventions and visiting the Panama-Pacific Exposition, the party will leave on Tuesday, August 24th, for the return trip, making stops at Los Angeles, Pasadena, San Diego, Salt Lake City, Pueblo, Colorado Springs, Denver, Kansas City and St. Louis, arriving at Eastern Cities Monday, September 6th.

CINCINNATI FLORISTS' SOCIETY.

This society's annual meeting at Max Rudolph's place last Monday afternoon was well attended. Max Rudolph was elected president, C. E. Critchell, vice-president; Alex Ostendarp, secretary; J. Chas. Murphy, treasurer, and R. Witterstaetter, director. A relief committee consisting of Frank Deller, J. Chas. Murphy and Ray Murphy was appointed to solicit subscriptions to a relief fund to use in helping florists whose places were damaged by last Wednesday's storm and who need help on that account. The society subscribed a hundred dollars to this fund. After the meeting the members sat down to a luncheon as the guests of Mr. and Mrs. Rudolph.

Mr. Rudolph's greenhouse establishment was in good condition and the uniform excellence of the stock in the various houses showed the reason why he always cuts blooms of the highest grade.

The annual outing of the society will be held on Wednesday, July 21st, at Coney Island. The outing committee consisting of Max Rudolph, C. E. Critchell, Henry Scharz and Wm. Sunderman has arranged for the usual list of athletic contests and promise all who attend a royal good time.

AMERICAN SWEET PEA SOCIETY.

President Morse's Address — The Sweet Pea in California.

When I was elected President of the American Sweet Pea Society a year ago, I hoped that the members and friends throughout the Eastern States could be present with us for the regular annual convention. However, since Mr. Bunyard found it impossible to be present himself, and as it seems impossible to get a quorum of members present, we decided to have a separate meeting in conjunction with out exhibit.

On June 11th, this exhibit was held in the Palace of Horticulture at the Exposition and was a grand success. There were some thirty entries, representing amateurs, professional gardeners and seed growers. There were some twelve hundred vases displayed; in fact, nearly every new variety of Spencer was represented.. The Exposition officials recognized the day by sending their special commissioner, who presented me as President, with a bronze tablet in memory of the event and designated June 11th on all of their programs as "Sweet Pea Day." They also furnished Cassassa's band, one of the best in the city and composed of 40 pieces, and we had a beautiful concert in connection with the exhibition.

We had expected to have the flowers exhibited only one day, but so great was the demand for more time, that we allowed the exhibition to stand three days, Friday, Saturday and Sunday, and kept the room open until 10 o'clock at night, although the building is usually closed at 6 o'clock. It was impossible to estimate the number of visitors, but there were literally thousands upon thousands present and all seemed amazed at an exhibit of such beautiful and magnificent flowers. We allowed nothing to be displayed but sweet peas.

Although California grows fully 95 per cent of all the sweet pea seeds used in the world, flower shows and exhibitions are seldom given. Sweet peas first began to be grown for seed in about 1886, when there were only about seven varieties. The acreage has steadily increased until for the past five years there has been no less than 2000 acres planted for sweet pea seed alone and all in what is known as the coast valley, from San Francisco south to Los Angeles. It is safe to say that no less than one million pounds a year is the average yield of the California seed farms and these farms are represented by some ten or twelve large seed growers. A great many new varieties have been originated in California but as the growers are largely wholesale dealers only, the novelties are introduced by seed dealers in other parts of the country. While probably only half of the acreage is devoted to Spencer varieties, the other half is made up largely of Grandiflora named varieties and mixtures. These latter are still popular for large planters.

Sweet Pea seed in California is usually planted in December and January and the fields are in full bloom in June. Harvest begins about August 1st. A great deal of development work is still being done and the large seed farms operate very large areas of what they call "workshops" where selections made from crosses and hybrids are being tried out. A great deal of time is now being spent on the development of the early flowering or Christmas Spencer types. As these are very shy seeders they are not handled much as yet in a wholesale way. I estimate that fully 50 per cent of all the California crop goes to Great Britain; some 10 per cent goes to Germany and France and other European countries, and about 40 per cent is consumed at home.

My firm has quite an elaborate exhibition at the Exposition Grounds, where we are growing sweet peas on the Cordon system, or the British exhibition plan. These plants were started in pots in the fall; the ground was prepared in the fall and by disbudding and proper feeding we have been able to grow some enormous blossoms, quite equal to any I have ever seen in Great Britain. Needless to say they are creating a great deal of interest.

We are hoping that the exhibition given last month is but the beginning of an annual sweet pea exhibit, which will be held as one of the features of the American Sweet Pea Society and will be held under its auspices. All members of the Sweet Pea Society are cordially invited to visit the seed farms should they ever be in California during the blossoming period, which begins about May 15th, and ends July 1st.

My best wishes to the Society for a long and useful career.

PITTSBURGH FLORISTS' AND GARDENERS' CLUB.

The closing meeting for the summer season on July 6th at the Fort Pitt Hotel was a very pleasant little affair. There were not a great many present, as the vacation season is calling, but those who were present had much to enjoy.

T. Tyler, gardener for C. D. Armstrong, showed four pots of Cattleya Gaskelliana in profuse bloom. He also showed a flower of Vanda Batemanii which is very rarely seen in bloom. The judging committee awarded to the cattleyas a cultural certificate. P. S. Randolph & Sons, Verona, Pa., showed a collection of ferns. to one of which, a new one, Nephrolepis Verona. was awarded a first-class certificate, also for a new sport of Teddy, Jr. Thanks were given to President Neil McCallum for his display from West End Park and his interesting descriptive talk. He also gave a history of the Crimson Rambler rose.

Wm. E. Niece, of Grove City, Pa., spoke in regard to vegetable humus, a large deposit of which, several feet in thickness, had been discovered in the vicinity of Grove City, and which analysis had shown to be very unusually rich in nitrogen. He asked the privilege of sending each member a 100-lb. sack for testing purposes, which was gladly accepted. One of the younger members, P. S. Randolph, Jr., having taken to himself a charming wife in the last few months, called on the boys to share his happiness by partaking of a pleasant little spread. Everybody wished the young couple long life and happiness.

There will be no meeting in August.

H. P. JOSLIN, Secretary.

AMERICAN ROSE SOCIETY.

The American Rose Society at its annual meeting in Boston endorsed the Cleveland Flower Show as its representative for a rose show this fall. The committee selected to attend to this work was: Guy Bate, Chairman, Newton Falls, Ohio; L. L. Lamborn, Alliance, Ohio, and E. B. George, Painesville, Ohio. These gentlemen constitute an official committee to represent the American Rose Society in accordance with the above action. The report that comes back at the present time is—that the exhibition of roses from the middle West will be of the first order. The list of premiums for the exhibition is quite liberal also.

With this month of July the newly elected officers assume their places, viz.: president, S. S. Pennock, 1612 Ludlow St., Phila., Pa., succeeding Wallace R. Pierson of Cromwell. Conn.; vice-president, Louis J. Reuter, Westerly, R. I., succeeding Robert Pyle of West Grove, Pa. The hold-overs are the treasurer, Harry O. May, Summit, N. J., and secretary, Benj. Hammond, Beacon, N. Y. The executive committee for the ensuing year stands as follows: August F. Poehlmann, Morton Grove, Ill.; John H. Dunlop, Richmond Hill, Ontario; Robert Simpson, Clifton, N. J.; Eber Holmes, Montrose, Mass.; Wallace R. Pierson, Cromwell, Conn.; Robert Pyle, West Grove, Pa.

An executive committee meeting will be held at the office of President S. S. Pennock, 1612 Ludlow St., Phila., Pa., at 2 p. m., on July 20. At this meeting consideration will be given to the coming International Flower Show in Philadelphia, also to the affiliation of local societies and the test gardens.

Four different affiliated societies have had a set of medals for their June shows. The paid membership of the American Rose Society is twenty more than we had at this time last year.

BENJAMIN HAMMOND, Secretary.

AMERICAN GLADIOLUS SOCIETY.

The schedule for the Annual Show of the American Gladioli Society is being distributed and may be had free upon application to H. Youell, Secretary, 538 Cedar St., Syracuse, N. Y. Cash amounting to $650.00 is offered in prizes besides two gold medals, seven silver medals, four bronze medals, four silver cups, one cut glass vase. The Newport Horticultural Society offers $100.00 in special prizes to the growers of Rhode Island only. The exhibitions at Newport and Atlantic City will be the largest ever held. Space for trade exhibits is being rapidly taken. The Newport exhibition will be held on August 18 and 19.

LADIES' S. A. F.

Mrs. John Vallance, 81 Glen avenue, Oakland, Cal., has been appointed by Mrs. W. F. Gude, president, as chairman of the introduction committee for convention week at San Francisco, Cal., August 17-20. Also the board of directors, Mrs. M. W. Colen (Indiana), chairman, are recommending by a majority vote of letters sent to the secretary, that the present officers and board be retained for 1916.

MRS. CHAS. H. MAYNARD, Secy.

FLORISTS' CLUB OF WASHINGTON.

Plans were discussed at the meeting of the Florists' Club for the holding of what is expected will be the most successful outing in its history. This affair will be given on Wednesday, July 21, at Great Falls, Va., and special trains will leave from Georgetown, commencing at 2 P. M. The general committee in charge consists of O. A. C. Oehmler, chairman; George W. Hess, W. W. Kimmel, George C. Shaffer and William Marche. President George H. Cooke is chairman of the joke inspectors; George Shaffer, arrangements; Edward S. Schmid, prizes; J. Richards, refreshments; Harry Lewis, lost children; Fred H. Kramer, keeper of the zoo; William Ernest, chairman humepatocharox; William F. Gude. band leader (the band, however, is colored); W. W. Kimmel, badges; William Marche, transportation; Lloyd Jenkins. information; C. Milton Thomas, sports; Theodore Diedrich, dancing.

A short talk was given by Richard Vincent, Jr., on the use of flower boxes in the decoration of buildings. He also spoke of the proposed dahlia show to be held in New York City and suggested that those of the local florists growing these flowers make an exhibit at that time.

William F. Gude spoke on the coming convention of the S. A. F. and mapped out the course of travel for the benefit of those who may desire to go. He urged that all go who could possibly do so, telling of the many advantages offered by such a trip both with respect to pleasure and educational value.

The Club accepted the invitation of Edward S. Schmid to become his guest for the September meeting, at which time he will give his annual crab feast. The florists of Baltimore are also to be invited and Mr. Schmid stated that the entertainment features will be most elaborate. A buffet luncheon followed the business meeting.

CHICAGO FLORISTS' CLUB.

A banquet was an important part of the program at the Club meeting at the Bismark, July 8. It marked the welding together again of the two clubs, which until three years ago. when the Cook Co. Florists' Association was formed. had been one club. The business session was very brief, nearly every item being laid over till the next meeting. The usual speeches on such occasions were omitted and a splendid talk on salesmanship, by Harry Newman Tolles, was the chief event of the evening. following the banquet. Everyone enjoyed the talk and wished for more of the same kind. Before closing. each member was urged to bring one new member into the club.

The arrangements are nearing completion for the florists' annual picnic, which occurs Sunday, July 25, at Morton Grove, in St. Paul's Park. Trains leave the Union Station at 9.15 A. M. and 12.40. 2.05. 3.05 and 5.15 P. M. A committee will see that florists using the first two trains will have reduced rates. The usual games will be pulled off in the afternoon and prizes awarded.

ST. LOUIS FLORIST CLUB.

The July 8th meeting of the Florist Club was by far the most interesting and well attended meeting of the year. When President Bourdet called the meeting to order at 2 P. M. there were nearly fifty members present and all officers, including some who have not been present for some time. Chairman Rowe of the trustees reported that his committee had everything in readiness for the annual picnic to be held Thursday, July 22, at Remona Park. J. F. Ammann, chairman of the Carnation Society meeting, reported that he had arranged with the Planters Hotel for headquarters for the meeting and exhibition and that the dates were fixed for January 26-27, 1916, and with the assurance of all in the trade of their support the meeting will be a great success.

Joseph Houser, of Webster Grove, invited the members to hold their August meeting at his place, which was accepted. Letters of sympathy were ordered sent to the families of C. Bergestermann and E. Schray.

The nomination of officers resulted as follows: President, Jules Bourdet; vice-president, W. S. Wells, Dave Geddis and W. E. Rowe; secretary, J. J. Beneke and William Ossick; treasurer, William C. Smith and Joseph J. Windler; three-year trustee, W. W. Ohweiller, George H. Pring and W. E. Agle. The treasurer's report showed the club in splendid financial condition. The annual meeting takes place Thursday, August 12.

GARDENERS' AND FLORISTS' CLUB OF BALTIMORE.

A motion of the Gardeners' & Florists' Club of Baltimore, to thank the mayor for securing professors of landscape gardening and plant diseases from College Park, Maryland Agricultural College, to instruct city yard flower growers, was recently passed; also one thanking the Park Board for the beautiful condition of Druid Hill Park. The discussion finally led to a motion that the club make a tour of inspection of Baltimore's chain of parks. It was carried. Today, July 12, the trip was made, and the members turned out by the score. The line of autos was led by the City Park auto with the Park Board members. Richard Vincent, Jr. was early at the starting point with a great quantity of fine dahlias. Each auto was decorated and every occupant wore a dahlia. The following parks were visited: Wynans, Druid Hill, Gwynn's Falls. Carroll, Federal Hill, Fort McHenry, Patterson and Clifton. All these parks were found in magnificent condition. Mr. Hamilton, the new president of the club, is a real live wire and has enthused the members so that the meetings are better attended than heretofore.

WESTCHESTER AND FAIRFIELD HORTICULTURAL SOCIETY.

At the July meeting of this society a fine display was on the exhibition tables. A cultural certificate was awarded to Wm. Morrow for Eucharis amazonica. Honorable mention to O. A. Hunwick for Centaurea macrocephala; Robert Grunnert, for Spencer sweet peas; Joseph Tiernan, for hardy border carnations and Clarkia

elegans. The summer show committee reported a substantial sum realized from this exhibition. The fall show committee reported progress. The premium list of the fall show is considerably increased by the receipt of a number of very fine offers from friends of the society. The outing committee reported that the annual outing and games will be held at Edwards Rye Beach Inn, Rye Beach, N. Y. Games will start promptly at 10.30 A. M. A shore dinner will be served at 1 P. M. Those requiring dinner tickets will please notify Wm. J. Sealey, Byram Shore, Portchester, N. Y. Dinner tickets are $1.50 a person. Don't forget the date, August 11. The next meeting will be held August 13.

P. W. POPP.

AMERICAN CARNATION SOCIETY.

We are desirous of getting into communication with the parties named below. We will consider it a favor, if they will drop us a postal, giving present address. Would appreciate the same from anyone else who might know the present whereabouts of any of these parties. The addresses given are in most cases several years old and mail addressed to them has been returned.

A. E. Boyce, Wellesville, N. S.; A. R. Walker, Flint, Mich.; M. Winandy, Chicago, Ill.; J. Scott, West Newton, Mass.; Aug. Rahner, Villisca, Iowa; Otto Mailander, Niles Centre, Ill.; E. McConnell, Sharon, Pa.; W. L. Lewis, Marlboro, Mass.; S. Lenton, Piru City, Cal.; H. B. Knight, Jersey City, N. J.; Ingleside Nurseries, Alhambra, Cal.; C. J. Haettel, Redondo Beach, Cal.; C. M. Frick, Philadelphia, Pa.; E. J. Cloud, Avondale, Pa.; Thos. Carroll, Sutor, Mo.; Jas. Allen, Paterson, N. J.; W. C. Jennings, Philadelphia, Pa.; F. C. Harwood, Torquay, England; F. W. Gooding, Middlesex, England; A. Smith, London, England; W. J. Smith, London, England; G. West, Berkshire, England.

A. F. J. BAUR, Sec'y.

Indianapolis, Ind.

CHICAGO GRAND FLORAL FESTIVAL.

The fall flower show executive committee met at the city offices of Poehlmann Brothers Company, July 12. There were present A. Henderson, August Poehlmann, Arnold Ringier, George Asmus, E. A. Kanst, Edward Goldenstein, C. W. Johnson, W. J. Keimel, N. P. Miller, H. S. Wilkerson and M. Barker. The report of S. J. Vaubhan on poster was presented and full power was given this committee to proceed as may seem best in the matter of securing suitable design. Plans covering the trade space to be sold in the Coliseum and annex were discussed at length and arrangements made to issue diagram and regulations. Appropriations aggregating approximately one thousand dollars were made in the gardeners' classes and the preliminary premium list was ordered printed. Chicago Grand Floral Festival was settled upon as the official name of the exhibition.

M. BARKER.

The next meeting of the Albany Florists' Club will be held at Henkes Bros., Newtonville.

White Plains, N. Y.—The Gedney Farm Company has leased for a term of years to William H. Moon Company, nurserymen, of Morrisville, Pa., a tract of land adjoining the Gedney Farm Hotel.

BOSTON SWEET PEA SHOW.

The Sweet Pea Show of the Massachusetts Horticultural Society on July 10 and 11 could hardly be called a "sweet pea" show, for these particular flowers were in a minority, and had it not been for the exhibitors of hardy garden flowers the display would have been rather limited in extent. For this condition the weather was wholly to blame, the terrific rain storms of the preceding days having practically ruined the sweet peas all over the state. There were some splendid blooms, however, from two or three exhibitors, those of Ed. Jenkins, of Lenox, and Mrs. T. J. Emery being particularly good as to quality and variety. Wells Beach Sweet Pea Farms was another sweet pea exhibitor to whom a word of commendation is due for the manner in which the varieties were labelled.

R. & J. Farquhar & Co. made a very extensive and brilliant display of border perennials. Also an imposing table of blooms of Lilium myriophyllum which showed this sterling novelty in perfection and permeated the whole hall with its agreeable perfume. Julius Heurlin showed a hybrid lily (L. philadelphicum, × L. bulbiferum) bearing a very numerously flowered spike of orange-yellow upright blooms. The Eastern Nurseries were represented by a grand collection of herbaceous perennial flowers. A good display of garden flowers and well-bloomed plants of Oncidium flexuosum was staged by H. Stewart, gardener for Miss Cornelia Warren, Waltham.

Very attractive indeed were the exhibits of novelty baskets arranged with sweet peas and gypsophila, by Penn the Florist and Boston Cut Flower Co., the former being shown on a background of purple velvet and the latter on soft green velvet. Trachelium cæruleum, shown by Faulkner Farm, attracted notice on account of its delicate beauty.

Awards for Plants and Flowers.

Sweet Peas.—Twenty-five sprays, white: 1st, Edwin Jenkins, 2d, Mrs. T. J. Emery; crimson or scarlet, 1st, Edwin Jenkins, 2d, Mrs. T. J. Emery; carmine, 1st, Edwin Jenkins, 2d, Mrs. T. J. Emery; yellow, 1st, Edwin Jenkins, 2d, Col. Charles Pfaff; blue, 1st, Edwin Jenkins, 2d, Mrs. T. J. Emery; blush, 1st, Edwin Jenkins, 2d, Mrs. T. J. Emery; deep pink, 1st, Edwin Jenkins, 2d, Mrs. T. J. Emery; cream pink, 1st, Mrs. T. J. Emery, 2d, Mrs. T. J. Emery; orange, 1st, Edwin Jenkins, 2d, Mrs. T. J. Emery; lavender, 1st, Edwin Jenkins, 2d, Mrs. T. J. Emery; purple, 1st, Edwin Jenkins, 2d, Col. Charles Pfaff; maroon, 1st, Edwin Jenkins, 2d, Mrs. T. J. Emery; picotee-edged, 1st, Edwin Jenkins, 2d, Mrs. T. J. Emery; striped or flaked red or rose, 1st, Edwin Jenkins, bicolor, 1st, Edwin Jenkins, 2d, Mrs. T. J. Emery; striped or flaked blue or purple, 1st, Edwin Jenkins, 2d, Mrs. T. J. Emery. Decoration of sweet peas: 1st, Penn, the Florist, silver medal; 2d, Boston Cut Flower Co., bronze medal. Iris Kaempferi—Collection; 1st, Dr. Harris Kennedy, 2d, Miss Cornelia Warren, 3d, Miss Cornelia Warren.

Gratuities—Wells Beach Sweet Pea Farm, display of sweet peas; Gertrude Schulz, bouquets and vases of sweet peas; Jackson Dawson, single hollyhocks; Miss Cornelia Warren, hemerocallis, veronica, hydrangea, snapdragon delphinium; T. C. Thurlow's Sons Co., herbaceous flowers; Mrs. E. M. Gill, display of flowers.

Silver medals—R. & J. Farquhar & Co., display of herbaceous plants; Eastern Nurseries, display of herbaceous plants; George McViu, Odontoglossum harvengtense.

First class certificate—Julius Heurlin, Hybrid lily (Lilium Philadelphicum, bulbiferum).

Certificate of honorable mention—R. & J. Farquhar & Co., Lilium regale.

Cultural certificate—Faulkner Farm, Trachelium cœruleum.

AN ESTATE WHERE GARDENING FLOURISHES.

ROCK GARDEN AND ROSE GARDEN
George E. Barnard Estate, Ipswich, Mass.

On Friday, July 9, the garden committee of the Massachusetts Horticultural Society visited the estate of Mr. George E. Barnard at Ipswich, Mass. This is one of the steadily advancing places in eastern Massachusetts. Several years ago it was awarded the Hunnewell triennial prize as the best kept garden visited by the committee but it is now greatly improved from that time and will doubtless continue to improve, as its owner, who is still in the prime of life, has retired from active business and devotes his time and energies to the beautifying of his extensive grounds, a work of which he is very fond and in which he is ably seconded by his superintendent, George C. Butler.

The place has been in Mr. Barnard's possession about twelve years. Previously it was an old farm, with much natural beauty in the lay of the land but neglected and unkempt. The house which has been greatly enlarged, was built in 1812, which is quite recent as compared with many of the residences in this ancient town.

The flower gardens are laid out on the most generous order, long sweeping borders skirting expansive lawns of beautiful finish and merging into the evergreen plantations and woodlands very impressively. 40,000 perennials and 50,000 annuals were used in the planting this year. There is a rose garden, the plan of which impressed every one with its dainty simplicity and convenience, being cut out in scroll pattern in the lawn, without gravel walks, and affording close inspection of every plant without encroaching on the beds.

The grounds follow the shore of the Concord river and the flower garden proper occupies the site of a reclaimed meadow. A sloping hillside has been converted into an extensive rock garden which has been laid out with a charming abandon and exuberance of material and together with the aquatic pools at its base, will in due time

take rank as a fine example of this fascinating branch of ornamental gardening.

It would be a great thing for horti-

A WALK IN THE PERENNIAL GARDEN
George E. Barnard Estate, Ipswich, Mass.

culture if there were more gentlemen of the type of Mr. Barnard who finds his keenest enjoyment in his garden and who is as charming and companionable in his personality as his estate is interesting and inspiring for the garden lover.

ECHINOPS RITRO.

The plant which is so strikingly depicted in our cover illustration this week is so well known as a hardy border subject that any particular description of it here would be superfluous. Its odd metallic blue flowers and beautiful pinnate lobed foliage never fail to attract attention. The plant is of the easiest culture and shows to best advantage when a number are grouped together as in the picture.

BRITISH HORTICULTURE.

At an exhibition of the Royal Horticultural Society, on June 22nd, a new delphinium, shown by A. Fergusson, was labelled "Souvenir de Lieutenant Warneford," in compliment to the plucky young British aviator whose daring exploit destroyed a German Zeppelin, and who met his death a few days afterwards in a flying accident. Another new delphinium from the same exhibitor was named "The Queen of the Belgians." Amongst the new orchids was one exhibited by J. G. Fowler, called "Queen Elizabeth." "Nowadays it is quite the fashion to give novelties a topical war name," a florist stated at the show. He pointed out several specimens marked with such names as Louvain and other places where battles have been fought.

A Florist's Hints.

"There is nothing of more serious importance to a seller of flowers than the careful keeping of his stock, and there is no doubt that the most terrible bogey man of our lovely business is named 'Waste.'" This is the opinion of R. F. Felton, in an informative article appearing in the "Fruit Trades' Journal." "From morn to night he is always staring us in the face, and it is our first duty to ourselves to do everything possible to keep him out of our establishments at all cost. The first start in this direction confronts us the very moment we open our market boxes. We are all rather apt to overlook the fact that these flowers which are perfectly fresh from our point of view have been cut at least 15 hours, and during that time they have been either on rail or road standing about the market; now it does not require any great reasoning power to determine that they are a little tired, to say the least, of it, and, therefore, instead of taking them out of the boxes, dumping them in vases, and selling them, they should have an hour or so of perfect rest. They do not get in a flower shop window, especially if it is like mine, due south and west. The first thing to do is to see that their stems are cut with a sharp knife; next see that all superfluous leaves are removed, as these leaves require feeding, and take their share of the sap before it gets to the flower, and moreover these lower leaves soon decay in the water and turn it sour. They should then be put in a cool place for an hour if possible."

W. H. ADSETT.

FIELD CULTURE OF CARNATIONS.

A paper by Ira Landis, before the Lancaster County Florist Club.

As soon as the soil can be gotten into shape early in April we like to commence planting into the field. Assuming that the soil has been well manured and properly prepared with three men and a few boys, the planting proceeds nicely. We always use two lines and draw a rake along each row to make the soil mellow and the planting easy.

Where a great many thousand are grown I believe it advisable to plant in beds of about five rows each, fifteen inches apart and ten inches between the plants and cultivate by hand. We plant in rows thirty inches apart and ten inches in the row and cultivate with a horse. This method of cultivation I prefer to the hand cultivator where space is not limited as the deep cultivation helps the soil to retain moisture for a greater period. Care must be taken not to cultivate too close to the plants so as to injure the roots. Cultivate about every two weeks and as soon as possible after a rain with a fine toothed harrow in order to leave the soil nice and mellow.

As soon as the plants have become thoroughly established and their flowering shoots begin to push up, the pinching back or topping must be attended to and the stock gone over about every two weeks. About August 1 this topping must be discontinued if you want early blooms and start with in the spring the greater part of it should be ready to plant into the house early in August.

In the discussion that followed Mr. Landis' paper, it was generally conceded by the fifteen or more carnation growers present that the cultivation by horse was an advantage on account of the greater depth the horse harrow had over the hand cultivation. It was also brought very strongly that early planting was an advantage and that some of the best results were obtained where the planting had been done so early that the plants had a pretty hard freeze after being planted out. B. F. Barr citing an instance where the thermometer went below 28 for several nights after planting out, and Frank Kohr, an instance where the plants were snowed under a few days after they had been planted, with beneficial results to the plants in both cases. W. B. Girvin said he planted about 22,000 to the acre, cultivating by horse power and was looking for a motor power cultivator to take the place of the horse. He believed in planting as early as the soil could be gotten into shape, which differs in some localities.

SEED TRADE

AMERICAN SEED TRADE ASSOCIATION
Officers—President, J. M. Lupton,
Mattituck, L. I., N. Y.; First Vice-Presi-
-dent, Kirby B. White, Detroit, Mich.;
Second Vice-President, F. W. Bolgiano,
Washington, D. C.; Secretary-Treasurer,
C. E. Kendel, Cleveland, O.; Assistant
Secretary, S. F. Willard, Jr., Cleveland,
O. Cincinnati, O., next meeting place.

Shenandoah, Ia.—The Ratekin Seed
Company have changed their name to
the Ratekin Seed House, capital stock,
$75,000.

Lexington, Ky.—C. S. Brent, Inc.,
have changed their firm name to C. S.
Brent Seed Company. Liability is
fixed at $100,000.

Value of imports of horticultural
material to port of New York for week
ending July 3, was as follows: fertilizer, $1,453; clover seed, $15,073;
grass seed, $1,309; trees and plants,
$335.

CATALOGUES RECEIVED.

J. Bolgiano & Son, Baltimore, Md.—
Special Vegetable Seed List, July 1,
1915. John Baer Tomato and Long
Lost Lettuce are special features.

Chas. Reuter, New Orleans, La.—
Fall List of Reuter's "Peerless" Seeds.
Looks good and reads comprehen-
"Ask the man who plants them."

A. T. Boddington, New York.—Mid-
summer Garden Guide. Contains a
list of strawberry plants, bulbs for fall
planting, seasonable seeds, insecticides, implements and sundries. A
business publication.

H. G. Hastings Co., Atlanta, Ga.—
Seed Catalogue No. 50, for Fall, 1915.
An excellent publication for the agri-
cultural or horticultural planter in the
South. Illustrated cover in colors—
strawberries predominating.

We have been receiving, regularly,
each week and each month respectively The Pennock-Meehan Weekly and
Pennock-Meehan Monthly, sent out
from the headquarters of that enterprising firm at 1620 Ludlow St., Philadelphia. The "Weekly" is a comprehensive folder telling of the weekly
offerings of flowers at wholesale and
timely supplies of florists' plants, supplies and ribbons. The "Monthly" is devoted to florists' plant stock. The current issue lists field grown carnations,
early flowering chrysanthemums, geraniums, bay trees, ferns, etc., and
strikes us as an excellent business
getter.

Little Compton, Mass.—William
Dickson, superintendent and landscape gardener at "Sea Lands" farm,
the estate of John E. McGowan, of
New York, has resigned his position,
and with his family has returned to
Providence.

PUBLICATIONS RECEIVED.

How to Lay Out Suburban Home
Grounds. By Herbert J. Kellaway,
Landscape Architect.

This is a new edition of a book that
has already made a place for itself in
this country and proved most helpful
to the rapidly growing legion of attractive home makers. Landscape
architecture is today recognized as
one of the fine arts. The application
of this new art is becoming more universal as the days and years go by,
not only in the large public and private undertakings, but even, about the
modern moderate home, for which
this work was especially written as an
inspiration. That it has accomplished
much in making the home surroundings beautiful is the best reason for
the believing that this new edition
will be helpful. It embodies a number of new features, four new chapters having been added. They give
suggestions as to the kind of trees to
plant, the use of shrubs for the
beautifying of grounds, and planting
of perennials, vines and annuals.
Taking the book in its new edition
as a whole, it is both suggestive and
practical, and one that may well be
studied by all desirous of making the
most of their grounds, be they even of
very modest dimensions, from the
standpoints of beauty and usefulness.

The subject of harmonious planting
and arrangement of grounds in relationship to buildings and environment
is as yet but faintly understood in its
fundamentals. This book with its
well-founded maxims and practical
rules for guidance will go far to prevent costly mistakes and to eliminate
regrets and dissatisfaction in later
years. There are fourteen comprehensive chapters, forty-one half-tone
plates and fifteen plans and maps.
Cloth $2.00 net, postpaid. John Wiley
& Sons, Inc., New York, are the publishers. Copies can be supplied by
Horticulture.

Market Gardening. By F. L. Yeaw,
an Elementary Text Book and a
Practical, Reliable and Handy Guide
for all Growers of Vegetables.

The purpose of this little manual
which has just been published by John
Wiley & Sons, Inc., New York, is to furnish, in a, condensed and usable form,
information concerning methods and
best practices for growing and marketing the commoner vegetables. It
considers in detail, methods for the
propagation, preparation of the soil
for planting, cultivation, harvesting
and marketing of twenty-three of the
more common and hardy vegetables.
In addition, much valuable information is given concerning soils, fertilizers, moisture requirements, seeds, germination, the preparation and care of
hot beds and the storing and packing
of vegetables. A special chapter is devoted to the location, planning and
care of home and school gardens.

It is estimated that the income
from the sale of vegetables is about
twice that produced from the great
fruit industries. Market gardening is
certainly important enough to justify
the preparation of this neat little
volume of 108 pages, at the modest
price of 75 cents net. It is well
printed on fine heavy paper and there
are thirty figures. A copy should be
in the possession of everyone who
grows garden vegetables for commercial purposes or home use.

Personal

L. Merton Gage, of gladiolus fame,
is taking a vacation in Bristol, Vt.,
and neighborhood.

Antoine Leuthy of Roslindale, Mass.,
has been suffering from an attack of
ptomaine poisoning.

A. C. Ruzicka, of late on the Iselin
estate, Glen Head, N. Y., has now
taken charge of the rose growing establishment of Nason & Sons, Murray
Hill, N. J.

Mr. and Mrs. Thomas B. Meehan, of
East Gorgas Lane, Mt. Airy, announce
the engagement of their daughter,
Rosa Denham Meehan, to Harold Aubrey Tyson of Germantown, Pa.

Edw'd Davies, recently superintendent for Paul Moore, Convent Sta., N.
J., will now take charge of the W. H.
Wellington estate, Wayland, Mass. A
new range of conservatories is being
erected here by the Pierson U-Bar Co.

W. E. Chappell, the genial secretary
of the Florists' and Gardeners' Club of
Rhode Island is off on a water trip to
Jacksonville, Fla., a vacation much
needed as his health has been badly
impaired since his nervous breakdown
last spring.

Mr. Alex. Forbes, president of J. F.
Noll & Co., Newark, N. J., who was
operated on for appendicitis in the
Orange Memorial Hospital, Orange, N.
J., was able to leave that institution
on the 10th inst., and is now recuperat-
ing at home.

We read in our English exchanges
of the dangerous illness of William
Wells, Sr., of Merstham, Surrey. A
serious operation was performed on
June 23, the result of which looked
very dubious for a time, but latest reports are more encouraging and it is
hoped that his robust constitution will
pull him through safely.

John Garlate, for 18 years in the
employ of Samuel Smith, a florist at
Jamestown, R. I., learned a few days
ago he had become wealthy through
the recent death of an uncle in Brazil,
who left his entire fortune, estimated
at $400,000, to Garlate. The estate in-
cludes coffee plantations and vast land
holdings. Mr. Garlate, who is 40 years
old, came to this country 18 years ago.

We are delighted to learn through
the columns of our California contemporary that Edwin Lonsdale is not being forgotten by the craft in his days
of tedious illness. The Pacific Garden
says:

Those who have gone through a similar
experience know that to be remembered
at such times by friends is a benediction.
If within reach of the institution, take
him a bouquet, or a choice potted plant,
and present it with a friendly greeting.
The kindly act will bring sunshine to his
soul, and a blessing on the bend of the
giver.
A bouquet to the living is worth more
than a carload of flowers to the dead. A
word of cheer in the ear yet sensitive to
sound is worth more to the heart of the
hearer than the most eloquent eulogy ever
proclaimed is to one whose ear is sealed
against sound by the reaper whose name is
Death.
Yes. visit Lonsdale and let him know
that you appreciate his services to the
horticultural world.

Of Interest to Retail Florists

FLORISTS AS ADVERTISERS AND BOOK-KEEPERS.

(An address by R. C. Kerr, before the Texas State Florists' Association.)

I want to say before I begin my paper proper, that this is a friendly criticism, and the gun shoots as far back toward me as it goes forward toward you; and I want to give you the benefit of the lesson that I received. I suppose there are no two features of our business that are more neglected than those pertaining to advertising and book-keeping. There is no line of business that needs a thorough system of book-keeping, and judicious advertising, more than the florist business.

How many florists in Texas today know whether or not their greenhouse is a paying proposition, if they are not keeping accurate records? While visiting over the state the past year, I was amazed at the great amount of wasted room in the greenhouses of Texas. Are your greenhouses producing 50c. per square foot each year? If not, then they are a losing proposition. All over and above this amount is profit. On the average cost of labor, stock and fuel, the above figure is a fair estimate by an authority. How are we to know whether or not we get these results unless a system of book-keeping is used to show what is produced?

The reason this subject is so vitally interesting to me at this particular time is that about six months ago we had an auditor complete a new set of books—and I want to tell you we have had some eye-openers. I am frank to say that our greenhouses up to that time had never made us one dollar. We are now culling out the stock that is unprofitable and adding more stock that has showed profit.

This is not so with our greenhouses alone, as we have had many leaks in our store. The auditor opened up a complete set of books for the store, that shows what each department is doing; for instance—funeral work, plants, decorating, miscellaneous, etc. We have found out what is the average cost of each delivery; the percentage of the cost of advertising, and other things of this nature that there was no way of getting at before. It is positively staggering on investigation, to find the great losses we have been suffering and to think that we did business in such a reckless manner. There is no other business that can be conducted so badly as the way some of us conduct the florist business, and have it last a year's time.

Another matter I want to touch upon, is that of our credit. Many of the florists are very careless with their credits. Did you ever figure what you can save in one year's time, by discounting your bills? If not, do so, and you will find it will run into a nice sum. Then, too, you can face the world with a smile, and say you owe no one.

I had a very prominent florist from Central Texas tell me he owed no one except his banker. The florist is what I call a good business man. The florists

NEWS ITEMS FROM EVERYWHERE

CHICAGO.

Anna Troeger, bookkeeper for Berger Bros., of Philadelphia, called on friends in the trade here last week. She was on her way to the exposition.

Charlie Hunt had the misfortune to injure an eye while putting up a hook for a bird cage in his home a short time ago. He is just home from the hospital and last report states that there is little probability of saving the eye.

The West Side store of Schiller, the Florist, had a narrow escape from destruction last week. At 7.30 P. M. it was discovered that flames were coming from the roof of the building adjoining their conservatories, used as a laundry. Broken glass and the disturbance always caused by a fire resulted. The money loss amounted to only $25.

George Rozakles, who has a retail store at 17 Madison St., left on the 13th for his old home in Sparta, Greece. He came to this country when only a boy and is very proud of his naturalization papers which show that he has been an American citizen for 21 years. He will be gone for three months and his daughter will have charge of the store during his absence.

Why not a prize for the best hints on "How to lengthen the flower season"? The florists' dull season has gradually become longer, till now it includes one-half of June and all of October or until automobiling season is over. For over four months the trade now depends upon funeral work. Is there not some way to induce flower lovers to buy flowers in summer.

At Zech & Mann's, the stock of carnations is remarkable for the substance of its flowers and the stiffness of the stems. Almost as good as the winter cuts are the July offerings and they have a justifiable pride in the fact that not a complaint has come from long distance shipments to Winnipeg and other points this season. Some Mrs. Ward carnations were seen that in every respect would be considered good in cold weather.

In a trip through Frank Oechslin's plant growing establishment, a bed of 5,000 poinsettia cuttings are just ready to be taken from the sand. The man in charge said that not more than 25 out of the bed had failed to root. The benches that had held bedding stock are now all filled with Bostons, Whitmani and other ferns. A large stock of cyclamen are making an especially good showing. The heat of mid-day is tempered by the use of adjustable cloth shades in the cyclamen houses. Mr. and Mrs. Oechslin are now at the Panama Exposition.

It speaks well for the men in the trade that so many are thinking of taking a course of study in salesmanship. The two speakers on this subject, who have recently addressed the Chicago Florists' Club, have been men of convincing power, and their arguments and illustrations are common talk in the downtown stores during the quiet times of the day. The florists' business, more than many others, needs study, for anyone, even a few years in the trade, can see the change in conditions which must be met.

P. J. Foley returned July 12 from a ten days' trip through the south west, in which he "participated" in the Texas State Florists' Association meeting at Fort Worth. As the captain of the visitors' baseball team he distinguished himself and did credit to his home city. Mr. Foley had on exhibition at Fort Worth a section of a model greenhouse and samples of the various castings used in his method of construction. He reports the florists of the Lone Star State as very much awake to the opportunities of their state.

PHILADELPHIA.

Mr. and Mrs. John Burton were on an automobile trip through Long Island for about a week. Hempstead and Garden City are among the bright spots in the reminiscences.

The Henry A. Dreer Co. have completed their planting in front of Convention Hall, Broad and Lehigh. Cannas, pennisetum, and double petunias are dominant features of the lay out. The Giant Phoenix canariensis has also been used with good effect.

The Colflesh boys have bought a piece of property at "The Hook" near Ridley Park. The supposition is that they intend to build there in the near future. Their present location is at 53rd and Woodland avenue, where property has become too valuable to be used for greenhouse purposes.

The Philadelphia-Frisco Line has been established and their first steamer will sail from this port July 26th. She is the "Walter D. Noyes" 7000 tons and will take the Panama route. O. G. Hempstead & Sons are the agents. This will be a convenience and a saving for shippers from this point and no doubt the line will also carry passengers.

The Kelly St. Business Men's Association will make an auto pilgrimage on the 19th inst. Among other places to be visited are the Shallcross Asparagus Farm near Bustleton; the Burton greenhouses at Chestnut Hill; and the Dwyer residence at Overbrook. A dinner will be given at Dooner's on the same evening at 7 p. m., with Judge Campbell as host.

We had a pleasant visit from Mr. Farquhar, of Boston, and his nursery manager this week. A visit to Commodore John Westcott, to the Andorra Nurseries, and a joy ride through the park, were features of the occasion.

"The rich man had his motor car,
  His country and his town estate,
He smokes a fifty-cent cigar
  And jeers at fate.

But 'though my lamp burns low and dim,
  'Though I must toil for livelihood.
Think you that I would change with him?
  You bet I would."

CLEVELAND.

W. A. Manda of So. Orange, N. J., who was in the city a few days ago is very much interested in the coming big Cleveland Flower Show and according to the statements he made, the entire East is watching the progress our show committees are making. "They are all waiting for the final premium list" was his significant comment.

All retailers report a general slowing up of business, as compared with the past few weeks. Smith & Fetters were the exception, because they had the one big wedding of the week. This wedding received much notice in the local papers by the fact that the groom composed his own wedding march. The father of the bride is one of the suburban street cars magnates of Cleveland.

The annual picnic of the Cleveland Florists' Club is to be held Friday, July 23rd at Willoughbeach Park. This park is twenty miles east of the city on the banks of Lake Erie. The men in charge of the picnic are to meet this week and it is announced that a splendid program is to be prepared with plenty of interesting prizes for the athletic events. A complete announcement will be made next week.

F. J. Schoen, manager of the Jas. Eadie Co. store is receiving congratulations on his Fourth of July window. It was a very large wire globe representing the World. In it were two white pigeons symbolizing peace with little American flags and red, white and blue ribbons entwined around the globe. When Mr. Schoen was ready to take out the window he discovered that Mrs. Dove of Peace was contentedly setting on some eggs and refused to be disturbed. "You can look for additions to the 'peace party' before very long," says Mr. Schoen.

The premiums committee of the Cleveland Flower Show, composed of Herbert Bate, Frank A. Friedley, and J. Curnow of Akron, have made an announcement that will interest the assistants in every greenhouse. They have decided to give a special prize of $5.00 in every important class and sweepstakes all the way through their final list which will be ready to mail September 1st. There will be at least fifty of these special prizes all of which will go to the section man in charge of the bench on which prize winners were grown and from which they were picked. This incentive for the men with the hose will mean more first prizes for his employer, if his efforts are successful, and it will mean $5.00 for the assistant, in addition to the big prize.

SAN FRANCISCO.

The regular monthly meeting of the Pacific Coast Horticultural Society was postponed from the first Saturday in the month to the 10th, as several members were spending the holiday week-end out of town.

The local trade has been advised by the American Express Co., which a short time ago inaugurated refrigerator car service between San Francisco and Chicago, to be maintained semi-weekly, the car leaving San Francisco, Wednesday and Saturday, that it has found it expedient to have these refrigerator cars run through to New York City and the service is being maintained accordingly. While some local concerns are already making use of this service to good advantage, the greatest benefit will probably be derived this fall in getting violets to the eastern markets.

The program for the entertainment of visiting ladies at the coming convention of the Society of American Florists is well in hand by the local Ladies' Auxiliary, organized recently, and it is expected practically all of the important details will be decided upon at a meeting next week to be held at the home of Mrs. J. A. Axell, wife of Manager Axell of the E. W. McLellan Co.

There is a movement among local florists toward getting their shops in excellent shape for the convention. This week Joseph's on Grant avenue is receiving a coat of fresh paint, and the Francis Floral Co. expects to renovate its establishment on Powell and Sutter streets before the end of the month.

NEW YORK.

Kervan & Co., dealers in florists' greens supplies, have leased the property at 115 West 28th street, for ten years and will spend about $15,000 in altering the building to suit their needs. They will continue their establishment at 119 West 28th street.

The twentieth anniversary of the appropriation by the City of New York of 250 acres of land in Bronx Park for the use of the New York Botanical Garden will be commemorated at the Garden during the week commencing September 6, 1915. Botanists from all parts of North America are invited to attend. A very elaborate program is planned, including addresses, reading of papers, inspection of the grounds and buildings, with lunch at the Garden each day from Monday till Thursday. On Friday, Sept. 10, there will be a visit to the pine barrens of New Jersey and on Saturday there will be a trip to Long Island, including the Brooklyn Botanic Garden.

WASHINGTON, D. C.

William Marche is spending considerable time during the summer at Melrose Gardens, formerly the estate of Senator Elliott, purchased by him some time ago. The gardens cover four acres and are surrounded by magnificent trees. The property is improved by an attractive eighteen-room mansion. This is one of the show places of Hyattsville, Md., in which town it is located.

George C. Shaffer and family will spend their vacation at Atlantic City, N. J., leaving here the latter part of the month.

STORM DAMAGE IN CINCINNATI.

The severe storm last Wednesday did considerable damage to some of the greenhouse places around town in Price Hill and Ft. Thomas, Ky. In the latter place Ed. Fries suffered a loss of five houses while Henry Goebel lost two. Chas. Pfeiffer's Sons, Lou. Pfeiffer's Sons and Wm. Speck in Newport also suffered some damage. In Price Hill the storm demolished five houses for Mrs. Chas. Witterstaetter, three for Wm. Taylor, one for Herbert Greensmith, one for Frank Kramer, and blew in the west end of the Deller and Witterstaetter range. All suffered some damage or other to their dwellings, barns, boiler houses and outdoor crops.

BUSINESS TROUBLES.

Chatham, N. J.—Samuel Lum was declared bankrupt on June 29 in the United States District Court and his case was referred to Referee Atwood L. DeCoster for administration. According to Corra N. Williams, who represents the petitioning creditors, Lum owes his creditors about $50,000. His assets include the equity in his greenhouses and a vacant piece of property in Main street, Chatham. The bankrupt has been a resident of Chatham for twenty years and for the major part of that time he was reputed wealthy. He kept no books in his business, according to Mr. Williams, and his true financial status has not yet been determined.

NEWS NOTES.

Andover, Mass.—Walter Holden has gone out of business.

Albion, Mich.—F. E. Hubert has purchased the greenhouse range of Carl Jacobs.

Twin Falls, Ida.—Lindahl & Peterson are the successors of the Twin Falls Floral Co.

Temple, Tex.—The Temple Seed & Floral Company has been sold to the Ferndale Greenhouses.

Bennington, Vt.—Burt, the florist, of Greenfield, Mass., has closed his store here for the summer months.

Rockland, Mass.—Lyle Lothrop has leased the flower shop of Mrs. W. T. Wilson, who will remove to Brockton.

Springfield, Mass.—Frank J. Cartier has leased a range of greenhouses in this city and will conduct a wholesale and retail business.

Glen Olden, Pa.—J. Wm. Colflesh's Sons have purchased an 18 acre tract at Elmwood & Ashland avenues from Walter Webb, on which they will erect a range of greenhouses.

Baltimore.—The blight of apple and pear trees is very extensive in the state—even Keffer pear trees being badly affected. Blight is also affecting English ivy, Japanese maples and some varieties of hydrangeas.

Boston.—Thomas Roland estimates his total crop of tomatoes from his big house in Revere at one hundred tons. As soon as the tomatoes are finished he will replace them with 25,000 roses of the various popular market varieties.

Cincinnati.—Mr. and Mrs. Thomas Windram leave this week for a trip to Idaho and Seattle, Washington.

Arthur Becher expects to leave at the end of this week on a trip to the Pacific Coast to visit his brother.

Lou. Davis, of P. J. Olinger's place, goes to Memphis, Tenn., and Arkansas for his vacation.

Flower Market Reports

BOSTON Summer quietude still rules. "Nothing doing" in either wholesale or retail circles although there are faint zephyrs which promise to work up into a good blow shortly. It is full time that the shore resorts should be heard from and we hope to have a more interesting report to send out next week. The glut of carnations has been of unusual volume up to the present time but they are beginning to shorten up now and values which have been too absurd to quote will quickly rebound to a reasonable figure. Roses continue good, but saleable in quantity only at prices too low for the quality. Gladioli are quite a feature of the market now being extremely plentiful, and some of them are of splendid quality. Pink Beauty is really the aristocrat of the gladiolus field at present and sells at a substantial advance over the price obtainable for other sorts. Sweet peas are not very good as a rule, owing to the unfavorable weather but the finer varieties are in evidence in most of the cuts. Lilies are very cheap.

BUFFALO The past week has been a very quiet one, and the cut flower sales are not very flourishing, the surplus being carried along from day to day. Roses are still good. Some excellent Shawyer, Maryland, Double White Killarney, Taft, Sunburst and Mock are had although there is too much of the ordinary mildewed quality. A good lot of carnations are still in sight but with prices very uneven. Beauties have no sale and lilies are still plentiful. Gladioli are coming in more plentiful each day, the southern stock shipping very unsatisfactorily. Outdoor peas, candytuft, sweet william and other stock has had only very small demand.

CHICAGO Never did a better quality of summer flowers come into this market than is coming now. Customers have every inducement to buy, for the assortment is large and every concession is made to please and prices are very low. Each day brings a new cut, heavier than the demand calls for, while leftover stock remains on the counters and in the ice boxes. How to move it to advantage is a question no one can answer. Peonies are still in storage and daily sales are too slow to warrant the taking out of many at a time. Gladioli are selling very poorly this summer, though the stock offered is extra fine. Carnations are near the top in quality and near the lowest notch in price. Occasional bunches are received in a sleepy condition, but the great bulk of them are firm and of good color. All kinds of roses are offered in large quantities, Mrs. Russell still holding the lead in price. The sensational prices, this week, 8 cents per doz., at which roses are offered at the big department stores, is cutting heavily into the regular sales of florists.

CINCINNATI Plenty of good stock that would have been welcome in other years is coming into the market, but the business is so slow that only a part of it sells. Locally at the time of this writing there is little business. Shipping business holds up fairly well. The rose supply is good and generally able to more than take care of present needs. The market is glutted with lilies and gladioli, neither of them is finding the sale they should find for this time of the year. Asters are plentiful and up to this time meet with no especially strong demand.

NEW YORK It is not easy to find anything to say that is worth saying concerning the wholesale flower trade as it exists at present. It is, indeed, a very feeble existence and there is no movement worth chronicling. Generally speaking the supply is lessening from day to day, but the average quality of material coming in is unusually good for this date. The outing of the Florists' Club and the excursion to the Sweet Pea Show at Newport, have interjected a little variety into the monotony of the listless days this week. Preparations for San Francisco will next ensue and in the meantime let us hope that the market will wake up once more.

PHILADELPHIA The week after the Fourth turned out, as was to be expected, pretty slow. Business was at a very low ebb and much more stock came in than there was any use for. This was particularly true of low-grade material, which covered 85 per cent. of the arrivals. In roses, the market was well stocked with American Beauty, which was of good quality and went fairly well. After it the best sellers were Russell, Jonkheer and Double White Killarney. There are a few good cuts of carnations still coming, but most of these are poor and buyers seem to prefer good asters instead. The asters are better than usual for so early, the copeous rains having been very favorable to their development. Gladioli are fine but redundant, far more than the market can absorb. Centaurea imperialis continues abundant and of fine quality; C. cyanus also. Plenty of other outdoor stock: hydrangea, coreopsis gaillardia, phlox, feverfew,

(Continued on page 89)

WHOLESALE FLOWER MARKETS — TRADE PRICES—Per 100
TO DEALERS ONLY

	BOSTON July 15		ST. LOUIS July 19		PHILA. July 12	
Roses						
Am. Beauty, Special	10.00 to	16.00	20.00 to	30.00	18.00 to	30.00
" " Fancy and Extra	6.00 to	8.00	10.00 to	15.00	10.00 to	16.00
" " No. 1	8.00 to	4.00	8.00 to	8.00	3.00 to	8.00
Killarney, Richmond, Extra	2.00 to	4.00	3.00 to	5.00	3.00 to	5.00
" " Ordinary	.50 to	1.00	2.00 to	3.00	1.00 to	2.00
Hillingdon, Ward, Sunburst, Extra	2.00 to	6.00	3.00 to	6.00	3.00 to	5.00
" " " Ordinary	.50 to	1.00	3.00 to	4.00	1.00 to	2.00
Arenberg, Radiance, Taft, Extra	2.00 to	6.00	...... to		6.00 to	8.00
" " " Ordinary	.50 to	1.00	...... to		2.00 to	4.00
Russell, Hadley, Ophelia, Mock	2.00 to	8.00	5.00 to	6.00	3.00 to	12.00
Carnations, Fancy	1.00 to	1.50	2.00 to	3.00	2.00 to	3.00
" Ordinary	.25 to	.50	.75 to	1.00	.75 to	1.00
Cattleyas	15.00 to	25.00	35.00 to	40.00	15.00 to	35.00
Dendrobium formosum	...... to		40.00 to	50.00	...... to	50.00
Lilies, Longiflorum	2.00 to	4.00	4.00 to	5.00	6.00 to	10.00
" Rubrum	...... to	2.00	...... to		...... to	3.00
Lily of the Valley	2.00 to	3.00	3.00 to	4.00	2.00 to	4.00
Daisies	.50 to	1.00	.50 to	.90	.25 to	.50
Stocks	...... to		4.00 to	5.00	10.00 to	15.00
Snapdragon	2.00 to	4.00	2.00 to	4.00	1.00 to	2.00
Gladioli	1.00 to	4.00	2.00 to	4.00	2.00 to	5.00
Sweet Peas	.15 to	.50	.25 to	.50	.25 to	.50
Gardenias	10.00 to	12.00	10.00 to	12.00	12.00 to	15.00
Adiantum	.50 to	1.00	1.00 to	1.25	.75 to	1.00
Smilax	10.00 to	12.00	20.00 to	25.00	...... to	20.00
Asparagus Plumosus, Strings (100)	25.00 to	50.00	35.00 to	50.00	...... to	50.00
" & Spren. (100 Bchs.)	25.00 to	35.00	15.00 to	20.00	25.00 to	50.00

Flower Market Reports

(Continued from page 81)

candytuft, achillea, etc. The market for greens such as asparagus and smilax is at low ebb. There is far too much of it for the demand.

Trade dropped **SAN FRANCISCO** off somewhat during the Fourth of July holidays, particularly in the more refined work for fancy bouquets, on account of the many city residents spending the week-end out of town or at the Exposition, and business continued quiet most of the week. All flowers arrived in abundance making it very difficult to clean up supplies. A large over-supply of carnations was the most notable feature, and the consequent low prices had a demoralizing effect upon other staple lines. Much of the surplus was taken by street venders at extremely low prices which enabled them to make such attractive offers that it undoubtedly took considerable business from the florists. However, this situation will not last much longer as growers are beginning to pull up some of their carnation plants and the supply will shortly be much curtailed. Sweet peas are plentiful and cheap. The offerings of gladioli show better average quality, and the really fine stock demands high prices. Some extra fine specimens of Geisha dahlias are coming in from Marin County, but the supply is limited and Delice continues as the principal feature in the dahlia market, the latter variety being offered in ample quantity and of fine quality as well. There are plenty of hydrangeas, both cut and potted, but their movement is rather slow, owing to the surplus of cheaper flowers. Shasta daisies figure largely in the daily offerings. Asters have not appeared as yet. In roses there is plenty of good stock. Long-stemmed American Beauties clean up readily. Killarney shows the effect of the hot weather more than some of the other varieties and is less popular. Russell, Ophelia and Irish Elegance are offered freely, but Cecile Brunner is a little less plentiful. Hanging baskets for porches have sold well.

The wholesale market **ST. LOUIS** is in a most deplorable condition. All the wholesale commission men are crowded up with all kinds of seasonable stock and the demand is so little that not half of the daily shipments can be disposed of. Correct price quotations are not possible. Great quantities of roses and carnations are coming in, of which only the first grades bring anything like a price and many in the other grades go for almost nothing. The many thousands of gladioli spikes that come from Kirkwood each morning find hard sailing these dull days. Asters sell better than any other flowers now

There seems to be **WASHINGTON** no let up at all in the amount of stock that is coming into the local market. This is particularly true of roses. Demand is limited to the requirements of a small amount of funeral work which comes spasmodically here and there, and if some of the shippers get even a small fraction of that which they expect in the way of returns they will be doing exceedingly well. Washington is more of a winter resort and the summer business cannot very well be boosted as was evidenced by the results obtained from several sales during the past few days whereby the advertisers failed to do enough business to pay for the space they used in the daily papers. The carnation season is pretty nearly over. There are some few coming from the north, but these reach here in very poor condition and it is a waste of time and money to fool with them. This is an unusual season with respect to dahlias, for owing to the cool weather these flowers were blooming in June, something never before known even to the oldest inhabitants, and they are now very plentiful. They are meeting with a fair sale, replacing to a large extent many of the other flowers which have been on the market-throughout the year. Some exceptionally fine America gladioli are to be had but on account of the immense quantities flooding the market and the lack of a heavy demand the price is exceptionally low. Gardenias are still excellent. There is but a limited sale on orchids and American Beauty roses move slowly. All high priced stock is tabooed.

NEW CORPORATIONS.

Boston, Mass.—Hoffman, Inc. Incorporators, Sidney Hoffman, James D. McQuaid. Capital $10,000.

Louisville, Ky.—Jacob Schulz Company, florists, capital stock, $12,000, Incorporators, Geo. E. and Anna Schulz, Mary Sheedy, C. M. Quirey, Karl Rabe and F. J. Keitig.

Rochester, N. Y.—Home Planters' Supply Co., Inc. Horticultural produce and supplies. Capital $35,000. Incorporators, M. E. Fricker, F. L. Pearce, R. D. Luetchford, all of Rochester.

NEW YORK QUOTATIONS PER 100. To Dealers Only

MISCELLANEOUS	Last Half of Week ending July 10 1915		First Half of Week beginning July 12 1915	
Cattleyas	6.00	to 20.00	8.00	to 20.00
Lilies, Longiflorum	1.00	to 2.00	1.00	to 2.00
" Rubrum	1.00	to 2.00	1.00	to 2.00
Lily of the Valley	.50	to 2.00	.50	to 2.00
Daisies	......	to .50	......	to .50
Stocks	......	to 1.00	......	to 1.00
Snapdragon	.50	to 1.00	.50	to 1.00
Gladioli	1.00	to 2.00	1.00	to 2.00
Peonies	2.00	to 3.00	1.00	to 3.00
Sweet Peas	.10	to .80	.10	to .15
Corn Flower	......	to .25	......	to .25
Gardenias	8.00	to 12.00	8.00	to 12.00
Adiantum	.50	to .75	.50	to .75
Smilax	6.00	to 12.00	6.00	to 12.00
Asparagus Plumosus, strings (per 100)	15.00	to 35.00	15.00	to 35.00
" & Spren (100 bunches)	10.00	to 20.00	10.00	to 20.00

DURING RECESS.

New York Florists' Club Outing.

The Fifteenth Annual Outing of the New York Florists' Club was enjoyed by about 250 of the members and their families and friends, on Wednesday, July 14, at Witzel's Point View Grove, College Point. It was a very pleasant affair, with fine weather conditions and altogether a great improvement over last year's trip to Glen Island. There were no accidents or untoward incidents to mar the perfect enjoyment of the occasion by all who participated. The attendance would undoubtedly have been larger had it not been for the pilgrimage to Newport, R. I., by many of the more active members of the club. The program of sports was well carried out and the prizes for the different athletic events were numerously competed for.

VISITORS' REGISTER.

Berlin, Md.—J. K. M. L. Farquhar, Boston.

Cincinnati—Mrs. Shull, Roanoke, Va.; Mrs. Gelach, Piqua, Ohio; Mr. Thomas, Indianapolis, Ind.

San Francisco—Louis Nash, park commissioner, St. Paul, Minn.; Mr. and Mrs. Frank Oechslin, Chicago, Ill.

Washington, D. C.—Sidney H. Bayersdorfer, of H. Bayersdorfer & Co., Philadelphia, Pa.; E. P. Scholtz, Charlotte, N. C.; Richard Vincent, Jr., White Marsh, Md.

Boston—W. O. Roy, Montreal, Canada; H. A. Naldrett, representing Kelway & Son. Langport, Eng.; Mr. Anderson, representing A. L. Randall, Chicago; Chas. D. Weathered, New York; Mr. Newell of Newell & Ustler, Apopka, Fla.

Philadelphia—Mr. Hayman, Hayman Greenhouses, Clarksburg, W. Va.; John K. M. L. Farquhar, Boston, Mass.; John Van Leeuwen, Dedham, Mass.; Mr. McDonald, representing Hastings & Co., Atlanta, Ga.; Mr. Fowler, representing J. Van Lindley Nursery Co., Greensboro, N. C.; Robt. H. Greenlaw, New England representative of Pennock-Meehan Co.

Buyer's Directory and Ready Reference Guide

Advertisements under this head, one cent a word.   Initials count as words.

Display advertisers in this issue are also listed under this classification without charge. Reference to List of Advertisers will indicate the respective pages.

Buyers failing to find what they want in this list will confer a favor by writing us and we will try to put them in communication with reliable dealers.

ACCOUNTANT
R. J. Dysart, 40 State St., Boston.
For page see List of Advertisers.

APHINE
Aphine Mfg. Co., Madison, N. J.
For page see List of Advertisers.

APHIS PUNK
Nicotine Mfg. Co., St. Louis, Mo.
For page see List of Advertisers.

ASPARAGUS
ASPARAGUS PLUMOSUS NANUS.
5,000 strong 3 and 4 in. pots ready for benching. 4 in. pots at $8.00 per 100, $75.00 per 1,000; 3 in. pots at $5.00 per 100, $50.00 per 1,000; 2¼ in. pots at $3.00 per 100, $22.50 per 1,000. MIAMI FLORAL CO., Dayton, Ohio.

ASPARAGUS SPRENGERI.
8,000 good 3 and 4 in. plants ready for benching. 4 in. pots at $8.00 per 100, $75.00 per 1,000; 3 in. pots at $5.00 per 100, $50.00 per 1,000; 2¼ in. pots at $3.00 per 100, $22.50 per 1,000. MIAMI FLORAL CO., Dayton, Ohio.

AUCTION SALES
Elliott Auction Co., New York City.
For page see List of Advertisers.

AZALEAS
P. Ouwerkerk, Hoboken, N. J.
For page see List of Advertisers.

BAY TREES
August Rolker & Sons, New York.
For page see List of Advertisers.

BAY TREES—Standard and Pyramids. All sizes. Price List on demand. JULIUS ROEHRS CO., Rutherford, N. J.

BEDDING PLANTS
A. N. Pierson, Inc., Cromwell, Conn.
For page see List of Advertisers.

R. Vincent, Jr. & Sons Co., White Marsh, Md.
For page see List of Advertisers.

Wood Bros., Fishkill, N. Y.

BEGONIAS
Julius Roehrs Company, Rutherford, N. J.
For page see List of Advertisers.

Thomas Roland, Nahant, Mass.
For page see List of Advertisers.

A. M. Davenport, Watertown, Mass.
For page see List of Advertisers.

Begonia Lorraine, $12.00 per 100, $110.00 per 1,000; Begonia Glory of Cincinnati, $15.00 per 100, $140.00 per 1,000. JULIUS ROEHRS CO., Rutherford, N. J.

BOILERS
Kroeschell Bros. Co., Chicago.
For page see List of Advertisers.

King Construction Co., North Tonawanda, N. Y.
"King Ideal" Boiler.
For page see List of Advertisers.

Lord & Burnham Co., New York City.
For page see List of Advertisers.

Hitchings & Co., New York City.

BOXES—CUT FLOWER FOLDING
Edwards Folding Box Co., Philadelphia.
For page see List of Advertisers.

Folding cut flower boxes, the best made. Write for list. HOLTON & HUNKEL CO., Milwaukee, Wis.

BOX TREES
BOX TREES—Standards, Pyramids and Bush. In various sizes. Price List on demand. JULIUS ROEHRS CO., Rutherford, N. J.

BULBS AND TUBERS
J. M. Thorburn & Co., New York City.
For page see List of Advertisers.

Ralph M. Ward & Co., New York City.
Lily Bulbs.
For page see List of Advertisers.

John Lewis Childs, Flowerfield, L. I., N. Y.
For page see List of Advertisers.

August Rolker & Sons, New York City.
Holland and Japan Bulbs.
For page see List of Advertisers.

R. & J. Farquhar & Co., Boston, Mass.
For page see List of Advertisers.

S. S. Skidelsky & Co., Philadelphia, Pa.
For page see List of Advertisers.

Chas. Schwake & Co., New York City.
Horticultural Importers and Exporters.
For page see List of Advertisers.

A. Henderson & Co., Chicago, Ill.
For page see List of Advertisers.

Burnett Bros., 98 Chambers St., New York.
For page see List of Advertisers.

Henry F. Michell Co., Philadelphia, Pa.
For page see List of Advertisers.

Roman J. Irwin, New York City.
Hardy Lilies.
For page see List of Advertisers.

Fottler, Fiske, Rawson Co., Boston, Mass.
Summer Flowering Bulbs.

Joseph Breck & Sons Corp., Boston, Mass.
Bulbs for Early Forcing.
For page see List of Advertisers.

GREAT REDUCTION IN PRICES Of HOLLAND BULBS of all kinds. Send for Price List. THOMAS COGGER, 229 Laurel St., Melrose, Mass.

C. KEUR & SONS, HILLEGOM, Holland. Bulbs of all descriptions. Write for prices. NEW YORK Branch, 8-10 Bridge St.

CAMELLIAS
Julius Roehrs Co., Rutherford, N. J.
For page see List of Advertisers.

CANNAS
R. Vincent, Jr. & Sons Co., White Marsh, Md.
For page see List of Advertisers.

Wood Bros., Fishkill, N. Y.

Canna Specialists.
Send for Canna book.
THE CONARD & JONES COMPANY, West Grove, Pa.

CARNATIONS
F. Dorner & Sons Co., Lafayette, Ind.
For page see List of Advertisers.

Wood Bros., Fishkill, N. Y.

Leo Niessen Co., Philadelphia, Pa.
Field Grown Carnation Plants.
For page see List of Advertisers.

CARNATIONS—Continued
250,000 Field-Grown Carnation Plants. Grown in Soil Especially Suited for Carnations.
Quality Guaranteed to Please You.
July and Later Delivery.
Order Early.

	100	1000
PINK—		
Mrs. C. Edward Akehurst	$12.00	$100.00
Pink Sensation	12.00	100.00
Good Cheer	12.00	100.00
Alice	12.00	100.00
Enchantress Supreme	8.00	70.00
Peerless Pink	8.00	70.00
Gorgeous	8.50	70.00
Pink Delight	7.50	65.00
Philadelphia	8.00	70.00
Glorious	7.00	60.00
Mrs. C. W. Ward	7.00	55.00
Northport	7.00	55.00
Enchantress	7.00	55.00
Rose-pink Enchantress	7.50	60.00
Dorothy Gordon	7.00	55.00
Rosette	7.50	60.00
Winona	7.00	55.00
Winsor	7.00	55.00
VARIEGATED—		
Benora	8.00	70.00
RED—		
Champion	8.00	75.00
Princess Dagmar	8.00	70.00
Beacon	7.50	60.00
Comfort	6.00	45.00
The Herald	8.00	75.00
Pocahontas	8.00	70.00
St. Nicholas	8.00	70.00
Harlowarden	7.00	55.00
Victory	7.00	55.00
Eureka	7.00	55.00
Bonfire	7.50	65.00
WHITE—		
Matchless	8.00	70.00
White Wonder	7.50	60.00
White Enchantress	7.00	55.00
White Perfection	7.00	55.00
Alma Ward	7.00	55.00
YELLOW—		
Yellow Prince	8.00	70.00
Yellowstone	8.00	70.00

Write for complete price list of bedding and greenhouse plants.
S. S. PENNOCK-MEEHAN CO., 1608-1620 Ludlow St., Philadelphia, Pa.

CARNATION STAPLES
Split carnations quickly, easily and cheaply mended. Pillsbury's Carnation Staple, 1000 for 35c.; 3000 for $1.00 post paid. I. L. PILLSBURY, Galesburg, Ill.

Supreme Carnation Staples, for repairing split carnations, 35c. per 1000; 3000 for $1.00. F. W. WAITE, 85 Belmont Ave., Springfield, Mass.

CARNATION SUPPORTS
Carnation Support Co., Connersville, Ind.

CHRYSANTHEMUMS
Poehlmann Bros. Co., Morton Grove, Ill.
For page see List of Advertisers.

Wood Bros., Fishkill, N. Y.
Chrysanthemums Rooted Cuttings.
For page see List of Advertisers.

Chas. H. Totty, Madison, N. J.
For page see List of Advertisers.

R. Vincent, Jr., & Sons Co., White Marsh, Md.
Pompon Chrysanthemums.
For page see List of Advertisers.

THE BEST 1915 NOVELTIES.
The Cream of 1914 Introductions.
The most popular Commercial and Exhibition kinds; also complete line of Pompons, Singles and Anemones. Trade list on application. ELMER D. SMITH & CO., Adrian, Mich.

For List of Advertisers See Page 63

COCOANUT FIBRE SOIL
20th Century Plant Food Co., Beverly, Mass
For page see List of Advertisers.

CROTONS
F. R. Pierson Co., Tarrytown, N. Y.

CYCLAMENS
CYCLAMEN — Separate colors; finest strain; extra strong plants; 3-inch pots, $10.00 per 100, $90.00 per 1,000. JULIUS ROEHRS CO., Rutherford, N. J.

CYCLAMEN.
Best strain of colors:
Xmas Red, Wonder of Wandsbek (best Salmon), Rose of Marienthal, Glowing Dark Red, White with Red Eye, Pure White.
Strong plants, out of 2¼-in. pots, at $5.00 per 100, $40.00 per 1000. Satisfaction guaranteed. Cash with order, please.
J. H. FIESSER,
709-735 Hamilton Ave., North Bergen, N. J.

DAHLIAS
Send for Wholesale List of whole clumps and separate stock; 40,000 clumps for sale. Northboro Dahlia and Gladiolus Gardens. J. L. MOORE, Prop, Northboro, Mass.

NEW PAEONY DAHLIA
John Wanamaker. Newest, Handsomest, Best. New color, new form and new habit of growth! Big stock of best cut-flower varieties. Send list of wants to
PEACOCK DAHLIA FARMS, Berlin, N. J.

DECORATIVE PLANTS
Robert Craig Co., Philadelphia, Pa.
For page see List of Advertisers.

Woodrow & Marketos, New York City.
For page see List of Advertisers.

S. S. Skidelsky & Co., Philadelphia, Pa.
For page see List of Advertisers.

Bobbink & Atkins, Rutherford, N. J.
For page see List of Advertisers.

A. Leuthy & Co., Roslindale, Boston, Mass.
For page see List of Advertisers.

DRACAENAS
F. R. Pierson Co., Tarrytown, N. Y.

Julius Roehrs Co., Rutherford, N. J.
For page see List of Advertisers.

ENGLISH IVY
English Ivy from soil, 20 to 30 in., $3.00; from pots, 12 to 15 in., $4.00. CHAS. FROST, Kenilworth, N. J.

FERNS
H. H Barrows & Son, Whitman, Mass.
For page see List of Advertisers.

Robert Craig Co., Philadelphia, Pa.
For page see List of Advertisers.

F. R. Pierson Co., Tarrytown, N. Y.

FERTILIZERS
20th Century Plant Food Co., Beverly, Mass
Coconut Fibre Soil.
For page see List of Advertisers.

Stumpp & Walter Co., New York City.
Scotch Soot.
For page see List of Advertisers.

Pulverized Manure Co., Chicago, Ill.
Wizard Brand Cattle Manure.

FLORISTS' LETTERS
Boston Florist Letter Co., Boston, Mass.
For page see List of Advertisers.

FLORISTS' SUPPLIES
N. F. McCarthy & Co., Boston, Mass.
For page see List of Advertisers.

Reed & Keller, New York City.

S. S. Pennock-Meehan Co., Philadelphia, Pa.
For page see List of Advertisers.

H. Bayersdorfer & Co., Philadelphia, Pa.
Up-to-Date Summer Novelties.
For page see List of Advertisers.

Welch Bros. Co., Boston, Mass.
For page see List of Advertisers.

FLOWER POTS
W. H. Ernest, Washington, D. C.
For page see List of Advertisers.

A. H. Hews & Co., Inc., Cambridge, Mass.
For page see List of Advertisers.

Hilfinger Bros., Ft. Edward, N. Y.
For page see List of Advertisers.

FOLIAGE PLANTS
A. Leuthy & Co., Roslindale, Boston, Mass.
For page see List of Advertisers.

FUCHSIAS
Fuchsias—Black Prince, Speciosa, double purple and white, Rooted Cuttings, $1.00 per 100; 2¼-in., $2.00 per 100.
W. J. BARNETT, R. D. 07, Sharon, Pa.

FUNGINE
Aphine Mfg. Co., Madison, N. J.
For page see List of Advertisers.

GALAX
Michigan Cut Flower Co., Detroit, Mich.
For page see List of Advertisers.

GERANIUMS
R. Vincent, Jr., & Sons Co.
White Marsh, Md.
For page see List of Advertisers.

GLADIOLUS
John Lewis Childs, Flowerfield, L. I., N. Y.
For page see List of Advertisers.

GLASS
Sharp, Partridge & Co., Chicago.

Parshelsky Bros., Inc., Brooklyn, N. Y.
For page see List of Advertisers.

Royal Glass Works, New York City.
For page see List of Advertisers.

Greenhouse glass, lowest prices. JOHN-STON GLASS CO., Hartford City, Ind.

100 boxes 16 x 24 double glass. $3.00 per box, f. o. b. Foxboro. V. S. POND CO., Foxboro, Mass.

GLASS CUTTERS
Smith & Hemenway Co., New York City.
Red Devil Glass Cutter.
For page see List of Advertisers.

GLAZING POINTS
H. A. Dreer, Philadelphia, Pa.
Peerless Glazing Point.
For page see List of Advertisers.

GOLD FISH
Gold fish, aquarium plants, snails, castles, globes, aquarium, fish goods, nets, etc., wholesale. FRANKLIN BARRETT, Breeder, 4815 D St., Olney, Philadelphia, Pa. Large breeding pairs for sale. Send for price list.

GREENHOUSE BUILDING MATERIAL
King Construction Co., N. Tonawanda, N. Y.
For page see List of Advertisers.

Parshelsky Bros., Inc., Brooklyn, N. Y.
For page see List of Advertisers.

Metropolitan Material Co., Brooklyn, N. Y.

Lord & Burnham Co., New York City.
For page see List of Advertisers.

A. T. Stearns Lumber Co., Neponset, Boston.
Pecky Cypress.

GREENHOUSE CONSTRUCTION
King Construction Co., N. Tonawanda, N. Y.
For page see List of Advertisers.

Foley Greenhouse Mfg. Co., Chicago, Ill.
For page see List of Advertisers

Metropolitan Material Co., Brooklyn, N. Y.

Lord & Burnham Co., New York City.
For page see List of Advertisers.

Hitchings & Co., New York City.

A. T. Stearns Lumber Co., Boston, Mass.

GREENHOUSE MATERIAL
Rosemere Conservatories, Dorchester, Mass.
Second Hand.

GUTTERS
King Construction Co., N. Tonawanda, N. Y.
King Channel Gutter.
For page see List of Advertisers.

Metropolitan Material Co., Brooklyn, N. Y.
Iron Gutters.

HAIL INSURANCE
Florists' Hail Asso. of America.
J. G Esler, Saddle River, N. J.

HARDY FERNS AND GREEN GOODS
Michigan Cut Flower Exchange, Detroit, Mich.
For page see List of Advertisers.

Knud Nielsen, Evergreen, Ala.
Natural Green Sheet Moss, Fancy and Dagger Ferns and Huckleberry Foliage.
For page see List of Advertisers.

The Kervan Co., New York.
For page see List of Advertisers.

HARDY PERENNIALS
Bay State Nurseries, No. Abington, Mass.
For page see List of Advertisers.

P. Ouwerkerk, Hoboken, N. J.
For page see List of Advertisers.

Palisades Nurseries, Sparkill, N. Y.
For page see List of Advertisers.

HEATING APPARATUS
Kroeschell Bros. Co., Chicago.
For page see List of Advertisers.

Lord & Burnham Co., New York City.
For page see List of Advertisers.

HOT-BED SASH
Parshelsky Bros., Inc., Brooklyn, N. Y.
For page see List of Advertisers.

Foley Greenhouse Construction Co., Chicago, Ill.
For page see List of Advertisers.

Lord & Burnham Co., New York City.
For page see List of Advertisers.

A. T. Stearns Lumber Co., Neponset, Mass

HOSE
H. A. Dreer, Philadelphia, Pa.
For page see List of Advertisers.

HYDRANGEAS
F. R. Pierson Co., Tarrytown, N. Y.

INSECTICIDES
Aphine Manufacturing Co., Madison, N. J.
Aphine and Fungine.
For page see List of Advertisers.

Lemon Oil Co., Baltimore, Md.
Standard Insecticides.
For page see List of Advertisers.

Nicotine Mfg. Co., St. Louis, Mo.
Aphis Punk and Nikoteen.
For page see List of Advertisers.

Roman J. Irwin, New York City.
Nico Fume Liquid and Paper.
For page see List of Advertisers.

IRRIGATION EQUIPMENT
Geo. N. Barrie, Brookline, Mass.
For page see List of Advertisers.

KIL-WORM AND KIL-WEED POISON
Lemon Oil Co., Baltimore, Md.
For page see List of Advertisers.

LEMON OIL
Lemon Oil Co., Baltimore, Md.

LILY BULBS
Chas. Schwake & Co., New York City.
Horticultural Importers and Exporters.
For page see List of Advertisers.

In writing to Advertisers kindly mention Horticulture

For List of Advertisers See Page 63

SWEET PEA SEED

Ant. C. Zvolanek, Lompoc, Calif.
Gold Medal of Honor Winter Orchid Sweet
Peas.
For page see List of Advertisers.

S. Bryson Ayres Co.,
Sunnyslope, Independence, Mo.
For page see List of Advertisers.

VEGETABLE PLANTS

Celery plants, Golden Self Blanching
(French Strain), Giant Pascal, White
Plume and Winter Queen, fine plants,
ready for field, $2.00 per 1000; $1.50 in
10,000 lots cash. BRILL CELERY GAR-
DENS, Kalamazoo, Mich.

CELERY PLANTS.

White Plume, Boston Market, Giant Pascal, Golden Self-blanching, $3.00 per 1000.
BRECK-ROBINSON NURSERY CO., Lexington, Mass.

VENTILATING APPARATUS

The Advance Co., Richmond, Ind.
For page see List of Advertisers.

The John A. Evans Co., Richmond, Ind.
For page see List of Advertisers.

VERMICIDES

Aphine Mfg. Co., Madison, N. J.
For page see List of Advertisers.

VINCAS

F. R. Pierson Co., Tarrytown, N. Y.

WEED DESTROYER

Pino-Lyptol Chemical Co., New York City.

WIRED TOOTHPICKS

W. J. Cowee, Berlin, N. Y.
For page see List of Advertisers.

WIREWORK

Reed & Keller, New York City.
For page see List of Advertisers.

WILLIAM E. HEILSCHER'S WIRE
WORKS, 264 Randolph St., Detroit, Mich.

WHOLESALE FLORISTS

Albany, N. Y.

Albany Cut Flower Exchange, Albany, N. Y.
For page see List of Advertisers.

Baltimore

The S. S. Pennock-Meehan Co., Franklin
and St. Paul Sts.
For page see List of Advertisers.

Boston

N. F. McCarthy & Co., 112 Arch St. and
31 Otis St.
For page see List of Advertisers.

Welch Bros. Co., 226 Devonshire St.
For page see List of Advertisers.

Patrick Welch, 262 Devonshire St., Boston,
Mass.
For page see List of Advertisers.

Brooklyn

Wm. H. Kuebler, 28 Willoughby St.
For page see List of Advertisers.

Buffalo, N. Y.

William F. Kasting Co., 383-87 Ellicott St.
For page see List of Advertisers.

Chicago

Poehlmann Bros. Co., Morton Grove, Ill.
For page see List of Advertisers.

Cincinnati

C. E. Critchell, 34-36 Third Ave., East.
For page see List of Advertisers.

Detroit

Michigan Cut Flower Exchange, 38 and 40
Broadway.
For page see List of Advertisers.

WHOLESALE FLORISTS—Continued

New York

H. E. Froment, 148 W. 28th St.
For page see List of Advertisers.

James McManus, 105 W. 28th St.
For page see List of Advertisers.

W. F. Sheridan, 133 W. 28th St.
For page see List of Advertisers.

P. J. Smith, 131 West 28th St., N. Y.
For page see List of Advertisers.

Moore, Hentz & Nash, 55 and 57 W. 26th St.
For page see List of Advertisers.

Charles Millang, 55 and 57 West 26th St.
For page see List of Advertisers.

W. P. Ford, New York
For page see List of Advertisers.

The S. S. Pennock-Meehan Co., 117 West
28th St.
For page see List of Advertisers.

Traendly & Schenck, 436 6th Ave., between
26th and 27th Sts.
For page see List of Advertisers.

Badgley, Riedel & Meyer, Inc., New York.
For page see List of Advertisers.

Woodrow & Marketos, 37 & 39 West 28th St.
For page see List of Advertisers.

George C. Siebrecht, 109 W. 28th St.
For page see List of Advertisers.

John Young & Co., 53 West 28th St.
For page see List of Advertisers.

M. C. Ford, 121 West 28th St.
For page see List of Advertisers.

Guttman & Reynor, Inc., 101 W. 28th St.,
New York.
For page see List of Advertisers.

Philadelphia

Leo, Niessen Co., 12th and Race Sts.
For page see List of Advertisers.

Edward Reid, 1619-21 Ranstead St.
For page see List of Advertisers.

The S. S. Pennock-Meehan Co., 1608-20
Ludlow St.
For page see List of Advertisers.

Stuart H. Miller, 1617 Ranstead St.
For page see List of Advertisers.

Richmond, Ind.

E. G. Hill Co.
For page see List of Advertisers.

Rochester, N. Y.

George B. Hart, 24 Stone St.
For page see List of Advertisers.

Washington

The S. S. Pennock-Meehan Co., 1216 H St.,
N. W.
For page see List of Advertisers.

New Offers In This Issue

BODDINGTON'S GIGANTIC PANSIES

Arthur T. Boddington, New York City.
For page see List of Advertisers.

FERNS IN FLATS

McHutchison & Co., New York City.
For page see List of Advertisers.

GREENHOUSE CONSTRUCTION

S. Jacobs & Sons, Brooklyn, N. Y.
For page see List of Advertisers.

IMP SOAP SPRAY

Eastern Chemical Co. Boston, Mass.
For page see List of Advertisers.

SUMMER ROSES

S. S. Pennock-Meehan Co., Philadelphia,
Pa.
For page see List of Advertisers.

THE KENILWORTH GIANT PANSY.

Chas. Frost, Kenilworth, N. J.
For page see List of Advertisers.

HELP WANTED

Orchid Grower Wanted

Send References and State
Wages Expected, to

A. A. M. Care Horticulture

SITUATIONS WANTED

GARDENER desires position. Age 35,
life experience under glass and outside.
Married, no family. Excellent references.
W. P., care of HORTICULTURE.

FOR SALE

FOR SALE—Fresh from factory, new;
10 x 12, 16 x 18, 16 x 24, double thick. A
and B qualities. Market dropped. Now is
the time to buy and save money. PAR-
SHELSKY BROS., INC., 215-217 Havemeyer St., Brooklyn, N. Y.

THE PRACTICAL BOOK

OF

Outdoor Rose Growing

FOR THE HOME GARDEN

by

GEORGE C. THOMAS, JR.

Elaborately Illustrated with 96 Perfect
Reproductions in Full Color of All
Varieties of Roses, and a Few Half-
tone Plates. Octavo, Handsome Cloth
Binding, in a Slip Case. $4.00 net.
Postage Extra.

We have sold a number of copies of
this sterling book. One purchaser
writes as follows:

HORTICULTURE, Boston, Mass.

Dear Sir: Some time ago we ordered
a copy of Thomas' Book on Roses. We
promised to send you postage as soon
as we learned the amount. The book
was so good that we forgot all about
postage until today. Please forgive our
lapse of memory.

We loaned it to a friend and he likes
it so well we're afraid that we will
have to buy another.

New York. Respectfully,
A. R.

Every rose grower should possess a
copy of this book.

IT IS THE REAL THING

Order From

Horticulture Publishing Co.

BOSTON.

In writing to Advertisers kindly mention Horticulture

HORTICULTURE INDISPENSABLE

The following examples of many approving letters received at the office of HORTICULTURE during the past few weeks, show why HORTICULTURE is so valuable as an advertising medium. Intensive circulation is HORTICULTURE'S best quality and practically every reader is a possible customer for the advertiser.

Gentlemen:—Last week's HORTICULTURE is not received. Have you scratched me off your list, or what is the matter? Appreciate your paper more than any of half a dozen I am receiving, and don't want to miss any copies. Will you please investigate?
Yours truly,
Missouri.   A. B. K.

Gentlemen:—It is getting late in the season and we wish to discontinue the advertisements which we carry in your paper. We would say that the advertisements which we have carried in your paper have brought us good results, and we feel that the money so expended was well invested.
Yours truly,
Standard Thermo Company,
S. C. LORD, President.

Kindly discontinue my advertisement in the classified ad. section of HORTICULTURE, rendering bill to date. Yours is a very good advertising medium. We have rid ourselves of practically all our surplus stock, and are therefore obliged to discontinue.
Very truly yours,
Mass.   A.

Here is my dollar for the 1915 trip with HORTICULTURE. HORTICULTURE is all right.
New York.   P. F.

Editor Horticulture:
Dear Sir — Enclosed please find $1.00, my subscription to your valuable paper for another year. Cannot do without it.
Conn.   O. A. H.

Dear Horticulture:
We can't keep house without you, and you can't travel without money, therefore I enclose money order to keep you coming for 1915.
Yours admiringly,
Iowa.   E. S.

We were satisfied with the results from the HORTICULTURE ad., and may be able to give you some further business in the future.
Sincerely yours,
National Floral Corporation,
By Hugo Mock, Pres.

Enclosed is post office order to pay for HORTICULTURE two years more. I like HORTICULTURE very much and hope to read it many more years.
N. Y.   S. F.

One of the many good features of HORTICULTURE is, that those who contribute to its columns always "say something" when they write. I take this opportunity to offer sincere congratulations. "May your shadow never grow less."
Sincerely yours,
New York.   P. F.

Editor HORTICULTURE:
Dear Sir:—I have been a subscriber to HORTICULTURE only about five weeks. I find in HORTICULTURE a paper of much importance. I hope to be a reader of it for the long future.
Mass.   A. B.

"HORTICULTURE is the finest paper under the sun."
New Jersey.   A.

Editor HORTICULTURE:
Dear Sir: — I have always been deeply interested in the letters of contributors in your paper, and find them very helpful.
Respectfully,
N. Y.   C. C.

"HORTICULTURE is grand. Keep it up."
San Jose, Cal.   B.

Dear Sirs — Enclosed please find one dollar for another year of the HORTICULTURE. My time is not up yet, but it won't be long. All I can say about your paper is that it is the best of its kind, and I read them all.
R. I.   J. B.

Enclosed are two dollars in payment for your very valuable paper. I find its contents timely and instructive.
Sincerely,
Conn.   C. S.

Gentlemen: — My paper did not arrive as usual on Saturday. It is all I have to look forward to each week; do not allow that to fail me. Kindly send one along at express rate.
Yours truly,
N. J.   G. W.

Gentlemen:—Will you please discontinue my classified gladioli advertisement now running in your paper? I am sold out of nearly all varieties, especially those called for by your readers, and hope to have as good success with you next year.
Yours truly,
Mass.   R. W. S.

When Writing to Advertisers Please Mention Horticulture

Coming Events

SHOWS.

Greenwich, Conn., July 18-19.—Westchester and Fairfield Horticultural Society, summer show.

Winnetka, Ill., July 22.—Summer exhibition of Lake Shore Hort. Society.

Lenox, Mass. July 27-28.—Summer exhibition of Lenox Horticultural Society.

Newport, R. I., Aug. 12, 13, 14.—Mid-summer exhibition of Newport Garden Club and Newport Horticultural Society.

Cleveland, O., Aug. 13-14.—Gladiolus Society of Ohio exhibition.

Newport, R. I., Aug. 18-19.—Fifth annual exhibition of the American Gladiolus Society.

Atlantic City, N. J., Aug. 26-29.—American Gladiolus Society exhibition.

Lewiston, Me., Aug. 27-28.—Fall exhibition in Lewiston City Hall of Lewiston and Auburn Gardeners' Union. Chas. S. Allen, President, Auburn, Me.; Mrs. Geo. A. Whitney, Secretary, 151 Winter St., Auburn, Me. Meetings first Friday in each month.

Rochester, N. Y., Aug. 30 to Sept. 11.—Rochester Exposition and Flower Show.

Hartford, Conn., Sept. 22-23.—Annual Dahlia exhibition of the Connecticut Horticultural Society, Unity Hall. Pratt St. Alfred Dixon, Sec., Wethersfield.

Cleveland, O., Nov. 10-14.—Annual show and meeting of Chrysanthemum Society of America. In conjunction with the Cleveland Flower Show. Chas. W. Johnson, Sec., 2226 Fairfax Ave., Morgan Park, Ill.

Cleveland, O., Nov. 10-14. — Cleveland Flower Show. The only show of national scope in the United States this fall. F. A. Friedley, Sec., 356 Leader Building.

MEETINGS.

Toronto, Ont., July 20.—Gardeners' and Florists' of Ontario, St. George's Hall, Elm St. Geo. Douglass, Sec., 180 Merton St., Toronto.

Newark, N. J., July 20.—Essex County Florists' Club, Kreuger Auditorium, 25 Belmont Ave. John Crossley, Sec., 37 Belleville Ave.

Washington, D. C., July 21.—Outing of Florists' Club of Washington, at Glen Falls, Va.

Chicago, July 22.—Chicago Florists' Club Picnic, Morton Grove, St. Paul's Park.

Twin Cities, St. Paul, Minn., Aug. 21-23.—Annual convention of the Association of American Cemetery Superintendents, Minneapolis and St. Paul. Secretary, Vellett Lawson, Jr., Supt. of Elm Root Cemetery, River Grove, Ill.

Hartford, Conn., Sept. 10.—Regular meeting Conn. Horticultural Society, County Bldg., Trumbull St. Alfred Dixon, Sec., Wethersfield.

CONVENTIONS TO BE HELD IN AUGUST IN SAN FRANCISCO.

August 12-14.—Thirteenth Annual Convention: The Pacific Coast Association of Nurserymen. President, John Vallance, 81 Glen avenue, Oakland; secretary-treasurer, C. A. Tonnesen, Tacoma, Washington.

August 17-14.—Fifth Annual Meeting: The California Association of Nurserymen. President, Fred H. Howard. Ninth and Olive streets, Los Angeles; secretary-treasurer, Henry W. Kruckeberg, 237 Franklin street, Los Angeles.

August 16.—Nurserymen's Day at the Panama-Pacific International Exposition.

August 17-19.—Annual Meeting: The American Rose Society. President, S. S. Pennock, Philadelphia, Pa.; secretary, Benjamin Hammond, Beacon, N. Y.; treasurer, Harry O. May, Summit, N. J.

August 17-20.—Thirty-first Annual Meeting: Society American Florists and Ornamental Horticulturists. President, Patrick Welch, Boston; vice-president, Daniel Macrorie, San Francisco; secretary, John Young, 53 W. Twenty-Eighth street, New York City; treasurer, W. F. Kasting, Buffalo, N. Y.

The National Association of Gardeners. President, John W. Everitt, Glen Cove, N. Y.; secretary, M. C. Ebel, Madison, N. J.

The Florists' Telegraph Delivery. President, Irwin Bertermann, Indianapolis, Ind.; secretary, Albert Pochelon, Detroit, Mich.

The Florists' Hail Association of America. President, E. G. Hill, Richmond, Ind.; secretary, John G. Esler, Saddle River, N. J.

August 18-20.—Annual Meeting: The American Association of Park Superintendents. President, G. X. Amrhyn, New

Haven, Conn.; secretary-treasurer, Roland W. Cotterill, Seattle, Wash.

August 18-25.—Thirty-fourth Biennial Session: The American Pomological Society, Berkeley, Cal. President, L. A. Goodman, Kansas City, Mo.; California vice-president, Henry W. Kruckeberg, 237 Franklin street, Los Angeles; executive committee, George C. Roeding, Fresno; secretary, E. R. Lake, 2033 Park Road, N. W., Washington, D. C.

A PEST CONQUERED.

It has been demonstrated at the Arnold Arboretum that the abominable pest known as the lace fly, which has defaced and done so much injury to the rhododendrons within the past few years, can be successfully combatted with a few sprayings of Imp soap solution on the underside of the foliage. This insect first made its appearance on Rhododendron maximum, but soon spread its depredations to the hybrids and the Kalmias and has been known to attack hawthorns and other shrubs growing in association with the rhododendrons. Whale oil soap has been used, but Imp soap is said to be better.

Obituary

Mrs. John A. Macrae.

Lula A. Macrae, wife of John A. Macrae, florist, of 1255 Smith street, Providence, R. I., died on Sunday, July 4, aged 53 years. She leaves, besides her husband, two sons and two daughters.

William Hill.

William Hill, well known as a florist in Toronto, Ont., for the past thirty-five years, died on June 21, after a long and painful illness. He leaves a widow, two daughters and four sons, two of the latter now carrying on the business.

F. Zimmermann.

Franz Zimmermann, for forty-two years engaged in the florist business at College Point, died on July 11, at his home, Fifteenth street, that village. He was seventy-two years old. He was prominent in civic affairs along the north shore of Long Island. He is survived by five sons and two daughters.

John Lambert.

John Lambert, the well known east end florist, passed away on July 6 at his home, 72 Jepson street, Fall River, Mass., following an illness of 11 weeks' duration. Deceased was 61 years old and was born in Ashton-under-Lynn, England. He came to this country about 30 years ago and for a time worked at the Oak Grove cemetery. For the past fifteen years, however, he had been engaged successfully in the florist trade and was very well known and highly regarded in the eastern section where he had resided ever since coming to Fall River. Besides a widow, there are left to mourn his loss, two sons and two daughters.

GREENHOUSES BUILDING OR CONTEMPLATED.

Milton, Pa.—W. Bruce Clinger, additions.

Bemidji, Minn.—W. A. Elliott, range of houses.

Valley Falls, R. I.—John J. Kelley, rebuilding.

North Weymouth, Mass.—Wm. B. Dasha, additions.

Springfield, Mass.—Benjamin F. James, additions.

Williamsport, Pa.—Williams Floral Co., range of houses.

Elmira, N. Y.—John B. Rudy, additions and alterations.

Wayland, Mass.—W. H. Wellington, range of U-Bar houses.

Beverly, Mass.—Perlie K. Cole, 3 Burton avenue, one house.

Sandwich, Ill.—Sandwich Greenhouses, Main street, one house.

Frankfort, Ind.—H. O. Meikel, one house. Geo. Switzer, one house.

Newburyport, Mass.—C. J. McGregor, Chapel street, enlarging.

Philadelphia, Pa.—Michaelson Bros., 56th and Walnut streets, three houses.

Fort Worth, Tex.—Drumm Seed & Floral Co., additions and alterations.

West Hoboken, N. J.—Geo. Giatras, 463 Summit avenue, two houses each 22 x 100.

Binghamton, N. Y.—J. W. Eldred, one house. H. S. Hopkins, 12 Floral avenue, additions.

Louisville, Ky.—H. Kleinstarink, three houses each 25 x 175. F. Walker Co., house 20 x 90.

Chicago Heights, Ill.—G. A. Weberg, Chicago road and Main street, additions and alterations.

Greenhouse building in Canada does not seem to be affected in the least by the war, judging by the number of contracts filed by the Toronto office of Lord & Burnham Co., as given in the news columns of our Canadian contemporary. The list is as follows: Sir John C. Eaton, Toronto, extensive range of houses; Sir Wm. Mulock, Toronto, two houses; Maj. W. H. Merritt, St. Catherines, three houses; Gordon K. Fraser, Hamilton, conservatory; Fred Magee, Port Elgin, N. B., conservatory. Also the following commercial establishments: Wm. Mousley & Sons, Weston, Ont., house, 51 x 300; A. Carriere, house, 50 x 100; R. L. Dunn, St. Catherines, two houses, 25 x 120; H. Newsome, St. Thomas, house, 60 feet long.

Vol. XXII
No. 4
JULY 24
1915

HORTICULTURE

William Gray
President-elect, American Sweet Pea Society

Published Every Saturday at 147 Summer Street, Boston, Mass.
Subscription, $1.00

LIST OF ADVERTISERS

FOR BUYERS' DIRECTORY AND READY REFERENCE GUIDE
SEE PAGES 116, 117, 118, 119

NOTES ON CULTURE OF FLORISTS' STOCK

CONDUCTED BY

John J. M. Farrell

Questions by our readers in line with any of the topics presented on this page will be cordially received and promptly answered by Mr. Farrell. Such communications should invariably be addressed to the office of HORTICULTURE.

"If vain our toil, we ought to blame the culture, not the soil."—*Pope.*

Bulb Compost

With the pressure of other duties there is a likelihood of the compost heaps being somewhat neglected in that they are allowed to become overgrown with rank weeds, which will soon eat away much of their richness. Keep the compost pile clean and you will find it to be money well invested. It will be some time before the French or Dutch bulbs arrive but it is better to prepare a pile of compost for them now rather than when they are on the place. It is much better to leave out bone and all chemical fertilizers. These are more likely to be harmful than helpful. If you stacked up a pile of sod and cow manure last fall chop this down and throw it in a heap. Bulbs like a light and rather rich soil. One-third of the whole should be decayed manure. If you have any spent hotbed manure or such as has been used in the make-up of a mushroom bed either of these is excellent for bulbs. A few shovels of soot and some sharp sand should also be added. Turn the pile over twice or thrice to thoroughly mix it.

Eucharis amazonica

Where you mean to start growing Eucharis amazonica now is a good time to begin. Plants that were started last winter and are now in 4 or 5-inch pots are the best. A perfectly sound bench should be chosen, as a bench of eucharis is good for years, the plants becoming more and more floriferous as they get crowded in the course of time. You can also use old clumps that have been divided up. The divided plants will take about a year to get established, and will not flower until then. Give them a good sod soil with about one-third of well decomposed cow manure. They can be planted as close as 5 or 6 inches apart. When established plants have made a good growth for about two months grant them a rest by shortening up on the supply of water for about four to six weeks, but not so severe as to show any bad effects on the foliage. By this process flowers will form instead of leaves. After this rest apply abundance of water. A temperature of 60 to 65 degrees at all times is needed.

Gardenias

Gardenias should now be advancing well in growth. These plants will want all the air possible now, so on all favorable opportunities give them ventilation without allowing drafts to strike them. Gardenias that were benched early in June will now be very active and must have every encouragement to promote a quick and sturdy growth. Give a good syringing in the morning and right after dinner-time. Examine the plants two or three times a day so none of them will remain dry, or, on the other hand, saturated for any length of time, both conditions being very detrimental. Give them a dusting of very fine bone, first over the surface and then a light mulch of well rotted cow manure. Damping down will now be necessary two or three times a day. Give them fumigations about every ten days.

Orchids

All cattleyas that have completed their growth should be placed at the coolest end of the house or where they can be given a fair amount of air. The quantity of water should be lessened until only enough is given to keep the plants from shrivelling. Cattleyas that are in active growth will require an abundance of water at the roots with a light syringing overhead two or three times a day. Damp the floors and benches well twice a day so as to create a humid atmosphere. All other orchids of the many species that will now be finishing up their growth should be removed to a cooler house that is very lightly shaded so as to prevent a second growth. Later you can give them more airy, cool, dry and sunny quarters which will induce them to ripen up their growth. Very little water will be needed at the roots during this rest, but give a gentle syringing over the plants on bright days which will help to keep the growths in good condition.

Poinsettias

We shall now be propagating poinsettias about as fast as we can get the young growth. Never let them wilt for want of water or from sunshine. Keep the sand saturated and guard against sun and draughts and ninety-five per cent. will root. Cuttings of poinsettias can be inserted until the middle of August and the late ones while they will not make large bracts are really preferable for making up into pans owing to their dwarfness. If the sand is sharp so that water passes away freely there should be little trouble from damping off. In putting in cuttings during this hot weather trim the leaves off quite close and let the cuttings lie in a pail of water half an hour to help plump them up. Be sure to examine the cuttings frequently and just as soon as they have made roots an inch long pot them. If left longer the roots will be broken, the cuttings will soon harden and never make as satisfactory plants as if potted more promptly. Any compost suitable for carnations or chrysanthemums will grow first-class poinsettias. Plants in pots should not receive any shade when once they have become established in their first pot.

Starting Hollyhocks

Now is the time to make a sowing of hollyhocks. The seed can be either sown out of doors or in a cold frame. The cold frame will prove to be the best. Here they can be watered and shaded and given general care. When large enough they can be planted out into other frames and kept there until next spring when they can be set out in the open.

Next Week:—Antirrhinums; Aspidistras; Chrysanthemums; Lorraine Begonias; Sweet Peas; Manure for Winter.

HORTICULTURE

VOL. XXII   JULY 24, 1915   NO. 4

PUBLISHED WEEKLY BY
HORTICULTURE PUBLISHING CO.
147 Summer Street, Boston, Mass.

Telephone, Oxford 292.
WM. J. STEWART, Editor and Manager.

SUBSCRIPTION RATES:
One Year, in advance, $1.00; To Foreign Countries, $2.00; To Canada, $1.50.

ADVERTISING RATES:
Per Inch, 30 inches to page..................... $1.00
Discounts on Contracts for consecutive insertions, as follows:
   One month (4 times), 5 per cent.; three months (13 times), 10 per cent.; six months (26 times), 20 per cent.; one year (52 times), 30 per cent.
Page and half page space, special rates on application.

Entered as second-class matter December 8, 1904, at the Post Office at Boston, Mass., under the Act of Congress of March 3, 1879.

CONTENTS   Page

It is said that by effecting economies in management the nine principal express companies have been able to wipe out the deficit which the parcels post caused. We might also add—and we believe the flower shippers will agree—that the

Express service improved

service rendered by the express people has been much improved. The arrogance of monopoly has largely disappeared as a consequence of the competition established by the people after a long and hard-fought struggle. The lesson seems to have been a good one, for extravagance and oppression have both been largely eliminated and it would seem that the express companies are really making an effort to serve the public and give satisfaction to their patrons. Thus not only the people but the express companies themselves are substantial gainers in the end.

The uses of adversity

W. H. Wyman's acknowledgment of the usefulness of the various moths, scales and other pestiferous enemies of the nurseryman's stock as effective agencies in promoting general cleanliness is unquestionably in keeping with the facts. New England has suffered from the inroads of these insects and the restrictive legislation brought about by them to a greater degree than any other section of this country. The result is an unremitting watchful care over every foot of nursery ground. Neglected corners under existing conditions would be simply suicidal and so it has come to pass that the nurseries of New England are models of cleanliness excelled by none in the world.

"Sweet are the uses of adversity,
Which like the toad, ugly and venomous,
Wears yet a precious jewel in his head;
And this our life, exempt from public haunt,
Finds tongues in trees, books in the running brooks,
Sermons in stones, and good in everything."

Working toward new ideals

The plans of the Cleveland florists for their big flower show three months hence, seem to be maturing on advanced lines and with a prospect that some new light will be thrown on the old problem of how to enlist the interest and co-operation of the retail florists in a public flower show and to profit by their experience and ability in making the show a success from a decorative and artistic standpoint. The prospectus for the gladiolus show at Atlantic City next month which we publish this week gives evidence that in this enterprise, also, the decorative possibilities of that flower are not to be neglected. All of which is very encouraging and practical evidence that the gospel which HORTICULTURE has been so zealously preaching for years has not been preached in vain. Long standing custom and deep rooted indifference are not overcome in a day and plenty of patience and persistence will still be needed before our exhibitions shall properly fill their place as advanced exponents of the uses of flowers. The reluctance of the retail trade, generally, to enter as competitors where prizes are offered for floral decorative work, was sharply in evidence at the Newport sweet pea show last week, where, in five classes for such work, only two florists competed. The floral exhibition should be in the vanguard of floral progress. There the newest and best in floral art should make its debut always. Plant and flower growers stand in the way of their own best interests when they fail to insist that in the planning for all exhibitions of their products, adequate provision shall be made in the schedule for demonstration of the many happy ways in which flowers may be used and enjoyed.

ROSE GROWING UNDER GLASS

CONDUCTED BY

Arthur C. Ruzicka

Questions by our readers in line with any of the topics presented on this page will be cordially received and promptly answered by Mr. Ruzicka. Such communications should invariably be addressed to the office of HORTICULTURE.

Tying

The earlier planted houses will now need tying, especially the teas, as these should not be allowed to lie around too long. With Beauties we like to let them lie as long as is possible without doing them harm. If they are tied up right after they are planted, they will not break at the bottom so well. This, of course, must not be carried too far, and as soon as it becomes hard to keep them clean of spider, they should be tied up at once. In tying the Beauties to wires, make sure that the breaks are well distributed. Also figure so that when the mother shoot grows up, and bears a bud, it can be cut right down to the bottom, providing the plant has sufficient breaks to get along without it. We find that it pays to do this, as the original shoot seldom bears any flowers to speak of, and if so they are short and of inferior quality. With teas it is different, and these we tie to stakes almost exclusively, preferring this method to the wires. With stakes the teas can be tied much better, and being better tied can easily be kept clean of spider. It is also much easier to get between them to mulch, to clean, to tie or to do anything at all. It is better to keep them low too, as the sap has that much less hard wood to go through, and the flowers are better and more of them. Beauties should never be tied to stakes, even in conservatories on private estates. The wires will look fully as good and better, and the plants will not be so likely to get red spider or spot, and do better all the way around.

Manure

It is very important that the manure to be used for mulching early in the fall be bought now, so that it can be heaped and turned over a few times to bring it into shape for mulching. If this is not done, the manure is likely to be too green, and that is bad for the plants, especially in the fall. In the spring it can be used without so much danger, as if it should take off some leaves, the damage would not be felt, but in the fall it would nearly ruin the plants. In heaping the manure, if no concrete platform is on the place and no provision made to take care of the leaching, pile up about six or twelve inches of sod and then heap the manure on top of this. This sod will take care of all the liquid that may leach out of the pile, and later the sod can be used as mulch or for some other suitable purpose. Most large places have their own dairies, and all that is usually needed is better facilities for handling the manure. However, growers are waking up to the fact that it is poor economy to have the manure pile near a brook or something and have the liquid go to waste. And it is not only waste; in most states it would be a violation of the law, as the liquids from manure would pollute the water. Each stable should be equipped with a covered concrete platform to take care of the manure, and this should drain into a water-tight concrete or brick cesspool out of which the liquid manure can be pumped either back on the pile or into the houses, to be used. With the low cost of concrete, and the fact that the cistern and platform can be built by the men on the place, makes us believe that the manure saved in one year after the system is put in would nearly pay for it. Manure is a hard thing to get if it is necessary to buy it, and growers who are fortunate to have a good supply of their own should surely take care of it. Business nowadays demands saving in every possible way, and the greatest loss the florist usually has is the loose way in which manure is handled.

Coal

Right now is a good time to stock up with coal. We find that we can get better prices now then later. The difference is not so great, yet there is a saving. We know several places that are looked upon as prosperous where the cellars are already stocked with the coal for the winter. With bad business, it may not always be possible to lay out the cash so far in advance but where it can be done it has a great many advantages.

The Boilers

Fires will be out on most places by this time, as the weather we have recently had does not call for heat, but for ice. Therefore as soon as a chance can be had, see that the boilers are cleaned, and oiled a little. Any cheap oil will do, and it will save the boilers a good deal. The boiler itself never suffers much all the while it is in use, but left to stand dirty in a damp cellar, it rusts very rapidly, and wears more in one summer than in three winters of firing. Clean out all soot as much as possible and put the oil on with a syringe. The outside of the boiler does not matter so much, as this is not so likely to suffer. While the work is being done it is well to see that everything is all right for the coming season, and should there be any grates or other parts of the boilers needed, order them at once so as to have them on hand. Later when they are ordered in a hurry they generally are a long time coming, and then when they do come they are generally parts from a boiler too small or will not fit, and the delay may mean a dose of mildew or other trouble.

AMERICAN SWEET PEA SOCIETY

The seventh annual meeting of this society was held at Newport, R. I., on Thursday afternoon, July 15. In the absence of President C. C. Morse and Vice-President A. M. Kirby, William Sim was asked to preside. Addresses of welcome to the society were made by President William MacKay on behalf of the Newport Horticultural Society and Mr. Sheffield for the Newport Garden Association. President Morse's address was read as it appeared in our issue of July 17. Secretary Bunyard made a general report of progress for the year, and the report of the treasurer was favorable. Prof. A. C. Beal made a detailed report on the Trial Grounds at Cornell University. J. Harrison Dick gave a valuable lecture on the Sweet Pea, its history, literature, diseases and culture and its future possibilities, and Geo. W. Kerr gave a talk on Sweet Peas for Amateurs.

Officers were elected as follows: President, William Gray, Newport, R. I.; vice-president, George W. Kerr, Doylestown, Pa.; secretary, H. A. Bunyard; treasurer, A. T. Boddington; recording secretary, J. H. Pepper; executive committee member, W. Atlee Burpee. Bar Harbor, Me., was selected as the next meeting place.

Response of President-Elect Gray.

It is with a deep sense of the honor you have conferred upon me, and of responsibility as well, that I accept the office of President of the American Sweet Pea Society.

While our exhibitions are growing more successful from a horticultural standpoint, I am sorry the financial end does not look so bright and I strongly appeal to the florist, gardener and amateur to help the good work along by becoming members of the American Sweet Pea Society. The gardener is the one to get the amateur interested by giving freely of his advice in regard to methods of growing, etc. In every community the gardener can take at least one amateur under his guidance and help arouse the amateur spirit which is so latent on this side of the Atlantic. This is right in line with the work of horticultural societies — the promotion of horticulture. Some of our seed firms do not realize the possibilities in this movement and should do all they can to help the good work along. With all pulling together the Society could be put on a basis where it would not be compelled to accept the invitation of other horticultural societies to enable it to hold exhibitions.

Our conventions in my mind should be made up of delegates from the different horticultural societies instructed by a vote of their respective societies, as to the best time and place to hold an exhibition. A place and date could thus be arrived at that would be satisfactory to the majority. I promise to do all I can to help the work along and I thank you for the honor that you have conferred upon me.

THE EXHIBITION.

The Seventh Annual Exhibition of the American Sweet Pea Society, with the co-operation and support of the Newport Horticultural Society and the Newport Garden Association, was held at the Casino, Newport, R. I., on Thursday and Friday, July 15 and 16, and was nothing short of a triumph from the standpoint of quality, extent and completeness. The arrangement was all that was possible, considering the rather restricted quarters for an exhibition of such magnitude. In many of the classes there were numerous entries and the judges had no easy job on their hands. Standing out prominently in extent and splendor Burpee's big display was easily the crowning feature of the main hall. The stage was occupied by R. & J. Farquhar & Co., with a lavish display of blooms of Lilium myriophyllum (regale) in an effective setting of palms and other greenery, the whole making an effective foil for the sea of sparkling color that filled the hall. The wide veranda which formed the entrance passageway to the main hall from the Casino grounds presented a wonderful sight, the equal of which has never been seen in any exhibition in this country, and those who have seen sweet pea shows abroad say it excelled even those. There were thirty large tubs of growing sweet peas, each specimen six to ten feet high and three to four feet through, loaded with bloom. These brought glory to the Newport growers whose chances in the cut flower classes were killed by unpropitious weather. In the cut flowers Ed. Jenkins from Lenox made a tremendous sweep, as will be seen by the list of awards which follows.

H. A. Dreer had a fascinating exhibit of nymphæas, arranged in a tank in the form of a horseshoe. This included several brilliant novelties. It was in charge of J. S. Hay. In their sweet pea display the variety Royal Purple was grand. W. A. Manda had an interesting and varied collection of new and rare stove and greenhouse plants. which attracted much attention. Bobbink & Atkins had a stand of cut roses and hardy garden perennials.

On Thursday a party from the Gardeners' and Florists' Club of Boston, 115 in number, under the guidance of Secretary W. N. Craig, visited the show and made the tour of some of the prominent estates. The trade visitors from New York and vicinity were quite numerous. Among the places inspected by the out-of-town people none attracted more attention and interest than the Mrs. H. D. Auchincloss estate where the rose garden, wild garden and rock garden under the care of Superintendent Mahan exemplify the highest attainments in their respective fields.

LIST OF AWARDS.

Section A—Private Gardeners.

Peter Henderson & Co.'s Prizes—12 vases, distinct varieties: 1st, Giraud Foster, supt. Edwin Jenkins; 2nd, Mrs. Robt. Winthrop, supt. S. W. Carlquist; 3rd, A. C. James, gard. J. H. Grentorex.

Thorburn Cup—12 vases of 12 Spencers: 1st, Giraud Foster.

Arthur T. Boddington Prizes—1st and challenge cup for collection, 25 varieties, Giraud Foster; 2nd, A. C. James.

Weeber & Don Prize—For vase of 100 sprays mixed, arranged for effect: Mrs. W. W. Sherman, gard. Andrew Ramsey.

Mount Desert Nurseries Prize—For vase of one variety, any color: Mrs. Thos. J. Emery, gard. A. L. Dorward.

Joseph Breck & Sons Prizes—For 3 vases Spencers: Mrs. Robt. Winthrop.

Henry A. Dreer Prize—For Vase of Royal Purple: Giraud Foster. Vase of Margaret Madison Improved: 1st, Mrs. H. D. Auchincloss, gard. John Mahan; 2nd, R. Pulitzer, gard. F. Hitchman.

Hitchings & Company's Cup—For 8 vases of Spencers: 1st, Giraud Foster; 2nd, Col. Chas. Pfaff, gard. Geo. Melvin.

Sutton & Sons' Cup—For table of Sweet Peas: Mrs. Thos. J. Emery.

The Carter's Tested Seeds, Inc., Prizes—For 6 tubs of Sweet Peas, any color, to be exhibited in bloom: 1st, Miss Edith Wetmore, gard. S. Johnson; 2nd, Stuart Duncan.

American Sweet Pea Society's Prizes—For display for effect, covering a round table, about four feet across: Society's silver medal and 1st, Mrs. W. G. Weld, gard. James Watt; 2nd and bronze medal, Mrs. W. B. Leeds, gard. Wm. Gray.

Section B — Private Gardeners and Amateurs.

W. Atlee Burpee & Co.'s Prizes—For 12 vases 12 varieties: 1st and silver cup, Giraud Foster; 2nd, Lester Leland, gard. E. H. Wetterlow.

Stumpp & Walter Co.'s Prizes—For 6 vases, 6 Spencers: 1st, A. N. Cooley; 2nd, Mrs. French Vanderbilt, gard. Daniel Hay; 3rd, Mrs. Rob't Winthrop.

H. F. Michell Co.'s Prizes—Silver medal for 6 vases, 6 Spencers: Col. Chas. Pfaff.

Michell Seed House bronze medal—For 25 blooms "Illuminator:" A. N. Cooley, gard. Ed. Edwards.

Michell Seed House silver medal—For vase Spencers, mixed: A. N. Cooley.

Thomas J. Grey Co.'s Cut Glass Bowl—For centerpiece for table: 1st, Mrs. W. W. Sherman; 2nd, Mrs. T. J. Emery.

Watkins & Simpson Prize—For six vases Spencer, six varieties: Giraud Foster.

Section C—Amateurs

who do not employ a gardener regularly. John Lewis Childs' prizes and American Sweet Pea Society's prizes won by about six competitors.

Section D—Retailers.

Decoration for table of eight covers: 1st, Alfred T. Bunyard, with canopy design of pink sweet peas and gypsophila; 2nd, J. G. Leikens, with branching design of pink sweet peas. Mantel Decoration: 1st, J. G. Leikens with white and lavender peas and Farleyense ferns; Bunyard exhibit disqualified for use of material not specified in schedule. Bridal Bouquet of Sweet Peas: 1st, A. T. Bunyard; 2nd, J. G. Leikens. Hamper of Sweet Peas: 1st, J. G. Leikens. Corsage of Sweet Peas: 1st, A. T. Bunyard; 2nd, J. G. Leikens.

Section E—School Children.

The Mrs. E. B. Auchincloss prizes and American Sweet Pea Society prizes, seven classes won by four competitors.

Section F—Open and Miscellaneous.

The C. C. Morse & Co.'s Cup—For the finest and most meritorious display (open to the seed trade only): 1st, W. Atlee Burpee & Co.

Jerome B. Rice Seed Co.'s Prizes—For 1915 Novelty Sweet Peas: 1st, Giraud Foster; 2nd, Mrs. Robt. Winthrop.

Lord & Burnham Co., gold watch—For the best display of Sweet Peas, arrangement to count: 1st, John G. Stalford; 2nd, Oscar Schulz.

Silver medal for best collection of Pea Novelties appearing in 1915 catalogs only: W. Atlee Burpee & Co.

Sweet Peas not yet in commerce: Silver medal to W. Atlee Burpee & Co., for Fiery Cross; certificates of merit to W. Atlee Burpee & Co., for Cherub and President.

National Sweet Pea Society of Great Britain Prize—For the largest and most meritorious exhibit of Sweet Peas: Gold medal to W. Atlee Burpee & Co.

Newport Garden Association Special Prizes (open to all)—For tub of any white, cream or cream-yellow variety: 1st, Stuart Duncan; 2nd, Miss Edith Wetmore; 3rd, Mrs. T. J. Emery. Tub of any scarlet, crimson, rose of carmine: 1st, Mrs. W. G. Weld; 2nd, Mrs. T. J. Emery. Tub of any lavender, mauve, purple or blue: 1st, Stuart Duncan; 2nd, Mrs. T. J. Emery. Tub of any pink, orange or salmon: 2nd, Mrs. T. J. Emery. Display arranged on table space of 3 ft. by 10 ft. Only the artistic arrangement of the exhibit considered in judging: 1st, silver cup, Mrs. W. G. Weld; 2nd, Mrs. T. J. Emery; 3rd, John Fletcher.

Newport Horticultural Society Special Prizes (open to all)—Sixteen classes, for 25 sprays in specified colors, of which Giraud Foster won thirteen 1sts. The other 1sts were Mrs. French Vanderbilt, two; Mrs. Robt. Winthrop, one. Winners of 2nds were Miss Edith Wetmore, Mrs. T. J. Emery, Mrs. Robt. Winthrop, Miss Alice Veltelts, gard. W. J. Watson; Giraud Foster, Robt. W. Goelet. 3rds were also awarded in most classes. The F. R. Pierson cup for most winning entries in this section was won by Giraud Foster, who also won The Garden Magazine medal of achievement for the finest vase in this section with the variety Doris Usher.

Section G, for Amateurs Only—Nine regular classes all fully competed for and awarded. R. & J. Farquhar & Co.'s prizes for 6 distinct varieties, open to private growers only: S. W. Colquist, gard. to Mrs. Robt. Winthrop. The William B. Scott & Co.'s prizes and Broadway Hardware Co.'s prizes were awarded to exhibits from children's gardens.

Newport Garden Club prizes for private gardeners and amateurs—Table Decoration: Silver cup and 1st, Mrs. Thos. J. Emery. Display for effect on round table: 1st, Mrs. W. Watts Sherman; 2nd, Mrs. H. Mortimer Brooks, gard. James Bond.

Special Awards.

Neil Ward, Lonsdale, L. I., certificate of merit for collection of sweet peas.

W. A. Manda, So. Orange, N. J., certificate of merit for collection of plants.

R. & J. Farquhar & Co., Boston, certificate of merit for collection of plants and cut flowers.

Henry A. Dreer, Inc., Philadelpila, certificate of merit for collection of water lilies.

Henry A. Dreer, Inc., honorable mention for collection of sweet peas.

Bobbink & Atkins, Rutherford, N. J., honorable mention for collection of perennials.

Miltonia Conservatories, Providence, R. I., certificate of merit for collection of cut cattleyas.

Oscar Schultz, Newport. R. I., honorable mention for Japanese iris.

Mr. Robinson, cultural certificate for Rose Ophelia.

WILLIAM GRAY,

President-Elect of The American Sweet Pea Society

The gentleman whose portrait adorns our cover page this week stands very high in the gardening fraternity as an able exponent of the best cultural skill and the American Sweet Pea Society will have an efficient and earnest president for the coming year.

Mr. Gray has been superintendent of the estate of Mrs. William B. Leeds at Newport, R. I., for the past five years. He is a native of Edinburgh, Scotland, having been born on the Arbarthnot estate "Mavis Bank," on April 20, 1874, where his father was gardener at that time, the profession of gardening having been followed by father and sons through several generations. The family came to America in 1883 and settled in Middletown. N. Y., where the father secured the position of florist at the State Hospital. After leaving school Mr. Gray served apprenticeship under his father and followed this up with an experience as assistant gardener on several private places in the vicinity of New York and in Newport. He then became head gardener to Horace Russell at Southampton and after five years' service there assumed the position he now holds.

SOCIETY OF AMERICAN FLORISTS AND ORNAMENTAL HORTICULTURISTS

Preliminary program for the Thirty-first Annual Convention, to be held in The Civic Center Auditorium, San Francisco, Cal., August 17, 18, 19, 1915.

First Day, Tuesday, August 17.

OPENING SESSION.

2 P. M.—Opening exercises in Hall H, east side, Fourth Floor, Civic Center Auditorium. Address of Welcome, by Hon. Jas. Rolph, Jr., Mayor of San Francisco; Response, by W. F. Gude; President Welch's Address; Reading Minutes of Executive Board; Report of the Secretary; Report of the Treasurer; Reports of State Vice-Presidents; Consideration of Invitations for Meeting Place for 1916.

EVENING SESSION.

8 P. M.—Balloting for Meeting Place for 1916, at St. Francis Hotel; Reception to President Welch, at the St. Francis Hotel. Music; Dancing; Refreshments. Strictly informal.

Second Day, Wednesday, August 18.

MORNING SESSION

9 A. M.—Meeting of The Florists' Telegraph Delivery.

10.30 A. M.—Annual Meeting of The Ladies' Society of American Florists. Session S. A. F. and O. H.; Report of the National Flower Show Committee; George Asmus, Chairman; Discussion; Nomination of Officers for 1916; Report of the Judges of the Trade Exhibition and the Convention Garden; Report of the Committee on the President's Address; Discussion.

AFTERNOON SESSION.

2 P. M.—Bowling Contest of The Ladies of the S. A. F.

2 P. M.—Session S. A. F. and O. H.; Discussion, "Are Not Insurance Rates on Modern Greehouse Establishments Too High, in view of the lighter risks accruing from better and less dangerous construction?" Led by Wm. F. Kasting; Report of the Committee on National Publicity—Irvin Bertermann, Chairman; Discussion.

Third Day, Thursday, August 19.

MORNING SESSION

9 A. M.—Meeting of The Florists' Hail Association.

10 A. M.—Time alloted for Meetings. Rose, Carnation. Chrysanthemum and Gladiolus Societies if desired.

11 A. M.—Election of Officers of the S. A. F. and O. H. for 1916; Polls open from 11 A. M. to 12 M.

AFTERNOON SESSION.

2 P. M.—Question Box; Deferred Business.

2 P. M.—Annual Bowling Tournament, S. A. F. and O. H., at Gramp alleys, 924 Market St.

Essays.

In view of the many and varied attractions of the Convention and Convention City, the Executive Board decided that it would be unwise to take up the time of the convention with the reading of essays. Realizing, however, the value of the presentation of essays at the Society's conventions, the secretary was instructed to invite essays from various gentlemen willing to pre-

pare them, such invitations and the number of them to be within his discretion, the essays to be furnished to the trade papers for publication during the convention period, and to be printed as part of the proceedings of the convention.

The following essays are presented: "Is it Advisable for the Society of American Florists and Ornamental Horticulturists to Establish a National Credit and Collection Department?" by August F. Poehlmann, Morton Grove, Ill.

"The Problems Attending the Establishment of Permanent Convention Gardens," by Theodore Wirth, Superintendent of Parks, Minneapolis, Minn.

"The Necessity of National Publicity to Advance the Interests of Commercial Floriculture in the United States," by Albert Pochelon, Detroit, Mich.

Fourth Day, Friday, August 20.

S. A. F. and O. H. Day at the Panama-Pacific International Exposition.

The Secretary's office will be near the main entrance of Halls H, I and J, east side, fourth floor, in the Civic Center Auditorium, where all members should report as soon as possible after their arrival in San Francisco. Members who have not paid their 1915 assessment can make payment at this office and receive the official badge button, but the work of the office will be greatly facilitated if members will make remittances to the secretary prior to the convention.

The address of the secretary from July 15 is care of Daniel MacRorie, 430 Phelan Bldg., San Francisco.

PACIFIC COAST HORTICULTURAL SOCIETY.

At the monthly meeting of the Pacific Coast Horticultural Society various matters of mutual interest were discussed, including preparations for the Fall Flower Show, the S. A. F. Convention, and a Fall Picnic. H. Plath announced that the prize list for the Fall Flower Show is much in demand, which shows that considerable interest is manifest in that event. On behalf of the program committee, Mr. Plath reported that the souvenir program is practically ready. A communication was read from the secretary of the Gardeners' Association, outlining plans for their convention. In regard to the Fall Picnic, the committee proposed to wait until September and recommended that it be held in Grand Canyon Park. A standing invitation was extended from Messrs. James, Plath and Fotheringham. present Jury on garden exhibits at the Exposition. to hold field day at the gardens on Saturday afternoons while their work is in progress. Much interest was shown in the evening's exhibits. An exhibit of Mrs. Francis King gladiolus from F. Pelicano took 90 points; a showing of Primula obconica from H. Plath was rated at 90 points; and a large display of statice from J. Gill took 80 points.

DURING RECESS

TWO PICNICS.

The two group pictures on these pages were taken on the occasion of the New York Florists' Club and the Greek-American Florists' outings, respectively. Each of these events constitutes an annual red letter day in the summer memories of those who participate, especially the ladies and children for whose pleasure they are primarily intended. Pretty good looking bunch—both of them—are they not? A close inspection will no doubt convince our readers who have any eye for structural beauty that the an-

Married Ladies' Race, 200 ft.: , Mrs. A. G. Handel; Mrs. L. T. Rodman; Mrs. Schwartz. Men's Race, 300 ft.: Edw. Mauda; N. B. Irwin; A. Demeusy, Jr. Potato Race for Ladies: Lilian Schwake; Jennie Mamitsch. Growers' Race (under 50 years), 300 ft.: P. J. Wright; Alfred Zeller; J. M. Kemper. Fat Men's Race: Edw. Manda; E. W. Housemau; Philip Mauker. Sack Race: Jos. Manda; John A. Kennedy; Emil Schloss. Standing Broad Jump (Boys under 18): Hank; E. Manda. Standing Broad Jump (Men members): Al. Rigo; Gus Marshall; C. Begerow. Wholesalers' Race, 300 ft.: N. B. Irwin; A. Demeusy; L. T. Rodman. Ladies' Bowling: Mrs. J. Duley; Mrs. George Mustoe. Men's Bowling (Members only): F. Grumbach; Ed. Holt; J. A. Manda; A. J. Guttman. Handsomest Girl Baby (under 2 years): Wilhelmina Manker.

tion Co.; Mr. Koeplitz representing the Sefton Box Co.; J. D. Keohane representing the H. F. Michell Co.; S. S. Pennock and Mr. Price representing their company; from Coatsville, James Brown and wife; from Chester County E. C. Marshall and family, Percy Bernard and Mr. Ludwig, Wm. Swayne and wife and Mr. Ladley and wife.

Rocky Springs Park was the place and could be reached by trolley for a nickle, but from the number of autos in evidence the average florist scorns a trolley, and turns up his nose at any thing so cheap as a nickle. The young-

NEW YORK FLORISTS' CLUB OUTING

cient Greek goddesses and classical beauties had nothing on their daughters of the present day.

At the Florists' Club Outing which was held on Wednesday, July 14, a long program of games and amusements was carried out. The names of the winning contestants were as follows:

Girls' Race (under 5 years), 100 ft.: Viola Greer. Boys' Race (under 5), 100 ft.: A. J. Handel; R. Schwartz. Boys' Race (5 to 7), 100 ft.: Harry Grumbach; Jerome Trepel; John McCarthy. Girls' Race (7 to 9), 200 ft.: Irene Mustoe; Mary Smith; Martha Schmutz. Boys' Race (7 to 9), 200 ft.: Howard Brown; Carl Giesler. Girls' Race (9 to 11), 200 ft.: Carrie Peterson; Mary O'Conner; Frances Esck. Boys' Race (9 to 11), 200 ft.: Robt. Hildenbrand; Aug. Walhel; Francis Smith. Girls' Race (11 to 13), 250 ft.: Anna Schwake; Agnes Wright; Phyllis Geisler. Boys' Race (11 to 13), 250 ft.: Jos. Walter; Cornelius Begerow; Robt. Mayer. Girls' Race (13 to 15), 250 ft.: Eloise Schmutz; Ida Grumbach; Mary Walter. Girls' Race (15 to 17), 300 ft.: Selma Guttman; Jennie Mamitsch; Lillian Schwake. Boys' Race (15 to 17), 300 ft.: Geo. Walter; William Wright. Young Men's Race, 300 ft.: Harry Walter; Wm. Bogert; Wm. Manda. Young Ladies' Race, 200 ft.: Christine Neilson; Olive Iler; Minnie Weise.

LANCASTER COUNTY FLORISTS' CLUB.

The third Thursday of each month we have the use of the Chamber of Commerce rooms but in spite of the fact that we pay rent we do not use them for July and August and instead have our picnic on the date of the July meeting and through the courtesy of our president a meeting and afternoon of sports at his farm, one of the many delightful places to spend a hot half day and evening, around this section of the world. It's a good scheme, try it out, Philadelphia, and you will have a big attendance to record for the summer.

Although our membership is limited in number we had at the July meeting (or picnic) in round numbers about 200 people, among them being T. J. Nolan representing the King Construc-

sters were made happy by the distribution of tickets that entitled them to any of the various amusements and the way those kids got rid of tickets was a revelation to the men who got them and to the men who contributed toward their purchase, the latter getting the most enjoyment out of it.

After lunch the fun began. Three strong games were going all the time on the Lancaster Quoit Club grounds which were given to us for the day, Mrs. A. M. Herr again showing her skill at this amusement. The following list of sports were pulled off under the able direction of Frank Kohr, Elmer Weaver and Harry Rohrer.

Boys' potato race, Edward E. Rohrer; Girls' do, 1st Anna Myers, 2nd, Katerine Siehert; Men's do, 1st E. S. Rutt, 2nd J. D. Keohane; Egg race, Miss Anna Mayers; Three-legged race, 1st Martin Good and Frank Bare; 50 yd. dash for men, Lloyd Weaver; 50 yd. dash for boys, Paul Weaver; 25 yd. dash for ladies, Miss Ida Miller; 25 yd. dash for girls, Miss Ruth Bare; Fat men's race, T. J. Nolan.

The tug of war was won through the leadership of S. S. Pennock and the superior strength of T. J. Nolan for their side as the local men were not up to the wrinkles and seemed just a bit tired after the strenuous week the most of them had getting houses into shape and other little (?) jobs this hot weather. After a chicken dinner a general good time was had, those who wanted to danced, and those who did not dance enjoyed the evening crowd from the city.

All of this for a dollar. Can you beat it? Any club wanting to give a successful picnic for a little bit of money should get into communication with our committee. For a few hundred dollars they might be induced to take charge of your outing.

ALBERT M. HERR.

Lancaster, Pa.

GARDENERS' AND FLORISTS' CLUB OF BOSTON.

Annual Picnic and Games.

As we are busy getting ready for the

"THE NURSERY BUSINESS AS A BUSINESS PROPOSITION."

(A Paper read before the American Association of Nurserymen, at Detroit, by Mr. W. H. Wyman).

No one who is in the nursery business today, or who has a fair knowledge of the history of the business, can doubt that it is a proposition. Comparatively few, out of the many who call themselves nurserymen, have attained a reasonable degree of success; while many more have a name to live, but in reality are leading a precarious existence; while still others have entirely fallen out and cast their wreckage upon the shoulders of too many with whom they have had to do. In this business, a few only succeed while the great majority come far short of success, if they do not utterly fail. It may be said that the same is true of every business.

Why Some Succeed.

With that proposition we are not

lives up to his obligations, providing he has a fair amount of business sagacity, he can succeed. But if on the other hand he tries a short cut to success, forfeiting his word and disregarding his obligations, his doom is sealed. The picture is not overdrawn. A few succeed in the nursery business, while many fail. Why it is? Is it because of its peculiarities? Is it hedged about by obstacles so many and so great as to make success almost unattainable?

Some of the Obstacles.

The fact that some succeed proves that the difficulties, however great, are not unsurmountable. What should the business world think of a shoe manufacturer who should take an order for a thousand cases of shoes, and who did not know just what it would cost to manufacture those shoes? Such a manufacturer would be ruled out of the business. It is of

NEW YORK GREEK AMERICAN FLORISTS' OUTING

press the members of the Gardeners' and Florists' Club and their families and friends are enjoying their annual outing at Cunningham Park, East Milton. Mass., under the efficient management of the following named officials and committees:

Ring Master—W. J. Kennedy. Starter—Peter M. Miller. Clerk—W. N. Craig. Judges—James Methven, Andrew K. Rogers, Frank Allison, Duncan Finlayson, Geo. M. Anderson, John Duguid, Peter Fisher, M. A. Patten, Wm. Sim, A. F. Barney, Robert Cameron, James Brown. Umpires—William J. Patterson for Men; Thomas H. Westwood for Boys; F. E. Palmer for Ladies. Committee—Peter M. Miller, Wm. J. Kennedy, Andrew K. Rogers, Wm. J. Patterson, Geo. M. Anderson, Jas. Methven, Chairman, Committee on Entertainment—G. W. Hamer.

Never was a finer day provided for an outing. Bright, cool and bracing weather, and everything in the landscape green and clean after the recent rains. The story of the athletic events and names of the winners will appear next week.

to concern ourselves now. We are nurserymen, and if I rightly comprehend the import of this organization, we are here for improvement. We have come together from all over this great country, to clasp hands in friendly intercourse; to exchange ideas as well as wares, and to be inspired, if possible, to greater and nobler attainments in our avocation.

One ambition animates every one of us. We all want to succeed and this is true of every man, strange as the proposition may seem. Some may be led to doubt that assertion, but I aver that it is true. All men court success; but from your view-point they could not, if they studied diligently, do that which would more surely bring defeat, than by continuing on in the course they are pursuing. By way of illustration: suppose a young man starts in business without capital—he will be given a chance. Everybody will help a fellow to make a start. Brotherly kindness is not dead. If he deals on the square and

no use to manufacture shoes, or trees, unless it can be done at a profit. And to do it at a sure profit, the cost of production must be ascertained with a reasonable degree of certainty.

In the case of most manufactured articles, that is a comparatively easy task; but not so in the nursery business. The superficial method of figuring costs is the one most generally employed whenever such an attempt is made. That is, an acre of land will yield a given number of plants, it costs so much to set them out, so much to cultivate the land per year, so much to bud or graft them, and so much more to dig and put them on the market. But that is not enough. The rental of the land, or the depletion of the soil in case one owns his land; the losses incurred by climatic conditions, such as excessive rain or no rain, frosts, hail and snow, and many more such natural contingencies must not be left out of account. Then again the depreciation of tools, machinery and buildings must not be overlooked; interest on the investment and a list of overhead charges all enter into the cost of production.

Unforeseen Contingencies.

Neither is this all. Thirty years ago this catalogue of expenses would have been about all that would have had to be considered; not so now. Insect pests, save the old tent caterpillar, were unknown. Even a quarter of a century ago who had heard of, or much less seen, the San Jose scale, the brown-tail, gipsy or leopard moth, or the white pine blister rust? I did not; but now all of us are familiar with some if not all of them; and we know too that these things add to the cost of production; they must not be regarded as unmitigated evils, any more than weeds should be. Weeds compel cultivation and hence growth; pests compel cleaning up of the nursery and its surrounding; they conduce to cleanliness. I venture the assertion that never in the history of the nursery business in this country, were there so many tidy, well-kept nurseries as there are today; and in a large measure, the pests are responsible for this state of things. While all this and even more is true, the fact remains that these pests, so-called, have added very materially to the cost of production.

Determining Total Costs

All of these things must be taken into account in determining costs, and when all have been taken into account we can arrive at the cost of production only relatively at best. But that relative cost makes a basis at which to begin. In our schooldays, we wrestled with algebraic propositions, with known and unknown quantities in the equation represented by such characters as X, Y and Z. Now we wrestle with problems known as costs, and costs that are unknown. In the one case we could determine the value of the unknown by the known values, but not so with such unknown quantities as storms, drought, wind and hail. These unknown quantities must be determined not by algebraic process, but by liberal additions. A safe way is that of the druggist, who adds to the cost price his two per cent. If we figure that a given plant cost (using the known values) $20 per 1,000 to produce it, I have regarded it a safe proposition to multiply that by two. In some instances that would seem excessive; in others it would fall below the actual cost. On the whole I believe it is a safe rule to follow in determining costs. But we must not stop here, when we have considered this side of the equation, for it is at this point that, with many, the tug-of-war begins.

(To be continued)

BRITISH HORTICULTURE.

Meritorious New Roses.

At the summer show of the National Rose Society in London awards were made to a batch of new introductions, which attracted considerable attention. G. Paul & Sons, secured a gold medal for Paul's Lemon Pillar, a meritorious addition. Wm. Paul & Son, Ltd., obtained a gold medal for Paul's Scarlet Climber. They also received certificates of merit for Queen of Fragrance, a pink H. T., which gained the Clay

PROF. H. B. DORNER.

The above picture shows our esteemed young friend H. B. Dorner, back among the flowers at the University greenhouses at Urbana, Ill. The look of quiet content on his face speaks for itself of the song in his heart, for he has just returned from his wedding trip.

cup last year for fragrance, and for Titania, a garden H. T. of a coppery red tint. Hugh Dickson added to his long list of successes by securing a certificate for Princess Charming, a small H. T., of an orange buff shade. Cherry Page, which received a certificate, is a garden H. T. of bright cherry red color, and was shown by W. Easlea who was also successful with Lady Bowater, a white exhibition H. T. B. R. Cant & Sons, gained certificates for Cupid, a single pink rose, Florence S. Paul, an exhibition H. T. with deep pink petals, and Sallie, a cream tinted exhibition H. T. S. McGredy & Sons were awarded a certificate for Flame of Fire, a garden rose of deep rich apricot, suffused with orange. Queen Alexandra, another certificated rose shown by Rev. J. H. Pemberton, is an excellent single.

R. H. S. Summer Show.

A brilliant feast of color was seen at the summer show of the Royal Horticultural Society, held in the grounds of Holland House, Kensington, on July 6 and two following days. According to Sir Harry Veitch, one of the society's veterans, in spite of the war the show was as good as, and possibly better, than the best which had previously been held. Orchids made a gorgeous and costly show, the contributors including Sir Jeremiah Colman, Gurney Fowler, Charlesworth & Co., and Sander & Sons. Mr. Fowler's exhibit included an imposing new hybrid odontoglossum, Georgius Rex, which was the chief attraction in the orchid tent, and was coveted and admired by the numerous visitors. Another special feature was the display of eremuri, the largest and finest ever seen in this country, arranged by H. Wallace & Co. The Coronation Cup

was secured by Blackmore & Langdon, whose begonia collection furnished a bright splash of color in one of the marquees. Roses of course, made a grand show, some excellent specimens of the Wichuraiana hybrids being well in evidence, whilst old favorites and newcomers were seen as cut blooms and in pots. The Clay challenge cup, was won by B. Cant & Son. Gold medals were awarded to Lord North, Sir Jeremiah Colman, W. Paul & Son, B. Cant & Son, A. Dickson & Son, Dobbie & Co., A. F. Dutton, Wallace & Co., and Blackmore & Langdon.

W. H. Adsett.

NASSAU COUNTY HORTICULTURAL SOCIETY.

At the meeting of the Nassau County Horticultural Society, Glen Cove, N. Y., Wednesday, July 14, first prizes were awarded Jas. Holloway for raspberries, W. D. Robertson for currants, R. Jones for peaches. President Westlake's special ($5.00) for sweet peas was won by H. Jones. Jas. Holloway was awarded a cultural certificate for a collection of outdoor fruit, 12 varieties.

An invitation was received from the Oyster Bay Horticultural Society to join them in their annual outing August 17. Further particulars of this event will be given at a later date.

The competition at our next meeting will be on 12 spikes gladioli, 6 ears of sweet corn and 12 mixed asters.

At the Sweet Pea Show held in the Glen Cove Neighborhood Building, July 8, the following were among the successful exhibitors: Mrs. C. F. Cartledge, gard. W. Noonin; Ralph Pulitzer, gard. F. Hitchman; Mrs. J. H. Ottley, gard. J. M. Dow; H. C. Smith, gard. A. Walker.

James Gladstone, Cor. Sec'y.

LENOX HORTICULTURAL SOCIETY.

There was a fine display of sweet peas at the Lenox Horticultural Society's meeting, Wednesday evening, July 14. George Foulsham, supt. to W. B. O. Field, and Edwin Jenkins, supt. to Giraud Foster, were both awarded a diploma, each display comprising about 30 varieties and showing a high degree of culture. E. J. Norman was awarded a first class certificate for a new rambler rose named Annie Norman.

The number of entries in the competition for school gardens has beat all previous records, and has gone over the hundred mark.

For the Society's Summer Show to be held July 27 and 28, Messrs. Arthur Herrington, of Madison, N. J., Robert Scott, Pittsfield, and Fred Heeremans, Lenox, have consented to act as judges. Gordon McMillan, Harold Bryant and William Spratt will act as committee of arrangements.

Louis Barnet, Asst. Sec.

PATENTS GRANTED.

1,144,464. Fertilizer Distributor Attachment. Joseph H. Crumpler, Magnolia, Ark.

1,144,542. Hedge Trimmer. Louis Hammel, Philadelphia, Pa.

1,144,663. Plant Cover. Leonard J. Merriman, Wilmington, N. C.

1,145,266. Plant Protector. George W. Roberts, Vicksburg, Miss.

SEED TRADE

Value of imports of horticultural
goods at the port of New York for
week ending July 10, is given as follows: Manure salt $8821; fertilizer
$103; clover seed $9435; trees and
plants $276.

On Thursday, July 15 the heads of
departments and other officials of the
Peter Henderson & Co., store to the
number of about thirty enjoyed an
outing by auto to Coney Island, with
dinner at Guffanti's, speeches and a
record good time altogether.

ATLANTIC CITY GLADIOLUS SHOW

All arrangements are now perfected
for the Gladiolus Show at Atlantic
City. The show will be held at the
Royal Palace Casino, situated on the
Boardwalk, and facing the ocean from
three sides, so that the hall is as cool
as one could wish for.

The dates are August 26, 27, 28 and
29. Admission from 10 A. M. until
6 P. M. 15 cents; from 6 P. M. until
10 P. M. 25 cents.

On each afternoon of the first three
days a lecture will be given. (1) by
Max Schling, New York, on "How to
arrange flowers artistically." (2) by
Arthur Cowee, Berlin, N. Y., on "The
varieties of Gladiolus." (3) by Maurice
Fuld, New York, on "How best to grow
the Gladioli by the amateur." The
fourth day being Sunday the lecture
has been omitted. Every evening from
8 to 10 music will be rendered by
Schwab's Orchestra, the best in Atlantic City.

The hall has been spaced into exhibitors' spaces, each measuring 6 by
20 feet. Every exhibitor must try to
break away from the old methods of
exhibiting, and display his flowers in
an original and artistic way, so that
the entire show will be a thing of
beauty. Exhibitors are charged rental
of $20 for each space, but the committee pledges itself to refund this
amount if the returns from the show
warrant it. A number of spaces are
unengaged, and applications should be
made at once to Maurice Fuld, 1
Madison avenue, N. Y. City. The committee is confident, that if the weather
conditions are favorable, our show will
draw an attendance of 100,000 people
during the four days, so that the exhibitors have a splendid guarantee of
making their exhibit profitable.

The committee from the very first
has planned this exhibit for the exclusive benefit of the American growers and dealers, and they will encourage all exhibitors to book as much
business as they possibly can. Appli-
cations from foreign firms, both for
space for exhibit and advertising in
the souvenir bulletin, have been refused.

A special souvenir bulletin and program is in the course of construction,
and the committee is glad to announce
that the advertising space in this bulletin has been completely covered, and
that further applications must be refused. The bulletin will contain as
contributors, the names of every prominent gladiolus grower and 10,000 of
same will be published which will be
sold at the exhibition at 10 cents each.
The entire week will be known in Atlantic City, as Gladiolus Week. This
has been originated by the Publicity
Bureau, and the Hotelmen's Association of Atlantic City, who are co-operating with our committee to make the
show a tremendous success.

The growers from all over the country will contribute in the neighborhood of 100,000 spikes of cut gladioli,
which will be furnished free of charge
to all the beach front hotels, who will
use them to decorate their dining
rooms. In return the hotels will prominently advertise our show on their
daily menus. As a further advertising campaign, the newspapers of Atlantic City will help us, and lithograph
display signs will be prominent in the
lobbies of the hotels, and in all the
shop windows along the boardwalk.

The committee will gladly help those
attending the show, to arrange hotel
accommodations for them. For the
benefit of those who are rather handicapped in the knowledge of arranging
flowers artistically, an artist has been
engaged who will help every exhibitor
to accomplish what he is after. The
hall will be open the day previous to
the show, and a carpenter and sign
painter will be on hand, to be of further assistance.

    MAURICE FULD, Chairman; MRS. B.
HAMMOND TRACY, ARTHUR COWEE,
GEORGE W. KERR.
      Special Exhibition Committee.

Newburgh, N. Y.—The directors of
the Yuess Gardens Company have
elected the following officers for a
year: President, W. Stanley Murtfeldt; vice-president, Percy W. Herbert; treasurer, O. J. Cathcart; secretary, R. Harry Cathcart, Jr.

Of Interest to Retail Florists

THE CLEVELAND SHOW.

Many Retailers Planning to Exhibit.

A plan for having many retail displays in the Cleveland Flower Show
has been worked out by the "retail display" committee in charge of all retail
work in connection with this coming
big event, and was submitted to the
members of the Cleveland Florists'
Club at their last meeting, held on
Monday, July 12th.

The plan is to allot to each florist an
equal amount of space and allow them
to exhibit table decorations, corsage
work, brides' bouquets, etc., basket arrangements, and general decorative effects. Each exhibitor will change his
display each day, and feature a different flower, using the official flower of
the day, chrysanthemums coming the
first day, and followed by roses and
then carnations.

This plan has been well received by
the members and the committee expect between twenty and thirty retailers to participate in the show. The
"retail displays" committee is composed of Frank Ritzenthaler, of Knoble
Bros. Co., C. M. Wagner, and C. E.
Russell of Jones-Russell Co., who
serves as chairman.

NEWS NOTES.

San Francisco, Cal.—The Jordan
Park Floral Company has been purchased by F. E. Stratton.

Swarthmore, Pa.—B. Schilder has
purchased the entire business of the
firm of Schilder & Lefebre.

Davenport, Ia.—Miss Mary A. Tier-
ney has purchased the florist business
of the Bills Floral Co., 102 West Second St.

Newton, Mass.—H. W. Cotton, the
florist, of Centre St., has bought the
John C. Clarke greenhouse business on
Mt. Ida St.

Newburyport, Mass.—A storehouse
and packing room are being added to
the equipment of Carl D. Hale, florist,
Main street.

Alden, N. Y.—Miller & Stroh have
dissolved partnership and J. B. Miller
will hereafter conduct the business in
his own name.

Schenectady, N. Y.—Julius Eger, the
State St. florist, is having an addition
30 by 36 constructed in the rear of his
place of business.

San Francisco, Cal.—The Metzner
Floral Co. succeeds the Richard Deiner
Company, 320 Market St., with nurs-
eries at Mountain View.

Boston. — Representing seventy-two
claims of a total value of $32,000, Alex-
ander I. Stoneman was elected trustee in the case of first meeting of the
creditors of Sidney Hoffman before
Referee Gibbs of the United States
Bankruptcy Court for Norfolk County.
His bond was fixed at $4,900. Mr. Stone-
man also served as receiver.

NEWS ITEMS FROM EVERYWHERE

CHICAGO.

F. Mallinson of Chas. Samuelson's had the misfortune to lose his father and mother-in-law, Friday July 17, in an automobile accident.

The sympathy of the trade is extended to Mr. and Mrs. Burmeister, florists of the Rosehill Cemetery on the death of their child on July 15.

Bruno Bandel of the Morton Grove factory of the Poehlmann Bros., will be compelled to leave the manufacture of florists' supplies and return to his native land to fight.

Mrs. P. J. Foley has returned from a three weeks' sojourn at St. Joseph, Mich., where she took the celebrated baths for rheumatism. She has completely recovered her former health.

Wm. Cook who was in the florist business here many years ago, called upon old acquaintances last week, on his way from the exposition in San Francisco to his home in the south.

Fred Ottenbacher of the Zech & Mann staff is enjoying his vacation. Joe Eringer comes next and Allie Zech, head of the firm since his father's death will stick to the store till the last.

Wm. Wolf of A. Lange's is at the West Side Hospital, where he is recovering from the effects of a fall from a step-ladder, in the store. It is doubtful if he will be about again for several weeks.

J. E. Pollworth, of the Chicago Feed and Fertilizer Co., will represent his firm at the convention at San Francisco. Among the salesmen recently added to their force are H. E. Humiston, Omaha, Neb., a graduate of the State Agricultural College; M. R. Jones, Kansas City, Kas., and M. A. Sanders, Cincinnati, all practical men.

Announcement was made of the engagement of John Walsh, and Miss Julia A. Faber, at a dinner party at the Bismarck Gardens, July 17. The bride to be, lives at Minock, Ill. and John is the popular young salesman for the Chicago Flower Growers' Association. The date of the wedding is not stated, but it is strongly suspected that when John returns from his vacation that he will not be alone.

With a supply of peonies that bids fair to reach into August, and a steady arrival of gladioli since cold weather and carnations still good, which are usually out of the way of asters, it is not surprising that there is not sale for all the flowers this summer. Summer roses now are about perfect, Mrs. Russell, Milady and Sunburst being a trio of splendid summer bloomers. What has been done to increase the demand correspondingly?

"What's in a name?" Chicago Grand Floral Festival is the new name for the fall flower show. It is harder to say than the old title, but florists will gladly make the effort if it will help assure that important event success. All the department committees are working with zest and a "pull together" spirit prevails. The fall flower show is thought by many to have a direct effect upon flower sales during the winter season and the constant increase in flower supply calls for every effort to increase demand.

The Foley Greenhouse Manufacturing Co. has the order for the new conservatories to be built for Wm. Wrigley, Jr., at his summer home at Lake Geneva, Wis. (This is the man whose name is said to be in the mouths of more people than that of any other, for he is the chewing gum magnate). This firm has just completed two new houses, 40 x 225 feet, for Fred Schram at Crystal Lake, Wis. The building of the power house was included. These houses are now planted and the heating system is being tested. The new greenhouse at the Chicago "Bridewell," also erected by the Foley people, is nearly completed.

After the joint meeting of the committee from the Chicago Florists' Club and the Chicago Park Association, it was discovered that the eastern delegations they were planning to entertain jointly, would be in Chicago four days apart. The park superintendents will be here August 8, and the florists August 12. All florists visiting Chicago en route to the convention at San Francisco, will be entertained by the Chicago Florists' Club, with an automobile ride through the parks and other places of interest in the city, ending with a dinner at the Bismarck Gardens. Ample time will be allowed to prepare for the 10 P. M. train. All visitors are invited to meet at the Auditorium Hotel, at 1.30 P. M. sharp.

During the summer months when the fertilizer dealers are having their dull season they are by no means idle. The whole subject of fertilizers, especially the so-called "commercial" kinds, are being studied as probably they never have before and the flower or vegetable grower who wants to get the greatest percent of profit out of his benches will find the fertilizer trade ready to meet his questions with an intelligent exposition of the whole subject. With competition becoming more keen each year and the areas of glass more extensive, it is business policy to make each foot of bench room produce to its utmost capacity. Many of the men now engaged in this important branch of the business have studied at our state agricultural colleges and done soil research work.

CINCINNATI.

Chas. Dudley, Jr., and R. T. Virgin. both of Parkersburg, W. Va., recently stopped in this city. They are on a trip down the Ohio in a canoe.

Mrs. P. J. Olinger and children, left for Evanston, Ill., to spend the balance of the summer. Mr. Olinger accompanied them as far as New Castle, Ind.

Max Rudolph, C. E. Critchell, Alex Ostendarp, J. Chas. Murphy and R. Witterstaetter, Directors of the Cincinnati Florists' Society, at a Board meeting held on Monday afternoon, decided not to hold the regular meeting of the Society in August as very many of the members plan to be away at that time.

PITTSBURGH.

Rumor says that constructive work is to begin early in the fall on a large and handsome greenhouse on the S u rre Hill estate of Andrew W. Mellon.

T. Hart Given, president of the Farmers' National Bank, is about to have built a fine greenhouse on his grounds on Morewood Heights and Wilkins avenue.

At the annual tree planting of the Congress of Women's Clubs of Western Pennsylvania Superintendent of Parks George W. Burke was among fifty for whom trees were named.

The West End Park under the regime of Neil McCallum is so unique in its representation of an English garden that numerous East End and North Side people make the long trip in order to see its beauty. Mr. McCallum has the distinction of being the president of both the Florists' Club of Pittsburgh and the Botanical Society of Western Pennsylvania. Although of Scottish race, he is a native of London, England, and for many years was a resident of Australia, going there when only fifteen.

The Garden Club of Allegheny County will hold its August meeting on the 14th at Rachelwood Farm, the summer home of Mr. and Mrs. James R. Mellon. This estate, which really embraces a chain of nine farms, is located in the heart of the Allegheny Mountains, eleven miles from Ligonier. Mrs. William Thaw, Jr., recently entertained the members at her Sewickley Heights place, to hear Mr. Strassburger, of Philadelphia, talk on Rock Gardens; the Methods of Making and the Flowers to Grow. This was followed by a visit to Mrs. Thaw's rock garden, just completed by Mr. Strassburger.

CLEVELAND.

Some florists in this section are having considerable trouble with rust on snapdragon. Some have lost whole batches outside and some lots in the greenhouses are looking pretty sick.

Al Barber and George Bate returned from their fishing trip and reported a fine time. George then took Herman Knoble and Frank Friedley and their families down from July 17th to 22nd. Al. Lingren spent a few days at Detroit. Harry Jones of the Jones-Russell Co. and Mr. MacDiarmid motored to Detroit last week.

The Cleveland Cut Flower Company is erecting two new houses at Newton Falls, Ohio; one house 49 by 400, Lord & Burnham construction, for roses, which is almost finished and ready for planting, and one house 24 by 200 for carnations which is to be built immediately. The Cleveland Cut Flower plant on Eddy Rd. is being torn down and the glass, tile benches and pipe are being shipped to Newton Falls, to be used in the new houses. Guy Bate who is in charge of the Newton Falls plant has his young stock in excellent shape to plant as soon as possible.

SAN FRANCISCO.

Daniel MacRorie has just returned from an outing in the Yosemite Valley with his father, Malcolm MacRorie, who is here from New Jersey.

John Young, secretary of the Society of American Florists, arrived in San Francisco a few days ago, expecting to remain until after the Convention.

The Ladies California Floral Society, recently organized in this city, held a social gathering at the home of Mr. and Mrs. J. A. Axel on the evening of July 14. Several members of the Pacific Coast Horticultural Society attended with their wives, there being about 35 present all told. Music was furnished, light refreshments served and the time passed very pleasantly. Several new members were enrolled.

The San Francisco and Oakland houses of Hogan-Kooyman & Co. will hereafter be operated independently, G. E. Hogan, Albert E. Evers, and C. Kooyman having dissolved partnership. Under the new arrangement, Messrs. Hogan and Evers take over the retail business in Oakland, and Mr. Kooyman becomes sole owner of the wholesale business in San Francisco. Both establishments have been going ahead nicely, but there has been no vital connection between them since the wholesale department was moved from Oakland to San Francisco a year ago in March, at which time Mr. Kooyman assumed full charge of the San Francisco store and the other partners took charge of the Oakland shop. Both firm names will be changed shortly.

PHILADELPHIA.

Mr. and Mrs. John Burton and grandson have been on a visit to John N. May, Summit, N. J.

The Truly-Rurals will have a week-end fishing trip at the Commodore's, July 30, 31 and August 1.

Campbell Bros., Pennlynn, suffered a loss of about fifty boxes of glass in the hailstorm which struck that section on July 13. Bill Comfort says he never saw such big 'uns. Some of them "large as hens' eggs."

KANSAS CITY.

Sam. Murray is jubilant over the increased business in his new establishment—very much better than last year.

This neighborhood has had no lack of rainfall. In fact, since last autumn the amount of rain has been the heaviest in many years. The country was never more beautiful and green than at the present time.

Never was a more cool and delightful spring. May, June and July, up to the present date have been simply ideal and as a consequence the florists have had a superb supply of garden flowers — delphiniums particularly — and gladioli are very fine as are also the dahlias which are now blooming in abundance.

HARTFORD, CONN.

One of West Hartford's oldest business industries changed hands last week when Carl Peterson took possession of the Whiting greenhouses on a lease for a term of years. Mr. Peterson has had charge of the greenhouses for the past eighteen years, and during the past ten years has been the manager for Miss Helen F. Whiting.

Mr. Peterson had his first horticultural experience in his native home in Sweden. He came to this country in 1893 and worked for A. N. Pierson in Cromwell and for Robt. Simpson in New Jersey, after which he took charge of the Whiting establishment. He is vice-president of the Conn. Horticultural Society.

NEW BEDFORD, MASS.

H. V. Sowle has just added a fine refrigerator to his store equipment.

The bedding plant season is about over, and business is reported as being quiet.

Post & Gray, with their employees, visited the show of the American Sweet Pea Society in Newport, July 16.

Joseph Peirce of Cottage street is away on a short vacation, and Samuel Rusitsky is spending three months in the mountains of Kentucky.

Richard Noftz has given up his attractive little store on William St. and is now doing all his business from his greenhouses in Kempton St.

WASHINGTON.

Superintendent George W. Hess, of the Botanic Gardens, has gone to New Iberia, La., the summer home of Senator Robert F. Broussard, where he will spend his vacation.

Mr. and Mrs. John Gutman, of Anacostia, last week suffered the loss of their daughter, Annie E. Gutman, aged eighteen years, who died following an attack of typhoid fever. Many expressions of sympathy were sent to the bereaved parents for Miss Gutman was one of the best liked of the members of the younger set of the city.

Otto Bauer, manager of the Pennock-Meehan store, returns next week from a vacation spent at North Beach where his family is staying during the summer. Fred W. Meyer, of Leapley & Meyer, also spent his vacation at North Beach. Frederick T. Leapley has returned from a week in Montgomery County, Md.

VISITORS' REGISTER.

New York—J. C. Vaughan, Chicago; J. K. M. L. Farquhar, Boston.

Cleveland, O.—Martin Reukauf, representing H. Bayersdorfer & Co., and Frank Farney, both of Philadelphia.

Boston — Vernon T. Sherwood, Charlestown, N. H.; A. E. Thatcher and John Stafford, Bar Harbor, Me.; E. J. Harmon, Portland, Me.

Philadelphia—Benj. Hammond, Beacon, N. Y.; Louis J. Reuter, Westerly, R. I.; W. R. Pierson, Cromwell, Conn.; Edwin A. Seidewitz, Baltimore, Md.

Cincinnati—Julius Dilloff, representing Schloss Bros., and Victor Morgan, representing Lord & Burnham Co., New York City; J. F. Keller, Lexington, Ky.: Chas. Dudley, Jr., and R. T. Virgin, Parkersburg, W. Va.

Chicago—James Cole, Peoria, Ill.; Martin Reukauf, representing H. Bayersdorfer & Co., and Mrs. Reukauf, Philadelphia; Mr. Cullett of Cullett & Sons, Lincoln, Nebraska; D. M. H. Underhill, Davenport, Ia.; Carl Hagenberger, West Mentor, Ohio.

Newport, R. I.—On Thursday, July 22, E. H. Wilson of the Arnold Arboretum, gave a stereopticon lecture on Japan, before the Newport Garden Club at the residence of Mrs. Hoffman.

Flower Market Reports

BOSTON There is still a heavy excess supply of flowers in this market and the growers have to be content with a very meagre return for their product. Hot weather last week affected many things unfavorably and quality, on the average, shows a falling off. Roses, carnations, sweet peas and lilies are all more or less off in color, size and form. The great elephant for the wholesale markets just now is the gladiolus. The influx has hardly got under way yet, either. What it will mean when the height of the crop is on may, perhaps, be imagined.

CHICAGO Asters are the latest addition to the stock of summer flowers. The blooms are small, but have so far met with better sale than could reasonably be expected in a market already glutted. Peonies are still here and some of the wholesalers have a large quantity still in storage. They are said to be keeping well—too well as one of the dealers remarked. Roses are a shade less in evidence this week. The hot sun following so much cloudy and wet weather burned the plants in some houses badly and some are suffering more or less from mildew. There is no danger, however, of orders being turned down for lack of stock. Every kind of summer flower that grows out-of-doors is in crop and competes with the products of the greenhouses. Ferns are selling for $1.00 per 1000.

CINCINNATI July business has not been anything to brag about. The supply has continued very heavy while business has not been good enough to bring about anything like a substantial price. Prices on all flowers are relatively lower than at this time last year. Lilies are in a glut and there is no sign of immediate relief from this condition of the market. Only the outdoor roses are having any kind of sale and this is because of their keeping qualities. Other roses including American Beauties, even though very good in quality are having a very poor market. Asters are now coming in heavy. So far they have been selling pretty well. For a few days last week ferns were rather scarce owing to the difficulty in getting shipments through on time.

NEW YORK All the wholesale places are still carrying large surpluses of flowers the sale for which is so light that the income from many shipments will scarcely cover express charges, packing, etc. Roses and carnations show the effect of the recent hot days and sweet peas the effect of the heavy rain storms. Receipts of carnations are falling off rapidly. Asters are seen on all sides now, but quality is yet lacking. Some dahlias are already in evidence. Of gladioli there is an overwhelming supply and the varieties are of a higher type than this market has been accustomed to in former years. Lilies are also in heavy supply and have to be sold very low to unload. Cattleyas are still in excess of requirements. Coreopsis, centaureas, hydrangeas and a variety of other garden flowers all help to load up the tables and ice boxes.

PHILADELPHIA Business slow. Enormous over-supply, especially of outdoor stock. Asters and gladioli never so plentiful as this year. All Europe must have been dumped on the gladiolus growers, to judge from the quantities coming in. Prices down out of sight and carloads for the dump on Saturday. Roses of all kinds have receded in quality since the hot spell set in. Carnations, also, are running down rapidly both in quality and quantity. Asters are very plentiful and the demand is fair. Lily of the valley and longiflorum lilies move off about as usual. The quality is a little under standard.

ST. LOUIS The local wholesale market is still over-crowded and the retailers cannot possibly consume a quarter of the consignments that are coming in daily. Roses are mostly small and short stemmed and sell as low as $5 per thousand. Very few fancies are to be had with the exception of Beauties. Gladioli are a great glut. Common mixed colors go at $4 per thousand, while selects bring only $1 per hundred. Never was there a season when so many gladioli were seen in this market. Carnations go slow and low. Asters, sweet peas, lily of the valley, lilies and tube roses are all in plenty with small demand.

Continued on page 1

WHOLESALE FLOWER MARKETS — TRADE PRICES—Per 100 TO DEALERS ONLY

	BOSTON July 22				ST. LOUIS July 12				PHILA. July 19			
Roses												
Am. Beauty, Special	10.00	to	18.00		20.00	to	30.00		15.00	to	20.00	
" " Fancy and Extra	6.00	to	8.00		10.00	to	15.00		10.00	to	12.00	
" " No. 1	1.00	to	3.00		5.00	to	8.00		2.00	to	6.00	
Killarney, Richmond, Extra	2.00	to	4.00		3.00	to	5.00		2.00	to	5.00	
" " Ordinary	.50	to	1.00		2.00	to	3.00		1.00	to	2.00	
Hillingdon, Ward, Sunburst, Extra	2.00	to	4.00		5.00	to	6.00		3.00	to	6.00	
" " Ordinary	.50	to	1.00		3.00	to	4.00		1.00	to	2.00	
Arenberg, Radiance, Taft, Extra	2.00	to	4.00		.....	to	.....		4.00	to	8.00	
" " " Ordinary	.50	to	1.00		.....	to	.....		2.00	to	4.00	
Russell, Hadley, Ophelia, Mock	2.00	to	8.00		5.00	to	6.00		2.00	to	10.00	
Carnations, Fancy	1.00	to	1.50		2.00	to	3.00		1.00	to	2.00	
" Ordinary	.35	to	.50		.75	to	1.00		.50	to	1.00	
Cattleyas	12.00	to	15.00		35.00	to	40.00		10.00	to	25.00	
Dendrobium formosum	.....	to	.....		40.00	to	50.00		25.00	to	35.00	
Lilies, Longiflorum	2.00	to	4.00		4.00	to	5.00		6.00	to	10.00	
" Rubrum	.....	to	.....		.....	to	.....		.....	to	.....	
Lily of the Valley	1.00	to	3.00		3.00	to	4.00		1.00	to	4.00	
Daisies	.50	to	1.00		.50	to	.50		.....	to	.....	
Stocks	.....	to	.....		.....	to	.....		.....	to	.....	
Snapdragon	1.00	to	3.00		2.00	to	4.00		1.00	to	2.00	
Gladioli	.50	to	2.00		3.00	to	4.00		2.00	to	4.00	
Sweet Peas	.15	to	.50		.25	to	.50		.0	to	.35	
Gardenias	10.00	to	12.00		10.00	to	12.00		.....	to	.....	
Adiantum	.50	to	1.00		1.00	to	1.75		.75	to	1.00	
Smilax	10.00	to	12.00		10.00	to	12.00		.....	to	20.00	
Asparagus Plumosus, Strings (100)	25.00	to	50.00		35.00	to	50.00		30.00	to	50.00	
" " & Spren. (100 Bchs.)	25.00	to	35.00		15.00	to	20.00		25.00	to	35.00	

Flower Market Reports

(Continued from page 113)

SAN FRANCISCO

The most important feature in the local flower market the past week was the putting into effect of an arrangement among the Japanese carnation growers to pool their crops instead of each grower marketing his supplies independently as has been the custom here. Under the new plan all carnations brought to the market are carefully graded into five grades by a committee representing the growers. This week special selected was quoted at 50 cents a bunch and the other grades were quoted three for $1, 25 cents, 15 cents and 10 cents a bunch, respectively. This move toward the standardization of carnation values was heralded with favor by all branches of the trade and beneficial results were felt immediately. Most other stock continues rather plentiful. Sweet peas are hardly so much in evidence, however, and good stock demands fair prices. Asters are beginning to arrive from down the peninsula, but the supply is still limited and the quality is nothing extra as yet. Many varieties of gladioli and dahlias are offered and the really fine stock demands high prices. Cut hydrangeas show fine quality. Shasta daisies, marguerites, scabiosas, mignonette, gaillardias, statice, and other seasonables are abundant. Roses are hardly so plentiful and prices are a shade firmer. Easter lilies are off the market, and some nice Lilium rubrum are making their appearance.

WASHINGTON

Funeral work last week was exceptionally heavy and the business was more than welcomed by the stores which otherwise would have done practically nothing. Stock cleaned up better than it had for several weeks although large quantities found its way to the refuse heaps. Asters have started to come in quantities and it is now but a matter of a few days when they will be very plentiful. Thus far they have met with a very good demand and large orders have been received from out-of-town. Gladioli are exceptionally fine and this is in part serving as a substitute for roses and carnations. Gardenias are still very good and plentiful but there is but a very light demand for them. Ordinary varieties of roses are nearly off the market but there are plenty of good Radiance, Mock and Kaiserin. Carnations are nearly off crop. There is practically no call for snapdragon. Sweet peas fail to meet with any sale.

GARDENERS' AND FLORISTS' CLUB OF BOSTON.

The visit of the Gardeners' and Florists' Club to the Newport Sweet Pea Show, on Thursday, July 15, was a most enjoyable occasion. Special cars were provided for the trip and some 115 were in the party. The visitors were met at the train by members of the Newport Society and shown the Ocean Drive in drays, stopping at the estates of Edward J. Berwind, Governor R. Livingstone Beeckman, William Storrs Welles and Charles F. Hoffman, after which they were given a shore dinner.

NEW YORK QUOTATIONS PER 100.   To Dealers Only

MISCELLANEOUS	Last Half of Week ending July 17 1915			First Half of Week beginning July 19 1915		
Cattleyas	8.00	to	20.00	8.00	to	20.00
Lilies, Longiflorum	1.00	to	2.00	1.00	to	2.00
" Rubrum	1.00	to	2.00	1.00	to	2.00
Lily of the Valley	.50	to	2.00	.50	to	2.00
Daisies	.....	to	.50	.....	to	.50
Stocks	.....	to	1.00	.....	to	1.00
Snapdragon	.50	to	1.00	.50	to	1.00
Gladioli	.50	to	1.50	.50	to	1.50
Asters	.50	to	1.00	.50	to	1.00
Sweet Peas	.10	to	.15	.10	to	.15
Corn Flower	.....	to	.25	.....	to	.25
Gardenias	8.00	to	12.00	8.00	to	12.00
Adiantum	.50	to	.75	.50	to	.75
Smilax	6.00	to	12.00	6.00	to	12.00
Asparagus Plumosus, strings (per 100)	15.00	to	15.00	15.00	to	35.00
& Spren (100 bunches)	10.00	to	20.00	10.00	to	90.00

PERSONAL.

George Corbett & Son of College Hill, Cincinnati, have retired from business.

David Welch, of Welch Bros., Boston, is enjoying a short vacation at The Samoset, Rockland, Me.

Geo. E. Lindeman, florist, Pleasant St., Fall River, Mass., is recovering at his home after having undergone an operation.

The employees of Barnes Bros. Nursery Company learning that one of their number, Allan McDonald, of Yalesville, Conn., was about to remove to Massachusetts to open a branch office for Barnes Bros., have presented him with a handsome silver coffee service with best wishes for success and happiness.

Mr. and Mrs. Martin Reukauf of Philadelphia are making the trip to the coast together combining business and sight seeing. At Chicago they will be joined by Sydney Bayersdorfer who will accompany them the rest of the way and visit the exposition with them. Mr. Reukauf says business has been very good for him so far since he left the East, quite up to an average year.

CLEVELAND FLORISTS' CLUB.

The last meeting of the Florists' Club was well attended. It was voted to have a blackboard placed in the club room where the members can indicate upon it whatever plant stock of any kind they may have to sell or are willing to buy, which should be a good help to members.

The picnic should be a big success judging by the interest evinced. There is a large list of prizes for the races, games, etc., and the committee say that they will have some new stunts. It was decided to play indoor baseball instead of the outdoor game, club members only to be allowed to participate. Members, their families and personal friends may take part in the other stunts.

BUSINESS TROUBLES.

Kalamazoo, Mich.—Kalamazoo Floral Co., assets, $785.69, liabilities, $1,170.

Atlanta, Ga.—Atlanta Floral Co., 97 Peachtree St. A settlement of 60c. on the dollar is looked for.

Samuel Lum, of Chatham, N. J., has filed a schedule of his assets and liabilities with Referee Atwood L. De Coster in Bankruptcy Court. According to the florist's estimate, his assets are $96,428 and his liabilities $65,975. Although apparently solvent, Lum has not contested the involuntary bankruptcy proceedings started against him a month ago. Real estate valued at $96,129 comprises the bulk of the assets. Liens amounting to $23,000 are held against the property by creditors. Of the liabilities $21,666 are secured.

A meeting of the creditors of Reilly Brothers retail nurserymen of Dansville, N. Y., was held on July 14, and it was voted to accept the offer made by the Reilly Brothers.

The composite agreement provides for the formation of a corporation having as directors for the first year some of the biggest creditors. An immediate dividend of ten per cent. is to be paid the creditors and preferred stock for the remaining 90 per cent. of their claims is to be issued to them in the new corporation. After preferred stock has been issued to creditors to cover 90 per cent. of their claims, common stock will be issued to the Reilly Brothers for the balance of the capital stock. The capitalization will be $50,000. This method of settlement eliminates the expensive proceedings connected with having a receiver appointed and a subsequent sale of the business and its assets to satisfy the creditors.

The Holyoke & Northampton (Mass.) Florists' & Gardeners' Club will hold their annual Chrysanthemum Show Wednesday and Thursday, November 3 and 4 in Windsor Hall. They will also hold a picnic in August.

Buyer's Directory and Ready Reference Guide

Advertisements under this head, one cent a word.　Initials count as words.

Display advertisers in this issue are also listed under this classification without charge. Reference to List of Advertisers will indicate the respective pages.

Buyers failing to find what they want in this list will confer a favor by writing us and we will try to put them in communication with reliable dealers.

ACCOUNTANT
R. J. Dysart, 40 State St., Boston.
For page see List of Advertisers.

APHINE
Aphine Mfg. Co., Madison, N. J.
For page see List of Advertisers.

APHIS PUNK
Nicotine Mfg. Co., St. Louis, Mo.
For page see List of Advertisers.

ASPARAGUS
ASPARAGUS PLUMOSUS NANUS.
5,000 strong 3 and 4 in. pots ready for benching. 4 in. pots at $8.00 per 100, $75.00 per 1,000; 3 in. pots at $5.00 per 100, $50.00 per 1,000; 2¼ in. pots at $3.00 per 100, $22.50 per 1,000. MIAMI FLORAL CO., Dayton, Ohio.

ASPARAGUS SPRENGERI.
8,000 good 3 and 4 in. plants ready for benching. 4 in. pots at $8.00 per 100, $75.00 per 1,000; 3 in. pots at $5.00 per 100; $50.00 per 1,000; 2¼ in. pots at $3.00 per 100, $22.50 per 1,000. MIAMI FLORAL CO., Dayton, Ohio.

AUCTION SALES
Elliott Auction Co., New York City.
For page see List of Advertisers.

AZALEAS
P. Ouwerkerk, Hoboken, N. J.
For page see List of Advertisers.

BAY TREES
August Rolker & Sons, New York.
For page see List of Advertisers.

BAY TREES—Standard and Pyramids. All sizes. Price list on demand. JULIUS ROEHRS CO., Rutherford, N. J.

BEDDING PLANTS
A N. Pierson, Inc., Cromwell, Conn.
For page see List of Advertisers.

R. Vincent, Jr. & Sons Co., White Marsh, Md.

BEGONIAS
Julius Roehrs Company, Rutherford, N. J.
For page see List of Advertisers.

Thomas Roland, Nahant, Mass.
For page see List of Advertisers.

A. M. Davenport, Watertown, Mass.
For page see List of Advertisers.

Begonia Lorraine, $12.00 per 100, $110.00 per 1,000; Begonia Glory of Cincinnati, $15.00 per 100, $140.00 per 1,000. JULIUS ROEHRS CO., Rutherford, N. J.

BOILERS
Kroeschell Bros. Co., Chicago.
For page see List of Advertisers.

King Construction Co., North Tonawanda, N. Y.
"King Ideal" Boiler.
For page see List of Advertisers.

Lord & Burnham Co., New York City.

Hitchings & Co., New York City.
For page see List of Advertisers.

BOXES—CUT FLOWER FOLDING
Edwards Folding Box Co., Philadelphia.
For page see List of Advertisers.

Folding cut flower boxes, the best made. Write for list. HOLTON & HUNKEL CO., Milwaukee, Wis.

BOX TREES
BOX TREES—Standards, Pyramids and Bush. In various sizes. Price List on demand. JULIUS ROEHRS CO., Rutherford, N. J.

BULBS AND TUBERS
J. M. Thorburn & Co., New York City.
For page see List of Advertisers.

Ralph M. Ward & Co., New York City.
Lily Bulbs.
For page see List of Advertisers.

John Lewis Childs, Flowerfield, L. I., N. Y.
For page see List of Advertisers.

August Rolker & Sons, New York City.
Holland and Japan Bulbs.
For page see List of Advertisers.

R. & J. Farquhar & Co., Boston, Mass.
For page see List of Advertisers.

S. S. Skidelsky & Co., Philadelphia, Pa.
For page see List of Advertisers.

Chas. Schwake & Co., New York City.
Horticultural Importers and Exporters.
For page see List of Advertisers.

A. Henderson & Co., Chicago, Ill.
For page see List of Advertisers.

Burnett Bros., 98 Chambers St., New York.
For page see List of Advertisers.

Henry F. Michell Co., Philadelphia, Pa.
For page see List of Advertisers.

Roman J. Irwin, New York City.
Hardy Lilies.
For page see List of Advertisers.

Fottler, Fiske, Rawson Co., Boston, Mass.
Summer Flowering Bulbs.
For page see List of Advertisers.

Joseph Breck & Sons Corp., Boston, Mass.
Bulbs for Early Forcing.
For page see List of Advertisers.

GREAT REDUCTION IN PRICES Of HOLLAND BULBS of all kinds. Send for Price List. THOMAS COGGER, 229 Laurel St., Melrose, Mass.

C. KEUR & SONS, HILLEGOM, Holland. Bulbs of all descriptions. Write for prices. NEW YORK Branch, 8-10 Bridge St.

CAMELLIAS
Julius Roehrs Co., Rutherford, N. J.
For page see List of Advertisers.

CANNAS
Canna Specialists.
Send for Canna book.
THE CONARD & JONES COMPANY, West Grove, Pa.

CARNATION STAPLES
Split carnations quickly, easily and cheaply mended. Pillsbury's Carnation Staple, 1000 for 35c.; 3000 for $1.00 post paid. I. L. PILLSBURY, Galesburg, Ill.

Supreme Carnation Staples, for repairing split carnations, 35c. per 1000; 3000 for $1.00. F. W. WAITE, 85 Belmont Ave., Springfield, Mass.

CARNATIONS.
F. Dorner & Sons Co., Lafayette, Ind.
For page see List of Advertisers.

Leo Niessen Co., Philadelphia, Pa.
Field Grown Carnation Plants.
For page see List of Advertisers.

250,000 Field-Grown Carnation Plants. Grown in Soil Especially Suited for Carnations. Quality Guaranteed to Please You. July and Later Delivery. Order Early.

PINK—	100	1000
Mrs. C. Edward Akehurst..	$12.00	$100.00
Pink Sensation	14.00	120.00
Good Cheer	12.00	100.00
Alice, first grade	16.00	140.00
Alice, second grade	15.00	125.00
Enchantress Supreme	8.00	70.00
Peerless Pink	8.00	70.00
Gorgeous	8.50	70.00
Pink Delight	7.50	00
Philadelphia	8.00	
Gloriosa	7.	
Mrs. C. W. Ward	7.00	
Northport	7.00	
Enchantress	7.00	
Rose-pink Enchantress	7.50	
Dorothy Gordon	7.50	
Rosette	7.50	
Winona	7.00	65.00
Winsor	7.00	60.00
VARIEGATED—		
Benora	8.00	70.00
RED—		
Champion	8.00	75.00
Princess Dagmar	8.00	70.00
Beacon	7.50	60.00
Comfort	6.00	45.00
The Herald	8.00	75.00
Pocahontas	8.00	70.00
St. Nicholas	8.00	70.00
Harlowarden	7.00	55.00
Victory	7.00	55.00
Eureka	7.00	55.00
Bonfire	7.50	65.00
WHITE—		
Matchless	8.00	70.00
White Wonder	7.50	60.00
White Enchantress	7.00	55.00
White Perfection	7.00	55.00
Alma Ward	7.00	55.00
YELLOW—		
Yellow Prince	8.00	70.00
Yellowstone	8.00	70.00

Write for complete price list of bedding and greenhouse plants.
S. S. PENNOCK-MEEHAN CO.,
1608-1620 Ludlow St.,　　Philadelphia, Pa.

CHRYSANTHEMUMS
Poehlmann Bros. Co., Morton Grove, Ill.
For page see List of Advertisers.

Wood Bros., Fishkill, N. Y.
Chrysanthemums Rooted Cuttings.
For page see List of Advertisers.

Chas. H. Totty, Madison, N. J.
For page see List of Advertisers.

R. Vincent, Jr., & Sons Co., White Marsh, Md.
Pompon Chrysanthemums,
For page see List of Advertisers.

THE BEST 1915 NOVELTIES.
The Cream of 1914 Introductions.
The most popular Commercial and Exhibition kinds; also complete line of Pompons, Singles and Anemones. Trade list on application. ELMER D. SMITH & CO., Adrian, Mich.

COCOANUT FIBRE SOIL
20th Century Plant Food Co., Beverly, Mass.
For page see List of Advertisers.

For List of Advertisers See Page 95

CYCLAMENS

CYCLAMEN — Separate colors; finest strain; extra strong plants; 3-inch pots, $10.00 per 100, $90.00 per 1,000. JULIUS ROEHRS CO., Rutherford, N. J.

DAHLIAS

Send for Wholesale List of whole clumps and separate stock; 40,000 clumps for sale. Northboro Dahlia and Gladiolus Gardens, J. L. MOORE, Prop, Northboro, Mass.

NEW PAEONY DAHLIA

John Wanamaker, Newest, Handsomest, Best. New color, new form and new habit of growth. Big stock of best cut-flower varieties. Send list of wants to PEACOCK DAHLIA FARMS, Berlin, N. J.

DECORATIVE PLANTS

Robert Craig Co., Philadelphia, Pa.
For page see List of Advertisers.

Woodrow & Marketos, New York City.
For page see List of Advertisers.

S. S. Skidelsky & Co., Philadelphia, Pa.
For page see List of Advertisers.

Bobbink & Atkins, Rutherford, N. J.
For page see List of Advertisers.

A. Leuthy & Co., Roslindale, Boston, Mass.
For page see List of Advertisers.

DRACAENAS

Julius Roehrs Co., Rutherford, N. J.
For page see List of Advertisers.

ENGLISH IVY

English Ivy from soil, 20 to 30 in., $3.00; from pots, 12 to 15 in., $4.00. CHAS. FROST, Kenilworth, N. J.

FERNS

H. H. Barrows & Son, Whitman, Mass.
For page see List of Advertisers.

Robert Craig Co., Philadelphia, Pa.
For page see List of Advertisers.

McHutchison & Co., New York City.
Ferns in Flats.
For page see List of Advertisers.

FERTILIZERS

20th Century Plant Food Co., Beverly, Mass.
Cocoanut Fibre Soil.
For page see List of Advertisers.

Stumpp & Walter Co., New York City.
Scotch Soot.
For page see List of Advertisers.

Pulverized Manure Co., Chicago, Ill.
Wizard Brand Cattle Manure.
For page see List of Advertisers.

Hardwood Ashes for sale. GEO. L. MUNROE & SONS, Oswego, N. Y.

FLORISTS' LETTERS

Boston Florist Letter Co., Boston, Mass.
For page see List of Advertisers.

FLORISTS' SUPPLIES

N. F. McCarthy & Co., Boston, Mass.
For page see List of Advertisers.

Reed & Keller, New York City.
For page see List of Advertisers.

S. S. Pennock-Meehan Co., Philadelphia, Pa.
For page see List of Advertisers.

H. Bayersdorfer & Co., Philadelphia, Pa.
Up-to-Date Summer Novelties.
For page see List of Advertisers.

Welch Bros. Co., Boston, Mass.
For page see List of Advertisers.

FLOWER POTS

W. H. Ernest, Washington, D. C.
For page see List of Advertisers.

A. H. Hews & Co., Inc., Cambridge, Mass.
For page see List of Advertisers.

Hilfinger Bros., Ft. Edward, N. Y.
For page see List of Advertisers.

FOLIAGE PLANTS

A. Leuthy & Co., Roslindale, Boston, Mass.
For page see List of Advertisers.

FUCHSIAS

Fuchsias—Black Prince, Speciosa, double purple and white, Rooted Cuttings, $1.00 per 100; 2¼-in., $2.00 per 100.
W. J. BARNETT, R. D. 67, Sharon, Pa.

FUNGINE

Aphine Mfg. Co., Madison, N. J.
For page see List of Advertisers.

GALAX

Michigan Cut Flower Co., Detroit, Mich.
For page see List of Advertisers.

GERANIUMS

R. Vincent, Jr., & Sons Co.
White Marsh, Md.
For page see List of Advertisers.

GLADIOLUS

John Lewis Childs, Flowerfield, L. I., N. Y.
For page see List of Advertisers.

GLASS

Sharp, Partridge & Co., Chicago.
For page see List of Advertisers.

Parshelsky Bros., Inc., Brooklyn, N. Y.
For page see List of Advertisers.

Royal Glass Works, New York City.
For page see List of Advertisers.

Greenhouse glass, lowest prices. JOHNSTON GLASS CO., Hartford City, Ind.

100 boxes 16 x 24 double glass, $3.00 per box, f. o. b. Foxboro. V. S. POND CO., Foxboro, Mass.

GLASS CUTTERS

Smith & Hemenway Co., New York City.
Red Devil Glass Cutter.
For page see List of Advertisers.

GLAZING POINTS

H. A. Dreer, Philadelphia, Pa.
Peerless Glazing Point.
For page see List of Advertisers.

GREENHOUSE BUILDING MATERIAL

King Construction Co., N. Tonawanda, N. Y.
For page see List of Advertisers.

Parshelsky Bros., Inc., Brooklyn, N. Y.
For page see List of Advertisers.

Metropolitan Material Co., Brooklyn, N. Y.
For page see List of Advertisers.

Lord & Burnham Co., New York City.

A. T. Stearns Lumber Co., Neponset, Boston.
Pecky Cypress.
For page see List of Advertisers.

GREENHOUSE CONSTRUCTION

King Construction Co., N. Tonawanda, N. Y.
For page see List of Advertisers.

Foley Greenhouse Mfg. Co., Chicago, Ill.
For page see List of Advertisers.

S. Jacobs & Sons, Brooklyn, N. Y.
For page see List of Advertisers.

Metropolitan Material Co., Brooklyn, N. Y.

Lord & Burnham Co., New York City.

Hitchings & Co., New York City.
For page see List of Advertisers.

A. T. Stearns Lumber Co., Boston, Mass.
For page see List of Advertisers.

GUTTERS

King Construction Co., N. Tonawanda, N. Y.
King Channel Gutter.
For page see List of Advertisers.

Metropolitan Material Co., Brooklyn, N. Y.
Iron Gutters.

HAIL INSURANCE

Florists' Hail Asso. of America.
J. G. Esler, Saddle River, N. J.
For page see List of Advertisers.

HARDY FERNS AND GREEN GOODS

Michigan Cut Flower Exchange, Detroit, Mich.
For page see List of Advertisers.

Knud Nielsen, Evergreen, Ala.
Natural Green Sheet Moss, Fancy and Dagger Ferns and Huckleberry Foliage.
For page see List of Advertisers.

The KerVan Co., New York.
For page see List of Advertisers.

HARDY PERENNIALS

Bay State Nurseries, No. Abington, Mass.
For page see List of Advertisers.

P. Ouwerkerk, Hoboken, N. J.
For page see List of Advertisers.

Palisades Nurseries, Sparkill, N. Y.
For page see List of Advertisers.

HEATING APPARATUS

Kroeschell Bros. Co., Chicago.
For page see List of Advertisers.

Lord & Burnham Co., New York City.

HOT-BED SASH

Parshelsky Bros., Inc., Brooklyn, N. Y.
For page see List of Advertisers.

Foley Greenhouse Construction Co., Chicago, Ill.
For page see List of Advertisers.

Lord & Burnham Co., New York City.

A. T. Stearns Lumber Co., Neponset, Mass.
For page see List of Advertisers.

HOSE

H. A. Dreer, Philadelphia, Pa.

INSECTICIDES

Aphine Manufacturing Co., Madison, N. J.
Aphine and Fungine.
For page see List of Advertisers.

Lemon Oil Co., Baltimore, Md.
Standard Insecticides.
For page see List of Advertisers.

Nicotine Mfg. Co., St. Louis, Mo.
Aphis Punk and Nikoteen.
For page see List of Advertisers.

Eastern Chemical Co. Boston, Mass.
Imp Soap Spray.

Roman J. Irwin, New York City.
Nico Fume Liquid and Paper.
For page see List of Advertisers.

IRRIGATION EQUIPMENT

Skinner Irrigation Co., Brookline, Mass.
For page see List of Advertisers.

KIL-WORM AND KIL-WEED POISON

Lemon Oil Co., Baltimore, Md.

LEMON OIL

Lemon Oil Co., Baltimore, Md.
For page see List of Advertisers.

LILY BULBS

Chas. Schwake & Co., New York City.
Horticultural Importers and Exporters.
For page see List of Advertisers.

R. M. Ward & Co., New York, N. Y.
Japanese Lily Bulbs of Superior Quality.
For page see List of Advertisers.

Corp. of Chas. F. Meyer, New York City.
Meyer's Brand Giganteums.
For page see List of Advertisers.

LILIUM MYRIOPHYLLUM

R. & J. Farquhar & Co., Boston, Mass.
For page see List of Advertisers.

LILY OF THE VALLEY

Chas. Schwake & Co., Inc., New York City.
Hohmann's Famous Lily of the Valley Pips.
For page see List of Advertisers.

McHutchison & Co., New York City.
For page see List of Advertisers.

Loechner & Co., New York City.
Lily of the Valley Pips.
For page see List of Advertisers.

In writing to Advertisers kindly mention Horticulture

LIQUID PUTTY MACHINE
Metropolitan Material Co., Brooklyn, N. Y.
For page see List of Advertisers.

MASTICA
F. O. Pierce Co., New York City.
For page see List of Advertisers.

NATIONAL NURSERYMAN
National Nurseryman Publishing Co., Inc.,
Rochester, N. Y.
For page see List of Advertisers.

NIKOTEEN
Nicotine Mfg. Co., St. Louis, Mo.
For page see List of Advertisers

NIKOTIANA
Aphine Mfg. Co., Madison, N. J.
For page see List of Advertisers

NURSERY STOCK
P. Ouwerkerk, Weehawken Heights, N. J.
For page see List of Advertisers.

W. & T. Smith Co., Geneva, N. Y.
For page see List of Advertisers.

Bay State Nurseries, North Abington, Mass.
Hardy, Northern Grown Stock.
For page see List of Advertisers.

Bobbink & Atkins, Rutherford, N. J.
For page see List of Advertisers.

Framingham Nurseries, Framingham, Mass.
For page see List of Advertisers.

August Rolker & Sons, New York City.
For page see List of Advertisers.

NUT GROWING.
The Nut-Grower, Waycross, Ga.
For page see List of Advertisers.

ONION SETS
Schilder Bros., Chillicothe, O.
Onion Seed—Onion Sets.
For page see List of Advertisers.

ORCHID FLOWERS
Jas. McManus, New York, N. Y.
For page see List of Advertisers.

ORCHID PLANTS
Julius Roehrs Co., Rutherford, N. J.
For page see List of Advertisers.
Lager & Hurrell, Summit, N. J.

PALMS, ETC.
Robert Craig Co., Philadelphia, Pa.
For page see List of Advertisers.
August Rolker & Sons, New York City.
For page see List of Advertisers.
A. Leuthy & Co., Roslindale, Boston, Mass.
For page see List of Advertisers.

PANDANUS VEITCHI
Julius Roehrs Co., Rutherford, N. J.
For page see List of Advertisers.

PANSY SEED
Chas. Frost, Kenilworth, N. J.
The Kenilworth Giant Pansy.
For page see List of Advertisers.
Arthur T. Boddington, New York City.
Boddington's Gigantic Pansies.
For page see List of Advertisers.

PEONIES
Peonies. The world's greatest collection.
1200 sorts. Send for list. C. BETSCHER,
Canal Dover, O.
French Peonies can be shipped with
celerity and security via Bordeaux-New
York. Catalogues free. DESSERT, Peony
Specialist, Chenonceaux (T. & L.), France.

PECKY CYPRESS BENCHES
A. T. Stearns Lumber Co. Boston, Mass.
For page see List of Advertisers.

PIPE AND FITTINGS
Kroeschell Bros. Co., Chicago.
For page see List of Advertisers
King Construction Company,
N. Tonawanda, N. Y.
Shelf Brackets and Pipe Hangers.
For page see List of Advertisers.

PLANT AND BULB IMPORTS
Chas. Schwake & Co., New York City.
For page see List of Advertisers.

August Rolker & Sons, New York City.
For page see List of Advertisers.

PLANT TRELLISES AND STAKES
Seele's Tieless Plant Stakes and Trellises. H. D. SEELE & SONS, Elkhart, Ind.

PLANT TUBS
H. A. Dreer, Philadelphia, Pa.
"Riverton Special."
For page see List of Advertisers.

POINSETTIAS.
A. Henderson & Co., Chicago, Ill.
For page see List of Advertisers.

POINSETTIAS—10,000 TRUE TYPE XMAS
RED.
Shipped in 2½ in. paper pots at $5.00 per
100; $50.00 per 1,000. MIAMI FLORAL CO.,
Dayton, Ohio.

RAFFIA
McHutchison & Co., New York, N. Y.
For page see List of Advertisers.

RHODODENDRONS
P. Ouwerkerk, Hoboken, N. J.
For page see List of Advertisers.

Framingham Nurseries, Framingham, Mass.
For page see List of Advertisers.

RIBBONS AND CHIFFONS
S. S. Pennock-Meehan Co., Philadelphia, Pa.
For page see List of Advertisers.

ROSES
Poehlmann Bros. Co., Morton Grove, Ill.
For page see List of Advertisers.

P. Ouwerkerk, Hoboken, N. J.
For page see List of Advertisers.

Robert Craig Co., Philadelphia, Pa.
For page see List of Advertisers.

W. & T. Smith Co., Geneva, N. Y.
American Grown Roses.
For page see List of Advertisers.

Bay State Nurseries, North Abington, Mass.
For page see List of Advertisers.

August Rolker & Sons, New York City.
For page see List of Advertisers.

Framingham Nurseries, Framingham, Mass.
For page see List of Advertisers.

A. N. Pierson, Inc., Cromwell, Conn.
For page see List of Advertisers.

Wood Bros., Fishkill, N. Y.
For page see List of Advertisers.

THE CONARD & JONES COMPANY.
Rose Specialists.
West Grove, Pa. Send for offers.

SEASONABLE PLANT STOCK
R. Vincent, Jr. & Sons Co., White Marsh,
Md.
For page see List of Advertisers.

SEED GROWERS
California Seed Growers' Association.
San Jose, Cal.
For page see List of Advertisers.

SEEDS
Carter's Tested Seeds,
Seeds with a Pedigree.
Boston, Mass., and London, England.
For page see List of Advertisers.

Schilder Bros., Chillicothe, O.
Onion Seed—Onion Sets.
For page see List of Advertisers

Joseph Breck & Sons, Boston, Mass.
For page see List of Advertisers.

Kelway & Son,
Langport, Somerset, England.
Kelway's Celebrated English Strain Garden
Seeds.
For page see List of Advertisers.
J. Bolgiano & Son, Baltimore, Md.
For page see List of Advertisers.

SEEDS—Continued
A. T. Boddington, New York City.
For page see List of Advertisers.

Chas. Schwake & Co., New York City.

Michell's Seed House, Philadelphia, Pa.
New Crop Pansy Seeds.
For page see List of Advertisers.

W. Atlee Burpee & Co., Philadelphia, Pa.
For page see List of Advertisers.

R. & J. Farquhar & Co., Boston, Mass.
For page see List of Advertisers.

J. M. Thorburn & Co., New York City.
Seeds for Present Sowing.
For page see List of Advertisers.

S. Bryson Ayres Co., Independence, Mo.
Sweet Peas.
For page see List of Advertisers.

Loechner & Co., New York City.
For page see List of Advertisers.

Ant. C. Zvolanek, Lompoc, Cal.
Winter Flowering Sweet Pea Seed.
For page see List of Advertisers.

S. S. Skidelsky & Co., Philadelphia, Pa.
For page see List of Advertisers.

W. E. Marshall & Co., New York City.
Seeds, Plants and Bulbs.
For page see List of Advertisers.

August Rolker & Sons, New York City.
For page see List of Advertisers.
Burnett Bros., 98 Chambers St., New York.
For page see List of Advertisers.
Fottler, Fiske, Rawson Co., Boston, Mass.
Aster Seed.
For page see List of Advertisers.

SKINNER IRRIGATION SYSTEM
Skinner Irrigation Co., Brookline, Mass.
For page see List of Advertisers.

SPHAGNUM MOSS
Live Sphagnum moss, orchid pest and
orchid baskets always on hand. LAGER
& HURRELL, Summit, N. J.
Sphagnum Moss—10-bbl. bales, $1.90;
5-bbl. bale, 90c. Laurel, 90c. bag. Get
prices on large lots. JOS. H. PAUL, P. O.
156, Manahawkin, N. J.
Sphagnum Moss—Clean, dry, 85c. per
5-bbl. bale; 10 bales, $8.00. Cash, please.
GEORGE THOREN, Mayetta, N. J.

STOVE PLANTS
Orchids—Largest stock in the country—
Stove plants and Crotons, finest collection.
JULIUS ROEHRS CO., Rutherford, N. J.

SWEET PEA SEED
Ant. C. Zvolanek, Lompoc, Calif.
Gold Medal of Honor Winter Orchid Sweet
Peas.
For page see List of Advertisers.
S. Bryson Ayres Co.,
Sunnyslope, Independence, Mo.
For page see List of Advertisers.

VEGETABLE PLANTS
Celery plants. Golden Self Blanching
(French Strain), Giant Pascal, White
Plume and Winter Queen, fine plants,
ready for field. $1.50 per 1000; $1.00 in
10,000 lots cash. BRILL CELERY GAR-
DENS, Kalamazoo, Mich.

VENTILATING APPARATUS
The Advance Co., Richmond, Ind.
For page see List of Advertisers.
The John A. Evans Co., Richmond, Ind.
For page see List of Advertisers.

VERMICIDES
Aphine Mfg. Co., Madison, N. J.
For page see List of Advertisers.

WEED DESTROYER
Pino-Lyptol Chemical Co., New York City.
For page see List of Advertisers.

WIRED TOOTHPICKS
W. J. Cowee, Berlin, N. Y.
For page see List of Advertisers.

For List of Advertisers See Page 95

THE GLASS MEN

The National Association of Window Glass Manufacturers will hold their fifth annual meeting at Atlantic City, N. J., on July 27, 28 and 29, at the Hotel Traymore. To judge from one of the photographs herewith reproduced at least two of the members of the organization are already somewhat familiar with the pastimes of the great seaside resort. Of the two happy looking gentlemen so comfortably ensconced in the wheelchair preparatory to a boardwalk stroll the one on the left is O. C. Teague, president of the National Association. His companion is genial Ed. Flood, whom many of our readers already know as the eastern representative of the Johnston Brokerage Co., the largest distributors of

Left—O. C. Teague, President National Association of Window Glass Manufacturers. Right—Ed. Flood of Johnston Brokerage Co.

J. R. JOHNSTON

President, Johnston Brokerage Co., and Secretary of National Association of Window Glass Manufacturers.

glass in this country, selling most of the product of the hand-blown glass factories.

We also present a portrait of J. R. Johnston, president of the Johnston Brokerage Co., and secretary of the National Association.

It may interest some of our friends whose duty it is to plan convention programs for florists and kindred organizations to see how the glass men do it when they foregather, so we present the program complete for their meeting.

Tuesday, July 27th, 1915

Forenoon—Registration: Business Session, 9 A. M. to 12 M.: Officers' Reports; Roll Call; Papers by Members; Talks by Guests; Wheel Chair ride for ladies, 10 to 12.

Afternoon—Flying Machines by special

arrangement with Professor Jacqwith, 3 P. M. from Inlet.

Evening—Theatre Party, 8.15 prompt, Keith's Vaudeville.

Wednesday, July 28th, 1915.

Forenoon—Usual Business Session, 9 to 12; Address and Papers; Reports of Committees; Nomination and Election of Directors; Wage Committee.

Afternoon—Fishing and Sailing; Flying Machine, 3 P. M. from Inlet.

Evening—Theatre Party, Musical Comedy, Appolo Theatre.

Thursday, July 29th, 1915.

Forenoon—Meeting, 9 to 12; Addresses; Election of Officers; New Business.

Afternoon—Golf Tournament, Country Club; Professor Jacqwith, Flying Machine.

Stenographer will be in Committee rooms for use of members and their friends. Parlors for Ladies provided. Maid, etc.

Some one of our party will accompany Prof. Jacqwith in his Hydro-aeroplane each day. A fifteen minute journey at great height over ocean and along beach. Exhilerating, and we hope harmless.

Those desiring to sail or fish please advise Secretary or members of Entertainment Committee.

Theatre tickets for entire party are reserved and will be distributed first day of conference.

Two Handsome Trophies have been provided for Golf Tournament, handicaps and details to be arranged by special committee.

On behalf of their good friends and profitable patrons, the greenhouse men, we extend congratulations and best wishes that the glass men may have the time of their lives. We confess we cannot get along without them. May they thrive and prosper.

but with due consideration for the pockets of the greenhouse men, when they talk about prices and lay schemes for next season's campaign. When they soar in those Atlantic City aeroplanes we hope the sensation of flying high will not unduly inflate their ideas of the greenhouse man's limit, but rather produce a feeling of sympathy for the poor mortal who must stay on the earth and who, when he has made a few dollars, is sure to "put it all into sash."

GREENHOUSES BUILDING OR CONTEMPLATED.

LeRoy, Ill.—L. L. Fry, house 48x90.

Hamilton, Md.—A. Beckman, alterations.

Providence, R. I.—Frey Bros., house 30x80.

Paxtang, Pa.—J. F. Harstick, rebuilding.

Salem Turnpike, Ct.—T. H. Peabody, 90 ft. house.

Bethel, Pa.—E. L. Shrigman, King house, 18x50.

Hambleton, W. Va.—H. E. Hoefner, house 20x100.

North Irwin, Pa.—James A. Jacobs, house 30x110.

Bristol Pa.—Jacob Schmidt, Otter St., house 70x100.

Montague, Mich.—Fruitvale Nurseries, two houses.

Detroit, Mich.—Thos. Brown, vegetable house 82½x600.

Contoocook, N. H.—Clarence V. Thompson, house 20x50.

St. Catherines, Ont.—R. L. Dunn, two houses each 25x120.

Speonk, N. Y.—South Shore Floral Co., King house, 35x150.

Champaign, Ill.—J. E. Yeats, East Springfield St., one house.

Portland, Me.—W. T. & H. T. Sawyer, 110 Coyle St., house 24x60.

Pleasant Hill, Mo.—Geo. M. Kellogg Flower & Plant Co., rebuilding.

Gobton, Pa.—Mrs. Herman Schoezenbach, two houses each 21x100.

South Richmond, Va.—Forest Hill Gardens, Lord & Burnham house.

Hartford, Ct.—Mrs. H. Thompson, Strawberry Hill, range of houses.

Albany, N. Y.—Executive mansion, range of houses. Lord & Burnham Co.

Greenwich, Conn.—Jesse I. Strauss, large range of houses. Lord & Burnham Co.

Newark, N. J.—Trauth, the Florist, 475 Orange St., house 23x100; two houses each 18x100.

Urbana, O.—R. H. Murphy's Sons, Oakland St., six houses, each 20x100; one house 13x200.

Fall River, Mass.—Oak Grove Cemetery, addition 25 x 100 with corridor; by the Weathered Company.

Wenona, Ill.—Wenona Greenhouses, Wm. Metzger, proprietor, house 25x75.

Newton Falls, O.—Cleveland Cut Flower Company, rose house 49x400; carnation house 24x200. Lord & Burnham construction.

STORM DAMAGE IN NEW JERSEY

A series of severe electrical storms accompanied by heavy hail did great injury in Morris, Union and Somerset counties, New Jersey, on July 13, and did considerable damage as it swept over the country around Summit, Madison, Chatham, Murray Hill, etc., especially the hail, as quite a number of lights were broken on all the greenhouse places in these towns. More than one hundred lights of glass were broken by hail in the greenhouse of Fred Nason, Murray Hill, New Providence. The greenhouses of Marcus L. Force of Morristown were riddled by hail and flowers and vegetables destroyed ruthlessly. At Westfield, Herder Bros. were heavy losers. Their greenhouses were completely wrecked and contents ruined.

At Springfield a dwelling in course of erection by the Jacobsen Floral Co. on Westfield Ave., was badly damaged. At Madison, truck gardens were either cut to pieces or the vegetables torn up by the roots and swept away. This along with the greenhouses that were wrecked and the wheat and oat crops that were destroyed runs the damage up to $100,000.

CATALOGUE RECEIVED.

A. H. Hews & Co., Inc., North Cambridge, Mass.— Catalogue and List Prices of Flower Pots and Red Earthenware Specialties, 1915 edition. This is a little 16 page publication, but it represents the largest factory of its kind in the world. Moreover it signalizes the completion of 150 years of business at the same stand, so the establishment of A. H. Hews & Co. is not alone the largest, but the oldest manufacturer of red flower pots in the world. The catalogue is illustrated with cuts showing the shapes of plain and fancy florists' earthenware with complete lists and prices of all sizes and is a very handy little reference book to have around the office and potting shed.

NEWS NOTES.

Fulton, Ia.—Chas. Stoll has purchased the John Kirman range of greenhouses.

Muncie, Ind.—Wm. M. Treffenger has leased the Carnes Greenhouses, 1126 South Jefferson St., and will conduct them under the name of the Southside Greenhouses.

Vol. XXII
No. 5
JULY 31
1915

HORTICULTURE

Miltonia vexillaria

Published Every Saturday at 147 Summer Street, Boston, Mass.
Subscription, $1.00

LIST OF ADVERTISERS

FOR BUYERS' DIRECTORY AND READY REFERENCE GUIDE
SEE PAGES 148, 149, 150, 151

NOTES ON CULTURE OF FLORISTS' STOCK

CONDUCTED BY

John J. M. Farrell

Questions by our readers in line with any of the topics presented on this page will be cordially received and promptly answered by Mr. Farrell. Such communications should invariably be addressed to the office of HORTICULTURE.

"If vain our toil, we ought to blame the culture, not the soil."—*Pope.*

Antirrhinums

For winter or spring flowering the antirrhinums are an excellent and profitable crop. For early flowering, through November and December, it is necessary to bench the plants about the first week in August. I find they do best with a minimum of 48 to 50 degrees in winter. Plant a foot apart each way if the stock was raised from cuttings. Pinch back the shoot as it pushes up to flower and allow four to five shoots to start from near the ground. Rub out all weak, useless growths. Three or four good spikes to a plant will pay better than three times that number of inferior ones. Stake the plants to keep them erect and rub off the side growths on flowering stems.

Aspidistras

It is a good plan to propagate a lot of aspidistra, as they are bound to come in very useful. Break up densely grown clumps leaving two or three leaves with each piece. For these divided pieces you can use 4 or 5-inch pots. Give them fibrous loam three parts, well rotted cow manure one part. Place in a house where they can be shaded and kept rather close and they will soon start new roots, after which place them near the glass and do not keep them too densely shaded. When started now they will make fine stock for early spring sales. They do fine in a temperature of from 55 to 60 degrees at night.

Chrysanthemums

Faithful attention to cultural details of apparently little importance is essential to success with chrysanthemums under glass. The very first and main aim should be to encourage a healthy faultlessly clean and withal exuberant growth of the plants before the buds are actually forming. All this stock, even the latest made and benched lots, is now or should be by this time well forward in growth, needing daily attention to watering, weeding, syringing, staking and tying while the earliest planted should have its complete scheme of stake, string and wire support fully adjusted, mulched to prevent rapid drying out of soil and closely watched as regards formation and eventual taking of buds. See that all houses have plenty of ventilation at all times. Fumigate once a week or not later than every ten days for fly.

Lorraine Begonias

These will need lots of attention from this out. Give them a place quite close to the glass which should not be too heavily shaded. Where possible give them shade during the hottest hours of the day with a lattice that can be removed after 3 or 4 P. M. and need not be put on again until 9 o'clock in the morning, or may be left off entirely on cloudy days. When given this treatment it is surprising how much more stocky and better the plants will be by late fall. Give them a shift before they become pot bound until they are in their flowering size. Use a compost of equal parts of fibrous loam, leaf mold and well decayed cow manure. Keep the air humid by wetting down paths and beneath the benches. When the plants begin to crowd give them a fresh stand with plenty of room between for light and air. Ventilate so as to avoid any sudden fluctuations in the temperature.

Sweet Peas

Do not buy cheap seed but be sure to get the best that is on the market. For early flowering seed should be sown by the end of this month. If the space on the benches is not ready sow in 4 or 5-inch pots and then plant out in four or five weeks. The best place to grow these along is in a cold frame where they can have plenty of air and be handy for water and syringing. They can be kept shaded until they come up which I think is better to hasten germination, but after that they will need full sun. To do well they should have at least eight inches of soil, but where you have a solid bed plant them there and you will never regret it. Whether in bench or solid bed give them a rich compost. They will grow very well in fibrous loam two parts, well rotted cow manure one part. and a little bone meal. Just as soon as they show any signs of climbing give them supports.

Manure for Winter

It takes some time to get a pile of good manure so it is always better to start early about this work. The grower who always makes it a point to have plenty of good manure in his shed for future use can rely on having fine crops. So turn this over in your mind now and make plans for later on.

Next Week:—Callas; Carnations; Cattleyas; Primulas; Seeds to Sow; Propagating Sand.

Two Little Known Perennials of Sterling Merit

Salvia virgata nemorosa is a plant all too little known in the catalogues of the nurseries of this country. Most of the stock used here is imported each year from Europe and as a result the supply is inadequate. It is hard to find a reason for this with a plant of such ease of propagation. It can be very easily raised from cuttings given the same treatment as those of any herbaceous perennial plant. These cuttings root readily in heat if they are rather soft and in a growing state. After well rooted the plants should be potted up and kept in pots until sold or until permanently planted out. The flower is one of the most delightful of the whole Sage family being a beautiful soft blue, and it is a deplorable fact that its use in American gardens should be limited by the supply, as is evidently the case.

Another perennial of value, often overlooked by planters is Nepeta Mussini, which flowers light blue during May and June. It will thrive in any ordinary light sandy soil and is easily propagated from seed or by division. It is a rapid grower and very soon covers the ground. Those plants which one finds in the market are ordinarily of a rather high price, even at wholesale, a fact for which I can see no reason, when it is so easy to procure a good stock of plants.

Here again I would recommend that the plants be grown in pots, for with all herbaceous plants, excepting perhaps peonies and the like, a potted plant suffers less of a set back when transplanted, ships in better condition over greater distances, and is more convenient to handle than the ordinary nursery clump. By this method the shipping season may be prolonged with greater safety and incidentally the gross receipts from sales are materially increased. Plants when sent out from pots should be as well pot-bound as possible to insure their holding their ball of soil which is essential to successful transplanting and the use of the now cheap and serviceable paper pot is of great advantage when the plants are to be shipped by freight or express. Potted plants ship over reasonable distances by freight as safely as by express, provided a little wet moss is placed among the pots to retain moisture. In packing the plants the open slatted crate seems to be the best way, for the expressman sees at a glance that carelessness on his part means a job to pick up the pieces and the weak top of the crate indicates that no weight can be put on top of the box. Hence the plants receive proper treatment and plenty of air and less rot and burning up will be found in such a shipment.

Hubert M. Canning.

Jamaica Plain, Mass.

Miltonia vexillaria
See Cover Illustration.

Miltonia vexillaria is well known and it certainly is one of the best spray orchids for either commercial or private use. Its flowering season extends from early April until the later part of July. The flowers, if kept cool and dry will keep in good condition four weeks and longer. The color varies in different plants from nearly white with a touch of pink in the center of the sepals and petals to deep pink and rose. Some varieties have a deep carmine blotch on the lip, others only a few radiating lines of a dark rose color in addition to the usual yellow blotch which surrounds the yellow crest. However, all of them are beautiful and well worth the little trouble it takes to grow them. They don't seem to care what compost they grow in, for I have seen excellent plants grown in osmunda fibre, others in peat and moss and others in moss alone. For the last few years I have used nothing but clean live sphagnum moss, which is kept growing and is replaced with fresh as soon as it shows signs of decay.

Miltonias are nearly always active and, therefore, require no special resting season. The only time they rest is when in full bloom and then less water is given at the root and the plants are kept in a cool, dry place where no damping down is done. Each plant is then allowed to get quite dry before water is again applied. At all other times the plants require an abundant supply of water and once a week or ten days an application of weak liquid manure. As the bulbs commence to swell and the flower spikes push forth this may be increased to double the usual strength until the flowers begin to expand. After that no more feeding is done until the new growths, which will push forth soon after the flowers are past, are well under way. Any dividing or repotting should be done at that time as then the roots are most active and will quickly take hold of the new compost.

Miltonia vexillaria is not over particular as to temperature. Some grow them cool, some warm and some in intermediate temperature. I prefer the latter with partial shade in summer and plenty of fresh air at all times. The atmosphere is kept damp during the growing season by frequent damping of the floors and between the pots.

Miltonia Roezlii requires a little more heat, but M. Bleuiana, a cross between the two, will do well under the treatment advised for M. vexillaria.

M. J. Cope

ROSE GROWING UNDER GLASS

CONDUCTED BY

Arthur C Ruzicka

Questions by our readers in line with any of the topics presented on this page will be cordially received and promptly answered by Mr. Ruzicka. Such communications should invariably be addressed to the office of HORTICULTURE.

Care of Old Plants

Old plants that have just been cut off and planted again in the benches will require every possible care to bring them to their first growth, after which they will be easier to handle, although to make them pay they must never be neglected for an instant. We find that it pays to give these plants even less soil than we would give young plants, for if the weather in the fall and winter should be very dark, less trouble will be experienced with the drying out of the benches. It is well to have plenty of well decayed manure in the soil as they will take more feed than young plants, and if not fed enough will produce a great many short-stemmed flowers, mostly No. 2's, and these are not very profitable to the grower. Syringe twice daily right after they are planted, being very careful to do the work quickly, so as not to get too much water on the benches. To do this right, the walks must be in good condition, so that the man with the hose can walk right along watching the plants and his work without having to look ahead to see that he does not walk into a hole, or slip on the slimy earth walks sometimes tolerated in greenhouses. A coat of sand is the very best these walks could get, with a little lime added to help kill the green. Ashes we would not recommend where pipes touch the walk, as these eat through the pipes in a very little time.

When syringing the plants that have already broken into leaf, see that they are wet enough, otherwise the foliage will likely be burned, and that is bad for plants that are just starting. As soon as there is enough growth to hide the main stalks, stop syringing, and syringe only as often as necessary to keep the plants clean, choosing the forenoon of bright clear days. Watering will also play an important part in starting old plants, and if done very carefully, the loss from plants dying will be very small.

Lime

In the early planted houses, where the plants have attained some size, it will be necessary to use a little lime every night when the plants are watered or syringed in the day time. Some nights are very cool and foggy, and if no lime is used the plants will likely suffer under the leaves from the moist air that stays around the bottom, and will be more apt to get mildew or spot. It is very good to use a little lime at night after a thunder storm in the afternoon, especially if the rain beat in. Use lime in old leaky houses when a shower comes up in the afternoon. Growers will say it is not necessary to use lime except for Beauties, but we like to use it for all roses, as there is very little expense attached to it, and the benefit is many times the small outlay.

Liquid Manure

It is still too early to use this on plants that are not well rooted, but any houses that have been grown for summer blooming should receive liberal doses. Do not mix any strong chemicals into it, using only a good lot of cow manure. If nitrate and other strong fertilizers are added, the plants are bound to get a little soft, and are likely to get a dose of mildew. If the liquid manure is not very strong, add a little bonemeal to it but nothing else.

Mulching

Watch the early planted houses, and see that the roots do not suffer by being exposed to the rays of the sun. Beauties especially will be working well to the surface now, and a protecting mulch of manure will do wonders in giving the plants color and keeping them in good growing condition. The roots that suffer most are the young tender feeders that supply the plant with food. These will appear right on the surface if the plants are mulched, and growers should be careful not to scratch the benches over deeply, as this would destroy all the tender roots and thus set the plants back. Protect all the roots for they are very important to the growing plant. If the plants have poor roots, the feed, water, etc., that is given them will largely be wasted, as they will have no way to take it up. Get the soil full of roots and keep these alive by careful watering and feeding, taking care to give the necessary mulching when it is required.

HYDRANGEAS AT ARNOLD ARBORETUM.

Hydrangea radiata. A form of *Hydrangea arborescens* (var. *grandiflora*), with large globose heads of sterile flowers, has become immensely popular in this country since its discovery a few years ago in one of the western states, and it can now be seen in many suburban gardens. A much more beautiful American species, however, is *Hydrangea radiata*, which is now in flower in the Shrub Collection. It is a native of mountain slopes in North and South Carolina, and is a round-topped shrub with large leaves very dark green above and silvery white below, and broad heads of flowers surrounded by a ring of while neutral flowers. It is one of the handsomest of all the Hydrangeas which are perfectly hardy in this climate, and although once a popular garden plant it is now rarely found in collections.

Hydrangea paniculata. More conspicuous now in the collection is the early-flowering form of *Hydrangea paniculata* (var. *praecox*). The most generally planted form of *Hydrangea paniculata* is that in which all the flowers are sterile, known as *Hydrangea paniculata grandiflora*. This plant produces large clusters of white flowers which turn rose color in fading, and will not be in bloom for several weeks. The variety *praecox*, which is one of the forms of the wild plant, has ray flowers surrounding the clusters of sterile flowers. There are two or three forms of the variety *praecox* in the collection differing in the size of the flower-clusters and in the size of the ray flowers. The handsomest and earliest of these was raised from seeds collected by Professor Sargent in Hokkaido where it grows into a small tree sometimes twenty or thirty feet tall.—*Arnold Arboretum Bulletin.*

During the next month several interesting plants will flower in the Arnold Arboretum. Among trees may be mentioned the Chinese *Koelreuteria paniculata*, the American and Asiatic forms of *Aralia spinosa*, the Japanese *Acanthopanax ricinifolium* and *Sophora japonica*; and among shrubs the Pepper-bush of the eastern United States (*Clethra alnifolia*), which has been largely used in the roadside plantations, and *Panax sessiliflorus* from eastern Siberia.

The Arboretum Bulletins will now be discontinued until autumn.

HORTICULTURE

VOL. XXII   JULY 31, 1915   NO. 5

PUBLISHED WEEKLY BY
HORTICULTURE PUBLISHING CO.
147 Summer Street, Boston, Mass.
Telephone, Oxford 292.
WM. J. STEWART, Editor and Manager.
SUBSCRIPTION RATES:
One Year, in advance, $1.00; To Foreign Countries, $2.00; To Canada, $1.50.

Entered as second-class matter December 8, 1904, at the Post Office at Boston, Mass., under the Act of Congress of March 3, 1879.

CONTENTS   Page

We are now right in the middle of the vacation and recreation period. The custom which has become so general among the various local florists' organizations of providing simple games and athletic contests as features of a special day of outdoor enjoyment once a year is a most commendable one and by bringing together families which have so much in common many life-long friendships are created between those who might otherwise never have met one another. We are disposed to devote a considerable space just now to the details of these out-

Play time

ings and we feel confident that our readers will find no fault with the brief digression from the serious things of life. "All work and no play" is not to be recommended as a steady diet.

We occasionally find in the public print an item that gives especial gratification because it marks some progressive step in one or another direction. Such a note is that from Bridgewater, Mass., wherein the tree warden of that town, in support of claims for the loss of trees by escaping illuminating gas, makes the assertion that the destruction of good healthy shade trees on property decreases its valuation at least twenty per cent. That is good doctrine and we hope it will be affirmed in the court should court action be found necessary to collect compensation in this instance. Gas and electric companies will not be so careless regarding injury to trees, public or private, when the public come to a full realization of their rights and a proper estimate of the intrinsic value of growing trees as property and as material assets in computing the worth of a town from a practical as well as an esthetic standpoint. Massachusetts has good tree warden laws and as a rule her towns have been blessed with good earnest officials who have performed the duties of their position in a most able, conscientious and public spirited manner.

Protecting the trees

Among those gentlemen who have been endeavoring to round-up delegations to attend the San Francisco S. A. F. Convention from the leading eastern sections it seems to be now a foregone conclusion that the number in attendance will be very meagre as compared with the hopes, predictions and promises so freely expressed a few months ago. The real reason for this condition is easily thought out and will be obvious to anybody with some knowledge of the course of business in most floricultural lines during the year since the meeting in Boston which so jauntily accepted the invitation to the Golden Gate and painted for us such rosy pictures of car loads of happy convention pilgrims westward bound in August, 1915. It would be a mistake to charge this miscarriage of plans entirely to indifference on the part of the S. A. F. members regarding the Society, the Convention, the Panama-Pacific Exposition or the brethren of San Francisco who with characteristic hospitality have been busy devising ways and means for extending entertainment and a big welcome to their visitors. We have no doubt of the sincerity of the majority of those who originally voiced their intention of going to San Francisco but have now "backed down." This is emphatically a year burdened with unforeseen complications, and which demands close application and attention to one's business. Not that the future looks so very unpromising as that its aspects are so ill-defined and uncertain that they cannot safely be neglected. It is for us to be thankful, however, that the situation is not much worse, for whatever temporary perplexities we are called upon to face in this momentous time they cannot for a moment be weighed against the conditions which prevail across the sea. The heart of the great horticultural host all over the country will be with the S. A. F. during its gala week in San Francisco to a degree equalled by no previous similar event. There will be intense interest in the story of the proceedings and, fully realizing this, HORTICULTURE has made arrangements for a very full telegraphic story of the convention doings in its convention week issue. *They will all read it and they will read it all.*

Thwarted plans

CLUBS AND SOCIETIES

AMERICAN SWEET PEA SOCIETY.

Report of the Sweet Pea Trial Grounds,
by Prof. A. C. Beal.

During the past year we were able to resume our trials with the winter-flowering sweet peas. Although we did not come into possession of the necessary greenhouse space in time to sow them for the early crop, we were able to plant during October and therefore had an excellent crop of flowers during midwinter and spring. In fact, last year's crop was the best we have ever had.

A large collection of varieties were received from Mr. Zvolanek and a few varieties from other seedsmen. Some of the older varieties were grown for comparison, and altogether there were sixty varieties in the collection. Among the newer sorts the following are very promising:

BRIDAL VEIL. A large to very large, much-waved white flower.

KING OF ENGLAND. A large waved flower, of a bright glowing crimson color. In our experience this variety is the best red for greenhouse culture.

REV. FATHER KELLY. A large to very large, much-waved lavender flower. Some of the standards show tints of mauve-rose, but change to the same color as the wings. The exact color is not given in the "Repertoire des Coleurs" being less red than 188 (1) and less blue than 201 (1).

BELGIAN HERO. A large waved flower with the standard salmon-carmine and wings purple-rose. This would be called by the trade an orange-pink. When grown in late spring or summer this variety, unless shaded, shows the blackened veins common to flowers of this color; but in winter this variety was free from this defect. When well grown it is a fine variety.

MORNING STAR. A very large much-waved flower with the standard bright mauve-rose and wings violet-rose. These are the approximate colors, as the real colors lie between the two and the flower is more nearly a self than is indicated.

MRS. CALVERT. A large waved deep pink flower. The standards are mauve-rose and the wings pale lilac-rose. A beautiful flower.

POLAR LIGHT. A large waved flower; standard lilac-rose, wings darker.

WAVED CHRISTMAS PINK. Appears to be a decided improvement on the widely-grown Christmas Pink.

The above are the best of the collection for commercial culture, but there are others of considerable promise which we have not space to describe as Pacific, Montenegrin, President Wilson and Polar Bear.

The above varieties were free from rogues, and all the varieties indicate a very great advance in the winter-flowering section.

Of the varieties received from other growers, Selma Swenson is a large to very large waved, pale lilac-rose with light violet-rose wings.

This season in the open ground we have seventy varieties of comparatively recent introduction, and about an equal number of the oldest varieties.

The latter we are growing to secure seed so that we may keep them for a few years. It is probable that the plants at Cornell are the only existing plants of some of these old varieties which are so interesting to those of us who wish to note the progress in the evolution of sweet peas. These, of course, were sown in the open ground.

The new varieties referred to were not received until the latter part of March, probably because of the war, and were sown in pots at once. Had we been able to forecast April conditions this year, we should have sown them in the open because when we did transplant we had a dry period which tended to check the plants.

They are now beginning to bloom, although the amount of growth is less than usual. It is too early to estimate the real worth of these varieties. What I shall say, therefore, is only tentative and subject to revision. At present we consider:

STARK'S GIANT BUFF. This with us is the largest waved variety of its class.

DUCHESS OF PORTLAND (Dobbie, 1915). A very large cream-pink.

ALFRED (Dobbie, 1915). A good sized clear pale lavender.

BLUE PICOTEE (Dobbie). Appears to surpass all other blue Picotees.

ROBERT SYDENHAM. The first flowers of this have proved a disappointment to us for it burns. We have had very unusual weather in that we have had frequent heavy rains alternated with bright sun. Possibly settled weather would result in better flowers, although the fault is not an uncommon one among the varieties of this color section.

STARK'S SOFT SALMON. Is a pretty thing; but we wish to see more of it.

KING WHITE. Is the leading exhibition white, and WEDGEWOOD appears likely to supplant the other waved blues.

Brooklands' Queen, Sincerity, Dobbie's Orange, Spitfire and others may prove desirable.

We hope that conditions may be better this fall and that we can receive seeds earlier next year for outdoor growing.

In closing let me urge the members of this society to use their influence to get varieties for the trial grounds. This fall we shall have better facilities for testing winter-flowering sweet peas than we have ever had before. We shall have a new modern house forty feet wide at our disposal, and the tests will be made under commercial conditions as we plan to use the house and crop as an object lesson in growing winter-flowering sweet peas. If we can secure all the varieties now in the trade for trial with our present notes, we can later issue another publication bringing the subject up-to-date.

The Cleveland Flower Show committee report the A. L. Randall Company of Chicago have taken prominent space, and that they have many inquiries from other live dealers and manufacturers.

AMERICAN ROSE SOCIETY

The executive committee of the American Rose Society met at the office of President S. S. Pennock, Philadelphia, on Tuesday, July 20. The appointment of Emil Buettner, Park Ridge, Ill., and John H. Dunlop, Richmond Hill, Ontario, as judges for the rose exhibits at the Cleveland Flower Show to be held in the Coliseum in Cleveland from November 10 to 15, was confirmed. Robert Scott & Sons of Sharon Hill, Pa., offer a special prize of $25 at this show.

The Hartford Rose Garden Committee, consisting of John F. Huss, Wallace R. Pierson and Alex. Cumming, Jr., report:

On the 25th of June the new roses of the test garden at Elizabeth Park, Hartford, Conn., were closely examined and silver medals were awarded as follows:

Conard & Jones Co., West Grove, Pa.—Climbing American Pillar. Scored 85 points. Highly recommended as pillar rose.

A. N. Pierson, Inc., Cromwell, Conn.—Killarney Queen. Scored 85 points. Recommended as a grand bedding rose.

Hoopes, Bro. & Thomas Co., West Chester, Pa.—Purity, Hybrid Wichuriana. Scored 87 points. A splendid grower that is recommended for every collection and garden.

Hoopes, Bro. & Thomas Co., West Chester, Pa.—Climbing American Beauty. Scored 87 points. A grand profuse bloomer deserving to be recommended for every garden.

Hugh Dickson, Ltd., Belfast, Ireland.—Lady Pirrie. Scored 85 points. Recommended as a splendid bedding rose.

Edward Kress, 2506 North Ave., Baltimore, Md.—Registered as Defiance. Scored 85 points. Highly recommended as a most excellent bedding rose.

There have been added a number of new varieties of American origin this spring which will be watched with great interest in the future, and more are promised for the planting in coming fall. Much interest has been especially devoted to this test garden by the lovers of roses, and the garden has been unusually well visited this season.

John F. Huss, Wallace R. Pierson, Alex. Cumming, Jr., Committee.

The National Flower Show to come off in Philadelphia next spring is gaining a good deal of attention and interest from the rose growers around Philadelphia.

The Waban Rose Conservatories presented for registration two new roses, as follows:

Mrs. Bayard Thayer—A sport from Mrs. Charles Russell. Flower is large and full. Color outside of petals deep rose, inside clear silver pink. Foliage large and very dark green, perfectly flat, has no tendency to curl as is sometimes the case with Mrs. Charles Russell.

Mrs. Moorfield Storey—A seedling. General McArthur X Joey Hill. A large full rose with heavy dark foliage. Color shell pink deeper towards the center, tip of petals deep rose.

There were directed to be accepted and published in accordance with the rules of the American Rose Society.

The Cleveland Rose Show was discussed and the desirability of holding a meeting in that city during the show was advocated, and a motion made to that effect was carried.

BENJAMIN HAMMOND, Sec'y.
Beacon, N. Y.

AMERICAN ASSOCIATION OF PARK SUPERINTENDENTS.

The eastern members who are to join the tour to San Francisco will start from New York, via the Penna. R. R., at 11.04 A. M. on Saturday, August 7. All eastern and southern delegates will converge at Chicago, the party leaving there via C. M. & St, P. R. R. on Sunday at 6.30 P. M. Arrival in San Francisco is scheduled for Monday P. M., August 16. The program of meetings and entertainments is as follows:

Informal Reception and Dance. Tuesday evening, August 17, at St. Francis Hotel. Wednesday, August 18, Morning—Opening Ceremonies; Address of Welcome by Mayor Jas. Rolph; Response by President Amryhn; Admission of New Members; Reports of Officers; Appointment of Committees; Introduction of Resolutions. Amendments to Constitution, etc. Afternoon—Reports of Committees; New Business; Papers and Addresses; Question Box; Election of Officers. Evening—Stereopticon Lectures; Address and Papers; Undulshed Business; Closing Ceremonies.
Thursday, August 19—Steamer trip around San Francisco Bay in forenoon; luncheon at Oakland, followed by auto tour of Oakland, Alameda and Berkely as guests of Board of Park Directors of Oakland: return to San Francisco about 6 P. M. by steamer. Evening—Stag smoker for the gentlemen at the Elks Club. Theatre party for the ladies.
Friday, August 20—All day auto tour of inspection over the parks, playgrounds and boulevards of San Francisco; also the pictruresque rural section known as "The Peninsula," luncheon being served enroute, the ride terminating at the Panama-Pacific Exposition. Evening—At the amusement features on "The Zone."
Saturday, August 21—This date left open for inspection of the Exposition exhibits, etc. Party leaves for San Diego Exposition and points eastward at 7.45 A. M. Sunday, August 22.

Papers and addresses are promised by the following:
Hon. Samuel Hill, President Pacific Highway Association.—Mr. Hill is an international character in road building, an extensive traveler and his illustrated lecture on "Good Ronds" is a revelation in various ways.
E. B. DeGroot, Director of Physical Education, San Francisco.—Mr. DeGroot is regarded as America's most eminent playground authority, having built up the wonderful South Park recreation centers in Chicago. His topic will be "The Drift of Organised Recreation."
J. H. Prost, City Forester of Chicago.—Mr. Prost will present a stereopticon lecture showing the wonderful work accomplished with trees in Chicago.
L. P. Jensen, of St. Louis, will present a paper on "Public Parks as Preservers of Native Plants."
Ernst Strehle will present a paper on the St. Louis Park Department Association, a unique and successful organization.
And others.

AMERICAN CARNATION SOCIETY.

Attention A. C. S. Members.

The Department of Floriculture of the University of Illinois is conducting experiments for the purpose of determining the cause of, and a remedy for the disease known as yellows among carnations. These experiments were started last year and have advanced far enough to promise definite results. There is perhaps no work in which the members of the A. C. S. could be more vitally interested, on account of the prevalence of this disease and the damage it is doing the carnation industry.

In order to carry on these experiments successfully and to arrive at definite conclusions, they require material from all sections of the country and to that end we ask that all members of the A. C. S. forward to them a limited number of each variety showing these light spots (in the red and

VANGUARD OF THE S. A. F. AT SAN FRANCISCO.

Here we have the picture of a special committee engaged in making preliminary arrangements for the visitors to the 31st Annual Convention of the S. A. F., taken at the famous Cliff House facing the Pacific Ocean. The occupants of the front seat are Secretary John Young of New York and

crimson sorts the spots are dark purplish) in the leaves.

The experimental benches will be planted during the first two weeks of August and these specimens should be forwarded during that time. Label each variety plainly.

The names of those sending in material will not be made public, so that no apprehension need be felt along that score.

Address all packages to Department of Floriculture, University of Illinois, Urbana, Ill.

A. F. J. BAUR, Sec'y.

AMERICAN DAHLIA SOCIETY SHOW.

Museum of Natural History, New York City, Sept. 24, 25, 26, 1915.

When the doors of this grand building are opened to the public on Sept. 24, we expect to have the greatest variety and best collection of dahlias ever gotten together anywhere in all their different types and classes. New seedlings and some of the newer varieties that have been either grown here or imported and not hitherto exhibited, will be shown for the first time at this meeting. There will be some seven hundred or eight hundred varieties grown by Prof. F. H. Hall, of the New York Experiment Station at Geneva, with other trial and experiment lots from other sections. We shall aim to have some one present who will explain the planting, growing and handling of dahlias for the garden. The Executive Committee have requested the retail florists to put up an exhibit of their decorative art and skill in showing the possibilities of this beautiful, many colored and exquisitely shaped flower. Each and every one will be given space free of charge to put up whatever they wish in table decorations, bouquets, baskets and vases of any design that will show the possibilities of the dahlia for ornamental and design work in its season.

The American Dahlia Society is the youngest society claiming notice, but is vigorous for its age and growing.

Vice-president Dan. MacRorie of San Francisco. In the second seat are C. W. Ward of Eureka, Cal. and R. C. Kerr of Houston, Texas. In the rear seat are C. P. Mueller of Wichita, Kans., and C. C. Grayson of Eureka, Cal. Standing, Ed. Sceery, Paterson, N. J.

The society is backed by good and experienced men who understand their business and will make an earnest effort to win the good opinion of their fellow craftsmen as well as the rest of the American public, especially the lovers of the beatiful dahlias.

RICHARD VINCENT, JR., Pres.

SOUTHAMPTON, N. Y., EXHIBITION.

It can safely be promised that the ninth annual exhibition of the Southampton Horticultural Society, to be held on Wednesday and Thursday, August 4 and 5, will be a real record-breaker.

Trade exhibits are promised from Bobbink & Atkins, Rutherford, N. J., roses and hardy perennials; Henry A. Dreer, Philadelphia, aquatics; W. A. Manda, So. Orange, N. J., roses and dahlias; Oak Park Nurseries, Patchogue, evergreens; Swan River Nurseries, Patchogue, evergreens; also exhibits of varied assortments from Guilfoyle, Frankenbach, Stumpff, Thomas Smith, Wm. F. Halsey and other local houses.

The prize list figures $735 outside the village competition, which is $105 more or $840 in all.

NEW YORK STATE FAIR.

The seventy-fifth annual New York State Fair will be held September 13-18, 1915, at Syracuse. An advance prize list for the flower department has been received. The commissioner in charge of this department is Charles S. Wilson, Albany, and David Lumsden, of Ithaca is superintendent.

The premiums are comprehensive and liberal. For roses in the professional classes alone they amount to over $400, of which $100 is offered for the best collection and display of roses consisting of 500 blooms and at least 12 distinct varieties. A second prize, $50, and a third, $25, are also offered in this class. Large sums are also offered for groups of stove and greenhouse plants, etc. Floral designs, gladioli, asters, carnations, dahlias, etc., are all liberally provided for.

DURING RECESS

PICNIC OF GARDENERS' AND FLORISTS' CLUB OF BOSTON.

As mentioned in a general way in our last week's issue, the annual picnic of the Boston Club on Thursday, July 22, was a pronounced success. About 500 florists with ladies and children participated. There were no accidents or other happenings to interfere with the perfect enjoyment of a perfect day. The games were well contested and a few extra ones were thrown in for good count. Below are the names of the winners of the prizes:

Base Ball—Commercial vs. Private Gardeners. Captains: William J. Iliffe, Private; William Mix, Commercial. Won by Commercials, 6 to 1.
Base Ball—Boys. Captains: Robert Smith, Philip Roland. Roland team won, 6 to 4.
Quoit Match. Captain: A. K. Rogers. 1st, M. Brown; 2nd, John Edgar; 3rd, K. Finlayson.
50-Yard Race for Girls, 13 and under—Mary Urann, Mary Flood, Alice Brown.
50-Yard Race for Boys under 8—Norman Craig, Arthur Rogers.
100-Yard Race for Single Ladies—Edith Iliffe, Alice Iliffe, Jessie Rogers.
50-Yard Race for Girls under 8—Ruth Brown, Margaret Craig.
50-Yard Race for Boys, 13 and under—T. Roland, P. Whyte, J. Douglas.
Egg and Spoon Race for Married Ladies—Mrs. J. Coles, Mrs. J. H. Flood.
Potato Race for Boys under 15—Thos. Roland, Victor Heurlin.
Flag Race for Girls under 15—Mary Urann, Margaret Iliffe.
Fat Men's Race—J. L. Smith, J. Methven; D. Iliffe and Nell Boyle tied for 3rd.
Base Ball—Married vs. Single Ladies: Mrs. F. Palmer's team, 1; Mrs. W. J. Paterson's team, 11.
Half-mile Race for Members—H. L. Pree, C. A. Stellberger.
50-Yard Race for Boys and Girls under 6—Julia Boyle, F. Kinkaid.
Needle Threading Race for Ladies over 50—Mrs. John Lally, Mrs. David Craig.
100-Yard Race for Members—C. A. Stellberger, H. L. Pree, W. J. Iliffe.
Sack Race for Boys under 16—W. Westwood, John Dogins.
Three-legged Race for Men—Stellberger and Eisenhardt, Palmer and Westwood.
Three-legged Race for Boys under 18—Sawyer and Westwood, Roland and Heurlin.
Sack Race for Members—H. L. Pree, C. A. Stellberger.
Obstacle Race—Theo. Palmer, A. McAuley.
Tug-of-war—Commercial vs. Private Gardeners. Captains: James Wheeler, John L. Smith. Won by Privates.
Special Race. Boys 8 and under—Nelson Bartsch, Norman Craig.
Race for Ex-presidents—P. M. Millet, T. J. Grey, Geo. M. Anderson.
Ladies' Tennis Match—Misses L. E. and F. Palmer, 6; Mrs. W. J. Paterson and Miss Eisenhardt, 2.
Married Ladies' Race—Mrs. J. F. Coles, Mrs. H. F. Woods, Mrs. J. F. Flood.

CLEVELAND FLORISTS' CLUB PICNIC.

The big event of the week was the annual picnic of the Cleveland Florists' Club. This proved to be the best one the club has ever held, both from the standpoint of attendance and general satisfaction. It was held at Willoughbeach Park located on Lake Erie, 18 miles east of Cleveland. There were about 250 in attendance. The two ball games proved very exciting and held the interest of the crowd. The first was indoor base ball. It was won by the retail men, the score being 9-7. The second game was regulation base

ball, won by the wholesalers after a hard fought battle. The long program of miscellaneous athletic events and races proved very interesting and provided much enjoyment for the crowd. Fred Witthuhn said he would have won the fat man's race if his breath had held out for the full distance. As it was he landed third place. The last event provided lots of fun for the boys who participated and the onlookers. About 15 boys each buried his face in a quarter of a big juicy watermelon and kept it there until nothing remained but the rind. Strange to say these boys did not care for any of the picnic lunch after finishing this event.

The Scores.

Indoor Baseball—Wholesale, 7; Retail, 9. Wholesale—H. Bate, Al Lingruen, Kerr, Wilson, S. Berthold, Talcott, Baird, Geo. W. Smith, C. Bastian, Rotter.
Retail—A. Barber, Tim Smith, C. Graham,

ham, Williams, F. Ritzenthaler, Clarence Meyers, E. Burger, Shoemacher, R. Hughes.
Baseball—Wholesale, 13; Retail, 12.
Wholesale—C. Williams, Rotter, P. Smith, Jr., Talcott, R. Hughes, P. Piggott, A. Lingruen, E. Burger, Bales.
Retail—C. J. Graham, Shoemacher, Al Barber, Heil, A. Graham, Jr., Tim Smith, Clarence Meyers, Baird, Rotter.
Bottle Race—Edith Heiss, Elenore Schoen, Madeline Smith.
Men's Sartorial Race—A. Williams, J. Brown, E. Burger.
Ladies' Sartorial Race—Nettie Smith, Mrs. Hepler, Ruth Monk.
Watermelon Eating Contest—Oscar Bauer, R. Talcott, J. Brown.
Fat Ladies' Race—Mrs. Kelch, Mrs. Hippler, Mrs. King.
Fat Men's Race—Kenneth Wilson, H. King, C. Bennett.
Married Ladies' Race—Mrs. Steinbrenner, Mrs. King, Mrs. Greiner.
Single Ladies' Race—E. Weis, Ruth Monk, Miss Buchle.
Married Men's Running Race—Harry Brook, Steve Berthold, L. G. Baird.
Single Men's Running Race—E. Burger, C. Muchinson, Chas. Rosenbnum.
Standing Broad Jump—E. Burger, Al Lingruen, Steve Berthold.
Hop, Skip and Jump Race—Harry Brooks, A. Williams, Al Lingruen.
Girls' Running Race, under 8 years—Marion Hepler, Alice Albrecht, Thelma Steinbrenner.

Boys' Running Race, under 8 years—Hal Schoen, Gene Smith, Herbert Bate, Jr.
Boys' Running Race, 8 to 12 years—Don Smith, Ray Schoen, Jacob Brown.
Girls' Running Race, 8 to 12 years—Helen Hart, Helen Bate, Madeline Smith.
Growers' Race—E. Burger, Al Lingruen.
Cock Fight—Harry Brooks, R. W. Talcott, R. Hughes.

FLORISTS' CLUB OF WASHINGTON.

The annual outing of the Florists' Club of Washington, held last Wednesday at Great Falls, Va., will go down into the club's history as another of the famous events which serve to lighten the cares and worries of the florists and bring sunshine into the lives of the little ones.

Despite the predictions of the weather man of forty days of continued rain, the day broke fair and cool, making possible the holding of a large number of athletic events. Charlie Chaplin, the famous comedian, had got wind of the outing and had loaned his facial and physical makeup to Samuel Ball, who created a great deal of merriment. The fun started when the special cars left from Georgetown. Identification tags were distributed that no one might get lost. Then came corsage bouquets for the ladies, boutonnieres for the men, and popcorn and peanuts for the kiddies.

Upon arriving at the Great Falls station the first number on the program was the refreshment booth events, awaiting the assault of the three hundred florists, their families and friends.

In addition to the races, quoit and baseball games, there was dancing, followed by movies and finally fireworks.

The schedule of games and the winners were as follows: Potato race for girls—1st, Rose Minder; 3d, Mary Higbee; for small girls—1st, Helen Barry; 2d, Elizabeth Dove; 3d, Mary Higbee; for small girls—1st, Helen Barry; 2d, E. Marche; 3d, M. Dauphin; for boys—1st, Edgar Burnham; 2d, Granville Gude; 3d, Teddy Schmid; open to all—1st, A. Ford; 2d, E. Smith. Potato race for ladies—1st, Miss D. B. Barry; 2d, Mrs. J. Richards. Flag race for girls—1st, Rose Minder; 2d, Mary Higbee; 3d, Mary Clark. 100-yard dash for men—1st, F. G. Weaver; 2d, Arthur Shaffer. 50-yard dash for ladies—1st, Miss Victoria Wilbur; 2d, Miss A. Barry; 3d, Miss Marie Coli. 100-yard dash for boys—1st, Herbert Moreland; 2d, George Hostetter. Three-legged race for boys won by Albert Ford and Harry Kimmel; for men, Albert Schnell and F. G. Weaver. The 100-yard dash for members of the club brought out a big lineup. This was a real race and taxed the energies of Harry Ley, who won, and George C. Shaffer who secured 2d.

A half-dozen pieces of jewelry and fine china were the inducements offered to the ladies to try their skill in depositing balls in a basket. The main prize was a handsome diamond sunburst, valued at $26, of which was won from a field of more than fifty by Miss Bernice Rigby, in the contest for married women Mrs. George C. Shaffer was 1st. Mrs. David J. Grillbortzer 2d and Mrs. George H. Cooke 3d, while the score of the single ladies showed the following winners: 1st, Miss Marie

Coll; 2d, Miss D. B. Barry; 3d, Miss Phillips. R. L. McLellan was the winner in the quoits, singles; George C. Shaffer, 2d; William Clark, 3d. In the doubles R. L. McLellan and J. J. Barry were the winners, with George C. and Arthur J. Shaffer, 2d.

The baseball teams from the downtown stores won by a number of timely hits and good field work. Their opponents were picked from the Anacostia greenhouses. The score was 10 to 5. The teams were composed as follows: Storemen—Charles E. Scarborough (captain), p.; R. W. Doty, c.; I. Rosnosky, 1st b.; Frank Good, 2d b.; B. Carrick, 3d b.; John Cook, s. s.; E. Draper, c. f.; Thomas Featherstone. r. f.; James Daly, l. f. Greenhouse team—Edward Henning, s. s.; Elmer Padgett (captain), 2d b.; John Carroll, c. f.; Leslie Dix, 3d b.; H. Sauber, p.; Samuel Ball, c.; Walter Gordon, l. f.; John Smith, r. f.

Those who served on the general entertainment committee were O. A. C. Oehmler. chairman; George W. Hess, George C. Shaffer, William Marche, George H. Cooke, Edward S. Schmid, Jake Richards, David J. Grillbortzer, Theodore Diedrich, William F. Gude, Harry Lewis. William H. Ernest, Lloyd Jenkins, Otto Bauer, G. Milton Thomas, Clareuce L. Linz and Fred H. Kramer.

ST. LOUIS CLUB PICNIC.

The St. Louis Florists' Club annual picnic held on Thursday, July 22, in Romona Park, was one of the most successful ever given and brought out the largest crowd yet. Chairman Rowe estimated the crowd at over five hundred, which speaks well. Everything they did was delightful, the music was delightful, the prizes were handsome and in all the contests the entries were large. There were some new and pleasing games and all were carried out to the letter. The winners were as follows:

75 yard dash for men—1st, Oscar Ruff, 2nd, J. R. McAlister.
Flag race, girls—1st, Miss Dahm; 2nd, Helen Borkern.
Backward walk for growers—1st, Gus Hartman; 2nd, W. Ogle.
Necktie contest for ladies—1st, Miss Erlinger, 2nd, Jesse Sanders.
Ball scramble for boys—1st, and 2nd won by Gussie and John Cerny.
Calico contest for ladies—1st, Mrs. Richie; 2nd, Mrs. Wm. Edwards.
Guinea catch, open to all—1st and 2nd won by the Williams Bros.
50 yard dash for boys—1st, E. Clobes; 2nd, W. Weinberger.
Time walk for married ladies—1st, Mrs. W. J. Pilcher; 2nd, Mrs. Lorenze.
Ball throwing contest for girls—1st, Miss M. Ninsheimer; 2nd, Miss A. Woods.
Wives only—1st, Mrs. Geo. Pring; 2nd, Mrs. Rowe.
Needle threading contest for growers Rowe.
50 yard dash, men—1st, Joe Hauser; 2nd, J. J. Beneke.
Cigar race, 14 boxes of cigars in a row. A race of some 30 men, at 100 yards, the first 14 to win.
Clock guessing contest—Fredie Strohmeyer.
Seed guessing contest—W. J. Pilcher.
Tug of war between single and married ladies—married ladies won.
Tug of war, growers versus retailers—won by Joe Hauser's team of growers.
The base-ball game between teams made up of growers and retailers the growers again came out winners by a score of 22 to 20, only five innings. H. Berning and Al Gunns were the umpires and ran the game like veterans.

TWIN CITY FLORISTS' CLUB.

On Tuesday, July 20th. the St. Paul and Minneapolis florists disported

Display at Panama-Pacific Exposition, Winning the Gold Medal of Honor.

Thirty-nine separate varieties of orchid sweet peas are planted in this bed. As the ground was not finished in time, the seed was sown the last week in January; they began to bloom the middle of April and promise to be still covered with blossoms for a considerable time yet.

The sub-soil all over the Exposition garden is quicksand, filled only about 10 to 15 inches with sandy loam, mixed with one-third old horse and cow manure and occasionally sprinkled with lime and bone meal. The flowers are picked mostly every day and exhibited in the Horticultural Building, and are a great attraction to thousands

themselves to Spring Park, Lake Minnetonka for a day's outing. It is estimated that they had a gathering of about three hundred. The St. Paulites defeated the Minneapolitans in a base ball game 11 to 4, and a number of races for all ages were run off. A boat ride was a most enjoyable feature, as was swimming, bowling and dancing. Henry Krinke a sixty-year-old florist of St. Paul won the first prize for the best old-fashioned waltz.

The Winners

Children's Race—1st, Kenneth Steath, Mpls.; 2nd, Albert Stern, Mpls.; 3rd, Gladys Sordren, Mpls.; 4th, Eugene Olsen, St. Paul; 5th, Mary Bolsky, Merriam Park.
Boys' Race—1st, George Olson, St. Paul; 2nd, Robert Stern, Mpls.; 3rd, Warren Olsen, St. Paul.
Young Men's Race—1st, Charles Heard, St. Paul; 2nd, George Patterson, Mpls.; 3rd, George Rowan, St. Paul.
Girls' Race—1st, Elsie Purogel, St. Paul; 2nd, Edna Gustafson, St. Paul; 3rd, Helen Olson, St. Paul.
Young Ladies' Race—1st, Bertha Anderson, Mpls.; 2nd, Dorothy Anderson, Mpls.; 3rd. Florence Mediel, St. Paul.
Ladies' Race—1st, Mrs. W. D. Desmond, Mpls.; 2nd, Mrs. L. W. Gray, St. Paul; 3rd, Mrs. Jake Gazzetti, Mpls.
Men's Race—1st, H. R. Purogel, St. Paul; 2nd, Lawrence Kilroy, Mpls.; 3rd, Frank Kennedy, Mpls.
Fat Man's Race—1st, F. A. Bayley, St. Paul; 2nd, Frank Penas, St. Paul; 3rd, Louis Danelik, Mpls.
Tug of War between Minneapolis and St. Paul, won by St. Paul. Tug of War between Ladies of St. Paul and Minneapolis, won by Minneapolis.
Base Ball game—Nine innings. Score 11-4 in favor of St. Paul.
Prize Waltzers—1st, Mrs. W. D. Desmond, Mpls.; Mr. Henry Krinke, St. Paul; 2nd, Mr. and Mrs. C. F. Rice. Mpls.; 3rd, John Rovik and Minnie Althoss, Mpls.

of visitors daily. According to the Exposition official report, this sweet pea exhibit is mostly admired by the visitors in the Exposition Garden.

In the picture is seen Wm. A. Leslie, the practical grower who has charge of the sweet peas. as well as of many other horticultural exhibits. Mr. Leslie is under the direct supervision of the landscape architect, Carl Purdy, who is now the Superintendent of the Exposition Horticultural Garden.

Both these gentlemen are hard and practical workers and many exhibitors in the Horticulture section as well as the general public have reason to be thankful for the excellent work they have accomplished.

CHICAGO FLORISTS' PICNIC.

The big picnic scheduled for July 25, at St. Paul's Park, Morton Grove, was not the success it would have been, on account of the boat disaster of the previous day. With over a thousand deaths in the city a gloom prevailed which made pleasure seeking distasteful to many. Had it not been for the preparations which had been made for the event it would have been called off, and notwithstanding the fact that all purchases had been made, the abandoning of the picnic would have met the approval of many. However, the trains and autos brought out a fair number and the usual picnic program was carried out.

CINCINNATI FLORISTS' SOCIETY.

The annual outing of the Cincinnati Florists' Society at Coney Island was a very successful affair due to the untiring efforts of the committee in charge. The baseball team captained by Chas. Windram won the ball game by the close score of 2-1, while P. Jackson was first in the bowling and C. E. Critchell was second.

THE ANNUAL MEETING OF THE

FLORISTS' HAIL ASSOCIATION

Will be held at the Civic Center Auditorium, Hayes and Larkin Sts., San Francisco, California, at 9 a. m. Thursday, August 19, 1915

JOHN G. ESLER, Sec.

THE LURE OF MAINE AND OF THE MARITIME PROVINCES.

Eastward Ho! is turning the tide of vacationists away from more distant lands. It is turning the tide toward Maine and its thousand charms. For there are found summer pleasures of every kind, fitted to every taste and desire.

For the lover of woods and lakes there are wonderful tramps through a beautifully rugged and wild country. There are mountains to climb, lakes to be crossed, rivers to follow, streams to ford, "carries" to enjoy, old Indian landmarks to be discovered. The entire region is filled with Indian lore. For the canoeist there are chains of lakes and rivers to be traveled—innumerable trips into wild and uninhabited country.

For the lover of the sea, there is the journey there and back, bold sea cliffs with the waves beating at their feet, the whispering of the sea breeze in the tree tops, the tang of the salt air, the sailing, the surf bathing, the Islands and bays.

For those who desire seclusion there are spots in the lake country where silence and peace and rest can be had.

Here also the fisherman and huntsman will find fish and game to their taste.

And for those who in summer are fond of social gayety, the distinction and elegance of the fashionable summer resort, there are noted places where the elite of America assemble. Eastward Ho! is the call of Maine, the Maine coast and the lake country, and the call of the rugged Maritime Provinces of New Brunswick, Nova Scotia, Prince Edward Island, Newfoundland.—*From "All the Way by Water," published by the Eastern Steamship Company.*

PERSONAL.

W. E. Chappell of Providence, R. I., has returned from the south after a four months' rest, greatly improved in health.

Mr. and Mrs. D. F. Roy of Marion, Mass., will accompany the members of the Association of Park Superintendents on the excursion to San Francisco.

OBITUARY.

Oliver Crissman.

While on his way to the Lutheran Sunday School, Sunday, July 4th, Oliver Crissman, of Punxsutawney, Pa., was struck by a train and killed instantly. Mr. Crissman was 70 years of age and early in life had been a landscape architect. Meanwhile he established the Crissman Greenhouses. He is survived by one son and four daughters.

Robert Robertson of Fitchburg, Mass., sends us a stalk of sweet peas, bearing the unusual number of eight flowers. The peduncle is slightly fasciated. The variety is one of the white grandifloras.

SEED TRADE

AMERICAN SEED TRADE ASSOCIATION
Officers—President, J. M. Lupton,
Mattituck, L. I., N. Y.; First Vice-President, Kirby B. White, Detroit, Mich.;
Second Vice-President, F. W. Bolgiano,
Washington, D. C.; Secretary-Treasurer,
C. E. Kendel, Cleveland, O.; Assistant
Secretary, S. F. Willard, Jr., Cleveland,
O. Cincinnati, O., next meeting place.

Prospects for Belgian Shipments.

William F. Gude, as the representative of the S. A. F. and O. H., last week had a conference with Robert F. Rose, of the Office of the Foreign Trade Advisers of the State Department, with a view to obtaining information as to what might be expected in the matter of securing permits from Great Britain for the exportation from Belgium of seeds and ornamental plants and was informed that the State Department is now doing everything possible to facilitate matters and there is nothing further that can be done. Since June 15, following which the British Embassy has been unable to issue permits under which Belgian goods could go forward, the State Department has been following a different method of procedure. In each case is brought to attention the matter is transmitted to the American Consul General at London with instructions to co-operate with the Belgian Minister there. A telegram is also sent to the American consul stationed nearest to the location of the seed producer with instructions to ascertain whether or not the producer is Belgian and if the Germans would benefit through the transaction. This information is furnished to the American consul general and the entire matter is then placed before the British foreign office. This procedure has been followed in a number of cases lately and the State Department officials have high hopes that they will meet with favorable consideration at the foreign office.

Notes.

The value of imports of horticultural material at the port of New York for the week ending July 17, is given as follows: Nitrate of soda, $212,024; fertilizer, $164; clover seed, $3,283; grass seed, $15,018; trees and plants, $330.

We have noticed some reports to the effect that radish crops in Michigan would be almost total failures. Messrs. Isbell & Co. inform us they are glad to say that although forced to plow up one or two small fields, the prospects are that they will harvest a fair radish crop at least.

We have received from S. M. Isbell & Co., seed growers of Jackson, Mich., sets of post cards and blotters with cuts of some of the fields of crops being grown for seed for them and showing various processes of perfecting and curing cucumber, watermelon and other seeds of which Michigan is a prominent source of supply.

EXPRESS RATES INCREASED.

Washington, D. C.—The florist trade of the country is facing an increase of from one to five cents on each shipment over the lines of the Adams, American, Wells Fargo and Southern express companies. The Interstate Commerce Commission has granted the petition of these companies to rearrange the express rate basis. The following shows the proposed increases on first-class shipments. It is stated that certain weight will, however, differ slightly from the figures given due to the disposition of fractions, and not all shipments over 85 pounds will be increased:

1 to 5 pounds	each 5 cents
6 to 29 pounds	each 4 cents
30 to 49 pounds	each 3 cents
50 to 70 pounds	each 2 cents
71 to 99 pounds	each 1 cent

The increase on second-class rates will be one-fourth less than the amounts stated. The increase in the rates covering shipments of plants will be from fifty to one hundred per cent higher than the figures given above.

The change in the rate structure will net the companies involved more than five million dollars per annum. It is claimed that for the year 1915, the companies will suffer a deficit of over two million dollars.

PUBLICATIONS RECEIVED.

Market Gardening by F. L. Yeaw, an Elementary Text Book and a Practical, Reliable and Handy Guide for all Growers of Vegetables.

The Brooklyn Botanic Garden Record for this quarter, contains among other things an illustrated article on Rare Cycads from Australia by Dr. C. Stuart Gager.

Transactions of the Iowa Horticultural Society, 1914. Vol. 49. This Society sets a shining example which some other so-called State "Horticultural" Societies might copy with great advantage to the people of their respective states. This volume of nearly 500 pages is a real treasury of horticultural and botanical information, covering in a wide range of topics connected with orcharding, home gardening ornamental and vegetable, tree planting and care, study of native plants, etc., showing that the Iowa State Society exists and works for every phase of horticulture without bias for any. We know some florists in Iowa whose names do not appear on the list of members. We would respectfully suggest that this is one organization well entitled to their support. Wesley Greene, Des Moines, is secretary.

Bernardsville, N. J.—The fifth annual show of the Bernardsville Horticultural and Agricultural Society has been announced for September 1 and 2 in Bernard's Inn auditorium. The pick of the fruit, flowers and vegetables grown on the estates of millionaires in this vicinity will be on exhibit.

The number of visitors recorded at the Missouri Botanical Garden during June, 1915, was 20,989. The Bulletin for July contains useful contributions on Cannas and Water Gardens.

Saratoga, N. Y.—Extensive improvements have recently been under way at the John Ralph greenhouses on Woodlawn avenue. A new system of overhead irrigation has been installed through the garden, and work is in progress on the office and work room which are to have a new metal ceiling, and will be repainted and refinished.

H. F. Michell Company have received a very flattering letter from Zieger & Sons of Germantown, Pa., complimenting them on the artistic planting and great beauty of their plantation of evergreens, crotons, etc., adjoining Convention Hall on Broad street, Philadelphia.

Of Interest to Retail Florists

HOW TO TREAT YOUR COMPETITORS.

A paper read before the Texas State Florists' Association by H. O. Hanna.

This is a friendly talk, part from experience, part from hearsay. We are here for our mutual benefit to cure the defects and to encourage in being and doing the right thing at the right time.

Your competitor is your best friend —you may say "a friend in disguise." He keeps you from being sordid, arrogant, selfish and perhaps unaccommodating. Hence, treat him fair, square, honorable, just, truthful and considerate. Remember the success of his business may often add to your success. No firm is going to sell all the flowers; each have their friends, and there is a place for him. Do your best, give the best flowers and plants; keep the most attractive store; arrange your flowers the most artistic; excel in all your decorations. Be original, be inventive, but never be a "copy cat," using your competitor's brain. Set the pace and let him follow.

Strive to excel. Make your own price and be sure to make it so it will leave you a profit. You owe this to your business and to your competitor and if he is a man he will do likewise. Be on good terms, visit him and his store, and never do anything that would cause you to avoid his presence or his confidence. Never do anything that will cause him to ask you why or wherefore the cause thereof. Honor and truthfulness should govern your acts toward him. Sell all the stock you can, but do it in the right way. Never, no never, let the thought occur to you to cut the price or quality to keep your competitor from making the sale. That is dishonorable.

If you are making prices on a large job of decorating, wedding, party or hall and you find out his prices and take same for almost half his price. making no money for yourself, but robbing him, this is almost "grand larceny." In furnishing figures for such occasions tell them, "We are not figuring against our competitor, but will make it complete and guarantee satisfaction." This is what we do, and if the other fellow wants it for glory, we do not. We are in business for money, and will seek glory and honor on other fields. We often cheapen work until the other fellow gets it, your customer knowing cheap price often means cheap work.

Never treat your competitor in any way that he will censure you either to your face or to your back. My competitors have never come to me and accused me in any way of being unfair to them, or to the trade. Truth prevails and lasts. Special sales for surplus is legitimate and honorable, but to make floral wreaths for 50c. or to sell carnations continuously for 25c. or 35c. per dozen, is disastrous, cheapens

the goods, and can be no profit, or if
any, very little. It costs in Texas to
grow flowers, and to buy we all know
there is a cost and expense. The trade
wants good stock and is willing to pay
for it.

Never pull crepe against your competitor nor allow your agents to do so.
This is dishonorable and unworthy of
your profession. Remember you sell
God's most gracious gift to man in all
its sweetness and beauty—hence do
not cheapen it nor tarnish it by little-
ness or unworthy act. Never, never,
cut your price, solely to keep your
competitor from making the sale.
That is almost petty theft.

Tell the truth and expect it of your
competitor. Never tell that an azalea,
poinsettia or primrose will bloom all
summer in order to make a sale. That
is lying, and your competitor may be
honorable. These things are done. I
have known clerks to tell customers
theirs was the only flower store, when
there was one almost across the street.
For shame, you may some time make
a sale by misrepresenting but a clear
conscience is more than a few pennies.

We have R. R. Commissions to make
the railroads "toe the mark," not to
cut the prices, or to make rebates, and
in many places florists need similar
regulating. Permit me to say that we
have two competitors, and we are on
friendly terms; trade, loan or sell anything the other needs. I appreciate
accommodating my competitors.

Never cheapen your goods by giving
away a flower or corsage to almost
every one that enters your store, trying to buy their trade. There are
times to give judiciously. Flowers
have value. Neither the dry goods
men, nor the grocer nor the druggist,
continuously give away their goods.
Then why should you? Don't make
yourself cheap nor your stock common.
Flowers have value and dignity, if I
may use the word.

NEW FLOWER STORES.

Chicago—John Meyer, who has been
a vender of flowers in this city for
some time has now opened a store at
2029 W. Chicago Ave.

Chicago—Herman H. Wenk and H.
Nelles have opened a retail flower
store at 302 W. North Ave., to be
known as the Plaza Flower Shop.

NEWS NOTES.

Greenwich, N. Y.—Frank H. Westinghouse, Academy street, has purchased the greenhouse and florist business of P. H. Hulst.

Rhinbeck, N. Y.—Charles R. Traver,
was elected president of the Violet
Growers' Mutual Association at the
annual meeting held in the Town
building, Saturday evening, July 10.

Lowell, Mass.—The office building of
the McManmon Company, florists,
Marshall avenue, was badly gutted and
the roof burned off Wednesday, July
21st. The damage will probably
amount to several hundred dollars.

NEWS ITEMS FROM EVERYWHERE

CHICAGO.

Word has been received from Frank Oechslin saying that they were enjoying their western outing but that a man needed an overcoat, as it was so cold.

As a background, the windows of the George Wienhoeber store had two large wreaths of green and purple last Monday, out of respect to the great number of dead in the city.

Phil McKee made a visit to Lincoln last week to see how the big Gullett range is progressing. On his return he left immediately for a business trip for his firm which is finding the season a busy one for greenhouse builders.

James J. Marsh, president of the Farmers' and Florists' Fertilizer Co., left this week for a business trip to Davenport and other cities of the middle west. Mr. Marsh reports business as very good.

The J. C. Moninger Co. received a telegram from Wilcox & Sons, of Council Bluffs, Ia., saying that they had suffered a large loss of glass from a hail storm which struck their plant on July 18th.

It seems now as if the peonies lasted so long this season that they might help out with the great need for flowers this week. Those who have been wishing to see them all used up by July 15th are most glad now to know there is a good supply left in the storage houses.

It is gratifying to note one new user of flowers in a large way the past week. The largest cafeteria in the city, The Harmony, gave a flower to each of its patrons on July 26th. As the daily attendance averages from three to five thousand, it meant the use of many flowers, but better still, the example was a good one. All of the tables were provided with a small bouquet and each employee wore a flower.

The August flower show at Garfield Park Conservatories will include 800 lily plants of several varieties. Just now the main bed in the big show room is filled with blooming plants of Nicotiana hybrids and along the side beds the beautiful gloxinias and begonias are found. The old time favorite achimenes are there too and appeal to those who love the flowers of a generation ago. An interesting group of plants rarely seen in bloom in August is the Campanula Vidalii, native of the Canary Islands.

A rare sight at the Garfield Park Conservatories is thirty foot plants of Kentia Forsteriana bearing fruit. The clusters are about ten feet from the ground and hang directly from the trunk. The fruit is about the size and shape of a sweet acorn and when cut open resembles white wax. Mr. Koch gave a scientific explanation of the process of fertilization in this familiar palm which seldom bears fruit outside of its native country.

Another novelty was a Ricinus Zanzibarensis 25 ft. high, now three years old. This is commonly grown as an annual but is in reality a perennial. Mr. Koch explained that it rests in winter.

D. L. Harris, president of the Pulverized Manure Co. finds so far that business has not been affected by the European disturbances. He thinks the probabilities are that the growers will find that the use of so much potash is not so necessary as they have been led to believe, but that proper cultivation of the soil will largely take its place. Mr. Harris is very optimistic on the outlook for the fertilizer business in the near future, though now it is more or less affected by local conditions, as in the south owing to the loss of the cotton market. The Pulverized Manure Co. has just completed its third plant, which is located in Kansas City, Mo. The second one is in St. Louis, Mo., while the main plant is here in Chicago. Their manufactured tonnage has been the largest this year in the ten years of their existence.

A delegation of the St. Louis Association of Park Employees and their ladies, numbering twenty-two, visited Chicago, arriving Sunday, July 25th, and leaving for home July 28th. Among the number were General Supt. Ernst Strehle; head gardener for the city of St. Louis, John Moritz; landscape gardener Board of Education, Hugo Schaff; Supervisor of Play Grounds, Mr. Kidians. They were met by Rudolph Schiele of the Northside Parks and Wm. O'Carrall of the University of Chicago. Sunday afternoon August Koch conducted them through Garfield Park and its conservatories. Monday morning a tour of the South Parks was made and Monday afternoon they visited Morton Grove and inspected the greenhouse establishment of Poehlmann Bros. Co. The visitors expressed themselves as much pleased with what Chicago has to offer in the way of parks and public play grounds.

Chicago is grief stricken over the terrible calamity of the capsized Eastland. Florists were singularly free from loss, although some were aboard the boat and some lost relatives. One of the fortunate to escape was Joe Eringer of Zech & Mann's. With his fiancee and four other young ladies he climbed over the rail on to the hull of the boat as it careened to the other side and they made their escape without getting into the water at all. Chas. Stehlek who is employed at Concordia Cemetery, lost a son and the young lady who was to have been his bride. Eleanor Hahn, of A. Lange's retail store was among those rescued from the river but her relatives were lost. Wm. Wichtendahl, of Maywood's growers lost a brother on the boat. Among F. Oechslin's force George Kirchoff was refused admission as the boat was filled and thereby his life was probably saved. The accident, which cost over a thousand lives, naturally made a sudden change in the flower market, and on the afternoon of the same day (Saturday) increased demand for flowers began to be noticed. On Sunday it was more apparent and by Monday every florist in the city was making up flowers for the many funerals, which will be held throughout the week.

BOSTON.

E. Allan Peirce is entertaining his friend William Whiting of New York City.

The fishing trip in Boston harbor by a number of the dealers and salesmen in the Flower Exchange has been postponed until Thursday, August 5.

Mr. and Mrs. P. Welch, accompanied by Mr. and Mrs. T. J. Grey, will start on their western trip on Wednesday, August 4, expecting to reach San Francisco a few days before the Convention date.

David Welch of Welch Bros., Boston, has returned from his holiday at Rockland, Me., where he indulged liberally in his favorite exercise of horseback riding, looking the picture of robust health and virility.

ST. LOUIS.

The C. Young & Sons Co. have bought a new site on Oliver street road. A new range of houses will be built this summer. The old site is now mostly surrounded with buildings and is practically useless for growing and the land is too valuable for this purpose.

The Retail Florists' Association met July 19 at the Mission Inn Garden. J. F. Ammann was to be the speaker of the evening but Mr. Ammann failed to come. Secretary Weber reports that all the summer meetings will be held at the garden, the next meeting taking place Monday evening, August 16.

San Francisco—July and August are the months holding the records for conventions in San Francisco during the exposition period, August having the largest number and July next. Lodge conventions have brought many visitors the past week and among them are several florists. J. R. Steinhauser of Pittsburg, Kan., is here with the Shriners and Elks. Carl Baum of Knoxville, Tenn., is here also, as well as Samuel Lundy of Denver, Colo.; R. C. Kerr of Houston, Tex.; Chas. P. Mueller of Wichita, Kan., and Vincent Gorly of St. Louis, Mo., has just left for the southern part of the state after spending several days in San Francisco. He expects to remain in the state until after the S. A. F. convention.

Mrs. J. Wessell, secretary of the Ladies' California Floral Society, has resumed her duties with Pelicano, Rossi & Co., after a short vacation. She says the women are taking considerable interest in their new organization.

Cincinnati — Mr. and Mrs. J. A. Peterson, Miss Ada Kresken and Lawrence Kresken have signified their intention of attending the S. A. F. convention and the Frisco Fair.

Wm. Gear has the formal opening of his new store on Saturday the 31st of this month.

Flowers by Telegraph

Leading Retail Florists Listed by Towns for Ready Reference. Orders transferred by telegram or otherwise to any of the firms whose address is here given will be promptly and properly filled and delivered.

Albany, N. Y.—Danker.

Albany, N. Y.—H. G. Eyres, 11 N. Pearl St.

Albany, N. Y.—The Rosery, 23 Steuben St.

Boston—Thos. F. Galvin, 1 Park St.

Boston—Penn, the Florist, 37-43 Bromfield St.

Buffalo, N. Y.—S. A. Anderson, 440 Main St.

Buffalo, N. Y.—Palmer's, 304 Main St.

Chicago—William J. Smyth, Michigan Ave. and 31st St.

Cleveland, O.—J. M. Gasser Co., Euclid Ave.

Cleveland, Ohio—Adam Graham & Sons, 5523 Euclid Ave.

Denver, Col.—Park Floral Co., 1643 Broadway.

Detroit, Mich.—J. Breitmeyer's Sons, corner Broadway and Gratiot Ave.

Houston, Tex.—Kerr. The Florist.

Kansas City, Mo.—Samuel Murray, 1017 Grand Ave.

New London, Conn.—Reuter's.

Newport, R. I.—Gibson Bros., Bellevue Ave.

New York—David Clarke's Sons, 2139-2141 Broadway.

New York—Alex. McConnell, 611 5th Ave.

New York—Young & Nugent, 42 W. 28th.

New York—Dards, N. E. corner 44th St. and Madison Ave.

New York—Max Schling, 22 W. 59th St.

New York—G. E. M. Stumpp, 761 Fifth Ave.

New York—Thos. F. Galvin, Fifth Ave., at 46th St.

New York—Myer, 609-611 Madison Ave.

New York—A. T. Bunyard, 413 Madison Ave.

New York—National Floral Corporation, 220 Broadway.

Norwich, Conn.—Reuter's.

Omaha, Neb.—Hess & Swoboda, 1415 Farnum St.

Rochester, N. Y.—J. B. Keller Sons, 25 Clinton Ave., N.

St. Louis, Mo.—Fred C. Weber, 4320-28 Olive St.

St. Paul, Minn.—Holm & Olson, Inc.

Tarrytown-on-Hudson, N. Y.—F. R. Pierson Co.

Toronto, Can.—J. H. Dunlop, 96 Yonge St.

Washington, D. C.—Gude Bros., 1214 F St.

Washington, D. C.—F. H. Kramer, 915 F St., N. W.

Westerly, R. I.—Reuter's.

Worcester, Mass.—Randall's Flower Shop, 3 Pleasant St.

LIBERTY BELL FLOAT DECORATION,
By Pelicano Rossi & Co.

The principal feature of the celebration in San Francisco on July 17th, commemorating the arrival of the Liberty Bell from Philadelphia, was the handsome float carrying it from the downtown business section to the Exposition grounds. Angelo J. Rossi was chairman of the parade committee, and his company carried out the decoration of the float, which was one of the largest cutflower decorations ever seen in this city. Ten thousand American Beauty roses were used, six thousand carnations and quantities of cornflowers. The roses shrouded the truck and supports of the bell, and red and white carnations and cornflowers were used for the representation of a flag, five by eight feet, appearing on either side, as well as for five shields around the float. Mr. Rossi says it took fifteen men about forty-eight hours to complete the job.

Flower Market Reports

BOSTON There is no flower business to speak of this week. Summer resort orders are beginning to materialize at the wholesale houses, but these calls are not large and they take only the selected stock and make no impression on the general market condition which is exceedingly dull. Gladioli are the strongest item on the list, but the asters are rapidly moving up to the firing line. Some of the gladioli are the finest ever seen here. America, Mrs. Pendleton, Mrs. Wigman, Halley and other high-class sorts, with flowers measuring five inches across are bringing from $4.00 to $6.00 per 100, while the common grades stick at $1.00. Aster quality is improving. In roses the Hadley and Ophelia are coming in fine form, and sell fairly well. In fact, all roses are of satisfactory quality, everything considered. Carnations have practically quit the game for the present. Sweet peas are very poor, due to the many heavy rains. Lilies too plentiful.

BUFFALO The market is full of gladioli. There is a good quantity of carnations. Roses were still plentiful up to a few days ago. Lilies have not been so abundant for some time. It would seem that every grower has gone into the lily growing business and all crops are on at the same time. Asters are gradually coming on and the season's outlook is promising. Some choice stock is now received though not in heavy supply. Beauties are still plentiful, but sales lacking. The best roses are Shawyer, Maryland and Double White Killarney. The latter has sold exceptionally well of late. The recent rains have helped them along considerably.

CHICAGO The awful tragedy of the week end exemplified the old adage "It's a poor wind that blows no one good." With the summer business dependent so largely upon funeral work, a thousand deaths in the city quickly changed market conditions. The wholesalers felt the change first, but a few hours after the overturning of the excursion boat in the Chicago River, and as the days went by flowers cleaned up as they had not done before in weeks. The rose supply was shorter because of the very wet season causing an unusual amount of mildew with many growers. Prices advanced rapidly in proportion to the demand and even very short stemmed roses brought three cents. Carnations are not in very good condition and asters are still short in stem for the most part, but the great number of designs helped to work off all of them to advantage. The stock of peonies in storage came in very handily and this week will probably see the last used up. Gladioli have not been much in favor this year and the pails have stood on the counters waiting for customers who did not come, but they served to help out in the sudden strain put upon the market. Ferns have been looked upon so long as a staple that cannot fail, that this midsummer experience is a new one. The constant rain in

northern Wisconsin has flooded the fern land and a shortage is the result.

CINCINNATI Local business is very dull. The supply of stock of all kinds is very heavy while the demand is not at all active. As a result the market is overloaded and prices are low. The cut of roses is large but business in them is not very active. Gladioli are having a very bad season as far as sales are concerned. They are very plentiful. Asters are now coming in very heavy and are backing up. Lilies are excellent and offered in large quantities. Other offerings include some very fine hardy hydrangeas, pond lilies and auratums.

NEW YORK The amount of business being done in the wholesale market is still very small with no tangible evidence to indicate any early improvement. Gladioli are the heaviest product now offered and every available

place is crowded with them. America, Halley, Mrs. King, Pink Beauty and others of the newer varieties have practically supplanted the old favorite kinds formerly grown in quantity for this market. Holland grown bulbs of American varieties at slaughter prices have simply broken the back of the gladiolus market here and elsewhere. Roses are not very abundant nor very good but there are enough. Carnations are about down and out but there are asters in plenty. These are really good for so early and the outlook for good asters was never better. As to what they will bring—"that's another story." Cattleyas are much reduced in quantity and it is possible to get an occasional good figure for really good flowers. Lilies continue to come in far beyond the capacity of the market, the low figures prevailing for some weeks past still continuing. Dahlias of particularly good finish are seen here and there. Everything else is in adequate supply.

(Continued on page 1:)

WHOLESALE FLOWER MARKETS — TRADE PRICES—Per 100 TO DEALERS ONLY

	BOSTON July 29		ST. LOUIS July 26		PHILA. July 26	
Roses						
Am. Beauty, Special	10.00 to	12.00	20.00 to	30.00	15.00 to	30.00
" " Fancy and Extra	6.00 to	8.00	10.00 to	15.00	8.00 to	12.00
" " No. 1	1.00 to	3.00	5.00 to	8.00	3.00 to	5.00
Killarney, Richmond, Extra	2.00 to	4.00	3.00 to	5.00	4.00 to	6.00
" " Ordinary	.50 to	1.00	2.00 to	3.00	1.00 to	2.00
Hillingdon, Ward, Sunburst, Extra	2.00 to	4.00	5.00 to	6.00	4.00 to	6.00
" " " Ordinary	.50 to	1.00	3.00 to	4.00	1.00 to	2.00
Arenberg, Radiance, Taft, Extra	2.00 to	4.00	...... to	......	4.00 to	6.00
" " " Ordinary	.50 to	1.00	...... to	......	1.00 to	2.00
Russell, Hadley, Ophelia, Mock	2.00 to	8.00	5.00 to	6.00	3.00 to	8.00
Carnations, Fancy	.75 to	1.00	2.00 to	3.00	...... to	......
" Ordinary	.50 to	.75	.75 to	1.00	1.00 to	2.00
Cattleyas	20.00 to	25.00	35.00 to	40.00	30.00 to	50.00
Dendrobium formosum	...... to	......	40.00 to	50.00	...... to	......
Lilies, Longiflorum	2.00 to	4.00	4.00 to	5.00	5.00 to	8.00
" Rubrum	...... to	2.00	...... to	......	4.00 to	6.00
Lily of the Valley	1.00 to	3.00	3.00 to	4.00	2.00 to	3.00
Daisies	.50 to	1.00	.30 to	.50	...... to	......
Asters	.50 to	1.00	...... to	......	1.00 to	2.00
Snapdragon	1.00 to	3.00	2.00 to	4.00	...... to	......
Gladioli	1.00 to	6.00	3.00 to	4.00	1.00 to	3.00
Sweet Peas	.15 to	.20	.25 to	.50	.50 to	.75
Gardenias	10.00 to	25.00	10.00 to	12.00	...... to	......
Adiantum	.50 to	1.00	1.00 to	1.25	1.00 to	1.50
Smilax	10.00 to	12.00	10.00 to	12.00	10.00 to	12.00
Asparagus Plumosus, Strings (100)	25.00 to	50.00	35.00 to	50.00	25.00 to	50.00
" & Spren. (100 Bchs.)	25.00 to	35.00	15.00 to	20.00	35.00 to	50.00

Flower Market Reports

(Continued from page 145)

PHILADELPHIA

Very little improvement is noted over the poor conditions reported in your previous issue. There is still a large over-supply, but the roses are easing up a little and it looks as if the gladiolus crop would be past the worst by the 31st. The asters are of excellent quality and becoming a more important factor in the market as the days roll by. The cut is very large and more than ample for all demands. Carnations are getting scarcer and of course the quality corresponds. Lily of the valley and lilies are normal, both as to supply and demand. Good delphinium is still a feature—mostly the Belladona. Orchids have slacked up a little in supply. The greens market is only fair.

SAN FRANCISCO

Business for the past week has been excellent according to reports from both the wholesale and retail florists. Many visitors are here to attend one or more of the various conventions and gatherings in session at this time, while others are attracted solely by the wonders of the Exposition. Many festivities are in order and the florists are sharing in the benefits. There is much call for decorative work, and counter trade for cut flowers is very satisfactory, much better in fact than ever before for the month of July. Prospects are good for August, also, as that month holds the record for the largest number of conventions during the Exposition period. Stock continues plentiful, but the surplus does not amount to much. The carnation situation is much improved since the new market system went into effect, as it seems to be working out nicely. Asters show improvement both in quantity and quality, but the offerings are still under standard and the prices are rather low. Within two weeks, however, good quality is expected, as the first arrivals are never so good here as the flowers coming in a little later. Sweet peas are still in ample supply, and show fair quality. Some fine specimens of gladioli are being shown, but the supply of the best stock is limited. Dahlias are plentiful with a heavy demand. Both cut and potted hydrangeas are moving well. Much coreopsis is being used, as well as large quantities of godetias, scabiosas, stocks, etc. Roses have cleaned up closely the past week, especially American Beauties, which were in rather light supply and much in demand. Tiger lilies are arriving quite freely and are readily absorbed. Gardenias are still plentiful, but orchids have been rather scarce for over a week.

ST. LOUIS

There is no great amount of business in the flower line. The retailers are having their troubles with dull business; the wholesalers are having theirs in disposing of the large amount of stock that comes in daily. This is pronounced to be the poorest summer the trade has had for many years back. Prices on everything are cheap. All grades suffer alike, but extra quality has the call and poor stock is dumped as a rule. Second and third grade roses and carnations

NEW YORK QUOTATIONS PER 100. To Dealers Only

MISCELLANEOUS		Last Half of Week ending July 24 1915		First Half of Week beginning July 26 1915	
Cattleyas		12.00 to	35.00	12.00 to	35.00
Lilies, Longiflorum		1.00 to	2.00	1.00 to	2.00
" Rubrum		1.00 to	2.00	1.00 to	2.00
Lily of the Valley		.50 to	2.00	.50 to	2.00
Daisies		...... to	.50	...... to	.50
Snapdragon		.50 to	1.00	.50 to	1.00
Gladioli		.50 to	1.00	.50 to	1.00
Asters		.50 to	1.00	.50 to	1.00
Sweet Peas		.10 to	.15	.10 to	.15
Corn Flower		...... to	.25	...... to	.25
Gardenias		10.00 to	20.00	12.00 to	25.00
Adiantum		.50 to	.75	.50 to	.75
Smilax		6.00 to	12.00	6.00 to	12.00
Asparagus Plumosus, strings (per 100)		15.00 to	35.00	15.00 to	35.00
" & Spren (100 bunches)		10.00 to	20.00	10.00 to	20.00

are very plentiful, while select stock is just the reverse. Gladioli, asters, hydrangeas and a lot of other outdoor truck is crowding up the market to its capacity daily.

VISITORS' REGISTER.

Cleveland, O.—George Hampton, representing J. Neidinger, Philadelphia.

Newport, R. I.—P. Welch, J. K. M. L. Farquhar and W. J. Stewart, Boston.

Boston—Dr. Geo. E. Stone, Amherst, Mass.; James McGregor, Dublin, N. H.; D. F. Roy, Marion, Mass.

Chicago—Mrs. Ella Kaber of Kaber Floral Co., La Porte, Ind.; M. J. Yopp, Yopp Seed Co., Paducah, Ky.; Jos. W. Heacock, Wyncote, Pa.; Roger Peterson of J. A. Peterson & Sons, Cincinnati, O.

Cincinnati—John A. Werncke, New Albany, Ind.; Fred Rupp, Lawrenceberg, Ind.; Martin Weber, Brookville, Ind.; Wm. Rogers and son, Dayton, Ohio; Mrs. Floyd Anderson and son and Mrs. Geo. Lampert, Xenia, Ohio; Sydney Bayersdorfer, representing H. Bayersdorfer & Co., Philadelphia, Pa.

Philadelphia—J. Horace McFarland and O. E. Beckley, Harrisburg, Pa.; David Geddes, St. Louis, Mo. (late of Pittsburgh); Mrs. L. H. D. Moore, Lancaster, Pa.; Raymond V. Kester, Williamsport, Pa.; H. A. Naldrett, representing Kelway & Son, Langport, England; J. W. Langenbach and Mr. Newkirk, Albion, N. Y.

St. Louis—Julius Dillhoff, representing Schloss Bros., New York; Robt. Newcomb, representing Vaughan's Seed Store, Chicago. Miss Paula Hunkel and Miss Cora Heiber, Milwaukee, Wis., stopped over here a few days last week on their way home from a Pacific Coast trip. Miss Hunkel is a sister of H. V. Hunkel of Holton & Hunkel.

The annual Vincent Dahlia Show will take place at White Marsh, Md., on Sept. 28 to October 2.

BUSINESS TROUBLES.

Johnson Seed Co., Philadelphia, Pa.—Adjudged involuntary bankrupt, July 19. Liabilities, $18,000; assets, nominal, $28,000.

St. Paul Minn.—St. Paul Floral Co., Frank Gustafson, prop. Liabilities. $4,099.53; assets, $2,692.42.

Henry G. Martin, florist at 39 Genesee street, Utica, N. Y., has filed petition in bankruptcy in United States court this city, placing his debts at $2,614 and his assets at $1,098 consisting of stock valued at $100; fixtures, $646 and $322, in accounts due him by 100 Uticans. Among the florist trade creditors are Brant Bros., $219 and S. A. Pinkstone $165, both of Utica.

J. Woodward Manning, a landscape architect, of Wilmington, Mass., filed a voluntary petition in bankruptcy admitting liabilities of $29,547.71. Of this amount $20,000 is a secured claim held by Joseph J. Bond of Reading. There are more than 70 unsecured claims aggregating $9,547.71. The petitioner's assets amount to $42,150 and include encumbered real estate valued at $37,150 and personal property, covered by a bill of sale to Joseph J. Bond, valued at $5,000.

Bridgewater, Mass.—Seventeen stately shade trees, many of them over 100 years old, have been killed by gas leaking through alleged faulty mains in Bridgewater, and citizens, who say many of the trees are priceless, have brought claims against the Brockton Gas Company, demanding in some cases $1000 per tree.

The gas company has signified its willingness to remove the dead trees and plant others in their place, besides offering a substantial cash bonus, but Tree Warden Robert McNelan claims the trees to be worth much more than what is offered. He asserts that the loss of good healthy shade trees on property decreases the valuation at least 20 per cent.

Buyer's Directory and Ready Reference Guide

Advertisements under this head, one cent a word.   Initials count as words.

Display advertisers in this issue are also listed under this classification without charge. Reference to List of Advertisers will indicate the respective pages.

Buyers failing to find what they want in this list will confer a favor by writing us and we will try to put them in communication with reliable dealers.

ACCOUNTANT
R. J. Dysart, 40 State St., Boston.
For page see List of Advertisers.

APHINE
Aphine Mfg. Co., Madison, N. J.
For page see List of Advertisers.

APHIS PUNK
Nicotine Mfg. Co., St. Louis, Mo.
For page see List of Advertisers.

ASPARAGUS
ASPARAGUS PLUMOSUS NANUS.
5,000 strong 3 and 4 in. pots ready for benching. 4 in. pots at $8.00 per 100, $75.00 per 1,000; 3 in. pots at $5.00 per 100, $50.00 per 1,000; 2½ in. pots at $3.00 per 100, $22.50 per 1,000. MIAMI FLORAL CO., Dayton, Ohio.

ASPARAGUS SPRENGERI.
8,000 good 3 and 4 in. plants ready for benching. 4 in. pots at $8.00 per 100, $75.00 per 1,000; 3 in. pots at $5.00 per 100; $50.00 per 1,000; 2½ in. pots at $3.00 per 100, $22.50 per 1,000. MIAMI FLORAL CO., Dayton, Ohio.

AUCTION SALES
Elliott Auction Co., New York City.
For page see List of Advertisers.

AZALEAS
P. Ouwerkerk, Hoboken, N. J.
For page see List of Advertisers.

BAY TREES
August Rolker & Sons, New York.
For page see List of Advertisers.

BAY TREES—Standard and Pyramids. All sizes. Price List on demand. JULIUS ROEHRS CO., Rutherford, N. J.

BEDDING PLANTS
A N. Pierson, Inc., Cromwell, Conn.
For page see List of Advertisers.

BEGONIAS
Julius Roehrs Company, Rutherford, N. J.
For page see List of Advertisers.

R. Vincent, Jr., & Sons Co., White Marsh, Md.
For page see List of Advertisers.

Thomas Roland, Nahant, Mass.
For page see List of Advertisers.

A. M. Davenport, Watertown, Mass.
For page see List of Advertisers.

Begonia Lorraine, $12.00 per 100, $110.00 per 1,000; Begonia Glory of Cincinnati, $15.00 per 100, $140.00 per 1,000. JULIUS ROEHRS CO., Rutherford, N. J.

BOILERS
Kroeschell Bros. Co., Chicago.
For page see List of Advertisers.

King Construction Co., North Tonawanda, N. Y.
"King Ideal" Boiler.
For page see List of Advertisers.

Lord & Burnham Co., New York City.
For page see List of Advertisers.

Hitchings & Co., New York City.

BOXES—CUT FLOWER FOLDING
Edwards Folding Box Co., Philadelphia.
For page see List of Advertisers.

Folding cut flower boxes, the best made. Write for list. HOLTON & HUNKEL CO., Milwaukee, Wis.

BOX TREES
BOX TREES—Standards, Pyramids and Bush. In various sizes. Price List on demand. JULIUS ROEHRS CO., Rutherford, N. J.

BULBS AND TUBERS
J. M. Thorburn & Co., New York City.
For page see List of Advertisers.

Ralph M. Ward & Co., New York City.
Lily Bulbs.
For page see List of Advertisers.

John Lewis Childs, Flowerfield, L. I., N. Y.
For page see List of Advertisers.

August Rolker & Sons, New York City.
Holland and Japan Bulbs.
For page see List of Advertisers.

R. & J. Farquhar & Co., Boston, Mass.
For page see List of Advertisers.

S. S. Skidelsky & Co., Philadelphia, Pa.
For page see List of Advertisers.

Chas. Schwake & Co., New York City.
Horticultural Importers and Exporters.
For page see List of Advertisers.

A. Henderson & Co., Chicago, Ill.
For page see List of Advertisers.

Burnett Bros., 98 Chambers St., New York.
For page see List of Advertisers.

Henry F. Michell Co., Philadelphia. Pa.
For page see List of Advertisers.

Roman J. Irwin, New York City.
Hardy Lilies.

Fottler, Fiske, Rawson Co., Boston, Mass.
Summer Flowering Bulbs.

Joseph Breck & Sons Corp., Boston, Mass.
Bulbs for Early Forcing.
For page see List of Advertisers.

GREAT REDUCTION IN PRICES of HOLLAND BULBS of all kinds. Send for Price List. THOMAS COGGER, 229 Laurel St., Melrose, Mass.

C. KEUR & SONS, HILLEGOM, Holland. Bulbs of all descriptions. Write for prices. NEW YORK Branch, 8-10 Bridge St.

CAMELLIAS
Julius Roehrs Co., Rutherford, N. J.
For page see List of Advertisers.

CANNAS
Canna Specialists.
Send for Canna book.
THE CONARD & JONES COMPANY, West Grove, Pa.

CARNATION STAPLES
Split Carnations quickly, easily and cheaply mended. Pillsbury's Carnation Staple, 1000 for 35c.; 3000 for $1.00 post paid. I. L. PILLSBURY, Galesburg, Ill.

Supreme Carnation Staples, for repairing split carnations, 35c. per 1000; 3000 for $1.00. F. W. WAITE, 85 Belmont Ave., Springfield, Mass.

CARNATIONS.
F. Dorner & Sons Co., Lafayette, Ind.
For page see List of Advertisers.

Leo Niessen Co., Philadelphia, Pa.
Field Grown Carnation Plants.
For page see List of Advertisers.

250,000 Field-Grown Carnation Plants. Grown in Soil Especially Suited for Carnations.
Quality Guaranteed to Please You.
July and Later Delivery.
Order Early.

PINK—	100	1000
Mrs. C. Edward Akehurst	$12.00	$100.00
Pink Sensation	14.00	120.00
Good Cheer	12.00	100.00
Alice, first grade	16.00	140.00
Alice, second grade	15.00	125.00
Enchantress Supreme	8.00	70.00
Peerless Pink	8.00	70.00
Gorgeous	8.50	70.00
Pink Delight	7.50	65.00
Philadelphia	8.00	70.00
Gloriosa	7.00	60.00
Mrs. C. W. Ward	7.00	55.00
Northport	7.00	55.00
Enchantress	7.00	55.00
Rose-pink Enchantress	7.50	60.00
Dorothy Gordon	7.00	55.00
Rosette	7.50	60.00
Winona	7.00	55.00
Winsor	7.00	55.00
VARIEGATED—		
Benora	8.00	70.00
RED—		
Champion	8.00	75.00
Princess Dagmar	8.00	70.00
Beacon	7.50	60.00
Comfort	6.00	45.00
The Herald	8.00	75.00
Pocahontas	8.00	70.00
St. Nicholas	8.00	70.00
Harlowarden	7.00	55.00
Victory	7.00	55.00
Eureka	7.00	55.00
Bonfire	7.50	65.00
WHITE—		
Matchless	8.00	70.00
White Wonder	7.50	60.00
White Enchantress	7.00	55.00
White Perfection	7.00	55.00
Alma Ward	7.00	55.00
YELLOW—		
Yellow Prince	8.00	70.00
Yellowstone	8.00	70.00

Write for complete price list of bedding and greenhouse plants.
S. S. PENNOCK-MEEHAN CO., 1608-1620 Ludlow St.,   Philadelphia, Pa.

CHRYSANTHEMUMS
Poehlmann Bros. Co., Morton Grove, Ill.
For page see List of Advertisers.

Wood Bros., Fishkill, N. Y.
Chrysanthemums Rooted Cuttings.
For page see List of Advertisers.

Chas. H. Totty, Madison, N. J.
For page see List of Advertisers.

R. Vincent, Jr., & Sons Co., White Marsh, Md.
Pompon Chrysanthemums,
For page see List of Advertisers.

THE BEST 1915 NOVELTIES.
The Cream of 1914 Introductions.
The most popular Commercial and Exhibition kinds; also complete line of Pompons: Singles and Anemones. Trade list on application. ELMER D. SMITH & CO., Adrian, Mich.

COCOANUT FIBRE SOIL
20th Century Plant Food Co., Beverly, Mass.
For page see List of Advertisers.

For List of Advertisers See Page 127

In writing to Advertisers kindly mention Horticulture

For List of Advertisers See Page 127

New Offers In This Issue

ASTERS.
S. S. Pennock-Meehan Co., Philadelphia, Pa.
For page see List of Advertisers.

ANNUAL MEETING.
Florists' Hail Association,
John G. Esler, Sec'y, San Francisco, Cal.
For page see List of Advertisers.

BOSTON AND WHITMANI FERNS.
Roman J. Irwin, New York City.
For page see List of Advertisers.

FLOWERS BY TELEGRAPH.
Gibson Bros., Newport, R. I.
For page see List of Advertisers.

MICHELL'S FLOWER SEEDS.
Henry F. Michell Co., Philadelphia, Pa.
For page see List of Advertisers.

NEW CATALOGUE OF CUT FLOWERS, PLANTS AND SUPPLIES.
Poehlmann Bros. Co., Chicago, Ill.
For page see List of Advertisers.

NURSERY STOCK FOR FALL PLANTING.
Chas. G. Curtis Co., Callicoon, N. Y.
For page see List of Advertisers.

In writing to Advertisers kindly mention Horticulture

Coming Events

SHOWS.

Boston, Aug. 7-8.—Gladiolus and Phlox Exhibition, Massachusetts Horticultural Society.

Newport, R. I., Aug. 12, 13, 14—Mid-summer exhibition of Newport Garden Club and Newport Horticultural Society.

Cleveland, O., Aug. 13-14.—Gladiolus Society of Ohio exhibition.

Newport, R. I., Aug. 18-19.—Fifth annual exhibition of the American Gladiolus Society.

Atlantic City, N. J., Aug. 26-29.—American Gladiolus Society exhibition.

Boston, Aug. 28-29.—Exhibition of the Products of Children's Gardens, Massachusetts Horticultural Society.

Lewiston, Me., Aug. 27-28.—Fall exhibition in Lewiston City Hall of Lewiston and Auburn Gardeners' Union. Chas. S. Allen, President, Auburn, Me.; Mrs. Geo. A. Whitney, Secretary, 151 Winter St., Auburn, Me. Meetings first Friday in each month.

Rochester, N. Y., Aug. 30 to Sept. 11.—Rochester Exposition and Flower Show.

Boston, Sept. 11-12.—Dahlia and Fruit Exhibition, Massachusetts Horticultural Society.

Hartford, Conn., Sept. 22-23.—Annual Dahlia exhibition of the Connecticut Horticultural Society, Unity Hall, Pratt St. Alfred Dixon, Sec., Wethersfield.

Boston, Oct. 2-3.—October Show Massachusetts Horticultural Society.

Orange, N. J., Oct. 4.—Tenth Annual Dahlia, Fruit, Gladioli and Vegetable Show of N. J. Floricultural Society. Geo. W. Strange, Sec., 94 Jackson St.

Oyster Bay, L. I., N. Y., Oct. 5-6.—Dahlia Show of the Oyster Bay Hort. Society. Chrysanthemum Show, Nov. 2. Andrew R. Kennedy, Westbury, L. I., secretary.

Glen Cove, L. I., Oct. 7.—Dahlia Show of Nassau Co. Hort. Soc. Fall Show of Nassau Co. Hort. Soc., Oct. 28 and 29.

Poughkeepsie, N. Y., Oct. 28-29.—Annual flower show of Duchess County Horticultural Society, N. Harold Cottam, Sec., Wappingers Falls.

Boston, Nov. 4, 5, 6, 7.—Grand Autumn Exhibition, Massachusetts Horticultural Society.

New York, N. Y., Nov. 3, 4, 5.—Annual Chrysanthemum Show of the American Institute, Engineering Societies Building.

Tarrytown, N. Y., Nov. 3-4-5.—Chrysanthemum Show in the Music Hall.

New York, N. Y., Nov. 4-7.—Annual Autumn exhibition of Hort. Soc. of New York, Museum of Natural History.

Chicago, Ill., Nov. 9-14.—Fall Flower Show of the Chicago Florists' Club and Horticultural Society of Chicago, to be held in the Coliseum.

Cleveland, O., Nov. 10-14.—Annual show and meeting of Chrysanthemum Society of America. In conjunction with the Cleveland Flower Show. Chas. W. Johnson, Sec., 2226 Fairfax Ave., Morgan Park, Ill.

Cleveland, O., Nov. 10-14.—Cleveland Flower Show. The only show of national scope in the United States this fall. F. A. Friedley, Sec., 356 Leader Building.

MEETINGS.

Twin Cities, St. Paul, Minn., Aug. 24-28.—Annual convention of the Association of American Cemetery Superintendents, Minneapolis and St. Paul. Secretary, Vellett Lawson, Jr., Supt. of Elm Root Cemetery, River Grove, Ill.

Hartford, Conn., Aug. 27.—Regular meeting Conn. Horticultural Society, County Bldg., Trumbull St. Alfred Dixon, Sec., Wethersfield.

CONVENTIONS TO BE HELD IN AUGUST IN SAN FRANCISCO.

August 12-14.—Thirteenth Annual Convention: The Pacific Coast Association of Nurserymen. President, John Vallance, at Glen avenue, Oakland; secretary-treasurer, C. A. Tonneson, Tacoma, Washington.

August 12-14.—Fifth Annual Meeting: The California Association of Nurserymen. President, Fred H. Howard, Ninth and Olive streets, Los Angeles; secretary-treasurer, Henry W. Kruckeberg, 237 Franklin street, Los Angeles.

August 16.—Nurserymen's Day at the Panama-Pacific International Exposition.

August 17-19.—Annual Meeting: The American Rose Society. President, S. S. Pennock, Philadelphia, Pa.; secretary, Benjamin Hammond, Beacon, N. Y.; treasurer, Harry O. May, Summit, N. J.

August 17-20.—Thirty-first Annual Meeting: Society American Florists and Ornamental Horticulturists. President, Patrick Welch, Boston; vice-president, Daniel MacRorie, San Francisco; secretary, John Young, 53 W. Twenty-Eighth street, New York City; treasurer, W. F. Kasting, Buffalo, N. Y.

The National Association of Gardeners. President, John W. Everitt, Glen Cove, N. Y.; secretary, M. C. Ebel, Madison, N. J.

The Florists' Telegraph Delivery. President, Irwin Bertermann, Indianapolis, Ind.; secretary, Albert Pochelon, Detroit, Mich.

The Florists' Hail Association of America. President, E. G. Hill, Richmond, Ind.; secretary, John G. Esler, Saddle River, N. J.

August 18-20.—Annual Meeting: The American Association of Park Superintendents. President, G. X. Amrhyn, New Haven, Conn.; secretary-treasurer, Roland W. Cotterill, Seattle, Wash.

August 23-25.—Thirty-fourth Annual Session: The American Pomological Society, Berkeley, Cal. President, L. A. Goodman, Kansas City, Mo.; California vice-president, Henry W. Kruckeberg, 237 Franklin street, Los Angeles; executive committee, George C. Roeding, Fresno; secretary, E. R. Lake, 2033 Park Road, N. W., Washington, D. C.

CALOSOMA BEETLE FOE TO GIPSY MOTH.

Insect Imported for the Purpose, Most Successful in Attacking Pest.

The calosoma beetle, which was introduced into New England in order to combat the gipsy moth, is declared by entomologists in the United States Department of Agriculture to have firmly established itself in its new environment. The first of these green beetles was sent from Europe in 1905. Between then and 1910 a little over 4,000 of the insects were shipped to this country. They have multiplied and spread with extraordinary rapidity and are now so abundant that many people in New England are familiar with their appearance and habits.

Investigations show that these insects, both as beetles and as larvae, consume enormous quantities of the gipsy moth larvae. They are able to climb the trees upon which their prey are feeding and are most active during the periods when the gipsy moths are abundant. The calosoma beetle, in fact, seems to be admirably adapted in every way to destroying the gipsy moth. It is not apparently injured by the wilt disease which is so prevalent in its prey, and neither is it apparently affected by the sprays used to control the gipsy moth. At the present time it is regarded as the most important of the natural enemies of this widespread pest. A new professional paper of the United States Department of Agriculture, Bulletin 251, contains a detailed description of the calosoma beetle, its distribution, life history and habits.

The third annual flower show of the Gladiolus Society of Ohio, will take place August 13-14, 1915, at the Assembly room of the Hollenden Hotel, Cleveland. The premium list has just been received from the secretary, Wilbur A. Christy, Warren, Ohio. It shows thirty-two important classes, including medals, silver cups and certificates. Copies may be had by addressing the secretary.

"THE NURSERY BUSINESS AS A BUSINESS PROPOSITION."

(A Paper read before the American Association of Nurserymen, at Detroit, by Mr. W. H. Wyman).

(Continued from page 104)

Unwise Policies.

Nurserymen are beset by dangers from without and foes from within their own camp. It is for the elimination of some of these deterrent factors that I beg every one of you to give due consideration. The plunger is a party to be avoided. The man who sells 10,000 Viburnum plicatum at a profit, year after year, starts in to increase that product by propagating 100,000. That is the man I would style a plunger, and the man who should be dissuaded from such folly. I simply use Viburnum plicatum as an illustration. The market calls for about such a number of plants of a given species. The number increases from year to year as the volume of nursery business increases; and every growing concern has a right to increase its plantings; but it has no moral right to propagate any article so much in excess of the legitimate demand that it is compelled, in order to unload, to do so at any price regardless of cost. I say we have no moral right to such a course. There may be no written law forbidding me to sell an article for any price I please; but there is a moral law that forbids my doing so. No man has a right deliberately to destroy the opportunities of livelihood and of gain for any other man. Such a course works hardship to the many and ruin to a possible few. The course of the plunger leads from bad to worse. It is loading the dice in the game of business. It is to invite financial disaster upon the perpetrator and disaster upon others.

The logical result of plunging in production is price-cutting at the selling end. The grocer who begins his career by cutting prices below a reasonable percentage of profit, works no good to a community. He is the man who should be shunned. He disturbs values and throws legitimate business out of the normal. He may run along for a while and make a big bluster in his community; but the day is sure to come when he, in a night, like the Arab of the desert, will fold his tent and get away, or, what may be worse, have his tent folded for him by order of the courts.

The result is, legitimate business has suffered; the public has become bewitched by the bargain counter idea in trade, and no one has been benefited. The legitimate child of plunging in production is price-cutting, that works no good to any and much harm to all. It may be urged that price-cutting is sometimes indulged in by those who do little if any producing. That is true. Hawkers and dry goods houses cut under the nurseryman in selling a few articles such as roses, California privet and the like; but they are in a class by themselves,

some plunger or inconsiderate nurseryman?

The Wiser Course.

These are evils which we should set ourselves to correct. I fancy I hear some one saying, "what shall be done when everybody has gone wild in production; when such a condition prevails again, as that which pertained the past season, as in the case of apple trees?" Probably no one will learn anything from his folly in the past, and the majority will cut and slash prices again, should occasion arise; and advertise far and wide, "Apples for five cents to the trade, and ten cents to the public, and if not ten cents, then anything." This is what has happened within six months, and it is what will probably happen until we nurserymen become sane and sensible business men. Under such circumstances, what

When writing to Advertisers kindly mention Horticulture

and for this very nuisance the nurserymen are themselves responsible. What nurseryman will lower the dignity of his business by considering for one moment the prices at which these people, who have no investment in the business, but who sell stock they have been able to procure from should we do? We should be men and have some "esprit de corps" for our craft. We should set our price where it will give us a reasonable profit, and we should stick to that price when once it has been established. In that event we may not sell all of our stock, quite true; but we shall get as much money for what we sell at a reasonable price, as we shall for all of it, sold at any ridiculously low price, and we shall not have ruined our prospects for another year.

The Disposition of the Surplus.

What do, then with the surplus? By all means burn it. The bonfire is one of the best paying propositions in such a case. When prices are so reduced, it follows that quality suffers. When selling so cheaply everything must go. When there is an overabundance, the highest standards of quality should be maintained. There is no time when an article cannot be marketed at a profit, if only men will hold themselves to the proposition that they will not sell unless it can be done at a fair percentage of gain. This does not follow that we have got to come together in convention and attempt to set a price on our wares; nothing of the kind. To attempt that would be to invite disaster. But we can, every one of us, say that if we cannot sell our stock at a profit, we will not sell at all. The result will be that if we hold to that proposition we shall all sell enough of our stock so that we shall all make some money, even if we are obliged to burn a part of it. If we cannot make money we are inviting disaster, and the quicker we hoist the white flag and go out of business the better for what possessions we may have and for the business in which we are engaged.

Quality Always Counts.

In the event of, each man fixing his price based upon the cost, plus a reasonable profit, there would be no uniformity of price, and that is what we do not want. That would work injustice, for there is not and never can be a uniformity in quality of stock and of service. In the nature of things these cannot be standardized, for the personal element enters into them.

When I purchase stock of a given size of one party, I am willing to pay more than I would for the same size stock from some other party. In the one case, I know that the name of the concern carries with it a degree of quality that I can depend upon. And this leads me to the crux of the whole matter. Our rivalry should not

be in cutting prices to gain business, but in perfecting the quality of our stock and quality of our service.

**GREENHOUSES BUILDING OR
CONTEMPLATED.**

Southwick, Mass.—Edward Gillett, one house.

Joliet, Ill.—C. Sterling, three houses, each 25 x 125.

Dighton, Mass. — W. W. Macker, house 18 x 50.

Buffalo, N. Y.— J. Bates, Dranke street, one house.

East Providence, R. I.—K. J. Murphy, range of houses.

Nashua, N. H.—W. W. Powers, Berkeley street, one house.

Pullman, Wash.—Washington State College, house 20 x 125.

Grand Rapids, Mich.—Henry Smith, rebuilding three houses.

Sharon, Pa. — John Murchie, South Irvine avenue, rebuilding.

Fairmont, Minn.—John McCullough, three houses each 25 x 125.

Pawtucket, R. I.—Wm. A. Forbes, Meadow street, house 20 x 50.

New York, N. Y.—C. C. Trepel, 89th and Broadway, house 40 x 100.

West Summit, N. J.—Albert E. Jackson, Springfield avenue, house 30 x 226.

Hartford, Ct.—Robert Marchant, 13 Huntington street, Lord & Burnham house, 18 x 76.

West Mentor, O.—Carl Hagenburger, reconstruction of four Moninger houses, each 24 x 110.

Washington, N. J.—Alonzo J. Bryan, East Washington avenue, additions and alterations. Wm. Sweeney, Belvidere avenue, house 16 x 30.

You Will Find It
In the Handy Hand Book

Anything you want for your greenhouse, from
glazing nails to a complete iron frame house,
you will find listed, described and in most cases
pictured in our Handy Hand Book.

THE only thing left out is the prices, and they are there; but if you are a grower they are not the prices for you. We will give you special discounts bringing them right down to rock bottom. We do it that way because market prices on materials are continually changing. To give you full benefit of all such changes, we keep changing our discounts accordingly. Keeping, as we do, not only up to the times but all the time ahead of the times, we are continually making

changes. To keep our Handy Hand Book right up with these changes, we make it with loose leaves, so that the old things can be taken out and new ones put in.

Ten chances to one your present book may not be up-to-date. You had better send for another and make sure. And while we think of it—how about your heating? Doesn't it need looking over and putting in apple-pie order for fall? Let us give you a figure for doing it. If you want to talk it over, say when and where and we'll be there.

There has been a lot of advertising talk of late about certain hair-splitting points concerning fire travel. All of which you are not going to bother your head about. Economy is what you want and it's what you get when you get a Burnham.

You know we have made several very radical changes in our greenhouse construction, which very naturally you want to know all about. They are not published yet. Write us about it and we will write you about it.

Lord & Burnham Co.

SALES OFFICES:

NEW YORK	BOSTON	PHILADELPHIA	CHICAGO	ROCHESTER	CLEVELAND
42nd Street Bldg.	Tremont Bldg.	Franklin Bank Bldg.	Rookery Bldg.	Granite Bldg.	Swetland Bldg.

TORONTO, CANADA, Royal Bank Bldg.   FACTORIES : Irvington, N. Y. Des Plaines, Ill. St. Catharines, Ontario.

Vol. XXII
No. 6
AUGUST 7
1915

HORTICULTURE

View in Rose Garden of Miss Sarah B. Fay, Woods Hole, Mass.

Published Every Saturday at 147 Summer Street, Boston, Mass.
Subscription, $1.00

LIST OF ADVERTISERS

**FOR BUYERS' DIRECTORY AND READY REFERENCE GUIDE
SEE PAGES 180, 181, 182, 183**

NOTES ON CULTURE OF FLORISTS' STOCK

CONDUCTED BY

John J. M. Farrell

Questions by our readers in line with any of the topics presented on this page will be cordially received and promptly answered by Mr. Farrell. Such communications should invariably be addressed to the office of HORTICULTURE.
"If vain our toil, we ought to blame the culture, not the soil."—*Pope.*

Callas

To flower well during the early winter callas should be started now. Shake off all the old soil and pot into 6 or 7-inch pots in fibrous loam three parts and well decayed cow manure one part with good drainage. Place in a cold frame until the first week in September. Any that are soft and flabby or show spots of mouldy decay and perhaps have already started a thin, spindly bit of growth should be discarded. New roots are cheap enough and most growers use none but fresh roots every year. Callas, although mighty thirsty when doing their best, are not aquatic plants and overwatering is harmful, so care should be exercised at this stage as they make roots slowly and are very likely to receive too much water.

Carnations

No further delay should be allowed in getting the houses refilled. Just now most carnation growers are busily engaged in replanting their houses or at least refilling the benches preparatory to replanting. It is surprising how quickly a plant will respond to the effects of moisture when it is dry and I think it is better to let the plant draw its first moisture from the new soil rather than to saturate it before planting. If your carnation field in close to the house do not dip the roots in water but get them planted just as soon as you can. If, however, they will have to be out of the soil four or five hours it is better to dip them.

Cattleyas

It is always safer to allow plants of this genus to get quite dry between waterings. Have you ever noticed how healthy a plant will look when it has been overlooked for several days at a time when you were soaking the other plants around it? If not, try the experiment and it will demonstrate how easy it is to overwater orchids, even in the summer months. On clear, warm days a syringing will be beneficial. Be sure, however, that the foliage is dry before nightfall. Do not close the ventilators at night if the nights get rather cool. Never mind if the temperature drops to 55 degrees, it will not hurt the plants half so much as shutting up the house and creating a stuffy atmosphere. Always keep the ventilators open as these orchids want air and the surest way to ruin them and make them send out quantities of roots into the air rather than into the pots is to keep them close and stuffy.

Primulas

Now is a good time to make a sowing of primulas that will bloom good from the end of February and until Easter. From the date of sowing until the time of blooming primulas usually require about seven months. In sowing use shallow boxes or seed pans filled not quite full with a mixture of light loam, leaf mold and sand. If the seeds are soaked in water for a day and night more even germination will be obtained. If the seeds are fresh, which is of vital importance, the young seedlings will be ready for pricking out in five or six weeks from time of planting. For this instead of pots use flat boxes or seed pans filled with a mixture of one part common soil and two parts of peat. When the young plants have three or four leaves pot them in small pots rather loosely and not too deep. These primulas can be placed in a frame where they can have lots of air.

Seeds to Sow

Now that we are coming to the end of summer we will have to think of seed sowing. Pansies intended for outdoor blooming next spring, English daisies and forget-me-nots may be sown now. They can be sown in a frame where the top surface has been made fine and light by the addition of some leaf mold and sand. Myosotis dissitiflora is one of the best forget-me-nots for early blooming and it pays to have a few at least of Giant Flowering Bellis. Transplant the little ones when large enough to handle to about four inches apart and they may remain that way without much protection through the winter.

Propagating Sand

This is the time of the year to lay in propagating sand. From now on there will always be something to propagate. Figure out how much you may need of this very important article and place the order. Prepare a place under shelter where it can be kept dry and clean.

Next Week:—Chrysanthemums; Mulching Mixture; Roman Hyacinths; Poinsettias; Stock Geraniums; Supply of Leaf Mold.

A Beautiful Rose Garden

Our cover illustration this week gives a glimpse into the rose garden of Miss S. B. Fay at Woods Hole, Mass. This garden contains what we believe to be the finest collection of roses in this country. It is under the care of the renowned rose hybridist, M. H. Walsh, and here are to be seen unrivalled examples of the adaptability of his wonderful hybrid Ramblers to arch and pergola use. Excelsa, Debutante, Sweetheart and Lady Gay are among the varieties that so gaily festoon the arches seen in the picture but at the time the photograph was made they were not yet bloomed out into their full glory. Through the vista may be seen the plantation of Hybrid Teas, which is worth going a long distance to see because of the great number of varieties under cultivation and of the luxuriance of their growth and perfection of the blooms. Woods Hole has a remarkably fine climate for rose growing. It is, in fact, the ideal spot in which to bring to perfection the Queen of Flowers and the rose loving proprietor of this beautiful garden and her skillful gardener have taken fullest advantage of it. Roses growing in this Rose Eden never experience what a really dry atmosphere is and scorched or discolored petals are here practically unknown.

HORTICULTURE

VOL. XXII   AUGUST 7, 1915   NO. 6

PUBLISHED WEEKLY BY

HORTICULTURE PUBLISHING CO.

147 Summer Street, Boston, Mass.

Telephone, Oxford 292.

WM. J. STEWART, Editor and Manager.

SUBSCRIPTION RATES:

One Year, in advance, $1.00; To Foreign Countries, $2.00; To Canada, $1.50.

ADVERTISING RATES:

Per inch, 30 inches to page.................................... $1.00
Discounts on Contracts for consecutive insertions, as follows:
One month (4 times), 5 per cent.; three months (13 times), 10 per cent.; six months (26 times), 20 per cent.; one year (52 times), 30 per cent.
Page and half page space, special rates on application.

Entered as second-class matter December 8. 1904, at the Post Office at Boston, Mass., under the Act of Congress of March 3, 1879.

CONTENTS

The Philadelphia Record of Sunday, July 25,
A good start presents a fine picture of the plantations that have been made in the grounds around Convention Hall in that city, together with a detailed description of the plans and schedule for the National Flower Show to be held there next spring. The plantings have been done by H. A. Dreer and H. F. Michell Company. They are intended as a sort of "curtain raiser" to prepare the people of Philadelphia for the great attractions which are in prospect for them.

No doubt, also, these enterprising firms will benefit considerably by the publicity they will acquire through this course and no one will begrudge it to them. It certainly is an excellent thing for the S. A. F. and should prove a material help in the advertising campaign which must be vigorously carried on when the time comes.

International affiliation The Canadian florists are having their annual convention this week at London, Ont., and, judging from the very full program provided for the three days as scheduled, they will have had a most useful and enjoyable occasion, with business well interspersed with recreation and hospitality. The political line dividing the two countries should not be a barrier to a closer fraternal relationship than now exists between the Canadian florists' association and our own S. A. F. and there are many reasons why some sort of practical affiliation, without disturbance of existing autonomy, would be of mutual advantage. There have been several occasions in the past when the prospect for a closer co-operative understanding seemed quite favorable and it should not be a difficult problem now to formulate some feasible plan in that direction which would be acceptable to all concerned.

Wait for the "Special" The eleventh annual Convention Number of HORTICULTURE is now in course of preparation and will, as far as we can make it, fill a worthy place in the line of uniformly successful Convention issues. As will be seen in the announcement on another page of this paper we have decided to depart on this occasion from the time-honored custom of putting out the Convention Number in advance of the Convention. On account of the peculiar conditions existing this year we propose to hold that issue back until the end of the Convention week, making a special feature of the report from San Francisco which we shall aim to have as complete as possible. That this number will all be eagerly perused by the trade generally, especially those east of the Mississippi, goes without saying, and its consequent value to the advertising trade will be exceptionally good. We hope our readers will wait until the progressive advertisers have spoken through HORTICULTURE's Convention Number before placing their orders for fall goods.

Where beauty should rule Those of our readers who are engaged in the greenhouse business, either retail or wholesale, should take to heart and act upon the thoroughly wholesome and sagacious advice given by Mr. Ruzicka in this issue on the value of tidiness and cheerful adornment of the grounds surrounding the rose houses. As Mr. Ruzicka truly says, it is a valuable asset for any man seeking a position, that he hails from a place where this feature has not been overlooked. We believe that this will be more and more emphatically true as time goes along. The rude shacks with grounds uncared for which in bygone years were to be seen so frequently on the outskirts of any of the large cities are fast disappearing and the dignity and standing of the flower business has been vastly advanced by the character of the buildings of to-day and their better kept surroundings. There is yet room for much improvement, however, and it should be the determination of every greenhouse owner or manager that no establishment of any kind whatsoever should ever be suffered to outdo his own domain in external neatness and floral embellishment.

ROSE GROWING UNDER GLASS

CONDUCTED BY

Arthur C Ruzicka

Questions by our readers in line with any of the topics presented on this page will be cordially received and promptly answered by Mr. Ruzicka. Such communications should invariably be addressed to the office of HORTICULTURE.

Scratching Over Benches

This should be done with care, for it is far more important than most greenhouse workers realize, and if done carelessly and in an offhand manner considerable harm may result. In the first place, the soil should never be broken up too fine. Let the surface stay lumpy and rough. It will be much easier to water, and the soil will stay open much better if it is left this way then when the lumps are all crushed fine, and the surface of the soil left smooth. Never scratch too deeply after the plants are rooted, as if this is done, a large number of the fine surface roots will be destroyed, and the plants checked, to say the least. Avoid using weeders, and other various devices used to scratch among the plants. Unless these are handled by well experienced men, more damage than good will result from their use. We find that the average unskilled man will dig around the plants far too deeply, taking out big chunks of sod and tearing these to pieces without any consideration for the welfare of the plants. Keep the benches rubbed over to keep the weeds all down, and the surface of the soil all open, but do not scratch too deeply.

Watering

As soon as the plants begin growing, and the roots start working in the soil, the area that is watered must be increased, so that the plants do not suffer. The new roots pushing out from the original ball will be very tender, and when they come in contact with the hot dry soil they will die, and this must not happen, as it is very important to keep the plants going all the time. To see how the roots are progressing, scratch the earth away here and there, and see how far they have penetrated into the new soil. Try to keep the soil wet just half an inch or so beyond this circle. When the plants happen to be quite dry, as sometimes occurs during these hot summer days, take care not to wet the foliage when watering, as it is apt to burn the same as it would when the plants are dry and are syringed. It is best to train all men to water without wetting any leaves at all, no matter what the weather is, and then the grower is always on the safe side. There is no sense in splashing the water all over the place for this work is as important as any other in rose growing and should be done equally as neatly and as well.

Staking and Tying

With the late planting this year there will still be a good many houses to be staked and tied. It is well to dip the ends of all stakes into good metallic paint, dipping only the portion that is to go into the soil. Dip the stakes ten or twenty at a time, doing the work outside in the hot sun, rather than in the potting shed. As soon as the stakes are dry they can be used. Do not use tar or any preparation containing tar or creosote, as the latter are harmful and although the little tar that would go on the end of a stake may not harm the plant seriously, it is best not to take any chances. See that the stakes are placed all on one side of the plants, and as nearly straight as possible. It may not make much difference in the returns whether the stakes are straight or not, but it adds much to the appearance of the place, and if this work is not done neatly, it is bound to suggest carelessness on somebody's part, for it does not take any longer to do the work neatly. In tying the plants the first time, it is well to use good strong white cord, as these first knots will have to weather the syringing, etc., for a whole year, and it is not nice to have the cords break toward spring and the plants lay all over. Another point to watch is to see that the plants are not bunched too much. If this is done they are bound to lose leaves or else be difficult to keep clean of spider and spot. Beauties should never be tied to stakes, as they will suffer in the long run, and cannot be handled nearly so well as when they are tied to wires. Be sure to use five wires to the four rows of plants, as less than that is unhandy in all the operations that follow. Be sure that the wood is well distributed when tying the first time. This will have an effect on number of roses cut, and the better the growth is distributed, the better chance there is for more roses. If Beauties are tied while they are still single stems, they should all be tied on a slant to the north, not using the front wire at all. This will help let the sun strike the foot of the plants where they are bound to break, whereas if they were tied up straight, or else slanted south, these bottom breaks would not have as much show as they should have. The above refers to plants in houses running east and west, or nearly so.

Perennials

It is not too late yet to sow some seed of the favorite perennials, cultural directions for which will be found elsewhere in HORTICULTURE, and the few dollars invested in these plants will be well spent, for the place that looks bright and cheerful with flowers here and there around the outside of the packing sheds and greenhouses, is always the one that is most prosperous, and the men employed on a place like that are proud of it as a rule and have little trouble to secure positions in case they have to leave. A Dorothy Perkins rose, or other varieties of this type planted here and there to climb over a fence which would otherwise be an eyesore, will do wonders in changing the looks of the place. Most of this work can be done without neglecting anything inside; in fact, we have known cases where men would be glad to do the work at noon or at night, just to see the place look better. It is well worth trying, and as soon as the men become interested in the work, it will be a simple matter to keep the place in shape.

CARNATIONS IN THE SOUTH

(A paper read before The Texas State Florists' Association by Bird Forrest of Waxahachie, Tex.)

"Growing Carnations for Profit," means growing them so as to get the very largest possible returns from the plants with the smallest possible outlay, consistent with growing good stock, and the profits will be larger if you err on the side of more attention than is absolutely necessary, than they will if you are a few hours late in watering, a few days late in putting on supports, or cultivating, and neglect the red spider till he gets hold.

Our conditions are entirely different in many respects, to those of our brothers further north. Our stock must be rooted much earlier to be established in the pots before the sun gets too hot, and to be ready for our earlier planting in the field. Also the period when there are no outdoor flowers is much shorter here. So, we must use every effort to get as much as possible out of our stock during our shorter period. This makes it necessary that we have heavy, stocky plants to bench; plants that will get right to work; that we give them the best of soil in the benches, and constant care and attention; to see that they are planted just the right depth; that they get enough, and still not too much water; that weeds and grass are kept pulled out, and soil frequently stirred. Effective supports should be put on early. Given good plants at benching time, the year's returns depend on constant and prompt attention to the needs of the plants.

The varieties of carnations we now grow, originated in a cooler climate than ours. The cool nights come earlier in the fall and start the plants off vigorously while ours are sweltering in the heat. This disadvantage can be overcome to some extent by close attention to watering and spraying. Can't some of you more experienced growers breed up a strain of carnation that will be, you might say, native to our climate and more resistant to our hot, dry summer atmosphere? The proposed greenhouse at College Station would be useful along this line. Our greatest enemies to the carnation are red spider and stem rot. Red spider is easily handled by promptly spraying with arsenic every spot where they appear; one pound to ten pounds sugar made to a thick syrup or paste with warm water (not cooked). One ounce of this mixture to one gallon of water, put on with compressed air sprayer will keep them cleaned out. The mixture is not strong enough to be dangerous, as you would have to eat a big bunch of stems to get enough to hurt you. The past two years we have practically eliminated stem rot in the greenhouses by having our soil clean, clean benches and proper attention to watering at benching time.

We firmly believe in cement benches as the very best way to handle carnations inside. Our benches are cast in one piece, five feet wide, six inches deep, with plenty of drainage holes. When changing the soil several years ago, we emptied one bench, cleaned and whitewashed it, and filled it as we emptied the next one; that is, a man would carry out a bucket of old soil from bench number 2 and bring back a bucket of new soil for bench number 1, using the same bucket. This we found would leave a small quantity of old soil with the new—enough to transfer any disease or fungus that might be in the soil. We had an attack of club root four years ago. We then adopted the method of cleaning soil out of the entire house, washing the benches good and then giving them a thorough whitewashing. Also whitewashing shovels and buckets before handling the new soil to fill the benches. This almost eliminated the trouble, but we still had a little of it. We thought possibly the infection was carried on the carnation support stakes of which there is one to every plant. So, last season, in addition to other precautions, we soaked the stakes in whitewash. The past season we have been entirely free of it. Infection can also be carried in freesia and gladiolus bulbs that are grown in carnation benches. But these can easily be cleaned by washing in formaldehyde solution. In cleaning ours, we also put them in a candy bucket and poured a teaspoonful of carbon bisulphide on them; putting a paper over the top to keep the fumes in. One or the other, or both of these plans effectively cleaned them.

No form of bench can be so easily cleaned and disinfected as the one piece cement bench. Also, it lasts a lifetime and cost of material is less than the cost of lumber to make the same bench. A cement bench five feet wide with three rows of legs spaced four feet apart costs less than thirty-five cents per running foot, including labor, gravel at $1.00 per yard, cement at 50c. per sack. We have on exhibition here a set of pictures of a cement bench in course of construction with notes on same. We will be glad to give any information wanted to those inquiring. No, we don't want to sell you one, but just to help along. This may be considered a digression from the subject in hand, but we believe anything that tends to lessen the cost of production is pertinent to the subject, and cement benches that never need repairs, do not decay, do not hold bugs, insects and fungus diseases from year to year are certainly an item when it comes to keeping down expenses. To get back to carnations, these are a few of the things we have found essential: Healthy stock from which to take cuttings (we do not like to pull leaves off the cuttings or top them as both leave open wounds), an absolutely clean cutting bench, with good drainage and clean sand. Also we have better success without bottom heat. Cuttings spaced far enough apart to see the sand freely between each one; watered well when put in, and sprinkled lightly every sun-shiny day. Covered with papers the first two weeks on sun-shiny day; papers put on about 9.30 or 10.30 A. M., and taken off about 3.00 P. M. Our best plants have always come from cuttings put in sand December 10th, to January 1st.

Close attention to the little plants in pots to see that they are kept in good shape (we keep them in a cool house), planting to the field March 10th to 20th; kept perfectly clean and plowed at least once a week. To get shapely plants, this is the most important time. Keep them topped and standing straight up. Benched June 25th to July 10th. See that they are not planted deeper than they were in the field. If planted deeper it is an invitation to stem rot. We plant ours seven rows across a five-foot bench, eleven inches between the rows. We have had excellent success planting in soil made by high water, deposited along the creek. Any soil that will grow bloodweeds twelve to fifteen feet high, will grow good carnations. We haul our soil up one year ahead, put in layers five loads of soil to one of manure. Manure from cotton seed meal fed cattle. This turned over twice to get it in good shape.

In conclusion, let me say that if you have good carnations and plenty of them and any kind of market for them, the profit will show up all right.

ONE WOBURN GROWER.

We have never seen a more promising field of fine asters than that of C. B. Johnson at Woburn, Mass. The "astermums" are especially handsome and are already producing heavily. Mr. Johnson, who is known as a very successful carnation grower, is busy transplanting from the field to the houses. He grows about 25,000 in which the varieties White Perfection, White Wonder, Matchless, Beacon, Harry Fenn and Benora figure most prominently. Philadelphia he will discard as a poor keeper and this will be his last year with White Wonder, White Perfection proving to be a much better keeper and shipper. In the matter of plants Matchless is far in the lead. Mr. Johnson has a large plantation of candytuft in frames, seed sown June 15th, which is expected to give an abundant and useful fall crop at a time when fine white flowers will be needed. It is a great pleasure as well as very instructive to inspect such a place as Mr. Johnson's where every foot of ground is made to yield to its full capacity and resourceful intelligent industry is paving the way to prosperity and affluence.

CLUBS AND SOCIETIES

LENOX HORTICULTURAL SOCIETY.

The Lenox (Mass.) Horticultural Society held their midsummer exhibition in the Town Hall, July 27 and 28, and there was as usual a keen competition both in fruit and cut flowers. The leading feature was the great display of sweet peas which occupied half the hall. William B. Osgood Field secured 1st in the big class of 24 vases distinct varieties, gard. G. Foulsham; 2nd, Giraud Foster, gard. E. Jenkins. Both exhibits were of high quality. In the single vases of each variety Giraud Foster took leading place. The perennials were also a catching feature of the show. Miss Adele Kneeland took 1st with 12 varieties, some of the latest novelties being included; gard. E. Etherington. In the group of 12 annuals, Charles Lanier took 1st; gard. A. H. Wingett. A selection of gladioli was shown by Arthur Cooley of Pittsfield who secured all the leading prizes in that class; gard. E. Edwards. For the collection of indoor fruit F. E. Lewis, gard. F. Smith was 1st; Mrs. R. Winthrop, gard. S. W. Carlquist, 2nd. Vegetables also were well contested. For collections of 18 varieties, Carlos De Heredia, gard. George Thompson was 1st. Collection of 12 varieties, Mrs. R. Winthrop, gard. S. W. Carlquist, 1st. There was also a fine display of phloxes, antirrhinum, asters, stocks, begonias, etc. A. N. Cooley was awarded a diploma for an exhibition of gladioli, also a first-class certificate for the varieties Europa and Baltimore. R. & J. Farquhar & Co., Boston, staged a new single chrysanthemum, named Mrs. Charles Daniels. W. Tricker of Arlington, N. J., exhibited a new lavender nymphaea, named Mrs. Woodrow Wilson and was awarded a first-class certificate. Mrs. Warren Salisbury exhibited a new candytuft and was awarded a diploma. The judges were Arthur Herrington of New Jersey, Robert Scott, Pittsfield, Fred Heermans of Lenox.

LEWIS BARNEY, Asst. Sec'y.

OYSTER BAY HORTICULTURAL SOCIETY.

The monthly meeting of the Oyster Bay, N. Y., Horticultural Society was held on Wednesday evening, July 28th. The attendance was the largest of the season. The exhibition tables carried fine exhibits of gladioli, dahlias, phlox, asters, stocks, etc., also an interesting lot of vegetables and fruit. Certificates of merit were awarded Chas. Milburn for Ten Weeks Stock, La France; Jas. Duthie for 26 varieties of dahlias. Honorable mention to Jas. Duckham for phlox; John T. Ingram, Gladiolus America; John Sorosick, Gladiolus Mrs. Francis King; Jas. Duckham, gladiolus; Frank Kyle for onions and string beans; F. Oliver for marrow squash; Arthur Patten, asters, "Snowdrift," society's prize; blackberries, society's prize; J. G. Marmarole, cucumbers, society's prize. Thanks of society to Harry Gibson for gladiolus.

The Outing Committee reported that the outing will be held on August 17th at the Sagamore Hotel, Oyster Bay, rain or shine, tickets for adults $1.50, children 50c. After the dinner there will be athletic contests for children, etc., for which many prizes have been offered by interested parties. The Nassau Co. Horticultural Society is expected to join us in this outing.

Prizes for the Autumn Show were received from Messrs. J. P. Morgan, E. F. Whitney, W. E. Roosevelt, I. C. Moore, C. O. Iselin, J. A. Garver, Howard C. Smith, M. L. Schiff.

We extend an invitation to all our friends and neighbors to join in our outing.

A. R. KENNEDY, Sec'y.

PRESIDENT WELCH STARTS FOR "THE COAST."

President P. Welch, with Mrs. Welch and Thos. J. Grey and wife, started on

PATRICK WELCH
President Society of American Florists.

the first lap of their Convention trip on Wednesday, August 4, taking the 10 A. M. train from Boston for Chicago, via Albany. Mr. Welch carried with him letters of introduction from the mayor of Boston to the mayors of San Francisco, Seattle and Chicago, and several other officials of national repute whom he might meet on the way. He also carried a much-prized resolution of parting good wishes, adopted by a little coterie of intimate friends in the Boston "old guard" fraternity, at an informal lunch given Mr. Welch at the Parker House on the evening previous to his departure. Although the unusual convention conditions this year deprived President Welch of the company of many of his eastern friends yet it can be truly said that no S. A. F. president ever started off to a convention followed by more sincere good wishes or greater personal esteem from the members of the society. And it goes without saying that his reception in San Francisco and en route to and from the Convention will be an ovation of which any man might well be proud.

SOCIETY OF AMERICAN FLORISTS AND ORNAMENTAL HORTICULTURISTS.

Department of Plant Registration.

Public notice is hereby given that the Oak Grove Greenhouse, Tuskegee, Ala., offers for registration the following Coleus. Any person objecting to the use of the proposed name or registration is requested to communicate with the Secretary at once. Failing to receive objection to the registration the same will be made three weeks from this date.

Raiser's Description.

Coleus Yellow Trailing Queen—An excellent variety for boxes, baskets or vases; it droops and hands down two feet or more in a large clump. Center of leaves bright yellow, then around that bright olive green border with deeply serrated edge. Sport from Trailing Queen or Beauty. Has all the good qualities of its parent except color which makes it a trailing mate. A very attractive novelty.

The Waban Rose Conservatories, Natick, Mass., offer for registration the roses described below. Any person objecting to the use of the proposed names or registrations, is requested to communicate with the Secretary at once. Failing to receive objection to the registration the same will be made three weeks from this date.

Raiser's Description.

Mrs. Bayard Thayer.—A sport from Mrs. Charles Russell. Flower is large and full. Color outside of petals deep rose, inside clear silver pink. Foliage large and very dark green, perfectly flat, has no tendency to curl as is sometimes the case with Mrs. Chas. Russell.

Mrs. Moorfield Storey.—A seedling. General McArthur × Joey Hill. A large full rose with heavy dark foliage. Color, shell pink, deeper towards the centre, tip of petals deep rose.

The A. T. Pyfer & Company, Chicago, Ill., offer for registration the following seedling Shasta Daisy. Any person objecting to the use of the proposed registration is requested to communicate with the Secretary at once. Failing to receive objection to the registration the same will be made three weeks from this date.

Raiser's Description.

Parentage: Leucanthemum Maxima Triumph × Leucanthemum Princess Henry. Flower four inches in diameter. Very robust and a heavy producer. Name: Mrs. H. G. Selfridge.

WESTCHESTER AND FAIRFIELD HORTICULTURAL SOCIETY.

The annual outing and games of this society will take place at Edwards' Rye Beach Inn, Rye Beach, N. Y., on Tuesday, August 10. Games will start promptly at 10.30 A. M. A feature will be an excellent shore dinner at $1.50 a person. Those desiring dinner tickets will kindly secure them as early as possible that ample provisions may be made. Tickets may be had by applying to W. J. Sealey, Byram Shore, Portchester, N. Y. Entertainment will be provided for the ladies and little folks. A large crowd is anticipated.

　　　　　　　　P. W. Popp, Cor. Sec'y.

ST. LOUIS MEETINGS FOR AUGUST

The various meetings of clubs and associations for the balance of this month are as follows: Florist Club at Joe Hauser's Dahlia farm in Webster Grove, Thursday, August 12. Annual election of officers.

The Ladies' Florists' Home Circle will be entertained by Mrs. Otto G. Koenig at her home, on Wednesday, August 11.

Retail Florists' Association, August 19, at the Mission Inn Garden, and Mr. Ammann has promised to deliver an address.

CLUB AND SOCIETY NOTES.

The annual meeting and election of officers of the American Gladiolus Society will be held at the Casino, Newport, R. I., August 18 at 7.30 P. M., by order of the president.

　　　　　　　　H. Youell, Sec'y.

The next exhibition of the Massachusetts Horticultural Society will be held at Horticultural Hall, Saturday and Sunday, August 7 and 8. The principal features of this show will be gladioli, phloxes, China asters and seasonable annual flowering plants. Summer fruits and vegetables are now maturing and apples, pears, peaches and plums appear on the schedule for the first time this season. The collection of vegetables will also attract interested attention.

The exhibition is free and will open Saturday from 12 to 6 and on Sunday from 2 to 6 o'clock.

The monthly meeting of the Florists' Club of Washington, D. C., was held last Tuesday evening. In the absence of President Cooke, William F. Gude presided. The feature of the evening was the talk of Charles S. Dulaney on the subject of artificial cooling of florists' ice boxes and the manufacture of ice. Mr. Dulaney showed the florists how they could more than cut their ice bills in half. The outing committee rendered a preliminary report. The outing, previously reported in these columns, was declared to have been the most successful in the history of the club. A buffet supper followed the meeting.

Coming Events

SHOWS.

Boston, Aug. 7-8.—Gladiolus and Phlox Exhibition, Massachusetts Horticultural Society.

Newport, R. I., Aug. 12, 13, 14.—Mid-summer exhibition of Newport Garden Club and Newport Horticultural Society.

Cleveland, O., Aug. 13-14.—Gladiolus Society of Ohio exhibition.

Newport, R. I., Aug. 18-19.—Fifth annual exhibition of the American Gladiolus Society.

Atlantic City, N. J., Aug. 26-29.—American Gladiolus Society exhibition.

Boston, Aug. 28-29.—Exhibition of the Products of Children's Gardens, Massachusetts Horticultural Society.

Lewiston, Me., Aug. 27-28.—Fall exhibition

GENERAL COLLECTION OF GLADIOLI BY METZNER FLORAL CO. AT PANAMA PACIFIC

in Lewiston City Hall of Lewiston and Auburn Gardeners' Union. Chas. S. Allen, President, Auburn, Me.; Mrs. Geo. A. Whitney, Secretary, 151 Winter St., Auburn, Me. Meetings first Friday in each month.

Rochester, N. Y., Aug. 30 to Sept. 11.—Rochester Exposition and Flower Show.

Boston, Sept. 11-12.—Dahlia and Fruit Exhibition, Massachusetts Horticultural Society.

Hartford, Conn., Sept. 22-23.—Annual Dahlia exhibition of the Connecticut Horticultural Society, Unity Hall, Pratt St. Alfred Dixon, Sec., Wethersfield.

Boston, Oct. 2-3.—October Show Massachusetts Horticultural Society.

Orange, N. J., Oct. 4.—Tenth Annual Dahlia, Fruit, Gladioli and Vegetable Show of N. J. Floricultural Society. Geo. W. Strange, Sec., 84 Jackson St.

Oyster Bay, L. I., N. Y., Oct. 5-6.—Dahlia Show of the Oyster Bay Hort. Society. Chrysanthemum Show, Nov. 2. Andrew R. Kennedy, Westbury, L. I., secretary.

Glen Cove, L. I., Oct. 7.—Dahlia Show of Nassau Co. Hort. Soc. Fall Show of Nassau Co. Hort. Soc., Oct. 28 and 29.

Poughkeepsie, N. Y., Oct. 28-29.—Annual flower show of Duchess County Horticultural Society, N. Harold Cottam, Sec., Wappingers Falls.

Boston, Nov. 4, 5, 6, 7.—Grand Autumn Exhibition, Massachusetts Horticultural society.

New York, N. Y., Nov. 3, 4, 5.—Annual Chrysanthemum Show of the American Institute, Engineering Societies Building.

Tarrytown, N. Y., Nov. 3-4-5.—Chrysanthemum Show in the Music Hall.

New York, N. Y., Nov. 4-7.—Annual autumn exhibition of Hort. Soc. of New York, Museum of Natural History.

Chicago, Ill., Nov. 9-14.—Fall Flower Show of the Chicago Florists' Club and Horticultural Society of Chicago, to be held in the Coliseum.

Cleveland, O., Nov. 10-14.—Annual show and meeting of Chrysanthemum Society of America. In conjunction with the Cleveland Flower Show. Chas. W. Johnson, Sec., 2226 Fairfax Ave., Morgan Park, Ill.

Cleveland, O., Nov. 10-14.—Cleveland Flower Show. The only show of national scope in the United States this fall. F. A. Friedley, Sec., 336 Leader Building.

MEETINGS.

Twin Cities, St. Paul, Minn., Aug. 24-28.—Annual convention of the Association of

American Cemetery Superintendents, Minneapolis and St. Paul. Secretary, Vellett Lawson, Jr., Supt. of Elm Root Cemetery, River Grove, Ill.

Hartford, Conn., Aug 27.—Regular meeting Conn. Horticultural Society, County Bldg., Trumbull St. Alfred Dixon, Sec., Wethersfield.

CONVENTIONS TO BE HELD IN AUGUST IN SAN FRANCISCO.

August 12-14.—Thirteenth Annual Convention: The Pacific Coast Association of Nurserymen. President, John Vallance, 51 Glen avenue, Oakland; secretary-treasurer, C. A. Tonneson, Tacoma, Washington.

August 12-14.—Fifth Annual Meeting: The California Association of Nurserymen. President, Fred H. Howard, Ninth and Olive streets, Los Angeles; secretary-treasurer, Henry W. Kruckeberg, 287 Franklin street, Los Angeles.

August 16.—Nurserymen's Day at the Panama-Pacific International Exposition.

August 17-19.—Annual Meeting: The American Rose Society. President, S. S. Pennock, Philadelphia, Pa.; secretary, Benjamin Hammond, Beacon, N. Y.; treasurer, Harry O. May, Summit, N. J.

August 17-20.—Thirty-first Annual Meeting: Society American Florists and Ornamental Horticulturists. President, Patrick Welch, Boston; vice-president, Daniel MacRorie, San Francisco; secretary, John Young, 53 W. Twenty-Eighth street, New York City; treasurer, W. F. Kasting, Buffalo, N. Y.

The National Association of Gardeners. President, John W. Everitt, Glen Cove, N. Y.; secretary, M. C. Ebel, Madison, N. J.

The Florists' Telegraph Delivery. President, Irwin Bertermann, Indianapolis, Ind.; secretary, Albert Pochelon, Detroit, Mich.

The Florists' Hail Association of America. President, E. G. Hill, Richmond, Ind.; secretary, John G. Esler, Saddle River, N. J.

August 18-20.—Annual Meeting: The American Association of Park Superintendents. President, G. N. Amrhym, New Haven, Conn.; secretary-treasurer, Roland W. Cotterill, Seattle, Wash.

August 23-25—Thirty-fourth Biennial Session: The American Pomological Society, Berkeley, Cal. President, L. A. Goodman, Kansas City, Mo.; California vice-president, Henry W. Kruckeberg, 287 Franklin street, Los Angeles; executive committee, George C. Roeding, Fresno; secretary, E. R. Lake, 2033 Park Road, N. W., Washington, D. C.

SWEET PEA CULTURE.

In the couse of a lengthy paper on the Sweet Pea read before the American Sweet Pea Society, at Newport, R. I., on July 15, J. Harrison Dick had the following to say regarding the modern methods of culture of the Sweet Pea.

A successful English gardener summed up the routine of Sweet Pea culture in the following words: "Trench deeply, manure liberally, plant thinly, stake quickly, water early, and dispod promptly."

I offer the following as my conclusions as to the most essential points in Sweet Pea cultivation for summer blooms namely, planting as early as it is at all safe to do so. The Sweet Pea is a hardy annual, withstanding very severe weather, and requires a long season for its early root growth in order to strike deeply and so secure a supply of moisture and nourishment during the hot days of summer. The second point I would emphasize is the need of entire liberty and freedom for each plant. One of the most fatal things is to cause attenuated growth, or to prevent the maximum development of leaf and stem growth; these build up a robust, disease-resistive plant, and lay the foundation for large, long-stemmed, solid, bright colored, fragrant blooms. Thirdly, I think all tendrils or nearly all, should be nipped off at an early stage, together with quite a considerable amount of lateral growth, but not all. Given enough space, a number of branches may be allowed to develop, the laterals from them however, being nipped. Fourthly, the need of the utmost care in keeping the plants free of aphis or other insect pests from the start. Aphis is far more dangerous than most of us are aware of. No carnation grower would for a moment neglect fumigating or spraying if he desired anything like a successful crop of first-class blooms. A few aphids in the growing point of a shoot will do enough harm in a couple of days to upset the energies of a healthy vine for some time, and may have paved a way for the entrance of disease germs. As to feeding and watering, they are largely subsidiary, although the manuring of the ground ought to receive careful attention at the time of digging and trenching; afterward, very little feeding should be necessary and watering must be done with judicious care. The late Henry Eckford never watered his peas at all I believe, but relied upon surface cultivation. Water, however, may be necessary occasionally, then a thorough soaking of all the ground should be given.

Work for the Future.

The sweet pea is a plastic flower, else it could never have created such world wide interest. It has a future as large as the United States—and that is literally true, for although it is grown in every state and territory, we want to feel that it is not only grown and prized in every state, but in every section and in every suburban homeplot. There is a great and grand field to be tilled, in a double sense, by the American Sweet Pea Society, which certainly won't be neglected. Yet in the progress of time if the fragrance of our flower gradually diminishes and is only known to posterity through the records of today, who shall bear the blame? The Sweet Pea scentless! What a travesty and tragedy. Yet again, whose could be the blame? The raisers, the growers? No, only our Sweet Pea Society which awarded 25 points to a novelty for length of stem, 25 for color, 20 for size, 15 for substance, 15 for number of flowers on a stem and not one for fragrance! But we will prefer to regard this as too hypothetical to become a fact.

Those who know most about the sweet pea are the most optimistic as to the possibility of its further development. As a society we have before us the improvement of the doubles; the strengthening of the Winter Spencers; the betterment of the Cupids; the quest of a blue that will equal Salvia patens; a yellow that will rival the Buttercup. We have, indeed, as much work as will keep us all busy for the next ten years. Then we can take stock again.

BEGONIA AND ASTER TROUBLES.

Editor HORTICULTURE:

Will you please tell Mr. Farrell what is the cause of the buds on potted tuberous-rooted Begonias dropping off just as they seem ready to open. They are in 7-inch pots with good soil, have been in the shade with plenty of moisture; would too much shade, too much moisture or too rich soil cause it? Plants are large and look healthy. I also have trouble with Late Branching Asters, of which a great many are coming "blind" this year. The crown turns white and leaves are wrinkled and misshapen. If Mr. Farrell will answer in an early issue of HORTICULTURE I will be extremely obliged.

Yours very truly,

T. A. L.

Mass.

In answer to the foregoing inquiry I would say that the dropping of buds on tuberous-rooted begonias can be traced to a good many causes. Poor drainage which will always result in a cold and over-wet soil will cause the trouble. Overwatering in any kind of soil should always be guarded against, as well as letting them become too dry at the roots. Either of these extremes will make the buds drop. Again the dropping can be caused by excessive plant food in the compost or by heavy liquid feeding which will produce very healthy looking foliage but to the deferioration of right bud formation. Too heavy shading would also cause the trouble. Which of these applies in this instance will have to be found out by the grower and then means taken to overcome it. Judicious watering, ventilation, etc., will in the end place the plants in better condition to digest the food that is in the soil. Do not keep the air of the house too moist as it always causes the plants to make a very soft growth which is not good for the flowering. Your asters are probably troubled with aster blight. It can only be prevented by timely spraying with ammoniacal carbonate solution, which can be made by dissolving one ounce of copper carbonate in a pint of ammonia. To every gallon of water add half an ounce and spray your asters every ten days. They should be sprayed from the time they are planted out up till they flower.

JOHN J. M. FARRELL

BRITISH HORTICULTURE.

National Sweet Peas.

There was an excellent and varied display at the 15th annual show of the National Sweet Pea Society, held in London, on July 13th. The Burpee Cup presented to the Society by W. Atlee Burpee & Co., for a display of waved sweet peas, only attracted one competitor, Miss Baird, St. James, West Malvern. For a bunch of seedling sweet peas not in commerce 15 competitors entered novelties. The prize was awarded to Dr. Hammond T. Hinton, Heytesbury, Wilts, for J. B. Lowe, a variety with scarlet standards and pink wings. Awards of merit were made to the following new varieties: Tea Rose, buff and deep cream, and Margaret Fife, heliotrope with blue wings, from A. Malcom, Duns, Scotland. Victory, mauve, from R. Bolton, Warton, Carnforth, Lancashire. Dora, scarlet and cream, from Dobbie & Co., Edinburgh. The new introductions seen at the trials in Essex and at the show indicate that the specialists are still doing their utmost to excel all past efforts. Mrs. E. Wright, exhibited by R. Bolton, is a bold bloom, of the waved section, with a pure white ground. The wings and standards are edged with deep lavender blue. Old Rose (Dobbie & Co.) is a useful addition to the varieties which lend themselves to table decorations. The President (A. Dickson & Sons) is an excellent orange scarlet. Cream Ground Mrs. Cuthbertson (E. W. King & Co.) has a delightful combination of apple blossom red over a cream ground. Constance Acomb (Robert Sydenham, Ltd.,) has a cream ground, the wings and standard being suffused with lilac.

Carnation Show.

The National Carnation and Picotee Society held its annual show in London, on July 22nd. The show was smaller than usual. The production of new fancies, bizarres and flakes still continues, and some very charming combinations of tints have been obtained by the hybridists.

Editor HORTICULTURE:

Dear Sir—Please find enclosed a check for Two Dollars to pay for your paper beginning June 1st, 1915, for two years. I find HORTICULTURE very interesting and instructive. Wishing you every success in your endeavors to accomplish such an up-to-date paper.

Yours truly,

J. W. S.

Mass.

SEED TRADE

AMERICAN SEED TRADE ASSOCIATION
Officers—President, J. M. Lupton, Mattituck, L. I., N. Y.; First Vice-President, Kirby B. White, Detroit, Mich.; Second Vice-President, F. W. Bolgiano, Washington, D. C.; Secretary-Treasurer, C. E. Kendel, Cleveland, O.; Assistant Secretary, S. F. Willard, Jr., Cleveland, O. Cincinnati, O., next meeting place.

Convention Joys.

Echoes of the recent seedsmen's convention at San Francisco are heard in the way of enthusiastic expressions of appreciation of the almost prodigal hospitality shown the visiting seedsmen by the California seed growers, and it will doubtless be many long days before the memory of the good time the seedsmen enjoyed in the Golden State will be forgotten.

California Seed Crops.

We have mentioned in recent issues that the onion seed crop would undoubtedly prove very disappointing, some estimates placing deliveries as low as 25 to 40 per cent. We think, however, that this is rather low and believe that when actual deliveries are made they will come pretty close to 50 per cent. This undoubtedly will mean a very great shortage, but probably there will be enough to meet the demand at a considerably advanced price over recent years. Nearly all other California crops are reported to be promising, especially sweet peas which will evidently prove a bumper crop.

Vine Seeds.

Vine seeds are still an uncertain quantity. Cucumbers are very late, two and sometimes three replantings having been necessary to secure a good stand. Still if the chinch bugs and other insect pests will only give the plants a chance we will, no doubt, get a very good crop of cucumber seed. Muskmelons are less promising and indications are that there will be a considerable shortage of certain varieties. This estimate of cucumbers and muskmelons will cover conditions both in Nebraska and at Rocky Ford, Colorado. At the latter place we are advised that the shipment of melons to the markets will probably not exceed 25 per cent. of normal. Whether the shortage will be serious enough to affect prices remains to be seen.

Beans and Seed Peas.

Garden beans in both Michigan and New York State are rather late, but in the former state the stand is the best for several years, and there is every indication of at least a full average crop. Conditions are not quite so favorable in New York State owing in large measure to too much rain. The seed pea crops both in Michigan, Wisconsin, Montana and Idaho are very promising, though in the last named states, rather late. They have not

yet passed the danger point either of frost or wet weather during the threshing season. These two factors have to be considered in estimating the crop, but assuming that conditions are normal there will be an abundance of most of the leading varieties of pea seed with probably a considerable surplus of some sorts left in the hands of the growers. Speaking of the pea crop it may not be amiss to say that the canners this year are having a very large pack and of fine quality. The extra fine quality will undoubtedly help in putting the peas into consumption, but prices will inevitably rule very low, and very few will be able to realize cost on their surplus. This, of course, is very unfortunate not only for the canner but for the seedsmen and seed growers, as a ready market for the canned products at profitable prices usually means an active demand for the various varieties of seed used by the canners, and this demand is likely to be more or less disappointing the coming season. Inquiry among the canners shows quite conclusively that there was a considerable reduction in acreage from that of a year ago, an average of at least 20 per cent, but the greatly increased yield will probably result in as large a pack the country over as last year, but, as already stated, fortunately of much higher quality.

Important Action on Belgian Plant Embargo.

The following resolution was unanimously adopted by the Horticultural Importers' Association at a special meeting held at New York July 22, 1915.

WHEREAS, The British "Order in Council" effective March 15, 1915, was intended to stop the export trade of the nations at war with Great Britain, but is at present so interpreted by the British authorities as to also stop the exportation of Azaleas and other Belgian Plants to the United States, because they are grown in that part of Belgium now occupied by the enemies of Great Britain, and

WHEREAS, This interpretation of the "Order in Council" by the British authorities will do incalculable damage to the interests of the American Florists and the Belgian growers, without unfavorably affecting the interests of the enemies of Great Britain, since it is generally known that Azaleas are only grown in the vicinity of Ghent, Belgium, and that the enemies of Great Britain also must get them there, and

WHEREAS, It can be clearly shown that these Azaleas and other Belgian Plants are of Belgian production and origin, exclusively grown by Belgians for Belgian interests, and that none other than Belgians get any revenue or benefit from their sale. Therefore be it

RESOLVED, That the Horticultural Importers' Association respectfully requests our State Department to use its influence to have the British authorities permit these shipments of Azaleas and other Belgian Plants and Bulbs to be exported here the coming fall dating from August 20, and be it also

RESOLVED, That the Secretary of this

Association be instructed to present this resolution personally to the Department of State at Washington.

JAS. McHUTCHISON, Sec'y.
17 Murray street, New York City.

Notes.

Boulder, Col.—A new seed store was opened on July 16th by J. D. Long.

East Jordan, Mich.—The Everett B. Clark Seed Company are building an addition to their seed warehouse.

The value of horticultural imports at the port of New York for the week ending July 24, 1915, is given as follows: Nitrate of soda, $306,530; fertilizer, $187; clover seed, $10,200; grass seed, $1,103; trees and plants, $1,719.

Louisville, Ky.—The Ross Seed Company was dissolved July 19, Wm. Ross selling his interest to the remaining partners, A. S. Chescheir and Chas. D. Foss. Business will be continued under the name of the Ross Seed Company.

NEW CORPORATION.

Oshkosh, Wis.—Wisconsin Seed & Fertilizer Co., capital stock, $1,000. Incorporators, Carl and Henry Rowecamp and A. Ross.

Personal

Henry Mazelle, proprietor of the Glenmere Flower Shop, Rand street, Lynn, Mass., and Miss Bertha Rose, were married July 18th.

Mr. and Mrs. Lewis E. Wood of Fishkill, N. Y., announce the engagement of their daughter Florence to Myers Brownell, Jr., of Brinckerhoff.

Mr. and Mrs. William Kleinheinz announce the marriage of their daugh-

Bridal Bouquet, Kleinheinz Wedding.

ter Anna to Mr. Charles A. Mitchell on Tuesday, July 27, at Ogontz, Pa. Miss Kleinheinz is the daughter of Wm. Kleinheinz, superintendent of the estate of P. A. B. Widener. The wedding party was given a reception and lunch by Mr. Kleinheinz, the table and

Bridesmaid's Parasol, Kleinheinz Wedding.

hall being lavishly adorned with flowers and plants. The bridal bouquet which is shown in the illustration consisted of Cattleyas Gaskelliana and Dowiana aurea with Sweetheart roses and lily of the valley arranged by Miss Minnie Wilhelm of Ogontz. The bridesmaid, Miss Stella Reed, carried a para-

sol decorated with orchids and pink roses, as shown in the cut. Wm. Kleinheinz, Jr. was best man. The happy couple went to Baltimore and thence by boat to Jacksonville, Fla., where they will reside.

NEWS ITEMS FROM EVERYWHERE

CHICAGO.

P. J. Foley is back from a business trip and says the greenhouse business is "picking up."

Mr. and Mrs. F. Oechslin returned Monday from their three weeks' trip. They pronounce the West in general and the exposition in particular as splendid places for a vacation.

T. McAllister, who is in charge of the plant department at A. Lange's, has left for an extended trip through the west and will be at San Francisco in time for the Convention.

Ed. Enders, for many years buyer for Chas. A. Samuelson, left on Saturday last for a tour of the western states which will include a visit to the apple orchard of his employee. He will be away for several weeks.

The florists of Chicago and vicinity had a big flower sale on the 4th of August, the proceeds of which are to go to the Eastland survivors. The committee to handle the project were J. L. Raske, W. P. Kyle, A. Chronis, Eric Johnson and Conelia Ryan.

Mr. and Mrs. Jas. G. Hancock and daughters Belle and Miriam left August 3 for a month in the west. They went via the Canadian Pacific and will visit friends in Seattle before going to San Francisco, where they will meet their daughter Franc, who has been studying at the University of California.

ST. LOUIS.

C. C. Sanders, of the Sanders Nursery leaves this week for a month's western trip which will end at San Francisco during the S. A. F. Convention.

Supt. Ernest Strehl and the 25 park employees who visited Chicago last week returned home much pleased with their trip and the hospitality of the Chicago Park employees and the members of Poehlmann Bros. Co.

Albert Gumz, vice-president of the Windler Wholesale Floral Co., and his bride were tendered a big surprise party at the home of W. A. Rowe in Kirkwood on Saturday, July 31, by about 50 of their friends. Congratulations and numerous presents were forthcoming and a number of friends who visit the wholesale houses each morning clubbed in with a handsome cut glass set and china closet. The evening was spent in a most enjoyable manner.

SAN FRANCISCO.

The E. W. McClellan Co. are moving from 18 Lick Place to 451 Bush street, just across from the California flower market.

The local market has been well supplied with very nice tritoma brought in by Schwerin Bros., from Visitacion Valley, South San Francisco.

Daniel MacRorie of the MacRorie-McLaren Co., has returned from a visit to the San Diego exposition and Los Angeles with his father, and has taken up his residence at Burlingame for the next two months.

The Francis Floral Co. is making some improvements at its Powell street shop, which will add to the general appearance of the place, and provide better facilities in the packing and shipping room at the rear.

The MacRorie-McLaren Co. has about completed the laying out of a large garden at the home of Hiram Johnson, Jr., on Russian Hill, said to be the highest point in San Francisco. The garden bed is made on solid rock.

F. J. Bertrand, chairman of the Hotel committee of the S. A. F. Convention, says he is now receiving many inquiries about accommodations and is already making a good many reservations, which bids fair for a large attendance at the Convention. Preparations are practically complete here.

Mr. McLaren of the MacRorie-McLaren Co., has just returned from Ashland, Ore., where he had been for some little time laying out the Lafayette Park of over a thousand acres. The job included the architectural embellishments of the park as well as the landscaping.

WASHINGTON.

Frank Slye, of the Center Market, has just returned from a two weeks' stay at his country home in Bushwood, Md.

Milton J. Redman, of the S. S. Pennock-Meehan store, left last Saturday for a ten days' stay at Atlantic City, N. J.

Miss Minnie E. Shea, bookkeeper for S. S. Pennock-Meehan Company, has left the city for a three weeks' visit in Springfield, Mass.

Miss Jessie Windsor, with Gude Bros. Company, acquired an excellent coat of tan during her month's vacation at Colonial Beach, Va.

Peter T. Leapley, father of Frederick Leapley, of Leapley & Meyer, died last week at the age of sixty years. The sympathy of the entire trade is with the family of the deceased in their bereavement.

PHILADELPHIA.

George Edmondson late with Burnett Bros., N. Y. City, has joined the Dreer staff as assistant to J. Otto Thilow in the vegetable seed department.

It is reproted that the outlook for a reorganization and continuance of the Johnson Seed Co.'s business, now in receivership, is not encouraging.

The Truly Rural Association held their annual fishing trip at Waretown, N. J., on July 30, 31 and Aug. 1. One baby member was added to the ranks this year—Charles L. Seybold, Superintendent of Parks, Wilkesbarre, Pa., and received a warm baptism from the old timers.

CINCINNATI.

J. T. Conger has returned from a visit to his son at Wichita, Kansas.

Mr. and Mrs. Frank Kyrk have returned from their honeymoon trip.

Wm. Mayhall of E. G. Gillett's was at home sick the first part of this week.

Ed. Bossmeyer, of C. E. Critchell's is having his vacation during the current fortnight.

Gus. Brunner has left for a trip through the northern states. His first stopping place is Petoskey, Mich.

Northampton, Mass.—Edward J. Canning, Northampton, Mass., announces that he will offer a fall and winter course of twelve weeks to ambitious young men for the study of practical landscape gardening, drawing plans, etc., and a critical study of trees, shrubs, vines and herbaceous perennials used in the art of landscape gardening. The course will be divided into two terms of six weeks each, the first term beginning November 9, and ending December 23, 1915; the second term beginning January 4, and ending February 17, 1916. Mr. Canning has had a long experience at landscape gardening and teaching. He is a graduate of the Royal Botanic Gardens, Kew, London, England. He was for nineteen years curator of the Botanic Gardens and instructor in horticulture and practical landscape gardening at Smith College, Northampton, Mass., and for a time instructor in plant materials at the Massachusetts Agricultural College, Amherst, Mass. He is now in business as a practical landscape architect.

VISITORS' REGISTER.

San Francisco—Henry Penn and wife, Boston, Mass.; H. Bayersdorfer and wife, Philadelphia, returning from Japan.

Cincinnati—F. J. Farney, of M. Rice & Co., Phila.; G. A. Beckman, Middletown, Ohio; Wm. Gardner, New Castle, Ind.; Carl Baum, Knoxville, Tenn.

Philadelphia—Antoine Leuthy, Roslindale, Mass.; P. Joseph Lynch, of Heller Bros. Co., New Castle, Ind.; Paul Klingsporn, Chicago Flower Growers' Ass'n., Chicago, Ill.; Charles L. Seybold, Wilkes Barre, Pa.; D. Scott Geddis, Mgr. Flower Dept., Scruggs-Vandervoort-Barney, St. Louis, Mo.

Washington—I. Rosnosky, representing H. F. Michell Co. Phila., Pa.; F. T. Corey, Fredericksburg, Va.; Robert Shoch, representing M. Rice & Co., Phila., Pa.; S. T. Pletcher, Zanesville, Ohio; Frank C. Hargett, Frederick, Md.; Charles E. Meehan, of the S. S. Pennock-Meehan Co., Phila., Pa.

NEW FLOWER STORES.

Providence, R. I.—John Burke, Strand bldg., Washington street.

Houston, Tex.—Glenwood Florists, H. S. Sisk, proprietor. 2610 Washington avenue, succeeding Kerr branch.

Henry R. Comley, one of Boston's leading retail florists, writes us in enthusiastic approval of the sentiments expressed in the article by H. O. Hanna, which appeared in our issue of July 31 under the heading "How to Treat Your Competitor."

BUSINESS TROUBLES.

Ludington, Mich.—Elmer L. Brillhart, proprietor Lake View Greenhouses; liabilities, $8,512.97; assets, $13,000, which includes property heavily mortgaged.

WHOLESALE FLOWER MARKETS — TRADE PRICES—Per 100 TO DEALERS ONLY

Roses	CINCINNATI Aug. 2		CHICAGO July 26		BUFFALO Aug. 2		PITTSBURG Aug. 2	
Am. Beauty, Special	20.00	to 25.00	20.00	to 30.00	20.00	to 25.00	20.00	to 25.00
" " Fancy and Extra	12.00	to 15.00	15.00	to 20.00	12.00	to 15.00	12.50	to 20.00
" " No. 1	5.00	to 10.00	8.00	to 15.00	6.00	to 10.00	4.00	to 10.00
Killarney, Richmond, Extra	3.00	to 4.00	6.00	to 10.00	5.00	to 7.00	6.00	to 8.00
" " Ordinary	2.00	to 2.00	2.00	to 6.00	4.00	to 2.00	2.00	to 4.00
Hilingdon, Ward, Sunburst, Extra	3.00	to 4.00	4.00	to 8.00	6.00	to 9.00	.....	to 6.00
" " " Ordinary	1.00	to 2.00	2.00	to 4.00	2.00	to 6.00	.....	to 4.00
Arenberg, Radiance, Taft, Extra	3.00	to 4.00	.....	to	6.00	to 8.00	6.00	to 8.00
" " " Ordinary	1.00	to 2.00	.....	to 10	2.00	to 6.00	.....	to 4.00
Russell, Hadley, Ophelia, Mock	2.00	to 6.00	2.00	to 15.00	3.00	to 10.00	6.00	to 10.00
Carnations, Fancy	1.00	to 2.00	2.00	to 3.00	1.00	to 2.00	.....	to 1.00
" Ordinary	.50	to .75	1.00	to 2.00	.75	to 1.00	.....	to .50
Cattleyas	25.00	to 50.00	35.00	to 50.00	25.00	to 50.00	40.00	to 50.00
Dendrobium formosum	.....	to	40.00	to 50.00	.....	to	.....	to .....
Lilies, Longiflorum	5.00	to 8.00	8.00	to 10.00	5.00	to 8.00	.....	to 8.00
" Rubrum	3.00	to 6.00	.....	to	3.00	to 4.00	.....	to 3.00
Lily of the Valley	3.00	to 4.00	2.00	to 4.00	.....	to 4.00	3.00	to 4.00
Daisies	.25	to .75	.50	to 1.50	1.00	to 1.50	.....	to .....
Snapdragon	1.00	to 3.00	2.00	to 4.00	2.00	to 3.00	.....	to .50
Gladioli	1.00	to 2.00	2.00	to 4.00	4.00	to 5.00	1.00	to 4.00
Asters	1.00	to 2.00	1.00	to 2.00	.40	to 1.50	1.00	to 2.00
Sweet Peas	.25	to .50	.25	to .50	.25	to .95	.....	to .....
Gardenias	.....	to	.....	to	20.00	to 25.00	.....	to .....
Adiantum	.....	to 1.00	1.00	to 1.25	1.00	to 1.25	.75	to 1.25
Smilax	8.00	to	15.00	to	.....	to 15.00	12.00	to 15.00
Asparagus Plumosus, Strings (100)	.....	to 50.00	25.00	to 50.00	40.00	to 50.00	20.00	to 40.00
& Spren. (100 bchs.)	.....	to 25.00	25.00	to 35.00	25.00	to 35.00	20.00	to 50.00

Flower Market Reports

BOSTON — Both shipping in and shipping out have been seriously impeded by the storms of the past few days. We cannot recall a parallel at this season of the year. We even hear of snowstorms in western Pennsylvania and the lowest temperatures in fifty years at a corresponding date. There is a great abundance of asters, gladioli and sweet peas in market. Most of the latter are badly injured by the heavy and continuous rain and will have to make a new growth before the flowers are marketable. Prices are maintained about as quoted last week, with some stiffening in the case of white roses. Carnations run very small and asters are called for as a substitute for the forlorn specimens coming in at present from the old plants. Lilies are quite abundant. Lily of the valley in adequate supply.

CHICAGO — The demand caused by the Eastland disaster used up practically all the flowers that the Chicago market could supply during the closing week of July. There were more or less of garden flowers, of the less attractive varieties left over, but so great was the demand that the market cleaned up every day all roses, carnations, etc. August opens with the prospect of a quiet month and with the usual summer stock curtailed by the continued damp and cloudy weather. Roses have been particularly affected and many of the growers are having their troubles with mildew, as well as having their cut limited. Carnations are being replanted and the limited amount of really good ones is not larger than is needed daily. Asters are more plentiful each day and the stems getting longer. No real fancy stock is offered as yet. Gladioli in the best three varieties are selling slowly and the poorly colored sorts not at all. Miscellaneous stock and green are not coming as fast as earlier in the summer.

CINCINNATI — Business is very quiet. The supply is not as large as it was but at that is still more than sufficient to take care of all present demands. Relatively speaking the shipping business is better than the local business. The cut of roses continues heavy but as a whole are not as good as they were. Some pretty good American Beauties may be had. The cut of asters and gladioli has shortened considerably but is still more than needed. Lilies too have shortened but are still plentiful. They include many blooms of the highest quality. Auratum and Rubrum lilies meet with a limited call. Other offerings include dahlias, snapdragon, pond lilies and carnations.

NEW YORK — The market is laboring under the burden of bad weather, and an over abundance of gladioli, asters and other field-grown flowers which have no fixed value, cannot be cleared out, and are a burden to the wholesaler. Carnations are still coming in and meet with an indifferent demand. The supply of roses of all varieties is more than ample to meet the meager requirements of the retail trade. American Beauties are very plentiful and cheap. Of the smaller varieties good white roses and some long stemmed colored roses are selling moderately well but there is a limit to the number that can be disposed of at a price and the surplus goes for anything that can be realized. Orchids are few in number and the best of them are selling. Lily of the valley is moving very slowly and if carried over has no staying qualities, but goes to pieces. On the whole, there is little in the way of business to look forward to this month, for the prospects are good for a full supply of roses and outdoor stock with a falling off in business.

PHILADELPHIA — Conditions have not improved any since our last report. There is far too much outside stock coming in for what little business there is. All the growers seem to have been doubling up on their production this year and yet they apparently expect the wholesalers to get as good prices for it as last year and also to sell it all. They just break the market, that's all, and get little or nothing for themselves or anybody else. Local new-crop American Beauty roses have commenced to arrive sparingly. They are of good quality but the northern-grown flowers still lead the procession. Other roses are in fair supply, but of course most of them have suffered from the hot weather. Asters are very, very plentiful, with prices much in the buyers' favor. Carnations poor in quality and getting scarcer. There are a few tuberose arrivals—mostly southern-grown. Early cosmos, statice and liatris are among the new items noted among this week's arrivals.

(Continued on page 170)

WHOLESALE FLOWER MARKETS — TRADE PRICES—Per 100 TO DEALERS ONLY

	BOSTON Aug. 5		ST. LOUIS Aug. 2		PHILA. July 26	
Roses						
Am. Beauty, Special	12.00 to	20.00	30.00 to	40.00	15.00 to	20.00
" " Fancy and Extra	6.00 to	10.00	20.00 to	25.00	8.00 to	12.00
" " No. 1	1.00 to	3.00	10.00 to	15.00	3.00 to	5.00
Killarney, Richmond, Extra	2.00 to	4.00	5.00 to	6.00	4.00 to	6.00
" " Ordinary	.50 to	1.00	2.00 to	3.00	1.00 to	3.00
Hilldegon, Ward, Sunburst, Extra	2.00 to	4.00	5.00 to	6.00	4.00 to	6.00
" " Ordinary	.50 to	1.00	2.00 to	3.00	2.00 to	3.00
Arenberg, Radiance, Taft, Extra	2.00 to	4.00	...... to		4.00 to	6.00
" " Ordinary	.50 to	1.00	...... to		2.00 to	3.00
Russell, Hadley, Ophelia, Mock	2.00 to	6.00	6.00 to	8.00	3.00 to	8.00
Carnations, Fancy	.75 to	1.00	2.00 to	3.00	...... to	
" Ordinary	.50 to	.75	1.00 to	1.50	1.00 to	2.00
Cattleyas	20.00 to	50.00	35.00 to	50.00	30.00 to	50.00
Dendrobium formosum	...... to		...... to		...... to	
Lilies, Longiflorum	2.00 to	4.00	6.00 to	8.00	5.00 to	8.00
" Rubrum	...... to	6.00	4.00 to	5.00	4.00 to	6.00
Lily of the Valley	1.00 to	3.00	3.00 to	4.00	2.00 to	3.00
Daisies	.50 to	1.00	.20 to	.25	...... to	
Snapdragon	1.00 to	2.00	3.00 to	4.00	...... to	
Gladioli	1.00 to	1.50	1.50 to	2.50	1.00 to	3.00
Asters	.15 to	.75	1.00 to	3.00	1.00 to	2.00
Sweet Peas	.15 to	.20	.15 to	.25	.50 to	.75
Gardenias	10.00 to	15.00	...... to		...... to	
Adiantum	.50 to	1.00	1.00 to	1.25	1.00 to	1.50
Smilax	10.00 to	12.00	12.00 to	15.00	10.00 to	12.00
Asparagus Plumosus, Strings (100)	25.00 to	50.00	35.00 to	50.00	35.00 to	50.00
" & Spren. (100 Bchs.)	25.00 to	35.00	30.00 to	35.00	35.00 to	50.00

Flower Market Reports
(Continued from page 177)

SAN FRANCISCO — Chrysanthemums have put in their appearance which is unusually early here. The second or third week in August is their normal time. So far the Golden Glow is the only variety offered. The quality is very fair for first arrivals, and the supply is readily absorbed at firm prices. The supply of carnations has dropped off abruptly, the demand exceeding the supply the last few days, which has stiffened up prices for good stock considerably. Gladioli are not so much in evidence, and receipts of sweet peas are falling off rapidly. Asters are seen on all sides and the quality is much improved over the earlier offerings. They clean up closely. Lilium rubrum is very plentiful and the specimens are of a higher type than this market has been accustomed to in former years. The downtown florists are featuring these lilies prominently in their displays, and a good demand is reported. Some nice amaryllis is appearing, but the supply is limited. The market is well supplied with tritoma, which shows excellent quality and is very popular. Roses are not so plentiful this week, and the average quality is down, really fine stock being quite scarce. Centaureas, coreopsis, hydrangeas and a variety of other garden flowers are still plentiful. Orchids continue in light supply.

ST. LOUIS — The wholesale market is still crowded up with stock and with the retail business at a standstill all over town the commission men have found it not easy to rid themselves of the consignments. Roses are in heavy supply in the second grades, but in the fancy goods the supply is short. Beauties are about enough for the demand. Gladioli are shortening up somewhat and prices have stiffened up. Asters sell well in lighter shades and dark purple. Lily of the valley and lilies have their usual good demand, as do smilax and asparagus.

WASHINGTON — There is an excessive over-production of stock of all kinds with the one exception of carnations which are now practically off the market. Those to be had are undesirable and for them there is no sale. Asters are being received in enormous quantities and are replacing to a large extent the dahlias which have been adversely affected by the heat. It seems that the plants are running heavily to foliage and growth. Washington is passing through the hottest period of the season and the city is sweltering in a torrid wave from which there seems no relief. This has caused a marked falling off in business and were it not for funeral work there would be absolutely nothing doing at the retail stores. The exchanges and wholesale houses are complaining of slow business and of the fact that hardly twenty-five per cent of the stock which they receive from the growers finds a purchaser. The heat has effectually killed off the sweet pea crop but its loss is not felt with the influx of other flowers. It is a hard matter to find an outlet even for the finest of roses and the prevailing prices are very low. Gladioli coming into the market in very large quantities are of exceptional quality and there is some demand at low prices. There is little or no call for the more expensive flowers such as orchids and American Beauty roses.

NEW YORK QUOTATIONS PER 100.   To Dealers Only

MISCELLANEOUS	Last Half of Week ending July 31 1915			First Half of Week beginning Aug. 2 1915		
Cattleyas	12.00	to	50.00	12.00	to	50.00
Lilies, Longiflorum	1.00	to	3.00	1.00	to	3.00
" Rubrum	1.00	to	2.00	1.00	to	2.00
Lily of the Valley	.50	to	3.00	.50	to	3.00
Daisies	......	to	.50	......	to	.50
Snapdragon	.50	to	1.00	.50	to	1.00
Gladioli	.50	to	1.50	.50	to	1.60
Asters	.25	to	1.50	.25	to	1.00
Sweet Peas	.10	to	.15	.10	to	.15
Corn Flower	.....	to	.15	.....	to	.15
Gardenias	12.00	to	25.00	12.00	to	25.00
Adiantum	.50	to	.75	.50	to	.75
Smilax	6.00	to	12.00	6.00	to	12.00
Asparagus Plumosus, sprigs (per 100)	15.00	to	35.00	15.00	to	35.00
& Spren (100 bunches)	10.00	to	30.00	10.00	to	30.00

Buyer's Directory and Ready Reference Guide

Advertisements under this head, one cent a word.   Initials count as words.

Display advertisers in this issue are also listed under this classification without charge. Reference to List of Advertisers will indicate the respective pages.

Buyers failing to find what they want in this list will confer a favor by writing us and we will try to put them in communication with reliable dealers.

ACCOUNTANT
R. J. Dysart, 40 State St., Boston.
For page see List of Advertisers.

APHINE
Aphine Mfg. Co., Madison, N. J.
For page see List of Advertisers.

APHIS PUNK
Nicotine Mfg. Co., St. Louis, Mo.
For page see List of Advertisers.

ASPARAGUS
ASPARAGUS PLUMOSUS NANUS.
5,000 strong 3 and 4 in. pots ready for benching. 4 in. pots at $8.00 per 100, $75.00 per 1,000; 3 in. pots at $5.00 per 100, $50.00 per 1,000; 2½ in. pots at $3.00 per 100, $22.50 per 1,000. MIAMI FLORAL CO., Dayton, Ohio.

ASPARAGUS SPRENGERI.
8,000 good 3 and 4 in. plants ready for benching. 4 in. pots at $8.00 per 100, $75.00 per 1,000; 3 in. pots at $5.00 per 100; $50.00 per 1,000; 2½ in. pots at $3.00 per 100, $22.50 per 1,000. MIAMI FLORAL CO., Dayton, Ohio.

AUCTION SALES
Elliott Auction Co., New York City.
For page see List of Advertisers.

AZALEAS
P. Ouwerkerk, Hoboken, N. J.
For page see List of Advertisers.

BAY TREES
August Rolker & Sons, New York.
For page see List of Advertisers.

BAY TREES—Standard and Pyramids. All sizes. Price List on demand. JULIUS ROEHRS CO., Rutherford, N. J.

BEDDING PLANTS
A. N. Pierson, Inc., Cromwell, Conn.
For page see List of Advertisers.

BEGONIAS
Julius Roehrs Company, Rutherford, N. J.
For page see List of Advertisers.

R. Vincent, Jr., & Sons Co., White Marsh, Md.
For page see List of Advertisers.

Thomas Roland, Nahant, Mass.
For page see List of Advertisers.

A. M. Davenport, Watertown, Mass.
For page see List of Advertisers.

Begonia Lorraine, $12.00 per 100, $110.00 per 1,000; Begonia Glory of Cincinnati, $15.00 per 100, $140.00 per 1,000. JULIUS ROEHRS CO., Rutherford, N. J.

BOILERS
Kroeschell Bros. Co., Chicago.
For page see List of Advertisers.

King Construction Co., North Tonawanda, N. Y.
"King Ideal" Boiler.
For page see List of Advertisers.

Hitchings & Co., New York City.
For page see List of Advertisers.

Lord & Burnham Co., New York City.

BOXES—CUT FLOWER FOLDING
Edwards Folding Box Co., Philadelphia.
For page see List of Advertisers.

Folding cut flower boxes, the best made. Write for list. HOLTON & HUNKEL CO., Milwaukee, Wis.

BOX TREES
BOX TREES—Standards, Pyramids and Bush. In various sizes. Price List on demand. JULIUS ROEHRS CO., Rutherford, N. J.

BULBS AND TUBERS
J. M. Thorburn & Co., New York City.
For page see List of Advertisers.

Ralph M. Ward & Co., New York City.
Lily Bulbs.
For page see List of Advertisers.

John Lewis Childs, Flowerfield, L. I., N. Y.
For page see List of Advertisers.

August Rolker & Sons, New York City.
Holland and Japan Bulbs.
For page see List of Advertisers.

R. & J. Farquhar & Co., Boston, Mass.
For page see List of Advertisers.

S. S. Skidelsky & Co., Philadelphia, Pa.
For page see List of Advertisers.

Chas. Schwake & Co., New York City.
Horticultural Importers and Exporters.
For page see List of Advertisers.

A. Henderson & Co., Chicago, Ill.
For page see List of Advertisers.

Burnett Bros., 98 Chambers St., New York.
For page see List of Advertisers.

Henry F. Michell Co., Philadelphia, Pa.
For page see List of Advertisers.

Fottler, Fiske, Rawson Co., Boston, Mass.
Summer Flowering Bulbs.
For page see List of Advertisers.

Joseph Breck & Sons Corp., Boston, Mass.
Bulbs for Early Forcing.
For page see List of Advertisers.

C. KEUR & SONS, HILLEGOM, Holland. Bulbs of all descriptions. Write for prices. NEW YORK Branch, 8-10 Bridge St.

CAMELLIAS
Julius Roehrs Co., Rutherford, N. J.
For page see List of Advertisers.

CANNAS
Canna Specialists.
Send for Canna book.
THE CONARD & JONES COMPANY,
West Grove, Pa.

CARNATION STAPLES
Split carnations quickly, easily and cheaply mended. Pillsbury's Carnation Staple, 1000 for 35c.; 3000 for $1.00 post paid. I. L. PILLSBURY, Galesburg, Ill.

Supreme Carnation Staples, for repairing split carnations, 35c. per 1000; 3000 for $1.00. F. W. WAITE, 85 Belmont Ave., Springfield, Mass.

CARNATIONS
F. Dorner & Sons Co., Lafayette, Ind.
For page see List of Advertisers.

Leo Niessen Co., Philadelphia, Pa.
Field Grown Carnation Plants.
For page see List of Advertisers.

CHRYSANTHEMUMS
Poehlmann Bros. Co., Morton Grove, Ill.
For page see List of Advertisers.

Wood Bros., Fishkill, N. Y.
Chrysanthemums Rooted Cuttings.
For page see List of Advertisers.

Chas. H. Totty, Madison, N. J.
For page see List of Advertisers.

R. Vincent, Jr., & Sons Co., White Marsh, Md.
For page see List of Advertisers.

Pompon Chrysanthemums,
For page see List of Advertisers.

THE BEST 1915 NOVELTIES.
The Cream of 1914 Introductions.
The most popular Commercial and Exhibition kinds; also complete line of Pompons, Singles and Anemones. Trade list on application. ELMER D. SMITH & CO., Adrian, Mich.

COCOANUT FIBRE SOIL
20th Century Plant Food Co., Beverly, Mass.
For page see List of Advertisers.

CYCLAMENS
CYCLAMEN — Separate colors; finest strain; extra strong plants; 3-inch pots, $10.00 per 100, $90.00 per 1,000. JULIUS ROEHRS CO., Rutherford, N. J.

CYCLAMEN—THE BEST STRAINS.
If you want quality, order now.

	100	1000
2½-in., ready for 4-in	$8.00	$75.00
3-in.	12.50	100.00
4-in.	25.00	.....

Write for copy of
Our Monthly Plant Bulletin.
S. S. PENNOCK-MEEHAN CO.,
1608-20 Ludlow St.,   Philadelphia, Pa.

DAHLIAS
Send for Wholesale List of whole clumps and separate stock; 40,000 clumps for sale. Northboro Dahlia and Gladiolus Gardens. J. L. MOORE, Prop, Northboro, Mass.

NEW PAEONY DAHLIA
John Wanamaker. Newest, Handsomest, Best. New color, new form and new habit of growth. Big stock of best cut-flower varieties. Send list of wants to PEACOCK DAHLIA FARMS, Berlin, N. J.

DECORATIVE PLANTS
Robert Craig Co., Philadelphia, Pa.
For page see List of Advertisers.

Woodrow & Markeros, New York City.
For page see List of Advertisers.

S. S. Skidelsky & Co., Philadelphia, Pa.
For page see List of Advertisers.

Bobbink & Atkins, Rutherford, N. J.
For page see List of Advertisers.

A. Leuthy & Co., Roslindale, Boston, Mass.
For page see List of Advertisers.

DRACAENAS
Julius Roehrs Co., Rutherford, N. J.
For page see List of Advertisers.

FERNS
H. H. Barrows & Son, Whitman, Mass.
For page see List of Advertisers.

Robert Craig Co., Philadelphia, Pa.
For page see List of Advertisers.

McHutchison & Co., New York City.
Ferns in Flats.
For page see List of Advertisers.

Roman J. Irwin, New York City.
Boston and Whitmani Ferns.
For page see List of Advertisers.

For List of Advertisers See Page 127

For List of Advertisers See Page 127

GARDENERS' ESSAY CONTEST.

The essay committee of the National Association of Gardeners request the following publicity for the contest of the President Everitt gold prize.

Contestants must have their essays in the hands of the chairman, Wm. H. Waite, P. O. Box 290, Madison, N. J., not later than October 1st. The essay must be signed with non de plume, and must bear no evidence of the author's identification and be mailed in a plain envelope, carefully addressed to the chairman of the committee.

The contestant will place his name and full address, stating the position he holds, in a separate envelope, writing the non de plume he signed to his essay on the outside of this envelope, and mail same in a separate envelope to M. C. Ebel, Secretary, National Association of Gardeners, Madison, N. J. This envelope is not to be opened until the judges have rendered their decision on the contest. Write your essay distinctly and use one side of paper only. These rules must be strictly followed to avoid disqualification.

The subjects have been arranged in four classes, as follows:

Class 1. Prize $35 gold—Subject: Horti-

culture as a Profession, from the standpoint of a gardener.

Class 2. Prize $25 gold—Subject: The Proper Grouping and Culture of Trees, Shrubs, Perennials and Annual Bedding Plants in the Ornamentation of Private Grounds.

Class 3. Prize $20 gold—Subject: Preparation of Ground for and General Treatment of Hardy Herbaceous Perennials. Naming a list of species (limited to one hundred) providing a succession of flowers throughout the entire season.

Class 4. Prize $20 gold—Subject: How to Secure a Year's Vegetable Supply with the Aid of Cold Frames or Hotbeds (but no greenhouses), Including Soil Preparation.

This essay competition is open to professional gardeners who are engaged in the capacity of superintendents, head gardeners or assistant gardeners. A competitor is entitled to enter in one class only. The broadest latitude will be allowed in dealing with each subject. The essays are limited to 3,000 words each.

The contest will close on October 1, the judges to report their decision at the next convention of the Association, to occur the first week of December. The Essay Committee will appoint five judges, consisting of three gardeners and two representatives of the horticultural press.

Contestants will address William H. Waite, Chairman of Essay Committee, National Association of Gardeners, P. O. Box 290, Madison, N. J., for further particulars.

HAILSTORM HAVOC.

The houses of the Pikes Peak Floral Company, Colorado Springs, after the storm of July 18, 1915.

CATALOGUES RECEIVED.

V. Lemoine & Son, Nancy, France—New List of Herbaceous Peonies, including some fine novelties.

Stumpp & Walter Co., New York—Midsummer Catalogue of Strawberry Plants, Perennial Flower Seeds, Lawn Sprinklers, Insecticides, etc., etc.

Royal Tottenham Nurseries, Dedemsvaart, Holland, wholesale catalogue, quoting current prices upon a full line of Herbaceous Perennials, Aquatics, Rock-plants, etc., for fall or spring shipment from there. This is, we believe the most complete catalogue issued by any firm in the same line and it offers items not readily procurable elsewhere. It is well to keep it on file for future reference. McHutchison & Co., New York, are the sole American representatives of this house. Mr. McHutchison states that prices are lower than usual this season, while freight rates are not advanced over those of normal seasons and that there is practically no doubt that Holland shipments will be made.

Norristown, Pa.—Mrs. William H. Catanese announces that she will continue the flower and seed business of her late husband.

IMPORTS OF POTASH SALTS.

The following table shows the quantity and value of the imports of potash into the United States during the month of June and the six months ending June, 1914 and 1915. The items are so grouped as to show the potash salts used chiefly as fertilizers and other potash salts. The ton given is the long ton of 2,240 pounds.

Articles	June—				Six months ending June—			
	1914		1915		1914		1915	
	Tons	Value	Tons	Value	Tons	Value	Tons	Value
Fertilizer salts:								
Kainit	17,891	$85,786	2,860	$65,205	257,253	$1,200,037	6,646	$94,818
Manure salts....	33,151	365,530	......	......	114,820	1,480,090	12,456	170,328
Sulphate of potash.	10,473	552,701	1,095	131,092	37,786	1,460,336	9,301	537,323
Muriate of potash.	5,060	126,631	320	48,273	108,759	3,753,076	56,435	2,384,371
Other potash salts:	Pounds		Pounds		Pounds		Pounds	
Carbonate of potash	1,385,750	41,137	588	41	11,252,825	323,895	8,396,622	261,275
Hydrate of potash.	740,930	31,249	7,000	937	4,203,568	150,562	2,023,942	98,803
Nitrate of potash.	479,881	17,061	......	......	1,858,926	52,960	6,855	400
Cyanide of potash.	22,400	3,558	......	......	298,377	40,920	825,527	124,934
Other potash salts.	540,295	50,835	11,275	8,150	3,244,686	291,910	2,075,535	205,729

PUBLICATIONS RECEIVED.

The Page Company of Boston, have just issued two new books of fiction which will fit in admirably for the vacation season. Anne of the Island is a delightful story by L. M. Montgomery, similar in character to and in fact a sequel to the widely read Anne of Green Gables by the same author which has passed its 40th printing. It will be given a warm welcome by the thousands and thousands of girls all over the country who have been yearning for more about Alice. Its chapters teem with simple but snappy humor and just enough of romance to fill the chinks and from first to last its characters are, to the reader, very real and unmistakably alive human beings. As a vacation gift for your own or somebody's else daughter you will make no mistake in selecting Anne of the Island. 326 pages, with frontispiece in full color. Net $1.25; carriage paid $1.40.

Our Little Macedonian Cousin of Long Ago is the latest addition to the popular Little Cousin series, by Julia Darrow Cowles. It tells the story of Nearchus, "a Boy of Macedonia and Companion of Alexander." While making no claim to historical accuracy the typical life of a Macedonian youth in the days of long ago is portrayed in true accord with the spirit and trend of Macedonian history and the boy who is fortunate enough to secure a copy of the book will not only be well entertained, but will have gained a good insight into the customs of a country and an era which in due time he will be called upon to take up more seriously in his school work. 106 pages, cloth finely illustrated in tints. Price 60 cents.

Editor HORTICULTURE:

Dear Sir—Please find enclosed a check for Two Dollars to pay for your paper beginning June 1st, 1915, for two years. I find HORTICULTURE very interesting and instructive. Wishing you every success in your endeavors to accomplish such an up-to-date paper,

Yours truly,

J. W. S.

Mass.

NEWS NOTES.

Southington, Conn.—Frederick Francis and John Olson have purchased the Goodison greenhouse property on Bristol street. Mr. Olson formerly had the business and had sold it to Mr. Goodison. Mr. Goodison expects to move to Wallingford.

Chatham, N. J.—Creditors of Samuel Lum, a florist, were deadlocked over the election of a trustee in bankruptcy, and Referee Atwood L. DeCoster had to take a hand in the appointment of Harry A. May of Summit, who has been serving as receiver. The contest over the election lasted for four hours. Three candidates were nominated. They were Mr. May, Henry Hentz, Jr., of Madison and William G. Badgley of Chatham. After a tentative vote was taken Mr. Hentz's nominators agreed to cast his vote for Mr. May. On the first vote thirty-four claims, amounting to $19,287, were cast for Mr. Badgley, and twelve claims totaling $15,800 were voted for Mr. May.

PATENTS GRANTED.

1,146,287. Garden Rake. A. B. Shaw. Medford, Mass.

1,146,663. Automatic Lawn Sprinkler. Friedrich C. Stetter, Attleboro, Mass.

1,146,891. Plant Support. William F. Maas, Cincinnati, Ohio, assignor to Peter Igoe, Jr., Brooklyn, N. Y.

1,147,926. Manufacture of Fertilizers. William B. Chisolm, Charleston, S. C.

MASTICA

Used for glazing greenhouses, per gal. $1.35
Machines for using same, each 1.25

GLAZING POINTS

The Peerless Glazing Points are very desirable for florists' use.
Per box of 1000 .... $0.60
5 boxes of 1000, per box .... .55

ZINC POINTS

Made from pure zinc. Put up in one pound
packages ....25c. per pound
(SAMPLES FREE)

GEO. H. ANGERMUELLER
Wholesale Florist
1324 Pine Street   St. Louis, Mo.

GREENHOUSES BUILDING OR CONTEMPLATED.

Batavia, N. Y.—J. Bates, one house.

Milldale, Ct.—Nicholas Grillo, one house.

Hamden, Ct.—Robert Johnstone, rebuilding.

Yardley, Pa.—Charles Cadwallader, one house.

Brattleboro, Vt.—Carroll N. Bond, one house.

Hartford, Ct.—Edward W. Newton, rebuilding.

Ridgetown, Ont.—D. A. Leitch, house 30 x 125.

Springfield, O.—Reeser Plant Company, one house.

Lebanon, Pa.—J. F. Vavrous & Sons, two houses.

Springfield, N. J.—Jacobson Floral Co., range of houses.

Catskill, N. Y.—Geo. H. Person, Jefferson Heights, one house.

Ellsworth, Me.—Miss M. A. Clark, Park street, carnation house, 20 x 70.

New Haven, Ct.—Mrs. Minnie Prepenhausen, 65 Goffe street, one house.

Urbana, O.—R. H. Murphy's Sons, Oakland street, six houses, each 20 x 100.

Philadelphia, Pa.—H. A. Miller, Chew street and Washington Lane, house 22 x 86.

Vol. XXII
No. 7
AUGUST 14
1915

HORTICULTURE

Corner in a Formal Garden at Bar Harbor, Me.

Kenarden Lodge, Estate of Mrs. John Stewart Kennedy, gard. W. T. Burton.

LIST OF ADVERTISERS

FOR BUYERS' DIRECTORY AND READY REFERENCE GUIDE
SEE PAGES 212, 213, 214, 215

NOTES ON CULTURE OF FLORISTS' STOCK

CONDUCTED BY

John J. M. Farrell

Questions by our readers in line with any of the topics presented on this page will be cordially received and promptly answered by Mr. Farrell. Such communications should invariably be addressed to the office of HORTICULTURE.

"If vain our toil, we ought to blame the culture, not the soil."—*Pope.*

Chrysanthemums

Keep the chrysanthemums growing right along now. Give plenty of fresh air day and night with an abundance of water, syringing several times daily and wetting down the walks. See that the plants are kept clean by spraying with some good insecticide and light fumigations every ten days. From this out it will be necessary to keep up a diligent fight against the black fly.

Mulching Mixture

In preparing mulch make it rich. I would let it consist of two parts of well-decomposed cow manure to one part of fibrous soil. Where you want to use bone meal or other fertilizer this can be added at any time. Having this mulch in good condition and in a handy place under cover constitutes one of the first elements of success in growing good flowers. Chop it quite fine and make it up into a neat pile and let it stand for about three weeks and then turn it over three or four times at intervals of about every ten days, after which run it through a ¾-inch screen and then store it away where the rain and snow will not reach it.

Roman Hyacinths

Get the flats and pans together so that when the bulbs arrive you will be all ready to care for them. When planting see that they have proper drainage. Use any good compost. See that the top of each bulb is pushed down level with the soil, and the soil made moderately firm. Give them a thorough watering and place in the bulb cellar or outside. If outside see that they are set level and covered with about 4 or 5 inches of soil. If they become dry they will need some extra waterings.

Poinsettias

Lose no time now in getting in poinsettia cuttings.

Poinsettias can be propagated up to the first week in September and make fair stock, but those that are rooted about this time will be better. Give good care when the cuttings are placed in sand, such as shading, watering and spraying. The one point to remember is not to let them flag. When rooted pot off into small pots using a mixture of fibrous loam, leaf mold and enough of sand to make it open. Keep rather close and spray often, with a fair amount of shade. After this keep them well up to the glass where they can have full sunshine. When they get pot-bound shift into 3-inch pots and plunge in ashes.

Stock Geraniums

See that geraniums are labeled true to name. Just now when they are all blooming and at their best it is well to see if any have not come true. It is an easy matter at this date to label or tag any that are not true to name. Much future annoyance can be saved now but only an expert would be able to separate them after the flower has gone. Geraniums left over can be made into fine stock plants by giving them a shift into 5 or 6-inch pots. These will be harder, shorter-pointed and less liable to damp off than field-grown stock. I think the failure to get a greater number of geraniums into flower by Decoration Day is in great part due to the sappy condition of our fall cuttings. When grown this way, they being more under the control of the grower, he can root practically every tip.

Supply of Leaf Mold

Every florist should lay in a good supply of leaf mold before the bad weather sets in. Now is a good time to get it. Leaf mold can be used in so many ways to good advantage that the good grower should always have a good amount on hand.

Next week:—Cyclamen; Bouvardias; Mignonette; Paper White Narcissus; Propagating Geraniums; Housing Tender Stock.

HORTICULTURE

VOL. XXII   **AUGUST 14, 1915**   **NO. 7**

PUBLISHED WEEKLY BY
HORTICULTURE PUBLISHING CO.
147 Summer Street, Boston, Mass.

Telephone, Oxford 292.
WM. J. STEWART, Editor and Manager.

SUBSCRIPTION RATES:
One Year, in advance, $1.00; To Foreign Countries, $2.00; To
Canada, $1.50.

ADVERTISING RATES:

Per inch, 30 inches to page.................................... $1.00
Discounts on Contracts for consecutive insertions, as follows:
   One month (4 times), 5 per cent.; three months (13 times), 10
per cent.; six months (26 times), 20 per cent.; one year (52 times),
30 per cent.
   Page and half page space, special rates on application.

Entered as second-class matter December 8, 1904, at the Post Office
at Boston, Mass., under the Act of Congress of March 3, 1879.

CONTENTS

Preparedness We take opportunity to again commend to our readers the very practical advice given by Mr. Ruzicka in his rose notes. The warning to get ready and well prepared now to meet the prospective emergencies of winter may not be needed by some readers of HORTICULTURE but we all know that there are many who procrastinate until too late and some time or another have to pay dearly for their indifference and improvidence. The admonition applies to any and all growers as well as to the rose men. "Preparedness" has taken on a startling national significance within the past few months. It is not without its application as a business policy.

The Convention Secretary Young, who has exceptional facilities for correctly estimating the probable attendance at the San Francisco Convention of the S. A. F., writes from the front a very optimistic letter, stating that the outlook for a favorable representation is daily becoming brighter, notwithstanding the accepted fact that the attendence from the far East will be very light. There is so much to be seen in California that is of interest to florists and the gardening fraternity generally that anyone making the effort to be present on this auspicious occasion will be well repaid for making the trip and, as the time approaches, many wavering individuals are pretty sure to come to a favorable decision and pack up for the journey to the Coast. HORTICULTURE'S sincere wishes for a numerously attended and otherwise successful and profitable 31st Convention are extended to the grand old S. A. F. and the brethren of the Golden West.

A trade booster Once a year when the Society of American Florists assembles in national convention HORTICULTURE honors the occasion by dressing up a little and coming out as a special edition. The trade buyers are all interested in the doings of the big organization which for the past thirty-one years has stood in the foremost position in America as the representative of floricultural progress. Our issue for this year is scheduled to appear next week. It will contain full information of the proceedings at San Francisco and will be in all respects the equal of any of its predecessors in publicity value for those trade advertisers who are sufficiently discerning and wide-awake to take advantage of the opportunity offered. There is yet time for the late comers to get in line but please do not delay further. If you have any specialty about which you would like to apprise the active and intelligent trade buyers, there is no better way to "get there" than through the columns of HORTICULTURE'S Convention Number.

"Robbing Peter to pay Paul" Commenting on the reported intention of the fraternal organizations of Waterbury, Conn., to limit their expenditures for floral tributes in memory of dead members to a small amount, the Meriden Record comes out with an editorial condemning the lavish use of flowers for funeral purposes and urging that "the money which is expended on short-lived blooms should be devoted toward relieving material want." It states that according to estimates of Chicago florists more than $100,000 had been spent on flowers for victims of the Eastland disaster and uses this grossly exaggerated estimate as an argument in support of its contention that much suffering and privation might have been averted by a better use of the money. This is another instance of the boomerang mischief which is always sure to result from these inflated yarns which stupid florists here and there are so prone to give out and the sensational reporter so eager to circulate. Whatever virtue there may be in these repeated propositions to divert money from flower buying to "relieving suffering" is completely counteracted by the impossibility of enforcing such diversion. We see no reason to believe that if the florists of the country were despoiled of half their business the amount contributed for charity would be appreciably increased. As we have repeatedly urged, it is full time that the S. A. F. should raise its voice against these hostile attacks upon a worthy industry.

ROSE GROWING UNDER GLASS

CONDUCTED BY

Arthur C. Ruzicka

Questions by our readers in line with any of the topics presented on this page will be cordially received and promptly answered by Mr. Ruzicka. Such communications should invariably be addressed to the office of HORTICULTURE.

Storms

The storms that have swept over the country recently, show that it is always best to be ready to meet all emergencies, have all drains clear at all times and have some glass and putty on hand, with the tools. Even the brads that are used to fasten the glass should not be overlooked as these are very important. A large place should have a large quantity of glass on hand. This may look as if a lot of money was laying idle, but we look at it as cheap insurance. In case of cold weather, and heavy glass breakage, the place with everything right there will be all repaired while the other places are figuring how much glass it will take to repair, and then ordering the same, and waiting for it to arrive. There are always a number of these rush orders, and there is always delay in receiving the needed glass and materials for repairs. Right now is the time to study out just how you would handle the place in case of a heavy snow storm of the kind that do damage, and at the same time see how well equipped you are to do the work. There is no time to get ready when the storm comes, as every minute then counts, and besides every stick of wood, etc., is snowed under very deep, or else frozen so that it is impossible to rig up any way of removing the snow from the wide houses, and we know what may happen if it keeps piling on and on as it will when the fall is heavy, and a wind blowing. Of course the houses are very strong, and never a one got damaged yet, but—. A grower with a lot of the old three-quarter span houses that are badly in need of repair, should see that they are properly braced now, while there is time to do it. We know of an instance where timely bracing saved several of these old houses from going down during the winter, and the returns from these houses for that season were enough to nearly pay for rebuilding them the following summer. To be real successful in business nowadays you have to be ready to meet any emergency, without stopping two or three days to think it over.

Picking Leaves on Beauties

With the unusual rainstorms and cloudy weather which prevails all over the country this summer, it will be wise to take especial care to see that all the leaves that touch the soil on the Beauty plants are removed as soon as the plants are of any size. About the time they are tied is a good time. It is best to do this in two or three pickings, as the plants will not feel it so much then, and it will be better all the way around. It would harm the plants to remove the leaves half way up to the first wire, so care should be taken to take only the leaves that lie on the soil or come in contact with it in such a way that they are always wet on the under side. These are very apt to get the first spot and then spread it to the rest of the plant, and from there to the plants surrounding. In doing this it is well to give the benches a little rubbing over and at the same time see that there is no big spot left anywhere in the house. Growers will say that it is all "tommy rot" or something similar, but we look upon this stray spot here and there as we would on a wolf among a lot of sheep. No matter how tame the wolf may seem he is still a wolf and will do damage sooner or later, so it is best to remove the wolf and thus nip the trouble in the bud, as we say.

Mildew

With showers coming two or three times a day and as many times in the night, it will take quite a little managing to run the houses just right, and avoid trouble with mildew. It is very important that the houses should not be put down too soon before the shower, and that they should not be kept closed too long after the shower has passed and the sun is shining. It is best not to put the houses down too low at first, unless the shower threatens to be a bad one, and by no means close the houses up tight the first time the vents are put down. It is only during very severe storms that it is necessary to close the house down tight, as most showers are pretty quiet after the first blow of wind, which generally is without rain. Houses with only one set of vents should have all end doors open and all obstructions removed so that men can go through one house and enter the next one through the far end door. The time thus gained is a wonderful help, especially if the shower comes quicker than was expected. Repair all broken glass at once, so there are no drafts, and should there be any plants that had a dose of mildew because of draughts of cold air coming in through broken glass, see that these are dusted with powdered sulphur or sprayed with Fungine. In using sulphur, do not apply it by throwing it on with hands, but use a good bellows or a good powder gun. Avoid late watering or syringing and make sure some lime is used at night. This will all help in preventing mildew, and "prevention is better than cure," always.

Larkspurs and Astilbes

Our cover illustration this week shows a corner of the beautiful Italian flower garden at Kenarden Lodge, the summer estate of Mrs. J. S. Kennedy at Bar Harbor, Me. Flowers and verdure at Bar Harbor are noticeably more brilliant and sparkling in color than those in places not favored with the prevalent moist sea atmosphere which is characteristic of Bar Harbor. Larkspurs, as seen in the picture, grow and flower grandly. In the foreground are seen some of the new hybrid astilbes which are a specialty of the Mt. Desert Nursery and were shown by that establishment so effectively at the National Flower Show in New York year before last. Just beyond is a group of that sterling novelty Lilium regale or myriophyllum.

The Kennedy estate under the care of W. T. Burton is the leading show place of Bar Harbor and the visitors to the noted seaside resort next year on the occasion of the Sweet Pea Society's meeting and exhibition will find in this masterpiece of gardening art and emerald lawns one of its chief attractions.

SOCIETY OF AMERICAN FLORISTS

AND

ORNAMENTAL HORTICULTURISTS

Preliminary program for the Thirty-first Annual Convention, to be held in The Civic Center Auditorium, San Francisco, Cal., August 17, 18, 19, 1915.

First Day, Tuesday, August 17.

OPENING SESSION.

2 P. M.—Opening exercises in Hall H, east side, Fourth Floor, Civic Center Auditorium. Address of Welcome, by Hon. Jas. Rolph, Jr., Mayor of San Francisco; Response, by W. F. Gude; President Welch's Address; Reading Minutes of the Secretary; Report of the Treasurer; Reports of State Vice-Presidents; Consideration of Invitations for Meeting Place for 1916.

EVENING SESSION.

8 P. M.—Balloting for Meeting Place for 1916, at St. Francis Hotel; Reception to President Welch, at the St. Francis Hotel. Music; Dancing; Refreshments. Strictly informal.

Second Day, Wednesday, August 18.

MORNING SESSION.

9 A. M.—Meeting of The Florists' Telegraph Delivery.

10.30 A. M.—Annual Meeting of The Ladies' Society of American Florists. Session S. A. F. and O. H.; Report of the National Flower Show Committee; George Asmus, Chairman; Discussion; Nomination of Officers for 1916; Report of the Judges of the Trade Exhibition and the Convention Garden; Report of the Committee on the President's Address; Discussion.

AFTERNOON SESSION.

2 P. M.—Bowling Contest of The Ladies of the S. A. F.

2 P. M.—Session S. A. F. and O. H.; Discussion, "Are Not Insurance Rates on Modern Greenhouse Establishments Too High, in view of the lighter risks accruing from better and less dangerous construction?" Led by Wm. F. Kasting. Report of the Committee on National Publicity—Irwin Bertermann, Chairman; Discussion.

Third Day, Thursday, August 19.

MORNING SESSION.

9 A. M.—Meeting of The Florists' Hall Association.

10 A. M.—Time alloted for Meetings, Rose, Carnation, Chrysanthemum and Gladiolus Societies if desired.

11 A. M.—Election of Officers of the S. A. F. and O. H. for 1916; Polls open from 11 A. M. to 12 M.

AFTERNOON SESSION.

2 P. M.—Question Box; Deferred Business.

2 P. M.—Annual Bowling Tournament, S. A. F. and O. H., at Gramp alleys, 924 Market St.

Essays

In view of the many and varied attractions of the Convention and Convention City, the Executive Board decided that it would be unwise to take up the time of the convention with the reading of essays. Realizing, however, the value of the presentation of essays at the Society's conventions, the secretary was instructed to invite essays from various gentlemen willing to prepare them, such invitations and the number of them to be within his discretion, the essays to be furnished to the trade papers for publication during the convention period, and to be printed as part of the proceedings of the convention.

The following essays are presented:

"Is it Advisable for the Society of American Florists and Ornamental Horticulturists to Establish a National Credit and Collection Department?" by August F. Poehlmann, Morton Grove, Ill.

"The Problems Attending the Establishment of Permanent Convention Gardens," by Theodore Wirth, Superintendent of Parks, Minneapolis, Minn.

"The Necessity of National Publicity to Advance the Interests of Commercial Floriculture in the United States," by Albert Pochelon, Detroit, Mich.

Fourth Day, Friday, August 20.

S. A. F. and O. H. Day at the Panama-Pacific International Exposition.

The address of the secretary is care of Daniel MacRorie, 430 Phelan Bldg., San Francisco.

OFF FOR SAN FRANCISCO.

The joint party of the Park Superintendents' and Gardeners' Association leaving New York for San Francisco on Saturday, August 7, consisted of Fred C. Green, Providence, R. I.; Her-mann W. Merkel and John J. Walsh of New York, N. Y.; Oscar W. Karlson, Riverdale, N. Y.; Charles Haible and William H. Coldwell, Newburgh, N. Y.; John D. McEwen and wife, Queens, N. Y.; Oscar Boehler, West Hoboken, N. J.; E. W. Schoneberger, Madison, N. J.; Robert Williamson, Greenwich, Conn.; A. Bieschke, wife and child, Noroton, Conn.; Miss Una Keith, Bridgeport, Conn.; W. R. Pierson, Cromwell, Conn.; David F. Roy and wife, Marion, Mass.; Joseph C. Forbes, New Bedford, Mass. Theodore Wirth and wife joined the party at Minneapolis. Others were to join at Spokane, Seattle and Portland. M. C. Ebel, who organized the party was obliged to give up the trip owing to sickness. He traveled with them as far as Philadelphia and they parted from him with much regret.

President Welch's party bound for the Convention, numbering four when starting from Boston had grown to twelve when leaving Chicago. Mr. Welch reports a very enjoyable visit in Chicago where hospitality without limit was extended by representatives of the Florists' Club, the trade and the park officials.

CLEVELAND FLOWER SHOW.

Six well-known gentlemen, authorities and veterans from the standpoint of judging exhibitions, have been selected by the premium committee of the Cleveland Flower Show to serve as their official judges. They are as follows: J. F. Ammann, Edwardsville, Ill.; Emil Buettner, Park Ridge, Ill.; Michael Bloy, Detroit, Mich.; Eugene Dailledouze, Brooklyn, N. Y.; John H. Dunlop, Toronto, Canada; Wm. Nicholson, Framingham, Mass.

Chairman Herbert Bate, of the premium committee, states that his committee is hard at work on getting the final premium list in shape to place in the hands of the printer so that it will be mailed early in September. Frank A. Freidley, of the James Eadie Company, representing the commercial growers, and J. Curnow, of Akron, representing the private growers, together with Mr. Bate compose the premium committee.

WAYS AND MEANS COMMITTEE OF THE PACIFIC COAST HORTICULTURAL SOCIETY
In Connection With S. A. F. Convention

Top row, left to right B. Myer, M. Poss, F. Bertrand; middle row, left to right—Wm. Kettlewell, J. Axel, A. J. Rossi, D. Raymond, V. Podesta; bottom row, left to right—J. R. Fotheringham, Walter Hoffnghoff, H. Plath, T. Taylor.

NORTH SHORE EXHIBITION.

The annual summer flower show of the North Shore (Mass.) Horticultural Society opened Wednesday afternoon, August 4, despite a deluge that flooded the tent where the exhibit was held on the estate of Mrs. R. C. Winthrop, West Manchester. The show was continued another day, however, but with no success as far as the weather was concerned.

Among the more notable displays was that of Mrs. H. L. Higginson, who had a number of small exhibits, and won first prize for the best specimen plant lilium auratum and first prize for best dinner table decoration, a rustic arrangement with a miniature tea garden for a centerpiece.

Mrs. W. D. Denegre, gard. H. Clark, took second prize for table decoration in sweet peas. Miss Pauline Croll also entered a table decoration in snapdragon. Mrs. F. P. Frazier won several prizes, including a first for artistically arranged table of hardy herbaceous flowers and first for specimen plant petunia (Rosy Morn). Mrs. Lester Leland. gard. E. Wetterlow, received many prizes, including a first for best table of flowers arranged for effect. for which Mrs. S. P. Blake took second. Mrs. Leland took first for 12 distinct varieties of specimen plants

and Mrs. Lathrop Brown second. Mrs. Leland also received a silver medal for a magnificent group of begonias. first prize for 12 achemines and a certificate for a new geranium.

The vegetable displays were particularly good, Mrs. C. S. Hanks taking first prize for a table very artistically arranged. A silver cup was given to Mrs. Frank B. Bemis for a general collection, and a special prize was awarded Mrs. H. L. Higginson.

The school garden competition was spirited and upwards of 75 prizes were distributed in this section.

Certificates of merit were awarded for new geranium named Mrs. Lester Leland, by Eric Wetterlow; standard heliotrope, by Mrs. T. J. Coolidge, Jr., gard. Gustave Ericsen; Pink Mallow, by Mrs. H. S. Grew 2nd, gard. James McIlheneny; display of fruit, by William Allen. Silver medal to Col. Chas. Pfaff for Epidendrum rismatocarpum.

W. T.

There will be an exhibition, mainly of gladioli. of the Horticultural Society of New York, on Saturday and Sunday. August 21 and 22. at the Museum Building, New York Botanical Garden. An invitation is extended to all interested to take part in the exhibition. Schedules are now ready and will be sent on application to the secretary. George V. Nash, New York Botanical Garden, Bronx Park, N. Y. City.

GEORGE V. NASH, Sec'y.

AMERICAN ROSE SOCIETY.

For the fall exhibition of the American Rose Society to be held in Cleveland, November 10th to 14th, the following prizes have been offered:

Twenty-five dollars by A. N. Pierson, Inc., Cromwell, Conn., for the best 50 blooms of Hadley roses.

Silver cup from The Lamborn Floral Co., Alliance, O.

Silver medal from Vaughan's Seed Store, New York and Chicago.

Ten dollars in cash from "The House of Burpee," Philadelphia. Pa.

Robert Scott & Son, Sharon Hill, Pa., $25 for 50 Killarney Brilliants.

These prizes are specials in addition to those of the regular list and in all probability there will be a number more added. Much interest is arising in this exhibition, and there are two prizes to be offered for the best unnamed rose that will be placed upon exhibition.

BENJAMIN HAMMOND, Sec.

Philadelphia—John Burton and party of about fifteen Montgomery county celebrities spent the week-end at Forked River August 1st. An interesting diversion of the outing was a friendly visit on Saturday evening to the Truly Rurals and the Commodore at Waretown.

AN EFFECTIVE VINE COMBINATION.

Actividia arguta is slowly but surely coming into use as one of the most rapid growing and desirable hardy climbers where a large space is to be quickly covered with a dense growing vine. It is equally useful for more restricted use as in the example shown herewith, frequent cutting back of the rampant growth being only required. Its thick dark green foliage seems to be immune against all insect attacks and its flowers are beautiful and sweet scented although short-lived. The latter disqualification may be adequately offset by planting Hall's honeysuckle so that it entwines and blossoms among the actinidia foliage. The contrast of the small pale foliage and white flowers with the heavy dark leaves of the latter is very effective and the two vines get along nicely together year after year. The picture shows the gate posts at the entrance to the cottage of the editor of HORTICULTURE at Winchester, Mass.

LITTLE ADS. BRING BIG RETURNS

Obituary

R. J. Groves.

R. J. Groves, the oldest florist in Atchison, Kan., died July 16, aged 83 years. He had been in business in Atchison since 1861. The business, known as the Groves Floral Co., was turned over in July to his daughters.

Alfred C. Burkhardt.

Alfred C. Burkhardt, florist, of Portland, Ore., died suddenly July 28 of heart failure. He was born in Switzerland, but came to this country in 1872 and entered the florist business with his brother Gustave. He is survived by his wife and six daughters.

William H. Westcott.

William H. Westcott, a pioneer florist of Philadelphia, died suddenly on the 5th inst. at his residence in Roxboro. He had a greenhouse plant there which he built in recent years after parting company with his brother, John Westcott, with whom he was associated at Ridge and Lehigh avenues for an extended period. Previous to that he had greenhouses at Second and Tioga street which he conducted successfully in the old-fashioned, conservative way for half a lifetime and brought up his family there. William Westcott was a quiet, easygoing man, and did not take much part in public affairs. But he was up to a few years ago, after an operation at a hospital, a faithful and constant member of the Florists' Club and the S. A. F., and there were but few of their meetings or celebrations but were graced by his genial, quiet, smiling presence. He was 72 years of age and a native of Philadelphia. Interment took place on the 9th inst. at Greenmount cemetery. A special meeting of the Florists' Club was held on the 6th inst. at which appropriate resolutions were passed and ordered sent to the family. The club also ordered that a floral design representing the club membership be sent and that its execution should be entrusted to the loving hands of the deceased's brother, Commodore John Westcott.

SEED TRADE

AMERICAN SEED TRADE ASSOCIATION

Officers—President, J. M. Lupton, Mattituck, L. I., N. Y.; First Vice-President, Kirby B. White, Detroit, Mich.; Second Vice-President, F. W. Bolgiano, Washington, D. C.; Secretary-Treasurer, C. E. Kendel, Cleveland, O.; Assistant Secretary, S. F. Willard, Jr., Cleveland, O. Cincinnati, O., next meeting place.

Crimson Clover Seed

There is apparently a larger supply of crimson clover seed on hand at the present time than in any previous year and much of it is of poor quality, according to specialists of the U. S. Department of Agriculture. While this would indicate that the price should be normal or less than normal it is rapidly advancing.

The greater part of the crimson clover seed sowed in the United States is normally imported from France and Austria. In the fall of 1914 conditions of trade with Europe were such that there appeared to be danger of a short supply of seed for this summer's planting. The desire of the seed trade to secure as much seed as possible, together with the improvement in trade facilities with France during the winter and spring, resulted in the importation of 12,000,000 pounds during the year ending June 30, 1915, as compared with 7,500,000 pounds the year previous and 1,500,000 pounds in 1910.

During May and June much seed of poor quality has been imported, more than 1,000,000 pounds made up of several lots, germinating from 29 per cent. to 62 per cent. Buyers should therefore be sure of the quality of the seed they buy. Crimson clover seed of a bright greenish yellow color usually germinates well, while a brownish color indicates poor germination. All lots containing brownish or brown seeds should be carefully tested for germination to determine the proportion that may be expected to grow in the field under favorable conditions and the rate of seeding should be adjusted accordingly.

Crop Damage in Massachusetts.

Damage amounting to several millions of dollars has been done to the crops of Massachusetts as the result of the extraordinary rainfall of the last few weeks, according to Secretary Wheeler of the Massachusetts State Board of Agriculture.

Mr. Wheeler, who has just returned from a trip about the State, declared that the agricultural situation has not been so bad since 1817, which was known as the "starvation" year. He declared that the State's annual $12,-000,000 hay crop will be cut in half this year, that the potato crop has been virtually destroyed and that the squash, cranberry, onion and tobacco crops have been unusually hard hit. The outlook for the onion and tobacco crops in the Connecticut valley, he declared, is particularly discouraging. He stated that he saw farms of five acres that were planted with potatoes where not a leaf was showing. Hay is selling now for $12 a ton, or higher, he said, than at any time since the Civil war.

Mr. Wheeler said that the situation might be helped if September is fine. To date, he stated, the fruit growers have not suffered a great deal, but that they will if the rain continues.

He accounted for the low price of garden truck by the light season in the hotel business. The weather, he asserted, has kept people away from the beach hotels, which ordinarily require tremendous quantities of vegetables to support them.

Notes.

D. F. Lomason, of the D. M. Ferry Co., of Detroit, Mich., was in St. Louis last week attending to his yearly collection of unsold seeds.

The value of imports of horticultural material at the port of New York for the week ending July 31, 1915, is given as follows: Manure salt, $2,327; sulphate of potash, $3,701; fertilizer, $216; clover seed, $6,256; grass seed, $1,690; palm seed, $2,646; trees and plants, $5,576.

NO QUARINTINE OF CHESTNUT NURSERY STOCK.

Following a public hearing on the subject, the Federal Horticultural Board has determined not to quarantine chestnut nursery stock for the purpose of preventing the distribution of the chestnut bark disease. The board announced that the disease spreads slowly and opportunity has already existed for several years for the distribution of this disease in small quantities to areas where extensive new plantings of chestnut are being inaugurated. Recommendation is made that plantings of chestnut stock be carefully inspected for the presence of the disease.

NEW CORPORATIONS.

Pittsburgh, Pa.—Elliott Nursery Co. Incorporators: J. Wilkinson Elliott, Thos. M. and Rhea F. Elliott.

Rochester, N. Y. — Howe-Campbell Nursery Co. Capital stock $1,000. Incorporators: Cora M. Graham, John M. Campbell and T. H. Howe.

Oswego, N. Y.—The Penfold Greenhouses have been purchased by C. A. Tanner.

Of Interest to Retail Florists

NEW FLOWER STORES.

Springfield, O.—Al. Bradford.

Donora, Pa.—C. Warren Kinder.

Rock Springs, Wyo.—L. B. West-
holder.

New Haven, Ct.—Morris Herz, 262
York street.

Oakfield, N. Y.—James J. Bates, 50
Drake street.

Milwaukee, Wis.—Edward Stewart,
661 Third street.

New York, N. Y.—Adolph Mayer,
1062 Madison avenue.

Hannibal, Mo. — Griffen's Flower
Shop, 316 Broadway.

Detroit. ·Mich.—Detroit Floral Co.,
703 Woodward avenue.

St. Louis, Mo.—Edward H. Pieper,
23rd and Salisbury streets.

Great Falls, Mont.—Geo. T. Barker,
612 South Second avenue.

Chicago, Ill.—O. H. Breyfogle, Halsted and 120th streets.

Chicago, Ill. — Chas. Lompos, Masonic Temple, about September 15.

Philadelphia, Pa.—Chas. H. Grakelow, Broad and Cumberland streets,
about October 1.

PERSONAL.

Edgar M. Mack, floral decorator for
the Coombs Flower Shop, Hartford,
Ct., and Ethel May Hodgkins were
married August 1 and are now on a
wedding trip in Maine.

Lars Lindahl, florist, 26 Vinson
street. Worcester, Mass., has been
elected treasurer of the Worcester
Workingmen's Association, an organization formed with a view of reducing
the cost of living.

NEWS NOTES.

Lewiston, Me.—The addition to the
office of T. J. Allen, the Pine street
florist, has been completed.

New Haven, Ct.—Mrs. Schneider has
purchased the florist business of Alfred T. Ostermann, 123 Church street.

East Saugus, Mass.—Louis Gerrar-
ranzo, an employee of William Sim at
Cliftondale, was held up and robbed
of $3 August 3 while on his way home.

CATALOGUE RECEIVED.

M. Rice Co., Philadelphia, Pa.—Portfolio of Florists' Supplies and Wedding
Suggestions. A comprehensive and finely printed illustrated list.

BUSINESS TROUBLES.

Randolph, Mass.—Marcus L. Tirrell.
florist; liabilities $454, no assets.

NEWS ITEMS FROM EVERYWHERE

WASHINGTON.

The Washington Floral Company has recently completed the installation of a large electrical sign bearing the words "Flowers at Popular Prices" above their store.

That Frank E. Miller, an employee of J. H. Small & Sons, is still in the land of the living is due to the capture of a crazy negro who recently threatened to take his life unless the small sum of $12 was immediately forthcoming.

William F. Gude and Mrs. Gude and their two daughters, and Mr. and Mrs. Christian Schellhorn and Theodore Diedrich left Washington on August 11 fo attend the convention at San Francisco. They will be joined at that place by Adolph Gude, Jr., who has been employed on the sweet pea range of A. C. Zvolanek, in Lompoc Valley.

Walter Hawley, with Gude Bros. Company, and Mrs. Hawley are visiting relatives in Brooklyn, N. Y. Henry Gottenkenny, with the same firm, and Mrs. Gottenkenny and their two children are spending their vacation in Fairfax County, Va. Mr. and Mrs. James Dalgleish and their daughter are spending a month's vacation at Arlington, Vermont.

Government officials are doing their part to have the coming encampment of the G. A. R. a great success. Special floral designs have been laid out on the lawns of the Capitol and other government buildings. These designs include the insignia of the veterans, the Women's Relief Corps and other organizations that will participate in the encampment. Seventy-five thousand foliage plants went into the making of the several badges of the various army corps that have been laid around the Sherman statue just south of the Treasury Building. William F. Gude is at the head of the band of workers having the encampment in charge. Associated with him are a number of florists, several of whom hold positions on very important committees.

There is the usual complaint of summer dullness, but it is interesting to note that nearly all of the leading florists of the city have informed the Washington representative of the HORTICULTURE that compared with a similar period of last year, July and the early part of August is entirely up to standard. The florists of the National Capital have learned to look for additional means of outlet and in this way

have brought about increased demands for their stocks. Last year was the worst in the history of the jewelry business of the National Capital. The reason was that the florists went after the holiday business with a vim and won. This does not mean only Christmas, Thanksgiving Day, Easter and New Year's, but every other occasion. Flowers replaced candy to a remarkable extent and other lines suffered equally as much. The flower business here has grown to a marked extent in the last two years and the end is not yet—the live ones are ever reaching out after new opportunities. More advertising space is weekly occupied by the florists than ever before; more attention is being paid to window displays, and there is exacted from some of the clerks an efficiency heretofore undreamt of, and all of these efforts are bringing results.

ST. LOUIS.

W. C. Smith, president of the W. C. Smith Floral Co., and Mrs. Smith, left last week for a two weeks' stay in the Ozark Mountains.

President J. S. Wilson, of the Missouri Horticultural Society, says the prospects are good for the annual meeting of the society being held here in November.

It was James Young and not C. Young & Sons Co. who bought the tract of land on the Olive street road recently. Mr. Young says he will build a range of houses on this at once and place his son Charles in charge as manager.

A very small delegation of members will go to the San Francisco convention. They include Frank A. Windler, J. J. Windler, C. C. Saunders and Vincent Gorly. This is the smallest delegation that ever represented St. Louis at an S. A. F. convention.

R. J. Windler, of Rogers Park, Chicago, was here a few days last week to attend the wedding of his brother, Joseph J., to Miss Paula Poss, which took place August 4. R. J. returns home Thursday, and the happy couple left for San Francisco to spend their honeymoon.

The St. Louis County Growers' Club held its meeting August 4. They decided to ask the proprietors of the five wholesale houses to meet with them at their meeting in September, at which great pressure will be exerted to have them reconsider their Sunday closing, which so far has availed them nothing.

SAN FRANCISCO.

At the regular August meeting of the Pacific Coast Horticultural Society, S. B. Mitchell will deliver a lecture on "Iris."

It is rumored here that Kansas City will be favored for the next meeting place of the S. A. F., as the 1914 convention was held in the far East and this year's will be held in the far West.

John A. Evans, of Richmond, Ind., has joined the advance guard which is here awaiting the convention. Mr. McCabe, of the A. L. Randall Co., arrived a few days ago, also, and expects to remain for the festivities.

Mrs. Hosp and her three daughters, who are in the florist business in Bakersfield and Riverside, Cal., are in San Francisco combining business and pleasure. H. A. Hyde, of Watsonville, Cal., was a recent visitor also.

Secretary John Young, of the S. A. F., who has been here the last fortnight concluding arrangements for the convention, says the convention garden is coming out nicely and will compare very favorably with those of former years.

Preparations are complete for the celebration of "Nurserymen's Day" at the exposition, on Aug. 16, which will conclude the joint conventions of the California Nurserymen's Association and the Pacific Coast Association of Nurserymen.

The most important move in the local wholesale trade in a long time took place the past week when the E. W. McLellan Co. occupied its new place, which provides much better facilities than were available at the old location. Arrangements have been made with about fifty growers to take space in the establishment besides themselves.

CINCINNATI.

Al. Horning is visiting his mother in Toledo, Ohio.

P. J. Olinger is spending the current week at Evanston and Aurora, Ill.

Burglars broke into the store of C. E. Jones at 905 E. McMillan street and attempted to pry open the safe.

Exhibitors at the Carthage Fair this week include Henry Schwarz, T. Ben, George and Fred Bachmeier. All have made extensive preparations for the affair.

BOSTON.

Andrew Christensen started alone for San Francisco on August 11, going via the northern route and planning to return by the southern.

Ed Welch and family have gone to their cottage at Old Orchard Beach for the summer. David Welch is left as sole director of the store on Devonshire street and fills this position with a graceful dignity which seems to ripen and mellow as time passes.

A furious thunder storm accompanied by a fusilade of small hailstones and the heaviest deluge of rain in this rain-soaked season, visited this city and suburbs on Monday, August 9th. It was particularly severe in Woburn, Winchester and other suburban districts on the north side.

Ever-industrious George Hamer is back at the Flower Exchange after two weeks' vacation, more than ever a shining example of perpetual motion. E. A. Stickel, who has represented Montrose Greenhouses for a considerable period, has got through. The long-talked-of fishing trip materialized last Tuesday when a party of thirteen from the Exchange went down the bay to the Graves, as guests of Wallace Greenwood of Winthrop, on his boat. "Bill" Hastings won the pool with the largest fish and second honors were shared between Billy Mix of the Edgar place and Louis Ginsburg. Between 75 and 100 fish of all races and persuasions were captured by the party.

Doorway florists in Lynn must procure a state license or go out of business, according to a ruling of Judge Lummus, who on August 10 found Harry Feinzig of Boston guilty of violating the laws regulating itinerant venders. The board of control caused Feinzig to be arrested, to make a test case. He was not fined, but his conviction is intended to stand as a warning to others who set up temporary flower stands for the sale of flowers. Since early spring many persons have rented small shops or secured permission to erect stands in doorways, and sold flowers. The florists of the city contended that this business was of a temporary or transient nature, and required a state license.

CHICAGO.

The Chicago florists held a sale of flowers for the benefit of the survivors of the Eastland disaster. The flowers were donated by the wholesale houses of Chicago, and the sum realized was $305.00.

At the Florists' Club meeting last Thursday, arrangements for the Flower Show were discussed, but nothing definite was settled. Vaughan's Seed Store exhibited a vase of delphiniums. There was an attendance of about 40.

NEWS NOTES.

Ravenna, O.—S. P. Pike has leased the Mellen Greenhouses on West Main street.

Forest City, Ia.—J. H. Rine and son, H. B. Rine, of Humboldt, Ia., have purchased the Hill City Greenhouses.

Woburn, Mass.—Lightning entered the boiler room of the greenhouses of R. F. Anderson, 71 Middle street, on August 9, and besides wrecking the place partly paralyzed the left side of one of the workmen.

VISITORS' REGISTER.

Cleveland, O.: J. K. M. L. Farquhar, Boston, Mass.

West Pembroke, Me.: W. H. Wilder, Somersworth, N. H.

Hallowell, Me.: Mr. and Mrs. Paul R. Brooks, Lawrence, Kans.

Chicago: Harry Balsley, Detroit, Mich.; L. B. Brague, Hinsdale, Mass.

Boston: S. Prentiss Baldwin, Cleveland, O.; Gerhard Bleicken, Plymouth, Mass.

St. Louis: F. J. Farney, Phila.; D. F. Lomason, Detroit, Mich.; R. J. Windler, Chicago.

Cincinnati: Gus. Kohlbrand, Chicago, Ill.; L. B. Salmlow, New York City; Jos. Hill, Richmond, Ind.

Buffalo, N. Y.: H. P. Knoble, Frank A. Friedley and Herbert Bate, all of Cleveland, O.; A. Albert, Philadelphia.

Philadelphia: Mr. and Mrs. Eble, New Orleans, La. (honeymoon trip); Mr. Weiss, Roanoke, Va.; Mr. Dicks, representing Cooper, Taber Co., London, Eng.; Theo. Edwards, Bridgeton, N. J.; Geo. C. Shaffer, wife and son, Washington, D. C.

WHOLESALE FLOWER MARKETS — TRADE PRICES—Per 100 TO DEALERS ONLY

Roses	CINCINNATI Aug. 9		CHICAGO July 26		BUFFALO Aug. 9		PITTSBURG Aug. 9	
Am. Beauty, Special	20.00 to	25.00	20.00 to	30.00	20.00 to	25.00	20.00 to	25.00
" " Fancy and Extra	12.00 to	15.00	15.00 to	20.00	12.00 to	15.00	12.50 to	15.00
" " No. 1	6.00 to	10.00	8.00 to	15.00	6.00 to	10.00	4.00 to	10.00
Killarney, Richmond, Extra	3.00 to	4.00	6.00 to	10.00	5.00 to	7.00	6.00 to	8.00
" " Ordinary	2.00 to	3.00	2.00 to	6.00	2.00 to	4.00	2.00 to	4.00
Hillingdon, Ward, Sunburst, Extra	4.00 to	6.00	4.00 to	8.00	6.00 to	9.00	...... to	6.00
" " Ordinary	2.00 to	3.00	2.00 to	4.00	2.00 to	6.00	...... to	4.00
Arenberg, Radiance, Taft, Extra	4.00 to	6.00	...... to		6.00 to	8.00	6.00 to	8.00
" " Ordinary	2.00 to	3.00	...... to		2.00 to	6.00	...... to	4.00
Russell, Hadley, Ophelia, Mock	3.00 to	6.00	5.00 to	15.00	5.00 to	10.00	6.00 to	10.00
Carnations, Fancy	1.00 to	2.00	2.00 to	3.00	1.00 to	2.00	...... to	1.00
" " Ordinary	.50 to	.75	1.00 to	2.00	.75 to	1.00	...... to	.50
Cattleyas	25.00 to	50.00	35.00 to	50.00	25.00 to	50.00	40.00 to	50.00
Dendrobium formosum	...... to		40.00 to	50.00	...... to		...... to	
Lilies, Longiflorum	6.00 to	10.00	8.00 to	10.00	5.00 to	8.00	...... to	8.00
" Rubrum	3.00 to	6.00	...... to		3.00 to	4.00	...... to	3.00
Lily of the Valley	...... to	4.00	2.00 to	4.00	...... to	4.00	3.00 to	4.00
Daisies	.25 to	.75	.50 to	1.50	1.00 to	1.50	...... to	
Snapdragon	1.00 to	3.00	2.00 to	4.00	3.00 to	6.00	...... to	3.00
Gladioli	1.00 to	4.00	2.00 to	4.00	1.00 to	5.00	2.00 to	4.00
Asters	1.50 to	2.00	1.00 to	2.00	.40 to	1.50	.50 to	8.00
Sweet Peas	.25 to	.50	.25 to	.50	.15 to	.25	...... to	
Gardenias	...... to		...... to		20.00 to	25.00	...... to	
Adiantum	...... to	1.00	1.00 to	1.25	1.00 to	1.25	.75 to	1.25
Smilax	...... to	15.00	10.00 to	15.00	...... to	15.00	10.00 to	15.00
Asparagus Plumosus, Strings (100)	...... to	50.00	40.00 to	50.00	40.00 to	50.00	20.00 to	40.00
& Spren. (100 bchs.)	...... to	25.00	25.00 to	35.00	25.00 to	35.00	20.00 to	50.00

Flower Market Reports

BOSTON The flower supply was shortened up somewhat during the stormy period early in the week but with the coming of brighter weather the surplus began to pile up again and the temporary activity ceased. What little business is being done at present is confined to funeral work and some insignificant seaside shipping calls. Asters and gladioli are being very heavily overstocked. Gladioli are excellent but are far in excess of the needs and the situation is further handicapped by the large quantities of this flower being shipped direct to consumers all through this section by large New York growers, at 35 to 50 cents a hundred. Asters are far from first quality as a rule. Sweet peas are practically useless from the effects of the recent heavy rainstorms. Small short-stemmed roses from young plants have commenced to come in this week. There is practically no market for them. Cattleyas are now very few and they bring the top price.

BUFFALO Trade has not improved much. There has been a rather heavy supply of carnations and roses. Lilies continue plentiful, in fact too many to command any price. Floral work was only lightly scattered. Gladioli were plentiful and mostly of the ordinary quality. America has had the best sales. Friday and Saturday brought on a heavy supply of asters and the quality was good though the outlet was blocked. On Monday, 9th, the market opened up brisk. The supply of roses was short and a general demand for floral work helped the day.

CHICAGO August has brought the usual midsummer dullness. Local demand is down to bed rock. There is a little spurt now and then for funerals and shipping to outside points is fairly active, these orders cleaning up the market in certain lines pretty well, particularly as regards good shipping quality of roses. Roses in medium to longer length are not at all too plenty. Some fine Russells are coming in and meeting with a brisk demand. Ophelia and Sunburst are also in active call. Killarney Brilliant is among the best in the line of pink and can be had in fairly good length. Pink and White Killarney also are of fair quality, but the bulk of the receipts are in the shorter grades. Thanks to the cool weather which has prevailed most of the time, Richmond is keeping up in good shape. We note some very good Milady and a few Hoosier Queen. Carnations are still hanging on, some

whites being unusually good for the season. Lilies are seen in quantity and good quality, but move slowly. Lily of the valley is rather short in supply. As to gladioli and asters, the market is so badly glutted that the wholesale men find it an impossibility to move the stock at anything like a decent price. In fact, a large amount of the daily receipts can't be sold at any price—this in spite of the fact that both are on the whole of very good quality. Shasta daisies, so abundant the last month or more, are nearly cut out. Other garden flowers such as coreopsis, gaillardia, calendula, larkspur, etc., are seen in abundance. A few good dahlias have made their appearance but meet with an indifferent demand.

CINCINNATI Business is a little better but not yet good enough to cause a very material stiffening in prices. The supply is large and able

to cope with all present needs. Shipping business is pretty fair. The general quality of the gladioli is not as good as it was. Asters are just between seasons, the early and late, while rose offerings include but a limited amount of fancy blooms. Lilies, longiflorum, rubrum and auratum are excellent and plentiful. Early dahlias, snapdragon and pond lilies may also be had. Greens are plentiful. The house-grown asparagus is excellent.

NEW YORK This market has been depressed to the limit during the past week. Very little of the stock coming in is moved in any legitimate channel and then at best very sluggishly. The number of gladioli and asters being sent in to find a market which does not really exist is beyond computation, but the

(Continued on page 217)

WHOLESALE FLOWER MARKETS — TRADE PRICES — Per 100 — TO DEALERS ONLY

Roses	BOSTON Aug. 12		ST. LOUIS Aug. 9		PHILA. Aug. 10	
Am. Beauty, Special	12.00 to 20.00		30.00 to 40.00		15.00 to 20.00	
" " Fancy and Extra	6.00 to 10.00		20.00 to 25.00		6.00 to 12.00	
" " No. 1	1.00 to 3.00		10.00 to 15.00		3.00 to 5.00	
Killarney, Richmond, Extra	2.00 to 5.00		5.00 to 6.00		4.00 to 6.00	
" " Ordinary	.50 to 1.00		2.00 to 3.00		1.00 to 2.00	
Hillingdon, Ward, Sunburst, Extra	2.00 to 4.00		5.00 to 6.00		4.00 to 6.00	
" " Ordinary	.50 to 1.00		2.00 to 3.00		1.00 to 2.00	
Arenberg, Radiance, Taft, Extra	2.00 to 4.00		.... to		4.00 to 6.00	
" " Ordinary	.50 to 1.00		.... to		1.00 to 2.00	
Russell, Hadley, Ophelia, Mock	2.00 to 10.00		6.00 to 8.00		3.00 to 8.00	
Carnations, Fancy	.75 to 1.00		2.00 to 3.00		.... to	
" Ordinary	.50 to .75		1.00 to 1.50		1.00 to 2.00	
Cattleyas	20.00 to 50.00		35.00 to 50.00		30.00 to 50.00	
Dendrobium formosum	.... to		.... to		.... to	
Lilies, Longiflorum	8.00 to 4.00		6.00 to 8.00		5.00 to 8.00	
" Rubrum	.... to 2.00		4.00 to 5.00		4.00 to 6.00	
Lily of the Valley	1.00 to 3.00		3.00 to 4.00		2.00 to 3.00	
Daisies	.50 to 1.00		.20 to .5		.... to	
Snapdragon	.25 to 1.00		3.00 to 4.00		.... to	
Gladioli	1.00 to 1.50		1.50 to 2.50		1.00 to 3.00	
Asters	.50 to 1.00		1.00 to 3.00		1.00 to 2.00	
Sweet Peas	.15 to .20		.15 to .5		.50 to .5	
Gardenias	10.00 to 25.00		.... to		.... to	
Adiantum	.50 to 1.00		1.00 to 1.75		1.00 to 1.50	
Smilax	10.00 to 12.00		12.00 to 15.00		10.00 to 15.00	
Asparagus Plumosus, Strings (100)	25.00 to 50.00		35.00 to 50.00		35.00 to 50.00	
" & Spren. (100 Bchs.)	25.00 to 35.00		20.00 to		35.00 to 50.00	

Flower Market Reports

(Continued from page 200)

receipts for it all are easily counted. Cattleyas are scarce but have no regular call, the demand being only intermittent. Lilies continue very abundant. Small roses from young planted houses come in by myriads but are hardly worth the time required to pack them which might easily be spent to better advantage. Asters are of all types and sizes and degrees of quality, many being badly bedraggled by exposure to wind and weather. Much rain has fallen, which has been very injurious to all outdoor flowers.

There was a **PHILADELPHIA** slight improvement last week in the general situation here. The overdose of outdoor stock has eased up a little and the demand is rather better. There is a noticeable shortening up in the gladiolus crop which helps very considerably in improving the tone. The early asters are now about over, and as these were more notable for quantity than quality as a rule their demise will not be regretted. They are being followed by the midseason sorts, which are much superior and all that can be asked for as to quality. In the rose market, American Beauty is in fine supply and is selling right well, the northern-grown stock still having a little the best of it as against the new crop locals. Other roses are not so plentiful as they were and as a rule are but medium as to quality. Carnations are few and poor. Cattleyas and other orchids scarce. Plenty of lilies of fine quality. These are showing up as a summer flower better than ever and are being more and more appreciated by the retailer. They are splendid shippers and keepers and are useful and appropriate for many purposes. The second crop of delphiniums is now in and meets with favor. Fine flowers but not so long-stemmed as the first cuts.

Little change **SAN FRANCISCO** has taken place in the local flower market either in conditions, prices or outlook. All seasonables are plentiful, but supplies clean up closely from day to day. German Day at the Panama-Pacific exposition, Thursday, created an unusual demand for cornflowers, which stripped the market early in the day. When the supply began to run short offers of $1 were made for bunches that brought only 25 cents in the morning. Chrysanthemums are more plentiful. Monrovia and Golden Glow being offered in considerable quantity, and a few October Frost have appeared during the last day or two. The supply of asters shows good quality, and though abundant, finds a ready market. The large majority of dahlias show the effect of hot weather, but a limited supply of excellent stock is still arriving from Marin County. Gladioli are a little more plentiful than they were last week and the really fine offerings bring high prices. Francis King is most in evidence and shows best average quality. America is on the down grade and Panama appears sparingly. Sweet peas are scarce and few of the

arrivals are up to standard. The same is true of carnations, the supply being very light, as growers are pulling up their old plants. Roses are quite good for this time of the year, especially Ophelia, and no difficulty is experienced in cleaning up the best and moderate offerings. Lilies continue to dominate the market. Very fine specimens of rubrum and auratum are shown everywhere, and some cold storage giganteum appeared the last few days. Neither orchids or gardenias are in very heavy supply, but the offerings come nearer filling the demand than they did a week or so ago.

The market was all to **ST. LOUIS** the bad last week. Buyers were few and those who did buy bought little. The weather was remarkably cool all week and stock at the wholesale market looked better than at any time this summer. Prices are very low in all grades, especially in outdoor grown stock, including tuberoses and gladioli, which are coming in daily in big lots from our home growers. Roses are many and in big lots sell cheap. Carnations are not so many, but asters take their place.

The local market, **WASHINGTON** as is usual at this time of the year, is overstocked with all sorts of flowers and although the quality in the main is good, it is impossible to find an outlet for much more than one-fourth of the supply. Nothing is scarce except orchids and these are at a premium. Asters show the effect of the recent rainstorms, which have beaten down the plants and spotted the flowers. Some very good stock brings a fair price, but the bulk of the asters go to the street venders at five cents per hundred and less. New crop roses are naturally very short-stemmed and worthless except for funeral work, but there are plenty of good roses to be had, especially in Ophelia, Taft, Kaiserin and American Beauty. Dahlias are not yet quite up to standard. The market can get along very well without them, however, and this same may be said of carnations.

BELGIAN PLANT SHIPMENTS WILL BE PERMITTED.

With reference to fall shipments of azaleas and other Belgian plants, which were under embargo by the British authorities, we are pleased to be able to now advise definitely that shipments will arrive this fall on schedule time from Belgium, unless the German authorities intervene or the progress of the war disrupts the present arrangements.

The plan worked out is that permits are given by the British authorities to individual Belgian shippers, when proof is submitted that the stock is of Belgian origin and production, for Belgian interests, and that the enemies of Great Britian do not get any revenue or benefit from the sales. The proceeds of the sales remain in control of the British authorities so long as the Belgians remain under control of the Germans.

It was largely by reason of the pressure brought to bear on the British authorities by the Belgian shippers that permission was given. The Belgian shippers through their powerful organization—"The Chambre Syndicale des Horticulteurs Belges"—protested direct to the British authorities, and in this protest we understand they were assisted by the British National Organization of Florists.

From our side, protest to the embargo was made through the State Department by the N. Y. Horticultural Importers' Association, assisted by individual importers and backed by the powerful Merchants' Association of N. Y. The combined pressure, strong but just, caused the British authorities to investigate, with the result that Belgian shippers who have secured permits can ship their orders to the United States.

This decision is important to florists who depend largely upon azaleas for their Christmas and Easter sales, but still more so to the Belgian shippers, since the United States is practically the only market left open to them.

McHutchinson & Co.

NEW YORK QUOTATIONS PER 100.　To Dealers Only

MISCELLANEOUS		Last Half of Week ending Aug. 7 1915			First Half of Week beginning Aug. 9 1915		
Cattleyas		30.00	to	50.00	25.00	to	50.00
Lilies, Longiflorum		2.00	to	3.00	2.00	to	3.00
" Rubrum		1.00	to	2.00	1.00	to	2.00
Lily of the Valley		.50	to	2.00	.50	to	2.00
Daises		.....	to	.50	.....	to	.50
Snapdragon		.50	to	1.00	.50	to	1.00
Gladioli		.50	to	1.50	.50	to	1.50
Asters		.25	to	1.00	.25	to	1.00
Sweet Peas		.10	to	.15	.10	to	.15
Corn Flower		.....	to	.25	.....	to	.25
Gardenias		12.00	to	25.00	12.00	to	25.00
Adiantum		.50	to	.75	.50	to	.75
Smilax		6.00	to	12.00	6.00	to	12.00
Asparagus Plumosus, strings (per 100)		15.00	to	35.00	15.00	to	35.00
" & Spren (100 bunches)		10.00	to	10.00	10.00	to	10.00

Buyer's Directory and Ready Reference Guide

Advertisements under this head, one cent a word.   Initials count as words.

Display advertisers in this issue are also listed under this classification without charge. Reference to List of Advertisers will indicate the respective pages.

Buyers failing to find what they want in this list will confer a favor by writing us and we will try to put them in communication with reliable dealers.

ACCOUNTANT
R. J. Dysart, 40 State St., Boston.
For page see List of Advertisers.

APHINE
Aphine Mfg. Co., Madison, N. J.
For page see List of Advertisers.

APHIS PUNK
Nicotine Mfg. Co., St. Louis, Mo.
For page see List of Advertisers.

AUCTION SALES
Elliott Auction Co., New York City.
For page see List of Advertisers.

AZALEAS
P. Ouwerkerk, Hoboken, N. J.
For page see List of Advertisers.

BAY TREES
August Rolker & Sons, New York.
For page see List of Advertisers.

BAY TREES—Standard and Pyramids. All sizes. Price List on demand. JULIUS ROEHRS CO., Rutherford, N. J.

BEDDING PLANTS
A. N. Pierson, Inc., Cromwell, Conn.
For page see List of Advertisers.

BEGONIAS
Julius Roehrs Company, Rutherford, N. J.
For page see List of Advertisers.

R. Vincent, Jr., & Sons Co., White Marsh, Md.
For page see List of Advertisers.

Thomas Roland, Nahant, Mass.
For page see List of Advertisers.

A. M. Davenport, Watertown, Mass.
For page see List of Advertisers.

Begonia Lorraine, $12.00 per 100, $110.00 per 1,000; Begonia Glory of Cincinnati, $15.00 per 100, $140.00 per 1,000. JULIUS ROEHRS CO., Rutherford, N. J.

BOILERS
Kroeschell Bros. Co., Chicago.
For page see List of Advertisers.

King Construction Co., North Tonawanda, N. Y.
"King Ideal" Boiler.
For page see List of Advertisers.

Lord & Burnham Co., New York City.
For page see List of Advertisers.

Hitchings & Co., New York City.

BOXES—CUT FLOWER FOLDING
Edwards Folding Box Co., Philadelphia.
For page see List of Advertisers.

Folding cut flower boxes, the best made. Write for list. HOLTON & HUNKEL CO., Milwaukee, Wis.

BOX TREES
BOX TREES—Standards, Pyramids and Bush. In various sizes. Price List on demand. JULIUS ROEHRS CO., Rutherford, N. J.

BULBS AND TUBERS
J. M. Thorburn & Co., New York City
Wholesale Price List of High Class Bulbs.
For page see List of Advertisers.

Ralph M. Ward & Co., New York City.
Lily Bulbs.
For page see List of Advertisers.

John Lewis Childs, Flowerfield, L. I., N. Y.
For page see List of Advertisers.

August Rolker & Sons, New York City.
Holland and Japan Bulbs.
For page see List of Advertisers.

R. & J. Farquhar & Co., Boston, Mass.
For page see List of Advertisers.

S. S. Skidelsky & Co., Philadelphia, Pa.
For page see List of Advertisers.

Chas. Schwake & Co., New York City.
Horticultural Importers and Exporters.
For page see List of Advertisers.

A. Henderson & Co., Chicago, Ill.

Burnett Bros., 98 Chambers St., New York.
For page see List of Advertisers.

Henry F. Michell Co., Philadelphia, Pa.

Joseph Breck & Sons Corp., Boston, Mass.
Bulbs for Early Forcing.
For page see List of Advertisers.

C. KEUR & SONS, HILLEGOM, Holland. Bulbs of all descriptions. Write for prices. NEW YORK Branch, 8-10 Bridge St.

Fottler, Fiske, Rawson Co., Boston, Mass.

CAMELLIAS
Julius Roehrs Co., Rutherford, N. J.
For page see List of Advertisers.

CANNAS
Canna Specialists.
Send for Canna book.
THE CONARD & JONES COMPANY,
West Grove, Pa.

CARNATION STAPLES
Split carnations quickly, easily and cheaply mended. Pillsbury's Carnation Staple. 1000 for 35c.; 3000 for $1.00 post paid. I. L. PILLSBURY, Galesburg, Ill.

Supreme Carnation Staples, for repairing split carnations, 35c. per 1000; 3000 for $1.00. F. W. WAITE, 85 Belmont Ave., Springfield, Mass.

CARNATIONS
F. Dorner & Sons Co., Lafayette, Ind.
For page see List of Advertisers.

Leo Niessen Co., Philadelphia, Pa.
Field Grown Carnation Plants.
For page see List of Advertisers.

CHRYSANTHEMUMS
Poehlmann Bros. Co., Morton Grove, Ill.
For page see List of Advertisers.

Wood Bros., Fishkill, N. Y.
Chrysanthemums Rooted Cuttings.
For page see List of Advertisers.

Chas. H. Totty, Madison, N. J.
For page see List of Advertisers.

CHRYSANTHEMUMS—Continued
R. Vincent, Jr., & Sons Co., White Marsh, Md.
Pompon Chrysanthemums.
For page see List of Advertisers.

THE BEST 1915 NOVELTIES.
The Cream of 1914 Introductions.
The most popular Commercial and Exhibition kinds; also complete line of Pompons, Singles and Anemones. Trade list on application. ELMER D. SMITH & CO., Adrian, Mich.

COCOANUT FIBRE SOIL
20th Century Plant Food Co., Beverly, Mass.
For page see List of Advertisers.

CYCLAMENS
CYCLAMEN — Separate colors; finest strain; extra strong plants; 3-inch pots, $10.00 per 100, $90.00 per 1,000. JULIUS ROEHRS CO., Rutherford, N. J.

CYCLAMEN—THE BEST STRAINS.
If you want quality, order now.

	100	1000
2½-in., ready for 4-in	$8.00	$75.00
3-in.	12.50	100.00
4-in.	25.00	

Write for copy of
Our Monthly Plant Bulletin.
S. S. PENNOCK-MEEHAN CO.,
1608-20 Ludlow St.,   Philadelphia, Pa.

DAHLIAS
Send for Wholesale List of whole clumps and separate stock; 40,000 clumps for sale. Northboro Dahlia and Gladiolus Gardens, J. L. MOORE, Prop, Northboro, Mass.

NEW PAEONY DAHLIA
John Wanamaker, Newest, Handsomest, Best. New color, new form and new habit of growth. Big stock of best cut-flower varieties. Send list of wants to PEACOCK DAHLIA FARMS, Berlin, N. J.

DECORATIVE PLANTS
Robert Craig Co., Philadelphia, Pa.
For page see List of Advertisers.

Woodrow & Marketos, New York City.
For page see List of Advertisers.

S. S. Skidelsky & Co., Philadelphia, Pa.
For page see List of Advertisers.

Bobbink & Atkins, Rutherford, N. J.
For page see List of Advertisers.

A. Leuthy & Co., Roslindale, Boston, Mass.
For page see List of Advertisers.

DRACAENAS
Julius Roehrs Co., Rutherford, N. J.
For page see List of Advertisers.

FERNS
Henry A. Dreer, Philadelphia, Pa.
Dreer's Fern Flats.
For page see List of Advertisers.

H. H Barrows & Son, Whitman, Mass.
For page see List of Advertisers.

Robert Craig Co., Philadelphia, Pa.
For page see List of Advertisers.

McHutchison & Co., New York City.
Ferns in Flats.
For page see List of Advertisers.

Roman J. Irwin, New York City.
Boston and Whitmani Ferns.
For page see List of Advertisers.

For List of Advertisers See Page 191

FERTILIZERS

20th Century Plant Food Co., Beverly, Mass.
Coconant Fibre Soil.
For page see List of Advertisers.

Stumpp & Walter Co., New York City.
Scotch Soot.
For page see List of Advertisers.

Pulverized Manure Co., Chicago, Ill.
Wizard Brand Cattle Manure.

Hardwood Ashes for sale. GEO. L.
MUNROE & SONS, Oswego, N. Y.

FLORISTS' LETTERS

Boston Florist Letter Co., Boston, Mass.
For page see List of Advertisers.

FLORISTS' SUPPLIES

N. F. McCarthy & Co., Boston, Mass.
For page see List of Advertisers.

Reed & Keller, New York City.
For page see List of Advertisers.

S. S. Pennock-Meehan Co., Philadelphia, Pa.
For page see List of Advertisers.

H. Bayersdorfer & Co., Philadelphia, Pa.
Up-to-Date Summer Novelties.
For page see List of Advertisers.

Welch Bros. Co., Boston, Mass.
For page see List of Advertisers.

FLOWER POTS

W. H. Ernest, Washington, D. C.
For page see List of Advertisers.

A. H. Hews & Co., Inc., Cambridge, Mass.
For page see List of Advertisers.

Hilfinger Bros., Ft. Edward, N. Y.
For page see List of Advertisers.

FOLIAGE PLANTS

A. Leuthy & Co., Roslindale, Boston, Mass.
For page see List of Advertisers.

FUCHSIAS

Fuchsias—Black Prince, Speciosa, double
purple and white. Rooted Cuttings, $1.00
per 100; 2¼-in. $2.00 per 100.
W. J. BARNETT, R. D. 67, Sharon, Pa.

FUNGINE

Aphine Mfg. Co., Madison, N. J.
For page see List of Advertisers.

GALAX

Michigan Cut Flower Co., Detroit, Mich.
For page see List of Advertisers.

GERANIUMS

R. Vincent, Jr., & Sons Co.
White Marsh, Md.
For page see List of Advertisers.

GLADIOLUS

John Lewis Childs. Flowerfield, L. I., N. Y.
For page see List of Advertisers.

GLASS

Sharp, Partridge & Co., Chicago.
For page see List of Advertisers.

Parshelsky Bros., Inc., Brooklyn, N. Y.
For page see List of Advertisers.

Royal Glass Works, New York City.
For page see List of Advertisers.

Greenhouse glass, lowest prices. JOHN-
STON GLASS CO., Hartford City, Ind.

GLASS CUTTERS

Smith & Hemenway Co., New York City.
Red Devil Glass Cutter.
For page see List of Advertisers.

GLAZING POINTS

H. A. Dreer, Philadelphia, Pa.
Peerless Glazing Point.
For page see List of Advertisers.

Geo. H. Angermueller, St., Louis, Mo.
For page see List of Advertisers.

GREENHOUSE BUILDING MATERIAL

King Construction Co., N. Tonawanda, N. Y.
For page see List of Advertisers.

Parshelsky Bros., Inc., Brooklyn, N. Y.
For page see List of Advertisers.

Lord & Burnham Co., New York City.
For page see List of Advertisers.

A. T. Stearns Lumber Co., Neponset,
Boston.
Pecky Cypress.

Metropolitan Material Co., Brooklyn, N. Y.

GREENHOUSE CONSTRUCTION

King Construction Co., N. Tonawanda, N. Y.
For page see List of Advertisers.

Foley Greenhouse Mfg. Co., Chicago, Ill.
For page see List of Advertisers.

Lord & Burnham Co., New York City.
For page see List of Advertisers.

Hitchings & Co., New York City.

A. T. Stearns Lumber Co., Boston, Mass.

Metropolitan Material Co., Brooklyn, N. Y.

GUTTERS

King Construction Co., N. Tonawanda, N. Y.
King Channel Gutter.
For page see List of Advertisers.

Metropolitan Material Co., Brooklyn, N. Y.
Iron Gutters.

HAIL INSURANCE

Florists' Hail Asso. of America.
J. G. Esler, Saddle River, N. J.
For page see List of Advertisers.

HARDY FERNS AND GREEN GOODS

Michigan Cut Flower Exchange, Detroit,
Mich.
For page see List of Advertisers.

Knud Nielsen, Evergreen, Ala.
Natural Green Sheet Moss, Fancy and Dag-
ger Ferns and Huckleberry Foliage.
For page see List of Advertisers.

The Kervan Co., New York.
For page see List of Advertisers.

HARDY PERENNIALS

R. & J. Farquhar & Co., Boston, Mass.
For page see List of Advertisers.

Bay State Nurseries, No. Abington, Mass.
For page see List of Advertisers.

P. Ouwerkerk, Hoboken, N. J.
For page see List of Advertisers.

Palisades Nurseries, Sparkill, N. J.
For page see List of Advertisers.

HEATING APPARATUS

Kroeschell Bros. Co., Chicago.
For page see List of Advertisers.

Lord & Burnham Co., New York City.
For page see List of Advertisers.

HOT-BED SASH

Parshelsky Bros., Inc., Brooklyn, N. Y.
For page see List of Advertisers.

Foley Greenhouse Construction Co.,
Chicago, Ill.
For page see List of Advertisers.

Lord & Burnham Co., New York City.
For page see List of Advertisers.

A. T. Stearns Lumber Co., Neponset, Mass.

HOSE

H. A. Dreer, Philadelphia, Pa.
For page see List of Advertisers.

INSECTICIDES

Aphine Manufacturing Co., Madison, N. J.
Aphine and Fungine.
For page see List of Advertisers.

Nicotine Mfg. Co., St. Louis, Mo.
Aphis Punk and Nikoteen.
For page see List of Advertisers.

Eastern Chemical Co., Boston, Mass.
Imp Soap Spray.
For page see List of Advertisers.

IRIS

R. & J. Farquhar & Co., Boston, Mass.
For page see List of Advertisers.

John Lewis Childs, Inc.,
Flowerfield, L. I., N. Y.
Hardy Lilies.
For page see List of Advertisers.

IRRIGATION EQUIPMENT

Skinner Irrigation Co., Brookline, Mass.
For page see List of Advertisers.

LILACS

White and purple lilacs for fall planting.
Large size to bloom, $2.00 per dozen.
Smaller size 1½ to 2½ ft., $1.00 per dozen.
Common Yellow day lily for massing, $1.00
per 100. C. E. B. Spalding, Schodack-on-
Hudson, N. Y. Spalding Gardens.

LILY BULBS

Chas. Schwake & Co., New York City.
Horticultural Importers and Exporters.
For page see List of Advertisers.

R. M. Ward & Co., New York, N. Y.
Japanese Lily Bulbs of Superior Quality.
For page see List of Advertisers.

Corp. of Chas. F. Meyer, New York City.
Meyer's T. Brand Gigantenms.
For page see List of Advertisers.

John Lewis Childs, Inc.,
Hardy Lilies.
Flowerfield, L. I., N. Y.
For page see List of Advertisers.

LILY OF THE VALLEY

Chas. Schwake & Co., Inc., New York City.
Hohmann's Famous Lily of the Valley Pips.
For page see List of Advertisers.

McHutchison & Co., New York City.
For page see List of Advertisers.

Loechner & Co., New York City.
Lily of the Valley Pips.
For page see List of Advertisers.

LIQUID PUTTY MACHINE

Metropolitan Material Co., Brooklyn, N. Y.
For page see List of Advertisers.

MASTICA

F. O. Pierce Co., New York City.
For page see List of Advertisers.

Geo. H. Angermueller, St. Louis, Mo.
For page see List of Advertisers.

NATIONAL NURSERYMAN

National Nurseryman Publishing Co., Inc.,
Rochester, N. Y.
For page see List of Advertisers.

NIKOTEEN

Nicotine Mfg. Co., St. Louis, Mo.
For page see List of Advertisers.

NIKOTIANA

Aphine Mfg. Co., Madison, N. J.
For page see List of Advertisers.

NURSERY STOCK

P. Ouwerkerk, Weehawken Heights, N. J.
For page see List of Advertisers.

W. & T. Smith Co., Geneva, N. Y.
For page see List of Advertisers.

In writing to Advertisers kindly mention Horticulture

For List of Advertisers See Page 191

New Offers In This Issue

ADVANCE SASH-OPERATING DE-
VICES AND GREENHOUSE
FITTINGS
Advance Co., Richmond, Ind.
For page see List of Advertisers.

BURPEE'S WINTER-FLOWERING
SPENCER SWEET PEAS
W. Atlee Burpee & Co., Philadelphia, Pa.
For page see List of Advertisers.

FREESIA PURITY AND CALLA
BULBS
Santa Cruz Bulb & Plant Co., Santa
Cruz, Cal.
For page see List of Advertisers.

GREENHOUSE CONSTRUCTION
S. Jacobs & Sons, Brooklyn, N. Y.
For page see List of Advertisers.

PLANTLIFE INSECTICIDE.
The Plantlife Co., New York City.
For page see List of Advertisers.

SPECIAL OFFER TO FLORISTS
Skinner Irrigation Co., Brookline, Mass.
For page see List of Advertisers.

In writing to Advertisers kindly mention Horticulture

Coming Events

SHOWS.

Newport, R. I., Aug. 18-19.—Fifth annual exhibition of the American Gladiolus Society.

Atlantic City, N. J., Aug. 26-29.—American Gladiolus Society exhibition.

Lewiston, Me., Aug. 27-28.—Fall exhibition in Lewiston City Hall of Lewiston and Auburn Gardeners' Union. Chas. S. Allen, President, Auburn, Me.; Mrs. Geo. A. Whitney, Secretary, 151 Winter St., Auburn, Me. Meetings first Friday in each month.

Rochester, N. Y., Aug. 30 to Sept. 11.—Rochester Exposition and Flower Show.

Boston, Sept. 11-12.—Dahlia and Fruit Exhibition, Massachusetts Horticultural Society.

Providence, R. I., Sept. 16-17.—September Exhibition, Rhode Island Horticultural Society, Narragansett Hotel.

Hartford, Conn., Sept. 22-23.—Annual Dahlia exhibition of the Connecticut Horticultural Society, Unity Hall, Pratt St. Alfred Dixon, Sec., Wethersfield.

Boston, Oct. 2-3.—October Show Massachusetts Horticultural Society.

Orange, N. J., Oct. 4.—Tenth Annual Dahlia, Fruit, Gladioli and Vegetable Show of N. J. Floricultural Society. Geo. W. Strange, Sec., 84 Jackson St.

Oyster Bay, L. I., N. Y., Oct. 5-6.—Dahlia Show of the Oyster Bay Hort. Society. Chrysanthemum Show, Nov. 2. Andrew R. Kennedy, Westbury, L. I., secretary.

Glen Cove, L. I., Oct. 7.—Dahlia Show of Nassau Co. Hort. Soc. Fall Show of Nassau Co. Hort. Soc. Oct. 28 and 29.

Poughkeepsie, N. Y., Oct. 28-29.—Annual flower show of Duchess County Horticultural Society. N. Harold Cottam, Sec. Wappingers Falls.

Boston, Nov. 4, 5, 6, 7.—Grand Autumn Exhibition, Massachusetts Horticultural Society.

New York, N. Y., Nov. 3, 4, 5.—Annual Chrysanthemum Show of the American Institute, Engineering Societies Building.

Tarrytown, N. Y., Nov. 3-4-5.—Chrysanthemum Show in the Music Hall.

New York, N. Y., Nov. 4-7.—Annual Autumn exhibition of Hort. Soc. of New York, Museum of Natural History.

Chicago, Ill., Nov. 9-14.—Fall Flower Show of the Chicago Florists' Club and Horticultural Society of Chicago, to be held in the Coliseum.

Cleveland, O., Nov. 10-14.—Annual show and meeting of Chrysanthemum Society of America. In conjunction with the Cleveland Flower Show. Chas. W. Johnson, Sec., 2226 Fairfax Ave., Morgan Park, Ill.

Cleveland, O., Nov. 10-14.—Cleveland Flower Show. The only show of national scope in the United States this fall. F. A. Friedley, Sec., 356 Leader Building.

Providence, R. I., Nov. 11-12.—November Exhibition, Rhode Island Horticultural Society, Narragansett Hotel.

MEETINGS.

Twin Cities, St. Paul, Minn., Aug. 24-28.—Annual convention of the Association of American Cemetery Superintendents. Minneapolis and St. Paul. Secretary, Bellett Lawson, Jr., Supt. of Elm Root Cemetery, River Grove, Ill.

Hartford, Conn., Aug 27.—Regular meeting Conn. Horticultural Society, County Bldg., Trumbull St. Alfred Dixon, Sec., Wethersfield.

CONVENTIONS TO BE HELD IN AUGUST IN SAN FRANCISCO.

August 12-14.—Thirteenth Annual Convention: The Pacific Coast Association of Nurserymen. President, John Vallance, 84 Glen avenue, Oakland; secretary-treasurer, C. A. Tonneson, Tacoma, Washington.

August 12-14.—Fifth Annual Meeting: The California Association of Nurserymen. President, Fred H. Howard, Ninth and Olive streets, Los Angeles; secretary-treasurer, Henry W. Kruckeberg, 237 Franklin street, Los Angeles.

August 16.—Nurserymen's Day at the Panama-Pacific International Exposition.

August 17-19.—Annual Meeting: The American Rose Society. President, S. S. Pennock, Philadelphia, Pa.; secretary, Benjamin Hammond, Beacon, N. Y.; treasurer, Harry O. May, Summit, N. J.

August 17-20.—Thirty-first Annual Meeting: Society American Florists and Ornamental Horticulturists. President, Patrick Welch, Boston; vice-president, Daniel MacRorie, San Francisco; secretary, John Young, 53 W. Twenty-Eighth street, New York City; treasurer, W. F. Kasting, Buffalo, N. Y.
The National Association of Gardeners,

President, John W. Everitt, Glen Cove, N. Y.; secretary, M. C. Ebel, Madison, N. J.
The Florists' Telegraph Delivery, President, Irwin Bertermann, Indianapolis, Ind.; secretary, Albert Pochelon, Detroit, Mich.
The Florists' Hail Association of America. President, E. G. Hill, Richmond, Ind.; secretary, John G. Esler, Saddle River, N. J.

August 18-20.—Annual Meeting: The American Association of Park Superintendents. President, G. X. Amrhym, New Haven, Conn.; secretary-treasurer, Roland W Cotterill, Seattle, Wash.

August 22-25.—Thirty - fourth Biennial Session : The American Pomological Society, Berkeley, Cal. President, L. A. Goodman, Kansas City, Mo.; California vice-president, Henry W. Kruckeberg, 237 Franklin street, Los Angeles; executive committee, George C. Roeding, Fresno; secretary, E. R. Lake, 2033 Park Road, N. W., Washington, D. C.

PUBLICATION RECEIVED.

The Principles of Floriculture.—By Edward A. White, Professor of Floriculture in the N. Y. State College of Agriculture at Cornell University, and formerly at the Mass. State College, Amherst. This book is the latest addition to the Rural Text Book Series, edited by Dr. L. H. Bailey and published by The MacMillan Company of New York. The names of Prof. White and Dr. Bailey in connection with it will at once fix the position of this volume in the estimation of our readers. As would be expected, its chapters give abundant evidence of close application and painstaking work in its preparation. There are nineteen chapters comprising no less than 750 distinct topics and filling 454 pages, minutely indexed. There are 52 illustrations and it would seem that every question that could possibly present itself in regard to the cultural needs, the growing and marketing of plants and flowers, both wholesale and retail, the construction and heating of greenhouses, soils, diseases, etc., etc., is fully answered in this really remarkable book. We do not hesitate to assert that it will acceptably meet the needs of the flower growers and to unreservedly recommend it as an indispensable manual. At the very low price of $1.75 it is sure to have a wide sale.

Copies can be supplied from the office of HORTICULTURE.

During Recess

N. Y. Florists' Bowling Club Outing.

President Meissem has appointed the writer, historian of this very enjoyable picnic party. On Wednesday, July 28th on the 1 P. M. Sandy Hook Boat, there assembled the following named gentlemen: John Meissem, Wm. H. Siebrecht, Sr., Wm. P. Ford, H. C. Reidel, Chas. W. Scott, Peter Jacobson, Wm. Duckham, Chas. H. Totty, Roman J. Irwin, and the writer. Each in the best of spirits, weather ideal, the party leaving all cares and prejudices behind, entered into the realm of harmony.

The sale to the Highlands was a perfect tonic. Upon landing, the party entrained for Highland Beach, and was met by Joseph Fenrich with his car and best smile. Joe Fenrich and W. P. Ford had been delegated to work out the plan for the party, and what follows will reveal how well they succeeded.

In two autos we proceeded down along the Jersey Coast, through Seabright, Red Bank, West End, Long Branch, Deal Beach, Allenhurst, Asbury, Ocean Grove, Etc. The writer confesses to inability to adequately describe the beauties of that section of country, its beautiful homes, magnificent and artistic gardens and grounds, also Mr. Fenrich's beautiful home at Bradley Beach, where Mrs. Fenrich and her husband entertained us royally for an hour. Mr. Irwin took a photograph of the party. We next stopped at Lakewood for some very welcome refreshments, then drove around Mr. George Gould's estate, Georgian Court, a veritable dreamland. We continued through real country to Toms River, where more timely refreshments were had, and arrived at Forked River, our destination. After a good dinner we explored the town a bit and made purchases of fishing paraphernalia, etc., and passed the evening playing cards. The next morning found everyone masqueraded, Ford looking like the banker, Siebrecht the rich farmer, Totty and Duckham like lawyers, Scott a miner, Fenrich as healthy as a butcher, Meissem the veteran fisherman. Jacobson, a boat builder, Irwin and Reidel like enthusiastic young fishermen. After breakfast, a stage conveyed us to the boat landing. The Evelyn is a gasoline yacht, constructed for long cruising, well built and comfortable. All hands got busy with their tackle, and soon we reached the fishing grounds, where the weakfish made some more welcome than others, and one humorous incident after another followed. About 100 fish were caught, Scott and Meissem having about 50 per cent of the total catch to their credit.

The first disappointment was the announcement by Messrs. Totty and Duckham, that they were obliged to leave us that evening, so retaining a few of the weakfish for our breakfast, the remainder were duly packed into a basket, and we weepingly escorted the two to the railroad station, and bid them God speed. That evening was spent playing cards and planning for the morrow. Meissem, Scott. Reidel, Siebrecht and Jacobson arose at 3 A. M. to go pickerel fishing in the Forked River. It is very pleasing to note such real enthusiasm and joy, and it is a sign of fine character to be able to transform into a perfect boy now and then. The four men returned in time for breakfast, three of them loaded with fish stories, and one with a real pickerel.

This proved the big day, however. After sailing for twenty miles, we arrived off the Barnegat Light. Trolling for bluefish, only two or at the most three men can have a line, as otherwise the lines would get tangled. The more experienced in the party very willingly gave the others a chance at the sport. When it came the writer's turn to hold the line he was lucky enough to get three with the assistance of others, one being an 8-pounder. Off the Whistling buoy, Reidel distinguished himself by catching two big sea bass at one haul, with rod and reel. All the others caught some bass, fluke, sharks, sea robins, skates, etc. We got seven large bluefish in all. It was a glorious day indeed, a deep and pleasing memory to all. The same autos conveyed us back to Lakewood, and thence we proceeded to Asbury by way of Pt. Pleasant, Sea Girt, Belmar, Avon, Bradley, Ocean Grove and were obliged to part from Mr. Fenrich, who had constantly looked to our comfort with the skill and grace of a perfect host. Almost before we knew it the brakeman called Jersey City, and after crossing the ferry, we parted to go to our homes. Let us hope that next year will find all well, young and enthusiastic, and that we may repeat this most pleasant of all picnic parties.

A. J. Guttman.

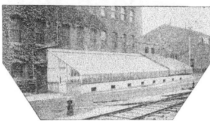

Vol. XXII
No. 8
AUGUST 21
1915

HORTICULTURE

Daniel MacRorie
President-elect Society of American Florists and Ornamental Horticulturists.

CONVENTION NUMBER

LIST OF ADVERTISERS

FOR BUYERS' DIRECTORY AND READY REFERENCE GUIDE
SEE PAGES 262, 263, 264, 265

CARNATIONS

Field Grown — Fine Stock

Matchless, Enchantress Supreme, $8.00 per 100; $70.00 per 1000.

Enchantress, British Triumph, White Wonder, Pink Delight, $7.00 per 100; $60.00 per 1000.

Lady Bountiful, Lady Northcliff, White Winsor, Pink Winsor, $6.00 per 100; $50.00 per 1000. Special rates on large lots.

WOOD BROTHERS
FISHKILL, N. Y.

FERNS IN FLATS
ALL VARIETIES

We ship by express during July and August, stock ready for 2½-inch pots in flats of about 110 clumps, which can be divided.

Price, $2.00 per flat.
20 or more flats, $1.75 each.

Packing included.

Order now while we have full list of Varieties to select from.
Write for Illustrated Folder.

McHUTCHISON & CO.
17 Murray Street,   NEW YORK

POINSETTIAS

JUNE AND JULY DELIVERY

True type, fine plants, packed in paper pots.

Per 100, $5.50; per 1000, $50.00

A. HENDERSON & CO.
Box 158   CHICAGO

LILY BULBS

RALPH M. WARD & CO.
71 MURRAY ST., - NEW YORK

BEGONIAS

CINCINNATI .... $18.00 per 100
LORRAINE .... $14.00 per 100
Good Strong Plants, 2½-inch Pots; Ready for 3½-inch pots.

THOMAS ROLAND, Nahant, Mass.

A. N. Pierson, Inc.
CROMWELL, CONN.

Bedding Plants and Roses

HOLLAND NURSERIES

BEST HARDY RHODODENDRONS, AZALEAS, CONIFERS, CLEMATIS M. F. ROSES, SHRUBS, AND HER BACKOUS PLANTS

P. OUWERKERK, 216 Jane St., Weehawken Heights P. O. No. 1, Hoboken N. J.

When writing to advertisers kindly mention HORTICULTURE.

DARWIN TULIPS

Ariadne. Bright rosy crimson, shaded scarlet, blue base. Very large and fine.
Baronne de la Tonnaye. Carmine rose shaded soft pink. Early forcer.
Clara Butt. Clear pink flushed salmon. Fine late forcer.
Dream. Very fine pale lilac.
Europe. Bright fiery scarlet white base. Very fine.
Gesneriana Lutea. Pure golden yellow. While not a Darwin it is identical in style.
Glow. Bright scarlet with a white base. Good forcer or bedder.
Gretchen. Pale rose ground flushed white. Very fine appearance.
Kate Greenaway. Large perfect pure white, shaded pale lilac.

La Candeur. Almost pure white shaded lilac blush.
Mr. Farncomb Sanders. Brilliant dark rosy red. White base. Very large.
Madam Krelage. Bright lilac rose bordered pale silvery rose.
Massachusetts. Very large perfect formed flower. Bright pink.
Painted Lady. Creamy white, tinged lilac when planted out. Pure white when forced.
Pride of Haarlem. Magnificently formed immense flowers, brilliant deep salmon rose, shaded scarlet, blue base.
Rev. Ewbank. Brilliant heliotrope lilac. Best of its color.
Wm. Copeland. Uniform lilac rose.
Mixed. Well balanced assortment.

$1.00 per 100; $8.00 per 1000.

HYACINTHS

King of the Blues. Blue.   L'Innocence. White.
Grand Maitre. Blue.   Moreno. Fine rose.
La Grandesse. White.   Gertrude. Pale rose

$2.00 per 100; $18.00 per 1000.

SPANISH IRIS

Belle Chinoise. Yellow. | Chrysolora. Yellow.
British Queen. White. | King of Blues. Blue.

$0.50 per 100; $4.00 per 1000.

RAYMOND W. SWETT
Saxonville, Mass.

ELLIOTT
AUCTION COMPANY

Disposes of anything in the way of green goods at their sales at

42 Vesey St., New York

Try us out. Prompt returns

BOBBINK & ATKINS
Nurserymen, Florists and Planters
RUTHERFORD,   NEW JERSEY

BOSTON FERNS 2¼ in. $4.00 per 100, $35 1000.
ROOSEVELT, 3¼ in. $6 per 100, $40 per 1000.
WHITMANI COMPACTA, 3¼ in. $6 per 100, $40 per 1000.
250 at 1000 rates.

H. H. BARROWS & SON, Whitman, Mass.
Palms, Ferns, Decorative and Foliage Plants

Orders taken now for IMPORTED AZALEAS

On hand a splendid stock of Ferns in leading sorts. Also Cocos, Asparagus for Jardinieres.

A. LEUTHY & CO.
Roslindale   Boston, Mass.

CARNATIONS

F. DORNER & SONS CO.
LA FAYETTE, IND.

POT GROWN
STRAWBERRY PLANTS

10 Best Varieties at

$2.50 per 100

WILFRID WHEELER
CONCORD, MASS.

Strawberry Plants

500,000 potted and over two million layer plants in all leading varieties, including Fall Bearers. Write for prices.

T. J. DWYER & CO.
Box 7.   Cornwall, New York

CHARLES H. TOTTY
CHRYSANTHEMUMS
MADISON, N. J.

Boston and Whitmani Ferns

Strong Plants, 4 inch, $20.00 per 100
Strong Plants, 5 inch, 40.00 per 100
Heavy Plants, 6 inch, 50.00 per 100

ROMAN J. IRWIN
108 West 28th St., New York

When writing to advertisers kindly mention HORTICULTURE.

NOTES ON CULTURE OF FLORISTS' STOCK

CONDUCTED BY

John J. M. Farrell

Questions by our readers in line with any of the topics presented on this page will be cordially received and promptly answered by Mr. Farrell. Such communications should invariably be addressed to the office of HORTICULTURE.
"If vain our toil, we ought to blame the culture, not the soil."—*Pope.*

Cyclamen

Now is the time to think of next year's cyclamen. First of all procure the best strains as they pay the best in the end. Do not take mixtures; they will probably contain some good colors but others will be included which no one will want. At the holidays the red shades are always in keen demand and while whites and pinks do not then move so quickly they are salable if grown cool until Easter. Do not omit the salmon pinks; they do not carry as large flowers as some other varieties, but the color is decidedly taking. The first half of September is the best time to make a sowing of cyclamen seeds. If given proper treatment plants started now will prove one of the best investments for the Christmas trade of 1916. Either pans or flats may be used for the soil, but be sure the drainage is good. Cyclamen should always be grown as near the glass as possible, for if the least drawn they lose much of their beauty.

Bouvardias

Many kinds of florist's stock can only be grown to perfection during the warmer season in open field rows. Bouvardias are such, but they are equally as sensitive as other plants to untoward weather conditions such as may now be expected. All bouvardias should be lifted before the nights become too cold. These plants do well in five inches of soil. A good compost is three parts fibrous loam to one of well decayed cow manure. Bouvardias recover slowly after being lifted from the field, unless the job is assigned to careful hands. Though quite resentful in this respect they are in no way particular as to the grade of soil used in potting and in any fair sample of good florists' compost they will do nicely. If this work is attended to properly the plants will show no bad effects. It is easy with almost any temperature to get the first crop of bouvardias but not so easy to get them to make a growth and a profitable crop of flowers in midwinter.

Mignonette

It is now time to sow the main crop of mignonette. To flower well after the new year the seed should be planted before the first of September. When planted later than this they do not move along very fast. They can be sown in 2½ or 3-inch pots. Any house that can be kept at about 45 degrees during the cold weather will suit mignonette. New soil three parts, leaf mold one

part and some sand will be a good compost. Place in a frame and keep shaded until they show signs of coming up, when they should have full sun. They should be kept moist at all times as they will not stand to be allowed to dry out too often. Keep a lookout for the greenworms and fly.

Paper White Narcissus

"Any old soil" for these bulbs is wrong. Use good, sweet soil, have proper drainage in flats and don't plant too closely. The more space between the bulbs the better, for only by so doing can you expect to produce flowers on stiff stems. A deep cold frame is a good place for the bulbs after being planted. Cover the frame with boards or other material to prevent the sun from drying out the flats. By the middle of October the first batch can be brought to the violet house, or anywhere that there is plenty of sunshine and the temperature can be kept down; for the cooler you grow the paperwhites the better for them. Keep them always moist at the roots, for when allowed to dry out they receive a check which will show in the blooms.

Propagating Geraniums

A good plan for growers who have any large stock plants to cut from is making a clean sweep at this time, putting in all the cuttings needed for the coming season's stock, and then done with it. Those having at their disposal but a limited space in greenhouse or garden save a reasonable number of good stock plants from spring sales. Take well-ripened tips, three or four inches long, as short-jointed as possible, cut or break off at or below a node or joint, trim off the lower leaves firmly, insert into sand. It will do no harm to let them wilt. Give one good watering after insertion and keep them a little on the dry side ever afterward. Some growers root their geraniums in two-inch pots, using any kind of good sandy earth, but I have found the regular propagating bed to be the better place for them. If you are short of stock plants you had better start now as you will then be able to get another batch of cuttings in September.

Housing Tender Stock

We are soon coming to the end of August and whatever tender stock you may have out should be in the greenhouse by that time for after the end of this month the nights become too cool for hot-blooded plants. So start early with this work.

Next Week—Bulb Stock for Winter; Carnations; Chrysanthemums; Decorative Plant Stock; Marguerites; Stevia.

HORTICULTURE

VOL. XXII   AUGUST 21, 1915   NO. 8

PUBLISHED WEEKLY BY

HORTICULTURE PUBLISHING CO.
147 Summer Street, Boston, Mass.

Telephone, Oxford 292.

WM. J. STEWART, Editor and Manager.

SUBSCRIPTION RATES:

One Year, in advance, $1.00; To Foreign Countries, $2.00; To Canada, $1.50.

ADVERTISING RATES:

Per inch, 30 inches to page................................. $1.00
Discounts on Contracts for consecutive insertions, as follows:
One month (4 times), 5 per cent.; three months (13 times), 10
per cent.; six months (26 times), 20 per cent.; one year (52 times),
30 per cent.
Page and half page space, special rates on application.

Entered as second-class matter December 8, 1904, at the Post Office at Boston, Mass., under the Act of Congress of March 3, 1879.

CONTENTS   Page

The address by President Welch to the Society of American Florists and Ornamental Horticulturists compares favorably with the best presidential messages of his predecessors. That old worn-out question "What has the S. A. F. done for the profession?" is not only answered by Mr. Welch but he has also given a most forceful presentation of what the Society can do, should do and will do if rightly supported by those who would be the greatest beneficiaries. It is a paper which will read well to the practical man and make a strong appeal to his business judgment, clean-cut and healthy in its sentiments and reflecting the best thought of the leading exponents of organized usefulness. We hope our readers all will do Mr. Welch, and the great association for which he speaks, the honor and justice of a careful reading of his thoughtful message.

The President's Message

The preliminary schedule for the 1916 exhibitions of the Massachusetts Horticultural Society which we publish in this issue mark a quite radical step in the activities of this old but alert organization. The usual Spring Exhibition taking place in March has been reduced in scope and prize appropriations and its importance minimized as compared with a new and very ambitious show to be held in May, at which, in addition to a number of valuable cups and medals, some four thousand dollars in cash prizes will be awarded. One reason for curtailing the March exhibition is the very laudable purpose not to detract from the National Flower Show which is scheduled to take place during that month at Philadelphia or to divert the attention of large exhibitors from that important event. Doubt has been expressed by some as to the practicability of attracting sufficient public support for such an enterprise so late in the spring season but, with commendable courage, the Society has cast the die and will test it out and we hope to see the project heartily seconded and supported by the leading plant and flower growers of the country, all of whom are invited to compete. We commend to all such a careful reading of the schedule the dissemination of which has been hastened in order to give intending exhibitors as much time as possible for preparatory work.

Big May Show for Boston

Taking it for granted that the dominant motive behind the Convention Garden feature of the annual meetings of the S. A. F. is to educate the public and stimulate the desire for a better and more general use of plants and flowers, then the suggestion of President Welch and others that these gardens after having been once established should be made permanent, seems most appropriate and to the point. Under any conditions the job of locating, planting and care of such an undertaking is very far from being a sinecure and if permanency as a cared-for public reservation is to be considered in all cases it will mean plenty of serious business for the newly constituted Convention garden committee. The preparatory work and general layout for an enduring affair which will be creditable to all concerned and accomplish the purpose for which

A point for careful consideration

ROSE GROWING UNDER GLASS

CONDUCTED BY

Arthur C Ruzicka

Questions by our readers in line with any of the topics presented on this page will be cordially received and promptly answered by Mr. Ruzicka. Such communications should invariably be addressed to the office of HORTICULTURE.

Syringing

Syringing will play an important part in the growing of roses from now on, much more important than ever before. Before attempting to syringe make sure that the plants are wet enough, so that the leaves will not burn afterward. We find that it is best to syringe as quickly as possible, with good pressure, holding the hose in front of you, and walking forward instead of backward as has been the custom to do. Then we go over the plants twice, syringing them from one side and then from the other, but very quickly, so as not to wet the benches enough to make much difference in drying out. The benches should not be found soaked after syringing, as by doing the work with a little care the water can be thrown so that most of it will go across the benches into the walks. With Beauties, especially in the earlier planted houses, it will be necessary to shake the plants so that they will be sure to dry off properly for the night. This is more important than may seem, as the houses will dry very little at night now, for with so much rain the air is very damp and dew is heavy. Later when it is cool enough to run steam the houses will dry much better at night, but the days will be shorter, so it will be even more important to have the houses dry for the night. There should be no spider anywhere at this time of the year, and if there is a trace of it, make sure that the place is marked and special care taken to clean it out. If it promises to be bad at all, get some good insecticide and apply it with a brass greenhouse syringe so that it gets well under the leaves where the spiders stay. Applying it with a sprayer will not be as good, as the spray will be too coarse and it will be difficult to reach under the leaves.

Painting

With the heavy showers that came almost daily, painting this year has been almost impossible for a month or so. However, the weather is more promising now, and all hands that can be spared should take the work up in earnest. It does not pay to let the houses go unpainted. Remove as much of the old paint as can be taken off without cutting into the wood, and if the houses have not been painted a long time, better figure on two coats, using the paint thick enough to keep it from running, but no thicker for the first coat. Use pure white lead and raw oil only, avoiding all turpentine or drier, unless a shower threatens or the painting is done in a place where water has to be sprinkled soon after the painting. Then a little drier can be used, but not too much. With the hot weather, there will be no trouble to make the paint dry and it will wear much better if only oil and lead are used. If the houses are painted two coats, let the puttying go until just before the second coat is applied. The first coat will help show up the cracks and then the putty will stick better, for the wood will then be saturated with paint, and will not draw the oil out of the putty, leaving it dry, and ready to fall out much sooner than it should. All houses painted on the inside should also be done on the outside, for if they are not the water will come in and freeze in the winter and thus push and loosen the putty so that the houses will leak again the first season after painting. Aim to have the putty very thin—so thin in fact that it cannot be handled with the hands. It will work into the holes better and then give the wood a chance to take up some oil without leaving the putty dry. To do this a lump of putty can be placed on a piece of glass and then taken off as needed with a putty knife. Avoid using too much white lead in the putty, as this makes it very hard, and although it will stick better it is almost impossible to remove it when repairing broken glass. If plain putty is used with very little white lead, and the houses kept painted, it will last good, and there will be little trouble to remove it should it be necessary to do some repairing. In glazing, keep the glass the bowed side up. There is a theory that if the glass is reversed the water will run down the center of the glass instead of running down along the bar. This does not work however, for the water will not run over the laps, but will condense there until there is enough to push it to the bar, and it will then run down alongside of the bars, no matter which way the glass is turned. In a recent hailstorm the number of lights broken in a house glazed bowed side down was nearly twice as large as the breakage in the house glazed properly. There is always a little spring or give to a glass when placed bowed side up, whereas if placed the other way it breaks with the least pressure. Use good rust-proof zinc points, not the three-cornered things used in glazing house windows, but the special greenhouse brads, for sale by greenhouse builders. Avoid getting paint on your hands. Lead is poisonous and the hands should always be kept clean. There is no excuse for having more paint on your person than on the greenhouse. Men doing considerable painting should be especially careful, as no ill effects are felt until the system is saturated with lead, and then the person will collapse all of a sudden. Put the paint where it should be put, and do not waste it by letting it fly all over.

---

it was created will necessarily be quite a different matter from that of merely making ready for a temporary display to be dismantled at the end of the season. If this attractive proposition is to be incorporated as one of the Society's accepted functions and properly carried out then the necessity for selecting the Convention City two years in advance instead of, as heretofore, one year ahead becomes obvious. We are pleased to see that

President Welch has attached so great importance to this question in his address. The selection of a Convention location will certainly have to be done with much more deliberation and careful investigation than it has been under the hit-or-miss custom in vogue for the past few years, if the installing of a permanent outdoor garden is to become an established feature of every Convention.

SOCIETY OF AMERICAN FLORISTS

AND

ORNAMENTAL HORTICULTURISTS

A Lively and Enthusiastic Convention

Daniel MacRorie Chosen Standard Bearer for 1916

Houston, Texas, Selected as Next Convention City

An Elaborate Reception by the Pacific Coast People to the National Society

OFFICERS ELECTED

PRESIDENT—Daniel MacRorie, San Francisco, Calf.
VICE-PRESIDENT—Robert C. Kerr, Houston, Texas.
TREASURER—William F. Kasting, Buffalo, N. Y.
SECRETARY—John Young, New York City.

OFFICERS FOR 1915.

PRESIDENT, Patrick Welch, Boston, Mass.

VICE-PRESIDENT, D a n i e l MacRorie, San Francisco, Cal.

SECRETARY, John Young, 53 W. 28th street, New York City.

TREASURER, Wm. F. Kasting, Buffalo N. Y.

Executive Committee.

The President, Vice-President, Secretary, Treasurer and junior ex-President, together with the following Directors:

For One Year—Thomas Roland, Na- hant, Mass., August F. Poehlmann, Morton Grove, Ill.

For Two Years—J. J. Hess, Omaha, Neb., J. A. Peterson, Cincinnati, O.

For Three Years—Wm. R. Nicholson, Framingham, Mass., Robert C. Kerr, Houston, Tex.

Additional members of the Executive Board, complying with the amendments adopted at the Boston Convention, to serve one year:

H. H. Bartsch, president Gardeners' and Florists' Club of Boston.

Wallace R. Pierson, president of the American Rose Society.

S. J. Goddard, Framingham, Mass.,

president of the American Carnation Society.

Irwin Bertermann, president of The Florists' Telegraph Delivery.

Harry A. Bunyard, president of the New York Florists' Club.

George Burton, president of the Florists' Club of Philadelphia.

Washington Representative.

W. F. Gude, 1214 F Street, N. W., Washington, D. C.

National Flower Show Committee.

George Asmus, Chairman, Chicago, Ill.; W. N. Rudd, Morgan Park, Ill.; Thomas Roland, Nahant, Mass.; Chas.

EXPOSITION MEMORIAL AUDITORIUM
The Convention and Exhibition Hall of the S. A. F. & O. H. in San Francisco, Cal., Aug. 17-20, 1915.

H. Totty, Madison, N. J.; Adolph Farenwald, Roslyn, Pa.; Wm. P. Craig, Philadelphia, Pa.

1915 Convention Advisory Committee.

Daniel MacRorie, San Francisco, Cal.; H. Plath, San Francisco, Cal.; Angelo J. Rossi, San Francisco, Cal.

Other Officers.

Botanist—Prof. J. F. Cowell,* Buffalo, N. Y.

Pathologist—Prof. H. H. Whetzel, Cornell University, Ithaca, N. Y.

Entomologist—Prof. W. E. Britton, State Entomologist, New Britain, Conn.

Chairman Committee on Sports—Chas. E. Critchell, Cincinnati, O.

S u p e r i n t e n d e n t o f T r a d e Exhibition —John Young, 53 W. 28th St., New York City.

S u p e r i n t e n d e n t of Convention G a r d e n—Daniel MacRorie, 430 Phelan Bldg., San Francisco, Cal.

Sergeant - at - Arms — Daniel Raymond.

* *Deceased.*

Tariff and Legislative Committee.

W. F. Gude, Chairman, Washington, D. C.; James McHutchison, 17 Murray St., New York City; Wm. F. Kasting, Buffalo, N. Y.; Ralph M. Ward, New York City; Julius Roehrs, Rutherford, N. J.; Wm. H. Siebrecht, Jr., Long Island City, N. Y.

Committee on School Gardens.

Benjamin Hammond. Chairman, Beacon, N. Y.; Irwin Bertermann. Indianapolis, Ind.; Gust. X. Amrhyn, Supt. of Parks, New H a v e n. Conn.; Michael Barker, Chicago, Ill.; Leonard Barron, Garden City, N. Y.

On Tuesday morning the proceedings were ushered in with a trip around the Bay on the U. S. revenue cutter Unalga, participated in by visiting and local florists, gardeners, park superintendents a n d others, including many ladies. Refreshments were served on board the boat returning at noon.

OPENING SESSION.

The opening exercises took place in Hall H. east side of the fourth floor of the Civic Center Auditorium. The hall was handsomely decorated with boxwood trees, palms, ferns, asters and garden lilies. Vice-president MacRorie introduced the several speakers, the first item on the program being an address of welcome by Hon. James Rolph, Jr., Mayor of San Francisco. It was an elaborate and graceful speech recounting the city's new birth after the great disaster of earthquake and fire, and voicing a warm welcome to the land of sunshine and bright flowers. He spoke in great praise of the work

of John McLaren who presides over the horticultural interests of the city and had transformed the wilderness of shifting sand dunes to beautiful Golden Gate Park.

Wm. F. Gude responded on behalf of the visitors to the Mayor's words of welcome, acknowledging with deep gratitude the cordial reception received. Mr. Gude, continuing said: "As practical florists, it may be that we appreciate more than the average visitor to your shores, your floriculture and horticulture, and, from the expressions I have heard already, every member here present of our Society has experienced a double pleasure—that of

PATRICK WELCH

President Society of American Florists and Ornamental Horticulturists

the thrill which prevades every citizen, and the practical feeling of the florist when he considers how you have seized on, and multiplied the advantages given you by Nature."

PRESIDENT'S ADDRESS.

President P. Welch received an ovation as he stepped forward to read his address. The message in full was as follows:

Ladies and Gentlemen:

On any occasion the members of this Society, especially those residing east of the Rockies, could have visited this city with pleasure and profit, but at this time when the great Panama-Pa-

cific 'International Exposition is being held here, we deem ourselves most favored.

It is needless for me to say that I am honored as the presiding officer of this great National Society, one of the few in the United States possessing a charter issued under a special act of the National Congress and signed by the President.

This great opening of our Convention proves that we are not an association of New Yorkers, New Englanders, Pennsylvanians or Virginians, but confirms our boast that we are a national association in representation as well as in name.

We should and we do feel proud of our profession for the wonderful progress it has made. According to the last available census—that of 1899-1909—the sale of plants and flowers advanced from 18,-758,864 in 1899 to 34,-872,329 in 1909, an increase of 91 per cent. The total number of establishments i n t h e United States in our business in 1909 was 10,614.

The leading states in value of flowers and plants produced are—New York, $5,110,000; Pennsylvania, $3,761,-000; Illinois, $3,681,000; New Jersey, $2,839,000; Massachusetts, $2,432,-000; Ohio, $2,357,000; California, $1,374,000; I n d i a n a, $1,202,000; Michigan, $1,132,000; Connecticut, $1,042,000.

Membership.

A society gains much of its influence and usefulness from a large membership, and while the Society of American Florists and Ornamental Horticulturists has been adding strength to its membership, I feel we can do much more in that direction. What work can be more pleasant than the gathering together in one great organization of all our business association in this country?

Experience has shown us that what is everybody's business is not attended to by anyone, and so I say, let the increasing of the membership be an individual matter of pride to us all. We all have a high estimate of the benefits derived from membership in our society; let us memorialize it during the coming year by doubling our membership list.

This is an age of co-operation and affiliation and what was formerly advanced individually is now accomplished only by thorough organization. If we are to perform the mission of this society we can only be satisfied when we have joined to its ranks every man engaged in floriculture and horticulture, whether he is doing business in the North, South, East or West of this grand country of ours.

Every state in the Union in which we have members is wisely entitled to a National Vice-President; wisely, I say, because every state has then at least one national officer within its limits. One of the principal duties of the Vice-President is to increase the membership in his state, therefore I urge the Vice-Presidents during this year to conduct active, spirited campaigns for new members in our society. Very few men join an organization such as ours without being invited, and anyone on being informed of the progress which this society has made in the last thirty years will hardly hesitate to become a member when he is invited.

We are proud indeed of the position of our Society today with two thousand members and $30,000 balance in our Treasury, thanks to the wise, discreet and courageous policy displayed by our officers. I feel that with a little effort on the part of our Vice-Presidents especially, our membership can be materially advanced and our usefulness increased accordingly.

The National Flower Show.

For the past six years we have witnessed the success of the National Flower Show and recognized its great value as a medium for educating the public in the love and admiration for horticulture and floral products. It has proved a safe financial enterprise for the society. To insure the continuance of the National Flower Show and in keeping with the ambitions of the society, it is necessary that the best and most efficient members should be placed on that committee.

There is no branch of the work which the S. A. F. has undertaken to put through that calls for co-operation with all other interests as much as the work of the Flower Show Committee— co-operation with the Rose, Carnation, Sweet Pea and Gladiolus Societies, the Private Gardener and all other kindred organizations. What can be accomplished through co-operation in other fields can likewise be accomplished here. All that is required is to emphasize the benefits that are to be derived and the determination to secure them. We have always been successful in securing the aid and support of the horticultural interests in the city where the National Flower Show has taken place and that we must always continue to have, for without it we cannot have a full measure of success.

There is no better agency for horticultural advancement than the one which has for its end a National Flower Show once in two years.

School Gardens.

I am much impressed with the work accomplished in the past by the permanent committee on School Gardens under the leadership of its able and efficient chairman Mr. Benjamin Hammond. This work is of much practical benefit and interest to the boys and girls of this nation, bringing health and strength to growing children. Its installation in school districts throughout the country would bring thrift to many a rising family. The School Garden affords much pleasure and broadens mentality. The training tends to improve home surroundings. A little instruction in this line helps to form habits of thrift and economy. Every member should assist in this work with a hope that it may create an interest in your town or city and be of inestimable value to the future welfare of commercial floriculture.

The Convention Gardens.

Our convention gardens of Minneapolis and Boston have undoubtedly met with the approval of the great majority of our members and the profession in general. Their value from an educational and commercial point of view is recognized by all and the question before us now is: "How can we best continue this important work, in what way and manner can we improve and advance its scope and how can we secure for those gardens permanent existence in the cities where we establish them?"

In the way of advancement it should be made possible to improve upon the plan of the Boston Garden. I should like to see those gardens designed and executed in such a way that they will represent good garden landscape effects, as well as good plant cultivation. It is necessary that all proper planting material and appurtenances known to good garden architecture be employed in the creation of those gardens, where each individual plant or group of plants would be given its proper place in the garden as a whole. This, I realize, cannot be done in one short season and would require not less than two years of planning and execution. To make this possible it would be necessary to select the convention city two years ahead of the meeting in place of one and I want to advance the question at this time, as to why this could not be done.

If the convention garden work can be enlarged upon, along the lines of this suggestion, I believe that the secretary and the local authorities of the convention cities, having the execution of the plans in charge, should have the assistance of a permanent committee of the S. A. F. members consisting of three members well versed and experienced in this work. They shall be appointed by the president, one for three years, one for two years and one for one year. Each president thereafter would make an appointment annually.

In this connection I recommend that after the appointment of this committee the first question they should consider would be an amendment to the constitution providing for the choice of the annual convention city two years in advance. Their recommendation should be submitted to the Executive Board for consideration before being acted upon by the National Convention.

Legislation.

The pioneers in commercial floriculture took conditions as they found them, surmounted difficulties and conquered many obstacles. They did it in their own way without any great assistance from legislation, but that method can no longer go on. We must see to it, that no hostile laws are put upon the statute books. Legislation emanating either from Congress or from any of our State Legislatures, may be helpful, or result in great injury unless prevented by the active work of our legislative committee.

The requirements of this committee call for a reasonable annual appropriation to be used when needed to encourage favorable and prevent hostile legislation. I would recommend that the chairman be given power to secure counsel in Washington or in any of our states, to appear before national or local legislative committees and make known our needs whenever in his judgment this may be necessary.

I would also recommend that our representative in Washington should in the future be given the same privilege that is accorded all other executive members, namely, the right to vote on all questions that may be brought up for adjustment before the Executive Board at the annual meeting. At present he is required to attend all meetings of this Board, but is denied the right to vote which is depriving the society of the benefits that would accrue from the exercise of this privilege by a member whose judgment and experience is of great value to the society.

Co-operation.

The parent society has ever been renowned for her many activities in behalf of advanced horticulture. It has played an important role with patience, zeal and determination, to the end that co-operation between the allied societies should be a fitting and notable achievement. To the committee comprising Messrs. Theodore Wirth, George Asmus and William F. Kastings, we owe a debt of gratitude for their labor, loyalty, unfailing patience and persistence.

The first practical step towards real affiliation with the kindred societies and florists' clubs throughout the country was passed at the last convention in Boston. Under the terms of this amendment the New York, Boston and Philadelphia Florists' Clubs, the Telegraph Delivery Association, the American Rose and Carnation Societies are now represented on the Executive Board by their President. This increase in the Board ought to prove of great value to this society and contribute much toward a liberal policy between the clubs and the parent society.

The wisdom and success of having the various minor organizations made a sectional portion of the S. A. F. & O. H. is no better exemplified than in the instance of the Florists' Telegraph Delivery and the consequent effects upon the parent body. This organization has grown immensely within the past four years. Approximately two hundred and thirty-five firms have joined the Florists' Telegraph Delivery and resultantly members of these firms are also members of our National Society.

The benefits from this important branch of the flower business are not retained by the retailer alone, but are passed on through the various branches to the humblest employee of the grower. This certainly makes it worth while for every retailer of standing to join and receive the benefits of its workings and also to assist the national association which has helped materially in its formation. We ought to make every effort possible to induce other clubs throughout the country to become interested in this movement.

I would recommend that the constitution be amended so that the members before taking their seat in the Executive Board have the consent of the majority of the club or society they represent.

Publicity.

It is needless to point out the value of publicity for the dissemination of proper knowledge and educating the public in the more general use of horticultural products. It is necessary for the society to organize a "Publicity Bureau," whose work would be along the lines of a campaign, directed primarily for the annual increase of the sale of flowers, plants and plant products, through new and varied channels and also to take means to prevent any society, corporation or individual from decrying the use of these products for special occasions. We very often learn of repeated attempts made to discourage the use of our

feel that the results would justify a reasonable expenditure annually for the maintenance of such a committee.

National Credit and Collection Department.

I am forcibly reminded by a large number of the members of our Society of the pressing necessity for creating a national bureau of credits, a central office where credit information can be kept and references obtained. The commercial interests of our business have grown to such an extent during the past fifteen years as to call for a more up-to-date standard of business practice.

There ought not to be any objection to such a movement as it is highly probable that it would do a great deal of good and there is but little danger that it would do any harm. It should, however, be carefully guarded so that it could be used mutually by both

of the country, to consider this subject and report at the meeting of the Executive Board in 1916.

American Products.

There is a constantly growing sentiment in this country among those who have given the subject study that the time has now arrived when a large part if not the whole of the horticultural products which have been grown and imported from Europe should be grown in this country. This is something I have had in mind for some time past.

We should not seek to take advantage of the unfortunate conditions existing in Europe at the present time, and this society will do its part toward helping to maintain the commercial honor of the United States so that we shall emerge from this war period with the love and admiration of all nations concerned.

Our climate, soil and other condi-

| WILLIAM F. KASTING | JOHN YOUNG | ROBERT C. KERR |
| Treasurer Society of American Florists | Secretary Society of American Florists | Director and Vice-President-elect Society of American Florists |

products. Such cases should be taken up by the Publicity Bureau and every means possible taken to offset the effects of such adverse influences.

I am very much in favor of a standing committee of five members whose duty it shall be to co-operate with the retailers, wholesalers and producers so that our business shall be brought before the public in a much more favorable and effective light than it has been in the past.

We should have recourse to the leading daily papers throughout the country, which I believe will gladly publish from time to time articles on Commercial Floriculture. This will have a wonderful effect for it will bring before the American people the merits of our business and the enjoyment derived from the use of our products.

The hour has come when we should give this question our best thought and action. I think greater benefits can be secured from aggressive work of this nature than any we can engage in. I

debtor and creditor. The slightest intimation that a creditor was benefiting to any extent at the expense of the debtor would create dissatisfaction and lead to serious results. The preservation of the rights of commercial life, liberty and the pursuit of trade should be upheld and not interfered with.

It is apparent, however, that ways and means should be considered and adopted by which the financial standing, honesty and integrity of the commercial florists could be measured, determined and circulated among our members to the end that honest, upright, just and creditable business men may be singled out from the unjust and unscrupulous operators. I regard this problem a fundamental one, and believe it should be considered and adopted only after a very careful study.

I would suggest the appointment of a committee of nine members to be elected from the large floral centers

tions are, according to our best authorities well adapted for the growth of palms, bulbs, nursery stock, etc., which now go to make a total of imports of $2,000,000 annually.

I recommend that a permanent committee of three be appointed to study this problem and seek the advice and counsel of the United States Department of Agriculture, and devise ways and means by which those interested in taking up this work which ought to bring about good results, and report annually to the society in convention.

Voting.

Experience has taught us that our present system of electing officers at our annual convention occupies too much time. It is wrong to ask a man to stand in line for half an hour and some times longer before he can cast a ballot for the choice of officers.

As a remedy for this condition I would suggest that a list of the members be alphabetically arranged in four

SOME BUSY MEN AT THE CONVENTION

F. J. BERTRAND
Chairman Hotel Committee

WALTER A. HOFINGHOFF
Chairman Ladies' Entertainment

H. PLATH
Pres. Pacific Coast Hort. Soc. and Chairman of Finance Committee

books:—Book No. 1 to include all names beginning with the letter "A" and ending with the letter "D." Book No. 3 to include all names of members beginning with the letter "E" and ending with the letter "K." Book No. 3 to include all names beginning with the letter "L" and ending with the letter "R." Book No. 4 to include all names beginning with the letter "S" and ending with the letter "Z." It will be necessary that one teller for each book be appointed to check names, also one to receive the ballots.

This calls for an amendment of our by-laws which I hope will be passed and made effective at the opening session of our next annual convention.

Finish.

The trade and commerce in seeds, plants and flowers are of such national magnitude and importance that they are justly classed among the great business interests in this country. There is no more charming art and occupation than the cultivation of flowers, plants and fruit-bearing trees. There is no calling more conducive to human welfare than that of the horticulturist.

Today let us applaud the work of our chosen officers for what they have done in the past but let us make this applause count by seeing that the good work continues. Let us see to it, that the society is built up, its influence increased by the combined efforts and with the co-operation and assistance of all kindred organizations, so that the next generation can look with pride on the work accomplished and take for their motto the inspiring words of Edward Everett Hale "Look up and not down, look out and not in, look forward and not back and lend a hand."

J. R. FOTHERINGHAM
Chairman Reception Committee

E. JAMES
Chairman Advertising Committee

ANGELO J. ROSSI
Chairman Program Committee

REPORTS.

Secretary John Young's report was the next article on the program. It was followed by the report of Treasurer W. F. Kasting and both were appreciatively applauded.

SECRETARY'S REPORT.

Secretary John Young read his annual report, as follows:

At the time of our last convention the florist trade, in common with many other industries, was feeling the effect of conditions brought about by the regrettable war precipitated in Europe, and while these conditions have not improved by any means, we have become somewhat accustomed to them, and we shall congratulate ourselves that business has not been much worse. Some localities have felt the depression more than others, while in other communities business has been near to the normal point. The cut flower section has felt the decline perhaps more keenly than other sections of the business, but preparations for another season have been pushed along in an atmosphere of cheerfulness, with the hope that the business horizon will clear before the end of the year.

Exhibition

Our trade exhibition has suffered this year from causes beyond control. The florists' supply trade has been unable to make the usual showing, for the reason that imported goods are just now a very poor possibility, and our own manufacturers have not had time to adjust themselves to circumstances, at least as far as the production of novelties in various lines is concerned. Distance, and cost of transportation to San Francisco are other factors which have tended to cut down our exhibits. Notwithstanding, our trade exhibition is this year most creditable, and the interest in has provoked quite as strong as at previous conventions.

Membership.

The bulk of our increase in membership is provided by California and the Pacific coast states. While it is not unusual for the Society to experience a large influx of members from a convention city and nearby territory, the business standing of those initiated this year is extraordinarily high in the aggregate, and your secretary hopes this means that the names of these new members will long remain on our membership roll, reminding us that their interest in the society and its work was not merely of a "passing" character.

The following have sent in one or more names for membership since the last convention:

Daniel MacRorie, 102; Florists' Telegraph Delivery, 24; J. F. Hahmann, 15; E. T. Mische, 11; W. R. Nicholson, 5; J. J. Hess, 3; Patrick Welch, J. F. Huss, F. H. Holton, Florists' Hail Asso., Harry S. Betz, 2 each; J. W. Duncan, 3; J. H. Dick, L. M. Gage, A. Farenwald, 1 each.

We have lost through death:

P. R. Quinlan, August 27, 1914; Peter Bohlender, September 8, 1914; W. L. Palinsky, October 10, 1914; Godfrey Aschmann, October 28, 1914; J. B. Steussy, September 2, 1914; D. Y. Mellis, November 21, 1914; John Monson, December 29, 1914; Richard Groves, January 30, 1915; Wm. B. Pat-

terson, March 16, 1915; H. Frank Darrow, February 21, 1915; John Zech, April 29, 1915; Professor J. F. Cowell, May 1, 1915; Simon Rodh, April 19, 1915; E. J. Welch, Jr., May 17, 1915; Chas. F. Krueger, June 4, 1915; Samuel Thorne, July 4, 1915.

Plant Registration.

The following plants have been registered:

No. 612—Nov. 7, 1914. Begonia Mrs. J. A. Peterson, by J. A. Peterson, Cincinnati, O.

No. 613—Nov. 28, 1914. Geranium La Favorite X Detroit, by Charles Borrmann, Buffalo, N. Y.

No. 614—Dec. 5, 1914. Canna Pocabontas (Bronze Olympic), by Conard & Jones Co., West Grove, Pa.

No. 615—Dec. 5, 1914. Canna Flag of Truce, by Conard & Jones Co., West Grove, Pa.

No. 616—Dec. 5, 1914. Canna Dragon, by Conard & Jones Co., West Grove, Pa.

V. PODESTA
Chairman Sports Committee

No. 617—Dec. 5, 1914. Canna Princeton, by Conard & Jones Co., West Grove, Pa.

No. 618—Dec. 5, 1914. Canna Gaiety, by Conard & Jones Co., West Grove, Pa.

No. 619—Dec. 26, 1914. Asparagus hybrida gracilis, by F. W. Fletcher, Auburndale, Mass.

No. 620—Feb. 13, 1915. Carnation Mrs. R. E. Loeben, by R. E. Loeben. Gloversville, N. Y.

No. 621—Feb. 13, 1915. Salvia Red Cross, by the Swiss Floral Co., Portland, O.

No. 622—May 15, 1915. Canna City of Portland, by Conard & Jones Co., West Grove, Pa.

No. 623—June 22, 1915. Violet Anne Evans, by Frank D. Pelicano, San Francisco, Cal.

No. 624—June 22, 1915. Violet Quaker Lady, by Frank D. Pelicano, San Francisco, Cal.

No. 625—July 31, 1915. Coleus Yellow Trailing Queen, by Oak Grove Greenhouses. Tuskagee, Ala.

No. 626—July 31, 1915. Daisy Mrs.

G. H. Selfridge, by A. T. Pyfer & Co., Chicago, Ill.

No. 627—July 31, 1915. Rose Mrs. Bayard Thayer, by The Waban Rose Conservatories, Natick. Mass.

No. 628—July 31, 1915. Rose Mrs. Moorfield Storey, by Waban Rose Conservatories, Natick, Mass.

Secretary's Financial Statement, Jan. 1 to June 30, 1915.

Dues, 1913.	5 at $3.00	....	$ 15.00
Dues, 1914.	20 at 3.00	....	60.00
Dues, 1915.	678 at 3.00	....	2,034.00
Dues, 1916.	1 at 3.00	....	3.00
Fees and dues, new members. 100 at $5.00		....	500.00
Life members. 18 at $25.00		....	450.00
A. T. Boddington. Account Convention Garden (1914)		....	$0.00
Account Trade Exhibition Boston Convention (1914)		....	30.00
Interest, etc.			
Tri-State Loan & Trust Co.—Account Dunkelberg Mortgage		....	125.00
Tri-State Loan & Trust Co.		....	37.50
			$3,344.50

Remitted to Wm. F. Kasting, treasurer:

General fund	....	$2,627.00
Permanent fund	....	612.50
Cash on hand	....	105.00
		$3,344.50

TREASURER'S REPORT.

The report of Treasurer W. F. Kasting was next presented, showing the total receipts and disbursements for the year 1914 and the balances of the several funds:

Permanent Fund.

Jan. 1 to Dec. 31, 1914.		
Balances per report	....	$15,704.03
Cash received as follows:		
From interest	....	1,161.16
From life members	....	950.00
		$17,815.19

General Fund.

Jan. 1 to Dec. 31, 1914.		
Balance as per report	....	$13,386.74
Cash received as follows:		
From dues and members	....	4,621.00
From exhibitions	....	5,393.85
From sale of buttons	....	101.25
		$23,502.84

Jan. 1 to Dec. 31, 1914.		
Cash disbursed as per Treasurer's report	....	9,330.36
Less amount refunded	....	203.99
		$14,376.48

Special Fund.

Jan. 1 to Dec. 31, 1914.		
Balance as per report	....	$ 1,527.80
Received from interest	....	62.02
Total	....	$33,781.49

The foregoing funds are invested as follows:

Permanent Fund.

Dunkelberg Bond and Mortgage	$ 5,000.00
City & Surburban Realty Co.	1,500.00
Germania Saving Bank, Pittsburgh, Pa.	726.00
Peoples Bank, Buffalo, N. Y.	6,455.31
American Savings Bank	3,918.97
	$17,590.28

General Fund.

American Savings Bank, Buffalo, N. Y.	4,896.83
German American Bank, Buffalo, N. Y.	3,436.48
Peoples Bank, Savings Account, Buffalo, N. Y.	3,305.60
Peoples Bank, Checking Account.	2,989.22
Less outstanding checks	16.85
	$14,611.30

Special Fund.

Manufacturers & Traders National Bank	1,569.82
Total	....	$33,781.49

TREASURER'S SEMI-ANNUAL REPORT.

January 1st, to July 30th, 1915.

Jan. 1, '15—Balance in Permanent Fund	$17,815.19
Receipts to July 30	1,192.31
Balance in Permanent Fund	$19,007.50
Jan. 1, '15—Balance in General Fund	$14,376.48
Receipts to July 30	2,732.00
	$17,108.48
Disbursements to July 29th	5,347.28
Balance in General Fund	$11,761.20
Jan. 1, '15—Balance in Special Fund	$1,589.82
Interest	31.94
Balance in Special Fund	$1,621.76
Total Balance	$32,390.46

..Invested. as follows:

Permanent Fund.

Dunkelberg Bond & Mortgage, Fort Wayne, Ind	$5,000.00
City & Suburban Realty Co., Fort Wayne, Ind	1,500.00
Germania Savings Bank, Pittsburg, Pa.	740.52
American Savings Bank, Buffalo, N. Y.	4,250.52
Peoples' Bank, Buffalo, N. Y.	6,496.46
Bankers' Trust Co., Buffalo, N. Y.	1,020.00
	$19,007.50

General Fund.

American Savings Bank, Buffalo N. Y.	$4,843.56
German-American Bank, Buffalo, N. Y.	3,505.54
Peoples' Bank (Savings account), Buffalo, N. Y.	3,270.08
Peoples' Bank (Checking account), Buffalo, N. Y.	142.02
	$11,761.20

Special Fund.

Manufacturers' and Traders' Bank, Buffalo, N. Y.	$1,621.76
	$32,390.46

Bond and Mortgage at 5% interest.
Pittsburg & Buffalo Savings Banks at 4% interest.
Peoples' Bank on Savings account, 4% interest.
Peoples' Bank on Checking account, 3% interest on quarterly balances.

Respectfully submitted,
W. F. KASTING, Treasurer.

The report of the Legislative Committee given by W. F. Gude created much interest. The committee was continued with power to combat the harmful legislation complained of, especially that requiring inspection of low pressure small capacity greenhouse boilers and requiring licensed engineers to operate them. President Welch recounted the success achieved by the Massachusetts florists in killing proposed legislation of this character in that state as applied to horticulturists. The report of the committee follows.

REPORT OF COMMITTEE ON LAW AND LEGISLATION.

Your committee had but two propositions referred to it during the past year. One of these propositions was brought up by J. A. Petersen of Cincinnati, Ohio, who complained of the classifications of express rates in reference to plants shipped in pots and plants shipped out of pots, insisting that there should be a lower rating on plants shipped in pots or tubs. The matter was promptly taken up with the Interstate Commerce Commission, and the Commission, in turn, corresponded with the several transportation companies, requesting an expression of their views. After receiving all the data that could be reasonably obtained, including copies of the correspondence between the Interstate Commerce Commission and the express companies, your committee reached the conclusion that, as the express companies seemed to be losing money on the present rates, it was an inopportune time to attempt to bring about a reduction of our rates. In other words, your committee felt that it would be the part of wisdom to "let well enough alone," and that an agitation of this matter at that time might result in our rates being raised, rather than lowered, under the authority given the Interstate Commerce Commission by Congress, in March last, to revise or change the express rates.

Subsequently, your committee received notice from the Interstate Commerce Commission that a hearing would be given on the question of express rates, May 26, 1915. Feeling that the florists should be represented, your committee had A. Leftwich Sinclair, an attorney, appear at this hearing, as counsel for our Society. In his reports, attached hereto, Mr. Sinclair explains the purpose and scope of the hearings attended by him and points out the procedure which will have to be followed, if our Society wishes to obtain a formal hearing on the question of the rating of plants. Mr. Sinclair also suggests that, before filing the necessary petition with the Interstate Commerce Commission, our Society should arrange for a conference with the representatives of the various express companies with a view to an amicable adjustment of this matter.

The other question referred to your committee relates to legislation concerning boiler inspection. It appears that, from time to time, numerous bills are introduced in the state legislatures to require the inspection and regulation of boilers. It has been suggested that, within the next year or so, there will probably be a large number of bills of this character introduced in the state legislatures, and that our Society should provide machinery by which we can resist the passage of legislation which would work a hardship on our industry. As illustrating the vicious character of some of these bills, your committee is informed that, only a short time ago, there was introduced in the legislature of the State of Pennsylvania a bill requiring every owner of a low pressure heating boiler to pay $5.00 a year for the inspection of that boiler, if his boiler should be over four feet of grate area and carry over ten pounds of pressure. Had that bill passed, every florist in the State of Pennsylvania would have been obliged to pay to that state the sum of $5.00 a year, or more, depending on the number of boilers in use.

Your committee is also informed that there are statutes in force in several of the states which provide that every steam boiler carrying over ten pounds of steam pressure must be in charge of a licensed engineer, and that a movement is on foot looking to the enactment of similar laws throughout the country.

All such propositions, in the opinion of your committee, should be fought by our society with all the force at its command. It is, therefore, recommended that the scope of your committee be enlarged, without delay, so that the committee can keep in touch with proceeding of the State Legislature, as well as those of Congress, and be prepared to resist the passage of all bills found to be detrimental to the members of our society.

If the foregoing recommendation of your committee is adopted, your committee should be authorized to arrange for a reporting service of some kind, and to employ counsel to represent the society, whenever, in the judgment of your committee the services of counsel are required.

Mr. Gude presented an addenda to the foregoing report stating that most important action the committee had been called on to take referred to fall shipments of azaleas and other Belgian plants at present under embargo by British authority, which, being exclusively of Belgian origin and production and the enemies of Great Britain getting no revenue or benefit from their sale, the embargo while not helping British would work considerable harm to both Belgian shippers and American importing florists. The U. S. trade advisors had informed committee how to proceed in the matter of securing permits for the importation of azaleas, etc., from British authorities and the committee has good reason for believing that these shipments will arrive this fall on schedule time. Definite information will be given in the trade papers as soon as an official decision is rendered by the British authorities.

(A favorable decision on this matter was published in HORTICULTURE for August 14—Ed.)

The report of Mr. Gude as Washington representative of the S. A. F. follows in full.

REPORT OF WASHINGTON REPRESENTATIVE, WM. F. GUDE.

The past year has been one of watchful waiting rather than strenuous action in the National Capital, so far as the interests of our Society are concerned. The demands on your representative there have not been excessive, from which I assume that the florists of our country have no fault to find with the laws enacted by Congress during the year.

In the early part of the winter a communication was received by your representative in which objection was raised to the classification of express rates on potted plants and plants not in pots. Another communication was received, in relation to bills introduced in the State Legislatures, providing for the inspection and regulation of steam boilers. Both of these communications were referred to the Committee on Legislation and will, doubtless, be dealt with by that committee in its annual report.

The most important event of the year, both locally and nationally, was the formal dedication of the Rose Gardens, at Arlington Farms, on June 2nd, 1915. Some fifty odd florists came from different cities, as far away as Boston, to be present at the ceremonies. A meeting of the American Rose Society was called in the rooms of the American Institute of Banking, where the party met on the date mentioned. After this meeting, they went in automobiles to the Arlington Farms, three miles away, in a downpour of rain. While the Gardens were in full bloom and showed up well, the drenching rain storm, which had lasted three days, had a very depressing effect on the general beauty of the Gardens. After viewing the Gardens, the party returned to the city, where the formal dedication took place and interesting addresses were made by officers of the National Government, the President of the Rose Society, and others.

After the dedicatory exercises had been concluded, the party went by automobiles to Twin Oaks, the home of Mrs. Charles J. Bell, daughter of the late Mrs. Gardner G. Hubbard, donor of the Gardner Hubbard Memorial Medal. Mrs. Bell had extended a kind invitation to the party to inspect her rose gardens. The party was most cordially received by Mrs. Bell and an

Other reports were presented, including the minutes of the Executive Board meeting last winter. Reports of State Vice Presidents were not read but ordered printed as usual.

MEETING PLACE FOR 1916.

Invitations were extended for Houston, Texas, championed by W. W. Coles of Kokomo, Ind., and backed by telegrams from various officials and the Florists' Club of that city; from New York, presented by A. T. Delamare, representing the N. Y. Florists club and several business organizations; by William Allen seconded by R. M. Ward and others for New Orleans, La. After considerable spicy oratory nominations

Francis Hotel. The result gave Houston, Texas, 105 votes, New York 28 votes and New Orleans 12 votes. Houston was accordingly declared winner amidst much cheering.

PRESIDENT'S RECEPTION.

The President's Reception, in all cases one of the most popular of the convention features, was held according to program in the St. Francis Hotel. President and Mrs. Welch were assisted in receiving by a brilliant line of local and visiting society officials and others. There was music, dancing and refreshments, and the affair will go down into history as a most delightful success.

THE CONVENTION CITY
A Vista Looking North Through the Court of Four Seasons Toward San Francisco Bay.

hour and a half was pleasantly and profitably spent at her beautiful home. The affair was voted a big success and one of the most interesting events in the annals of floriculture and horticulture.

I am pleased to state that the pride taken in the S. A. F. and O. H. by the florists of the National Capital, is surpassed by no other city in the Union, and is attested by the presence here today of nearly a dozen members of this Society, from Washington, three thousand miles away.

With hearty greetings and best wishes to all, I remain, as ever,

Yours for service,

WM. F. GUDE.

closed on Houston, New York and New Orleans.

President Welch made the following appointments: J. G. Esler, judge of election; H. Plath and Dan Raymond, tellers. Committee on president's address, George Asmus, Henry Kruckeberg, Ed J. Fancourt, C. W. Ward, H. Plath. Judges of trade exhibition, Frank Pelicano, Albert Stein, W. F. Judges of convention garden, Theodore Wirth, John Pilkington, John Morley, William Hertrieb.

TUESDAY EVENING SESSION.
Houston Wins.

Balloting for choice of convention city for 1916 took place at the St.

WEDNESDAY'S SESSION.

The first business following the formal announcement of the result of the ballot for next Convention City was the presentation of the report of the National Flower Show Committee by George Asmus, chairman.

REPORT OF THE NATIONAL FLOW-
ER SHOW COMMITTEE.
By Chairman George Asmus.

Since making my last report to the Convention in Boston a year ago, matters pertaining to the Show in Philadelphia next spring have progressed rapidly and favorably. At a meeting held in Philadelphia last November the general local organization work was drafted and chairmen of committees carefully selected. They are as follows:

Committee on Press, Publicity and Advertising, W. F. Therkildson; Securing Exhibits. William Kleinheinz; Decorations, John Habermehl; Special Premiums, Wm. P. Craig; Special Features, Chas. Grakelow; Lease and Contracts, A. Farenwald; Music, Leo Niessen; Printing, S. S. Pennock; Concessions. Henry F. Michell; Trade Tickets, E. J. Fancourt; Lectures, J. Otto Thilow; Bureau of Information, Frederick Cowperthwaite; Secretary and Treasurer, A. A. Niessen; Committee-at-Large, George Burton, Louis Burk, Robert Craig.

These gentlemen appointed from among the craft in Philadelphia, others to serve on these committees. The chairmen of these committees form what is known as a Local Executive Committee to carry out in detail the work of the show. Such committees have met from time to time, about once a month, and are enthusiastic about the coming exhibition. Through the generosity of H. F. Michell Co. and H. A. Dreer the grass plots in front of the big Convention Hall, where the show is to be held, have been tastefully planted and serve as a beautiful advance guard of what will happen in the near future in the building. There recently appeared in the Philadelphia Record about a half page, showing the building, in front and grounds, as treated by the above mentioned firms. This shows the good work that is being done by the Publicity Bureau of which Mr. Therkildson is the head.

I also wish to mention the good work of Mr. Farenwald and the Committee on Lease and Contracts. By their earnest efforts the rental for this mammoth building has been secured at the low rate of $100 per day. We have been able to secure the co-operation of the American Carnation Society, this being the 25th year since the organization of that Society, the same to be celebrated by a silver jubilee to be held at Philadelphia in connection with the show. Their premium list has been prepared by them and, underwritten by the Society, will be published in the next edition of the "Premium List" which will go out some time this fall. By this time The American Rose Society will have their list completed and same will also be a part of the next schedule.

The plant growers, of whom there are so many in the vicinity of Philadelphia, are already making preparations. The Pennsylvania Horticultural Society have joined hands and have appointed a committee of three to work in conjunction and act as part of the Local Executive Committee. The guaranteed funds of $10,000 has been completed and contains the usual country-wide list of guarantors. William P. Craig, Chairman of Committee on Special Premiums, reports a very large list of donors and expects to more than double what he now has in the near future.

The size of the building, which will enable all of the show to be on one floor, should work out very favorably, and then the large balcony with its great seating capacity will prove to be a feature of the show that will appeal to the public as there seems to be a delight to sit among the flowers and

listen to the music. The installation of heat for the building has been cared for and will be installed at a very normal cost. The total premium list, as offered, is $15,000, the largest sum ever offered in this country at a flower show.

I will conclude my report by saying that in my estimation the coming exhibition in Philadelphia will, from all standpoints eclipse anything ever before attempted in this country, and I have no doubts about the financial success. This annual Convention of the Society not being held in the east this year or next will no doubt help to sell space at the National Flower Show, as the records of previous exhibitions show that the attendance by the trade at the past exhibitions have been greater than at the convention and it is at a season of the year when the buyer is usually in the market for his spring or Easter business.

Secretary Young stated that all prospects are favorable and he can see a bright augury for the National Flower Show in the whole-hearted cooperation which is assured in Philadelphia. A ladies' organization has been started in Philadelphia and preliminaries are developing satisfactorily in all respects.

COMMITTEE ON PRESIDENT'S ADDRESS.

The committee on President's address made a well-considered report favorably endorsing all the recommendations made by President Welch. They recommended the appointment of a special committee to draft proposed amendments to the Constitution for submission to the executive board and on their approval to be voted on at the next Convention, covering the president's views as to the selection of the Convention City two years in advance, the employment of counsel to assist the legislative committee, making the Washington representative an ex-officio member of the executive board, providing that directors be elected instead of appointed and that executive board members from affiliated organizations shall furnish credentials of their election. The president's publicity recommendation was endorsed and adopted, also his recommendation as to a committee of nine to consider how best to handle national credits and collections, but the committee to incur no expense and report to the executive board. This recommendation was adopted after a very full and interesting discussion generally participated in, the consensus of opinion being that this matter requires careful handling because it treads dangerous ground and probably would be best if conducted by some affiliated body not directly involving the parent organization. The recommendation to improve voting methods was also endorsed and referred to a special committee to draft the proper constitutional amendment. The general acceptance of the president's recommendations was a signal recognition of his ability, zeal and devotion which fact the committee in concluding its report called attention to.

NOMINATION OF OFFICERS.

Vice-President Daniel MacRorie was unanimously nominated for the presi-

dency, the nomination being made by W. F. Gude and seconded by H. W. Kruckeberg. W. W. Coles nominated and J. J. Hess seconded Robert C. Kerr of Houston, Texas, for vice-president and George Asmus nominated W. F. Kasting for treasurer, no other candidates being presented for either of these offices. For the position of secretary John Young was nominated by J. A. Peterson, seconded by W. W. Coles, and John R. Fotheringham by D. Raymond, seconded by H. A. Hyde.

VARIOUS MATTERS.

Robert Pyle moved resolutions of sympathy to Edwin Lonsdale, now in the hospital at Los Angeles, which were carried unanimously by a rising vote. Benjamin Hammond moved a similar resolution to Wallace R. Pierson in the hospital in San Francisco, which was seconded by J. J. Hess and carried by an unanimous rising vote. W. F. Kasting moved resolutions on the death of Prof. J. F. Cowell, Botanist of the Society to be formulated by a special committee and chair appointed E. G. Hill, Theo. Wirth and George Asmus to report on Thursday. Ex-President Wirth presented an invitation from the Association of Park Superintendents to attend a stereopticon lecture by Hon. Sam'l B. Hill, president of the Columbia Highway Association, and the invitation was accepted for Wednesday afternoon. Consequently the business scheduled for Wednesday afternoon was proceeded with at the forenoon session—viz., the discussion, "Are Not Insurance Rates on Modern Greenhouse Establishments Too High, in view of the lighter risks accruing from better and less dangerous construction?" led by Wm. F. Kasting, and the report of the committee on National Publicity by Irwin Bertermann, chairman. Mr. Bertermann's report, which follows, was referred to the executive committee to be treated in line with previous action on President's recommendations.

REPORT OF COMMITTEE ON PUBLICITY.

National publicity, a much talked of problem hard to solve, yet with wonderful possibilities and a great future, particularly in the field of the florists' profession.

As a sequence to the talk of Mr. Philip Breitmeyer during the Executive Board meeting at Chicago, March 2, our president appointed the following gentlemen, George Burton, Irwin Bertermann and W. F. Kasting as a committee to deal with the problem. Little has been done further than making the following report which we trust may have a stimulating effect in an undertaking the National Society stands much in need of.

Large appropriations for the furtherance of publicity throughout the land are impractical from a financial standpoint and unless carefully safeguarded and given detail attention, there is so much liability that a large percentage of the same be wasted.

Advertising experts of the larger cities have in several instances made suggestions to prominent members of the S. A. F. in regard to national publicity. In the main, their ideas were practical and would no doubt bring results, but it was also very evident that the cost of the same was at no time in accord with the measure of direct returns receivable by the florist fraternity. In fact, one prominent expert had it that $25,000 would be a very reasonable sum with which to start in the city of New York. This, of course sounds well and no doubt would be of immense value, but at the same time it would be impossible to carry such a project forward through the country.

One of the self-evident features that has brought itself clearly to the front in the past few years is the following: that the great national flower shows given in larger centers, the extensive advertising campaigns of the larger individual firms of the country and the national publicity campaign of the Florists' Telegraph Delivery show that there is a great wealth of strength in the S. A. F. and O. H. itself; that we have a strong advertising feature to stand on within our organization.

There are approximately two thousand of the better florists throughout the country closely united, willing and only whiting the proper call to send forth the proper issues before the public. It is true that one florist hasn't the strength in the smallest fraction of a large newspaper, but one individual florist has within himself the power to carry forward a campaign which will interest thousands of people. The florists of a large city like Chicago alone, if properly united on a single subject can place the same before its immense population. This is shown in the newspaper features of united florist advertising in Detroit, Cleveland and Philadelphia newspapers.

It is the firm belief of this committee that if any special line of advertising be taken up and set before the members of this organization in the proper manner, the advertising will be carried throughout the breadth of the country and the expense from the parent source be entirely within the reasonable bounds to be expected.

A few hundred dollars expended by this organization, or obtained collectively from individuals, in properly placing an outline before its members and in aiding them to carry it out will within a reasonable time make its appearance as a national message to the flower buying public. This has been clearly demonstrated through the efforts of the Florists' Telegraph Delivery, each individual member using feature advertising on his letter heads, on a majority of one million folders or in his advertising space in newspapers and periodicals. This same plan can easily be carried forward as there is not a member who is not willing to aid the parent association and himself in such a manner. The sum of money expended at the start whether it be one thousand dollars or five thousand dollars, will easily return to the source in the way of strength and influence or in membership itself, for every one connected will be pleased with the results and satisfied with the good accomplished.

We say confidently that if the Society of American florists wants its members to sell a particular flower next Christmas or if it wants a certain line featured or if it has any publicity of any special nature in mind, it can safely do so through its membership and at a cost that is less than one-twentieth of what would be

charged by any professionals who are interested in doing the work without the aid of two thousand florists themselves. It did not take long for Madame Russell rose to be known generally—Why? Because thousands of florists boosted it. Neither would it take long for any worthy publicity to reach the public if handled along the same lines.

The coming great Philadelphia show will in itself add a stimulus to the local flower business and with an advertising secretary of the S. A. F. acting with its members themselves, publicity space could be procured for a few dollars that could not be had for a larger sum in a direct manner. Many new, also immensely worthy exhibits will be shown there and great good will come to this organization and financial benefit to the trade if this be used as a small instance, by every florist in his dealing with the public.

A telegram of greetings and congratulations from J. C. Vaughan was read. Vice-President MacRorie announced that on Friday morning at 10 o'clock the Exposition authorities would present a placque to the S. A. F., this to be followed by an address by C. W. Ward of Eureka. The lecture on Wednesday afternoon was much enjoyed by all who attended. It presented magnificent views of road building, mountain scenery and wonderful light effects well worth the trip to the Coast.

THURSDAY'S SESSION.

At the opening of the session Mr. Fotheringham asked to have his name as candidate for secretary withdrawn and that John Young be unanimously elected. This was agreed to and there being no contest for any office all the candidates on the ticket were elected by unanimous vote. A query from the question box as to the best way to increase the supply of carnations for Mother's Day was spiritedly discussed by many members. C. W. Ward extended an invitation to visit with him the redwood forest which it is proposed be set aside for bird protection. R. Vincent, Jr., invited all to visit the Dahlia Show in New York next September. John McLaren and Hans Plath, being called upon, addressed the Convention in words of compliment and good fellowship. President Welch responded appreciatively and several other members spoke, including Robert Pyle who urged the advisability of systematic effort to produce in this country new roses and other plants so as to become independent of Europe.

JUDGES' REPORT

The judges of the trade exhibits reported recommending a gold medal to R. Diener, for improved gladioli; bronze medal and certificate of merit to H. Bayersdorfer & Co., for their elaborate and instructive display of new and novel baskets and supplies; honorable mention to M. Rice Co., for florists' accessories and novelties; highly commending exhibit of A. L. Randall Co.; certificate of merit to S. S. Pennock Meehan Co., for novel ribbons and baskets; bronze medal to Domoto Bros. for new double hydrangea; certificate of merit to ¡The Ferneries for ferns and palms; bohor-

able mention to H. J. Kessel for new ferns; certificate of merit to Superior Nursery Co., for ferns; certificate of merit to Advance Co., for ventilating apparatus and greenhouse accessories; silver medal to J. A. Peterson for new Begonia Mrs. J. A. Peterson; bronze medals to John A. Evans Co., for detachable pipe hangers, Mrs. F. J. Reidy for dahlias and Herbert & Fleishauer for fine asters; honorable mention to Swiss Floral Co., for rare petunias.

Obituary resolutions on Prof. J. F. Cowell were adopted. Speeches by the elected candidates followed, W. W. Coles speaking for R. C. Kerr. Prof. E. A. White also addressed the meeting in an interesting manner on the education of young men in horticulture. After several other felicitous talks by various members adjournment was in order, the only further business being to receive the placque and pass final resolutions at the Exposition Grounds on Friday morning.

REPORT OF THE WM. R. SMITH MEMORIAL COMMITTEE.

On account of the general depression in business all over the United States, and further on account of various other disturbances throughout the world, which affect us generally, the Memorial Committee thought best not to push this project during the past year. The following statement shows the money collected to date:

Received since last meeting.

Aug., 1914.		
15. Vaughan's Seed Store, Chicago		$75.00
23. M. A. Patten, Tewksbury, Mass.		10.00
" J. H. Dillon, Boston, Mass.....		5.00
" Chas. Lenker, Freeport, N. Y.		5.00
" Wm. Jurgens, Freeport, N. Y.		5.00
" Wm. Nilsson, New York, N. Y.		10.00
" Theo. Standt, Rockville, Conn.		10.00
" Henshaw & Fenrich, New York, N. Y.		5.00
" Albany Florist Club, Albany, N. Y.		10.00
" Chas. L. Seybold, Wilkesbarre, Pa.		5.00
" C. E. Critchell, Cincinnati, Ohio		10.00
" Ladies' S. A. F.		25.00
Sept.		
7. Poehlmann Bros. Co., Morton Grove, Ill.		50.00
12. Wm. L. Rock Flower Co., Kansas City, Mo.		10.00
" Geo. W. Hess & Employees U. S. Botanic Gardens, Washington, D. C.		15.00
Nov.		
9. Kentucky Society of Florists..		10.00
John McLaren, San Francisco, Cal.		50.00
Daniel MacRorie, San Francisco, Cal.		50.00
		$300.00
1915.		
Cash previously acknowledged.....		$1416.00
Interest credit to date		64.03
Total cash		$1830.03
Expenditures, stationery, postage, etc.		85.35
Balance in Munsey Trust Co., Washington, D. C.		$1745.28
Amount pledged, not yet collected		625.00

Your committee feels hopeful of receiving some goodly sums from influential citizens and a liberal support from the Congress of the U. S.

Your committee has not decided what form of a memorial to suggest as their decision will no doubt be largely governed by the amount of subscriptions collected and Government influence that they may be able to secure.

WM. F. GUDE, Chairman.

THE TRADE EXHIBITION.

This important department of the Convention showed up finely—much better than was generally looked for, on account of the great distance away from the headquarters of the many exhibitors who have been accustomed to make large displays in previous years. The Advance Company of Richmond, Ind., was represented by R. E. Jones with his usual exhibit of greenhouse ventilating apparatus and other fittings. Sidney Bayersdorfer and Martin Reukauf were on hand with an excellent array of florists' supplies in full assortment from H. Bayersdorfer & Co., Philadelphia. Hugo Plath of San Francisco showed ferns in variety. H. J. Kessel of San Francisco, Ideal maiden hair ferns. C. F. Gutting, representing the Superior Nurseries, Los Angeles, new fern "Superior." Herbert & Fleishauer, McMinnville, Oregon, new improved asters. John A. Evans Co., Richmond, Ind., 20th Century ventilating apparatus, etc. Richard Diener, Colma, Cal., thirty-two new varieties of gladiolus. J. A. Peterson, Cincinnati, Ohio, usual display of begonias. A. L. Randall Co., Chicago, florists' and nurserymen's supplies. The Rice Company, Phila., Pa., florists' supplies and ribbons. S. S. Pennock-Meehan Co., Philadelphia, represented by E. J. Fancourt and J. R. Fotheringham, a comprehensive line of florists' ribbons, chiffon, baskets, etc. MacRorie McLaren Co., San Francisco, phalaenopsis. Mrs. Reidy, dahlias. Swiss Floral Company, Portland, Oregon, represented by J. G. Bacher, new forms of petunias originated by themselves.

LIST OF EXHIBITORS IN THE CONVENTION GARDEN, SAN FRANCISCO.

Hans Plath, 250 sq. ft.; Eric James, 250 sq. ft.; Santa Barbara Nursery Co., 250 sq. ft.; Frank Pelicano, 250 sq. ft.; Cottage Gardens Nursery Co., 2500 sq. ft.; Domoto Bros., 1500 sq. ft.; Howard & Smith, 1500 sq. ft.; MacRorie, McLaren Co., 1000 sq. ft.; Henry Turner, 500 sq. ft.; W. Atlee Burpee & Co., 750 sq. ft.; Hillsborough Nurseries, 500 sq. ft.; W. F. Kasting Co., 300 sq. ft.; Ferrari Bros., 250 sq. ft.; Fred Grohe, 200 sq. ft.; Chas. H. Totty, 500 sq. ft.; H. A. Dreer, 200 sq. ft.; Swiss Floral Co., 100 sq. ft.; Vaughan's Seed Store, 1000 sq. ft.; Hogan & Kooyman, 100 sq. ft.; E. Gill Nursery Co.

Among the many kind telegrams from San Francisco received at the office of HORTICULTURE during the convention the following one from Prof. A. H. Nehrling, of Amherst Agricultural College, was particularly gratifying:

"I send you greetings from San Francisco and the S. A. F. convention. The opening session was the most interesting and enthusiastic I have ever attended. Our president handled all matters in a creditable manner and Massachusetts may well be proud of him".　　　A. H. NEHRLING."

A report of the third annual exhibition of the Gladiolus Society of Ohio, also the address of President Paul Huebner before the Railroad Gardeners' Association and several other items which we have in type are crowded out this week but will appear next week.

LADIES' S. A. F.

Greetings by President Mrs. William F. Gude.

Ladies of the S. A. F.:

It is with much pleasure that I welcome you to this, the ninth annual session of the Ladies' S. A. F. and I extend to you all a cordial and heartfelt greeting. We are assembled here to consider the work of the past year and to make plans for the future. May our deliberations be guided by wisdom and may this session be so filled with good work that nothing will mar the harmony of the occasion. May our past experiences help us to improve our present opportunities. Keeping in mind at all times the saying that it is good for men to dwell together in unity and practicing that, it is even better for women to meet and confer together in harmony, sincerity and devotion to our cause, assisting the men in their able calling by enabling us to make them brighter and happier by the inspiring influences gathered at these meetings. And so when we return to our homes from this convention may we all feel better and happier for having met, refreshed in health and spirit and better enabled to pursue our duties for the coming year. May good health, happiness and prosperity ever abide with you.

FLORISTS' HAIL ASSOCIATION.

The annual report of Secretary John G. Esler for the year ending August 1, 1915, gives in detail the amount of insurance on glass in the different states as well as the number of hail storms and the losses paid in each. The figures show an insurance upon 40,411,003 square feet of glass.

The total receipts for the year ending August 1, 1915, and including last year's balance, as per Treasurer's Report, are $61,590.90.

The total expenditures, as per Treasurer's Report, for the year ending August 1, 1915, are $24,860.78.

The cash balance on hand is $36,730.12, of which $1,713.90 belongs to the Reserve Fund.

The Reserve Fund now amounts to $35.713.90, of which $34,000.00 is invested in first class municipal bonds, and $1,713.90 cash in hands of the Treasurer.

The amount of interest collected on bank deposits for the year is $431.44.

The amount of interest collected on Reserve Fund investments for the year is $1,347.50.

Twenty-two hundred losses have been adjusted since the organization of the F. H. A., involving a total expenditure of nearly $317,000.00.

The number of members at date of closing is 1621.

An equivalent of 110,276 square feet of single thick glass was broken by hail, for which the Association paid $5,513.80; and an equivalent of 196,733 square feet of double thick glass was broken, which cost the Association $13,771.28.

The F. H. A. liabilities at the close of this report are a number of unadjusted losses, the proofs of which are not at hand.

Treasurer Heacock's report was presented at the same time and was in accordance with the foregoing figures.

The Florists' Hail Association re-

elected the old officers also C. L. Washburn, Fred Burki and Chas. P. Mueller as directors for three years.

AMERICAN ASSOCIATION OF PARK SUPERINTENDENTS.

News of the S. A. F. Convention monopolizes our reading columns to such an extent this week that the fact of the 17th annual convention of the American Association of Park Superintendents occurring in San Francisco on the same dates as the former has been temporarily side-tracked. But the number of members in attendance from all parts of the country is quite large and the program of the meetings is elaborate and covers many important matters of business as well as a series of inspection tours and entertainments of more than usual interest. The park superintendents leave San Francisco on Sunday morning for the San Diego Exposition.

We hope to present a more detailed account of the proceedings of the association in a later issue.

NATIONAL ASSOCIATION OF GARDENERS.

There was a very light attendance at the meeting of the National Association of Gardeners on Wednesday afternoon in the S. A. F. Hall. Vice-President W. S. Rennie of Ross, Calif., presided, President J. W. Everitt and Secretary M. C. Ebel being unable to attend. Addresses were made by Theodore Wirth and Richard Vincent, Jr., expresidents of the S. A. F.

FLORISTS' TELEGRAPH DELIVERY.

The meeting of this organization was held on Wednesday forenoon, August 18, as scheduled. In the absence of President Bertermann, also Secretary Pochelon, Wm. F. Gude, vice-president, conducted the meeting. All the officers were re-elected. Frank D. Pelicano of San Francisco, Frank X. Stuppy of St. Joseph, Mo., and August Lange of Chicago were chosen directors for a three-year term, succeeding Philip Breitmeyer, E. Weinhoeber and George Asmus, whose terms had expired. The reports showed a healthy condition financially, and a gratifying increase in membership. J. J. Hess urged that the utmost care should be exercised in scrutinizing the qualifications of all candidates for membership. The committee on revised constitution was continued.

The Gladiolus and Phlox exhibition at Horticultural Hall, Boston, on August 7 and 8 was an attractive affair although not very extensive. Some of the displays were of a very high order of merit, notwithstanding the stormy weather which had used outdoor vegetation very roughly. C. F. Fairbank's one hundred vases of gladioli arranged for effect was a superb display the equal of which has never been seen here and well entitled to the special silver medal bestowed. Phloxes from R. & J. Farquhar & Co., Blue Hill Nurseries and others were fair, considering the untoward circumstances. Herbaceous perennial flowers, greenhouse plants, fruit and vegetables were staged by the usual contributors.

CLUBS AND SOCIETIES

SOUTHAMPTON HORTICULTURAL SOCIETY.

The ninth annual exhibition of the Southampton Horticultural Society was held in the Park Grounds in Southampton, N. Y., on July 28 and 29.

The entries this year were a record and the competition in some cases was very keen, as most of the classes were filled. The display of flowers were, according to the oldest members of the society, the best ever seen at Southampton, both in number and quality; in fact, according to various experts, the exhibition was spoken of as the best of its kind ever held on the Island. This exhibition is one of the annual events of the fashionable society that flocks to the colony at Southampton for the summer and the success of the exhibition is due to a large extent to their active assistance.

The most sought for prize is that offered by the Southampton Garden Club of $25, for best 12 varieties of hardy perennials. This was won by Mrs. Pomery, gard. J. Cassidy. Other noteworthy exhibits were 12 gloxinias by Mrs. Horace Russell, gard. Wm. McCord, and the display of vegetables tastefully arranged by Mrs. W. G. Curtis, gard. J. Johnson; without doubt this latter was the most talked of exbibit. The display of water lilies by H. A. Dreer was deserving of great praise as also were the many groups by the various nurserymen and florists, including C. E. Frankenbach & Sons, local; G. E. Stumpp & Co., Southampton and New York; Oak Park Nursery Co., Patchogue; Swan River Nursery Co., Patchogue, and John Lewis Childs, Flowerfield, L. I. The judges were John Canning of Ardsley, J. Malcolm of Shinnecock Golf Club, Southampton, and W. Halsey, florist, Southampton.

WESTCHESTER AND FAIRFIELD HORTICULTURAL SOCIETY.

Despite the intense heat of the past week, the regular monthly meeting of this society was well attended. Honorable mention was accorded to Owen A. Hunwick for a fine specimen plant of Torenia Fourneiri gr.-fl. The outing committee made their final report, and was discharged with a vote of thanks. The fall show will be held in the Casino at Stamford, Ct., Nov 5-6. Letters were read from several good friends of the society offering substantial prizes. Messages were read from several of our members enroute to the Coast to

attend the convention. All report having a splendid time. The next meeting will be held Sept. 10, when we anticipate a fine display of seasonable flowers.　　　　　　P. W. POPP.

PACIFIC COAST HORTICULTURAL SOCIETY.

As the monthly meeting of the Pacific Coast Horticultural Society held Aug. 7th, was the last regular meeting before the S. A. F. Convention, final preparations for that event took up most of the time. Reports were made by the different committee chairmen, which showed that all arrangements for the convention had been well looked after. Announcement was made that a permanent organization to be known as the Ladies' Auxiliary of the Pacific Coast Horticultural Society has been organized by the ladies connected with the trade in this vicinity. Members of the society were invited to attend the convention of the Pacific Coast Nurserymen's Association, Aug. 12, 13 and 14. A lecture on "Iris" by S. B. Mitchell was very well received. The evening's exhibits made a splendid showing. A fine display of hybrid seedling gladioli by Mr. Diener was rated at 99 points. A sample of Nephrolepis tuberosa by H. Plath took 80 points. An exhibit of late Crawford peaches by Mr. Shilling was rated at 75 points, and a collection shown by F. T. Pelicano including four samples of cactus dahlias and a vase each of gladiolus Niagara and dahlia Hampton Court was judged at 70 points.

VISITORS' REGISTER.

Chicago—J. Papas, Des Moines, Ia.

New York—Louis J. Reuter, Westerly, R. I. -

Newport, R. I.—Leonard Barron, Garden City, N. Y.

Rockland, Me.—Cap't Burnett Landreth, Philadelphia.

Cincinnati: J. E. Morichard, representing S. S. Pennock-Meehan Company, Philadelphia, Pa.

St. Louis.—Samuel Seligmann, New York; H. Balsley, of Detroit Flower Pot Co., Detroit, Mich.; Max Feinstein, Phila. Pa.; Joseph M. Stern, of Cleveland, Ohio.

Washington.—I. Rosnosky, representing H. F. Michell, Phila. Pa.; Harry Quint, Boston, Mass.; Mr. and Mrs. Charles Eble, Jr., New Orleans, La.; Charles E. Barton, Norwalk, Ohio.

Philadelphia—Wm. Gibson, Idle Hour Nurseries, Macon, Ga.; George Horsman, representing Holmes Seed Co., Harrisburg, Pa.; Alexander Forbes and Alexander Forbes, Jr., Newark, N. J.; William J. Stewart, Boston, Mass.

Boston—William Plumb, New York; David Burpee and W. Atlee Burpee, Jr., of W. Atlee Burpee & Co., Philadelphia, accompanied by Edward Bromfield of "Good Housekeeping," all homeward bound from a fortnight's vacation in Camden, Me.; Montague Free, Botanic Garden, Brooklyn, N. Y.; Leonard Barron, Garden City, N. Y. .

THE ATTRACTIONS OF THE MAINE SEA COAST.

In our notes last week on one of the foremost examples of fine gardening at Bar Harbor, Me., we referred incidentally to the treat that is in store for all who make the trip to that famous "down-east" resort on the occasion of the meeting and exhibition of the American Sweet Pea Society which will probably be held there next July. There will be not only the attraction of the beautiful summer estates which abound in the several famed "Harbors" of Mt. Desert but the sublime panorama of rugged coast, islands, reefs and sombre evergreen forests which help to make every minute of the sail from Boston to Bar Harbor a never-to-be-forgotten delight.

On each occasion that we have made the trip to Bar Harbor by either of the several routes provided by the Eastern Steamship Corporation we are more and more deeply impressed by the matchless scenery of the Maine coast. One may go direct by the Bangor steamer from Boston to Rockland, there transferring to the Bar Harbor boat which winds its way around and through the picturesque islands of Penobscot Bay, with the highlands of Mt. Desert in view for hours, passing at Southwest Harbor, far-famed Somes' Sound unriveled in its placid loveliness by any other view on the Atlantic coast. Even. the renowned Hudson River with its wonderful scenery has nothing on the surf-lashed crags of the Mt. Desert coast from Seal Harbor to Bar Harbor. Between Boston and Rockland there is a choice of several routes, via Portland with its magnificent harbor and among the romantic islands and the swirling "hellgates" of Casco Bay, or via the Bath line, and Seguin light which guards the mouth of the great Kennebec river. One may go by either of these routes and return by another and we have no doubt that the steamship people will be ready with an ideal itinerary when the time comes to get ready for the sweet pea show. Sweet peas grow grandly on Mt. Desert. In common with all other outdoor flowers their colors have a rare purity and sheen, due to the moist and often misty atmosphere, and the lawns present a picture of purest emerald. Few there are who realize until they see it the gorgeous brilliancy of a field of roses, phloxes, irises, peonies, delphiniums or aconites in this soft atmosphere. The Mt. Desert Nurseries have quantities of all these garden favorites and a myriad other gems of the herbaceous garden. During the present month one of the most impressive sights is a section of Arend's wonderful hybrid astilbes, of which there are nine or ten distinct varieties, ranging from pure white to deep pink. The flower spikes rise to a height of from three to five feet.

While on the subject of Bar Harbor gardening we must not skip John Stalford, who has a well-managed commercial place. Melons under glass are one specialty with Mr. Stalford. He has five houses of them in bearing at the present time, one house having 170 of these fruits, each suspended in a net. After the melons are gathered the house will be filled with carnations.

MASSACHUSETTS HORTI-CULTURAL SOCIETY.

The Massachusetts Horticultural Society announces the preliminary schedule of prizes to be offered at the exhibitions to be held at Horticultural Hall, Boston, in March and May, 1916. The list is as follows:

March Exhibition.

PLANTS.

Acacias. To cover not less than 150 sq. ft., 1st, $75; 2nd, $40. One specimen plant, 1st, $10.

Anthuriums. Three plants, 1st, $10; 2nd, $5.

Callas. Display, 1st, $15; 2nd, $8.

Camellias. Four plants in bloom, 1st, $12; 2nd, $6.

Cinerarias. Grandiflora type. Six plants, 1st, $12; 2nd, $6. One specimen plant, 1st, $4. Stellata type. Six plants, 1st, $12; 2nd, $6. One specimen plant, 1st, $4.

Cyclamens. Ten plants, 1st, $25; 2nd, $12. Six plants, 1st, $15; 2nd, $8.

Cytisus. Six plants, 1st, $15; 2nd, $8.

Ericas. Six plants. Not less than three varieties, 1st, $15; 2nd, $8.

Freesias. Six pots or pans, 1st, $8; 2nd, $4.

Gardenias. Four plants, 1st, $10; 2nd, $5.

Hardwooded Greenhouse Plants other than Acacias, Azaleas, and Ericas, 1st, $15; 2nd, $8.

Hyacinths. Six pans not exceeding ten inches in diameter, 1st, $10; 2nd, $6. One pan not exceeding ten inches, 1st, $4; 2nd, $2. Bed to cover not over twenty-five sq. ft. arranged for color effect. Sand will be provided in which to set the pots. Pots can be used for edging, 1st, $30; 2nd, $10.

Lilacs. Display covering not less than 150 sq. ft., 1st, $25; 2nd, $12.

Liliums. Twelve pots. One or more varieties, 1st, $15; 2nd, $8.

Lily of the Valley. Six pots or pans, not over 8 inches, 1st, $6; 2nd, $4.

Narcissuses. Large Trumpet. Twelve pots, 1st, $15; 2nd, $8. Four pots, 1st, $6; 2nd, $3. Short Trumpet. Twelve pots, 1st, $10; 2nd, $5.

Palms. Six plants in pots or tubs, 1st, $20; 2nd, $10.

Primulas. Acaulis, 1st, $6; 2nd, $4.

Polyantha Hybrids, 1st, $6; 2nd, $4.

Schizanthus. Six plants, 1st, $12; 2nd, $8. Three pans each color, white, red, pink, yellow, and any other color, 1st, $6; 2nd, $3. Bed to cover not over 25 sq. ft. arranged for color effect. Sand will be provided in which to set the pots. Pots can be used for edging, 1st, $30; 2nd, $10.

General Display of Spring Bulbous Plants. To be arranged with foliage plants, 1st, $40; 2nd, $20.

Artistic Display of Foliage and Flowering Plants not exceeding 250 sq. ft., 1st, $50; 2nd, $25.

Forced Hardy Shrubs to cover not more than 150 sq. ft., 1st, $25; 2nd, $12.

AMATEUR CLASSES.

Hyacinths. Six plants in one or more pots or pans, 1st, $5; 2nd, $3.

Narcissuses. Twelve plants in one or more pots or pans, 1st, $5; 2nd, $3.

Orchids. Group of plants arranged for effect with ferns or other foliage plants to cover not less than 50 sq. ft., 1st, $30; 2nd, $15.

Collection of Forced Bulbs covering not more than 12 sq. ft., 1st, $10; 2nd, $8.

Tulips. Twelve plants in one or more pots or pans, 1st, $5; 2nd, $3.

FLOWERS.

Camellias. Twelve blooms, 1st, $5; 2nd, $3.

Carnations. Any named variety admissible. Fifty blooms each, white, red or crimson, pink, yellow and variegated, 1st, $8; 2nd, $4.

Freesias. One hundred sprays, 1st, $4; 2nd, $2.

Gladioli. Colvillei type. Three vases, 25 spikes each, 1st, $5; 2nd, $3.

Mignonette. Twelve spikes, 1st, $4; 2nd, $2.

Orchids. Cut flowers, arranged for effect, to cover 24 sq. ft., 1st, $20; 2nd, $10.

Roses. Any named variety admissible. Twenty-five blooms each, white, red, pink, yellow and any other color, 1st, $12; 2nd, $6.

Sweet Peas. Twenty-five blooms each, white, scarlet, pink, lavender and any other color, 1st, $4; 2nd, $2.

Violets. One hundred blooms each, single and double, 1st, $4; 2nd, $2.

May Exhibition.

PLANTS.

Abutilons. Six plants, 1st, $15; 2nd, $8.

Achimenes. Eight plants, 1st, $10; 2nd, $5.

Amaryllis. Twelve plants, not less than six varieties, 1st, $15; 2nd, $8. Six plants, not less than three varieties, 1st, $8; 2nd, $4.

Antirrhinums. Eight plants, 1st, $12; 2nd, $6.

Astilbes. Twelve plants, not less than four varieties, 1st, $20; 2nd, $10. Six plants, not less than three varieties, 1st, $10; 2nd, $5.

Azaleas. Indica. To cover not more than 200 sq. ft., 1st, $100; 2nd, $50. Indica. Four plants, 1st, $50; 2nd, $25. Ghent or Mollis. Eight plants, not less than three varieties, 1st, $20; 2nd, $10. Ghent or Mollis. Four plants, not less than two varieties, 1st, $10; 2nd, $5. Any other variety, four plants, 1st, $10; 2nd, $5.

Calceolarias. Large flowering varieties. Eight plants, 1st, $15; 2nd, $8. Stewartii. Six plants, 1st, $15; 2nd, $8.

Canterbury Bells. Eight plants, 1st, $15; 2nd, $10. Pyramidalis. Eight plants, 1st, $15; 2nd, $10.

Ericas. Six plants, 1st, $15; 2nd, $8.

Ferns. Six plants in variety, 1st, $25; 2nd, $15. Hardy Ferns. 25 plants, not less than 12 varieties, 1st, $15; 2nd, $8. Tree fern, one specimen, 1st, $10; 2nd, $5.

Fuchsias. Eight plants, 1st, $25; 2nd, $15.

Gloxinias. Twelve plants, 1st, $15; 2nd, $8.

Heliotrope. Standard. Six plants, 1st, $15; 2nd, $8.

Hydrangeas. Group to cover not less than 150 sq. ft., 1st, $75; 2nd, $40. Four plants, not less than two varieties, 1st, $25; 2nd, $12.

Fuchsias. Four plants, 1st $12; 2nd, $8.

Kalmias. Eight plants, 1st, $20; 2nd, $10.

Marguerites. Six plants, 1st, $20; 2nd, $10.

Palms. Two specimens, any variety, 1st, $15; 2nd, $8.

Pelargoniums. Show. Twelve plants, not less than six Varieties, 1st, $25; 2nd, $10. Six plants, not less than three Varieties, 1st, $10; 2nd, $5. Zonale, eight plants, 1st, $20; 2nd, $10.

Lilies. Collection covering 50 sq. ft., 1st, $50; 2nd, $25.

Orchids. Group arranged for effect, covering 200 sq. ft., cut foliage or pots admissible, 1st, gold medal and $200; 2nd, silver medal and $100. Group arranged for effect, covering 100 sq. ft., cut foliage or pots admissible (for private growers only), 1st, silver cup and $100; 2nd, $50. Six plants, six varieties, 1st, $20; 2nd, $10.

Rhododendrons. Group not exceeding 300 sq. ft., 1st, $100; 2nd, $50. Four plants, not less than two varieties, 1st, $50; 2nd, $25. One specimen plant, 1st, $15.

Roses. Group to cover not more than 200 sq. ft., all classes admissible, 1st, $100; 2nd, $50. Four Varieties, 1st, $30; 2nd, $25. Specimen plant, 1st, $10. Hybrid Roses, twelve plants, not less than six varieties, 1st, $20; 2nd, $10. Six plants, not less than three Varieties, 1st, $10; 2nd, $5. Hybrid Tea Roses, twelve plants, not less than six varieties, 1st, $20; 2nd, $10. Six plants, not less than three varieties, 1st, $10; 2nd, $5. Baby Ramblers, twelve plants, 1st, $20; 2nd, $10.

Schizanthus. Six plants, 1st, $12; 2nd, $6.

Streptocarpus. Twelve plants, 1st, $10; 2nd, $5.

Verbenas. Eight plants in pots or pans, 1st, $10; 2nd, $5.

Wistarias. Four plants, 1st, $25; 2nd, $10.

Artistic Display of Flowering and Foliage Plants, to cover not less than 200 sq. ft., 1st, cup and $100; 2nd, silver medal and $50.

Display of Herbaceous and Alpine Plants. Arranged to produce natural effects, covering not more than 200 sq. ft., 1st, $100; 2nd, $50. To cover not more than 100 sq. ft., 1st, $50; 2nd, $35.

Stove or Greenhouse Flowering Plants. Six plants, 1st, $50; 2nd, $25. Foliage plants, six plants, 1st, $40; 2nd, $20. Flowering Plant, one specimen, 1st, $10; 2nd, $5. Display of Dwarf and Japanese Plants, 1st, $75; 2nd, $40.

FLOWERS.

Antirrhinums, six Vases. 25 spikes each, not less than three varieties. One Vase, one or more varieties, 1st, $5; 2nd, $3.

Carnations. Fifty blooms each, white, red or crimson, pink, yellow and variegated, 1st, $25; 2nd, $15, each color. Display, covering not more than 100 sq. ft., any material in arrangement admissible, 1st, $100; 2nd, $50. Display of 100 Carnations, one or more Varieties admissible. 1st, $25; 2nd, $10.

Gladioli. Vase of 100 spikes, one or more Varieties, 1st, $15; 2nd, $10.

Iris, Spanish. Six Vases, 25 blooms each, not less than three varieties, 1st, $10; 2nd, $5.

Marguerites. One hundred blooms each, white and yellow, 1st, $8; 2nd, $5.

Narcissuses. Ten Vases, ten Varieties, ten blooms each, 1st, $10; 2nd, $5.

Pansies. Display, 1st, $10; 2nd, $5.

Roses. Display, covering not more than 100 sq. ft., 1st, $100; 2nd, $50. Hybrid Teas, fifty blooms each, white, red, pink, yellow, 1st, $25; 2nd, $15. Twelve blooms each, white, red, pink, yellow (for private gardeners only), 1st, $6; 2nd, $4, each color.

Sweet Peas. Display to cover not more than 50 sq. ft., 1st, $35; 2nd, $20.

Tulips. Twelve Vases, twelve Varieties, ten blooms each, 1st, $8; 2nd, $5. Six Vases, six varieties, ten blooms each, 1st, $5; 2nd, $3. Display of Darwin Tulips, not less than 100 sq. ft., 1st, $50; 2nd, $25. sq. ft. (for private growers only), 1st $25; 2nd, $15.

In addition to the spring exhibitions, a large show will be held in November, 1916. Also there will be fortnightly exhibitions throughout the year, on the first and third Saturdays of every month, when seasonable plants, flowers, fruits and Vegetables may be brought in for suitable recognition. Full details of all the exhibitions of the year will be printed later in the annual schedule of the Society, copies of which are freely sent on request.

WM. P. RICH, Secretary.
Horticultural Hall, Boston.

SEED TRADE

AMERICAN SEED TRADE ASSOCIATION
Officers—President, J. M. Lupton,
Mattituck, L. I., N. Y.; First Vice-President, Kirby B. White, Detroit, Mich.;
Second Vice-President, F. W. Bolgiano,
Washington, D. C.; Secretary-Treasurer,
C. E. Kendel, Cleveland, O.; Assistant
Secretary, S. F. Willard, Jr., Cleveland,
O. Cincinnati, O., next meeting place.

Pea Outlook Dubious.

Since our last crop report was published, conditions have changed more or less for the worst, with respect to certain crops. Peas in Montana and Idaho are not as promising as two weeks ago, and particularly in Idaho. What with hail storms, frosts and latterly a shortage in the water supply the pea crop in Idaho has deteriorated and unfortunately it affects the longpod, late varieties, such as Alderman, Duke of Albany, Telephone, etc., though of course all of the late or medium late varieties are more or less affected. The extent of the damage probably will not be definitely known until threshing time. Had the damage fallen on the canners' varieties, such as Horsford's Market Garden, Alaska, Advancer, or Admiral, it would not have been an unmixed evil as there was a considerable carry-over of one or two of the canners' sorts, and prospects for a full average crop of all of the varieties this year. This means a demoralized market, with no fixed, nor anything approaching fixed minimum prices on any of the varieties, though Alaska promises to be the firmest. Another and very important factor, is the condition of the canned pea market. With a considerable surplus in the hands of the canners, with jobbers buying very sparingly, either because they look for lower prices or are already overstocked the immediate future at least does not look very rosy to the average pea-packer, and prospects for another year, are not any too bright. The growers and dealers in seed peas know only too well what this portends, and view the future with many misgivings.

A Disquieting Feature.

There is another feature of the business much more disquieting, that is, that the canners expect to be, and insist on being babied. A prominent pea seed grower said not long since, that during the years of short crops, when he could deliver only 25 to 50 per cent. on his contracts, that he experienced far less trouble than now when he is delivering 100 per cent. When the deliveries were short, there were of course vigorous kicks, but it ended there. Now, the canner insists on throwing a considerable part of all of his future order back on the seed growers and making him carry the load, and this is especially true if spot seed can be bought at a lower figure than the price of "futures."

It is of course not our intention to indict the entire list of pea canners, nor even a majority of them, but what we have said unfortunately does apply to a considerable number. The canner of this class justifies his action often by saying that the jobber imposes the same conditions on him, but two wrongs do not make a right, and every man, be he canner or engaged in any other business, should feel in honor bound when he makes a contract to accept the fortunes of war as he expects the other fellow to do. This is a condition which seed growers and dealers are likely to learn more about to their sorrow the coming autumn and winter.

Beans and Corn.

Beans are not so near maturity as peas, and the final results cannot be calculated so nearly, but beans have not improved—in fact, they have deteriorated, but that is as far as we can go at this time. Corn is still a source of anxiety to growers, and it depends on how early Jack Frost pays his customary visit the coming autumn as to what sort of corn crop is harvested. We have learned of no radical changes in other seed crops from last reports in HORTICULTURE.

The European Situation.

Several inquiries as to what we know of the European situation have come to us. These inquiries have to do less with the volume of the crops than with the chances of getting them into this country. To all such we must say we don't know. It would require a seer to even prognosticate the future in this line. The actions of the allies will doubtless be governed by expediency, and in any event we can hope for but little from Germany or Austria-Hungary. Considerable quantities of seeds from Germany came through by way of Holland, Denmark and other neutral countries last season, but whether these sources will be open or closed the coming autumn and winter is a question only the future can answer.

The Lily of the Valley Situation.

Owing to the fact that German lily of the valley pips cannot be exported this season, even by way of neutral ports as was the case last year, the Danish pips have been taken up so rapidly that prices are being advanced on account of the limited quantity available. Higher values for the coming season are inevitable.

Notes.

Clarinda, Ia.—The Berry Seed Co. has increased its capital stock from $75,000 to $150,000.

David Adam has taken a position with Burnett Bros., Chambers St., New York.

Lexington, Ky.—C. S. Brent, Inc.,
have changed their firm name to C. S. Brent Seed Co., with liability fixed at $100,000.

Alexander Forbes of Newark, N. J., has recently come out of the hospital after an operation for appendicitis. He is recovering satisfactorily, but is not yet very strong.

Samuel T. Freeman & Co. will sell at public auction on the premises, 217 Market street, Philadelphia, the goodwill, stock and fixtures of the Johnson Seed Co., commencing at 10 A. M. Tuesday, August 24.

The value of horticultural imports at the Port of New York for the week ending August 7, 1915, is given as follows: Manure salt, $3,364; nitrate of soda, $159,505; Clover seed, $8,839; grass seed, $114; trees and plants, $2,956.

Providence, R. I.—Hamlin Johnson, former seed merchant of this city, observed his 90th birthday Monday at his home in Seekonk, near Hunt's Mills. Monday a party of about 50 relatives and friends paid him a surprise visit at the Johnson homestead on Fall River avenue, and the celebration proved to be a most enjoyable affair. Mr. Johnson was born in Brooklyn, Conn., and came to Providence when a young man. He was employed as bookkeeper with the Oliver Johnson Company in his younger days, and in 1879 opened a seed and farm implement store at 6 Exchange place. He sold this business in 1890, and retired about the time that his wife died. Fifty years ago he located at his present home in Seekonk and for a number of years had a greenhouse there.

NEW CORPORATIONS.

Seattle, Wash.—Orpheum Floral Co., capital stock, $5,000. Incorporators, D. A. Fetta and F. T. Rosaia.

Great Falls, Mont. — Great Falls Floral Co., capital stock, $25,000. Incorporators, H. L. and Ella G. Byrum, and John Hodley.

Philadelphia, Pa.—Jos. G. Neidinger Co., florists' supplies, capital stock, $75,000. Incorporators, Joseph G. and John Neidinger, and Joseph Hampton.

Meriden, Conn.—The Meriden Nursery, Fruit & Orchard Developing Company, to develop and operate farms, nurseries, orchards, etc., with an authorized capital stock of $50,000. The incorporators are: Joseph N. Nettleton of Meriden, Berkley C. Stone of Middletown and John N. Nettleton of Meriden.

Of Interest to Retail Florists

TO BLOCK THE FAKIR.

The following letter from Secretary William H. Day, Jr., of the Chamber of Commerce, of Lynn, Mass., sent last week to Chief of Police Thomas M. Burckes, is self-explanatory:

"Chief of Police Thomas M. Burckes,

"Dear Sir: In behalf of the Lynn Chamber of Commerce, I desire to compliment both you and Sealer of Weights and Measures Charles P. Murray, on recent decisions obtained from Judge Lummus on test case brought against residents from nearby towns for disposing of flowers from doorways on Market street.

"The Lynn Chamber of Commerce, in general, and the retail merchants, in particular, have no objections to anyone earning a living, but have long felt that the disposing of fruits and flowers by outsiders from doorways, alleyways and yards has been a menace to our regular merchants and a nuisance to our city. It is my understanding that new ordinance now being drafted gives to the board of control supervision over itinerant vendors, the same as over hawkers or peddlers and it is sincerely hoped by the Chamber of Commerce that you will continue your efforts until these vendors are either put out of business or on a plane with other legitimate merchants whose taxes help to make possible our city government.

"Very truly yours,

(Signed)
"LYNN CHAMBER OF COMMERCE,
"W. H. Day, Jr.,
"Acting Secretary."

NATIONAL FLORAL CORPORATION.

The National Floral Corporation has sent us samples of some of the window display slips which they are furnishing to members of their organization. These are about 5x25 inches in size and bear inscriptions such as "American Beauty Day;" "Fresh Violets Just Received;" "Love Insurance—Buy Flowers;" "Saturday Flowers Make Sunday Gladness," "Chrysanthemums Are in Season," etc., attractively printed in red and green. This new organization already has forty-three retail florists enrolled as members.

NEW FLOWER STORES.

Cincinnati, O.—Louis Roth, 15th and Vine streets.

Chicago, Ill.—Arthur F. Keenan, 1220 East 63d street.

Janesville, Wis.—Chas. Rathjen, 413 W. Milwaukee street.

Springfield, Ill.—Colonial Flower Shop, 409 E. Washington street.

Buffalo, N. Y.—Allen Flower Shop, Wm. Norman, proprietor, Allen and Franklin streets.

NEWS ITEMS FROM EVERYWHERE

NEW YORK.

Phil. Kessler has returned to the mountains for another week's vacation with his family

W. P. Ford has been rusticating as time and business would permit, down in Chester County, Pa.

Miss Rose Grafmann, bookkeeper and cashier for J. K. Allen is spending two weeks at Rockaway Beach.

Twenty-eighth street seems rather lonesome without John Young. His return from San Francisco will be a welcome event.

J. K. Allen has stretched an awning over the open area in the rear of his wholesale flower store and finds it an admirable place for the gladiolus blooms, which are coming in by the thousands at present.

Hadley rose is said by some to be a difficult variety to grow. A. S. Burns, Jr., does not find it so. He says it wants plenty of room and when so planted it will give a big account for itself. His success with this superb rose is well demonstrated in the quantity and quality of the shipments to P. J. Smith every morning.

C. C. Trepel's new greenhouse 48 by 100, on the roof of his new building, 89th street and Broadway is nearing completion. It is an iron frame structure and one of the best examples of Jacobs & Sons' construction. It will be connected with the street by elevator service. C. C. Trepel is enjoying a well-earned vacation in Oxford.

Francis Scott Key is a leading specialty on the tables of W. F. Sheridan daily. It is a tough fibred bloom and is a favorite with buyers because of the amount of handling it will bear without injury, but the growers are cutting it in a too mature condition. The same criticism applies to Ophelia, a rose that is divested of much of its beauty when allowed to spread out too much.

Quite a number of the horticultural trade advertisers have placed their advertising business in the hands of the Tuthill Ad. Agency at 1133 Broadway. The latest addition to Mr. Tuthill's growing family is the National Florists' Corporation. The country is overrun with advertising agencies. A few of them are helpful to their clients and appreciated by the magazines and foremost among these in matters horticultural we would place the Tuthill for intelligent, conscientious and effective service.

Anyone who has not visited the block on West 28th street, between Broadway and Sixth Ave., for several years, would scarcely recognize the place. Once the busy centre of the great cut flower industry of the metropolis, the majority of the stores on both sides of the street occupied by wholesale flower dealers, it is now largely a series of buildings and stores to rent. A few of the flower establishments are still there, but many have betaken themselves to other quarters, leaving the old haunts vacant, all because of the rapacity of landlords, who set out to grasp everything and who now are paying the penalty for their greed. There is a certain satisfaction in seeing the plight the landlords have brought upon themselves.

CHICAGO.

A. J. Zech and wife will leave Saturday night for two weeks' vacation in Wisconsin.

J. C. Schubert, who formerly had a retail store in Chicago is reported ill at the Kennilworth Sanitarium.

B. Juergens and son, Wallie, from Peoria, Ill., passed through Chicago this week en route to New York to spend their vacation.

C. L. Washburn and wife are back from California, and Mr. and Mrs. O. P. Bassett are expected to arrive in Chicago Saturday. They are making the trip by auto from Pasadena, California.

SAN FRANCISCO.

H. A. Avansino of the Fairmont Floral Co., Powell street florists, is spending a vacation at his beautiful summer home in Fairfax.

Arrangements have been completed by Mr. and Mrs. R. D. Paul for reopening the Hanford Floral Shop in the Ashby Theater Building, Hanford, Cal.

A handsome bowling trophy arrived the first of the week from the Aphine Manufacturing Co., Madison, N. J., to be awarded for the highest individual score in the contest between the Society of American Florists and Ornamental Horticulturists, the National Association of Gardeners and the American Association of Park Superintendents.

The Spokane Florist Co., of Spokane, Wash., has secured a new location, having taken a five year lease on a store in the new Mohawk Block on Riverside street, between Howard and Stevens, which is nearing completion. The shop is to be nicely fitted up. The main floor will have a floor space of 23 by 90 feet.

PHILADELPHIA.

Harry Bayersdorfer and family are sojourning in Atlantic City at present, Mr. Bayersdorfer coming up daily to business in Philadelphia.

E. H. Wilson, of the Arnold Arboretum, will deliver his lecture on the flora of northern China before the Pennsylvania Horticultural Society, next January. Secretary Rust says this will be the first of an interesting series now being arranged for the coming year.

On the opening day of the Convention the following telegram was sent from this city to San Francisco:

"To P. Welch, President S. A. F., San Francisco, Cal.—Greetings from special meeting, Stewart, Westcott, Watson, Forbes, Michell and others of Philadelphia, New York and Boston. May wisdom guide you, and may you have a successful convention. Sorry we are not with you in person as we are in spirit.
　　　　THE OLD GUARD."

WASHINGTON.

Mrs. G. Supper, who is employed at the Gude Bros. store, started last Saturday on a four weeks' vacation. With Mr. Supper, she will soon leave for one of the popular summer resorts.

A telegram from the Washington delegation which went to attend the convention of the S. A. F. and O. H. at San Francisco, tells of the safe arrival of the party, all of whom are very enthusiastic at the efforts made by associations and individual florists all along the line to entertain them.

Mr. and Mrs. Henry Pfister were scheduled to leave Switzerland, during the week for the United States, according to a postal card just received by Albert Schnell. They have been abroad for a number of months and would have returned earlier were it not for the fact that great difficulty is experienced in securing transportation.

Detlef Witt, who was connected with his brother in business at Silver Hill, Md., for about two and a half years, is a member of the army stationed in Russia. Mr. Witt returned to Germany with his father about a year ago with the intention of taking charge of the latter's farm in Holstein. Early in the spring he was called on to take his place in the German army and was assigned to a regiment of infantry.

Carlos J. Jensen, representing L. Daehnfeldt, Ltd., of Odense, Denmark, last week conferred with the Foreign Trade Advisers of the State Department with a view to securing their aid in obtaining a modification of the British embargo, as set forth in the Order in Council of March 11 and subsequent regulations, in order that it may be made possible to secure the shipment of seeds to the United States from this country to Denmark. This firm has seed gardens in the San Jose valley of California, in Denmark and in Germany. Unmolested exportation from Denmark is permissible under England's restrictions only where it can be proven that they are Danish products. This is a hard matter to do in the case of the seeds grown in Germany. With respect to shipments of seeds from and to Denmark, this can only be accomplished where it is guaranteed to the British authorities that they will not be re-exported to enemy countries.

PITTSBURGH.

George C. McCallum of the McCallum Co., left last Saturday to spend his vacation in Ohio.

Mr. and Mrs. Julius W. Ludwig, of the Ludwig Floral Company, left last Thursday to visit relatives at Milwaukee.

B. L. Elliott, president of the John Bader Co., with his wife and daughter have returned from an extended trip in California.

Harry Ackermann, secretary of the Ziegar Co., left Thursday night to spend three weeks with his family who are occupying a cottage at Ocean City on the Jersey Coast.

OUR MOTTO FOR PROGRESSIVENESS

"Customers must be satisfied," has made our unexcelled delivery possible. Send us your next order for Washington, D. C., and vicinity if you appreciate quality, quantity and mode of good conduct.

GUDE BROTHERS CO.

Members of the F. T. D.

Florists and Floral Decorators

Washington, D. C.

James J. Higgins, of the Mrs. E. A. Williams Co., with his family, is spending a few weeks in Chicago and Duluth. Miss Brunner, the bookkeeper, is expected next Monday from her vacation spent at Wildwood, New Jersey.

Catherine Friel, head saleswoman for Ray J. Daschbach, left Thursday to spend a month at Atlantic City. George Cresby, the greenhouse foreman, has just returned from a two weeks' trip to the same resort.

Fred Burki, president of the Pittsburgh Cut Flower Co., accompanied by his family, has just returned from an automobile trip to Niagara Falls and points en route. T. P. Langhans, secretary, has joined his family at Atlantic City for a few weeks. William A. Clarke, has also returned from his vacation spent at the family cottage at Chautauqua Lake.

S. J. Frampton, of the J. P. Weaklin Co., is to return on Monday from a vacation trip at Clarion, Pa. J. M. McGrew, of the same company, has returned with his little son Murray from a sojourn at his farm near Ashtabula, Ohio. Edward Weaver, also with the Weaklin Co., has returned from a three weeks' vacation spent in the mountains near Connellsville, with his family.

Mr. and Mrs. E. C. Ludwig and their neice, Miss Strasser, returned on Thursday from a two weeks' sojourn at Atlantic City. Their sons, De-Forest, and Edward E. Ludwig are expected Monday from an automobile trip to Frostburg, Maryland. John Hoffman and Rudolph Zilka, employees of the same company are spending their vacation at various points along Lake Erie.

NEWS NOTES.

Bay City, Mich. — Boehringer Bros. have purchased the Bay City Flower Store.

Pascoag, R. I. — R. A. Buxton Greenhouses have been sold to Edward F. Lovejoy.

Steubenville, O. — E. E. McCausland has purchased the greenhouse range of G. L. Huscroft.

Texarkana, Ark. — The State Line Floral Company has been purchased by Herbert D. Enoe.

St. Louis, Mo. — Louis Volkmann has purchased the greenhouse range and store at 5415 Easton avenue.

Bergenfield, N. J. — H. E. Fischer will conduct the florist business at the Bergenfield Nurseries under the firm name of H. E. Fischer & Sons.

During Recess

WESTCHESTER AND FAIRFIELD HORTICULTURAL SOCIETY.

The annual outing was held Tuesday, Aug 10, at Rye Beach Inn, Rye Beach, N. Y., the weather was ideal and a very large number of the members, their wives, families and friends formed a happy and care-free party. The horticultural trade and press were well represented, also there was a large delegation from Tarrytown Horticultural Society and several from Glen Cove. The games were interesting and amusing, and there was an excellent shore dinner. "Breaking the flower pots" proved a humorous and amusing pastime. A tug-of-war between the members from Westchester county and those from Fairfield county was a laughable event.

List of Winners.

Tug of War, won by Fairfield Co. Quoit Match, won by Westchester, 23-18. Wheelbarrow Race: 1st, Neil McInnes and Colin Aitcheson; 2nd, Wm. Whittin and Alex. Clarkson. Race for single women: 1st, Marie Addis; 2nd, Annie Peters. 100-yard dash for gardeners: 1st, W. J. Seeley; 2nd, Wm. Whittin. Throwing hammer: 1st, Thos. Aitcheson; 2nd, Wm. Whittin. Race for gardeners' wives: 1st, Mrs. McArdle; 2nd, Mrs. Stuart. Running high jump: 1st, Wm. Whittin; 2nd, Patrick Danakey. Blind-fold race: 1st, Neil McInnes; 2nd, Lizzie Aitcheson. Mixed race: 1st, Colin Aitcheson; 2nd, Wm. Whittin. Football kick for women: 1st, Mrs. Gueronsprey; 2nd, Mrs. Stuart. Baseball throw for women: 1st, Miss Isabelle Flaherty; 2nd, Mrs. Peterson. Fat men's race: 1st, Thos. Bell; 2nd, Jas. Stuart. Boys' race: 1st, Wm. Morrow; 2nd, Joseph Morrow. Girls' race: 1st, Bettie Scott; 2nd, Agnes Aitcheson. Girls' race (not over 7 years): 1st, Agnes Aitcheson; 2nd, Isabelle Wynne. Boys' race (not over 7 years): 1st, Edwin Wynne; 2nd, Willie Peterson. Boys' race (not over 12 years): 1st, Leo Troy; 2nd, Axel Peterson.

P. W. POPP, Cor. Sec'y.

ROCHESTER FLORISTS' ASSOCIATION.

The grand picnic of this association was scheduled for Thursday of this week, our "press day," and consequently we can only conjecture what has happened. But knowing the Rochester "bunch" so well as we de we feel quite safe in saying that the affair was a glorious, howling success. We know that the stunts' committee have been very busy for weeks inventing new and striking novelties in that line. After the boys get through and have recovered we are looking for a veracious account of the proceedings, and shall give it space as soon as it comes.

On Saturday, August 21, the Michell Seed House baseball team journeys to Riverton, N. J., to play the Henry A. Dreer nine. The Michell boys have defeated some of the strongest amateur teams in Philadelphia and vicinity, and will be accompanied by at least fifty loyal rooters. They expect to make the trip in the Michell Company's two big auto trucks, and will bring along all sorts of noise-producing instruments to make things lively on the Jersey side. The last two games played by the rival seed houses were won by the Michell team, but the Dreer boys will try hard to win this year.

Cincinnati — The prizes at the floral exhibit at the Carthage Fair last week were pretty thoroughly distributed between T. Ben George, Henry Schwarz and Fred Backmeier.

Mr. and Mrs. C. E. Critchell are planning an auto trip through Indiana for the latter part of this week.

ALLIE ZECH.

Allie Zech is probably the youngest man in the wholesale flower business in Chicago. Upon the death of his father, the late John Zech, he succeeded him as head of the firm of Zech

ALLIE ZECH

& Mann, one of the best known of the Chicago wholesale commission houses. Mr. Zech has a number of years' experience to his credit, as he was right hand man to his father, who was known as one of the most capable men in the trade. This firm stands well with the trade of Chicago and has the disposition of some of the best cut flower stock coming into the Chicago market.

PERSONAL.

John S. Doig has been appointed head gardener to Mrs. J. M. Sears, Southborough, Mass.

P. J. Donahue, of Boston, has just returned from a two weeks' vacation at Oak Bluffs, Martha's Vinyard.

Charles Richardson of the Wyndhurst greenhouses, Lenox, Mass., has accepted a position in the Brookside greenhouses at Great Barrington.

Edward W. Breed of Clinton, Mass., president of the Worcester County Horticultural society, and Mrs. Breed, have returned after a trip to the Panama-Pacific Exposition.

St. Louis.—Miss Julia Mottell, cashier of the Nicotine Mfg. Co., had a tussle with a robber last week when she was returning from the bank with the weekly payroll. Miss Mottell wrenched herself from his grasp, thus saving the money. She is a basket ball champion and an athlete and surprised the robber with her strength. Her boss, J. S. Carter, is away attending the S. A. F. convention with the St. Louis delegation.

Obituary

John M. Clark.

Information comes to us briefly of the death of John M. Clark, secretary of the Leonard Seed Company of Chicago, which occurred on Sunday morning, August 15, after an operation for ulcers of the stomach. Further particulars next week.

Nicholas Hallock

Nicholas Hallock, well-known to the older generation of seed growers and florists of New York and Long Island, died of pneumonia on August 5, while on a visit to relatives in Seattle, Washington. Mr. Hallock was a native of Milton, Ulster County, N. Y., and was 88 years of age at the time of his death.

James L. Green.

James L. Green, an old employee of the S. S. Pennock-Meehan Co., died on the 10th inst. at 6166 Upland street, West Philadelphia, aged 75. He was with the company eight or ten years and retired on the pension list some three years ago owing to impaired health and infirmities due to advanced years.

Fred B. Barrington.

Fred B. Barrington a well-known florist, died on August 14 at the Addison Gilbert Hospital, Gloucester, Mass., after several days illness. He was born in Cambridge and was 56 years old. He came here about 25 years ago and succeeded to the florist business of the late Seth Cole. He leaves a wife and a son.

Henry Arnold.

Henry Arnold, head designer in the Back Bay establishment of Thos. F. Galvin, Boston, died at the Eliot Hospital on Tuesday morning, August 17, after a three days' illness with acute Bright's disease. Mr. Arnold was formerly located in Rochester, where he worked for Vick and for Wilson, and has been with Galvin for the past eight years, a competent and well-liked employee. His age was 51 years. He was unmarried.

WHOLESALE FLOWER MARKETS — TRADE PRICES—Per 100 TO DEALERS ONLY

Roses	CINCINNATI Aug. 16		CHICAGO July 26		BUFFALO Aug. 16		PITTSBURG Aug. 16	
Am. Beauty, Special	20.00 to 25.00		20.00 to 30.00		20.00 to 25.00		20.00 to 25.00	
" " Fancy and Extra	12.50 to 15.00		15.00 to 20.00		12.00 to 15.00		12.50 to 15.00	
" " No. 1	6.00 to 10.00		8.00 to 15.00		6.00 to 10.00		4.00 to 10.00	
Killarney, Richmond, Extra	4.00 to 5.00		6.00 to 10.00		5.00 to 7.00		6.00 to 8.00	
" " Ordinary	2.00 to		3.00 to 6.00		2.00 to 4.00		2.00 to 4.00	
Hillingdon, Ward, Sunburst, Extra	4.00 to 6.00		4.00 to 8.00		6.00 to 9.00		to 6.00	
" " " Ordinary	2.00 to 3.00		2.00 to 4.00		2.00 to 5.00		2.00 to 4.00	
Arenberg, Radiance, Taft, Extra	4.00 to 6.00		to		6.00 to 8.00		6.00 to 8.00	
" " " Ordinary	2.00 to		to		2.00 to 6.00		to 4.00	
Russell, Hadley, Ophelia, Mock	2.00 to 8.00		5.00 to 15.00		5.00 to 10.00		6.00 to 10.00	
Carnations, Fancy	1.00 to 2.00		2.00 to 3.00		1.00 to 2.00		1.00 to 2.00	
" Ordinary	to .75		1.00 to 2.00		.75 to 1.00		to .50	
Cattleyas	25.00 to 50.00		35.00 to 50.00		25.00 to 50.00		40.00 to 50.00	
Dendrobium formosum	to		40.00 to 50.00		to		to	
Lilies, Longiflorum	8.00 to 10.00		8.00 to 10.00		5.00 to 8.00		to 8.00	
" Rubrum	3.00 to 6.00		to		3.00 to 4.00		to 3.00	
Lily of the Valley	to 4.00		2.00 to 4.00		to 4.00		3.00 to 4.00	
Daisies	to .50		.50 to 1.00		1.00 to 1.50		to	
SnapDragon	1.00 to 3.00		2.00 to 4.00		3.00 to 5.00		to .50	
Gladioli	2.00 to 5.00		2.00 to 4.00		4.00 to 5.00		2.00 to 4.00	
Asters	1.00 to 3.00		1.00 to 4.00		2.00 to 4.00		2.00 to 3.00	
Sweet Peas	to		.25 to .50		.15 to .75		to	
Gardenias	to		to		20.00 to 25.00		to	
Smilax	to 15.00		10.00 to 15.00		to 15.00		12.50 to 15.00	
Asparagus Plumosus, Strings (100)	to 50.00		40.00 to 50.00		40.00 to 50.00		20.00 to 40.00	
" & Spren. (100 bchs.)	to 25.00		25.00 to 35.00		25.00 to 35.00		20.00 to 50.00	

Flower Market Reports

BOSTON It is a very dull and lifeless market this week. There is an excess of flowers, of course, and with no trade outlet the only fate for much of the shipments to the wholesale markets is the cart which carries away refuse. Quality is all right but that alone does not make trade, and this is the deadest August Boston florists have ever had to face. Roses have not been very heavily overstocked, but are not beginning to heap up as the new planted stock comes along. It is the gladioli, asters, lilies and miscellaneous outdoor products that makes most of the trouble.

BUFFALO Business is very weak. The receipts of gladiolus have been very heavy and with no outlet, there being no set price and everything having to be forced. The early crop of asters is nearly over, with some fine stock of the branching type slowly coming in, though the sales on these, too, have been very slow. There are enough roses. Carnations are about done for. Lilies are still plentiful and sales also slow. There is very little floral work to consume hardly any portion of the receipts, and most of the merchants are taking vacations right in their own stores.

CINCINNATI Business was rather dull last week. Not even the opening and close were very active. A large supply of good stock is coming into the wholesale houses. Shipping business is only fair. Rose offerings include some very good American Beauties, Taft and Radiance. Carnations from the young stock are beginning to come in and up to this time have found a very ready market. Late asters may now be had in all colors in quantities. Gladioli are coming along steadily and are plenti-

WHOLESALE FLOWER MARKETS — TRADE PRICES—Per 100 TO DEALERS ONLY

	BOSTON Aug. 19		ST. LOUIS Aug. 16		PHILA. Aug. 16	
Roses						
Am. Beauty, Special	12.00 to	20.00	30.00 to	40.00	20.00 to	25.00
" " Fancy and Extra	6.00 to	10.00	20.00 to	25.00	12.00 to	18.00
" " No. 1	1.00 to	3.00	10.00 to	15.00	6.00 to	10.00
Killarney, Richmond, Extra	2.00 to	4.00	5.00 to	6.00	1.00 to	6.00
" " Ordinary	.50 to	1.00	2.00 to	3.00	.50 to	1.00
Hillingdon, Ward, Sunburst, Extra	2.00 to	4.00	5.00 to	6.00	3.00 to	6.00
" " Ordinary	.50 to	1.00	2.00 to	3.00	2.00 to	3.00
Arenberg, Radiance, Taft, Extra	2.00 to	4.00	..... to	.....,	3.00 to	6.00
" " Ordinary	.50 to	1.00	..... to	.....	2.00 to	3.00
Russell, Hadley, Ophelia, Mock	2.00 to	8.00	6.00 to	8.00	2.00 to	10.00
Carnations, Fancy	.75 to	1.00	2.00 to	3.00	1.00 to	2.00
Ordinary	.50 to	.75	1.00 to	1.50	.50 to	1.00
Cattleyas	20.00 to	50.00	35.00 to	50.00	20.00 to	35.00
Dendrobium formosum	10.00 to	.....	..... to	.....	..... to	.....
Lilies, Longiflorum	2.00 to	4.00	6.00 to	8.00	5.00 to	8.00
Rubrum	1.00 to	2.00	4.00 to	5.00	..... to	.....
Lily of the Valley	1.00 to	3.00	3.00 to	4.00	1.00 to	4.00
Daisies	.50 to	1.00	.30 to	.25	..... to	.....
Snapdragon	.75 to	1.00	3.00 to	4.00	..... to	.....
Gladioli	1.00 to	1.50	1.50 to	2.50	1.00 to	3.00
Asters	.25 to	1.00	1.00 to	3.00	.50 to	2.00
Sweet Peas	.15 to	.20	.15 to	.25	.20 to	1.50
Gardenias	10.00 to	15.00	..... to	.....	..... to	.....
Adiantum	.50 to	1.00	1.00 to	1.75	..... to	1.00
Smilax	6.00 to	12.00	10.00 to	15.00	15.00 to	20.00
Asparagus Plumosus, Strings (100)	25.00 to	50.00	50.00 to	50.00	35.00 to	50.00
& Spren. (100 Bchs.)	25.00 to	35.00	20.00 to	35.00	25.00 to	50.00

ful. Other offerings include auratum and rubrum lilies, dahlias and pond lilies.

NEW YORK Great drifts of asters, white, blue, lavender and pink, characterize the entire wholesale cut flower district this week. They are of all types and qualities, some very good and some very bum but on the whole much better than those offered a week ago. Gladioli seem not quite so numerous as they were but there are still plenty of them and they have to be offered very low to get a taker. Roses are looking pretty good, even the little midgets from young stock showing clean foliage and bright color. Cattleyas are very few but even those are not readily disposed of, there being no trade that demands them. The trading at present is of the "catch-as catch-can" sort and there is nothing in the situation that warrants any synopsis.

PHILADELPHIA There is but little change in the business situation here. The slight improvement previously reported continued and with some diminution of receipts and there was rather less unsold stock. This refers mostly to indoor crops. There is still a little too much outdoor stock. Asters continue good as a rule, although there are still some tailenders of the inferior early-flowering varieties coming in. There are not nearly so many gladioli. Quality continues excellent. Roses are in fair supply, but rather soft and do not keep very well. Among the best are Russells and Beauties. Carnations are practically over for the time being and what few keep coming in are of poor quality. Orchids are still very scarce. There are a few gardenias, but they are mostly of southern origin and the demand for them is slow. Lilies are still plentiful, with prices

(Continued on page 61)

Flower Market Reports

(Continued from page 259)

reasonable. These find favor with the retailers for design work and various decorative uses, as they keep and ship better than most flowers at this season, when nearly everything is lacking in substance and virility.

SAN FRANCISCO Business continues are above the average here for this time of the year, owing to the increased counter trade caused by the large number of visitors in town for the exposition and the large amount of decorative work connected with the many conventions and exposition festivities. Stock is still plentiful. Asters are offered in all colors and quantities of them are being sold. The supply of chrysanthemums is increasing rapidly, but the offerings find a ready market at firm prices. Gladioli are offered quite freely and the fine stock moves readily. While dahlias are on the decline, some excellent specimens are still to be seen which demand a good price. Carnations are exceedingly scarce, and the quality is so poor on the average that they demand little attention. The light offerings of sweet peas show poor quality also. Amaryllis is appearing abundantly, and some zinnias are being brought in. There is little change in the rose situation. Stock is not over-plentiful, and the quality of some varieties is hardly up to standard. Russell and Hadley show some improvement. Wonderful tiger lilies are to be seen everywhere, and the offerings of rubrum and auratum show excellent quality also. A good many double sunflowers are being used.

ST. LOUIS The wholesale market is in the same old rut as for the last few weeks. Everything is plentiful and prices at their lowest. Business conditions in general are bad and, of course, the florists have to suffer their share. As to stock at the wholesale market we can only say that everything in season is plentiful. Roses and asters are more than the trade can handle and most any price will buy them in big lots. Gladioli were about to go up in price a little when along came outside consignments. Lily of the valley, lilies, tuberose stalks and carnations field grown are plentiful.

WASHINGTON There has been no improvement in trade here during the past ten days. Very little of the stock coming in can be moved at any price. Enormous quantities of asters are being sent in, only to be eventually carted away as refuse. The supply of gladioli has decreased to some extent, but the demand has fallen off

---

NEW YORK QUOTATIONS PER 100.　To Dealers Only

MISCELLANEOUS	Last Half of Week ending Aug. 14 1915		First Half of Week begining Aug. 16 1915	
Cattleyas	20.00	to 50.00	20.00	to 50.00
Lilies, Longiflorum	1.00	to 3.00	1.00	to 3.00
Rubrum	1.00	to 2.00	1.00	to 2.00
Lily of the Valley	1.00	to 2.00	1.00	to 3.00
Daisies	....	to .50	....	to .50
Snapdragon	.50	to 1.00	.50	to 1.00
Gladioli	.50	to 1.00	.50	to 1.00
Asters	.15	to 1.50	.15	to 1.00
Sweet Peas	.10	to .15	.10	to .15
Corn Flower	....	to .25	....	to .25
Gardenias	12.00	to 25.00	12.00	to 25.00
Adiantum	.50	to .75	.50	to .75
Smilax	4.00	to 8.00	4.00	to 8.00
Asparagus Plumosus, strings (per 100)	15.00	to 30.00	15.00	to 30.00
& Spren (100 bunches)	10.00	to 30.00	10.00	to 30.00

in proportion. Lilies continue very abundant. Carnations are few and very poor. Cattleyas and other orchids are scarce and it is hard to get these at a price. Some few good dahlias are to be had, but on the whole the heat has badly affected this flower and has put all the life into foliage. Among the roses are some very good Hoosier Beauty. This flower is finding great favor with some of the retailers and the sale has been boosted to quite an extent. On the whole roses are very good for this time of the year, but with a sluggish market. American Beauty from the North are very good. Snapdragon and water lilies are seen in the stores.

ROCHESTER'S BIG FLOWER SHOW.

The attractive proposition made by the management of the Rochester, N. Y., Exposition Flower Show has invited the attention of the best known growers in the country, as had been expected. With no charge for space and the promise of adequate service, and a daily average attendance of over 20,000, it would have been surprising if the big growers had not responded to the invitation to send exhibits to the Rochester Show. August 30 to September 11 are the dates. The management of the Flower Show is to be an annual event. The Exposition itself is on a permanent basis. It is held at the City's own exposition park, and is now in its eighth year. The park has ten large fireproof buildings, and one of the best has been assigned to the Flower Show. A committee of the Rochester Florists' Association is co-operating with the management and hopes to make the Rochester Show a

meeting place for florist and grower, seedsman and importer. They believe that there is need for such an exhibition, as it will give the florists a chance to see, without traveling the country over, what the growers have to offer in new and standard varieties of plants and flowers. That the plan has every promise of success is evidenced by the permanency of the Exposition itself, which is practically under municipal auspices.

A personal invitation has been sent to every florist in New York state, as well as in some adjoining states, informing them of the names of the exhibitors and suggesting that they combine business with pleasure by arranging to spend an early fall vacation in the Flower City and, at the same time, see what the growers have to offer.

Following is a list of the exhibitors already entered: J. K. Alexander, East Bridgewater, Mass.; C. Betscher, Canal Dover, O.; John Lewis Childs, Flowerfield, L. I.; Wilbur A. Christy, Warren, O.; Henry A. Dreer, Inc., Philadelphia; R. & J. Farquhar & Co., Boston; A. E. Kunderd, Goshen, Ind.; Burt Olney Greenhouses, Albion, N. Y.; A. N. Pierson, Inc., Cromwell, Ct.; F. R. Pierson, Tarrytown, N. Y.; Geo. L. Stillman, Westerly, R. I.; N. Harold Cottam & Son, Wappinger Falls, N. Y. and the following Rochester houses: Edward Brockman, George H. Hart, W. T. Logan, Henry P. Neun, Salter Bros., P. Schlegel & Sons, Jacob Thomann & Sons, James Vick's Sons, H. E. Wilson, Geo. T. Boucher and J. B. Keller's Sons Co.

New York, N. Y.—Lecakes will move September 1st into the store formerly occupied by J. K. Allen, 106 W. 28th street.

Buyer's Directory and Ready Reference Guide

Advertisements under this head, one cent a word.   Initials count as words.

Display advertisers in this issue are also listed under this classification without charge. Reference to List of Advertisers will indicate the respective pages.

Buyers failing to find what they want in this list will confer a favor by writing us and we will try to put them in communication with reliable dealers.

ACCOUNTANT

R. J. Dysart, 40 State St., Boston.
For page see List of Advertisers.

ACHILLEA

"Pearl." Fine Seedlings, $3.00 per 1,000, cash. JAMES MOSS, Wholesale Grower, Johnsville, Pa.

APHINE

Aphine Mfg. Co., Madison, N. J.
For page see List of Advertisers.

APHIS PUNK

Nicotine Mfg. Co., St. Louis, Mo.
For page see List of Advertisers.

ASTERS

ASTERS—Invincible, Henderson's seed, and as fine and healthy plants that grow; in white, pink, purple, rose and blue, $3.00 per 1,000; 5,000 or more, $2.50 per 1,000. Cash. JAMES MOSS, Wholesale Grower, Johnsville, Pa.

AUCTION SALES

Elliott Auction Co., New York City.
For page see List of Advertisers.

AZALEAS

P. Ouwerkerk, Hoboken, N. J.
For page see List of Advertisers.

BAY TREES

August Rolker & Sons, New York.
For page see List of Advertisers.

BAY TREES—Standard and Pyramids. All sizes. Price list on demand. JULIUS ROEHRS CO., Rutherford, N. J.

BEDDING PLANTS

A. N. Pierson, Inc., Cromwell, Conn.
For page see List of Advertisers.

BEGONIAS

Julius Roehrs Company, Rutherford, N. J.
For page see List of Advertisers.

R. Vincent, Jr., & Sons Co., White
Marsh, Md.
For page see List of Advertisers.

Thomas Roland, Nahant, Mass.
For page see List of Advertisers.

A. M. Davenport, Watertown, Mass.
For page see List of Advertisers.

Begonia Lorraine, $12.00 per 100, $110.00 per 1,000; Begonia Glory of Cincinnati. $15.00 per 100, $140.00 per 1,000. JULIUS ROEHRS CO., Rutherford, N. J.

BOILERS

Kroeschell Bros. Co., Chicago.
For page see List of Advertisers.

King Construction Co., North Tonawanda, N. Y.
"King Ideal" Boiler.
For page see List of Advertisers.

Hitchings & Co., New York City.
For page see List of Advertisers.

Lord & Burnham Co., New York City.

BOXES—CUT FLOWER FOLDING

Edwards Folding Box Co., Philadelphia.
For page see List of Advertisers.

Folding cut flower boxes, the best made. Write for list. HOLTON & HUNKEL CO., Milwaukee, Wis.

BOX TREES

BOX TREES—Standards, Pyramids and Bush. In various sizes. Price List on demand. JULIUS ROEHRS CO., Rutherford, N. J.

BULBS AND TUBERS

Santa Cruz Bulb & Plant Co., Santa Cruz, Cal.

Freesia Purity and Calla Bulbs.
For page see List of Advertisers.

J. M. Thorburn & Co., New York City Wholesale Price List of High Class Bulbs.
For page see List of Advertisers.

Ralph M. Ward & Co., New York City.
Lily Bulbs.
For page see List of Advertisers.

John Lewis Childs, Flowerfield, L. I., N. Y.
For page see List of Advertisers.

August Rolker & Sons, New York City.
Holland and Japan Bulbs.
For page see List of Advertisers.

R. & J. Farquhar & Co., Boston, Mass.
For page see List of Advertisers.

S. S. Skidelsky & Co., Philadelphia, Pa.
For page see List of Advertisers.

Chas. Schwake & Co., New York City.
Horticultural Importers and Exporters.
For page see List of Advertisers.

A. Henderson & Co., Chicago, Ill.
For page see List of Advertisers.

Burnett Bros., 98 Chambers St., New York.
For page see List of Advertisers.

Henry F. Michell Co., Philadelphia, Pa.
For page see List of Advertisers.

Joseph Breck & Sons Corp., Boston, Mass.
Bulbs for Early Forcing.
For page see List of Advertisers.

C. KEUR & SONS, HILLEGOM, Holland. Bulbs of all descriptions. Write for prices. NEW YORK Branch, 8-10 Bridge St.

Fottler, Fiske, Rawson Co., Boston, Mass.
For page see List of Advertisers.

CAMELLIAS

Julius Roehrs Co., Rutherford, N. J.
For page see List of Advertisers.

CANNAS

Canna Specialists.
Send for Canna book.
THE CONARD & JONES COMPANY, West Grove, Pa.

CARNATION STAPLES

Split carnations quickly, easily and cheaply mended. Pillsbury's Carnation Staple, 1000 for 35c.; 3000 for $1.00 post paid. I. L. PILLSBURY, Galesburg, Ill.

Supreme Carnation Staples, for repairing split carnations, 35c. per 1000; 3000 for $1.00. F. W. WAITE, 85 Belmont Ave., Springfield, Mass.

CARNATIONS

F. Dorner & Sons Co., Lafayette, Ind.
For page see List of Advertisers.

Leo Niessen Co., Philadelphia, Pa.
Field Grown Carnation Plants.
For page see List of Advertisers.

Carnations, field grown, $6.00 per 100. Cash. White and Pink Enchantress Mrs. Ward, Perfection, Fenn, Winsor, Queen, Lawson, Beacon. CHAS. H. GREEN, Spencer, Mass.

CHRYSANTHEMUMS

Poehlmann Bros. Co., Morton Grove, Ill.
For page see List of Advertisers.

Wood Bros., Fishkill, N. Y.
Chrysanthemums Rooted Cuttings.
For page see List of Advertisers.

Chas. H. Totty, Madison, N. J.
For page see List of Advertisers.

R. Vincent, Jr., & Sons Co., White Marsh, Md.
Pompon Chrysanthemums.
For page see List of Advertisers.

THE BEST 1915 NOVELTIES.
The Cream of 1914 Introductions.
The most popular Commercial and Exhibition kinds; also complete line of Pompons, Singles and Anemones. Trade list on application. ELMER D. SMITH & CO., Adrian, Mich.

COCOANUT FIBRE SOIL

20th Century Plant Food Co., Beverly, Mass.
For page see List of Advertisers.

CYCLAMENS

CYCLAMEN — Separate colors; finest strain; extra strong plants; 3-inch pots, $10.00 per 100, $90.00 per 1,000. JULIUS ROEHRS CO., Rutherford, N. J.

DAHLIAS

Send for Wholesale List of whole clumps and separate stock; 40,000 clumps for sale. Northboro Dahlia and Gladiolus Gardens. J. L. MOORE, Prop, Northboro, Mass.

NEW PAEONY DAHLIA
John Wanamaker, Newest, Handsomest, Best. New color, new form and new habit of growth. Big stock of best cut-flower varieties. Send list of wants to PEACOCK DAHLIA FARMS, Berlin, N. J.

DECORATIVE PLANTS

Robert Craig Co., Philadelphia, Pa.
For page see List of Advertisers.

Woodrow & Marketos, New York City.
For page see List of Advertisers.

S. S. Skidelsky & Co., Philadelphia, Pa.
For page see List of Advertisers.

Bobbink & Atkins, Rutherford, N. J.
For page see List of Advertisers.

A. Leuthy & Co., Roslindale, Boston, Mass.
For page see List of Advertisers.

DRACAENAS

Julius Roehrs Co., Rutherford, N. J.
For page see List of Advertisers.

FERNS

Henry A. Dreer, Philadelphia, Pa.
Dreer's Fern Flats.
For page see List of Advertisers.

H. H Barrows & Son, Whitman, Mass.
For page see List of Advertisers.

Robert Craig Co., Philadelphia, Pa.
For page see List of Advertisers.

McHutchison & Co., New York City.
Ferns in Flats.
For page see List of Advertisers.

Roman J. Irwin, New York City.
Boston and Whitmani Ferns.
For page see List of Advertisers.

FERTILIZERS

20th Century Plant Food Co., Beverly, Mass.
Cocoanut Fibre Soil.
For page see List of Advertisers.

Stumpp & Walter Co., New York City.
Scotch Soot.
For page see List of Advertisers.

For List of Advertisers See Page 223

FERTILIZERS—Continued
Pulverized Manure Co., Chicago, Ill.
Wizard Brand Cattle Manure.
For page see List of Advertisers.

Hardwood Ashes for sale. GEO. L. MUNROE & SONS, Oswego, N. Y.

FLORISTS' LETTERS
Boston Florist Letter Co., Boston, Mass.
For page see List of Advertisers.

FLORISTS' SUPPLIES
N. F. McCarthy & Co., Boston, Mass.
For page see List of Advertisers.

Reed & Keller, New York City.
For page see List of Advertisers.

S. S. Pennock-Meehan Co., Philadelphia, Pa.
For page see List of Advertisers.

H. Bayersdorfer & Co., Philadelphia, Pa.
Up-to-Date Summer Novelties.
For page see List of Advertisers.

Welch Bros. Co., Boston, Mass.
For page see List of Advertisers.

FLOWER POTS
W. H. Ernest, Washington, D. C.
For page see List of Advertisers.

A. H. Hews & Co., Inc., Cambridge, Mass.
For page see List of Advertisers.

Hilfinger Bros., Ft. Edward, N. Y.
For page see List of Advertisers.

FOLIAGE PLANTS
A. Leuthy & Co., Roslindale, Boston, Mass.
For page see List of Advertisers.

FUCHSIAS
Fuchsias—Black Prince, Speciosa, double purple and white, Rooted Cuttings, $1.00 per 100; 2¼-in., $2.00 per 100.
W. J. BARNETT, R. D. 57, Sharon, Pa.

FUNGINE
Aphine Mfg. Co., Madison, N. J.
For page see List of Advertisers.

GALAX
Michigan Cut Flower Co., Detroit, Mich.
For page see List of Advertisers.

GERANIUMS
R. Vincent, Jr., & Sons Co.
White Marsh, Md.
For page see List of Advertisers.

GLASS
Sharp, Partridge & Co., Chicago.
For page see List of Advertisers.

Parshelsky Bros., Inc., Brooklyn, N. Y.
For page see List of Advertisers.

Royal Glass Works, New York City.
For page see List of Advertisers.

Greenhouse glass, lowest prices. JOHNSTON GLASS CO., Hartford City, Ind.

GLASS CUTTERS
Smith & Hemenway Co., New York City.
Red Devil Glass Cutter.
For page see List of Advertisers.

GLAZING POINTS
H. A. Dreer, Philadelphia, Pa.
Peerless Glazing Point.
For page see List of Advertisers.

Geo. H. Angermueller, St. Louis, Mo.
For page see List of Advertisers.

GOLD FISH
Gold fish, aquarium plants, snails, castles, globes, aquarium, fish goods, nets, etc., wholesale. FRANKLIN BARRETT, Breeder, 4815 D St., Olney, Philadelphia, Pa. Large breeding pairs for sale. Send for price list.

GREENHOUSE BUILDING MATERIAL
King Construction Co., N. Tonawanda, N. Y.
For page see List of Advertisers.

Parshelsky Bros., Inc., Brooklyn, N. Y.
For page see List of Advertisers.

GREENHOUSE BUILDING MATERIAL—Continued
A. T. Stearns Lumber Co., Neponset, Boston.
Pecky Cypress.
For page see List of Advertisers.

Lord & Burnham Co., New York City.

Metropolitan Material Co., Brooklyn, N. Y.

GREENHOUSE CONSTRUCTION
King Construction Co., N. Tonawanda, N. Y.
For page see List of Advertisers.

Foley Greenhouse Mfg. Co., Chicago, Ill.
For page see List of Advertisers.

Hitchings & Co., New York City.
For page see List of Advertisers.

A. T. Stearns Lumber Co., Boston, Mass.
For page see List of Advertisers.

S. Jacobs & Sons, Brooklyn, N. Y.
For page see List of Advertisers.

Lord & Burnham Co., New York City.

Metropolitan Material Co., Brooklyn, N. Y.

GUTTERS
King Construction Co., N. Tonawanda, N. Y.
King Channel Gutter.
For page see List of Advertisers.

Metropolitan Material Co., Brooklyn, N. Y.
Iron Gutters.

HAIL INSURANCE
Florists' Hail Asso. of America.
J. G Esler, Saddle River, N. J.
For page see List of Advertisers.

HARDY FERNS AND GREEN GOODS
Michigan Cut Flower Exchange, Detroit, Mich.
For page see List of Advertisers.

Knud Nielsen, Evergreen, Ala.
Natural Green Sheet Moss, Fancy and Dagger Ferns and Huckleberry Foliage.
For page see List of Advertisers.

The Kervan Co., New York.
For page see List of Advertisers.

HARDY PERENNIALS
R. & J. Farquhar & Co., Boston, Mass.
For page see List of Advertisers.

Bay State Nurseries, No. Abington, Mass.
For page see List of Advertisers.

P. Ouwerkerk, Hoboken, N. J.
For page see List of Advertisers.

Palisades Nurseries, Sparkill, N. Y.
For page see List of Advertisers.

HEATING APPARATUS
Kroeschell Bros. Co., Chicago.
For page see List of Advertisers.

Lord & Burnham Co., New York City.

HOT-BED SASH
Parshelsky Bros., Inc., Brooklyn, N. Y.
For page see List of Advertisers.

Foley Greenhouse Construction Co.
Chicago, Ill.
For page see List of Advertisers.

A. T. Stearns Lumber Co., Neponset, Mass.
For page see List of Advertisers.

Lord & Burnham Co., New York City.

HOSE
H. A. Dreer, Philadelphia, Pa.

INSECTICIDES
Aphine Manufacturing Co., Madison, N. J.
Aphine and Fungine.
For page see List of Advertisers.

Nicotine Mfg. Co., St. Louis, Mo.
Aphis Punk and Nikoteen.
For page see List of Advertisers.

Eastern Chemical Co., Boston, Mass.
Imp Soap Spray.
For page see List of Advertisers.

The Plantlife Co., New York City.
Plantlife Insecticide.
For page see List of Advertisers.

IRIS
R. & J. Farquhar & Co., Boston, Mass.
For page see List of Advertisers.

John Lewis Childs, Inc.,
Flowerfield, L. I., N. Y.
For page see List of Advertisers.

IRRIGATION EQUIPMENT
Skinner Irrigation Co., Brookline, Mass.
For page see List of Advertisers.

LILY BULBS
Chas. Schwake & Co., New York City.
Horticultural Importers and Exporters.
For page see List of Advertisers.

R. M. Ward & Co., New York, N. Y.
Japanese Lily Bulbs of Superior Quality.
For page see List of Advertisers.

Corp. of Chas. F. Meyer, New York City.
Meyer's T. Brand Giganteums.
For page see List of Advertisers.

John Lewis Childs, Inc.,
Hardy Lilies.
Flowerfield, L. I., N. Y.
For page see List of Advertisers.

LILY OF THE VALLEY
Chas. Schwake & Co., Inc., New York City.
Hohmann's Famous Lily of the Valley Pips.
For page see List of Advertisers.

McHutchison & Co., New York City.
For page see List of Advertisers.

Loechner & Co., New York City.
Lily of the Valley Pips.
For page see List of Advertisers.

LIQUID PUTTY MACHINE
Metropolitan Material Co., Brooklyn, N. Y.
For page see List of Advertisers.

MASTICA
F. O. Pierce Co., New York City.
For page see List of Advertisers.

Geo. H. Angermueller, St. Louis, Mo.
For page see List of Advertisers.

NATIONAL NURSERYMAN
National Nurseryman Publishing Co., Inc.,
Rochester, N. Y.
For page see List of Advertisers.

NIKOTEEN
Nicotine Mfg. Co., St. Louis, Mo.
For page see List of Advertisers.

NIKOTIANA
Aphine Mfg. Co., Madison, N. J.
For page see List of Advertisers.

NURSERY STOCK
P. Ouwerkerk, Weehawken Heights, N. J.
For page see List of Advertisers.

W. & T. Smith Co., Geneva, N. Y.
For page see List of Advertisers.

Bay State Nurseries, North Abington, Mass.
Hardy, Northern Grown Stock.
For page see List of Advertisers.

Bobbink & Atkins, Rutherford, N. J.
For page see List of Advertisers.

Framingham Nurseries, Framingham, Mass.
For page see List of Advertisers.

August Rolker & Sons, New York City.
For page see List of Advertisers.

Chas. G. Curtis Co., Callicoon, N. Y.
Nursery Stock for Fall Planting.
For page see List of Advertisers.

NUT GROWING
The Nut-Grower, Waycross, Ga.
For page see List of Advertisers.

ONION SETS
Schilder Bros., Chillicothe, O.
Onion Seed—Onion Sets.
For page see List of Advertisers.

ORCHID FLOWERS
Jas. McManus, New York, N. Y.
For page see List of Advertisers.

ORCHID PLANTS
Julius Roehrs Co., Rutherford, N. J.
For page see List of Advertisers.

Lager & Hurrell, Summit, N. J.

PALMS, ETC.
Robert Craig Co., Philadelphia, Pa.
For page see List of Advertisers.

August Rolker & Sons, New York City.
For page see List of Advertisers.

A. Leuthy & Co., Roslindale, Boston, Mass.
For page see List of Advertisers.

PANDANUS VEITCHI
Julius Roehrs Co., Rutherford, N. J.
For page see List of Advertisers.

PANSY PLANTS
PANSIES—The Big Giant Flowering
Kind—$3.00 per 1,000; $25.00 for 10,000. If
I could only show the nice plants, hundred
of testimonials and repeat orders, I would
be flooded with new business. Cash.
JAMES MOSS, Wholesale Grower, Johnsville, Pa.

PANSY SEED
Chas. Frost. Kenilworth, N. J.
The Kenilworth Giant Pansy.
For page see List of Advertisers.

Arthur T. Boddington Co., Inc.,
New York City.
Boddington's Gigantic Pansies.
For page see List of Advertisers.

PEONIES
Peonies. The world's greatest collection.
1200 sorts. Send for list. C. BETSCHER,
Canal Dover, O.

French Peonies can be shipped with
celerity and security via: Bordeaux-New
York. Catalogues free. DESSERT, Peony
Specialist, Chenonceaux (T. & L.), France.

RARE PEONIES—Therese, Mons. M. Cahusac, $3.00 each. Send for list of largest
collection of Continental and European varieties, Marcelle, Dessert, Solange, Tourangelle, Primevere, Mignon, Alsace Lorraine, Baroness Schroeder, etc. D. W. C.
RUFF, Buena Vista Gardens, St. Paul,
Minn.

PECKY CYPRESS BENCHES
A T Stearns Lumber Co., Boston, Mass.
For page see List of Advertisers.

PIPE AND FITTINGS
Kroeschell Bros. Co., Chicago.
For page see List of Advertisers.

King Construction Company,
N. Tonawanda, N. Y.
Shelf Brackets and Pipe Hangers.
For page see List of Advertisers.

PLANT AND BULB IMPORTS
Chas. Schwake & Co., New York City.
For page see List of Advertisers.

August Rolker & Sons, New York City.
For page see List of Advertisers.

PLANT TRELLISES AND STAKES
Seele's Tieless Plant Stakes and Trellises. H. D. SEELE & SONS, Elkhart, Ind.

PLANT TUBS
H. A. Dreer, Philadelphia, Pa.
"Riverton Special."
For page see List of Advertisers.

POINSETTIAS
A. Henderson & Co., Chicago, Ill.
For page see List of Advertisers.

RAFFIA
McHutchison & Co., New York, N. Y.
For page see List of Advertisers.

RHODODENDRONS
P. Ouwerkerk, Hoboken, N. J.
For page see List of Advertisers.

Framingham Nurseries, Framingham, Mass.
For page see List of Advertisers.

RIBBONS AND CHIFFONS
S. S. Pennock-Meehan Co., Philadelphia, Pa.
For page see List of Advertisers.

ROSES
Poehlmann Bros. Co., Morton Grove, Ill.
For page see List of Advertisers.

P. Ouwerkerk, Hoboken, N. J.
For page see List of Advertisers.

Robert Craig Co., Philadelphia, Pa.
For page see List of Advertisers.

W. & T. Smith Co., Geneva, N. Y.
American Grown Roses.
For page see List of Advertisers.

Bay State Nurseries, North Abington, Mass.

August Rolker & Sons, New York City.
For page see List of Advertisers.

Framingham Nurseries, Framingham, Mass.
For page see List of Advertisers.

A. N. Pierson, Inc., Cromwell, Conn.
For page see List of Advertisers.

Wood Bros., Fishkill, N. Y.
For page see List of Advertisers.

THE CONARD & JONES COMPANY,
Rose Specialists.
West Grove, Pa. Send for offers.

SEASONABLE PLANT STOCK
R. Vincent, Jr. & Sons Co., White Marsh
Md.
For page see List of Advertisers.

SEED GROWERS
California Seed Growers' Association.
San Jose, Cal.
For page see List of Advertisers.

SEEDS
Carter's Tested Seeds,
Seeds with a Pedigree.
Boston, Mass., and London, England
For page see List of Advertisers.

Schilder Bros., Chillicothe, O.
Onion Seed—Onion Sets.

Joseph Breck & Sons, Boston, Mass
For page see List of Advertisers.

Kelway & Son,
Langport, Somerset, England.
Kelway's Celebrated English Strain Garden
Seeds.
For page see List of Advertisers.

J. Bolgiano & Son, Baltimore, Md.
For page see List of Advertisers.

A. T. Boddington Co., Inc., New York City.
For page see List of Advertisers.

Chas. Schwake & Co., New York City
For page see List of Advertisers.

Michell's Seed House, Philadelphia, Pa.
New Crop Flower Seeds.
For page see List of Advertisers.

W. Atlee Burpee & Co., Philadelphia, Pa
For page see List of Advertisers.

R. & J. Farquhar & Co., Boston, Mass
For page see List of Advertisers.

J. M. Thorburn & Co., New York City
For page see List of Advertisers.

S. Bryson Ayres Co., Independence, Mo.
Sweet Peas.
For page see List of Advertisers.

Loechner & Co., New York City.
For page see List of Advertisers.

Ant. C. Zvolanek, Lompoc, Cal.
Winter Flowering Sweet Pea Seed
For page see List of Advertisers.

S. S. Skidelsky & Co., Philadelphia, Pa
For page see List of Advertisers.

W. E. Marshall & Co., New York City.
Seeds, Plants and Bulbs.
For page see List of Advertisers.

August Rolker & Sons, New York City.
For page see List of Advertisers.

SEEDS—Continued
Burnett Bros., 98 Chambers St., New York.
For page see List of Advertisers.

Fottler, Fiske, Rawson Co., Boston, Mass.
Seeds for the Florist.
For page see List of Advertisers.

SKINNER IRRIGATION SYSTEM
Skinner Irrigation Co., Brookline, Mass.
For page see List of Advertisers.

SPHAGNUM MOSS
Live Sphagnum moss, orchid peat and
orchid baskets always on hand. LAGER
& HURRELL, Summit, N. J.

Sphagnum Moss—10-bbl. bales, $1.90;
5-bbl. bale, 90c. Laurel, 90c. bag. Get
prices on large lots. JOS. H. PAUL, P. O.
156, Manahawkin, N. J.

STOVE PLANTS
Orchids—Largest stock in the country—
Stove plants and Crotons, finest collection.
JULIUS ROEHRS CO., Rutherford, N. J.

STRAWBERRY PLANTS
Wilfrid Wheeler, Concord, Mass.
Pot Grown.
For page see List of Advertisers.

SWAINSONA
R. Vincent, Jr., & Sons Co., White
Marsh, Md.
For page see List of Advertisers.

SWEET PEA SEED
W. Atlee Burpee & Co., Philadelphia, Pa.
Burpee's Winter-Flowering Spencer Sweet
Peas.
For page see List of Advertisers.

Ant. C. Zvolanek, Lompoc, Calif.
Gold Medal of Honor Winter Orchid Sweet
Peas.
For page see List of Advertisers.

S. Bryson Ayres Co.,
Sunnyslope, Independence, Mo.
For page see List of Advertisers.

A. T. Boddington Co., Inc., New York City.
For page see List of Advertisers.

SWEET PEAS—Send 25 cents for ounce
pkt. new Spencer Sweet Peas, and get a
large pkt. Early Sweet Peas, extra.
BUFORD REID, Sherman, Miss.

NEW WINTER FLOWERING VARIETIES
SWEET PEA SEED.
MRS. A. A. SKACH—A beautiful shell pink.
Will not fade and has splendid keeping
qualities. Per oz., $1.75; 4 oz., $6.50; 1
lb., $18.00.
MRS. M. SPANOLIN—Black-seeded, of the
purest white color. Has won a number of
first prizes. Per oz., $2.00; 4 oz., $7.00;
1 lb., $25.00.
VENUS—White with slight pink blush, one
of the best. Per oz., $2.00; 4 oz., $7.00;
1 lb., $25.00.
LAVENDER ORCHID—Lavender pink, very
large. Per oz., $2.00; 4 oz., $7.00; 1 lb.,
$25.00.
WHITE ORCHID—A true white. Per oz.,
$1.75; 4 oz., $6.00; 1 lb., $18.00.
MRS. JOS. MANDA—A light shell pink
with extra long stem. Flowers ruffled,
becoming a brighter pink the longer he
are kept. Per oz., $2.00; 4 oz., $7.00; 1 lb.,
$25.00.
ORCHID BEAUTY—Dark rose, blushed
with orange. Per oz., $1.75; 4 oz., $6.00;
1 lb., $18.00.
ORANGE ORCHID—Begins to bloom in
March. One of the best if sown late.
During December and January the color
is more rose. True. Per oz., $4.00; 4 oz.,
$7.00; 1 lb. $25.00.
YARRAWA—Spencer, early winter flowering, bright rose pink, seed sown August
1st will flower November 15th. ¼ oz.,
$1.00; 1 oz., $3.50; ¼ lb., $12.50.
All other varieties, with prices, on
application.
S. S. PENNOCK-MEEHAN CO.,
1608-20 Ludlow Street,   Philadelphia, Pa.

VENTILATING APPARATUS
The Advance Co., Richmond, Ind.
For page see List of Advertisers.

The John A. Evans Co., Richmond, Ind.
For page see List of Advertisers.

For List of Advertisers See Page 223

New Offers In This Issue

**AETNA BRAND TANKAGE FER-
TILIZER.**
Farmers & Florists Fertilizer Co.,
Chicago, Ill.
For page see List of Advertisers.

**BODDINGTON'S MATCHLESS
CINERARIAS.**
Arthur T. Boddington Co., Inc.,
New York City.
For page see List of Advertisers.

CARNATIONS.
Wood Bros., Fishkill, N. Y.
For page see List of Advertisers.

**DARWIN TULIPS, HYACINTHS AND
SPANISH IRIS BULBS.**
Raymond W. Swett, Saxonville, Mass.
For page see List of Advertisers.

**EASTERN HEADQUARTERS FOR
FLORISTS' SUPPLIES AND
CUT FLOWERS.**
N. F. McCarthy & Co., Boston, Mass.

**FERNS FOR DISHES AND DECORA-
TIVE PLANTS.**
Frank Oechslin, Chicago, Ill.
For page see List of Advertisers.

FLOWERS BY TELEGRAPH.
The Florists' Telegraph Delivery
Association.
Albert Pochelon, Secretary, Detroit, Mich.
For page see List of Advertisers.

FLOWERS BY TELEGRAPH.
Samuel Murray, Kansas City, Mo.
For page see List of Advertisers.

New Offers In This Issue

FLOWERS BY TELEGRAPH.
National Floral Corporation, New York City.
For page see List of Advertisers.

**GREENHOUSE BOILERS AND
HEATING.**
Kroeschell Bros. Co., Chicago, Ill.
For page see List of Advertisers.

GREENHOUSE CONSTRUCTION.
John C. Moninger Co., Chicago, Ill.
For page see List of Advertisers.

GREENHOUSE CONSTRUCTION.
Foley Greenhouse Mfg. Co., Chicago, Ill.
For page see List of Advertisers.

**GREENHOUSE CONSTRUCTION
MATERIAL.**
A. Dietsch Co., Chicago, Ill.
For page see List of Advertisers.

HAND-MADE GREENHOUSE GLASS.
Johnston Brokerage Co., Pittsburgh, Pa.
For page see List of Advertisers.

**HENDERSON'S SUPERIOR BULBS
FOR FALL PLANTING.**
Peter Henderson & Co., New York City.
For page see List of Advertisers.

JUNIPERUS PROSTRATA.
Mt. Desert Nurseries, Bar Harbor, Me.
For page see List of Advertisers.

MAGIC BRAND MANURES.
Chicago Feed & Fertilizer Co.,
Union Stock Yards, Chicago, Ill.
For page see List of Advertisers.

NEW FLORISTS' SUPPLIES.
H. Bayersdorfer & Co., Philadelphia, Pa.
For page see List of Advertisers.

**NEW NEPHROLEPIS JOHN WANA-
MAKER.**
Robt. Craig Co., Philadelphia, Pa.
For page see List of Advertisers.

**OUR MOTTO, FOR PROGRESSIVE-
NESS.**
Gude Bros. Co., Washington, D. C.
For page see List of Advertisers.

PANSY SEED.
Fottler, Fiske, Rawson Co., Boston, Mass.
For page see List of Advertisers.

**ROCHESTER'S EXPOSITION AND
FLOWER SHOW.**
Geo. B. Hart, Chairman of Committee,
Rochester, N. Y.
For page see List of Advertisers.

**ROSES, CARNATIONS, ETC., PLANT-
ING STOCK.**
Poehlmann Bros. Co., Chicago, Ill.
For page see List of Advertisers.

STRAWBERRY PLANTS.
T. J. Dwyer & Co., Cornwall, N. Y.
For page see List of Advertisers.

SUMMER FLOWERS.
S. S. Pennock-Meehan Co., Philadelphia, Pa.
For page see List of Advertisers.

WHOLESALE FLORISTS.
Zech & Mann, Chicago, Ill.
For page see List of Advertisers.

WHOLESALE FLORIST.
Chicago Flower Growers' Association,
Chicago, Ill.
For page see List of Advertisers.

WIZARD BRAND MANURES.
The Pulverized Manure Co., Chicago, Ill.
For page see List of Advertisers.

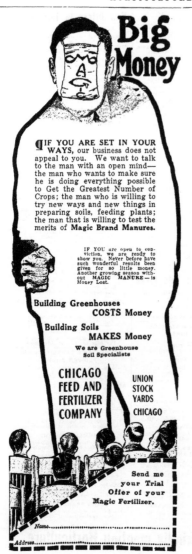

Big Money

¶IF YOU ARE SET IN YOUR WAYS, our business does not appeal to you. We want to talk to the man with an open mind—the man who wants to make sure he is doing everything possible to Get the Greatest Number of Crops; the man who is willing to try new ways and new things in preparing soils, feeding plants; the man that is willing to test the merits of **Magic Brand Manures.**

IF YOU are open to conviction, we are ready to show you. Never before have such wonderful results been given for so little money. Another growing season without MAGIC MANURE — is Money Lost.

Building Greenhouses
    COSTS Money

Building Soils
    MAKES Money

We are Greenhouse
Soil Specialists

CHICAGO FEED AND FERTILIZER COMPANY

UNION STOCK YARDS CHICAGO

Send me your Trial Offer of your Magic Fertilizer.

Name..

Address...

The Lorain Ave. Greenhouse Co., a new corporation of West Park, Ohio, a suburb of Cleveland have placed an order with the John C. Moninger Co. of Chicago, for eight greenhouses 30 ft. x 300 ft. of the new style "bolted thru" construction. The plant will also be equipped with a modern fireproof boiler and packing room. Tomatoes and cucumbers will be the principal crops grown. Chas. C. Christensen of Rocky River, a veteran vegetable grower, is president of the new firm. H. M. Berner represented the John C. Moninger Co. in the transaction.

WANTS, FOR SALE, Etc.

GREENHOUSES BUILDING OR CONTEMPLATED.

Lorain, O.—Tony Carek, one house.

Eureka, Ill. — Earl Ewing, one house.

Newark, N. J.—R. P. Plebany, one house.

Lancaster, Wis.—Chas. Stratton, additions.

Merrill, Wis.—Paul, the florist, additions and alterations.

Wellesley Hills, Mass. — Thomas Capers, house 35 x 300.

Scranton, Pa. — St. Peter's Cathedral, King house 18 x 25.

Canajoharie, N. Y.—Joseph Traudt, additions and alterations.

Bucyrus, O. — F. J. Norton, West Charles street, rebuilding.

Lincoln, Neb.—Griswold Seed Co., South 15th street, one house.

St. Louis, Mo.—John Nyflot, 7319 Florissant avenue, one house.

New Haven, Ct.—Alfred Nyren, 530 Townsend avenue, rebuilding.

Garrett Park, Md. — David Bisset, two violet houses, each 25 x 150.

Moosehart, Ill.—Moosehart Greenhouses, two Foley houses, each 40 x 300.

Saginaw, Mich. — Chas. Frueh & Sons, Genesee avenue, range of houses. Roethke Floral Co., rebuilding.

JAMES B. FOLEY.

A rising young man in one of the allied trades in Chicago is James Foley, who, like his father, bids fair to be a

JAMES B. FOLEY

big man in more ways than one. He is treasurer and director in the Foley Greenhouse Manufacturing Co, and although a very young man has the backing of seven years of practical work. While his education has been largely in the school of experience he has taken advantage of the opportunities offered by one of Chicago's largest technical schools, and so is well equipped to take a prominent place in the construction and manufacture of greenhouse materials.

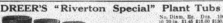

Your Hurry Calls on Fittings or Boilers We Can Fill at Once

IT will soon be the time of the year when all of a sudden you find out that your old boiler won't stand the racket for another season, and you must have one to replace it in a hurry.

It's also the time when you find your coils need new fittings here and there.

At all times we endeavor to ship all orders as promptly as possible, but at just that time **of year** our shipping department has instructions to "**rush all boilers and fittings.**"

So no matter whether you write, wire or phone, your order will be filled and sent on its way immediately on its receipt.

However, what do you need now?

Hitchings *and* Company

NEW YORK	BOSTON	PHILADELPHIA
1170 Broadway	49 Federal Street	40 S. 15th Street

General Offices and Factory, Elizabeth, N. J.

HORTICULTURE

Clematis paniculata

Published Every Saturday at 147 Summer Street, Boston, Mass.
Subscription, $1.00

LIST OF ADVERTISERS

FOR BUYERS' DIRECTORY AND READY REFERENCE GUIDE
SEE PAGES 296, 297, 298, 299

NOTES ON CULTURE OF FLORISTS' STOCK

CONDUCTED BY

John J. M. Farrell

Questions by our readers in line with any of the topics presented on this page will be cordially received and promptly answered by Mr. Farrell. Such communications should invariably be addressed to the office of HORTICULTURE.
"If vain our toil, we ought to blame the culture, not the soil."—*Pope.*

Carnations

Let the plants have the benefit of a full circulation of air all around. Keep the ventilators wide open and if possible the doors, especially on hot days. Sunlight and fresh air are what the plants need before fire heat touches them. Cultivating, cleaning and watering are the main things to be attended to now. You can overdo the watering but not the other two. It is needless to say that no weeds should ever be allowed to get established among the plants; don't wait for them to come nor neglect the removing of every bad leaf on the plants. Give the soil a thorough soaking when it is in need of it and don't repeat it until it dries out—not dust dry for that would stunt the growth if repeated and be as wrong as to continuously keep it in a wet state.

Chrysanthemums

Make it a rule to look over the benches every morning and water where needed, but only where needed as saturation all the time will work ruin now. Syringe only in the morning now and on clear days, so that before night fall all the superfluous water will have time to dry up. Give attention to disbudding and liquid feeding. Keep on feeding until the flowers show color. If we run into a spell of damp and rainy weather have a little heat run through the pipes. Keep the plants clear of all by-growth, so the full strength will be carried to the bloom. Keep them clear of fly by timely fumigation done carefully.

Decorative Stock

Now is a good time to go over your stock and see what you are short of. Lay in a supply of Phoenix Roebelenii, Areca lutescens, Cocos Weddelliana, Latania borbonica and Kentias, also ferns, Pandanus and Aspidistra. Scan the advertisements in HORTICULTURE and place your order early. Money invested in a good stock of these and the half dozen other plants usually found at the retailers' always comes back with good interest. Give the palm house a good cleaning, then fill it up and make things attractive for the opening of another season—the best one you ever had. Only by carrying a good supply of salable stock can we expect to do business.

Marguerites

Suitable cuttings are not procurable on marguerites during the hot months but are now to be had and a good batch should be placed in sand at once. These can be grown into nice bushy plants in 6-inch or 7-inch pots for spring sales. When rooted they can be potted into 2½ or 3-inch pots using any good rose or carnation compost. When they will stand the sun place them in the highest house. To keep them growing they will want a winter temperature of from 50 to 55 degrees night. These should not be allowed to suffer from want of a shift and be sure to give them a rich soil. If your old plants were carried over in the field lift and pot them during the present month. Be sure each has a good ball attached and keep them well watered and shaded for a few days until they cease wilting. In a couple of weeks they will have to be housed.

Bulb Stock for Winter

To make bulb growing pay a careful study is absolutely necessary to prevent waste of material. The smaller retail grower depends to a large extent on the Dutch bulbs to furnish him flowers during the first four months of the year. Roman hyacinths and the paperwhites are the next thing on the program to be planted out for flowers from Christmas on.

Stevia

Do not leave it too late before lifting the stevia as the least bit of frost will injure it. For a week after they are lifted they will want some shade and careful handling, but after this give them full light and in a cool house as they do not like to be grown too warm.

Next Week:—Cattleyas; Cinerarias for Easter; Freesias; Tulips; Winter Flowering Geraniums; Watch Out for Frost.

Clematis paniculata

This popular climbing vine is too well known to our readers to require any detailed notes in connection with the picture which adorns our title page this week. The residence shown is that of Edward Harris, Weymouth, Mass. The extent to which this Clematis varies when raised as usual from seed is perhaps not generally realized. Most are fragrant, but some have no fragrance, some are purest white—others creamy, while they vary greatly in size of individual flowers and in form of truss, some being in long scattered racemes—others almost flat heads. The most interesting fact, however, to be remembered is the wide variation in the time of blooming of different plants, a difference of two or three weeks being possible, and thus it is easy to assure customers of a long extended flowering period by classifying nursery stock as early or late blooming.

HORTICULTURE

VOL. XXII   AUGUST 28, 1915   NO. 9

PUBLISHED WEEKLY BY
HORTICULTURE PUBLISHING CO.
147 Summer Street, Boston, Mass.
Telephone, Oxford 292.
WM. J. STEWART, Editor and Manager.

SUBSCRIPTION RATES:
One Year, in advance, $1.00; To Foreign Countries, $2.00; To
Canada, $1.50.

Entered as second-class matter December 8, 1904, at the Post Office
at Boston, Mass., under the Act of Congress of March 3, 1879.

CONTENTS   Page

After looking upon the pictures of the
Houston wrecked greenhouses at Houston, Texas,
grit which appear in this issue we believe every
one of our readers will heartily second our
feeling of deep sympathy for all who suffered in this

grevious disaster. It requires some courage in the face
of such a visitation as has befallen Mr. Kerr to take
so philosophical a view of his loss as is expressed in
his letter. The vice-president elect of the S. A. F. has
evidently a goodly portion of "gritty sand" in his
make-up.

Of the several flowers now in the public eye,
The which have responded readily to the art of
gladiolus the hybridist, none have made more
rapid and sensational improvement than
the gladiolus. The exhibitions of this flower at various
places during the present season have brought out material which is nothing short of marvelous and one of the
most interesting facts in this connection is that the
varieties showing the greatest advancement over the old
types are the productions of American specialists. Unfortunately for these earnest workers the emoluments
from their triumphs have been and are likely to be very
very small so long as conditions are such that foreign
growers can swamp our markets with stock of our own
best production at prices with which home competition
is next to impossible.

HORTICULTURE feels a bit proud
One lesson of the fact that, although much
of the Convention farther removed from San Francisco than any of its competitors,
it was able to give to its readers the most complete
account and latest news of the Convention proceedings
of any published last week. The record of the Convention, summed up, would appear to fully justify the judgment of those members at the Boston Convention who
were responsible for the acceptance of the invitation to
take the Society to the far-away Pacific Coast. We
might say, however, that as it appears to us, the un-
questioned success of the San Francisco Convention lies
not so much in the amount of direct practical work
accomplished as in the evidence presented of the firm
grasp which the national organization now holds upon
the progressive horticultural interests of the country and
in the demonstration of the rapid growth and spread
of this sentiment of loyalty which is now in progress.

With the big Exposition beckoning and
The part every spare moment crowded with enter-
of wisdom tainment of some kind, it was not to be
expected that any great measure of seri-
ous work could be accomplished at San Francisco and
it is no surprise that the principal business done by a
Convention primarily bent on sight-seeing seems to have
been the good-natured approval and passing on to the
Executive Board of the various projects so earnestly
thought out and formulated for months previously and
recommended by the President for the organic and
structural strengthening of the Association and the systematic development of its channels for usefulness. Obviously it is too much to expect from a gathering made
up as S. A. F. Conventions are, that calm deliberation
and far-seeing judgment which should underlie every
important enactment by such an institution. Consequently the inclination to avoid the hazards of hasty
action, by first submitting momentous matters to responsible officials for leisurely, thoughtful consideration,
is the part of wisdom. In our humble opinion, an application of a goodly portion of the same conservative
reasoning will be in order when the time comes to decide
whether the selection of two directors each year shall
be cast into the impetuous politics of a convention election or entrusted, as hitherto, to the president-elect to
appoint after he has had several months' opportunity to
study the immediate needs of the Society.

ROSE GROWING UNDER GLASS

CONDUCTED BY

Arthur C. Ruzicka

Questions by our readers in line with any of the topics presented on this page will be cordially received and promptly answered by Mr. Ruzicka. Such communications should invariably be addressed to the office of HORTICULTURE.

Lime

If the soil used in making sod heaps had the least trace of acid in it, it will not be very long after planting that the houses will need a light dose of lime. If green appears here and there on the surface of the soil, and the plants have not the dark color that they should have, or are a little soft, it is a sure sign that lime ought to be applied. Use pure air slacked lime, prefering lime bought in barrels and slacked at home, to any mixture that is on the market as agricultural lime. To slack a barrel of lime quickly, dump it into a large box and then sprinkle a can or two of water over it. Avoid using too much water as the lime might remain damp, and although it would be just as good for applying to the benches it would be worthless to blow around the houses at night and it is best to have the lime so that it can be used for both purposes at the same time. When applying have the lime cold and free from unslacked lumps. Do not apply too much all at once but just enough to whiten the benches nicely. We find it best to apply it right after watering, after the benches have dried off just a little, then going over the surface and rubbing the lime in a little. Avoid going deep, as the roots are sure to be disturbed, and this would harm the plants. After this the plants can be watered when they require it, which will be a little sooner, for the lime and the rubbing over of the surface will make them dry out a little quicker. Do not apply lime if the benches have just been mulched or if they have just received a dressing of bonemeal, soot, or sheep manure. The lime coming into contact with the last named fertilizers would release a large portion of the ammonia and other fertilizing elements, and these, suddenly turned into gases would be sure to harm the plants.

Blackspot

When tying or cutting, in fact when doing anything at all around the plants, always watch out for spot. Wherever it appears see that it is picked off at once, and then see that the foliage is dry at night as it should be. Also see that the rain does not beat in when showers come up and should it happen that the houses are open and do get wet, care for the plants properly. This applies especially to Beauties which are more apt to get it than any other rose we grow. When tying, distribute the wood well so that it is not bunched up too much, shutting out air and making it easy for the disease to gain a foothold. Once it gets in it will not be very easy to rid the plants of it, and only by good culture and keeping the plants growing all the time will they eventually grow out of it. It is well to apply a spray of the ammoniacal copper carbonate mixture if the attack promises to be bad at all. This is no cure, by any means, but it will do a good deal to keep the spot from spreading. Avoid overwatering at all times, at the same time being careful not to dry the plants out so that they will get a bad setback. Beauties are very particular in this respect, and once severely checked it is a big undertaking to get them going right again. If the first few spots that appear are removed at once the danger of their spreading will be very small. Keep right after it.

Fumigation

As soon as the plants begin cutting, the use of tobacco stems for smoking should be stopped at once and other materials used to keep out the always-on-hand greenfly. It is strange where these little rascals come from, for no matter how clean the house was they will be sure to appear unless it is smoked or sprayed regularly. Try to spray or fumigate the night before syringing. If it is raining so much the better for then the houses are sure to be tight. If hydro-cyanic acid gas is used be very careful to inform every one of the fact or else lock the house, or better still have a sign on chains stretched across the door, with the word, "Cyanide." That ought to be sufficient warning for every one to keep out. The gas is very poisonus and it does not take very much of it to kill a person, so great care should be taken in using it. It is very good, however, and very effective and will clean out insects quicker than anything we know. Even snails and sow bugs were found dead in the morning under the benches after it had been used the night before. Avoid using it too strong and be sure to figure out the volume of air in your houses instead of guessing at it. You will then know just what you are doing and there will be no harm done by using too much of the deadly gas. Make sure that the houses are wet enough, no matter what is used for fumigation or spraying, otherwise the foliage is likely to get scorched and this is bad for the plants, for they are still young and need all the leaves that they can hold.

The Boilers

Katydids are already singing at night, and they are the very first sign that frost will soon be here. It may not be true that frost will be here in six weeks, but nevertheless with their song they serve as a reminder of what we should prepare for. Are the boilers all right? Have they been looked over? Have all the necessary repairs arrived? All these things should be attended to at once. Clean all flues well and see that the smoke pipes are good enough to last all winter. Every loose joint in these interferes with the draft so they should all be made tight with asbestos. Make sure the dampers work well and that the grates are in good condition. If poor at all order a new set, keeping the old for emergency. Make sure that the ash pit under the boiler is deep enough. Shallow boiler pits are responsible for more grate troubles than all the flaws that may be in the grates themselves. Try to have at least a foot of air between the grates and the highest level of ashes ever in the pit. This will keep the grates cool and avoid their burning out. We once had occasion to see a new set of grates burned out the very first time a fire was made in a steam boiler, all because the ash pit was not deep enough and the grates had no chance to cool, for the heat reflected from the ashes was terrific. It is better to have the ash pit deeper than to have it too shallow. It can still be changed if it is not deep enough. It will also make a big difference in the draft if there is plenty of air space under the grates. See to it now that the boilers are all in good shape for the coming cool, and ever-getting-colder nights.

CONVENTION REPORT CONCLUDED

HORTICULTURAL COLLEGE EDUCATION.

An interesting communication from Prof E. A. White of the Department of Floriculture at Cornell University was presented at the meeting on Thursday morning. Prof. White said he was proud to have been a pioneer in courses in Floriculture for young men at State Colleges. He was pleased with the change of sentiment among practical men regarding the value of such courses. He said that he does not believe the establishment of a school of floriculture, as a W. R. Smith memorial, to be practical, because of the high cost of establishment and maintenance and the difficulty in locating such a school to meet the needs of students in different states in which culture conditions vary. He recommends instead the establishing of an endowment fund for floricultural training in a few important educational institutions in different parts of the country where floriculture is now well taught. The apprenticeship system extant abroad is not practical here. Better courses may be developed in the agricultural colleges than at present if the florists will co-operate. Many American gardeners cannot grow plants successfully because they are ignorant of them. A young man should take theoretical work in summer and practical range work in winter. It is difficult to get successful florists to permit students on ranges. He recommends three years' theoretical work and one year in an up-to-date commercial range.

THE SMOKER.

Thursday night's smoker was a big enjoyable affair, Angelo Rossi presiding. There was a very large attendance, with music, vaudeville and a boxing contest. W. F. Kasting made a speech, presenting to Daniel MacRorie President Welch's prize offered to the member securing the largest number of new members during the year. The president-elect responded, stating that he would make the same offer next year and urging all to meet him at Houston in 1916. Mr. Rossi called upon President Welch who made a very clever speech, asserting that all Californians are but imported easterners and that the east can, if necessary, furnish plenty of more good timber but it will not be needed as there is already talent enough in the far west to elevate horticulture to the highest standard. He said he would take great pride in carrying back to Boston the news of California's achievements and California's hospitality.

FRIDAY'S SESSION.

The session on Friday morning was held at the Panama Pacific Exposition, President Welch in the chair. A handsome bronze plaque was presented to the S. A. F., with appropriate sentiments, by Commissioner General Chas. A. Vogelsang. The plaque was received on behalf of the Society by C. W. Ward, who made an address giving the history, growth and standing of the S. A. F. Park Commissioner Shearer of Los Angeles extended an invitation to attend a barbecue there on August 26th. A magnificent beaten silver dinner service was presented to President Welch, the presentation speech being made by Hans Plath. President Welch responded in words of grateful appreciation. It was announced that the Ladies' reception would be held in the California Building on Friday afternoon. E. G. Hill then read the report of the committee on final resolutions after which the convention adjourned.

FINAL RESOLUTIONS.

Whereas, The officers and members of the Society of American Florists and Ornamental Horticulturists in 31st annual convention assembled, in the city of the Golden Gate during its exposition year, have enjoyed to the utmost that magnificent hospitality which is peculiar to the California coast and have had every want anticipated, every convenience and comfort afforded by our hosts of San Francisco and the Pacific Coast, and

Whereas, The manifold labors incident to the preparations for this convention and our entertainment while here have been most efficiently performed and have been contributed to by so many of the citizens here as well as by our brothers in the trade and allied industries that it would be invidious to select individuals out of the many deserving mentioned, therefore, be it

Resolved, That individually and collectively we the visiting members of the Society and our ladies with grateful appreciation tender our unstinted thanks to our hosts one and all including His Honor Mayor James Rolph, Jr., the officials of the Pan-American Pacific International Exposition, the various committees of the city and state local organizations, the nurserymen of this locality, and all others who have contributed to make our stay here so enjoyable that we will carry home remembrances of the many kindnesses shown us which will linger like the perfume of the California flowers blooming beneath its cloudless skies.

REPORT OF COMMITTEE ON PRESIDENT'S ADDRESS.

Your committee to whom was assigned the duty of making report on recommendations contained in the annual address of President Welch beg to submit the following as their con-

GROUP OF SOCIETY OF AMERICAN FLORISTS AND ORNAMENTAL HORTICULTURISTS MEM

clusions and recommendations as to some of its salient features, to wit:

Convention Garden.

Your committee approves of the idea of changing the time of selecting convention city so that the selection shall be made two years in advance, and would suggest that a committee of three be appointed to draft necessary changes in the by-laws to carry out this idea and present such proposed amendments to the next meeting of the Executive Board for approval and subsequent submission to the entire membership as represented at the convention. We heartily endorse the statement of the president of the importance from both an educational and cultural point of view of the establishment of Convention Gardens.

Legislation.

With respect to the recommendation as to employment of counsel to assist the Legislative Committee, this having been already acted upon by the convention, necessitates no further action.

Washington Representative.

We endorse and recommend your concurrence in the recommendation of the President that the Washington representative of this society be made ex-officio a member of the Executive Board; and further recommend that the same committee as above provided for be entrusted also with the duty of drafting a suitable amendment to the constitution to carry this recommendation into effect.

Election of Directors.

We endorse the recommendation of the president favoring the election instead of the appointment of the two annually retiring members of the Board of Directors; and further recommend the concurrence of the convention in the same and the reference to the same committee hereinbefore provided for to draft suitable amendment to the constitution to carry this into effect.

Credentials for Affiliated Board Members.

We endorse and recommend concurrence in the following: That only the president of a subsidiary society or club be entitled to represent such society or club under the plan of affiliation on the Executive Board and he cannot take his seat on the Executive Board without credentials from his organization properly attested by the secretary thereof; and further recommend the drafting of suitable amendment to the constitution of this society to carry same into effect as hereinbefore provided by committee.

Publicity.

We endorse and recommend concurrence in the recommendation of the president to have a Committee on Publicity and suggest that the Executive Committee at its next meeting make a suitable appropriation to carry this into effect.

National Credits and Collections Bureau.

We have carefully considered the recommendation of our president with regard to the desirability of a more effective means of handling credits and collections, and believe that this work might well be taken up by a separate organization affiliated with this society as there is an urgent need as indicated by President Welch for some better machinery of a protective nature than is now available to us.

This question is one of such vital importance and involves such detail that we are not prepared during the limited time during the convention period to make any further or more definite recommendation for your adoption than the foregoing.

Development of American Products.

Believing firmly and unequivocally in the solidarity of the American people of this United States, we note with approval the utterances of President Welch as to encouraging American products and endorse any movement tending to develop self-reliance and independence where such development will beneficially affect our trade and avocation.

Improved Voting Method in Annual Elections.

We endorse and recommend concurrence in the following recommendation of President Welch, and their submission to the same committee as hereinbefore provided for to incorporate in a proposed amendment to the constitution, to wit:

That for election purposes a list of the members of this society be alphabetically arranged in four books:

Book No. 1 to include all names beginning with the letter "A" and ending with the letter "D."

Book No. 2 to include all names of members beginning with the letter "E" and ending with the letter "K."

Book No. 3 to include all names beginning with the letter "L" and ending with the letter "R."

Book No. 4 to include all names beginning with the letter "S" and ending with the letter "Z."

One teller be appointed to check the names listed in each book, also one to receive the ballots.

Your committee in conclusion believe that we voice the unanimous approval of this organization of the spirit of devotion to the highest interests of this society which permeates the President's address and commend the zeal and devotion that he has evinced therein.

All of which is respectfully submitted.

RESOLUTIONS ON DEATH OF J. F. COWELL.

Whereas, in the removal by death during the past year of Prof. J. F. Cowell, Buffalo, N. Y., the Society of American Florists and Ornamental Horticulturists has been deprived of the valued services of one whose contributions to the work of the society were always freely given in his capacity as Botanist, and whose services were greatly appreciated by us; therefore,

Be it Resolved: That this Society tender to those near and dear who mourn his loss our sincere sympathy in their bereavement; and that a copy of this resolution be officially attested by our Secretary and forwarded to the family of the deceased.

E. G. Hill, Theodore Wirth, George Asmus, Committee.

We have received a very optimistic letter from Vice-President-elect R. C.

BERS PHOTOGRAPHED AUGUST 17, 1915, IN FRONT OF CIVIC AUDITORIUM, SAN FRANCISCO.

Kerr, concerning the selection of Houston for the 1916 convention. He says, in part:

"We appreciate this great honor, and I assure you that we are going to try hard to make this the greatest Convention the S. A. F. has ever held. We propose to give it a great deal of publicity and pull hard for a large attendance, as our future work will show. We have the support of the Chamber of Commerce, the City of Houston and the Rotary Club, as well as the other Civic organizations.

"We want to call attention to the fact that we have one of the largest auditoriums in the South for convention and exhibition purposes. We have a citizenship which has left nothing unturned to make our visitors enjoy their stay here. We have many side attractions which makes it worth while for conventions in Houston. These matters will . be taken up from time to time. I want to express for Texas and the florists of the South our gratefulness for this convention.

"The convention came as a complete surprise. We really did not figure on getting it for next year. We did not have a single Texas representative on the ground, to my knowledge, although I have not received the details of the nomination. However, I will learn all this later."

LADIES' S. A. F.

The annual business meeting of the Ladies' S. A. F. was held at San Francisco on August 18, forenoon, the president, Mrs. W. F. Gude, of Washington, D. C., in the chair. The meeting opened with an address of welcome by Mrs. F. H. Howard, of Los Angeles, who spoke as follows:

Dear Ladies:—On behalf of the members of our organization I extend to you all our happiest and most heartfelt greetings in this the 31st annual convention of the S. A. F. held in the city of San Francisco.

. It is the first time in its history that a meeting has been held in California, and I am sure it is the first time many of the ladies present have set foot on the golden shores of the Pacific. We trust that you will enjoy the trip with an ever increasing pleasure as the scenes of our state's beauty so infuse themselves to you, that the recollections will be pleasant ones and linger long in your memory.

Our members in the state are but few, but our hearts are big and we extend to you all a truly western welcome, always looking forward to the time when the pleasure of meeting you again in some other state shall be ours. I thank you.

An appreciative response was voiced by Mrs. R. Vincent, Jr., of White Marsh, Md. The address of Mrs. Gude, which was published in HORTICULTURE last week, followed.

The following officers were elected: President, Mrs. John Vallance, Oakland, Cal.; vice-president, Mrs. W. W. Coles, Kokomo, Ind.; second vice-president, Mrs. Robert C. Kerr, Houston, Texas; treasurer, Mrs. A. M. Herr, Lancaster, Pa.; secretary, Mrs. George W. Smith, Cleveland, Ohio; special committee, Mrs. J. G. Hancock, Chicago, chairman.

CLUBS AND SOCIETIES

RAILWAY GARDENING ASSOCIATION.

At the meeting of this Association held in Detroit, Michigan, Aug. 17-20, officers for the ensuing year were chosen as follows: President, J. A. Byrne, B. & O., Relay, Md.; vice-presidents, C. W. Eichling, Q. & C., New Orleans, La., and R. J. Rice, M. C., Niles, Mich.; secretary, Chas. E. Lowe, P. R. R., Sewickley, Pa.; treas., J. K. Wingert, C. V., Chambersburg, Pa. New Orleans was chosen for the next meeting. The address of Pres. Paul Huebner follows:

President's Address.

It certainly gives me great pleasure to greet you on this auspicious occasion, the ninth annual meeting of our association, and to see so many of my fellow members gracing the occasion from far and near. It certainly shows a keen interest in our chosen profession and I congratulate you. I also wish to congratulate you on the splendid work you have accomplished during the past nine years. The progress has been marked in all sections of the country and we have come to be a power for progress such as we hardly dared to hope for in our modest beginning. This is true not only of the Atlantic Coast, but all over the country to the far Pacific. Those of you who have visited the western roads not only in this country, but in Canada, can testify to the vast improvement in railroad gardening in recent years. I feel proud of the honor you have done me in electing me your president and it goes without saying that I have been anxious to do everything in my power to further the interests of our profession and place it on a still higher standard.

In the way of practical suggestions for appropriate action at this Convention I would call your attention to the following features of organization:

First, the permanent committees upon the several subjects under which all of our work may be grouped. It is intended that the membership in these committees be slightly changed each year, but that a broad scheme for the systematic development of each topic be followed continuously, working from the most general aspects of the subject gradually into the details and collecting all available information upon each phase of the subject as we progress, as was stated in my recent letters to chairmen of committees. In this way we should ultimately accumulate a large and orderly mass of facts of everyday value to railway gardeners, especially, but also to gardening people in general, and such results should warrant a distinctive recognition of our association for practical achievements.

That indeed should be the sphere or slogan of our association, achievements along lines of practical, horticultural work under a great variety of natural conditions. In order to accomplish a respected standing for our association in horticultural circles the conscientious effort of every member to produce the best possible report upon each topic that is assigned to them is absolutely necessary. Each problem should receive thorough investigation in libraries as well as in the ground and among fellow gardeners, and the report should be a complete and concise statement of the facts of practical value thus obtained.

Second, the suggestion has been made that for our future meetings we follow the points of the compass in successive years; this is our northern meeting, let next year be our southern meeting, then an eastern and then a western meeting. Further, that the date of meeting be determined largely by the climate of the place where we will meet, later for northern situations and vice versa. Consideration should also be given, in this regard, to timing the meetings so that we shall see some feature of horticultural interest, during the meeting, that meetings shall not be fixed closer than six months from the previous meeting and that, so far as possible, the meetings shall be held during our least busy season. I should like to have a full discussion of this matter with a possible determination of our meeting places and dates for the remaining three years of this cycle.

In conclusion, gentlemen, I wish to thank you in advance for your kind co-operation in the sessions to follow this, and for your careful and conscientious work on the various committees. May wisdom and harmony prevail in all our doings and may you all enjoy yourselves not only from the professional standpoint but in every other way, so that when we return to our homes we may all feel the wiser and the happier for our experiences at Detroit.

AMERICAN GLADIOLUS SOCIETY.

The sixth annual exhibition of the American Gladiolus Society which was held at Newport, R. I., in the Casino Theatre, was the grandest show of gladioli that has ever taken place in America. The wonderful collections of the best standard varieties, and the great number of the newer sorts was a revelation to all, both amateur and professional admirers of these beautiful flowers, and the quality of the blooms has never been equalled at any of our former exhibitions.

The stage was filled entirely with a magnificently arranged exhibit by Charles Francis Fairbanks of Boston, which was not for competition, and the Newport Horticultural Society bestowed on him a silver medal. Other splendid exhibits were staged by B. Hammond Tracy, Wenham, Mass.; William Sim, Cliftondale, Mass.; Knight & Struck, New York City; Arthur Cowee, Berlin, N. Y., and John Lewis Childs, Flowerfield, L. I. Mrs. B. Hammond Tracy exhibited a superb basket in competition for the silver cup, but it was disqualified because it contained one more spike of flowers than specified in the schedule. The judges were James Wheeler, Natick, Mass.; J. Leestraten, Saxonville.

Mass.; Wm. Anderson, Sterling, Mass.; Bruce Butterton, James Robertson and Andrew S. Meikle, Newport.

Awards.

In the competition calling for six spikes of one variety in each color class the winners of 1st prize were C. F. Fairbanks, A. E. Griffin, R. W. Swet of Saxonville, and B. Hammond Tracy. In the special classes for vases of specified varieties, Madison Cooper and C. W. Brown were winners, many of these classes not being competed for.

The Kunderd gold medal for the best collection of Kunderd Varieties was won by Clark W. Brown of Ashland, Mass., and the silver medal by P. W. Popp, Mamaroneck, N. Y. The Michell silver medal for Hollandia was won by C. F. Fairbanks, and bronze medal by R. W. Swett. Merton Gage won the Fairbanks prize for best seedling never before exhibited. John Lewis Childs was 2nd, and R. W. Swett, 3rd. The Garden Association's prizes for 25 spikes in six color classes were won by John Lewis Childs, R. W. Swett, C. W. Brown, C. F. Fairbanks and B. Hammond Tracy. B. Hammond Tracy captured the Burpee prize for best collection of ten Varieties, and C. W. Brown got the Thomann prize for best vase of new white seedling. Carter's Tested Seeds prizes went to H. E. Meader, Dover, N. H., and R. W. Sweet. The Hitchings silver cup for the most artistically arranged basket of blooms was won by J. G. Leikens, Newport. There were many classes for private gardeners and amateurs but not more than half of these were filled. Miss Fanny Foster won the silver trophy cup offered by The Modern Gladiolus Grower, and T. A. Havemeyer the Tracy cup. The Fairbanks prize for best collection and display was won by R. H. Tracy, William Sim getting 2nd. Silver medal for exhibit 3 spikes each variety, was awarded to C. F. Fairbanks, and bronze medal to Madison Cooper. The Kunderd gold medals, in tbe Amateur Classes, was won by C. F. Fairbanks.

The judges awarded the following Certificates: L. Merton Gage, Natick, Mass., for Mrs. Dr. Norton; R. W. Swett, Saxonville, for Lieberfeur; John Lewis Childs, Flowerfield, for Newport; John Schupers & Co., New York, for Seedling No. 3/7229. Honorable mention to Chamberlain & Co. for general display; A. E. Kunderd for Primulinus hybrids; W. Atlee Burpee for seedlings; Knight & Struck Co., S. E. Spencer, T. A. Havemeyer, H. A. Dreer, A. H. Austin & Co., and T. E. Gonger for general display. C. M. Bugbolt, Cultural Certificate for Europa.

GLADIOLUS SOCIETY OF OHIO.

The third annual exhibition of the Gladiolus Society of Ohio was held in the Hollenden assembly room, Cleveland, Ohio, on Friday and Saturday, August 13 and 14. This is the third consecutive year that this society has met in the "Sixth City." The showing was the best ever made, there being a number of very good seedlings in evidence.

The Cleveland Florists' Club handled the local arrangements of the show in excellent manner and as a result the public attended in large numbers. Twelve thousand invitations were issued and mailed to friends and customers of the club members.

Interesting table decorations were shown by Jones-Russell Co., The J. M. Gasser Co., Westman & Getz, The Jas. Eadie Co., Smith & Fetters and Knoble Bros. Several tables were filled with well arranged baskets by A. M. Albrecht, Jones-Russell, Westman & Getz, Knoble Bros., Ohio Floral Co., The Jas. Eadie Co., Charlesworth & Son, and The J. M. Gasser Co. A prime attraction was a brides' bouquet of white gladioli, shown on a standard, by A. M. Albrecht.

The prize for the best display by any one exhibitor was awarded to The Austin Co. Other prize winners in the commercial section were J. Thomann & Sons, Perkins King Co., R. E. Huntington, Bidwell & Fobes, Munsell & Harvey, Madison Cooper, C. Betscher, J. F. Rychlik, E. E. Stewart and Wayside Gardens. Three certificates for new varieties never shown before were awarded to The Austin Co. and one to J. Thomann & Sons.

The judges were W. C. Werner, of Painesville, O. and F. W. Griffin of Cleveland.

Table Decorations by Leading Retailers of Cleveland, at the Annual Exhibition of the Gladiolus Society of Ohio.

At the annual meeting held on Saturday morning it was unanimously decided to hold the 1916 meeting and show in Cleveland. The election of officers was postponed to come up at an adjourned meeting to be held in Cleveland, Nov. 11th, during the Cleveland Flower Show.

ST. LOUIS FLORIST CLUB.

The St. Louis Florist Club held one of those much enjoyed outdoor meetings on Thursday afternoon, August 12, at Joseph Hauser's Dahlia Farm in Webster Groves. The secretary's notice for the meeting, headed with,

"Before green apples blush,
Before green nuts embrown,
Why one day in the country
Is worth a month in town,"

brought one of the largest outdoor meetings the club ever held. They inspected the dahlia fields and were much impressed with Mr. Hauser's new single red and other new varieties.

Mrs. M. M. Ayers, the only lady member of the club, sent in her resignation, which was accepted and she was placed on the honorary member list.

Walter Weber, of the Weber Nursery Co., extended an invitation to meet at their place in the country in September, which was accepted with thanks. The election of officers for the ensuing year took place. Jules Bourdet, president, and J. J. Beneke, secretary, were re-elected by unanimous vote. E. S. Wells and David Geddis fought it out for vice-president, and Mr. Wells was re-elected. W. C. Smith and J. J. Windler opposed each other for the treasurership and Mr. Smith was re-elected. W. W. Ohlweiter, trustee for a three-year term, was elected by unanimous vote, and W. A. Rowe and F. A. Windler will serve with him. This closed a most interesting meeting. Mr. and Mrs. Hauser then invited all to partake of a bounteous lunch. They were assisted by Mrs. Hauser's sister, Mrs. Grossart and Mrs. Pilcher.

AMERICAN ASSOCIATION OF PARK SUPERINTENDENTS.

The convention of park superintendents, coincident with that of the S. A. F., at San Francisco, was a very busy and enjoyable affair, one of its greatest educational features being the many opportunities offered for visits and inspection of the many local and national public reservations in San Francisco and on the way to and from that city. Addresses, discussions and stereopticon lectures crowded the business hours and everything went off smoothly under the guiding hand of President Amrhyn and his official retinue. Officers were elected as follows: President, Emil T. Mische; vice-presidents, J. W. Thompson, J. F. Walsh, Alex. Stuart, E. P. Griffin, L. P. Jansen, E. V. Goebel; secretary-treasurer, R. W. Cotterill. John McLaren was elected to the office of honorary president. New Orleans was chosen for the convention of 1916.

Table Decoration by the J. M. Gasser Co., at the Exhibition of the Gladiolus Society of Ohio.

SEED TRADE

Beans Deteriorating.

Reports reaching us within a few days indicate that the bean crop is deteriorating every day, and this applies particularly to wax pod sorts, although green pods are also hard hit. This situation has been brought about as a result of excessive rains, and the damage comes so late there seems little hope of recovering. In fact, there is none, and if deterioration should cease now the crop situation would be almost as serious as last year.

There is much pessimism about corn, and it will require a long open autumn free from frost to mature the crop. Both growers and dealers are reluctant to accept orders for this season's crop, or even old corn, as it is liable to be worth much more a few months hence. The same may be said of beans and peas, particularly beans. We may say here that the reports on the bean crops given herewith are mainly from Michigan, and while our information is not as authentic, we believe conditions in New York State are little better. In fact it would be an ill informed or rash grower or dealer who would accept orders for beans in the present circumstances. These dealers who have failed to cover their requirements will pay heavy toll for their procrastination, and they will find little sympathy anywhere.

Tomatoes.

Tomatoes are very late but there is little cause for anxiety here. A total failure of the crop no doubt would prove embarrassing, but that is wholly improbable, and a considerable shrinkage in the output of both seed and canned tomatoes would be far from an unmixed evil. It is regrettable that a considerable shortage did not occur in canned peas and the seed, also, of the canning varieties.

This is a good time for jobbing houses to go slowly. Crop conditions affecting most staples produced in this country are either bad or doubtful, while the European situation is an unknown quantity.

Crop Report on Dutch Vegetable Seeds.

The annual crop-report of Sluis & Groot, seedgrowers and merchants, of Enkhuizen, Holland, has been received in which they state that although the winter was very mild but a small percentage of the biennials did set seed, generally speaking. By a continuous wet period in the preceding autumn, the plants were much weakened and the following spring brought no recovery for even then the weather was not at all favorable. Drought, cold and, worst of all, considerable frost in May and June kept the vegetation backward and many items could not be replanted, and under the circumstances many growers simply ploughed up those poor looking fields. They con-

clude that there will be in almost all articles a shortage more or less. Of the following items they give a more detailed account.

Cauliflower—Scarcely better than average.

Cabbage and Red Cabbage—Small plantings in general and some varieties almost totally failing, especially Red Cabbage.

Savoy, Brussels Sprouts and Borecole—Little better than the foregoing.

Turnip and Swedes—Sufficiently planted but much ploughed up. In some districts the seed-pods are fearfully eaten by worms. Many sorts will give but a small crop.

Kohlrabi—Almost total failure.

Mangels and Sugar Beets—Although the stand is fair and in some places good, the total yield will be small.

Beets—As with Mangels and Sugar Beets, much has been lost in consequence of the persistent drought, especially on the light grounds.

Radish and Winter Radish—Small acreage; though the stand may be considered good, the crop will not answer the usual demand.

Onion—Dutch flat yellow excepted, all sorts fail, so to speak. Of the Dutch blood-red there is some left, but Zittau is a total failure. Up till now the stand of what is left is very good.

Garlic Bulbs—Small acreage. Stand pretty good.

Parsley—Sufficiently sown, but only little remained. Here and there very weak in consequence of the drought.

Chervil—Very little left. Average stand.

Spinach—We expect in general but a small crop.

Cucumber—Of our local sorts scarcely sufficient is planted, of others very little. In some districts late frosts have done much harm. Generally speaking the stand is poor.

Peas—Extraordinarily small acreage, especially little of the wrinkled varieties. Average stand. There is a general expectation of a small crop.

Dwarf Beans—The variety "Best of All," white seeded, was sown on a very large scale. Of other leading sorts the acreages are scarcely normal and of the by-sorts even very small. Up till the present the stand is pretty good, on average.

Running Beans—Very small plantings, especially of the improved long-podded sorts.

Broad Beans—Insignificant area sown. Stand not bad.

Parsnip—Small plantation. Stand not bad.

Scorzonera—Average plantation. Stand good.

Cornsalad—Dutch large seeded was but little sown. Of the other varieties only small patches, which look well.

Celery—Very small crop.

Flower Seeds—In consequence of the persistent drought in spring and even partly still in summer, planting conditions were very bad for the Annuals and scarcely a middling-crop is to be expected. The sown articles have partly suffered from late frosts, especially Nasturtiums. Nasturtium Tom Thumb insufficient. May be Nasturtium Tall may produce a middling crop. Myosotis and some other Biennials did not very well run to seed. The Perennials promise a average crop.

Spades Versus Shovels.

The Treasury Department has made a ruling that is expected to go a long way toward solving the perplexities of customs men regarding the difference, for classification purposes, of spades and shovels. Up to this time there has been a wide variation in the practice at the several ports in returning these articles for duty. It is announced that following an investigation the department has decided upon these rules:

Spades, both long-handled and D-handled and whether polished or black, are chiefly used for agricultural purposes, while ordinary shovels, both polished and black, and whether long-handled or D-handled, are chiefly used for purposes other than agriculture. In view of this conclusion, customs officials will hereafter pass free of duty as agricultural implements, under Paragraph 391, spades of the kinds mentioned above, while shovels, either pol-

ished or black, long-handled or D-handled, are to be assessed at 20 per cent. ad valorem as manufactures of metal, under Paragraph 167.

Notes.

Montgomery, Ala.—Greil Bros. Co. will open a wholesale seed department about September 1.

The value of imports of horticultural material at the Port of New York for week ending August 14 is given as follows: Grass seed, $15,478; palm seed, $583; trees and plants, $22,373.

TO PROMOTE SOIL FERTILITY KNOWLEDGE.

Believing that they can render material assistance in the upbuilding and maintaining of soil fertilizers, the Chicago Feed & Fertilizer Co. have employed practical greenhouse men in their research and laboratory department, and in the handling of correspondence pertaining to questions arising on soil requirements and plant foods.

Their object is to demonstrate the practicability of making up soil mixtures and build up soils that are deficient in plant foods through the addition of fertilizers or commercial manures as the season progresses. In connection with this work they are taking into consideration the uses of stable manures and legumes, supplemented by commercial manures that carry nitrogen, phosphoric acid and potash and also the scientific uses of floricultural lime to meet the greenhouse soil's particular needs.

This work is under the direction of J. E. Pollworth, who has surrounded himself with graduates of the floricultural course of the University of Illinois and Massachusetts, also three leading growers who have held responsible positions with large greenhouse establishments and who are well versed in the practical uses of commercial manures as practiced at this time among the most successful greenhouse establishments.

CATALOGUES RECEIVED.

S. G. Harris, Tarrytown, N. Y.—Price List of Fall Bargains in Fall Planting Stock—Including Trees, Herbaceous Perennials and Bulbs.

Peter Henderson & Co., New York, N. Y.—Catalogues and Price List of Wheats, Grasses, Clovers, Etc., Etc., for Fall Sowing." An unique and very interesting publication, illustrated in blue ink.

W. B. Whittier & Co., Framingham Nurseries, Framingham, Mass.—Trade Price List of Evergreens for August and September Planting. This list includes, besides the desirable conifers in all sizes a fine line of hardy hybrid and native rhododendrons.

SAN FRANCISCO.

Domoto Bros. are bringing in some nice cyclamen plants, which, they say, are in good demand.

Fred Broock, of New Ulm, Minn., has been visiting the Pacific Coast trade for several weeks.

Wm. Hutchins, grower on Fruitvale avenue, Fruitvale, Cal., is being congratulated by his many friends in the trade upon his recent marriage.

In honor of the convention, the Art Floral Co. arranged a special bridal display at its Powell-street shop, which attracted much attention.

The winning of the handsome bowling trophy of the Aphine Manufacturing Co. by Victor Podesta is a source of satisfaction to the San Francisco trade.

While attending the S. A. F. convention, Geo. W. Smith, of Cleveland, O., succeeded in working up considerable interest in the coming Cleveland Flower Show.

E. R. Chappelle and wife, of Portland, Ore., returned the first of the week from a motoring trip to the San Diego exposition and are visiting the exposition here for a few days.

F. T. Schlotzhauer, proprietor of the Francis Floral Co., reports very good success with his new line of bisque baskets. He says they were much admired by the eastern visitors. He is working on a new line for fall.

WASHINGTON, D. C.

Mrs. Beatrice Moss has returned to the store of F. H. Kramer after a short absence at Atlantic City, N. J.

James Daly has returned to the city from a three weeks' vacation, two weeks of which were spent at his former home, Providence, R. I.

Gude Bros.' store interior has been redecorated in white and green. William F. Gude is expected to arrive back during the coming week from the west. After leaving San Francisco they went to Los Angeles, and stops will be made at all of the large cities on the way back.

Invitations are soon to be sent out to the members of the Florists' Club of Washington by Edward S. Schmid to attend his annual crab feast on Tuesday evening, September 7. This promises to be the greatest event in the history of the club. Music and vaudeville will provide the evening's entertainment, which will be given in the conservatory of the store of Fred H. Kramer.

NEW FLOWER STORES.

Aberdeen, S. D.—E. C. Siebrecht.

Cleveland, O. — J. F. Brotz, 9724 Lorain avenue.

Springfield, O.—Leman Bradford, 106 East High street.

Atlantic City, N. J.—W. R. Thomas, Egg Harbor Flower Shop.

Tampa, Fla.—Knull Floral Co., removing to 408 Tampa street.

Kenosha, Wis. — Lewis Turner & Sons, Park avenue and Main street.

Chicago, Ill.—Drexel Flower Shop, Arthur Weatherwax, proprietor, 823 47th street; Daniel Branch, 313 E. 51st street.

During Recess

Lancaster County Florists' Club.

On Thursday, Aug. 19th, the regular car for Elizabethtown was filled with florists bound for the Avondale Farm and nurseries of our President, B. F. Barr. We had as guests, B. H. Farr, President of The American Peony Society; H. C. Huesman and F. H. Laucks from Reading, Mr. and Mrs. C. E. Smith and Mr. and Mrs. August Shaeffer of York, Pa., and Dennis Connor of The Lord & Burnham Co.

After an inspection of the nursery, bowling on the green, croquet, cards, quoits and conversation were indulged in. In the bowling Jacob Fleer carried the honors for the greatest number of points. In the first match between teams made up by B. F. Barr and Albert M. Herr, the Herr team won out with flying colors and in the match between teams made up by Geo. Goldbach and Rudolph Nagle, the Goldbach team won out. In croquet, J. Ralph and J. Rutter Hess from the Gap showed Ira Landis from Paradise and Chas. B. Herr from Strasburg that the Gap is not a sleepy town in spite of its name. In the quoits, Willis Girvin of Leola and Mr. Shaeffer of York, showed they had some science and knowledge of other things than those pertaining to the florists' business. In cards, I think Elmer Weaver of Ronks won the booby, and in conversation H. A. Schroyer, Frank L. Kohr, A. F. Strickler and Dennis Connor seemed to be in the lead.

About six o'clock, Mrs. B. F. Barr took the party in charge and fed us royally, ably assisted in the serving by Rodney Eshlemen and Chas. B. Herr. Japanese lanterns were then lit all over the lawn and a half hour of general sociability followed, after which a unanimous vote of thanks was extended to Mr. and Mrs. B. F. Barr for their generous hospitality.

The regular meeting was called to order at 7.30 P. M. A report was heard from the dahlia Show Committee that they had secured 800 square feet of space in the main building at The Lancaster County Fair grounds, about half of which will be reserved for out-of-the-county trade exhibits, as this will be an exceptional opportunity for the dahlia growers to show their products to several hundred thousand people. Volunteers were asked for to help at this show and there will be two or more members of the club in attendance all the time to make it educational and advertise the dahlia. The date is Sept. 8th to Oct. 1st, inclusive.

Mr. Farr was scheduled for an address on Peonies, but unfortunately was unable to stay for the evening meeting. Frank Suter made an elegant display of dahlias and received the thanks of the club.

The meeting will long be remembered as one of the red letter days for the year 1915 by those who were with us.

ALBERT M. HERR.

Rochester Florists' Association.

The Rochester Florists' Association Outing, held on Thursday, August 19th, at Salmon's Grove, was "a rattling good time." Pretty much everybody was on the job at the time dinner was served at 1.30 and relished an excellently gotten up and well served repast.

Stunts were pulled off during the feast. C. H. Vick, president of the Association, was presented with a fitting remembrance by the boys, in the absence of the ladies (which he had been in favor of inviting to the outing, but the committee had voted against) in the shape of a very delicate reminder of femininity. H. E. Bates, vice-president of the Association was also remembered fittingly, being given a pair of baby sandals and he is still wondering if the token was a reminder that the job's shoes were too big for him. John House, the venerable standby of the Florists' Association, was presented with a garden set, he being the oldest and fattest man there. Charlie Chaplin was on deck to give the occasion the touch of up-to-dateness.

After the refreshments everybody was called to the baseball field to witness a ball game between the single men captained by Harry Glenn and married men captained by George Boucher. We say witness a ball game but in reality it was a slaughter. The two umpires, Lavigne and Bates, were called upon at regular intervals to get off the grounds before there was bloodshed, but they either misunderstood the temper of the crowd or the players reconsideration for they stayed until the last.

Chas. Schomberg, the official score keeper, called for roll after roll of paper and finally through sheer exhaustion of both players and those who witnessed the game, time was called. The official score was given out as 22 runs for the single men and 15 runs for the married men.

The sports were under the leadership of Harry Glenn.

Following were the events:

50 yd. dash—H. Salmon, Cuff Buttons; C. Vick, Bot. Wine. 100 yd. dash—W. Briggs, Umbrella; W. Rypma, 25 cigars. 3-leg race—W. Rypma, Flash Lt. Eastern; Elder, Knife. Shoe race—Elder, Safety rasor; W. Gommel, 25 cigars. Walking race—G. Cramer, Barometer; J. Brown, Feather Duster. Shoe race—Geo. M. Desmith, Ball glove; F. Bohnke, Baseball. Backward race—Elder, Necktie; C. Vick, Note book. Quoits—Ed. Vick, Thermos Bottle; Elder, Umbrella; Lavigne, Tobacco; Thomas, Cigars. Ball Game—Single men. 50 cigars.

Holyoke and Northampton Club.

The third annual outing and field day of the Holyoke and Northampton Florists' and Gardeners' Club was held in Smith's Ferry, Wednesday afternoon, Aug. 18. There were about 100 present, including members and families from Holyoke, Northampton and Amherst, in addition to guests from Springfield, Westfield and Greenfield.

The greenhouse of Gallivan Bros. and the residence of D. J. Gallivan were the principal headquarters for the outing, although by courtesy of the Holyoke Canoe Club, the sports and bake took place on the club grounds.

The assemblage enjoyed an outdoor bake at 1 o'clock, after which the sports program took place. The married men, represented by a team of nine, proved far superior to the single men in the tug-of-war, but the single men redeemed their lost honors by emerging from a baseball game with a 12 to 8 victory to their credit. Summary:

100-yard dash, unmarried women—Won by Miss Fowles of Amherst; Miss Doris Kellogg of Smith's Ferry, 2nd. 100-yard dash, married women—Won by Mrs. Thomas Bray of Holyoke; Mrs. Keyes of Florence, 2nd. 100-yard dash, unmarried men—Won by Michael Gee. 100-yard dash, married men—Won by G. H. Sinclair of Holyoke; R. F. Carey of South Hadley, 2nd. 100-yard dash, boys—Won by Dawson Bray, son of Thomas Bray, Holyoke.

The committee of arrangements for

GEORGE E. M. STUMPP'S SUMMER ESTABLISHMENT AT SOUTHAMPTON, N. Y.

The accompanying cut shows the summer establishment of G. E. M. Stumpp at Southampton, Long Island, which has proven to be a most successful venture. The store at the right has a front of fifty feet and depth of seventy-five feet, and besides a large stock of cut flowers and plants. There are numerous novelties for the table and porch, together with useful ornaments for the lawn and summer home.

In front of the house in the center, which Mr. Stumpp occupies, there is a lily pond encircled by a driveway.

the outing was G. H. Sinclair. George Rackliffe, Thomas Bray and D. J. Gallivan, all of Holyoke, and Edward Fowles of Amherst.

Connecticut Nurserymen's Annual Outing.

The morning of August 19, 1915 dawned bright and clear and everything looked good to the members of the Connecticut Nurserymen's Association, their "better halfs," and enthusiastic friends, as they motored to the annual summer outing, held this year at Lake Compounce. On arrival at this beautiful summer resort the autos were parked, greetings exchanged, after which a base ball game was played with Messrs. Burr and Campbell as captains. Burr's team, nicknamed the "Berberry Thunberglis" were defeated by Campbell's "Forsythias" by a heavy margin. The features of the game were Burr's coaching, Hunt's batting, Hoyt's catching, Campbell's pitching and Wilson's stealing bases. Dinner was partaken of, after which the party visited the points of scenic interest about the lake, grounds and mountain. A short business session was called later on, and one new member added to the association.

All present voted it a most enjoyable occasion.

The annual outing of the New York and New Jersey Association of Plant Growers will take place Tuesday, September 7th. The steamer "Commander" has been specially chartered. The party will get a three-hour sail on the Sound to Valley Grove at Northport, L. I., where a good meal will be awaiting them.

VISITORS' REGISTER.

Chicago, Ill.—Mrs. Thaden, Cincinnati, O.

Boston: Paul M. Pierson, Scarborough, N. Y.

Milwaukee, Wis.: H. E. Philpott, Winnipeg, Can.

Washington, D. C.—Morris Cohen, of New York; Julius A. Dilhoff, New York; I. Rosnosky, representing H. F. Michell Co., Phila; Mr. and Mrs. Fred H. Meinhardt, St. Louis, Mo.: Arthur Niessen, Phila; W. W. Woodruff, Lowgap, N. C.

PREPARING FOR THE NATIONAL FLOWER SHOW.

The Dreer Garden and Lawn in Front of Convention Hall, Philadelphia.

The accompanying illustration is from a photograph of the Dreer Gardens and Lawn in front of Convention Hall, Philadelphia. These gardens have a 90 ft. frontage and 45 ft. depth. At the rear and next to the building they have planted a large, irregular border, 90 feet long, varying in depth from 10 to 16 feet, the rear being planted with Canna Louis Reverchou. and in front of these is Canna Gustav Gumpper, and the entire bed is bordered with Pennisetum Ruppellanum. The two large oval beds contain Dreer's Single Fringed Petunias. Between these there is a large specimen plant of Phoenix sylvestris.

The gardens and lawn are now in a flourishing condition and are creating a great deal of comment which will undoubtedly bear fruit when the great National Flower Show opens its doors next March.

AN IDEAL GLADIOLUS.

L. Merton Gage may justly be proud of his new Kunderd gladiolus Mrs. Dr. Norton. In our estimation it is one of the finest varieties yet introduced and it was entirely reasonable and appropriate that it won the first prize and certificate of merit at Newport. Its color, a beautiful pale rose pink, deeper flushed at the extremities of the petals and illumined by a faint glow of primrose yellow on the lower segments, is very captivating. In size and arrangement of blooms on the spike it is an ideal gladiolus.

PERSONAL.

Wallace R. Pierson is at the Adler Sanitarium, San Francisco, recovering from an operation for appendicitis. He was taken sick on the way to the Convention.

Harry A. Barnard, of Stuart Low & Co., Bush Hill Park, Enfield, England, started from Liverpool on the S. S. St. Louis, Saturday, August 21st, on his annual visit to the United States. His headquarters on arrival in New York will be the Hotel Albert.

Editor HORTICULTURE:

Dear Sir—HORTICULTURE'S Convention Number reached us this morning.. "A Great Number."

We send our congratulations.

Yours very truly,

KROESCHELL BROS. CO.

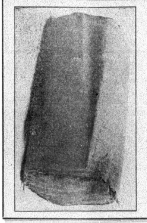
Flower Market Reports

BOSTON — This week is characterized by a very stagnant market. Last week was poor but this week seems even worse, although the presence of many distinguished guests of the city and state might have been expected to start up a little trade. Gladioli continues to dominate everything and they are selling "for a song." Many superb varieties are in evidence. One named Schwaben, which S. E. Spencer is sending in seems to have particularly caught the popular fancy and it, at least, can be sold. Asters are abundant, of course, many of them poor and a few of them excellent. Lily of the valley is in short supply and the initiated will have no trouble in surmising the reason. Lilies are in sufficient supply but not so badly overstocked as they were. Of roses, there are more than enough and they are very good indeed for the season.

BUFFALO — There has been no improvement in market conditions thus far. Stock is plentiful and there is very little business. Gladioli have not shortened up and asters of ordinary quality have been plentiful. The late branching asters are gradually coming in and some choice ones are seen and have had a fair sale: Lilies continue plentiful and sales slow. Roses are enough to supply all needs and lily of the valley and other stock is coming in normal supply. Asparagus, smilax and greens are also plentiful with no special demand.

CHICAGO — The market condition has changed very little from last week. Local demand is very light. There is just a little stir now and then for funeral stock. Supply is more than ample for all demands. On the whole roses in

most lines are clearing up fairly well, the cut at present being rather light though a prospect for an early increase in the output is apparent. Beauties have been moving well; most of the call is for medium 24 to 30 inch and these in most cases realize as good a return as the long-stemmed stock. Some very fine Russells may be had of various lengths of stem. Ophelia and Sunburst are fine and meet with good demand. There are more Killarneys, both pink and white. Of the longer lengths, good flowers of shipping quality are rather scarce. Short Wards are hard to move. Hoosier Beauty is seen at a number of houses and meets with ready sale. This appears to be a rose of great promise. Some good Maryland and Richmond may be had. Gladioli are still much in over supply, in spite of the fact that a number of growers report being pretty well cut out and a good many others having stopped shipping to this

market on account of the extremely low prices that have been realized. The later varieties of asters are now in full swing and have cleared, fairly well and some very fine greenhouse-grown stock is seen. Chrysanthemum "Golden Glow" is shown in increasing numbers but they move rather slow. There is a good demand for lily of the valley which is a scarce article. Very few orchids are seen. Lilies are quite plenty and move none too well. There is a fair market for green goods, especially Asparagus plumosus sprays. Ferns move slowly. New crop carnations have made their appearance though in short stems as yet, but the quality of bloom is good.

CINCINNATI — The tail end of the Galveston storm hit this vicinity at the end of last week and the heavy rains probably caused very considerable damage to the outdoor cut flower

(Continued on page 301)

WHOLESALE FLOWER MARKETS — TRADE PRICES—Per 100
TO DEALERS ONLY

	BOSTON Aug. 26		ST. LOUIS Aug. 23		PHILA. Aug. 23	
Roses						
Am. Beauty, Special	15.00 to	20.00	30.00 to	40.00	...... to	25.00
" " Fancy and Extra	6.00 to	10.00	20.00 to	25.00	15.00 to	20.00
" " No. 1	1.00 to	3.00	10.00 to	15.00	10.00 to	12.50
Killarney, Richmond, Extra	2.00 to	4.00	5.00 to	6.00	4.00 to	6.00
" " Ordinary	.50 to	1.00	2.00 to	3.00	2.00 to	3.00
Hillingdon, Ward, Sunburst, Extra	2.00 to	4.00	5.00 to	6.00	5.00 to	6.00
" " Ordinary	.50 to	2.00	2.00 to	3.00	2.00 to	4.00
Arenberg, Radiance, Taft, Extra	2.00 to	4.00	...... to	......	4.00 to	6.00
" " Ordinary	.50 to	1.00	...... to	......	2.00 to	4.00
Russell, Hadley, Ophelia, Mock	2.00 to	8.00	6.00 to	8.00	3.00 to	12.00
Carnations, Fancy	.75 to	1.00	1.00 to	1.50	...... to	1.50
Ordinary	.50 to	.75	.50 to	.75	...... to	1.00
Cattleyas	35.00 to	75.00	35.00 to	50.00	50.00 to	75.00
Dendrobium formosum	...... to	......	.... to	......	...... to	75.00
Lilies, Longiflorum	2.00 to	5.00	6.00 to	8.00	8.00 to	12.50
Rubrum	...... to	2.00	4.00 to	5.00	.... to	2.00
Lily of the Valley	2.00 to	4.00	3.00 to	4.00	2.00 to	4.00
Daisies	.50 to	1.00	.10 to	.25	...... to	1.00
Snapdragon	.25 to	1.00	3.00 to	4.00	...... to	......
Gladioli	.50 to	1.00	2.00 to	3.00	1.00 to	3.00
Asters	.25 to	1.00	.75 to	2.00	.50 to	2.00
Sweet Peas	.15 to	.50	.15 to	.25	.25 to	.75
Gardenias	10.00 to	15.00	...... to	......	...... to	......
Adiantum	.50 to	1.00	1.00 to	1.25	...... to	1.00
Smilax	6.00 to	12.00	12.00 to	15.00	15.00 to	20.00
Asparagus Plumosus, Strings (100)	25.00 to	50.00	35.00 to	50.00	...... to	50.00
" & Spren. (100 Bchs.)	25.00 to	35.00	35.00 to	50.00	...... to	50.00

Flower Market Reports

(Continued from page 203)

crops. The supply in the market is as heavy as it was while the demand for stock, although steady, has shown no marked improvement. The rose cut is heavier and better than it was. Carnations, too, are a little more plentiful than at the last writing. The gladiolus supply is steady and more than able to take care of the present demand. Aster receipts include large supplies in the various colors. Lilies are not very plentiful.

NEW YORK The flower trade situation here shows no improvement, with few exceptions. Lilies and lily of the valley are going better owing to a decreased supply and to an unusual amount of funeral work. Orchids are in very limited supply; the few there are of best quality are selling at top figures. Roses are in larger supply and in quality and length of stem are notable for August. Of course there are thousands of the short grades but never have there been so many good roses to be had in midsummer. The sale of these is limited, however. Asters are still plentiful but gladioli are not so abundant. General business is very dull.

PHILADELPHIA Friday and Saturday of last week were pretty good days but business was rather slow until then. Roses have sold better, especially in the higher grades, these being rather on the scarce side. There are some excellent Russells also some good White Killarneys and Sunbursts. The new crop local Beauties have greatly improved and are now preferred to the northern grown as they arrive in better condition. The hot weather is against even fine stock coming from a distance. The oversupply of lilies is past for the time being and prices have hardened up very considerably. Too many asters and much of the stock not top notch. The many heavy showers nearly every day and then the blaze of sunshine following has been apt to blister the flowers and make them spotty and unsalable to a large degree. Gladioli are selling better—at least there are not so many to throw away at the wind-up of the week's business. The orchid market continues firm with supply slightly increased. Vandas and oncidiums add a little variety to the cattleya standbys. There are oceans of white hydrangea heads and other outdoor flowers.

SAN FRANCISCO Usual midsummer dullness has failed to materialize here, as shown by the fact that stocks cleaned up as closely the past week as any time since the first of the year. Most lines are plentiful and where slightly short substitutes can be made, so the situation is highly satisfactory all around. Scabiosas, marigolds, mignonette, marguerites, gypsophilas, coreopsis and other summer flowers continue to move in exceptionally large quantities. Small sunflowers are popular. Chrysanthemums are more in evidence from day to day and the quality is excellent for the opening of the season. Monrovia, Golden Glow and October Frost are offered quite freely now, and Unaka, the large pink

variety, and the large yellow Crocus will probably put in an appearance next week. A limited amount of new carnations have arrived the last few days, which, however, do not attract much attention as the stems are short. Old cuttings are very scarce and the quality very poor. The supply of asters is enormous, but they all seem to find an outlet, as no surplus is reported in any quarter. Gladioli are hardly so plentiful, although some very nice Mrs. Francis King are still offered, as well as fine Niagara and a few Panama. On the other hand the supply of dahlias has increased somewhat and the quality, if anything, averages better than it has for two or three weeks. Some of the rose offerings are nothing extra in quality and good stock is easily disposed of at firm prices. Not much improvement is expected before the middle of September. Rubrum lilies are plentiful, good quality and cheap. Orchids are in a little better supply, but more could be sold if available. Gardenias clean up particularly well on account of the scarcity of orchids.

ST. LOUIS It is difficult to write up the market as it really is and the prices obtained for stock. Business among the retailers was at a standstill, so the wholesalers have had a hard time in disposing of their consignments, which have been heavy of late. There are plenty of roses of all kinds, asters, field-grown carnations, tuberoses and gladioli. The latter have shortened up since the week previous, with the price a few cents higher this week.

WASHINGTON This has been a slightly better market for cut flowers during the past week or ten days and conditions are more hopeful. The glut of gladioli and asters is about over and those being received are in better quality. Roses have improved and are now coming in with longer stems. Dahlias have not as yet made their appearance in quantities sufficient to menace the sale of other stock. Carnations are decidedly off. Gardenias are not very plentiful and orchids are extremely scarce, with prices very high. The retailers report

many queries regarding prices for decorations and even the placement of orders for execution during the latter part of September and early in October and the prediction is made that business during the fall season will be very good.

PHILADELPHIA NOTES.

Mr. and Mrs. Abram L. Pennock are spending a vacation at Ocean City, N. J., with their son Samuel S. Pennock and his family. Abram L. will be 88 on his next birthday.

Paul Huebner of the Reading R. R. system has just returned from the R. R. Gardeners' Convention at Detroit and speaks enthusiastically of the splendid reception given the delegates by the local trade—members of the Florists' Club and others. He says they had a very successful meeting and much good work was accomplished.

The House of Michell has sent out a large number of personal invitations to attend a special inspection trip to their nurseries and perennial gardens, at Andalusia, on Wednesday, September 8th. They have provided a special train, leaving Broad Street Station at 11.30 A. M. on that date. "Recognition tags" to be worn visibly on the lapel of the coat will be distributed so that no one may miss the special train. Refreshments will be served, as well as free transportation.

ROCHESTER TAKES THE STAGE.

All roads lead to Rochester next week, when the results of the zealous campaign by the members of the Florists' Association will, we sincerely hope, materialize in a floral and horticultural exhibition worthy of the occasion. A large trade display is assured and a representative attendance of florists and their allies is expected from far and near. The exposition, of which the horticultural show is a part, will be open from August 30 till September 11. A daily attendance of over 20,000 is counted upon.

The wholesale florists of St. Louis have agreed to close their places at 6 P. M. every week day and to remain closed on Sundays all winter.

NEW YORK QUOTATIONS PER 100. To Dealers Only

MISCELLANEOUS	Last Half of Week ending Aug. 21 1915			First Half of Week beginning Aug. 23 1915		
Cattleyas	25.00	to	75.00	25.00	to	75.00
Lilies, Longiflorum	3.00	to	6.00	3.00	to	6.00
" Rubrum	1.00	to	2.00	1.00	to	2.00
Lily of the Valley	2.00	to	4.00	2.00	to	4.00
Daisies		to	.50		to	.50
Snapdragon	.50	to	1.00	.50	to	1.00
Gladioli	.50	to	2.00	.50	to	2.00
Asters	.15	to	1.00	.25	to	1.00
Sweet Peas	.10	to	.15	.10	to	.15
Corn Flower		to	.25		to	.25
Gardenias	12.00	to	25.00	12.00	to	25.00
Adiantum	.50	to	.75	.50	to	.75
Smilax	4.00	to	8.00	4.00	to	8.00
Asparagus Plumosus, strngs (per 100)	15.00	to	30.00	15.00	to	30.00
" " & Spren (100 bunches)	20.00	to	30.00	20.00	to	30.00

Buyer's Directory and Ready Reference Guide

Advertisements under this head, one cent a word.   Initials count as words.

Display advertisers in this issue are also listed under this classification without charge. Reference to List of Advertisers will indicate the respective pages.

Buyers failing to find what they want in this list will confer a favor by writing us and we will try to put them in communication with reliable dealers.

ACCOUNTANT
R. J. Dysart, 40 State St., Boston.
For page see List of Advertisers.

ACHILLEA
"Pearl." Fine Seedlings. $3.00 per 1,000, cash. JAMES MOSS, Wholesale Grower, Johnsville, Pa.

APHINE
Aphine Mfg. Co., Madison, N. J.
For page see List of Advertisers.

APHIS PUNK
Nicotine Mfg. Co., St. Louis, Mo.
For page see List of Advertisers.

ASTERS
ASTERS—Invincible, Henderson's seed, and as fine and healthy plants that grow; in white, pink, purple, rose and blue, $3.00 per 1,000; 5,000 or more, $2.50 per 1,000. Cash. JAMES MOSS, Wholesale Grower, Johnsville, Pa.

AUCTION SALES
Elliott Auction Co., New York City.
For page see List of Advertisers.

AZALEAS
P. Ouwerkerk, Hoboken, N. J.
For page see List of Advertisers.

BAY TREES
August Rolker & Sons, New York.
For page see List of Advertisers.

BEDDING PLANTS
A. N. Pierson, Inc., Cromwell, Conn.
For page see List of Advertisers.

BEGONIAS
Julius Roehrs Company, Rutherford, N. J.
For page see List of Advertisers.

R. Vincent, Jr., & Sons Co., White Marsh, Md.
For page see List of Advertisers.

Thomas Roland, Nahant, Mass.
For page see List of Advertisers.

A. M. Davenport, Watertown, Mass.
For page see List of Advertisers.

                 Per 100
BEGONIA LORRAINE, 2½ in......$12.00
               3 in...... 20.00
               4 in...... 35.00
               5 in...... 50.00
BEGONIA CINCINNATI, 2½ in...... 15.00
               3 in...... 25.00
               3½ in...... 30.00
               4½ in...... 40.00
JULIUS ROEHRS CO., Rutherford, N. J.

BOILERS
Kroeschell Bros. Co., Chicago.
For page see List of Advertisers.

King Construction Co., North Tonawanda, N. Y.
"King Ideal" Boiler.
For page see List of Advertisers.

Lord & Burnham Co., New York City.
For page see List of Advertisers.

Hitchings & Co., New York City.

BOXES—CUT FLOWER FOLDING
Edwards Folding Box Co., Philadelphia.
For page see List of Advertisers.

Folding cut flower boxes, the best made. Write for list. HOLTON & HUNKEL CO., Milwaukee, Wis.

BOX TREES
BOX TREES—Standards, Pyramids and Bush, in various sizes. Price List on demand. JULIUS ROEHRS CO., Rutherford, N. J.

BULBS AND TUBERS
Santa Cruz Bulb & Plant Co., Santa Cruz, Cal.
Freesia Purity and Calla Bulbs.
For page see List of Advertisers.

J. M. Thorburn & Co., New York City
Wholesale Price List of High Class Bulbs.
For page see List of Advertisers.

Ralph M. Ward & Co., New York City.
Lily Bulbs.
For page see List of Advertisers.

John Lewis Childs, Flowerfield, L. I., N. Y.
For page see List of Advertisers.

August Rolker & Sons, New York City.
Holland and Japan Bulbs.
For page see List of Advertisers.

R. & J. Farquhar & Co., Boston, Mass.
For page see List of Advertisers.

S. S. Skidelsky & Co., Philadelphia, Pa.
For page see List of Advertisers.

Chas. Schwake & Co., New York City.
Horticultural Importers and Exporters.
For page see List of Advertisers.

A. Henderson & Co., Chicago, Ill.
For page see List of Advertisers.

Burnett Bros., 98 Chambers St., New York.
For page see List of Advertisers.

Henry F. Michell Co., Philadelphia, Pa.
For page see List of Advertisers.

Joseph Breck & Sons Corp., Boston, Mass.
Bulbs for Early Forcing.
For page see List of Advertisers.

Raymond W. Swett, Saxonville, Mass.
Darwin Tulips, Hyacinths and Spanish Iris Bulbs.

Peter Henderson & Co., New York City.
Henderson's Superior Bulbs for Fall Planting.

C. KEUR & SONS, HILLEGOM, Holland. Bulbs of all descriptions. Write for prices. NEW YORK Branch, 8-10 Bridge St.

Fottler, Fiske, Rawson Co., Boston, Mass.

CANNAS
Canna Specialists.
Send for Canna book.
THE CONARD & JONES COMPANY, West Grove, Pa.

CARNATION STAPLES
Split carnations quickly, easily and cheaply mended. Pillsbury's Carnation Staple, 1000 for 35c.; 3000 for $1.00 post paid. I. L. PILLSBURY, Galesburg, Ill.

Supreme Carnation Staples, for repairing split carnations. 35c. per 1000; 3600 for $1.00. F. W. WAITE, 85 Belmont Ave., Springfield, Mass.

CARNATIONS.
Wood Bros., Fishkill, N. Y.
For page see List of Advertisers.

F. Dorner & Sons Co., Lafayette, Ind.
For page see List of Advertisers.

Leo Niessen Co., Philadelphia, Pa.
Field Grown Carnation Plants.
For page see List of Advertisers.

Carnations, field grown. $6.00 per 100. Cash. White and Pink Enchantress Mrs. Ward. Perfection, Fenn, Winsor, Queen, Lawson, Beacon. CHAS. H. GREEN, Spencer, Mass.

CHRYSANTHEMUMS
Chas. H. Totty, Madison, N. J.
For page see List of Advertisers.

R. Vincent, Jr., & Sons Co., White Marsh, Md.
Pompon Chrysanthemums,
For page see List of Advertisers.

For Sale—800 Yellow Bonnaffons, transplanted, 3 branches, $35.00 takes the lot. Apply to W. H. TOMLINSON, 355 Centre St., Dorchester, Mass. Tel., 22477 Dorchester.

THE BEST 1915 NOVELTIES.
The Cream of 1914 Introductions.
The most popular Commercial and Exhibition kinds; also complete line of Pompons, Singles and Anemones. Trade list on application. ELMER D. SMITH & CO., Adrian, Mich.

COCOANUT FIBRE SOIL
20th Century Plant Food Co., Beverly, Mass.
For page see List of Advertisers.

DAHLIAS
Send for Wholesale List of whole clumps and separate stock; 40,000 clumps for sale. Northboro Dahlia and Gladiolus Gardens, J. L. MOORE, Prop, Northboro, Mass.

NEW PAEONY DAHLIA
John Wanamaker, Newest, Handsomest, Best. New color, new form and new habit of growth. Big stock of best cut-flower varieties. Send list of wants to PEACOCK DAHLIA FARMS, Berlin, N. J.

DECORATIVE PLANTS
Robert Craig Co., Philadelphia, Pa.
For page see List of Advertisers.

Woodrow & Marketos, New York City.
For page see List of Advertisers.

S. S. Skidelsky & Co., Philadelphia, Pa.
For page see List of Advertisers.

Bobbink & Atkins, Rutherford, N. J.
For page see List of Advertisers.

A. Leuthy & Co., Roslindale, Boston, Mass.
For page see List of Advertisers.

Frank Oechslin, Chicago, Ill.
Ferns for Dishes.

DRACAENAS
2,000 Dracaena Indivisa, 2¼ in. pot plants, $2.50 per 100; $20.00 per 1000, to clean out. Apply to W. H. TOMLINSON, 355 Centre St., Dorchester, Mass. Tel., 22477 Dorchester.

FERNS
Henry A. Dreer, Philadelphia, Pa.
Dreer's Fern Flats.
For page see List of Advertisers.

H. H. Barrows & Son, Whitman, Mass.
For page see List of Advertisers.

Robert Craig Co., Philadelphia, Pa.
For page see List of Advertisers.

McHutchison & Co., New York City.
Ferns in Flats.
For page see List of Advertisers.

Roman J. Irwin, New York City.
Boston and Whitmani Ferns.
For page see List of Advertisers.

Frank Oechslin, Chicago, Ill.
Ferns for Dishes.

FERTILIZERS
20th Century Plant Food Co., Beverly, Mass.
Cocoanut Fibre Soil.
For page see List of Advertisers.

Stumpp & Walter Co., New York City.
Scotch Soot.
For page see List of Advertisers.

For List of Advertisers See Page 275

FERTILIZERS—Continued

Pulverized Manure Co., Chicago, Ill.
 Wizard Brand Cattle Manure.

Farmers & Florists Fertilizer Co.,
 Chicago, Ill.
Aetna Brand Tankage Fertilizer.

Chicago Feed & Fertilizer Co.,
 Magic Brand Manures.
Union Stock Yards, Chicago, Ill.

Hardwood Ashes for sale. GEO. L.
MUNROE & SONS, Oswego, N. Y.

FLORISTS' LETTERS

Boston Florist Letter Co., Boston, Mass.
 For page see List of Advertisers.

FLORISTS' SUPPLIES

N. F. McCarthy & Co., Boston, Mass.
 For page see List of Advertisers.

Reed & Keller, New York City.
 For page see List of Advertisers.

S. S. Pennock-Meehan Co., Philadelphia, Pa.
 For page see List of Advertisers.

H. Bayersdorfer & Co., Philadelphia, Pa.
 Up-to-Date Summer Novelties.
 For page see List of Advertisers.

Welch Bros. Co., Boston, Mass.
 For page see List of Advertisers.

FLOWER POTS

W. H. Ernest, Washington, D. C.
 For page see List of Advertisers.

A. H. Hews & Co., Inc., Cambridge, Mass.
 For page see List of Advertisers.

Hilfinger Bros., Ft. Edward, N. Y.
 For page see List of Advertisers.

FOLIAGE PLANTS

A. Leuthy & Co., Roslindale, Boston, Mass.
 For page see List of Advertisers.

FUCHSIAS

Fuchsias—Black Prince, Speciosa, double
purple and white, Rooted Cuttings, $1.00
per 100; 2½-in., $2.00 per 100.
W. J. BARNETT, R. D. 67, Sharon, Pa.

FUNGINE

Aphine Mfg. Co., Madison, N. J.
 For page see List of Advertisers.

GALAX

Michigan Cut Flower Co., Detroit, Mich.
 For page see List of Advertisers.

GERANIUMS

R. Vincent, Jr., & Sons Co.
 White Marsh, Md.
 For page see List of Advertisers.

GLASS

Sharp, Partridge & Co., Chicago.
 For page see List of Advertisers.

Parshelsky Bros., Inc., Brooklyn, N. Y.
 For page see List of Advertisers.

Royal Glass Works, New York City.
 For page see List of Advertisers.

Johnston Brokerage Co., Pittsburgh, Pa.
 Home-Made Greenhouse Glass.

Greenhouse glass, lowest prices. JOHN-
STON GLASS CO., Hartford City, Ind.

GLASS CUTTERS

Smith & Hemenway Co., New York City.
 Red Devil Glass Cutter.
 For page see List of Advertisers.

GLAZING POINTS

H. A. Dreer, Philadelphia, Pa.
 Peerless Glazing Point.
 For page see List of Advertisers.

Geo. H. Angermueller, St. Louis, Mo.
 For page see List of Advertisers.

GREENHOUSE BUILDING MATERIAL

King Construction Co., N. Tonawanda, N. Y.
 For page see List of Advertisers.

Parshelsky Bros., Inc., Brooklyn, N. Y.
 For page see List of Advertisers.

**GREENHOUSE BUILDING MATERIAL—
Continued**

A. T. Stearns Lumber Co., Neponset,
 Boston.
 Pecky Cypress.

Lord & Burnham Co., New York City.
 For page see List of Advertisers.

Metropolitan Material Co., Brooklyn, N. Y.
 For page see List of Advertisers.

A. Dietsch Co., Chicago, Ill.

GREENHOUSE CONSTRUCTION

King Construction Co., N. Tonawanda, N. Y.
 For page see List of Advertisers.

Foley Greenhouse Mfg. Co., Chicago, Ill.
 For page see List of Advertisers.

Lord & Burnham Co., New York City.
 For page see List of Advertisers.

Metropolitan Material Co., Brooklyn, N. Y.
 For page see List of Advertisers.

Hitchings & Co., New York City.

A. T. Stearns Lumber Co., Boston, Mass.

S. Jacobs & Sons, Brooklyn, N. Y.

John C. Moninger Co., Chicago, Ill.

GUTTERS

King Construction Co., N. Tonawanda, N. Y.
 King Channel Gutter.
 For page see List of Advertisers.

Metropolitan Material Co., Brooklyn, N. Y.
 Iron Gutters.
 For page see List of Advertisers.

HAIL INSURANCE

Florists' Hail Asso. of America.
J. G. Esler, Saddle River, N. J.

HARDY FERNS AND GREEN GOODS

Michigan Cut Flower Exchange, Detroit,
 Mich.
 For page see List of Advertisers.

Knud Nielsen, Evergreen, Ala.
Natural Green Sheet Moss, Fancy and Dag-
 ger Ferns and Huckleberry Foliage.
 For page see List of Advertisers.

The Kervan Co., New York.
 For page see List of Advertisers.

HARDY PERENNIALS

R. & J. Farquhar & Co., Boston, Mass.
 For page see List of Advertisers.

Bay State Nurseries, No. Abington, Mass.
 For page see List of Advertisers.

P. Ouwerkerk, Hoboken, N. J.
 For page see List of Advertisers.

Palisades Nurseries, Sparkill, N. Y.
 For page see List of Advertisers.

HEATING APPARATUS

Kroeschell Bros. Co., Chicago.
 For page see List of Advertisers.

Lord & Burnham Co., New York City.
 For page see List of Advertisers.

HOT-BED SASH

Parshelsky Bros., Inc., Brooklyn, N. Y.
 For page see List of Advertisers.

Foley Greenhouse Construction Co.,
 Chicago, Ill.
 For page see List of Advertisers.

Lord & Burnham Co., New York City.
 For page see List of Advertisers.

A. T. Stearns Lumber Co., Neponset, Mass.

HOSE

H. A. Dreer, Philadelphia, Pa.
 For page see List of Advertisers.

INSECTICIDES

Aphine Manufacturing Co., Madison, N. J.
 Aphine and Fungine.
 For page see List of Advertisers.

Nicotine Mfg. Co., St. Louis, Mo.
 Aphis Punk and Nikoteen.
 For page see List of Advertisers.

INSECTICIDES—Continued

Eastern Chemical Co. Boston, Mass.
 Imp Soap Spray.
 For page see List of Advertisers.

The Plantlife Co., New York City.
 Plantlife Insecticide.
 For page see List of Advertisers.

IRIS

R. & J. Farquhar & Co., Boston, Mass.
 For page see List of Advertisers.

John Lewis Childs, Inc.
 Flowerfield, L. I., N. Y.
 For page see List of Advertisers.

IRIS—Splendid stock. Send for List and
let us figure on your wants. GEO. N.
SMITH, Wellesley Nurseries, Wellesley
Hills, Mass.

IRRIGATION EQUIPMENT

Skinner Irrigation Co., Brookline, Mass.
 For page see List of Advertisers.

JUNIPERUS PROSTRATA

Mt. Desert Nurseries, Bar Harbor, Me.

LILY BULBS

Chas. Schwake & Co., New York City.
Horticultural Importers and Exporters.
 For page see List of Advertisers.

R. M. Ward & Co., New York, N. Y.
Japanese Lily Bulbs of Superior Quality.
 For page see List of Advertisers.

Corp. of Chas. F. Meyer, New York City.
 Meyer's T. Brand Giganteums.
 For page see List of Advertisers.

John Lewis Childs, Inc.,
 Hardy Lilies.
 Flowerfield, L. I., N. Y.
 For page see List of Advertisers.

LILY OF THE VALLEY

Chas. Schwake & Co., Inc., New York City.
Hohmann's Famous Lily of the Valley Pips.
 For page see List of Advertisers.

McHutchison & Co., New York City.
 For page see List of Advertisers.

Loechner & Co., New York City.
 Lily of the Valley Pips.
 For page see List of Advertisers.

LIQUID PUTTY MACHINE

Metropolitan Material Co., Brooklyn, N. Y.
 For page see List of Advertisers.

MASTICA

F. O. Pierce Co., New York City.
 For page see List of Advertisers.

Geo. H. Angermueller, St. Louis, Mo.
 For page see List of Advertisers.

MUSHROOM SPAWN

MUSHROOM SPAWN.
Let us quote you on your requirements
of Mushroom Spawn for the present season.
Buy from the Makers and get select stock
at lowest prices. We have had 30 years'
experience.
CANADIAN MUSHROOM GROWERS, Ltd.,
 Lindsay, Ont.

NATIONAL NURSERYMAN

National Nurseryman Publishing Co., Inc.,
 Rochester, N. Y.
 For page see List of Advertisers.

NIKOTEEN

Nicotine Mfg. Co., St. Louis, Mo.
 For page see List of Advertisers.

NIKOTIANA

Aphine Mfg. Co., Madison, N. J.
 For page see List of Advertisers.

NURSERY STOCK

P. Ouwerkerk, Weehawken Heights, N. J.
 For page see List of Advertisers.

W. & T. Smith Co., Geneva, N. Y.
 For page see List of Advertisers.

SWEET PEAS—Continued

NEW WINTER FLOWERING VARIETIES SWEET PEA SEED.

MRS. A. A. SEACH—A beautiful shell pink. Will not fade and has splendid keeping qualities. Per oz., $1.75; 4 oz., $6.00; 1 lb., $18.00.

MRS. M. SPANOLIN—Black-seeded, of the purest white color. Has won a number of first prizes. Per oz., $2.00; 4 oz., $7.00; 1 lb., $25.00.

VENUS—White with slight pink blush, one of the best. Per oz., $2.00; 4 oz., $7.00; 1 lb., $25.00.

LAVENDER ORCHID—Lavender pink, very large. Per oz., $2.00; 4 oz., $7.00; 1 lb., $25.00.

WHITE ORCHID—A true white. Per oz., $1.75; 4 oz., $6.00; 1 lb., $18.00.

MRS. JOS. MANDA—A light shell pink with extra long stem. Flowers ruffled, becoming a brighter pink the longer they are kept. Per oz., $2.00; 4 oz., $7.00; 1 lb., $25.00.

ORCHID BEAUTY—Dark rose, blushed with orange. Per oz., $1.75; 4 oz., $6.00; 1 lb., $18.00.

ORANGE ORCHID—Begins to bloom in March. One of the best if sown late. During December and January the color is more rose. True. Per oz., $4.00; 4 oz., $7.00; 1 lb., $25.00.

YARRAWA—Spencer, early winter flowering, bright rose pink, seed sown August 1st will flower November 15th. ¼ oz., $1.00; 1 oz., $3.50; ¼ lb., $12.50.

All other varieties, with prices, on application.

S. S. PENNOCK-MEEHAN CO., 1608-20 Ludlow Street, Philadelphia, Pa.

VENTILATING APPARATUS

The Advance Co., Richmond, Ind.
For page see List of Advertisers.

The John A. Evans Co., Richmond, Ind.
For page see List of Advertisers.

VERMICIDES

Aphine Mfg. Co., Madison, N. J.
For page see List of Advertisers.

WEED DESTROYER

Pino-Lyptol Chemical Co., New York City.

WINTER FLOWERING SWEET PEAS

Arthur T. Boddington, New York City.
For page see List of Advertisers.

W. Atlee Burpee & Co., Philadelphia, Pa.
Burpee's Winter-Flowering Spencer Sweet Peas.

WIRED TOOTHPICKS

W. J. Cowee, Berlin, N. Y.
For page see List of Advertisers.

WIREWORK

Reed & Keller, New York City.
For page see List of Advertisers.

WILLIAM E. HEILSCHER'S WIRE WORKS, 264 Randolph St., Detroit, Mich.

WHOLESALE FLORISTS
Albany, N. Y.

Albany Cut Flower Exchange, Albany, N. Y.
For page see List of Advertisers.

Baltimore

The S. S. Pennock-Meehan Co., Franklin and St. Paul Sts.
For page see List of Advertisers.

Boston

N. F. McCarthy & Co., 112 Arch St. and 31 Otis St.
For page see List of Advertisers.

Welch Bros. Co., 226 Devonshire St.
For page see List of Advertisers.

Patrick Welch, 262 Devonshire St., Boston, Mass.
For page see List of Advertisers.

WHOLESALE FLORISTS
Brooklyn

Wm. H. Kuebler, 28 Willoughby St.
For page see List of Advertisers.

Buffalo, N. Y.

William F. Kasting Co., 383-87 Ellicott St.
For page see List of Advertisers.

Chicago

Poehlmann Bros. Co., Morton Grove, Ill.
For page see List of Advertisers.

Cincinnati

C. E. Critchell, 34-36 Third Ave., East.
For page see List of Advertisers.

Detroit

Michigan Cut Flower Exchange, 38 and 40 Broadway.
For page see List of Advertisers.

New York

H. E. Froment, 148 W. 28th St.

James McManus, 105 W. 28th St.
For page see List of Advertisers.

W. F. Sheridan, 133 W. 28th St.
For page see List of Advertisers.

P. J. Smith, 131 West 28th St., N. Y.
For page see List of Advertisers.

Moore, Hentz & Nash, 55 and 57 W. 26th St.
For page see List of Advertisers.

Charles Millang, 55 and 57 West 26th St.
For page see List of Advertisers.

W. P. Ford, New York

The S. S. Pennock-Meehan Co., 117 West 28th St.
For page see List of Advertisers.

Traendly & Schenck, 436 6th Ave., between 26th and 27th Sts.
For page see List of Advertisers.

Badgley, Riedel & Meyer, Inc., New York.
For page see List of Advertisers.

Woodrow & Marketos, 37 & 39 West 28th St.
For page see List of Advertisers.

George C. Siebrecht, 109 W. 28th St.
For page see List of Advertisers.

John Young & Co., 53 West 28th St.
For page see List of Advertisers.

M. C. Ford, 121 West 28th St.
For page see List of Advertisers.

Guttman & Raynor, Inc., 101 W. 28th St., New York.
For page see List of Advertisers.

Philadelphia

Leo, Niessen Co., 12th and Race Sts.
For page see List of Advertisers.

Edward Reid, 1619-21 Ranstead St.
For page see List of Advertisers.

The S. S. Pennock-Meehan Co., 1608-20 Ludlow St.
For page see List of Advertisers.

Stuart H. Miller, 2617 Ranstead St.
For page see List of Advertisers.

Richmond, Ind.

E. G. Hill Co.
For page see List of Advertisers

Rochester, N. Y.

George B. Hart, 24 Stone St.
For page see List of Advertisers.

Washington

The S. S. Pennock-Meehan Co., 1216 H St., N. W.
For page see List of Advertisers.

New Offers In This Issue

AZALEA SHIPMENTS WILL COME.
McHutchison & Co., New York City.
For page see List of Advertisers.

BEGONIAS LORRAINE AND CINCINNATI.
Julius Roehrs Co., Rutherford, N. J.
For page see List of Advertisers.

BODDINGTON'S GIGANTIC CYCLAMEN SEED.
Arthur T. Boddington Co., Inc., New York City.
For page see List of Advertisers.

LILIUM HARRISII BULBS.
F. R. Pierson Co., Tarrytown, N. Y.
For page see List of Advertisers.

SPHAGNUM MOSS.
S. S. Pennock-Meehan Co., Philadelphia, Pa.
For page see List of Advertisers.

WANTS, FOR SALE, Etc.

HELP WANTED

ASSISTANT WANTED Sept. 1st for greenhouses; experienced in grapes, roses, carnations, etc., and outside flowers. Wages $60 per month with room. State nre, references and nationality. JOSEPH LEE, Windholme Farm, Islip, L. I., N. Y.

SITUATIONS WANTED

GARDENER—Scotch Canadian, 45. Can care for flowers, fruit, lawns, vegetables and greenhouse. No liquor or tobacco. Hard worker, has taken care, alone, of five acres of market garden this summer. Will be free after first frost. Family of two girls. Permanent place desired. Write L. P. MacLENNAN, Malletts Bay, Vermont.

SITUATION WANTED by gardener, English, as head in private place. Experienced in all branches of horticulture under glass and outside, the growing of stove and greenhouse plants, orchids, fruit under glass, vegetable and flower garden, alpine and herbaceous plants. Married, no family. Good references. "J.," care HORTICULTURE, Boston.

TO LET

TO LET—at Jamaica Plain. A steam-heated store suitable for Florist. Apply to JOHN R. SAWYER, 367 Centre street, Jamaica Plain, Mass.

FOR SALE

FOR SALE—Second hand copy of B. S. Williams' Orchid Growers' Manual, good as new. Edition 1885. "A. D.," care HORTICULTURE.

FOR SALE—Fresh from factory, new; 10 x 12, 16 x 18, 16 x 24, double thick. A and B qualities. Market dropped. Now is the time to buy and save money. PARSHELSKY BROS., INC., 215-217 Havemeyer St., Brooklyn, N. Y.

In writing to Advertisers kindly mention Horticulture

THE GREAT STORM IN HOUSTON, TEXAS.

THE RUINS OF THE KERR GREENHOUSES AFTER HOUSTON STORM

1.—A Close View of the Wreck of the Kerr Plant.   2.—Showing the Destroyed Fern House.

3.—General View of the Ruins.

4.—Showing Destruction of Steel Tower Which Supported a 15,000 Gallon Tank.   5.—Showing One Corner of the Wrecked Greenhouse.

The accompanying pictures show how completely the greenhouses of R. C. Kerr were demolished by the great storm of last week. Mr. Kerr informs us that his losses at the nursery will amount to about five thousand dollars. H. H. Kuhlmann's losses are heavy, about the same as Kerr's. Mr. Cotney's store was destroyed and the family was caught in the wreck. Mr. Cotney was hurt to some extent, but not very seriously. W. T. Hauser lost

about one-half of his greenhouses, which will amount to about $3,000. The Brazoe Greenhouses suffered very little—only three or four hundred glass lights being broken. The greenhouses being modern stood the storm very well.

Downtown the Forestdale Store suffered the loss of three big plate glass windows and considerable damage to the stock. Mr. Kerr's conservatory and store were only slightly damaged due to the protection of several large brick buildings. Two plate glass windows were broken out of Kuhlmann's downtown store. The Gulf Florist (a small greenhouse in the business center) was badly damaged. Henry Blecker at the Glenwood Cemetery, had the top blown off of his store, and some damages to his greenhouse.

Mr. Kerr, in a letter to HORTICULTURE, says, that this storm was a blessing in disguise to the florists of Houston. "While our losses are a little heavy, we will soon recover, and after talking it over, I believe everyone will construct only modern houses. In a year or two from now you will see modern greenhouses around Houston instead of the old shacks they have been using for the

last ten or fifteen years. In the course of a week or so all the wreckage will be cleared away, and preparations will be made by spring for the erection of the new greenhouses. It is the consensus of opinion that it is too late to do anything this fall except what is necessary for the protection of the stock on hand.

Houston will be in better trim for the Convention on account of this storm, as we will not have these old unsightly greenhouses to show our visitors, and it is needless to say the impression will be far better for Houston."

BOSTON SPRING SHOW.

In the prize list for the exhibition to be held in March, 1916, as printed in our issue of last week an omission occurred in the paragraph of prizes for tulips. The paragraph should read as follows:

Schizanthus. Six plants, 1st, $12; 2nd, $6.
Tulips, three pans each color, white, red, pink, yellow, and any other color, 1st, $6; 2nd, $3. Bed to cover not over 25 sq. ft. arranged for color effect; sand will be provided in which to set the pots; pots can be used for edging, 1st, $20; 2nd, $10.

Obituary

George E. Luffman.

George E. Luffman of Glen Iris, Birmingham, Ala., died suddenly on Sunday, August 15, at his home in Birmingham, aged 58 years and 4 months. He leaves a widow and three daughters, one of whom, Mrs. Amy L. Lambly of Spokane, Wash., is a life member of the S. A. F. Mr. Luffman was a landscape gardener and florist, deeply attached to his calling. He was in business in Philadelphia a good many years ago.

Thomas A. Ivey.

Thomas A. Ivey, of Port Dover, Ont., lost his life on the night of August 14 in a collision between a taxicab in which he was riding and a locomotive. He was a widely-known florist throughout Canada, with a large area of glass in Port Dover and wholesale and retail branches in Montreal, Hamilton and elsewhere. He leaves a widow, three daughters and four sons, the sons being associated in the business. He was 68 years of age.

Lawrence W. Kervan.

Lawrence W. Kervan of the Kervan Company, dealing in evergreens and florists' supplies at 119 West 28th street, New York City, died Tuesday night, August 24, in Roosevelt Hospital as the result of an operation for hernia, performed the previous Thursday.

Mr. Kervan was born in New York City, February 21, 1843, and was a Civil War veteran, having served three years in the Fifth Connecticut Regiment. After living a number of years in Florida he returned to New York seventeen years ago and engaged in the selling of evergreens and ferns, building up the large and prosperous concern known as the Kervan Company.

Mr. Kervan was highly esteemed in the trade for his integrity and straightforwardness and a most likable personality won him many warm friends. He is survived by a widow and four sons, three of whom were associated with him in business.

Funeral services were held at his home, No. 7 West 108th street, on Thursday evening, August 26. Interment was in Montague, Mass., the burial place of Mrs Kervan's family.

Frank Frank, florist, 1561 3rd Avenue, New York, has lost his young daughter, Rita, aged 22 months.

THE LATE JOHN MACDILL CLARK.

The death of John Macdill Clark, secretary of the Leonard Seed Company of Chicago, was briefly announced in our issue of last week. Mr. Macdill had been unwell for about three weeks. Becoming worse, he was operated upon at the West Suburban Hospital three days before his death, when it was discovered that he was suffering from ulceration of the stomach and recovery was impossible.

Mr. Clark was born in Kirkcudbright, Scotland, May 8, 1860. He came to this country with his parents at the age of 7 years and received his education in the public schools of New York. He first worked for a clothing firm, but soon left this position for one with the seed house of A. D. Cowan, New York. After this he worked successively for the Robert Buist Co., of Philadelphia, and Vaughan's Seed Store, Chicago, until January 1, 1885, when he cast his lot with S. F. Leonard, and when the Leonard Seed Co. was incorporated in 1891 he was chosen secretary.

For many years Mr. Clark had been prominent in the seed trade as an expert in types, bringing a practical knowledge and experience to bear on the subject that gained for him a high place in the esteem and confidence of seed trade and agricultural circles. He was a member of the farmers' institute of the eighth congressional district, and for several years had been one of its directors. His business associates pay him the respect of stating that to his even temper, untiring efforts and close attention to detail, together with his efficient co-operation with the rest of the organization, is due to no small extent the unfaltering advance of the house. In his more than thirty years' connection with the company there has never been a moment of friction. His associates will not try to fill his place; they will merely learn to do without him.

NEWS NOTES.

Shelburne Falls, Mass.—P. R. Burtt, who recently bought the original Fife greenhouses, is renovating them with a view to opening up the florist business again there.

Beverly Farms, Mass.—Frank E. Cole is running the once famed Spaulding gardens as a commercial enterprise, under the name of North Shore Nurseries and Florist Company, and is very successful with it.

NEWS NOTES.

Independence, Ia.—Ray Whitney has purchased the Ibling greenhouses.

Webster City, Ia.—A. E. Flindt has leased the greenhouses of the Curtis Floral Company on Second street.

Atlantic Highlands, N. J.—Wm. H. Bennett has purchased the Hillside Greenhouses from his father, John Bennett, who will in the future devote all his attention to his nursery and landscape interests.

GREENHOUSES BUILDING OR CONTEMPLATED.

Zimbrota, Minn.—S. B. Scott, Dietsch house.

Nappanee, Ind.—Norton Gibson, one house.

Kansas City, Mo.—W. J. Barnes, additions.

Columbus, O.—H. C. Phelps, range of houses.

Punxsutawney, Pa.—R. M. Campbell, additions.

Philadelphia, Pa.—Chas. Grakelow, one house.

Clarks Summit, Pa.—L. E. Jennings, one house.

Prairie du Chien, Wis.—C. C. Case, one house.

Saginaw, Mich.—Desner & Fisher, two houses.

Newburyport, Mass.—C. J. McGregor, enlarging.

Cromwell, Ct.—Magnus Pierson, house 15x150.

Allegon, Mich.—O. E. Hall, Otsego road, one house.

Dayton, O.—W. S. Kidder, Grand Ave., one house.

Honesdale, Pa.—J. H. Storyman, King house, 18x50.

Worcester, Mass.—Chas. Greenwood, May St., one house.

Patchogue, N. Y.—J. K. Vanderveer, Jr., King house, 46x130.

Bristol, Pa.—Jacob Schmidt, range of seven houses, each 70x100.

Tarrytown-on-Hudson, N. Y. — Nathan Brewer & Son, one house.

Philadelphia, Pa.—Michaelson Bros., Walnut and 58th Sts., house 36x96. J. L. Nichols, 5435 North Water St., house 50x100.

Frederick, Md.—Frederick's educational botanical gardens will be formally opened on Thursday evening, September 2, when the Governor of Maryland and leading officials of the United States government will come to Frederick and participate in the official ceremonies.

The botanical gardens reflect credit to this community. They are not only a valuable asset to the community, but an illustration of co-operative community work. Mayor Fraley has worked tirelessly with the assistance of Frank C. Hargett, the superintendent, in making these gardens a successful venture.

The officers of the gardens: Executive committee, William F. Gude, Washington; George W. Hess, Washington; Richard Vincent, Jr., White Marsh, Md.; Mayor Lewis H. Fraley, Frederick, Md.; Frank C. Hargett, superintendent.

There is now a movement on foot to secure a public park, a part of which will be devoted to the further development of these gardens.

Vol. XXII
No. 10
SEPT. 4
1915

HORTICULTURE

Special Convention Display

Art Floral Co.'s Store, San Francisco. Showing Rear of Store

Published Every Saturday at 147 Summer Street, Boston, Mass.
Subscription, $1.00

LIST OF ADVERTISERS

FOR BUYERS' DIRECTORY AND READY REFERENCE GUIDE
SEE PAGES 328, 329, 330, 331

NOTES ON CULTURE OF FLORISTS' STOCK

CONDUCTED BY

John J. M. Farrell

Questions by our readers in line with any of the topics presented on this page will be cordially received and promptly answered by Mr. Farrell. Such communications should invariably be addressed to the office of HORTICULTURE. "If vain our toil, we ought to blame the culture, not the soil."—*Pope.*

Cattleyas

We are likely to have a good deal of warm, humid and cloudy weather before September closes and it behooves us to see to it that the shading over the cattleyas is not too dense. Those who can afford roller or other movable shades have a great advantage in being able to give their plants a maximum of light when it is most needed. Watering should be done in the morning. Plants such as C. labiata, Trianæ, Mossiæ, Percivaliana and others in active growth, will need a liberal supply more than C. Gaskelliana, Dowiana and others which are just starting into growth. A spraying each clear afternoon should be given the cattleyas. Do it sufficiently early so that it will dry before nightfall. Night temperatures are variable during September. As a general rule it can run from 60 to 65 degrees. Some nights it will be higher and it will do no harm if it falls to 58 degrees on cool evenings. It is not a good plan to shut the house up tightly on a cool night. Leave some air on to keep the atmosphere buoyant.

Cinerarias for Easter

Cineraria seed should be sown any time from the middle of September but no later. Sow in a well screened compost of new loam and peat or leaf mold half and half and a little sand. Have the pans well drained with plenty of crocks, upon which spread some sphagnum moss. Fill the pans to within half an inch and press firm and absolutely level. Water thoroughly before sowing and cover each pan with a pane of glass and place in cold frame under heavy shading, to be made lighter after the plants are up. When large enough, prick out into other pans or flats, and when they have made three or four leaves they can be potted into 2 or 2½-inch pots, using a compost of fibrous loam three parts, leaf mold and cow manure one part each and enough sand to keep it open.

Freesias

Give these little bulbs a good place well up to the glass. Keep the soil moist but not overwet. Provide proper supports to keep them upright. The earliest batch should now be several inches high and to get them

in flower as early as possible they should be moved into a sunny house where a winter minimum of 52 to 55 degrees is maintained. It is often possible to use shelves for them, providing saucers where the plants are in pans to prevent drying out later in the season.

Tulips

With the arrival of September it is time to think of tulips. Tulips are more in demand in pans or pots than any other Dutch bulbs. Use a light but moderately rich compost. Two-thirds decayed loam, one-third old hotbed or mushroom manure, with a fair addition of leafmold and plenty of sharp sand will be found suitable, and it is all the better if it is prepared well beforehand. It is safer not to add bone or any chemical fertilizers to soil for bulbs, as it is more likely to injure than to improve the plants. Water thoroughly and place outside and cover with about five or six inches of soil. With some protection they can stay here until wanted. Tulips do not force well until after January.

Winter Flowering Geraniums

Geraniums for winter use should not be allowed to get potbound between shifts. Should they show starvation in their blooming pots, a dusting of fine bone or other fertilizer or weak nitrate of soda water will tone them up. Give an occasional spraying overhead. The regular winter blooming geraniums being grown in pots should have the strong leading shoots pinched as they show any tendency to "run away," also keep all flower spikes picked off. Dead leaves and weeds should be removed and the plants frequently spread out while growing. They like a freely ventilated house. In a musty, ill-ventilated one they will develop bacteria. Let them dry out once in a while and when watering give them enough so as to soak the ball thoroughly.

Watch Out for Frost

While some growers are so crowded that it is next to impossible for them to house all their stock in a hurry it must be remembered that from this out we are liable to have a touch of frost at any time in some of our northern states. See that stock is brought together so they can be given protection at any moment.

Next Week: Carnations; Geranium Cuttings; Lifting Hydrangeas; Midseason Sweet Peas; Preparing Soil; Starting Firing.

ROSE GROWING UNDER GLASS

CONDUCTED BY

Arthur C. Ruzicka

Questions by our readers in line with any of the topics presented on this page will be cordially received and promptly answered by Mr. Ruzicka. Such communications should invariably be addressed to the office of HORTICULTURE.

Starting the Fires

It has been necessary to start the boilers much sooner than we expected, the cool snap arriving last week, with the thermometer down to 54 outside. A steam pipe through the houses made them feel much more comfortable, and the roses looked as though they appreciated the little heat. The houses should not be allowed to go much below 64, as it is too early in the season to run them at the regular night temperature, and then this cool weather will not last, and there may be nights when it will be hot and the houses will stay around 70. There is nothing in that hardening the plants up, by letting them go without heat, and allowing the houses to drop down to 56. This is all right in the middle of the winter but just now the roses should have heat so that they will make as much growth as possible. They should not be forced, by any means, but kept going all the time with nothing done that might check them in any way. It will pay in the long run to start the fires as soon as it gets cool, even though the night fireman has to be put on the job. It is poor economy to try to save ten dollars or perhaps a little more on the night man's wages, and lose two or three times the amount in the houses.

Ventilation

Do not close up the houses at night because of a cool night. Keep as much air on as possible, and with a steam pipe here and there it will not be necessary to reduce the air very low at night. Eight inches of air in clear weather is none too much and the wider houses should have more. All side ventilators had better be kept closed from now on unless they are looked after by a well skilled grower, and if this is the case he will know when to open them and when to leave them closed. The practice of putting the houses up full, first thing in the morning, should now be stopped and the thermometer used in deciding when the air is needed. It will be best not to put full air on until the houses reach a temperature of 78 degrees. In the cross houses where asparagus or smilax is grown the greens will grow much better if they are kept a little warmer. We find it best to keep these warm until they are almost ready to ship, and then run them cool to harden them off for the market.

Sulphur

As soon as the steam is turned on it will be well to apply a least bit of sulphur to the pipes, every ten or twenty feet as may be needed. This can be done even though there is no mildew to be seen. The gentle fumes resulting will destroy a good deal of fungus, and will not harm the plants or flowers in any way. Care should be taken, however, not to have more then five pounds of steam in the pipes when the sulphur is applied as otherwise it will evaporate too quickly and the fumes would become too strong and would be apt to bleach the flowers even though they did no harm to the foliage. For applying the sulphur we find nothing handier than the common indurated fibre rose jar and some sort of a brush. This must not be too big or too far gone or it will waste a good deal of the sulphur. Add enough water to the sulphur to make easy to apply and it will be better to have a little more water rather than to have the mixture too thick. If there is a crop of roses it will be well to add a little lime to the sulphur, say about one-third. This will keep the sulphur on the pipes longer and prevent it from evaporating too soon, so that the fumes will be much milder and will not be apt to bleach the flowers.

Repairs

If all the broken glass has not been repaired as yet no time should be lost in doing so now. The cool nights of last week would cause cold air to come in on the plants where it was not wanted, and they would likely get specked with mildew as a result. It is best to do the work right when repairing. Some growers have a habit of just sticking the glass in without any putty, leaving the rest of the work for some future day. This day seldom comes and the chances are that the glass gets broken again very shortly or else cracks because it does not lay properly. Do not be afraid to use the glass cutter. A good one can be had for ten cents, and with a little practice on some old glass anyone can become quite an expert at this business so that there is really no excuse for laps in the glass as wide as two inches. The lap should never be more than a quarter of an inch and less is better. If the lap is too wide, dirt will collect between the panes and dark strips will cast shadows over the plants. Then, too, water will get in in the winter and freeze thus breaking one or both panes quite often. Be sure to remove all surplus putty even though you have to get a ladder from the inside to do so. The work will never look finished if the putty is left sticking out after the glass is put in. It is well to paint over the putty a day or so after it is put in, for it will then stay put much better.

Wires

The earlier planted houses of Beauties will now take their last set of wires, and it is best not to wait too long in stretching these. We generally stretch them at the same time that the second tier is put on, unless we are rushed with other work. At any rate, do not let the plants lie around after the first wires are put on as they will come to harm if they are not kept tied up properly. With teas it is much the same. Those early houses on wires will have to get their second set before the tops get too high, as it will then be difficult to put the wires in.

Indigofera decora

The Indigoferas may well be classed among the prettiest and most graceful garden shrubs. They belong to the family Leguminosae and derive their name from indigo, referring to the use of certain species in producing the well known dye.

Indigofera decora, a native of southern China, is, I think, one of the finest of the genus, and although it dies to the ground each winter in the vicinity of Boston it deserves more general planting, for each spring it sends up quantities of new shoots which, early in June, are covered with terminal racemes of large white flowers. These shoots attain a height of from one and one-half to two feet and are well clothed with bluish green compound leaves of a fine texture.

Indigofera kirilowi, a close relative of the above, is another plant deserving of attention. This species, a native of Korea, from whence it was brought by Mr. J. G. Jack, is, if anything, hardier than I. decora for it does not die back each year. It is a fast growing species forming a spreading mass from one to two feet in height with bluish green foliage and rosy pink flowers of the same size as those of I. decora and borne also in terminal racemes. In the Arnold Arboretum it has proven to be one of the best shrubs of its class, remaining in bloom during several weeks.

Among the other species of Indigofera, which have proven hardy or half hardy at the Arnold Arboretum, are I. Gerardiana, a native of the Himalayas, which dies back each year but comes up again like I. decora, and I. amblyantha, a plant of entirely different habit, having slender stems and axillary clusters of small flowers, rose colored, and continuing in bloom for two or three months. The foliage is smaller than on other species. I. amblyantha was introduced from western China by E. H. Wilson. There he found it growing on cliffs above

rivers in altitudes of up to six thousand feet above the sea.

The Indigoferas may be propagated from seed or by firm cuttings of young shoots inserted in sandy or peaty soil under glass in slight heat in summer. These plants give promise of becoming valuable material for the use of the landscape gardener when they become better known. The foliage is of a texture which harmonizes well with many other shrubs and they make an attractive addition to the shrubbery, especially since their blooming period is later than most of our native shrubs. Their use should be encouraged where conditions warrant planting shrubs of their class.

Hubert M. Canning

Jamaica Plain, Mass.

A PEST OF THE RHODODENDRON.

Editor HORTICULTURE.

Dear Sir: If possible I would like to get some information about a pest which destroys Rhododendrons. In the last couple of years I have lost quite a few of the rarer kinds. At first I could not account for it, but on close examination I found that in every case an inch or so below the ground the bark had been eaten off the stem. Although I repeatedly examined the plants I was never able to find anything that was likely to do it. Soaking the ground with Vermine did not prevent it. Dutch gardeners tell me that it is done by the larva of a bug they call Mobium which comes from Holland. The bug also eats the leaves during the night, which is probably correct, as I have observed that parts of the leaves have been eaten, but that is done at an earlier time. At the present time I have not been able to see any.

If there is any remedy against this pest I would very much like to know it.

Yours truly,
Aug. J. Pauls.

Palisades Park, N. J.

Editor HORTICULTURE.

We have had the trouble which Mr. Pauls writes about, for years. We find it is caused by a little white grub about the size of a grain of wheat, and no doubt the larvae of the bug mentioned—mobium. We know of no remedy. So far our trouble has been confined to nursery beds, none having yet appeared in the larger plantations in the grounds. It is not confined, however, to rhododendrons. Yews are great favorites with the grub, and large plants 3-4 feet high have been killed by it. It eats all the bark off the roots to the ground level, and it is hard to detect, for the plants do not appear to show its work until it is all but finished. Occasionally I have detected its work and moved the plants, and saved them. So far the only way we have successfully combatted the grub has been changing the place every two years, for it takes about this time from the laying of the eggs for the grub to become dangerous. It is practically a fixture—has no locomotion and so moving saves the plants for a while.

We find it attacks all Ericaceæ—Azaleas, Kalmias, Leucothoes, Andromedas, Zenobia, Oxydendron and many others.　　　T. D. Hatfield.

Wellesley, Mass.

LANDSCAPE GARDENERS SCARCE IN MISSOURI.

Landscape gardeners are scarce in Missouri. From fifteen to twenty applications have been on file in the Landscape Gardening Department at the University of Missouri during the last year. At least seven of these positions remain unfilled at the present time. The work includes supervision of grounds about institutions and parks, planting, designing, care of arboretums and nurseries.

Horace F. Major, assistant professor of Landscape gardening at the University, says that there are great opportunities in this profession. So great are the opportunities, he says, that untrained men are calling themselves landscape architects and are turning to this profession.

About a dozen students are taking the advanced courses in this work at the university. A greater number are taking the more elementary courses. Many university women are taking the work. A course in floriculture, which consists of the care of house plants and gardens, is given especially for women. A course in landscape gardening takes up the principles underlying the ornamentation of public and private grounds. Other courses are given in the history of landscape gardening, theory and principles of landscape design and engineering, elementary landscape design, and ornamental plants. Considerable work is given for graduate students.

HORTICULTURE

VOL. XXII   SEPTEMBER 4, 1915 .   NO. 9

PUBLISHED WEEKLY BY

HORTICULTURE PUBLISHING CO.

147 Summer Street, Boston, Mass.

Telephone, Oxford 292.

WM. J. STEWART, Editor and Manager.

SUBSCRIPTION RATES:

One Year, in advance, $1.00; To Foreign Countries, $2.00; To Canada, $1.50.

Entered as second-class matter December 8, 1904, at the Post Office at Boston, Mass., under the Act of Congress of March 3, 1879.

CONTENTS

A theory upset

Nature not infrequently seems possessed of a desire to overturn and discredit our cherished theories and show us how far we are yet from understanding the rules of her game. Just as some of our inquiring scientists had about reached the conclusion that a vigorous bombarding of the atmosphere might be productive of local conditions conducive to the precipitation of rain, here we are in the most peaceful section of the globe —where in these "safe and sane" times the exploding of anything bigger than a squib, even on the glorious Fourth, is liable to put us in durance vile—treated to the most remarkable series of downpours ever recorded here, while over in war-torn Europe where bombarding has been a daily pastime for over a year nothing out of the ordinary in this respect has been reported.

After the deluge

We hear of rotting potato crops, mildewed hay fields and widespread injury to many other products of the husbandman's industry as a result of the unprecedented soaking to which the land has been subjected during this unusual summer. Our attention was recently called by a Philadelphia friend to the shoots of ailantus sprouting up through the pavement on one of that city's principal thoroughfares. No old time-frayed reflection on Philadelphia is here intended; we only record it as one interesting consequence of the summer's deluge. It is, perhaps, pertinent to say here that the growths above mentioned are not found in front of any one of the firms that advertise in HORTICULTURE! However this great wet-down may affect us individually, it nevertheless behooves us to be thankful for the good that is to be found in everything, no matter how unpromising it may appear. So let us feast our eyes on the rare green fields and lawns which greet us on all sides, which even the verdant Emerald Isle at its best cannot excel; the luxuriant vigor of trees, shrubs and every other growing thing which goes to make our gardens and landscape presumable reproductions of the first Paradise. It may be that another half century may pass before such a visitation shall come our way again.

The S. A. F.

Some little apprehension has been expressed by members of the Society of American Florists that the action of the Society in holding the successive conventions in territory remote from its centres of activity and main body of its supporters hitherto, is liable to result in a serious shrinkage in membership eastward and that the accretions from the west will not be sufficient to counterbalance this loss. We hope and believe that these fears will prove to have been groundless, and it is our opinion that the majority of the thoughtful, far-sighted members of the organization share this view. The S. A. F. is becoming too influential, too strong financially, to suffer any serious defection in its membership roll due to convention location. The activities of the organization are no longer confined to the proceedings of the annual gathering but spread over the entire year and all indications point to bigger doings in the near future. In consequence of this substantial advancement, membership in the S. A. F. is coming to be regarded as something to be proud of, whether one does or does not appear in person at every convention. Many agencies are working to that end and the prospects are favorable for a much larger numerical representation of the profession in its ranks rather than otherwise and this is as it should be.

Obituary

Edwin Lonsdale.

The news of the passing away of Edwin Lonsdale will bring sorrow home to the hearts of a host of friends who loved him. Mr. Lonsdale's death was not unexpected as it has been well known for some time that there was practically no possibility of recovery from the malady from which he was suffering. The news has just reached us that he passed away on Wednesday afternoon, September 1, at the Naturopathic Institute, Los Angeles, Cal.

Edwin Lonsdale was a native of Litchfield, Staffordshire, England; born on October 6, 1845, and educated in horticulture by apprenticeship and service in several places of note, in-

EDWIN LONSDALE

cluding Enville Hall gardens, Staffordshire, and Hanover Lodge, Regents Park, London. At the age of 24 he came to America and was employed at Syracuse, N. Y. in market gardening; at Germantown, Pa., with the late Thomas Meehan; at San Francisco, with Miller and Sievers, and San Jose, Cal., with Levi P. Sanderson. At the age of 30 he visited his old home in England where he married Miss Sarah Burton, sister of John Burton of Philadelphia. Returning he established himself as a florist in Philadelphia and five years later went into partnership with John Burton. Later, on the dissolution of the firm, he resumed business on his own account. This he gave up in 1904 and became superintendent of Girard College. Five years later he accepted the position of manager for W. Atlee Burpee & Co., at their seed farms in Lompoc, Cal., where he continued until overcome by the illness which resulted in his death.

Edwin Lonsdale was one of the pioneer members of the Society of American Florists. He served as secretary of that organization in 1887 and as president in 1896. He was also officially connected with the Penna. Horticultural Society and the Florists' Club of Philadelphia, serving as president of the latter. He was the first president of the American Carnation Society, holding that office for three consecutive years.

Mr. Lonsdale was one of the best informed and well-read men in American commercial horticulture. His name is linked with many movements for the advancement of his profession and the improvement of those specialties in florists' flowers in which he took a direct interest. Some of the finest varieties of crotons ever produced in the world were raised by him. Carnations Helen Keller, Mrs. Cleveland and Grace Battles were produced and introduced by him, also the zonal geranium La Pilot.

In his personality, Edwin Lonsdale was one of the most lovable men the Almighty ever put upon this Earth. True hearted and loyal, he was a shining example of manly nobility. Words fail when we try to express how dearly we loved him. They will bring him home to Chestnut Hill where he may sleep with his daughters in Ivy Hill Cemetery—those daughters so cruelly torn from them in that awful drowning accident at Ocean City a number of years ago and the remaining one who followed them a year or two later.

John Mackenzie.

John Mackenzie, formerly gardener for W. Emerson Cox and later with E. B. Dane when Mr. Dane bought the Cox estate, died on August 25th at the Massachusetts General Hospital, following an operation for hernia. Mr. Mackenzie had been doing job gardening of late, temporarily, for R. & J. Farquhar & Co. He leaves a widow and a large family, most of them grown up.

PUBLICATION RECEIVED.

The Complete Club Book for Women. By Caroline French Benton. A companion volume to "Woman's Club Work and Programs." If women must have their own clubs — and why shouldn't they?—then here is a book that they will find helpful, or, we might say indispensable. The volume embraces in its 300 pages the last word in proper organization and management. A model Constitution is offered which any club may adapt to its own needs. Condensed rules of order and examples of programs, etc., are also given. But all this fills only a minor place in the contents of the book under consideration. Chapters are devoted to Community Improvement, The Business of Systematic Housekeeping, Literature, History. Educational Systems, How to Make a Year Book, A Study of Songs, A Study of the American Colonies, Child Labor, Famous Buildings. Great Men and Women in History, etc., etc., topics selected for their educational and uplifting character. Organizations taking their inspiration from this unique volume will unquestionably fill a useful place in their respective communities. The publication is just off the press of The Page Company, Boston. Price $1.25 net or $1.40 carriage paid.

Personal

James Macfarlane of Werden. N. Y., has been appointed instructor in floriculture at New Hampshire Agricultural College, Durham, N. H.

M. F. Byxbee, the florist of So. Norwalk, Conn., is ill with typhoid fever. Health Officer W. J. Tracey is investigating to learn the source of contagion.

Miss Elizabeth Clucas daughter of Mr. and Mrs. R. W. Clucas, and Mr. John Young Telfer will be married at Sparkill. N. Y., on Wednesday, September 15.

J. F. Ammann, secretary of the Illinois State Florists' Association, left St. Louis with Mrs. Ammann on August 28th for Peoria, where a meeting of the executive board of the association was held on Tuesday, August 31st.

A DEFORMED BRANCH.

The accompanying photograph is a good example of a fasciated branch

and was found on Amorpha virgata, growing in the shrub collection in the Arnold Arboretum. This branch was the only one on the plant which was so deformed, the others being normal. In the case of this particular branch the growth at the crown of the plant was normal, but about a foot away the whole structure started to flatten out and continued so to the end of the branch, where it seemed to split up into many small immature leaflets. As will be noticed, the branch is approximately an inch and three-quarters wide for a great deal of its length and about one-quarter of an inch thick. The curious way in which the leaves have disposed themselves is very interesting. The bush on which this occurred is a handsome specimen about nine feet high and has a spread of over six feet. The branch was one of the lower ones but with just as much space in which to develop as the rest on the same level.

HUBERT M. CANNING.

BUSINESS TROUBLES.

Chattanooga, Tenn. — Chattanooga Floral Co., East Main street, voluntary bankrupt; assets, $4,200; liabilities, $2,435.66.

SOCIETY OF AMERICAN FLORISTS

REPORT OF THE ENTOMOLOGIST, SOCIETY OF AMERICAN FLOR- ISTS AND ORNAMENTAL HORTICULTURISTS.

By W. E. Britton, Ph. D., State Entomol- ogist of Connecticut.

Chrysanthemum Pests.

All who have been troubled by the chrysanthemum leaf miner or mar- guerite fly, *Phytomyza chrysanthemi* Kowarz., should obtain Bulletin No. 157 of the Massachusetts Agricultural Ex- periment Station, Amherst, Mass., is- sued recently.

For the past twenty-five years this insect has caused damage to composite plants in the northern states. The adult is a two-winged fly which lays an egg in an incision just under the epidermis of the leaf. This egg hatches in five days and the larva mines in the parenchyma of the leaf for about two weeks when it trans- forms to the pupa stage inside the leaf. Two weeks later the adult emerges. There are ten generations each year.

Spraying the plants with nicotine solution is a remedy. If "Black Leaf 40" is the kind used it should be di- luted at the rate of about 1 part in 400 parts of water or roughly 2 tea- spoonfuls in a gallon.

Another chrysanthemum pest new to our continent is the Chrysanthe- mum midge, a European insect which has recently caused much damage in some large commercial greenhouses in Michigan. The presence of this in- sect was recorded by Dr. E. P. Felt, State Entomologist of New York, in Florists' Exchange, Vol. XXXIX, page 859, April 10, 1915. It causes a swell- ing on the main stem near the surface of the ground, galls or enlargements on the mid-ribs of the leaves, and close ill-shaped heads which ruin the plant for commercial purposes. It will prob- ably be difficult to control this pest.

Further injury to chrysanthemums may be here recorded by a mite, *Tar- sonemus pallidus* Banks, mentioned in my report of last year. This time it occurred in October in a commercial greenhouse at Hartford, Conn., and many of the petals had withered and turned brown.

A New Pest of Pine Trees.

During the past year one of the de- structive European saw-flies Diprion (Lophyrus) simile Hartig, has been found in this country, where it has apparently become established. The insect passes the winter in its cocoons on or under leaves and rubbish near the ground. There are apparently three broods each year in Connecticut, the cocoons of the first and second broods often being formed on the twigs. The larvae are about an inch long, greenish yellow with brown markings, and have the appearance characteristic of sawfly larvae. They feed upon the needles of several spe- cies of pine, including the white pine, Austrian pine, *Pinus densiflora, P. ex- celsa,* and *P. flexilis.* It will doubtless be found to attack other species as well.

The eggs are laid in longitudinal in- cisions in the needles and are placed end to end.

The cocoons are brown oval bodies about three-eights of an inch long and of a tough leathery texture.

The adults have a wing-spread of from about half an inch in the male to three-fourths of an inch in the female. The male is black, but the female has yellow thorax and abdomen.

Though this insect occurs in four towns in Connecticut it will probably be found in other states. Just how it was brought to this country is not known but probably cocoons came over on nursery stock and either passed the inspectors or perhaps came in before the inspection system was established. Parasites of this sawfly have been ob- served in Connecticut. Spraying the pine trees with lead arsenate (3 lbs. in 50 gallons of water) is the best remedy.

A preliminary illustrated account of this insect may be found in the Jour- nal of Economic Entomology, Vol. 8, page 379, June 1915.

A Juniper Web Worm.

Several samples have been received by the writer of juniper twigs webbed together by this insect. On rearing the adult it proved to be *Dichromeris marginellus* Fabr. Dr. E. P. Felt* has recorded this insect from Long Island and from the Hudson River Valley in New York State. This is also a Eu- ropean species which has appeared in the United States during the past few years. The real damage from it will be in ornamental plantings in parks and on private grounds, and doubtless may be prevented by a thorough spray- ing of lead arsenate early in spring and again late in summer.

*Report N. Y. State Entomologist, 26, page 35, 1910.

REPORT OF THE SCHOOL GARDEN COMMITTEE.

Benj. Hammond, Chairman.

Our country is so large that to na- tionalize any movement is no small work, and to hold the interest of each section in any particular work or ob- ject is difficult, but one effort to stir up common interest certainly meets with a well nigh universal apprecia- tion, and that is—"School Gardening." The florists of this country are in a trade that helps greatly to develop beauty all around, and in the efforts made by the Society of American Flor- ists and Ornamental Horticulturists to stimulate interest in some practical labor by teaching in our schools a lit- tle gardening and floriculture, the an- swers come from many points which show without question that the effort is having a helpful result.

This season our letter sent to every school board or school superintendent where is located a member of the S. A. F. and to each and every state com- missioner of education, had, as a lead- ing picture the beautiful statue and surrounding of Washington in the Grand Avenue Park at Milwaukee.

This picture with its spirit of emula- tion represented by the mother and her boy as she directs his attention to Washington as his pattern, certainly seemed to strike a responsive chord.

In one place where efforts are made to have the children interested in gar- dening the report comes—"the chil- dren want flower seeds, and the flower beds wherever started set an example. The demand comes for geraniums, coleus, dahlias and roses."

The newspapers of the country are paying more and more heed to this flower gardening, and small yards of the cities show the effect.

Schools can never take the place of parental oversight and encouragement. In one dark back yard overshadowed by other buildings two boys came to invite us "to come see our garden." Sure enough those youngsters had dug up a bit of waste ground, planted it, weeded and watered the ten or dozen feet square which looked like an irrigated patch near Denver, Col., so prolific it was, and those lads were pleased. This kind of work aids to develop American citizens of character. In many villages and small towns im- provement societies exist, and these, societies are usually excellent sup- porters of the florist craft directly and indirectly. By small prizes well distributed the children are encour- aged to keep up the home yards.

In San Francisco this year Superin- tendent Thomas L. Heaton has been busy in his efforts for a School Gar- den Exhibit at the Exposition. In San Diego and Los Angeles these cities of the Pacific Coast stand out boldly in the common efforts of the school au- thorities to fix up and look nice, and to encourage the children gardening at home. This year in Los Angeles we learn in a letter recently received from Morris M. Rathbun that cash prizes ranging from five dollars ($5.00) to the individual student home gar- dener to five hundred dollars ($500) for the school making the best show- ing in the Exposition year in 1915 were distributed. This work cleaned up many neglected lots, turning waste places into beauty spots. Los Angeles to do this work well employed an ex- pert teacher florist, and this work and its effects is seen in many of the cities and towns of the Pacific Coast. At Portland, Oregon. work of this kind is being carried on under the direc- tion of a landscape artist from Chicago who is specially employed to give in- struction in this line.

In every State in the American Union this good work is being carried on. School Gardening has its greatest application in our great cities. School Gardening aims to take hold and in- terest the city boys. At a flower show held in New York City in the Museum of Natural History, the school children came in classes to view the exhibits. There were children born in congested sections of New York and some of them never had been in the country, and their wonder at seeing so many flowers was expressed without reserve. In the city of Philadelphia the

committee in charge of the garden all School Garden work is well organized, and the back yards of the thousands of little houses reveal a taste and industry of great importance to any one. No one city probably is doing more by organized effort to make up home and public gardening instruction than is Toronto, Ontario. Here is a climate the opposite in its make-up to that of Southern California, yet the same appreciation of the beautiful and the value of economic thrift is evidenced in both sections. Down the Ohio river, in city after city its entire length, this school gardening and home gardening is being carried on. At Evansville, Ind., our old friend and pioneer member of the society, J. D. Carmody, has encouraged this sort of work and lately given valuable land for garden and park use. This illustration serves simply to show the interest in this great work. It is one that grows, and no craft can do more to encourage it and profit by it than the florists of America, and in so doing the homes of the people of America are made the more beautiful.

FROM THE S. A. F. CONVENTION CITY OF 1916.

One week has passed since the storm, and the florists have about cleaned up the wreckage, and are beginning to rebuild. After checking up the stock we find the damage to extend to about 25 to 35 per cent. In about two or three weeks we will not know we had a storm. Everybody is working a large force of men and will soon have things straightened out.

All the florists are enthusiastic over the S. A. F. Convention for next summer. Very shortly we shall name our committees, and get busy early in the game. We propose to make this a record breaking Convention for the Society. I firmly believe it will come right up to the best Convention the S. A. F. has ever known, if it is not a record breaker. In view of the line of publicity, we are going to give the Convention the coming year, it will stir up interest throughout the United States, and very few of the members will feel like staying at home.

As far as trade exhibits are concerned, we have a large auditorium, and I am sure it is going to be packed to its capacity. I cite you for example our Texas State Florists' Association, which is as yet a small organization, and we were unable to stir up enough interest to fill a good sized building with exhibits. Now compare, if you please, the Texas State Florists' Association and the great S. A. F. and you will have in comparison the kind of an exhibit we shall have at the 1916 S. A. F. Convention in Houston.

R. C. KERR, Vice-Pres., S. A. F.

The premium list for the Maryland State Horticultural Society and affiliated organizations has been received. Among the special features are a "Maryland Week" Essay Contest, and a "Club Exhibit" Contest, intended for farmers' clubs and granges. etc. Prospects are for the largest and best exhibition in the history of the organizations. Copies of the schedule may be obtained from Thomas B. Symons, Secretary, College Park Md.

THE PROBLEMS ATTENDING THE ESTABLISHMENT OF PERMANENT CONVENTION GARDENS.

(Paper by Theodore Wirth.)

There can be no question as to the importance and desirability of arranging for Convention Gardens wherever our annual meetings are to be held. The usefulness and value of such gardens as a medium of publicity and education will not be doubted by any one who gives the subject due consideration.

There is, to the best of my knowledge and belief, no great difficulty in establishing such a garden for each convention, and the only real problem, it seems to me, is to make it permanent. This necessarily is a question which, in the main, must be solved by the local promotors of the garden. The same spirit that was employed in its creation, should be able to solve the question of its future existence, permanency and growth.

I have, in the past, presented the question whether or not it would be possible to select the Convention City two years in advance, instead of one, in order to provide for two years' growth of the hardy material, which could be used to advantage in the planting of the garden.

Personally, I wish this could be done, because I realize the great and resulting benefits that would accrue; and I believe that all plantsmen will agree with me. There can be no doubt but that the value of the gardens, from every point of view, would be greatly enhanced by this additional time given them in preparation; and that the interest of professionals and the public alike, before and after, as well as during, the Convention, would be correspondingly increased.

However, if this plan is not deemed feasible, there is still one advantage open with the present arrangement, which has not been made use of in our past undertakings along this line.

If our brother florists and horticulturists of the city ambitious of securing the next Convention are real anxious to have the best garden thus far made, they will select a piece of land for that purpose, far in advance, and will submit a well arranged plan to the Convention at which they make their bid for the next meeting. If they land the prize, they should prepare the grounds at once, and secure without delay all planting material that can be transplanted to advantage in the fall. In this way, most of the perennials, shrubs, and trees will be well established in the spring, and make a very good showing by Convention time.

Early solicitation amongst prospective exhibitors is, for many reasons absolutely necessary. A time limit should be set for allotment of space in the garden, and the special attention of such prospective exhibitor must be called to this. All space not applied for by a certain date, should then be offered to nearby and local growers with a slightly extended time limit. This limit should be set so as to give the committee in charge an opportunity to secure suitable planting material for filling the unsold spaces in the garden in good time. It is absolutely necessary, in my opinion, to give the necessary power and means, and to concentrate the actual direction and

supervision in one active, experienced, dependable man. Tell this man to go ahead, and then do not interfere with him; but give him all the assistance he needs, when he asks for it. I believe it would be a good investment, generally speaking, to send him on a two months' trip to visit personally the principal growers in all parts of the country for the purpose of soliciting exhibits. Let him start right at the Convention. The right man will thereby awaken the general interest of the trade and secure the desired support. Correspondence would not be nearly as effective.

I cannot lay too much stress on the necessity of giving all exhibits the best possible attention and care, and of guarding the interests of the exhibitor in every possible way. Be sure that he gets the space he bought; that his plants are properly labeled, and his firm's name is properly displayed. Give him all he is entitled to and as much more as you can.

It is too much to expect that very many distant firms will keep up their exhibits after the Convention year. Yet some of the wide-awake and progressive growers will undoubtedly be glad to permanently make use of our gardens and thus exhibit their goods and special novelties in different parts of the country at the same time. In most instances, it will, therefore, become desirable and necessary, after the first year, to change the layout of the garden and to devote the larger part of the grounds to hardy material, and a much smaller portion to the tender annual bedding plants. This we have now done at Minneapolis and the new layout will be as beautiful and instructive to our people from now on as the real Convention Garden was to us professionals two years ago.

The Convention Garden must, in my opinion, always be created and maintained under the auspices of the National Society. The price for space should, if at all possible, be the same wherever the Garden is, and same should be high enough to defray the expense of maintenance. The chairman of the local garden committee should be appointed a member of a similar committee of the National Society and as such could act as the executive officer of both committees.

The garden should be located on public land in order to make its future existence possible and I know of no good reason why every city park administration should not only be willing, but really anxious, to cooperate with us in the establishment of such trial and exhibition grounds which cannot help but be of educational value to the people of their city.

Our esteemed President, Mr. P. Welch, has assigned to me the subject herein presented, but I am not sure that I have covered the ground to his entire satisfaction. There are really no great problems, no great obstacles, that I can see, attending the establishment of permanent Convention Gardens ,and I believe that if the old saying—' where there is a will, there is a way"—is applied at all times, there can never be any doubt as to our ability to establish such Convention Gardens wherever we may go, and to make them successful in every instance.

BOSTON.

The directors of A. H. Hews & Co., Inc., in acknowledgment of conscientious and faithful service of Thomas J. Benwell, for fifty years associated with the company, have presented him with a flower pot filled with gold.

Fottler, Fiske, Rawson Co. have a splendid display of dahlia blooms of all classes in their show window. There are fully 200 varieties, all under number and a crowd of admirers, some with note book and pencil, is constantly in evidence.

Park Commissioner Charles D. Gibson is one of the latest recruits to the military encampment at Plattsburg, N. Y. In order that Commissioner Gibson might join the citizen-soldiers, Mayor Curley has granted him a leave of absence from Sept. 6 to Oct. 8.

President Welch and Mrs. Welch have arrived home all safely from their month's tour of the country, full of enthusiasm over the success of the San Francisco Convention and the many courtesies enjoyed at every stopping place on the route, going and coming.

R. & J. Farquhar & Co. have a field of 50,000 phloxes in bloom at their Dedham nurseries at the present time and it makes a gorgeous sight. There are a good many seedlings of much merit among them. We were particularly impressed with one vivid scarlet which in brilliancy far outranks the old favorite Coquelicot.

R. & J. Farquhar & Co. are enlarging their seed establishment by taking in the building No. 8 and 9 South Market street, adjoining their old quarters. There are four stories with basement. All the floors are being thoroughly renovated and equipped. Part of one floor will be used for a draughting room in connection with their landscape planting department.

The directors of the American Forestry Association flashed through Boston's parkways, saw Boston's mid-summer finery in a series of quick glimpses, snatched a bite of breakfast at the Algonquin Club, and caught an afternoon train for the White Mountains at the North Station on Tuesday, Aug. 31. Among the visitors were Dr. Henry S. Drinker, president of Lehigh University; Prof. H. H. Chapman of Yale; S. B. Eliot of the Pennsylvania State Forestry Commission; P. S. Ridsdale, secretary of the association; Alfred Gaskell, New Jersey State Forester; and Charles Quincy of New York.

The Boston trade will not lack for fine home grown plant stock during the coming season judging from what is already in sight at Thomas Roland's Nahant greenhouses. There are upwards of 4000 Erica melanthera planted out in the fields and 10 more in pots plunged in frames. The latter are the best for Christmas blooming. A house now full of early chrysanthemums mostly Golden Glow will be filled up with plants which are now outside as soon as the flowers have been cut. Begonia Lorraine and cyclamens are many and there is a good stock of ardisias, which are scarce this year. Crotons are being pushed as a specialty and there is a grand stock of that finest of all crotons, Reidii. Mr. Roland finds that the red foliaged varieties sell much better than the yellow. Mr. Roland's place might be aptly termed "the place of no bugs," everything looks so spotless and trim.

PHILADELPHIA

The latest advice from the sick bed of our good old friend George Anderson is: "A little better this morning (Aug. 30), but not able to sit up yet, and cannot see anyone." Mr. Anderson has been ill for three weeks. Something wrong with the circulation—which does not respond readily to medical treatment. One side of the body has been entirely numb and useless.

Horticulturists, flower specialists and vegetable gardeners, of Norwood, assembled last night in the headquarters of the Norwood Horticultural Society to receive prizes for the best-kept place in the borough. There were ten prizes offered, six of which were contributed by the Henry F. Michell Company, seed merchants, of Philadelphia. The judges, all of whom are authorities on flower and vegetable raising, were Fred Cowperthwaite, C. Vander Breggen and Mr. Michell. (Here follow the names of the winners.)

The Norwood Horticultural Society is an enterprising organization and has done much to boost the "town beautiful" campaign in Delaware County. Dr. John A. Borneman is president of the society.
—*Phila. Public Ledger.*

We cant' have too much of this kind of thing. Grand for the business everywhere. And I am pleased to see the tendency on the increase as the years roll by   G. C. W.

The death of Edwin Lonsdale, recorded in another column of this paper, recalls the many social and convivial occasions in the early days of the Florists' Club of Philadelphia when "Ned's" buoyant personality, merry laugh and jolly humor counted for so much. "The Brave Old Duke of York" as sung by him, never failed to bring down the house and receive encore after encore. But let Ned tell about it in his own artless way:

"I remember the first time I ever sang that song. It was a long time ago, before the club was organized or anything, back in '81 or '82—somewhere along there—and the boys didn't know each other very well. Craig and Fancourt, I think, were the committee and they were getting up a supper. I said to Craig that day, 'I know a kind of a nice little song and I'll sing it for you tonight if you like; it's a simple little thing and I guess they'll like it. It's got a chorus.' Well, when the time came, I thought he would just call me up and ask me to sing, but he told them I had volunteered to sing a song and I didn't like that; it didn't please me a bit. I thought he would just ask me to sing it."

SEED TRADE

AMERICAN SEED TRADE ASSOCIATION
Officers—President, J. M. Lupton.
Mattituck, L. I., N. Y.; First Vice-President, Kirby B. White, Detroit, Mich.;
Second Vice-President, F. W. Bolgiano,
Washington, D. C.; Secretary-Treasurer,
C. E. Kendel, Cleveland, O.; Assistant
Secretary, S. F. Willard, Jr., Cleveland,
O. Cincinnati, O., next meeting place.

Syracuse, N. Y.—The Fairview Seed Farms have been merged with the F. B. Mills Seed Co.

Faribault, Minn. — O. J. Stark has purchased the Faribault Seed Co. and will continue the business under that name.

The Blue Ribbon stock farm near Clayton, Mo., was purchased last week by Arthur Schisler of the Schisler & Kaercher Seed Co. The farm comprises 377 acres, all under cultivation except thirty acres, and will be used by the firm as a seed experiment station. Mr. Schisler says the price paid for the farm was $60,000. Their store is now located at 708 N. Fourth street, St. Louis, where they do a general seed business.

The St. Louis Seed Co.'s employees held their annual picnic on Sunday, Aug. 29, at Waterloo, Ill., and with their families spent a most pleasant day. This is an annual affair given by the officials of the company, who pay all expenses. A splendid chicken dinner was served and the usual number of games took place. Miss Frese won the ladies' egg race, Ray Pantler the men's race, Mrs. Martin Moran the time-walking race, Miss Frese the young ladies' race, Mrs. Ripple the married ladies' race, Freddie Henselmeyer won the little boys' race, and Mrs. Blase the ladies' ball-throwing contest. The tug-of-war was won by the shipping force. Jeff Payne won the boys' race, Sylvester Pantler the cigar race and Miss Mildred Sonderman the calico contest. Miss Frese for the third time was declared a winner, this time in the needle-threading contest. The ball game was won by the office force from the salesmen by a score of 6 to 3.

DURING RECESS

The program for the Michell outing, Andalusia, Pa., on Sept. 8, is as follows:—

11.45 A. M.: Special train leaves Broad Street Station for Andalusia, stopping at North Philadelphia. 1.00 P. M.: Refreshments at the nurseries. 2.00 P. M.: Inspection of nurseries and grounds. 3.00 P. M.: Official photograph. 3.15 P. M.: Address by prominent speakers. 3.30 P. M.: Sports—Fat Man's Race, open to all over 180 pounds; Thin Man's Race; Three Legged Race; Wheelbarrow Race; Sack Race; Potato Race; Broad Jump; Ladies' Race; Hop, Step and Jump; Pie Eating Contest; Tug of War.
Prizes for Men—1st, Box of Cigars; 2nd, Pocket Knife.
Prizes for Ladies—1st, Box of Handkerchiefs; 2nd, Hand Bag.
5.30 P. M.: Special train leaves Andalusia, making stops at North Philadelphia, West Philadelphia and Broad Street.
Music will be furnished by the Imperial Band of Philadelphia.

BRITISH HORTICULTURE.

Seeds for Serbia.

Following the recommendation of the Society's special commissioner, the Council of the Royal Horticultural Society has decided to send out to Serbia seeds to the value of £500 for distribution amongst the distressed small farmers. The Royal Horticultural Society is appealing for further contributions to the Allies' War Relief Fund. Many of the nurserymen in Belgium and France have been ruined by the war, and they will need all the financial assistance which can be given them by their confreres in this country.

Thirty-five Miles of Glasshouses.

Recently I had the pleasure of visiting one of the chief English centres of the glasshouse industry, viz., Worthing, in Sussex. Here are grown tons of grapes, tomatoes, cucumbers, and flowers for the London and provincial markets. Some indication of the extent of the industry can be gathered when it is stated that if the glasshouses were placed end to end they would reach 35 miles. In the height of the season on three days a week the packages despatched average from 2,500 to 3,000 per day. Worthing, owing to its favorable climate, is able to place strawberries on the market at Christmas, when big prices are made, as well as securing the trade for grapes when they are the luxury of the wealthy. The cost of growing is minimized to the lowest possible limit, whilst a rapid succession of crops keeps the growers busy all the year round. In the spring a big business is done with peas, beans. marrows, and other early vegetables, and in the autumn there is a tremendous out-put of cut bloom. Another branch of growing associated with the district is the culture of green figs. One of the show places which attracts many visitors is a garden in the old-world village of West Tarring, where Sir Thomas a'Becket is supposed to have planted the first fig tree introduced into this country. The remains of a fine old White Marseilles tree in the garden is stated to have been planted by Sir Thomas. **W. H. ADSETT.**

CATALOGUES RECEIVED.

W. Atlee Burpee & Co., Philadelphia, Pa.—Folder of Fiery Cross Sweet Pea.

Vaughan's Seed Store, Chicago—Bulbs and Hardy Plants for Autumn, 1915.

William Elliott & Sons, New York—Trade Catalogue and Price List for Autumn, 1915, of "Giant-Flowering Bulbs and Seeds."

Henry F. Michell Co., Philadelphia, Pa.—Wholesale Price List of Bulbs. Etc., for Sept., Oct. and Nov., 1915. Pretty near everything is included in this wide-awake catalogue; 72 pages with cover.

John C. Moninger Co., Chicago, Ill. —"Moninger Proof Book." A valuable treatise on the science of greenhouse building and the problems that must be met and mastered. Fully illustrated. 48 pages.

W. E. Marshall & Co., New York City—Fall Bulb List for 1915. A very effective catalogue, strong on nice varieties of Darwin and Cottage tulips and similar things that are in demand for exhibitions and other choice uses.

Hitchings & Co., Elizabeth, N. J.— Hitchings' Supply Book, 1915 Edition. Everybody who reeds HORTICULTURE knows who Hitchings & Co. are. They also know something of what that firm is doing and has been doing for more than a generation towards the upbuilding of floriculture under glass. But the contents of this book of 116 pages has a been a revelation to many as to the extent of the industry in which Hitchings & Co. have made so honorable a record, in the designing, building and equipping of a greenhouse. The firm manufactures every item in the multitude of parts used, most of the work being done by employees who have grown up with them in the business. The book is splendidly illustrated, has many tabulated lists, charts and diagrams, all of which will be found extremely useful for anyone having a greenhouse or intending to have one. Copies will be sent to all who apply.

FORCING CUCUMBERS.

Editor HORTICULTURE:
Could you give me any information as to how to prepare the ground for a bed of cucumbers in a hot house for winter growing, and when is the best time to plant?
Los Angeles, Cal.
W. J. S.

The ground for cucumbers should be composed of 60 per cent. turfy loam and 40 per cent. fresh horse droppings. This compost should be turned over several times to prevent heating. Start the seeds in pots—say, three seeds to a 4-in. pot, and as they develop pull out the two weakest plants. When the first two rough leaves have grown to about three or four inches turn the plants out of the pots, being careful not to break the ball, and plant in the bed made of the compost as above directed. The bed should be eight or nine inches deep. Maintain a humid atmosphere at all times, which will prevent red spider, the greatest pest of the cucumber. At no time should the temperature fall below 70 degrees Farenheit.

News Items

SAN FRANCISCO.

The shop at 1328 Polk street has
changed hands, Yamato the Florist being succeeded by Warlow's Flower
Shop.

A. J. Burt of Spokane, Wash., is
among the last of the conventionists to
get away. He is still in San Francisco
visiting the exposition and picking up
new ideas for his business.

C. Kooyman has improved the appearance of his wholesale establishment on St. Ann street, by adding
large glass cases in the front of the
store for the display of supplies. He
reports a good shipping demand for
calla bulbs.

Special prizes for asters and sweet
peas in baskets and dahlias in addition to the regular prizes will be
offered this year by the Spokane Floral Association, which will be in charge
of the flower show at the Spokane,
Wash., Interstate Fair, September 13
to 18.

The Ladies' Auxiliary of the Pacific
Coast Horticultural Society met in the
Phelan Building, on the afternoon of
August 25, at which time plans were
consummated for the holding of regular meetings on the last Tuesday of
each month, alternate meetings to be
held in conjunction with the men to
get their co-operation and interest.

A jolly party of conventionists accompanied Chas. W. Ward to Eureka,
Cal., for a ten-days' hunting and fishing trip, leaving here immediately
after the S. A. F. festivities were over.
Most of the time will be spent at the
famous Ah-Pah ranch. In the party
are Daniel MacRorie, Frank Pelicano,
H. Plath, Peter Rock, Frank Shearer
and John Morley, park superintendent
of Southern California; Mr. Urquhart
of the Panama-Pacific Exposition and
Prof. Stephens of the University of
California.

NEW YORK.

Percy Richter of 55 W. 26, formerly
employed by E. Asmus as salesman,
has taken the position of manager for
the United Cut Flower Co., of 111
West 28th.

Hitchings & Co. have erected at
Bound Brook, N. J., for Charles
Smith's Son of Woodside, a greenhouse
48x400. Asparagus plumosus has already been planted and it required
36,000 plants to fill the house. The
product will be handled by Phil. Kessler, with whom this is a specialty.

Phil. Kessler gave his annual outing
to the boys of the Coogan Building on
Thursday, Aug. 26th. About twenty of
them indulged in a base ball game and
bowling, and after that enjoyed a fine
spread of eatables such as Phil. Kessler
delights to provide, under the trees at
Fuhrer's Park, at Elmhurst. All had
a good time and went home at about
7 P. M. There were three prizes for
bowling and these were won by: A.
Radice, 1st, 172; D. Cantillion, 2nd,
172; J. Cook, 3rd, 149.

CLUBS AND SOCIETIES

AMERICAN ROSE SOCIETY.

A meeting of the American Rose Society was held at 10 o'clock Thursday morning, August 19, at the Civic Center Auditorium at San Francisco, Cal. In the absence of Wallace R. Pierson, due to his illness, Robert Pyle, of West Grove, Pa., was made chairman pro tem, Benjamin Hammond, secretary, being in attendance.

Action was taken confirming the action of the Executive Committee with reference to the publication of the Annual Bulletin, which will be in charge of the J. Horace McFarland Company, Harrisburg, Pa., with Mr. McFarland as editor, and Mr. Hammond, chairman of the Bulletin Committee; the scope to be practically doubled, and circulation to be obtained through the medium of offers in florists' catalogues as well as through affiliated societies. Action was taken inviting affiliation of the Pacific Coast Rose Society and general approval was expressed of the adoption of such a policy.

It is usual at these meetings of the Rose Society to install the officers-elect; but Mr. S. S. Pennock took office at the last meeting of the Executive Committee in Philadelphia. The absence of Ex-President Pierson was universally regretted.

Among those present were Professor Beal of Cornell, and Professor Mulford, of Washington, D. C. The meeting adjourned to reconvene at the Cleveland Flower Show in November.

GARDENERS' AND FLORISTS' CLUB OF BOSTON.

The club will hold a field day at the nurseries of the Breck-Robinson Co., Lexington, Mass., on Sept. 11. Transportation will be provided for all members and friends, who can take the train leaving the North Station, Boston, at 1.51 P. M. The train stops at the nurseries. Those preferring to travel via electric cars can take a Cambridge tunnel train at Park street, transferring at Harvard Square to an Arlington, Lowell or Lexington car, all of which pass the nurseries.

Club meetings at Horticultural Hall will be resumed on Sept. 21. There will be special exhibits of gladioli and dahlias. Several prominent members, some of whom have recently visited the Pacific slope, will give vacation experiences which should prove interesting.   W. N. CRAIG, Sec.

AMERICAN SWEET PEA SOCIETY.

A committee appointed by President Gray, to pass upon the sweet peas grown in Newport on account of C. C. Morse & Co., California, have awarded certificates to the following varieties: Jessie Cuthbertson, New Miriam Beaver and Duplex W. T. Hutchins.

(Signed)
JAMES ROBERTSON, WILLIAM MACKAY, CHRISTIAN M. BOGHOLT, Com.

CONNECTICUT HORTICULTURAL SOCIETY.

On Friday evening, Aug. 27, this society held its first regular meeting

succeeding the usual two-months vacation. Vice-President Hollister presided. A collection of asters by G. Ogren, gard. for Mrs. W. H. Bulkeley, was awarded a certificate of merit.

The subject of bleaching celery was brought up for discussion, one member advocating the paper collar, so-called, inasmuch as one man could cover more plants in one hour by its use than he could hill-up in a day. The chairman stated that the elm leaf beetle was not in evidence around Hartford this year. He had found eggs but they were dead.

At the close of the meeting the executive committee went into session to discuss plans for the Dahlia Show

MRS. JOHN VALLANCE
President-Elect Ladies' Society of American Florists.

to be held the latter part of September. By the entries already received this show will be the best ever held in Hartford. The society will hold its next regular meeting on September 10.
     ALFRED DIXON, Sec'y.

ST. LOUIS MEETINGS FOR SEPTEMBER.

St. Louis County Growers' Association, September 1.
St. Louis Florist Club, Thursday afternoon, Sept. 9, at Nursery, Mo., on the grounds of the H. J. Weber Nursery Co.
The Lady Florists' Home Circle, Wednesday afternoon, Sept. 8, at the home of Mrs. John L. Koenig, 2307 Clarence avenue.
Retail Florists' Association, Monday evening, Sept. 20.

A NEW ASSOCIATION.

Prof. H. C. Irish was selected secretary of a new association which was formed here last week to be known as the American Association of Apple Growers. This meeting was held at the Planters Hotel, St. Louis. The following compose the Executive Committee: H. M. Dunlop of Savoy, Ill., chairman,

Thos. Bregger of Champaign, Ill., Prof. W. A. Ruth of Urbana, Ill., H. W. Funk of Normal, Ill., and T. C. Wilson of St. Louis, Mo. This committee will hold a conference in St. Louis next March, when plans will be made to enlarge the association and a call for a general convention of apple growers to be held next August.

CLUB AND SOCIETY NOTES.

The dahlia growers of Attleboro, Mass., have organized with Charles Sleeper, president; George L. Cobb, secretary; W. C. Corey, treasurer.

The Twentieth Annual Flower Show of the Morris County Gardeners' and Florists' Society will be held Oct. 28-29, 1915, in Assembly Hall, Madison, N. J.   EDWARD REAGAN, Sec'y.

The regular monthly meeting of the Oyster Bay, N. Y., Horticultural Society was held on Wednesday evening, Aug. 25th. On the exhibition tables there were a fine lot of flowers, fruit and vegetables. Prizes and diplomas were won by Alfred Walker, Henry Gibson, James Duckham, Frank Petroccia, Katrine Hoyt, Chas. Milburn and John T. Ingram.

Prizes were received from the following for the fall shows: A. T. Boddington Co., P. D. Cravath, Wm. L. Swan, Stumpp & Walter Co., P. Henderson & Co., A. N. Pierson, Inc.; Weeber & Don, A. Strauss, Geo. S. Brewster, Mrs. W. R. Coe, J. M. Thorburn Co., Mrs. W. D. Straight. A prize of fifteen dollars was donated to the National Dahlia Society. Schedules for the Dahlia Show to be held in October are now ready and can be obtained by sending to the secretary for same.

     A. R. KENNEDY, Sec'y.

COMING EVENTS.

Shows.

Rochester, N. Y., Aug. 30 to Sept. 11.— Rochester Exposition and Flower Show.

Boston, Sept. 11-12.—Dahlia and Fruit Exhibition, Massachusetts Horticultural Society.

Providence, R. I., Sept. 16-17.—September Exhibition, Rhode Island Horticultural Society, Narragansett Hotel.

New Haven, Conn., Sept. 16-17.—Eighty-third annual exhibition of the New Haven County Horticultural Society to be held in Harmonie Hall. W. C. McIntosh, Sec., 925 Howard Ave., New Haven.

Hartford, Conn., Sept. 22-23.—Annual Dahlia exhibition of the Connecticut Horticultural Society, Unity Hall, Pratt St. Alfred Dixon, Sec., Wethersfield.

Portland, Ore., Sept. 23-25.—Annual Show of the Northwest National Dahlia Society.

New York, N. Y., Sept. 24-26.—American Dahlia Society's first exhibition. Museum of Natural History.

Boston, Oct. 2-3.—October Show Massachusetts Horticultural Society.

Orange, N. J., Oct. 4.—Tenth Annual Dahlia, Fruit, Gladioli and Vegetable Show of N. J. Floricultural Society. Geo. W. Strange, Sec., 84 Jackson St.

Oyster Bay, L. I., N. Y., Oct. 5-6.—Dahlia Show of the Oyster Bay Hort. Society. Chrysanthemum Show, Nov. 2. Andrew R. Kennedy, Westbury, L. I., secretary.

Glen Cove, L. I., Oct. 7.—Dahlia Show of Nassau Co. Hort. Soc. Fall Show of Nassau Co. Hort. Soc. Oct. 28 and 29.

Red Bank, N. J., Oct. 27-28.—Annual Flower Show of the Monmouth County Horticultural Society. H. A. Kettel, Sec., Fair Haven, N. J.

Poughkeepsie, N. Y., Oct. 28-29.—Annual flower show of Duchess County Horticultural Society. N. Harold Cottam, Sec., Wappingers Falls.

Boston, Nov. 4, 5, 6, 7.—Grand Autumn Exhibition, Massachusetts Horticultural society.

New York, N. Y., Nov. 3, 4, 5.—Annual Chrysanthemum Show of the American Institute, Engineering Societies Building.

Tarrytown, N. Y., Nov. 3-4-5.—Chrysanthemum Show in the Music Hall.

New York, N. Y., Nov. 4-7.—Annual Autumn exhibition of Hort. Soc. of New York, Museum of Natural History.

Chicago, Ill., Nov. 9-14.—Grand Floral Festival of the Chicago Florist's Club and Horticultural Society of Chicago, to be held in the Coliseum.

Cleveland, O., Nov. 10-14.—Annual show and meeting of Chrysanthemum Society of America. In conjunction with the Cleveland Flower Show. Chas. W. Johnson, Sec., 2220 Fairfax Ave., Morgan Park, Ill.

Cleveland, O., Nov. 10-14. — Cleveland Flower Show. The only show of national scope in the United States this fall. F. A. Friedley, Sec., 356 Leader Building.

Cleveland, O., Nov. 10-14.—The American Rose Society Fall Exhibition and Meeting in connection with the Cleveland Flower Show, Coliseum.

Providence, R. I., Nov. 11-12.—November Exhibition, Rhode Island Horticultural Society, Narragansett Hotel.

Baltimore, Md., Nov. 16-20.—Maryland Week Exhibition, Fifth Regiment Armory.

Madison, N. J., Oct. 28-29.—The twentieth annual flower show of the Morris Co. Gardeners' and Florists' Society, Assembly Hall.

Houston, Tex., Nov. 15-20.—State Flower Show.

A SAN FRANCISCO FLOWER STORE

SPECIAL CONVENTION DISPLAY
By Art Floral Co., San Francisco, Showing Front of Store.

In the accompanying picture and the frontispiece of this issue, we present interesting views of one of San Francisco's leading florist stores as decorated for Convention week in honor of the visit of the Society of American Florists. This was by the Art Floral Company at its Powell street shop and was one of the most notable displays made for the occasion. The sides of the store, which do not appear in the pictures shown were lined with lattice work with two panels set in on each side. In each panel was the figure of a girl carrying a bouquet, painted on heavy cardboard and set against a background of ferns, with 16 electric lights illuminating each

from behind the edge of the panel. The first figure was a bride carrying phalaenopsis and the frame of the lattice around her panel was adorned with white hydrangeas. Next came the bridesmaid carrying a bouquet of Ophelia roses, with roses of the same kind used around the panel. On the opposite side was the Senorita, dressed in yellow, carrying Ward roses, with yellow chrysanthemums forming the panel decoration. The other figure was the Corsage girl. She carried an appropriate bouquet of orchids, and rubrum lilies were used to good advantage around her panel. The moral effect was very striking and was the subject of much favorable and well merited comment.

Flower Market Reports

BOSTON Colder weather than usual at this season has retarded crops in some lines and to that extent reduced the daily oversupply which has encumbered the wholesale markets for the past month or more. Roses are distinctly benefited in consequence and there are none too many on some days. The outdoor product, such as gladioli, asters, gypsophila, etc., is still in somewhat obtrusive evidence on the sales counters. Asters are much better than they were, some of the long-stemned branching stock being very handsome. Gladioli are fine also but their abundance makes them almost an eyesore and it is not easy to admire anything which persists in accumulating until it is in everybody's way. Some of the growers have evidently overdone the gladiolus business and spoiled the game not only for themselves but everybody else. Lily of the valley is good property just now. Lilies are having a fair market. Of cattleyas there are very few in evidence. Seaside and mountain shipping trade is dwindling and should the cool weather continue, it will soon come to its finish.

CHICAGO Very cool weather prevailed the past week. In consequence there was a marked lessening of stock in every line. Beauties are active, the select long ones bringing $3.00 per dozen. The rose market in general is good for this season of the year, and the quality was never better. Some especially fine Killarney Brilliant is offered; these run in all lengths up to 36 inch stems. Russell continues fine and so does Ophelia and Sunburst. Pink and white Killarney show a marked improvement. In the red varieties, Hoosier Beauty and Milady are the best. Richmond also may be had of very good quality. Bulgaria, which for a number of years has been one of our very best sellers, in summer, is in very little demand this season. Ophelia apparently has taken its place to a considerable extent. Carnations continue scarce and short in stem. The market in asters is quite active. Some very fine stock is offered. The glut in gladioli for the present, at least, seems to be over although there is plenty for all demands, but prices have advanced somewhat, particularly on the better grades. Chrysanthemums are increasing; besides Golden Glow we now have Smith's Advance in white. Lilies are quite plentiful and move rather slow. Lily of the valley is still very scarce, the wholesale houses finding it difficult to fill orders at times. Dahlias are more plentiful but this market has never taken much of a fancy to this flower. In miscellaneous garden stuff there is gaillardia, gaura, tuft, cornflowers, coreopsis, daisies, etc. Demand for green goods is fairly active.

NEW YORK The arrival of September finds the flower market in normal condition as to supply, but still a little behind hand as to demand. New roses are gradually improving in quality and the outlook seems good for an unprecedented variety and perfection of roses for the coming season. Lilies are selling fairly well, for a change. Gladioli are still plentiful. Asters sell very well, the later varieties coming in very fine. Carnations are not yet in evidence. A good many dahlias are seen and they are good. A few chrysanthemums have made their appearance, as a sort of reminder that fall is approaching and the next symptom due to develop will be the irrepressible annual scout from "up-the-Hudson" with the first bunch of violets. Little activity is apparent as yet in the wholesale district and the amount of business done after 10.30 A. M. is very small.

PHILADELPHIA Stock cleaned up pretty well last week except on the poorer grades of asters. It was hard to move the latter at any price and many of them remained unsold at the end of the week. Gladioli are selling better and the supply is considerably shorter. The demand is particularly good for America, this one being especially fine at present. Cattleyas are still scarce and there are not many other orchids arriving—the Oncidium varicosum being the most conspicuous. Roses continue to improve in quality, the leaders at present being Russells, Sunbursts and Beauties. The latter hung fire early in the week but recovered later. Sweet peas are best from northern points and are as good as could be expected, but the demand is only so-so. What few carnations arriving are mostly from field-grown. No new indoor as yet. Golden Glow chrysanthemums are to be seen around, also some dahlias, but it is too early for these yet. They will go better after the middle of September. Same may be said of tritomas. Lots of the latter to be seen but they meet with little attention. Much outdoor stock is still coming in—except what they call "small stuff"—achillea, feverfew candytuft, etc.

(Continued on page 327)

WHOLESALE FLOWER MARKETS — TRADE PRICES—Per 100 TO DEALERS ONLY

	BOSTON Sept. 2		ST. LOUIS Aug. 30		PHILA. Aug. 23	
Roses						
Am. Beauty, Special	12.00 to 20.00	30.00 to 40.00	..... to 25.00
" " Fancy and Extra	6.00 to 10.00	20.00 to 25.00	15.00 to 20.00
" " No.	1.00 to 3.00	5.00 to 8.00	10.00 to 12.50
" " No. 2	4.00 to 10.00	20.00 to 15.00	3.00 to 12.00
Russell, Hadley	2.00 to 4.00	5.00 to 6.00	4.00 to 6.00
Killarney, Richmond, Hillingdon, Ward, Extra	.50 to 1.00	2.00 to 3.00	2.00 to 3.00
Arenburg; Radiance, Taft, Key, Extra	2.00 to 4.00	5.00 to 6.00	5.00 to 6.00
" " " Ordinary	.50 to 1.00	2.00 to 3.00	2.00 to 4.00
Ophelia, Mock, Sunburst, Extra	2.00 to 4.00	..... to	4.00 to 6.00
" " " Ordinary	.50 to 1.00	..... to	2.00 to 4.00
Carnations, Fancy	.75 to 1.00	1.00 to 1.50	..... to 1.50
Ordinary	.50 to .75	.50 to .75	..... to 1.00
Cattleyas	35.00 to 75.00	35.00 to 50.00	50.00 to 75.00
Dendrobium formosun	..... to	..... to	..... to 75.00
Lilies, Longiflorum	4.00 to 6.00	6.00 to 8.00	8.00 to 12.50
" Rubrum	..... to	4.00 to 5.00	..... to 2.00
Lily of the Valley	3.00 to 4.00	3.00 to 4.00	2.00 to 4.00
Daisies	.50 to 1.00	.80 to .25	..... to .....
Violets	..... to	..... to	..... to .....
Snapdragon	.50 to 1.00	3.00 to 4.00	..... to .....
Gladioli	.50 to 1.50	2.00 to 3.00	1.00 to 3.00
Chrysanthemums	.25 to 1.00	.75 to 2.00	.50 to 2.00
Sweet Peas	.15 to .30	.15 to .25	.50 to .75
Gardenias	10.00 to 25.00	..... to	..... to .....
Adiantum	.50 to 1.00	1.00 to 1.25	..... to 1.00
Smilax	6.00 to 12.00	12.00 to 15.00	15.00 to 20.00
Asparagus Plumosus, Strings (100)	25.00 to 50.00	50.00 to	..... to 50.00
" & Spren, (100 Bchs.)	25.00 to 35.00	20.00 to 35.00	..... to 50.00

Flower Market Reports

(Continued from page 321.)

SAN FRANCISCO

Still there are no complaints among the local florists about slow business. Everyone seems to be busy and stock offerings fill all requirements nicely with very little surplus. A few violets made their initial appearance the past week, but the supply is very limited and the offerings so far have been snapped up so quickly that many of the shops have not shown any as yet. Their arrival is earlier this season than usual, as has been the case with most other varieties of flowers, the growers having forced their plants on account of the exposition. New crop carnations are coming in quite freely, and the quality is good except that stems are still a little short. Sweet peas are about off the market. The average quality of chrysanthemums is rapidly improving and the offerings clean up readily. Dahlias are holding their own wonderfully well, both in quantity and quality, while gladioli are scarce and off quality. Much amaryllis is being used, and there is a fair outlet for zinnias. Asters are at their height now, the quality is excellent and the demand steady. A slight falling off in supply is looked for in the next week or two. Lilies are in good supply and meet with a fair demand, rubrum being seen in greatest quantity, although considerable auratum and tigrium are still to be seen at many shops. Lily of the valley cleans up closely. The rose market shows improvement, but the quality on the whole is none too good, the percentage of short stock running rather high. Really fine offerings are hardly sufficient for the demand, which makes them clear readily at satisfactory prices. Orchids are unusually fine but scarce.

ST. LOUIS

Our market is still in an overcrowded condition. There has been considerable demand for white flowers all week, but outside of this call for funeral work business has been dull all summer. The cool weather has made better trade. Roses are mostly all short stems and plenty of them. The few fancy long ones sell clean daily. Carnations will be few until the middle of the month. Gladioli have shortened up greatly, also tuberoses and asters. Dahlias and cosmos are the flowers now to crowd up the market. Lily of the valley has had a big call all week, also lilies, both rubrums and longiflorums. A few chrysanthemums are in, with slow call as yet.

WASHINGTON

Unlike the more northern cities, Washington is still without the early chrysanthemums this year. It has been found that the early varieties mature too quickly in this climate and the results obtained from them has in previous seasons proven very unsatisfactory. Their loss is in no wise felt, however, as the market is still glutted with asters and the cool weather promises to bring in a large supply of dahlias at an early date. The supply of gladioli has decreased and the ratio of sale has correspondingly increased. There are plenty of longiflorum lilies. None of the florists are placing orders for orchids in more than half-dozen lots and it is extremely difficult to get more than that amount at any one time. Rubrum lilies were sent in last week and have met with fairly ready sale. The situation with respect to roses remains as previously reported. The sale of white roses was made better last week by reason of an increased number of wedding decorations. This added business produced the first shortage of lily of the valley since early in June. It is reported by the exchanges that shippers have cut their consignments in half of late, probably with a view to stretching out the pips which they now have on hand. This is giving to the growers a much better average return from their consignments and assures a continued and even supply. American Beauty roses are meeting with slightly better sale.

WASHINGTON.

During the past week the interior of the Leo Niessen Co.'s store has been repainted and now presents a very attractive appearance.

The Civil Service Commission has just announced that an examination will be held on September 28 to secure eligibles for positions as quarantine inspectors in the office of the Federal Horticultural Board. These positions carry an annual salary of $2,400. Further information can be obtained by writing to the Commission.

A window display contest, open to merchants in all lines of business in Washington, will be held by the Retail Merchants' Association on September 27, on which date the fiftieth annual encampment of the Grand Army of the Republic will commence. Prizes amounting to $50 are offered. All windows will be darkened during the day. At eight o'clock in the evening a signal will be given and all curtains will be raised and windows illuminated displaying their contents. A number of florists are contemplating entering in to the contest, honorable mention therein meaning considerable to them by way of advertising.

Louis L. Bowdler has brought suit in the Supreme Court against Annie E. Murphy, the former owner of the property occupied by him as a retail flower store, to recover damages of $20,000 for breach of contract. He alleges that a clause in the lease provided that it should not be sold during his tenancy without giving him the privilege of making the purchase at a price equal to that offered by any other person. He states that the building was sold for $75,000, whereas it was worth $95,000 to him, without the notice of sale provided for. He further sues for $1,000 covering inconvenience caused by the closing of a hallway to which he was to have had full use.

It is stated in Washington that Great Britain has so modified the provisions of her Order in Council of March 11, which practically closed the seas to all commerce in German, Austro-Hungarian and Belgian goods, whereby merchandise produced in those countries and bought and paid for by American importers prior to March 1, or delivered f. o. b. in neutral countries prior to March 15, will be granted permits guaranteeing safe conduct across the ocean. This will probably mean that American importers of ornamental plants will be able to secure their Christmas supplies in ample time. It is declared that there is already in the hands of the Trade Advisers a vast volume of evidence which will be placed before the proper British authorities immediately upon the confirmation of the report that England has granted these concessions.

KANSAS CITY.

Samuel Murray had as guests last Sunday President P. Welch and Mrs. Welch and friend of Boston, on their way home from California. The party arrived several hours late, thus curtailing somewhat the hospitalities prepared for them, but they were in good hands and were given an opportunity to see some of the attractions of Kansas City under most congenial circumstances and company.

NEW YORK QUOTATIONS PER 100.　To Dealers Only

MISCELLANEOUS	Last Half of Week ending Aug. 28 1915				First Half of Week beginning Aug. 30 1915		
Cattleyas	25.00	to	75.00		25.00	to	75.00
Lilies, Longiflorum	3.00	to	6.00		3.00	to	6.00
Rubrum	1.00	to	2.00		1.00	to	2.00
Lily of the Valley	2.00	to	4.00		2.00	to	4.00
Daisies	.....	to	.50		.....	to	.50
Snapdragon	.50	to	1.00		.50	to	1.00
Gladioli	.50	to	1.00		.50	to	1.00
Asters	.15	to	1.00		.15	to	1.00
Sweet Peas	.10	to	.15		.10	to	.15
Corn Flower	.....	to	.25		.....	to	.25
Gardenias	12.00	to	25.00		12.00	to	25.00
Adiantum	.50	to	.75		.50	to	.75
Smilax	4.00	to	8.00		4.00	to	8.00
Asparagus Plumosus, strings (per 100)	15.00	to	30.00		15.00	to	30.00
& Spren (100 bunches)	10.00	to	20.00		10.00	to	20.00

Buyer's Directory and Ready Reference Guide

Advertisements under this head, one cent a word.　　Initials count as words.

Display advertisers in this issue are also listed under this classification without charge. Reference to List of Advertisers will indicate the respective pages.

Buyers failing to find what they want in this list will confer a favor by writing us and we will try to put them in communication with reliable dealers.

ACCOUNTANT

R. J. Dysart, 40 State St., Boston.
For page see List of Advertisers.

ACHILLEA

"Pearl," Fine Seedlings, $3.00 per 1,000, cash. JAMES MOSS, Wholesale Grower, Johnsville, Pa.

APHINE

Aphine Mfg. Co., Madison, N. J.
For page see List of Advertisers.

APHIS PUNK

Nicotine Mfg. Co., St. Louis, Mo.
For page see List of Advertisers.

ASTERS

ASTERS—Invincible, Henderson's seed, and as fine and healthy plants that grow; in white, pink, purple, rose and blue, $3.00 per 1,000; 5,000 or more, $2.50 per 1,000. Cash. JAMES MOSS, Wholesale Grower, Johnsville, Pa.

AUCTION SALES

Elliott Auction Co., New York City.
For page see List of Advertisers.

AZALEAS

P. Ouwerkerk, Hoboken, N. J.
For page see List of Advertisers.

McHutchison & Co., New York City.
Azalea Shipments Will Come.

BAY TREES

August Rolker & Sons, New York.
For page see List of Advertisers.

BEDDING PLANTS

A. N. Pierson, Inc., Cromwell, Conn.
For page see List of Advertisers.

BEGONIAS

Julius Roehrs Company, Rutherford, N. J.
For page see List of Advertisers.

R. Vincent, Jr., & Sons Co., White Marsh, Md.
For page see List of Advertisers.

Thomas Roland, Nahant, Mass.
For page see List of Advertisers.

A. M. Davenport, Watertown, Mass.
For page see List of Advertisers.

			Per 100
BEGONIA LORRAINE,	2½	in	$12.00
	3	in	20.00
	4	in	35.00
	5	in	50.00
BEGONIA CINCINNATI,	2½	in	15.00
	3	in	25.00
	3½	in	30.00
	4½	in	40.00

JULIUS ROEHRS CO., Rutherford, N. J.

BOILERS

Kroeschell Bros. Co., Chicago.
For page see List of Advertisers.

King Construction Co., North Tonawanda, N. Y.
"King Ideal" Boiler.
For page see List of Advertisers.

Hitchings & Co., New York City.
For page see List of Advertisers.

Lord & Burnham Co., New York City.

BOXES—CUT FLOWER FOLDING

Edwards Folding Box Co., Philadelphia.
For page see List of Advertisers.

Folding cut flower boxes, the best made. Write for list. HOLTON & HUNKEL CO., Milwaukee, Wis.

BOX TREES

BOX TREES—Standards, Pyramids and Bush. In various sizes. Price List on demand. JULIUS ROEHRS CO., Rutherford, N. J.

BULBS AND TUBERS

Santa Cruz Bulb & Plant Co., Santa Cruz, Cal.
Freesia Purity and Calla Bulbs.
For page see List of Advertisers.

J. M. Thorburn & Co., New York City
Wholesale Price List of High Class Bulbs.
For page see List of Advertisers.

Ralph M. Ward & Co., New York City.
Lily Bulbs.
For page see List of Advertisers.

John Lewis Childs, Flowerfield, L. I., N. Y.
For page see List of Advertisers.

August Rolker & Sons, New York City.
Holland and Japan Bulbs.
For page see List of Advertisers.

R. & J. Farquhar & Co., Boston, Mass.
For page see List of Advertisers.

S. S. Skidelsky & Co., Philadelphia, Pa.
For page see List of Advertisers.

Chas. Schwake & Co., New York City.
Horticultural Importers and Exporters.
For page see List of Advertisers.

A. Henderson & Co., Chicago, Ill.
For page see List of Advertisers.

Burnett Bros., 98 Chambers St., New York.
For page see List of Advertisers.

Henry F. Michell Co., Philadelphia, Pa.
For page see List of Advertisers.

Joseph Breck & Sons Corp., Boston, Mass.
For page see List of Advertisers.

Fottler, Fiske, Rawson Co., Boston, Mass.
For page see List of Advertisers.

C. KEUR & SONS, HILLEGOM, Holland.
Bulbs of all descriptions. Write for prices.
NEW YORK Branch, 8-10 Bridge St.

CANNAS

Canna Specialists.
Send for Canna book.
THE CONARD & JONES COMPANY, West Grove, Pa.

CARNATION STAPLES

Split carnations quickly, easily and cheaply mended. Pillsbury's Carnation Staple, 1000 for 35c.; 3000 for $1.00 post paid. I. L. PILLSBURY, Galesburg, Ill.

Supreme Carnation Staples, for repairing split carnations, 35c. per 1000; 3000 for $1.00. F. W. WAITE, 85 Belmont Ave., Springfield, Mass.

CARNATIONS

Wood Bros., Fishkill, N. Y.
For page see List of Advertisers.

F. Dorner & Sons Co., Lafayette, Ind.
For page see List of Advertisers.

Leo Niessen Co., Philadelphia, Pa.
Field Grown Carnation Plants.
For page see List of Advertisers.

CARNATIONS—Continued

Carnations, field grown, $6.00 per 100. Cash. White and Pink Enchantress Mrs. Ward, Perfection, Penn, Winsor, Queen, Lawson, Beacon. CHAS. H. GREEN, Spencer, Mass.

CHRYSANTHEMUMS

Chas. H. Totty, Madison, N. J.
For page see List of Advertisers.

R. Vincent, Jr., & Sons Co., White Marsh, Md.
Pompon Chrysanthemums.
For page see List of Advertisers.

THE BEST 1915 NOVELTIES.
The Cream of 1914 introductions.
The most popular Commercial and Exhibition kinds; also complete line of Pompons, Singles and Anemones. Trade list on application. ELMER D. SMITH & CO., Adrian, Mich.

COCOANUT FIBRE SOIL

20th Century Plant Food Co., Beverly, Mass.
For page see List of Advertisers.

CYCLAMENS

The Best Strains.
Eight Varieties.　　　　　Very Fine.
If you want quality, order now.

	100	1000
2½ in.	$7.00	$60.00
3 in.	9.00	80.00
4 in.	20.00	

Write for copy of our monthly plant bulletin.
S. S. PENNOCK-MEEHAN CO., 1608-1620 Ludlow St., Philadelphia, Pa.

DAHLIAS

Send for Wholesale List of whole clumps and separate stock; 40,000 clumps for sale. Northboro Dahlia and Gladiolus Gardens. J. L. MOORE, Prop, Northboro, Mass.

NEW PAEONY DAHLIA
John Wanamaker, Newest, Handsomest, Best. New color, new form and new habit of growth. Big stock of best cut-flower varieties. Send list of wants to PEACOCK DAHLIA FARMS, Berlin, N. J.

DECORATIVE PLANTS

Robert Craig Co., Philadelphia, Pa.
For page see List of Advertisers.

Woodrow & Marketos, New York City.
For page see List of Advertisers.

S. S. Skidelsky & Co., Philadelphia, Pa.
For page see List of Advertisers.

Bobbink & Atkins, Rutherford, N. J.
For page see List of Advertisers.

A. Leuthy & Co., Roslindale, Boston, Mass.
For page see List of Advertisers.

FERNS

Henry A. Dreer, Philadelphia, Pa.

H. H. Barrows & Son, Whitman, Mass.
For page see List of Advertisers.

Robert Craig Co., Philadelphia, Pa.
For page see List of Advertisers.

McHutchison & Co., New York City.
Ferns in Flats.
For page see List of Advertisers.

Roman J. Irwin, New York City.
Boston and Whitmani Ferns.
For page see List of Advertisers.

FERTILIZERS

20th Century Plant Food Co., Beverly, Mass.
Cocoanut Fibre Soil.
For page see List of Advertisers.

For List of Advertisers See Page 307

In writing to Advertisers kindly mention Horticulture

For List of Advertisers See Page 307

New Offers In This Issue

THE NECESSITY OF NATIONAL PUBLICITY TO ADVANCE THE INTERESTS OF COMMERCIAL FLORICULTURE IN THE UNITED STATES.

(A Paper by A. Pochelon, Presented at the San Francisco Convention.)

This subject has been given to me and I shall try to treat it from the standpoint of Secretary of The Florists' Telegraph Delivery, an association which has done a great deal of work in the way of publicity. So far, of course, every member has been doing his or her share in their different localities to draw their patrons, or would-be patrons' attention to the telegraph or out-of-town service, and the results gained in the past few years have been very much beyond expectation.

This much for the introduction of the points which I will bring out now. If the florists throughout the country can be indorsed by a national advertising campaign drawing the public's attention to The Florists' Telegraph Delivery shops all over the country, and the public impressed that F. T. D. does not only stand for telegraph orders, but for the best service, prompt pay, sure and honest delivery—that means progress.

Immediately after reading the above lines you may think that I am too much F. T. D., but that is not at all so. Just remember that every good retail florist in the United States and Canada has the same right to join the F. T. D. and work with us, not alone for his or our benefit but for the good of the florist trade.

Today you may consider the F. T. D. a pretty good organization of the sales department in the florists' trade and if you want to make a start for a national campaign, you have to get a body of retailers who are businesslike enough to see the benefit of such a campaign and who will have to get up a fund to spend for this advertising and this fund must be guaranteed before any attempt at spending it is made. This campaign must go through periodicals as well as local daily papers.

For many years this relaying of orders has been, you might say, limited to steamer deliveries in New York or for funeral work, but the day is here when this relaying can be applied to every occasion for which we sell flowers in our shops. Many a retailer has shipped flowers from his town for one hundred or more miles and felt that he would rather make the sale than relay the order; has he gained anything by so doing? No, he has hurt the florist trade; in almost every instance, these shipments have arrived poorly, where, if the man in the respective town would have made this delivery the patron would have received the full value for his money beside advertising the florist out-of-town service.

Do not forget for one moment that you may do $10,000 worth of advertising and then not be able to deliver the goods right and faithful. By such methods you will do more harm than good to the florist trade. I, therefore, advise, first of all, before any national advertising campaign is undertaken to investigate who can handle and deliver the goods the best and so back up his

advertising. I would hate to think that an order sent by me to a brother florist in another town would not be handled as conscientiously as I would want to fill it myself.

There is absolutely no doubt in my mind that our florist trade is still one of the least advertised trades, but it seems a lot of retailers are waiting for someone outside the trade to advertise their goods and you may rest assured they surely will have a long wait coming.

If we had five hundred retailers around the country like Henry Penn and a few others whom I could name who have spent money on a large scale for advertising and yet doing this cautiously, the whole florist trade would gain a lot, but just now instead of being thankful to such men what do a great many narrow, jealous retailers do? They knock, criticise and run down the many advertising florists; at the same time forgetting that if all the people they have made flower buyers of, would go back to their shops for everything they need, they could not handle the business. Many a man or woman have I induced to use flowers on their tables and if all would come and trade with me alone I would not care to handle all that amount of business.

Let each retailer make up his mind to cultivate a want for flowers at occasions where people now do not think of using flowers, instead of watching with jealous eyes his florist neighbor's store and criticising his way of doing business, and we all will be better satisfied aside from being better men and better florists.

I think it is folly for the New York men to dictate to the man in Detroit how to advertise; it is a much safer way for each man to study a plan or system of how he can get the most publicity in his locality. After this is done an indorsement by a national campaign is absolutely in order but before that it would be throwing away money. National advertising is a good deal like co-operation advertising. It is up to a few to do the work to the best of their ability and even after they can show the best results it is hard for the few to collect the money from the others.

There is absolutely no doubt in my mind that Mother's Day would never have become the great benefit to the florist trade had it not been for the florists in different localities taking this proposition in hand and following it up so that some day I hope Mothers' Day will become the same as Easter or Christmas is to the florist trade. Yet, ask the fellows who do the actual work and see and hear what they have to say about plugging to get even a hearing with some of their brother florists. You might be surprised when I tell you they sometimes almost have to beg and plead for the other fellows to come in with them, aside from doing the hard work, and I venture to say right here that if they were not successful and got results they would never be forgiven and even the best of us can make a misjudgment sometimes.

Cleveland is going to have a big Flower Show next fall and the way they go at the advertising is a study worth while being appreciated by a great many. In the florist trade not just one or two individuals will get the largest benefit from some and the men who are doing the work should be honored and appreciation shown by their brother florists and I sincerely hope they will get this without any curtailing.

If publicity and advertising in the florist trade will keep on increasing as it has within the last five years I can safely state that in another five years the trade will be on more of a business basis than it is now. The time has past where a merchant or business man could not be a florist unless he was a graduate from a greenhouse. Today the most prominent retail florists have graduated from merchants' office or business institutions.

The grower, of course, does not like this as well, but let the grower raise a pretty plant, or cut flowers, then add the artistic taste of the up-to-date retailer, and let him place it in his method on the market, and watch the success.

The success of the Ford automobile organization is not so much the mechanic who puts it together but the merchant's ways of publicity. You will find that the largest part of the publicity was studied out by not so much the practical and theoretical man as the man with the most modern up-to-date business ideas.

Of course, I have to come back to my first saying that advertising must first start by getting up an article which will stand on its merits, and which you can fully back up before you reach out for the publicity. I could keep on writing on these lines, but the same substance will always lead me back to my first saying, that before we can think of a national advertising campaign we must have, first of all, representative retailers in every town who will back up our preaching and give the best of service, followed up with a prompt payment of their bills and not allow them to run along for three, four or six months, or even longer. It is to be regretted that there are many florists in this country who seem to forget that prompt payments of bills is one of the greatest reputations a man can get.

Yours in hope that within the next few years advertising publicity will be increased so that no town will ever be able to report in the florists' trade papers about a glut or overstock of the market. It is up to the retailers to get rid of the grower's production, and not up to the grower.

RED SPIDER REMEDIES.

Koster & Co., of Boskoop, Holland, write in reply to an inquiry by one of our correspondents, that they fight red spider on azaleas, blue spruce and other conifers, etc., with a preparation called there Emulgated Carbolineum. They syringe thoroughly with this in early spring before the buds swell. They claim to have had very fine results and have practically eradicated red spider from their nurseries, whereas previous to its use they were badly overrun.

We understand that this preparation, or a similar material (Carbolineum), has been tried in this country but it did not seem to take very well. Prof. Surface, economic zoologist of the Pensylvania Agricultural Department at Harrisburg, is authority for the statement that any preparation

that has sulphur in it will kill red spider. In a bulletin issued last March he said:

Among the very common pests of plants are those commonly known as Mites or Red Spiders. As a matter of fact they are not Spiders, although they belong to the same general order of animate life as do the Spiders. Neither are they always red, as, in fact, they are generally grayish or whitish. These pests are properly called Mites. There are several species of them, some of which are the most serious pests of vegetation, while others attack stored fruits, and still others are the common Red Lice of poultry.

Those Mites which attack vegetation generally accompany Mildew, and where the leaf or other part of the plant looks powdery or whitish, as though it were more or less covered with flour, the plant disease known as Mildew is doubtless the cause, and Mites are generally present.

Mites on plants are also best destroyed by spraying with dilute lime-sulfur solution or the self-boiled lime-sulfur formula. One part of strong lime-sulfur solution in ten gallons of water is generally enough to have the desired effect for Mites and Mildew of growing vegetation. The spraying should be done with an up-turned nozzle held beneath, the leaves of the plants, in order to strike the under side of the leaves, and also turned so as to cover the upper side. A few varieties of plants may be so tender as to require a dilution which is a little greater, but most plants when in leaf will stand even a stronger application than this, which should consequently be made.

WIZARD BRAND MANURES

Unequalled for Greenhouse and Landscape Fertilizing

THE PULVERIZED MANURE CO.
31 Union Stock Yards, Chicago

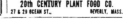

GREENHOUSES BUILDING OR CONTEMPLATED.

Leroy, Ill.—L. L. Fry, house, 48x90.

Wayzata, Minn.—John Bell, one house.

Sellersville, Pa.—Frank S. Jackson, addition.

Philadelphia, Pa.—J. L. Nichols, house, 50x100.

Worcester, Mass.—Chas. Greenwood, May street, one house.

Cudahy, Wis.—Cudahy Floral Co., Moninger house, 28x175.

Sioux City, Ia.—J. C. Rennison Co., three houses, each 30x300.

Wheeling, W. Va.—Albert Lash, S. Warwood avenue, one house.

Spencerport, N. Y.—H. E. Rogers & Son, Union street, one house.

Providence, R. I.—Albert Holscher, Hartford avenue, house, 20x110.

Newton Falls, O.—Cleveland Cut Flower Co., carnation house, 24x200.

Hackettstown, N. J.—Edward C. Boss has surrendered his lease on the Central street greenhouses. He will soon return to his former home in Stroudsburg, Pa.

Recent contracts closed for King Construction Co., by Wm. J. Muth in Philadelphia territory, are as follows:

Henry F. Michell Co., extensive improvements and alterations to the greenhouse plant at Andalusia, Pa., including the addition of three pipe-frame houses each 22 x 125 and connecting house 22 x 143. Fire-proof boiler house 22 x 43 with asbestos protected metal and concrete side walls. An entire new system of heating by the King Richcon system.

H. A. Dreer, Inc., Riverton, N. J., three houses 12 x 100 and one house 22 x 150.

Dingee & Conard Co., West Grove, Pa., two houses each 30 x 150.

Harry E. Cooper, West Grove, Pa. Material for house 50 x 150 feet long with connecting passageway.

Leonard H. Dudman, Manoa, Pa. Material for two houses 25 x 125 and new boiler.

Frank Jackson, Sellersville, Pa. Material for house 28 x 120.

George School, Bucks Co., Pa. House 16 x 25 for class work in botany.

Vol. XXII
No. 11
SEPT. 11
1915

HORTICULTURE

The Fern Garden

Published Every Saturday at 147 Summer Street, Boston, Mass.
Subscription, $1.00

LIST OF ADVERTISERS

**FOR BUYERS' DIRECTORY AND READY REFERENCE GUIDE
SEE PAGES 360, 361, 362, 363**

NOTES ON CULTURE OF FLORISTS' STOCK

CONDUCTED BY

John J. M. Farrell

Questions by our readers in line with any of the topics presented on this page will be cordially received and promptly answered by Mr. Farrell. Such communications should invariably be addressed to the office of HORTICULTURE.
"If vain our toil, we ought to blame the culture, not the soil."—*Pope.*

Carnations

There is more to the growing of carnations than to ventilate faithfully and water regularly. Keep your eyes open and take a walk through the houses whenever there is a chance. Hardly ever do we do this without finding something requiring attention. If there should happen to be a little let-up in the rush you couldn't take better advantage of it than to get the supports put in place for the carnations. Which is the best kind to use? The kind which in your judgment will hold the plants up well, make the cutting of flowers an easy matter and will let the sun and air into the rows. The winter months are not the ones to attempt to get a stunted plant into condition. If healthy field-grown plants have been housed, try to keep them so; get a bench full of live stock and busy tops by the middle of October. Look over the beds every day and water where they show dry. Keep on ventilating all day and even at night, as this tends to produce growth that is hard and robust.

Geranium Cuttings

Where a big amount of these cuttings are wanted, lose no time from this out. By rooting the cuttings in benches in sand, a greater number of plants can be raised in a given time than by either of the other methods and if at all times the cuttings are kept cool enough, good salable plants will be the result. Another method is that of putting the cuttings, to the number of fifty or more—the number depending on the size of the flats—into flats. This method, which is generally practiced by private growers and by some commercial growers also, possesses many points of advantage. Those adopting it should, however, count on losing ten per cent. of the cuttings put in if these are allowed as they often are to remain in flats three or four months. The cuttings should be thoroughly watered after being put in the flats and then shaded for a day or two.

Lifting Hydrangeas

It is now about time to lift field grown hydrangeas. Many make the mistake of lifting them too early, when the wood is not nearly matured; but as each location differs in temperature and other climatic conditions, in one or more particulars, it is impossible to advise as to the exact date for lifting and potting. Give the plants a good watering directly after potting. After the plants are potted they should be placed in as exposed a situation as can be found for them outdoors, until safety demands their removal to other quarters. A cool cellar is a good place for resting hydrangeas, but

care should be taken that frost does not reach them. You will need to look at them about every two weeks and see that they do not become dust dry.

Midseason Sweet Peas

A much larger number are planting sweet peas as a succession crop to chrysanthemums. The importance of these flowers commercially is yearly increasing as better varieties are introduced. Any florist who cares to plant sweet peas in benches can get good flowers for a long period if they are kept well fed and watered. It is, however, in solid beds that the really fine long-stemmed flowers are to be had. The finest sweet peas under glass are grown in solid beds, as in these they have a deeper root run and the roots are cooler and moister than is possible in raised benches. The soil must be thoroughly prepared. For best results trench the beds twelve to eighteen inches deep, working in plenty of well decayed cow manure. Be sure that the drainage is good. Sow the seed thinly, letting individual plants stand two or three inches apart in the rows. Some people prefer to sow the seed in the rows, other to start in flats of sand or fine loam and transplant singly.

Preparing Soil

The present is a good time to look to the turning over and preparing of the soil to be used for the coming season. The compost should have been got together some time ago but should be turned over and well broken up now so as to be in readiness when wanted. It is necessary that it be finely chopped so that the ingredients are evenly mixed. If barnyard manure was put in the compost at the time it was stacked up nothing else will be necessary. Bone meal or tankage (the later a mixture of blood, bone and the waste from slaughter houses which is dried and then finely ground up) we have found very good for this purpose. Either of these added to the compost at the rate of about fifty pounds to the yard of soil will make a good, strong soil and also has the advantage of causing the compost to heat sufficiently to destroy the larvæ or grubs of insects that would prove a detriment to the growth of the plants later.

Firing

There are quite a few growers that let all their warm-blooded stock go too long without fire heat. This is not a good plan as it always works harm when the nights become cool. I know some growers who start firing by the 20th of August within fifty miles of New York City. So it is safe to begin firing for this locality now.

Next Week: Canterbury Bells; Chrysanthemums; Gardenias; Lorraine Begonias; Violets; Ventilation.

ROSE GROWING UNDER GLASS

CONDUCTED BY

Arthur C. Ruzicka

Questions by our readers in line with any of the topics presented on this page will be cordially received and promptly answered by Mr. Ruzicka. Such communications should invariably be addressed to the office of HORTICULTURE.

Mulching

The houses that were planted a little earlier in the season and have made considerable growth must not be allowed to suffer from lack of mulching. After the plants have grown up nicely and the soil in the benches is full of roots it is best to keep sufficient mulch on to keep the surface of all benches rough so that water will not run all over when you water but will stay where it is applied. If this is not so then the benches will always have dry spots and some plants will fairly shrivel up for want of water while others are suffering from over watering. With liquid manure always on tap we do not depend on this mulch to give the plants much feed, although they do get a good deal out of it even at that. As soon as any bare spots appear in the benches more mulch is applied to these. It is better to do this than to mulch the whole house for the whole house may not need it and the plants would come to harm if mulched. Do not apply too much at the one time, especially if the manure that is used is not well decayed. Not only would a good deal of it be wasted but harm would likely result, for the ammonia and other gases from the manure would be almost sure to burn the leaves. Apply just enough to cover the surface of the benches nicely and when more is needed it can always be applied later.

Bonemeal

If bonemeal is to be used as fertilizer fall and early winter is the best time to use it, especially on places where the old greenhouse soil is not used on the fields for growing field crops. The bone, although a very good fertilizer and plant food, is rather slow in action, especially the coarser grades, and the plants will not get the full benefit if it is applied too late in the season. The best time is just before a mulch is applied, as very little of it will be lost then. It will mix in with the manure and the little roots will find it there when they are after it. And they will be, too, especially if the benches have not been heaped with soil which stays wet most of the time and gives the roots a poor chance to work.

Watering

Watering will play an important part in growing now and the plants that are growing well in only two or three inches of soil will have to be watched very closely as they will dry out in a few hours once they begin to go. These benches will all have to be watered oftener than those that carry six or more inches of soil. Should the plants be allowed to get too dry while they are growing it would check them quite a bit and should the soil be heavy and crack a good deal it would tear the roots as it did so. In the spring this would do little harm; in fact it would be a help to the plants as all the main roots that would lose their laterals would at once send out countless number of new roots and these would be far more active in securing water, nourishment and so

on. Now in the fall, however, with winter on it is best to make it as easy for the plants as possible and keep them going all the time, but not to force them to any extent.

Liquid Manure

It is still very early in the season but the early planted houses that have been cutting quite heavy and are growing well will not be hurt by a liquid manure now and then, being very careful not to use anything but good cow manure in making this. Make sure that the houses are wet enough before it is applied. Better water with clear water first and then apply the liquid later. Watch the plants carefully, and should they show any sign of becoming soft stop using the liquid at once and use no more until the plants starve a little.

Electricity in Rose Growing

Why so many places continue to use the old fashioned steam pumps, which require a lot of care and give unsatisfactory service at their best is more than we can see. The modern electric pump with a motor of sufficient size will not only do the work quicker and better, but pressure can be had on a minute's notice without stopping to get steam up for an hour or more. Once these pumps are started they will work unattended for a very long time. One place we know saves nearly a hundred dollars a month on their water bill by making use of a pump which takes water from a brook running past the place. This pump works for hours at a time without anyone looking at it. The water is pumped into a large concrete reservoir, and another pump with a large motor forces it for syringing when it is wanted. As many as twenty-five men use the hose at the same time, and there is good pressure for them all. The best part of it is that the pump is not damaged in any way should nearly all the faucets happen to be turned off at the same time. Pressure can be regulated by opening or closing the suction valve. Liquid manure can be handled as easily as clear water. Electric lights are very handy to have around, and a small electric motor with brushes to wash pots will clean them up as fast as the men can handle them. They will wash much quicker and save the brushes if the pots are allowed to soak a day or two before washing. A little caustic soda in the water will also help to clean them, but the amount used should be very small, as it will burn the hands of the men who have to handle the wet pots.

Some Practical Inquiries

Gentlemen:

I am a yearly subscriber to your paper. I wish to ask of Mr. Ruzicka, and if possible to get his answer in your next issue if I can use the ammoniated copper solution for Blackspot on Roses that have been sprayed with Fungine? The spot is not bad and is mostly on the old leaves; I use Fungine about once a week at this time of year to ward off mildew. I also wish he would give us some pointers on

THE FERN GARDEN

The present season has been very favorable to the ferns. Loving moisture and shade they have reveled in the overcast, weeping skies of the summer of 1915. To the uninitiated the number and beauty of the ferns which are absolutely hardy in any part of the United States would be a great surprise. Some of the many crested and feathered forms of the Asplenium Filex-fœmina for example are not excelled in striking beauty and diversity by any greenhouse fern in existence. For the plant lover there can be no more attractive spot than the rocky grotto where these dainty gems display their charms. They demand but little care after they have been once ensconced in congenial soil, sheltered from the sun rays and wind and provided with abundant moisture above and below. Their variety is infinite and their appeal to the artistic eye is irresistible. Some of these hardy sorts are evergreen but this is not material as they shrink from winter exposure and prefer to hug the ground under Nature's blanket of fallen leaves and snow during the inclement season.

The accompanying illustration and the one which serves as a frontispiece for this issue of HORTICULTURE are from photographs taken in the fern corner of the editor's little suburban garden in Winchester, Mass.

---

pruning the new rose Ophelia. How low may the first growths be pinched? By pinching off the flower bud and one leaf only, the next three eyes all start. Can these in their turn be pinched back to one good leaf one at a time to give a succession of blooms, or would it have been better to pinch back all strong shoots coming from low down on the plant, to one, two or three eyes from the ground while still soft? Plants are in raised benches and were planted last of June, first buds just showing color. We want plenty of cut flowers; long stems not required. An answer on these points will much oblige   J. E.

Norfolk. Ct.

The ammoniated copper solution can safely be used on the same plants that have been sprayed with Fungine, although the latter when used regularly will go a good ways to keep out blackspot. Do not apply the two at the same time, but use one one day and the other a day or so afterward. We find Ophelia a good mildew resisting rose. Regarding pinching this rose we never pinch any buds save the short breaks, after the plants have grown to a nice size. If the three eyes that break are at all strong it will be better to let them come on rather then pinch the strong shoots away down low. This is more so when you want more cut flowers and the stems so much. When all these three shoots come up on a stem, and bear a flower, more care will have to be taken in cutting, for if all

the three were to be cut so as to leave two eyes, or even one, and these were to break it would be too much for the one stem to carry. Usually the top break will bloom first and then it should be cut away down to the next break, without leaving any eyes at all. Then if the shoot is strong eyes can be left on the next two, but should the shoot be inclined to be weak it may be better to cut the second flower down near the third break and then leave two good eyes on the stem when the third rose is cut. If the flowers are not wanted when these shoots begin to show bud they can be disbudded again, but this work should be done while the buds are still very small, just barely visible. Taken with one leaf when they are very small the break will grow right on and there will be no hard joint. Should any of these break with three eyes it will be best to remove the top break with a sharp knife right down to the second shoot. This will give the other two a better chance to form good flowers. In pinching we take the buds with one good leaf. If this were not done and the bud only taken the growth that the top eye would make would have a bud before it was more then two inches long which of course is not desirable. Should these breaks be taken away down as this method would not build up the plant very much.

HORTICULTURE

VOL. XXII   **SEPTEMBER 11, 1915**   **NO. 11**

PUBLISHED WEEKLY BY

HORTICULTURE PUBLISHING CO.

147 Summer Street, Boston, Mass.

Telephone, Oxford 292.

WM. J. STEWART, Editor and Manager.

SUBSCRIPTION RATES:

One Year, in advance, $1.00; To Foreign Countries, $2.00; To Canada, $1.50.

Entered as second-class matter December 8. 1904, at the Post Office at Boston, Mass., under the Act of Congress of March 3, 1879.

CONTENTS

Resources undeveloped

The fertilizer question is recognized as one of paramount importance as it now stands, its seriousness due not only to the fact that importations from Europe are (not possible but also to our unpreparedness to supply ourselves from our own resources. Quite at variance with our reputation abroad as a nation of shrewd commercial hustlers, in the matter of agricultural fertilizers as also in that of certain bulbs and plant stock we have been contenting ourselves hitherto with working on the lines of least resistance and now we find ourselves "up against it," whereas our natural resources and commercial possibilities are abundant and ample in both instances. "Where there's a will there's a way," is a proverb which we feel applies with pertinence to the fertilizer problem as it confronts this country. American enterprise seems to lag wofully in the handling of this all-important subject.

Cleveland's way

In advertising their big flower show as "the next horticultural exhibit of national scope" the Cleveland people have hit upon a slogan which should insure an interested reading of their prospectus by all in the horticultural industry who take a more than merely local interest in trade matters. The Ohio Horticultural Society and the Cleveland Garden Club, under whose direction jointly with the Cleveland Florists' Club the show will be given, include among their 200 members practically every wealthy owner of a large private estate within a 75-mile circuit of Cleveland. Dealers and manufacturers who are looking for business from such estates will no doubt be quick to recognize the opportunity thus presented and take advantage of it. The adoption of the trade exhibition feature should have an inspiring effect and the experiment, if successful, will have the result of opening up some new angles of vision for the horticultural jobbing trade.

Progress slow but sure

Movements for great reforms as a rule are apt to advance but slowly. The campaign to suppress the roadside billboard certainly means a great reform for it strikes at a great nuisance well-entrenched and difficult to reach. But it is making progress nevertheless, and it is possible that the high tide of this infliction has now passed. We read that a certain lady has adopted a method for getting rid of these disfigurements of the scenic beauty of Lenox, Mass., where she is a summer resident, by making long contracts for the lease of the land on which billboards have been located. This is of course an expensive proposition, but it has been successful to the extent that the approaches to Lenox station have been freed from the gaudy and obtrusive advertisements which stood there, and there can be no question that the improved appearance thus acquired will make a favorite impression with the people and do much to develop and crystalize that public sentiment without which no great general movement can make much headway. On Sept. 1st a statute went into force in the state of Rhode Island forbidding billboards or advertising signs of any description on "trees, poles, fences, stones or stumps" on the public highways. Here again, while the use of private property for advertising purposes is not interfered with, yet the good example set by the state will go far to influence private interests to join in the reform which is so much to be desired.

EDWIN LONSDALE

It was HORTICULTURE's sad privilege to be the only one of the trade journals to announce the death of Edwin Lonsdale in last week's issue. As an addenda to the quite complete life record and obituary notes there presented we have the honor to place before our readers, herewith, a few testimonials from men who knew and loved Ed. Lonsdale, as a garland worthy of his memory and a heart tribute to one of Nature's noblemen.

FROM PATRICK O'MARA.

The news of Edwin Lonsdale's death came as a shock, although not unexpected. The passing away of such a man leaves deep regret with all who had the pleasure of knowing him.

His work in horticulture was of great value to the cult and it will no doubt be fully dwelt upon by those who were in close touch with him.

It is the removal from among us of such a kindly, lovable man which will cause unusual sorrow throughout the trade for there was hardly another so universally beloved for sterling qualities of mind and heart.

Successful business men come and go without leaving a deep impression; but men such as Edwin Lonsdale leave behind them a memory which inspires others to do better things. Men such as he supply that "Touch of nature which makes the world akin." He will be deeply mourned and his memory will remain fresh and green for many a year. He loved the flowers and his life was like them, giving forth brightness and cheerfulness without stint.

PATRICK O'MARA.

New York.

FROM J. OTTO THILOW.

In the career of Edwin Lonsdale, the horticultural world is impressed with the persistent conformity of one's love for his vocation. In his exit from the stage of life's activities, we are impressed with the stern reality, that life is made up of coming and going. His friends and all who knew him, keenly feel the loss of one so genial, kind and affectionate and rigidly loyal to any trust imposed upon him, conforming to the wishes of those he served.

While Providence was kind in many ways, yet sorrow fell upon him when responsibilities were heavy, but he emerged from the weight of distress, resigned entirely to conditions over which he had no control. The genial Lonsdale has left his impress never to be erased from our memory. His sterling worth won for him honors he so well deserved.

J. OTTO THILOW.

Philadelphia.

FROM SARAH A. HILL.

We have always felt very closely attached to Mr. Lonsdale, and have been deeply pained over the series of misfortunes which have befallen him. Many a time we have wondered why they were permitted in his life and in the life of his dear, good wife. His memory will be cherished for many a year by a large circle of affectionate friends.

S. A. HILL.

Richmond. Ind.

FROM WILLIAM BURNS SMITH,
Ex-Mayor of Philadelphia.

* * * * * * * * * * * * *
* 　　　EDWIN LONSDALE.　　　 *
* Born, Oct. 6, 1815.　Died, Sept. 1, 1915. *
* * * * * * * * * * * * *

"And the stately ships go on,
　To their haven under the hill;
But O for the touch of a vanished hand
　And the sound of a voice that is still."
　　　　　　　　　—Tennyson.

Every light has its shadow and every sorrow its balm, and as we journey through life we meet occasionally people who impress themselves upon the tablets of our memory and leave a sweet and indelible impress of their personality, character and distinguished virtues.

This is the realm which Edwin Lonsdale created for himself. Here his magnetic personality and great heart filled with social qualities of good fellowship adorned him, and were reflected back in the hearts of his associates.

It was my good fortune to become acquainted with him soon after his arrival in Philadelphia, and I was at once impressed with his most excellent qualities. In organizations such as the Pennsylvania Horticultural Society, the Philadelphia Florists' Club and the Society of American Florists, abounding in men of cultured taste and sweet simplicity, it required more than ordinary capacity to make its mark, but here he was in his proper element. Dignified, humorous, logical and amiable he was the boon companion of all, and his personality, like the perfume of the roses he grew, was over all. Such men are worth much to the world and their departure leaves a void which cannot be effaced by the tears of affection or the most sincere love of our sorrowing hearts either expressed in words or by memoriam.

Adieu to the noble hearted, generous, social friend and companion, who made us all happy as he in his own inimitable way and led us into that old refrain—sweet with the memories of his dear personality, when we recall how he would re-commence after each assumed interruption, his good old song—

"Oh! The brave old Duke of York," &c.

The echo of his manly voice will steal in unbidden through the long years which will be consecrated to his memory and let us join with the poet Longfellow, when he says—

"The friends who leave us do not feel the
　　　sorrow
Of parting, as we feel it, who must stay
　Lamenting day by day.
And knowing when we wake upon the
　　　morrow,
We shall not find in its accustomed
　　　place
The one beloved face."

Farewell! Old friend, your memory is a sweet heritage.

WILLIAM BURNS SMITH.

"Sunset," Laurel Springs. N. J.

FROM PATRICK WELCH.

I am grieved to learn of the death of Edwin Lonsdale. While visiting in Los Angeles, Aug. 24, it was my intention to call on him but I was informed that he could not be seen. When I returned to Boston, Sept. 2, I learned of his death.

Edwin Lonsdale was a splendid type of a man and did much to advance horticultural interests in this country. He was a gentleman who had many excellent qualities—always a good natured, jolly, pleasant companion whose personality earned for him a host of friends who I am sure deeply regret his loss. I wish to express my sympathy for those whom he held dear.

PATRICK WELCH.

Boston.

FROM W. A. MANDA.

The body of the noblest of horticulturists is gone; no more the bright, smiling face to behold nor the wise and learned words to listen to, yet the never-fading memory will be with us all who had the fortune to know personally this man. Yes, man, every inch of him, a gentleman without a peer, horticulturist in all the different branches, of the highest standard, surpassed by none, deserving the first niche in the Hall of Fame of our profession. Modest to a fault, most unselfish, either privately or in business, devoting his whole life to his family and the profession he so loved, nobler in character and deeds than the Duke of York, with whose song he used to delight us on festive occasions, the best tribute we can offer is to follow his example and thus raise the standard of manhood and horticulture.

W. A. MANDA.

South Orange, N. J.

FROM GEORGE C. WATSON.

Good old Ned! He was a prince of good fellows. We ne'er shall see his like again. But Edwin Lonsdale was far more than a prince of good fellows —full of wit and geniality and human kindness! He was also an inspiration for every one he came in contact with. The most unselfish and tireless worker for the uplift I have ever known. He was always a leader in everything aiming to advance horticulture. He had initiative and enthusiasm and carried us all by storm. It was not only what he did himself; but what he made others do—a vastly more important thing. When I came to Philadelphia from Boston twenty-seven years ago Edwin Lonsdale was one of the first warm friends I made, and I am proud to say we remained so to the end. We worked together, played together, fought together during all these years and I feel today that I have lost a tried, true, trusted and loving comrade. Blessings on his memory. He made some noise in his day and generation, and the beauty of it is, it was all for the benefit of mankind.   GEORGE C. WATSON.

FROM ROBERT CRAIG.

Edwin Lonsdale will be remembered as one who had a great fund of information in all lines of horticulture, which he was always ready cheerfully to impart to ready listeners. He delighted to instruct young gardeners in the intricate processes of how to hybridize and to graft in the different methods with the best stocks for the various subjects. He had a hobby for importing, as soon as offered, any new plant that had promise of merit, so that his place at Chestnut Hill was always of interest to those who wished to see the latest introductions. As a man he had more good qualities than any one I ever knew. He was honorable, unselfish and always cheerful, although he had, in late years, to drink deeply of the cup of sorrow. He left for his friends a rich legacy of pleasant memories.

Philadelphia.   ROBT. CRAIG.

FROM JOHN WESTCOTT.

It is with deep sorrow that I write these few lines in memoriam, I and others having lost by death our dear old friend and companion, Ned Lonsdale. It was my privilege and pleasure to have known him for a great many years, not only in a business way, but socially. He was honest and true, and with his happy smile and sunny disposition it was always a real pleasure to meet him. He helped to brighten many a corner where he was, and the sincere and fervent prayer of one of his old chums is that he and the ones that he loved may find and occupy a bright and happy corner in Heaven.

Philadelphia.   JOHN WESTCOTT.

Obituary

George F. Thomas.

Salem, Mass., Sept. 7.—George F. Thomas, aged 75, was found lifeless in bed at his home, 23 Southwick street, today. He was a gardener. Three daughters and three sons survive him.

Thomas Alfred Hewitt Rivers.

British horticulture has lately lost one of its best known men in the death of T. A. H. Rivers, of the firm of Rivers & Son, nurserymen, Sawbridgeworth, Herts. Deceased, who was in his 52nd year, was the eldest son of the late Thos. Francis Rivers. In 1886 he went to Colorado, U. S. A., where he spent eight years in ranching and mining. In 1894 he returned to Sawbridgeworth and took an active part in the business. Mr. Rivers skillfully followed in the footsteps of his father and grandfather, who had done so much to forward the British fruit growing industry in the raising of new varieties. He was a member of the Management Committee of the Horticultural Club, and had acted as a steward at the festival of the Gardeners' Royal Benevolent Institution, besides usefully filling a number of public offices in his own particular district.—W. H. A.

ROCHESTER FLOWER SHOW

The Flower Show which is being held in Rochester in connection with the Rochester Industrial Exposition is making an excellent record.

Building No. 5 where the Floricultural Exhibit is held, lends itself particularly well to artistic treatment. The building is 100 ft. in width and a clear span, the roof being supported by an arched trussing and the center portion of the roof itself is glass. The trussing is most artistically decorated with smilax and large quantities have been used in this decoration. Suspended from each truss are great baskets covered with smilax and artificial wisteria. The side walls are masses of smilax and at each column are grouped a profusion of arborvitae. For the background the color scheme is beautiful as the difference in the two tones of green gives a very artistic effect.

As visitors enter the building from the main entrance, they are confronted with a beautiful display by the Rochester Park Board. It is of pyramid effect built up with palms, bedding plants, with a border of begonias, ferns and sod and the effect is most pleasing. Immediately to the right and at the end of the hall is a display by Schlegel & Sons who have a miniature pool well grouped with foliage, plants and palms. Farther along a very large and elaborate exhibit is made by James Vicks' Sons. Artistically grouped here are gladioli in beds, cannas in beds, dahlias, asters, perennial plants, annuals, flowering bulbs, etc. This exhibit has a riot of color and presents a splendid effect.

On the left are the exhibits of John House and Frank Lavigne, showing foliage and flowering plants. Next to them is the display of Jacob Thomann & Sons. Their exhibit of gladioli and particularly the "Rochester White" for which they took a silver cup from Cleveland, is a work of art. A bed of "Rochester White" circular in shape, is the foremost and center feature. George Boucher has an excellent exhibit of palms, foliage plants, ferns, etc., grouped in pyramid form with baskets of blooms to lend a touch of color. Next comes H. B. Wilson with foliage plants, palms, etc., massed. They are showing design work each day representing the different classes of this type of work which they do. Their floral horseshoe at the opening of the horse show elicited much pleasing comment. All the foregoing exhibitors are of Rochester.

Immediately in the center of the horticultural exhibit is an immense fountain filled with aquatic plants, by H. A. Dreer of Philadelphia. This exhibit is the center of attraction, as the basin is some 30 ft. in width, built up with rocks and richly colored foliage plants, from the center of which the fountain flows. The adjoining exhibit is also H. A. Dreer's and is composed entirely of decorative plants, palms, pandanus, dracaenas, ferns and crotons, with a profusion of cibotiums.

R. & J. Farquhar & Co. of Boston occupy most of the space in the center

dividing the flower exhibit from the fruit and vegetable section. They show paintings of their new Lilium myriophyllum. Their exhibit of scotch heather is attracting quite a little attention. A. N. Pierson of Cromwell, Conn. is showing cut roses, ferns, etc.

A most pleasing display of J. B. Keller & Sons, Rochester, consists of palms, decorative plants, roses in baskets, etc., the center feature being a table with a miniature fountain in the center and small favor decorations, etc. The Burt Olney Greenhouses, Albion, N. Y., show two massive beds of geraniums and numerous vases of roses. Their display is a demonstration of what can be done in the rose line in the lake country.

Next to J. B. Keller & Sons come the exhibits of George B. Hart of Rochester and Ed. Brockman of Irondequoit, Mr. Hart showing flowering plants, decorative stuff, cut flowers, etc., a beautiful display. Mr. Brockman is showing geraniums and various flowering plants which form a tastefully gotten up color scheme.

The Sunnyside Dahlia Farms show some of their new dahlias. Salter Bros., Rochester, make unique displays of baskets, together with cut flowers, small ferns, palms, etc. The Crescent Seed Farms show some splendid asters, and John Lewis Childs has a good display of plants, decorative material, etc. C. Kuer & Son make a display of bulbs, etc., with Thomas Cogger in charge. F. R. Pierson has, as usual, a fine exhibit of ferns, plants, etc.

Table decorations are being arranged each day by the various local florists, during the entire time of the Exposition.

The attendance at the Exposition has been very large and one can hear pleasing comments for the two big departments, the Horse Show and the Flower Show.

TEXAS STATE FLOWER SHOW.

Committees for the Texas State Flower Show, to be held in Houston, Tex., from November 17 to 20th, 1915, inclusive, have been appointed as follows:

R. C. Kerr, general chairman; A. L. Perrin, secretary; F. M. Carroll, treasurer.
Trade Display—W. J. Baker, Ft. Worth, chairman; H. O. Hannah, Sherman; Chas. Aff, Jr., Austin.
Exhibition and Hall—C. L. Brock, Houston, chairman; A. F. Koehle, Sherman; Bird Forrest, Waxahachie; E. E. Stone, Dickinson.
Premiums and Judges — Tom Wolf, Waco, chairman; Ed. Hall, Austin; J. E. McAdam, Ft. Worth.
Admission — F. M. Carroll, Houston, chairman; A. L. Perrin, Houston; C. H. Blecker, Houston.
Publicity — S. J. Mitchell, Houston, chairman; L. J. Tackett, Ft. Worth; Louis Oesch, Dallas.
Amateur Exhibits—R. G. Hewitt, Houston, chairman; W. T. Hauser, Houston; H. Dirken, Houston.
Entertainment — H. H. Kuhlmann, Sr., Houston, chairman, and all members of the Houston Florists' Club.
Decorations — H. H. Kuhlmann, Jr., chairman; John J. Boyle, Houston; Mrs. M. A. Hansen, Galveston; Mrs. F. L. Cotney.

The premium list and other data will follow shortly.

BRITISH HORTICUTURE.

New Carnations.

The following varieties have lately been registered by the Perpetual Flowering Carnation Society:

Chelsea—white penciled pink. King Albert—deep satin pink. Louvain—rosy salmon; by A. F. Dutton, Iver, Bucks.

Flaming June—sport from Mikado, geranium cerise. Golden Flag—yellow. Shepherdess—salmon. Souvenir — pale rose salmon; by Young & Co., Cheltenham, Gloster.

General Joffre—scarlet sport from Lady Northcliffe; by G. Clarke, Leighton Buzzard, Bucks.

King of the Belgians—deep crimson. Lord Kitchener—purple, striped crimson; by E. H. Coleman, Bognor, Sussex.

Mrs. A. L. Cross—sport from R. F. Felton; pink, flaked deeper pink by W. J. Douce, Rugby, Warwichshire.

Mrs. W. L. Aimslie—salmon pink by W. Hemus, Hanworth.

Peace—white sport from Lady Meyer by Newport Nurseries, Essex.

National Gladiolus Society.

This Society held its summer show in London, on August 4. The number of exhibits was smaller than usual, owing to the absence of entries from the Dutch and French growers. New varieties from the Society's trial ground were brought before the Committee, and the following received an award of merit:—

Vanessa, Nonpareil, Picotee, Mrs. Swainson, Princess Patricia, and Mrs. Robert Wordsworth, raised by Kelway and Sons, Langport, Somerset. Wil-helm Steinhausen, Erica von Barczay, raised by W. Pfitzer. White Giant, raised by Van Meerbeck and Co. Red Emperor, raised by K. Vethuys.

EDWIN JENKINS AND HIS SWEET PEAS

Royal Botanic Society's Affairs.

At the annual meeting of the Royal Botanic Society, some of the speakers contended that it was inadvisable that dog shows, for which the Society's grounds at Regent's Park were made use of, should be allowed to overshadow the main purport of the organization, which was to advance the cult of flora and not the canine race. The treasurer stated that the moment the Society's financial position was secure the Council would agree to get rid of the dog shows, and would revert to flower shows.

W. H. ADSETT.

EDWIN JENKINS AND HIS SWEET PEAS.

The recent exhibits of sweet peas at Boston and Newport by Edwin Jenkins of Lenox, Mass., were indeed the triumph of much care and attention to detail in cultivation. The photograph shows how Mr. Jenkins' sweet peas respond to the liberal treatment he gives them. The vines were grown to single stems and reached a height of eight to ten feet, with vigorous dark green foliage and flowers of magnificent size and depth of color.

The results accomplished bear out the principle that if a thing is worth growing it is worth growing well and anyone looking over this lot of plants could but gather inspiration to improve his own methods of culture and not feel satisfied until he had at least tried his best to attain such perfection as exemplified by the plants and flowers in the accompanying picture.

CHRIS SCHWAB, JR.

CLUBS AND SOCIETIES

PARK SUPERINTENDENTS' CONVENTION.

The seventeenth annual convention of the American Association of Park Superintendents was held in San Francisco Aug. 18-20. sessions being held in the new Municipal Auditorium.

About sixty park executives from forty cities of the United States and Canada were present and with ladies and visitors made up an attendance of over one hundred. The convention program provided one day of papers and discussions and two days of inspection tours of the recreation features at San Francisco, Oakland and Berkeley, as well as the landscape features of the Panama-Pacific Exposition and a number of private estates adjacent to San Francisco. Practically the entire convention party toured the Pacific Coast inspecting recreation features at Spokane, Seattle, Tacoma, Portland, Los Angeles and San Diego, including the Panama-California Exposition.

New Orleans was selected as the city in which the 1916 convention will be held, the time to be decided by the executive committee, but October as the month tentatively agreed upon.

The following officers were elected for the ensuing year: President, Emil T. Mische, Portland, Oregon; vice-presidents, J. W. Thompson, Seattle, Wash., John T. Walsh, New York City, Alexander Stuart, Ottawa, Canada, Emmett P. Griffin, East St. Louis, Ill., Eugene V. Goebel, Grand Rapids, Mich., L. P. Jensen, St. Louis, Mo.; secretary-treasurer, Roland Cotterill. Seattle.

Twenty-four new members were admitted to membership. The by-laws were amended to require five years' practical experience as a qualification for active membership and the admission fee was raised to $10.

R. W. COTTERILL, Sec'y.

GARDENERS' AND FLORISTS' CLUB OF BOSTON.

The club, on invitation of the Breck-Robinson Co., will hold a field day at their nurseries in Lexington, on Saturday, September 11, 1915. Transportation will be furnished to all who can take the train leaving the North Union Station at 1.51 P. M. Those who may prefer to go via electrics should take a Cambridge tunnel train at Washington or Park streets, transferring at Harvard Square to cars marked Lowell, Arlington Heights, or Lexington, all of which pass the nurseries.

We hope we may have a large attendance at this field day. Nurseries are specially attractive in September, and the weather is invariably comfortable. Ladies are always welcome on these occasions.

Club meetings will be resumed on September 21. A varied and attractive programme has been arranged for this meeting. Circulars will be forwarded in a few days.

W. N. CRAIG, Sec'y.
H. H. BARTSCH, Pres.

NEW HAVEN COUNTY HORTICULTURAL SOCIETY.

The New Haven County Horticultural Society, with headquarters in New Haven, Conn., is one of the best known societies of its kind in the Eastern states. It is an organization that had its inception over eighty-six years ago. In 1832 it was incorporated by the Connecticut Legislature and for over three-quarters of a century has held a commanding position in the horticultural field. Throughout its history it has been officered by some of the best men in the commercial life of New Haven—men who today subscribe liberally for the society's support.

The New Haven County Horticultural Society gives many exhibitions during the summer months, but the annual exhibition is held this year on September 16th and 17th. These annual exhibitions have become famous for showing the largest and best displays of dahlias, gladioli, etc., in this section of the country. Last season over four thousand specimens were shown. The society is planning for a still larger exhibition this fall and at the present time it looks as if its plans will mature successfully. In the schedule of prizes just issued is the society's "New Classification of Dahlias." Interested persons can obtain a copy by addressing W. C. McIntosh, secretary, 925 Howard avenue, New Haven, Conn.

The list of prizes is complete. Section A, for professionals only, has eleven classes for dahlias, one for cosmos and one for gladioli. Section B, for amateurs only, has five classes for dahlias, three for dahlias, one for asters and two for gladioli. Section C, open to all, has twenty-one classes—all dahlias. Section D, open to all, has four classes for asters. Section E, open to all, consists of special prizes and has eight classes, principally dahlias and gladioli. Section F, open to all except where noted, has twenty-nine classes for fruits and vegetables. Section G, open to all, has four classes for bees.

Among the contributors to the prizes are Peter Henderson & Co., Stumpp & Walter Co., Pierson U-Bar Co., and J. M. Thorburn & Co. of New York City; Carter's Tested Seeds, Inc., and R. & T. Farquhar & Co. of Boston, Mass.; Henry F. Michell Co., W. Atlee Burpee & Co. and Henry A. Dreer of Philadelphia, Pa.; Hitchings & Co. of Elizabeth, N. J., and Bobbink & Atkins of Rutherford, N. J.; S. D. Woodruff & Sons of Orange, Conn.; W. W. Wilmore of Denver, Col., and Elm City Nursery Co. of New Haven, Conn. Lord & Burnham Co. of New York City contribute a gold medal which is presented to the member of the society making the highest number of points at the bi-weekly exhibits throughout the year.

FLORISTS' CLUB OF PHILADELPHIA.

The regular monthly meeting was held in the club room, Horticultural Hall, on Tuesday evening, and in spite of the warm humid night there was a very good attendance, the attraction being an informal talk by Robert Pyle of the Conard & Jones Company, West Grove, Pa., upon his observations along horticultural lines on the Pacific Coast while visiting the two expositions. Mr. Pyle entertained the club for one hour, giving a good account of the planting, and of all the chief things that were used for producing effect at the two expositions. He stated that the month of August was really the worst month of the whole year to go to California, as anything not under irrigation was dried up and brown, it being practically their winter season. He stated that some wonderful results were attained in the plantings of the past three and four years. He dwelt at some length upon the color scheme which was carried out with such telling effect at San Francisco, even the uniform of the guards being made to accord with the color scheme of buildings, and the black asphalt walks were covered with red sand in order to harmonize. The planting in the different courts was all made to harmonize with the surroundings. Yellow narcissi were followed by yellow tulips and these were followed by yellow iris; in another court rhododendrons were followed with hydrangea, in another court peonies were followed by gladioli, all in proper colors to harmonize with the buildings surrounding them. To an eastern man many things were a disappointment; for instance, cannas that make such a splendid showing in the East, although they make good growth on the Pacific Coast, suffer from the strong winds that blow all the flowers to pieces. The speaker seemed to be most impressed during his twenty-five days' travel with the flora and scenery of the Canadian Rockies, through which he passed on his return, and stated that anyone going to the far West should make his trip so as to pass through these regions either in going or coming back, and should stop off and spend a day at Lake Louise and another at Banff.

This being nomination night of the club, all the present officers were renominated. George Burton, president: John C. Gracey, vice-president; George Craig, treasurer, and David Rust, secretary.

The secretary announced with much feeling the death of Edwin Lonsdale, and stated that at the request of the president of the club he had prepared suitable resolutions as follows:

"In the death of Edwin Lonsdale the Florists' Club has lost another of its original landmarks. He was a charter member, and the first secretary of the club. He served as secretary in 1886 and 1887, and again from October, 1898 to May 1907. He was president in 1894, 1895, being the second president

of the club, the first president of the club having held office for eight years. He was at all times deeply interested in all the affairs of the club, and when not holding office was always on important committees. His work was greatly appreciated and he was held in such high esteem by our members that when he decided to go to California, a testimonial banquet was given him on October 28th, 1909. This was attended by eighty-three of our members together with three prominent florists of New York and three from Boston. This banquet was the most successful ever given by the club, and we know that it was greatly appreciated by Edwin Lonsdale, and he went forth to his new work with bright hopes for the future, and now we are brought face to face with the fact that he has been taken away from us by death, therefore, be it

RESOLVED, That the members of the Club desire to put on record their sense of loss and to extend to his widow their sympathy.

Edwin Lonsdale was a diligent and faithful worker for the interests of the Club. In his intercourse with members of the Club, he was always courteous, kind and modest, and thus endeared himself to us all. He did much to advance the interests of Horticulture, and was always ready to help along anything that would benefit our cause.

RESOLVED. That these resolutions be spread on the minutes and a copy sent to Mrs. Lonsdale."

The reading of these resolutions was listened to with marked attention and they were at once approved by the club.

The outlook for the meetings for the coming season is a very bright one. There will be a very prominent lecture at the October meeting, a ladies' night and entertainment in November, together with interesting matters pertaining to the National Flower Show at every meeting.

Both Robert Craig and Adolph Farenwald gave a detailed account of what was being done for the National Flower Show. A contract for heating the building has been let, the advertising campaign is well on its way, and the city authorities are now working in harmony with the flower show committees, and everything looks promising for a successful exhibition.

DAVID RUST, Sec'y.

ST. LOUIS COUNTY GROWERS' ASSOCIATION.

The County Growers' Association held a very pleasant meeting on Wednesday night, Sept. 1, at the Eleven Mile House. They had extended an invitation to the five wholesale houses to send representatives for a conference, and Messrs. Berning, Kuehn, Smith, Windler and Anger muller were present. It was mutually agreed that the wholesalers are to keep open daily and remain closed on Sunday for the coming season.

CLUB AND SOCIETY NOTES.

The Cincinnati Florists' Society will hold its regular meeting next Monday evening.

The Montreal Horticultural Society and Fruit Growers' Association of the Province of Quebec, held its annual exhibition in the Winter Club rink, on Wednesday and Thursday, September 8 and 9. The mayor officially opened the exhibition on Wednesday evening. The exhibits included plants, and vases of cut flowers, fruits and vegetables, a large number of prizes being offered both to professional gardeners and amateurs.

PERSONAL.

Mrs. Charles Millang and daughter are at Bethlehem, N. H., until about October 10.

Richard Brett has been obliged to resign his position at Islip, N. Y. His address is now 275 Sheppard Ave., East Orange, N. J.

Marriage intentions have been filed by Harold J. Gladd, a florist of Rye, N. Y., and Miss Jane E. Crosby, a trained nurse of New York city.

NEWS NOTES.

Hackettstown, N. J.—Alonzo D. Herrick and Arthur L. Ross, the latter formerly with Siebrecht & Sons, have leased the Center Street Greenhouses.

Peoria, Ill.—At a meeting of the executive board of the Illinois Florists' Association, Moline was named as the next annual meeting place of the Association.

SEED TRADE

The Bean Crop.

Since issuing our last crop news,
later information fully confirms the
rather pessimistic information we
gave out at that time regarding the
bean crop, as frost has aided in the destruction of what remained of the
crop. So serious is the situation as reported by several growers, that already a number of wax-pod varieties
are classed as crop failures, and some
of the green-pods as nearly so. Fortunately there is some mitigation of this
situation, in the fact that the demand
for seed beans from truck farmers and
market gardeners, particularly in the
south, promises to be much lighter
than usual. This is due in great measure to the light demand for green
beans the past summer, and the very
low prices secured. As a consequence hundreds of acres were allowed
to ripen, and of course the seed will be
saved. This condition has seemed so
serious to many southern seed merchants that they have made application to their growers for permission to
cancel a large part of their contracts
for beans. Such requests have been
granted with alacrity, as the growers
realize that under the most favorable
conditions that can possibly be expected their deliveries will be very unsatisfactory. It is hardly necessary to say
that the dealers who are thus seeking
to escape from their contracts are not
well informed on crop conditions, as
every bushel of seed beans will be
worth double the normal price. As a
further evidence of the bad conditions
of the bean crop, we are informed that
hundreds of acres are being plowed up

in Michigan, and winter wheat planted
instead. A considerable acreage of
beans were planted in Wisconsin the
past season, but we are advised that
while better than the average in Michigan, the crop is very poor both in yield
and samples. It may be well to say
here that average samples of this
year's crops are likely to be much inferior to last, owing to last year's
shortage being due to drought, while
this year's is due to excessive rain, developing anthracnose to an alarming
extent. To this disease, coupled with
a lack of humus in the soil, is due the
failure of the bean crop quite as much
as to weather conditions. The growers are said to be making every possible effort to overcome these conditions.

Notes.

The value of horticultural imports
at the port of New York for the week
ending August 28 is given as follows:
Fertilizer, $171; clover seed, $4388;
grass seed, $3820; trees, bulbs and
plants, $65,886.

Corn has made good progress during
the past two weeks, and it seems that
the light frosts which have visited
many sections of the middle west, did
little if any damage and the outlook is
much more encouraging. Vine seeds
are also promising much better.

W. B. Van Eyk, for nine years U. S.
representative for G. W. Van Gelderen,
Boskoop, Holland, has gone in as a
partner and the house will now be
known as Van Gelderen & Co. The
new firm will take charge of all the
assets and liabilities of the old house.

The Jerome B. Rice Seed Co. inform
us that they are developing seed stock
free of anthracnose but it is a slow
process, and requires much painstaking care to accomplish the desired results. However, they are much encouraged by conditions already attained and intend to continue until
completely successful. We assume
other growers are working along the
same lines, but none of them have told

us how they are going to put humus
in the soil. May be they know; we
hope so.

NEW CORPORATIONS.

Terre Haute, Ind.—Hoermann Seed
Store, capital stock, $5,000. Incorpor-
ators, Frank Hoermann, L. J. Quinlan
and M. E. Hoermann.

Council Bluffs, Ia.—Shugart-Ouren
Seed Co., capital stock increased from
$50,000 to $100,000. C. G. Ouren, president, J. P. Davis, secretary.

Buffalo, N. Y.—Kenmore Floral Co.,
capital stock, $10,000. Incorporators,
Wm. G. Tyler, C. W. Donoghue and W.
Smith.

The Agricultural and Mechanical
College of Texas has provided a corres-
poundence course in Agricultural Jour-
nalism, 10 lessons, by S. G. Rubinow.
The aim of this course will be to prepare students for writing articles for
agricultural journals and magazines.
Emphasis will be placed upon style
and make up of articles, "leads," appropriate subjects, seasonal material,
etc. The character of the leading agricultural papers and journals will be
discussed with particular reference to
the kind of material they desire. Students will be expected to prepare articles of various kinds and will be constantly referred to concrete examples
in various publications.

I want to congratulate you on the
continued improvement of Horticulture. It is first class in its high-class
contributions and other "number one"
qualities. Very truly yours,
      A. E. KUNDERD.

Goshen, Indiana.

CHICAGO Send Your Orders to WILLIAM J. SMYTH

Member Florists' Telegraph Delivery Association

Michigan Ave. at 31st Street

Prompt Auto Delivery Service

THOS. F. GALVIN

INC.

NEW YORK 561 Fifth Ave. Vanderbilt Hotel

BOSTON 1 Park Street 799 Boylston Street

Deliveries to Steamers and all Eastern Points

CLEVELAND

A. GRAHAM & SON

5523 Euclid Ave.

Will take good care of your orders

Members of F. T. D. Association.

WASHINGTON

915 F ST. N. W.

F. H. KRAMER

Auto delivery of Designs and Flowers to any address in Washington.

Stock and Work First Class

ALBANY, N. Y.

EYRES

Flowers or Design Work

DELIVERED IN ALBANY AND VICINITY ON TELEGRAPHIC ORDER

11 NORTH PEARL STREET, ALBANY, N. Y.

ST. LOUIS, MO.

FRED C. WEBER

4326-28 Olive St.

Member Florists Telegraph Delivery Association
NOTICE INITIALS. We have one store only

THE J. M. GASSER COMPANY,

CLEVELAND

Euclid Avenue

Kerr

ORDERS FOR TEXAS

The Florist HOUSTON, TEXAS

Member F. T. D. Association.

The Far-Famed Flowers of

TORONTO

Delivered on mail or telegraph order for any occasion, in any part of the Dominion.

JOHN H. DUNLOP

94 Yonge St., - - TORONTO, ONT.

Flowers by Telegraph

Leading Retail Florists Listed by Towns for Ready Reference. Orders transferred by telegram or otherwise to any of the firms whose address is here given will be promptly and properly filled and delivered.

Albany, N. Y.—H. G. Eyres, 11 N. Pearl St.
Albany, N. Y.—The Rosery, 23 Steuben St.
Albany, N. Y.—William C. Gloeckner, 97 State St.
Boston—Thos. F. Galvin, 1 Park St.
Boston—Penn, the Florist, 37-43 Bromfield St.
Buffalo, N. Y.—S. A. Anderson, 440 Main St.
Buffalo, N. Y.—Palmer's, 304 Main St.
Chicago—William J. Smyth, Michigan Ave. and 31st St.
Cleveland, O.—J. M. Gasser Co., Euclid Ave.
Cleveland, O.—Adam Graham & Sons, 5523 Euclid Ave.
Denver, Col.—Park Floral Co., 1643 Broadway.
Detroit, Mich.—J. Breitmeyer's Sons, corner Broadway and Gratiot Ave.
Houston, Tex.—Kerr, The Florist.
Kansas City, Mo.—Samuel Murray, 1017 Grand Ave.
New London, Conn.—Reuter's.
Newport, R. I.—Gibson Bros., Bellevue Ave.
New York—David Clarke's Sons, 2139-2141 Broadway.
New York—Alex. McConnell, 611 5th Ave.
New York—Young & Nugent, 42 W. 28th.
New York—Dards, N. E. corner 44th St. and Madison Ave.
New York—Max Schling, 22 W. 59th St.
New York—G. E. M. Stumpp, 761 Fifth Ave.
New York—Thos. F. Galvin, Fifth Ave., at 46th St.
New York—Myer, 609-611 Madison Ave.
New York—A. T. Bunyard, 413 Madison Ave.
New York—National Floral Corporation, 220 Broadway.
Norwich, Conn.—Reuter's.
Omaha, Neb.—Hess & Swoboda, 1415 Farnum St.
Rochester, N. Y.—J. B. Keller Sons, 25 Clinton Ave., N.
St. Louis, Mo.—Fred C. Weber, 4326-28 Olive St.
St. Paul, Minn.—Holm & Olson, Inc.
Tarrytown-on-Hudson, N. Y.—F. R. Pierson Co.
Toronto, Can.—J. H. Dunlop, 96 Yonge St.
Washington, D. C.—Gude Bros., 1214 F St.
Washington, D. C.—F. H. Kramer, 915 F St., N. W.
Westerly, R. I.—Reuter's.
Worcester, Mass.—Randall's Flower Shop, 3 Pleasant St.

A F. T. D. WINDOW.

W. C. Gloeckner has sent us an interesting picture of what he describes as the most talked-of window in Albany, N. Y. It demonstrates the activities of the F. T. D. florists very impressively and had so strong a pull on the public that Mr. Gloeckner says he booked an average of three orders a day while this window display was on.

"The Telegraph Florist"

Member of Florists' Telegraph Delivery

37-43 Bromfield St., Boston, Mass.

REUTER'S

Members Florists Telegraph Delivery

STORES IN

New London and Norwich, Conn. and Westerly, R. I.

We cover the territory between

New Haven and Providence

Orders for New York. Write or Phone to:

MAX SCHLING

22 West 59th Street, - Adjoining Plaza Hotel

Best Florists in the States as References.
EUROPEAN ORDERS EXECUTED.
Members of the Florists' Telegraph Association.

HESS & SWOBODA

FLORISTS

Telephones 1501 and L 1582

1415 Farnum St.,

OMAHA, NEB.

NEW FLOWER STORES.

Minot, N. D.—George Valker.
Bemus Point, N. Y.—A. D. Heath.
Boston, Mass.—Max Fishelson, Winter street.
Springfield, O.—L. Bradford, 106 E. High street.
Meriden, Ct.—E. B. Gallivan, 170 Pratt street.
Dayton, O.—E. E. Schaffer, 5th and Main streets.
Aberdeen, S. D.—B. F. Siebrecht, 305 S. Main street.
Shelburne Fall, Mass.—P. R. Burtt, Fife greenhouses.
West Bend, Wis.—Mrs. Fred Kesting, Regner block.
Little Rock, Ark.—Paul M. Palez, removing to 604 Main street.
Arlington Centre, Mass.—John McKenzie, Whittemore Block.
Dallas, Tex.—Ernest Rische and Charles Choller, Elm street.
Omaha, Neb.—Lewis Henderson, removing to Fontenelle Hotel building.
Bridgeton, N. J.—Adolph Hespelt, South Laurel street, succeeding Mrs. Jennie Ingles.
Chicago, Ill.—R. L. & D. Nelson, 1528 Hyde Park Blvd.; Joseph Papacek, 3222 S. Market street.

NEWS ITEMS FROM EVERYWHERE

SAN FRANCISCO.

Mr. Kuentzel is preparing to open a new florist shop at 1462 Sutter street.

W. S. Marshall, president of the Marshall Nursery Co., Fresno, Cal., has just returned after an extended visit in the east. He was gone about three months, most of which he spent in New York.

At the Chas. Navlet stand at the rear of the ground floor of the Emporium, an early opening of the bulb season is reported. The tourist trade is being catered to especially and with very good returns. A large shipment of Holland bulbs is expected about the middle of the month.

C. W. Ward of Eureka, Cal., is preparing to extend the Cottage Garden Nurseries at Humboldt and C strets, which he operates, having purchased the remainder of the Eden tract adjoining his property. He has already completed plans for two more greenhouses to be erected shortly on the newly acquired property.

The party of florists and nurserymen who went up into Humboldt County as the guests of Chas. W. Ward, following the convention. returned the first of the week after a most enjoyable outing. Daniel MacRorie, H. Plath and Frank Pelicano, who made the trip, have apparently all turned ardent admirers of the northern part of the state. Mr. Pelicano says he had no idea there was such scenery in this part of the country. Going up they spent two days at Eureka, Mr. Ward making sure that they saw all the principal points of interest near the city before they left on the 100-mile automobile trip up the coast, which culminated in a 30-mile ride up the Klamath River in canoes paddled by Indians. They camped at the mouth of Ah-Pah creek for a week, there being sixteen in the party which left Eureka.

WASHINGTON, D. C.

Edward Bowers, who has been employed at the store of the S. S. Pennock-Meehan Company practically since it was opened here, has resigned, it is said, to accept employment with the Hammond Company, Inc., Richmond, Va.

William J. Boas & Co., Philadelphia, have brought suit against Z. D. Blackistone for flower boxes sold to the latter during the period from January 25 to July 16, inclusive, amounting to $622.46, in addition to which interest is claimed.

The Interstate Commerce Commission has authorized a refund of $223.94 by the railroad companies to J. A. Morris & Son. of Los Angeles, Cal., covering an unreasonable rate charged upon dormant shrubs and plants imported and forwarded from Jersey City to Los Angeles last November. The Commission has also authorized a refund to

the Aberdeen Fruit Commission Company on account of an unreasonable rate applied to a shipment of Christmas trees from Trego, Wis.

George W. Hess has practically completed the restoration of the Bartholdi fountain in the Botanic Gardens, so that it now is as it was during the Centennial Exposition. It will be illuminated at night during the fiftieth annual encampment of the G. A. R., which commences September 27. Special flower beds are being set out around it for this occasion. W. F. Gude, who is chairman of the committee of citizens in charge of this encampment, desires that all visiting florists register at his store during their stay in the city. Mr. Hess, who was largely instrumental in the establishment of the botanical garden at Frederick, Md., which was formally opened on September 2, is having designed a handsome gold medal for use as a first prize in competition under the auspices of this garden.

ST. LOUIS.

E. A. Kalish, of Kalish Bros. Floral Co., F. C. Weber, Jr., Frank Windler, C. C. Sanders and Vincent Gorly have returned from their summer vacations.

Wiliam Gray has left the employ of the Mullanphy Florists Co. and left for Kansas City, Mo., where he has associated himself with Larkins the Florist.

M. S. Newman's store which was closed for the past two months is again open for business. Miss Newman has as yet not returned home from her summer trip to Colorado. Miss Armstrong is in charge until her return.

C. H. Thompson, botanist at the Missouri Botanical Garden for the past sixteen years, has resigned his position to become assistant professor of horticulture at Amherst, Mass. Mr. Thompson has many friends here in the trade.

William Seeger, president of the Mullanphy Florists' Company, was married on August 31 to a charming widow, Mrs. B. K. Ranford of Chattanooga, Tenn. Mr. Seeger and Mrs. Ranford had known each other only twenty-four hours.

On Saturday, Sept. 4, Superintendent of Parks E. Strehle escorted twenty-five members of the Park Superintendents' Association on their way home from San Francisco, through all the parks and show gardens and a dinner was enjoyed at Sunset Inn.

Cincinnati—Mr. and Mrs. E. G. Gillett again have as their guests Mr. and Mrs. C. J. Ohmer and Master Jim Ohmer of West Palm Beach, Fla.. who have just returned from an auto tour through Ohio.

P. J. Olinger went to Chicago, Ill., last Saturday. He and Mrs. Olinger who have been spending some time with relatives at Evanston, Ill.. will return to this city at the end of this week.

CLEVELAND.

C. E. Russell, of the Jones-Russell Co., is spending his vacation at home, superintending the rebuilding of a portion of his residence, as more room is necessary to accommodate his family, which is increasing in numbers.

The Gasser Company has now under construction a $10,000 store building at 527 Huron road on a site leased several months ago. The work is being pushed rapidly. The store will be occupied for their wholesale business and will be much more central than their old location.

F. C. W. Brown, manager of the Gasser Co., accompanied by F. C. Bartels, manager of the greenhouses of the Gasser Co., left on August 28th. taking the water trip to Toronto, where they will visit the Canadian Exposition and some of the large growers near Toronto, including the Dale estate.

Among the magnet events that will draw all live commercial and private growers and retail and wholesale florists to Cleveland, November 10 to 14, are the following: Annual Exhibition and Convention of the Chrysanthemum Society of America; Fall Exhibition and Meeting of the American Rose Society; Adjourned Meeting of the Florists Telegraph Delivery Association; Adjourned Meeting of the Gladiolus Society of Ohio.

Michael Bloy of Detroit, who was in the city from Sunday until Tuesday, was kept busy by the various members of the Cleveland Florists' Club seeing the improvements and additions that have been made to the Sixth City, since he was a resident here eight or ten years ago. On Tuesday Herb. Bate and Frank Friedley accompanied Mr. Bloy to Storrs & Harrison Co.'s plant at Painesville, and they also called upon Carl Hagenberger and Merkel Bros. at Mentor, and inspected the private estate of James Corrigan at Wickliffe. Mr. Bloy is to be one of the judges in the coming flower show.

Herbert Bate spent a few weeks down at the Lakes south of Cleveland, and is now back on the job, getting the final premium list for the big November Flower Show shaped up. A lot of fine special prizes are being received from the owners of private estates in and near Cleveland, all of which will go to make the premium list more interesting to the growers. Mr. Bate figures on not less than 500 prominent dealers and growers in attendance. The campaign for the next four weeks will be to get exhibitors that have been withholding their decision regarding taking display space for trade exhibits; telling us how much space they really want and arranging for it before it is too late for them to get the full advantage of having time enough to make plans to get the best results out of the show.

NEW YORK.

The New York Florists' Supply Company are about to move from 127 West 28th street to 103 W. 28th.

Harry A. Barnard, amiable and earnest representative for Stuart Low & Co., is at the Hotel Albert, New York City, and any communications about choice material such as that firm has been supplying to discriminating buyers in past years will receive a prompt and zealous attention if sent to that address any time during September and October.

The Elliott Auction Company have received a full quota of Dutch bulb consignments and will offer them in handy lots at auction at their rooms, 42 Vesey street, on Tuesday, September 14. To make this sale particularly interesting a fine collection of palms, ferns, dracaenas and other foliage plants by local growers of repute will be offered at the same time.

In the official report of the Panama-Pacific Exposition, New York State wins the bulk of awards. The landscape treatment surrounding the New York State Building was awarded a gold medal, the only prize given for landscape treatment in the entire Exposition. This work was done by Siebrecht & Son, of the Rose Hill Nurseries, and all the stock for the landscape work was shipped from this city last December. The plans were made by Henry A. Siebrecht, Jr., and the work was executed by Henry A. Siebrecht, Sr., who was four and a half months in California.

PHILADELPHIA

George Anderson continues to improve a little and the family are now a bit more hopeful in their reports.

The last rites over Edwin Lonsdale were held on Wednesday, Sept. 8th, from the residence of his brother-in-law, John Burton, at Chestnut Hill, and were largely attended by representatives from all branches of the trade as well as many personal friends. Interment was in the Lonsdale family lot at Ivy Hill Cemetery.

AMERICAN DAHLIA SOCIETY.
New York Show Promises to Be a Great Success.

A tremendous amount of enthusiasm is being shown in every section of the country in The American Dahlia Society, which was formed in New York City in May by Ex-President Vincent of the Society of American Florists and other dahlia lovers. It is the pleasure of the secretary to advise that over a hundred dahlia lovers have joined as charter members, and that there is every prospect of this number being increased to 250 before the annual meeting.

The annual meeting will be held during the first show of the organization on September 24th, 25th and 26th, at the Museum of Natural History in New York City. Here will be held what is expected to be the largest and grandest dahlia show ever held in the United States. Expectations are that over $300 will be offered for competition at this show. Copies of the preliminary schedule have been issued, and may be obtained by writing to either George V. Nash, secretary of the Horticultural Society of New York, Bronx Park, or Joseph J. Lane, secretary, The American Dahlia Society, 11 West 32nd street, New York City. John Young, secretary of the Society of American Florists will take charge of the Exhibition.

Among other things which are being done to promote interest in this show and make it a success, may be mentioned the fact that the executive board at its last meeting, authorized the secretary to prepare 2500 double post cards, to be sent out through the co-operation of dahlia dealers in various parts of the country to the best customers of the dahlia. These 2500 cards have already been mailed, and great returns are looked forward to. This card is an urgent appeal to the dahlia lover to join The American Dahlia Society, now in its infancy, and so get charter membership. All joining before September 24th become charter members. The dues are $1

for initiation, $2 for active membership and $1 for associate membership. It is stated in this post card that it is the intention of the society to publish an information bulletin for members as soon as the events of the organization permit. As has been stated previously, President Vincent has offered to supply the dahlia blooms to any florist who will enter into the competition for the various prizes offered for dahlias shown in use for decoration.

The Michell Seed House of Philadelphia, have offered gold, silver and bronze medals. The Society of American Florists has recognized the society, and also offered one of their medals for competition for showings of new and rare varieties of dahlias. Peter Henderson & Co., H. A. Bunyard Co., Stumpp & Walter Co., Fottler, Fiske, Rawson Co., The Garden Magazine, John Lewis Childs Co., Henry A. Dreer and W. Atlee Burpee Co., have all contributed prizes and the Horticultural Society of New York has offered $100. Everything points to this being one of the most successful individual flower shows that has ever been held in this country. Intense enthusiasm is being manifested among the trade, and the amateurs are certainly doing their share to make it a successful show. An attempt is being made to get together flowers from all the growers possible and to make an exhibition of one flower of each of as many varieties as possible. This, I believe, will be of very great interest to the visitors.

It is expected that guides will be on the floor of the Exhibition to inform and help visitors in acquainting themselves with the dahlia and the varieties. The secretary and the executive board are desirous of securing prompt and early co-operation from the trade and from amateurs in general, and will appreciate hearing from those who are willing to co-operate. As the show will be held September 24th, 25th and 26th, prompt action is necessary.

JOSEPH J. LANE, Sec'y.

Marietta, O.—J. W. Dudley & Sons of Parkersburg, W. Va., have taken over the retail store of the Marietta Floral Company, and assumed charge at once.

Flower Market Reports

BOSTON — A combination of excessively sultry summer weather this week in combination with the Jewish New Year abstinence from business has had a decidedly soporific effect upon business at the time of our going to press. The holidays will pass, but the weather is not so easily predicted and so we are in some doubt as to the outlook for the balance of this week. It is a fact, however, that the few cold days last week seemed to have a decidedly stimulating influence and the markets where flowers are wholesaled took on a lively hue quite in contrast with the drowsy inactivity which has blanketed the district since General Humidity opened headquarters in Boston. Nothing needs to be said about the stock on sale. It is asters, asters, asters. Gladioli are materially shortened up. Cattleyas are still scarce, but every day shows a loosening up of the stringency and the prices tend downwards. Quality of roses is excellent.

BUFFALO — A marked improvement was shown in business conditions on Friday and Saturday of last week. There was nothing stirring earlier in the week though a heavy supply of all stock was received and the outlet hard to find. Roses were a little scarce for a few days but the supply on these is now again normal and demand a trifle better. A few weddings have helped things along and lily of the valley, white roses and other wedding material have had a slightly improved demand.

CHICAGO — Bright and warm weather the first part of last week caused a largely increased supply of roses. Beauties more than doubled in quantity. The market held up stiff, however, until the end of the week, when prices began to sag, particularly in open stock. Good sound shipping stock held its own at current quotations. Roses are offered in all lengths and in quality are the best this market ever saw at this season of the year. The list includes all the novelties as well as the standard sorts. Shipping demand continues quite active and in local circles also there is a little more life. On the whole, stock is clearing at fairly good prices. Asters continue in active demand and are clearing well, really fancy stock being often short of demand. Gladioli are much less in evidence and as to quality leave much to be desired. Most of the stock is short in stem excepting Mrs. Francis King, which is still very good. Carnations are in good demand, the offering being very light; the quality is improving. Chrysanthemums are quite plenty and move slowly. Orchids are hard to find and lily of the valley continues extremely scarce. Green goods have enjoyed an active demand, plumosus and Sprengerii especially. This week opened with cool weather and a steady downpour of rain with prospects of decreasing supplies.

WHOLESALE FLOWER MARKETS — TRADE PRICES—Per 100 TO DEALERS ONLY

Roses	BOSTON Sept. 9		ST. LOUIS Sept. 6		PHILA. Sept. 7	
Am. Beauty, Special	12.00 to 20.00		20.00 to 25.00		..... to 25.00	
" " Fancy and Extra	6.00 to 10.00		12.00 to 40.00		15.00 to 20.00	
" " No. 1	1.00 to 3.00		3.00 to 8.00		10.00 to 12.50	
Russell, Hadley	4.00 to 10.00		10.00 to 15.00		3.00 to 12.00	
Killarney, Richmond, Hillingdon, Ward, Extra	2.00 to 4.00		5.00 to 6.00		4.00 to 6.00	
" " " " Ordinary	.50 to 1.00		1.00 to 3.00		1.00 to 3.00	
Arenburg: Radiance, Taft, Key, Extra	2.00 to 4.00		5.00 to 6.00		5.00 to 6.00	
" " " " Ordinary	.50 to 1.00		2.00 to 3.00		1.00 to 4.00	
Ophelia, Mock, Sunburst, Extra	2.00 to 4.00		..... to 6.00		4.00 to 6.00	
" " " Ordinary	.50 to 1.00		..... to 1.00		1.00 to 4.00	
Carnations, Fancy	.75 to 1.00		1.50 to 2.00		..... to 1.50	
" Ordinary	.50 to .75		.50 to 1.00		..... to 1.00	
Cattleyas	35.00 to 75.00		35.00 to 75.00		50.00 to 75.00	
Dendrobium formosum	..... to 25.00		25.00 to		..... to 50.00	
Lilies, Longiflorum	4.00 to 8.00		6.00 to 8.00		8.00 to 10.00	
" Rubrum	..... to 2.00		2.00 to 3.00		..... to 2.00	
Lily of the Valley	3.00 to 4.00		3.00 to 4.00		3.00 to 4.00	
Daisies	.50 to 1.00		.20 to .75		..... to	
Violets	..... to		..... to		..... to	
Snapdragon	.50 to 1.00		3.00 to 4.00		..... to 2.00	
Gladioli	1.00 to 3.00		2.00 to 3.00		1.00 to 3.00	
Asters	.25 to 1.00		.75 to 2.00		.25 to 1.00	
Chrysanthemums	6.00 to 12.00		..... to 12.00		..... to 12.00	
Sweet Peas	.15 to .30		.15 to .25		.50 to .75	
Gardenias	10.00 to 25.00		..... to		..... to	
Adiantum	.50 to 1.00		1.00 to 1.25		..... to 1.00	
Smilax	6.00 to 12.00		12.00 to 15.00		15.00 to 20.00	
Asparagus Plumosus, Strings (100)	25.00 to 50.00		35.00 to 50.00		25.00 to 50.00	
" & Spren. (100 Bchs.)	25.00 to 35.00		20.00 to 35.00		..... to	

CINCINNATI — The supply is holding up well and is giving us more than the usual share of flowers we are accustomed to having as the middle of September approaches. This supply is more than sufficient for present needs although shipping business is good. The receipts in asters are very heavy and generally very good. The offerings in roses are large and of a much better quality than they were. The shorter ones are not selling very well. Carnations are coming in steadily and show some improvement in quality. Lilies are plentiful. Other offerings include gladioli, dahlias and cosmos in quantity.

NEW YORK — A tour of observation around the wholesale district at any time during the past week would not tend to inspire anyone with a great desire to get into the wholesale flower business or even into the flower growers domain. The Jewish holidays now on do not tend to improve the situation which has been anything but encouraging for some time past. Aside from the asters, which are now at their height, the quantity of desirable material in sight is not very large but it is far beyond the requirements of the drowsy market. Gladioli continue to shrink in number. Cattleyas are moving the other way and probably will soon be down to panic prices as the labiatas begin to come forward. There are heaps of lilies, lots of roses and a supply of dahlias of rather medium quality which increases in volume daily. Chrysanthemums are gradually coming into line as staples of the market and they are very nice in quality but this does not seem to accelerate their movement. Like everything else they seem loth to move

(Continued on page 360)

Flower Market Reports

(Continued from page 357)

SAN FRANCISCO Very little change has occurred in the stock offerings since our last report. The supply of asters has dropped off rather abruptly and the best offerings are readily absorbed at higher prices. Carnations show improvement, but the stems of the new crop are still short. Sweet peas are a negligible quantity, the supply being limited and the quality poor. Dahlias continue to arrive in ample supply. Minnie Berger, Delice, Geisha and Mrs. Kitwell are to be seen everywhere and show excellent quality. Lots of them are being sold at fair prices. There is a drop in the supply of gladioli, while amaryllis floods the market. Lots of zinnias are appearing, but they do not move so well as many other kinds of flowers. Chrysanthemums are beginning to play an important part in the daily business. The quality is improving rapidly, and the supplies are now sufficient for all requirements. There is plenty of Golden Glow, October Frost and Monrovia and other varieties are beginning to arrive. So far the supply has all been consumed in the local market, but shipments will start about the middle of the month. Violets are improving, but they are still very soft with little prospect of eastern shipments starting much before the middle of October. A real scarcity of lily of the valley was felt the past week. Lilium speciosum rubrum still appears in great quantity and maintains its popularity well. Roses show better quality, but good stock is still rather scarce.

ST. LOUIS The daily market during the last week was all that could be expected of it at this time of the year. Business is reported poor in all parts of the city by the retail florists. The wholesale market is kept well supplied with stock. Prices are low in all grades. Roses are many. Carnations are coming along fine and show marked improvement, color, size and stems. Lilies and lily of the valley sold well all week. Asters are too many. Gladioli and tuberoses are nearing their end and dahlias, cosmos and chrysanthemums are coming on.

WASHINGTON The general tone of business shows some little improvement over last week—in fact, better this year than last. Many orders for future dates have already been placed and it is predicted that during the coming season business will be exceptionally good. There is still far more stock to be had than the market can possibly consume. Dahlias are making their presence felt by reason of the quantities in which they are received, but it looks as though asters were about on the wane and the majority of these flowers are below A1 quality. The dahlias themselves are not of the best by reason of the earliness of their season. Huge quantities of all flowers daily go to the refuse piles, even including roses which for this season of the year are quite good. American Beauty roses from the north

are quite in favor. Lily of the valley are short in supply, yet there is no lack. Carnations are again coming in but with short stems and comparatively small flowers and no one seems to want them. Early chrysanthemums have made their appearance in small quantities.

VISITORS' REGISTER.

Cleveland, O.—Michael Bloy, Detroit, Mich.

St. Louis, Mo.—J. Prost, city forester, Chicago.

Colorado Springs, Colo.—Mr. and Mrs. J. G. Hancock, Chicago.

Boston—Carl Jurgens, Newport, R. I.; W. A. Manda, South Orange, N. J.; F. R. Pierson, Tarrytown, N. Y.; A. E. Thatcher, Bar Harbor, Me.

Philadelphia—F. J. LeClair, representing Julius Roehrs Co., Rutherford, N. J.; A. Langjahr, New York City; James Brown, Coatesville, Pa.; W. J. Stewart, Boston, Mass.; Robert Pyle, West Grove, Pa.

Cincinnati—George Hampton, of Jos. G. Neidinger Co., Phila.; Milton Alexander, representing Lion & Company, New York; S. Geller, Brooklyn, N. Y.; Mrs. Wm. Gerlach, Jr., Piqua, Ohio; W. C. Lawrence, Atlanta, Ga.; J. G. Botkin, Urbana, Ohio; J. T. Hudegen, Aurora, Ind.

Washington—William E. McKissick and A. Niessen, Philadelphia; Robert Schoch, representing M. Rice & Company, Philadelphia; A. J. Pykes, of the Van Lindley Company, Greensboro. N. C.; Mrs. Pykes, and Charles Niemann, of Vaughan's Seed Store, New York.

BUSINESS TROUBLES.

The Santa Cruz Bulb and Plant Co., Santa Cruz, Cal., is reported as being embarrassed and its business is under attachments from a number of creditors.

The Cowee gladiolus farm at Berlin, N. Y., has been made use of for some time past as a scenic setting for some movie photo plays. No more beautiful setting could be imagined for a rural romance than the resplendent fields of blooming gladioli on the Cowee farm.

NEW YORK QUOTATIONS PER 100. To Dealers Only

MISCELLANEOUS	Last Half of Week ending Sept. 4 1915				First Half of Week beginning Sept. 6 1915			
Cattleyas	25.00	to	60.00		25.00	to	90.00
Lilies, Longiflorum	3.00	to	6.00		3.00	to	5.00
Rubrum	7.00	to	8.00		1.00	to	2.00
Lily of the Valley	2.00	to	4.00		2.00	to	3.00
Daisies		to	.50		.....	to	.50
Snapdragon		to	1.00		.50	to	1.00
Gladioli	.50	to	1.00		.50	to	2.00
Asters	.15	to	1.00		.15	to	1.00
Sweet Peas	.10	to	.15		.10	to	.15
Corn Flower	.....	to	.25		.....	to	.25
Gardenias	12.00	to	25.00		12.00	to	25.00
Adiantum	.50	to	.75		.50	to	.75
Smilax	4.00	to	8.00		4.00	to	8.00
Asparagus Plumosus, strings (per 100)	15.00	to	30.00		15.00	to	30.00
& Spren (100 bunches)	10.00	to	20.00		10.00	to	20.00

COMING EVENTS.

Shows.

Boston, Sept. 11-12.—Dahlia and Fruit Exhibition, Massachusetts Horticultural Society.

Providence, R. I., Sept. 16-17.—September Exhibition, Rhode Island Horticultural Society, Narragansett Hotel.

New Haven, Conn., Sept. 16-17.—Eighty-third annual exhibition of the New Haven County Horticultural Society to be held in Harmonie Hall. W. C. McIntosh, Sec., 925 Howard Ave., New Haven.

Hartford, Conn., Sept. 22-23.—Annual Dahlia exhibition of the Connecticut Horticultural Society, Unity Hall, Pratt St. Alfred Dixon, Sec., Wethersfield.

Portland, Ore., Sept. 23-25.—Annual Show of the Northwest National Dahlia Society.

New York, N. Y., Sept. 24-26.—American Dahlia Society's first exhibition, Museum of Natural History.

Boston, Oct. 2-3.—October Show Massachusetts Horticultural Society.

Orange, N. J., Oct. 4.—Tenth Annual Dahlia, Fruit, Gladioli and Vegetable Show of N. J. Floricultural Society. Geo. W. Strange, Sec., 84 Jackson St.

Oyster Bay, L. I., N. Y., Oct. 5-6.—Dahlia Show of the Oyster Bay Hort. Society. Chrysanthemum Show, Nov. 2. Andrew K. Kennedy, Westbury, L. I., secretary.

Glen Cove, L. I., Oct. 7.—Dahlia Show of Nassau Co. Hort. Soc. Fall Show of Nassau Co. Hort. Soc., Oct. 28 and 29.

Red Bank, N. J., Oct. 27-28.—Annual Flower Show of the Monmouth County Horticultural Society. H. A. Kettel, Sec., Fair Haven, N. J.

Poughkeepsie, N. Y., Oct. 28-29.—Annual flower show of Duchess County Horticultural Society. N. Harold Cottam, Sec., Wappingers Falls.

Boston, Nov. 4, 5, 6, 7.—Grand Autumn Exhibition, Massachusetts Horticultural society.

New York, N. Y., Nov. 3, 4, 5.—Annual Chrysanthemum Show of the American Institute, Engineering Societies Building.

Morris County, N. J., Oct. 28-29.—The twentieth annual flower show of the Gardeners and Florists Society, Assembly Hall, Madison, N. J., Edward Reagan, secretary, Morristown, N. J.

Tarrytown, N. Y., Nov. 3-4-5.—Chrysanthemum Show in the Music Hall.

New York, N. Y., Nov. 4-7.—Annual Autumn exhibition of Hort. Soc. of New York, Museum of Natural History.

Chicago, Ill., Nov. 9-14.—Grand Floral Festival of the Chicago Florist's Club and Horticultural Society of Chicago, to be held in the Coliseum.

Cleveland, O., Nov. 10-14.—Annual show and meeting of Chrysanthemum Society of America. In conjunction with the Cleveland Flower Show. Chas. W. Johnson, Sec., 2226 Fairfax Ave., Morgan Park, Ill.

Cleveland, O., Nov. 10-14.—Cleveland Flower Show. The only show of national scope in the United States this fall. F. A. Friedley, Sec., 356 Leader Building.

Buyer's Directory and Ready Reference Guide

Advertisements under this head, one cent a word.   Initials count as words.

Display advertisers in this issue are also listed under this classification without charge. Reference to List of Advertisers will indicate the respective pages.

Buyers failing to find what they want in this list will confer a favor by writing us and we will try to put them in communication with reliable dealers.

ACCOUNTANT
R. J. Dysart, 40 State St., Boston.
For page see List of Advertisers.

ACHILLEA
"Pearl," Fine Seedlings, $3.00 per 1,000, cash. JAMES MOSS, Wholesale Grower, Johnsville, Pa.

APHINE
Aphine Mfg. Co., Madison, N. J.
For page see List of Advertisers.

APHIS PUNK
Nicotine Mfg. Co., St. Louis, Mo.
For page see List of Advertisers.

ARAUCARIAS
Henry A. Dreer, Philadelphia, Pa.
For page see List of Advertisers.

AUCTION SALES
Elliott Auction Co., New York City.
For page see List of Advertisers.

AZALEAS
P. Ouwerkerk, Hoboken, N. J.
For page see List of Advertisers.

BAY TREES
August Rolker & Sons, New York.
For page see List of Advertisers.

BEDDING PLANTS
A. N. Pierson, Inc., Cromwell, Conn.
For page see List of Advertisers.

BEGONIAS
Julius Roehrs Company, Rutherford, N. J.

R. Vincent, Jr., & Sons Co., White Marsh, Md.
For page see List of Advertisers.

Thomas Roland, Nahant, Mass.
For page see List of Advertisers.

A. M. Davenport, Watertown, Mass.
For page see List of Advertisers.

		Per 100
BEGONIA LORRAINE,	2½ in.	$12.00
	3 in.	20.00
	4 in.	35.00
	5 in.	50.00
BEGONIA CINCINNATI,	2½ in.	15.00
	3 in.	25.00
	3½ in.	30.00
	4½ in.	40.00

JULIUS ROEHRS CO., Rutherford, N. J.

BOILERS
Kroeschell Bros. Co., Chicago.
For page see List of Advertisers.

King Construction Co., North Tonawanda, N. Y.
"King Ideal" Boiler.
For page see List of Advertisers.

Hitchings & Co., New York City.

Lord & Burnham Co., New York City.
For page see List of Advertisers.

BOXES—CUT FLOWER FOLDING
Edwards Folding Box Co., Philadelphia.
For page see List of Advertisers.

Folding cut flower boxes, the best made. Write for list. HOLTON & HUNKEL CO., Milwaukee, Wis.

BOX TREES
BOX TREES—Standards, Pyramids and Bush. In various sizes. Price List on demand. JULIUS ROEHRS CO., Rutherford, N. J.

BULBS AND TUBERS
Arthur T. Boddington Co., Inc., New York City.
Christmas Forcing Bulbs—Ready for Delivery.
For page see List of Advertisers.

J. M. Thorburn & Co., New York City.
Wholesale Price List of High Class Bulbs.
For page see List of Advertisers.

Ralph M. Ward & Co., New York City.
Lily Bulbs.
For page see List of Advertisers.

John Lewis Childs, Flowerfield, L. I., N. Y.
For page see List of Advertisers.

August Rolker & Sons, New York City.
Holland and Japan Bulbs.
For page see List of Advertisers.

R. & J. Farquhar & Co., Boston, Mass.
For page see List of Advertisers.

S. S. Skidelsky & Co., Philadelphia, Pa.
For page see List of Advertisers.

Chas. Schwake & Co., New York City.
Horticultural Importers and Exporters.
For page see List of Advertisers.

A. Henderson & Co., Chicago, Ill.
For page see List of Advertisers.

Burnett Bros., 98 Chambers St., New York.

Henry F. Michell Co., Philadelphia, Pa.
For page see List of Advertisers.

Joseph Breck & Sons Corp., Boston, Mass.
For page see List of Advertisers.

Fottler, Fiske, Rawson Co., Boston, Mass.

C. KEUR & SONS, HILLEGOM, Holland.
Bulbs of all descriptions. Write for prices.
NEW YORK Branch, 8-10 Bridge St.

CANNAS
Canna Specialists.
Send for Canna book.
THE CONARD & JONES COMPANY, West Grove, Pa.

CARNATION STAPLES
Split carnations quickly, easily and cheaply mended. Pillsbury's Carnation Staple, 1000 for 35c.; 3000 for $1.00 post paid. I. L. PILLSBURY, Galesburg, Ill.

Supreme Carnation Staples, for repairing split carnations, 35c. per 1000; 3000 for $1.00. F. W. WAITE, 85 Belmont Ave., Springfield, Mass.

CARNATIONS.
Wood Bros., Fishkill, N. Y.
For page see List of Advertisers.

F. Dorner & Sons Co., Lafayette, Ind.
For page see List of Advertisers.

Leo Niessen Co., Philadelphia, Pa.
Field Grown Carnation Plants.
For page see List of Advertisers.

F. R. Pierson, Tarrytown, N. Y.
Carnation Matchless.
For page see List of Advertisers.

Littlefield & Wyman, North Abington, Mass.
New Pink Carnation, Miss Theo.
For page see List of Advertisers.

CARNATIONS—Continued
Carnations, field grown, $6.00 per 100. Cash. White and Pink Enchantress Mrs. Ward, Perfection, Fenn, Winsor, Queen, Lawson, Beacon. CHAS. H. GREEN, Spencer, Mass.

CHRYSANTHEMUMS
Chas. H. Totty, Madison, N. J.
For page see List of Advertisers.

R. Vincent, Jr., & Sons Co., White Marsh, Md.
Pompon Chrysanthemums,
For page see List of Advertisers.

THE BEST 1915 NOVELTIES.
The Cream of 1914 Introductions.
The most popular Commercial and Exhibition kinds; also complete line of Pompons, Singles and Anemones. Trade list on application. ELMER D. SMITH & CO., Adrian, Mich.

COCOANUT FIBRE SOIL
20th Century Plant Food Co., Beverly, Mass.
For page see List of Advertisers.

CYCLAMENS
The Best Strains.
Eight Varieties.   Very Fine.
If you want quality, order now.

	100	1000
2½ in.	$7.00	$60.00
3 in.	9.00	80.00
4 in.	20.00	

Write for copy of our monthly plant bulletin.
S. S. PENNOCK-MEEHAN CO., 1608-1620 Ludlow St., Philadelphia, Pa.

DAHLIAS
Send for Wholesale List of whole clumps and separate stock; 40,000 clumps for sale. Northboro Dahlia and Gladiolus Gardens. J. L. MOORE, Prop, Northboro, Mass.

NEW PAEONY DAHLIA
John Wanamaker. Newest, Handsomest, Best. New color, new form and new habit of growth. Big stock of best cut-flower varieties. Send list of wants to PEACOCK DAHLIA FARMS, Berlin, N. J.

DECORATIVE PLANTS
Robert Craig Co., Philadelphia, Pa.
For page see List of Advertisers.

Woodrow & Marketos, New York City.
For page see List of Advertisers.

S. S. Skidelsky & Co., Philadelphia, Pa.
For page see List of Advertisers.

Bobbink & Atkins, Rutherford, N. J.
For page see List of Advertisers.

A. Leuthy & Co., Roslindale, Boston, Mass.
For page see List of Advertisers.

FERNS
H. H. Barrows & Son, Whitman, Mass.
For page see List of Advertisers.

Robert Craig Co., Philadelphia, Pa.
For page see List of Advertisers.

McHutchison & Co., New York City.
Ferns in Flats.
For page see List of Advertisers.

Roman J. Irwin, New York City.
Boston and Whitmani Ferns.
For page see List of Advertisers.

FERTILIZERS
20th Century Plant Food Co., Beverly, Mass.
Cocoanut Fibre Soil.
For page see List of Advertisers.

For List of Advertisers See Page 339

In writing to Advertisers kindly mention Horticulture

NURSERY STOCK—Continued

Bay State Nurseries, North Abington, Mass.
Hardy, Northern Grown Stock.
For page see List of Advertisers.

Bobbink & Atkins, Rutherford, N. J.
For page see List of Advertisers.

Framingham Nurseries, Framingham, Mass.
For page see List of Advertisers.

August Rolker & Sons, New York City.
For page see List of Advertisers.

Chas. G. Curtis Co., Callicoon, N. Y.
Nursery Stock for Fall Planting.
For page see List of Advertisers.

NUT GROWING.

The Nut-Grower, Waycross, Ga.
For page see List of Advertisers.

ONION SETS

Schilder Bros., Chillicothe, O.
Onion Seed—Onion Sets.
For page see List of Advertisers.

ORCHID FLOWERS

Jas. McManus, New York, N. Y.
For page see List of Advertisers.

ORCHID PLANTS

Julius Roehrs Co., Rutherford, N. J.
For page see List of Advertisers.

Lager & Hurrell, Summit, N. J.
For page see List of Advertisers.

PALMS, ETC.

Robert Craig Co., Philadelphia, Pa.
For page see List of Advertisers.

August Rolker & Sons, New York City.
For page see List of Advertisers.

A. Leuthy & Co., Roslindale, Boston, Mass.
For page see List of Advertisers.

PANSY PLANTS

PANSIES—The Big Giant Flowering
Kind—$3.00 per 1,000; $25.00 for 10,000. If
I could only show the nice plants, hundred
of testimonials and repeat orders, I would
be flooded with new business. Cash.
JAMES MOSS, Wholesale Grower, Johnsville, Pa.

PANSY SEED

Chas. Frost, Kenilworth, N. J.
The Kenilworth Giant Pansy.
For page see List of Advertisers.

Fottler, Fiske, Rawson Co., Boston, Mass.

PEONIES

Peonies. The world's greatest collection.
1200 sorts. Send for list. C. BETSCHER,
Canal Dover, O.

PEONIES? Try us once and if not satisfied tell us why. GEO. N. SMITH, Wellesley Nurseries, Wellesley Hills, Mass.

RARE PEONIES—Therese, Mons. M. Cabusac, $3.00 each. Send for list of largest
collection of Continental and European varieties. Marcelle, Dessert, Solange, Tourangelle, Primevere, Mignon, Alsace Lorraine, Baroness Schroeder, etc. D. W. C.
RUFF, Buena Vista Gardens, St. Paul,
Minn.

PECKY CYPRESS BENCHES

A. T. Stearns Lumber Co., Boston, Mass.

PHLOX

PHLOX—Coquelicot, Eclaireur, Rosen-
berg, Independence, Lothair, etc. GEO. N.
SMITH, Wellesley Nurseries, Wellesley
Hills, Mass.

PIPE AND FITTINGS

Kroeschell Bros. Co., Chicago.
For page see List of Advertisers.

King Construction Company,
N. Tonawanda, N. Y.
Shelf Brackets and Pipe Hangers.
For page see List of Advertisers.

PLANT AND BULB IMPORTS

Chas. Schwake & Co., New York City.
For page see List of Advertisers.

August Rolker & Sons, New York City.
For page see List of Advertisers.

PLANT TRELLISES AND STAKES

Seele's Tieless Plant Stakes and Trellises. H. D. SEELE & SONS, Elkhart, Ind.

PLANT TUBS

H. A. Dreer, Philadelphia, Pa.
"Riverton Special."

RAFFIA

McHutchison & Co., New York, N. Y.
For page see List of Advertisers.

RHODODENDRONS

P. Ouwerkerk, Hoboken, N. J.
For page see List of Advertisers.

Framingham Nurseries, Framingham, Mass.
For page see List of Advertisers.

RIBBONS AND CHIFFONS

S. S. Pennock-Meehan Co., Philadelphia, Pa.
For page see List of Advertisers.

ROSES

Poehlmann Bros. Co., Morton Grove, Ill.
For page see List of Advertisers.

P. Ouwerkerk, Hoboken, N. J.
For page see List of Advertisers.

Robert Craig Co., Philadelphia, Pa.
For page see List of Advertisers.

W. & T. Smith Co., Geneva, N. Y.
American Grown Roses.
For page see List of Advertisers.

Bay State Nurseries, North Abington, Mass.
For page see List of Advertisers.

August Rolker & Sons, New York City.
For page see List of Advertisers.

Framingham Nurseries, Framingham, Mass.
For page see List of Advertisers.

A. N. Pierson, Inc., Cromwell, Conn.
For page see List of Advertisers.

THE CONARD & JONES COMPANY.
Rose Specialists.
West Grove, Pa. Send for offers.

SEASONABLE PLANT STOCK

R. Vincent, Jr., & Sons Co., White Marsh
Md.
For page see List of Advertisers.

SEED GROWERS

California Seed Growers' Association,
San Jose, Cal.
For page see List of Advertisers.

SEEDS

Carter's Tested Seeds.
Seeds with a Pedigree.
Boston, Mass., and London, England.
For page see List of Advertisers.

Schilder Bros., Chillicothe, O.
Onion Seed—Onion Sets.
For page see List of Advertisers.

Joseph Breck & Sons, Boston, Mass.
For page see List of Advertisers.

Kelway & Son,
Langport, Somerset, England.
Kelway's Celebrated English Strain Garden
Seeds.

J. Bolgiano & Son, Baltimore, Md.
For page see List of Advertisers.

A. T. Boddington Co., Inc., New York City.
For page see List of Advertisers.

Chas. Schwake & Co., New York City
For page see List of Advertisers.

Michell's Seed House, Philadelphia, Pa.
New Crop Flower Seeds.
For page see List of Advertisers.

SEEDS—Continued

W. Atlee Burpee & Co., Philadelphia, Pa.
For page see List of Advertisers.

R. & J. Farquhar & Co., Boston, Mass.
Giant Cyclamen Seed.
For page see List of Advertisers.

J. M. Thorburn & Co., New York City.
For page see List of Advertisers.

S. Bryson Ayres Co., Independence, Mo.
Sweet Peas.
For page see List of Advertisers.

Loechner & Co., New York City.
For page see List of Advertisers.

Ant. C. Zvolanek, Lompoc, Cal.
Winter Flowering Sweet Pea Seed.
For page see List of Advertisers.

S. S. Skidelsky & Co., Philadelphia, Pa.
For page see List of Advertisers.

W. E. Marshall & Co., New York City.
Seeds, Plants and Bulbs.
For page see List of Advertisers.

August Rolker & Sons, New York City.
For page see List of Advertisers.

Burnett Bros., 98 Chambers St., New York.
For page see List of Advertisers.

Fottler, Fiske, Rawson Co., Boston, Mass.
Seeds for the Florist.

SKINNER IRRIGATION SYSTEM

Skinner Irrigation Co., Brookline, Mass.
For page see List of Advertisers.

SPHAGNUM MOSS

Live Sphagnum moss, orchid peat and
orchid baskets always on hand. LAGER
& HURRELL, Summit, N. J.

Sphagnum Moss, 12 bbl. bale, burlap,
$2.50; 4 bales. $9.50; 5 bbl. bale, $2.00; 4
bales, $7.50, in burlap. Get prices on large
lots. JOS. H. PAUL, P. O. Box, 156,
Manahaukin, N. J.

STOVE PLANTS

Orchids—Largest stock in the country—
Stove plants and Crotons, finest collection.
JULIUS ROEHRS CO., Rutherford, N. J.

STRAWBERRY PLANTS.

Wilfrid Wheeler, Concord, Mass.
Pot Grown.
For page see List of Advertisers.

SWAINSONA

R. Vincent, Jr., & Sons Co., White
Marsh, Md.
For page see List of Advertisers.

SWEET PEA SEED

Ant. C. Zvolanek, Lompoc, Calif.
Gold Medal of Honor Winter Orchid Sweet
Peas.
For page see List of Advertisers.

S. Bryson Ayres Co.,
Sunnyslope, Independence, Mo.
For page see List of Advertisers.

VENTILATING APPARATUS

The Advance Co., Richmond, Ind.
For page see List of Advertisers.

The John A. Evans Co., Richmond, Ind.
For page see List of Advertisers.

VERMICIDES

Aphine Mfg. Co., Madison, N. J.
For page see List of Advertisers.

VIOLETS

FIELD-GROWN VIOLET PLANTS.

	100	1000
Princess of Wales	$5.00	$45.00
Lady Campbell	5.00	45.00
Marie Louise	5.00	45.00
Gov. Herrick	5.00	45.00
Farquhar	5.00	45.00
La France	5.00	45.00

Write for copy of our monthly plant
bulletin.
S. S. PENNOCK-MEEHAN CO.,
1608-1620 Ludlow St., Philadelphia, Pa.

For List of Advertisers See Page 339

WIRED TOOTHPICKS
W. J. Cowee, Berlin, N. Y.
For page see List of Advertisers.

WIREWORK
Reed & Keller, New York City.
For page see List of Advertisers.

WILLIAM E. HEILSCHER'S WIRE
WORKS, 264 Randolph St., Detroit, Mich.

WHOLESALE FLORISTS
Albany, N. Y.

Albany Cut Flower Exchange, Albany, N. Y.
For page see List of Advertisers.

Baltimore

The S. S. Pennock-Meehan Co., Franklin
and St. Paul Sts.
For page see List of Advertisers.

Boston

N. F. McCarthy & Co., 112 Arch St. and
31 Otis St.
For page see List of Advertisers.

Welch Bros. Co., 226 Devonshire St.
For page see List of Advertisers.

Patrick Welch, 262 Devonshire St., Boston,
Mass.
For page see List of Advertisers.

Brooklyn

Wm. H. Kuebler, 28 Willoughby St.
For page see List of Advertisers.

Buffalo, N. Y.

William F. Kasting Co., 383-87 Ellicott St.
For page see List of Advertisers.

Chicago

Poehlmann Bros. Co., Morton Grove, Ill.
For page see List of Advertisers.

Detroit

Michigan Cut Flower Exchange, 38 and 40
Broadway.
For page see List of Advertisers.

New York

H. E. Froment, 148 W. 28th St.
For page see List of Advertisers.

James McManus, 105 W. 28th St.
For page see List of Advertisers.

W. F. Sheridan, 133 W. 28th St.
For page see List of Advertisers.

P. J. Smith, 131 West 28th St., N. Y.
For page see List of Advertisers.

Moore, Hentz & Nash, 55 and 57 W. 26th St.
For page see List of Advertisers.

Charles Millang, 55 and 57 West 26th St.
For page see List of Advertisers.

W. P. Ford, New York
For page see List of Advertisers.

The S S. Pennock-Meehan Co., 117 West
28th St.
For page see List of Advertisers.

Traendly & Schenck, 436 6th Ave., between
26th and 27th Sts.
For page see List of Advertisers.

Badgley, Riedel & Meyer, Inc., New York.
For page see List of Advertisers.

Woodrow & Marketos, 37 & 39 West 28th St.
For page see List of Advertisers.

George C. Siebrecht, 109 W. 28th St.

John Young & Co., 53 West 28th St.
For page see List of Advertisers.

M. C. Ford, 121 West 28th St.
For page see List of Advertisers.

WHOLESALE FLORISTS
New York—Continued

Guttman & Reynor, Inc., 101 W. 28th St.,
New York.
For page see List of Advertisers.

Philadelphia

Leo, Niessen Co., 12th and Race Sts.
For page see List of Advertisers.

Edward Reid, 1619-21 Ranstead St.
For page see List of Advertisers.

The S. S. Pennock-Meehan Co., 1608-20
Ludlow St.
For page see List of Advertisers.

Stuart H. Miller, 1617 Ranstead St.
For page see List of Advertisers.

Richmond, Ind.

E. G. Hill Co.
For page see List of Advertisers.

Rochester, N. Y.

George B. Hart, 24 Stone St.
For page see List of Advertisers.

Washington

The S. S. Pennock-Meehan Co., 1216 H St.,
N. W.
For page see List of Advertisers.

New Offers In This Issue

ASTERS.

S. S. Pennock-Meehan Co., Philadelphia, Pa.
For page see List of Advertisers.

ARECAS, KENTIAS, ETC.

Joseph Heacock Co., Wyncote, Pa.
For page see List of Advertisers.

**AUCTION SALES OF BULBS AND
FOLIAGE STOCK.**

Elliott Auction Co., New York City.
For page see List of Advertisers.

MAGIC MANURES.

Chicago Feed & Fertilizer Co., Chicago, Ill.
For page see List of Advertisers.

NEW CROP CYCLAMEN SEED.

Henry F. Michell Co., Philadelphia, Pa.
For page see List of Advertisers.

**ORCHIDS — ACACIAS — PALMS—
ROSES—NURSERY STOCK.**

Stuart Low & Co., Harry A. Barnard, representative, Hotel Albert, New York City.
For page see List of Advertisers.

**SPECIAL OFFER GREENHOUSE
SASH.**

Lord & Burnham Co., New York City.
For page see List of Advertisers.

THE NUT-GROWER

The unique monthly publication which furnishes reliable
and interesting up-to-date information regarding the value
of pecans and other edible nuts
and how to grow them for profit.

Subscription, $1.00 per year

Sample Copy Free

THE NUT-GROWER
WAYCROSS, GA.

In writing to Advertisers kindly mention Horticulture

GREENHOUSES BUILDING OR CONTEMPLATED.

Penbrook, Pa.—Snyder & Hass, additions.

Wichita, Kan.—F. Kuechenmeister, rebuilding.

Columbia, Mo.—Sunnyslope Greenhouses, addition.

Dolgeville, N. Y.—R. B. Poole, State street, one house.

Bound Brook, N. J.—Chas. Zvolanek, additions and alterations.

Providence, R. I.—Johnston Bros., Hope street., house 32x152.

New Haven, Ct.—Frank Lawrence, East Main street, one house.

Wilmington, Del.—C. W. Griffith, 9th and Tatnall streets, one house.

Needham, Mass.—Paul E. Richwagen, Rosemary street, one house.

Kalamazoo, Mich.—G. Van Bochove & Bro., Rose Hill, range of houses.

New Ulin, Minn.—Boock Greenhouses, Third North street, one house.

Buffalo, N. Y.—Jerry Brookins, Orchard Park, Lord & Burnham house 70x150.

San Francisco, Cal.—C. W. Ward of Eureka, Cal., two houses, one 24x80 and one 29x80.

Terre Haute, Ind.—Heini & Weber, one house. Davis Gardens, three houses each 72x600.

"FREE SASH."

At this season of the year this sounds good. We have just discovered it on the outside back cover of this paper. You'd better look for it, and while we hate to advise anybody to tear even a corner off from any page of HORTICULTURE, yet the interests of our readers are our first consideration and "for just this once" we will say—Tear off that corner and get the coveted yellow slip.

FREAKISH FACTS AND FACTLESS FREAKS.

Compiled from Our Exchanges.

A white carnation for Mothers' Day cost 15 cents, and in some cases Mother would much rather have had the 15 cents.
—Boston Record.

With fields of corn that appears to be 15 feet high, Oklahoma is short of enough tall men to harvest the crop and may have to supply its lads with ladders.
—Boston Traveler.

Perhaps the best example of a truly reckless person is the householder who buys "mushrooms" from an unknown pedler who says he gathered them in the fields.
—Boston Traveler.

Prof. H. G. Walters, of Langhorne, Pa., has a peach tree which bears grafts as follows: Two of apple, three of rose, two of cedar and one each of hemlock, blackberry, lilac, plum and cherry.
—Boston Traveler.

Luling, Tex., Aug. 29.—W. H. Hipple had on exhibition here a mammoth peapod measuring 2 feet 9 inches in length, of the new asparagus variety. It contained a large number of peas of uniform size. It is said the pod is a very delicious table dish when used as a snap bean. This is the first season this variety of pea has been planted in this section, and it is proving to be very prolific.
—Boston Post.

Last Friday morning W. D. Howard found that the money drawer of his greenhouses on South Main street, had been broken open during the night and 10 cents taken, the only money left in the drawer. Suspicion rested on two young boys seen about the premises, and after being questioned by Chief Murphy, they confessed the act. The boys' parents were notified and the punishment received should be a warning against similar misdeeds in the future.
—Milford (Mass.) Gazette.

Frank Deborn and Vincent Pannello, who say they live in Fall River, will spend the next 30 days in the House of Correction because they helped themselves to some fruit in the yard in the rear of 46 Walnut street. Neponset. Sunday night. The men were arraigned in the Dorchester court yesterday on the charge of larceny. According to their story, they were walking from Fall River to Boston to see the Italian consul and could not resist the pangs of hunger when they passed the orchard in Neponset.
—Boston Post.

An alligator pear tree has been insured by Lloyd's for $30,000. This makes an American tree, situated in Los Angeles County, Cal., the most valuable tree in the world, even outstripping the centuries old date palms of Arabia. Through the enterprise of Lloyd's of London this tree is insured against damage by wind or rain.

This Avacado tree grows on a fruit ranch in Whittier, Cal. Last year it produced 3,000 pears, which brought the owner an average of 50 cents apiece. Besides the pears, which are used extensively for salads, the owner received $1,500 for the bud wood.
—Ex.

THOMAS J. BENWELL.

We mentioned in our issue of last week the gift of a purse of gold to Thomas J. Benwell by A. Hews & Co., in recognition of his fifty years' faithful service in the employ of the company. We now present a portrait of Mr. Benwell, familiar to a generation of flower pot buyers in and around Boston as local salesman for that well known concern.

Mr. Benwell was born in Birmingham, England, on December 15, 1851. He came to this country in infancy with his parents, who settled in Cambridge, Mass., and was educated in the Cambridge public schools. At the age of 14 he went to work for H. Hews & Son and learned the fundamentals of the pottery art. The concern was a modest one in those days, the entire force consisting of H. and A. H. Hews —father and son—and two boys, of which Benwell was one. All hands worked at the wheel and in delivering orders, etc., as necessity demanded. Five thousand flower pots was considered a fair week's sales, all being hand made. Last year's output was twenty million. Clay ground sufficient for the wants of the firm for the next fifty years has recently been secured and we

THOMAS J. BENWELL

hope that popular "Tom" Benwell may live to see the greater part of that clay supply used up.

On May 13, 1902, Mr. Benwell met with an awful accident. His clothing got entangled with some shafting in the factory and before he was finally released from the machinery his right arm, muscles of the shoulder and flesh on his chest had been slowly torn away and ground up, fifteen minutes having elapsed before his panic stricken fellow workmen managed to shut off the power and release what was left of him. On his return from the hospital he was given by Mr. Hews the option of a continuation of his salary without work for the remainder of his life, but he preferred to stay in the harness and, as he says, "work his life out rather than to rust out."

Masury, O.—Ely & Lloyd have purchased the Service Greenhouses.

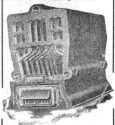

Offer of Free Sash

This Tells How To Get Yours

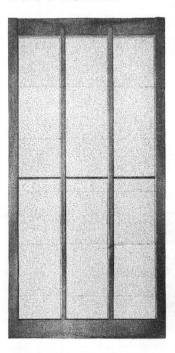

A WEEK from today we will send through the mails a special offer on our Sash That Last.

In addition to a special price we will give a certain number of sash away free.

In order to get the sash free, you **must send in your order on the yellow order slip** enclosed along with each offer we are sending to every grower on our list.

Are you on our list—that's the question.

The way to make sure is to tear off the coupon below; sign your name and address and mail to us.

It is the surest way of your being surely sure of your getting in on this Sash Free offer.

LORD & BURNHAM CO.

Send me your special free Sash offer and Yellow Order Slip.

Name................................

Address...............................

....

Lord & Burnham Co.

SALES OFFICES:

NEW YORK   BOSTON   PHILADELPHIA
42nd Street Bldg,   Tremont Bldg.   Franklin Bank Bldg.

CHICAGO   ROCHESTER   CLEVELAND
Rookery Bldg.   Granite Bldg.   Swetland Bldg.

TORONTO, CANADA, Royal Bank Bldg.

FACTORIES : Irvington, N. Y. Des Plaines, Ill.
St. Catharines, Canada

Vol. XXII
No. 12
SEPT. 18
1915

HORTICULTURE

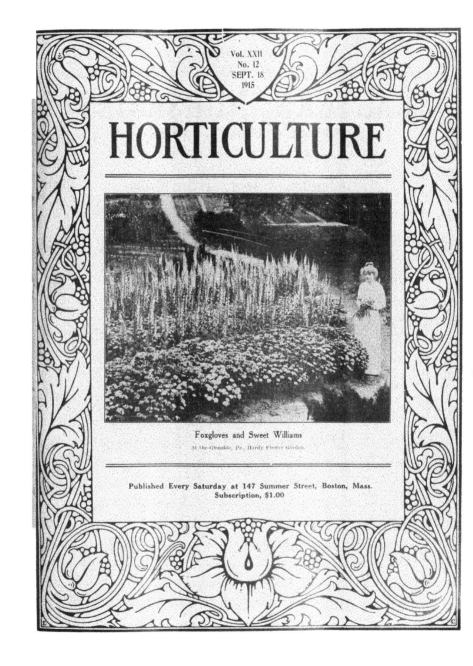

Foxgloves and Sweet Williams

At the Glenside, Pa., Hardy Flower Garden.

Published Every Saturday at 147 Summer Street, Boston, Mass.
Subscription, $1.00

LIST OF ADVERTISERS

FOR BUYERS' DIRECTORY AND READY REFERENCE GUIDE
SEE PAGES 392, 393, 394, 395

NOTES ON CULTURE OF FLORISTS' STOCK

CONDUCTED BY

John J. M. Farrell

Questions by our readers in line with any of the topics presented on this page will be cordially received and promptly answered by Mr. Farrell. Such communications should invariably be addressed to the office of HORTICULTURE.
"If vain our toil, we ought to blame the culture, not the soil."—*Pope.*

Canterbury Bells

Now is the proper time to lift and pot plants from the field. As a rule 7-inch and 8-inch pots will suffice, but extra large plants will need 8-inch and 10-inch pots. Give these plants a generous compost, stand them out doors in an open sunny spot and leave them there until sharp frost endangers the pots when they should be placed on a bed of coal ashes in a cold frame. Leave them exposed to the weather for some weeks yet. A few degrees of frost will do them no harm but cover with sashes when cold becomes keener. They can be buried in perfectly dry leaves and kept over winter in frames if desired. They can be started in gentle heat for spring flowering any time after the middle of December. There are no finer spring flowering plants for the country florist than Campanula Medium.

Chrysanthemums

What feeding is needed must be done during the next few weeks as it is impossible to continue feeding much after the buds show color. The question of feeding chrysanthemums is an especially important one and many otherwise good growers seem to be all at sea as to what and when and how much to feed their plants. I prefer a natural fertilizer such as cow or sheep manure. The proportion of natural fertilizer is at a rate of about a bushel to a barrel. This information is more for the small grower or beginner, as the big grower, with his large tanks and pumping supply, is able to figure out his own formula. This fertilizer can be allowed to stand in the barrel for a couple of days and after the water has been drawn off the barrel can be filled again. Where you use chemicals such as nitrate of soda, sulphate of ammonia and nitrate of potash, a safe proportion of any of these fertilizers is at the rate of a 4-inch pot to a 50 gallon barrel of water making sure that the crystals are all dissolved before applying to the plants. Give weekly fumigations for fly.

Gardenias

If the plants show any white roots on the surface give them a thin mulch of old decayed cow or horse manure but do not apply any liquid manure or chemicals; these may produce plants of great vigor but it will be only at the expense of buds. It is unwise to rush the plants in any way. From 60 to 65 degrees at night will suffice now and ventilation can be freely given. When watering soak the benches thoroughly but be sure to allow them to dry out tolerably well before applying any more. With a soil sufficiently porous so that water will pass away freely and with some bottom heat and a nice genial atmosphere there will not be any considerable number of buds dropping. One good syringing a week with the spray nozzle will take care of mealy bug but do it on clear warm days. The foliage should be allowed to dry before nightfall.

Lorraine Begonias

Probably you will have noticed how much faster the Lorraine begonias are now growing. They do not move much during the hottest summer weather but as soon as the nights are cooler they, in common with many other plants, make much more rapid headway. Give attention to ventilation now as the weather is more uneven both in sunshine and temperature. After the middle or 20th of September they will want to be in a house where they can have fire heat at night. The strongest plants should now be well established in 6-inch pots or pans and it is to be hoped that the necessary staking has not been forgotten. Be sure to use stakes which are light, painted green and as inconspicuous as possible. Keep the growths nicely tied up to them.

Violets

Scratch over the surface soil occasionally. Remove all weeds, runners and spotted or decaying foliage. If the plants are growing in raised benches do not allow rubbish to accumulate below them. Neatness, cleanliness, careful watering and ventilating and the keeping of a sweet atmosphere are what violets need. Double violets should have been all planted indoors some weeks ago and by this time will be well established. Ventilators can usually be kept wide open all the time until the middle of October and no fire heat should be necessary before that time. Violets do not, like artificial heat and were it possible to have a sufficient warmth without using it they would do all the better and be less susceptible to insect attacks. To know how and when to water denotes the experienced grower. It is just as great a fault in treatment to stint fast-growing plants in the needful amount of water as to keep the soil in a constantly saturated condition.

Next Week:—Allamandas; Palms; Ferns; Orchids; Poinsettias; Necessary Repairing.

HORTICULTURE

VOL. XXII   SEPTEMBER 18, 1915   NO. 12

PUBLISHED WEEKLY BY

HORTICULTURE PUBLISHING CO.

147 Summer Street, Boston, Mass.

Telephone, Oxford 292.

WM. J. STEWART, Editor and Manager.

SUBSCRIPTION RATES:

One Year, in advance, $1.00; To Foreign Countries, $2.00; To Canada, $1.50.

Entered as second-class matter December 8, 1904, at the Post Office at Boston, Mass., under the Act of Congress of March 3, 1879.

CONTENTS

"It seems to me there is abundant room for some artistic person with bold and original ideas to devise some really pleasing method of staging gladioli. The formality of long rows of vases filled with noble spikes of these gorgeous flowers is a drawback to the effectiveness of a large collection. Cannot Mr. Felton or some gifted artist show us something new in arrangement?"

The foregoing, clipped from the Horticultural Trade Advertiser of London, indicates that the flower industry in England, like that of our own country, is permitting its best opportunities for publicity and advancement to be lost through indifference or inability to show their products to the public in an attractive and impressive manner. The day of "long rows of vases" has gone by,

and exhibitions depending upon that worn-out and monotonous method of displaying flower exhibits are making a costly mistake.

About "overplanting" We have noticed in our exchanges recently some complaining about the overplanting of Hydrangea paniculata grandiflora as a garden ornament. We are inclined to take issue on this question. The hardy hydrangea is pre-eminently a "people's" shrub. It requires no coddling, is perfectly hardy, not particular as to location, soil or food, and practically free from troublesome insects. It blooms profusely and the flowers last a long time at the season when flowering shrubs are few. Why should not the people plant it abundantly? The critics fail to suggest anything that might be acceptably substituted for it. It is very true that not enough shrubs are planted and many of the most commendable ones for the home grounds are rarely seen in the gardens or exploited by the nurserymen. But that is another story, and is no ground for condemning the Hydrangea. For every garden in which this shrub flaunts its glorious white and pink tinted trusses there are scores where none are seen and in our humble opinion thousands more might be planted in every town before its abundance would be any blemish on the landscape. The real trouble is that in many instances they are set in the wrong place and wrongly grouped and in this respect we agree that criticism is in order and education in artistic arrangement and planting judgment is sorely needed. If every retail nurseryman were to maintain an exhibition plot where intelligent suggestions as to the proper placing and grouping of garden material might be seen it would result in the greatest revival the ornamental nursery business ever received.

Futility of spasmodic effort The paint and drug trade people naturally take a direct practical interest in the "Paint Up and Clean Up" campaigns which have been started more or less success in many places. They, however, express the conviction that the various plans for a clean-up day which have been advocated have little merit in them or permanent value to the trade. They are simply incidental and it is urged that to be effective and fully carry out their mission these efforts at civic improvement should be continuous, hammering away at the good work every day the year through. Limitations of activity to a single day or single week should be removed and a steady drive put in operation to impress on the public that there was something to interest them all the year around. We read with interest these views as expressed by the leading paint manufacturers and dealers, for they are in line exactly with what HORTICULTURE has been harping upon for years in regard to the flower trade. To the flower producer it is but a small matter that the florists whose business it is to turn his products into money should merely boost the sales for any one special day or occasion. What he needs is that the public shall be induced to use his goods every day and in increasing quantity. Like the paint and oil men, what concerns him is that a steady demand shall be built up for his products. In one respect, indeed, he is directly and permanently injured by the spasmodic exploiting by the retailer of any one special day or exclusive flower for any occasion which is sure to cause sharp fluctuations in market values and bring public criticism and disfavor upon the flower industry which in the long run overbalances by far any transient financial advantage that may have been reaped.

ROSE GROWING UNDER GLASS

CONDUCTED BY

[signature]

Questions by our readers in line with any of the topics presented on this page will be cordially received and promptly answered by Mr. Ruzicka. Such communications should invariably be addressed to the office of HORTICULTURE.

Manure for Mulching

The manure to be used for mulching will have to be turned over almost every week now. Do not add too much soil just yet, and if any coarse sod can be had do not use the soil at all, using the sod instead. Never add bone to the manure, or any fertilizer, as it would only waste a lot of it. Lime should never be added, as it would free a good deal of ammonia and nitrogen, and the manure would be worth just so much less. If there is no shed or other covered building to store the manure, put a layer of good coarse sod under it. This will take up whatever leaches and this sod can afterward be used wherever it is wanted for it will be very rich. In turning the manure over all straw, corn stalks if any, and coarse materials that would interfere with applying it, should be removed.

Packing Cut Roses for Shipment

Beauties and some of the free-growing Teas will now be cutting long-stemmed roses and these are best tied in the boxes when shipping to the market. Where the roses have to travel long distances this method is especially useful. It is very simple as after the long-stemmed roses are packed a piece of rope is run around the outside of the box and into the box through the side wherever wanted and the two ends are tied over the stems. This will keep them from sliding around and prevent their getting bruised and broken. It is also well to put two thicknesses of newspaper between the layers of stems every three rows or so. This will prevent the thorns from puncturing the leaves and will make the roses much more attractive when they reach the market. The thorny varieties should always be packed in this way for if the leaves are damaged the bud will not show off as it should and, therefore, will not bring the price that a bud with perfect leaves would. Where two layers of roses are packed in one box be very careful not to pack white in the bottom. The whites will show the bruises more readily and no matter how carefully the blooms are packed the bottom layer will always get bruised more or less. We would never advocate this method, save in packing short stuff such as No. 3 Beauties and roses that have very little market value. Of these we have very few, as they are all pinched at the proper time and they soon grow into number ones or extras.

Icing the Boxes

With the weather warmer than it has been all summer roses had better be iced after packing for shipment. Use a little more paper in the boxes and crush some ice which is afterward put in the end of the box around the stems. A little can be added here and there all through the box, being careful not to have it come into contact with the buds. The object of more paper in the boxes is to keep the roses cooler by keeping the heat out. This will make the ice last longer and the flowers will arrive in a much better condition.

Water in the Vases

This had better be changed daily and the jars scrubbed out at least once a week. If this is not done the water will become poluted and is bound to damage the bottom foliage on all the roses that are put into the water. It is also apt to poison the men that have to handle the roses after they are taken out of such water. The poisoning we hear about every now and then from rose thorns could easily be traced to bad water in the rose jars. Where there are plenty of jars on hand it will be a great help to set them out in the sun every now and then. This will sweeten them all the way through so that the water will not get bad so soon. This is the same with the barrels in which special Beauties are kept. Roll them out every now then and let the sun get at them. They should not be allowed to stay in the sun too long as they are likely to get too dry and spread so that it will take quite a while to get them tight again.

Watering the Bench Fronts

As the season advances the benches will not dry out evenly all over, as they have been doing all summer, and it will be necessary to water every now and then while the rest of the house will be wet enough. Watch these fronts so that they are never allowed to get too dry as the roses would soon show signs of check in their growth. Also see that they are mulched, or have some coarse material right on them all the time, for if the earth is allowed to lie exposed it will not be very encouraging for the roots to work in, and we shall need all the roots that we can get before very long. In watering it is best not to use too much pressure as this would wash the surface of the branches around too much and would be sure to hurt the plants. It will take a little longer to do the watering if the hose is not used full force but it will pay in the end. In watering it is best not to flood the benches too much as this would wash out a good deal of plant food, but at the same time enough water should be applied to wet the soil through thoroughly, letting the water drip through evenly all over. There should be no dry spots in the benches after they are watered.

NATIONAL ASSOCIATION OF GARDENERS

The summer meeting of the National Association of Gardeners was held in the Civic Center Auditorium, San Francisco, Cal., Wednesday, Aug. 18, 1915. In the absence of President John W. Everitt, of New York, Vice-President William S. Rennie, of California, presided.

Although the meeting was not as largely attended as some of the midsummer meetings have been in the East, what was lacking in numbers, however, was fully offset by the general interest and enthusiasm manifested by those present in the proceedings.

Mr. Rennie in welcoming the visiting members to California expressed his regrets at the inability of the president of the association to be on hand. He presented a message to the meeting from the president, however, in which the latter stated in part.

"Whether we come from the East, the West, the North or the South, as professional gardeners our aim should be to produce a broader development for ornamental horticulture which cannot fail to bring greater recognition to our profession, and which will ultimately result in increasing benefits to those in it.

"A strong national association of the gardeners, heartily supported by those who follow the profession, I believe, could be made most powerful and influential in its work for the good of the profession, although it may at times prove disappointing to individuals seeking direct benefits from it. It is, as you are aware, the policy of our association to develop along lines where it will serve its members and aid those striving to advance and better themselves in their calling. We have committees at work endeavoring to thrash out the problems with which an organization like ours is confronted in its development stage, and these committees, and also your officers, at all times court and welcome suggestions from members which may be valuable in aiding the progress of the organization."

Following the reading of the president's message, Vice-President Rennie called on the different members present for a few remarks, and in responding, Robert Williamson, of Greenwich, Conn., said:

"I am indeed glad to be here to meet with the gardeners of the West. I am somewhat disappointed that there are not more of our Eastern members present, as we expected to have a larger body with us, but, of course, we are rather young as an organization and on account of the distance being so great we must make allowance for so few of us here from a distance, but personally I am glad to have taken the trip to meet with the other gardeners here.

David F. Roy, of Marion, Mass., referring to President Everitt's message, said, "I can quite understand why it is that he is not here. Men in our position, if they want to succeed, find that one of the first requisites is that they must cater to the wishes of their employers."

L. P. Jenson, of St. Louis, Mo., in urging a campaign to increase the membership, remarked: "This is the first opportunity I have had to be with this body of gardeners. I hope in the future I will be with you often. It seems to me that the gardeners throughout the country do not know enough about it. I think we ought to make a strong effort to have our members throughout the country get in new members. In that way in a short time we would have a strong representative body of men throughout the United States.

W. T. Lee, of San Francisco, Cal., speaking on increased membership remarked, "It seems to me that as we develop and get more members we should have local organizations if it can be done, to affiliate with the central body in some way, so that we could meet once in a while. I understand that there are quite a number of members on the coast."

A. Bischke, of Noroton, Conn., speaking on the pleasures of the trip and the future of the association, said: "I am greatly surprised to see the strides that have been made by these great western cities; for instance, Minneapolis and Seattle. Then take Tacoma, with its giant trees; we have to take our hats off, to those trees, lakes and boulevards. We have nothing like them in the East. I think we should strive to start a propaganda in each community to develop our association right now. It should not be a local society. It should be a national organization. The more members we can get in, the better, and scattered all over the United States. Our profession is a great one. What would a city like Minneapolis or New York, or any of the greater cities, be without their parks, or without gardens and trees? They would be a barren waste."

Percy Ellings, of Menlo Park, Cal., secretary of the Menlo Park Horticultural Society, extended an invitation to the visiting gardeners to come to Menlo Park and be the guests of the society for a day, stating that they had made arrangements to take the gardeners all through the principal estates down on the Peninsula, and afterwards to treat them to a good old-fashioned Spanish barbecue.

Theodore Wirth, of Minneapolis, Minn., on being called on said in the course of remarks: "While I am a park superintendent now, I came to that position as a gardener, and I am proud to be a gardener and always have been proud of it and always will be. There are many possibilities in our profession, so many different ways to develop that it is certainly very important that we make more effort in the future than in the past to get together and enlarge the usefulness of the National Association of Gardeners. The only way that this can be done best in my opinion is through the formation of local organizations and having them represented by delegates to the national meetings wherever they may be held."

Vice-President Rennie next called on Richard Vincent, Jr., of White Marsh, Md., who said: "In regard to this matter before us, I am something like the boy who made his first trip out in the country. I may be a little green as to what the idea of this association is, but I think that the suggestion in regard to building up the organization is an excellent one. Every man who wants his organization to go ahead ought to put a little energy into it. It is only by thorough work that you can make this organization what it ought to be. It is now in its infancy, but it can and will grow if you will only put your shoulders to the wheel and give it a little push up hill."

Mr. Vincent was followed by some of the members of the Pacific Coast, and what they had to say indicated that they were thoroughly interested in the work that could be accomplished by an organization such as the National Association of Gardeners and that they might be counted on to give their support and co-operation.

An invitation was received at this time from the American Association of Park Superintendents to attend the illustrated lecture of Hon. Samuel E. Hill on "Good Roads" and the meeting adjourned to attend the lecture. It was intended to re-convene after the lecture, but owing to so many other attractions of the exposition city there was no re-convening and the meeting stood finally adjourned.

BIENNIALS AT GLENSIDE, PA.

The cover illustration represents a partial view of Foxgloves and Sweet Williams which, exposed to a lively traffic on two Philadelphia suburban pikes during last June attracted considerable public attention. Calculated to demonstrate to some extent their usefulness for floral mass-effects it also offered a good opportunity to study the attitude of the average visitor. The frequent question, "What are those beautiful flowers?" indicated less familiarity of even well-educated people with biennials than one would suppose. The fact that this class of plants do not flower "all summer" and as a rule do not last over two seasons, invariably brought to light by succeeding questions, did not seem to dampen the admiration for the display. But the most appealing feature to many interested callers was apparently the possibility of easy raising from seed. I am inclined to believe that from the purely business standpoint similar displays are likely to, first of all, benefit the seed trade. There is, however, not the least doubt in regard to their stimulating influence in general. To see a thing brings the desire to have it and the American garden owner, particularly when the quality warrants it, is, as a rule, quick to act.

Knowing the readers of HORTICULTURE to be well posted on the simple proceedings of growing biennials from seed I wish to call attention only to the matter of strains in seeds. From the very start the best should be just good enough for your planting and while foxgloves, for instance, "grow like weeds", to obtain strong evenly grown stock means systematic work and the necessary care. Keeping this strictly in mind and, acting accordingly, the matter is indeed an easy one.

Glenside, Pa.　　　RICHARD ROTHE.

During Recess

Florists' Club of Washington.

The members of the Florists' Club and their friends were the guests on the occasion of the September meeting of Edward S. Schmid and Fred H. Kramer at the crab feast annually tendered them in the Kramer conservatory, at 916 F street. This was to be the "florists' fun night" and all speaking was tabooed. This rule was vacated only in the case of Edward S. Schmid, Fred H. Kramer and George H. Cooke who made two-minute addresses of welcome, and by Richard Vincent, Jr., and Adolph Gude who sang "We're Glad Because We're Here" refrain. Charles A. Stevens acted as toastmaster.

The entertainment consisted of songs and recitations by J. Crosby McCarthy, songs by Kirk Miller who sang of how at the last crab feast the florists had missed going home "On the Five Fifteen" and had returned to finish the festivities, and songs by Sam Shreve, Gerald E. Fitzgerald, and Peter Latterner, for all of whom Jacques Heidenheimer was accompanist.

During the course of the evening the florists were visited by a Russian count and a German schoolmaster, each in native dress, the former in everyday life being Charles A. Stevens and the latter Fred H. Kramer. Mr. Kramer sang a funny little schoolroom song in which he was joined by nearly all of those present.

The big surprise of the evening was the arrival of members of the theatrical companies playing at the Casino and Gaiety theatres who joined them in the feast and later the popular song hits of the respective plays and skits in which they were appearing.

Among those present were George H. Cooke, Edward S. Schmid, E. F. Schmid, Fred H. Kramer, William F. Gude, Adolph Gude, Richard Vincent, Jr., Clarence L. Linz, George H. Shaffer, Otto Bauer, O. A. C. Oehmler, George W. Hess, Harry B. Louis, G. E. Anderson, R. L. Jenkins, C. A. Jackson, Jake Richards, David J. Grillbortzer, Otto Bauer, Samuel Simmons, William Marche, M. J. McCabe, Joe Leaman, Harry Ley, John Robertson, Sr., John Robertson, Jr., David E. Saunders, J. J. Barry, Harry Ley, G. Milton Thomas, Mendel Bedrend, Paul C.

Ziebel, J. Crosby McCarthy, Charles A. Stevens, Peter Latterner, John Shreve, C. P. Boss, Kirk C. Miller, G. W. Libbey, John F. Kleaver, J. W. W. Pickering, Daniel L. O'Brien, Gerald E. Fitzgerald, W. H. Childs, W. F. R. Philipps, Jacque Heidenheimer, Samuel Tapp, I. S. Goldsmith, George H. Emmons, Charles Bradley, Philip Goldstein, M. Graner, Dr. L. H. Vicks, James Quinn, the Grotto band, members of the theatrical companies and others.

The Michell Outing.

The Henry F. Michell Company, seed growers, of 518 Market street, Philadelphia, on Sept. 8, gave its second annual outing to nearly 1200 horticulturists, whom it entertained on its seed

PARK MEN AND PIGEONS AT SAN DIEGO

Left to right—John Morley, Supt. Parks, San Diego; Theo. Wirth, Supt. Parks, Minneapolis; F. C. Green. Supt. Parks, Providence.

The accompanying cut shows three distinguished members of the Association of Park Superintendents enjoying themselves on their trans-continental tour. John Morley the gentleman on the left is the man responsible for the grand planting about the San Diego Exposition, which has been so highly praised by all visitors. Theodore Wirth is too well-known to our readers and the public park profession all over the country for any further introduction here. F. C. Green, standing, is the popular superintendent of famous Roger Williams Park and other public reservations of Providence, R. I. California, Minnesota and Rhode Island fairly represent "both ends and the middle."

farm at Andalusia. Among the farmers and flower growers who made the trip were men from all parts of Pennsylvania and New Jersey, several from New York and Connecticut and one from Chicago.

At Andalusia station the throng formed in line, eight abreast, with the Imperial Band in its midst, and marched to the Michell farm, past canna beds of unusual brilliancy. A buffet lunch was served, and then most of the horticulturists set out on a tour of inspection through the grounds.

The floral display which attracted the greatest attention was an exhibition of cut flowers which included all the varieties seen in the beds outside, and many others as gay and more exotic. They were then taken through the fields where flowers are being grown for seed. In the horticultural reservation they were shown 45,000 blooming cannas, 75,000 blooming plox, 60,000 scarlet sage plants, 50,000 gladioli and 30,000 dahlias.

When the visitors had finished their tour of the flower-beds they were gathered on the lawn for addresses. Henry F. Michell, president of the company, welcomed his guests and announced that it rounded off the company's twenty-fifth anniversary. Brief addresses were also made by E. J. Berlet, president of the Walnut Street Business Men's Association, Prof. Fancourt and Robert Craig.

The addresses were followed by field sports. There were events for both men and women, and the day had its ludicrous climax in a pie-eating contest. Prizes of a very substantial sort were awarded to the winners. After the sports had been concluded the visitors went back to tour the gardens until the special train returned to bring them back to the city.

CONNECTICUT NURSERYMEN'S ASSOCIATION
Group of members on the baseball field at Lake Compounce.

CLUBS AND SOCIETIES

PITTSBURGH FLORISTS' AND GARDENERS' CLUB.

The meeting of this club, September 7, was Gladiolus Night, and in addition to the local exhibits there was a large display from Bidwell & Fobes, Kinsman, O., including some of the newer varieties. We have seldom had before the club an exhibit of gladioli of such all around excellence. Perhaps the least striking of all as shown was the much-advertised E u r o p a, the blooms being very small although they were certainly white. The Secretary was instructed to express the thanks of the club in a letter to Messrs. Bidwell & Fobes. Carl Becherer, gardener at Dixmont Hospital, showed double and single seedling dahlias. the most striking being a large, double-flowered peony dahlia, not yet named, and of a most beautiful deep rich pink. The Bureau of Parks, through Jno. W. Jones, foreman, showed red helianthus, they should make a very striking window decoration. They were grown from seed procured from England. Neil McCallum, president of the club, showed many interesting outdoor flowers and grasses from West End Park. Pasquale Fabozzi, gardener for J. C. Trees, showed gladioli and asters.

I. Roznosky, representing H.F.Michell Co., of Philadelphia, cheered the hearts of those present with his predictions of good fall trade and business. Messrs. Falconer and Knauff who have recently returned from vacation spent in visiting the principal cities of the west and middle west from San Francisco to Cleveland, agreed that in none of the parks of the cities visited did they see such fine specimens of bedding as we have in the Pittsburgh Parks, and on resolution it was carried by the club that the Superintendent of the Parks be requested to have pictures taken of the bedding for use in the trade papers.

H. P. JOSLIN, Sec'y.

PACIFIC COAST HORTICULTURAL SOCIETY.

This society held its regular monthly meeting Sept. 4th, with a large attendance. The session was taken up largely with aftermath of the S. A. F. convention. President H. Plath gave a very satisfactory report of the event, which was followed by a short talk from Daniel MacRorie, on matters pertaining to the convention. For the exhibition committee, H. Plath announced a dahlia show to be held on Sept. 18 and 19 in the Palace of Horticulture at the exposition, under the auspices of the California State Floral Society and the Alameda County Floral Society. He said eleven prizes would be open for professional growers. For the picnic committee Frank Pelicano recommended a Florists' Day at the Exposition instead of the usual picnic. Following the acceptance of J. Noordink to membership in the society, several more names were proposed by Daniel MacRorie, including Patrick Welch, Chas. Willis Ward, Wm. F. Kasting, V. J. Gorly and John Morley. The calling of the names

was greeted with applause, and then more applause when Mr. MacRorie added that some of them had asked for life membership. As there is no provision in the constitution for life membership, a committee was appointed to consider the matter of changing that part of the bylaws. Among the evening's exhibits were Victor Podesta's bowling trophy which took 105 points; a display of Delice and Kaiser Wilhelm dahlias by Frank Pelicano rated at 85 points, and Nephrolepis Piersoni Elegantissima, rated at 85 points.

ST. LOUIS FLORIST CLUB.

The St. Louis Florist Club had a fine day for their outdoor meeting Sept. 9, which was held on the grounds of the H. J. Weber & Sons Nursery Co. The members came out in large numbers. All those having touring cars placed them in service. The meeting was held in the large packing shed fitted up for the occasion. Frank, George, William and Walter Weber took the visitors in charge and escorted them through the grounds. This being installation meeting the chair ordered all committees to make final reports, as the new officers always begin with a clean slate. Ex-Presidents Pitcher and Windler installed the newly elected officers—Julius Bourdet, president; J. J. Beneke, secretary; W. C. Smith, treasurer. Vice-President Wells and Trustee Ohlweiler, owing to business engagements, were absent. After a general talk the meeting adjourned and the members were then invited to a fine lunch and cigars. After satisfying the inner man a second tour was made of the greenhouses and north side grounds. Before leaving for home there were three cheers for the hosts, and the day will long be remembered by those who took part.

MEDFORD (MASS.) HORTICULTURAL SOCIETY.

The annual fall exhibition of this society was held on Friday, Sept. 10. The Breck-Robinson Nursery Co. put up an excellent display of gladioli and cannas. Quite a collection of fine varieties of gladioli was also staged by the Brookland Gardens, S. E. Spencer, proprietor. This gentleman contributed a large part of the best basket of gladioli. Joseph Breck & Sons, Fotler, Fiske, Rawson Co., and Breck-Robinson Nursery Co., also contributed prizes. Fine dahlias were exhibited by Mrs. George B. Gill and Mrs. St. Dennis. The children's classes for flowers and vegetables were keenly contested. The ladies of the society devote a great deal of time and patience to this work and it is bearing fruit. The prize for the best kept home garden for the season was won by Mrs. Aykroid. Mrs. Bush's garden showed the greatest improvement. An Italian boy 13 years old had the best vegetable garden; a Chinese boy the best vase of flowers. Wm. N. Craig and Duncan Finlayson of Brookline were the judges.

NEW JERSEY FLORICULTURAL SOCIETY.

A regular meeting of this society was held at the house of Joseph A. Manda, West Orange, on Tuesday evening, Sept. 7, 1915. A letter was read from the National Association of Gardeners asking all local societies to affiliate so that should a member leave one society he would immediately become a member of another, without payment of further dues, on presentation of a card from the secretary of his society showing him to be in good standing. The society acted favorably on this proposition. Everything is completed for the Dahlia Show, Oct. 4, and schedules will be mailed on application to the secretary.

At the close of the meeting refreshments were enjoyed at the expense of Mr. Manda. A vote of thanks was recorded him and all spent a very pleasant evening. The awards were as follows:

Begonia McLance, Peter Hauck, Jr., gard. Max Schneider, 52 points; dahlias by same, 75 points. Cissus discolor, Wm. Barr, gard. Emil Panuska, 75 points. Coleus Cecil Brown, Mrs. Wm. Barr, certificate of merit. Display of orchids, Joseph A. Manda, first class certificate.

GEO. W. STRANGE, Sec.

GREYSTONE (R. I.) HORTICULTURAL SOCIETY.

This society held its Fifth Annual Exhibition on Saturday, Sept. 4, in the Whitehall Assembly Room.

For quantity as well as quality of the exhibits, the show was easily the best ever held here. John Lewis Childs sent a beautiful collection of gladioli which along with a very fine and comprehensive collection of asters from Henry A. Dreer of Phila., occupied the whole of the stage. The dahlias of Wm. Steel, Auburn, R. I., were the best shown in the open classes.

In the classes for members of the society only, R. J. Murray obtained the most points and won the medal offered by Messrs. Dobbie & Co., of Edinburgh. Ben Steed of Greystone won in both members and open classes with asters.

Cornelius Hartstra and John Marshall of Providence were the judges.

CLEVELAND FLORISTS' CLUB.

The annual meeting of the Cleveland Florists' Club held September 13th, resulted in part of the list of officers being changed. Herbert Bate, president; Al. Ligren, 1st vice-president; Claude Tyler, 2nd vice-president. The old standbys, both of whom have proved their value as faithful officers in the club for the past two years, were re-elected to their respective positions—for secretary, Frank A. Friedley and treasurer, Geo. W. Smith. These men have the handling of several thousand dollars annually, being the funds subscribed by the florists of Cleveland for co-operative advertising. Mr. Knoble assumes the chairmanship of the executive committee and will be assisted by Albert Barber, F. C. W. Brown, F. A. Wittbuhn and S. S. Pen-

tecost, who with the officers will compose the Board of Directors. There was a good attendance present, all of whom enjoyed the personally conducted tour as given by Frank Ritzenthaler and Fred Witthuhn who took the entire party over the route of their recent Southern and Western trip. Mr. Witthuhn only succeeded in reaching Texas, where he discontinued the trip because it was about time for the berths to be made up. He promises to continue his interesting story, pointing out many of the exciting and amusing adventures of their party.

CHICAGO FLORISTS' CLUB.

The regular meeting of the Chicago Florists' Club was held Sept. 9, at the Hotel Bismarck, about fifty being present. The meeting was more social than otherwise, no important business coming up. Discussion of the Amalgamation banquet to be given on October 7, the regular meeting night, followed. Mr. Tricker of Arlington, N. J., was a guest and gave a description of his method og growing nymphaeas. One variety Mrs. Woodrow Wilson which is a success in the New York market, he hopes to make equally successful in Chicago. Pres. Wm. J. Keimel and T. MacAllister both spoke of their impressions of the convention and the two fairs and were voted the thanks of the club for their interesting accounts. Several names were added to the membership and several new ones proposed.

MASSACHUSETTS HORTICULTURAL SOCIETY.

Dahlia and Fruit Exhibition.

This exhibition is one of the series of free summer shows at Horticultural Hall, Boston. It opened on Saturday, September 11 and closed on Sunday evening and was well attended by the public, whose infatuation with the dahlia continues unabated.

Dahlias were shown in brilliant array, all classes being well represented on tables that occupied the main part of the large exhibition hall. The flowers were superb, the season apparently having been favorable. New developments in the cactus, decorative and peony-flowered sections were noticeable but other classes seemed to simply hold their own with recent past shows. The principal winners in the dahlia classes were J. K. Alexander, W. D. Hathaway, George H. Walker, E. F. Dwyer, W. H. Symonds, Miss Fanny Foster, Lamont D. Litchfield, Mary C. Caswell, F. P. Webber and James Robertson. These were all represented by extensive displays, and most of the blooms were nicely labeled. Fottler, Fiske, Rawson Co. showed a very large collection, flowers mostly under number. Mrs. L. A. Towle, F. L. Tinkham, J. S. Bailey, Thos. M. Proctor, Riverside Dahlia Gardens, and H. F. Burt all had good displays and F. H. Snow staged some 25 excellent seedlings. A creditable basket of dahlia blooms was put up by the Boston Cut Flower Co. Luther C. Parker got honorable mention for a seedling decorative dahlia, an enormous flower of pale delicate pink.

The show was notable for many other things besides dahlias. Mt. Desert Nurseries made a beautiful and unique display of hardy perennials in branching bamboo stands, among them being enormous spikes of Lilium Henryi. This exhibit received honorable mention. T. D. Hatfield, gardener for Walter Hunnewell showed Buddleias from seed sown last March, the flowers borne on branches four feet high which certainly put this popular shrub in a new and impressive light. Blue Hill Nurseries showed among their hardy phloxes a fine seedling white named Mrs. Heurlin. J. K. Alexander was strong on gladioli. Geo. W. Page showed fall asters. Buddleia variabiles was staged by James Wheeler.

The fruit and vegetables display was very fine, the peaches being the best we have ever seen exhibited in Boston. Jennison's Floral Gardens showed a basket of the new everbearing strawberry Ideal, which was a great attraction, the berries being simply perfect. This variety was awarded a first-class certificate by the Massachusetts Horticultural Society last year.

The American Dahlia Society, in cooperation with the Horticultural Society of New York, will hold its Dahlia exhibition in the American Museum of Natural History, Central Park West and 77th street, New York City, on Sept. 24, 25 and 26. Copies of the schedule and further information may be had by addressing Joseph J. Lane, Secretary A. D. S., 11 West 32d street, New York City, or George V. Nash, Secretary Hort. Soc. of N. Y., Bronx Park, N. Y.

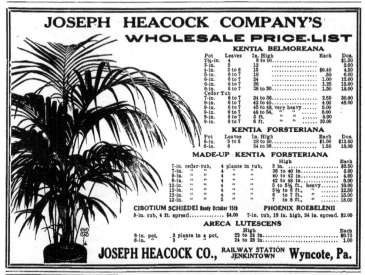

CLUB AND SOCIETY NOTES.

The Dayton (Ohio) Florists and Gardeners' Association met on Tuesday, Sept. 7.

The Minneapolis Florists' Club met in the Minneapolis Floral Co.'s establishment on September 14.

There was a large attendance at the regular meeting of the Cincinnati Florists' Society at Hotel Gibson on Monday evening. J. A. Peterson and John Van Leeuwen gave interesting talks, the former on the S. A. F. meeting at Frisco, the latter on Co-operation in Buying Among the Florists.

The New York Florists' Club held its first meeting for the season of '15 and '16 on Monday evening, September 13. Exhibits of dahlias and gladioli, a fine lecture on Gladioli with lantern slides, by Mrs. B. Hammond Tracy, of Wenham, Mass., a gratifying report of the Flower Show committee and the formulating of general plans for preliminary work on the big flower show for next spring furnished interest and instruction in plenty for the members who were present and to all

this must be added, last but not least, the ample provision made for the inner man's comfort by Chairman Phil Kessler and his vigilant House Committee.

The next meeting of the Gardeners' and Florists' Club of Boston will take place on Tuesday evening, September 21, when it is said a talk will be given by M. C. Ebel, of Madison, N. J.

The annual field day was held last Saturday afternoon at the nurseries of the Breck-Robinson Company at Munroe Station. The party of 100 came in a special car. Lunch was served in the large packing house. A. E. Robinson was master of ceremonies. After lunch Pres. Herman H. Bartsch of Waverley called the meeting to order. The other speakers were W. N. Craig of Brookline, Charles H. Breck of Boston, Ex-Pres. W. J. Kennedy of Chestnut Hill and Thomas J. Grey of Boston. It was a most interesting and enjoyable occasion.

The annual exhibition of the Andover (Mass.) Florists and Gardeners' Club, held in the Town Hall on September 10 and 11, was like its prede-

cessors, a very large and attractive show, creditable alike to the amateur gardeners of the town and the professional florists and gardeners who gave it encouragement. There was a long list of prizes in which the children were well remembered and there was plenty of competition. We should estimate that there was between four and five hundred running feet of table space filled to the limit. The stage was handsomely banked by J. H. Playdon, who officiated as manager, and there was a long table of dahlias, gladioli and Buddleias from Fottler, Fiske, Rawson Co. Everything else was from amateur sources. Nasturtiums, verbenas, gladioli, stocks, cockscombs, zinnias, asters, dahlias, balsams, centaureas, sweet peas, etc., certainly made a very gay picture and it was evident from the quality of the blossoms that the Andoverites go in for the best strains of seed the market affords.

The judges were J. Berndtson of Lawrence, Frank Leith of Haverhill and George Westland of North Andover, and they surely had a big afternoon's work laid out for them.

SEED TRADE

AMERICAN SEED TRADE ASSOCIATION

Officers—President, J. M. Lupton, Mattituck, L. I., N. Y.; First Vice-President, Kirby B. White, Detroit, Mich.; Second Vice-President. F. W. Bolgiano, Washington, D. C.; Secretary-Treasurer, C. E. Kendel, Cleveland, O.; Assistant Secretary, S. F. Willard, Jr., Cleveland, O. Cincinnati, O., next meeting place.

Clover Seed Acreage and Condition.

The acreage for clover seed in the United States this year is estimated to be about 114.5 per cent of last year's acreage, based upon reports to the Bureau of Crop Estimates of the United States Department of Agriculture. The condition of the crop on September 1, is estimated at 80.3 per cent of normal which compares with 77.3 per cent a year ago and 79.7 the average of the past ten years on September 1. These figures forecast a moderately larger crop this year than last year.

The acreage this year as compared with last year, and the condition on September 1 of this year and of last year, in percentage of normal in important States, are estimated respectively as follows: New York, 125, 88, 73; Pennsylvania, 95, 83, 84; Ohio, 108, 74, 78; Indiana, 130, 67, 74; Illinois, 125, 78, 70; Michigan, 106, 79, 84; Wisconsin, 95, 83, 88; Minnesota, 97, 84, 91; Iowa, 102, 87, 86; Missouri, 148, 79, 63; Kentucky, 140, 89, 55; Tennessee, 120, 88, 75; Idaho, 120, 94, 88; Oregon, 86, 84, 63;

American Seed and Nursery Stock for China.

(Commercial Attaché Juleau H. Arnold. Peking. Aug. 9).

It is suggested that American dealers in seeds and nursery stock furnish this office with a number of catalogues as we often receive inquires from residents in this country for American seed and nursery catalogues. The climate of Peking is dry and cold in the winter and damp and hot in the summer, with a temperature ranging between zero and 100 degrees Fahrenheit.

Notes.

D. D. P. Roy has opened a new seed store at 168 North Michigan avenue, Chicago.

Rochelle, Ill.—Augustus Caspers is going into the wholesale and mail order seed business.

Saginaw, Mich.—The branch store of the Grenell house will be managed by F. W. Mahan, of Watertown, N. Y.

Washington.—After years of vain efforts to make blue grass grow on the little plot in front of its building, the agriculture department is plowing the weeds up, to start again.

The value of imports of horticultural material at the Port of New York for the week ending September 4, is given as follows:

Sulphate of potash, $18,670; nitrate of soda, $231,857; clover seed, $31,510; grass seed, $10,999; trees, plants and bulbs, $180,404.

Louisville, Ky.—A fine store formerly occupied by a grocery concern has been secured by Hardin, Hamilton & Lewman for a seed store, in place of the temporary place they have been occupying since they were burned out.

The news that a certain well-known house in the trade are offering £300 a year for the services of an assistant manager caused a little excitement among some of the actual or would-be experts of the seed trade. Berths with such a salary are not going every day, neither are really good men for such positions as plentiful as grass-hoppers. It will be interesting to see who is the chosen candidate.

The above, clipped from the Horticultural Trade Advertiser of London, may interest our readers. In this country "berths" such as mentioned are more plentiful than men who are competent to fill them. And $1500 a year would hardly be sufficient inducement for the right man.

Editor HORTICULTURE:

I notice in the last issue of HORTICULTURE you credit us with informing you that we are developing a seed stock of beans free of anthracnose, by which we suppose you mean anthracnose resistant stock. Any stock of beans may be free of anthracnose under certain conditions of growth. Think you must have misunderstood your informant or had this bit of gossip second hand, for if we are anywhere within forty miles of accomplishing so worthy an object, I am unaware of it, much as I regret to say so. I hasten to enter this disclaimer for the reason that I do not want those of our friends who realize the responsibility assumed in making such a statement to be misadvised on the one hand, or, on the other, credit us with dealing with so serious a matter flippantly.

Very truly yours,
WILBUR BROTHERTON.
Jerome B. Rice Seed Co.

CATALOGUES RECEIVED.

N. A. Hallauer, Ontario, N. Y.—Peonies, Gladioli, Dahlias, Roses, Hardy Plants and Shrubs.

Sutton & Sons, Reading, England—"Sutton's Bulbs." An attractive well illustrated publication.

Thos. J. Grey & Co., Boston—Autumn Catalogue of Bulbs, Hardy Herbaceous Plants, Implements, Etc.

Heller Bros Co., New Castle, Ind.—"The Roses of New Castle," Autumn Edition. Hardy plants and bulbs for fall planting.

Good & Reese Co., Springfield, Ohio —Fall Trade List for Florists, Nurserymen and Dealers only. Close printed and "full of meat."

Conard & Jones Co., West Grove, Pa.—"New Floral Guide," Autumn, 1915. Bulbs, peonies, greenhouses and outdoor plants and shrubs.

F. W Kelsey Nursery Co., New York City—Wholesale Price List of Trees, Shrubs, Etc., for Fall, 1915, Planting and Reservation for Spring, 1916.

Przedpelski & Antoniewicz, Kieff, Russia—Price List No. 11 of Seeds of Russian Conifers, Trees and Shrubs. Special Catalogue for U. S. and Great Britain.

Storrs & Harrison Co., Painesville, Ohio—Autumn Catalogue, No. 3, for 1915. Bulbs, Seeds, Plants and Trees are well represented in this very comprehensive illustrated list.

Peter Henderson & Co., New York City—Autumn Catalogue. An up-to-date and interesting issue. Covers adorned with Giant Darwin and Cottage Tulips beautifully done in natural colors.

Kirke Chemical Co., Inc., Brooklyn, N. Y.—Folder of the Specialties of the Kirke System. Fertilizers, Insecticides and Spraying Specialties. Contains valuable tabulated planting lists for vegetables and flowers.

The Union Nurseries, Oudenbosch, Holland—Wholesale Catalogue of Forest and Ornamental Trees, Spring Flowering, Forcing and American Plants, Coniferae and Evergreens. McHutchison & Co., sole agents for America.

Peter Henderson & Co., New York City—Wholesale Catalogue for Florists and Market Gardeners for Autumn, 1915. This is a valuable wholesale list for the trade, covering seeds, bulbs, plants, tools, requisites, fertilizers, insecticides and books.

W. B. Whittier & Co., Framingham Nurseries, Framingham, Mass.—Fall Trade Price List for 1915, for Nurserymen, Dealers, Florists and Landscape Architects only. A splendid list of trees, shrubs, evergreens, vines and roses which we advise our readers to peruse.

Melrose, Mass.—Mayor Charles H. Adams urges that all citizens take particular care of grass plots at the edge of sidewalks. In many suburban cities are seen beautiful lawns, well cared for, but ending at the sidewalk's inner edge. The mayor believes the 100 miles of sidewalks in Melrose will be a thing of beauty if citizens will take pains to cut the grass on the outer edges.

Of Interest to Retail Florists

BATTLE OF FLOWERS AT WORCESTER.

One of the big features of the New England Fair at Worcester, Mass., last week was the parade of flower decorated autos and "battle of flowers."

When the hour arrived for the parade and judging, the grandstand was packed, and enclosures about the track were crowded. For an hour previous, all had been coming in decked in all the beautiful hues of New England flora. An international truck owned by Ross Bros: Co., promptly at 4.30 o'clock led the procession onto the track and 16 cars, covered with a wealth of flowers and occupied by handsomely gowned women and enthusiastic men followed. As the cars approached in front of the grandstand, each was given an ovation, while thousands of yards of serpentine streamers of bright colors were thrown at them from the stand.

As cars passed and repassed each other in front of the grandstand, armful after armful of handsome blossoms was hurled into the faces of the happy contestants. Basket after basket of confetti was emptied and hundreds of rolls of the streamers were unfurled until cars and occupants were buried beneath it and the track itself was carpeted with a four-inch depth of color that no artist could duplicate.

It was a stirring scene, novel to Worcester and the applause from the stand and track was tremendous. Each car had its suporters among the spectators. The appearance of the battleship Cadillac, entered by Walter D. Ross, was a signal for applause from all sides. Flying the stars and stripes, manned by men in the uniform of Uncle Sam's seamen, armed with a battery of four-inch guns, the Cadillac steamed through to victory, winning in each place where a win was possible, $170 in prizes.

Wm. Anderson and L. C. Midgeley were the judges. Second money in the touring car class, finally went to Arthur T. Hunting, West Boylston, for his Cadillac, handsomely trimmed with gladioli, asters, dahlias, goldenrod and asparagus. Henry A. Mower's Stanley steamer was adjudged winner of third money. The car was a mass of flowers, and on each side and on the hood were great butterflies made of red gladioli on a green background. Fifteen hundred blossoms were used by Harry I. Randall who designed the decorations and was a passenger in the car.

At the conclusion of the battle, Gov. David I. Walsh boarded the craft and was taken into the city, convoyed by all the other cars in the show.

Hampton Beach, N. H.—Sept. 9 was Governor's Day at the Hampton Beach carnival and nearly 20,000 persons attended. There was a parade of more than a mile of decorated automobiles. Silver cups were awarded to J. J. Comley, florist, of Newburyport, Messrs. Lane of Haverhill and Whitely of Lowell. Mr. Comley's machine was decorated with nearly 5000 flowers.

NEWS NOTES.

Chelsea, Mass.—Tower & Harney, florist, have removed to a new store at 440 Broadway.

Newburyport, Mass. — Comley, the florist, is adding a large glass room to his flower store at the corner of Pleasant and Titcomb streets.

Houston, Tex.—The Cotney Floral Co. are about to replace their old flower establishment, which was demolished in the great storm, with a fine modern store and work rooms.

Rutherford, N. J.—A plantation of standard roses at Julius Roehrs' Co.'s place is attractively blooming at present, and offers a good opportunity to compare the merits of the many varieties there represented. The conclusion pretty sure to be reached is that after all, Gruss an Teplitz has all the rest beaten as a standard rose. We noticed some good phloxes on a recent visit. Among the very finest were Chastity, white, dwarf; Champs Elysee, deep magenta; Geo. A. Strohlein, bright scarlet with dark eye; Mme. Paul Dutrie, pale lilac blush; Beranger, soft pink with darker eye; Baron von Dedem, deep pink, on scarlet tone.

St. Paul, Minn.—The annual chrysanthemum show at Como Park will mark the celebration of the opening of the immense greenhouse completed in the last year. Park Superintendent Fred Nussbaumer expects to have the building filled with its winter quota of flowers in October, including almost 100 varieties of chrysanthemums. Adolph Keiper, 318 Wabasha street, was the only successful candidate in a class of four who took the examination for head gardener. This is the second examination to be held, no one having passed the first. The head gardener will have charge of the greenhouse under Superintendent Nussbaumer's direction.

Andover, Mass.—J. H. Playdon is just completing a new greenhouse, 20 by 125 with Stearns Lumber Co. material. Emil Weber is foreman in charge of this place for the past 14 years and it is easy to see by the appearance of the stock and general surroundings that his reputation as a good grower is well merited. W. A. Trow, whose estate adjoins the Playdon establishment, is one of Andover's most ardent amateur gardeners—we should add that Mrs. Trow is also. They have a splendid field of dahlias of which many are seedlings raised on the place. Mr. Trow is an enthusiastic supporter of the club and the flower shows.

The Minnesota State Florists' Association held its annual meeting in St. Paul, on Thursday, September 9th at the Holm & Olson store.

NEW FLOWER STORES.

Aberdeen, S. D.—Siebrecht, 306 So. Main street.

Dayton, Ohio.—W. G. Mathews, Miami Hotel.

Chicago, Ill.—H. Munson, 1353 North Clark street.

Pittsburgh, Pa.—Carl Zilinski, Montooth Borough.

Northampton, Mass.—C. A. Rosander, 159 Main street.

Cleveland, Ohio.—R. B. Kegg & Co., Euclid avenue and 79th street.

Marlboro, Mass.—H. E. Pease of Worcester, agency at Burke's Specialty Shop.

Cleveland, O.—The Jones-Russell Company will open a branch store on October 1st in the Taylor Arcade.

Chicago, Ill.—The Rosery Florist, 6972 N. Clark street; Drexel Floral Co. 47th street and Drexel Boulevard.

The flower department of the New York State Fair opened at Syracuse, on Tuesday, September 14, with an excellent display both amateur and professional. David Lumsden is superintendent of this department.

NEWS ITEMS FROM EVERYWHERE

CHICAGO.

Mr. and Mrs. Louis Winterson have returned from two weeks at Deleran Lake, Wis.

Allie Zech is back from a fishing exposition at Tomahawk Lake, Wis., where he spent a fortnight.

Mr. and Mrs. Geo. Asmus are home and like all the rest think Chicago a pretty good place to live in after all.

Theodore Vogel, formerly known as "Teddy" is back in Chicago where he hopes to secure a position and again call Chicago his home.

W. Weatherwax formerly with W. J. Smyth, 31st and Michigan Ave., has opened a store at 47th St. and Drexel Boul, known as the Drexel Floral Co.

H. Perkins, 2nd, formerly of the Shaw Gardens, St. Louis, Mo., was in Chicago this week looking up materials for building. He will go into business in Pacific, Mo.

Miss Marguerite McNulty and Miss Parker are both back at their desks and pleased with their western outing which included some 6000 miles of continuous sight-seeing.

E. W. Siebrecht will sever his connection with the Fleischman Floral Co. in the Railway Exchange Bldg. and open a store at 6972 N. Clark St., to be known as the Rosery Florist.

Victor Young, manager of Geo. Wittbold & Co.'s retail store on N. Clark St. will go into business with Fred Ronsley, now doing business under the name of Ronsley the Florist, on Dearborn St.

The new warehouse now being built by Vaughan's Seed Store at Morton Grove, is nearing completion under the supervision of Albert Erickson. It is for storing onion sets and surplus seeds.

A Lange and family and Tom MacAllister are all back from the Pacific Coast. At this popular store four or five wedding orders per day have come in regularly since Sept. 1, and no dropping off as yet. The little colonial corsages are taking as well as ever at their stand in the Stevens Arcade.

C. B. Knickman was a welcome visitor here on his way back from the Pacific Coast this week. He found enough business there to keep him well past his usual schedule and says he is well pleased with the summer's work. This seems to be the general verdict of those who sought business in the West this summer, possibly because so few ventured to undertake it.

Jas. G. Hancock and family say that when they were crossing the Canadian Rockies they stopped at that pearl in the mountains, Lake Louise, on August 5th. Leaving the hotel they climbed the trail a thousand feet higher to Lake Agnes, then skirted the rocky side of the mountain above the water and continued to climb till snow line was reached. Very few flowers were passed on the trail but beyond that and growing not more than fifty feet from the ice snow packs, were quantities of wild flowers. Mr. Hancock gathered a collection of 20 varieties. There was nothing, however, that closely resembled the Edelweis of Switzerland.

Mr. and Mrs. Jas. G. Hancock and their daughters have returned from an extended trip through the West, going out via the Canadian Pacific then down the Coast as far as Mexico and home via the Grand Canyon of the Colorado, Colorado Springs, etc. One of the most unique things they saw was the Great American Desert covered with sage bush and cactus trees, broken up by orchards of apples and fields of hay. The great desert seems bound to give way to the conquest by water which engineers are solving with their irrigation projects. A "prairie schooner," and an automobile seen from the car window at the same time, crossing the desert seemed to link the past with the present.

The Outlook.

Judging from the number of debutantes, Chicago florists have reason to look forward to a good season just ahead. Social butterflies they may be, but they revel in roses, and social affairs of all kinds follow in their wake. This has been a busy summer for Cupid. Shut off from the usual outdoor sports by the daily downpour, the summer youth has used his time awooing and the florist reaps the benefit. From all the retailers comes the same report that September is making a record for weddings. Florists and fashion makers have apparently entered into a friendly conspiracy, for the fall suits seem to demand the return of the corsage for street wear, while for parties and evening affairs they are more popular than ever.

PROVIDENCE, R. I.

The September Exhibition of the Rhode Island Horticultural Society opened in the ball room of the Narragansett Hotel, Thursday, Sept. 16, for a two days' exhibit of dahlias, asters and gladioli in commercial and professional classes.

The Elmwood Dahlia Society of Providence held a dahlia show last week and prizes were taken by John Cade, 1st; William Ashcroft, 2nd; and James W. Speight, third. The judges were Thomas Gould, John Morrison and Thomas Stones.

The professional classes at the South County fair this week were well filled and keen competition was a result. A new feature was the big exhibit of gladioli by Carmichael Brothers of Shannock. George L. Stillman the Westerly "dahlia king," was also a large exhibitor.

PHILADELPHIA.

Charles R. O'Donnell representing Henry A. Dreer left on the 15th inst. on a business trip West.

Edwin J. Fancourt of the S. S. Pennock-Meehan Co., was reported to be at Butte, Montana, on the 15th inst. headed East, after a successful business tour of the Pacific Coast.

Howard M. Earl will leave on the 18th inst. for his second trip this season to California. We presume this is, in part, called for by the death of Mr. Lonsdale, their manager at the Floradale Farms, and the new arrangements made necessary thereby.

George Anderson is about the same; but for the first time in five weeks two of his brother craftsmen, John Burton and your scribe, were allowed in his sick room on the 14th inst. He looks natural enough, and was able to sit up to greet us. But can only speak a few syllables. The doctor says the lingual nerve ought to be the first to recover but its not there yet. Still, George knew us, and seemed glad to nod an acquiescence for a motor race with honorable Burton and smile at a cigar from thrifty scribe. This is not a very cheerful report but it is the best we dare give under the circumstances.

"God Almighty first planted a garden," said Bacon, and ever since Eden gardening has been a highly respectable business. Emerson said that "the earth laughs in flowers," and John Milton, blind though he was, spoke of "flowers of paradise," didn't intend, however, to reproduce Bartlett's familiar quotations, but to tell you something about Washington Atlee Burpee.

Here is a gentleman whose father was from the French Beaupres, whose mother's people, the Atlees, lived in England at the early home of the Washingtons, and himself born in Canada, works in Philadelphia and lives in Bucks County.

Besides that, he is probably responsible for more flowers than any other person in the land. Thousands of years ago it was commanded:

"In the morning sow thy seed and in the evening withhold not thine hand;" and Burpee is the man who grows the seeds you sow, hence I might almost christen him the godfather of flowers.

Yes, everybody hereabouts has heard of the wonderful Fordhook farms, near Doylestown; but bless you, brced as are their several hundred acres, they don't produce more than a fraction of all the seeds which this bucolic artist and poet distributes over the world.

"Do you buy seeds in Europe?" I asked him.

"I dislike and don't 'buy' because I don't buy seeds anywhere. I grow and sell them," was his answer.

Yes, Mr. Burpee not only raises tomato seeds in Bucks County, but cabbages in Denmark, beets, radishes and carrots in France, sweet peas in California and goodness alone knows how many other things in other parts of America. Each thing is grown where it will develop the best; but even so, Mr. Burpee takes nobody's say-so for a seed any more than Uncle Sam's mint will take your gold without assaying it.

The above is clipped from a lengthy article which appeared in the Philadelphia Ledger, September 11th, which is certainly pretty good work for a daily paper and very well put. But while it is true Burpee was born in Canada, he is not much of a Canadian—as all his people fore and aft are Philadelphia colonial from "seventeen something!"　　　　G. C. W.

CLEVELAND.

Wm. P. Craig, representing the Robert Craig Co., Philadelphia, was one of the visitors of the past few days. Mr. Craig reserved space in the Cleveland Flower Show where he is planning to put a feature exhibit.

Clarence Myers, of the Smith & Fetters Company, left on his vacation Monday. He chose a good time for vacating because of this being the hottest week of the summer. Trade is very inactive and stock is hanging on according to the wholesalers.

Schiller, the Florist (George Asmus?) of Chicago, was conducted by Mr. F. C. W. Brown, of the J. M. Gasser Co., through a tour of all the retail and wholesale houses in town. Mr. Schiller stated that he was going to try and get away to come to the Cleveland Flower Show if he could arrange it.

The Flower Show Committee is very much elated in securing a special prize from Mr. James W. Corrigan, one of the wealthy iron ore operators in Cleveland. This will be a silver cup valued at $500. The order has been placed with the Tiffany Company, New York, to design a special cup after a chrysanthemum. It is to be competed for by the private gardeners of Ohio only.

This is Style Show week in Cleveland and all the retail stores are full of the newest creations for milady. J. M. Gasser Company have taken advantage of the extensive publicity of all the dry goods stores by making a feature style show window. They have a model bride dressed in an American-created gown. At one side of the window is a very fine specimen of peacock which adds greatly to the attractiveness of the window.

WASHINGTON, D. C.

Stanley Holland has removed from 2406 Eighteenth street to his attractive new quarters, corner of Eighteenth and Columbia Road, N. W.

W. W. Kimmel has reopened his store on Fourteenth street, N. W., for the fall season. He had been spending the summer at Colonial Beach.

Local gossip has it that Henry Pfister will shortly re-enter the retail florist business and will be located in the vicinity of Connecticut and Rhode Island avenues, N. W.

The Civil Service Commission announces that an examination will be held on October 6 to secure eligibles for appointment to the position of assistant in shade tree insect work in the Bureau of Entomology of the Department of Agriculture. This position pays between $1,400 and $1,600 per annum.

Fred Leapley became infected with poison last week by the bite of an insect, probably a mosquito, and the irritation caused him to scratch his forehead just above the eye. He had been handling flowers and plants that had evidently just been sprayed and it was not long before the swelling became of a size as to necessitate him remaining home for several days.

Although the purchase of the property has not yet been consummated, the Leo Niessen Company state that before another year they will be in a building of their own. In addition to putting on an automobile delivery wagon, they intend increasing their store force to take care of their added business and other improvements, such as increasing the capacity of their ice boxes, are also to be made.

"It was an agreeable surprise to those of us who represented Washington and Baltimore at the recent Convention," said William F. Gude, who has recently returned from San Francisco, "to be entertained so royally all along the line. Through the courtesy of Mr. and Mrs. William L. Rock we had an excellent opportunity of touring Kansas City, Mo., by automobile. We were their guests at a dinner at the Muehlbach Hotel and later visited one of the theatres, and altogether spent a most enjoyable day in that

city. This is a sample of the entertainment provided for us at every place we stopped."

ST. LOUIS.

The Vanderwoorts Floral department worked a big force on Saturday night and Sunday decorating the store for their fall opening, which took place Monday, Sept. 13.

The Lady Florists held a pleasant meeting at the home of Mrs. John L. Koenig on Clarence avenue. All members were present and enjoyed a pleasant afternoon. Mrs. E. Schray will entertain them for the October meeting.

A new floral concern has made its appearance in St. Louis under the name of Young Bros. Floral Co. William C. Young and John Young, formerly with C. Young & Sons Co., have gone into the retail florists' business at 5504 Waterman avenue, the old West End branch of the C. Young & Sons Co.

The floral firms of Windler's, Wm. Schray & Sons, A. Brix and Max Pelletier were victims of many bogus telephone orders on Wednesday of the past week by a young West End woman to send floral baskets and plants to her birthday in the names of prominent brewery officials. The second order to the Windler store caused suspicion, and on investigation it was found to be bogus and caused the arrest of the woman, who was at the time entertaining her friends. The plants and floral offerings were ordered sent back and the woman held for fraud.

BUFFALO, N. Y.

Wm. F. Kasting has returned from the S. A. F. Convention, also Jas. Peak and Wm. Siever and family.

Al. Keltsch is now in the swim, having purchased a real Ford car, and can be seen at the wholesale house early in the morning.

Peter Hoffman, well known to the trade, is at the Deaconess Hospital. Mr. Hoffman had an operation performed which was successful and he is now gradually improving.

Flower Market Reports

BOSTON This market is suffering from the effects of the hottest days of the present summer. Much of the material comes to town in a bedraggled condition of collapse equalled only by the condition of those unfortunate mortals who must stick to their job, an almost hopeless one at present, of trying to turn the stuff into cash. There are heaps of asters and gladioli still, and roses and carnations are accumulating only to go into the discard daily. People have little need to purchase flowers at such a time. Better news next week.

BUFFALO Conditions have fallen back to summer days again, the weather being very hot and roses of new crops came in very much full blown. Asters have continued heavy throughout the week, though gladioli have shortened up and price on these are a trifle better. Chrysanthemums have made their appearance but no special demand. Lily of the valley, white roses and orchids had a slight demand and lilies moved a little better than a week previous. Dahlias are coming in; also carnation are seen, some very choice Enchantress and Perfection, and these have sold readily.

CHICAGO As the first fall month advances, summer heat prevails as if making up for lost opportunity. Asters are being hurried to a finish and the most of the stock remaining is of medium size, although a few of the larger ones are still left. Carnations are beginning to come more freely, but they are far from their best. The Queen of the Fall arrived two weeks ago and Golden Glow and Smith's Advance have no rivals as yet in the chrysanthemum world. Prices are not high and demand is not urgent. Gladioli are large and full, but sales are very slow indeed. A fair quantity of roses is coming each day and the local demand is generally conceded to be fair, but the outside trade is needed to use up the flowers. The supply of garden flowers is not so great as in some other seasons and this has helped to keep prices steady.

CINCINNATI After an unusually cool August, September has started to give us some real summer weather. This has apparently worked to a disadvantage in the florist business for it has brought in very heavy cuts while the demand for stock seemed to fall away. Shipping business, however, has been pretty good. The supply of roses is very heavy and the same is true of asters and lilies. Dahlias are beginning to come in very strong. They are excellent in quality. The aster and gladiolus situation is good and in a fairly large supply. A few chrysanthemums in yellow have made their appearance.

NEW YORK Whatever optimism might have been generated by last week's improved market tone was quickly and most effectively dissipated when this week's sizzling got to working. The unprecedented heat has created fierce havoc with most of the stock coming in and put a quietus on all demand. Lots of material has been received at the markets in useless condition. Quoting prices is a waste of time. There is no standard of values under present conditions.

PHILADELPHIA The hot spell has certainly "played hob" with the cut flower business here. Last Saturday there were hundreds of boxes of asters that had never yet been opened and could not be sold at any price. Gladioli were almost in the same boat. The stocks came piling in by the carload, without sense or reason—each grower seeming to think maybe his particular shipment would be lucky enough to get the preference on any little business agoing. The aster and gladiolus situation was certainly enough to drive any wholesaler to drink. Things were not quite so bad in the rose market. American Beauty keeps improving in quality and is selling at about normal prices for this season of the year. Russells are also very good and going well. Brilliant is the best of the Killarneys at present, but even that summer favorite will soon show effects if this torrid weather keeps on a few more days. Carnations are shaping up a little better. The moist summer has been particularly favorable to the dahlia crop. We have never seen them in finer form than this year. October Frost and Golden Glow are about the only chrysanthemums to be seen so far. Orchids are still very scarce. A few Dendrobium formosum added a little variety to the limited list last week.

SAN FRANCISCO The holidays of the past week drained this market of flowers, and some of the wholesalers say they could have sold more of some varieties had they been available. Labor Day and Admission Day, September 9th, were big days at the exposition, and the festivities in connection with both celebrations took many flowers, especially the Native Sons parade, which contained some of the most elaborate floats yet to appear during the exposition period. The Jewish holiday helped out considerably also by stimulating the demand for chrysanthemums and fancy basket arrangements, as well as general counter trade. Carnations are very scarce, it being difficult to fill orders at times.

(Continued on page 391)

WHOLESALE FLOWER MARKETS — TRADE PRICES—Per 100 TO DEALERS ONLY

	BOSTON Sept. 16	ST. LOUIS Sept. 13	PHILA. Sept. 6
Roses			
Am. Beauty, Special	12.00 to 20.00	30.00 to 25.00	..... to 25.00
" " Fancy and Extra	6.00 to 10.00	12.00 to 20.00	15.00 to 20.00
" " No. 1	1.00 to 3.00	3.00 to 8.00	10.00 to 12.50
Russell, Hadley	4.00 to 8.00	10.00 to 15.00	3.00 to 12.00
Killarney, Richmond, Hillingdon, Ward, Extra	1.00 to 4.00	5.00 to 8.00	4.00 to 6.00
" " " " Ordinary	.50 to 1.00	2.00 to 3.00	1.00 to 3.00
Arenburg: Radiance, Taft, Key, Extra	1.00 to 1.00	5.00 to 8.00	5.00 to 6.00
" " " " Ordinary	.50 to 1.00	1.00 to 3.00	1.00 to 4.00
Ophelia, Mock, Sunburst, Extra	2.00 to 4.00	..... to	4.00 to 6.00
" " " Ordinary	.50 to 1.00	..... to	1.00 to 4.00
Carnations, Fancy	.75 to 1.00	1.50 to 2.00	... to 1.50
" Ordinary	.50 to .75	.50 to 1.00	..... to 1.00
Cattleyas	35.00 to 50.00	35.00 to 75.00	50.00 to 75.00
Dendrobium formosum	..... to 25.00	..... to	..... to 50.00
Lilies, Longiflorum	4.00 to 6.00	6.00 to 8.00	8.00 to 10.00
" Rubrum	..... to 8.00	2.00 to 3.00	.... to 2.00
Lily of the Valley	2.00 to 4.00	3.00 to 4.00	3.00 to 12.00
Daisies	..... to 2.00	.80 to .75	..... to
Violets	..... to	..... to	..... to
Snapdragon	.50 to 1.00	3.00 to 4.00	..... to 2.00
Gladioli	1.00 to 2.00	2.00 to 3.00	1.00 to 3.00
Asters	.25 to 1.00	.75 to 2.00	.25 to 1.00
Chrysanthemums	8.00 to 12.00	..... to	..... to 12.00
Sweet Peas	.15 to .30	.15 to .25	.50 to .75
Gardenias	10.00 to 12.00	..... to	..... to
Adiantum	.50 to 1.00	1.00 to 1.25	..... to 1.00
Smilax	6.00 to 12.00	12.00 to 15.00	15.00 to 20.00
Asparagus Plumosus, Strings (100)	25.00 to 50.00	35.00 to 50.00	..... to 50.00
" & Spren. (100 Bchs.)	25.00 to 35.00	20.00 to 35.00	..... to 50.00

Flower Market Reports
(Continued from page 380)

The early violets are very popular and the limited supplies are readily absorbed. A good many asters are still appearing, but they offer no difficulties, as everything in this line cleans up closely. Chrysanthemums show more variety and better quality. Unakas are appearing quite freely in addition to October Frost, Golden Glow, Monrovia, Crocker and some of the smaller varieties which have been in for several weeks. Amaryllis is still plentiful and cheap. The supply of dahlias is abundant, but the demand seems to equal it every day. Small outdoor stock is decreasing in supply a little and the offerings find a ready outlet. Lots of flowering plants were brought in the past week which met with great popularity. Roses continue rather scarce with good stock demanding high prices. Orchids and gardenias are in light supply.

ST. LOUIS — The wholesale market received some hard knocks the past week owing to the hot weather when the demand slowed down and consignments came in bad shape. The retailers, too, say that trade was beginning to look up when along came the hot wave and stopped the demand. Roses are so plentiful that a great many are dumped. The great majority of them are of the Killarney varieties. Carnations, too, are away too many. There is also a lot of outdoor stuff still coming in, including a great raft of asters.

WASHINGTON — Business during the past week has been exceptionally flat. This is due in part to the return of hot weather. There has not been near enough business to clean up even a fraction of the flowers with which the market is flooded. The supply of gladioli has lessened considerable. Dahlias are improving to some extent and more of them are coming in but these, as well as asters, have been hit by the heat and their sales are draggy. A decrease in the receipts of lily of the valley was reported but this did not cause much of a hardship and allowed the dealers to clean up better on that which they received. Cattleyas still remain very scarce and high of price. Roses are very plentiful and some of them are exceptionally good. Carnations are increasing in quality and improving slightly in quality, but for them there is very little call. An oddity of the week was the receipt by a local firm of an order calling for 175 callas which, of course, could not be filled.

NASSAU CO. HORTICULTURAL SOCIETY.

At the meeting of this society at Glen Cove on Wednesday, Sept. 8, awards were made as follows—Muskmelon, 1st J. Robinson; celery, 1st R. Jones; tomatoes, 1st F. Hitchman.

Nephrolepis Smithii exhibited by J. W. Everitt was awarded a certificate of culture. Early flowering chrysanthemums by H. Goodband and outdoor fruit by J. Holloway received the thanks of the society.

The Dahlia Show will take place on Thursday, October 7. Schedules may be had by applying to Harry Jones, secretary.

JAMES GLADSTONE, Cor. Sec'y.

NEW YORK QUOTATIONS PER 100. To Dealers Only

MISCELLANEOUS		Last Half of Week ending Sept. 11 1915			First Half of Week beginning Sept. 13 1915		
Cattleyas		25.00	to	50.00	25.00	to	40.00
Lilies, Longiflorum		3.00	to	5.00	3.00	to	4.00
Rubrum		1.00	to	3.00	1.00	to	3.00
Lily of the Valley		2.00	to	3.00	1.00	to	3.00
Daisies		.....	to	.50	.....	to	.50
Snapdragon		.50	to	1.00	.50	to	1.00
Gladioli		.50	to	1.00	.50	to	1.00
Asters		.15	to	1.00	.25	to	1.00
Sweet Peas		.10	to	.15	.10	to	.15
Corn Flower		.....	to	.25	.....	to	.25
Gardenias		6.00	to	8.00	6.00	to	8.00
Adiantum		.50	to	.75	.50	to	.75
Smilax		4.00	to	8.00	4.00	to	8.00
Asparagus Plumosus, strings (per 100)		15.00	to	30.00	15.00	to	30.00
" & Spren. (100 bunches)		10.00	to	30.00	10.00	to	30.00

NEW YORK.

Frank Dinda of Farmingdale, Long Island, N. Y., is cutting flowers of his new orchid tinted seedling chrysanthemum, which Guttman & Raynor inform us they are selling at the exceptional price of $5.00 a dozen, wholesale. Frank Dinda has also a new seedling carnation, Olive Whitman, which is very fine at this early date.

Charles Millang is satisfied that he has solved the problem of the bundle boy and the street car restrictions with his Ford delivery car. Labor Day afternoon he spent in getting 1000 hydrangea heads in Bayside and distributing them in upper Broadway to the stores of the Colonial Florist. We had the pleasure of making the trip with him and could see plainly how impossible the transaction would have been without a motor wagon.

George Polykranas, the well-known manager for the United Cut Flower Co., has leased the store at 104 West 28th street for a wholesale and commission flower shop. He resigned from the United last December but remained with the firm until they were able to find a man to take his place. Mr. Polykranas has been in the retail flower trade for the past 25 years. Of his five sons two of them are his able assistants.

Bayside, N. Y.—Among the florist establishments of Bayside, one of the most interesting is that of Charles Thienel. Mr. Thienel has just had a new Lord & Burnham carnation house finished. A new boiler house and coal cellar ingeniously constructed under the concrete walk outside the houses has just been completed. Chrysanthemums and carnations are indoor specialties and outdoor the asters and hydrangeas, which are very fine, hold supremacy.

Frank Finger is another prosperous Bayside florist. Outdoor sweet peas are his leading specialty. There are three houses of carnations, very early, blooming quite profusely, and lots of chrysanthemums coming on. Branching asters have been grand for several weeks.

SAN FRANCISCO.

Adolphus E. Gude of Washington, D. C., and E. G. Hill of Richmond, Ind., returned to San Francisco a few days ago after visiting other parts of the state.

Just before his departure for the South, Wallace R. Pierson was guest of honor at a dinner given by a number of local florists. Mr. Pierson's friends will be glad to learn that he has fully recovered from the operation for appendicitis performed at a local hospital during the S. A. F. convention.

Angelo J. Rossi was chairman of the parade committee on Admission Day, and his house decorated one of the finest floats. It was a float for the Native Sons and Native Daughters, the main body of which, 26 feet long, was done with yellow chrysanthemums, while the lettering around the top was made of coreopsis and African marigolds. A big bear flag appeared on the sides, white carnations being used for the field, Minnie Burgle dahlias for the base, scabiosa for the bear and red carnations for the star.

NEW CORPORATIONS.

Joplin, Mo. — Joplin-Galena Greenhouse Co., capital stock $15,000.

Buffalo, N. Y.—Kenmore Floral Co., capital $10,000. W. G. Tyler, C. W. Donoghue and W. Smith, directors.

Buffalo, N. Y.—Kenmore Floral Co., 243 Walden avenue. Incorporators, H. W. Smith, S. W. Donaghue and W. G. Tyler; capital, $10,000.

Youngstown, O.—The Kay-Dimond Co. has been incorporated at $10,000. George Kay, R. W. Dimond, Blanche Kay, T. M. Fontaine and Elizabeth Fontaine are named as incorporators.

Bridgeport, Conn.—Patrick Byrnes, 50, landscape gardener, who has boarded at the home of Miss Mary L. Stafford at 439 Fairview avenue for several years, shot Miss Stafford last Friday morning in a fit of jealous rage. He is now held in bonds of $2,500 pending the recovery or death of the girl.

Buyer's Directory and Ready Reference Guide

Advertisements under this head, one cent a word.   Initials count as words.

Display advertisers in this issue are also listed under this classification without charge. Reference to List of Advertisers will indicate the respective pages.

Buyers failing to find what they want in this list will confer a favor by writing us and we will try to put them in communication with reliable dealers.

ACACIAS.
Stuart Low & Co., Harry A. Barnard, representative, Hotel Albert, New York City.
For page see List of Advertisers.

ACCOUNTANT
R. J. Dysart, 40 State St., Boston.
For page see List of Advertisers.

ACHILLEA
"Pearl," Fine Seedlings, $3.00 per 1,000, cash. JAMES MOSS, Wholesale Grower, Johnsville, Pa.

APHINE
Aphine Mfg. Co., Madison, N. J.
For page see List of Advertisers.

APHIS PUNK
Nicotine Mfg. Co., St. Louis, Mo.
For page see List of Advertisers.

ARAUCARIAS
Henry A. Dreer, Philadelphia, Pa.
For page see List of Advertisers.

ARECAS.
Joseph Heacock Co., Wyncote, Pa.
For page see List of Advertisers.

AUCTION SALES
Elliott Auction Co., New York City.
For page see List of Advertisers.

AZALEAS
P. Ouwerkerk, Hoboken, N. J.
For page see List of Advertisers.

BAY TREES
August Rolker & Sons, New York.
For page see List of Advertisers.

BEDDING PLANTS
A. N. Pierson, Inc., Cromwell, Conn.
For page see List of Advertisers.

BEGONIAS
Julius Roehrs Company, Rutherford, N. J.
For page see List of Advertisers.

R. Vincent, Jr., & Sons Co., White Marsh, Md.
For page see List of Advertisers.

Thomas Roland, Nahant, Mass.
For page see List of Advertisers.

A. M. Davenport, Watertown, Mass.

		Per 100
BEGONIA LORRAINE,	2½ in.	$12.00
	3 in.	20.00
	4 in.	35.00
	5 in.	50.00
BEGONIA CINCINNATI,	2½ in.	15.00
	3 in.	25.00
	3½ in.	30.00
	4½ in.	40.00

JULIUS ROEHRS CO., Rutherford, N. J.

BOILERS
Kroeschell Bros. Co., Chicago.
For page see List of Advertisers.

King Construction Co., North Tonawanda, N. Y.
"King Ideal" Boiler.
For page see List of Advertisers.

Hitchings & Co., New York City.
For page see List of Advertisers.

Lord & Burnham Co., New York City.

BOXES—CUT FLOWER FOLDING
Edwards Folding Box Co., Philadelphia.
For page see List of Advertisers.

Folding cut flower-boxes, the best made. Write for list. HOLTON & HUNKEL CO., Milwaukee, Wis.

BOX TREES
BOX TREES—Standards, Pyramids and Bush. In various sizes. Price List on demand. JULIUS ROEHRS CO., Rutherford, N. J.

BULBS AND TUBERS
Arthur T. Boddington Co., Inc., New York City.
For page see List of Advertisers.

J. M. Thorburn & Co., New York City.
Wholesale Price List of High Class Bulbs.
For page see List of Advertisers.

Ralph M. Ward & Co., New York City.
Lily Bulbs.
For page see List of Advertisers.

John Lewis Childs, Flowerfield, L. I., N. Y.
For page see List of Advertisers.

August Rolker & Sons, New York City.
Holland and Japan Bulbs.
For page see List of Advertisers.

R. & J. Farquhar & Co., Boston, Mass.
For page see List of Advertisers.

S. S. Skidelsky & Co., Philadelphia, Pa.
For page see List of Advertisers.

Chas. Schwake & Co., New York City.
Horticultural Importers and Exporters.
For page see List of Advertisers.

A. Henderson & Co., Chicago, Ill.
For page see List of Advertisers.

Burnett Bros., 98 Chambers St., New York.
For page see List of Advertisers.

Henry F. Michell Co., Philadelphia, Pa.
For page see List of Advertisers.

Joseph Breck & Sons Corp., Boston, Mass.
For page see List of Advertisers.

Fottler, Fiske, Rawson Co., Boston, Mass.
For page see List of Advertisers.

C. EBUR & SONS, HILLEGOM, Holland.
Bulbs of all descriptions. Write for prices.
NEW YORK Branch, 8-10 Bridge St.

CANNAS
Canna Specialists.
Send for Canna book.
THE CONARD & JONES COMPANY,
West Grove, Pa.

CARNATION STAPLES
Split carnations quickly, easily and cheaply mended. Pillsbury's Carnation Staple, 1000 for 35c.; 3000 for $1.00 post paid. I. L. PILLSBURY, Galesburg, Ill.

Supreme Carnation Staples, for repairing split carnations, 35c. per 1000; 3000 for $1.00. F. W. WAITE, 85 Belmont Ave., Springfield, Mass.

CARNATIONS.
Wood Bros., Fishkill, N. Y.
For page see List of Advertisers.

F. Dorner & Sons Co., Lafayette, Ind.
For page see List of Advertisers.

Leo Niessen Co., Philadelphia, Pa.
Field Grown Carnation Plants.

CARNATIONS—Continued
F. R. Pierson, Tarrytown, N. Y.
Carnation Matchless.
For page see List of Advertisers.

Littlefield & Wyman, North Abington, Mass.
New Pink Carnation, Miss Theo.
For page see List of Advertisers.

Carnations, field grown, $6.00 per 100. Cash. White and Pink Enchantress Mrs. Ward, Perfection, Fenn, Winsor, Queen, Lawson, Beacon. CHAS. H. GREEN, Spencer, Mass.

CHRYSANTHEMUMS
Chas. H. Totty, Madison, N. J.
For page see List of Advertisers.

R. Vincent, Jr., & Sons Co., White Marsh, Md.
Pompon Chrysanthemums.
For page see List of Advertisers.

THE BEST 1915 NOVELTIES.
The Cream of 1914 Introductions.
The most popular Commercial and Exhibition kinds; also complete line of Pompons, Singles and Anemones. Trade list on application. ELMER D. SMITH & CO., Adrian, Mich.

COCOANUT FIBRE SOIL
20th Century Plant Food Co., Beverly, Mass.
For page see List of Advertisers.

CYCLAMENS
The Best Strains.
Eight Varieties.   Very Fine.
If you want quality, order now.

	100	1000
2½ in.	$7.00	$60.00
3 in.	9.00	80.00
4 in.	20.00	

Write for copy of our monthly plant bulletin.
S. S. PENNOCK-MEEHAN CO.,
1608-1620 Ludlow St., Philadelphia, Pa.

DAHLIAS
Send for Wholesale List of whole clumps and separate stock; 40,000 clumps for sale. Northboro Dahlia and Gladiolus Gardens, J. L. MOORE, Prop, Northboro, Mass.

NEW PAEONY DAHLIA
John Wanamaker. Newest. Handsomest. Best. New color, new form and new habit of growth. Big stock of best cut-flower varieties. Send list of wants to PEACOCK DAHLIA FARMS, Berlin, N. J.

DECORATIVE PLANTS
Robert Craig Co., Philadelphia, Pa.
For page see List of Advertisers.

Woodrow & Marketos, New York City.
For page see List of Advertisers.

S. S. Skidelsky & Co., Philadelphia, Pa.
For page see List of Advertisers.

Bobbink & Atkins, Rutherford, N. J.
For page see List of Advertisers.

A. Leuthy & Co., Roslindale, Boston, Mass.
For page see List of Advertisers.

FERNS
H. H. Barrows & Son, Whitman, Mass.
For page see List of Advertisers.

Robert Craig Co., Philadelphia, Pa.
For page see List of Advertisers.

McHutchison & Co., New York City.
Ferns in Flats.
For page see List of Advertisers.

For List of Advertisers See Page 371

FERNS—Continued

Roman J. Irwin, New York City.
Boston and Whitmani Ferns.
For page see List of Advertisers.

ASPLENIUM NIDUS AVIS (Birds-nest fern).

Good strong healthy plants, 4 in. pots, $40.00 per 100; 5 in. pots, $75.00 per 100; 6 in. pots, $100.00 per 100. WM. K. HARRIS, 55th and Springfield Ave., W. Phila. delphia, Pa.

FERTILIZERS

20th Century Plant Food Co., Beverly, Mass
Coconut Fibre Soil.
For page see List of Advertisers.

Stumpp & Walter Co., New York City.
Scotch Soot.
For page see List of Advertisers.

Pulverized Manure Co., Chicago, Ill.
Wizard Brand Cattle Manure.
For page see List of Advertisers.

Chicago Feed & Fertilizer Co., Chicago, Ill.
Magic Manures.
For page see List of Advertisers.

Hardwood Ashes for sale. GEO. L. MUNROE & SONS, Oswego, N. Y.

FLORISTS' LETTERS

Boston Florist Letter Co., Boston, Mass.
For page see List of Advertisers.

FLORISTS' SUPPLIES

N. F. McCarthy & Co., Boston, Mass.
For page see List of Advertisers.

Reed & Keller, New York City.
For page see List of Advertisers.

S. S. Pennock-Meehan Co., Philadelphia, Pa.
For page see List of Advertisers.

H. Bayersdorfer & Co., Philadelphia, Pa.
For page see List of Advertisers.

Welch Bros. Co., Boston, Mass.
For page see List of Advertisers.

FLOWER POTS

W. H. Ernest, Washington, D. C.
For page see List of Advertisers.

A. H. Hews & Co., Inc., Cambridge, Mass.
For page see List of Advertisers.

Hilfinger Bros., Ft. Edward, N. Y.
For page see List of Advertisers.

FOLIAGE PLANTS

A. Leuthy & Co., Roslindale, Boston, Mass.
For page see List of Advertisers.

FUCHSIAS

Fuchsias—Black Prince, Speciosa, double purple and white. Rooted Cuttings, $1.00 per 100; 1½-in., $2.00 per 100.
W. J. BARNETT, R. D. 67, Sharon, Pa.

FUNGINE

Aphine Mfg. Co., Madison, N. J.
For page see List of Advertisers.

GALAX

Michigan Cut Flower Co., Detroit, Mich.
For page see List of Advertisers.

GERANIUMS

R. Vincent, Jr., & Sons Co.
White Marsh, Md.
For page see List of Advertisers.

Geraniums, rooted in Silica rock sand; show a better color and grow better. Let me have your order for Nutt, Ricard, Poitevine and La Favorite. $10.00 per 1000. Cash. JAMES MOSS, Johnsville, Pa.

GLASS

Sharp, Partridge & Co., Chicago.
For page see List of Advertisers.

Parshelsky Bros., Inc., Brooklyn, N. Y.
For page see List of Advertisers.

Royal Glass Works, New York City.
For page see List of Advertisers.

Greenhouse glass, lowest prices. JOHNSTON GLASS CO., Hartford City, Ind.

GLASS CUTTERS

Smith & Hemenway Co., New York City.
Red Devil Glass Cutter.
For page see List of Advertisers.

GLAZING POINTS

H. A. Dreer, Philadelphia, Pa.
Peerless Glazing Point.
For page see List of Advertisers.

Geo. H. Angermueller, St. Louis, Mo.
For page see List of Advertisers.

GOLD FISH

Gold fish, aquarium plants, snails, castles, globes, aquarium, fish goods, nets, etc., wholesale. FRANKLIN BARRETT, Breeder, 4815 D St., Olney, Philadelphia, Pa. Large breeding pairs for sale. Send for price list.

GREENHOUSE BUILDING MATERIAL

King Construction Co., N. Tonawanda, N. Y.
For page see List of Advertisers.

Parshelsky Bros., Inc., Brooklyn, N. Y.
For page see List of Advertisers.

A. T. Stearns Lumber Co., Neponset, Boston.
Pecky Cypress.
For page see List of Advertisers.

Metropolitan Material Co., Brooklyn, N. Y.
For page see List of Advertisers.

Lord & Burnham Co., New York City.

GREENHOUSE CONSTRUCTION

King Construction Co., N. Tonawanda, N. Y.
For page see List of Advertisers.

Foley Greenhouse Mfg. Co., Chicago, Ill.
For page see List of Advertisers.

Metropolitan Material Co., Brooklyn, N. Y.
For page see List of Advertisers.

Hitchings & Co., New York City.
For page see List of Advertisers.

A. T. Stearns Lumber Co., Boston. Mass.
For page see List of Advertisers.

Lord & Burnham Co., New York City.

GUTTERS

King Construction Co., N. Tonawanda, N. Y
King Channel Gutter.
For page see List of Advertisers.

Metropolitan Material Co., Brooklyn, N. Y
Iron Gutters.
For page see List of Advertisers.

HAIL INSURANCE

Florists' Hail Asso. of America.
J. G Esler, Saddle River, N. J.
For page see List of Advertisers.

HARDY FERNS AND GREEN GOODS

Michigan Cut Flower Exchange, Detroit Mich.
For page see List of Advertisers.

Knud Nielsen, Evergreen, Ala.
Natural Green Sheet Moss, Fancy and Dagger Ferns and Huckleberry Foliage.
For page see List of Advertisers.

The Kervan Co., New York.
For page see List of Advertisers.

HARDY PERENNIALS

Bay State Nurseries, No. Abington, Mass
For page see List of Advertisers.

P. Ouwerkerk, Hoboken, N. J.
For page see List of Advertisers.

Palisades Nurseries, Sparkill, N. Y.
For page see List of Advertisers.

HEATING APPARATUS

Kroeschell Bros. Co., Chicago.
For page see List of Advertisers.

Lord & Burnham Co., New York City.

HOT BED SASH.

Parshelsky Bros., Inc., Brooklyn, N. Y.
For page see List of Advertisers.

Foley Greenhouse Construction Co., Chicago, Ill.
For page see List of Advertisers.

A. T. Stearns Lumber Co., Neponset, Mass.
For page see List of Advertisers.

S. Jacobs & Sons, Brooklyn, N. Y.
For page see List of Advertisers.

Lord & Burnham Co., New York City.

HOSE

H. A. Dreer, Philadelphia, Pa.

INSECTICIDES

Aphine Manufacturing Co., Madison, N. J.
Aphine and Fungine.
For page see List of Advertisers.

Nicotine Mfg. Co., St. Louis, Mo.
Aphis Punk and Nikoteen.
For page see List of Advertisers.

The Plantlife Co., New York City.
Plantlife Insecticide.
For page see List of Advertisers.

IRIS

John Lewis Childs, Inc.,
Flowerfield, L. I., N. Y.
For page see List of Advertisers.

IRIS—Splendid stock. Send for List and let us figure on your wants. GEO. N. SMITH, Wellesley Nurseries, Wellesley Hills, Mass.

IRRIGATION EQUIPMENT

Skinner Irrigation Co., Brookline, Mass.
For page see List of Advertisers.

KENTIAS

Joseph Heacock Co., Wyncotte, Pa.
For page see List of Advertisers.

LILY BULBS

Chas. Schwake & Co., New York City.
Horticultural Importers and Exporters.
For page see List of Advertisers.

R. M. Ward & Co., New York, N. Y.
Japanese Lily Bulbs of Superior Quality.
For page see List of Advertisers.

Corp. of Chas. F. Meyer, New York City.
Meyer's T. Brand Giganteums.
For page see List of Advertisers.

John Lewis Childs, Inc.,
Hardy Lilies.
Flowerfield, L. I., N. Y.
For page see List of Advertisers.

LILY OF THE VALLEY

Chas. Schwake & Co., Inc., New York City.
Hohmann's Famous Lily of the Valley Pips
For page see List of Advertisers.

McHutchison & Co., New York City.
For page see List of Advertisers.

Loechner & Co., New York City.
Lily of the Valley Pips.
For page see List of Advertisers.

LIQUID PUTTY MACHINE

Metropolitan Material Co., Brooklyn, N. Y.
For page see List of Advertisers.

MASTICA

F. O. Pierce Co., New York City.
For page see List of Advertisers.

Geo. H. Angermueller, St. Louis, Mo.
For page see List of Advertisers.

NATIONAL NURSERYMAN

National Nurseryman Publishing Co., Inc., Rochester, N. Y.
For page see List of Advertisers.

NIKOTEEN

Nicotine Mfg. Co., St. Louis, Mo.
For page see List of Advertisers.

NIKOTIANA

Aphine Mfg. Co., Madison, N. J.
For page see List of Advertisers.

NURSERY STOCK

P. Ouwerkerk, Weehawken Heights, N. J.
For page see List of Advertisers.

W. & T. Smith Co., Geneva, N. Y.
For page see List of Advertisers

Bay State Nurseries, North Abington, Mass.
Hardy, Northern Grown Stock.
For page see List of Advertisers.

Bobbink & Atkins, Rutherford, N. J.
For page see List of Advertisers.

Framingham Nurseries, Framingham, Mass.
For page see List of Advertisers.

August Rolker & Sons, New York City.
For page see List of Advertisers.

Chas. G. Curtis Co., Callicoon, N. Y.
Nursery Stock for Fall Planting.
For page see List of Advertisers.

Stuart Low & Co., Harry A. Barnard, representative, Hotel Albert, New York City.
For page see List of Advertisers.

NUT GROWING.

The Nut-Grower, Waycross, Ga.
For page see List of Advertisers.

ONION SETS

Schilder Bros., Chillicothe, O.
Onion Seed—Onion Sets.
For page see List of Advertisers.

ORCHID FLOWERS

Jas. McManus, New York, N. Y.
For page see List of Advertisers.

ORCHID PLANTS

Julius Roehrs Co., Rutherford, N. J.
For page see List of Advertisers.

Stuart Low & Co., Harry A. Barnard, representative, Hotel Albert, New York City.

Lager & Hurrell, Summit, N. J.

PALMS, ETC.

Robert Craig Co., Philadelphia, Pa.
For page see List of Advertisers.

August Rolker & Sons, New York City
For page see List of Advertisers.

A. Leuthy & Co., Roslindale, Boston, Mass.
For page see List of Advertisers.

Stuart Low & Co., Harry A. Barnard, representative, Hotel Albert, New York City.
For page see List of Advertisers.

PANSY PLANTS

PANSIES—The Big Giant Flowering
Kind—$3.00 per 1,000; $25.00 for 10,000. If
I could only show the nice plants, hundred
of testimonials and repeat orders, I would
be flooded with new business. Cash.
JAMES MOSS, Wholesale Grower, Johnsville, Pa.

PANSY SEED

Chas. Frost, Kenilworth, N. J.
The Kenilworth Giant Pansy.
For page see List of Advertisers.

Fottler, Fiske, Rawson Co., Boston, Mass.
For page see List of Advertisers.

PEONIES

Peonies. The world's greatest collection
120 sorts. Send for list. C. BETSCHER,
Canal Dover, O.

PEONIES? Try us once and if not satisfied tell us why. GEO. N. SMITH, Wellesley Nurseries, Wellesley Hills, Mass.

PECKY CYPRESS BENCHES

A. T. Stearns Lumber Co., Boston, Mass.
For page see List of Advertisers.

PHLOX

PHLOX—Coquellcot, Eclaireur, Rosenberg, Independence, Lothair, etc. GEO. N. SMITH, Wellesley Nurseries, Wellesley Hills, Mass.

PIPE AND FITTINGS

Kroeschell Bros. Co., Chicago.
For page see List of Advertisers.

King Construction Company,
N. Tonawanda, N. Y.
Shelf Brackets and Pipe Hangers.
For page see List of Advertisers.

PLANT AND BULB IMPORTS

Chas. Schwake & Co., New York City.
For page see List of Advertisers.

August Rolker & Sons, New York City.
For page see List of Advertisers.

PLANT TRELLISES AND STAKES

Seele's Tieless Plant Stakes and Trellises. H. D. SEELE & SONS, Elkhart, Ind.

PLANT TUBS

H. A. Dreer, Philadelphia, Pa.
"Riverton Special."
For page see List of Advertisers.

RAFFIA

McHutchison & Co., New York, N. Y.
For page see List of Advertisers.

RHODODENDRONS

P. Ouwerkerk, Hoboken, N. J.
For page see List of Advertisers.

Framingham Nurseries, Framingham, Mass.
For page see List of Advertisers.

RIBBONS AND CHIFFONS

S. S. Pennock-Meehan Co., Philadelphia, Pa.
For page see List of Advertisers.

ROSES

Poehlmann Bros. Co., Morton Grove, Ill.
For page see List of Advertisers.

P. Ouwerkerk, Hoboken, N. J.
For page see List of Advertisers.

Robert Craig Co., Philadelphia, Pa.
For page see List of Advertisers.

W. & T. Smith Co., Geneva, N. Y.
American Grown Roses.
For page see List of Advertisers.

Bay State Nurseries, North Abington, Mass.
For page see List of Advertisers.

August Rolker & Sons, New York City.
For page see List of Advertisers.

Framingham Nurseries, Framingham, Mass.
For page see List of Advertisers.

A. N. Pierson, Inc., Cromwell, Conn.
For page see List of Advertisers.

Stuart Low & Co., Harry A. Barnard, representative, Hotel Albert, New York City.
For page see List of Advertisers.

THE CONARD & JONES COMPANY.
Rose Specialists
West Grove, Pa. Send for offers.

SEASONABLE PLANT STOCK

R. Vincent, Jr. & Sons Co., White Marsh, Md.
For page see List of Advertisers.

SEED GROWERS

California Seed Growers' Association.
San Jose, Cal.
For page see List of Advertisers.

SEEDS

Carter's Tested Seeds,
Seeds with a Pedigree.
Boston, Mass., and London, England.
For page see List of Advertisers.

Schilder Bros., Chillicothe, O.
Onion Seed—Onion Sets.
For page see List of Advertisers.

Joseph Breck & Sons, Boston, Mass.
For page see List of Advertisers.

Kelway & Son,
Langport, Somerset, England.
Kelway's Celebrated English Strain Garden Seeds.
For page see List of Advertisers.

SEEDS—Continued

J. Bolgiano & Son, Baltimore, Md.
For page see List of Advertisers.

A. T. Boddington Co., Inc., New York City.
For page see List of Advertisers.

Chas. Schwake & Co., New York City.
For page see List of Advertisers.

Michell's Seed House, Philadelphia, Pa.
New Crop Cyclamen Seeds.
For page see List of Advertisers.

W. Atlee Burpee & Co., Philadelphia, Pa.
Giant Cyclamen Seed.
For page see List of Advertisers.

R. & J. Farquhar & Co., Boston, Mass.
For page see List of Advertisers.

J. M. Thorburn & Co., New York City.
For page see List of Advertisers.

S. Bryson Ayres Co., Independence, Mo.
Sweet Peas.
For page see List of Advertisers.

Loechner & Co., New York City.
For page see List of Advertisers.

Ant. C. Zvolanek, Lompoc, Cal.
Winter Flowering Sweet Pea Seed.
For page see List of Advertisers.

S. S. Skidelsky & Co., Philadelphia, Pa.
For page see List of Advertisers.

W. E. Marshall & Co., New York City.
Seeds, Plants and Bulbs.
For page see List of Advertisers.

August Rolker & Sons, New York City.
For page see List of Advertisers.

Burnett Bros., 98 Chambers St., New York.
For page see List of Advertisers.

Fottler, Fiske, Rawson Co., Boston, Mass.
Seeds for the Florist.
For page see List of Advertisers.

SKINNER IRRIGATION SYSTEM

Skinner Irrigation Co., Brookline, Mass.
For page see List of Advertisers.

SPHAGNUM MOSS

Live Sphagnum moss, orchid peat and
orchid baskets always on hand. LAGER
& HURRELL, Summit, N. J.

STOVE PLANTS

Orchids—Largest stock in the country—
Stove plants and Crotons, finest collection.
JULIUS ROEHRS CO., Rutherford, N. J.

STRAWBERRY PLANTS

Wilfrid Wheeler, Concord, Mass.
Pot Grown.

SWAINSONA

R. Vincent, Jr., & Sons Co., White Marsh, Md.
For page see List of Advertisers.

SWEET PEA SEED

Ant. C. Zvolanek, Lompoc, Calif.
Gold Medal of Honor Winter Orchid Sweet
Peas.
For page see List of Advertisers.

S. Bryson Ayres Co.,
Sunnyslope, Independence, Mo.
For page see List of Advertisers.

VENTILATING APPARATUS

The Advance Co., Richmond, Ind.
For page see List of Advertisers.

The John A. Evans Co., Richmond, Ind.
For page see List of Advertisers.

VIOLETS

FIELD-GROWN VIOLET PLANTS.

	100	1000
Princess of Wales	$5.00	$45.00
Lady Campbell	5.00	45.00
Marie Louise	5.00	45.00
Gov. Herrick	5.00	45.00
Farquhar	5.00	45.00
La France	5.00	45.00

Write for copy of our monthly plant
bulletin.
S. S. PENNOCK-MEEHAN CO.,
1608-1620 Ludlow St., Philadelphia, Pa.

[For List of Advertisers See Page 371

New Offers In This Issue

A NEW CORSAGE RIBBON
S. S. Pennock-Meehan Co., Philadelphia, Pa.
For page see List of Advertisers.

BOSTON AND WHITMANI FERNS.
A. M. Davenport, Watertown, Mass.
For page see List of Advertisers.

**CARNATIONS—FIELD GROWN
PLANTS.**
Jas. Vick's Sons, Rochester, N. Y.
For page see List of Advertisers.

HIGH GRADE DAHLIAS.
The Leo Niessen Co., Philadelphia, Pa.
For page see List of Advertisers.

**SURPLUS LIST OF HARDY PEREN-
NIALS.**
Eastern Nurseries, Jamaica Plain, Mass.
For page see List of Advertisers.

**WINTER FLOWERING SWEET
PEA SEED.**
Arthur T. Boddington, Inc., New York City.
For page see List of Advertisers.

In writing to Advertisers kindly mention Horticulture

Obituary

Joseph H. Bechamps.

Joseph H. Bechamps, a well known florist of Bayside, N. Y., died at his home in Flushing on September 7, aged 76 years. He was a veteran of the civil war. He leaves three sons and three-daughters.

George Walther

George Walther one of the old-time Chicago retail florists, died on September 1. He was born in Germany and was 78 years of age at the time of his death. He retired from active work about two years ago leaving the business management to his daughter and son.

James Allen.

James Allen, gardener for A. D. Juilliard, Tuxedo Park, N. Y., died suddenly on August 17, aged 46. He was a native of Kent, England, and was classed as a very proficient gardener. He was active in the affairs of the Tuxedo Horticultural Society for many years.

Edward H. White

Edward H. White, a well known market gardener of Norwalk, Conn., committed suicide by hanging, early Saturday, Sept. 11, presumably because of the failure of his peach crop with which, it is said, he had speculated extensively. He was about seventy years old and leaves a son Fay O. White.

Fritz Starke.

Fritz Starke, who was until a few years ago, when he retired from business, a well known florist and nurseryman at Ravenswood, Long Island, N. Y., died at Dundee Lake, N. J., on Wednesday, Sept. 1, aged 63 years. He was a native of Westphalia, Germany, where he got his education as a gardener. He leaves a widow, three sons and two daughters.

Louis Forget

The British journals tell of the death in a hospital at Rennes, France, on August 10, of Louis Forget, a noted orchid collector for Sander & Sons for the past twenty-four years. The large consignments of the re-discovered Cattleya labiata which surprised the orchid world in the '90's were the result of Mr. Forget explorations in South and Central America, as well as many other rare and lovely gems among the Cattleyas and Laelias. His death was sudden, caused by heart failure.

Charles Jameson

Charles Jameson, 29, gardener for Mrs. Arthur Hale of Philadelphia, was drowned while bathing off Scarborough Beach at Narragansett Pier last Saturday afternoon. His home is in Hyde Park, N. Y. Mr. Jameson was swimming with late-season residents at the Pier when he was caught in a heavy undertow and carried out, the heavy seas of the past two weeks having made the beaches very treacherous.

William Goff, a companion, siezed Jameson by the hair to save him when a big wave wrenched him from Goff's grasp and the body was lost and has not been recovered. Goff and three other persons were saved by the police.

Patrick Norton.

Patrick Norton passed away at his home in Dorchester, Boston, Mass., on Thursday, September 9, aged 76 years, after a weary and painful illness extending over seven or eight years, and on Saturday was laid away in Calvary cemetery. He was born in Athlone, Ireland, and came to this country when one year old. He was educated in the Dorchester public schools and, when a young man, got employment in Hovey's Nurseries at Cambridge, under that able old gardener, C. M. Atkinson. After seven years Mr. Atkinson left to take charge of the famous Cushing estate at Belmont and Mr. Norton went with him as assistant foreman. Four years later Atkinson accepted the position of superintendent of Mt. Hope cemetery. Norton was offered the place on the Cushing estate but refused, preferring to leave and go into the florist business with his brother Michael as Norton Bros., adjacent to their old home in Dorchester. That was in 1864 and for over thirty-five years the firm carried on a successful business, with greenhouses in Dorchester where they grew Bousilene roses and violets, and a store in Boston during the greater part of that time. Upon the dissolution of the firm Mr. Norton retired from business.

Mr. Norton's activities were many and he was a strong leader in the affairs of the Massachusetts Horticultural Society, serving for many years in the capacity of chairman of the garden committee and of the committee of arrangements. It was in the latter capacity that he scored his most signal success—the great horticultural exhibition which was held in Music Hall during the S. A. F. Convention in Boston in 1890, an exhibition which to this day stands without a rival in this country as to quality and arrangement.

Patrick Norton was an able, genial, generous-hearted man, very popular among the leading men of the profession who were his contemporaries. Among his most intimate associates and admirers were such men as Peter Henderson, John Henderson, Michael Wiegand, Ernst Asmus, John N. May, John H. Taylor, Thomas Cartledge and other eminent horticulturists of New York and Philadelphia as well as the leading gardeners in and around Boston, most of whom have long since passed away. In fact, Mr. Norton's suave, tactful and kindly personality made him a great favorite wherever he went. The death of his only son about fifteen years ago made him heart-broken and since then he has never been the same man as before. He is survived by his widow and three daughters, and his brother M. H. Norton.

PATRICK NORTON.

VISITORS' REGISTER.

Detroit, Mich.—J. H. Snyder, Rhinebeck, N. Y.

Cleveland, O.—W. P. Craig, Philadelphia, Pa.

Providence, R. I.—S. H. Moore, New Haven, Conn.

Atlantic City, N. J.—William Walker and wife, Louisville, Ky.

Milwaukee, Wis.—Adolph and August Poehlmann, Morton Grove, Ill.

St. Louis, Mo.—A. T. Delamare, New York, Mr. and Mrs. Martin Reukauf, Philadelphia.

Cincinnati—Jos. Hill, Fred Lemon and Earl Mann, Richmond, Ind.; Geo. Lambert, Xenia Ohio; H. J. Vanderhorst, St. Mary's, O.

Boston—H. C. Neubrand, representing A. N. Pierson, Cromwell, Conn.; H. A. Barnard, representing Stuart Low & Co., Bush Hill Park, Enfield, Eng.

Washington, D. C.—Richard Vincent, Jr., White Marsh, Md.; H. Riebe, of the Berryhill Nursery, Harrisburg, Pa.; C. P. W. Nims, representing Hews & Co., Cambridge, Mass.; James W. Heacock, Wyncote, Pa.; L. A. Berckmans, Augusta, Ga.

Chicago—Mr. and Mrs. Eugene Dalledouze, Brooklyn, N. Y.; W. F. Kasting, Buffalo, N. Y.; H. Perkins, 2nd, Newark, N. Y.; C. W. Garrett, R. F. D. No. 1, Pacific, Mo.; C. B. Knickman, representing McHutchison Co., New York; C. F. Nawrocki, Ashland, Wis.; Sam. Seligman, New York; Wm. Tricker, Arlington, N. J.

Philadelphia—Sam'l Batchelor, Mamaroneck, N. Y.; John Bader, Pittsburgh, Pa.; John Heck, Reading, Pa.; R. W. Marvell, representing C. C. Higgins, Worthington, Ohio; Geo. F. Ekas, Baltimore, Md.; John L. Ratcliffe, Richmond, Va.; P. S. Randolph, Pittsburgh, Pa.; W. C. Lawrence, Lawrence Flower Co., Atlanta, Georgia; James Brown, Coatesville, Pa.; Samuel S. Pennock, Ocean City, N. J.

Jersey City, N. J.—Charles Reitman, Trenton, N. J., has filed a petition in the United States District Court against Bonnot Bros., of Jersey City, claiming that they are insolvent and asks that they be declared bankrupt. He alleges that they owe the New York Cut Flower Company $6,935, and that this claim has been assigned to him.

BASIS FOR EUROPEAN IMPORTATION PERMITS.

Editor HORTICULTURE:

Dear Sir: I am informed by the Merchants' Association of New York that it is stated unofficially by the Foreign Trade Advisers in behalf of The American importers that the incurring of liability for the payment of goods by the American importer prior to March 1, 1915, is to be the basis on which permits for shipments will be issued in future. No payment needs to have been made, but the American purchaser must show that he was legally bound to pay for the goods before that date. Evidence that will substantiate the above facts should be submitted to the Foreign Trade Advisers by interested houses as follows:

(a) An affidavit giving the history of the case and showing all the documentary evidences submitted:

(b) Either the original contract or certified copies of the same:

(c) Copies of order sheets, the original acceptances, invoices and consular invoices if available. In addition to these proofs all marks, numbers, value, and cost of goods, and the name and address of shipping agent in neutral port should be given.

Such evidence will be kept on file by the Foreign Trade Advisers and as soon as the Department of State is officially notified by the British authorities that such claims will be received and considered by the British Government, it is the purpose of the Foreign Trade Advisers to file these claims with the British Embassy in Washington in the order in which they are received by the Department of State. It would be well, therefore, that all interested houses should forward a sworn statement to Judge W. D. Fleming, Foreign Trade Adviser, Department of State, Washington, D. C., as soon as possible if they desire an early movement of their goods.

As soon as the Department of State receives official confirmation of the above, they will be notified.

Yours very truly,
New York.   CHAS. A. DARDS.

Horticulture Publishing Co.:

Enclosed please find check for $2.00 for two years' subscription to Horticulture. Can't get along without it."
T. P.

Rochester, N. Y., Sept. 15.

PERSONAL

John Scott, florist, of Huntsville, Ala., has been missing from his home for several weeks.

Miss Margaret Didier, granddaughter of M. Wieland, and Chas. Hilhoff were married on September 8, at Evanston, Ill.

Royal W. Smith, employed at the store of Hopkins, the florist, Brattleboro, Vt., and Miss Helen Leone, were married on Sept. 6.

Wallace R. Pierson, who has been in the hospital in San Francisco since the Convention, is recovering nicely and expects to get home about September 25.

George Piddington, of Andover, Mass., who was badly shaken by a fall from a tree which he was trimming three weeks ago, is still incapacitated from attending to his landscape gardening work.

Charles H. Pugh, a Westboro (Mass.) florist, was given a farewell banquet on Sept. 11, at Westboro Inn on the even of going to New Jersey to engage in the florist business. The banquet was given by Paul Brigham.

We are sorry to learn that William Wells the noted chrysanthemum grower of Merstham, England has had a set-back in his convalescence from the serious operation which he underwent some months ago. We sincerely hope to hear soon that he is again making hopeful progress toward complete recovery.

NEWS NOTES.

Los Angeles, Cal. — Arthur Falkentrayer is about to go into the nursery business.

Portland, Ore. — A municipal rose garden is being advocated by some of the daily newspapers.

Columbus, O. — The Livingston Seed Co. won first prize for table decoration at the State Fair. Mrs. H. A. Bell was 2nd, Indianola Floral Co. 3rd and Hardesty Floral Co. 4th.

Cromwell, Conn. — George Johannes and N. F. Higgins have formed a co-partnership in the florist business here. Mr. Higgins has a store on State street, Springfield, Mass., and greenhouses on Pine street.

GREENHOUSES BUILDING OR CONTEMPLATED.

Elgin, Ill. — Frank Asheman, plant house.

Wheeling, W. Va. — Albert Lash, one house.

Natick, Mass. — Paul E. Richwagen, one house.

Riverton, N. J. — H. A. Dreer, four houses.

Oakland, Cal. — Elmhurst Floral Co., one house.

Norwood, R. I. — Norwood Floral Co., one house.

Cromwell, Conn. — Magnus Pierson, one house.

Rutherford, N. J. — Julius Roehrs Co., plant house.

Andover, Mass. — J. H. Playdon, house 20 x 125.

Piedmont, Cal. — Sanborn, the Florist, one house.

Blue Point, N. Y. — J. K. Vanderveer, Jr. carnation house.

San Antonio, Texas. — Mr. Charles Albrecht, one plant house.

Brooklyn, N. Y. — Louis Schmutz, Clarkson street, two houses.

St. Louis, Mo. — J. Young & Sons, Olive Road, range of houses.

Chicago, Ill. — Lawndale Floral Co., 3212 W. 22nd street, one house.

Pawtucket, R. I. — Fred Hoffman, East avenue, two houses, each 38x85.

Birmingham, Ala. — Theo. Smith, range of houses and mushroom cellars.

Chicago, Ill. — T. Grabowski, 4523 Addison street, three Moninger houses.

PATENTS GRANTED.

1,152,093. Lawn Edger. Caleb A. Isaac, Los Angles, Cal.

Woonsocket, R. I. — Harry A. Jencks, a landscape gardener of New York City, and formerly of Woonsocket has presented plans for the beautifying the grounds surrounding the high school of Woonsocket. The cost as estimated by Mr. Jencks is $12,000. The finance committee of the City Council is considering an appropriation of $5000 for this work.

Vol. XXII
No. 13
SEPT. 25
1915

HORTICULTURE

Dipladenia splendens profusa

LIST OF ADVERTISERS

FOR BUYERS' DIRECTORY AND READY REFERENCE GUIDE
SEE PAGES 424, 425, 426, 427

NOTES ON CULTURE OF FLORISTS' STOCK
CONDUCTED BY

John J. M. Farrell

Questions by our readers in line with any of the topics presented on this page will be cordially received and promptly answered by Mr. Farrell. Such communications should invariably be addressed to the office of HORTICULTURE.
"If vain our toil, we ought to blame the culture, not the soil."—*Pope.*

Allamandas

Plants that were pruned last spring to within a joint or two and these when they had made two or three whorls of leaves pinched again, and so on during the summer will by this time have formed nice bushy specimens. Water may be withheld till they flag but do not allow the wood to shrivel. In fact allamandas can be so managed as to have them bloom at any time of the year by first resting the plants then pruning them back and then encouraging root action. If these plants are required for early flowering they should now be kept drier at the roots so as to harden and ripen up their wood. They will rest well in a temperature of 50 to 55 degrees, but when starting them into bloom keep them at 65 degrees and give an abundance of water as soon as they get into active growth. These plants are well worth to grow where yellow flowers are wanted; they adapt themselves beautifully to various forms of decorations.

Care of Palms

Now that the sun is losing its power we can discontinue shading. Get them inured to the sun by reducing the shading little by little until they are standing full sun. Syringings once a day during bright weather will now be enough. Root action is becoming less and less so they will not need so much moisture as a month back. For large palms it will be well not to run the temperature any higher than about 60 degrees night with about 10 degrees higher during bright weather. After the summer's heavy syringing and moving about the soil may be loose and they may have lost some of their compost. It will be well to go over them and replace any of this lost soil. Also give them a good cleaning by sponging the foliage.

Ferns

After some months of labor with the Boston fern and others of the same family we are now at the season when we will have to get them into shape for the winter and spring sales. Those who made a practice of planting out their Boston ferns during the summer months on benches should lose no time in getting the stock potted up. The average florist retailing his stock has use for Boston ferns from 4-inch pots on up to 12 inch pans and it is well to make up what will be needed

in the larger sizes when lifting the plants. There is no trouble in getting made-up plants established in a very few days if they are kept in a shady house, but don't let them remain there any longer than necessary. They can stand a good deal of sun and plants which have had a rather cool house and but little shade will be more satisfactory as house plants than soft stock. When potted up keep the atmosphere moist by damping down.

Orchids

Dendrobium nobile, and many Dendrobium hybrids should now have their growths completed and be ready for a ripening process in a cooler and dry house. Reduce the water supply considerably but spray overhead on clear, hot days, such as we often get in October and November. Dendrobium Phalænopsis Schroederianum is at its best under warm house culture, and should have a night temperature of 65 degrees when developing its flower spikes. This orchid succeeds best in quite small pans or baskets, which dry up rapidly, and, if time will permit, the best method of watering is dipping in a pail or tub. At this season twice a week will suffice. D Phalænopsis is more difficult to keep in good condition year after year. It does well in a hot, humid, old-fashioned stove-house.

Poinsettias

Keep the temperature where the poinsettias are, at about 60 degrees during the night, which can be raised 10 to 15 degrees more during sunshine. As they grow give the pots more room. Do not let them become crowded as they will draw up and grow lanky. On all bright mornings give them a light spray and keep the air of the house moist. When ventilating do it so as not to create any cold drafts or chilly atmosphere around the plants. From this out you will have to watch the waterings, as there is no plant more affected by careless watering than the poinsettia.

Necessary Repairing

All repairing that has been put off until now should be done without delay as the days are becoming shorter and the nights much cooler. This repairing will include putting in broken glass, replacing loose putty and painting where needed, and putting the boilers in the very best shape before the cold weather sets in.

Next Week:—Chrysanthemums; Christmas Cyclamen; Carnations; Christmas Lilies; Planting Trees and Shrubs; Wasted Bench Space.

HORTICULTURE

VOL. XXII   SEPTEMBER 25, 1915   NO. 13

PUBLISHED WEEKLY BY
HORTICULTURE PUBLISHING CO.
147 Summer Street, Boston, Mass.
Telephone, Oxford 292.
WM. J. STEWART, Editor and Manager.

Entered as second-class matter December 8, 1904, at the Post Office
at Boston, Mass., under the Act of Congress of March 3, 1879.

CONTENTS

Massachusetts' place — At the Panama Pacific Exposition the State of Massachusetts has once more demonstrated to the world her unrivalled industrial and educational resources and her ability to maintain her position of supremacy among her sister states. We learn from the report of the chairman of the Board of Managers that more first-class awards have been made at the Exposition to Massachusetts official exhibits and to the exhibits of Massachusetts industrial concerns than to any other state in the country—a fact which is all the more impressive when it is remembered that, with the exception of two of her neighboring New England states, Massachusetts is the most remote from the Exposition at the Golden Gate. Horticulturally as well as otherwise Massachusetts fares well. The first-class awards in that section are given as follows:

Medal of honor to State of Massachusetts, collective horticultural exhibit of trees and shrubs and flowers, arranged in landscaping design.
Medal of honor to Massachusetts exhibit of horticultural tools and demonstration.
Medal of honor to Bay State Nurseries, North Abington.
Gold medal to State Forester's Department.
Gold medal to State Highway Commission.
Gold medal to Harvard University, Cambridge, landscape architecture.
Gold medal to Massachusetts Agricultural College, Amherst.
Gold medal to R. &. J. Farquhar & Co., Boston.
Gold medal to Edward G. Gillette, Southwick.
Gold medal to New England Nurseries, Bedford.
Gold medal to Thomas Roland, Nahant.
Gold medal to Frederick J. Rea, Norwood.

Incidentally, we might be pardoned for mentioning the fact that HORTICULTURE hails from Massachusetts.

Horticulture's place — Any periodical looking for advertising support in any special field is liable to be called upon from time to time to furnish evidence as to its value as a publicity medium and business producer for the advertising trade. Numerical circulation, that greatly overworked weapon of the advertising agencies, while it may have a considerable bearing upon the value of a publication catering to the general public is in a journal with circulation restricted to people engaged in a distinct industry, by no means an infallible basis of estimate as to productive publicity value, but, in fact, is in many instances a secondary consideration as compared with quality and appeal to a desirable purchasing class of readers. It has been the aim of HORTICULTURE since its inception to maintain a high plane of excellence and to count first among its readers the most reliable, intelligent and worthy classes in the industries to which it caters. That we have met with a good measure of success in this respect will not be openly denied. HORTICULTURE has reason to feel proud also of the wide territory over which its influence extends. For the information of those who may not fully realize what this means we will state that in the morning mail of the day on which these lines were written subscription remittances were received at the office of HORTICULTURE from twenty-one states, viz: Michigan, Georgia, Virginia, Maine, Missouri, South Carolina, New Jersey, Wisconsin, Illinois, Massachusetts, Nebraska, Minnesota, Ohio, Pennsylvania, Maryland, New York, Indiana, Connecticut, Rhode Island, South Dakota and Florida, and Canada. Of the various enclosures referred to one was for five years in advance and three were for two years each. HORTICULTURE offers the advertising trade in horticultural, floral and allied industries a zealous and trustworthy advertising service and the evidence for any and all of the foregoing claims will be cheerfully opened to any intending advertiser desiring same.

"Abnormal" colors in the landscape — In connection with the question of propriety and taste in the use of certain trees and shrubs for garden and landscape adornment which was the subject of one of our editorial notes last week we are reminded by a friend about the clamor against the use of material bearing foliage other than straight green, which has been taken up as a sort of fashionable fad by some people. The blue spruce, purple beech and red or golden or variegated foliaged subjects have all come under wholesale interdiction by these critics as unnatural and abnormal and consequently objectionable to their artistic sensibilities. But is the glaucus foliage of the blue spruce really unnatural or its frosted effect among other trees a landscape disfigurement? Watch the purple beech bursting into a cloud of soft coppery color in springtime, then gradually maturing to bronzy

ROSE GROWING UNDER GLASS

CONDUCTED BY

Arthur C Ruzicka

Questions by our readers in line with any of the topics presented on this page will be cordially received and promptly answered by Mr. Ruzicka. Such communications should invariably be addressed to the office of HORTICULTURE.

Cutting Roses

It is very important that all roses should be cut properly, with attention paid to the leaving of eyes on the stems from which the flowers are cut. So early in the season, if the roses are cut carelessly, the plants will show the effects before the season is over. Leave two good eyes wherever possible, going down to one eye only in cutting a short rose that can be turned into a "number one" if cut a little lower. If the plant is well cut off it will pay to cut the bud out with one leaf, allowing the rest of the stem to remain. This will give the plant more foliage and give it a better chance to grow. This applies to plants that are surrounded by plants with plenty of growth especially; if all are pretty well cut off they have more show as all are about to start even for another crop and can be treated accordingly. The idea is to keep the plants as nearly even as possible so that water, feed, etc, can then be applied to the whole bench and all the plants will be in condition to take it. Although the roses can be left on a little longer, and so increase the size of the buds, care should be taken not to allow them to open too much. According to market reports there are many coming in that are far too open and therefore nearly given away. Even with ice boxes and iced shipments it is best to have the buds a little tight rather than too open.

Sand

On many places propagation begins very early, in fact as soon as it is cool enough to insure control of heat in the houses. For this reason it will be wise to secure a good supply of sand and have it on hand when it is wanted. There are sections of the country where sand is hard to get, and this applies to those places in particular. Where a good gravel pit is right on the place there is no better place to store sand than to leave it where nature put it. Protection from frost should be provided later; not too early, for if a heap of sand should be covered with leaves, straw, etc., from now on, fungus is liable to work into it and thus render it useless. In storing sand select a nice clean place where it will be fairly dry and where it will not be flooded every time it rains. Surface water collects impurities and it runs over the earth and these are not wanted in the sand.

A manure shed with a concrete floor is an ideal place as there is little danger of getting foreign matter into it from the bottom.

The Propagating House

If this holds last season's sand it should be removed at once allowing the air and light to sweeten the benches and the space under the benches before the new sand is applied. In cleaning this house do it even more thoroughly than when cleaning other greenhouses as it is very important to have everything clean and free from last year's soil and sand. Wash out the benches well and whitewash them at once. Then clean out once more under the benches and scatter some airslacked lime over the surface under the benches. This will help sweeten it and kill a good many germs and fungi that would otherwise winter over under there.

Watch for Spider

With the wet summer we are very apt to have a dark fall, and perhaps winter, and conditions may be such that the plants will not be syringed for two or three weeks at a time. Therefore, it will be well to go through the houses carefully taking note and marking all places that indicate that spider is present. These "nests," as they may be called, should receive a dose of good insecticide and an extra careful syringing whenever there is opportunity to do so. If there are none to be found so much the better but as a rule there will be a spot or two where spider can be found even with the most careful grower. Mark these spots and see that they are all clean before the season advances much more. It is especially necessary to see that all plants from which cuttings will be taken later are free from spider as well as other pests or diseases. If this is done far less trouble will be experienced with the cuttings and young stock later.

Ventilation in Cloudy Weather

Ventilation on cloudy or rainy days will have to receive more attention now and after than ever before as the plants are apt to get very soft if allowed to have too much heat on cloudy days. Keep the houses as cool as possible, not letting them go below 66 or 68, however. Keep air on at all times and give heat if necessary.

purple, when as if regretting its sombreness it decks itself with innumerable tips of young growth of bright red; then in the fall—away into November, when other deciduous trees are bare, when it takes on its dress of golden russet and luminous orange in the sunlight—is it not a charm to all rational beholders? Is the indiscriminate denunciation of such objects anything more than the whim of a biased mind grown into an unreasoning prejudice? Noting the exquisite transitions of color in the spring foliage as it breaks out in deep rose, or dusky gray, when the swamps are aflame with red maples, or speeding through country roads on an autumn afternoon entranced by the radiant coloring of crimson, gold and bronze, one wonders why it is that the slightest reproduction of these dashes of color

in a landscape picture at any other season of the year should be adjudged a violation of the principles of correct art or an affront to good taste. We overheard a lady, recently, condemning a well-placed clump of purple beeches on a certain estate as an evidence of faulty taste and we could not but notice the incongruous jumble of colors in her headgear and wonder how the lady's perceptions happened to be so esthetic as to gardens and so savagely crude as to hat adornment! In the selection of other than green trees, as in the matter of planting Hydrangeas, Spireas and other "too common" things on which adverse criticism is so often heard. "the eternal fitness of things" from all view points would, we think, be a good basis on which to rely. "A place for everything and everything in its place."

CLUBS AND SOCIETIES

NEW YORK STATE FEDERATION OF HORTICULTURAL SOCIE-TIES AND FLORAL CLUBS.

The annual meeting of this organization was held at the office of Commissioner Wilson at the State Fair Grounds, Syracuse, on Thursday, September 16th. There were present President W. F. Kasting, Vice-President Erl A. Bates, Secretary John Young, Treasurer W. A. Adams, and Messrs. F. R. Pierson, Tarrytown; C. H. Vick, Rochester; Prof. Lumsden, Ithaca, N. Y.; Messrs. Youell, Thorp, Bultman, Sheeran, Baker, Workman and Bard, all of Syracuse; Dr. Mills, president of the Syracuse Rose Society; Messrs. Moeller and Fall of Eastwood, and Maguire of Auburn; Prof. E. A. White, Ithaca. President W. F. Kasting occupied the chair.

The report of the committee appointed to consider the question of whether a State society would be more beneficial than the federation was received and discussed. The committee was of the opinion that a State federation of organized interests would accomplish more than a society made up of individual interests. The delegates present sharing the same opinion, the suggestion was adopted, and the committee discharged with thanks.

Some discussion ensued as to the advisability of changing the name of organization, so that it included "Horticultural Societies," and thus become better descriptive of the federation. and on motion of Mr. Pierson seconded by Dr. Bates, it was resolved that the name be changed to read "New York Federation of Horticultural Societies and Floral Clubs."

The subject of the movement to obtain an appropriation of $60,000 from the State for the erection of greenhouses for the purpose of carrying on experimental work with flowers and vegetables came up for discussion. President Kasting reported the vetoing of the bill passed by both houses, and expressed his opinion that the only course was to have the bill introduced again. After discussion it was resolved that a committee of three be appointed to meet with the trustees of Cornell University, and determine if possible upon the most adequate framing of a new bill. It was the concensus of opinion that the trustees of the university should add to their regular budget for State appropriations an amount sufficient to cover the cost of the proposed buildings. If this were not feasible, it was understood that a bill should be introduced as before. The president appointed Messrs. Pierson and Vick, with himself, as such committee.

The next subject for discussion was the necessity of a building at the State Fair embodying means for taking proper care of exhibits of plants, flowers, fruits and vegetables, the quarters now in use not being suitable for the necessary preservation of exhibits during the fair period. Many suggestions as to the best way to secure the required facilities were offered. It was very generally agreed upon that if a

suitable horticultural building were erected at the head of Empire Court the florists would see that a very creditable planting of flower beds around it was carried out, stock to be donated, and the only cost to be defrayed being the labor of planting and taking care of the beds. Such a planting would give this section of the grounds a parklike appearance, and render them pleasing to visitors, in striking contrast to their present appearance which was practically offensive. It was resolved that a committee of two be appointed to confer with the Western New York State Horticultural Society, the New York State Fruit Growers' Association, and the New York State Vegetable Growers' Association, and solicit their co-operation in an

WM. F. KASTING
Re-elected President of New York State Federation of Horticultural Societies and Floral Clubs.

effort to evolve ways and means for getting an appropriation for the erection of a suitable building. Dr. Bates and Mr. Kasting were chosen as such committee. The discussion lasted some time, and much enthusiasm was evident.

Election of officers for the ensuing year resulted as follows: President, Wm. F. Kasting, Buffalo; first vice-president, Dr. Erl A. Bates, Syracuse; second vice-president, Chas. H. Vick, Rochester; third vice-president, F. R. Pierson, Tarrytown; secretary, John Young, New York; treasurer, W. A. Adams, Buffalo. The chair appointed F. R. Pierson, chairman of the legislative committee, and George Thorp chairman of the State Fair committee, and they were given power to select their own committees.

The report of the treasurer showed a substantial balance in the treasury. The meeting adjourned until next February, when there will be a meeting in Ithaca, during Farmers' Week. It was the most interesting meeting held since the organization of the Federation.
JOHN YOUNG, Sec'y.

LANCASTER COUNTY FLORISTS' CLUB.

Sept. 16th, about 5 P. M., a telephone message notified the writer that Richard Vincent, Jr., and son Robert and two of their foremen were at the Brunswick, in response to a request from the writer also that they give us a talk on dahlias for this meeting of the club. It is characteristic of this firm that they never do anything by halves and we not only had a paper that was a gem from every point of view but we also had some 125 varieties of dahlias from White Marsh, Md., on exhibition, all correctly labeled and a revelation to some of our local people. Robert Vincent read the paper and told us the history of the dahlia from its earliest record down to the present day, with cultural notes and suggestions. Richard Vincent, Jr., told some of his experiences at the convention and invited us all to join the National Dahlia Society and come to the show in New York and also to their own show at White Marsh, Md., which unfortunately comes in the same week as our own show.

In addition to the flowers exhibited by our visitors we had a fine vase of dahlia blooms by David Rose, an amateur, who does not hesitate to pay the price for new varieties. Rudolph Nagle exhibited a very fine vase of chrysanthemums, Smith's Advance and a yellow sport from the same.

The Dahlia Show committee reported progress in all lines and asking for volunteers received the offer of the services of at least a dozen of the club members. Wild smilax was ordered for the decoration of the tables, vases contributed by several of the members and offers received from members having machines to collect these vases and help us in any other way, so that with such a unanimity of helpfulness it will not be our fault if the show is not a success.

The programme committee reported having a promise from Robert Pyle, of West Grove, Pa., for a talk for the October meeting and this report met with the enthusiasm that it deserved. The visiting committee reported as having nothing arranged but would probably make the first visiting trip of the season one to Reading during the week of their show.

The Vincents were given an unanimous vote of thanks for their generosity in coming all the way to Lancaster by automobile with such a fine exhibit of flowers and such a valuable paper, and we trust they recognized the fact that it was a real vote and not merely a perfunctory one.
ALBERT M. HERR.

GARDENERS' AND FLORISTS' CLUB OF BOSTON.

The Gardeners' and Florists' Club had its initial meeting for the season at Horticultural Hall, on Tuesday evening, September 21. The attendance was moderate, but as large as could reasonably be expected for the first of the season. It had been announced that M. C. Ebel, of Madison. N. J., would address the club, but a communication from that gentleman stated that his health would not permit of his being present. It had been expected also that President P. Welch would tell the club some interesting things about the recent convention in San Francisco and his experiences in the transcontinental trip, but he was obliged to be out of town for several days, so the meeting had to provide its own entertainment from among the members present—not a difficult matter considering the oratorical abilities of some of the regular attendants.

Reports were made showing that the annual picnic had been a success, with a surplus to turn into the treasury, that the field day, so-called, at Newport had been a revelation in many ways to those who had participated and that the visit to the Breck-Robinson Nurseries at Lexington had been a very enjoyable outing. Votes of thanks was unanimously extended to the Breck-Robinson Co. and the Newport Horticultural Society. A communication from the Nassau County (N. Y.) Horticultural Society suggesting a plan of blanket membership in the various societies was referred to the executive committee, as was also a proposition that the club provide a special premium to be awarded at one of the big shows of the Massachusetts Horticultural Society in 1916. The proposed renewal of the landscape gardening classes for the coming season was discussed and a report of last year's committee will be called for at the next meeting. It was voted to have the annual club banquet in February, 1916.

Eber Holmes, representing W. A. Manda, staged a number of dahlias, including Mrs. Minnie Burgess, scarlet, Albert Mande, lemon and pink, Veronica Manda, rose pink, Josef Manda, crimson, Gertrude Manda, rose, Mrs. A. I. Dupont, ruby red, South Orange Surprise, changeable bronze, salmon and white, and some ten seedling dahlias; also Rudbeckia Mandianum and Salvia Greggii. Unfortunately Mr. Manda's exhibit had suffered badly in transit. W. N. Craig exhibited from Faulkner Farm some beautiful hardy asters and a superb vase of Buddleia variabilis magnifica.

CHRYSANTHEMUM SOCIETY OF AMERICA.

Examining Committees.

President Wm. Kleinheinz announces the committees to examine new chrysanthemums for the ensuing year, which are as follows:

Boston—Wm. Nicholson (Chairman), James Wheeler, Alex. Montgomery. Ship flowers to Chairman, care W. J. Thurston, Manager, Boston Flower Exchange, 1 Winthrop Square and Otis St., Boston, Mass.

New York—Eugene Dailledouze (Chairman), Wm. H. Duckham, A. Herrington. Ship flowers to New York Cut Flower Co., 55 W. Twenty-Sixth St., care Chairman.

Philadelphia—A. B. Cartledge (Chairman), John Westcott, S. S. Pennock. Ship flowers to A. B. Cartledge, 1514 Chestnut St., Philadelphia.

Cincinnati—R. Witterstaetter (Chairman), James Allen, Henry Schwarz. Ship flowers to Chairman, Jabez Elliott Flower Market, care Janitor.

Chicago—N. J. Wietor (Chairman), George Asmus, Wm. E. Tricker. Ship flowers to Chairman, 162 N. Wabash Ave., Chicago.

Shipments should be made to arrive

Some of the gardeners and florists who with their ladies attended the field meeting of the Boston Gardeners' and Florists' Club on the grounds of the Breck-Robinson Nursery Co., September 11th.

by 2 P. M. on examination days to receive attention from the committee. Must be prepaid to destination and an entry fee of $2.00 should be forwarded to the Secretary not later than Tuesday of the week they are to be examined, or it may accompany the blooms.

Seedlings and sports are both eligible to be shown before these committees, provided the raiser has given them two years trial to determine their true character. Special attention is called to the rule that sports to receive a certificate must pass at least three of the five committees.

The committees will be in session to examine such exhibits as may be submitted on each Saturday during October and November, the dates of which will be October 2, 9, 16, 23, 30 and November 6, 13, 20, 27.

Due to annexation and the changing of street names the Secretary's address now is 2134 West 110th street, Chicago, Ill.

CHAS. W. JOHNSON, Sec'y.

SOCIETY OF AMERICAN FLORISTS AND ORNAMENTAL HORTICULTURISTS.

Department of Plant Registration.

Public notice is hereby given that as no objection has been filed, the following registrations become complete:

Violets, Anne Evans and Quaker Lady, by Frank D. Pelicano, 119 Gutenberg street, San Francisco, Cal.

Coleus Yellow Trailing Queen, by the Oak Grove Greenhouse, Tuskegee, Ala.

Roses, Mrs. Bayard Thayer and Mrs. Moorfield Storey, by the Waban Rose Conservatories, Natick, Mass.

Shasta Daisy, Mrs. H. G. Selfridge, by A. T. Pyfer & Co., Chicago, Ill.

JOHN YOUNG, Sec'y.

Sept. 17th, 1915.

ST. LOUIS FLORIST CLUB

Secretary Beneke reports an officers' meeting at the home of President Bourdet on Thursday night of last week for the purpose of laying plans for fall and winter. A nice lunch was provided by the host. As the next meeting is to be held on the grounds of the Bourdet Floral Co. they will be in shape to tell of the interesting things provided for the next few months. These monthly officers' meetings will continue throughout the winter, a week before each meeting.

LADIES' SOCIETY OF AMERICAN FLORISTS.

To the Members of the Ladies' Society of American Florists:

My report and paper which I was to send to the convention was forwarded by registered mail to San Francisco and reached there on Aug. 15. They were returned to me on Aug. 29. I mailed them to the president that she would understand I had kept faith with her and was not responsible for my report not being at the meeting. I feel that it is only right and proper that all should at least see the report and I have asked HORTICULTURE to print the same.

Respectfully yours,

MRS. ALBERT M. HERR,

Treas.

Treasurer's Report for Year Ending Aug. 6th, 1915.

Balance on hand Aug. 14th, 1914....$211.88
Received from dues, pins, etc....... 265.75
Received from one life member..... 10.00
　　　　　　　　　　　　　　　　　$487.63

DISBURSEMENTS.

W. R. Nicholson, bowling prize......	$25.00
W. F. Gude, Smith Memorial fund...	25.00
Copley-Plaza Hotel reception......	77.75
Topping & Co., printing............	9.25
Miller Jewelry Co., pins...........	37.50
Mrs. Maynard, postage and wreath for Mrs. Fetters..............	28.00
Halliday Bros., flowers for Mrs. Quick	2.00
H. F. Comley, flowers for Mrs. Montgomery	2.60
Topping & Co., printing............	11.75
Theo. Miller, flowers for Mrs. Herring	2.00
Topping & Co., printing............	7.50
DeLaMare Ptg. & Pub. Co., annual printing	37.50
M. S. Newman, wreath for Mrs. Berning	5.00
Miller Jewelry Co., pins...........	37.50
Mrs. Maynard, salary to Aug. 14th, 1915	50.00
Mrs. Maynard, postage, etc........	34.75
	$382.50

Receipts $487.63
Disbursements 382.50

Balance on hand Aug. 9th, 1915...$105.13
MRS. ALBERT M. HERR, Treas.

The Minnesota State Florists' Association has elected officers as follows: W. D. Desmond, Minneapolis, president; Max Kaiser, Merriam Park, vice-president; A. Lauritzen, Como Park, treasurer; Thomas C. Rogers, 409 Hennepin avenue, Minneapolis, secretary.

NEW HAVEN COUNTY HORTICULTURAL SOCIETY.

The New Haven County Horticultural Society held its annual exhibition Thursday and Friday of last week in Harmonie Hall, New Haven. At 8 A. M., Thursday, everything was ready for the admission of entries, and they came thick and fast. John Lewis Childs, Inc., of Flowerfield, N. Y., sent 78 vases of gladioli, each vase a different variety.

A. N., Pierson, Inc., of Cromwell, Conn., sent phloxes and five large vases of roses. P. W. Popp, of Mamaroneck, N. Y., showed dahlias and gladioli—a very artistic exhibit. The city of New Haven made an especially attractive display, through Gustave X. Amrhyn, superintendent of the park department. There were many beautiful dahlias, lilies, phloxes, tuberoses, pampas grass and myriads of polyantha roses. The finest and largest display, however, was by John H. Slocombe, the veteran dahlia specialist. He has served his day and generation and he has served it well. His exhibit occupied the whole of the stage and towered fifteen feet high in the rear. It comprised dahlias, gladioli, phlox, shasta daisies and cosmos.

For "collection of named gladioli," John Lewis Childs was 1st. P. W. Popp, 2nd. For "ten named varieties of gladioli," a special prize was awarded P. W. Popp.

The Lord & Burnham gold medal was awarded C. Louis Alling, of West Haven, for greatest number of points won in exhibits throughout the year at the bi-weekly meetings. The competition was very keen. C. Louis Alling is a young man who has made an enviable record as a dahlia grower. His dahlia winnings were five 1st prizes and six 2nd prizes.

W. F. Jost, who has six acres under dahlia cultivation in East Haven, won eight 1st and five 2nd. Mr. Jost's dahlia farm is up to date. He has about five hundred feet in length with patent sprinklers and other improvements. Alfred E. Doty, of Morris Cove, Conn., won three 1st and five 2nd in the dahlia class. Lester B. Linsley, of West Haven, won four 1st, one 2nd, and an Award of Recognition for a Dahlia Seedling of Merit, from seed in 1915. F. W. Dewhurst, of Milford, Conn., won four 1st for asters.

Others who were prize winners in the dahlia class were Joseph E. Wehner, Derby, Conn.; Herbert H. Clark, West Haven, Conn.; P. W. Popp, Mamaroneck, N. Y.; John Madzen, New Haven; A. W. Davidson, Ansonia, Conn.; Hubert R. Allen, West Haven; Nathan A. Miller, Branford, Conn.; Chas. C. Barnes, Fair Haven; W. J. Myers and Otto C. Unger, both of New Haven.

John H. Slocombe entered but few classes, preferring to rest on the laurels he obtained in former years. He took two first for yellow and pink dahlias respectively, 1st for cosmos, and a certificate of merit for a superior new dahlia. He also received an award of recognition for a meritorious dahlia seedling, from seed in 1915. He gained the Sanderson prize for the largest and best display of dahlias of

EUONYMUS VEGETUS.

This new Euonymus appears to be a sport from the well-known old species, radicans, but it is far superior on account of the large and more glossy foliage. It seems also to adhere better to smooth surfaces, such as frame buildings and brick walls, than the old variety. The handsome foliage is attractive winter and summer, and is not injured in the least by our rather severe winters; but the main attractions are the holly red berries which cover the plant from top to bottom after frost. The berries form in August and color in November, but have generally fallen before first of April. The vine has become unusually popular among those that know it, and in the near future will be demanded as freely

as the Crimson Rambler rose was when introduced and E. vegetus is not likely to suffer a decline as its foliage is proof against insects and mildew.

American origin. He also captured the Elm City Nursery Co.'s prize of twenty dollars for the "best vase of fifteen blooms, showing stem and foliage of an American seedling, not yet in commerce."

RHODE ISLAND HORTICULTURAL SOCIETY.

The Rhode Island Horticultural Society held its annual September exhibition of fruits and flowers on Thursday and Friday, Sept. 16-17, in the ballroom of the Narragansett Hotel, Providence. Exhibitors from all over the State had sent choice blooms and garden products, with the result that the ballroom was a mass of color.

The dahlias formed the largest part of the collection and they were arranged down the center of the room on a long stand. Many asters and gladioli were to be seen, the gladiolus displays of A. P. Lenzen and the Carmicheal Orchards being especially beautiful. Although many blooms of a fine quality were staged, the hot weather had affected the flowers so that the exhibition was not quite up to the standard of last year. The fruit classes were not all filled, but the exhibits entered were of the first order. The display of bees, wax and honey was unusually good. One of the features of the exhibition was the large number of entries of fruit and flowers received from school children.

The officers of the society are: Dr. H. H. York, president; Harold L. Madison, treasurer; Ernest K. Thomas, secretary. The exhibition committee are Eugene A. Appleton (chairman), Joshua Vose, Arthur Sellew, Cornelius Hartstra, Dr. H. W. Heaton, the president and secretary. The judges were William Gray of Newport and Henry C. Neubrand, of Cromwell, Conn.

CLUB AND SOCIETY NOTES.

The Dahlia Show at Newport. R. I., is on as we go to press this week.

The September meeting of the St.

Paul Florists' Club was held on Sept. 21, at O. R. Echhardt's store.

The St. Louis Retail Florists' Association held its monthly meeting on Monday night, Sept. 20th, at the Mission Inn Garden.

The next meeting of the Albany (N. Y.) Florists' Club will be held at the Albany Cut Flower Exchange on Thursday evening, October 7.

The Prize Schedule of the Morris County (N. J.) Gardeners' and Florists' Society's twentieth annual flower show has been issued and copies may be obtained from the secretary, Edward Reagan, Madison, N. J. The date of the show is October 28-29.

The third annual flower show of the Holyoke and Northampton Florists' and Gardeners' Club will be held in Windsor Hall, Dwight street, Holyoke, on November 3 and 4, 1915. The committee in charge consists of D. J. Gallivan, Edward Hennessy, G. H. Sinclair, James Whiting, Wm. Downer, Geo. Rackliffe and George Strugnell. A liberal schedule of prizes has been issued.

Among the principal prize winners at the Pennsylvania Horticultural Society show were John Little, gard. to C. N. Welch, Chestnut Hill; Wm. Robertson, gard. to John W. Pepper, Jenkintown; Michael J. Flynn, gard. to H. A. Poth, Wayne; David Ingram, gard. to Mrs. Jos. F. Sinnott, Rosemont; Robert Abernethy, gard. to Thos. McKean, Rosemont; James Bell, gard. to J. W. Geary, Chestnut Hill, and Robert J. Morrow, Chestnut Hill.

The plant and flower exhibit in connection with the 41st annual fair of the Washington County Agricultural Society last week at West Kingston,

R. I. surpassed any that the society has ever held. A magnificent showing of gladioli by Carmichael Brothers of Shannock and a large exhibit of dahlias by George L. Stillman of Westerly, were the features. The Carmichael exhibit was not in competition, and Mr. Stillman took the honors in the dahlia classes. The prize for the best greenhouse collection went to State Senator Rowland Hazard, of Peace Dale. The gorgeous display of gladioli from the Carmichael gardens has never been equalled in the 41 years of history of the society.   S. A. G.

DIPLADENIA SPLENDENS PRO-
FUSA.

The illustration which appears on the cover of HORTICULTURE this week shows a plant of Dipladenia profusa, which was grown from a cutting about eighteen years ago. At the time the picture was taken, there were about two hundred open flowers upon the plant. It is one of a pair that we have used many times in decorative work during the last dozen years. This Dipladenia is in flower from June until Christmas. It has been potted once every two years, during the last twelve years, but has been fed liberally with manure water during the year that it did not receive a shift. The potting compost has been equal parts of fibre of loam, osmunda fern root, sphagnum moss, sand, charcoal, with about a third of sheep manure, and a good sprinkling of chicken bone. This has been used in as rough a state as could

be conveniently worked around the ball of the plant. Plenty of good drainage is essential, so that the water may pass off freely. We rest the plants from December until February and prune back the weak wood to strong eyes, before starting into growth in the spring. We find that it is a good plan to pinch the points of the shoots after the flowers are set. This check makes the belated eyes start away, and catch up to the others. Stove temperature is advised for these plants in nearly all books on plants that I have read, but I find that they do far better when treated as a greenhouse plant. We have wintered them as low as forty and forty-five degrees and find that they do not require water so often, and

start into stronger growth when the resting period is over. In summer we never shade them but give all the ventilation possible. The individual blooms are useful for cut flower work, and make very pretty centerpieces. Their lasting qualities are good, the lovely pink flowers keeping in good condition for a week.
GEORGE F. STEWART.

Medford, Mass.

Milton, Mass.—Geo. M. Anderson, for the past twenty-five years superintendent of the Wayside Farm, has leased the greenhouses at No. 499 Centre street, Milton, and will open an up-to-date retail florist's establishment.

CHICAGO GRAND FLORAL FESTIVAL.

At a meeting of the executive committee of the Chicago Grand Floral Festival, held at the offices of the Poehlmann Bros. Co., September 16, much routine business was transacted, A. Henderson, W. N. Rudd, W. J. Keimel, N. P. Miller, George Asmus and M. Barker in attendance. Considerable space was reported sold in the trade exhibits' department, including a number of the prominent retailers. Arrangements were made to materially extend the private gardeners' section of the premium list so as to conform to the wishes of exhibitors. A number of additional committees were suggested which will be announced as soon as completed.

The preliminary premium list is now ready and copies may be had on application to N. P. Miller, 179-183 North Wabash avenue, Chicago. The exhibition will be held at the Coliseum, November 9-14, and the liberal prizes include the following:

Class 15A—Best display chrysanthemum cut flowers, one or more varieties, arranged for effect, to contain not less than 100 large blooms; foliage, smaller chrysanthemum flowers, plants and other accessories permitted. 1st, $200; 2nd, $150; 3rd, $100.

Class 76A—Best display cut roses, one or more varieties, arranged for effect, to contain not less than 500 flowers, foliage and other accessories. 1st, $125; 2nd, $90; 3rd, $60.

Class 31—Best group of chrysanthemum plants arranged for effect, to occupy not less than 150 sq. ft. 1st, $100; 2nd, $80; 3rd, $60.

Class 33—Best display orchids (not less than 25 plants). 1st, $100; 2nd, $50.

Class 46—Best group of palms and decorative plants to occupy not less than 150 square feet of space. 1st, $100; 2nd, $75; 3rd, $50.

M. BARKER,
Chairman Publicity Committee.

CLEVELAND SHOW TO SHARE PROFITS WITH EXHIBITORS.

The enterprising florists and growers of Cleveland are not to be outdone by the much advertised citizen of a sister Lake City in the matter of profit sharing. For the first time in the history of floral exhibitions the exhibitors are to reap a double reward from their part in the show. All trade exhibitors in the Cleveland Flower Show to be held at the Coliseum, November 10 to 15, will have returned to them twenty-five per cent. of the net profits of the show.

This action was taken by the executive committee, all Cleveland growers and dealers, when it appeared that the success of their venture was guaranteed. Not being interested in the show from a profit standpoint and being assured that their cash guarantee was safe from the sale of space, they decided to make the event truly co-operative, and to share the profits with the trade exhibitors who have responded so liberally in the matter of taking space in the show.

Widespread interest in the coming Cleveland Show indicates a record-breaking attendance. The prospect of good returns from admissions added to the large proportion of the Coliseum space already sold makes it certain that there will be a considerable sum in the fund to be returned to the trade exhibitors.

At an executive committee meeting of the Cleveland Flower Show, held in the Hollenden Hotel, Friday evening, September 17, the following important action was taken because the three associations—Ohio Horticultural Society, Cleveland Florists' Club and the Garden Club of Cleveland, guaranteeing the $12,500 expense of the Cleveland Flower Show—are not in the show business for an enormous financial gain, the trade exhibitors will receive an equal share of the possible total net profits likewise with the three associations, 25 per cent. of the net profits to be divided pro rata with all trade exhibitors. The share of each one, however, is not to exceed 50 per cent. of the total amount of cost of space occupied by each exhibitor.

This action was passed unanimously after financial report made by Chairman H. P. Knoble, who is directing the work of ten sub-committees in charge of the various details of the show.

The following were in attendance: H. P. Merrick of Lord & Burnham Co.; C. U. Russell, Jones-Russell Co.; Geo. Bate, Cleveland Cut Flower Co.; Herbert Bate, Cleveland Cut Flower Co.; F. C. W. Brown, J. M. Gasser Co.; Timothy Smith, Smith & Fetters Co.

The executive committee was represented by

Chairman S. Prentiss Baldwin of Gates Mills, O.; Wm. G. Mather, president of the Ohio Horticultural Society; H. P. Knoble, general chairman of all committees, and F. A. Friedley, secretary of the James Eadie Co.

It was predicted at the meeting, which was a very enthusiastic one, that the few remaining spaces would be taken immediately. When all the space is sold it will leave the committees free to devote all their time in developing the artistic side of the show and in spreading the publicity throughout the country among the trade.

THAT RHODODENDRON PEST.

Editor HORTICULTURE:

Dear Sir—I notice in your paper of Sept. 4th an item headed "A pest of the Rhododendron," in which Mr. Pauls, from Palisade Parks, N. J., complains that he has trouble with what we call in Holland "Mobiums," which come from Holland. That does not mean that Holland is the only place where this bug exists as I have seen places here which had more of the bugs on the square foot than we have in Holland on the square acre. Mr. Hatfield says it is caused by a little white grub about the size of a grain of wheat. They must have large grains of wheat in Massachusetts as when the larvae are full grown they are about an inch in length and live in winter time as larvae in the ground and prefer Taxus above anything else to feed on. In the summer they grow to black bugs of the size of peas and during the night attack the leaves of the Rhododendron and other plants, hiding themselves during the day time under the leaves on the surface of the ground. If the gentlemen will keep the ground clean of leaves and put a few small boards on the ground under the Rhododendrons or Taxus, they will find in the morning many bugs on the underside of the board and it is easy to get rid of this pest by a little trouble and attention.

Your respectfully,
F. OUWERKERK.
Weehawken, N. J.

FOURTH NATIONAL FLOWER SHOW, PHILADELPHIA, PA.

Preparations for the Fourth National Flower Show, to be held in Philadelphia, March 25th to April 2d next, are in active progress. Space in the areas set apart for the trade exhibits is being freely reserved, and at present the bookings amount to over $4,000 in the aggregate. One exhibitor who had engaged a liberal space recently increased his booking to 1,200 sq. ft. equivalent to a $1,200 stand.

Chairman George Asmus, of the National Flower Show Committee, will call a meeting of his committee shortly, at which the second preliminary schedule will be settled. The schedule will include the American Carnation Society's premiums and the Carnation section; this section will, it is expected, have more than usual prominence for the reason that the A. C. S. is to celebrate its twenty-fifth anniversary or Silver Jubilee at this show.

The Rose Society and American Sweet Pea Society premiums, with the sectional premiums, will also appear in the new schedule. Special prizes offered by H. A. Dreer, Inc., H. F. Michell Co., John Cook, Zanberger Bros. of Holland, and others will also be announced.

The Pennsylvania Horticultural Society has decided to abandon its customary Spring Show for 1916 and to throw its influence into the work of the National Flower Show, and to this end has appointed W. F. Therkildsen, Robt. Craig and David Rust a committee to act in conjunction with the National Flower Show Committee.

J. Otto Thilow, chairman of the lecture committee has the work of his committee well in hand and the lectures will be an important feature of the show. The Committee on special features and the other local committees are all making good progress and have their plans well on the way to completion.

Much favorable comment by the trade has been passed upon the two plantings outside the exhibition hall which have been very conspicuous this summer and have helped considerably to attract attention to the forthcoming show. H. A. Dreer, Inc., and H. F. Michell Co., who provided these plantings are to be commended for their interest and forethought.

Treasurer F. R. Newbold of the Horticultural Society of New York, who is taking a very active and kindly interest in the show, has obtained promises of assistance from the members of several ladies' garden clubs and societies, and he reports that all seem ambitious to even outdo the efforts of the ladies whose excellent assistance was such an important feature of the success of the 1915 New York Show.

That the show has the interest and attention of the trade in all its branches throughout the country is evident from the letters received at the secretary's office, and there is every prospect that the National Exhibition of 1916 will eclipse all preceding flower shows.

JOHN YOUNG, Sec'y.
Sept. 17th, 1915.

MASS. AGRICULTURAL COLLEGE NOTES.

The Mass. Agri. College began its new year last Wednesday. Classes began on Thursday. There have been some radical changes in the Horticultural Department. C. H. Thompson, formerly of the Missouri Botanical Gardens at St. Louis, has taken charge of the work in plant propagation and plant materials. This relieves Prof. Nehrling of considerable work and allows him to divert his entire attention to floriculture. Several new courses have also been introduced in the department of floriculture. The work in greenhouse construction which formerly came in Floriculture 1 (Greenhouse Management), has been placed in a separate course known as Floriculture 5. Floriculture 7, is a new course in palms and decorative plants while Floriculture 6, is also a new course in hardy perennials, annuals, and bedding plants. The department is better equipped than ever and looks forward to a very successful year.

Twenty-three students are enrolled in the floriculture courses. Mr. Thurston is back to continue graduate work in horticulture and will assist in the department as before.

In the market gardening department H. F. Thompson of Arlington has been promoted to head of the department, while A. S. Thomson, of Pennsylvania, has been engaged to assist in the work.

In the department of Botany some changes have been made. Botany 7, formerly known as Plant Pathology, has been changed to a course in the classification of the different fungi and economic fungi. The scope of Botany 5 (Plant Diseases), has been increased to meet the requirements of the individual student.

P. H. Elwood, hitherto engaged in extension work in Landscape Gardening, has accepted a position as head of the department of Landscape Gardening at the University of Ohio.

The flower show section of the annual Country Fair at Lincoln Park, New Bedford, Mass., last week was in the theatre building in charge of James Garthley, ex-gardener at the Rogers estate in Fairhaven, assisted by James Armstrong, gardener at the Converse estate at Marion.

Thomas W. Head, recently of Bergenfield, N. J., has accepted the position of superintendent of the J. Ogden Armour estate at Lake Forest, Ill.

SEED TRADE

AMERICAN SEED TRADE ASSOCIATION

Officers—President, J. M. Lupton, Mattituck, L. I., N. Y.; First Vice-President, Kirby B. White, Detroit, Mich.; Second Vice-President, F. W. Bolgiano, Washington, D. C.; Secretary-Treasurer, C. E. Kendel, Cleveland, O.; Assistant Secretary, S. F. Willard, Jr., Cleveland, O. Cincinnati, O., next meeting place.

Seed Corn.

Continued warm weather up to this date, much of it the warmest of the entire season, has probably saved the corn crop. This, at least, is the message from one of the leading seed corn growers. It may be well to add that the corn has a long line of vicissitudes to encounter before it is cured and becomes seed for planting. This applies particularly to sweet corn and especially if any considerable percentage is soft or "in the milk." A rainy, cold autumn will ruin a large percentage of such corn, causing it to mould, unless cured by artificial heat, which most of the progressive growers are now prepared to employ. However, the condition of the crop is vastly more satisfactory than appeared probable a month ago.

Beans.

There is nothing more definite to report regarding the bean crop than contained in Seed Trade Notes of two weeks ago. We are still hoping despite the pessimistic reports of the growers that conditions are really not as bad as they fear.

Peas.

No further particulars can be given of the pea crop. There are still fears of some shortage of the late long pod sorts, but this will probably prove a blessing to the dealers. We are advised that growers of green peas for the market realized very unsatisfactory prices this season, which, as in the case of beans, will probably have a restraining influence on demand. So far as we have ascertained either seed crops remain in status quo as last reported.

Garden Beets.

A large acreage of garden beets was grown for seed the past season. One grower estimated that more than 100,000 pounds more were grown in this country this year. We have no means of knowing how good this guess is. Possibly some of our readers can make a better estimate. So far as we can learn, dealers generally are not worrying about their supplies of beet or other biennials. Perhaps they have assured themselves on this point. The situation will doubtless develop within the next sixty days. We hope to give a general summary of the season's crops in a near issue of HORTICULTURE.

Notes.

The Door County Seed Co. have now occupied their new quarters on St. John street.

Black's Seeds is the title of a new company at Albert Lea, Minn., which succeeds Robert H. Black.

The value of horticultural imports at the port of New York, for week ending September 11, is given as follows: Clover seed, $13,000; grass seed, $10,420; fertilizer, $11,022; trees, plants and shrubs, $110,965.

Charles Johnson, American agent for Denaiffe & Son, La Menitre, France, has changed his main office address from Marietta, Pa., to 1905 Virginia street, Berkeley, Cal. His New York address, up to Oct. 10, will be Charles Johnson, Hotel Brevoort, New York. After that date it will be in care of American Express, 65 Broadway, New York. He is now on his annual business tour. Denaiffe & Son having resumed their business which was suddenly suspended a year ago by the calling into the French army of more than 600 employees, including every active head of the company.

CATALOGUES RECEIVED.

Livingston Seed Co., Columbus, Ohio.—Fall Catalogue of Bulbs and Plants for 1915.

J. F. Noll & Co., Newark, N. J.—Bulb Catalogue, Autumn 1915. Seeds, Plants, Bulbs, Fertilizers, Poultry Supplies.

Vincent Lebreton, Angers, France.—Wholesale Trade List for Autumn 1915 and Spring 1916. Complete nursery stock list with cable code, etc. McHutchinson & Co., N. Y., sole agents for U. S. and Canada.

Stumpp & Walter Co., New York.—"Bulbs for Autumn Planting." An elaborate and very attractive fall catalogue. Handsome covers and abundantly illustrated with half-tone engravings and four beautiful color plate.

Breck-Robinson Co., Lexington, Mass.—"Trees, Plants, Planting."—An exceptional publication in the arrangement of its plates and typographical make-up. Well printed, with practical cultural and descriptive notes and altogether a dignified and impressive manual of hardy planting material.

NEWS NOTES.

Beacon, N. Y.—Benjamin Hammond advertises that ten per cent of all sales made of Hammond's Cottage Colors for use on property located in the city of Beacon will be turned over to the treasurer of Highland Hospital.

Hartford, Conn.—A contract for 1,400 potted geraniums has been awarded to E. S. Drake of Fairfield avenue, by Charles A. Stedman Camp, Sons of Veterans, to be furnished for decoration of the graves of the veterans of the Civil War next Memorial Day. Because it has grown increasingly more difficult to secure flowers by the methods which have long been pursued in this city, the society, which now has charge of the Memorial Day celebration, decided to make a change last summer, and after much deliberation decided to buy potted plants next year.

The big conservatory in course of construction by Lord & Burnham in the Missouri Botanic Garden is nearing completion. Here the chrysanthemum show will be staged in November.

IMPORTATION OF BELGIAN PRODUCTS.

Horticulture Publishing Co:

I am in receipt of the following information from the Merchant Association of New York. Will you be kind enough to give it the necessary publicity through your paper, and oblige?

"Referring to previous correspondence relative to your desire to bring forward from Rotterdam goods of Belgian origin, I have to inform you that the Department has received from the American Ambassador at London the following telegram, dated September 8:

"'2769. September 8th. Foreign office today sends me printed form now being sent to all persons desiring to export goods of Belgian origin from Holland. Form as follows:

"'The Under Secretary of State for foreign affairs presents his compliments to Messrs. —— and, in reply to their letter of the ——, relative to the exportation from Belgium to —— of —— is directed by Secretary Sir E. Grey to state that his Majesty's Consular Officer at the port of shipment will be instructed to issue the necessary permit as soon as Messrs. —— have produced to the satisfaction of the Foreign Office ——.

"'One. A declaration or certificate from the competent Belgian local or municipal authority that the goods in question are of Belgian origin or manufacture; and

"'Second. A written guarantee from a bank in this country that the purchase money for the goods has been deposited with them, and will not be withdrawn, without the special authorization of his Majesty's Government, during the continuance of the occupation of Belgium by the enemy; or alternatively clear evidence that the purchase money was remitted to Belgium before the thirty-first of July, 1915, such as an affidavit of the bank in a neutral country through which the money was remitted.

"'Please request persons approaching Embassy in cases of this description to furnish documents set forth above.'

"Unless you have submitted to the office of the Foreign Trade Advisers the necessary undertaking as to payment and the required proof of the Belgian origin of the goods you desire to import I suggest that you do so at once."

Possibly statements similar to the above came to your attention in the daily press a day or so ago. We are passing this on to you for whatever it may be worth.

Yours very truly,

CHAS. A. DARDS.

New York.

Sharon, Pa.—The Murchie greenhouses on South Irvine avenue have been moved from their old location and are being rebuilt on a site on the opposite side of the street. When rebuilt there will be six new greenhouses, measuring 120 by 20 feet, with a lean-to of 12 by 120 feet. A new heating system will be installed, making the plant one of the most modern of this kind in this section.

NEWS NOTES.

West Haven, Conn.—David Kydd is
going into the nursery business.

Galesburg, Ill.—I. L. Pillsbury, of
carnation staple fame, has remodelled
his flower store and added a motor
truck to the equipment.

South Lyon, Mich.—W. E. Hastings
whose shipments of asters to the Detroit market amounted to about 300,000
this year, contemplates planting five
acres of asters next season.

Kalamazoo, Mich.—One of the most
attractive features of "Prosperity
week," October 4-9, will be the chrysanthemum show which will mark the
formal opening of Erb & Erb's flower
shop, 106 West Main street. The exact
day for the opening has not yet been
set, but that named will be one which
will least interfere with other attractions during the week.

The National Floral Corporation
comprises up-to-date a list of 51 leading florists in important cities in all
sections of the country. The first "National" advertising appeared in "Life"
for September 9 and 16 and we understand that space has been contracted
for in the Ladies' Home Journal for
December and the Saturday Evening
Post in four numbers during November and December.

NEWS ITEMS FROM EVERYWHERE

CHICAGO.

H. F. Halle, for many years at 801 Sheridan Road now has his store at 4753 Broadway.

Dutch bulbs which are now arriving in quantity are reported to be badly heated in many instances.

visited Mrs. Haas' father Judge Hutchinson.

Mr. and Mrs. E. Haas have returned from Davenport, Florida, where they visited Mrs. Haas' father Judge Hutchinson.

Smith's Advance chrysanthemum is having almost a clear field at this time for its usual companion Golden Glow is badly effected by the unusually hot weather.

The three-story building occupied by the Raedlein Basket Co. is being remodeled and the changes will include a fine new front with suitable show windows.

Mr. and Mrs. Chas. Fisk are now on their way home from a six-weeks' trip through the west, with California and their daughter's home as the objective point. Mr. Fisk is so pleased with the Pacific coast that he will likely make that country his permanent home.

Fritz Bahr opened a fine new store at Highland Park on Sept. 18th. The store is located in the down town district about four blocks from the greenhouses, and is equipped with high-class furnishings suitable to the trade he enjoys there. Many remembrances were sent by his numerous friends in the trade. An unique feature of the new store is the service room which is in the form of a cottage and occupies the middle portion of the store which is very deep. This cottage affords excellent opportunity for showing window boxes, etc.

NEW YORK.

The Dahlia Show at the Museum of Natural History on September 25, 26, 29 is expected to bring a great many horticultural visitors from out of town.

Geo. E. M. Stumpp reports a very successful season at Southampton and predicts that Southampton will before long outclass Newport as a summer resort. Mr. Stumpp is taking a great deal of interest in the New York Spring Flower Show and has signed up for almost one thousand dollars' worth of space.

The first meeting of the schedule committee of the New York Spring Show was held in the office of Secretary John Young and a good beginning made on the serious preparatory work. The re-election of the old officers and manager gives assurance of the ultimate success of the undertaking, financially and otherwise.

WASHINGTON, D. C.

George Field is beginning to cut some very fine Cattleya labiata and his Dendrobium formosum are due in the first of the coming week. The rose houses are taking on fine form.

Leapley & Meyer are dressing up their store and expect to have it take on a most attractive appearance prior

to the Grand Army celebration next week. The outside of the store has been painted a rich chocolate brown, while the interior has been decorated in several harmonizing shades of green. New cork linoleum which closely resembles a mottled stone flooring, has recently been laid and numerous other improvements have been made.

Mrs. J. A. Phillips, who conducts the flower store at the corner of Fourteenth and Harvard streets, is being congratulated on having won the distinction of being the most popular lady in the Mt. Pleasant and Columbia Heights districts and as a result being awarded a trip to California. 29,680 votes were cast in her favor. With her husband, Mrs. Phillips has been in the florist business in the neighbor-

MRS. J. A. PHILLIPS

hood of their present location for the past twelve years.

A number of the local florists and growers are again complaining of the worms which are stripping the fronds of their ferns and doing their work so quickly that a whole house may be cleaned out in short order unless prompt action is taken. These worms closely resemble cut worms and range in size from a quarter of an inch to an inch and a quarter. One florist states that he has obtained good results through the use of Persian insect powder. This can be put on the ferns in large quantities without injuring them and later washed off with a hose.

The second annual flower show under the auspices of the Falls Church, Va., Civic League is to be held October 1 and 2. Competition for prizes is open only to amateurs and no entrance fee is to be charged, nor will there be any admission fee charged to the exhibition. The purpose of the show is to encourage the beautification of homes. A large number of special prizes are offered by florists, nurserymen and seedmen of Washington, Phil-

adelphia and other cities. George W. Mess, of the Botanic Gardens, and George A. Comley, a Washington florist, have consented to act as judges; the third judge will be announced later.

BOSTON.

Ruane florist, Waltham, celebrated his fifth anniversary on September 15, by presenting a rose to every caller at his store.

The daily papers are praising Henry Penn for his philanthropy in sending to the hospitals as a gift on Wednesday, September 22, thirty-five thousand roses. Generosity of this kind is commendable as well as enterprising.

The annual meeting of the Boston Flower Exchange will be held on Saturday evening, October 23, at Young's Hotel. The annual banquet will be enjoyed at the same time by the stockholders and invited guests and will be, as usual, one of the "red-letter" events of the floricultural year in the Hub.

W. C. Ward of Quincy has sold out his business and is going down in Maine to lead the simple life and seek some return in comfort and recreation for his years of arduous work. We hope he will find it to be all he anticipates. The purchasers are W. Cahill, formerly employed by Fottler, Fiske, Rawson Co., and Charles Beasley, recently of New Jersey. The sale was dated September 1, but Mr. Ward agreed to stay a little while to "break them in." We are told that their first job in the breaking-in process was that of wheeling manure. Just imagine! But there's nothing like starting at "the bottom of the ladder" and the young firm may yet have occasion to thank Mr. Ward for his practical lesson in the fundamentals of successful floriculture.

PROVIDENCE, R. I.

Clifton W. Loveland, Assistant State Entomologist and Secretary of the Rhode Island League of Improvement Societies, has resigned his posts here and gone to Florida, where he is to take up the work.

William E. Chappell, a well-known florist of this city, has sufficiently recovered from his long illness to get back on the job. Last spring he suffered a severe nervous breakdown and for five months gave up business entirely. His trip to Florida was the most beneficial of all. Mr. Chappell looks for a busy season and is getting back into the harness to keep up with the procession.

The Florists' and Gardeners' Club of Rhode Island will hold its first meeting following the summer recess next Monday evening, in Swart's Lodge Hall, 96 Westminster street, when matters of business will come up and plans for the winter work will be discussed. A report of the committee on the annual outing of the club will be submitted and there will also be reports from members bearing on the vacation period.

PHILADELPHIA.

The "Old Guard" will hold their annual reunion at Commodore Westcott's bungalow, Waretown, N. J., week end of Oct. 1.

The sympathy of the many friends of Victor I. Ridenour the well known retail florist of Ridge Ave. and 32nd street goes out to him on the death of his father which occurred in Washington, D. C. on the 19th inst.

Growers about here are speaking enthusiastically of the new rose Mrs. Moorfield Storey which is already showing great promise. One of the largest plantings is that of William Munro at Garrettford. His stock looks very fine but he is not going to send any to market just yet. We may expect some about mid-October.

There were two dahlia shows here on Tuesday, 21st—one at Horticultural Hall, the other at Michells'. Both were quite interesting and instructive from a local standpoint. The society idea is the best to our mind as it keeps the commercial idea in the background and is therefore more convincing to the public.

Our attention has been called to a slip of the types and the proof reader on an item in last week's notes. For Fordbrook Farms read Fordhook Farms. The Phila. Ledger man may not have known any better but HORTICULTURE did, and Mr. Burpee will please accept our apology. Fordhook has a very interesting history in connection with the family forebears of the Burpees. We may tell the story some day.

John Deutscher, late head salesman for the Thomas Young establishment at Bound Brook, N. J., will start business on his own account at 1625 Ranstead street on or about the 25th of Sept. He will do a general wholesale commission business and will handle a full line in addition to the Bound Brook specialties. The title of the concern will be The Philadelphia Wholesale Cut Flower Exchange. A Mr. Glaser will be associated with Mr. Deutscher and is reported to be the financial backer of the new venture. Mr. Deutscher is well-known and well liked in the local trade here and has excellent prospects of making a good success. He had the advantage of several years experience in the New

York wholesale market before striking Philadelphia and this, added to his local experience, will be of distinct benefit in carving a foothold for himself here.

Condensed, up-to-date, thorough, may be truly said of the 450 page text-book or Commercial Floriculture by Professor White of Cornell, just published by the MacMillan Co., and editorially noticed in HORTICULTURE recently. We have had the pleasure of glancing through a copy and it is a monument of learning, accuracy and comprehensiveness. The professor has depended not only on his own profound knowledge of his subject, but he has also gone right to the recognized experts in every branch of the business and tells their story in their own words. The grower, the commission man, the retailer; all receive their proper share of treatment in every phase of their operations. This book should be in the hands of everyone connected with the business, young or old; but especially the younger element. The fine work of pioneers in this line, such as Henderson, Hunt, Scott and others are all retained where valuable; but all matter now superseded has been eliminated, so that the student may grasp the essentials of his particular branch in a nutshell. The price of the volume is $1.75 net. Copies can be supplied from the office of HORTICULTURE.

SAN FRANCISCO.

Podesta & Baldocchi are showing a fine lot of Irish Elegance roses, the first that have come in for some time.

John R. Fotheringham, who represents the S. S. Pennock-Meehan Company and several other houses on the Coast, is making a visit to the East.

Arthur Cann, who has conducted a flower shop at San Jose, Cal., for the last 19 years, and has been for five years at 51 S. First street, has just moved into a new store at S. First and San Antonio streets. Here he has a store about twice as large as the old one, and a large basement suitable for storage of supplies, in connection with his extensive seed business. The store is beautifully fitted up and conveniently arranged, with an office and basket-display room on the balcony and a comfortable writing-room on the ground floor.

PERSONAL.

Married at Worcester, Mass., Ralph M. Forbes, florist, and Miss Bessie A. Hildreth.

Louis Schultheis, of Scranton, Pa., goes to Honesdale as manager of the Maple City Greenhouses.

Lawrence Coy, of the Coy Seed Co., Valley, Neb., and Miss Margaret McCold were married on September 10.

Fred Reynolds of New Bedford, Mass., and Mrs. M. T. Edson of Chester, Vt., were married on September 22.

Homer Richey, who is associated with his father, William Richie, in the florist business at Albia, Ia., was elected president of the State Florists' Association at DesMoines last week.

VISITORS' REGISTER.

Montreal, P. Q.—Mr. and Mrs. Walter Sword of Lonsdale, R. I.

Chicago—W. P. Craig, Phila, Pa.; Mrs. M. E. Irby, Memphis, Tenn.; Mrs. Turbiville and Son, Memphis, Tenn.

St. Louis, Mo.—F. J. Farney, representing M. Rice Co., Phila.; Aug. A. Schwerin, Burlington, Iowa.

Boston — Paul Berkowitz, of H. Bayersdorfer & Co., Philadelphia; J. J. Karins, representing H. A. Dreer, Philadelphia.

New York—J. C. Vaughan, Chicago, Ill.; P. Welch, Boston; A. N. Pierson, Cromwell, Conn.; Charles W. Crouch and Mrs. Crouch, Knoxville, Tenn.; George L. Stillman, Westerly, R. I.; Cincinnati—Julius Dilloff of Schloss Bros. & Co., New York.; I. Bayersdorfer of H. Bayersdorfer & Co., Phila.; Mr. and Mrs. G. A. Bechman, Middletown, O.; Mrs. Lampert, Xenia, Ohio.

Philadelphia — Bates Butler, Elm Grove, West Virginia; Fred Heck, Heck Bros., Reading, Pa.; William Walker, Louisville, Ky.; Reinhold E. Schiller, Chicago, Ill.; C. P. W. Nimms, representing A. H. Hews & Co., Cambridge, Mass.

Washington, D. C.—I. Rosnosky, representing H. F. Michell Co., Phila., Pa.; Ralph M. Ward, New York; Henry Bomhoft, of Gullett & Sons, Lincoln, Ill.; Paul F. Dutz, New Castle, Pa.; Richard Vincent, Jr., and Thomas A. Vincent, White Marsh, Md., and Prof. Bert W. Anspon, College Park, Md.

WHOLESALE FLOWER MARKETS — TRADE PRICES—Per 100 TO DEALERS ONLY

Roses	CINCINNATI Sept. 20		CHICAGO Sept. 20		BUFFALO Sept. 20		PITTSBURG Sept. 23	
Am. Beauty, Special	20.00	25.00	20.00	25.00	20.00	25.00	15.00	20.00
" " Fancy and Extra	15.00	20.00	12.00	15.00	15.00	20.00	10.00	12.50
" " No. 1	6.00	10.00	5.00	10.00	6.00	8.00	6.00	8.00
Russell, Hadley	4.00	8.00	5.00	10	5.00	7.00	4.00	8.00
Killarney, Richm'd, Hill'don, Ward	4.00	6.00	4.00	6.00	5.00	7.00	6.00	8.00
" " " " Ord.	3.00	4.00	2.00	3.00	3.00	4.00	2.00	4.00
Arenburg, Radiance, Taft, Key, Ex.	4.00	6.00	4.00	6.00	5.00	6.00	6.00	8.00
" " " " " Ord.	3.00	4.00	2.00	3.00	3.00	5.00	2.00	4.00
Ophelia, Mock, Sunburst, Extra	4.00	6.00	6.00	8.00	4.00	7.00	6.00	8.00
" " " Ordinary	3.00	4.00	2.00	4.00	3.00	4.00		4.00
Carnations, Fancy	1.50	2.00	2.00	3.00		2.00		2.00
" Ordinary		1.00	1.00	2.00	1.00	1.25		1.50
Cattleyas		30.00	50.00	75.00	40.00	50.00	40.00	60.00
Dendrobium formosum				50.00			30.00	40.00
Lilies, Longiflorum	8.00	10.00	6.00	10.00	8.00	10.00	8.00	10.00
" Rubrum	4.00	8.00	2.00	4.00	2.00	4.00	2.00	4.00
Lily of the Valley		4.00	3.00	10	2.00	4.00	3.00	4.00
Daisies								1.50
Violets								
Snapdragon					1.00	2.00		
Gladioli	2.00	4.00	2.00	3.00	1.00	2.00	1.00	4.00
Asters	1.00	2.00	1.00	3.00	.50	1.50	1.00	3.00
Chrysanthemums	15.00	20.00	10.00	15.00	12.00	15.00	10.00	20.00
Sweet Peas								
Gardenias			20.00		25.00			
Adiantum		1.00	1.00	1.25	1.00	1.25	.75	1.25
Smilax		15.00	8.00	10.00		15.00	12.00	15.00
Asparagus Plumosus, Strings (100)		50.00	30.00	50.00	40.00	50.00	40.00	50.00
& Spren. (100 bchs.)		25.00	25.00	50	30.00	25.00	35.00	40.00

Flower Market Reports

BOSTON Seasonably cool weather gives renewed courage to a dispirited market and a cheerful buoyant air is noticed in the wholesale district. Values are still at lowest point on everything but quality is improving and quantity on some things that have encumbered the market is materially reduced. As soon as outdoor flowers have been finished up, by frost or otherwise, conditions will brace up, but until then not much permanent advancement can be expected. Cattleyas have suddenly become very plentiful and prices have been cut down fifty per cent.

BUFFALO Trade was on the quiet side up to last Friday, when things improved slightly, especially in the aster and gladiolus lines, which are gradually coming nearer to the end daily. The let up on supply caused the prices to build up. Roses are good. Excellent color is seen in Killarney, and there are some fine Maryland, Scott, Key and Ophelia, all of which have had a fair sale. Lilies are shortening up and prices are gradually getting better. There has been a call for yellow and white chrysanthemum, lily of the valley, white roses and orchids. Carnations are coming on in excellent shape. Shipping trade has been good and the outlook is for a good autumn business.

CHICAGO Trade in general has been fairly good the past week. There was a good supply of flowers and they cleared up well, especially all stock that was of first-class quality. The hot weather at the end of the week diminished the supply and at this writing good roses are not easy to get in large quantities. The number of telegrams coming into this market show the supply is short outside also. Asters are now about gone and as usual they are more in demand as they disappear. Early chrysanthemums are about all cut and the supply has not been large. All kinds of roses have been in sufficient supply till now and the present shortage is only for a few days. American Beauties are rather below demand. There is a scant supply of cattleyas and they are bringing good prices. Outdoor flowers are represented now by tritoma, larkspur, hardy phlox, gaillardia, etc. Fine smilax is now seen in the market but demand is slow.

CINCINNATI The change to cooler weather will probably bring about better market conditions for it will undoubtedly cut down the quantity of stock coming in and cause the supply to more nearly equal the demand. Roses are in large quantities and all seasonable varieties may be had. Carnations are coming in somewhat stronger and are of a much better quality. Both longiflorum and rubrum lilies are plentiful. Asters are in a heavy supply and good gladioli may still be had. Cosmos and dahlias are both excellent and plentiful. Wild smilax is meeting with a strong demand, caused by many fall opening decorations.

NEW YORK The wholesale business had been moving along very satisfactorily when its progress was interrupted by the very warm spell, then it went all to pieces and thus far has not recovered. Roses are now being sold in most cases in bulk—$1.00 a box, and so on. Dahlias have been very plentiful and cheap, with quality excellent. Gladiolus also good, although the recent storm put a good many of them out of commission. Carnations are getting more plentiful. The supply of Cattleya labiata already exceeds the demand and prices have fallen away down, blooms of indifferent quality being offered as low as 10 cents and the very best stopping at 25c. Gigas, of course, commands a better figure. Oncidiums are meeting with a good demand at $2.00 to $3.00 per 100. Southern asparagus, which has been coming in heavily all summer, has been received in bad condition of late on account of the hot weather. Asters less plentiful and not so good as they were.

PHILADELPHIA The two weeks' heat-wave broke here on the 17th and this week quite an improvement can be seen in the quality of the dahlias as to substance and finish. Other flowers also show the same effect although in lesser degree. The aster crop is on the wane, the local supplies being the final cuts from the field and not high-grade. There are some nice asters arriving, however, from greenhouse-grown plants and a limited quantity of field-grown from northern points which are also very good. Gladioli are nearly over. White roses sold well last week, also Russells and Scott Key. Beauties are rather draggy. Cosmos, tuberoses and tritomas are very plentiful—about three times as many as the market can absorb. Carnations are showing up a little better and there is no trouble in selling the few arriving with good stems, but the short-stemmed ones are hard to dispose of. Orchids are more plentiful and prices have eased up considerably. In chrysanthemums the Golden Glow seems to be the only one in sight in any quantity. Very few of the early white varieties are to be seen.

SAN FRANCISCO While the rush experienced early in the month has passed, the florists are still getting a lively business. It is now getting to the hot, dry time of year before the fall rains, and much of the outside stock is going off, both in quantity and quality, while little new is

(Continued on page 423)

WHOLESALE FLOWER MARKETS — TRADE PRICES — Per 100 TO DEALERS ONLY

	BOSTON Sept. 23	ST. LOUIS Sept. 20	PHILA. Sept. 20
Roses			
Am. Beauty, Special	12.00 to 20.00	20.00 to 25.00	15.00 to 20.00
" Fancy and Extra	6.00 to 10.00	12.00 to 20.00	8.00 to 15.00
" No. 1	1.00 to 3.00	3.00 to 8.00	6.00 to 10.00
Russell, Hadley	4.00 to 8.00	10.00 to 15.00	3.00 to 15.00
Killarney, Richmond, Hillingdon, Ward, Extra	1.00 to 4.00	5.00 to 6.00	1.00 to 6.00
" Ordinary	.25 to 1.00	1.00 to 3.00	1.00 to 3.00
Arenburg Radiance, Taft, Key, Extra	1.00 to 4.00	5.00 to 6.00	3.00 to 8.00
" Ordinary	.50 to 1.00	1.00 to 3.00	1.00 to 3.00
Ophelia, Mock, Sunburst, Extra	2.00 to 4.00	...... to	3.00 to 8.00
" Ordinary	.50 to 1.00	...... to	2.00 to 3.00
Carnations, Fancy	.75 to 1.00	1.50 to 2.00	1.50 to 2.00
" Ordinary	.50 to .75	.50 to 1.00	1.00 to 1.50
Cattleyas	15.00 to 25.00	35.00 to 75.00	40.00 to 60.00
Dendrobium formosum	...... to 25.00	...... to	40.00 to 50.00
Lilies, Longiflorum	4.00 to 6.00	6.00 to 8.00	8.00 to 12.50
" Rubrum	...... to 2.00	2.00 to 3.00	3.00 to 4.00
Lily of the Valley	2.00 to 4.00	3.00 to 4.00	3.00 to 4.00
Daisies	.50 to 1.00	.20 to .75	...... to ......
Violets	...... to	...... to	...... to ......
Snapdragon	.50 to 1.00	3.00 to 4.00	4.00 to 6.00
Gladioli	1.00 to 2.00	2.00 to 3.00	2.00 to 3.00
Asters	.25 to 1.00	.75 to 2.00	1.50 to 2.00
Chrysanthemums	8.00 to 12.00	...... to 12.00	12.00 to 15.00
Sweet Peas	.15 to .30	.15 to .25	...... to .75
Gardenias	10.00 to 12.00	...... to	...... to ......
Adiantum	.50 to 1.00	1.00 to 1.25	...... to 1.00
Smilax	6.00 to 12.00	12.00 to 15.00	...... to 6.00
Asparagus Plumosus, Strings (100)	25.00 to 50.00	35.00 to 50.00	...... to 50.00
" & Spren. (100 Bchs.)	25.00 to 35.00	30.00 to 35.00	...... to 50.00

Flower Market Reports

(Continued from page 421)

coming in, aside from chrysanthemums, of which there is now considerable variety, yellow predominating. Shipments to state points are increasing rapidly, but the heavy movement will not start till next month. Roses show little improvement. The best of the daily cut is spoken for in advance, and everything cleans up early in the day. The carnation market is still unsatisfactory, with very little stock and most of that poor. Good violets still command high prices, and it will be several weeks before much stock will appear. Asters are scarce and poor, and a week or so more will finish them. There are still a good many sunflowers, marigolds, gypsophilas, scabiosas, etc., but not so much as a few weeks ago. A few scattered lots of gladioli are still coming in. Dahlias are offered in abundance, the average quality good. Lilies, except cold storage stock, are about gone. There is all the amaryllis the market will absorb. The cut of gardenias is improving a little both in quality and quantity and finds a very good demand. Orchids are extremely scarce; there is practically nothing beyond an occasional spray of phalaenopsis, though a fine cut of cattleyas is expected within a few weeks. Some very fine cyclamen plants are coming on, but so far no great number have been brought to market. Greens are in strong demand. There is plenty of Asparagus plumosus, huckleberry is largely used, and some fine varieties of eucalyptus are receiving attention.

ST. LOUIS During the last week this market was demoralized; there was so much stock coming in and the demand being so slow that the bulk of the consignments were dumped or sold at so low a price that it about paid express charges to outside consignors. There is entirely too much second-grade stock coming in, while the extra fancy grades are very scarce at present.

WASHINGTON A change in the temperature seems to bid well for an increased business during this week. Last week showed something of an improvement with some few society events calling for decorations. The aster season is about over and the continued hot weather has had its effect upon dahlias. Chrysanthemums are coming in increased quantities and Golden Glow, with heavy heads and fairly long stems, are being offered. Gladioli are slowly leaving the market. In carnations an improvement is noted in the varieties now to be had and they are very good considering the season. Lily of the valley is selling better and the supply has increased slightly. Lilies are less plentiful and falling off in demand. Orchids are again to be had in small quantities.

Waltham. Mass.—Peirce Brothers donated 5,000 roses last week to be sold on Thursday afternoon and evening in the lobbies of the theatres and other public places for the benefit of the G. A. R. encampment.

NEW YORK QUOTATIONS PER 100. To Dealers Only

MISCELLANEOUS	Last Half of Week ending Sept. 18 1915	First Half of Week beginning Sept. 20 1915
Cattleyas	10.00 to 25.00	10.00 to 25.00
Dendrobium formosum	20.00 to 25.00	20.00 to 25.00
Lilies, Longiflorum	2.00 to 4.00	4.00 to 5.00
" Rubrum	1.00 to 2.00	2.00 to 3.00
Lily of the Valley	2.00 to 3.00	2.00 to 3.00
Daisies	...... to .50	...... to .50
Violets	...... to	...... to ......
Snapdragon	.50 to 1.00	.50 to 1.00
Gladioli	.50 to 2.00	.50 to 2.00
Asters	.25 to 1.00	.50 to 1.00
Chrysanthemums	6.00 to 8.00	6.00 to 8.00
Sweet Peas	...... to	...... to ......
Corn Flower	...... to .25	...... to .25
Gardenias	6.00 to 12.00	5.00 to 12.00
Adiantum	.50 to .75	.50 to .75
Smilax	8.00 to 10.00	8.00 to 10.00
Asparagus Plumosus, strings (per 100)	15.00 to 30.00	15.00 to 30.00
" & Sprm (100 bunches)	10.00 to 20.00	10.00 to 20.00

OBITUARY.

Mrs. Harry Krider.

Mrs. Harry Krider, better known perhaps to the New York trade under her maiden name of Miss Smedley died on September 10, of heart failure. As bookkeeper and cashier for J. K. Allen for a number of years previous to her marriage, Miss Smedley was deservedly popular with the trade because of her fidelity and agreeable personality.

Mrs. Johanna Barth.

Mrs. Johanna Barth, who for the past fifty-two years had conducted a flower shop at the entrance to the Mt. Olivet Cemetery in Bloomfield, N. J., died on September 11, at her home, 38 Division place, from a complication of ailments. She was the widow of Michael Barth and was seventy-four years old. Surviving her are four sons and two daughters.

Charles F. Hoffmeister.

Chas. F. Hoffmeister died at his home on September 17, after an illness that lasted for some months. He was in his 56th year. Mr. Hoffmeister had been connected with the florist business in Cincinnati, Ohio, for more than a score of years. First he was in the employ of his brother and sisters in the Hoffmeister Floral Co., and later had his own business in a retail store and later had a greenhouse plant of his own at Ft. Thomas, Ky. His wife, a daughter, Miss Marie A. Hoffmeister, and two sons, Chas H. and Otto H. survive him.

Alvin Burrows.

While swimming in the Eastern Branch, near the Anacostia Bridge, Washington, D. C., last week, Alvin Burrows, 20 years of age, of 1915 Good Hope Road, Anacostia, lost his life and nearly carried a companion. Norman Padgett, with him. These two and Clifton J. Smith all reside at the Good Hope Road address. Burrows was an employee of Fred H. Kramer, Padgett was employed at the Gude Bros. greenhouses, while Smith works at the steel plant. Burrows was seized with cramps and Padgett went to his rescue but was borne down by the drowning man. Smith soon arrived where the two youths were fighting for their lives and separating them towed Padgett to safety and then went back after Burrows but he could do nothing and the body was found later on at the foot of Eleventh street. Burrows was very popular among the younger employees of the various Anacostia greenhouses and was held in high esteem by his employers.

F. W. Harvey.

It is with great regret that we learn of the sudden death, following an operation, of Mr. F. W. Harvey, the editor of our contemporary, The Garden. Mr. Harvey had been suffering from an abscess on the brain, for which he underwent an operation. He was removed to the London Temperance Hospital on the 23rd ult., but succumbed early in the morning of the 31st. Early in life Mr. Harvey engaged in the business of market gardening, and later studied horticulture, Chelmsford, under Mr. C. Wakely. He was afterwards a member of the garden staff at Kew, where he remained until 1905, leaving to take up the position of sub-editor of The Gardener, under Mr. W. P. Wright, who was at that time editor. Here he stayed for about three years, and left to take up a similar position on The Garden, under the late E. T. Cook. He made the best use of the experience thus gained, and when, about four years ago, Mr. Cook left for America, Mr. Harvey was able to take up the position of editor thus vacated. Under his editorship The Garden has more than maintained its standard, and his loss will be deeply felt by the staff, with whom he worked in amity and harmony. Although his duties were onerous, Mr. Harvey found time to interest himself in matters connected with horticulture. He was chairman of the Sweet Pea Society in 1914, a member of the Floral Committee of the R. H. S., and a member of the Council of the National Rose Society. Mr. Harvey leaves a widow and one son. —*The Gardeners' Chronicle.*

Buyer's Directory and Ready Reference Guide

Advertisements under this head, one cent a word.   Initials count as words.

Display advertisers in this issue are also listed under this classification without charge. Reference to List of Advertisers will indicate the respective pages.

Buyers failing to find what they want in this list will confer a favor by writing us and we will try to put them in communication with reliable dealers.

ACACIAS.
Stuart Low & Co., Harry A. Barnard, representative, Hotel Albert, New York City.
For page see List of Advertisers.

ACCOUNTANT
R. J. Dysart, 40 State St., Boston.
For page see List of Advertisers.

ACHILLEA
"Pearl," Fine Seedlings, $3.00 per 1,000, cash. JAMES MOSS, Wholesale Grower, Johnsville, Pa.

APHINE
Aphine Mfg. Co., Madison, N. J.
For page see List of Advertisers.

APHIS PUNK
Nicotine Mfg. Co., St. Louis, Mo.
For page see List of Advertisers.

ARAUCARIAS
Henry A. Dreer, Philadelphia, Pa.
For page see List of Advertisers.

ARECAS.
Joseph Heacock Co., Wyncote, Pa.
For page see List of Advertisers.

AUCTION SALES
Elliott Auction Co., New York City.
For page see List of Advertisers.

AZALEAS
P. Ouwerkerk, Hoboken, N. J.
For page see List of Advertisers.

BAY TREES
August Rolker & Sons, New York.
For page see List of Advertisers.

BEDDING PLANTS
A. N. Pierson, Inc., Cromwell, Conn.
For page see List of Advertisers.

BEGONIAS
Julius Roehrs Company, Rutherford, N. J.
For page see List of Advertisers.

R. Vincent, Jr., & Sons Co., White Marsh, Md.
For page see List of Advertisers.

Thomas Roland, Nahant, Mass.
For page see List of Advertisers.

		Per 100
BEGONIA LORRAINE,	2½ in.	$12.00
	3 in.	20.00
	4 in.	35.00
	5 in.	50.00
BEGONIA CINCINNATI,	2½ in.	15.00
	3 in.	25.00
	3½ in.	30.00
	4½ in.	40.00
JULIUS ROEHRS CO., Rutherford, N. J.		

BOILERS
Kroeschell Bros. Co., Chicago.
For page see List of Advertisers.

King Construction Co., North Tonawanda, N. Y.
"King Ideal" Boiler.
For page see List of Advertisers.

Lord & Burnham Co., New York City.
For page see List of Advertisers.

Hitchings & Co., New York City.

BOXES—CUT FLOWER FOLDING
Edwards Folding Box Co., Philadelphia.
For page see List of Advertisers.

Folding cut flower boxes, the best made. Write for list. HOLTON & HUNKEL CO., Milwaukee, Wis.

BOX TREES
BOX TREES—Standards, Pyramids and Bush. In various sizes. Price List on demand. JULIUS ROEHRS CO., Rutherford, N. J.

BULBS AND TUBERS
Arthur T. Boddington Co., Inc., New York City.
For page see List of Advertisers.

J. M. Thorburn & Co., New York City
Wholesale Price List of High Class Bulbs.
For page see List of Advertisers.

Ralph M. Ward & Co., New York City.
Lily Bulbs.
For page see List of Advertisers.

John Lewis Childs, Flowerfield, L. I., N. Y.
For page see List of Advertisers.

August Rolker & Sons, New York City.
Holland and Japan Bulbs.
For page see List of Advertisers.

R. & J. Farquhar & Co., Boston, Mass.
For page see List of Advertisers.

S. S. Skidelsky & Co., Philadelphia, Pa.
For page see List of Advertisers.

Chas. Schwake & Co., New York City.
Horticultural Importers and Exporters.
For page see List of Advertisers.

A. Henderson & Co., Chicago, Ill.
For page see List of Advertisers.

Burnett Bros., 98 Chambers St., New York.
For page see List of Advertisers.

Henry F. Michell Co., Philadelphia, Pa.
For page see List of Advertisers.

Joseph Breck & Sons Corp., Boston, Mass.
For page see List of Advertisers.

Fottler, Fiske, Rawson Co., Boston, Mass.

C. KEUR & SONS, HILLEGOM, Holland.
Bulbs of all descriptions. Write for prices.
NEW YORK Branch, 8-10 Bridge St.

CANNAS
Canna Specialists.
Send for Canna book.
THE CONARD & JONES COMPANY, West Grove, Pa.

CARNATION STAPLES
Split carnations quickly, easily and cheaply mended. Pillsbury's Carnation Staple, 1000 for 35c.; 3000 for $1.00 post paid. I. L. PILLSBURY, Galesburg, Ill.

Supreme Carnation Staples, for repairing split carnations, 35c. per 1000; 3000 for $1.00. F. W. WAITE, 85 Belmont Ave., Springfield, Mass.

CARNATIONS.
Wood Bros., Fishkill, N. Y.
For page see List of Advertisers.

F. Dorner & Sons Co., Lafayette, Ind.
For page see List of Advertisers.

F. R. Pierson, Tarrytown, N. Y.
Carnation Matchless.
For page see List of Advertisers.

CARNATIONS—Continued
Jas. Vick's Sons, Rochester, N. Y.
Field Grown Plants.
For page see List of Advertisers.

Littlefield & Wyman, North Abington, Mass.
New Pink Carnation, Miss Theo.
For page see List of Advertisers.

Carnations, field grown, $6.00 per 100. Cash. White and Pink Enchantress Mrs. Ward, Perfection, Fenn, Winsor, Queen, Lawson, Beacon. CHAS. H. GREEN, Spencer, Mass.

CHRYSANTHEMUMS
Chas. H. Totty, Madison, N. J.
For page see List of Advertisers.

R. Vincent, Jr., & Sons Co., White Marsh, Md.
Pompon Chrysanthemums,
For page see List of Advertisers.

THE BEST 1915 NOVELTIES.
The Cream of 1914 Introductions.
The most popular Commercial and Exhibition kinds; also complete line of Pompons, Singles and Anemones. Trade list on application. ELMER D. SMITH & CO., Adrian, Mich.

COCOANUT FIBRE SOIL
20th Century Plant Food Co., Beverly, Mass
For page see List of Advertisers.

CYCLAMENS
The Best Strains.
Eight Varieties.   Very Fine.
If you want quality, order now.

	100	1000
2½ in.	$7.00	$60.00
3 in.	9.00	80.00
4 in.	20.00	

Write for copy of our monthly plant bulletin.
S. S. PENNOCK-MEEHAN CO., 1608-1620 Ludlow St., Philadelphia, Pa.

DAHLIAS
Send for Wholesale List of whole clumps and separate stock; 40,000 clumps for sale. Northboro Dahlia and Gladiolus Gardens, J. L. MOORE, Prop, Northboro, Mass.

NEW PAEONY DAHLIA
John Wanamaker, Newest, Handsomest, Best. New color, new form and new habit of growth. Big stock of best cut-flower varieties. Send list of wants to PEACOCK DAHLIA FARMS, Berlin, N. J.

DECORATIVE PLANTS
Robert Craig Co., Philadelphia, Pa.
For page see List of Advertisers.

Woodrow & Marketos, New York City.
For page see List of Advertisers.

S. S. Skidelsky & Co., Philadelphia, Pa.
For page see List of Advertisers.

Bobbink & Atkins, Rutherford, N. J.
For page see List of Advertisers.

A. Leuthy & Co., Roslindale, Boston, Mass.
For page see List of Advertisers.

EUONYMUS RADICANS.
Euonymus Radicans Vegetus—Three-year-old potted plants for immediate delivery; also three-year field-grown plants. $14.00 per 100, $2.00 per doz. Illustrated booklet, free for the asking. THE GARDEN NURSERIES, Narberth, Pa.

For List of Advertisers See Page 403

In writing to Advertisers kindly mention Horticulture

NURSERY STOCK

P. Ouwerkerk, Weehawken Heights, N. J.
For page see List of Advertisers.

W. & T. Smith Co., Geneva, N. Y.
For page see List of Advertisers.

Bay State Nurseries, North Abington, Mass.
Hardy, Northern Grown Stock.
For page see List of Advertisers.

Bobbink & Atkins, Rutherford, N. J.
For page see List of Advertisers.

Framingham Nurseries, Framingham, Mass.
For page see List of Advertisers.

August Rolker & Sons, New York City.
For page see List of Advertisers.

Chas. G. Curtis Co., Callicoon, N. Y.
Nursery Stock for Fall Planting.

Stuart Low & Co., Harry A. Barnard, representative, Hotel Albert, New York City.
For page see List of Advertisers.

NUT GROWING.

The Nut-Grower, Waycross, Ga.
For page see List of Advertisers.

ONION SETS

Schilder Bros., Chillicothe, O.
Onion Seed—Onion Sets.
For page see List of Advertisers.

ORCHID FLOWERS

Jas. McManus, New York, N. Y.
For page see List of Advertisers.

ORCHID PLANTS

Julius Roehrs Co., Rutherford, N. J.
For page see List of Advertisers.

Stuart Low & Co., Harry A. Barnard, representative, Hotel Albert, New York City.
For page see List of Advertisers.

Lager & Hurrell, Summit, N. J.
For page see List of Advertisers.

PALMS, ETC.

Robert Craig Co., Philadelphia, Pa.
For page see List of Advertisers.

August Rolker & Sons, New York City.
For page see List of Advertisers.

A. Leuthy & Co., Roslindale, Boston, Mass.
For page see List of Advertisers.

Stuart Low & Co., Harry A. Barnard, representative, Hotel Albert, New York City.
For page see List of Advertisers.

Jos. Heacock Co., Wyncote, Pa.
For page see List of Advertisers.

PANSY PLANTS

PANSIES—The Big Giant Flowering Kind—$3.00 per 1,000; $25.00 for 10,000. If I could only show the nice plants, hundred of testimonials and repeat orders, I would be flooded with new business. Cash. JAMES MOSS, Wholesale Grower, Johnsville, Pa.

PANSY SEED

Chas. Frost, Kenilworth, N. J.
The Kenilworth Giant Pansy.

Fottler, Fiske, Rawson Co., Boston, Mass.

PEONIES

Peonies. The world's greatest collection. 1200 sorts. Send for list. C. BETSCHER, Canal Dover, O.

PEONIES! Try us once and if not satisfied tell us why. GEO. N. SMITH, Wellesley Nurseries, Wellesley Hills, Mass.

PECKY CYPRESS BENCHES

A. T. Stearns Lumber Co., Boston, Mass.

PHLOX

PHLOX—Coquelicot, Eclaireur, Rosenberg, Independence, Lothair, etc. GEO. N. SMITH, Wellesley Nurseries, Wellesley Hills, Mass.

PIPE AND FITTINGS

Kroeschell Bros. Co., Chicago.
For page see List of Advertisers.

King Construction Company, N. Tonawanda, N. Y.
Shelf Brackets and Pipe Hangers.
For page see List of Advertisers.

PLANT AND BULB IMPORTS

Chas. Schwake & Co., New York City.
For page see List of Advertisers.

August Rolker & Sons, New York City.
For page see List of Advertisers.

PLANT TRELLISES AND STAKES

Seele's Tieless Plant Stakes and Trellises. H. D. SEELE & SONS, Elkhart, Ind.

PLANT TUBS

R. A. Dreer, Philadelphia, Pa.
"Riverton Special."

RAFFIA

McHutchison & Co., New York, N. Y.
For page see List of Advertisers.

RHODODENDRONS

P. Ouwerkerk, Hoboken, N. J.
For page see List of Advertisers.

Framingham Nurseries, Framingham, Mass.
For page see List of Advertisers.

RIBBONS AND CHIFFONS

S. S. Pennock-Meehan Co., Philadelphia, Pa.
For page see List of Advertisers.

ROSES

Poehlmann Bros. Co., Morton Grove, Ill.
For page see List of Advertisers.

P. Ouwerkerk, Hoboken, N. J.
For page see List of Advertisers.

Robert Craig Co., Philadelphia, Pa.
For page see List of Advertisers.

W. & T. Smith Co., Geneva, N. Y.
American Grown Roses.
For page see List of Advertisers.

Bay State Nurseries, North Abington, Mass.
For page see List of Advertisers.

August Rolker & Sons, New York City.
For page see List of Advertisers.

Framingham Nurseries, Framingham, Mass.
For page see List of Advertisers.

A. N. Pierson, Inc., Cromwell, Conn.

Stuart Low & Co., Harry A. Barnard, representative, Hotel Albert, New York City.
For page see List of Advertisers.

THE CONARD & JONES COMPANY, Rose Specialists
West Grove, Pa. Send for offers.

SEASONABLE PLANT STOCK

R. Vincent, Jr. & Sons Co., White Marsh Md.
For page see List of Advertisers.

SEED GROWERS

California Seed Growers' Association.
San Jose, Cal.
For page see List of Advertisers.

SEEDS

Carter's Tested Seeds.
Seeds with a Pedigree.
Boston, Mass., and London, England.
For page see List of Advertisers.

Schilder Bros., Chillicothe, O.
Onion Seed—Onion Sets.
For page see List of Advertisers.

Joseph Breck & Sons, Boston, Mass.
For page see List of Advertisers.

Kelway & Son,
Langport, Somerset, England.
Kelway's Celebrated English Strain Garden Seeds.
For page see List of Advertisers.

SEEDS—Continued

J. Bolgiano & Son, Baltimore, Md.
For page see List of Advertisers.

A. T. Boddington Co., Inc., New York City.
For page see List of Advertisers.

Chas. Schwake & Co., New York City
For page see List of Advertisers.

Michell's Seed House, Philadelphia, Pa
New Crop Cyclamen Seeds.
For page see List of Advertisers.

W. Atlee Burpee & Co., Philadelphia, Pa.
For page see List of Advertisers.

R. & J. Farquhar & Co., Boston, Mass.
Giant Cyclamen Seed.
For page see List of Advertisers.

J. M. Thorburn & Co., New York City
For page see List of Advertisers.

S. Bryson Ayres Co., Independence, Mo.
Sweet Peas.
For page see List of Advertisers.

Loechner & Co., New York City.
For page see List of Advertisers.

Ant. C. Zvolanek, Lompoc, Cal.
Winter Flowering Sweet Pea Seed.
For page see List of Advertisers.

S. S. Skidelsky & Co., Philadelphia, Pa.
For page see List of Advertisers.

W. E. Marshall & Co., New York City.
Seeds, Plants and Bulbs.
For page see List of Advertisers.

August Rolker & Sons, New York City.
For page see List of Advertisers.

Burnett Bros., 98 Chambers St., New York.
For page see List of Advertisers.

Fottler, Fiske, Rawson Co., Boston, Mass.
Seeds for the Florist.

SKINNER IRRIGATION SYSTEM

Skinner Irrigation Co., Brookline, Mass.
For page see List of Advertisers.

SPHAGNUM MOSS

Live Sphagnum moss, orchid peat and orchid baskets always on hand. LAGER & HURRELL, Summit, N. J.

STOVE PLANTS

Orchids—Largest stock in the country—Stove plants and Crotons, finest collection JULIUS ROEHRS CO., Rutherford, N. J

SWAINSONA

R. Vincent, Jr., & Sons Co., White Marsh, Md.
For page see List of Advertisers.

SWEET PEA SEED

Ant. C. Zvolanek, Lompoc, Calif.
Gold Medal of Honor Winter Orchid Sweet Peas.
For page see List of Advertisers.

S. Bryson Ayres Co.,
Sunnyslope, Independence, Mo.
For page see List of Advertisers.

Arthur T. Boddington, Inc., New York City.
Winter Flowering.

VENTILATING APPARATUS

The Advance Co., Richmond, Ind.
For page see List of Advertisers.

The John A. Evans Co., Richmond, Ind
For page see List of Advertisers.

VIOLETS

FIELD-GROWN VIOLET PLANTS.

	100	1000
Princess of Wales	$5.00	$45.00
Lady Campbell	5.00	45.00
Marie Louise	5.00	45.00
Gov. Herrick	5.00	45.00
Farquhar	5.00	45.00
La France	5.00	45.00

Write for copy of our monthly plant bulletin.
S. S. PENNOCK-MEEHAN CO.,
1608-1620 Ludlow St., Philadelphia, Pa.

For List of Advertisers See Page 403

Portland, Me.—Members of the Portland Florists' Association enjoyed a
delightful time with Alexander Skillin
at his home, Falmouth Foreside, Wednesday afternoon and evening, Sept.
15. There were 36 florists who accepted the invitation and during the
afternoon tennis, base ball and races
were enjoyed. At 4 o'clock on the
spacious lawn a delicious clam-bake
was served. Sports were participated
in afterwards until evening, when
music and cards afforded entertainment inside. The affair was a very
successful one and a vote of thanks
was extended Mr. and Mrs. Skillin for
their delightful entertainment and excellent supper.
The florists represented were Frank
L. Minott, Dennett's, Portland Flower
Shop, Talbot's, Conant of Westbrook,
Goddard of Deering Centre, Sawyer,
Clark, Nelson of South Portland and
Peterson of Scarboro.

In writing to Advertisers kindly mention Horticulture

PUBLICATIONS RECEIVED.

Bulletin of Peony News, No. 1, together with the Proceedings of the American Peony Society for 1914 and 1915. This is a 36-page pamphlet of much interest and practical value to the peony grower and dealer. Contains some excellent cultural notes on the peony from widely known specialists.

Proceedings of the Wisconsin State Horticultural Society.—This is the Annual Report for 1915, by F. Cranefield, secretary. A well-bound volume of 106 pages with several full page plates. A very useful feature is a careful descriptive list of trees and shrubs recommended as hardy and desirable for planting in Wisconsin, together with a "black list" of shrubs which have been tested on the grounds of the Experiment Station at Madison and found unsatisfactory.

Our Little Carthaginian Cousin and Our Little Norman Cousin of Long Ago, are two books especially designed for boys and girls, just sent out by The Page Company, Boston. These books are uniform with those previously published in the Little Cousin Series all of which have had a wide popularity as interesting and authentic accounts of the children and their manners, customs and surroundings in other countries in the olden time. The first named is The Story of Hanno, a Boy of Carthage, by Clara Vostrovsky Winlow, the time being about 2,000 years ago. The second is a Story of Normandy in the time of William the Conqueror, by Evalein Stein. Both are splendidly illustrated by John Goss with six full page plates in tints and expressive frontispiece in colors. The low price at which these instructive and entertaining books are sold—60 cents a volume—should insure a very large sale.

Sander's List of Orchid Hybrids—by Sander & Sons, St. Albans, England. This new and up-to-date issue of this work so indispensable to the orchid enthusiast, will be welcomed in all parts of the world where orchids are cultivated. It contains a complete list of the names and parentages of all the known Hybrid Orchids, whether introduced or artificially raised. The lists are arranged in tabular form so that all hybrids, derived from each species or hybrid, may be ascertained at a glance. The premier position so long held by Messrs Sander in the orchid world is the best guarantee of the exactness and reliability of the contents of this work, which must have entailed much pains-taking labor and zealous research. It comprises 158 pages and blank leaves are inserted to enable those who wish to do so to add new records from time to time. The price of the volume is 21 shillings in England. Parties wanting copies can get them through the office of HORTICULTURE, or by application direct

to Sander & Sons, St. Albans, England.

Manual on the Iris. By C. S. Harrison, York, Neb. Giving directions for their propagation and care, how to enlarge a wide field of profit and pleasure. Mr. Harrison is known far and wide for his devotion to the Iris, the Phlox and the Peony—indeed to any plant that will make itself at home and adorn the gardens in the semiarid regions. Mr. Harrison's attachment for these things finds vent in a command of beautiful sentiments, an almost poetic fervor and contagious enthusiasm. He believes in "something more than dollar chasing" and is in the business of nurseryman not alone for its emoluments but also because he loves the goods he handles and he has given freely of his time and ability to the missionary work of teaching others to love them. This iris book is very attractively illustrated with portraits of many of the finest varieties and an excellent picture of the author forms an appropriate frontispiece. The manual will fill a good and useful place.

The Holy Earth. By Dr. L. H. Bailey.—In this volume one of the foremost living authorities on rural life and agriculture presents his personal views, formed by many years of thought, study and contact, of man's relations to the soil, both physical and spiritual. In it he reveals rare poetic gifts of wisdom and expression. His style is captivating, his philosophy convincing, his enthusiasm infectious. The reader's mental vision is focussed upon himself as one of the teeming, tense and aspiring human race, as a factor in Nature's great plan and a participator in some far-reaching destiny. The Neighbor's Access to the Earth, The Sub-dividing of the Land, The Struggle for Existence, The Keeping of The Beautiful Earth. The Democratic Basis in Agriculture, A forest Background, The Open Fields, The Habit of Destruction—these are the titles of a few of the twenty-nine chapters which make up this literary gem. After reading it we realize more than ever before the responsibility which has been placed upon man to act rightly towards the earth and our obligations "to react and to partake, to keep, to cherish, and to operate" in every way possible to conserve the beauty and the utility of this Earth once pronounced "Good" by the Creator. "The Holy Earth" is published by Charles Scribner's Sons, New York. Price $1.00. HORTICULTURE can supply copies. If to be sent by mail add postage, 10c.

NEWS NOTES.

Elizabeth, N. J.—The Elizabeth Nursery Co. is putting up a storage house 30 x 60.

Bradford, Pa.—E. B. Sage has retired and C. Gunton becomes the new owner of the Red Rock Rosery.

Northfield, N. J.—John Siebel, manager of Hendrickson Farm Greenhouses, has resigned his position.

New Haven, Ind.—The New Haven Floral Co.'s greenhouses were badly damaged by the big storm of September 10.

Syracuse—The Quinlan Greenhouses were badly damaged by lightning in the big storm of Thursday, Sept. 9. The damage exceeded $2,000.

Salem, Ohio—W. L. Petit has just set up a reserve boiler for use in case of emergency. The weight of the boiler, which was made in Erie, Pa., is eighteen tons.

Rutherford, N. J.—Bobbink & Atkins have purchased fifty acres of additional land near Paterson, N. J. The land will be devoted exclusively to the culture of roses. The firm now occupies 350 acres of greenhouses and nurseries.

GREENHOUSE BUILDING OR CONTEMPLATED.

Champaign, Ill.—J. E. Yates, one house.

Salamacana, N. Y.—M. M. Dye, one house.

Pennsburg, Pa.—O. C. Trumbore, enlarging.

Black Duck, Minn.—J. W. Baney, enlarging.

Terre Haute, Ind.—Heinl & Weber, additions.

Joliet, Ill.—Clarence Sterling, range of houses.

Minneapolis, Minn.—C. I. Lindskoog, one house.

Baltimore, Md.—E. W. Heinbuck, one house.

West Haven, Conn.—E. L. Reinwald, one house.

Woodstock, Ill.—George Moncur, house 30 x 80.

Reading, Pa.—C. J. Huesman & Son, house 20 x 100.

Hartford, Conn.—Carl Pierson, house 20 x 100.

St. Matthew, Ky.—Nanz & Neuner Co., range of houses.

Springfield, Mass.—J. W. Adams Nursery Co., additions.

Pawtucket, R. I.—Wm. Forbes, Meadow street, one house.

Providence, R. I.—H. J. Doll, 609 Douglas avenue, one house.

Los Angeles, Cal.—Germain Seed Co., two houses, each 30 x 300.

Campaign, Ill.—John E. Yeats, range of houses in contemplation.

Pleasantville, N. J.—Chas. Eckley, removed from Frankford, Pa.

Newark, N. J.—Kimmerie & Minder, 488 So. Orange Cor., one house.

Quincy, Mass.—George A. Thompson, 82 Glencoe place, one house.

Oklahoma City, Okla.—Furrow & Co., range of houses in contemplation.

East Providence, R. I.—Jos. Koppelman, Pawtucket avenue, house .35 x 300.

Detroit, Mich.—E. A. Fetters, Woodward avenue, range of houses in contemplation.

PATENTS GRANTED.

1,152,402. Planter. David Draper, Rome, N. Y.
1,152,574. Weed-Remover. James Tomlin, Moro, Oreg.
1,152,531. Hedge Cutter. Herbert E. Marshall, New York, N. Y.
1,153,028. Plant and Flower Stand. Alvin Thos. Chalk, Baltimore, Md.
1,152,940. Weed-Destroying Machine. Patrick J. Gannon, Farmington, Minn.

Red Rock, Pa.—E. B. Sage has sold out his florist business.

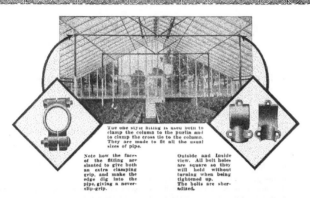

The one style fitting is used both to clamp the column to the purlin and to clamp the cross tie to the column. They are made to fit all the usual sizes of pipe.

Note how the faces of the fitting are slanted to give both an extra clamping grip, and make the edge dig into the pipe, giving a never-slip-grip.

Outside and inside view. All bolt holes are square so they will hold without turning when being tightened up. The bolts are sherardized.

New Design Malleable Fittings For Pipe Frame Houses

WITH half the weight of iron, these new design Malleable Fittings of ours are twice as strong as the cast iron ones.

There is such a "give" to these fittings, that you can draw the bolts up to the very last turn without the danger of snapping the casting.

They are made with a slanting face so that when the bolts are

Malleable split cross fitting taken apart.

Split cross fitting clamped to ridge column and cross ties.

drawn up, the fittings not only hold the pipe in a pinching grip, but the edges of the fitting bite into the pipe, giving a dig-in-grip.

Both of the two parts of the fitting are exactly alike. There is none of that bothersome chance of getting sides mixed.

Send for prices and any further facts you want.

Lord & Burnham Co.

SALES OFFICES:

NEW YORK	BOSTON	PHILADELPHIA	CHICAGO	ROCHESTER	CLEVELAND
42nd Street Bldg.	Tremont Bldg.	Franklin Bank Bldg.	Rookery Bldg.	Granite Bldg.	Swetland Bldg.

TORONTO, CANADA, Royal Bank Bldg.   MONTREAL, Transportation Bldg.

FACTORIES : Irvington, N. Y. Des Plaines, Ill. St. Catharines, Canada

Vol. XXII
No. 14
OCT. 2
1915

HORTICULTURE

View in a Rock Garden
At Thomas Roland's, Nahant, Mass.

EASTERN NURSERIES

JAMAICA PLAIN, MASS.

Special surplus list of Hardy Perennials or Old-Fashioned Flowers.

NURSERIES AT HOLLISTON, MASS.

Terms Cash, F. O. B. our Nurseries. Packing at cost. Subject to Prior Sales. Void after October 15th. Not less than 25 sold at these prices. When less than 25 of one kind is wanted, add 10% to the 100 rate.

STRONG STOCK, FIELD GROWN CLUMPS

	Per 100
500 Achillea Millefolium Roseum	$3.50
300 Achillea Tomentosum	4.00
500 Achillea The Pearl	3.50
400 Aconitum Acutum	4.00
200 Agrostemma Coronaria Walkeri	4.00
100 Double Hollyhocks, pink, white, dark red yellow	4.00
300 Anchusa Italica Dropmore	4.00
400 Anthericum Liliago	4.00
300 Aquilegia Coerulea	4.50
100 Aquilegia Coerulea Alba	5.00
300 Aquilegia Haylodgensis	4.50
600 Aquilegia Nivea Grandiflora	4.00
800 Arabis Alpina	4.00
500 Armeria Maritima Splendens	4.00
400 Artemesia Purshiana	3.50
500 Artemesia Stellariana	4.00
200 Asclepias Tuberosa	4.00
400 Asperula Hexaphylla	4.00
400 Aster Climax	8.00
400 Aster Miss Willmott	4.50
400 Aster NoVae Angliae	4.50
300 Aster Novelty	4.50
400 Aster Regina	4.00
500 Aster Sibericus	4.00
250 Aster Thomas Ware	4.50
100 Aster Top Sawyer	4.50
800 Baptisia Australis	5.00
250 Bettonica Grandiflora	4.00
300 Buddleia DaVidii	12.00
300 Buddleia Magnifica	11.00
600 Campanula Carpatica	4.50
900 Campanula Carpatica Alba	5.00
500 Cassia Marylandica	3.50
300 Centaurea Babylonica	4.50
100 Centaurea Dealbata	5.00
150 Centaurea Montana	4.50
190 Centaurea Montana Alba	5.50
300 Cerastium ArVense	4.00
300 Chrysanthemum Maximum	4.00
300 Chrysanthemum King Edward VII	4.50
500 Chrysanthemum Uliginosum	3.50
400 Lily of the Valley, clumps	10.00
400 Coreopsis Delphinifolia	3.50
330 Coreopsis Lanceolata	3.50
400 Coreopsis Rosea	3.50
300 Coreopsis Verticillata	3.50
300 Daphne Cneorum, 2 year	$8.00
200 Delphinium Chinensis	4.00
200 Delphinium Chinensis Album	4.00
250 Delphinium Formosum	4.00
200 Delphinium Formosum Coelestinum	
300 Dianthus Atrorubens	3.50
300 Dianthus Barbatus, pink, red, white	3.50
300 Dianthus Fragrans	3.50
400 Doronicum Caucasicum	3.50
500 Doronicum Plantagineum	3.50
300 Erigeron Coulteri	4.00
300 Eryngium Amethystinum	3.00
500 Festuca Glauca	3.50
400 Funkia Lancifolia	4.00
100 Gaillardia Grandiflora	4.00
400 Geranium Platypetalum	4.00
400 Geranium Sanguineum	4.00

	Per 100
400 Geum Triflorum	4.00
200 Gypsophila Repens	4.50
300 Helenium Autumnale Rubrum	5.00
300 Helenium Autumnale Hoopesii	4.00
400 Helenium H. S. Moon	3.50
350 Helianthus Maximiliana	3.50
900 Helianthus Miss Mellish	3.50
500 Helianthus Mollis	3.50
100 Helianthus Multiflorus	3.50
400 Helianthus Orgyalis	4.00
600 Helianthus Rigidus	4.00
400 Heliopsis LaeVis	4.00
500 Heliopsis Pitcheriana	3.50
1,200 Hemerocallis Dumortierii	3.50
500 Hemerocallis FulVa	3.50
150 Hemerocallis Kwanso	4.00
300 Hemerocallis Rutilans	4.00
1,000 Hemerocallis Thunbergii	4.50
500 Hesperis Matronalis Alba	3.50
500 Heuchera Brizoides	5.00
200 Hibiscus Moscheutos	4.50
500 Hypericum Adpressum	5.00
3,000 Hypericum Calycinum, small clumps	8.00
700 Iris Germanica, gold and purple	3.00
100 Iris Germanica, light blue, velvet white	4.00
660 Iris Germanica, yellow standards, bronze drops	4.00
400 Iris Germanica, yellow standards, purple drops	3.50
300 Iris Germanica Charlotte Patty	3.50
300 Iris Germanica Fairy Queen	4.00
700 Iris Germanica Garrick	3.50
300 Iris Germanica Madame Chereau	4.00
100 Iris Pallida Speciosa	12.00
800 Iris LaeVigata	5.00
900 Iris Gold Bound	5.00
400 Iris Pseudacorus	3.50
1,000 Iris Pumila Aurea	4.50
1,400 Iris Sibericus	3.50
500 Iris Siberica Alba	3.50
300 Iris Siberica Snow Queen	5.00
200 Iris Orientalis	5.00
570 Jasione Perenne	4.00
250 Lamium Maculatum Album	4.00
250 Liatris Scariosa	4.00
200 Liatris Spicata	4.50
200 Lotus Corniculata	4.50
100 Lychnis Haageana	5.50
400 Lysimachia Nummularia	3.50
900 Malva Moschata	3.50
400 Monarda Fistulosa Alba	3.50
1,100 Nepeta Mussini	4.00
400 Oenothera Fruticosa	4.50
400 Oenothera Fruticosa var. Youngii	4.50
300 Oenothera Glauca, var. Fraseri	4.50
450 Ornithogalum Umbellatum	4.50
10,000 Pachysandra Terminalis, 2½ in. pots	6.00
900 Pachysandra Terminalis, field-grown	7.00

	Per 100
1,000 Pentstemon Barbatus Torreyi	4.00
400 Pentstemon Confertus	4.00
400 Pentstemon Pubescens	4.00
500 Phalaris Arundinacea, Variegated	4.00
10,000 Phlox Paniculata in the following Varieties	4.00

(except where noted)

Albion, Antonin Mercie, Bouquet Fleuri, Colquelicot, Cyclone, Czarina, $3.50, Embrasement, Eugene Danzanvilliers, F. G. Von Lassburg, General Van Heutz, Hermione, Independence, $3.50, James Galloway, Jean D'Arc, Madame Pape Carpentier, Mrs. Cook, $3.50, Mrs. Arnold Turner, Ornament, Prof. Schlieman, Rijnstroom, Richard Wallace.

	Per 100
300 Phlox Reptans	4.00
400 Phlox Subulata Alba	4.00
200 Phlox Subulata, lilac	4.00
3,000 Phlox Subulata, pink	4.00
100 Phlox Suffruticosa Belle Pyramid	4.50
250 Phlox Suffruticosa Indian Chief	4.00
400 Phlox Suffruticosa Miss Lingard	4.00
500 Physostegia Virginica	3.50
800 Platycodon Grandiflorum	3.50
400 Potemonium Reptans	4.00
500 Polygonum Compactum	4.50
500 Potentilla Hybrida	5.00
900 Primula Polyanthus	6.00
400 Ranunculus Incana fl. pl.	3.50
400 Rudbeckia Hirta	4.00
400 Rudbeckia Golden Glow	3.00
500 Rudbeckia Subtomentosa	3.50
300 Ruellia Ciliosa	3.50
500 Sedum Acre	4.00
350 Sedum Braunii	4.00
800 Sedum Lydium Roseum	4.50
400 Sedum Sexangulare	3.50
200 Sedum Sieboldiana	4.00
400 Sedum Spectabilis	4.00
250 Sedum Variegated	4.00
900 Sedum Spurium Coccineum	3.50
600 Sedum Tevillum	3.00
400 Sempervivum Arachnoides	3.5
1,000 SemperViVum Globiferum	3.5
5,000 SemperViVum Tectorum	3.50
300 Silphium Perfoliatum	4.50
400 Senecio Clivorum	4.00
400 Solidago Tenuifolia	4.00
300 Spiraea Aruncus	4.00
1,000 Spiraea Filipendula	4.50
300 Stokesia Cyanea	5.
300 Stokesia Cyanea, white	5.
200 Thermopsis Caroliniana	5.00
400 Tradescantia Virginica	3.50
300 Trollius Europaeus	4.00
250 Tunica Saxifraga	4.50
500 Veronica Alpestris	4.00
500 Veronica Circaeoides	4.00
500 Veronica Gentianoides	4.00
300 Veronica Rupestris	4.00
400 Veronica Spicata Maxima	4.00
300 Vernonia Noveboracensis	4.00

LIST OF ADVERTISERS

NOTES ON CULTURE OF FLORISTS' STOCK
CONDUCTED BY

John J. M. Farrell

Questions by our readers in line with any of the topics presented on this page will be cordially received and promptly answered by Mr. Farrell. Such communications should invariably be addressed to the office of HORTICULTURE.
"If vain our toil, we ought to blame the culture, not the soil."—Pope.

Chrysanthemums

Keep everything clean. A little lime spread below the benches, especially in damp or cold houses, is of the greatest benefit at the time the flowers begin to open. This and plenty of ventilation prevents the petals from damping off. A moist atmosphere is not beneficial to the expanding flowers and to prevent this and yet supply sufficient moisture to keep the plants in good condition should be the object. Watering the benches should be attended to in the forenoon so as to give the foliage a chance to dry off properly before the close of the day. And always start the disbudding on top of the plant. If through carelessness or by accident you should break off the top of the plant there is a chance of getting a side shoot or bud to take the place of the one which was to be selected.

Christmas Cyclamen

In order to have well flowered plants for Christmas they should be well supplied with buds that can be readily seen by the 10th of October. Place all those wanted for the holidays on a light bench well up to the glass. Do not keep the atmosphere too moist as they will come along better with bud when the air is dryer. Give a night temperature of from 50 to 55 degrees with a rise of from 10 to 15 degrees with sunshine, but during dark weather about 5 degrees of a rise will be enough. Keep giving the pots more room from time to time so they will get the air and sun to each plant. Don't crowd them. Spray in the morning but not in the late afternoon as the foliage should be dry by night.

Carnations

No crop under glass is more impatient of neglect than this queen of flowers and any grower who fails to put his soul energy and skill into the subject had better be out of it. He must become an ardent and careful observer, noting every failure and trying to trace its cause. The act of searching for a cause will be the means of obtaining additional knowledge regarding the wants and character of each variety and also lead to a systematic study of the diseases to which they are liable and the most effectual method of combating such. A thorough knowledge of the theory of ventilation is also necessary to the carnation grower and the reduction to an exact science should be practiced as there is great danger to even the finest crops if indiscriminate ventilation is resorted to.

Christmas Lilies

The earliest Bermuda lilies should now be removed from the cold frame to a warm house. Some of them will have formed sufficient roots by this time. No actual forcing is necessary. If given an average temperature of 60 degrees they should be in plenty of time for Christmas. Water carefully so as not to sour the compost. Let them show signs of dryness first and then give enough water to soak the whole ball through. Frequent and slight waterings are dangerous. Syringe regularly. The grower can employ any degree from 55 to 75 degrees at night as he may see fit in order to get his lilies in at the right moment. Fumigating frequently, say about once a week, will keep the plants free of the pest. When the plants are from 15 to 20 inches high they ought to be staked and kept neatly but not tightly tied.

Planting Trees and Shrubs

At this season the nurseries are not overcrowded with orders and the stock will be freshly dug and not taken from storage sheds where it has been packed in sand for several months. The ground is usually more moist at this season than in spring and there is more time to do planting properly. Nearly all deciduous trees and shrubs can be just as well or better planted in fall than in spring. The roots, also, are far less likely to get dried up now than in spring. People are so much in the habit, however, of leaving all planting until spring that they rarely think of doing any now. Possible exceptions to the success of fall planting might be due to too dry a condition of the soil at planting time and the freezing up of the ground while the roots were inadequately supplied with moisture. Artificial watering would be necessary in such cases. Such shrubs as spiraeas, philadelphus, syringas, most of the viburnums, etc., do much better if planted in the fall.

Wasted Bench Space

Keep the greenhouse benches from end to end constantly in use. Wasted bench space is the direct cause of thousands of dollars loss annually in the florists' business. The grower who produces the largest amount in cut flowers and plants per annum in a given space is the best grower.

Next Week:—Care of Mignonette; Double Tulips for Easter; Ericas; Lilium Longiflorum; Phlox; Temperature.

HORTICULTURE

VOL. XXII   **OCTOBER 2, 1915**   **NO. 14**

PUBLISHED WEEKLY BY

HORTICULTURE PUBLISHING CO.
147 Summer Street, Boston, Mass.

Telephone, Oxford 292.

WM. J. STEWART, Editor and Manager.

SUBSCRIPTION RATES:

One Year, in advance, $1.00; To Foreign Countries, $2.00; To Canada, $1.50.

ADVERTISING RATES:

Per inch, 30 inches to page..................... $1.00
Discounts on Contracts for consecutive insertions, as follows:
One month (4 times), 5 per cent.; three months (12 times), 10 per cent.; six months (26 times), 20 per cent.; one year (52 times), 30 per cent.

Page and half page space, special rates on application.

Entered as second-class matter December 8, 1904, at the Post Office at Boston, Mass., under the Act of Congress of March 3, 1879.

CONTENTS

Revolutionizing show methods The extensive preparations being made for the big joint exhibition in Cleveland next month and the really stupendous operations in connection with the National Flower Show at Philadelphia next spring cannot fail to impress the observer with the fact that the public exhibiting of flowers and other horticultural products has taken a tremendous jump far and away beyond former methods and scope as an institution. Indeed, modern promotion methods have practically remodelled and revolutionized the whole business of creating and managing a metropolitan horticultural exhibition. The splendid enthusiasm developed among the best people of the city of Cleveland, the harmony with which the commercial and amateur elements are working together and the able manner in which plans have been perfected command admiration and furnish a most hopeful augury for a successful outcome.

The Dahlia Show The American Dahlia Society made quite a spectacular start in New York last week, as recorded in our news columns. The Dahlia is as well entitled to a special society as most of the flowers so honored and evidently needs the attention of the nomenclature surgeon even more than some of them and we hope that this new "drive," so auspiciously launched in the interest of the popular garden flower may meet with a full measure of success. President Vincent's recommendation of a series of consecutive shows in different cities in the same year certainly has the merit of ambitious originality and while it surely would entail a lot of executive work to carry it out yet it is well worth considering. It should not take long under such high pressure tactics to place the Dahlia Society numerically at the head of all special floral organizations in this country. Good team work is the main requirement now and this seems to be well assured.

The Dahlia One of the New York daily newspapers, in commenting on the Dahlia Show at the Museum of National History last week, made a deprecatory criticism on the name which the flower bears and expressed regret that some more pleasing name could not have been given to it than that of Dahlia. To our mind there are plenty of plants that have to go through life with much homelier and less appropriate generic names than the Dahlia. The name was given in honor of Andrew Dahl, a Swedist botonist and pupil of Linnæus, we are told, but it may not be generally known that this genus was first known among continental botanists as Georgina, a name which possibly might better suit the taste of the New York critic. In fact, the flowers were shown as Georginas at some of the earlier exhibitions of the Massachusetts Horticultural Society. We might mention here, also, that the Massachusetts Horticultural Society gave its first "Grand Dahlia Show" on September 23-26, 1840, on which occasion it is recorded that over 3,000 blooms were staged. So great was the interest manifested on that occasion that another prize show was given on October 10th of the same year, the premium list being financed from the entry receipts and it recorded that there were ten entries in each class.

"Handicaps" Our Chicago representative writes that the section at Marshall Field's big department store, formerly devoted to fresh flowers, is now filled up entirely with artificial flowers and that all the accessories which are usually found in a florist shop may be obtained at this store as well as at several others of similar character. The question arises as to what extent, if any, and in what manner this will affect the florist trade. Some retail store florists will rejoice, no doubt, at any sign of the abandonment by the department stores of the fresh flower field. Growers of flowers for market, however, will not be so keen in their approval. The sale of artificial flowers and, more especially, of artificial foliage plants, un-

ROSE GROWING UNDER GLASS

CONDUCTED BY

Arthur C. Ruzicka

Questions by our readers in line with any of the topics presented on this page will be cordially received and promptly answered by Mr. Ruzicka. Such communications should invariably be addressed to the office of HORTICULTURE.

The Night Temperature

As the days and nights grow colder it will be necessary to lower the heat in the houses at night, until it is down to the regular night temperature. Up to recently the houses were better off with the thermometers up to 64 or 65 at night but now it will be better to drop it down to 62, especially for the varieties of roses that are to be grown a little cooler than the rest. Keep air on all night, even if this does mean a little more coal burned. The plants will be much better off for it and will make it up before the season is over. An inch of air is about the least that the houses should have until frost comes, and then it will be safe to put them down to a crack unless it freezes quite hard, and then only should the vents be closed altogether.

Keeping Even Temperature

If the house was never tested for evenness of temperature and the roses do not seem to grow evenly, apply this test at once. Place several thermometers at different points, first making sure that these will all register the same, and then see just how the house does run. It may be necessary to cover pipes here and there, or else uncover some on the extreme end, but it will pay to see that the whole house runs as nearly even as it is possible to get it. It is not the fault of the greenhouse as a rule but of the conditions surrounding it. These differ as much as one place does from another and therefore each grower has to study his own situation before applying any remedy. If the houses suffer from heavy winds on the north, a wind-break of some quick-growing evergreen trees will prove very effective and will help save a little coal in the winter, and at the same time make the first house on the north run more evenly. This windbreak should not be planted too close to the houses as it will make them run much hotter in the summer. Avoid much trees on the east and west, as these will throw shade and that is not wanted, for the sooner the sun hits the plants in the morning and the longer at night the better for them.

Tying

Keep right after this and try to get over the plants weekly and tie them up. It is better to do this oftener as it will not take very long, but if the work is let go for a while it will be quite a proposition to tie the plants properly, especially if they are growing real good. Avoid tying the shoots too tight to the stake. There is no benefit in it and the chances are they will lose a good many leaves if they are bunched too much. In tying Beauties make sure that the shoots are on the same side

of the wires on the bottom as well as on top. Should they be tied on one side on the bottom and on the other side on top trouble will be experienced should it be necessary to bend down the tall breaks later. Take care to distribute the wood well, so that the plants get as much light and sun as possible. Needless to say, when tying to the wires the string should always be wrapped around the wire once before tying the knot, otherwise the shoots will slide from place to place when syringing, and will likely come to harm.

Picking Dead Leaves

There should not be very many of these as yet, but here and there there will be some. As soon as they are knocked off they should be picked up as time will permit. It is best to keep the benches clean until the season is half over at least, although the plants will do better if they receive good care right up to replanting time. This applies to plants that will be run another year especially as they will do much better the second year if they are properly cared for all through the first season. It will not take very long to pick up all these dead leaves, also watching for spot, and picking off any diseased leaves that may be found.

The Sod Heaps

Although there are a good many places where the sod heaps are not put up until spring it is much better to have them up in the fall. The spring generally brings a great deal of work and then too the sod is generally soaked and much heavier to handle. Just now, the sod is fairly dry and easily handled and if it lays over the winter composted with good manure it will be in fine condition for using next spring. Do not allow the men to use shovels to load the sod. It is better for the roses and better for the field to plow it up and then pick up what can be taken with the fork. The sod should not be plowed deeply, three or four inches being plenty. If done deeper it will take years to establish another turf over the field, and this takes time and costs money. It is best to use about half sod and half manure, as the latter will decay rapidly and by spring will be just about right. Avoid piling the sod in layers too thick. It is best to use about six inches of each, with about a foot of soil for the bottom layer. This method will insure the leachings from the manure going through all the sod and it will be far better for the roses than if the sod is piled in layers a foot and a half to two feet thick. If this is done only some of the sod will have a chance to absorb liquids, and the result will be that the soil resulting will be very uneven in fertility, which will cause trouble with the plants later.

---

questionably cuts into the fresh flower and plant business. But there is no industry known which has not competition of some sort to struggle against. Every one will not agree with us, we know, but it is our belief that the undertaker, for instance, is fully as heavy a handicap on the flower business as the artificial material dealer can possibly be. We have always felt that it was very unfortunate for the future welfare of the flower trade in its younger days that so many of the florists established themselves adjacent to a cemetery gate and adopted as their almost universal style of sign-board—"Wreaths, Crosses, Anchors, Bouquets."

AMERICAN DAHLIA SOCIETY

The first annual meeting of this young society was held according to schedule in the Museum of Natural History, New York City, on September 24 at 8 P. M. There was a good attendance. President R. Vincent, Jr., made a few introductory remarks explaining the purpose of the organization and read a paper on pertinent matters concerning its future activities. In refering to the several cities which had extended invitations for the Society to hold its exhibition with them next year, he advanced the proposition that the show be held in Rochester next year, another show in Philadelphia the following week and a third in New York the week after that. He believed that this would give great publicity to the Dahlia and would not be impossible of accomplishment.

Secretary Joseph J. Lane presented an informal report, showing a rapid growth in membership which, later on, he supplemented by the announcement that the list had now passed the two hundred mark. He reported good results from the sending out of double postal cards soliciting new members and said that 75 per cent. of the members consisted of amateurs.

Treasurer F. R. Austin also reported informally, showing a healthy balance in his hands. Quite a discussion followed on the question of issuing a regular bulletin and it was announced that No. 1 of Vol. 1 would be sent out this week, the edition to consist of 5000 copies, of which President Vincent and Mr. Stillman agreed to distribute one thousand each.

Election of officers resulted as follows:

President, R. Vincent, Jr.; secretary, J. J. Lane, of the Garden Magazine; treasurer; F. R. Austin; vice-presidents, W. W. Wilmore, Prof. Norton, Geo. L. Stillman, E. S. Brown; executive committee, Geo. W. Kerr, Jos. Duthie, I. S. Hendrickson, P. W. Popp, J. Harrison Dick.

Prof. F. H. Hall reported for the nomenclature committee that he had made an examination of dahlia catalogues and had listed in alphabetical order over 4500 names, all grown in America with few exceptions. Some were listed under four or five names and the situation appeared to be a bad one. On his suggestion a classification committee was elected as follows:

R. VINCENT, JR.,
President American Dahlia Society.

Prof. F. H. Hall, George Fraser, James Kirby, L. K. Peacock, Leonard Barron. The selection of location for the exhibition of 1916 was by vote left to the executive committee. There will be a meeting of the executive committee in New York at the time of the Chrysanthemum Show. A telegram of congratulation and good wishes was received from Mrs. Francis King.

Secretary Lane expects to cover the entire list of dahlia growers, amateur and commercial, in the distribution of the bulletin. The time limit for the admission of charter members has been extended to October 15.

THE EXHIBITION.

The exhibition at the Museum of Natural History was a genuine surprise in its extent and the public attendance, as well as the quality and interest of the exhibits which had suffered a severe handicap in the weather of the week preceding the show. The big foyer of the Museum building was devoted to the special exhibits by retail florists, of large vases, baskets, placques, etc., and presented a brilliant picture, the various possible uses of the dahlia in decorative work being well demonstrated. W. A. Manda was one of the largest exhibitors, filling practically the entire space of one of the long corridors. President Vincent, of course, was a very large exhibitor as was also Geo. H. Stillman. W. Atlee Burpee's big display arranged for effect was one of the features of the exhibition.

Seedlings that attracted attention were Mrs. H. R. Allen, a deep pink, closely resembling Antoine Rivoire, and Gold Fish, an orange and salmon decorative, by H. R. Allen, and Sunshine by C. H. Stout, a beautiful cream and salmon combination. W. A. Finger's collection was also very fine.

The judges were J. C. Clark of Dreer's, Phila.; Leonard Barron, Editor Garden Magazine; Prof. F. H. Hall, Geneva; G. W. Kerr, of Burpee's, Phila.; J. Harrison Dick, New York; Prof. J. B. Norton, Md. State Agricultural College; James Duthie, Oyster Bay; Prof. Geo. Fraser, Connecticut Agricultural College.

The attendance was 8,000 each day, Friday and Saturday, and 13,000 on Sunday.

THE AWARDS.

Commercial Classes.

100 varieties, one each, short stems: 1st, Geo. H. Walker, North Dighton, Mass.; 2nd, Geo. L. Stillman, Westerly, R. I.; 3rd, N. Harold Cottam & Son, Wappingers Falls, N. Y.; special to L. K. Peacock, Berlin, N. J.

50 varieties, do.: 1st, 2nd and 3rd, as above; special to W. A. Finger, Jr., Hicksville, N. Y.

In the classes for eight vases, 3 flowers each, the winners were W. A. Finger, W. A. Manda, South Orange, N. J., and C. Louis Alling.

Best collection of peony flowered varieties, Geo. L. Stillman.

The finest and most meritorious display of Dahlias—any, or all classes; grasses or other foliage allowed, quality and arrangement to count: Gold medal to W. Atlee Burpee, Philadelphia, Pa.; silver medal to R. Vincent, Jr. & Sons Co., White Marsh, Md.; bronze medal to W. A. Manda.

Dinner table decoration of dahlias: 1st, A. Kotmiller, 426 Madison Ave., New York; 2nd, Max Schling, 22 W. 59th St., New York; 3rd, Geo. E. M. Stumpp, 761 Fifth Ave., New York; highly commended, O. P. Chapman, Westerly, R. I.

Decorative design in dahlias: 1st, Geo. E. M. Stumpp, arrangement on placque, framed; 2nd, Max Schling, do.

Vase of dahlias arranged for effect: 1st, Max Schling; 2nd, G. E. M. Stumpp.

Basket of dahlias: 1st, A. Kotmiller; 2nd, Max Schling; 3rd, Young & Nugent,

Museum of Natural History, New York City, Where Meeting and Exhibition was Held.

42 W. 28th St., New York; 4th, G. E. M. Stumpp.

Bridal bouquet: 1st, Max Schling; 2nd, G. E. M. Stumpp.

Non-Commercial.

50 Varieties, 1 each, short stems: 1st, E. M. Townsend, gard. Jas. Duthie, Oyster Bay, N. Y.; 2nd, Wm. J. Matheson, gard. Jas. Kirby, Huntington, N. Y.; 3rd, Arthur Daly, 358 Fifth Ave., N. Y.

25 Varieties, do.: Arthur Daly, E. N. Townsend, Miss Eleanor F. Fullerton, Medford, N. Y., respectively. 12 Varieties, do.: E. N. Townsend, Arthur Daly, W. J. Matheson, respectively; special to Mrs. H. Darlington, gard. P. W. Popp, Mamaroneck, N. Y. Winners in other classes in this section were: Mrs. H. Darlington; Wm. Shillaber, gard. J. P. Sorenson, Essex Falls, N. J.; Miss Elizabeth Morehouse, Fairfield, Conn.; Mrs. C. H. Stout, Short Hills, N. J.; and John F. Anderson, Bernardsville, N. J.

In the six color classes, 1st prizes were won by W. A. Finger, R. Vincent, Jr. & Sons Co., Peacock Dahlia Farms. C. Lewis Alling and W. A. Manda, the last named being in the class for "any other color," with the new variety Mrs. Dupont. The "largest decorative bloom" prize was also won by Mr. Manda with the new variety, Albert Manda. Largest cactus bloom, W. A. Finger; largest peony bloom, Mrs. Darlington.

The pompon classes were won by C. L. Alling, N. H. Cottam and Wm. Shillaber.

Specials were awarded to W. A. Manda, Wm. Shillaber and Miss Morehouse in dahlia classes, Wm. Shillaber for display of annuals, Mrs. E. T. Burrows, Plainfield, N. J., for basket of dahlias, Bobbink & Atkins, Rutherford, N. J., for meritorious display, Prof. Hull, Geneva, and Geo. H. Stillman for special collections. The Garden Magazine Achievement Medal was awarded to Mrs. C. H. Stout for exhibit of seedling dahlia Sunshine.

DAHLIA SHOW AT SAN FRANCISCO.

One of the most successful flower shows ever arranged here was the Dahlia Show held September 18 and 19 under the auspices of the California State Floral Society and the Alameda County Floral Society in conjunction with the Department of Horticulture of the Panama-Pacific Exposition. Exposition visitors swarmed the building during the show, and much interest was shown in the awarding of the prizes, all of which, whether medals or cash, were given by the P. P. I. E. About 25 awards were made in the class open to growers. For the best collection of dahlias, the Lovers' Point Dahlia Garden received gold medal; Bessie Boston Dahlia Farm, silver medal; Miss Ruth Gleadell, bronze medal. For the best collection in at least four classes, the Bessie Boston Dahlia Farm took 1st and C. S. Quick 2nd. For best 24 cactus dahlias, the 1st went to the Bessie Boston Dahlia Farm and 2nd to Miss Ruth Gleadell. Frank Pelicano took 1st for 24 decorative and the Bessie Boston Dahlia Farm 2nd. Frank Pelicano was awarded 1st for vase of 50, with Delice and Burns & Co.. took 2nd with Geisha. For seedling dahlia never before exhibited in competition. Arthur Carter took silver medal; L. J. Fenton, bronze medal, and J. W. Gleadell, honorary mention. Frank Pelicano received bronze medal for the best this year's seedling, and L. J. Fenton honorary mention. Special awards of silver medals were given to J. W. Gleadell, L. J. Fenton, Bessie Boston Dahlia Farm and C. S. Quick for collections of seedlings. For an especially fine showing of 1,000 varieties, T. A. Burns was awarded a special medal of honor.

CLEVELAND FLOWER SHOW

The final premium list of the Cleveland Flower Show to be held at the Coliseum, Cleveland, Ohio, November 10 to 14, 1905, Wednesday to Sunday, inclusive, has been completed. This list includes the special prizes for the annual exhibition of the Chrysanthemum Society of America, for the fall exhibition of the American Rose Society, and for a special exhibition of carnations, all to be held under the joint direction and supervision of the Ohio Horticultural Society, Cleveland Florists' Club and Garden Club of Cleveland.

In connection with this great event will be held the annual exhibition and convention of the Chrysanthemum Society of America; fall exhibition and meeting of the American Rose Society; meeting of executive committee of the American Carnation Society; adjourned meeting of the Florists' Telegraph Delivery Association; adjourned meeting of the Gladiolus Society of Ohio.

The Chrysanthemum Society list of special prizes comprises 80 classes, the premiums offered being very liberal and including cups, medals and cash contributed by Hitchings & Co., H. A. Dreer, E. G. Hill Co., Wells and Totty, H. E. Converse, Lord & Burnham Co., Wm. Kleinheinz, Julius Roehrs Co., National Association of Gardeners, Alpine Mfg. Co., A. N. Pierson, Inc., Elmer D. Smith & Co., Michell's Seed House, John C. Moninger Co., Vaughan's Seed Store and a long list of Cleveland patrons of horticulture, also the Society of American Florists' medals for meritorious seedlings. Chrysanthemum prizes will be awarded on Wednesday, November 10.

The rose section, under the auspices of the American Rose Society, includes the premiums as listed from No. 81 to 117A, in which are represented as donors, Benj. Hammond; A. N. Pierson, Inc., Robt. Scott & Son, Lamborn Floral Co., Cleveland Cut Flower Co., W. Atlee Burpee & Co., Storrs & Harrison Co., and a large number of Cleveland firms and individuals, with munificent contributions. The rose awards will be made on Thursday, November 11.

The carnation section comprises classes 118 to 154A and these will be judged on Friday, November 12. The premiums are offered by such gentlemen of national prominence as Jos. H. Hill, president of the American Carnation Society, John D. Rockefeller, etc., and there is a tempting list of certificates of merit to be striven for, under the section of seedlings and sports.

In the general classes, stove and greenhouse plants, violets, cyclamen, antirrhinum, lilies, begonias, orchids, ferns, etc., are well provided for with liberal special premiums, up to a $100 silver cup for group of orchids. These classe are to be staged Wednesday.

An item of much local interest is the Corrigan Cup, valued at $500, to be competed for by private growers of Ohio only. This is class 263, 36 chrysanthemum blooms, 6 varieties, 6 blooms each, to be staged in two vases. Exhi-bitors may furnish their own vases. Any accessories and greens allowed. Arrangement to be considered. This cup is to become the temporary property of the winner for one year, to be returned to the Cleveland Flower Show Committee one month before the date of their next show. Before the cup becomes the permanent property of any private grower, he must win it three times at the Cleveland Flower Show.

One of the important and interesting features will be the non-competitive exhibit of table decorations, bride and bridesmaid bouquets, corsages asd basket arrangements by the leading retail florists of Cleveland and a number from New York, Boston, Philadelphia, Rochester, Buffalo, Pittsburgh, Cincinnati, Indianapolis and other leading cities.

Announcement for 100 Special Prizes.

The star (*) that precedes nearly 100 classes in the premium list signifies that in the classes so marked, $5.00 in gold will be given to the section man or actual grower of the stock taking first prize in that class.

In the non-commercial classes, a medal will be given instead of a cash prize. After the awards are made the exhibitors winning classes with stars (*) attached should register their growers' name or names with the exhibition committee as soon as possible to assist in the prompt distribution of these special prizes.

Prizes of this nature have never been offered in connection with any previous flower show to the knowledge of the committee.

The list of judges is as follows: Chrysanthemums, J. F. Ammann, Edwardsville, Ill.; Michael Bloy, Detroit, Mich.

Roses, Emil Buettner, Park Ridge, Ill.; John H. Dunlop, Toronto, Can.

Carnations, Eugene Dailledouze, Brooklyn, N. Y.; Wm. Nicholson, Framingham, Mass.

Address all correspondence to 356 Leader Bldg., Cleveland.

Address all shipments, care Frank A. Friedley, Cleveland Flower Show, Wigmore Coliseum, Cleveland, Ohio.

Bowling.

The following letter has been sent by C. J. Graham, chairman of the bowling tournament to the secretaries of all the Florists' Clubs in the country.

Dear Sir: During the week of our big Cleveland Flower Show we intend to hold a "Florists' National Bowling Tournament." As the S. A. F. Tournament this year was not well attended by the florists from the eastern and central states, we believe our Tournament will be more than welcomed by the bowlers of the trade.

We extend a cordial invitation to your city to enter one five-man team, as well as singles, in this Tournament. Members of the teams are not eligible to bowl in singles.

Liberal prizes will be offered. Prize list will be mailed within a few days. The high man on each team and the five men in the singles are to bowl off for a special trophy, the nature of which will be announced later.

Please bring this before your members as soon as possible and let us get your views on the subject. Also please call your members' attention to the number of national meetings to be held here.

CHICAGO GRAND FLORAL FESTIVAL.

Recent appointments include committee of ways, means and audit, with Peter Reinberg as chairman. The other members of this committee so far appointed are C. L. Washburn, Phillip Schupp, George Reinberg, N. J. Wietor, F. Hoerber, A. L. Randall, E. C. Amling, Ed. Meuret, J. H. Kidwell and Emil Beuttner. August Poehlmann has been elected treasurer. The committee on lectures has W. J. Keimel for chairman and it is proposed to arrange for an elaborate series covering subjects of public interest with stereoption views, this having been one of the taking features at previous Coliseum shows. A. I. Simmons has been appointed chairman of committee on music. August Koch has been appointed chief of the information bureau. H. B. Kennicott as chairman of the press committee is at work with his assistants preparing material for an elaborate publicity campaign in the local newspapers. Guy W. French, chairman of the Florists' Club special premiums committee reports highly satisfactory results from his first day's canvas.

Arrangements are under way for an elaborate display of vegetables in which various nearby horticultural organizations such as those of Lake Geneva, Lake Forest, Winnetka, etc., will be the contestants.

M. BARKER,
Chairman Pub. Com.

NATIONAL FLOWER SHOW NEWS.

Special Prize lists have been offered by Henry A. Dreer and Henry F. Michell Company for the National Flower Show. This is in addition to the regular prizes offered and there will no doubt be several other additional lists in the near future. W. Atlee Burpee & Co., expect to offer a list on sweet peas, but this is not yet made up.

There was a meeting of the Press and Publicity Committee in Mr. Therkildson's office last Thursday afternoon, the 23rd, and the plan for publicity was agreed upon. This committee is made up of a representative from each of the Philadelphia papers. By this means they expect to get some extraordinary publicity.

Poster stamps were agreed upon to be furnished to the several local firms for use in their correspondence prior to the Flower Show, as well as the design for the premium list cover. It was also decided that a design should be worked up for window cards, posters and programs, this design to be the same so as to get the cumulative value of keeping one design continually before the public.

The special prize list by H. A. Dreer, above referred to comprises 23 classes and amounting to about $250. It provides for hardy perennials, H. T. roses, amaryllis, ferns, hyacinths, tulips, narcissi, cornflower, lupines, nemesia, schizanthus, stocks and pansies. These are open to private growers only. Michell's list is also open only to private gardeners. It comprises no less than 46 gold, silver and bronze medals and cups, for various flowering plants, bulbs, sweet peas and other cut flowers, miniature lawns and gardens, etc., also cash prizes amounting to nearly $400

for bulbous exhibits, plant groups. mushrooms, etc., and liberal prizes for an arrangement of bulbous flowers to represent the American Flag in a frame 4 by 6 feet.

"BRINGING UP FATHER."

"The Commodore," (Mr. John Westcott of Philadelphia), is seventy-four, your scribe fifty-four years of age, so the thing looked easy three months ago, and was cheerfully tackled. But as the days roll by, this job of bringing up father begins to take on a different aspect.

To our mild admonitions the kid is pert. When we become a little stern, it becomes even impudent. When we really put our foot down, it offers to take its coat and lick us.

For instance: Today we had made up our mind to take in the Dreer Dahlia Show at Riverton. So we invited the child to Dooner's for lunch at noon, thinking that we could educate him a little in what was going on in the world. Instead of being modest as every young gentleman should be on the bill of fare, he ordered right and left and tucked his napkin under his chin with a wolfish grin and the most utter abandon. You can imagine how a thrifty person like ourselves would feel under such circumstances. But we could not say anything, on account of the waiter.

Well, we finally got to the ferry and there met ambassadors from the Dreer establishment—James Karins and John Ruppert. We greeted them with dignity and all would have been well but the kid had to run off on some side issue—some friend at the ticket office who had handed him candy about twenty years ago. Nearly lost train.

The youngster behaved pretty well until we got to Riverview. We got to the exhibition hall and threaded our way through—then out and in again, among immense crowds—and of course he had to get lost.

We finally came up to him hob-nobbing with Patrick O'Mara, young Peter Henderson and Jacob Eisele. We thought we were all right then, but as there were some myriads of automobiles and other conveyances coming and going, he got lost again, and it was only through the generalship of J. Otto Thilow and Emil Michel, (the latter the big chief of the show) that we finally caught up with the stray sheep and started in an automobile for Riverton.

After a visit to Mr. Ruppert's home at Riverton, all seemed well. But, across the street were the Dreer nurseries again, and we had to take a look through. The first thing here—well, that kid had to go crazy over James Davidson whom he seems to have known in a previous incarnation in Brooklyn N. Y. We had to drag sonny away by main force.

Then, having only twenty minutes left, we started for the new operations bulb warehouse, a new garage, and several other new things. But on the way who should pop up but James Taplin. Whew! such a gladness! such a handshaking and the minutes flying. However we finally caught the train and got back to Philadelphia safe and sound for which we are truly thankful.

One of the worst features of this case of bringing up father is that the kid insists on having the last word, will never admit he is wrong, and absolutely refuses to apologize.

We have a sheaf of notes about the best dahlias at this Dreer show, but that will have to wait. Sorry!

G. C. W.

Horticulture Publishing Co.,
Boston, Mass.

Gentlemen: It may interest you to know that I never really appreciated the value of Horticulture until last week's number failed to show up. Believe me I made quite a few extra trips to the P. O. without results. I was just in the act of mailing you a letter when I received your notice that another dollar is due, or, to be right, past due, which I did not know. Enclosed please find a dollar and please see that I get last week's issue.

Wishing you unlimited success I remain　　　　　C. B., Penna.

	Per doz.	Per 100			
Andre Lauries. Deep Tyrian rose	$1.50	$10.00	**L'Esclatante.** Brilliant red mid-season	2.00	15.00
Augustin D'Hour. Brilliant dark red	1.00	20.00	**L'Indispensable.** Delicate lilac pink	2.00	15.00
Arthemise. Violet rose with Solferino-rose shadings	2.00	15.00	**Lady Bramwell.** Fine silvery rose	2.00	15.00
Charlemagne. Lilac-white with blush centre	1.75	12.00	**Mme. Calot.** Delicate Hydrangea-pink	2.50	20.00
Canary. White with amber centre	1.75	12.00	**Mme. de Verneville.** White, touched carmine	2.00	15.00
Delachei. Deep crimson purple	2.00	15.00	**Mme. Bucel.** Bright silvery pink	2.50	25.00
Duke of Wellington. Fine sulphur-white	1.75	12.00	**Marie Jacquin.** White with yellow stamens	2.00	15.00
Duchesse de Nemours. Superb pure white	1.75	12.00	**Mme. Boulanger.** Handsome soft lilac-tinted white	5.00	40.00
Dr. Gallot. Brilliant late Tyrian rose	5.00	20.00	**Meissonier.** Rich purplish crimson	2.00	15.00
Duc de Cazes. Lively bright pink with light centre	1.75	12.00	**Mons. Jules Elie.** Very large lilac-rose with silvery reflex	6.00	45.00
Edouard Andre. Dark reddish-crimson	1.75	12.00	**Ne-Plus-Ultra.** Early pure purple	1.25	10.00
Edulis Superba. Brilliant pink, fragrant, early	2.50	18.00	**Princess Galatin.** Pale flesh color	2.00	15.00
Felix Crousse. The ideal self colored red	3.50	25.00	**Queen Victoria.** Popular rose-white	1.50	10.00
Francois Ortegat. Brilliant dark crimson	2.00	15.00	**Rosea Elegans.** Lilac-rose with cream centre	2.00	15.00
Festiva Maxima. The standard early white	2.50	20.00	**Virginie Modeste.** Lovely Hydrangea, salmon		
Louis van Houtte. Fine dark rose, medium	1.75	12.00	white centre	1.50	10.00

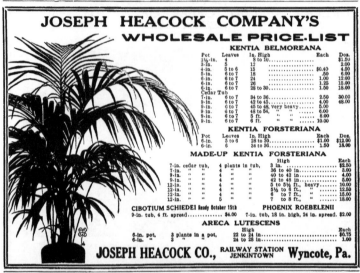

BRITISH HORTICULTURE.
Practical Sympathy.

The Royal Horticultural Society Council has decided to send to Serbia seeds to the value of £500 (pounds) which have been supplied by Hurst & Son, of London. The consignment has been shipped to the Co-operative Union in Serbia for distribution. It is largely owing to the secretary of the society (Rev. W. Wilks), to Mr. Arthur Sutton and other members of the subcommittee appointed to deal with the immediate needs of Serbia that the task of discovering exactly what these needs were and of contributing toward their satisfaction has been discharged so promptly.

Extension at Kew.

A new laboratory of plant pathology has been opened at the Royal Botanic Gardens, Kew, and will form a valuable addition to that institution. Mr. A. D. Cotton, assistant in the berberium, has been promoted to a first-class assistantship in the new laboratory, and W. B. Brierley, of Manchester University, has been appointed a first-class assistant.

The War and the Nursery Trade.

With a view to inducing the public to act upon the motto of "business as usual" as regards their gardens, the secretary to the Royal Horticultural Society has addressed another letter to the press, following one published on the same subject a few months ago. It is pointed out that the nursery and seed trade is very seriously depressed. The entire cessation of gardening will not only cause financial loss, but an irretrievable sacrifice of many years' labor spent in introducing new and improved varieties of fruits, vegetables and flowers. "They (the trade), rightly feel," the letter states, "that as they have catered for our highest happiness in times past, it is hardly right that they should now be brought to a position in which they can no longer even retain their employees' services. Most of their younger men have enlisted, and they ask not for the usual trade, but for just sufficient support to keep them going, and to meet current expenses, which cannot be suspended. The president and council feel that in drawing the attention of fellows to this trade aspect of the question they are but again advising that medium policy which in the long run is always the wisest, and fellows are urged not to forget this when framing their economies."

Dahlia Novelties.

A batch of dahlias has lately received awards of merit from the Floral Committee of the Royal Horticultural Society, acting conjointly with the National Dahlia Society. Stredwick & Sons, have added Herald, a variable collarette, deep pink with white collar. Miss Judd, cactus, lemon yellow, and Washington, cactus, with incurved florets of deep crimson. The name of Warneford, has been given to a pure white decorative flower, exhibited by J. West. Cheal & Sons, obtained awards for Primrose Queen, light yellow petals, and straw tinted collar, and for Yellow Star. Other varieties gaining awards were Caprice, from A. Turner—a decorative single, with white petals, tinted with maroon, and Scarlet Queen, from Dobbie & Co., a brilliant collarette.
W. H. Adsett.

MASS. AGRICULTURAL COLLEGE NOTES.

The Florists' and Gardeners' Club of M. A. C. held its first meeting of the year last Thursday. At that time the following officers were elected: C. E. Wildon, Melrose, president; H. H. Walkden, Westford, vice-president; Miss E. H. Chase, Holden, secretary-treasurer. The members of the program committee are H. H. Walkden, Westford; E. J. Cardarelli, Boston; W. P. Lyford, Natick.

A. S. Thurston has been spending a few days in the Arnold Arboretum during the past week in checking up a key to vines for Prof. R. W. Curtis of the Landscape Art Dept. at Cornell.

A perennial collection of 300 varieties and species has been begun at the college and will be added to extensively in the future. This perennial collection is a new feature inaugurated by Prof. A. H. Nehrling and bids fair to become one of the most attractive features in the Floriculture Dept. It will give an excellent opportunity for the study of perennials to which so much attention is being directed of late. Each species and variety is labeled with an aluminum label. The lettering was done by means of acid. Much of this lettering was done by W. H. Hatfield. '15. Brookline.

Merchantville, N. J.—J. A. Smith served as judge at the Annual Fall Show of the Merchantville Horticultural Society, on Friday, October 1, 1915. The Henry F. Michell Co. had a very fine exhibit of perennials from their nurseries, at Andalusia, Pa.

SEED TRADE

AMERICAN SEED TRADE ASSOCIATION

Officers—President, J. M. Lupton,
Mattituck, L. I., N. Y.; First Vice-President, Kirby B. White, Detroit, Mich.;
Second Vice-President, F. W. Bolgiano,
Washington, D. C.; Secretary-Treasurer,
C. E. Kendel, Cleveland, O.; Assistant
Secretary, S. F. Willard, Jr., Cleveland,
O. Cincinnati, O., next meeting place.

Shipments of Belgian Goods.

Horticulture Publishing Co.

I am in receipt of the following from
The Merchants' Association of New
York:

"I have to inform you that the Department has received from the American Ambassador at London the following telegram, supplementing that dated
September 8:

"'I have today received the following note from Sir Edward Grey, dated
September 16:

"'With reference to my note of the
7th ultimo, regarding the conditions on
which His Majesty's Government are
prepared to issue permits for the exports of goods of Belgian origin to
neutral countries, I have the honor to
inform Your Excellency that an agreement has now been reached with the
Belgian Government by which the deposit of documents covering the sale
and shipment of such goods with a
bank in the United Kingdom will be
accepted in lieu of the deposit of the
purchase money itself, in cases where
the latter condition is not practicable.'"

I am also in receipt of the following:
"The Department of State has sent
word to the Merchants' Association
that formal notification has come to
the Department from the British government to the effect that applications
for the release of goods of German or
Austrian origin, contracted for by the
American importer prior to March 1st,
last, would henceforth be received at
the British Embassy at Washington
when filed by the Foreign Trade Advisers of the Department of State.
That Department is now, therefore,
filing applications with the British Embassy for the release of such shipments. The assumption of liability to
pay for the goods before March 1st by
the American importer is now the
basis on which such permits are issued
by the British government. Hereafter,
all applications for the release of these
goods are to be filed at the British Embassy in Washington and not in London.

"Applications should be addressed to

Hon. W. B. Fleming, Foreign Trade
Adviser, Department of State, Washington, D. C., who will transmit them
to the British Embassy."

CHAS. A. DARDS.

The HORTICULTURE Publishing Co.

With regard to Fall shipments of
Azaleas and other plants from Belgium, we have been in constant cable
communication with our connections
in Belgium, Holland and London, but
the arrangements have been made and
upset so often that we feared to make
any definite statement. Now we can
say definitely that Fall shipments will
come. We review briefly the changes
as follows:

1. From June to August the shipments were included with the British
"Order in Council" goods and shipments were embargoed by the British
authorities and could not leave.

2. During August, all arrangements
were made with the British authorities, the embargo was lifted, permits
were given to individual Belgium shippers on the understanding that payments for the shipments be made in
England before the shipments left
Belgium.

3. Early in September—when shipments were ready to leave, the German authorities—learning that proceeds would not go directly into Belgium—prevented shipments from leaving Belgium.

4. Now arrangements have been
made with both the German and
British authorities and shipments are
now leaving Belgium.

The above refers exclusively to our
own shipments—we cannot speak for
all Belgium shippers, or all American
consignees. Within a few days we
expect to be able to advise you what
Belgium shipments have already left
Rotterdam. Yours truly,

McHUTCHISON & Co.

Value of imports of horticultural
merchandise at the Port of New York
for week ending September 18 is given
as follows: Clover seed, $43; grass
seed, $326; palm seed, $300; trees,
plants and bulbs, $163,740.

PUBLICATIONS RECEIVED.

The Bay State Nurseries of North
Abington, Mass., have just sent out a
little folder, "Why You Should Plant
in the Fall," being a reprint of an
article by A. E. Wilkinson, of Cornell
University, which appeared in the
Garden Magazine. It is a very convincing little document on lines on
which it would pay every nurseryman
to push.

Sixty-Second Annual Report of the
Secretary of the Massachusetts State
Board of Agriculture for 1914. — A
splendid volume of 700 pages, containing reports of meetings, lectures and
essays of much practical value, agricultural legislation, and reports of
State officials, including Nursery Inspector, Ornithologist, Dairy Bureau,
Apiary Inspector, Boys' and Girls' Club
Work, State Forester and Incorporated
Agricultural Societies, all finely illustrated with insert plates. Secretary
Wheeler has in this volume given the
people of the State the best agricultural report ever presented in Massachusetts.

PERTINENT ADVICE ON THE ASTER QUESTION.

There is no one connected with the
flower business who sees the question
from all sides as does the wholesale
commission man. To get the best
flowers to sell to the trade and to get
the best prices for those flowers he
must know a lot on the subject. A
recent discussion of the aster question
took place in one of Chicago's largest
wholesale commission houses and a
man long in the business of turning
flowers into money said that a few
things only were needed to turn the
growing of asters from a poor proposition to a paying one. When asked
what they were, he said that, first of
all, the grower must get away from
the idea of quantity to that of quality,
because people buy garden flowers
from a florist only when they can get
better ones than they can grow themselves. Next, loose types of asters
produce, in proportion, more imperfect
flowers and the grower should study
to have his proportion of imperfect
flowers reduced to a minimum. Then
there are too many dark asters for the
demand and more light tints should
take their places. Center buds should
be picked out as soon as they form and
not more than six blooms should be
allowed on any aster plant. Imperfect
flowers should not be sent into the
market but should be destroyed, as
they bring down the price by competing with good stock. Aster foliage
should be stripped from six to eight
inches of the stems. Asters should be
bunched with heads put even so customers can readily see the quality of
the flowers. He ended by remarking
that it is easier to sell good asters at
a good price than to sell poor ones at
any price.

Bloomfield, N. J.—J. J. Brozat, who
has a commodious flower store with
semi-conservatory glass front at 554
Bloomfield avenue, has seen seriously
ill for several weeks, but is now on
the road to recovery and expects to
be soon out again.

The name of the Providence Horticultural Company got incorrectly into
our column of New Flower Stores last
week. The business of this company,
of which Edward Mora Pope is proprietor is that of landscape gardening,
forestry, agricultural blasting and similar work, and the addresses at 107
Westminister street, Providence, R.
I., is their office and not a flower store.

Of Interest to Retail Florists

ROUGH USAGE OF FUNERAL TRIBUTES.

Editor HORTICULTURE:

May I trespass inside of your valuable paper to offer a protest as to the handling of funeral flowers by undertakers and I regret to say by some florists, when they are taken from house or church after the funeral services. The usual practice is to throw them promiscously into a vehicle, helter-skelter as quickly as possible and so that they will occupy as small a space as possible. The feeling seems to be that the show is over, the florist has done his work and the undertaker is in a hurry to complete his. Does the florist ever stop to consider the feelings of the mourners who have sent those flowers, some of whom frequently see the way their offerings are treated, or do they ever take a moment to consider the effect it is likely to have upon people who have sent or would send floral tributes to the departed when they see costly flowers treated like so much rubbish, the moment they have served their purpose? Is it good business to show so little regard for the flowers from which we florists get our living? Do they think that a customer who has given perhaps fifty dollars for a design and sees it treated with such carelessness will be likely to repeat an experience of this kind, or is he not more likely to say to himself, —I will send a letter of sympathy or just a few loose flowers, if that is the way my tribute is treated.

In these days when flowers are produced in great quantity and are placed before the public in a large measure by vendors who are neither florists by profession or by instinct, it is more than ever necessary for the florists who have stores with all the attendant heavy expenses, to be particularly watchful to keep up the veneration sentiment and love of flowers by the wealthy classes upon whom they have to rely for their support.

CHAS. A. DARDS.
New York.

NEW FLOWER STORES.

Ardmore, Okla.—Woerz Bros.

Delaware, O.—Rex Floral Co., 17 E. Winter street.

Philadelphia, Pa. — Al. Saxer, 4410 Frankford avenue.

Arlington, Mass. — John McKenzie, Whittemore block.

Reno, Nev.—The Flower Shop, Masonic Temple building.

York, Pa.—Chas. E. Smith, removing to 125 E. Market street.

Vancouver, B. C. — Ritchie Bros. & Co., 840 Granville street.

St. Joseph, Mich.—Norman Richardson. Union Bank building.

Lincoln, Neb. — Enslow Floral Co., Oscar H. Enslow, proprietor.

E. Cleveland, O.—Windermere Floral Co., J. H. Mickelson, proprietor.

Pittsburgh, Pa. — Woodville Floral Co., South Main street, West End.

Flowers by Telegraph

Leading Retail Florists Listed by
Towns for Ready Reference. Orders
transferred by telegram or otherwise
to any of the firms whose address is
here given will be promptly and properly filled and delivered.

Albany, N. Y.—H. G. Eyres, 11 N. Pearl St.
Albany, N. Y.—The Rosery, 23 Steuben St. llr
Albany, N. Y.—William C. Gloeckner, 97 State St.
Boston—Thos. F. Galvin, 1 Park St.
Boston—Penn, the Florist, 37-43 Bromfield St.
Buffalo, N. Y.—S. A. Anderson, 440 Main St.
Buffalo, N. Y.—Palmer's, 304 Main St.
Chicago—William J. Smyth, Michigan Ave. and 31st St.
Cleveland, O.—J. M. Gasser Co., Euclid Ave.
Cleveland, O.—Adam Graham & Sons, 5523 Euclid Ave.
Denver, Col.—Park Floral Co., 1643 Broadway.
Detroit, Mich.—J. Breitmeyer's Sons, corner Broadway and Gratiot Ave.
Houston, Tex.—Kerr, The Florist.
Kansas City, Mo.—Samuel Murray, 1017 Grand Ave.
New London, Conn.—Reuter's.
Newport, R. I.—Gibson Bros., Bellevue Ave.
New York—David Clarke's Sons, 2139-2141 Broadway.
New York—Alex. McConnell, 611 5th Ave.
New York—Young & Nugent, 42 W. 28th.
New York—Dards, N. E. corner 44th St. and Madison Ave.
New York—Max Schling, 22 W. 59th St.
New York—G. E. M. Stumpp, 761 Fifth Ave.
New York—Thos. F. Galvin, Fifth Ave., at 46th St.
New York—Myer, 609-611 Madison Ave.
New York—A. T. Bunyard, 413 Madison Ave.
New York—National Floral Corporation, 220 Broadway.
Norwich, Conn.—Reuter's.
Omaha, Neb.—Hess & Swoboda, 1415 Farnum St.
Rochester, N. Y.—J. B. Keller Sons, 25 Clinton Ave., N.
St. Louis, Mo.—Fred C. Weber, 4326-28 Olive St.
St. Paul, Minn.—Holm & Olson, Inc.
Tarrytown-on-Hudson, N. Y.—F. R. Pierson Co.
Toronto, Can.—J. H. Dunlop, 96 Yonge St.
Washington, D. C.—Gude Bros., 1214 F St.
Washington, D. C.—F. H. Kramer, 915 F St. N. W.
Westerly, R. I.—Reuter's.
Worcester, Mass.—Randall's Flower Shop, 3 Pleasant St.

VISITORS' REGISTER.

Culver, Ind.—E. G. Gillett and Clarence Ohmer, Cincinnati, O.

Pittsburgh, Pa.—Clarence J. Watson, representing the Niessen Co., Phila.

Boston — F. Lazenby, Plymouth, Mass.; Paul M. Pierson, Scarborough, N. Y.

Cincinnati—R. E. Blackshaw of A. L. Randall Co., Chicago; B. J. Dudley, Parkersburg, W. Va.

St. Louis—Guy Reyburn of A. Henderson Co., Chicago; Julius Dillhoff of Schloss Bros., New York; C. S. Ford representing Hermann Co., New York; Hart Lehmann, Cleveland, O.

New York—M. A. Vinson, publicity

agent for the Cleveland Flower Show; F. G. McDonald and W. A. McAlpine, Boston; Prof. F. H. Hall, Geneva, N. Y.; Louis J. Reuter, Westerly, R. I.; D. Ormiston Roy, Montreal; R. Vincent, Jr., White Marsh, Maryland; Geo. L. Stillman, Westerly, R. I.

Philadelphia—Percy Barnard, Northbrook, Pa.; James M. Thoirs and Raymond Thoirs, Camden, N. J.; Rear Admiral Aaron Ward, N. Y.; Robert Pyle of Conard & Jones Co., West Grove, Pa.; Milton Moss, Huntsville, Ala.; Antoine Leuthy, Roslindale, Mass.; Patrick O'Mara and Peter Henderson, New York.

Chicago—Anton Schultheis, College Point, N. Y.; P. M. Koster, Boskoop, Holland; S. W. Pike, St. Charles, Ill.; Ralph Bather, Clinton, Ia.; George Beyer, Toledo, Ohio; W. G. Matthews, Dayton, Ohio; Geo. Dysinger, Ionia, Mich.; Elsie Cole, Kokomo, Ind.; J. R. Fotheringham, San Francisco, Cal.

Washington—J. C. Anderson, Greensboro, N. C.; Winfried Roelker, New York, N. Y.; J. D. Bockmann, Phila., Pa.; S. S. Pennock, Phila., Pa.; T. A. Walne, Bristol, Pa.; R. E. Lassman, Watertown, Mass.; W. J. Baker, Phila., Pa.; Rear Admiral Aaron Ward, N. Y.; Robert Pyle, West Grove, Pa.; C. W. Ward, Eureka, Cal., and A. J. Vascellius and party of Paterson, N. J.

NEWS ITEMS FROM EVERYWHERE

CHICAGO.

George Perdikas underwent an operation for appendicitis at the German Hospital this week.

Bassett & Washburn take possession this week of their new home in the new La Moyne Bldg., at the corner of Wabash avenue and Lake street.

The Red Bud Flower and Sweet Shop is the name of a flower and candy shop to be opened October 2, at 155 N. State street. The proprietor is C. Lampas formerly with Geo. Perdikas.

The openings of some of the big State street stores are taking place this week and some orders for flowers were the result. One order for one thousand chrysanthemums helped clear the market on Monday.

Mrs. Frank Oechslin is at St. Joseph's Hospital where an operation was performed on the jaw bone, September 23. She is doing as well as could be expected following such a painful operation.

Ernest Farley cannot overcome his love of Chicago and is back again looking for a position here. Theodore Vogel has also returned and has his old place with Wm. J. Smythe at Michigan avenue and 31st street.

The many wholesale florists in the Atlas Block are house-cleaning this week and the building is being overhauled by the owners also. The result is spotless wood work and a general "ready for inspection" air prevails.

Robt. Huehnchen was run down by an automobile and severely bruised and cut about the head and body, on September 25. Mr. Huehnchen is father of Mrs. Meyers the Humboldt Park Florist and assists in buying for the store.

The first cuts of the George Elgar rose are being received by F. F. Benthey who handles the stock of F. J. Benthey of Newcastle, Ind., at Kennicott Bros. It is a very attractive little yellow rose, about the size of Cecil Brunner.

The Chicago Florists' Club will hold an amalgamation banquet, Oct. 7 at 8 P. M. This is the final ceremony in the welding together of the two clubs and the trade in general is glad that a spirit of good fellowship now exists and that one united club takes the place of two. The banquet is free to members and $2.00 per plate to others.

Harry H. Conn who has been connected with the flower business here for several years, has bought the C. V. Abeele greenhouses at 61st and Throop street. Mr. Abeele will go to Europe to try and locate his two brothers, whom he has not heard from since the outbreak of the war. The new name of the store will be the Englewood Florist.

Phil Schupp says he made no mistake in growing double white Killarney roses and discarding the single ones. He has some magnificent stock to back up his opinion and with not a trace of color. The foliage is very heavy and rich in color. Mr. Schupp who is manager for J. A. Budlong, who is an extensive grower of lily of the valley,

says he has had no advice yet concerning the lily of the valley shipments due to arrive here in November.

The Coliseum, so well known over the country as the home of the Chicago Flower Shows and which is booked again for this fall, had a narrow escape from destruction early Sunday morning. Buildings directly north were destroyed in a fire which cost half a million dollars and Grace church built in 1868 and for so many years adjoining the Coliseum came near carrying that building down with it. The north wall is injured but not seriously. Only the fact that the wind was to the north saved the building that means so much to Chicago florists.

WASHINGTON, D. C.

The next regular meeting of the Florists' Club is scheduled to be held Tuesday evening, October 5. A special entertainment will be provided following the close of the business meeting.

Miss Nellie Brueninger, of Gude Bros. Co., has returned from a two weeks' vacation at Atlantic City. Mrs. Supper, also with that concern, is again on duty after an absence from the store.

A number of the local florists entered in the window display contest held under the auspices of the Retail Merchants' Association during the encampment of the Grand Army of the Republic, but none were so fortunate as to secure a prize.

Harry Kennelly, one of the chauffeurs for Gude Bros. Co. was badly injured recently when the automobile which he was driving was struck by a trolley car, necessitating his removal to the Emergency Hospital. It was found that his shoulder was dislocated and he will be confined to his home for some time.

The Takoma Park Horticultural Association was last week organized for the purpose of beautifying generally that section of the city. It will have the close co-operation of the Citizens' Association and will number among its members many of the officials of the Department of Agriculture who live in that suburb. The association will begin immediately upon a program to stimulate interest in horticulture and plans will be made for a flower show next week. Homer Skeels, a landscape gardener, and Ben Y. Morrison were appointed members of the committee which will have the latter event in charge.

S. S. Pennock, Admiral Aaron Ward, and Robert Pyle, last week came to Washington to make an inspection of the rose garden at Arlington. While in Washington they were the guests of William F. Gude, who accompanied them on their trip. An appeal will shortly be made to rose growers to furnish the necessary plants to complete this place. An automobile trip was taken through Arlington cemetery, the grounds of the Department of Agriculture, and the private rose garden of Mrs. Charles J. Bell, where they were the personal guests of Mrs. Bell who conducted them through the famous rose arbor.

PHILADELPHIA.

Jno. H. Dodds is reported out again after a two weeks' illness which threatened typhoid in its early stages.

Mrs. Edwin Lonsdale writes—Sept. 16—from Lompoc, Cal., thanking the Florists' Club for their telegram and tokens of sympathy.

Rear Admiral Aaron Ward, a noted amateur rosarian of New York, and Robert Pyle, of West Grove, Pa., were the guests of Pres. S. S. Pennock on September 23rd. An auto visit among the rose growers was a feature.

The Henry F. Michell Co. had a very excellent display of perennials on Friday, September 24, 1915, at the Annual Fall Show of the Ridley Park Civic Association at Ridley Park, Pa. Frank B. Michell was in charge of the exhibit.

Mr. Woodward of the Philadelphia force of the Lord & Burnham Co,. left on a two weeks' business trip south. On his return he expects to go down New England way on his vacation. He is a yankee and loves his native stamping ground. There are many worse places.

Among the roses to be seen the past week or two, Prince d' Arenberg and Hoosier Beauty are receiving a welcome reception from the up-to-date buyers, always on the look-out for something finer and newer. As a cut flower they rank in size and form with Hadley—which is proving such a favorite in the crimson section.

The Henry A. Dreer Co. have doubled their office capacity on the second floor, 714-716 Chestnut street. All departments now have much needed room for rapidly increasing business. The latest devices for labor saving, filing, etc., are all there. Smiles are on the department chiefs now, as they enjoy their extra elbow room.

Arthur H. Lanser and Frank Alter have purchased the Krueger interest of the Reading Terminal Flower stand and will conduct same under the name of the Charles F. Krueger Co. Mr. Lanser is well known locally, having conducted a growing and retailing business at Wayne for years. Mr. Alter was the late Mr. Krueger's assistant. . .

The "Old Guards' Reunion" has been postponed to Oct. 8th (instead of Oct. 1st) to suit the convenience of such national characters and busy men as Wm. F. Gude of Washington, Dennis T. Connor and Daniel C. Donoghue of Philadelphia. Men who stand with President Woodrow Wilson on the platform receiving guests— and things like that—have to be given some consideration.

Edward Towill had on exhibition at Pennock-Meehan's on Sept 29th, three of his new seedling roses. The white one with the dark center appealed to us. Magnificent stem and beautiful foliage. Robert Craig thought the yellow one the best. The pink one is fine also. Mr. Towill says all three are great producers and on that account alone some of our present standbys will have to "sit up and take notice."

The Joseph Heacock Co. opened

their Philadelphia headquarters at 1526 Ranstead street on September 21st. Carl Corts, the manager, reports very good business for their first week of the new season. All the Heacock products, cut roses and other flowers, palms, ferns and foliage plants, are up to the usual high quality which has made them justly famous. This is what, combined with courteous and efficient service, keeps their old friends firmly with them—and is constantly making new.

The auto truck value was well illustrated last week when a load of sixty-four hundred pounds left Dreer's at Riverton, N. J., at 3 A. M., for New York City, arriving there at 3 P. M. and getting back to Riverton by 2 A. M. next morning. Time and labor at both ends, packing and unpacking, cartage, freight and other incidentals all saved and the goods got there in better shape. But the railroads will not welcome that sort of thing. There are more loads to go yet, if one may judge from the "set-aside" blocks at the Riverton Nurseries.

NEW YORK.

Myer Othile, formerly of Badgley, Riedel & Myer is about to start in the wholesale florist business for himself.

Thomas F. Galvin's flower window on Fifth avenue was devoted exclusively to dahlias and notices of the dahlia show for two days last week. It was a compliment fully appreciated by the dahlia show people.

The general committee of the New York Spring Flower Show met at the office of Secretary John Young on Monday afternoon, September 27 and practically completed the work on the schedule, which Mr. Young will now push along for early distribution.

M. A. Vinson, publicity manager for the Cleveland Flower Show has been in New York in the interest of that enterprise, especially to arrange details for shipping the gigantic hush chrysanthemum plants grown by John Canning of Ardsley. If this exhibit can be safely transported to Cleveland it will prove a strong attraction. Mr

PRIZE WINNING FLOAT.

Floral Float by Ross Bros., Worcester, Mass.

The auto float shown in the accompanying picture was fully described in a description of the "battle of flowers" at Worcester, Mass., which we published in our issue of September 18.

Canning's plants shown at the exhibition here last fall were fifteen or sixteen feet in diameter and railroad transportation of such is quite a problem.

John Young is one of the busiest men we know of. What with the secretaryship of the Society of American Florists and the New York Florists' Club, the work connected with the National Flower Show at Philadelphia and the New York Flower Show for next spring and the Dahlia Show just closed and a multitude of committee meetings, there is no idle moment in Mr. Young's day—yet he never fails to find a few leisure minutes to devote to members who call on him. John H. Pepper is temporarily assisting him at present in the clerical work.

There are dahlias and dahlias. Possibly they may be equally attractive at

It was entered by W. D. Ross and won first prize among sixteen competitors, amounting to $170, in addition to which it won a pair of Sterling tires valued at $100 and a silver cup from the Cadillac people.

the time they are cut from the plants—after that it's all in the packing. Dahlia growers who are disappointed over the prices obtained for their flowers in the wholesale market should take a trip to the city and see how their competitors pack their flowers and it will soon dawn upon them why it is that some growers get $2.00 or $3.00 per 100 while others don't realize that much per 1000. We saw some of L. K. Peacock's shipments at Langjahr's. They were packed like eggs and—well, such goods almost sell themselves.

Much favoring comment is heard among the florist trade of Boston and vicinity on the very entertaining talk given by Henry Penn before the Gardeners' and Florists' Club of Boston last week, giving his experiences and observations on his recent trip to California.

WHOLESALE FLOWER MARKETS — TRADE PRICES—Per 100 TO DEALERS ONLY

Roses	CINCINNATI Sept. 27		CHICAGO Sept. 27		BUFFALO Sept. 27		PITTSBURG Sept. 23	
Am. Beauty, Special	20.00	to 25.00	20.00	to 25.00	20.00	to 25.00	15.00	to 20.00
" " Fancy and Extra	15.00	to 20.00	15.00	to 20.00	15.00	to 20.00	10.00	to 12.50
" " No. 1	8.00	to 10.00	8.00	to 10.00	6.00	to 8.00	6.00	to 8.00
Russell, Hadley	4.00	to 8.00	5.00	to 15.00	4.00	to 7.00	4.00	to 8.00
Killarney, Richm'd, Hill'don, Ward	4.00	to 8.00	6.00	to 8.00	5.00	to 7.00	6.00	to 8.00
" " " Ord.	3.00	to 4.00	2.00	to 5.00	3.00	to 4.00	2.00	to 4.00
Arenburg, Radiance, Taft, Key, Ex.	4.00	to 8.00	6.00	to 8.00	5.00	to 6.00	6.00	to 8.00
" " " Ord.	3.00	to 4.00	2.00	to 5.00	3.00	to 5.00	2.00	to 4.00
Ophelia, Mock, Sunburst, Extra	4.00	to 8.00	6.00	to 8.00	4.00	to 7.00	6.00	to 8.00
" " " Ordinary	3.00	to 4.00	2.00	to 5.00	3.00	to 5.00	2.00	to 4.00
Carnations, Fancy	1.50	to 2.00	2.00	to 3.00	2.00	to 3.00	2.00	to 3.00
" Ordinary		to 1.00	1.00	to 2.00	1.00	to 2.00		to 1.50
Cattleyas	50.00	to 75.00	50.00	to 60.00	40.00	to 50.00	40.00	to 60.00
Dendrobium formosum			40.00	to 60.00		to	30.00	to 40.00
Lilies, Longiflorum	8.00	to 10.00	8.00	to 10.00	8.00	to 10.00	8.00	to 10.00
" Rubrum	4.00	to 8.00		to	4.00	to 8.00	6.00	to 8.00
Lily of the Valley		to 4.00	3.00	to 4.00	3.00	to 4.00	3.00	to 4.00
Violets		to		.50		.75		to
Snapdragon		to						to
Gladioli	3.00	to 4.00	2.00	to 3.00	1.00	to 2.00	1.00	to
Asters	1.00	to 2.00	1.00	to 3.00	.50	to 1.50	1.00	to 2.00
Chrysanthemums	15.00	to 20.00	10.00	to 25.00	10.00	to 15.00	10.00	to 20.00
Sweet Peas		to				to		to
Gardenias		to	20.00	to 25.00		to		to
Adiantum	1.00	to 1.00	1.00	to 1.25	1.00	to 1.25	.75	to 1.25
Smilax	12.50	to 15.00	8.00	to 15.00		to 15.00	12.00	to 15.00
Asparagus Plumosus, Strings (100)	25.00	to 50.00	25.00	to 50.00	25.00	to 50.00	40.00	to 50.00
" & Spren. (100 bchs.)		to 35.00	25.00	to 30.00	25.00	to 35.00	30.00	to 40.00

Flower Market Reports

BOSTON Market conditions have greatly improved within the past few days. It is quite an encouraging sign to find the tables in the wholesale markets at last free from accumulated surplus flowers and to learn that everything of acceptable quality finds a ready sale at a fixed price. This means two or three hundred per cent of an advance on gross receipts for many of the local growers. Chrysanthemums are increasing in number but not fast enough to fill the vacancy left by the retreating asters and gladioli. Of dahlias there are never very many seen in the wholesale markets here and so they are not interfering with the monopoly of the situation by the standard florist crops.

BUFFALO Trade is noticeably on the upward course and this, no doubt, is due to the shortening up and poor quality of the outdoor flowers. There are still asters, gladioli, marigolds, cosmos and other stock, but it is gradually becoming lighter each day. Roses have arrived in better shape since cooler weather set in and the demand has fallen on carnations and these are not coming in in quantity. Lilies, too, have had a better sale and everything indoor grown has had more sales. There are chrysanthemums, Golden Glow, Smith's Advance, and some dahlias of eastern consignments, which have taken well. There has never been a September month in which roses were finer than at present; double white Killarney good, pink Killarney grand color and excellent stems, Sunburst very choice, Ward, Maryland, Bonsilene all good, Scott, Key, Russell, Ophelia, beautiful color and excellent stems and the sales have been satisfactory throughout the week. Conditions are satisfactory to all and it is hoped that things will improve daily.

CHICAGO September closes with nearly all outdoor flowers gone and no surplus of any kind in the market. Out-of-town trade is very good and local sales have been better the past week. While there is no marked increase, the tendency has been to a good amount of steady business which has used up all the good stock at a fair price. Just at this writing carnations are scarce. Cold rain has prevented the opening of buds but stems are lengthening and when the sun comes out again regular cold weather stock will be seen. While asters locally grown are considered out of the race some are coming now from New York which, though short, are of good quality and size. Gladioli are nearing the close of the outdoor season and it has been a poor one financially, excepting for those who had a good early stock. American Beauty roses are coming of good quality and there are now reaching the four-foot mark. Other roses are about equal to the demand. Chrysanthemums are having an unusual experience, the early ones being badly hampered by the heat and the late ones held back by the dark days. The large number of weddings is using up all of the lily of the valley and making white orchids much in demand. Social events are starting early this fall, making an earlier revival of the flower business and of course meeting the approval of all in the trade. The supply of all kinds of green is excellent.

CINCINNATI Toward the end of last week the supply began to shorten rapidly but the first days of this week opened with receipts that were more than adequate for present needs. Roses are in a very large supply and generally are of a high quality. Carnations are fairly plentiful. The supply of lilies is about equal to the demand. Dahlias are very fine and there are many of them. Gladioli and asters have about run their course. Greens are plentiful. Wild smilax is enjoying a pretty good demand.

NEW YORK The impression one gets from a tour of the wholesale flower district this week is of a very uncertain character. Dealers are expectant rather than sanguine and the degrees of expectancy vary according to the man and his environment. Growers are gradually bringing their standard fall and winter crops forward so that estimates and forecasts as to quality and quantity can be made and the question of selling agencies is now to the front with some important changes in alignment already settled or soon to be. The fag end of the outdoor summer season supply still hangs on—asters, gladioli, hydrangeas, gypsophila, with odds and ends in variety, and lastly the dahlias which are seen in abundance but not always in salable shape—but a good frost will quickly wipe these off the boards and we shall then be down once again to the old standbys. Of the latter, roses are in moderate supply, stems and flowers small but buds well colored, uniform and indicating good culture and care-

(Continued on page 455)

WHOLESALE FLOWER MARKETS — TRADE PRICES—Per 100 TO DEALERS ONLY

	BOSTON Sept. 30		ST. LOUIS Sept. 27		PHILA. Sept. 27	
Roses						
Am. Beauty, Special	12.00	25.00	20.00	25.00	18.00	20.00
" " Fancy and Extra	8.00	10.00	12.00	20.00	12.00	16.00
" " No. 1	1.00	3.00	3.00	8.00	6.00	10.00
Russell, Hadley	4.00	8.00	10.00	15.00	3.00	15.00
Killarney, Richmond, Hillingdon, Ward, Extra	4.00	6.00	5.00	6.00	3.00	6.00
" " " " Ordinary	2.00	4.00	1.00	3.00	1.00	3.00
Arenburg; Radiance, Taft, Key, Extra	4.00	8.00	5.00	6.00	3.00	6.00
" " " " Ordinary	2.00	4.00	1.00	3.00	1.00	2.00
Ophelia, Mock, Sunburst, Extra	4.00	8.00	.....	to	3.00	6.00
" " " Ordinary	2.00	4.00	.....	10	2.00	3.00
Carnations, Fancy	2.00	3.00	1.50	2.00	1.00	3.00
Ordinary	1.00	2.00	.50	1.00	.50	1.00
Cattleyas	15.00	25.00	35.00	75.00	35.00	50.00
Dendrobium formosum	...10	25.00	...10	.....	..10	50.00
Lilies, Longiflorum	6.00	8.00	6.00	8.00	8.00	12.00
Rubrum		10	2.00	3.00	..10	.....
Lily of the Valley	3.00	4.00	3.00	6.00	2.00	4.00
Daisies	.50	1.00	.20	.25	..10	.....
Violets			.....	.....	..10	.....
Snapdragon	.50	1.00	3.00	4.00	..10	1.50
Gladioli	2.00	4.00	2.00	3.00	1.00	1.50
Asters	.25	1.00	.75	2.00	.50	1.00
Chrysanthemums	12.00	16.00	..10	12.00	8.00	15.00
Sweet Peas	.15	.30	.15	.25	..25	.....
Gardenias	10.00	12.00	..10	.....	..10	.....
Adiantum	.....	1.00	1.00	1.05	..10	1.00
Smilax	12.00	16.00	12.00	16.00	12.00	20.00
Asparagus Plumosus, Strings (100)	25.00	50.00	35.00	50.00	..10	50.00
" " & Spren. (100 Bchs.)	25.00	35.00	20.00	35.00	35.00	50.00

Flower Market Reports
(Continued from page 453)

ful handling; carnations are very poor indeed; lilies are of higher quality than at any time during the summer and there are lots of them; lily of the valley is of regal quality from some growers but there is plenty of the other kind; cattleyas are of varying quality and are moving with exasperating slowness; oncidiums, Dendrobium phalaenopsis, D. formosum giganteum help out on the variety of orchids; chrysanthemums are gradually asserting themselves and already show signs of accumulation which will seriously affect the returns if the asters and dahlias delay their exit much longer. There are quite a few changes, removals and new firms in the wholesale market district, mention of which will be found from time to time in our reading columns or in the advertising pages.

PHILADELPHIA Business continues to improve slowly here, as was to be expected. with the advent of cooler weather. Stocks of all kinds have decreased in quantity and as a rule have bettered in quality. There is an air of activity all around and a much better tone and feeling everywhere. In roses, American Beauty is back to its old place as leader and moves off nicely at about same prices as last year. Close seconds in the running are Ophelia and Russell. We have never seen Ophelia in finer form than it is at present. Crimson Queen and Hoosier Beauty are among the new ones that are attracting attention. Carnations are coming in better and selling right well. Orchids were plentiful; fine quality; demand not brisk. There is much more activity in the dahlia market since the cool weather set in. Asters and gladioli are practically over, although there are a few stragglers here and there. No change in the chrysanthemum situation—just a few of the early yellows and whites. The supply of lily of the valley and lilies has shortened up and the demand remains excellent. Tritomas are selling better, although it is still a little early for them.

PITTSBURGH After an unprecedented season of cold weather and rain, followed by a fortnight of dry weather and torrid heat, autumnal growing conditions are well-nigh perfect. Chrysanthemums have just started to come in, and as the early varieties go, are of exceptional good quality. Considering the early season, business is fine and the supply very heavy, with the disposal in proportion. Asters and gladioli have nearly run their course, but dahlias continue "Queen of the Day," both as to quality, quantity and favor. The McCallum Company which makes a specialty of these flowers is averaging 4,500 daily. All are specimen varieties, their dahlia man having made their growth almost a religion, saying nothing of science.

SAN FRANCISCO Flowers are hardly so plentiful as they were a few weeks ago. and with business keeping up nicely the supply is practically cleaned up from day to day. Several large decorations of a social nature took many flowers the past week, and a great deal of less desirable stock was used on floats in the big I. O. O. F. parade. Carnations are coming in a little better, but the supply is still limited and the offerings are readily absorbed notwithstanding rather poor quality. The supply of chrysanthemums is increasing rapidly and they meet with excellent demand. October Frost is getting scarce, but there are plenty other varieties to take its place. Queens are beginning to appear and show excellent quality. Rose Pink and Unaka are arriving freely and pompons are plentiful. The latter are very popular and bring top prices. Dahlias continue very satisfactory both in quantity and quality, and the demand shows no inclination to weaken. Gladiolus is holding out fairly well, and asters are still offered in considerable quantity, while the supply of amaryllis is abundant. Violets are coming in more freely, but the demand exceeds the supply by a large margin and heavier arrivals will be welcome to the trade. The rose market shows little change, summer roses being off crop and winter roses just beginning to appear. The quality is a little better this week, but there is not enough good stock to fill the demand. Gardenias are scarce, and the limited supply is readily absorbed. The same is true of orchids, although cattleyas promise to be plentiful in another week or two. The supply of small outdoor stock is gradually decreasing, after a very successful summer season.

ST. LOUIS The market is still overcrowded and has been so all week and with the retail business slow, the wholesalers have a hard time cleaning up their stock. Chrysanthemums of the white and yellow sorts are coming in more freely and sell better. Roses are most plentiful and down in price and only the fancy sorts sell with any degree of regularity. Carnations are looking better; still the quality is shy, also the stems. Outdoor stock is still coming in.

WASHINGTON A marked drop in the temperature last week created a scarcity of stock of all kinds. It is stated that not more than one-tenth of the number of dahlias generally to be had at this time of the year are now obtainable. Carnations are not as yet very plentiful, nor is the stock anything to boast of. Cattleyas are more plentiful and are bringing lower prices. Spray orchids are not in any great demand. There have not been nearly enough good white roses to go around for the past ten days. Funeral work has been quite heavy and the demand for white roses was greater than it has been for some time. Pink roses are more plentiful. American Beauty roses are very good and in fair demand. Lily of the valley is more plentiful but has been selling quite well.

PERSONAL.

Daniel J. Leary, florist, Baldwin street, Waterbury, Ct., and Miss Sadie V. Dougherty will be married Oct. 12.

John M. Hunter, the veteran gardener, of Englewood, N. J., has gone to California hoping to improve his health.

Irvington, N. J.—E. W. Fengar has two happy finds among his chrysanthemums. One is a bronze sport from Unaka and the other a pure white sport from Well's Late pink.

Lawrence Cotter, manager of Lakeview Rose Gardens at Jamestown, N. Y., has recently returned from a sanitarium. having been ill all summer. We hope the improvement now indicated will continue uninterrupted.

NEW YORK QUOTATIONS PER 100. To Dealers Only

MISCELLANEOUS	Last Half of Week ending Sept. 25 1915	First Half of Week beginning Sept. 27 1915
Cattleyas	10.00 to 25.00	10.00 to 25.00
Dendrobium formosum	20.00 to 25.00	20.00 to 25.00
Lilies, Longiflorum	3.00 to 5.00	4.00 to 5.00
Rubrum	2.00 to 3.00	2.00 to 3.00
Lily of the Valley	2.00 to 3.00	2.00 to 4.00
Daisies	...... to .50	...... to .50
Violets	...... to	...... to ......
Snapdragon	.50 to 1.00	1.00 to 2.00
Gladioli	1.00 to 2.00	1.00 to 3.00
Asters	.25 to 1.00	.50 to 1.00
Chrysanthemums	6.00 to 8.00	6.00 to 12.00
Sweet Peas	...... to	...... to ......
Corn Flower	...... to .25	...... to .25
Gardenias	5.00 to 16.00	5.00 to 16.00
Adiantum	.50 to .75	.50 to .75
Smilax	8.00 to 10.00	8.00 to 10.00
Asparagus Plumosus, strings (per 100)	15.00 to 30.00	15.00 to 30.00
& Spren (100 bunches)	10.00 to 20.00	10.00 to 20.00

Buyer's Directory and Ready Reference Guide

Advertisements under this head, one cent a word.   **Initials count as words**

Display advertisers in this issue are also listed under this classification without charge. Reference to List of Advertisers will indicate the respective pages.

Buyers failing to find what they want in this list will confer a favor by writing us and we will try to put them in communication with reliable dealers.

ACACIAS.
Stuart Low & Co., Harry A. Barnard, representative, Hotel Albert, New York City.
For page see List of Advertisers.

ACCOUNTANT
R. J. Dysart, 40 State St., Boston.
For page see List of Advertisers.

ACHILLEA
"Pearl," Fine Seedlings, $3.00 per 1,000, cash. JAMES MOSS, Wholesale Grower, Johnsville, Pa.

ADIANTUM
The Storrs & Harrison Co., Painesville, Ohio.
For page see List of Advertisers.

APHINE
Aphine Mfg. Co., Madison, N. J.
For page see List of Advertisers.

APHIS PUNK
Nicotine Mfg. Co., St. Louis, Mo.
For page see List of Advertisers.

ARAUCARIAS
Henry A. Dreer, Philadelphia, Pa.
For page see List of Advertisers.

ARECAS
Joseph Heacock Co., Wyncote, Pa.
For page see List of Advertisers.

ASPARAGUS
The Storrs & Harrison Co., Painesville, Ohio.
For page see List of Advertisers.

AUCTION SALES
Elliott Auction Co., New York City.
For page see List of Advertisers.

AZALEAS
P. Ouwerkerk, Hoboken, N. J.
For page see List of Advertisers.

BAY TREES
August Rolker & Sons, New York.
For page see List of Advertisers.

BEDDING PLANTS
A N. Pierson, Inc., Cromwell, Conn.
For page see List of Advertisers.

BEGONIAS
Julius Roehrs Company, Rutherford, N. J.
For page see List of Advertisers.

R. Vincent, Jr., & Sons Co., White Marsh, Md.
For page see List of Advertisers.

Thomas Roland, Nahant, Mass.
For page see List of Advertisers.

The Storrs & Harrison Co., Painesville, Ohio.
For page see List of Advertisers.

	Per 100
BEGONIA LORRAINE, 2½ in	$12.00
3 in	20.00
4 in	35.00
5 in	50.00
BEGONIA CINCINNATI, 2½ in	15.00
3 in	25.00
3½ in	30.00
4½ in	40.00

JULIUS ROEHRS CO., Rutherford, N. J.

BOILERS
Kroeschell Bros. Co., Chicago.
For page see List of Advertisers.

BOILERS—Continued
King Construction Co., North Tonawanda, N. Y.
"King Ideal" Boiler.
For page see List of Advertisers.

Lord & Burnham Co., New York City.

Hitchings & Co., New York City.
For page see List of Advertisers.

BOUGAINVILLEA
The Storrs & Harrison Co., Painesville, Ohio.
For page see List of Advertisers.

BOXES—CUT FLOWER FOLDING
Edwards Folding Box Co., Philadelphia.
For page see List of Advertisers.

Folding cut flower boxes, the best made. Write for list. HOLTON & HUNKEL CO., Milwaukee, Wis.

BOX TREES
BOX TREES—Standards, Pyramids and Bush, in various sizes. Price List on demand. JULIUS ROEHRS CO., Rutherford, N. J

BULBS AND TUBERS
Arthur T. Boddington Co., Inc., New York City.
For page see List of Advertisers.

J. M. Thorburn & Co., New York City. Wholesale Price List of High Class Bulbs.
For page see List of Advertisers.

Ralph M. Ward & Co., New York City. Lily Bulbs.
For page see List of Advertisers.

John Lewis Childs, Flowerfield, L. I., N. Y.

August Rolker & Sons, New York City. Holland and Japan Bulbs.
For page see List of Advertisers.

R. & J. Farquhar & Co., Boston, Mass.
For page see List of Advertisers.

S. S. Skidelsky & Co., Philadelphia, Pa.
For page see List of Advertisers.

Chas. Schwake & Co., New York City. Horticultural Importers and Exporters.
For page see List of Advertisers.

A. Henderson & Co., Chicago, Ill.
For page see List of Advertisers.

Burnett Bros., 98 Chambers St., New York.
For page see List of Advertisers.

Henry F. Michell Co., Philadelphia, Pa.
For page see List of Advertisers.

Joseph Breck & Sons Corp., Boston, Mass.
For page see List of Advertisers.

Fottler, Fiske, Rawson Co., Boston, Mass.
For page see List of Advertisers.

C. KEUR & SONS, HILLEGOM, Holland. Bulbs of all descriptions. Write for prices. NEW YORK Branch, 8-10 Bridge St.

CANNAS
Canna Specialists.
Send for Canna book.
THE CONARD & JONES COMPANY, West Grove, Pa.

CARNATION STAPLES
Split carnations quickly, easily and cheaply mended. Pillsbury's Carnation Staple, 1000 for 35c.; 3000 for $1.00 post paid. I. L. PILLSBURY, Galesburg, Ill.

Supreme Carnation Staples, for repairing split carnations, 35c. per 1000; 3000 for $1.00. F. W. WAITE, 85 Belmont Ave., Springfield, Mass.

CARNATIONS.
Wood Bros., Fishkill, N. Y.
For page see List of Advertisers.

F. Dorner & Sons Co., Lafayette, Ind.
For page see List of Advertisers.

F. R. Pierson, Tarrytown, N. Y.
Carnation Matchless.
For page see List of Advertisers.

Jas. Vick's Sons, Rochester, N. Y.
Field Grown Plants.
For page see List of Advertisers.

Littlefield & Wyman, North Abington, Mass.
New Pink Carnation, Miss Theo.
For page see List of Advertisers.

Carnations, field grown, $6.00 per 100. Cash. White and Pink Enchantress, Mrs. Ward, Perfection, Fenn, Winsor, Queen, Lawson, Beacon. CHAS. H. GREEN, Spencer, Mass.

CHRYSANTHEMUMS
Chas. H. Totty, Madison, N. J.
For page see List of Advertisers.

R. Vincent, Jr., & Sons Co., White Marsh, Md.
Pompon Chrysanthemums,
For page see List of Advertisers.

THE BEST 1915 NOVELTIES.
The Cream of 1914 Introductions.
The most popular Commercial and Exhibition kinds; also complete line of Pompons, Singles and Anemones. Trade list on application. ELMER D. SMITH & CO., Adrian, Mich.

COCOANUT FIBRE SOIL
20th Century Plant Food Co., Beverly, Mass
For page see List of Advertisers.

DAHLIAS
Send for Wholesale List of whole clumps and separate stock; 40,000 clumps for sale. Northboro Dahlia and Gladiolus Gardens. J. L. MOORE, Prop, Northboro, Mass.

NEW PAEONY DAHLIA
John Wanamaker, Newest, Handsomest, Best. New color, new form and new habit of growth. Big stock of best cut-flower varieties. Send list of wants to PEACOCK DAHLIA FARMS, Berlin, N. J.

DECORATIVE PLANTS
Robert Craig Co., Philadelphia, Pa.
For page see List of Advertisers.

Woodrow & Marketos, New York City.
For page see List of Advertisers.

S. S. Skidelsky & Co., Philadelphia, Pa.
For page see List of Advertisers.

Bobbink & Atkins, Rutherford, N. J.
For page see List of Advertisers.

A. Leuthy & Co., Roslindale, Boston, Mass.
For page see List of Advertisers.

DRACENAS
The Storrs & Harrison Co., Painesville, Ohio.
For page see List of Advertisers.

EUONYMUS RADICANS VEGETUS
Euonymus Radicans Vegetus—Three-year-old potted plants for immediate delivery; also three-year field-grown plants. $14.00 per 100, $2.00 per doz. Illustrated booklet. free for the asking. THE GARDEN NURSERIES, Narberth, Pa.

FERNS
H. H. Barrows & Son, Whitman, Mass.
For page see List of Advertisers.

Robert Craig Co., Philadelphia, Pa.
For page see List of Advertisers.

For List of Advertisers See Page 435

FERNS—Continued

McHutchison & Co., New York City.
Ferns in Flats.
For page see List of Advertisers.

A. M. Davenport, Watertown, Mass.
Boston and Whitmani Ferns.
For page see List of Advertisers.

Roman J. Irwin, New York City.
Boston and Whitmani Ferns.
For page see List of Advertisers.

The Storrs & Harrison Co., Painesville,
Ohio.
For page see List of Advertisers.

ASPLENIUM NIDUS AVIS (Birds-nest fern).
Good strong healthy plants, 4 in. pots,
$40.00 per 100; 5 in. pots, $75.00 per 100;
6 in. pots, $100.00 per 100. WM. K. HARRIS, 55th and Springfield Ave., W. Philadelphia, Pa.

FERTILIZERS

20th Century Plant Food Co., Beverly, Mass.
Cocoanut Fibre Soil.
For page see List of Advertisers.

Stumpp & Walter Co., New York City.
Scotch Soot.
For page see List of Advertisers.

Chicago Feed & Fertilizer Co., Chicago, Ill.
Magic Manures.
For page see List of Advertisers.

Pulverized Manure Co., Chicago, Ill.
Wizard Brand Cattle Manure.
For page see List of Advertisers.

FLORISTS' LETTERS

Boston Florist Letter Co., Boston, Mass.
For page see List of Advertisers.

FLORISTS' SUPPLIES

N. F. McCarthy & Co., Boston, Mass.
For page see List of Advertisers.

Reed & Keller, New York City.
For page see List of Advertisers.

S. S. Pennock-Meehan Co., Philadelphia, Pa.
For page see List of Advertisers.

Bayersdorfer & Co., Philadelphia, Pa.
For page see List of Advertisers.

Welch Bros., Boston, Mass.
For page see List of Advertisers.

FLOWER POTS

W. H. Ernest, Washington, D. C.
For page see List of Advertisers.

A. H. Hews & Co., Inc., Cambridge, Mass.
For page see List of Advertisers.

Hilfinger Bros., Ft. Edward, N. Y.
For page see List of Advertisers.

FOLIAGE PLANTS

A. Leuthy & Co., Roslindale, Boston, Mass.
For page see List of Advertisers.

FUNGINE

Aphine Mfg. Co., Madison, N. J.
For page see List of Advertisers.

GALAX

Michigan Cut Flower Co., Detroit, Mich.
For page see List of Advertisers.

GERANIUMS

GERANIUMS.
SINGLE.

	2 and 2½-in.		3-in.	
	100	1000	100	1000
Feuer	$3.50	$32.50	$5.00	$40.00
Granville	2.50	22.50	5.00	40.00
Mrs. E. G. Hill	2.50	22.50	5.00	40.00

DOUBLE.

Alph. Ricard	3.00	25.00	5.00	45.00
Beaute Poitevine	3.00	25.00	5.00	45.00
Berthe de Presilly	2.50	22.50	5.00	40.00
J. Viaud	2.50	22.50	5.00	40.00
La Favorite	2.50	22.50	5.00	40.00
Marq'se de Castellane	2.50	22.50	5.00	40.00
Miss F. Perkins	2.50	22.50	5.00	40.00
Mme. Landry	2.50	22.50	5.00	40.00
S. A. Nutt	2.50	22.50	5.00	40.00

Prices of rooted cuttings on application.
WRITE FOR COPY OF OUR
MONTHLY PLANT BULLETIN.
S. S. PENNOCK-MEEHAN CO.,
1608-1620 Ludlow St., Philadelphia, Pa.

GERANIUMS—Continued

R. Vincent, Jr., & Sons Co.
White Marsh, Md.
For page see List of Advertisers.

Geraniums, rooted in silica rock sand;
show a better color and grow better. Let
me have your order for Nutt, Ricard, Poitevine and La Favorite. $10.00 per 1000.
Cash. JAMES MOSS, Johnsville, Pa.

GLASS

Sharp, Partridge & Co., Chicago.
For page see List of Advertisers.

Parshelsky Bros., Inc., Brooklyn, N. Y.
For page see List of Advertisers.

Royal Glass Works, New York City.
For page see List of Advertisers.

Greenhouse glass, lowest prices. JOHNSTON GLASS CO., Hartford City, Ind.

GLASS CUTTERS

Smith & Hemenway Co., New York City.
Red Devil Glass Cutter.
For page see List of Advertisers.

GLAZING POINTS

H. A. Dreer, Philadelphia, Pa.
Peerless Glazing Point.
For page see List of Advertisers.

Geo. H. Angermueller, St. Louis, Mo.

GOLD FISH

Gold fish, aquarium plants, snails, castles, globes, aquarium, fish goods, nets, etc., wholesale. FRANKLIN BARRETT, Breeder, 4815 D St., Olney, Philadelphia, Pa. Large breeding pairs for sale. Send for price list.

GREENHOUSE BUILDING MATERIAL

King Construction Co., N. Tonawanda, N. Y.
For page see List of Advertisers.

Parshelsky Bros., Inc., Brooklyn, N. Y.
For page see List of Advertisers.

Metropolitan Material Co., Brooklyn, N. Y.
For page see List of Advertisers.

Lord & Burnham Co., New York City.

A. T. Stearns Lumber Co., Neponset, Boston.
Pecky Cypress.
For page see List of Advertisers.

GREENHOUSE CONSTRUCTION

King Construction Co., N. Tonawanda, N. Y.
For page see List of Advertisers.

Foley Greenhouse Mfg. Co., Chicago, Ill.
For page see List of Advertisers.

Metropolitan Material Co., Brooklyn, N. Y.
For page see List of Advertisers.

Lord & Burnham Co., New York City.

Hitchings & Co., New York City.
For page see List of Advertisers.

A. T. Stearns Lumber Co., Boston, Mass.
For page see List of Advertisers.

GUTTERS

King Construction Co., N. Tonawanda, N. Y
King Channel Gutter.
For page see List of Advertisers.

Metropolitan Material Co., Brooklyn, N. Y
Iron Gutters.
For page see List of Advertisers.

HAIL INSURANCE

Florists' Hail Asso. of America.
J G Esler, Saddle River, N. J.
For page see List of Advertisers.

HARDY FERNS AND GREEN GOODS

Michigan Cut Flower Exchange, Detroit, Mich.
For page see List of Advertisers.

Knud Nielsen, Evergreen, Ala.
Natural Green Sheet Moss, Fancy and Dagger Ferns and Huckleberry Foliage.
For page see List of Advertisers.

The Kervan Co., New York.
For page see List of Advertisers.

HARDY PERENNIALS

Bay State Nurseries, No. Abington, Mass.
For page see List of Advertisers.

P. Ouwerkerk, Hoboken, N. J.
For page see List of Advertisers.

Palisades Nurseries, Sparkill, N. Y.
For page see List of Advertisers.

Eastern Nurseries, Jamaica Plain, Mass.
Surplus List.
For page see List of Advertisers.

HEATING APPARATUS

Kroeschell Bros. Co., Chicago.
For page see List of Advertisers.

Lord & Burnham Co., New York City.

HOT BED SASH.

Parshelsky Bros., Inc., Brooklyn, N. Y.
For page see List of Advertisers.

Foley Greenhouse Construction Co., Chicago, Ill.
For page see List of Advertisers.

S. Jacobs & Sons, Brooklyn, N. Y.
For page see List of Advertisers.

Lord & Burnham Co., New York City.

A. T. Stearns Lumber Co., Neponset, Mass.
For page see List of Advertisers.

HOSE

H. A. Dreer, Philadelphia, Pa.

INSECTICIDES

Aphine Manufacturing Co., Madison, N. J.
Aphine and Fungine.
For page see List of Advertisers.

Nicotine Mfg. Co., St. Louis, Mo.
Aphis Punk and Nikoteen.
For page see List of Advertisers.

The Plantlife Co., New York City.
Plantlife Insecticide.
For page see List of Advertisers.

HYDRANGEAS

The Storrs & Harrison Co., Painesville, Ohio.
For page see List of Advertisers.

IRIS

John Lewis Childs, Inc.,
Flowerfield, L. I., N. Y.
For page see List of Advertisers.

IRRIGATION EQUIPMENT

Skinner Irrigation Co., Brookline, Mass.
For page see List of Advertisers.

KENTIAS

Joseph Heacock Co., Wyncote, Pa.
For page see List of Advertisers.

LILY BULBS

Chas. Schwake & Co., New York City.
Horticultural Importers and Exporters
For page see List of Advertisers.

R. M. Ward & Co., New York, N. Y.
Japanese Lily Bulbs of Superior Quality.
For page see List of Advertisers.

Corp. of Chas. F. Meyer, New York City
Meyer's T. Brand Giganteums.
For page see List of Advertisers.

John Lewis Childs, Inc.,
Hardy Lilies.
Flowerfield, L. I., N. Y.
For page see List of Advertisers.

LILY OF THE VALLEY

Chas. Schwake & Co., Inc., New York City
Hohmann's Famous Lily of the Valley Pips
For page see List of Advertisers.

McHutchison & Co., New York City.
For page see List of Advertisers.

Loechner & Co., New York City.
Lily of the Valley Pips.
For page see List of Advertisers.

LIQUID PUTTY MACHINE

Metropolitan Material Co., Brooklyn, N. Y.
For page see List of Advertisers.

In writing to Advertisers kindly mention Horticulture

LOPEZIAS, ETC.

LOPEZIAS, 3-in., 3c. Stock Geranium. $5.00 per 100. Coleus, assorted, $2.00. Pansy Giants, $3.00 per 1000. Hardy seedlings, all kinds. Hibiscus Hardy, $6.00 per 100. Hollyhocks, $2.00 per 100. Cash, please. S. P. VAN HEEST, Wortendyke, N. J.

MASTICA

F. O. Pierce Co., New York City. For page see List of Advertisers.

Geo. H. Angermueller, St. Louis, Mo.

NATIONAL NURSERYMAN

National Nurseryman Publishing Co., Inc., Rochester, N. Y. For page see List of Advertisers.

NIKOTEEN

Nicotine Mfg. Co., St. Louis, Mo. For page see List of Advertisers.

NIKOTIANA

Aphine Mfg. Co., Madison, N. J. For page see List of Advertisers.

NURSERY STOCK

P. Ouwerkerk, Weehawken Heights, N. J. For page see List of Advertisers.

W. & T. Smith Co., Geneva, N. Y. For page see List of Advertisers.

Bay State Nurseries, North Abington, Mass. Hardy, Northern Grown Stock. For page see List of Advertisers.

Bobbink & Atkins, Rutherford, N. J. For page see List of Advertisers.

Framingham Nurseries, Framingham, Mass. For page see List of Advertisers.

August Rolker & Sons, New York City. For page see List of Advertisers.

Stuart Low & Co., Harry A. Barnard, representative, Hotel Albert, New York City. For page see List of Advertisers.

NUT GROWING.

The Nut-Grower, Waycross, Ga. For page see List of Advertisers.

ONION SETS

Schilder Bros., Chillicothe, O. Onion Seed—Onion Sets. For page see List of Advertisers.

ORCHID FLOWERS

Jas. McManus, New York, N. Y. For page see List of Advertisers.

ORCHID PLANTS

Julius Roehrs Co., Rutherford, N. J. For page see List of Advertisers.

Stuart Low & Co., Harry A. Barnard, representative, Hotel Albert, New York City. For page see List of Advertisers.

Lager & Hurrell, Summit, N. J.

PALMS, ETC.

Robert Craig Co., Philadelphia, Pa. For page see List of Advertisers.

August Rolker & Sons, New York City For page see List of Advertisers.

A. Leuthy & Co., Roslindale, Boston, Mass. For page see List of Advertisers.

Stuart Low & Co., Harry A. Barnard, representative, Hotel Albert, New York City. For page see List of Advertisers.

Jos. Heacock Co., Wyncote, Pa. For page see List of Advertisers.

PANSY PLANTS

PANSIES—The Big Giant Flowering Kind—$3.00 per 1,000; $25.00 for 10,000. If I could only show the nice plants, hundred of testimonials and repeat orders, I would be flooded with new business. Cash. JAMES MOSS, Wholesale Grower, Johnsville, Pa.

PANSY SEED

Fottler, Fiske, Rawson Co., Boston, Mass. For page see List of Advertisers.

PEONIES

Peonies. The world's greatest collection. 1200 sorts. Send for list. C. BETSCHER, Canal Dover, O.

PECKY CYPRESS BENCHES

A. T. Stearns Lumber Co., Boston, Mass. For page see List of Advertisers.

PIPE AND FITTINGS

Kroeschell Bros. Co., Chicago. For page see List of Advertisers.

King Construction Company, N. Tonawanda, N. Y. Shelf Brackets and Pipe Hangers. For page see List of Advertisers.

PLANT AND BULB IMPORTS

Chas. Schwake & Co., New York City. For page see List of Advertisers.

August Rolker & Sons, New York City. For page see List of Advertisers.

PLANT TRELLISES AND STAKES

Seele's Tieless Plant Stakes and Trellises. H. D. SEELE & SONS, Elkhart, Ind.

PLANT TUBS

H. A. Dreer, Philadelphia, Pa. "Riverton Special." For page see List of Advertisers.

RAFFIA

McHutchison & Co., New York, N. Y. For page see List of Advertisers.

RHODODENDRONS

P. Ouwerkerk, Hoboken, N. J. For page see List of Advertisers.

Framingham Nurseries, Framingham, Mass. For page see List of Advertisers.

RIBBONS AND CHIFFONS

S. S. Pennock-Meehan Co., Philadelphia, Pa. For page see List of Advertisers.

ROSES

Poehlmann Bros. Co., Morton Grove, Ill. For page see List of Advertisers.

P. Ouwerkerk, Hoboken, N. J. For page see List of Advertisers.

Robert Craig Co., Philadelphia, Pa. For page see List of Advertisers.

W. & T. Smith Co., Geneva, N. Y. American Grown Roses. For page see List of Advertisers.

Bay State Nurseries, North Abington, Mass. For page see List of Advertisers.

August Rolker & Sons, New York City. For page see List of Advertisers.

Framingham Nurseries, Framingham, Mass. For page see List of Advertisers.

A. N. Pierson, Inc., Cromwell, Conn. For page see List of Advertisers.

Stuart Low & Co., Harry A. Barnard, representative, Hotel Albert, New York City. For page see List of Advertisers.

THE CONARD & JONES COMPANY. Rose Specialists. West Grove, Pa. Send for offers.

SEASONABLE PLANT STOCK

R. Vincent, Jr. & Sons Co., White Marsh, Md. For page see List of Advertisers.

SEED GROWERS

California Seed Growers' Association San Jose, Cal. For page see List of Advertisers.

SEEDS

Carter's Tested Seeds, Seeds with a Pedigree. Boston, Mass., and London, England For page see List of Advertisers.

Schilder Bros., Chillicothe, O. Onion Seed—Onion Sets. For page see List of Advertisers

Kelway & Son, Langport, Somerset, England. Kelway's Celebrated English Strain Garden Seeds. For page see List of Advertisers.

SEEDS—Continued

Joseph Breck & Sons, Boston, Mass. For page see List of Advertisers.

J. Bolgiano & Son, Baltimore, Md. For page see List of Advertisers.

A. T. Boddington Co., Inc., New York City. For page see List of Advertisers.

Chas. Schwake & Co., New York City For page see List of Advertisers.

Michell's Seed House, Philadelphia, Pa. New Crop Cyclamen Seeds. For page see List of Advertisers.

W. Atlee Burpee & Co., Philadelphia, Pa For page see List of Advertisers.

R. & J. Farquhar & Co., Boston, Mass. Giant Cyclamen Seed. For page see List of Advertisers.

J. M. Thorburn & Co., New York City For page see List of Advertisers.

S. Bryson Ayres Co., Independence, Mo. Sweet Peas. For page see List of Advertisers.

Loechner & Co., New York City. For page see List of Advertisers.

Ant. C. Zvolanek, Lompoc, Cal. Winter Flowering Sweet Pea Seed. For page see List of Advertisers.

S. S. Skidelsky & Co., Philadelphia, Pa. For page see List of Advertisers.

W. E. Marshall & Co., New York City. Seeds, Plants and Bulbs. For page see List of Advertisers.

August Rolker & Sons, New York City. For page see List of Advertisers.

Burnett Bros., 98 Chambers St., New York. For page see List of Advertisers.

Fottler, Fiske, Rawson Co., Boston, Mass. Seeds for the Florist For page see List of Advertisers.

SKINNER IRRIGATION SYSTEM

Skinner Irrigation Co., Brookline, Mass. For page see List of Advertisers.

SPHAGNUM MOSS

Live Sphagnum moss, orchid peat and orchid baskets always on hand. LAGER & HURRELL, Summit, N. J.

STOVE PLANTS

Orchids—Largest stock in the country. Stove plants and Crotons, finest collection. JULIUS ROEHRS CO., Rutherford, N. J.

SWAINSONA

R. Vincent, Jr., & Sons Co., White Marsh, Md. For page see List of Advertisers.

SWEET PEA SEED

Ant. C. Zvolanek, Lompoc, Calif. Gold Medal of Honor Winter Orchid Sweet Peas. For page see List of Advertisers

S. Bryson Ayres Co., Sunnyslope, Independence, Mo. For page see List of Advertisers.

VENTILATING APPARATUS

The Advance Co., Richmond, Ind. For page see List of Advertisers.

The John A. Evans Co., Richmond, Ind. For page see List of Advertisers.

VIOLETS

FIELD-GROWN VIOLET PLANTS.

	100	1000
Princess of Wales	$5.00	$45.00
Lady Campbell	5.00	45.00
Gov. Herrick	5.00	45.00
Marie Louise	5.00	45.00
Farquhar	5.00	45.00
La France	5.00	45.00

WRITE FOR COPY OF OUR MONTHLY PLANT BULLETIN. S. S. PENNOCK-MEEHAN CO., 1608-1620 Ludlow St., Philadelphia, Pa.

For List of Advertisers See Page 435

New Offers In This Issue

BOXWOOD.

Breck-Robinson Nursery Co., Lexington,
Mass.
For page see List of Advertisers.

**COLD STORAGE LILY OF THE
VALLEY.**

Chas. Schwake & Co., Inc., New York City.
For page see List of Advertisers.

DAHLIAS.

S. S. Pennock-Meehan Co., Philadelphia, Pa.
For page see List of Advertisers.

DARWIN BULBS AND HYACINTHS.

Raymond W. Swett, Saxonville, Mass.
For page see List of Advertisers.

**DREER'S SPECIAL OFFER OF HAR-
DY PHLOX AND HERBACE-
OUS PAEONIES.**

Henry A. Dreer, Philadelphia, Pa.
For page see List of Advertisers.

**DUTCH HYACINTHS AND TULIP
BULBS.**

Arthur T. Boddington Co., Inc.,
New York City.
For page see List of Advertisers.

FIELD GROWN VIOLET PLANTS.

Kidder Bros., Lincoln, Mass.
For page see List of Advertisers.

**JAPAN GROWN FREESIAS AND L.
FORMOSUMS.**

Yokohama Nursery Co., Ltd., New York City.
For page see List of Advertisers.

PELARGONIUM CLORINDA

John A. Fraser, Wellesley, Mass.
For page see List of Advertisers.

**STANDARD SPRAY MATERIALS—
SCALECIDE—GARDEN TOOLS,
ETC.**

B. G. Pratt Co., New York City.
For page see List of Advertisers.

WHOLESALE FLORISTS.

United Cut Flower Co., Inc.,
111 W. 28th St., New York City.
For page see List of Advertisers.

In writing to Advertisers kindly mention Horticulture

CLUBS AND SOCIETIES

CONNECTICUT HORTICULTURAL SOCIETY.

This society held its Annual Dahlia Show on September 22-23, in Unity Hall, Pratt street, Hartford. The entries were larger than usual and the dimensions of the hall were hardly equal to the occasion. Vice-President G. H. Hollister acted as superintendent of the exhibition. J. F. Huss decorated the stage, for which he received the prize for the exhibit of most general merit. He also got the Stumpp & Walter cup for best display of annuals. From New Haven we had as exhibitors Alfred E. Doty and John H. Slocombe; from West Haven, C. Louis Alling; and from Taunton, Mass., Henry F. Burt. There were also a number of growers for private estates around Hartford, among whom might be mentioned Niel Nelson and Nathaniel Slocombe, the latter of Farmington. The vegetable exhibit was unusually fine. J. F. Huss carrying off first money for the largest display. There was also a fine display of fruit, Warren S. Mason, of Farmington, having things his own way in this department and also carrying off the silver cup for perennials, valued at $25.

John H. Slocombe and Niel Nelson were 1st and 2nd on seedling dahlias, Mr. Nelson 1st for floral piece. Most of the regular dahlia prizes were taken by the parties above mentioned. There were galadioli, cosmos, asters, etc., in good quantity, from East Hartford Dahlia Gardens, A. Righenzi, H. L. Metcalfe, N. Slocombe, N. Nelson, W. S. Mason and J. F. Huss.

MAPLEWOOD DAHLIA SOCIETY.

The first annual show of the Maplewood Dahlia Society took place in the elegant hall of the Maplewood Field Club, Maplewood, N. J., from 1 P. M. till 10 P. M., followed by two hours of dancing and was favored with every success, good weather, good exhibits and plenty of them and from miles around, the judging being very hard owing to the good quality of flowers. The attendance was far beyond expectations. We have the list of winners in the 28 classes but unfortunately have no copy of the schedule and consequently are not able to tell what the awards represent. The list of winners, however, includes F. V. Braun, A. A. Earl, Mrs. W. F. Duel, Geo. Stevenson, Miss M. Commerford, Walter Lawrence, C. W. Groo, A. W. Pohlman, Mrs. A. G. Seymour, Frank E. Taylor, Mrs. C. W. Pollard, J. R. Le Count, J. H. Ayres, E. B. Phelps and Wm. Larbig.

The premiums which included 19 silver medals were mostly specials contributed by friends of the Society, including J. M. Thorburn & Co., Mrs. J. R. Le Count, Henry A. Dreer, H. F. Michell Co., H. B. Fraentzel, Walter Lawrence, John Le Count, F. & F. Nurseries, Geo. S. Salmon Co., Samuel H. Ross, Wm. H. Kemp, Mrs. F. F. Durand, Wm. H. Solph, C. Kessinger & Co., Chas. M. Decker & Bro., L. I. Dahlia Gardens, S. G. Memory, Mrs. W. M. Gray and Mrs. W. F. Deuel.

The special Manda prizes were won

by Hugo Volkening, Orange, N. J. The judges were William Reid, John Garvin and Dietrich and Kinsgrab.

LENOX HORTICULTURAL SOCIETY.

The annual exhibition of fruit, flowers and vegetables will be held in the Town Hall, Lenox, Mass., October 26 and 27. The schedule of prizes has been issued and copies may be had on application to the secretary, John Carman, Lenox, Mass. The following individuals and firms appear as donors of special prizes:

W. E. S. Griswold, silver cup, for collection of eighteen kinds of vegetables; W. H. Walker, silver cup, for six blooms of the new chrysanthemum Mrs. W. H. Walker; R. & J. Farquhar & Co., silver cup, for best collection of twelve kinds of vegetables; Hitchings & Co., silver cup, for best two bunches of grapes; Lenox Horticultural Society, silver cup, for best ten blooms of chrysanthemums, one variety; C. H. Totty, The Wells gold and bronze medals, for two blooms of Adele Griswold.

Cash prizes are offered by A. H. Hews Co., Frank Howard, Bon Arbor Chemical Co., H. A. Dreer, A. N. Pierson Co., W. E. Marshall, Scott Bros., Lord & Burnham Co., Peter Henderson & Co., Carter's Tested Seeds and John Wilk.

OYSTER BAY HORTICULTURAL SOCIETY.

At the monthly meeting of the Oyster Bay (N. Y.) Horticultural Society, the exhibition tables were well filled with fruit, flowers and vegetables. The society's prizes were awarded to Chas. Milburn for tomatoes, and to James Duthie for dahlias and apples. Honorable mention was given John Sorosik and Jos. Robinson for dahlias; Chas. Milburn for marigolds; Alfred Walker for gladioli; A. Yanuchi for celery. David Hothersall received a cultural certificate for roses and Chas. Milburn received the thanks of the society for antirrhinums. Prizes were received from I. Hicks & Son, Frost & Bartlett Co. and Vaughan's Seed Store. At the next meeting prizes will be awarded for chrysanthemums, cauliflower and celery. The Dahlia Show, to be held on October 5 and 6, bids fair to be the best in the history of the Society. Schedules for the Dahlia and Chrysanthemum Shows, to be held on November 2, are now ready. A. R. KENNEDY, Sec.

AMERICAN ROSE SOCIETY.

The Cleveland Flower Show is progressing and it seems as though there is likely to be considerable of an exhibit there. The interest in the rose exhibit is developing. Two more special prizes have been offered, one from Storrs & Harrison of $25, and another of $10 for the prettiest vase of cut roses, the decision to be made by a vote of lady visitors. There will also be a meeting of the American Rose Society held at that time in the Coliseum. Also an Executive meeting of the Committee in New York City, October 11.

BENJAMIN HAMMOND, Sec'y.
Beacon, N. Y.

ST. LOUIS CLUBS AND SOCIETIES.

The County Growers' Association meets on October 6 at the Eleven Mile House.

The Lady Florists' Home Circle meets Wednesday, October 13, at the home of Mrs. E. Schray.

The St. Louis Florist Club meets on the grounds of the Bourdet Floral Co. on Thursday afternoon, October 14. This is at the home of the club's president, Jules Bourdet.

The Retail Florists' Association meets on Monday, October 18, at the Mission Inn Garden.

HOUSTON, TEXAS.
State Flower Show.

The Flower Show promises to exceed last year's show by one hundred per cent. About fifty per cent. of the florists of the state expect to make exhibits. They realize the value of this from last year's show, and are all coming in on this year's show. Aside from this, all of the out-of-the-state exhibitors of last year and a great many additional are planning exhibits for this year, which shows they find it worth while.

We feel that the S. A. F. Convention for Houston in 1916 has a great deal to do with the added interest in our Flower Show here.

The S. A. F. Convention Outlook.

William C. Gloeckner, of Albany, N. Y. writes that he will organize a party from his city for the Houston Convention. He says that the florists of his city expect to take advantage of this opportunity to visit the South. It is more than likely that this party will go by boat from New York to New Orleans or Galveston—this however, will be decided later.

Mr. Gloeckner says—"Houston is a long way from home but I am going to do everything in my power to attend the Convention next year and I will try to get every florist in Albany to accompany me on this trip."

The indications are, plans being formed so early, that this is going to be a record-breaking convention.

R. C. KERR.

SAN FRANCISCO.

Donald McLaren has returned from a business trip in the northwestern part of the state.

C. Kooyman has on display this week a new seedling dahlia from Burns & Co., a clear white color and in form much like Minnie Burgle.

Daniel MacRorie expects to take a trip to the southern part of the state shortly with his sister who is visiting here from South Orange, N. J.

MacRorie, McLaren & Co. have just completed the renovation of the Hawaiian state building at the Exposition, supplying many tropical plants, palms, etc.

At the regular monthly meeting of the Ladies' Auxiliary of the Pacific Coast Horticultural Society next week, papers will be read on "Roses at the Exposition."

Robert Simpson, of Clifton, N. J., accompanied by his wife and children, arrived a few days ago to visit the Exposition, after spending a week at Yellowstone Park and a week at Portland.

Gustave A. Navlet, who for many years conducted a florist shop in Sacramento, Cal., prior to moving to Eureka about seven years ago, died in that city on September 16. The deceased was a brother of Charles C. Navlet, who conducts the flower and seed department in the Emporium in this city.

PITTSBURGH.

Mr. and Mrs. Julius W. Ludwig have returned from a three-weeks' visit with relatives in Milwaukee, Wis.

The E. C. Ludwig Company has just begun the building of an additional greenhouse, 25 by 200, at Mars, Pa.

Miss Abby Fuhr, the bookkeeper for the E. C. Ludwig Co., has been spending a two weeks' vacation on the Great Lakes.

William Lowe, the Diamond St. florist, and his brother, have returned from a trip to the Pacific Coast including the two Expositions.

Harvey C. Sheaff, manager for Mrs. E. A. Williams, is spending a month in visiting the cities of the Western Slope, returning home on October 6.

Mr. and Mrs. Victor Bergman, the former of Friedman & Bergman of Chicago, have returned home after spending a month with Mrs. Bergman's parents, Mr. and Mrs. Gustave Ludwig.

The branch house of the Zieger Company is soon to be removed from Penn avenue to North Highland avenue adjoining the Dovenshire market. Meanwhile important improvements and changes are being made in the branch house-to-be.

Mr. and Mrs. Edward L. McGrath, the former manager of the Blind Floral Co., have returned from a visit in Cleveland, O. The firm is adding materially to the appearance of its store room by two additional display cases, repainting and handsome new draperies.

S. J. or "Jack" Frampton, as he is more familiarly known to his friends, has left the G. P. Weaklin & Co., for the Zieger Co., where he has assumed the responsibilities of "outside man." Francis Smith formerly with O. R. Cramer of Uniontown succeeds Mr. Frampton at Weaklin's.

The Pennsylvania Railroad Company is beautifying its station and the approaches at Glencairn, Pa., following up the plan it adopted a few years ago. The banks where the road runs through a deep cut, have been sodded and flower beds added. Grass and flowers also adorn the walks in and about the station grounds. This work was done under the supervision of Nicholas Cassalucia, who has charge of the horticultural features of the railroad for sixty miles east of Pittsburgh.

Anthony W. Smith, Jr., has returned to business, following a week's illness. The A. W. Smith Company are known as extensive advertisers as "America's Largest Florists." Among their flowers the Smiths have on sale some attractive Bombay and brass cages containing Brazillian cardinals, parokeets and Tyrolese canaries.

Malden, Mass. — Bids have been called for by John G. Tilden, secretary of the Park Commissioners of Malden, for the erection of a comfort station and shelter on Ferryway Green, one of the fine playgrounds of which the city boasts. McNaughton & Robinson of Boston are the architects.

OBITUARY.

Martin H. Hess.

Martin H. Hess, 83 years old, retired florist, died at Lititz, Pa., on Sept. 14, from infirmities of age. His wife died last April. His survivors are a son and a brother, the Rev. Jonas Hess.

Albert H. Smith.

Albert Harrison Smith, for more than thirty years a traveling nursery stock salesman, mostly in Massachusetts territory, died September 24 at his home in Bangor, Me., aged 75 years. He is survived by his wife and two children.

William Murphy.

William Murphy, the well-known florist, of Cincinnati, Ohio, passed away on last Monday morning at his home at the age of 57. He had been seriously ill for the greater part of a year but at times rallied so that his family and many friends thought he would recover his health and be like his former self.

Mr. Murphy has been in the florist business for a period covering more than 33 years, first as a grower and for the last fifteen years as a wholesale commission florist. He was very successful in these enterprises. During this time he took a very active interest in the trade and its various organizations and functions in this vicinity, and he held positions of trust and responsibility in the Cincinnati Florist Society, local exhibitions, etc.

The deceased's wife, four daughters and his son W. Ray Murphy, who will continue his father's business, survive him.

GREENHOUSES BUILDING OR CONTEMPLATED.

Sharon, Pa.—John Murchie, rebuilding.

Tyone, Pa.—Engleman Bros., house 35x260.

Flushing, N. Y.—Otto Muller, house 30x100.

Grand Rapids, Mich.—Lewis Kunst, house 24x65.

Holliston, Mass.—Eastern Nurseries, house, 20x75.

Holland, Mich. — Henry Ebelink, house 20x130.

Fairmont, W. Va.—Lee Yost, 1409 Ninth St., house 18x60.

Elmira, N. Y.—G. T. Janowoski, 114 Esty street, King house.

Beverly, Mass.—P. E. Sanborn, Winthrop avenue, one house.

Hicksville, O. — Chas. Seibert, Defiance avenue, one house.

Hutchinson, Kan. — Koon Beck, Riverside Park, house 40x80.

Jamaica, N. Y.—A. L. Miller, five Lord & Burnham houses.

Baltimore, Md.—A. S. Richmond, East Erdman avenue, house 13x200.

Birmingham, Ala.—Huch Seales, two houses. Parker estate, carnation house.

Fort Smith, Ark. — Geo. Rye, 11th street and Garrison avenue, one house.

NEW CORPORATIONS.

Columbus, Ohio—Columbus Floral Co.; capital, $70,000 to $80,000; Chas. L. Reach.

BUSINESS TROUBLES.

Stoneham, Mass. — John L. White, florist; assets $2,512, liabilities $2,795. Moore Seed Company, of Philadelphia, is said to be the largest unsecured creditor, amount $653.00.

Vol. XXII
No. 15
OCT. 9
1915

HORTICULTURE

The Vincent Dahlia Show

View showing the arrangement of Dahlias at the annual exhibition in White Marsh,
Md., last week.

Published **Every Saturday** at 147 Summer Street, **Boston, Mass.**
Subscription, $1.00

LIST OF ADVERTISERS

FOR BUYERS' DIRECTORY AND READY REFERENCE GUIDE
SEE PAGES 488, 489, 490, 491

NOTES ON CULTURE OF FLORISTS' STOCK
CONDUCTED BY

John J. M. Farrell

Questions by our readers in line with any of the topics presented on this page will be cordially received and promptly answered by Mr. Farrell. Such communications should invariably be addressed to the office of HORTICULTURE.
"If vain our toil, we ought to blame the culture, not the soil."—*Pope.*

Mignonette

See that the plants are well supported to keep the stems upright. Keep all unnecessary side growths removed to throw the full strength into the flowering spike. Where the plants have been started early the bench will in most cases be filled with roots so now is a good time to give them a mulch of equal parts of soil and well rotted cow manure. This can be put on about half an inch deep. Don't put it on too heavy but follow with another mulch in five or six weeks. It will do them more good this way. On bright mornings they can be syringed. Look the beds over often for the dry spots and water them. Give light fumigation every week and plenty of ventilation when possible.

Double Tulips for Easter

Double tulips, such as Murillo, Salvator Rosa and Couronne d'Or are particularly good for pot and pan culture. 6 to 10-inch pans seem to be the best sellers. Any good compost will do. See that each pan or pot has good drainage. It is well to have quite a number in 4 and 5-inch pots, three bulbs in the former and five in the latter. These pans or pots can be placed in a deep frame and plunged and with some protection will do until about five weeks before Easter.

Ericas

These old favorites are coming to the front more and more as pot plants. For the Christmas holidays there is nothing better than Erica melanthera. Give them the coolest house as they will not require much pushing to be in on that date. Anywhere from 45 to 48 degrees night temperature will hold them in good shape. If there is any plant that likes lot of air it is the Erica. Give ventilation on all possible occasions, and remember to keep the compost in the pots in an even state of moisture all the time. If they do not soak through, which is often the case, plunge them in a tub of water and leave them there for a while.

Lilium longiflorum

Longiflorums for Easter can now be potted into 6-inch pots which will be large enough for the trade. Use good new soil, three parts, well rotted cow or horse manure one part, and see that each pot has plenty of drainage. Put in some cool place until they have made lots of roots; a cellar or a deep frame will suit them. Sometime before January they can be placed in a house that stands about 50 degrees at night. If there is not room in cellar or frame they can be placed on a high piece of ground and covered with about six inches of soil. When cold weather sets in they can have some long manure put over them for protection.

Phlox

From now on up to the end of October is the best time to make new borders or divide and replant old ones. When phloxes are grown commercially it is essential that the soil be spaded deep—or still better, trenched. Then apply a generous amount of well rotted manure. Any extra labor and fertilizer put into the preparation of the border will be repaid for some years afterward in results. It pays to trench the ground well for this perennial and have plenty of well decomposed manure thoroughly incorporated with the soil. Good varieties to plant are Nettie Stuart white shaded pink, White Swan, pure white and Rosy Gem clear rose. A few specially good forms of P. decussata are Independence, Le Cygne, Albatre, Jeanne D'Arc, all pure white; Le Soleil rose, Coquelicot, orange scarlet; General Chanzy scarlet; R. P. Struthers, salmon pink.

Temperature

We are now coming to the season when we can keep a more even temperature in our several departments. The cool house can be kept at from 45 to 50 for night with a rise during sunshine to 55 to 60 degrees. Intermediate house 55 to 60 at night, day 65 to 70 degrees. Warm house 60 to 65 degrees night temperature, day 70 to 75 degrees. This temperature is meant for a general run of florists' stock only.

Next Week:—Bouvardias; Crops to Take Place of Chrysanthemums; Bulbs for Outdoors; Forcing Gladioli; Preparing Sweet Pea Ground; Shamrocks for St. Patrick's Day.

PERRENNIAL DELPHINIUMS

The Larkspur is among the most beautiful and useful of our hardy perennial plants, and as a material for planting has for some few years been receiving ever increasing attention. Many beautiful hybrids have been raised varying in height and color and affording material for almost any color or height combination desired, either in the garden border or rockery.

The culture of Delphiniums is simple, in fact more simple than many of our herbaceous plants. Good cultivation of the soil around their roots will be found to be all that is necessary. The plants should not be overfed, being well satisfied with a good garden soil. A mulch of manure should never be put over or around them as they will merely rot away, or produce inferior flowers. If necessary to mulch in winter a few dry leaves will suit the purpose admirably.

Propagation of Delphiniums is accomplished best by seed. Of course in some of the hybrid varieties all plants will not come true, but the majority will. Seed should be sown as soon as ripe, for only a small percentage of seed will germinate after being kept a year. If sown as soon as ready plants will be produced before winter that can be planted out and will flower finely the following summer. Other means of propagation are by division or by cuttings of the young shoots in spring or autumn, potted separately and placed in a cold frame. These cuttings will make good plants by spring and will flower at the same time as the divisions. This is probably the best and safest way to propagate any particular variety.

In glancing through nurserymen's catalogues one will see many fine varieties listed, but there are a great many even more beautiful ones which have not as yet found their way into the United States in commercial quantities. The following is a small list of some of the most desirable varieties from the standpoint of the planter, including some of the species which are seldom grown in gardens, giving notes as to color, height, etc. This list, as will be seen is far from complete, but I trust may be helpful to some of my readers.

Delphinium cashmirianum, pale blue with flowers one to two inches across. Ht. 12-18 in.

Delphinium nudicaule, red; petals clear yellow, long spurred, a Californian species growing from 10-18 in. high.

Delphinium formosum, the old-fashioned garden Larkspur, of which a great many varieties exist.

Delphinium belladonna, another old variety with a profusion of transparent sky-blue flowers. This species does not often set fertile seed, although I notice some seedsmen offering it and claiming that they have managed to procure fertile seeds.

The following are all hybrids—some of belladonna, some of formosum type, and while a great many of them are offered in this country they are not procurable in any great quantity.

Antigone—Bright blue, lilac centre, fine for grouping.

Bleu Tendre—Silvery white single flowers flushed very light blue and carried on long spike. Ht. 4-5 ft.

King of Delphiniums—Enormous semi-double flowers on tall spikes to a height of 5 ft. Deep indigo blue with inner petals plum color; large white centre tipped purple.

Lizzie van Veen—Long spikes and unusually large single flowers; Cambridge blue with a white eye.

K. T. Caron—Gentian blue with conspicuous white eye; semi-double, very large spikes.

Mme. Violet Geslin—Large round flowers, blue, with lavender centre and white eye, semi-double.

Polar Star—Ivory white, semi-double on dwarf spikes of branching habit.

Mrs. Creighton—Semi-double; Oxford blue, dark plum colored centre and brown eye.

Queen Wilhelmina—Sky-blue, slightly veined rose, white eye.

Turquoise—Semi-double; turquoise blue slightly tinged rose.

Queen of the Blues—Gentian blue; 18 in.

Capri—Sky-blue, blooming over long period. 5 ft.

Lamartine—Prussian blue, with white eye.

Moerheimi—White; from June to frost. 5 ft.

Mr. J. S. Brunton—An improved belladonna with larger flowers in great quantity throughout the summer. 3 to 4 ft.

Persimmon—Sky-blue, of the belladonna type.

Mrs. Thompson—Belladonna hybrid; deep blue flowers with a brown bell.

Christine Kellway—Sky-blue and white eye.

Langport Blue—Five feet or more in height; bright blue.

Rev. W. Wilks—Deep purple flushed plum color with prominent dark eye; 4½ ft.

Sir George Newnes—Semi-double; cobalt blue, inner petals flushed plum color. 4½ ft.

Sir Walter Scott—Blue flushed violet with conspicuous black centre, 4½ ft.

Althos—Purple and violet with white centre, 5-6 ft.

True-Blue—Perhaps the richest colored of all; strong constitution, 5-6 ft.

General Baden Powell—Lavender tinted rose, with a brownish black eye. 4½ ft.

James Kellway—Violet blue; white eye. 5-6 ft.

Princess Maud—Sky-blue, veined rose, with white eye. Semi-double. 5½ ft.

Sir Trevor Lawrence—Sky-blue with inner petals flushed rose pink, white eye. 6 ft.

Rev. E. Lascelles—Of recent introduction. Violet-blue with white eye.

Statuaire Rude—Soft lavender with slight flush of rose. Semi-double and very large.

Carmen—A veritable giant, 8 ft in height. Gentian-blue flushed rose in centre, black eye.

E. Augustus Bowles—6 ft. brilliant blue with large dark centre.

Mona—Massive spikes, gentian-blue and heliotrope with white eye.

Perfection—Flowers large rose-mauve on massive spikes. 6 ft.

Progression—Semi-double with bright yellow centre.

Queen Mary—Azure with white and yellow centres.

Rozenlust—Rosy mauve, double.

Ustane—Double, circular flowers of rosy mauve with dark eye.

Duke of Connaught—Single flowers, 3 in. across, crimson purple with white centre, on 6 ft. stems.

Geneva—Branching stems; single; light blue with bright eye.

Julia—Cornflower blue and rose.

Lizzie—Branching spikes on five foot stems; single, sky-blue with cream centre.

Masterpiece—Gentian-blue and rose purple with white centre.

Nellie—Sky-blue and white.

Portia—Cornflower blue flushed rose with black centre. A tall single variety.

Queen of the Lilacs—Lilac with white eye, on tall stems. Single.

Nulli Secundus—White, new and rare. Bold spikes on 6 ft. stems. Flowers white except for dark eye.

Hubert M. Canning

Jamaica Plain, Mass.

ROSE GROWING UNDER GLASS

CONDUCTED BY

Arthur C. Ruzicka

Questions by our readers in line with any of the topics presented on this page will be cordially received and promptly answered by Mr. Ruzicka. Such communications should invariably be addressed to the office of HORTICULTURE.

Asparagus and Smilax

These two greens are so common on a rose growing establishment that a word or two on them will not be out of place in these columns. Where there is enough headroom in the cross houses smilax is usually grown, the remainder of the space being devoted to asparagus. If a little attention is given these greens the returns will be found a good deal more than if they are merely planted and watered once in a while. In the first place, these greens will thrive better if allowed a little more heat, then more moisture, not at the roots so much as in the air, so it will be well to damp down in the cross houses that are hot and dry as a rule. This should not be allowed to get into the rose houses, however, as roses have different habits and the wet warm atmosphere will not be beneficial to them. For fertilizer horse manure will be found better for asparagus and smilax than cow manure would be, and the greens will make a quicker growth if this is used. A little nitrate of soda every now and then as the plants need it will also hasten their growth. As a rule asparagus is not planted every year, but kept going as long as it will produce greens for cutting, and if this is the case with yours it will be well to use a little lime now while the chrysanthemums will be in season and greens will not sell so well. If the greens have been forced all summer it will be necessary to dry them off a little now applying a dose of lime to sweeten the soil and to kill what earth worms there may be in it. If there are too many of these they will be largely responsible for the plants not drying out well, as they fill the bottom layer of soil with slime and stop up the pores, thus preventing air from getting in much, and this will keep the soil wet and soggy. When applying the lime make sure that the greens are dry so that none of the lime will stick to the tops and thus render it useless for market. Lime can also be slacked and used in the form of liquid manure and if made strong enough will be even more effective in ridding the soil of worms. Sow bugs and thrips also bother asparagus and smilax, but these can be killed with Slug Shot for the first, and any good insecticide advertised in HORTI-CULTURE. The work of thrips on smilax can be noticed by the small white marks all over the bottom leaves, and often it is possible to catch the thrips at work.

Mildew

A little sulphur applied to pipes will generally rid the houses of this disease, but should the plants have become very soft because of being forced too much or for any other reason, mildew will set in the very first opportunity it gets and will be hard to eradicate for a while. In a case like that sulphur fumes would have to be made quite strong to kill the disease, and a continued use of this would be apt to bleach the flowers to a certain degree, depending on how long the plants are exposed to the fumes. In cases that promise to be bad at all, and with buds nearly showing color we would not use sulphur for the reasons stated but would spray the plants with Fungine, advertised elsewhere. Many growers use it regularly as a preventive, and where this can be done it is better than the sulphur treatment although a trifle more expensive. However, with careful attention paid to the ventilators and to the feeding of the plants there should be little trouble with mildew. Roses enjoy plenty of air so it is best to keep the air in the houses fresh and sweet, even though it does take a little coal to do it. Keep air on all night except in severe storms or when the temperature outside falls below 26.

Cover Crops

The proper preparation of soil for the roses before planting is playing a more important part in the growing every year, for, with keen competition, low prices for roses grown, high cost of labor and raw materials, growers cannot afford to let go anything that can be done to give them better roses and sooner, for the sooner the plants start cutting after planting the better. To have proper soil for the plants it will be necessary to look after the fields well, even if this does seem to be out of our line. The ground that is to be seeded to grass to grow sod in the future, should be plowed up as soon as possible and seeded to rye or wheat. It would have been better to have done this earlier as then a little winter vetch could be added, and this would enrich the soil a good deal by storing nitrogen which the bacteria on its roots take from the air. In the spring this can be plowed under and the field seeded to grass, or to some cover crop to be plowed under later, and the grass seeded in late summer. If the ground is weedy it would be well to let the weeds grow up and plow them under before they go to seed, repeating this operation until the soil is nearly free from weeds. Avoid using old greenhouse soil on lots where the sod is to be taken for the heaps in the near future. There are certain insects and fungi that take several years to die so it will be best to use the soil for fields where farm or garden crops are to be grown. Never allow any soil to lay exposed to the weather over winter. A large amount of plant food is wasted in this way every year, especially on sloping ground where the soil is bound to wash. All growers know the important part played by good soil in successful rose growing, and the ideal soil can seldom be had from natural fields. Most of the soil has to be made, so if this end has not been looked after in the past it can be turned into profit to look after the soil-growing fields, and beginning right now.

HORTICULTURE

VOL. XXII   **OCTOBER 9, 1915**   **NO. 15**

PUBLISHED WEEKLY BY

HORTICULTURE PUBLISHING CO.
147 Summer Street, Boston, Mass.

Telephone, Oxford 292.
WM. J. STEWART, Editor and Manager.

SUBSCRIPTION RATES:
One Year, in advance, $1.00; To Foreign Countries, $2.00; To
Canada, $1.50.

ADVERTISING RATES:

Per Inch, 30 Inches to page.......................... $1.00
Discounts on Contracts for consecutive insertions, as follows:
    One month (4 times), 5 per cent.; three months (13 times), 10
per cent.; six months (26 times), 20 per cent.; one year (52 times),
30 per cent.
    Page and half page space, special rates on application.

Entered as second-class matter December 8, 1914, at the Post Office
at Boston, Mass., under the Act of Congress of March 3, 1879.

CONTENTS

"Good Times" — Are the "good times" really here once more? It seems almost too good to be true. The improved tone of the flower market reports from practically all sections is very pleasing. The period of depression has been a long one, particularly in the eastern part of the country, and very dispiriting has been the tardy coming of the longed-for revival. Just to what extent the disappearance of the outdoor flowers and light cut of the indoor product at the present moment is responsible for the better conditions we can only conjecture but the hopeful activity which seems to be developing in all the commercial centres, in every line of trade, should and probably will include all the horticultural industries in its refreshing influence. HORTICULTURE hopes to see the flower people—growers and dealers, and those in all related lines come now into the enjoyment of a season of uninterrupted prosperity.

Ways and methods — Flower growers for the wholesale markets will now be considering the ways and means for disposing of their products to the best advantage during the coming season. Each has the right to conduct his business in such manner as pleases him best but we have always regarded the custom of a certain class of growers of shifting repeatedly during the season from one wholesale house to another for the purpose of playing the wholesale men against one another in the hope of extracting from them larger returns, as an unfortunate thing for the business, in which, however, not all the wholesalers themselves are entirely blameless. Any course which tends to stability and harmony now will help all around, and all should work hand in hand to place the business, as a whole, upon a more substantial basis than ever before. A long step to that end would be a closer personal relationship and acquaintance between growers, wholesalers and retailers in the same community. Their interests are closely interlocked and what makes for real permanent welfare for one makes for the prosperity of all.

Dahlia progress — After attending a few of the dahlia exhibitions this season one finds it increasingly difficult to distinguish between the various classes as hitherto defined. Even the expert finds it next to impossible to draw the line between "decorative" and "peony flowered" as represented by the new varieties constantly coming forward. We understand the Dahlia Society proposes to tackle this class problem, among its other ambitious aims, and see if something cannot be done to segregate the varieties under such distinguishing characteristics that the puzzling problems which judges and others have had to contend with will be eliminated. Our present system of classification is largely an inheritance from the time when regularity of outline, arrangement of petals, etc., was the supreme test by which a variety was approved or condemned—when a pointed petal was regarded as a fatal blemish and any suggestion of an open centre was almost a crime. The formalists of a generation or more ago would stand aghast could they see what are now regarded as worthy of admiration and honor among dahlias. "The world do move," and insofar as this applies to the dahlia, we think it is moving in the right direction.

HARDY VINES

We are indebted to The Garden Magazine, Garden City, N. Y., for the use of the accompanying cut, which shows so effectively the characteristics of some of the hardy vines which are worth growing for flower or foliage effects. Several of the vines shown are among the new species collected by E. H. Wilson in China and the cut is used as one of the illustrations in an article contributed by that gentleman to The Garden Magazine which appears in the September issue and which we commend to our readers as very interesting and instructive and well worth careful perusal.

Of Clematis montana rubens, Mr. Wilson says:

"The white flowered C. montana from Eastern Asia is an old favorite. A variety of this (C. montana var. rubens) with rose-colored flowers 2¼-3 inches across and dark foliage, which I had the pleasure of introducing to cultivation in 1900, is acclaimed by garden lovers to be one of the most beautiful of all the clematis. Around Boston it has not proved completely hardy but at Newport, R. I., some good examples may be seen."

It will not be out of place here to recall the fact that the first public mention of these new hardy vines in this country was made by Mr. Wilson in our issues of March 12 and 19, 1910, in a series of articles which he wrote for HORTICULTURE at that time. The several new species of Clematis, Rubus, Vitis and Actinidia which are now recognized as introductions of superior merit were there described and illustrations were shown of a number of them. On March 12 Mr. Wilson contributed some very interesting and hopeful notes on Clematis, stating that not fewer than sixty-five species occur in China, and mentioning Armandi and montana in its varieties rubens, Wilsoni and sericia as among the most promising.

ASPIDISTRA.

The aspidistra is one of the best of decorative foliage plants. Its value as a house plant lies in the fact that it is indifferent to neglect. It seems to be able to withstand hot air, gas and all the hard usage possible. Twenty years ago aspidistras were to be found in nearly every collection. They were familiar plants of our grandmothers. Today we see very few. One use, however, has been found for it and that is for renting purposes. It is also used to some extent in window boxes and vases in the city. It will thrive in dark places such as halls, etc.

China is the original home of this plant. The commonest species are A. lurida and a variegated form A. lurida variegata. The variegated form is more attractive and grown to a larger extent.

The plants may be propagated by division in early spring. They may also be propagated by cutting up the rhizomes into pieces one inch to an inch and a half long and planting in flats.

They will thrive in any fairly rich soil and are not particular as to temperature. A house kept at about 60 degrees is, however, best.

Amherst, Mass.   C. E. WILDON.

CLEVELAND FLOWER SHOW

All the nine committees in charge of the various branches of work in connection with the Cleveland Flower Show are each holding meetings of their own and beginning to get busy.

At a meeting of the general committees made up of the various chairmen, held at the Hollenden Hotel, October 1st, M. A. Vinson, secretary to the committees made a detailed report of his recent eastern trip. He explained the many details that were necessary to complete the arrangement with the New York Central R. R. for them to handle one of the large plants grown by Mr. John Canning, on the estate of Mr. Adolph Lewisohn, at Ardsley, N. Y. A definite decision regarding this shipment will be made this week upon the return of Mr. Lewisohn.

At the present time there are 46 representative firms included in our list of trade exhibitors, as follows:

F. R. Pierson; Tarrytown, N. Y.; Standard Pump & Engine Co., Cleveland; Fowler Mfg. Co., Cleveland; Hitchings & Co., Elizabeth, N. J.; Richmond Cedar Works, Richmond, Va.; Grasselli Chemical Co., Cleveland; Mentor Nurseries, Mentor, Ohio; Merkle & Son, Mentor, Ohio; Advance Co., Richmond, Ind.; Lord & Burnham Co., Cleveland; Stumpp & Walter Co., New York City; Henry A. Dreer, Philadelphia; Eagle Wire Works, Cleveland; H. F. Michell Co., Philadelphia; Julius Roehre Co., Rutherford, N. J.; A. N. Pierson, Inc., Cromwell, Conn.; Chas. Reep, Cleveland; Geo. Bowman Co., Cleveland; Chas. H. Totty, Madison, N. J.; M. Rice Co., Philadelphia; Robert Craig & Co., Philadelphia; H. Bayersdorfer & Co., Philadelphia; A. L. Randall Co., Chicago; Tajimi Co., New York City; Jos. Neidinger Co., Philadelphia; Sixth City Wire Co., Cleveland; Lion & Co., New York City; Jos. Stern Co., Cleveland; Arnold Paper Box Co., Chicago; J. L. Schiller, Toledo, O.; Storrs & Harrison Co., Painesville; Naumann Co., Cleveland; Chris Knuth, Euclid, O.; Ralph M. Ward & Co., New York; Scheepers & Co., New York; Florists' Telegraph Delivery Association, Cleveland; Wertheimer Bros., New York; Florists' Exchange, New York; Lutton Co., Jersey City; Reed & Keller, New York; Schloss Bros., New York; Bobbink & Atkins, Rutherford, N. J.; Russin & Handlng, New York; B. Hammond Tracy, Wenham, Mass.; D. D. Johnson, Chicago, Ill.; Pletcher & Leland, Zanesville, O.; S. S. Pennock-Meehan Co., Philadelphia, Pa.

Their locations are grouped so as to come before the retailers, commercial growers, or private growers, as they prefer.

The committees are most enthusiastic over the bright outlook for the success of the largest undertaking the Cleveland florists have ever handled. The out-of-town attendance of commercial and private growers is expected to be in the neighborhood of 600.

The following letter has been mailed to the secretaries of 115 Florists' Clubs and Societies in the United States and Canada:

Executive Office, 356 Leader Building,
Cleveland, October 2, 1915.
30 Days Before the BIG SHOW.
To Members of Every Florists' Club and Horticultural Society in the United States.
Ladies and Gentlemen:
We wish to extend an invitation to the members of your Club, to attend our big Flower Show to be held November 10th to 14th.
Your members can look upon this as a business trip because of the fact that they will see the exhibits of some fifty "live" growers, manufacturers and dealers in supplies of all kinds, and in that way they

will get in touch with the newest things on the market.
Please do not get an impression, however, that there will be no pleasure for your members coming to Cleveland. We just followed the old saying and placed business before pleasure, but assure you we have a good entertainment committee on the job.
We suggest that you appoint an "official chaperone" together with a transportation committee to work together and secure a large enough party to make a special car or several cars possible from your city to Cleveland.
The enclosed slip will tell you of five important meetings to be held during the Show. Thanking you for prompt action on this subject, we remain
Yours, for a big Cleveland Flower Show,
H. P. KNOBLE,
Chairman, General Committee.

CHICAGO GRAND FLORAL FESTIVAL.

At the regular meeting of the Chicago Grand Floral Festival executive committee, held at the Morrison Hotel, September 30, much progress was made with flower show business, those in attendance being A. Henderson, W. N. Rudd, W. J. Keimel, August Poehlmann, Peter Reinberg, N. P. Miller, Geo. Asmus, H. B. Kennicott, August Koch and Robert Brenton.

Nic. Wietor was elected vice-chairman of the ways, means and audit committee, E. F. Kurowski, chairman of the reception committee, Payne Jennings, chairman retail florists' committee, Robert Brenton, chairman special features committee, and A. Henderson, Geo. Asmus and N. P. Miller, committee of management. Guy W. French has been appointed manager.

Chairman Brenton has many novel attractions in preparation for this exhibition and it now seems certain these special features will draw large audiences.

Chairman Keimel promises an unusually interesting series of lectures, along popular lines with stereopticon pictures.

Chairman Vaughan, of the poster committee, reports the fine poster in the hands of the lithographer will be ready in good season.

August Koch, of the west side parks, was elected chief of the information bureau.   MICHAEL BARKER,
Chairman Publicity Committee.

GRAND NATIONAL FALL FLOWER SHOW.

Preparations for the Grand National Fall Flower Show to be held at the Palace of Horticulture Exposition grounds, San Francisco, October 21st to 26th, under the auspices of the Pacific Coast Horticultural Society in conjunction with the Chrysanthemum Society of America and the Department of Horticulture of the Panama-Pacific International Exposition are in active progress, and much interest is being shown in the event. H. Plath is manager and John R. Fotheringham, assistant manager, while the exhibition committee is composed as follows: Daniel MacRorie, T. Taylor, F. Pelicano, E. James, Angelo J. Rossi, D. Raymond, W. A. Hofinghof, Donald McLaren, Wm. Kettlewell, Wm. Munro, John R. Fotheringham, P. Ellings and M. Poss. A large number of prizes are offered, including many exposition

medals and cash prizes donated by the Panama-Pacific Exposition Co., as well as various special prizes contributed by members of the trade associations, etc. Awards will be made for eight classes of exhibits, including 112 different numbers. Principal attention is given to chrysanthemums, but other flowers will be entered for awards also. Several prizes are offered for roses, carnations, dahlias, orchids, etc. Competition is open to all in all classes, with two or three exceptions, and plants and flowers displayed do not necessarily have to be grown by the exhibitor. Among the special features four awards are to be made for the best table decoration to be competed for five successive days, chrysanthemums to be the principal feature the first day, roses the second, dahlias the third and any other flower the fourth and growing plants the fifth. From present indications the approaching show will be about the finest held here this year, —and there have been more shows than usual on account of the exposition.

INTERNATIONAL FLOWER SHOW NEW YORK.

The schedule of premiums to be offered at the International Flower Show to be held in the Grand Central Palace, New York, April 5th to 12th next, has been issued and copies may be obtained on application to the secretary.

The premiums offered are again on a very liberal scale, and there are some notable additions to the classes. In the section for commercial growers covering roses in pots and tubs, there are three prizes offered for a display of rose plants arranged as a rose garden covering 500 sq. ft., respectively $500, $300 and $200. In this class last year, there were but two prizes, $300 and $200.

Some important additions have been made to the classes covering bulbous plants. There is a class devoted to private growers covering a display of bulbs in flower to occupy 200 sq. ft., arranged for effect, prizes $150 and $100. There is also a class for dealers and seedsmen calling for a display of bulbs, etc., arranged as a Dutch bulb garden, covering 500 sq. ft., appropriate accessories permitted, prizes $250, $150 and $100, respectively.

In the commercial class covering a display of cut roses covering 200 sq. ft., the first prize is increased to $250 and the second prize in the new schedule is increased to $200. Bougainvilleas are to be features so as to form a distinct attraction among the groups of flowering plants, prizes of $75 and $50 being offered for a group arranged for effect covering 100 sq. ft.

A new feature is a class for a collection of new Holland plants covering 100 sq. ft., with prizes $50 and $25.

Rock gardens are to be another important feature, a commercial class for such gardens covering a space 10 ft. by 30 ft., suitable accessories permitted, having been introduced with prizes $250 and $150.

A very full and complete exhibition in the trade section is practically assured, the contracts already accepted aggregate in value upward of $10,000.

The entertainment features of the show will, it is expected be of the usual high standard and fully in accord with the purposes of the show.
JOHN YOUNG, Sec'y.

CLUBS AND SOCIETIES

MASSACHUSETTS HORTICULTURAL SOCIETY.

The October show of fruits and vegetables held at Horticultural Hall, Boston, on October 2 and 3 was one of the most elegant displays of really high class products of the fruit and vegetable garden ever staged by the Boston growers. The entire list was splendidly represented. We have never seen so fine peaches of local production and Jennison's Floral Garden scored a sensation with the Ideal strawberry, which we had occasion to mention two weeks ago. The collections of vegetables were arranged with much taste and the exhibits of salad plants were eagerly inspected by a throng of visitors. Dr. F. S. DeLuc won honorable mention for Improved Golden Bantam sweet corn and Jas. S. Bache's Golden Eagle sweet corn was accorded a vote of thanks.

Blue Hill Nurseries was the only exhibitor gaining recognition in the cut flower line. Honorable mention was accorded their seedling Phlox, Mrs. James Wheeler, a pale lavender rose flower. An attractive hardy hybrid aster shown by this exhibitor showed up well—A. Blue Hills (A. laevis X A. turbinellus.

The nominating committee of the Massachusetts Horticultural Society announces the following list of candidates for the various offices of the Society for the ensuing year, to be filled at the annual meeting November 13.

President, Richard M. Saltonstall; vice-president, Walter Hunnewell; trustees for 3 years, George E. Barnard, William C. Endicott, Arthur F. Estabrook, John K. M. L. Farquhar; nominating committee, Arthur F. Estabrook, Richard Hittinger, John G. Jack, Thomas Roland, John L. Smith.

In accordance with the By-laws of the Society two weeks are allowed for further nominations should any be desired.

Wm. P. Rich, Secretary.

NEW JERSEY FLORICULTURAL SOCIETY.

The 10th Annual Dahlia, Fruit and Vegetable Show was held in Orange, N. J., on Monday, Oct. 4th. The show was the greatest success ever held by the society. That the blooms were larger and quite surpassed the N. Y. show was the opinion of many present. W. A. Manda staged a wonderful collection of dahlias and carried off many of the prizes. P. W. Popp, gardener to H. Darlington, Marmaroneck, N. Y., took seven 1st prizes in all the large classes. A fine collection of fruit which took 1st prize was staged by William Reid, gardener to Sidney and A. M. Colgate, Orange, N. J. A close second for an equally fine collection was awarded to Wm. Shillaber, gard. J. P. Sorenson, of Essex Fells, N. J. The miniature gardens were quite a feature and caused quite some interest to the general public. A. J. Moulton was awarded first, gard. Alfred A. Thoma, and the Essex County Country Club, gard. Gustaf Christenson, second, although the competition was very close.

Peter Hauck, Jr., of East Orange won 1st with a fine centre piece of dahlias and on 25 show dahlias. Among the other winners were Wm. Barr, Llewellyn Park, Walter Lawrence, Mrs. C. H. Stout of Short Hills and Walter Gray.

A special silver medal was awarded to Sidney and Austin Colgate for a group of foliage and flowering plants. A fine display of annuals exhibited by Wm. Shillaber was awarded a first-class certificate. The vegetable classes were of extraordinary merit. The judges were Peter Duff, Alex. Robertson and W. A. Manda.

LANCASTER COUNTY FLORISTS' CLUB DAHLIA SHOW.

This club supervised the floral exhibit for the Fair Association this season, featuring dahlias as their part of the exhibit. The McCallum Co., S. S. Pennock-Meehan Co. and H. F. Michell Co. all sent liberal displays of dahlias and the Michell Co. sent an assortment of Phlox and other perennials that were much admired. It was due to these firms that we were enabled to fill the space assigned in the artistic manner in which we did. The table was eighty feet long by eight feet wide with a raised table of about eighteen inches in width and that height from the lower table. This was decorated with wild smilax by I. Landis and Thomas Fries in festoons and stringers and made a handsome table for staging the dahlias.

B. F. Barr added a few palms and a handsome basket of gladioli and chrysanthemums for the center. Frank Suter being the only one who grows dahlias as a commercial cut flower in this vicinity, made the best local exhibit and H. D. Rohrer had a very good collection. A. F. Strickler had some mixed bowls of short-stemmed flowers.

In the amateur class David Roar staged a mighty fine collection and secured all the prizes for this section. Adam Felsinger staged the best flowers of the show simply for exhibition. Frank Suter captured the cash prize for florists with the largest collection and the silver cup for sweepstake prize. Master Edward E. Rohrer, a grandson of H. D. Rohrer, captured 1st for three handsome baskets of straw flowers grown and arranged by himself. The judge was S. S. Pennock.

In competition with Barr's handsome basket was a design made of marigolds in a frame two inches deep and sixteen by sixteen in size, made up by using different colors in the style of a patchwork quilt and the wording of the schedule compelled it to have first prize and the basket second. This sort of thing we hope to be able to eliminate by another year if the Fair officials appreciate our efforts this season enough to let us have a real hand in running the flower end of the Fair.

Albert M. Herr.

FLORISTS' CLUB OF PHILADELPHIA.

Tuesday night, October 6, was "dahlia night" and Lawrence K. Peacock had just given a lecture. We challenged any of the rose, carnation or chrysanthemum growers to stand up in open meeting and defend the dahlia but no one responded. The dahlia has no more poetry in its make-up than a zinnia has—a turnip of a flower! That's the feeling it gives us. Mr. Manda's man made a good showing and Pennock Bros. made a decoration.

Last year's officers were re-elected. New committees were appointed for the coming year. A collation was furnished by the officers and everybody had a good time. Commodore Westcott did some talking; so did Adolph Farenwald. We don't think much of the new essay committee. Your scribe is one of this essay committee, so he ought to know. But seriously, it was a fine meeting. There was a good attendance and lots of vim and enthusiasm. The secretary reported 299 members. Let's root for 500. Under the able leadership of George Burton we can do lots in the next 12 months. Let's each bring in five more new ones and boost for Philly.

NEW YORK FLORISTS' CLUB.

President Harry A. Bunyard has appointed A. M. Henshaw, C. H. Totty and Roman J. Irwin a committee on transportation to Cleveland of those desirous of attending the Flower Show in that city, to take place November 10 to 14 next.

John Young, Sec'y.

CLUB AND SOCIETY NOTES.

The October meeting of the Cincinnati Florists' Society will be held next Monday evening, October 11th at Hotel Gibson.

The St. Louis Florist Club will hold an important meeting next Thursday afternoon, at 2 o'clock, on the grounds of the Bourdet Floral Co.

The Third Annual Flower Show of the Holyoke and Northampton Florist and Gardener's Club will be held in Windsor Hall, Dwight street, Holyoke, Mass., on November 3 and 4. There is a liberal prize schedule.

The new officers of the Minnesota State Florists' Association are as follows: President, W. D. Desmond, Minneapolis; vice-president, Max Kaiser, St. Paul; secretary, T. C. Rogers, Minneapolis; treasurer, A. Lauritzen, St. Paul; executive committee, O. J. Olson and S. D. Dysinger, St. Paul, and S. S. Cargill and Oscar E. Amundson, Minneapolis.

New England's big indoor country fair will be held in Mechanic's Hall, Boston, Oct. 23 to 30. The fair will be under the auspices of the fourth biennial Fruit Show Inc., and the Market Gardeners' Association. Exhibits of fruit, vegetables and flowers will be shown. The floral exhibition will be under the management of Norris F. Comley and liberal prizes will be awarded.

SEED TRADE

AMERICAN SEED TRADE ASSOCIATION

Officers—President, J. M. Lupton,
Mattituck, L. I., N. Y.; First Vice-President, Kirby B. White, Detroit, Mich.;
Second Vice-President, F. W. Bolgiano,
Washington, D. C.; Secretary-Treasurer,
C. E. Kendel, Cleveland, O.; Assistant
Secretary, S. F. Willard, Jr., Cleveland,
O. Cincinnati, O., next meeting place.

S. P. Dernison, well-known in the
East and Middle West is now representing Arthur T. Boddington Co., Inc.,
on the road.

Los Angeles, Cal.—Fire in the warehouse of the Germain Seed & Plant Co.
caused a loss of between $40,000 and
$50,000, fully covered by insurance.

Value of horticultural importations
at the Port of New York for the week
ending September 25, is given as follows: Grass seed, $2,448; fertilizer,
$2,075; trees, plants and bulbs, $127,-
712.

CATALOGUES RECEIVED.

J. J. Wilson Seed Co., Inc., Newark,
N. J.—"Quality" Bulbs for Autumn
Planting and Spring Flowering.

The Garden Nurseries, Narberth, Pa.
—Illustrated Pamphlet of the new
evergreen vine euonymus radicans
vegetus.

F. & F. Nurseries, Springfield, N. J.
—"Quality First" Trade List of Ornamental Nursery Stock for Fall, 1915.
A very complete list.

J. Bolgiano & Son, Baltimore, Md.—
Bolgiano's Bulb Book for 1915. A fine,
seductive catalogue with much that is
unique in its contents.

Joseph Breck & Sons Corporation,
Boston, Mass. — Autumn Catalogue,
1915, of High Grade Bulbs, a handsome
publication typographically and up to
date in its contents.

V. Lemoine & Son, Nancy, France.—
Autumn Catalogue for 1915. As ever,
this is one of the most interesting
catalogues published, for plant lover.
Some enticing novelties in shrubs are
listed.

William Elliott & Sons, New York,
N. Y.—"Flowering Bulbs." This Autumn Edition for 1915 is a worthy exponent of the best that is offered in
fall bulb stock. Attractively illustrated.

L. W. Goodell, Pansy Park, Dwight,
Mass.—Wholesale Price List of Pansy
Seeds. Mr. Goodell has made pansies
a specialty for over forty years and
his strains have an unsullied record.

J. Chas. McCullough Seed Co., Cincinnati, O.—Fall Catalogue, 1915, of
Bulbs, Nursery Stock, Seeds and Poultry supplies.

Eastern Nurseries, Jamaica Plain,
Mass.—Wholesale Trade List for Fall,
1915, and Spring, 1916. A 50-page catalogue, illustrated and very complete.
Contains offers of species and varieties
in ornamental evergreen and deciduous tree and shrub material which is
rarely to be found in wholesale nursery
catalogues. Anyone wishing to get
started into a line of rare and choice
things will do well to consult this
really superior list of trees, shrubs and
hardy herbaceous perennials.

FERTILE HOLLAND.

The whole area of Holland is 12,600
square miles (about the size of Maryland), which is occupied approximately as follows:

	Square Miles
Flowers and bulbs	30
Nurseries	85
Market gardens	195
Area most highly fertilized	310
Grain, potatoes and other field crops	3,400
Total area fertilized	3,710
Meadows	4,750
Parks and trees	1,000
Buildings, roads, canals, moors	3,140
Total	12,600

Considering the fertilized area of
3,710 square miles, or 2,374,400 acres,
the commercial fertilizer used averages more than 1,270 pounds per acre,
which is fully three or four times as
much as the average—where employed
at all—in the United States. When to
this is added the considerable amount
of home manures used, it is not difficult to understand the high agricultural productiveness of this little country.—*U. S. Commerce Report.*

PUBLICATION RECEIVED.

The Annual Report of the Public
Parks Board of Winnipeg, Canada, is
an attractive volume of 98 pages with
several full page illustrations. The
secretary's report shows receipts of
$173,489.27, and expenditures $169,377,-
04. The detailed report of the superintendent, G. Champion, shows that
Winnipeg's parks are well cared for
horticulturally.

Dear Sir: — Enclosed please find
check for $5.00 in payment for HORTICULTURE till April, 1920.
　　　　　Yours very truly,
Newport, R. I.　　　　　J. H. G.

UNIVERSITY OF ILLINOIS.

Eight new students have enrolled in
the course given in Floriculture. One
of the new members is doing graduate
work in Floriculture and the others
have registered for the regular undergraduate work. This makes a total of
twenty-three floricultural students of
which eight are seniors, two juniors,
four sophomores, eight freshmen, and
one a graduate student.

The courses given during the semester are as follows:

Greenhouse Construction, with an enrollment of 31.
Commercial Crops, with an enrollment of 5
Amateur Floriculture, "　"　"　" 43
Garden Flowers, "　"　"　" 31

Several changes were made in the
staff this year. W. K. Palmer of Berwyn, Ill., has been appointed to succeed Mr. Hutchinson, who now has
charge of a 350 acre farm recently acquired by the Department of Horticulture for nursery experiments. Mr.
Palmer graduated with the class of
1913 when he received the degree of
B. S. in Floriculture. Immediately after graduation he secured employment
with F. Dorner & Sons Company of
Lafayette, Ind., where he gained considerable knowledge of the work as
carried on by them. From Lafayette
Mr. Palmer went to Morton Grove, Ill.,
to work for Poehlmann Bros. From
here he went to Fleischman of Chicago, where he received much experience in retail work. Besides having
charge of the greenhouses, Mr. Palmer
also has charge of the course in commercial crops.

E. G. Lauterbach of Bushnell, Illinois, has been appointed to succeed C.
C. Rees as Assistant to Mr. Peltier in
Plant Pathology.

F. L. Washburn, of Bloomington,
visited the experimental greenhouses
on Wednesday of last week.

　　　　　　　　　　　A. G. H.

Of Interest to Retail Florists

NEW FLOWER STORES.

Dayton, O.—Dayton Floral Co., Mutual Hotel.

Delaware, O. — Rex Garden, Farm
and Floral Co.

Rockville, Ct.—Edward Lagan, Robertson block.

Red Rock, Pa.—C. Gunton, successor
to E. B. Sage.

Kansas City, Mo.—Patrick Larkin,
Hotel Muehlbach.

Providence, R. I.—E. M. Pope, 107
Westminster street.

Los Angeles, Cal.—Mrs. E. R. Powers, 652 South Hill street.

Louisville, Ky.—S. E. Thompson, removing to 607 South 4th street.

Fort Dodge, Ia.—North Floral Co.,
11th street and Central avenue.

Atlanta, Ga.—Dahl's Floral Shop, removing to 103 Peachtree street.

Portland, Me.—Eugene Davis, removing to Congress and Exchange Sts.

Indianapolis, Ind. — A. Reynolds,
Ohio street, succeeding Alfred Brandt.

Toronto, Ont.—John H. Dunlop, removing from 96 Yonge street to 8-10
West Adelaide street.

Philadelphia, Pa. — Tiswell Flower
Shop, 1722 North Broad street. Frank
Phillips, 410 South 52nd street. Haas,
the florist, 19th and Susquehanna avenue.

NEWS NOTES.

Moundsville, W. Va.—The front of
the Miller Flower Store has been torn
away and a new front is being erected.

Providence, R. I.—Nellie O'Connor,
formerly with Timothy O'Connor, has
opened a new flower store on Fair
street, East Side.

Newark, N. J.—George Penek, whose
main store is at 637 Broad street, has
now a branch store at 142 Belleville
avenue. Mr. Penek's brother Frank
is in charge of the Broad street store.

New Haven Conn.—Burglars entered
the floral shop of John N. Champion,
at 1026 Chapel street, sometime last
Saturday night and robbed the cash
register of its contents, about $14 in
change. It is believed the thief gained
entrance by means of a side door.

Toronto, Ont. — John H. Dunlop
opened his new store at 8-10 West Adelaide street to the public on Thursday,
October 7. The equipment of this establishment will rank with the best
retail stores in the country, every detail having been arranged by his manager, George M. Geraghty.

BUSINESS TROUBLES.

Denver, Col.—The Elitch-Long Gardens, florists, have been placed in the
hands of a receiver.

NEWS ITEMS FROM EVERYWHERE

CHICAGO.

Walter M. Rupp of J. C. Moninger Co., is receiving the congratulations of his many friends. The bride was Miss Dorothy M. Ashley.

Wm. Homberg, long connected with the Chicago trade and lately with J. A. Budlong, is now starting in the wholesale business for himself at 183 N. Wabash avenue.

At a meeting of the directors of the Grand Floral Festival to be held here in November, Guy French was appointed manager. Joe Biever will be assistant manager, which position he has acceptably filled on many former occasions. Two large silver cups are now displayed in the office of E. C. Amling, which are to be awarded at the festival. They are given, one by W. J. Keimel, president of the Chicago Florists' Club and the other by the Chicago Florists' Club.

Allie Zech is receiving some fine late asters from Petosky, Michigan. They arrive in splendid condition, packed without bunching, after the manner of packing roses or chrysanthemums, one hundred in a box, such as is used by retailers. They were sold as soon as received and except for re-shipping were not taken from the boxes. This way of handling asters pays the shipper well for the extra time. Good flowers packed this way easily receive double the price that the bunched ones bring.

As usual the greenhouses have been filled all summer with young Boston ferns, and now that they must give way to make room for other stock, the market is flooded with them. The department stores are coming to the rescue of the growers, if not to the retailer, and large sales are taking place at sensational prices. There is the usual call for blooming plants and the usual dearth of these at this season. Small cyclamens are coming into bloom and eagerly bought up despite their size. These, with Primula obconica, cover the field at this time but the early pot chrysanthemums will be here in limited quantities in a short time.

The parks are rapidly getting ready for their fall chrysanthemum exhibits. These affairs grow in popularity each year and the attendance is a great encouragement to the management. At Garfield Park Supt. Aug. Koch says another month will see the show in full swing. The shrubbery and bedding stock have both suffered from the rain this summer, particularly the latter. Geraniums reached a height of 30 inches, covered with foliage and until the few warm days near the close of the season were almost without blooms. The new venture of the West Side Park Board in placing half acre plots of land devoted to vegetables in Humboldt, Garfield and Douglas parks is regarded as satisfactory, especially in Douglas where both adults and pupils of the upper grades and of the High School were regular visitors. The plots were to show how different vegetables should be grown and in what succession.

NEW YORK.

The Florists' Club meeting on Monday evening, October 11, will be devoted especially to the chrysanthemum.

H. H. Burns, son of A. S. Burns, of Elmhurst, has opened a retail flower store at Madison avenue and 52nd street.

Myer Othile has acquired the store at 49 West 28th street, for his new wholesale venture and will open up shortly.

The Manda Floral Co., will have their first annual orchid show at 191 Valley Road, West Orange, N. J., on October 6 to 12 inclusive, from 8 A. M. to 5 P. M. daily.

The First Preliminary Schedule of the "International" Flower Show under the auspices of the Horticultural Society of New York and the N. Y. Florists' Club has been sent out. The show will be held at the Grand Central Palace, New York City, April 5 to 12, 1916. The prizes offered are very liberal, on a par with the prizes at previous spring shows under the same auspices. Complete schedule will be issued later. For additional schedules or information apply to John Young, Secretary, 53 West 28th street, New York City.

The first of a series of monthly flower shows and lectures on the subject of the cultivation of flowers will be held at the Country Life Permanent Exposition, Grand Central Terminal Building, on November 1 and 2. The first show will consist of a chrysanthemum exhibit. Charles H. Totty, of Madison, N. J., will deliver a lecture on the first day on the "Cultivation of Hardy Chrysanthemums."

Full particulars of the flower show and schedule may be obtained by applying to Robert H. Sexton, care Country Life Permanent Exposition, Grand Central Terminal Building, New York, N. Y.

Suitable prizes will be offered to private and amateur gardeners in competition and trade exhibits will be invited but not for competition. An invitation is extended to all garden lovers to attend the show and lecture, to which there will be no charge. The Country Life Permanent Exposition is an institution devoted to the promoting of country life and it believes that these monthly shows will prove both interesting and instructive.

PROVIDENCE, R. I.

The tax list compiled by the Board of Assessors of East Providence which was made public last week, contains the following florists who are assessed over $5,000: Joseph E. Koppleman, $16,350; Andrew J. Olsen, et ux, $5,200; Laurence Hay, $6,225.

J. W. Speight, of this city, won the prize for the best dahlia display at the Elmwood Dahlia Society's rooms last week, showing the Imp, Rev. D. Bridge and Cockatoo. The Imp was said to be the nearest to a black dahlia that is grown. Thomas English was the judge. S. A. G.

WASHINGTON.

Richard Vincent, Jr., lectured on the glories of the western trip incident to his attendance at the annual convention of the S. A. F. and O. H., before the Florists' Club at its October meeting. Mr. Vincent compared the retail stores of San Francisco with those of Washington, telling the members of the club that they will have to hustle considerably or they will find themselves surpassed by their brothers of the west coast. He spoke of the wonderful growth of dahlias, asters and sweet peas and of the great farms and ranches which he visited. William F. Gude also spoke of the beauties of the trip, and of the many entertainments provided for his party at the stops made en route. His experiences over the border line in Mexico and the Grand Canyon of Arizona were most interesting.

Following the business meeting there was an informal discussion on general trade and the condition of stock. Many complaints were heard of the poor quality at present in many lines. This, the florists stated, was due to the many and rapid changes of temperature. The members seemed agreed that the prospects for an increased fall and winter business were good. The growers severally reported that their houses were coming along in fine shape, giving promise of cuttings of exceptionally good stock at an early date.

SAN FRANCISCO.

The United Flower & Supply Co. reports heavy shipments of chrysanthemums out of the city the past two weeks.

The Aggeler & Musser Seed Co. was awarded gold medal for its seed exhibit at the Panama-California exposition at San Diego, Cal.

Mr. Warlow who opened for business on Polk street, near Pine, a few months ago has discontinued. It is understood he is looking for a new location.

C. Kooyman expects a large shipment of bulbs next week. He is shipping some chrysanthemums and expects to begin sending out violets about the 10th.

A special feature at the next meeting of the Pacific Coast Horticultural Society will be a lantern slide lecture on "Wood Decay of Ornamental Plants" to be delivered by Prof. W. T. Horne of the University of California.

BOSTON.

Jackson Dawson, of the Arnold Arboretum, celebrated his 74th birthday anniversary on October 5.

William Mix, well-known among the plant and flower fraternity of Boston, mourns the death of his father, which occurred at his home in Cambridge, on Monday, October 5. A handsome wreath of white chrysanthemums was sent by the Flower Exchange to the funeral on Thursday.

The Horticultural Club of Boston was entertained at its October meeting, Wednesday last, by E. H. Wilson, who gave a graphic account of his recent experiences in Japan, illustrated with beautiful stereopticon views. Among the guests on this occasion was John Dunbar, of the Rochester, N. Y., parks. The table was lavishly decorated with new dahlias by W. A. Manda, and a vase of the new rose Mrs. Bayard Thayer, by Alexander Montgomery.

PHILADELPHIA

Charles E. Meehan of the Pennock-Meehan Co. has not been seen around his usual haunts for a week back. They say he is off rusticating somewhere.

S. S. Pennock was one of the judges at the Lancaster Co. Flower Show last week. He went also to the Vincent , show at White Marsh, Maryland. A very busy man is Samuel.

Congratulations are in order to a new recruit in the wholesale cut flower trade. Walter Davis opened on the 4th inst at 1713 Ranstead street, succeeding John McIntyre. Mr. Davis has been twenty-eight years in the business in this city, having started at the Gracey store (then Goff & Magee) at 21st and Columbia avenue. For the past eleven years he has been associated with the Leo Niessen Co, so he knows retailing as well as wholesaling. An able man, of fine character and bound to succeed.

PITTSBURGH.

Miss Eliza McKinley has the sympathy of her many friends and acquaintances in the death of her mother, which took place in New York, where she was visiting relatives. Miss McKinley is the head saleswoman for Randolph & McClements, and one of the best known women in trade circles.

Mrs. E. A. Williams' entire force was on duty all of last Thursday night and Friday morning arranging the floral designs for the funeral of Mrs. Andrew Fleming. Seven hundred and fifty cattleyas were called into requisition, also 500 American Beauties, 1500 lilies of the valley and numerous clusters of chrysanthemums, roses, lilies and dahlias.

Hutchinson, Kans.—J. Ralph Soudu has started business here with three houses, two of them 27 x 110 and one 10 x 100, with office, etc., just completed, at 521 Eleventh avenue, east.

Obituary

Matthew Macnair.

Matthew Macnair of Providence, R. I., one of the city's leading and oldest florists, died very suddenly Sept. 29. Mr. Macnair had just left his store and was walking down the street with his son, Charles, when he suddenly collapsed and would have fallen headlong to the concrete walk had it not been

MATTHEW MACNAIR

for the protecting arm of his son. By an unusual coincidence, the funeral was held Saturday from the church in front of which Mr. Macnair died and the service was at 2.30, the same time that he was fatally stricken three days before. There was a large attendance of relatives, friends and former business associates present and many flowers were sent.

Mr. Macnair was widely known as a florist, having been in the business in this city for more than a quarter of a century. He was the founder and proprietor of the two stores that bore his

name, one at 322 Weybosset and another at 2 Broad street. He was born in Glasgow, Scotland, in 1845, and came to New York in 1870. About 25 years ago he started in the flower business in Providence with a store on Westminster street, removing three years later to Weybosset street. This venture was a success and in 1900 he opened a second store on Broad street. He was a firm believer in window advertising and his show windows were said to be the most attractive in the city.

Of a cheerful disposition, Mr. Macnair made many friends in and out of his professional calling. He was a great lover of music and was well-known for his Scotch songs. He was a member of the Arion Club of Providence, and frequently referred with happy recollections to his associations with Beecher's Choir of Brooklyn, N. Y. Mr. Macnair had traveled extensively in Europe. He leaves a widow, two sons, Charles and Thomas; also five brothers and two sisters. S. A. G.

NEW CORPORATIONS.

Portland, Ore. — Henry Clemmens, florist. Incorporators: Henry Clemmens, C. R. Langstaff and Julius Cohn.

Chicago, Ill. — National Plant & Flower Co., capital stock $10,000. Incorporators: Edward R. Newmann, Geo. S. Pines and Martin W. Reiss.

Stamford, Ct.—The Stamford Seed and Nursery Company has filed a certificate showing an increase of its capital stock from $15,000 to $20,000 and an increase of shares from 600 to 1,200, par value, $25, all common stock.

Cleveland, O. — Holmes-Letherman Seed Company, Canton, has been incorporated by George M. Letherman, H. L. Holmes, Jr., Edwin L. Gehman, H. W. Shriver and Minnie L. Letherman, with a capital of $25,000, in landscape gardening business.

NEWS NOTES.

New Castle, N. H. — The Eaton Greenhouses have been purchased by C. W. Lefeber.

Ludington, Mich.—Martin Lunde has purchased the greenhouses of the E. L. Brillhart bankrupt estate.

WHOLESALE FLOWER MARKETS — TRADE PRICES—Per 100 TO DEALERS ONLY

	CINCINNATI Oct. 4	CHICAGO Oct. 4	BUFFALO Oct. 4	PITTSBURG Sept. 23
Roses				
Am. Beauty, Special............	20.00 to 25.00	20.00 to 30.00	20.00 to 25.00	15.00 to 20.00
" " Fancy and Extra....	15.00 to 20.00	15.00 to 20.00	15.00 to 20.00	10.00 to 12.50
" " No. 1...No. 2........	6.00 to 10.00	5.00 to 10.00	6.00 to 8.00	6.00 to 8.00
Russell, Hadley...............	4.00 to 8.00	3.00 to 12.00	4.00 to 7.00	4.00 to 8.00
Killarney, Richm'd, Hill'don, Ward	5.00 to 8.00	8.00 to 12.00	5.00 to 7.00	6.00 to 8.00
" " Ord.	3.00 to 4.00	4.00 to 6.00	3.00 to 6.00	2.00 to 4.00
Arenburg, Radiance, Taft, Key, Ex.	5.00 to 8.00	8.00 to 12.00	5.00 to 6.00	6.00 to 8.00
" " Ord.	3.00 to 4.00	...... to	3.00 to 5.00	5.00 to 4.00
Ophelia, Mock, Sunburst, Extra	5.00 to 8.00	8.00 to 12.00	4.00 to 7.00	6.00 to 8.00
" " Ordinary	3.00 to 4.00	3.00 to 6.00	3.00 to 4.00	...... to 4.00
Carnations, Fancy.............	...... to 2.00	2.00 to 3.00	3.00 to 9.50	...... to 2.00
" " Ordinary.............	...... to 1.50	1.00 to 2.00	1.00 to 2.00	...... to 1.50
Cattleyas.............	50.00 to 60.00	40.00 to 50.00	40.00 to 50.00	40.00 to 60.00
Dendrobium formosum.............	...... to	40.00 to 50.00	...... to	30.00 to 40.00
Lilies, Longiflorum.............	10.00 to 12.50	10.00 to 12.00	8.00 to 10.00	8.00 to 10.00
" " Rubrum.............	4.00 to 10.00	...... to	3.00 to 4.00	3.00 to 4.00
Lily of the Valley.............	...... to 4.00	3.00 to 4.00	3.00 to 4.00	3.00 to 4.00
Daisies.............	...... to	.75 to 2.00	...... to	...... to 1.50
Violets.............	...... to	...... to	...... to	...... to ......
Snapdragon.............	...... to	...... to 5.00	1.00 to 2.00	...... to ......
Gladioli.............	8.00 to 4.00	2.00 to 4.00	2.00 to 3.00	2.00 to 4.00
Asters.............	1.00 to 2.00	1.00 to 3.00	.50 to 1.50	1.00 to 2.00
Chrysanthemum.............	12.50 to 15.00	12.00 to 25.00	8.00 to 20.00	10.00 to 25.00
Sweet Peas.............	...... to	...... to	...... to	...... to ......
Gardenias.............	...... to	15.00 to 25.00	...... to	...... to ......
Adiantum.............	...... to 1.00	1.00 to 1.95	1.00 to 1.25	.75 to 1.25
Smilax.............	12.50 to 15.00	15.00 to 18.00	...... to 15.00	12.00 to 15.00
Asparagus Plumosus, Strings (100)	25.00 to 50.00	40.00 to 50.00	40.00 to 50.00	40.00 to 50.00
" " & Spren. (100 bchs.)	...... to 25.00	25.00 to 30.00	25.00 to 35.00	30.00 to 40.00

Flower Market Reports

BOSTON A lively revival in flower trading is in progress here. Prices have taken on a "war baby" smile and the man who has anything to sell is happy to the limit. Unluckily for him, however, he hasn't very much to offer. Carnations have doubled in value since a week ago. Roses have taken a similar spurt. Chrysanthemums have not yet become plentiful enough to interfere and there will be no trouble until they do. The first violets have already appeared. The tables in the wholesale marts are bare, these days—quite an agreeable change for all, except the fellow who thrives on the surplus when there is any.

BUFFALO Heavy rain storms and frosty nights have ruined most all of the outdoor stock and there is at this time very little coming in, which has had a tendency to throw the demand toward carnations which are only coming in normal supply, the greater part being very short. Roses have been in fair quality and quantity and these too have moved more freely and at fair prices. Beauties have better sales also and lilies clean up well. Chrysanthemum sales are good. The market has improved wonderfully in the last week and business is still on the upward course.

CHICAGO October opens with a fair demand for flowers. Society events are taking place earlier than in former seasons and outdoor flowers are less in evidence than is frequently the case in the fall. The dearth of flowers in the surrounding country stimulates shipping trade and together the daily cut is used up. The supply is not large but compares well with that of average years. Carnations are coming in large quantities now but are still considered scarce. American Beauties from some of the growers are showing plenty of black spot, owing probably to the dark, damp days. An occasional bunch of violets reminds one that the season for that flower will soon be here. Some very good snapdragons are to be had. Roses of all kinds are coming and the quality is good but the best grades are not more than sufficient for regular trade. Of the smaller ones the supply is better. Some short-stemmed asters with rather large flowers are still coming and are sure to sell at sight. Chrysanthemums are still confined mostly to white and yellow, but a few pink are seen. A clear yellow known here as Yellow Frost, similar in size and form to October Frost, is taking well this week.

CINCINNATI With the end of the gladiolus and aster season the market shortened up very considerably and now there is just about enough stock to take care of the demand. The call for stock both locally and from out of town is brisk. Prices are somewhat better than they were up to the end of last week. The rose cut is large and includes many excellent blooms. Carnations are in a fair supply and move nicely. Longiflorum lilies are not very plentiful. The cut of rubrums is ample. Dahlia receipts are some of the best we have ever had.

DAHLIAS

Nothing more showy nor better value than Dahlias, with all their brilliant colorings and varieties.

With 24 hours notice, orders can be packed in original boxes at the Dahlia farms, thus insuring the blooms reaching our customers in perfect condition. Try a sample shipment. Special inducements on regular orders.

$1.00, $1.50, $2.00 per 100.
Novelties at $3.00 and $4.00 per 100.
Some splendid values at $15.00 per 1000.
CATTLEYAS, $5.00 per doz.; $35.00 per 100. As a Special, two doz. for $8.00.
VALLEY, Special, $1.00 per 100; Fancy, $3.00 per 100.

S. S. PENNOCK-MEEHAN CO.

The Wholesale Florists of Philadelphia

| PHILADELPHIA | NEW YORK | BALTIMORE | WASHINGTON |
| 1608-1620 Ludlow St. | 117 W. 28th St. | Franklin and St. Paul Sts. | 1216 H St., N. W. |

WHOLESALE FLOWER MARKETS — TRADE PRICES—Per 100 TO DEALERS ONLY

Roses	BOSTON Oct. 7		ST. LOUIS Oct. 4		PHILA. Oct. 4	
Am. Beauty, Special	12.00 to 25.00		20.00 to 30.00		18.00 to 25.00	
" " Fancy and Extra	6.00 to 10.00		12.00 to 15.00		12.00 to 16.00	
" " No. 1	3.00 to 5.00		3.00 to 10.00		6.00 to 10.00	
Russell, Hadley	4.00 to 12.00		8.00 to 12.00		4.00 to 15.00	
Killarney, Richmond, Hillingdon, Ward, Extra	4.00 to 8.00		6.00 to 8.00		4.00 to 8.00	
" " " Ordinary	2.00 to 4.00		3.00 to 4.00		2.00 to 3.00	
Arenburg; Radiance, Taft, Key, Extra	4.00 to 8.00		.... to		4.00 to 10.00	
" " " Ordinary	2.00 to 4.00		.... to		2.00 to 4.00	
Ophelia, Mock, Sunburst, Extra	4.00 to 8.00		6.00 to 10.00		4.00 to 8.00	
" " Ordinary	2.00 to 4.00		4.00 to 5.00		2.00 to 3.00	
Carnations, Fancy	2.00 to 3.00		1.50 to 2.00		.... to 2.00	
" Ordinary	1.00 to 2.00		.50 to .75		1.00 to 1.50	
Cattleyas	25.00 to 40.00		35.00 to 50.00		25.00 to 40.00	
Dendrobium formosum	.... to 40.00		.... to		.... to 50.00	
Lilies, Longiflorum	6.00 to 10.00		6.00 to 8.00		8.00 to 12.00	
" Rubrum	.... to 3.00		3.00 to 4.00		.. to 10.00	
Lily of the Valley	3.00 to 4.00		3.00 to 4.00		8.00 to 4.00	
Daisies	.50 to 1.00		.25 to .50		.... to	
Violets	.... to		.25 to .50		.15 to .50	
Snapdragon	2.00 to 2.00		3.00 to 4.00		.... to	
Gladioli	2.00 to 4.00		3.00 to 4.00		.... to	
Asters	.50 to 1.00		2.00 to 3.00		.... to	
Chrysanthemums	12.00 to 20.00		1.50 to 2.50		8.00 to 20.00	
Sweet Peas	.... to		.... to		.... to	
Gardenias	15.00 to 20.00		.... to		.... to	
Adiantum	.... to 1.00		1.00 to 1.25		.... to 1.00	
Smilax	12.00 to 16.00		12.00 to 15.00		.... to 20.00	
Asparagus Plumosus, Strings (100)	25.00 to 50.00		50.00 to 50.00		50.00 to 50.00	
" & Spren. (100 Bchs.)	25.00 to 35.00		20.00 to 35.00		35.00 to 50.00	

NEW YORK Early chrysanthemums are now coming in regularly.

It is very refreshing, as it is decidedly unusual, to be able to record that flowers are really scarce in the New York market. The consequence of this rare situation is a stiff advance in values, from the bargain counter plane up to a reasonable and proper standard. The rose is the leading item at present, the small blooms from young plants lacking size and stem, as yet, but being very acceptable in the prevalent stringency. Lily of the valley is in very scant supply and is selling at a higher price than it has at any time in recent years. The probability is that we shall have a similar story to tell about lily of the valley more than once during the coming winter. Cattleyas are plentiful but selling better than of late. Carnations, of course, feel the impulse of the refreshing activity and have doubled in price. Even dahlias are selling well at present writing.

PHILADELPHIA The improvement noted in our last report has continued, the upward tendency still prevailing with highly gratifying speed—and at this writing everybody looks more cheerful. The gloomy and worried countenances that have greeted your observer for many months are replaced by gladsome Polly Anna smiles. Long may this encouraging state of affairs continue. The rose market is in especially good shape. American Beauties are fine and Russells were never better for so early. Some of the latter brought as high as $2.00 per doz. (almost special Beauty price), which tells the tale as to their quality in few words. Jonkheer Mock is also in fine form; so is Ophelia and Hadley. Prices on carnations have stiffened up quite a little. Their big rival, the aster, is now out of the race. Besides that, there is improvement in the quality, and nothing in the shape of an oversupply. Dahlias continue a strong feature and large quantities of

(Continued on page 487)

Flower Market Reports
(Continued from page 485)

these are being moved daily. The early yellow and white chrysanthemums are more plentiful and have been supplemented by a good pink variety, Unaka, the past few days. Orchids plentiful and draggy. Gardenias scarce—in fact the old-timers say they have never seen them so scarce at this time of year as they are now.

The demand for **SAN FRANCISCO** flowers seemed to drop off a little here the past week without any apparent cause, unless it was a natural lull after the several weeks of activity in connection with special events of one kind and another, which took a good many flowers. Even with the slight falling off in demand there was no surplus of stock, however, as several varieties of flowers which have been very plentiful are going off crop, without enough new stock as yet to take their places. Asters are about out, dahlias are beginning to wane, and gladioli are getting rather scarce. The latter are in excellent demand and fine stock brings high prices. Violets go the rounds a little better now, but the quality is still not up to standard, a little rain and cool weather being needed to bring them to their best. A few are being shipped and a good many are being taken by the street venders. Chrysanthemums are coming in freely and good stock finds a ready outlet. Three or four varieties of pink are in ample supply with a very good demand, and there is plenty of yellow, but more white could be sold if available. The small outdoor Chinese chrysanthemums are quite popular. Roses are getting better every day, but there is still room for improvement in both quantity and quality. In view of the very light supply, everything sells and prices are well maintained. Orchids continue very scarce which helps to clean up gardenias very readily although the latter are in better supply. More good carnations could be sold. There is a good supply of greens, balanced by a good demand.

Stock of all kinds is **ST. LOUIS** not in so great abundance as it has been and the demand has been much better of late and prices have stiffened some. A great crop of chrysanthemums is looked for from local growers this season and already the consignments are quite heavy. The best roses have gone up a few cents, but the ordinary are still low. Carnations too slow, good blooms, but the most of them are short stems. Violets are looking better, the cooler weather has toned them up in color. There is still plenty of cosmos, gladioli, tuberoses, asters and dahlias coming from our local growers and seem to have a fairly good demand.

The cool weather **WASHINGTON** has brought a marked improvement to the cut flower market. There are a sufficient number of white roses to go the rounds, this is only made possible by the influx of white asters from the north. Local asters and gladioli

are off the market. Carnations are bringing $2 per hundred with a slightly higher price for selects. Of dahlias some excellent stock is now finding its way into the market and is meeting with a good demand at moderate prices. Cattleya labiata and spray orchids are very plentiful and there has been a slump in their movement causing a drop in the price. Chrysanthemums have improved wonderfully and are now moving nicely. American Beauty roses are good.

PERSONAL.

David Crawford, formerly gardener for J. W. Pybus, Pittsfield, Mass., has accepted a position with James Fraser, Morristown, N. J.

S. J. Reuter of Westerly. R. I., was remembered by the good wishes of many friends on Thursday, October 7, which was his sixty-fourth birthday anniversary. Mr. Reuter's health has improved much this summer and we hope he may see many more returns of the day.

NEW YORK QUOTATIONS PER 100. To Dealers Only

MISCELLANEOUS	Last Half of Week ending Oct. 2 1915	First Half of Week beginning Oct. 4 1915
Cattleyas	10.00 to 25.00	20.00 to 35.00
Dendrobium formosum	20.00 to 25.00	20.00 to 25.00
Lilies, Longiflorum	3.00 to 6.00	6.00 to 8.00
Rubrum	2.00 to 3.00	2.00 to 4.00
Lily of the Valley	2.00 to 3.00	3.00 to 4.00
Daises	to .50	to .50
Violets	to	to
Snapdragon	.50 to 1.00	1.00 to 2.00
Gladioli	1.00 to 2.00	1.00 to 3.00
Asters	.25 to 1.00	.50 to 1.00
Chrysanthemums	6.00 to 15.00	6.00 to 20.00
Sweet Peas	to	to
Corn Flower	to .25	to
Gardenias	5.00 to 20.00	5.00 to 15.00
Adiantum	.50 to .75	.50 to .75
Smilax	8.00 to 10.00	8.00 to 10.00
Asparagus Plumosus, strings (per 100)	30.00 to 40.00	15.00 to 20.00
& Spren (100 bunches)	15.00 to 20.00	15.00 to 25.00

THE VINCENT DAHLIA SHOW.

View showing the arrangement of Dahlias at the annual exhibition in White Marsh, Md., last week.

DURING RECESS.

Boston—The bowling enthusiasts of this neighborhood have got together in promising shape and have organized a florists' bowling league. There are eight teams of five men each, and they started business on Thursday evening, Oct. 7, in the following order, at the Boston alleys on Arch street and will continue the series every Thursday evening throughout the season.:

Teams.

Carbone vs. Florists' Exchange.
Flower Market vs. Robinson.
Zinn vs. Galvin.
Comley & Rosenthal vs. Wax.

The tickets are out for the annual social and dance of Farquhar's Nursery Employees, which will take place in Memorial Hall, Dedham. Mass., Friday evening, October 22.

Greensboro. N. C.—S. N. Griffith, formerly of the Greensboro Floral Co., is now associated with the Jennings Floral Co., McAdoo Hotel building.

Buyer's Directory and Ready Reference Guide

Advertisements under this head, one cent a word.   **Initials count as words.**

Display advertisers in this issue are also listed under this classification without charge. Reference to List of Advertisers will indicate the respective pages.

Buyers failing to find what they want in this list will confer a favor by writing us and we will try to put them in communication with reliable dealers.

ACACIAS.

Stuart Low & Co., Harry A. Barnard, representative, Hotel Albert, New York City.

ACCOUNTANT

R. Dysart, 40 State St., Boston.
For page see List of Advertisers.

ACHILLEA

"Pearl." Fine Seedlings, $3.00 per 1,000, cash. JAMES MOSS, Wholesale Grower, Johnsville, Pa.

ADIANTUM

The Storrs & Harrison Co., Painesville, Ohio.
For page see List of Advertisers.

APHINE

Aphine Mfg. Co., Madison, N. J.
For page see List of Advertisers.

APHIS PUNK

Nicotine Mfg. Co., St. Louis, Mo.
For page see List of Advertisers.

ARECAS.

Joseph Heacock Co., Wyncote, Pa.

ASPARAGUS

The Storrs & Harrison Co., Painesville, Ohio.
For page see List of Advertisers.

AUCTION SALES

Elliott Auction Co., New York City.
For page see List of Advertisers.

AZALEAS

P. Onwerkerk, Hoboken, N. J.
For page see List of Advertisers.

BAY TREES

August Rolker & Sons, New York.
For page see List of Advertisers.

BEDDING PLANTS

A. N. Pierson, Inc., Cromwell, Conn.
For page see List of Advertisers.

BEGONIAS

Julius Roehrs Company, Rutherford, N. J.
For page see List of Advertisers.

R. Vincent, Jr., & Sons Co., White Marsh, Md.
For page see List of Advertisers.

Thomas Roland, Nahant, Mass.
For page see List of Advertisers.

The Storrs & Harrison Co., Painesville, Ohio.
For page see List of Advertisers.

	Per 100
BEGONIA LORRAINE, 2½ in	$12.00
3 in	20.00
4 in	35.00
5 in	50.00
BEGONIA CINCINNATI, 2½ in	15.00
3 in	20.00
3½ in	30.00
4½ in	40.00

JULIUS ROEHRS CO., Rutherford, N. J.

BOILERS

Kroeschell Bros. Co., Chicago.
For page see List of Advertisers.

King Construction Co., North Tonawanda, N. Y.

"King Ideal" Boiler.

Lord & Burnham Co., New York City.
For page see List of Advertisers.

Hitchings & Co., New York City.

BOUGAINVILLEA

The Storrs & Harrison Co., Painesville, Ohio.
For page see List of Advertisers.

BOXES—CUT FLOWER FOLDING

Edwards Folding Box Co., Philadelphia.
For page see List of Advertisers.

Folding cut flower boxes, the best made. Write for list. HOLTON & HUNKEL CO., Milwaukee, Wis.

BOX TREES

BOX TREES—Standards, Pyramids and Bush. In various sizes. Price List on demand. JULIUS ROEHRS CO., Rutherford, N. J.

BOXWOOD

Breck-Robinson Nursery Co., Lexington, Mass.
For page see List of Advertisers.

BULBS AND TUBERS

Arthur T. Boddington Co., Inc., New York City.
Dutch Hyacinths and Tulip Bulbs.
For page see List of Advertisers.

J. M. Thorburn & Co., New York City
Wholesale Price List of High Class Bulbs.
For page see List of Advertisers.

Ralph M. Ward & Co., New York City.
Lily Bulbs.
For page see List of Advertisers.

John Lewis Childs, Flowerfield, L. I., N. Y.
For page see List of Advertisers.

August Rolker & Sons, New York City.
Holland and Japan Bulbs.
For page see List of Advertisers.

R. & J. Farquhar & Co., Boston, Mass.
For page see List of Advertisers.

S. S. Skidelsky & Co., Philadelphia, Pa.
For page see List of Advertisers.

Chas. Schwake & Co., New York City.
Horticultural Importers and Exporters.
For page see List of Advertisers.

A. Henderson & Co., Chicago, Ill.
For page see List of Advertisers.

Burnett Bros., 98 Chambers St., New York.
For page see List of Advertisers.

Henry F. Michell Co., Philadelphia, Pa.
For page see List of Advertisers.

Joseph Breck & Sons Corp., Boston, Mass.
For page see List of Advertisers.

Raymond W. Swett, Saxonville, Mass.
Darwin Bulbs and Hyacinths.
For page see List of Advertisers.

Fottler, Fiske, Rawson Co., Boston, Mass.

C. KEUR & SONS, HILLEGOM, Holland. Bulbs of all descriptions. Write for prices. NEW YORK Branch, 8-10 Bridge St.

CANNAS

Canna Specialists.
Send for Canna book.
THE CONARD & JONES COMPANY, West Grove, Pa.

CARNATION STAPLES

Split carnations quickly, easily and cheaply mended. Pillsbury's Carnation Staple, 1000 for 35c.; 3000 for $1.00 post paid. I. L. PILLSBURY, Galesburg, Ill.

Supreme Carnation Staples, for repairing split carnations, 35c. per 1000; 3000 for $1.00. F. W. WAITE, 85 Belmont Ave., Springfield, Mass.

CARNATIONS.

Wood Bros., Fishkill, N. Y.
For page see List of Advertisers.

F. Dorner & Sons Co., Lafayette, Ind.
For page see List of Advertisers.

F. R. Pierson, Tarrytown, N. Y.
Carnation Matchless.
For page see List of Advertisers.

Jas. Vick's Sons, Rochester, N. Y.
Field Grown Plants.
For page see List of Advertisers.

Littlefield & Wyman, North Abington, Mass.
New Pink Carnation, Miss Theo.
For page see List of Advertisers.

Carnations, field grown, $6.00 per 100. Cash. White and Pink Enchantress Mrs. Ward, Perfection, Fenn, Winsor, Queen, Lawson, Beacon. CHAS. H. GREEN, Spencer, Mass.

CHRYSANTHEMUMS

Chas. H. Totty, Madison, N. J.
For page see List of Advertisers.

R. Vincent, Jr., & Sons Co., White Marsh, Md.
Pompon Chrysanthemums.
For page see List of Advertisers.

THE BEST 1915 NOVELTIES.
The Cream of 1914 Introductions.

The most popular Commercial and Exhibition kinds; also complete line of Pompons, Singles and Anemones. Trade list on application. ELMER D. SMITH & CO., Adrian, Mich.

COCOANUT FIBRE SOIL

20th Century Plant Food Co., Beverly, Mass.
For page see List of Advertisers.

DAHLIAS

Send for Wholesale List of whole clumps and separate stock; 60,000 clumps for sale. Northboro Dahlia and Gladiolus Gardens, J. L. MOORE, Prop, Northboro, Mass.

NEW PAEONY DAHLIA
John Wanamaker. Newest, Handsomest, Best. New color, new form and new habit of growth. Big stock of best cut-flower varieties. Send list of wants to PEACOCK DAHLIA FARMS, Berlin, N. J.

DAISIES

DAISIES (Bellis), fine stock; Longfellow, $2.00 per 1000; Monstrosa, $3.00 per 1000. CLARK-FLORIST, 124 Washington Ave., Scranton, Pa.

DECORATIVE PLANTS

Robert Craig Co., Philadelphia, Pa.
For page see List of Advertisers.

Woodrow & Marketos, New York City.
For page see List of Advertisers.

S. S. Skidelsky & Co., Philadelphia, Pa.
For page see List of Advertisers.

Bobbink & Atkins, Rutherford, N. J.
For page see List of Advertisers.

A. Leuthy & Co., Roslindale, Boston, Mass.
For page see List of Advertisers.

Araucarias, 7 in. pots, 3 to 5 tiers, $1.00 each; Cyclamen, 4 and 5 in. pots, 15c. and 25c. each; Primulas Obconica, 3 and 4 in. pots, 5c. each; Begonias Chatelaine, 5 in. pans, 20c. each; Begonias Luminosa, 4 and 5 in. pots, 10c. and 15c. each; Asp. Sprengeri, 3 in. pots, $3.00 per 100; Asp. Plumosus, 3 in. pots, $4.00 per 100; Table Ferns, 2½ in. pots, $3.00 per 100; Jerusalem Cherries, 4 in. pots, 5c. each; Jerusalem Cherries, from field, 5 in. pots, 10c. each; Var. Vincas, from field, $5.00 per 100. Write for prices on Holland Bulbs of all kinds. ROSENDALE NURSERY & GREENHOUSES, Schenectady, N. Y.

For List of Advertisers See Page 467

DRACENAS

The Storrs & Harrison Co., Painesville, Ohio.
For page see List of Advertisers.

DRACAENAS

indivisa—Fine large plants, special offer to close out the lot.

	100	1000
2½ inch	$6.00	$50.00
4 "	12.50	100.00
5 "	20.00	
5½ "	25.00	
6 "	40.00	

WRITE FOR COPY OF OUR MONTHLY PLANT BULLETIN.
S. S. PENNOCK-MEEHAN CO.,
1608-1620 Ludlow St., Philadelphia, Pa.

EUONYMUS RADICANS VEGETUS

Euonymus Radicans Vegetus—Three-year-old potted plants for immediate delivery; also three-year field-grown plants. $14.00 per 100, $2.00 per doz. Illustrated booklet, free for the asking. THE GARDEN NURSERIES, Narberth, Pa.

FERNS

H. H Barrows & Son, Whitman, Mass.
For page see List of Advertisers.

Robert Craig Co., Philadelphia, Pa.
For page see List of Advertisers.

McHutchison & Co., New York City.
Ferns in Flats.
For page see List of Advertisers.

A. M. Davenport, Watertown, Mass.
Boston and Whitman Ferns.
For page see List of Advertisers.

Roman J. Irwin, New York City.
Boston and Whitman Ferns.
For page see List of Advertisers.

The Storrs & Harrison Co., Painesville, Ohio.
For page see List of Advertisers.

ASPLENIUM NIDUS AVIS (Birds-nest fern).

Good strong healthy plants, 4 in. pots, $40.00 per 100; 5 in. pots, $75.00 per 100; 6 in. pots, $100.00 per 100. WM. K. HARRIS, 55th and Springfield Ave., W. Philadelphia, Pa.

FERTILIZERS

20th Century Plant Food Co., Beverly, Mass. Coconut Fibre Soil.
For page see List of Advertisers.

Stumpp & Walter Co., New York City.
Scotch Soot.
For page see List of Advertisers.

Chicago Feed & Fertilizer Co., Chicago, Ill.
Magic Manures.
For page see List of Advertisers.

Pulverized Manure Co., Chicago, Ill.
Wizard Brand Cattle Manure.

FLORISTS' LETTERS

Boston Florist Letter Co., Boston, Mass.
For page see List of Advertisers.

FLORISTS' SUPPLIES

N. F. McCarthy & Co., Boston, Mass.
For page see List of Advertisers.

Reed & Keller, New York City.
For page see List of Advertisers.

S. S. Pennock-Meehan Co., Philadelphia, Pa.
For page see List of Advertisers.

H. Bayersdorfer & Co., Philadelphia, Pa.
For page see List of Advertisers.

Welch Bros. Co., Boston, Mass.
For page see List of Advertisers.

FLOWER POTS

W. H. Ernest, Washington, D. C.
For page see List of Advertisers.

A. H. Hews & Co., Inc., Cambridge, Mass.
For page see List of Advertisers.

Hilfinger Bros., Ft. Edward, N. Y.
For page see List of Advertisers.

FOLIAGE PLANTS

A. Leuthy & Co., Roslindale, Boston, Mass.
For page see List of Advertisers.

FORGET-ME-NOTS

FORGET-ME-NOTS—Just right in transplant, several varieties. Surplus at $2.00, $3.00 and $4.00 per 1000, according to variety. CLARK-FLORIST, 124 Washington Ave., Scranton, Pa.

FREESIAS

Yokohama Nursery Co., Ltd., New York City.
Japan Grown Freesias.
For page see List of Advertisers.

FUNGINE

Aphine Mfg. Co., Madison, N. J.
For page see List of Advertisers.

GALAX

Michigan Cut Flower Co., Detroit, Mich.
For page see List of Advertisers.

GADEN TOOLS

B. G. Pratt Co., New York City.

GERANIUMS

R. Vincent, Jr., & Sons Co.
White Marsh, Md.
For page see List of Advertisers.

Geraniums, rooted in Silica rock sand; show a better color and grow better. Let me have your order for Nutt, Ricard, Poitevine and La Favorite. $10.00 per 1000. Cash. JAMES MOSS, Johnsville, Pa.

GLASS

Sharp, Partridge & Co., Chicago.
For page see List of Advertisers.

Parshelsky Bros., Inc., Brooklyn, N. Y.
For page see List of Advertisers.

Royal Glass Works, New York City.
For page see List of Advertisers.

Greenhouse glass, lowest prices. JOHNSTON GLASS CO., Hartford City, Ind.

GLASS CUTTERS

Smith & Hemenway Co., New York City.
Red Devil Glass Cutter.
For page see List of Advertisers.

GLAZING POINTS

H. A. Dreer, Philadelphia, Pa.
Peerless Glazing Point.
For page see List of Advertisers.

GREENHOUSE BUILDING MATERIAL

King Construction Co., N. Tonawanda, N. Y.
For page see List of Advertisers.

Parshelsky Bros., Inc., Brooklyn, N. Y.
For page see List of Advertisers.

Metropolitan Material Co., Brooklyn, N. Y.
For page see List of Advertisers.

Lord & Burnham Co., New York City.
For page see List of Advertisers.

A. T. Stearns Lumber Co., Neponset, Boston.
Pecky Cypress.

GREENHOUSE CONSTRUCTION

King Construction Co., N. Tonawanda, N. Y.
For page see List of Advertisers.

Foley Greenhouse Mfg. Co., Chicago, Ill.
For page see List of Advertisers

Metropolitan Material Co., Brooklyn, N. Y.
For page see List of Advertisers.

Lord & Burnham Co., New York City.
For page see List of Advertisers.

Hitchings & Co., New York City.

A. T. Stearns Lumber Co., Boston, Mass.

GUTTERS

King Construction Co., N. Tonawanda, N. Y.
King Channel Gutter.
For page see List of Advertisers.

Metropolitan Material Co., Brooklyn, N. Y.
Iron Gutters.
For page see List of Advertisers.

HAIL INSURANCE

Florists' Hail Assn. of America.
J. G. Esler, Saddle River, N. J.
For page see List of Advertisers.

HARDY FERNS AND GREEN GOODS

Michigan Cut Flower Exchange, Detroit, Mich.
For page see List of Advertisers.

Knud Nielsen, Evergreen, Ala.
Natural Green Sheet Moss, Fancy and Dagger Ferns and Huckleberry Foliage.
For page see List of Advertisers.

The Kervan Co., New York.
For page see List of Advertisers.

HARDY PERENNIALS

Bay State Nurseries, No. Abington, Mass.
For page see List of Advertisers.

P. Ouwerkerk, Hoboken, N. J.
For page see List of Advertisers.

Palisades Nurseries, Sparkill, N. Y.
For page see List of Advertisers.

Eastern Nurseries, Jamaica Plain, Mass.
Surplus List.

HARDY PERENNIALS—Many varieties, fine stock, just in the pink of condition to transplant. Surplus $1.00 to $2.50 per 100, according to variety. CLARK-FLORIST, 124 Washington Ave., Scranton, Pa.

HEATING APPARATUS

Kroeschell Bros. Co., Chicago.
For page see List of Advertisers.

Lord & Burnham Co., New York City.
For page see List of Advertisers.

HOT BED SASH.

Parshelsky Bros., Inc., Brooklyn, N. Y.
For page see List of Advertisers.

Foley Greenhouse Construction Co., Chicago, Ill.
For page see List of Advertisers.

S. Jacobs & Sons, Brooklyn, N. Y.
For page see List of Advertisers.

Lord & Burnham Co., New York City.
For page see List of Advertisers.

A. T. Stearns Lumber Co., Neponset, Mass.

HOSE

H. A. Dreer, Philadelphia, Pa.
For page see List of Advertisers.

INSECTICIDES

Aphine Manufacturing Co., Madison, N. J.
Aphine and Fungine.
For page see List of Advertisers.

Nicotine Mfg. Co., St. Louis, Mo.
Aphis Punk and Nikoteen.
For page see List of Advertisers.

The Plantlife Co., New York City.
Plantlife Insecticide.
For page see List of Advertisers.

HYDRANGEAS

The Storrs & Harrison Co., Painesville, Ohio.
For page see List of Advertisers.

IRIS

John Lewis Childs, Inc.,
Flowerfield, L. I., N. Y.
For page see List of Advertisers.

IRRIGATION EQUIPMENT

Skinner Irrigation Co., Brookline, Mass.
For page see List of Advertisers.

KENTIAS

Joseph Heacock Co., Wyncotte, Pa.

L. FORMOSUMS

Yokohama Nursery Co., Ltd., New York City.
For page see List of Advertisers.

LILY BULBS

Chas. Schwake & Co., New York City.
Horticultural Importers and Exporters.
For page see List of Advertisers.

R. M. Ward & Co., New York, N. Y.
Japanese Lily Bulbs of Superior Quality.
For page see List of Advertisers.

Corp. of Chas. F. Meyer, New York City.
Meyer's T. Brand Giganteums.
For page see List of Advertisers.

John Lewis Childs, Inc.,
Hardy Lilies.
Flowerfield, L. I., N. Y.
For page see List of Advertisers.

LILY OF THE VALLEY

Chas. Schwake & Co., Inc., New York City.
Bohmann's Famous Lily of the Valley Pips.
For page see List of Advertisers.

McHutchison & Co., New York City.
For page see List of Advertisers.

Loechner & Co., New York City.
Lily of the Valley Pips.
For page see List of Advertisers.

For List of Advertisers See Page 467

In writing to Advertisers kindly mention Horticulture

A MODERN BUILT HOUSE.

Every grower who handles bulbs in quantity knows the trouble and expense of starting the bulbs and getting them ready for forcing. The methods of potting up the bulbs and placing in cold frames, covered with soil or litter or stable manure, which is the general practice in northern states, is usually very satisfactory in its results, but is very expensive and requires much labor only to be followed by more expense for labor in planting them in, especially in cold weather when they often have to be dug out of snow and ice. Those who force bulbs in large quantities have long felt the want of a better way of handling them so as to reduce expense and labor of winter handling.

About three years ago, Frank Oesch-

slin, of Chicago, who forces about 300,-000 tulips, hyacinths and daffodils in pots and pans for wholesaling and none for cut flowers, began experimenting with bulb houses. Since then he has had so many letters of inquiry from all over the country as to his method of construction, that he has kindly consented to give a detailed description of his bulb house, which, as it now stands, is giving perfect satisfaction. The accompanying cut is made from a flash light of the interior of the house, which measures 20x115 feet on the inside and is 8½ feet high, one half being underground. A house of this size will accommodate about a quarter million bulbs in pots and pans. The side walls are made of solid concrete, twelve inches thick. The floor is well drained, having sewer connection, with cement walks and six or eight inches of sand over clay bottom. One half of the roof is formed by a cottage, the balance made of reinforced concrete. supported by steel beams, making a very permanent structure. Ventilation is provided for by means of four-inch pipes running through the side walls near the top

and also by means of small doors in the walls. The house is fitted with pecky cypress movable shelves, four feet wide on each side and eight feet wide in the center, resting upon galvanized iron pipes that are joined to iron posts by means of split T's. The posts are about four feet apart and the cross-pipes are about ten inches apart, giving eight shelves. The house is equipped with a small hot-water boiler, but it has never been used as sufficient heat is maintained by small gasoline stoves and these were used only in severe weather. The bulbs are planted in pots and pans, usually in October, and after being thoroughly watered are placed at once upon the shelves and root growth starts immediately. The temperature is kept as low as possible during the fall and just about freezing during the winter. Watering is done as required, usually three or four times during the season. The house is fitted with electric lights for working, otherwise is kept perfectly dark. Root action is excellent and the bulbs are in the best of condition for forcing. This house has been used for two years and proved successful.

NEWS NOTES.

Ludington, Mich.—Two greenhouses, with their tools and stock, owned by E. L. Brillhart. a bankrupt, and valued at $8,000, were sold to Martin Lunde for $1,000 by court order.

Bloomfield, N. J. — When you say Bloomfield you naturally think of Peter Hauck, who is one of those far-sighted florists who cannot be prevented from making money. Just now his place, recently enlarged by the purchase of the Brozat greenhouse property adjoining, is largely in chrysanthemums and tomatoes. The chrysanthemums are very promising and among them is a yellow sport from Timothy Eaton which is practically a Chadwick flower on an Eaton plant. It stands for late propagation and can be planted very close. It is to be introduced later on. After the chrysanthemums, geraniums. in which Mr. Hauck is a large operator. will fill the houses—100,000 or more plants for spring sales.

Mr. Hauck grows only one tomato, an English variety known as Early Dumpleton. The first fruit is being picked now and the heavy part of the six tons expected will come in December when tomatoes are worth big money. We counted five tiers of blossoms on plants less than two feet tall which is a pretty good showing for Early Dumpleton.

When writing to advertisers kindly mention HORTICULTURE.

MASSACHUSETTS AGRICULTURAL COLLEGE NOTES.

A greenhouse, 24x33 feet, has just been completed for the agronomy department. It is the first greenhouse that the agronomy department has had the use of. In it students will be able to carry on experiments with soils, fertilizers, hays and grains, etc. The house is to be heated from the college power plant. The construction was in charge of Hitchings & Co.

A Plymouth man has recently invented a sure cure for all diseases of fruit trees. The name of this medicine is "Dextrogermiform." The inventor is demonstrating on the young Clark orchard at the college. The experiment is creating considerable interest among fruit growers.

PATENTS GRANTED.

1,154,173. Plant-Setting Machine. Solomon L. Bryant, Mt. Airy, N. C.
1,154,364. Weed-Cutting Machine. Oscar H. Bjur, Kennewick. Wash.
1,154,536. Wheel-Barrow. George S. Nichols, Freeport. Maine.
1,154,839. Garden Tool. John Wesley Bigford. Toronto, Ontario, Canada.
1,155,174. Self-Cleaning Rake. Joseph H. Ubelaker, Chicago, Ill.
1,155,313. Protector for Trees or Other Vegetation. Newton Hogan, Los Angeles, Cal.

GREENHOUSES BUILDING OR CONTEMPLATED.

Norwich, Ct.—T. H. Peabody, house, 30x75.
Felchville, Vt.—H. C. Hawkins, house 27 x 60.
Flint, Mich.—Hasselbring Floral Co., additions.
Wyomissing, Pa.—B. H. Farr, King house, 35x150.
Rome, N. Y.—E. J. Byam, Elm street, house, 32x150.
Williamsport, Pa.—W. J. Graham, house, 20x100.
Maryville, Mo.—State Normal College, one house.
Sinking Spring, Pa.—Harry E. Kiffer, King house, 18x24.
Waukesha, Wis.—Andrew Butchart, Broadway, additions.
Lafayette, Ind.—Fred Schilling, additions and alterations.
Pawtucket, R. I.—Wm. Hoffman, East Ave., two houses.
Cedar Rapids, Ia.—F. L. Diserens, two houses each 28x150.
Baltimore, Md.—A. Spath, Jr. & Son, Embla Park, house, 43x75.
Scranton, Pa.—Mrs. A. F. Conwell, Lincoln avenue, one house.
Grand Rapids, Mich.—H. S. Jordan, 1440 Union avenue, additions.
Beverly, Mass.—Robert S. Bradley, 691 Hale street, house, 19x82.
North Adams, Mass.—Dr. Vanderpool Adriance, conservatory 40 x 60.
Portland, Ore.—R. Riegelmann, Miles and Nevada streets, one house.
Newport, R. I.—Eleanor E. Widener, Coggeshall avenue, house, 24x84.
Williamsport, Pa. — Williamsport Floral Co., High street, range of houses.
East Orange, N. J.—Davis & Davis, Central avenue and Grove street, house, 17x100.
Ronks, Pa.—Chas. Weaver, King house, 42½x300. Ezra Miller, King house, 35x100.
Columbus, O.—E. H. Burkley and J. U. Cassidy, 237-245 Richardson avenue, one house.
Hartford, Ct.—J. W. Adams Co., Dover street, one house, H. P. Brooks, 755 Campbell avenue, one house.
Providence, R. I.—Johnston Bros., Rocbambeau Ave. and Hope St., range of 150-foot Lord & Burnham houses.
Newark, N. J.—Ernest Radany, 596 Central avenue, alterations. F. H. Kuehn, 621 Central avenue, additions.
Philadelphia, Pa.—Carl Moll, Gorgas lane and Ridge avenue, one house. John Wieland, 111 W. Luray street. house, 22x90.
Providence, R. I.—Chas. Hunt, Burnside street, one house. Richard Higgins, Academy street, alterations. Lawrence Hay, one house.

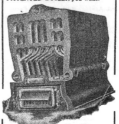

Vol. XXII
No. 16
OCT. 16
1915

HORTICULTURE

Field of Gladiolus America
At B. Hammond Tracy's, Wenham, Mass.

Published Every Saturday at 147 Summer Street, Boston, Mass.
Subscription, $1.00

LIST OF ADVERTISERS

FOR BUYERS' DIRECTORY AND READY REFERENCE GUIDE
SEE PAGES 520, 521, 522, 523

NOTES ON CULTURE OF FLORISTS' STOCK
CONDUCTED BY

John J. M. Farrell

Questions by our readers in line with any of the topics presented on this page will be cordially received and promptly answered by Mr. Farrell. Such communications should invariably be addressed to the office of HORTICULTURE.
"If vain our toil, we ought to blame the culture, not the soil."—*Pope.*

Bouvardias

Bouvardias that were lifted and planted out in a bench the end of August will by this time be making lots of roots into the new soil. Do not keep too low a temperature; 60 degrees at night, 70 to 75 on bright days and about 65 in cloudy weather will do. Water carefully and on bright mornings give a good syringing to help keep them clean of mealy bug and red spider. Fumigate lightly and often for green fly.

To Follow Chrysanthemums

The more quickly a chrysanthemum house is emptied, cleaned and replanted the better. Sweet peas, snapdragons, stocks, marguerites, violets, mignonette and pansies are among the many desirable things that might follow the chrysanthemums. For these crops the soil will not need to be removed. All that will be necessary is to add some bone meal and give it a dig over. The man who retails the stock he grows can always dispose of certain things in cut flowers which would never find a buyer on the wholesale market. Often the little odds and ends, as we might call them, bring better returns than some of the standard stock occupying the benches.

Tulips for Outdoors

It pays to grow an assortment of hardy bulbs for cutting, entirely apart from such as may be used for bedding. These follow the indoor crop and can hardly be dispensed with. When it comes to bulbs for bedding, tulips are the bulbs par excellence, and every year sees more and more of them planted. A well assorted mixture is often used and looks well, but beds of one solid color make the most pleasing and at the same time the most imposing show. Care should be taken to select varieties of uniform height which bloom together. By far the finest of all white bedding tulips is White Joost van Vondel; Flamingo and Rose Grisdelin, pink; Yellow Prince and Ophir d'Or, yellow; Belle Alliance, scarlet. and striped Joost von Vondel, rose flaked white, are of uniform height, and bloom together. The following

are inexpensive late tulips: Gesneriana lutea, Golden Crown, T. retroflexa, Bouton d'Or and Leghorn Bonnet. Among whites La Candeur is good; in scarlets, Gesneriana spathulata and Inglescombe Scarlet; in pink, Inglescombe.

Forcing Gladioli

Every florist who has a local trade should force a good batch of gladiolus. The Colvillei corms can be planted in flats or beds and will flower in from fourteen to sixteen weeks. When planting in benches, allow about five inches between the rows and two or three inches in the rows. The corms should be placed about three inches deep. There are many beautiful varieties in the smaller flowered or Colvillei section and for later forcing we have in addition to these the large flowered sorts. Give them a temperature of from 50 to 55 degrees at night. When they have made fairly good roots and top growth they will be greatly benefited by weekly doses of liquid manure, which will help the size of the flower.

Preparing Sweet Pea Ground

Now is the time to get the ground in condition for next spring. Good flowers may be had by merely manuring heavily and plowing deeply or spading the ground over, leaving it with a rough surface over winter. When flowers of a more fancy quality are desired, trenching should be resorted to. Dig out the trenches to the required depth, then place layers of well rotted manure and soil, mixing them as placed in the trenches. Some bone meal scattered through the compost will also be advantageous. Discard all stones, gravel and hard pan. This often means considerable work but a job well done will pay for itself better. Where you first plow it spread manure about two inches deep all over and plow under. In the spring add the bone and wood ashes.

Shamrock for St. Patrick's Day

Now is the time to sow the shamrock for the St. Patrick Day trade. There is more call for the shamrock every year. Prepare some flats and sow the seed not too thick. When large enough, pot them into small pots and grow them on in a cool house. About 45 degrees at night will be right.

Next Week:—Adiantums; Azalea mollis; Begonias; Lily of the Valley; Spiraeas; Outside Work.

HORTICULTURE

VOL. XXII   **OCTOBER 16, 1915**   **NO. 16**

PUBLISHED WEEKLY BY

HORTICULTURE PUBLISHING CO.

147 Summer Street, Boston, Mass.

Telephone, Oxford 292.

WM. J. STEWART, Editor and Manager.

SUBSCRIPTION RATES:

One Year, in advance, $1.00; To Foreign Countries, $2.00; To Canada, $1.50.

ADVERTISING RATES:

Per inch, 30 inches to page.............................. $1.00
Discounts on Contracts for consecutive insertions, as follows:
One month (4 times), 5 per cent.; three months (13 times), 10
per cent.; six months (26 times), 20 per cent.; one year (52 times),
30 per cent.
Page and half page space, special rates on application.   ;and

Entered as second-class matter December 8, 1914, at the Post Office at Boston, Mass., under the Act of Congress of March 3, 1879.

CONTENTS   Page

About
the Boston
fern

Ralph C. Benedict, in Brooklyn Botanic Garden leaflet No. 8, makes some state- ments regarding the "discovery" of the Boston fern which seem to us to be based on some misinformation. It is true that the now well-known arching form of Nephrolepis exaltata called Bostoniensis had its general distribution over the

country through the late F. C. Becker, of Cambridge, but that it was "first discovered" by Mr. Becker as stated in the leaflet is not correct. The truth is that this variety was well known to many Boston gardeners years previous to the time of its exploitation by Mr. Becker and was also recognized by certain New York plantsmen as a Boston form much to be preferred to the one which was being grown in and around New York. The matter is, of course, immaterial now so far as the trade is concerned but anything emanating from a scientific institution should be very exact and no doubt Mr. Benedict will be pleased to learn the facts in this case.

Two
bean diseases

The office of Information of the U. S. Department of Agriculture has sent out an instructive bulletin on the two prevalent bean diseases—anthracnose and bacterial blight—with directions as to the best methods of eradicating these troubles. In our seed trade notes this week will be found a summary of the instructions given out in the bulletin referred to. It will be noticed that home selection of seed is insisted upon and that no reference is made to the efforts being put forth by the growers for the seed trade to produce clean and disease resistant seed. We believe that the Department might derive great benefit and much valuable assistance in this and similar work by closer affiliation and intercourse with the practical men who are engaged commercially in seed growing than from our view point seems to be the case. No one can possibly have more forcible and cogent reason to maintain purity of product and freedom from taint of any kind than he whose business repute and prosperity is at stake.

Bulbs of
high degree

Not in any season within the memory of "the oldest inhabitant" have the tulips, hyacinths and other Dutch bulbs been so handsome to the eye as they are this year in the stocks shown in the seed stores. Should their dormant and unseen good qualities hold up to the standard indicated by their external appearance we may expect to see some superb blooms in the displays at the spring shows of 1916. Exhibition quality needs only to be supplemented by exhibition skill and exhibition opportunity to effect a winning combination such as rarely comes. Whether the high quality of the material so lavishly spread out on the seed store counters and shelves at present is due to the diversion to the United States of goods which the European consumer formerly monopolized or is the result of an unusually favorable season for the Holland bulb growers, matters little so long as we have the goods at our command and it is to be hoped that full advantage will be taken of this unprecedented opportunity to impress upon the public the beauties of these spring garden flowers, by means of the flower shows, and that thus the demand for the bulbs may be greatly increased. We can think of no better means for developing and enlarging this department of the seedsmen's business.

ROSE GROWING UNDER GLASS

CONDUCTED BY

Arthur C Ruzicka

Questions by our readers in line with any of the topics presented on this page will be cordially received and promptly answered by Mr. Ruzicka. Such communications should invariably be addressed to the office of HORTICULTURE.

Treatment for Blackspot

Mr. Arthur Ruzicka.

Dear Sir—We have read your report on rose-growing as was published in the HORTICULTURE under date of August 28th.

We are at present troubled with black-spot and some of our benches of Ophelia roses are affected. We would appreciate very much to receive from you full information regarding the mixture Ammonical Copper Carbonate. We would also like to know how this drug is to be applied, as we have never before used this. Any other information regarding the treatment of black-spot will be greatly appreciated.

Trusting you will favor us with an early reply, we remain, Yours very truly,

T. A. I. & SONS.

Regarding the use of copper carbonate as preventive for blackspot, to two ounces of pure copper carbonate add enough ammonia to thoroughly dissolve it. The mixture is then added to two gallons of water, well stirred, and applied at once. Glass jars should be used for dissolving the copper with the ammonia. Where a larger amount is necessary it can be mixed in a barrel, but we always mixed it in small quantities only, as it loses strength quite rapidly after mixing.

Further treatment for blackspot on Ophelia may be as follows: Keep the plants on the dry side for a while. This does not mean drying them out until they shrivel but let them get fairly dry before they are watered. Avoid syringing for a while as this will spread blackspot quicker than anything. Go over the plants carefully and pick off all leaves that are affected. This cannot be done if the plants are badly attacked but if the disease is taken in time it will be checked this way a great deal. After picking as many of the diseased leaves as can be safely taken apply the ammoniacal copper carbonate and keep the plants on the dry side. Give plenty of air, both night and day, and try to induce the plants to grow as much as possible. Never neglect to blow lime under them at night after watering, and if the weather is dark and rainy do this whether the plants are watered or not. If the benches do not dry out readily it may be that the soil is somewhat sour, and a top dressing of lime will be a great help towards drying the benches out. Use air-slacked lime, freshly slacked, and apply enough to nicely whiten the surface of the soil. This can be applied one day and the benches watered the next, or it can be allowed to lie for several days, after which it will have to be rubbed over to break up any caking that may have taken place. The copper carbonate can be applied two or three times a week if necessary. It will not cure the spot but will keep it from spreading by killing the spores that the mixture touches. When it will be safe to resume syringing, see that it is done quite early in the day so that all the plants will be dry before night comes. Also see that it is done quick and well, with good pressure, so that the whole house is not drenched from top to bottom, taking a long time to dry out. It will be well to blow a little lime around the house during the morning and afternoon of rainy or wet warm foggy days. This is done by walking backwards in the walks with the bellows, holding them up level with the shoulders and working them so that the dust will circulate freely through the house, at the same time not proving so irritating to the one who has to do the work. Through constant use of lime, and care in watering, we have never had a serious case of spot.

Watering

Be careful to see that the plants are not overwatered, more so the plants that have just finished a crop. These will be pretty well cut off and if they are kept too wet they will not break as strongly as they should. Keep plants like these on the dry side. Then again, plants that are covered with buds about ready to show color should never be allowed to become too dry as this would hurt the buds and they would likely be small and not well developed. If there are any poor plants among the others they will not take very much water, and therefore should be skipped when watering. To make sure this is done it is best to go around some time with a box of lime and scatter a little around each plant. Thus marked, they will be easier to avoid when applying water. Late planted roses should be kept on the dry side, so that they will make as much root as possible, but this does not mean that they should be dried out until the soil cracks. This would damage the present roots a good deal, not only tearing them where the soil cracks, but also killing a good many by the too dry a state of the soil. With cold frosty nights it will be necessary to use the tires more and the plants will dry out quicker, so they will take more watching. The soil often dries out in the bottom of the benches first, so when examining benches for watering it is best to reach down to the bottom. Be especially careful not to let a rapidly growing bench of Beauties get too dry as this would be apt to check their growth, and once they stop they will be hard to get going again. In using liquid manure make sure that the plants are wet enough before the liquid is applied. We generally water with clear water first and then apply enough liquid to go through the soil nicely, without running through too much. This takes a little longer but the work is well done and a good deal of manure is thus saved. We can water two houses with the liquid that would be needed to do one were it not for the clear water used before using the liquid manure.

THREE POPULAR GLADIOLI

LILY LEHMAN   PINK PERFECTION   NIAGARA

Grown by B. Hammond Tracy of Wenham, Mass., as three of the best for cut blooms.

THE FLORISTS' OPPORTUNITIES ON THE WESTERN COAST.

The holding of the convention in California this year has already proven a better policy than even its promoters dreamed of one year ago. All eyes in the horticultural world have been turned upon this great state, at a time when conditions in Europe are making it impossible to get plants from the districts which have formerly supplied us. C. W. Ward, of Cottage Gardens, Queens, N. Y., is developing very extensive nurseries at Eureka, Calif., three hundred miles north of San Francisco, where climatic conditions seem to be favorable for growing azaleas, rhododendrons and other plants which we have depended upon Belgium to produce. Other growers have taken up the growing of palms in other parts of the state and already this seems to be an assured success when the same knowledge and care is given it that is required in Belgium. This alone may revolutionize a large and growing industry in the U. S. One of the things first noticed by an eastern florist is the lack of glass on the western coast. The plants require protection from heat rather than from cold and lath houses afford this better than glass-covered ones. These houses are of the same general shape as the regular greenhouses but are apt to be longer and higher. Some glass is needed, however, for the young stock when first lifted from the field. Going farther north from San Francisco more and more glass is used, till, in Washington, comparatively large ranges are seen and in and about Seattle the greenhouses remind one of those in Chicago and vicinity.

Going south from San Francisco, Los Angeles affords the most opportunities for commercial possibilities in horticulture. Here everything grows with so little attention, except a good water supply, that the eye is often shocked with the riot of colors. Some experiments are being tried out here which will prove in the near future the possibilities of producing in Southern California many of the things that we have always bought in Europe. All the way down to the Mexican border (which seemed like the end of civilization) the coast suggests possibilities which will justify the term "Golden West," and offer the reward of dollars to the men and women who will learn to understand and apply the principles that will make nature their ally in commercialized horticulture.

M. B. HANCOCK.

South Orange, N. J.—W. A. Manda. is gradually getting his grounds into good shape after the chaos resulting from the elevation of the tracks of the D. L. & W. railroad, but alterations will not be fully carried out before next spring. The new dahlias are a prime popular attraction with their great blooms as large as peonies and will so continue as long as frost stays away. Mr. Manda has diverted the water in a brook which traverses his grounds so as to form an island approached by rustic bridges. which will be devoted to exotic plants exclusively as a tropical summer garden. A very extensive rock garden will be constructed also, and a pumping outfit will be installed to take water from the brook for greenhouse use. The greenhouses have been repainted and renovated and two large Kroeschell boilers are being put in to take the place of a number of small heaters. One cannot but observe the sturdy health and vigor of the cattleyas here, all of which have passed the summer outside up to the present time with no protection other than some cheese cloth.

CLEVELAND FLOWER SHOW

At a meeting of the private growers of Cleveland, held at the Hollenden Hotel, Friday, October 8, the wrappings were taken from a huge package and the magnificent Corrigan cup, one of the chief trophies offered for the Cleveland Flower Show, November 10 to 14, was exposed for the first time here. It had just arrived from Tiffany, New York, the makers, and although there was a spirited rivalry among the Ohio growers for this prize even before seeing it, there now is a spirit of contest that will keep every private grower on tiptoe until the close of the show.

Among the many novel advertising plans being carried out by the publicity committee of The Cleveland Flower Show is the use of the popular "poster stamps." These small stickers are reproductions, in miniature, of the poster cards used by the show and thousands of them are being added to the collections of the school children. It is the committee's aim to get the widest circulation possible of these stamps and a quantity will be sent to anyone, anywhere in the United States, upon request. The local growers and dealers connected with the show and all exhibitors will be provided with them for use upon their business correspondence between this time and the date of the show.

H. P. Knoble, general chairman, and Timothy Smith, of the admissions committee, will confer with Superintendent Frederick, of the Cleveland Public Schools, this week to arrange for free admission of the school children on mornings during the show, beginning the second day. There are about 200,000 children enrolled in Cleveland's schools and the committees hope to have each one take advantage of the educational features of the exhibition.

The private gardeners of Cleveland have become more enthusiastic than ever of the Cleveland show since the meeting held at The Hollenden last Friday. They were unanimous in voting the work of the premiums committee satisfactory. The premiums committee is composed of Herbert Bate, chairman, J. Curnow, of Akron, and Frank A. Friedley.

Permission has been granted the show committee to place bay trees along Euclid avenue from Public square to the Coliseum entrance, during the exposition. Each bay tree will support a small card directing the observer to the show. The publicity committee expect to make this the most attractive and novel scheme of street advertising that has been used in the city.

The entertainment committee is busy with the plans for the varied entertainment and arrangement of the business and semi-social program during show days. This committee, headed by G. W. Smith and his aids are. C. J. Graham, George Jacques, S. N. Pentecost, F. C. Witthuhn. The rooms of The Cleveland Florist Club, Hollenden Hotel, will be the meeting place of the various organizations, as well as the scene of many social events.

In discussing the plans of his committee, Chairman Smith said: "We expect to be able to announce the complete program within a few days. Provision will be made for the meetings of the Chrysanthemum Society of America, which has its annual exhibition and convention in conjunction with our show for the fall exhibition and meeting of The American Rose Society and the other important events. The executive committee of the American Carnation Society will have a place on the program, as will the Florists Telegraph Delivery Association, which comes for an adjourned meeting and the adjourned meeting of The Gladiolus Society of Ohio.

"Entertainment fitting the bringing together of the members of these important organizations will be arranged. Without interfering with the business sessions or the exposition we will provide amusement for the leisure hours that we hope will make all visitors remember Cleveland kindly."

NATIONAL FLOWER SHOW.

Philadelphia, March 25 to April 2.

Chairman George Asmus of the National Flower Show Committee has called a meeting of his committee to be held on Tuesday, October 19, at the Bellevue-Stratford Hotel, Philadelphia, at 10 A. M. At this meeting the schedule of the Rose, Carnation, Sweet Pea and Gladiolus Societies will be completed, and much other business relating to the show transacted. On the day previous to the meeting members of the National Flower Show Committee will meet the chairmen and members of the different local committees to talk over details of the work of preparation for the show, and if any member of the trade has a suggestion to make either in regard to schedule or anything else bearing upon the conduct of the show, it would be well to communicate with the management in order that it receive proper consideration. As all know, the National Flower Show Committee is composed of members of the S. A. F. and O. H. located widely apart, thus being representative of different communities, consequently it is not possible to have frequent meetings, and this opportunity to bring anything before the committee at this meeting should not be neglected.

Preparations in general are well advanced, and a great deal has been accomplished. Space in the trade section of the show is in good demand, reservations aggregating in value $6,000 or more having even at this early date been made. It is expected that every foot of space available for trade exhibits will be sold a long time ahead of the show dates. The greenhouse builders, plantsmen and others have made early selection of locations, and but a few of the choicer blocks of space are left.

The committee is now prepared to receive offers of special prizes from the trade, and others whose business brings them in touch with enterprises of this character. It need not be pointed out that the publicity to be derived from our special prize list is worthy of consideration by all; and again, there should be some feeling of pleasure to result from a helpful effort in anything which will advance horticultural interests. As the second preliminary schedule will go out shortly after the meeting of the National Flower Show Committee, donors of special prizes should communicate their wishes to the secretary without delay.

The all important business of selection of a design for the show poster has been taken up by Mr. Therkildson and his committee, and the result of their efforts will be presented at the forthcoming meeting. Some novel plans for publicity are expected to be evolved by this committee.

The plantings on the plots outside of Convention Hall this summer have, as Robert Craig says, furnished good subject matter for publicity for the show, and it is to be regretted that the approaching frosty season necessitates the withdrawal of the crotons, the beds of which have daily attracted thousands.

Looked at from every standpoint, the Fourth National Flower Show bids fair to more than warrant the slogan that it will be "The Greatest Horticultural Event of 1916," and then some more.　　JOHN YOUNG, Sec. 53 W. 28th St., New York City.

CHICAGO GRAND FLORAL FESTIVAL.

The regular meeting of the executive committee of the Chicago Grand Floral Festival was held at the Hotel Morrison, October 7. Routine business connected with the exhibition to be held at the Coliseum November 9-14, occupied the attention of the committee the greater part of the afternoon, and reports from chairmen of the various sub-committees showed substantial progress. Manager French announced that a large number of special prizes have already been secured and others promised. Arrangements are being made for extensive exhibits from the various park systems and plans for Robert Brenton's novel, flower-dance feature are going well.

The name of Prof. H. B. Dorner, of the University of Illinois, has been added to the lecture program, his subject being "Garden Flowers," with an extensive exhibit of stereopticon slides, and E. G. Hill, of Richmond, Ind., has promised a talk on garden roses.

Exhibitors in the non-competitive trade display will be given one trade ticket good the first day of the show for each square foot of space taken. E. F. Winterson has been appointed chairman of the trade tickets committee.　　M. BARKER, Chairman Publicity Com.

The Thirteenth Annual Exhibition of the Northern Westchester County Horticultural and Agricultural Society will be held at Civic Hall, Mt. Kisco, N. Y., on October 29, 30 and 31. The schedule contains fifty-six classes, of which seven are open to private gardeners only. Copies may be obtained by applying to M. J. O'Brien, Secretary, Mt. Kisco, N. Y.

CLUBS AND SOCIETIES

NEW YORK FLORISTS' CLUB.

The monthly meeting of this club on Monday evening, October 11, was well attended by a representative gathering of florists, gardeners, seedsmen and others from New York, New Jersey and other sections. The principal items of business as per the secretary's prospectus were the exhibition of chrysanthemums, payment of dues, S. A. F. and O. H. affiliation, Cleveland Flower Show and House Committee. Not the least among these attractions was the last named and ample justice was done by the members to the roast turkey, celery and approved accompaniments liberally distributed by Chairman Phil. Kessler and his loyal minions. There were ample reports, communications, etc., in ample supply, all of which in the harmonious atmosphere which prevailed received good natured approval. "The ayes have it" quoth the president as each was passed along. F. R. Pierson urged zealous activity on the part of the members in securing special premiums for the Spring Flower Show. F. L. Atkins for the Club and T. A. Havemeyer for the Horticultural Society, are the chairmen of the respective committees to receive these special premiums.

A. M. Henshaw told of the general arrangements in progress for the comfort of members proposing to go to the Cleveland Show and for the transportation of exhibits thereto.

The judges reported on the exhibits of chrysanthemums as follows:

Carnations Laura Weber by Chas. Weber, Victory and Prosperity Sport by Rowehl & Granz, vote of thanks. Seedling Dahlia Sunshine by Mrs. Stout, Short Hills, N. J., highly commended. Collection of dahlias all types, by P. W. Popp, highly commended. Collection of dahlias by W. A. Manda, all highly commended, the following six being given special mention: Mrs. Minnie Burgess, red; Perfection, cream color, certificate of merit; No. 16, deep salmon, certificate of merit; Joseph Manda, red; Albert Manda, pale yellow striped pink; Veronica Manda, variegated. Chrysanthemum Wm. Rigby, a sport of Mrs. G. Drabble and vase of bedding varieties by C. H. Totty, vote of thanks with request to see Wm. Rigby again. Chrysanthemum Marigold (Early Frost × Golden Queen) from A. N. Pierson, vote of thanks. Chrysanthemum Frank Dinda, a pink seedling by Frank Dinda, scored 85 points, commercial scale.

The following resolution reported by Patrick O'Mara was adopted:

Resolved that the New York Florists' Club have heard with the deepest regret of the sudden illness and death of Samuel Thorne. That we take this opportunity of expressing our sympathy with the family of our deceased life member, friend, patron and colleague in their bereavement.

We desire further to express our sense of the great loss which the city and community, as well as horticulture, have sustained in his decease.

He was a shining example for those who survive him, noted for his resolute industry, uncompromising integrity, wise enterprise, high public spirit, sage counsel and helpful attitude towards those who sought his advice. He was a man deserving of all honors, a conspicuous success in his field of endeavor, an encouragement for all who would follow his example.

We cherish his memory and gratefully testify to his many acts of practical help in our efforts to advance horticulture in this city.

Resolved, that our Secretary be instructed to send a copy of this resolution to the family of the deceased and cause same to be published in the horticulture press.

PATRICK O'MARA, CHARLES H. TOTTY, WALTER F. SHERIDAN.

PACIFIC COAST HORTICULTURAL SOCIETY.

The regular meeting of the Pacific Coast Horticultural Society held Saturday evening, October 2, was well attended and several interesting matters were taken up. The admission of several new members, some of national prominence, was a feature of the meeting. They included Wm. F. Kasting, of Buffalo, N. Y.; Patrick Welch, of Boston; Vincent Gorly, of St. Louis; Jas. Kirkman, of New York; Walter W. Coles, of Kokomo, Ind.; C. W. Ward, of Eureka, Cal.; Frank Sherrer, superintendent of parks of Los Angeles, Cal.; John Morley, park superintendent of San Diego, Cal.; A. C. Zvolanek, of Lompoc, Cal. The illustrated lecture on "Wood Decay of Ornamental Plants," presented by Prof. W. T. Horne of the Department of Plant Pathology of the University of California, was very well received. Members were urged to enter exhibits at once for the Grand National Show, October 21 to 26. They were invited to attend in a body the formal exercises to be held in the South Gardens in front of the Palace of Horticulture this Saturday afternoon in connection with Exposition Gardeners' Day at the Fair, at which time a handsome trophy will be presented to John McLaren on behalf of the people of San Francisco in recognition of his able services in the landscaping of the Exposition grounds. It was decided to observe Florists' Day at the Exposition on October 25. Among the evening's exhibits were three vases of dahlias by Frank Pelicano, which took 95 points, and one pot each of Ficus lutescens, Ficus utilis and Ficus pandurata by H. Plath, rated at 92 points.

AMERICAN CARNATION SOCIETY.

A meeting of the Board of Directors will be held at Cleveland, O., on Friday, November 12. The Cleveland Florists' Club rooms in the Hollenden Hotel will be placed at our disposal and the meeting will be called at 4.00 P. M. Any of our members who happen to be in Cleveland at that time are invited to be present.

A. F. J. BAUR, Secy.

Jos. H. HILL, Pres.

TEXAS NURSERYMEN'S CONVENTION.

The regular annual meeting of the Nurserymen's Association met in Waco, Sept. 28-29. All of the members of the association but ten and several nurserymen who are not members, were present. The meeting was one of the best that has been held by the nurserymen for several years. Some of the most important questions pertaining to the nursery business were brought before the convention and all were freely discussed. The association was welcomed to Waco by Mayor J. W. Riggins. Response to the welcome address was made by C. C. Mayhew, of Sherman.

The report of the secretary-treasurer, the president's annual address, reports of committees, appointment of committees and an address by J. H. Arbenz, of Sarita, on "The Nurserymen's Interest in a State Board of Horticulture," comprised the proceedings of the first session, Tuesday morning, September 28.

One of the most interesting and most important reports was made by the Legislative Committee. J. R. Mayhew, of Waxahachie, chairman of this committee, made an extensive report of the work·this committee has been doing. The greater portion of his report dealt with the Oklahoma Inspection Law. He stated that the feeling between the nurserymen in Texas and the Texas nursery inspectors was much better now than at any time in the past. He, however, introduced the matter of a proposed uniform inspection bill and a committee was appointed to report on this proposed bill, making recommendations to the association. The committee recommended that the Texas Nurserymen's Association indorse the proposed bill, which was done. A telegram was sent to the president of the Oklahoma Nurserymen's Association, informing him of the action taken by the Texas nurserymen, requesting that the Oklahoma nurserymen also approve the bill and seek its adoption.

The Tuesday afternoon session was full of interesting discussions. A paper was read by J. B. Baker on "Notes on New or Little Known Ornamentals." After the session, the nurserymen were taken in automobiles for a drive over the city and a barbecue was served at the Fish Pond club house. The Wednesday morning session was taken up by two addresses, reports of committees and election of officers. The address of Mr. Ed. L. Ayres, Chief Inspector of Orchards and Nurseries, on "Crown Gall and Other Diseases," was much appreciated by the nurserymen. He had quite a lot of specimens with which he illustrated his lecture. J. R. Mayhew addressed the association on "How can the Texas Nurserymen's Association Best Work in Co-operation with the National Association." He reviewed the history of both the organizations and showed how important benefits could be obtained. A strong appeal for a greater membership in the Texas Nurserymen's Association was made.

The election of officers resulted as follows: Will B. Munson, Dennison, president; J. M. Ramsey, Austin, vice-president; J. S. Kerr, Sherman, secretary-treasurer.

A strong resolution of thanks was tendered the local nurserymen and the people of Waco for their friendly reception and excellent entertainment given the nurserymen while in that city.

PITTSBURGH FLORISTS' AND GARDENERS' CLUB.

A good attendance of the club was present for Dahlia Night, Tuesday, Oct. 5, in the Assembly Room of the Fort Pitt Hotel. R. Vincent, Jr., & Sons, White Marsh, Md., made a display of dahlias not so large as they have shown before the club in some years, but all the blooms of a high order of merit. One of our Pittsburgh commission houses reported as the best selling dahlias Marguerite Bouchon and Souvenir de Douzon. A vote of thanks was awarded Messrs. Vincent & Sons. Carl Becherer showed a large assortment of dahlias. Among the cactus varieties he finds Floradora the most profuse bloomer, followed by Country Girl. His display was strong in Collarettes, which made a fine showing, and he also exhibited an attractive crimson seedling named for W. C. Beckert, our Pittsburgh seedsman. Mr. Becherer's display was awarded a cultural certificate, and further, in view of his constant and meritorious displays before the club, the secretary was instructed to send a letter of appreciation to the superintendent of the Dixmont Hospital of Mr. Becherer's work. Wm. Thompson, gardener for W. P. Snyder, Sewickley, Pa., showed a good vase of Delice and a large lot of other dahlias, some of them seedlings, for which he was given a cultural certificate. M. Curran, gardener for Mrs. Jos. Horne, Sewickley, showed two vases of seedling dahlias, one vase of standard varieties, also chrysanthemums which have been blooming with him since the middle of August. He was awarded a cultural certificate. T. Tyler, gardener for C. D. Armstrong was awarded a certificate of merit for orchids. The Pittsburgh Cut Flower Co. showed a spray of Cattleya labiata of great merit, for which they were awarded a certificate of merit. G. Wessenauer, Sewickley, received a cultural certificate for sprayed fruit.

H. P. JOSLIN, Secretary.

WESTCHESTER AND FAIRFIELD HORTICULTURAL SOCIETY.

An interesting and enthusiastic meeting of this society was held on Friday evening, Oct. 8th, at Greenwich, Ct. The fall show will be held in the Armory at Stamford, Conn., Nov. 5-6. The schedule lists many very valuable prizes. The names of the winners in the competition for the J. H. Troy prizes for the best list of 25 garden roses will be announced at the next meeting.

There was an interesting display on the exhibition tables. Strawberries "Superb" from Thos. Ryan received honorable mention. Carl Hawkenson

was highly commended for chrysanthemum Glory of the Pacific. Robert Grunnert showed September Morn roses, carnation Pink Sensation, and begonia Golden Shower, a meritorious exhibit that was highly commended. P. W. Popp was awarded a certificate of merit for dahlias in six types shown on long stems. Andrew Kennedy offers prizes for the best 25 carnations, assorted colors, shown at the next meeting to be held Nov. 12th.

P. W. POPP, Cor. Sec'y.

C. L. BROCK.

C. L. Brock has been appointed by President Welch as superintendent of the Convention Garden for Houston. The appointment this year is made a little in advance as conditions in the South for planting are such as to justify an early beginning. This will be of great advantage to the Convention Garden, giving more time to work up exhibits and give it more publicity.

Mr. Brock's appointment is considered a good one. He is superintendent of the parks of the city of Houston,

C. L. BROCK
Appointed Superintendent of Houston Convention Garden for 1916.

where large tracks of land are now being laid out for park use. Mr. Brock has displayed great ability in handling this work.

About twenty acres have been outlined for the Convention Garden, having already natural lakes and natural drainage, which makes this an ideal place for the purpose. Mr. Brock is now getting busy on his plans and more than likely will enroll as assistant Mr. Kessler of St. Louis, who is working in conjunction with Mr. Brock in laying out the other parks. He is a man of national reputation for work of this kind.

Exhibitors who anticipate making a display at the Convention should write Mr. Brock or Vice-President R. C. Kerr immediately for full information.

OYSTER BAY HORTICULTURAL SOCIETY.

The autumn show of the Oyster Bay Horticultural Society was held at Fireman's Hall, Oyster Bay, N. Y., on Oct. 5th and 6th. There were many beautiful displays of flowers, also very fine

collections of vegetables and fruits. Geo. Ashworth, James Hall and Geo. Wilson acted as judges.

First prizes in the dahlia classes were won by E. M. Townsend, gard. James Duthie; J. A. Blair, gard. John Devine; Mrs. W. R. Coe, gard. J. Robinson; Mrs. C. L. Tiffany, gard. F. J. Kyle; J. A. Garver, gard. J. Sorosick.

First prize winners in the other flower and plant classes were E. M. Townsend, Frank A. Gale, Howard C. Smith, gard. A. Walker; J. A. Garver, G. Bullock, gard. D. Hothersall; Albert Strauss, gard. M. O'Neill; Eastover Farm, gard. Henry Gibson.

First prize winners in the many vegetable classes were Mrs. W. R. Coe, Albert Strauss, E. F. Whitney, Supt. Jas. Duckham, H. C. Smith, gard. C. Erickson, Howard C. Smith, Mrs. C. L. Tiffany, Eastover Farm, W. A. Delano, gard. A. Yanuchi, E. F. Whitney and John T. Ingram.

In the fruit classes the following were first prize winners: E. M. Townsend, Mrs. W. R. Coe, Frank Petroccia, Albert Strauss.

ALBANY FLORISTS' CLUB.

As usual, at the monthly meeting of this club, on the evening of Thursday, October 7, there was a full attendance and much interest. Five long-distance visitors were present—Patrick Welch of Boston, president of the S. A. F.; Wm. J. Stewart of Boston, editor of HORTICULTURE; J. J. Karins of Philadelphia, minister plenipotentiary to the florist trade from the House of Dreer; C. S. Ford of New York and Mr. Bochman, representing H. F. Michell Co. of Philadelphia. After the opening business these visitors were called upon for speeches. Mr. Welch was listened to with close attention as he told some of his experiences at the recent convention in San Francisco and dilated on the advantages to the florist industry of organization and country-wide society and club co-operation. Mr. Stewart endorsed Mr. Welch's views and suggested that the S. A. F. might yet find some means of enlisting the larger and affiliation of the smaller florist clubs as it had now succeeded in doing with those of large membership.

Considerable interest was manifested in the coming Cleveland Flower Show and Messrs. Danker, Ed. Tracey and Henkes were appointed by the president as a special committee on the details for the trip of club members on that occasion.

The Albany Cut Flower Exchange at whose place the club holds its meetings, provided generous refreshments and a pleasant social hour was enjoyed after the meeting adjourned.

NASSAU COUNTY HORTICULTURAL SOCIETY.

The annual Dahlia show of this society was held in Pembroke Hall, Glen Cove, N. Y., Thursday, Oct. 7. Some very fine exhibits were staged and competition was very strong in almost every class. The class for table decoration was one of the main features of the show, there being eight entries in all. 1st prize was awarded to R. Jones, gard. for Percy Chubb; 2nd to J. Adler, gard. for H. Ladew; 3rd to H. Jones, gard. for Dr. Ayres. Among the principal winners in other classes were Mr. W. J. Matheson, gard. J. Kirby; Mrs. H. Darlington, gard. P.

W. Popp; Mrs. C. D. Smithers, gard. P. Charbonnard; Mrs. F. S. Smithers, gard. V. Cleres; Mrs. G. D. Pratt, gard. J. F. Johnston; Mrs. H. I. Pratt, gard. F. O. Johnson; F. W. Woolworth, gard W. D. Robertson; W. R. Coe, gard. J. Robinson; J B. Taylor, gard. G. Wilson; J. T. Pratt, gard. J. W. Everitt; Mrs. J. H. Otiay, gard. J. McDonald, and Mrs H. L. Pratt, gard. H. Gaut.

The judges were James Bell, Thomas Griffin and William Vert.

JAMES GLADSTONE, Cor. Sec.

NORTH SHORE HORTICULTURAL SOCIETY.

The North Shore Horticultural Society, Manchester, Mass., plans to break ground in the near future for the erection of a permanent building. The concrete structure will have a floor space of 60 by 80 feet, with several removable partitions for dividing the main floor into several small committee rooms.

William Till, head gardener on the estate of T. Jefferson Coolidge, is chairman of the building committee. Eric H. Wetterlow, head gardener of Mrs. Leslie Leland's estate, is vice-president of the Horticultural Society and is active in furthering the plans. He states that Ernest Longfellow has submitted a sketch for the building and that ground will be broken before cold weather.

A new building has been made imperative by the sale of Lee's Hall, where the horticultural shows have been held. A few weeks ago an attempt was made to hold the show under a tent on the estate of Mrs. Robert C. Winthrop, but rain handicapped the arrangements. It was decided that the only sure course was to have a home for the society.

PERSONAL.

Edward Andrews, formerly of Toledo, has entered the employ of Chas. Seibert, florist, Defiance, O.

After an illness of over nine weeks with typhoid fever, Morris F. Byxbee, the Harriet street florist, Norwalk, Ct., is able to be out again.

Robert Lickman, formerly of Edgewood Farm, Great Barrington, Mass., has taken the position of head gardener for H. H. Knapp, East Islip, L. I., N. Y.

The MacNiff Horticultural Co., seedsmen and horticulturists, have opened a retail branch store at No. 182 Fulton street, between Church street and Broadway, New York.

Coming Events

Shows.

Red Bank, N. J., Oct. 27-28.—Annual Flower Show of the Monmouth County Horticultural Society. H. A. Kettel, Sec., Fair Haven, N. J.

Morris County, N. J., Oct. 28-29.—The twentieth annual flower show of the Gardeners and Florists Society, Assembly Hall, Madison, N. J. Edward Reagan, secretary, Morristown, N. J.

Madison, N. J., Oct. 28-29.—The twentieth annual flower show of the Morris Co. Gardeners' and Florists' Society, Assembly Hall.

Poughkeepsie, N. Y., Oct. 28-29.—Annual flower show of Duchess County Horticultural Society. N. Harold Cottam, Sec., Wappingers Falls.

New York, N. Y., Nov. 3, 4, 5.—Annual Chrysanthemum Show of the American Institute, Engineering Societies Building.

Holyoke, Mass., Nov. 3-4.—Third Annual Flower Show, Holyoke and Northampton Florists' and Gardeners' Club, Windsor Hall.

Tarrytown, N. Y., Nov. 3-4-5.—Chrysanthemum Show in the Music Hall.

Boston, Nov. 4, 5, 6, 7.—Grand Autumn Exhibition, Massachusetts Horticultural society.

New York, N. Y. Nov. 4-7.—Annual Autumn exhibition of Hort. Soc. of New York, Museum of Natural History.

Chicago, Ill., Nov. 9-14.—Grand Floral Festival of the Chicago Florist's Club and Horticultural Society of Chicago, to be held in the Coliseum.

Cleveland, O., Nov. 10-14.—Cleveland Flower Show. The only show of national scope in the United States this fall. F. A. Friedley, Sec., 356 Leader Building.

Cleveland, O., Nov. 10-14.—The American Rose Society Fall Exhibition and Meeting in connection with the Cleveland Flower Show, Coliseum.

Cleveland, O., Nov. 10-14.—Annual show and meeting of Chrysanthemum Society of America, in conjunction with the Cleveland Flower Show. Chas. W. Johnson, Sec., 2226 Fairfax Ave., Morgan Park, Ill.

Providence, R. I., Nov. 11-12.—November Exhibition, Rhode Island Horticultural Society, Narragansett Hotel.

Baltimore, Md., Nov. 16-20.—Maryland Week Exhibition, Fifth Regiment Armory.

Houston, Tex., Nov. 17-20.—State Flower Show.

ROBERT DYSART
CERTIFIED PUBLIC ACCOUNTANT
Simple methods of correct accounting especially adapted for florists' use.

BOOKS BALANCED AND ADJUSTED

40 STATE ST. · · · · BOSTON

Telephone Main 58.

Obituary

John E. Walters.

John E. Walters, who for many years was employed as a florist, died last week at the home of his brother-in-law, J. L. Christian, Highland Park, Richmond, Va. Death was caused by tuberculosis, from which he had been a sufferer for some time. Mr. Walters is survived by his mother and two sisters.

Oglesby Paul.

Following an operation, Oglesby Paul, a widely known botanist and prominent in social circles, died on Tuesday, October 5, in a Boston hospital, having been taken there for treatment from his summer home at Saunderstown, Rhode Island. He was taken ill late in August and the best medical skill was employed without result. Mr. Paul was a son of the late Captain Frank W. Paul and a nephew of the late James W. Paul, of Drexel & Co. An aunt was the late Mrs. William Waldorf Astor. Born September 28, 1877, he graduated from the University of Pennsylvania in 1899 and took a post-graduate course in horticulture and agriculture at Harvard. In 1902 he was made landscape gardener of Fairmount Park, Philadelphia, to which he devoted much of his time. Many rare plants were secured by him for Horticultural Hall while on trips to tropical countries, and his reputation as a horticulturist was national. His widow survives him. The body was brought to the Paul home at Villanova, Pa., for burial Saturday afternoon, October 9.

George G. Goldbach.

George G. Goldbach, a prominent retail florist of Lancaster, Pa., died at the St. Joseph's Hospital Tuesday morning, October 6. About ten days previous to his death he scratched a pimple on his arm, soon afterwards the limb began to swell and blood poisoning set in, which gradually grew worse until it resulted in his death.

Mr. Goldbach was born in Leicester and always resided there. He started in business in the eastern end of the city some seventeen years back, building up for himself a very fine range of glass and along with it a good retail

trade, which increased so that a property was bought down town and re-arranged and a conservatory and fine store room added and a fine business is being built up at this location, 141 N. Duke street.

He was 37 years old and leaves a wife and three children and a host of friends to mourn his death, for he was one of those rare characters who make a friend of everyone who meets and learns to know them. He was a member of the Lancaster County Florists' Club. The funeral was held in St. Anthony's Church, the florists attending in a body, and the floral tributes were unusually handsome, some being sent from out of town firms.

Mrs. Goldbach will continue the business and the Florists' Club stand ready as a man to give her any assistance she may need.

SEED TRADE

The Bean Crop.

Notwithstanding strenuous efforts on our part to get something in the nature of definite information regarding the various seed crops, we are not able at this date to gratify the very natural desire of our readers for such information. The leading seed growers tell us that it is too early to be able to furnish definite figures as to what their deliveries will be, and, in addition, crop conditions this year are more puzzling than usual. We have been informed that the bean crop is no better than previous estimates, and with reference to the wax-pod varieties, it is very nearly an even bet between from two to three-fold or absolute crop failure. It seems to be settled already that several varieties will be returned as crop failures, but there is hope that a number of other varieties may return from a two to three-fold yield as already stated. Most of the green-pod varieties are in much the same condition, though there is some confidence expressed that Refugees, Red Valentines and Black Valentines may return a five or six-fold yield. There is nothing new in the news affecting Lima beans, and while there may be some shortage in the Fordhook and Burpee's Improved, there will probably be sufficient of the other varieties to meet ordinary requirements.

Peas.

As the situation develops it begins to look as if peas will not prove as abundant a crop as appeared probable a month ago. As threshing and hand picking extends, the shrinkage becomes much larger than anticipated. This is largely due to rain after harvest, and before the peas were threshed in Wisconsin and Michigan, and, in the northwest, to a shortage of water, which affected the late varieties especially, although yields in general are below average. It is expected that the growers of peas and beans will be issuing their preliminary estimates in the very near future, which will furnish the nearest to definite information obtainable up to this time.

Onion Sets and Seed.

As the price of onions and onion sets very largely determines the demand for onion seed, it may be well to take note of the existing situation. Reports from all sources indicate a very short crop of onions, of very inferior quality as a whole. A very large dealer in onions reported recently that in more than a week's canvass of one of the leading onion growing counties of Ohio, he had secured but three carloads of onions suitable for winter storage. Nearly all the onions he saw were so soft that he did not believe they would carry beyond the holidays, if they lasted that long. While the condition of onion sets is not so bad as large onions, it is serious enough

only generalize, although we assume to prevent dealers from naming spring prices, excepting at figures that seem unreasonably high to buyers. Taking the present conditions into careful consideration, the conclusion is unavoidable that both onions and onion sets will bring abnormally high prices next spring, and in consequence thereof a very heavy demand for onion seed.

We have recently seem some of the preliminary prices sent out by the wholesale houses on onion seed, and they are certainly radically higher than for several years past. Not an item was quoted below $1.25, and from that up to $2.50 in several hundred pound lots. We are assured by one or two wholesalers that these prices will look very reasonable sixty or ninety days hence. We are wondering what the retail price of onion seed will be this year, and especially what figures will be named by the leading catalog houses. No doubt this will be governed largely by their available stocks, but it would seem that conditions will justify rather strong prices.

Other Seed Crops.

We have stated in previous issues that practically all vine seeds will be short; but the extent of the shortage cannot be ascertained as yet. It seems, however, to be rather greater than expected some weeks ago.

A considerable shortage is reported in tomato seed, one or two leading growers claiming that their yield will not exceed 25 to 50 per cent of an average. This will mean a firming up in the price of tomato seed, but nothing that will be alarming.

The condition of corn has shown further improvement, and it is generally believed now, that barring early freezing weather, while the corn is still soft, that there should be a fair crop, although there is likely to be some shortage in two or three of the late varieties.

No reference has been made to seed corn of the sweet varieties, but we can say, in a general way, that there will be considerable of a crop of all the standard varieties, though prices because of quite a shortage will rule considerably higher than last year.

The radish seed crop of Michigan has proved a good one, but that of California has been rather light. We understand that the European crop is light, then again is the eternal question of whether we are going to get any of it, and if so, how much. This applies to practically all European seed crops. Even from neutral countries there will be some trouble experienced, as shipping facilities are much below normal and freight rates very much higher.

Wholesale Seedmen's League.

The meeting of the directors of the Wholesale Seedmen's League in New York last week is reported to have been a very interesting one, and the prices suggested on beans, vine seeds, biennials such as beets, mangels, carrots, turnips, etc., as well as onion seed and tomato seed, all confirm the predictions made in HORTICULTURE's Seed Trade Notes from time to time during the past two months. While we have no details of the meeting, or the prices suggested, we learn that they are higher than we expected and that on beans, as a whole, they are

probably the highest ever named by the wholesale trade of this country. We also understand that onion seed is considerably higher than any prices named for several years. We wish we could furnish detailed information, but this is not available and we can it will not be long before the trade in general will be advised of the prices suggested.

Those of our readers who thought our crop reports during August and September were rather pessimistic will probably acknowledge now that we knew of what we were speaking, and will appreciate the fact that HORTICULTURE's crop news is generally reliable.

How to Select Seed Beans.

(From Agri. Dept. Bulletin.)

Get seed from your own crop if possible. If there are no clean pods in your own crop try to secure clean pods from a more fortunate neighbor.

Select in the pod, not after threshing.

Pick pods free from all spots. Spots on the pods mean that anthracnose or bacterial blight may be hidden in the seemingly clean bean.

Thresh selected pods separately.

Examine your threshed seed carefully and throw out all doubtful-looking beans, especially those that are spotted or shriveled.

Rotate. Don't replant old bean ground next year. Clean seed and rotation are the best crop insurance.

If you have to buy your seed, make sure that it has been selected by the grower from disease-free pods. Examine purchased seed. Do not plant if the threshed seed looks suspicious.

Look ahead. Insure a supply of clean seed for 1917 by selecting seed from clean pods and planting it on clean land in 1916.

The trade in general will be sorry to learn of the serious illness of Mr. W. Atlee Burpee, who is now receiving treatment at a sanitarium in Pennsylvania. We are glad to say that the latest information to hand indicates some improvement in Mr. Burpee's condition.

News Items From Everywhere

ALBANY, N. Y.

By mutual agreement all flower stores in Albany close promptly at 6 P. M. every day.

The Arkay Florists who started business about two years ago on a prominent corner have already built up a prosperous business. "Jimmie" is a clever buyer and they handle a nice quality of goods.

Messrs. Wemple and Sanders are at the helm in the Eyres greenhouses and a fine stock of decorative material is being brought into shape for the winter requirement of the Pearl street store. Mr. Eyres whose health was poor last year is in "the pink of condition" now.

The Rosery's slogan is, "Our special auto service insures timely delivery." This is displayed on a card bearing the picture of a handsome bridal bouquet. Ed. P. Tracey bought out the interest of his partner E. T. Meany on October 1 and will continue the business under the title of The Rosery as heretofore.

The Albany Cut Flower Exchange has added a much needed convenience in an automobile for quick delivery of flowers to the trade in Albany, Troy, Schenectady and adjacent neighborhood. Business has started up with a gratifying activity and there is every evidence that this wholesale flower establishment has secured the good will and support of the trade in this section—growers and buyers, both. Manager Tom Tracey is ever on the wire.

Fred Danker, at whose store on Maiden Lane there is always something doing reports business as improving and the outlook more promising than for a long time past. Mr. Danker has an expressive poster bearing a cluster of roses in colors and the inscription, "Aren't you a little neglectful for not sending her some flowers recently? You know how she loves them." We might mention that Mr. Danker does not pack this legend away to be brought out on one particular day, but displays it every day in the year, which is good business.

SCHENECTADY, N. Y.

W. C. Eger. Schenectady's pioneer florist, is planning to give an exhibition in Turn Hall, on Thursday, Friday and Saturday, Nov. 11, 12 and 13.

Schenectady has a Florists' Club which holds meetings on the second Monday of each month. M. P. Champlin is president this year. Several of the members anticipate going to the Cleveland Flower Show in company with the Albany Club party.

Julius Eger has partially rebuilt his store. Tiled windows with lattice work walls and ceiling, a cement floor, drained so that water may be freely thrown about and an ingenious and novel arrangement whereby the office and refrigerator can be pushed around on rollers and their position changed at will, are among the new features.

NEWS ITEMS FROM EVERYWHERE

CHICAGO.

Amalgamation Banquet.

One of the pleasantest events in the history of the Chicago Florists' Club which covers twenty-eight years, was the banquet which again unites the two clubs. The kindest of feeling prevailed and after the dinner the speeches took on more or less of a personal nature and at the close all felt that a new era had begun for the club. Plates were reserved for over one hundred and the 7th of October will be a memorable one in the history of the Chicago Florists' Club.

Jack Frost.

The delight of the florist and the dread of those outside the trade took place October 7, when the tender outdoor flowers and vines received a nipping. The damage would not have been so great had it not been followed by two other nights and but little now remains of the fall flowers. The change is not so noticeable as in some other years, for the continued rains had gradually taken the life out of many plants, still the event means something to the florists and trade is bound to be benefited thereby.

One Way to Stimulate Trade.

The special efforts to stimulate trade in various parts of the city, so successfully carried out last year, are in full swing again now. The Northwest side had a big parade, street decorations, etc., last week and the Southwest side follows this week. In all these the florists have taken a part and from their reports it is evident they believe it pays to follow the example of merchants in other lines. Streets are hung with flags for miles and "Booster Week" is now a big factor in the revival of fall trade. The big night parade is the crowning feature.

Personal and Other Notes.

Miss M. Corneil is assistant bookkeeper in the supply department at Poehlmann Bros.

Mrs. Frank Oechslin is home from the hospital and is recovering slowly from an operation on her face.

Mrs. John Ravatzos was in Chicago this week looking for new ideas in the florists' work. They have retail stores in Winnipeg and Minneapolis.

Herbert Stone, manager of The Atlas, decorated some of the automobiles for the parade on 26th St., October 13. There are several wide-awake florists on the Southwest.

When Mr. and Mrs. Chas. B. Stevens of Plymouth, Mass., reached Chicago on their way back from the Pacific Coast they found an old acquaintance in Tim. Waters, the first since leaving home, they said.

Charles McKellar has this week big yellow pumpkins, lined up on one counter, rather drolly contrasting with the orchid display case just opposite. Some florists are using them for flower baskets to make unusual window attractions.

Poehlmann Bros. are making a feature of the Hanasha grass which comes from Japan. A large vase with samples of the colors turned out in their coloring factory, shows up well, and this will make a new offering among the decorative materials this season.

Nick Monsen of 3640 Fullerton Ave. has not been able to positively locate the cause of the destruction of his 8 by 12½ ft. plate glass window last Thursday evening. Judging from the appearance of the glass, a window bomb had been placed on it, but why such a thing should be done in his case, is a mystery.

John Kruchten attributes the unusual experience of growers with Golden Glow chrysanthemums this season to the hot weather a month ago. With his stock the high temperature, coming with the rain, dampened and decayed the inside of the flowers. This week finishes the early chrysanthemums and a good cut of midseason blooms is assured. Wm. J. McKee is now in charge of the books at the Kruchten office.

L. C. Collins, proprietor of the Parkside Greenhouses who has been ill is again able to be about. Mrs. Collins, who is in charge of the store says business is beginning to pick up and a trip through the greenhouses shows a fine supply of chrysanthemums both in pots and for cut flowers and a large number of extra fine Boston ferns. Mr. and Mrs. Collins are pioneer florists of the far South side, and with their son have built up a fine business.

SAN FRANCISCO.

Mark Ebel, florist, of Sacramento, Cal., was a recent visitor at the exposition, accompanied by Mrs. Ebel.

Mrs. Ray Paul, proprietor of the Hanford Floral Co., Hanford, Cal., opened her new shop in the Ashby Theater Building on October 4.

A special showing of orchids in handsome basket arrangements attracted much attention in the window of Joseph's shop on Grant avenue the past week.

Three cars of garden seed raised on the islands above Stockton were received this week by the Rohnert Seed Co. in Hollister, Cal. The seed is raised for the company under contract and is cleaned and repacked by it before being placed on the market.

The Ladies' Auxiliary of the Pacific Coast Horticultural Society has preparations well under way for a social meeting to be held on the evening of October 28. The program includes various entertainment features, and invitations have been extended to the members of the men's organization.

Frank Pelicano entertained several members of the local trade and other friends at his home in Ocean View last Sunday. After dinner the party spent the afternoon in his gardens, where all were much impressed by the splendid showing of dahlias. Over 8,000 blooms of Delice were out and about 12,000 blooms of Mrs. Kettlewell, besides quantities of Minnie Burgle. A good many pictures were taken by the visitors. A long auto ride concluded the day's outing.

ST. LOUIS.

The Mullanphy Florist Co. will vacate their present location and move to the corner of Eighth and Locust streets, a block from the old place.

Secretary Fred C. Weber, of the Retail Florists' Association, says that they would hold an important meeting next Monday night at the Mission Inn Garden.

Frank Sanders, late of Sanders Nursery floral store, has accepted a position with the Grand Leader department store, having charge of the floral and bulb department.

The Strohmeyer Floral Co. in St. Louis has closed its doors and discontinued business. F. Strohmeyer, who was president of the firm, has accepted a position with the M. M. Ayers Floral Co.

The Schakleford Nursery Co., who has been supplying the local trade with outdoor flowers all season, has bought a big tract of land adjoining them, which will be planted for next season's cut.

The County Growers' Association held a meeting on October 6 at the Eleven Mile House. A committee was appointed to meet with the Florist Club Committee and assist them in entertaining the members of the American Carnation Society when they meet here in January.

Secretary Beneke, of the Florist Club, says the prospects are good for a delegation from here next month to visit the Cleveland Flower Show and perhaps a bowling club to take part in the tournament, of which Charlie Graham has charge. This week's club meeting will decide this question.

PROVIDENCE, R. I.

William H. Tarbox the dahlia specialist of West Greenwich, made a novel exhibit at the Danbury, Conn., fair last week. Over 2000 asters were used in addition to dahlias, in an ingenious windmill form.

Miss Madge Tyree Banigan, a daughter of Mrs. Timothy Lucian O'Connor, was married Oct. 6, to Philip Fatio L'Engle of Atlanta, Ga., at the Church of the Transfiguration in Edgewood, R. I., followed by a reception at the home of the bride's parents. The rooms were beautifully decorated with lilies, American Beauty roses, Southern smilax, pink snapdragon and yellow chrysanthemums. Garlands of laurel were used in the veranda decorations.

Last Wednesday evening while the family was at dinner, a porch thief entered the home of Mrs. O'Connor and was preparing to get away with the costly wedding presents that were on the second floor. A maid who had been detailed to watch the gifts, heard the intruder and called Mr. O'Connor. As they entered the room upstairs the thief slid out the window and made his escape. Nothing was taken.

S. A. G.

NEW YORK.

The McCray Refrigerator Company have a New York office now at 7 and 9 West 30th street.

John P. Cleary is now engaged with C. C. Trepel at the Bloomingdale establishment on East 59th street.

Eugene Chatelle, of Vilmorin & Co., Paris, France, is expected to arrive in New York in latter part of October.

McHutchison & Co. have this week received by one steamer six delayed raffia shipments—659 bales. Some of these shipments of raffia have been in transit from Madagascar for more than six months.

Henry C. Riedel and Meyer Othile have formed a partnership as Riedel & Meyer, Inc., and on Monday, October 11, opened for business at 49 West 28th street. A large floral horseshoe in the window attested the good wishes of their friends.

As a result of the withdrawal of H. C. Riedel and Meyer Othile, the wholesale business of Badgley, Riedel & Meyer has been reorganized under the title of Badgley & Bishop and business will go on as heretofore at 34 West 28th street.

John Donaldson's case against the gas company for damages by leaking gas at his greenhouses at Elmhurst has been settled for $2700. Mr. Donaldson now fills the exalted and dignified office of chaplain in a new Lodge of Elks at Patchogue. He carries the responsibility with all due solemnity. Frivolous people should not intrude too far.

BOSTON.

James Fahey has resigned his position as buyer for Galvin. John Dowd, for ten years associated with Galvin's Back Bay store succeeds him. Mr. Fahey will henceforth give his time entirely to his duties as ball commissioner for the city of Boston.

P. Welch has been compiling information for the benefit of those who wish to go from Boston to the Cleveland Flower Show next month. The rate of fare from Boston to Cleveland via N. Y. Central R. R. is $15.50. For a party of ten traveling on one ticket the fare will be $14.40 each. Berths

are $3.50 for lower and $2.80 for upper. Trains leave Boston at 2 and 4.25 P. M., due in Cleveland at 7.20 and 10.52 A. M. respectively.

Chester I. Campbell's big Indoor Country Fair will open Saturday evening, October 23, and will end Saturday evening, October 30, at Mechanics' Building. Several acres of floor space will be given over to displays of New England grown apples, fruit, vegetables and flowers. A wonderful exhibit will be made by the Boston Market Gardeners' Association. The floral exhibit will be made by the Boston Co-operative Flower Market.

A flower garden in a coal hod was one of the prize winners in the North End Garden Association competition. Five hundred residents of the North End have cultivated some kind of roof, window or backyard garden this past summer. Fifty of these were given prizes. A first prize goes to the small gardener who has raised his, or her, flowers under the most difficult conditions. Another prize goes to the most unique garden—this to a small Italian girl who hung her garden out of a tenement window in a coal hod.

PITTSBURGH.

Harvey C. Sheaff, manager for Mrs. E. A. Williams, returned on Monday morning from a five weeks' trip to the Pacific Coast.

O. J. Parker of Scobie & Parker, and family, have returned from a four months' sojourn at Prout's Neck on the Maine coast.

The monthly meeting of the Garden Club of Allegheny County was held on Friday of last week at Penn Sylvan Farm, country place of Mr. and Mrs. Harvey Childs, Jr.

Judging from the exterior view, Randolph & McClements might be having what the milliners and department shop people term their "Fall Opening" this week. On the marble shelf of the display windows are three tall silver vases of oncidiums and cattleyas. In the background are large bowls of yellow chrysanthemums and ferns flanked by clusters of lilies and cardinal dahlias.

Tuesday evening John R. Bracken, assistant landscape architect for the

A. W. Smith Company, gave a stereopticon lecture in the opening session of the course of "Landscape Architecture and Ornamentation of Home Grounds," of which Norman S. Grubbs, and Mr. Bracken are the instructors. The following afternoon the latter addressed the New Era Club on the subject of "The Ornamentation of Home Grounds."

WASHINGTON.

William F. Gude and George W. Hess spent the week end at Barnegat Bay as the guests of Commodore Westcott.

Florists and commission merchants must renew their licenses if they desire to continue in business after October 31, on which day the old licenses expire, according to the announcement of the assessors of taxes.

The Alexandria (Va.) board of civil service examiners will hold an examination to secure eligibles for the positions of assistant in poisonous plant investigations and assistant in dry land aboriculture.

In a recent statement to the press, Secretary of the Treasury McAdoo announced that "In reply to many inquiries I have received about the revenue measures that will be proposed in the next Congress, I have determined to recommend that the emergency revenue act which expires by limitation on December 31, 1915, be extended until peace is restored in Europe. * * *" This act provides for a tax of $20 upon all commission merchants, $10 upon all custom house brokers, as well as stamp taxes on express and freight receipts, telephone (for more than 15-cent calls) and telegraph messages.

PHILADELPHIA.

The dahlias are dead. A sharp frost on October 10 over in Jersey. Your scribe will feel better from now on.

The "old guards" are all back from their three days' outing at Barnegat. They were favored with fine weather, good fishing and unlimited hospitality. No one got seasick to speak of and no rudders were lost this time.

Flower Market Reports

BOSTON — There are evidences to show that the brief famine for flowers in this market is nearly over. Warm June-like weather is driving the chrysanthemums along rapidly and the carnations are also coming in better and more numerous. Roses are letting down a little in price although it is true that some of the largest growers are off crop for the time being. American Beauty has difficulty in maintaining top figures. The quality of roses generally is very good. A few violets are in but they are inferior yet. The first sweet peas of the new crop are coming in, grandiflora varieties only.

BUFFALO — The past week proved to be one that seldom occurs at this time of the season. White roses are about equal to the demand, there being a cleanup on these daily and so on with everything along the line. Chrysanthemums have been coming in fair supply, also dahlias, cosmos, asters and everything sell out before the day is over. There has been a heavy demand for wedding flowers which used considerable carnations, roses, lily of the valley and lilies. Business is really brisk and it is hoped that same will continue.

CHICAGO — A general scarcity of stock prevails. With the coming of the first frosts and the shortening up of practically all staples in cut flowers, Chicago florists have had a week of new experiences. The "25c. a dozen" signs disappeared from the sidewalks, and the stores that attract by sensational prices are not heard from now. The retailer who has a large trade in cheap funeral designs is hit the worst for he cannot raise materially on his prices without offending customers and there is really no cheap stock to be had. Asters are gone, chrysanthemums just coming and not enough carnations to bring the price within the design limit. The counters look very empty and only some bright sunshine can bring along the flowers. The early chrysanthemums are about over. Those who lost out on their Golden Glow will soon have the midseason varieties to offer. So far the crop is backward but with favorable weather there will be no lack of the big favorites later. A good supply of all kinds of green, including southern smilax, helps out.

NEW YORK — The short supply of flowers which at the present time exists in all sections of the country has had a most exhilarating effect on the wholesale district here. The hard times of the recent summer season are all apparently forgotten and every denizen of the wholesale establishment seems charged with some of the ginger of the "good old times." The loquacious buyers who have had things all their own way ever since last spring are discomfited, as they realize that arguments, pleadings and expostulations will avail them nothing while present conditions prevail, and they are only too glad to crowd around the crates of dahlias, once displaced, but now a centre of attraction as soon as received. We might here mention that specimen dahlia blooms cut with long stalks and properly packed and shipped by W. A. Manda to John Young have been selling for six and eight dollars a hundred. Chrysanthemums have already reached that stage of quality where they have their flowers hooded in tissue paper and are carried heads down with great care. Roses are better each day and carnations show a slow but steady improvement. Violets of exceptionally good quality for so early a date are now in evidence.

PHILADELPHIA — What they call the "wind-up" of the week — the Friday Saturday sales—were especially good here. October 8 and 9, accentuating the upward tendency of prices which has been noticeable for some time back. Roses were scarce and went up fully ten per cent. Carnations were more plentiful and also went up fully thirty per cent. As a rule when supply increases prices go down, but that did not happen in this carnation situation this time. Senator Heacock is a great exponent of the law of supply and demand being infallible. Someone would better ask him to explain this. Dahlias are over, except in a few protected spots. The chrysanthemum is much more of a factor now. The finer varieties are arriving and show better class and finish than anything we have had so far and also gives us greater selection to choose from. Altogether it has been a very satisfactory week since last report, and the "stabbed-to-the-heart" buyer has to take a back seat for the minute.

(Continued on page 516)

WHOLESALE FLOWER MARKETS — TRADE PRICES—Per 100 TO DEALERS ONLY

Roses	BOSTON Oct. 14		ST. LOUIS Oct. 11		PHILA. Oct. 11	
Am. Beauty, Special	12.00	25.00	25.00	35.00	25.00	30.00
" " Fancy and Extra	8.00	10.00	15.00	20.00	15.00	20.00
" " No. 1	3.00	5.00	3.00	10.00	10.00	12.00
Russell, Hadley	4.00	10.00	8.00	15.00	4.00	18.00
Killarney, Kichmond, Hillingdon, Ward, Extra	4.00	8.00	8.00	10.00	4.00	8.00
" " " Ordinary	1.00	3.00	4.00	6.00	2.00	3.00
Areuburg, Radiance, Taft, Key, Extra	4.00	8.00	....	....	4.00	8.00
" " " " Ordinary	1.00	3.00	....	....	....	....
Ophelia, Mock, Sunburst, Extra	4.00	8.00	8.00	10.00	6.00	8.00
" " " Ordinary	1.00	3.00	4.00	6.00	3.00	5.00
Carnations, Fancy	2.00	3.00	3.00	3.00	3.00	4.00
" Ordinary	1.00	2.00	1.00	1.50	2.00	3.00
Cattleyas	20.00	30.00	35.00	50.00	25.00	40.00
Dendrobium formosum	....	25.00	....	....	....	50.00
Lilies, Longiflorum	8.00	10.00	8.00	12.00	12.00	18.00
" Rubrum	....	3.00	4.00	6.00	....	....
Lily of the Valley	3.00	4.00	3.00	4.00	2.00	5.00
Daisies	.50	1.00	.25	.50	....	....
Violets	....	.50	.35	.50	....	....
Snapdragon	1.00	2.00	3.00	5.00	3.00	5.00
Gladioli	1.00	2.00	2.00	3.00	....	....
Asters	.50	1.00	1.00	2.00	1.00	2.00
Chrysanthemums	6.00	10.00	10.00	25.00	10.00	25.00
Sweet Peas	....	1.00	.50	.75	....	1.00
Gardenia	15.00	25.00	....	....	....	25.00
Adiantum	....	1.00	1.00	1.25	....	1.00
Smilax	12.00	16.00	12.00	15.00	15.00	20.00
Asparagus Plumosus, Strings (100)	25.00	50.00	35.00	50.00	20.00	50.00
" " & Spren. (100 Bchs.)	25.00	35.00	25.00	35.00	35.00	50.00

Flower Market Reports
(Continued from page 517)

PITTSBURGH Floriculture is going through the unsatisfactory period following the early frosts, when the outside flowers are damaged, if not absolutely destroyed, and those inside are lacking in quantity, if not quality. There is a general complaint of scarcity of stock, the supply scarcely paralleling the demand, although on the whole there is no marked advance in prices. The stock of carnations is anything but heavy, and chrysanthemums are coming in slowly and likewise, not opening readily. Apropos of this, the A. W. Smith Company has a contract to supply fifty thousand of the "baby" variety, yellow and white, for a Tag Day benefit to be held today in behalf of the Sunshine Babies' Home. At the time of writing, it looks a little doubtful if the babies will receive the benefit of the full fifty thousand.

SAN FRANCISCO While not quite so active as during September, when the city was full of tourists and many conventions were in progress, the demand for flowers continues on a satisfactory basis. As the supply is not excessive, prices are fairly well maintained, extra fine stock bringing top figures, in some instances. The shipping demand is increasing daily, which helps out to a considerable extent also. Chrysanthemums are the feature of the market, much variety being shown in the offerings with average quality a little above normal and the demand good. A large cut of Portola is beginning to arrive, and Wm. Turner, as well as several other new varieties are coming in quite plentifully to replace the earlier varieties going off crop. Violets are still too soft for shipping, except in a small way, but the local demand is pretty well supplied. Some nice America gladiolus continues to arrive, but it does not move so well as the more seasonable offerings. The lighter supply of dahlias finds a ready demand. The average quality of the roses is gradually getting better, and stocks clean up closely. Cyclamen plants are offered freely, and sell readily. The orchid situation has improved very noticeably the past week, several of the downtown shops making ample showings the last few days. The demand is good also, following the long scarcity.

ST. LOUIS The big frost cut out all outdoor stock and the undue shortage of indoor stock caught the local trade unawares at the end of the last week. The cold weather has toned up the stock, which is showing a great improvement in quality. Prices are advanced, some to almost double what they were early in the week. This was Festival Week and the retailers had a great deal more business than usual, and this week the shortage and higher prices inconvenienced them much. Fancy grades in roses, as well as ordinary stock, also chrysanthemums, carnations, lilies, violets, etc., are cleaning up satisfactorily.

WASHINGTON Washington and the surrounding territory had the first real touch of frost last week. Flower and truck gardens in many places were about at an end and the frost completed the work, relieving the market places of quantities of outdoor stock which have been competing with the products of the greenhouses. Local conditions have shown a decided improvement and business is brisk. Local stock is fast coming into form and will be in fine shape by the end of next week. The first of the single violets are in. American Beauty and all the Killarney roses are very good. Ophelia, Radiance, Mock, Taft and Ward are in good demand. There has been an exceptionally heavy call for the lily of the valley and not enough to go around. Daily shipments of lily of the valley have decreased until now the volume is half of what it was at this time last year. Carnations are not yet in their best shape, but the demand for them has been so heavy that even the very poorest clean up. Lilies also have a good call. Cattleya labiata are not in so great a supply as they were and the price has stiffened somewhat. Chrysanthemums can now be had in pink as well as in yellow and white, although the two latter dominate the market.

NEW CORPORATIONS.

Shenandoah, Ia.—Ratekin Seed Co.; capital stock, $75,000.

New York, N. Y.—G. H. Stuber. Bronx, to deal in horticultural supplies; capital stock, $10,000.

Canton, O.—Holmes-Letherman Seed Co., 126 Cleveland avenue, N. W.; capital stock, $25,000. Incorporators, G. M. Letherman. H. L. Holmes, Jr., E. L. Gehman, H. W. Shriver and Mrs. G. M. Letherman.

Uniontown, Pa.—W. R. Barton has assumed control of the Cramer greenhouses, near Leith, of which he was proprietor until eight years ago when Mr. Cramer took charge of same. J. H. Thompson, who has been manager of the greenhouses for a number of years, will continue in that capacity.

NEW YORK QUOTATIONS PER 100. To Dealers Only

MISCELLANEOUS	Last Half of Week ending Oct. 9 1915		First Half of Week beginning Oct. 11 1915	
Cattleyas	10.00 to	25.00	15.00 to	25.00
Dendrobium formosum	20.00 to	25.00	20.00 to	25.00
Lilies, Longiflorum	4.00 to	8.00	6.00 to	8.00
" Rubrum	1.00 to	3.00	1.00 to	4.00
Lily of the Valley	2.00 to	4.00	3.00 to	5.00
Daisies	..... to	.50	..... to	.50
Violets	..... to	.50	..... to	.50
Snapdragon	1.00 to	2.00	1.00 to	2.00
Gladioli	1.00 to	2.00	1.00 to	2.00
Asters	.25 to	1.00	.50 to	1.00
Chrysanthemums	6.00 to	15.00	6.00 to	20.00
Sweet Peas	..... to	.75		
Corn Flower	..... to	.75	..... to	.....
Gardenia	8.00 to	20.00	8.00 to	25.00
Adiantum	.50 to	.75	.50 to	.75
Smilax	8.00 to	10.00	8.00 to	10.00
Asparagus Plumosus, strings (per 100)	30.00 to	40.00	35.00 to	50.00
& Spren (100 bunches)	15.00 to	20.00	15.00 to	25.00

During Recess

BOSTON FLORISTS' BOWLING LEAGUE.

The Boston Bowling League is proving a big success and much interest is manifested in the Thursday evening meets. Scores for Thursday, October 9, were as follows:

Carbone, 1230, vs. Florists' Exchange, 1168
Galvin, 1221, vs. Zinn, 1178
Pansies, 1222, vs. Wax, 1160
Cooperative Market, 1190, vs. Robinson, 1175

The standing up to date is as follows:

	W.	L.
Carbone	4	0
Galvin	4	0
Coop. Market	3	1
Pansies	3	1
Robinson	1	3
Wax	1	3
Flor. Exch.	0	4
Zinn	0	4

It having been found that Wax would be unable to play a full team, McAlpine and McDonald have taken their place and will succeed to the score made by Wax up to present time. Visitors will be welcome at the Boston alleys on any Thursday night.

West Orange, N. J. — The Manda Floral Co. (Joseph Manda) had a public exhibition of orchids last week which attracted a throng of visitors. Cattleya labiata made a fine display and under Mr. Manda's skillful manipulation, will so continue until Christmas. Cattleyas in general seem to find an ideal home here as do also the Vanda coerulea and Cypripedium Sanderæ. Of the last named Mr. Manda has 1000 plants. Among the novelties here are a yellow Miltonia candida, Brasso-Cattleya Leemaniæ and an attractive sport from Swainsona with flowers of cattleya pink color, which has been named Mrs. Joseph Manda and will be introduced next season.

Buyer's Directory and Ready Reference Guide

Advertisements under this head, one cent a word.   Initials count as words.

Display advertisers in this issue are also listed under this classification without charge. Reference to List of Advertisers will indicate the respective pages.

Buyers failing to find what they want in this list will confer a favor by writing us and we will try to put them in communication with reliable dealers.

ACCOUNTANT
R. Dysart, 40 State St., Boston.
For page see List of Advertisers.

ACHILLEA
"Pearl," Fine Seedlings, $3.00 per 1,000, cash. JAMES MOSS, Wholesale Grower, Johnsville, Pa.

ADIANTUM
The Storrs & Harrison Co., Painesville, Ohio.
For page see List of Advertisers.

APHINE
Aphine Mfg. Co., Madison, N. J.
For page see List of Advertisers.

APHIS PUNK
Nicotine Mfg. Co., St. Louis, Mo.
For page see List of Advertisers.

ASPARAGUS
The Storrs & Harrison Co., Painesville, Ohio.
For page see List of Advertisers.

Asparagus Sprengeri, fine 2¼-in., $2.50 per 100; $20.00 per 1000. Cash. M. F. BYXBEE, Norwalk, Conn.

AUCTION SALES
The MacNiff Horticultural Co., New York City.
Plants Sales by Auction.
For page see List of Advertisers.

Elliott Auction Co., New York City.
For page see List of Advertisers.

AZALEAS
P. Ouwerkerk, Hoboken, N. J.
For page see List of Advertisers.

BAY TREES
August Rolker & Sons, New York.
For page see List of Advertisers.

BEDDING PLANTS
A. N. Pierson, Inc., Cromwell, Conn.
For page see List of Advertisers.

BEGONIAS
Julius Roehrs Company, Rutherford, N. J.
For page see List of Advertisers.

R. Vincent, Jr. & Sons Co., White Marsh, Md.

Thomas Roland, Nahant, Mass.
For page see List of Advertisers.

The Storrs & Harrison Co., Painesville, Ohio.
For page see List of Advertisers.

	Per 100
BEGONIA LORRAINE, 2¼ in	$12.00
3 in	20.00
4 in	35.00
5 in	50.00
BEGONIA CINCINNATI, 2½ in	15.00
3 in	20.00
3½ in	30.00
4½ in	40.00

JULIUS ROEHRS CO., Rutherford, N. J.

BOILERS
Kroeschell Bros. Co., Chicago.
For page see List of Advertisers.

King Construction Co., North Tonawanda, N. Y.
"King Ideal" Boiler.
For page see List of Advertisers.

Lord & Burnham Co., New York City.

Hitchings & Co., New York City.
For page see List of Advertisers.

BOUGAINVILLEA
The Storrs & Harrison Co., Painesville, Ohio.
For page see List of Advertisers.

BOXES—CUT FLOWER FOLDING
Edwards Folding Box Co., Philadelphia.
For page see List of Advertisers.

Folding cut flower boxes, the best made. Write for list. HOLTON & HUNKEL CO., Milwaukee, Wis.

BOX TREES
BOX TREES—Standards, Pyramids and Bush. In various sizes. Price List on demand. JULIUS ROEHRS CO., Rutherford, N. J.

BOXWOOD
Breck-Robinson Nursery Co., Lexington, Mass.
For page see List of Advertisers.

BULBS AND TUBERS
Arthur T. Boddington Co., Inc., New York City.
For page see List of Advertisers.

J. M. Thorburn & Co., New York City
Wholesale Price List of High Class Bulbs.
For page see List of Advertisers.

Ralph M. Ward & Co., New York City.
Lily Bulbs.
For page see List of Advertisers.

John Lewis Childs, Flowerfield, L. I., N. Y.
For page see List of Advertisers.

August Rolker & Sons, New York City.
Holland and Japan Bulbs.
For page see List of Advertisers.

R. & J. Farquhar & Co., Boston, Mass.
For page see List of Advertisers.

S. S. Skidelsky & Co., Philadelphia, Pa.
For page see List of Advertisers.

Chas. Schwake & Co., New York City.
Horticultural Importers and Exporters.
For page see List of Advertisers.

A. Henderson & Co., Chicago, Ill.
For page see List of Advertisers.

Burnett Bros., 98 Chambers St., New York.
For page see List of Advertisers.

Henry F. Michell Co., Philadelphia, Pa.
Dutch Bulbs.
For page see List of Advertisers.

Joseph Breck & Sons Corp., Boston, Mass.
For page see List of Advertisers.

Raymond W. Swett, Saxonville, Mass.
Darwin Tulips and Hyacinths.
For page see List of Advertisers.

Fottler, Fiske, Rawson Co., Boston, Mass.
For page see List of Advertisers.

C. KEUR & SONS, HILLEGOM, Holland. Bulbs of all descriptions. Write for prices. NEW YORK Branch, 8-10 Bridge St.

CANNAS
Canna Specialists.
Send for Canna book.
THE CONARD & JONES COMPANY, West Grove, Pa.

CARNATIONS
Wood Bros., Fishkill, N. Y.
For page see List of Advertisers.

F. R. Pierson, Tarrytown, N. Y.
Carnation Matchless.
For page see List of Advertisers.

CARNATIONS—Continued
F. Dorner & Sons Co., Lafayette, Ind.
For page see List of Advertisers.

Jas. Vick's Sons, Rochester, N. Y.
Field Grown Plants.
For page see List of Advertisers.

Littlefield & Wyman, North Abington, Mass.
New Pink Carnation, Miss Theo.
For page see List of Advertisers.

700 Pink Enchantress, 800 White Enchantress, 500 Mrs. Ward, $5.00 per 100. 500 Winsor, 250 Lawson, $4.50 per 100. 200 Queen, $4.00 per 100. Cash. CHAS. H. GREEN, Spencer, Mass.

CARNATION STAPLES
Split carnations quickly, easily and cheaply mended. Pillsbury's Carnation Staple, 1000 for 35c.; 3000 for $1.00 post paid. I. L. PILLSBURY, Galesburg, Ill.

Supreme Carnation Staples, for repairing split carnations, 35c. per 1000; 3000 for $1.00. F. W. WAITE, 85 Belmont Ave., Springfield, Mass.

CHRYSANTHEMUMS
Chas. H. Totty, Madison, N. J.

R. Vincent, Jr., & Sons Co., White Marsh, Md.
Pompon Chrysanthemums.
For page see List of Advertisers.

THE BEST 1915 NOVELTIES.
The Cream of 1914 Introductions.
The most popular Commercial and Exhibition kinds; also complete line of Pompons, Singles and Anemones. Trade list on application. ELMER D. SMITH & CO., Adrian, Mich.

COCOANUT FIBRE SOIL
20th Century Plant Food Co., Beverly, Mass.
For page see List of Advertisers.

DAHLIAS
Send for Wholesale List of whole clumps and separate stock; 40,000 clumps for sale. Northboro Dahlia and Gladiolus Gardens, J. L. MOORE, Prop., Northboro, Mass.

NEW PAEONY DAHLIA
John Wanamaker, Newest, Handsomest, Best. New color, new form and new habit of growth. Big stock of best cut-flower varieties. Send list of wants to PEACOCK DAHLIA FARMS, Berlin, N. J.

DECORATIVE PLANTS
Robert Craig Co., Philadelphia, Pa.
For page see List of Advertisers.

Woodrow & Marketos, New York City.
For page see List of Advertisers.

S. S. Skidelsky & Co., Philadelphia, Pa.
For page see List of Advertisers.

Bobbink & Atkins, Rutherford, N. J.
For page see List of Advertisers.

A. Leuthy & Co., Roslindale, Boston, Mass.
For page see List of Advertisers.

Araucarias, 7 in. pots, 3 to 5 tiers, $1.00 each; Cyclamen, 4 and 5 in. pots, 15c. and 25c. each; Primulas Obconica, 3 and 4 in. pots, 5c. and 8c. each; Begonias Chatelaine, 5 in. pans, 20c. each; Begonias Luminosa, 4 and 5 in. pots, 10c. and 15c. each; Asp. Sprengeri, 3 in. pots, $3.00 per 100; Asp. Plumosus, 3 in. pots, $4.00 per 100; Table Ferns, 2½ in. pots, $3.00 per 100; Jerusalem Cherries, 4 in. pots, 6c. each; Jerusalem Cherries, from field, 5 in. pots, 10c. each; Var. Vincas, from field, $5.00 per 100. Write for prices on Holland Bulbs of all kinds. ROSENDALE NURSERY & GREENHOUSES, Schenectady, N. Y.

For List of Advertisers See Page 499

DRACENAS

The Storrs & Harrison Co., Painesville, Ohio.
For page see List of Advertisers.

DRACAENAS

Indivisa—Fine large plants, special offer to close out the lot.

	100	1000
2½ inch	$6.00	$50.00
5 "	12.50	100.00
5½ "	20.00	
6½ "	25.00	
6 "	40.00	

WRITE FOR COPY OF OUR MONTHLY PLANT BULLETIN.
S. S. PENNOCK-MEEHAN CO.,
1608-1620 Ludlow St., Philadelphia, Pa.

EUONYMUS RADICANS VEGETUS

Euonymus Radicans Vegetus—Three-year-old potted plants for immediate delivery; also three-year field-grown plants, $14.00 per 100, $2.00 per doz. Illustrated booklet, free for the asking. THE GARDEN NURSERIES, Narberth, Pa.

FERNS

H. H. Barrows & Son, Whitman, Mass.
For page see List of Advertisers.

Robert Craig Co., Philadelphia, Pa.
For page see List of Advertisers.

McHutchison & Co., New York City.
Ferns in Flats.
For page see List of Advertisers.

A. M. Davenport, Watertown, Mass.
Boston and Whitmani Ferns.
For page see List of Advertisers.

Roman J. Irwin, New York City.
Boston and Whitmani Ferns.
For page see List of Advertisers.

The Storrs & Harrison Co., Painesville, Ohio.
For page see List of Advertisers.

ASPLENIUM NIDUS AVIS (Birds-nest fern).
Good strong healthy plants, 4 in. pots. $40.00 per 100: 5 in. pots, $75.00 per 100; 6 in. pots, $100.00 per 100. WM. K. HARRIS, 55th and Springfield Ave., W. Philadelphia, Pa.

FERTILIZERS

20th Century Plant Food Co., Beverly, Mass
Cocoanut Fibre Soil.
For page see List of Advertisers.

Stumpp & Walter Co., New York City.
Scotch Soot.
For page see List of Advertisers.

Chicago Feed & Fertilizer Co., Chicago, Ill.
Magic Manures.
For page see List of Advertisers.

Pulverized Manure Co., Chicago. Ill.
Wizard Brand Cattle Manure.
For page see List of Advertisers.

FLORISTS' LETTERS

Boston Florist Letter Co., Boston, Mass.
For page see List of Advertisers.

FLORISTS' SUPPLIES

N. F. McCarthy & Co., Boston, Mass.
For page see List of Advertisers.

Reed & Keller, New York City.
For page see List of Advertisers.

S. S. Pennock-Meehan Co., Philadelphia, Pa.
For page see List of Advertisers.

H. Bayersdorfer & Co., Philadelphia, Pa.
For page see List of Advertisers.

Welch Bros. Co., Boston, Mass.
For page see List of Advertisers.

FLOWER POTS

W. H. Ernest, Washington, D. C.
For page see List of Advertisers.

A. H. Hews & Co., Inc., Cambridge, Mass.
For page see List of Advertisers.

Hilfinger Bros., Ft. Edward, N. Y.
For page see List of Advertisers.

FOLIAGE PLANTS

A. Leuthy & Co., Roslindale, Boston, Mass.
For page see List of Advertisers.

FREESIAS

Yokohama Nursery Co., Ltd., New York City.
Japan Grown Freesias.
For page see List of Advertisers.

FUNGINE

Aphine Mfg. Co., Madison, N. J.
For page see List of Advertisers.

GALAX

Michigan Cut Flower Co., Detroit, Mich.
For page see List of Advertisers.

GADEN TOOLS

B. G. Pratt Co., New York City.
For page see List of Advertisers.

GERANIUMS

R. Vincent, Jr., & Sons Co.
White Marsh, Md.
For page see List of Advertisers.

Geraniums, rooted in Silica rock sand; show a better color and grow better. Let me have your order for Nutt, Ricard, Poitevine and La Favorite, $10.00 per 1000. Cash. JAMES MOSS, Johnsville, Pa.

GLASS

Sharp, Partridge & Co., Chicago.
For page see List of Advertisers.

Parshelsky Bros., Inc., Brooklyn, N. Y.
For page see List of Advertisers.

Royal Glass Works, New York City.
For page see List of Advertisers.

Greenhouse glass, lowest prices. JOHNSTON GLASS CO., Hartford City, Ind.

GLASS CUTTERS

Smith & Hemenway Co., New York City.
Red Devil Glass Cutter.
For page see List of Advertisers.

GLAZING POINTS

H. A. Dreer, Philadelphia, Pa.
Peerless Glazing Point.
For page see List of Advertisers.

GOLD FISH

Gold fish, aquarium plants, snails, castles, globes, aquarium, fish goods, nets, etc., wholesale. FRANKLIN BARRETT, Breeder, 4815 D St., Olney, Philadelphia, Pa. Large breeding pairs for sale. Send for price list.

GREENHOUSE BUILDING MATERIAL

King Construction Co., N. Tonawanda, N. Y.
For page see List of Advertisers.

Parshelsky Bros., Inc., Brooklyn, N. Y.
For page see List of Advertisers.

Metropolitan Material Co., Brooklyn, N. Y.

Lord & Burnham Co., New York City.

A. T. Stearns Lumber Co., Neponset, Boston.
Pecky Cypress.
For page see List of Advertisers.

GREENHOUSE CONSTRUCTION

King Construction Co., N. Tonawanda, N. Y.
For page see List of Advertisers.

Foley Greenhouse Mfg. Co., Chicago, Ill.
For page see List of Advertisers.

Metropolitan Material Co., Brooklyn, N. Y.

Lord & Burnham Co., New York City.

Hitchings & Co., New York City.
For page see List of Advertisers.

A. T. Stearns Lumber Co., Boston, Mass.
For page see List of Advertisers.

GUTTERS

King Construction Co., N. Tonawanda, N. Y.
For page see List of Advertisers.

Metropolitan Material Co., Brooklyn, N. Y.
Iron Gutters.

HAIL INSURANCE

Florists' Hail Asso. of America.
J. G. Esler, Saddle River, N. J.
For page see List of Advertisers.

HARDY FERNS AND GREEN GOODS

Michigan Cut Flower Exchange, Detroit, Mic
For page see List of Advertisers.

Knud Nielsen, Evergreen, Ala.
Natural Green Sheet Moss, Fancy and Dagger Ferns and Huckleberry Foliage.
For page see List of Advertisers.

The Kervan Co., New York.
For page see List of Advertisers.

HARDY PERENNIALS

Bay State Nurseries, No. Abington, Mass.
For page see List of Advertisers.

P. Ouwerkerk, Hoboken, N. J.
For page see List of Advertisers.

Palisades Nurseries, Sparkill, N. Y.
For page see List of Advertisers.

HEATING APPARATUS

Kroeschell Bros. Co., Chicago.
For page see List of Advertisers.

Lord & Burnham Co., New York City.

HOT BED SASH

Parshelsky Bros., Inc., Brooklyn, N. Y.
For page see List of Advertisers.

Foley Greenhouse Construction Co.,
Chicago, Ill.
For page see List of Advertisers.

S. Jacobs & Sons, Brooklyn, N. Y.
For page see List of Advertisers.

Lord & Burnham Co., New York City.

A. T. Stearns Lumber Co. Neponset, Mass.
For page see List of Advertisers.

HOSE

H. A. Dreer, Philadelphia, Pa.

INSECTICIDES

Aphine Manufacturing Co., Madison, N. J.
Aphine and Fungine.
For page see List of Advertisers.

Nicotine Mfg. Co., St. Louis, Mo.
Aphis Punk and Nikoteen.
For page see List of Advertisers.

The Plantlife Co., New York City.
Plantlife Insecticide.
For page see List of Advertisers.

HYDRANGEAS

The Storrs & Harrison Co., Painesville, Ohio.
For page see List of Advertisers.

IRIS

John Lewis Childs, Inc.,
Flowerfield, L. I., N. Y.
For page see List of Advertisers.

IRRIGATION EQUIPMENT

Skinner Irrigation Co., Brookline, Mass.
For page see List of Advertisers.

LILIUM FORMOSUM

Yokohama Nursery Co., Ltd., New York City.
For page see List of Advertisers.

LILY BULBS

Chas. Schwake & Co., New York City.
Horticultural Importers and Exporters
For page see List of Advertisers.

R. M. Ward & Co., New York, N. Y.
Japanese Lily Bulbs of Superior Quality.
For page see List of Advertisers.

Corp. of Chas. F. Meyer, New York City
Meyer's T. Brand Giganteums.
For page see List of Advertisers.

John Lewis Childs, Inc.,
Hardy Lilies.
Flowerfield, L. I., N. Y.
For page see List of Advertisers.

LILY OF THE VALLEY

Chas. Schwake & Co., Inc., New York City
Hohmann's Famous Lily of the Valley Pips
For page see List of Advertisers.

McHutchison & Co., New York City.
For page see List of Advertisers.

Loechner & Co., New York City.
Lily of the Valley Pips.
For page see List of Advertisers.

Lily of the Valley Pips, $5.00 per 1000;
Clumps, $8.00 per 100. Dahlia Clumps, $2.00
per 100. Write HENRY SCHAUMBERG,
Hammonton, N. J.

LIQUID PUTTY MACHINE

Metropolitan Material Co., Brooklyn, N. Y.
For page see List of Advertisers.

LOPEZIAS, ETC.

Lopezia racemosa covered with thousands of red flowers. A continuous
bloomer which makes them valuable as
cut flower and pot lant. $3.00 per 100 out
of 2 inch. E. H. BAUDISCH, 753 Hamilton
Ave., North Bergen, N. J.

LOPEZIAS, 3-in., 3c. Stock Geranium,
$5.00 per 100. Coleus, assorted, $2.00.
Pansy Giants, $3.00 per 1000. Hardy seed-
lings, all kinds. Hibiscus Hardy, $6.00
per 100. Hollyhocks, $2.00 per 100. Cash,
please. S. P. VAN HEEST, Wortendyke,
N. J.

MASTICA

F. O. Pierce Co., New York City.
For page see List of Advertisers.

NATIONAL NURSERYMAN

National Nurseryman Publishing Co., Inc.,
Rochester, N. Y.
For page see List of Advertisers.

NIKOTEEN

Nicotine Mfg. Co., St. Louis, Mo.
For page see List of Advertisers.

NIKOTIANA

Aphine Mfg. Co., Madison, N. J.
For page see List of Advertisers.

NURSERY STOCK

P. Ouwerkerk, Weehawken Heights, N. J.
For page see List of Advertisers.

W. & T. Smith Co., Geneva, N. Y.
For page see List of Advertisers

Bay State Nurseries, North Abington, Mass.
Hardy, Northern Grown Stock.
For page see List of Advertisers.

Bobbink & Atkins, Rutherford, N. J.
For page see List of Advertisers.

Framingham Nurseries, Framingham, Mass.
For page see List of Advertisers.

August Rolker & Sons, New York City.
For page see List of Advertisers.

NUT GROWING.

The Nut-Grower, Waycross, Ga.
For page see List of Advertisers.

ORCHID FLOWERS

Jas. McManus, New York, N. Y.
For page see List of Advertisers.

ORCHID PLANTS

Julius Roehrs Co., Rutherford, N. J.
For page see List of Advertisers.

Lager & Hurrell, Summit, N. J.

PALMS, ETC.

Robert Craig Co., Philadelphia, Pa.
For page see List of Advertisers.

August Rolker & Sons, New York City.
For page see List of Advertisers.

A. Leuthy & Co., Roslindale, Boston, Mass.
For page see List of Advertisers.

PANSY PLANTS

PANSIES—The Big Giant Flowering
Kind—$3.00 per 1,000; $25.00 for 10,000. If
I could only show the nice plants, hundred
of testimonials and repeat orders, I would
be flooded with new business. Cash.
JAMES MOSS, Wholesale Grower, Johnsville, Pa.

PANSY SEED

Fottler, Fiske, Rawson Co., Boston, Mass.
For page see List of Advertisers.

PEONIES

Henry A. Dreer, Philadelphia, Pa.
Dreer's Special Offer or Hardy Paeonies.
For page see List of Advertisers.

Peonies. The world's greatest collection.
1200 sorts. Send for list. C. BETSCHER,
Canal Dover, O.

PECKY CYPRESS BENCHES

A. T. Stearns Lumber Co., Boston, Mass.
For page see List of Advertisers.

PELARGONIUM CLORINDA

John A. Fraser, Wellesley, Mass.

PHLOX

Henry A. Dreer, Philadelphia, Pa.
For page see List of Advertisers.

PIPE AND FITTINGS

Kroeschell Bros. Co., Chicago.
For page see List of Advertisers.

King Construction Company,
N. Tonawanda, N. Y.
Shelf Brackets and Pipe Hangers.
For page see List of Advertisers.

PLANT AND BULB IMPORTS

Chas. Schwake & Co., New York City.
For page see List of Advertisers.

August Rolker & Sons, New York City.
For page see List of Advertisers.

PLANT TRELLISES AND STAKES

Seele's Tieless Plant Stakes and Trellises. H. D. SEELE & SONS, Elkhart, Ind.

PLANT TUBS

H. A. Dreer, Philadelphia, Pa.
"Riverton Special."
For page see List of Advertisers.

PRIMULAS

	100	1000
Obconica, 2½ inch	$4.00	$30.00
Malacoides, 2½ inch	4.00	30.00

WRITE FOR OUR MONTHLY PLANT
BULLETIN.
S. S. PENNOCK-MEEHAN CO.,
1608-1620 Ludlow St., Philadelphia, Pa.

RAFFIA

McHutchison & Co., New York, N. Y.
For page see List of Advertisers.

RHODODENDRONS

P. Ouwerkerk, Hoboken, N. J.
For page see List of Advertisers.

Framingham Nurseries, Framingham, Mass.
For page see List of Advertisers.

RIBBONS AND CHIFFONS

S. S. Pennock-Meehan Co., Philadelphia, Pa.

ROSES

Poehlmann Bros. Co., Morton Grove, Ill.
For page see List of Advertisers.

P. Ouwerkerk, Hoboken, N. J.
For page see List of Advertisers.

Robert Craig Co., Philadelphia, Pa.
For page see List of Advertisers.

W. & T. Smith Co., Geneva, N. Y.
American Grown Roses.
For page see List of Advertisers.

Bay State Nurseries, North Abington, Mass.
For page see List of Advertisers.

August Rolker & Sons, New York City.
For page see List of Advertisers.

ROSES—Continued

Framingham Nurseries, Framingham, Mass.
For page see List of Advertisers.

A. N. Pierson, Inc., Cromwell, Conn.
For page see List of Advertisers.

THE CONARD & JONES COMPANY,
Rose Specialists.
West Grove, Pa. Send for offers.

SCALECIDE

B. G. Pratt Co., New York City.
For page see List of Advertisers.

SEASONABLE PLANT STOCK

R. Vincent, Jr. & Sons Co., White Marsh
Md.
For page see List of Advertisers.

SEED GROWERS

California Seed Growers' Association.
San Jose, Cal.
For page see List of Advertisers.

SEEDS

Carter's Tested Seeds,
Seeds with a Pedigree.
Boston, Mass., and London, England
For page see List of Advertisers.

Kelway & Son,
Langport, Somerset, England.
Kelway's Celebrated English Strain Garden
Seeds.
For page see List of Advertisers.

Joseph Breck & Sons, Boston, Mass.
For page see List of Advertisers.

J. Bolgiano & Son, Baltimore, Md.
For page see List of Advertisers.

A. T. Boddington Co., Inc., New York City.
For page see List of Advertisers.

Chas. Schwake & Co., New York City
For page see List of Advertisers.

Michell's Seed House, Philadelphia, Pa.
For page see List of Advertisers.

W. Atlee Burpee & Co., Philadelphia, Pa.
For page see List of Advertisers.

R. & J. Farquhar & Co., Boston, Mass.
Giant Cyclamen Seed.
For page see List of Advertisers.

J. M. Thorburn & Co., New York City.
For page see List of Advertisers.

S. Bryson Ayres Co., Independence, Mo.
Sweet Peas.
For page see List of Advertisers

Loechner & Co., New York City.
For page see List of Advertisers

Ant. C. Zvolanek, Lompoc, Cal.
Winter Flowering Sweet Pea Seed.
For page see List of Advertisers.

S. S. Skidelsky & Co., Philadelphia, Pa.
For page see List of Advertisers.

W. E. Marshall & Co., New York City.
Seeds, Plants and Bulbs.
For page see List of Advertisers.

August Rolker & Sons, New York City.
For page see List of Advertisers.

Burnett Bros., 98 Chambers St., New York.
For page see List of Advertisers.

Fottler, Fiske, Rawson Co., Boston, Mass.
Seeds for the Florist.
For page see List of Advertisers.

SKINNER IRRIGATION SYSTEM

Skinner Irrigation Co., Brookline, Mass.
For page see List of Advertisers.

SPHAGNUM MOSS

Live Sphagnum moss, orchid peat and
orchid baskets always on hand. LAGER
& HURRELL, Summit, N. J.

SPRAYING MATERIALS

B. G. Pratt Co., New York City.
For page see List of Advertisers.

STOVE PLANTS

Orchids—Largest stock in the country.
Stove plants and Crotons, finest collection.
JULIUS ROEHRS CO., Rutherford, N. J.

For List of Advertisers See Page 499

SWEET PEA SEED

Ant. C. Zvolanek, Lompoc, Calif.
Gold Medal of Honor Winter Orchid Sweet
   Peas.
For page see List of Advertisers.

S. Bryson Ayres Co.,
   Sunnyslope, Independence, Mo.
For page see List of Advertisers.

W. Atlee Burpee & Co., Philadelphia, Pa.
Three "Superfine" New Spencers for 1916.

VENTILATING APPARATUS

The Advance Co., Richmond, Ind.
For page see List of Advertisers.

The John A. Evans Co., Richmond, Ind.
For page see List of Advertisers.

VERMICIDES

Aphine Mfg. Co., Madison, N. J.
For page see List of Advertisers.

WIRED TOOTHPICKS

W. J. Cowee, Berlin, N. Y.
For page see List of Advertisers.

WIREWORK

Reed & Keller, New York City.
For page see List of Advertisers.

WILLIAM E. HEILSCHER'S WIRE
WORKS, 264 Randolph St., Detroit, Mich.

WHOLESALE FLORISTS
Albany, N. Y.

Albany Cut Flower Exchange, Albany, N. Y.
For page see List of Advertisers.

Baltimore

The S. S. Pennock-Meehan Co., Franklin
   and St. Paul Sts.
For page see List of Advertisers.

Boston

N. F. McCarthy & Co., 112 Arch St. and
   31 Otis St.
For page see List of Advertisers.

Welch Bros. Co., 226 Devonshire St.
For page see List of Advertisers.

Patrick Welch, 262 Devonshire St., Boston,
   Mass.
For page see List of Advertisers.

Brooklyn

Wm. H. Kuebler, 28 Willoughby St.
For page see List of Advertisers.

Buffalo, N. Y.

William F. Kasting Co., 383-87 Ellicott St.
For page see List of Advertisers.

Chicago

Poehlmann Bros. Co., Morton Grove, Ill.
For page see List of Advertisers.

Detroit

Michigan Cut Flower Exchange, 38 and 40
   Broadway.
For page see List of Advertisers.

New York

H. E. Froment, 148 W. 28th St.
For page see List of Advertisers.

James McManus, 105 W. 28th St.
For page see List of Advertisers.

W. F. Sheridan, 133 W. 28th St.
For page see List of Advertisers.

P. J. Smith, 131 West 28th St., N. Y.
For page see List of Advertisers.

Moore, Hentz & Nash, 55 and 57 W. 26th St.
For page see List of Advertisers.

Charles Millang, 55 and 57 West 26th St.
For page see List of Advertisers.

W. P. Ford, New York.
For page see List of Advertisers.

The S. S. Pennock-Meehan Co., 117 West
   28th St.
For page see List of Advertisers.

Traendly & Schenck, 436 6th Ave., between
   26th and 27th Sts.
For page see List of Advertisers.

Badgley & Bishop, Inc., New York.
For page see List of Advertisers.

Woodrow & Marketos, 37 & 39 West 28th St.
For page see List of Advertisers.

WHOLESALE FLORISTS
New York—Continued

George C. Siebrecht, 109 W. 28th St.
For page see List of Advertisers.

John Young & Co., 53 West 28th St.
For page see List of Advertisers.

M. C. Ford, 121 West 28th St.
For page see List of Advertisers.

United Cut Flower Co., Inc., 111 W. 29th St.
For page see List of Advertisers.

Guttman & Reynor, Inc., 101 W. 28th St.,
   New York.
For page see List of Advertisers.

Philadelphia

Leo. Niessen Co., 12th and Race Sts.
For page see List of Advertisers.

Edward Reid, 1619-21 Ranstead St.
For page see List of Advertisers.

The S. S. Pennock-Meehan Co., 1608-20
   Ludlow St.
For page see List of Advertisers.

Philadelphia Wholesale Flower Exchange,
   1625 Ranstead St., Philadelphia, Pa.
For page see List of Advertisers.

Richmond, Ind.

E. G. Hill Co.
For page see List of Advertisers.

Rochester, N. Y.

George B. Hart, 24 Stone St.
For page see List of Advertisers.

Washington

The S. S. Pennock-Meehan Co., 1216 H St.,
   N. W.
For page see List of Advertisers.

New Offers In This Issue

AMERICAN BEAUTY ROSES.

The Leo Niessen Co., Philadelphia, Pa.
For page see List of Advertisers.

BEANS WANTED.

The J. Chas. McCullough Seed Co.,
   Cincinnati, Ohio.
For page see List of Advertisers.

BERLIN VALLEY PIPS

Dudley Hartford, Bedford, Mass.
For page see List of Advertisers.

CHRYSANTHEMUMS.

S. S. Pennock-Meehan Co., Philadelphia, Pa.
For page see List of Advertisers.

FLOWERS BY TELEGRAPH

Danker,
40 and 42 Maiden Lane, Albany, N. Y.
For page see List of Advertisers.

**GERANIUMS, BEDDING AND VEGE-
TABLE PLANTS.**

R. Vincent, Jr. & Sons Co.,
White Marsh, Md.
For page see List of Advertisers.

HOT BED SASH.

S. Jacobs & Sons, Brooklyn, N. Y.
For page see List of Advertisers.

LILIUM MYRIOPHYLLUM.

R. & J. Farquhar & Co., Boston, Mass.
For page see List of Advertisers.

SCALECIDE.

B. G. Pratt Co., New York City.
For page see List of Advertisers.

WHOLESALE FLORISTS.

Riedel & Meyer, Inc., 49 West 28th St.,
New York City.
For page see List of Advertisers.

WHOLESALE FLORISTS.

Badgley & Bishop, Inc., New York City.
For page see List of Advertisers.

In writing to Advertisers kindly mention Horticulture

EFFECT OF THE WAR ON AMERICAN INDUSTRIES

The blow in the face received by American industries through conditions brought about by the European war has acted as a tonic, has forced the nation to create new branches and enlarge the scope of existing phases of manufacture, opened the way to utilize, on a vast scale, great natural resources of the United States, and induced manufacturers and merchants to expand their markets into foreign fields with prospects of permanent results, says the Bureau of Foreign and Domestic Commerce, of the Department of Commerce, in a forecast of the effect of the war on the industrial future of the country.

American ingenuity has been applied with success to the making of articles previously imported, and among those who have shown conspicuous ability in meeting the situation, an important place is given to Thomas A. Edison, "American's scientific wizard," who has had a great part in the enterprise and initiative required to build, at a moment's notice, some of the new American manufactures required by the emergency.

A review of the chief industries ministering particularly to the temporary needs of the belligerents across the Atlantic shows that the final outcome will be a very material addition to the manufacturing plant of the United States. Part of this plant will be simply anticipatory of the normal growth of the country's mechanical equipment; part must lie idle in time of peace, but is a distinct asset in the national preparation for an adequate defence against attack; the remainder furnishes at once products needed in the healthy expansion of the chemical industry of the country.

Less conspicuous and spectacular, but of far greater permanent value, is the impulse given to the manufacture on American soil, with American raw materials, of a variety of articles for which we have hitherto been dependent upon foreign skill and enterprise. In a more or less uncomfortable way, we have suddenly been brought to recognize the unwisdom, the folly, of shipping vast amounts of the crude material of our farms, forests, and mines 3000 miles across the ocean, and buying it back in a manufactured form, at a vastly enhanced price. We have likewise come to recognize the absurdity of allowing many natural products of the tropics, of South America, of the Far East, to find their way to Europe, and of paying foreign intelligence and skill to transform them into articles of daily need in our lives.

American ingenuity, adaptation, inventive talent, scientific attainments, and general enterprise have promptly rallied to meet widespread demands, and establish on our own soil the permanent manufacture of a number of wares, some of minor, others of major importance. The return of peace will see them well rooted and able to withstand foreign competition.

The Bureau of Foreign and Domestic Commerce points to the course of events that followed the cutting off by war of the aniline imports from Germany and the supply of potash from the same source, with the resulting tremendous impulse given to the expansion of domestic manufacture. It also calls attention to the fact that, side by side with the increased production of artificial colors, has come the realization by dyers of textiles that the possibilities of the natural dyestuffs have been sadly neglected during the past few decades. The facility and exactness with which the coal tar colors can be employed, the endless diversity of tints and shades readily secured by their aid, have led the modern generation of dyers to disregard, in great measure, those time-honored vegetable dyes, for centuries the only available source of color, which still give their charm and value to the choice products of Oriental looms. The present "dye-stuff famine" has brought them again into prominence. Not so easily applied as the aniline dyes, they still have their especial merits. As a result the American works engaged in the preparation of extracts from the yellow oak of the Alleghanies, from the logwood of Jamaica, from the redwood of Brazil, from the cutch of India, are providing in enormous amounts the substitutes for the more brilliant, but often more fugitive, hues of the coal-tar products.

In the future, natural dystuffs will occupy a more important position in the textile world, and a more ample recognition will be accorded to the highly perfected processes of recent years, ensuring their fastness upon the animal and vegetable fibres. At the same time, we can look forward with confidence to the evolution of a genuine American coal-tar color industry.

Of the domestic potash supply it is stated that large amounts of the compounds of this element are present in the vast beds of kelp floating on the waves of the Pacific, close to the western littoral of the country, that each year the waters of the Pacific coast are producing a crop in which potash salts possessing a normal value of more than $90,000,000 are readily available for use in agriculture and the arts. Now a dozen companies are engaged in the campaign. Not only the inexhaustible supplies in the waters of the Pacific, but also the remarkable deposits in the arid waste about Searles Lake in California, and the valuable alunite of Utah are being rapidly transformed into standard, commercial grades. A year or two, hence we may be able to fertilize our broad acres with American potash exclusively, while another year or two may see us free from dependence upon dyes of foreign make.

The Bureau advises the business men of the United States that the present time is opportune for them to study the Latin American markets, to get in touch with the people of the countries, and thus to open the way for extensive business operations. In other countries also there are unprecedented opportunities for the extension of foreign trade, and with the indications that we are entering upon a period as a creditor nation, we are in a position, as never before, to invest our capital in industries and developments in foreign countries.

It does not believe that the cost of production in the warring countries of Europe will be lowered as a result of the war, or that there will be danger from that source to the holding of new markets already gained. Experience has shown that it is apt to be higher instead of lower after the close of a war, with higher interest rates, higher wages, and higher prices in the warring countries. Surveying the whole field, it may justly be said that the world's conflict has been of unmeasured value to American industry as a whole.

Visitors' Register

Boston—A. J. Loder, Bangor, Me.; George Emslie, Barre, Vt.; C. Gebicke. Burlington, Vt.

Philadelphia—W. F. and Adolphus Gude, George W. Hess, Washington, D. C.; T. Malbrano and wife, Johnstown, Pa.

Pittsburgh: E. J. Fancourt, representing the Pennock-Meehan Company of Phila.; Martin Reukauf, representing H. Bayersdorfer & Co., Phila.

New York—Robert Pyle, West Grove, Pa.; S. S. Pennock, Phila, Pa.; L. J. Reuter, Westerly, R. I.; J. Horace McFarland, Harrisburg, Pa.; P. Welch, Boston.

Washington, D. C.—Antoine Wintzer, West Grove, Pa.; S. S. Pennock, Phila, Pa.; H. Cheeseman, New York, N. Y.; L. C. Vinson, Cleveland, Ohio; I. Rosnosky, representing H. F. Michell Co., Phila.

Albany, N. Y.—F. J. Dolansky, Lynn, Mass.; Simon Guldemond, representing John Guldemond Sons, Hillegom, Holland; George Ruigrok, Hillegom, Holland; C. S. Ford, representing A. Herrmann, New York; J. J. Karins, representing H. A. Dreer, Phila., Pa.; Mr. Bochman, representing H. F. Michell Co., Phila., Pa.

Chicago—C. C. Kurzdurfer, Davenport, Ia.; Robert. C. Smallwood of A. N. Pierson, Inc., Cromwell, Conn.; Mr. and Mrs. Chas. B. Stevens, Plymouth, Mass.; H. A. Barnard, representing Stuart Low & Co., Bush Hill Park, Enfield, Eng.; George Franks, Champaign, Ill.; Mrs. Chas D. Bradley, Fort Wayne, Ind.; Frank M. Smith, Los Angeles, Calif.; Mrs. John Rovatzos, Minneapolis, Minn.

MASSACHUSETTS AGRICULTURAL COLLEGE NOTES.

The Stockbridge Club held its first meeting last Tuesday (Oct. 5).

The Extension Service of the M. A. C. announces that the correspondence courses in Agriculture and Home Economics will open Oct. 1. Registration is restricted to citizens or property holders of Massachusetts. Persons interested should address E. H. Forbush, Amherst, Mass.

The Floricultural classes are getting practice work in floral decoration this month in anticipation of the annual fall flower show. The senior classes are working with basket designs and several very good ones have been made. The junior classes are making a special study of table decorations.

President Kenyon L. Butterfield, has decided to remain president of this college. Last spring, it will be remembered, he was approached on the matter of taking up the presidency of Michigan State College, his alma mater. His action on the matter has been received joyfully by the students.

Professor Waugh is arranging for an exchange professorship with Professor R. R. Root of the University of Illinois. Nothing definite has been arranged yet, but it is not likely that the exchange will be for a month and will come sometime before the Christmas holidays.

Value of horticultural imports at the port of New York for week ending October 2, 1915: Sulphate of potash, $2,471; nitrate of soda, $39,316; clover seed, $26; grass seed, $2,888; trees, bulbs and plants, $194,261.

FREAKISH FACTS AND FACTLESS FREAKS.

Culled mostly from the columns of our exchanges.

The unusual size of some game fish caught in irrigation ditches in Washington led to the belief that they had fattened themselves by eating alfalfa, and an investigation proved the theory correct.
—*Ex.*

Those millions and millions of wild asters that paint the New England fields blue, just now, are so highly esteemed in some parts of the country that single roots sell to flower lovers for 25 cents each.
—*Boston Post.*

Had that South Carolina "Burbank" who is on the way toward growing cotton of any shade desired developed his scheme a few years earlier, doubtless we should not now be hearing much complaint because of the shortage of German dyestuffs.
—*Boston Traveler.*

There will be some splash in the Atlantic ocean this week—all caused by John Scally, city representative of M. Rice & Co., taking his daily dips in the cool wet. The ocean will be the goat for one whole week.
—*Would-be Correspondent for Horticulture.*

About 15 minutes ride from the State House, one may see a scene reminiscent of the old farming days of Boston. From early morn may be seen a herd of about 50 cows grazing on the side of Parker Hill, Roxbury, with a modern hospital on one side of the hill and an old church on the other for environment.
—*Boston Post.*

It has been a long time since I have met a woman so well posted on all kinds of flowers and vegetable growing as Mrs. C. S. Eastwood, who has charge of the Arlington school gardens, the Battery street school garden, and the roof garden at South Bay Union. Among other hints she gave me was this one which flower lovers may well treasure away in their memory for use

another planting time, it seems to me. She said that one of the most successful dahlia growers she had ever met told her that he had made a practice of securing all the fish heads he could from the fish market near his home; and when he planted his dahlia roots he had put a fish head under each bulb, and the fish constituted a fertilizer that he had found to be unsurpassed. It works well with other kinds of plants, too.
—*Boston Post.*

Carlisle, Pa.—On the so-called "Mc" Allister Farm," now conducted by Charles F. Pillsbury, two Williams and Gravenstein trees and a crab apple tree are in bloom. During a recent hail storm that swept this section of the county the Williams and Gravenstein apple trees were stripped of their fruit. Shortly afterward Mr. Pillsbury noticed that apple buds were opening up all over the trees, and today they are in full bloom again for the second time this season. The crab apple tree is a prolific bearer and has blossomed twice in one season in previous years.

A new species of dahlia, with a wide scarlet stripe down its white leaves, and a centre of yellow, grown by Julius Weiss, florist of the State Hospital, Trenton, was shown for the first time at the Michell outing at Andalusia. Weiss explained that it was called Helvetia, the "Swiss Dahlia," because its leaves looked like a Swiss flag and he added that he had put himself to the trouble of discovering it for patriotic reasons.— *Doylestown Intelligencer.*

GREENHOUSES BUILDING OR CONTEMPLATED.

Clinton, Ind.—Herman G. Hershey, rebuilding.

Hicksville, O.—Chas. W. Seibert, house, 30x95.

Pontiac, Mich.—Pontiac Floral Co., house, 35x275.

Sunbury, Pa.—E. H. Luckart, Water street, additions.

Norwich, Ct.—T. H. Peabody, Salem turnpike, house, 30x75.

Richmond, Ind.—Hammond & Co., Brook road, one house.

Attica, N. Y.—Rocco Farnelli, 908 Broad street, one house.

Aurora, Ill.—Aurora Greenhouse Co., two houses, each 28x150.

Fairchance, Pa.—A. M. Frederick, Jr., vegetable house, 40x134.

Rochdale, Mass.—Elbridge S. Carleton, Dale street, conservatory.

Providence, R. I.—Butler Hospital, Blackstone boulevard, one house.

Lincoln, Neb.—E. S. Gunn, for many years connected with the Griswold Seed Company, has started in business for himself under the name of the Gunn Seed Co.

Reconstructed Construction House of Griffin Bros., Torresdale, Pa.

Hand Wheel and Tell-Tale Device used exclusively on our Ridge Ventilating Apparatus.

This house of Griffin Bros. is 40 ft. wide and 200 ft. long.

NOT ASSEMBLERS
BUT MANUFACTURERS

THERE are a lot of greenhouse, as well as automobile builders, who are assemblers. They do not make their parts; they buy them here, there and everywhere; and put them together.

We are not assemblers; **we are manufacturers.**

With but a few minor exceptions, we make everything we sell. Consequently, it is made particularly for the particular purpose for which it is to be used.

Take for example our boilers; we don't buy them. We make them. We make them so they will be made the way a greenhouse boiler should be made. They are not the regular house-heating boilers, bought of some outside firm who cast our name on the door.

It's the same, even with a somewhat minor thing like our Tell-Tale Ventilating Apparatus.

We don't buy it of some recording machine company. It is made right in our own factory. A glance at the pointer will tell exactly how wide the ridge sash is opened.

And so we could go right through our house, and show you how practically everything in the construction and equipping of our houses is made by us, for our houses.

That's one of the big reasons why you can depend on depending on Hitchings. And remember, that we go anywhere for business, or to talk business.

Hitchings and Company

General Offices and Factory: Elizabeth, N. J.

NEW YORK	BOSTON	PHILADELPHIA
1170 Broadway	49 Federal Street	40 S. 15th Street

Vol. XXII
No. 17
OCT. 23
1915

HORTICULTURE

Lasiandra (Pleroma) macranthum

HARDY PHLOX, MRS. JENKINS

LIST OF ADVERTISERS

FOR BUYERS' DIRECTORY AND READY REFERENCE GUIDE
SEE PAGES 552, 553, 554, 555

NOTES ON CULTURE OF FLORISTS' STOCK
CONDUCTED BY

John J. M. Farrell

Questions by our readers in line with any of the topics presented on this page will be cordially received and promptly answered by Mr. Farrell. Such communications should invariably be addressed to the office of HORTICULTURE.
"If vain our toil, we ought to blame the culture, not the soil."—*Pope.*

Adiantum

Adiantum cuneatum and Croweanum will need a temperature of at least 55 to grow well. This temperature will grow all intermediate ferns but for stove species about 65 degrees at night will be required. Examine the beds every day for dry spots, which should be watered. They will have to be kept moist at the roots, but not continually wet. The weather now will make it quite hard to ventilate right but always make it a point to give air whenever possible. When the growth becomes strong give them a mulch and weak liquid manure water once a week.

Azalea mollis

Do not fail to get a supply of these azaleas as they are very fine for forcing during late winter and spring. As soon as received they should be potted up as they do not gain anything by lying around. Pot firm and with good drainage and place where they can be kept cool such as a deep cold-frame. Here they can remain dormant until wanted for forcing. Take a good look at the list of these azaleas and you will be able to pick out some very fine and charming colors. By the end of January you can bring some of them in and force them along. A well flowered plant will always find a ready buyer. It takes from six to eight weeks to force them into bloom in a temperature of from 55 to 60 degrees.

Begonias

Attractive four-inch begonias of the best kinds from the semperflorens class may be had by next spring if they are started now from cuttings. The time when most of our Rex and flowering begonias can successfully be propagated is not limited to any certain seasons but we have found now to be the most convenient month in which to work up a supply. We then can rely on steadily held bottom heat, which is an essential—at least a helpful factor—in leaf and cutting propagation to be carried on with dispatch and no loss worth considering. Some kinds of shrubby begonias, however, only furnish good cuttings in early spring. These plants are given something of a rest from the present on and their propagation is deferred until the time mentioned.

Lily of the Valley

Until the beginning of the new year cold storage pips take the place of the newly imported lily of the valley for forcing. After that the latter proves fairly satisfactory though somewhat slow and often furnished but sparingly with foliage. The nearer we come to the end of the present cold storage supply the less time it takes to force the pips into bloom. The latter from start to finish takes about three or four weeks under a temperature of from 75 to 80 degrees with sand kept well soaked and the air in the house also kept charged with moisture to the extent of being just perceptible to one entering the house. By putting in batches every three weeks you can keep up a steady supply for cutting purposes. When the bells begin to open be very careful about watering as they will damp if allowed to remain wet through the night. At the start keep the atmosphere damp but when the bells begin to open let the atmosphere become much drier.

Spiraeas (Astilbe)

Prominent among plants forced into bloom for early spring and Easter are spiraeas. There is no immediate need of potting them at their arrival if root balls hold firm, as is the rule. For the present they may be heeled in frames covered lightly with loose litter to prevent freezing of the soil into a solid mass and left until after the holiday rush is over. The roots should then have a good soaking, the plants brought in, potted up and slowly accustomed to artificial heat. One may easily figure on fully three months of steady forcing in an intermediate house to have spiraeas in presentable trim for the Easter trade and on considerable less time if the finished plants are wanted for the usual late spring business. Spiraeas when in good growth and perfecting their bloom are ever thirsty and must not be allowed to reach a state approaching dire need of water.

Outside Work

Get all protecting material together for the frames. Fix up all breakages in glass not already repaired. Do not neglect to look over the houses outside for leaks and broken glass and repair without delay. Large tubs of oleander, agapanthus, etc., should be given a cool shed if there is not room in some of the cool houses. Chionadoxa, scillas and other similar small bulbs can be planted now between shrubbery and herbaceous borders and make a fine show in the spring.

Next Week:—Carnations; Cocos; Ixias; Pot Roses for Easter; Shrubs for Spring Forcing; Violas, Daisies, Aubrietias Myosotis, etc. In Frames.

ROSE GROWING UNDER GLASS
CONDUCTED BY
Arthur C. Ruzicka

Questions by our readers in line with any of the topics presented on this page will be cordially received and promptly answered by Mr. Ruzicka. Such communications should invariably be addressed to the office of HORTICULTURE.

Syringing

Because the plants are growing very freely, have a good color and are apparently free from all disease, is no reason why they should not receive a good syringing once a week at least. Spider if not watched will work havoc and the chances are that it will spread a good deal before it is discovered and then it will be a proposition to clean it out, especially with the winter months coming on. Syringe very quickly with high pressure for the less water that is thrown around the houses the better for the plants. Be careful to go into all the corners well, around all braces, and then between faucets where the hose meet. After the benches are syringed go over them and shake the plants as much as possible without taking too much time, so that they will be sure to dry off well before night. Then do not neglect the lime, which is more necessary this year than ever before. It will also be well to carry a trifle more air at night after syringing so as to dry out the air as quickly as possible.

Manure

If the supply of this is bought up locally, little here and a little there, there should be no let up in getting all the manure that can be secured. It will be needed before the season is over. Once it starts going it will be used rapidly and an exhausted supply may cut the crop down a good deal. A concrete platform with drainage arranged into the manure tank or cistern near the manure shed is ideal, but if it is not to be had the manure will have to be stored outside. Pile it in square heaps, not too high, and have these arranged so that the manure can be turned over every so often. A little straw in the manure will not do any harm, but it must not be too coarse. It would be well to see the dairymen from whom the supply is secured, and get them to cut their bedding short, so that it will be better for the greenhouse. Watch the piles carefully so that the manure will not burn. If piled high and if it is not very wet it is very apt to burn, and it is of very little value then. To prevent this a good wetting down will be necessary, but should not be done unless the heap shows signs of heating.

Visit the Market

Every time there is a little time to spare it will do the growers good to go to their market and pay a visit to their wholesale florist and watch how their stock arrives. Usually a good many things can be learned in this way that will be of benefit. The wholesale florist may not have much time to entertain the grower but that matters little. The buyers are all anxious to get back to their stores and they must be waited on at once or they will look for their supply elsewhere. Time is usually a very precious thing and a visit to the market will prove to the grower the importance of having all roses properly packed, all slips properly added, and boxes plainly marked. Even proper tying will help to save time.

The Retail Trade

Growers could no doubt do a little more retail work if they had the proper supplies on hand. Most places are located so that if the growers were in position to offer to the public real flower service they could work up a good deal of new trade without in the least taking any from the regular retail stores. Wire designs of the several standard kinds should always be kept on hand, as should ribbons, tinfoil, toothpicks, and many other knick-knacks that go to make up the florists' supplies. Moss can generally be secured locally and enough of it should be picked and kept right on hand all the time. A supply should be picked now to do for the winter, as later with snow and ice on the ground it will be quite difficult to get. Some nice green cord and colored wax paper put a pretty touch to the flowers and makes the work of opening the packages a delightful task. Never use old drygoods boxes for the retail trade. They are all right to ship flowers to people in the trade but should never be used for retail flowers. We know of several cases where florists lost trade merely because of the use of boxes that formerly contained underwear. Neat boxes tied with ribbon or nice tape make anyone proud to carry them unwrapped anywhere, and wherever they are carried they advertise by suggesting to people that flowers are for all occasions, and are usually more appreciated than any other gift.

Lasiandra (Pleroma) macranthum

Lasiandra macranthum, better known as Pleroma macranthum by old-type gardeners, is a beautiful and effective warm greenhouse subject, possibly the most desirable of the many species on account of its large deep violet purple flowers. A denizen of Brazil, like most of its compeers, it is a strong grower requiring ample quarters for its full development. It is adapted best to pillar and trellis trained specimens. It is particularly effective when trained to a cross section end of the greenhouse, thus showing off its large deep blue flowers to perfection.

The individual flowers do not last long, but this short-coming is made up by an abundance of successive flowers taking their place for an indefinite period. For cut flower purposes it is not well fitted, as the flowers will wilt early after severing the branchlets from the plant.

The subject of this note, like many other beautiful members of Queen flora's family is less in evidence nowadays than in former times, for some inscrutable reason.

N. Finlayson

CYPRIPEDIUM ROTHSCHILDIANUM

Among the large family of ladies' slippers one finds some very interesting and peculiar members, one of them being C. Rothschildianum. A glance at the accompanying picture will plainly show the characteristics by which it differs from the ordinary run of cypripediums, chief among them being the singularly shaped staminode, with its whorls, of white-tipped hairs which gives the flower a very fantastic appearance. The main color of the flowers is a deep chocolate brown laid over a dull green ground. This cypripedium will succeed under the treatment usually given the warm growing section of the genus and the warmest place one can find for it will not be any too warm. Small receptacles will be found best and as a compost a good quality of osmunda fibre with the addition of a little fibrous loam or live sphagnum moss, but fibre alone will do should it be difficult to obtain the latter two ingredients. It will be found well to grow them suspended from the roof of the warm house, shading them but slightly during the warm summer months. Cypripediums should never be allowed to remain dry at the roots for any length of time and the atmosphere in which they are growing should be charged with moisture at all times by frequently damping down the walks and between the plants and on all bright days the plants may be sprayed overhead to keep down insect pests.

M. J. Cope

Naugatuck, Conn.

CYPRIPEDIUM ROTHSCHILDIANUM

BRITISH HORTICULTURE.

The Horticultural Trades Association.

At the annual meeting of this Association, a satisfactory report was presented of the year's working. W. Cuthbertson, of Dobbie & Co., Edinburgh, president; C. A. Pearson, secretary, and the members of the Council were re-elected. E. A. Bunyard, W. Thomson, and E. Merryweather were appointed to fill vacancies on the Council. The president alluded to the severe loss the Association had sustained by the deaths of D. W. Thomson, of Edinburgh, a member of the Council and T. A. H. Rivers, a former president, and on his proposal a vote of sympathy with the relatives was passed.

Autumn Roses.

A splendid array of blooms was seen at the autumn show of the National Rose Society, in London, on Sept. 16. A high standard prevailed throughout, the competition in most of the classes being exceedingly keen. The Cory cup, presented by Reginald Cory for the best new seedling climbing rose shown at all or any of the Society's shows this year was won by Wm. Paul & Son, with Paul's Scarlet Climber, a meritorious variety, which has previously received honors at the Society's summer show, and at the R. H. S. show at Chelsea. The chief award in the premier class for 36 blooms of exhibition roses, was obtained by Alex. Dickson & Sons. Amongst the new introductions, S. M. McGredy & Son, the well-known Irish raisers, received a gold medal for Golden Emblem, a decorative garden rose, of the Rayon d'Or type. The same firm were awarded certificates for Modesty, a H. T., pink, flushed, creamy white, National Emblem, velvety crimson H. T., and Tipperary, a deep saffron yellow H. T.

National Dahlia Society.

Owing to the Crystal Palace being in the hands of the military authorities the venue of the dahlia show was transferred to the Royal Horticultural Hall, in London. The Cory cup, given for a group of decorative garden dahlias, was taken by W. Treseder, Ltd., of Cardiff. Collarette dahlias, which appear to be increasing in popularity, produced a good show. Cheal & Son, gained the first prize in singles with a fine display.   W. H. Adsett.

SOLANUMS

Solanums may be propagated by cuttings, although seeds are more commonly used commercially. January is perhaps the best time to plant the seeds. Cuttings may be taken from old cut-down plants that have started into growth. They are inserted in sand with bottom heat. They will root quickly and are planted singly into pots. When well established the tips are pinched back to induce a bushy growth.

The seedlings should be planted into pots as soon as possible. In June they are planted out into the open ground. Here they may remain until September giving them careful cultivation frequently. If for any reason the plants can not be set into the open field, give them an airy house in order to insure the moving of the pollen to fertilize the flowers.

In September the plants are potted up. The soil used consists of three parts loam, one part well-rotted cow manure, or leaf mold, and a little sand. Plenty of drainage should be put in each pot. When the plants need it a little liquid manure may be applied from time to time.

Solanum Pseudo-capsicum is the "Jerusalem Cherry," an old fashioned plant reaching a height of three to four feet and bearing an abundance of scarlet or yellow fruit. It is often seen in window gardens. Solanum capsicastrum attains a height of but two feet. It has orange red or scarlet fruit and is also used in window gardens. This is known also as the "Winter Cherry." These two are the species commonly used for Christmas sale. There are many other Solanums and some are of value to the florist. For sub-tropical gardens we have S. robustum, S. giganteum, and S. Warscewiczii.

Solanum crispum has very fragrant, bluish-purple flowers produced abundantly in large corymbs. It grows to a height of fourteen feet against a wall and is moreover, hardy.

S. Wendlandii, S. jasminoides, S. Seaforthianum, and S. pensile make fine greenhouse climbers. The first is one of the best climbers grown. It has bright, blue-purple flowers borne in enormous terminal clusters. It may be propagated by cutting the old vine into short pieces and inserting in sand.
    C. E. Wilton.

Amherst, Mass.

HORTICULTURE

VOL. XXII   **OCTOBER 23, 1915**   **NO. 17**

PUBLISHED WEEKLY BY

HORTICULTURE PUBLISHING CO.
147 Summer Street, Boston, Mass.

Telephone, Oxford 292.
WM. J. STEWART, Editor and Manager.

SUBSCRIPTION RATES:
One Year, in advance, $1.00; To Foreign Countries, $2.00; To
Canada, $1.50.

Entered as second-class matter December 8, 1914, at the Post Office
at Boston, Mass., under the Act of Congress of March 3, 1879.

CONTENTS

We rise to express cordial approval of the
Getting experiment formulated by the essay com-
out of the mittee of the Florists' Club of Philadel-
rut phia to promote the interest and instructive value of the meetings of that body
during the coming season. It is greatly to be regretted
that in so many club and society meetings the time is
frittered away in cursory talk or controversy on mere
routine details and the decadence of interest and falling off in attendance from which clubs often suffer

may generally be traced to just this cause. We expect
that when the proposed meetings have taken place in
Philadelphia we shall have the pleasure of making a
report thereon which will indicate so great a success
as to arouse the officers and members of similar organizations elsewhere to new activities on bold progressive
lines. Read the Philadelphia prospectus on another
page and see what you think of it.

Mr. Ruzicka's advice in this issue to
An ex- the rose growers to visit the market
cellent sugges- from time to time and see how their
tion stock arrives is good. The grower of
any kind of flowers for the wholesale
market owes it, not only to himself but to his dealer
to make frequent visits to the latter's place of business
—not for any purpose of espionage but to acquire a
better knowledge of the conditions which affect and
control the disposition of his product, to observe and
compare his own goods alongside of those of his competitor, to get wise as to lacks and leaks and, in general,
to take counsel with his selling agent so that he may
co-operate intelligently with him to the end that his
product may reach the market in such quality and condition as will assure its sale at the best possible price.
Every wholesaler welcomes such opportunities to enlighten his growers as to the conditions which he as
their selling representative has to contend with. Every
wholesaler will tell you that he can "get along" better
always with growers who thus take a sincere personel
interest in becoming familiar with what is going on in
the exacting and often erratic business of wholesale
flower marketing than with the man who stays away
and consequently is apt to form hasty and often un-
warranted conclusions as to the ability or integrity of
his agent.

An editorial note in one of our esteemed
About contemporaries particularly identified with
the gypsy the nursery interests, states that investiga-
moth tions carried on by the U. S. Department
of Agriculture "have resulted in the conclusion that the wind is chiefly responsible for the
spread of the gypsy moth. We do not remember having
seen the statement by the Department of Agriculture
to which the foregoing quotation refers but we do know
a little about the pest in question and we do think that
somebody is "away off" and disseminating misleading
ideas. We cannot imagine a wind that could blow
gypsy caterpillars very far and as the female moth is
incapable of flying and lays her eggs within a few
inches at most of the crevice where she emerged from
her cocoon it is not easy to conceive of her being blown
away by anything less than a bomb. Our contemporary,
referring to the fact that the gypsy moth has not become established to any extent outside of the quaran-
tined district, naively remarks that either the nursery
stock sent out from that area was clean or the gypsy
moth will not thrive far from its present quarters. Our
advice to you, brother, is not to take any chances on its
thriving, but just settle down fairly and squarely on
the proposition that the nursery stock was clean. The
moth visitation has been a blessing in disguise to the
nurserymen of New England as HORTICULTURE has already remarked several times. Cleanliness has, per-
force, become a cardinal virtue with them during
these trying years and as a result the stock they send
out is the cleanest of the clean. If the gypsy moth gets
a foothold outside of its present limits we do not think
it will be either by means of the wind or by infested
New England nursery stock.

SCHOOL GARDENS.

A school garden has been defined as a plot or section of ground where children may be taught how to care for growing plants. This plot or section is not necessarily a part of the school, but may be in the form of the public garden or playground, or even in the home yard or garden.

Frederick Froebel, the founder of the Kindergarten, says, "It is of the utmost importance that children should acquire the habit of cultivating a plot of ground long before the school life begins. Nowhere as in the vegetable kingdom can his action be so clearly traced by him, entering in as a link in the chain of cause and effect."

Children will take an active interest in anything which they can watch develop. The planting of seeds takes on a new mystery when the seed is "mine," and great is the joy when the first tiny green leaves appear.

It is necessary that the child be taught that the proper care must be given to the little seedling as well as to the larger plant and that this care must be exercised continuously. What is more disappointing than to have a fine lot of plants in good condition and by forgetting the necessary drink of water to find them looking as if they were dead? Here is where the school garden steps in and the child is taught to till the ground, plant the seed, watch against enemies of all kind, and to give the plants the proper amount of water and sunshine.

In many places, especially in large cities, there is not sufficient available space to give even a small plot to every one who applies, but in nearly every schoolyard there is a portion covered with grass. Here many lessons of responsibility, care of public property, etc., can be taught by allowing the children to look after this spot of green, keeping it free from paper and weeds and where there are flowers, keeping them in good growing condition.

I know of no better place to teach a child "property rights" than right in the garden. If this lesson were impressed on a child from the time he is wanting to take or use everything in sight, regardless of ownership, when he comes where there are other children that have equal rights there will not be the constant harassing of others. In a garden in which each child or set of children can have a plot this cannot be too strongly emphasized, for what child, be he careful or careless, will not resent, and justly, too, the injuring of his plants in any way?

If you members of the Ladies' Society of American Florists are living in a town in which you do not have School Gardens "get out and push." Get the Parent-Teachers' Association, the Civic Club, or any other club that is interested in Child Welfare, at work and have these gardens. Too much cannot be said about the help which they give the children and the idle ground is made to "blossom like a rose" instead of producing the usual crop of weeds.

In my home town, Lancaster, Pa., the first garden was staraed by the principal of a public school, and she has practically reformed the neighborhood in

View in Geranium House at Homewood Cemetery, Pittsburgh, Pa.

Plant Stand Used at Homewood Cemetery.

which this school is situated. The school was built on the edge of a public dumping ground. A fine large building with an unusual amount of ground space. The teacher started by beautifying the lawn. The children became so enthusiastic they got the fathers to hunt up the proper authorities and had the dump closed. At the back of the building some ground was procured and a tennis court and baseball diamond were laid out, for this teacher believes that "all work and no play make Jack a dull boy." The remainder was laid out in sections and the children of the higher grades were given an opportunity to have vegetable gardens as well as flower gardens. Now this school, which stood for two months stark and bare on the edge of a dump, is, the whole year round, a source of beauty and joy, not only to

The house shown in the first picture is 25 by 100 feet, one of a range of very useful plant houses. The second picture shows a section of the coleus house, with a portrait of Walter Jordan, the gardener for the cemetery. The plant stand speaks for itself in both pictures.

the children but to the whole neighborhood and the passerby.

Since this fine example has been set, public gardens have been opened in four sections of the city, in which for the sum of five cents any boy or girl can rent a small plot on which can be raised plants according to the individual taste. How the children enjoy these gardens, the work and the chance of showing them off. What splendid opportunity to get in close touch with Nature! Here the lessons of neatness, neighborly kindness, helpfulness, fair play and the love of labor are the more firmly impressed because of the spirit of recreation which enters into all the work.

May I appeal to you, florists, florists' wives, daughters and mothers to become interested in this work and help put in practice in your home towns? This will not be wasted energy; for every garden opened will be the means of keeping many uncared-for children off the streets and teaching them clean living. The florist clubs can assist you very much to carry out this movement. The Lancaster Florist Club gives nearly all the seeds used in our public gardens. Each year they make a liberal donation of both flower and vegetable seeds to the persons having the work in charge.

We cannot afford to look only on the dollar-and-cents side of our trade, but if we can implant in the hearts of the boys and girls the love of plants and flowers, it will eventually make returns to some florist, and what helps one is, in nearly every case, of benefit to the trade at large.

In one of the trade papers I saw the following and treasured it, never ex-

(Continued on page 550)

CLUBS AND SOCIETIES

GARDENERS' AND FLORISTS' CLUB OF BOSTON.

Lecture by E. H. Wilson.

The members of this club spent a most enjoyable evening on Tuesday, October 19, listening to the portrayal by E. H. Wilson, of the natural and horticultural features of Japan as observed by him on his second expedition to the Flowery Kingdom. Mr. Wilson's address was illustrated by a series of colored lantern slides of great beauty and the lecture was full of not only interesting but instructive information. Japan is very rich in woody floral resources, the number of species indigenous there exceeding that found in any other section of the northern hemisphere. The Japanese display great fondness for tree bloom, but, with possibly three exceptions, they care nothing for herbaceous flowers. These exceptions are the irises, peonies and moon flowers. Highest in their affection stand the cherries, and the time of cherry blooming is turned into a series of holidays and great rejoicing. Regarding the Japan cherries Mr. Wilson said that a principal cause of their frequent failure in this country is that they are worked on an unsuitable stock. He recommended Prunus Sargentii as well adapted for use as a grafting stock. Moutan peonies, which give such unsatisfactory results usually, do so because they are grafted on a very vigorous stock which suckers and in a very few years kills out the grafted variety. He advised the roots of the herbaceous peony as a preferable stock, but the process of producing a plant by this method is much more tedious and the Japs find it commercially unremunerative. Incidental to his remarks on the longiflorum lily industry Mr. Wilson predicted that the "Regal Lily" of China will eventually take the place of the longiflorum as an Easter specialty. It was a surprise to learn that the art of Japanese gardens really originated in China. Mr. Wilson predicted a bright future for Azalea Kaempferi as a forcing subject for florists' use.

Other Business.

It was announced that the annual club banquet will take place at the New American House on February 9.

On the proposition from the Association of Gardeners for a plan of affiliating membership it was voted that any visitor from other bodies would be made welcome but could not enjoy the privilege of voting until he had become a regular member of the club.

A $50 silver cup was appropriated for award at the Spring Show of the Mass. Horticultural Society for twelve cyclamen plants, three or more colors.

A letter was received from Max Schling, of New York, in response to the invitation to address the club on this occasion, regretting his inability to comply at present and the loss to him in missing the opportunity to meet the members and get acquainted. An invitation for members to visit the Cleveland Flower Show was cordially received.

The exhibits of the evening included a group of seedling dahlias from W. A. Manda, a collection of flowering and foliage plants from W. W. Edgar Co., Buddleias from W. N. Craig, and a large vase of the pink carnation novelty Miss Theo from Littlefield & Wyman.

AMERICAN ROSE SOCIETY.

The Executive Committee of the American Rose Society held a meeting in New York City, President Pennock presiding. The matter of the annual bulletin, with the proceedings for 1915 was gone over, with the plan of making improvement in this publication. The J. H. McFarland Co., of Harrisburg, made a proposition to issue the same in a much better form than heretofore, and this proposition was accepted, and the same will come out after the first of January, embodying the transactions of the year, with colored illustrations.

The matter of cost of affiliated membership was gone over with some detail. At present the affiliated membership is ten cents for each member, and after careful consideration it was moved that the associate membership be changed from ten cents to twenty-five cents per member; this change to be put into effect January 1, 1916.

The premium list for the exhibit of 1916, to be held in Philadelphia at the National Flower Show from March 25, to April 2, was submitted and gone over carefully, covering roses in pots and tubs, table decorations, blooms by commercial growers and blooms by private growers. The total amount of premiums to be awarded is $2,500. The final adjustment of the schedule of prizes was referred to a committee of Messrs. Pennock and Reuter to arrange.

C. T. Tansill of the Washington Test Garden Committee tendered his resignation. Wm. F. Gude of Washington, was selected to fill the vacancy, and Mr. Gude has accepted the position. A new rose was reported for registration and the same was referred for proper consideration.

The Cleveland Flower Show to be held from November 10 to 14, was carefully gone over and arrangement made to call a regular meeting of the Society at that time, for the consideration of any matters pertaining to the best interests of the Society.

The Cleveland Flower Show has placed at the disposal of the American Rose Society, the sum of $700 in prizes. There has been added to that a special prize of $25 by Robert Scott & Son, of Sharon Hill, Pa., for 50 blooms of Killarney Brilliant rose, A. N. Pierson, Inc., offers $25 for the best 50 blooms of the rose Hadley and Benjamin Hammond offers a cash prize of $10 for the prettiest exhibition of roses, same to be decided by vote of the lady visitors, a silver cup is offered by the Lamborn Floral Co., of Alliance, O., a silver medal, by Vaughan's Seed Store of New York and Chicago, and $10 in cash by W. Atlee Burpee & Co.

The judges for the American Rose Society at the Cleveland show are Emil Buettner of Park Ridge, Ill., and John H. Dunlop of Toronto, Ont.

BENJAMIN HAMMOND, Sec'y.

FLORISTS' CLUB OF PHILADELPHIA.

The Essay Committee made the following report at the October Meeting.

NOVEMBER MEETING.

Debate: "Is it good for the business at large to keep flower vendors off the street."

Affirmative, assigned to William Graham.

Negative, assigned to Robert A. Craig.

In the event of the negative vote winning, the Club to prepare a petition and present to councils to remove present restrictions back to their old-time status for the good of the business in general and in conformity with the principles of liberty the world over.

DECEMBER MEETING.

Debate: "Is it wise for the producer to depend entirely on the enterprise of the retailer for marketing his products."

Affirmative, assigned to Chas. H. Grakelow.

Negative, assigned to W. Frank Therkildson.

In the event of the negative winning, steps to be taken by the Club at this meeting to put the suggestions of the speaker into practise, for the general benefit but not to the disadvantage of any one branch of the trade.

JANUARY MEETING.

Debate: "Is a grower or his agent entitled to sell both at wholesale and retail."

Affirmative, assigned to Wm. H. Taplin.

Negative, assigned to Arthur A. Niessen.

In the event of the negative winning, the Club shall pass a resolution defining the proper ethics to be observed by its members, in regard to the question.

RULE OF DEBATE.

It is the understanding that the principal speakers shall have the floor first, in rebuttal and sur-rebuttal, after which the subject is open to general discussion from the floor, at the conclusion of which a vote shall be taken.

The report of the Essay Committee was on regular motion approved.

DAVID RUST, Sec'y.

ST. LOUIS FLORIST CLUB.

The Florist Club held its last outdoor meeting on Thursday afternoon, October 14, at the home of its president. The meeting was the largest on record, no less than eighty members greeting the officers, as well as a number of visitors, and it was a fine compliment to President Bourdet, who at the opening was presented with a handsome gavel by the lady members of his family. A letter from the Cleveland Florists' Club inviting the members to Cleveland next month was read and acted upon by the chair appointing Messrs. Geddis, Berning and Pilcher a transportation committee.

W. T. Wells as vice-president and

W. W. Ohlweiler as trustee were installed into office. There was a discussion on corsage bouquets in which several of the retailers took part and made things interesting for awhile. Messrs. Janiecke and Windler were appointed to consider and report at the next meeting as to the advisability of holding a flower show next spring. The treasurer's report showed that the club's finances are in a healthy condition.

After adjournment the president invited all to a fine lunch on the lawn. At the end a rousing vote of thanks was extended Mr. Bourdet and his family for their splendid afternoon hospitality.

CLUB AND SOCIETY NOTES.

The next regular meeting of the Cleveland Florists' Club will be held Monday, November 1. This will be a big "live" meeting because it will be the last meeting before the big Cleveland Flower Show.

FRANK A. FRIEDLEY, Sec'y.

The First Annual Convention of the Western Walnut Association will be held at the Imperial Hotel, Portland, Oregon, November 3 and 4, 1915. The programe for the meeting, which contains some instructive cultural topics, may be obtained by writing to the secretary.   H. V. MEADE,
Orenco, Ore.

Under the auspices of the Committee on Gardens of the Massachusetts Horticultural Society a visit will be made to the Arnold Arboretum, Jamaica Plain, on Wednesday, October 27, 1915. Professor John G. Jack, of the Arboretum staff, will conduct the party, pointing out and describing the various fruiting trees and berried shrubs. Members of the Society and their personal friends are cordially invited to be present on this occasion. The party will assemble at the Forest Hills entrance to the Arboretum at 10 o'clock A. M., and the visit will occupy two hours. WILLIAM P. RICH, Sec'y.

CLEVELAND FLOWER SHOW.

The display of orchids from the Dale Estate, Brampton, Ont., will be one of the features of the Cleveland exhibit. Other exhibits coming from beyond the borders of the United States include one procured by Ambassador W. C. Sharp, at Paris. This will embrace, it is expected, selections from the private conservatories of President Poincare. Hawaii is sending a collection of twenty-four hibiscus blooms selected from the horticultural station at Honolulu. The Japanese contribution will be a miniature Japanese garden designed by Mr. Tange, Japanese Tea Merchant of Cleveland, who also conducts a landscaping concern to meet the demand for Japanese gardens throughout this part of the country.

CHICAGO GRAND FLORAL FESTIVAL.

Space is now well taken in the non-competitive trade section of the Grand Floral Festival, to be held in the Coliseum, November 9-14. The few good locations remaining will be sold to the first applicants. The rate for space is very low, 30 cents per square foot in the main hall and 20 cents per square foot in the annex, the minimum for space being $25. Applications for space in this section should be addressed as early as possible to A. Henderson, 369 River street, Chicago.

The jurors for the show thus far appointed include E. A. Kanst, superintendent of Lincoln Park, chairman; J. J. Hess, Omaha, Neb.; James S. Wilson, Des Moines, Ia.; W. A. Kennedy, Milwaukee, Wis.; J. E. Matthewson, Sheboygan, Wis.; John Reardon, Ames, Ia.; A. J. Smith, Lake Geneva, Wis.; Donald McNaughton, Lake Forest; Edward Boulter, Winnetka; August Koch, West Park System; H. N. Bruns, A. Lange, Ernst Wienhocber and Chas. A. Samuelson.

A large array of special prizes in the form of cups, trophies, etc., has been secured, including a magnificent series donated by the greenhouse building concern located in this vicinity and valued at $500.

H. B. Howard and James Morton have been added to the executive committee and both were on hand at the last meeting, October 14.

MICHAEL BARKER,
Chairman Publicity Committee.

MARKET FLOWER SHOW.

An exhibition will be held at Mechanics Building, Boston, Mass., on October 23 to 30, 1915, under direction of Boston Co-operative Flower Market. The following schedule of prizes is offered by Chester I. Campbell.

Roses: American Beauties and other varieties, not less than 100 flowers, $25; Ophelia; 50 Russell; 50 Hadley or any red; 50 Killarney or any pink variety; 50 any pink variety not Killarney; 50 Killarney white or any other white; 50 Sunburst or any other yellow; Cecil Brunner and other Pollyantha roses, display not less than 100, $10 in each class.

Roses grown from 40,000 feet of glass or less—25 Ophelia; 25 Russell; 25 Hadley or any red; 25 Killarney or any pink variety; 25 Killarney white or any other white, $5 in each class.

Carnations—50 white, 1st prize, $5, 2nd prize $3; 50 red, 1st prize, $5, 2nd

prize, $3; 50 pink, 1st prize, $5, 2nd prize, $3; 50 variegated, 1st prize $5, 2nd prize, $3; vases, 100 mixed, 1st prize $10, 2nd prize, $5; 6 vases or more, 25 flowers each, 1st prize, $15, 2nd prize, $10.

Chrysanthemums—Vase of 50, white, 1st prize, $8, 2nd prize, $3; 50 yellow, 1st prize, $8 2nd prize, $3; 50 pink, 1st prize, $8, 2nd prize, $3; 100 mixed, $15; display of Pompons, $10; display in pots, $25.

Miscellaneous—Display of violets, 1st prize, $5, 2nd prize, $3; display of pansies, $3; 100 lily of the valley, 1st prize, $6, 2nd prize, 4; display of bachelor's buttons, $2; display of callas, $2; general display of cut flowers, 1st prize, $10, 2nd prize, $5; group of commercial foliage and flowered plants and other foliage, 1st prize, $35, 2nd prize, $25; display of nursery stock (evergreens and bay-trees), 1st prize, $25, 2nd prize, $15; table decorations, 3 prizes, 1st, $35, $25, $15.

New York, N. Y.—The first of the series of monthly flower shows and lectures will be given at the Country Life Permanent Exposition, over the Main Waiting Room in the Grand Central Terminal. Charles H. Totty, of Madison, N. J., will deliver a lecture on "Hardy Chrysanthemums," on Monday afternoon, November 1, at 3 o'clock. A special musical program will be provided in the Music Hall at 4 P. M., on Monday and Tuesday. Competition open to all private and amateur gardeners. Trade exhibits are invited but not for competition. No admission charged.

The Eighty-fourth annual exhibition of The American Institute of the City of New York, will be held on Wednesday, Thursday and Friday, November 3, 4, and 5, at the Engineering Building, 25 to 33 West Thirty-ninth street. Chrysanthemums, orchids, roses, carnations, ferns, palms, fruits and vegetables are all liberally provided for in the prize schedule.

GARDENERS' DAY AT THE EXPOSITION.

The principal feature of the formal programme in commemoration of "Gardeners'" or "Landscape Engineers' Day" at the Exposition on October 9th, was the presentation of a handsome trophy to John McLaren in recognition of his able services in connection with the landscaping of the exposition grounds. The exercises were held on a platform erected at the east entrance of the Palace of Horticulture. The speaker's stand was almost hidden from view with the many floral pieces brought by an admiring public. When McLaren stepped on the platform, the Exposition band struck up a medley of Scotch melodies, and the audience arose spontaneously and cheered. Mayor Jas. Rolph, Jr., made a hurried trip from his ranch in the Santa Clara mountains that he might be present to help honor McLaren for his wonderful work in the beautification of San Francisco and the Exposition. The cup presented by him was a huge silver trophy, mounted on a pedestal of Italian marble. It was purchased with the dimes contributed by thousands of friends and admirers. Donald McLaren, his son and assistant, was presented with a special plaque by the Exposition. Nor did this end the presentations. On behalf of the school Children of San Francisco, little Margaret O'Connor presented the landscape expert with several baskets and a wreath of flowers. The ceremonies were attended by many gardeners, nurserymen and florists, about thirty members of the Pacific Coast Horticultural Society attending in a body. The great day was rounded into a perfect memory in the evening, when Mr. and Mrs. McLaren received a few friends at "The Lodge" in Golden Gate Park. During the dinner hour a handsome silver vase arrived. It was a present from the Bohemian Club to Jon McLaren and Mrs. McLaren.

Coming Events

Shows.

San Francisco, Cal., Oct. 21-26.—The Pacific Coast Horticultural Society, in conjunction with the Chrysanthemum Society of America, and the Department of Horticulture of the P. P. I. E.

Red Bank, N. J., Oct. 27-28.—Annual Flower Show of the Monmouth County Horticultural Society. H. A. Kettel, Sec., Fair Haven, N. J.

Madison, N. J., Oct. 28-29.—The twentieth annual flower show of the Gardeners and Florists Society, Assembly Hall, Madison, N. J. Edward Reagan, secretary, Madison, N. J.

Poughkeepsie, N. Y., Oct. 28-29.—Annual flower show of Duchess County Horticultural Society. N. Harold Cottam, Sec., Wappingers Falls.

Glen Cove, L. I., Oct. 28-29.—Fall show of Nassau Co. Hort. Soc.

Pasadena, Cal., Oct. 28-30.—Eighth annual Fall exhibition of the Pasadena Horticultural Society.

Oyster Bay, L. I., N. Y., Nov. 2.—Chrysanthemum show of the Oyster Bay Horticultural Society. Andrew R. Kennedy, Westbury, L. I., secretary.

Holyoke, Mass., Nov. 3-4.—Third Annual Flower Show, Holyoke and Northampton Florists' and Gardeners' Club, Windsor Hall.

New York, N. Y., Nov. 3, 4, 5.—Annual Chrysanthemum Show of the American Institute, Engineering Societies Building.

Tarrytown, N. Y., Nov. 3-4-5.—Chrysanthemum Show in the Music Hall.

Boston, Nov. 4, 5, 6, 7.—Grand Autumn Exhibition, Massachusetts Horticultural society.

Syracuse, N. Y., Nov. 4-6.—Chrysanthemum Show.

New York, N. Y., Nov. 4-7.—Annual Autumn exhibition of Hort. Soc. of New York, Museum of Natural History.

Chicago, Ill., Nov. 9-14.—Grand Floral Festival of the Chicago Florist's Club and Horticultural Society of Chicago, to be held in the Coliseum.

Cleveland, O., Nov. 10-14.—Cleveland Flower Show. The only show of national scope in the United States this fall. F. A. Friedley, Sec., 356 Leader Building.

Cleveland, O., Nov. 10-14.—The American Rose Society Fall Exhibition and Meeting in connection with the Cleveland Flower Show, Coliseum.

Cleveland, O., Nov. 10-14.—Annual show and meeting of Chrysanthemum Society of America. In conjunction with the Cleveland Flower Show. Chas. W. Johnson, Sec., 2226 Fairfax Ave., Morgan Park, Ill.

Providence, R. I., Nov. 11-12.—November Exhibition, Rhode Island Horticultural Society, Narragansett Hotel.

Baltimore, Md., Nov. 16-20.—Maryland Week Exhibition, Fifth Regiment Armory.

Houston, Tex., Nov. 17-20.—State Flower Show.

President Irwin Bertermann has called a meeting of the Florists' Telegraph Delivery at the Cleveland Flower Show, Nov. 11, 1915, at 9 A. M., at the Hotel Statler, and any member who can possibly make it should attend this meeting for their own interest as well as our association's benefit.　ALBERT POCHELON, Sec'y.

A WORD TO THE WISE.

In a personal letter from John Wanamaker to the undersigned, Mr. Wanamaker says "My idea of advertising is much higher than merely to sell goods. It is to educate our own people and to some extent, whoever reads what is upon our page." This is worth quoting as it emphasizes a fact that many in our business do not fully realize—namely, that advertising in its highest sense should have an educative character in addition to establishing a reputation of high standing. The selling of one's products is a national consequence. Advertising is a deeper study than many people think. John Wanamaker is a past master in the art and has been for nearly fifty years. A careful study of his methods from day to day and year to year is an object lesson for everybody who has the acumen to absorb their points and apply them. In our business Burpee is a good second.

Try to make your advertising attractive and interesting. Try to appeal to the personal element to which all are responsive. And when possible use a picture of some kind to attract attention. Children will stop to look at a picture. Men are but children for a larger growth. And don't do it just one time and imagine the whole world is gazing at you. Keep everlastingly at it.　G. C. WATSON.

SEED TRADE

Canary Onions and Onion Seed.

(Consul George K. Stiles, Teneriffe, Canary Islands, Sept. 4.)

The 1915 export season for Canary Island onions and onion seed closed, so far as shipments to the United States are concerned, on August 28, showing small reduction from last year's figures in the quantities of seed exported. However, a slight increase in prices has made the values approximately the same, so that shippers and growers are well satisfied with the general results. Onions for Porto Rico made a decided gain.

As declared at the Teneriffe consulate, the value of the onion seed exported to the United States in 1915 was $40,828, against $43,293 in 1914; to Porto Rico $973, against $2,548; or a total of $41,801, against $45,841. Onion shipments to Porto Rico (there being none to the United States) were valued at $13,435, as compared with $7,963 last year, this gain being sufficient to 'offset the loss on the seed exports and leave a favorable balance of $1,432 for the present year.

The question of securing the necessary bottoms for shipments to the United States turned out to be (as was forecast in Commerce Reports for July 26) the most serious problem of the 1915 crop.

The Crop Situation.

There have been no new developments in the crop situation during the past week, excepting that our prediction of very high prices for onions next spring have been confirmed by one of the largest dealers and shippers of onions in the country. He stated that onions next March would bring a higher price than for twenty years past. The same opinion seems to be quite general about onion sets, at least, that they will be higher next spring than for several years.

One exception to the statement that there had been no change in the crop situation is the announcement that late varieties of sweet corn will be very short, one or two estimates placing deliveries on contracts not above 40 to 50 per cent., and this is based on the crop curing well as harvested. Should there be any serious damage as a result of unfavorable weather causing the soft corn to mould, prices are likely to rule higher than now seems probable.

Because of the unfavorable crop situation several of the larger wholesale houses are declining to quote prices on most lines of seeds in quantities. In fact they have refused recently to accept orders even in very small quantities for many items, and this probably accounts in large measure for the few salesmen representing the larger houses who are now on the road. One of the oldest members of the trade

stated recently that he had never known a season when such a condition prevailed 'and it was very conclusive of the extreme shortage of many items and the generally unsettled situation.

The news that our old friend Eugene Schaettel is over here again canvassing the trade for Messrs. Vilmorin, Andrieux & Co., will be received with pleasure by the trade, as Mr. Schaettel has been always a most popular and welcome visitor. We may be able to get some information from Mr. Schaettel through our correspondents, and we know that anything he may offer will be read with interest by the trade.

The value of imports of horticultural material at the Port of New York for the week ending October 9, is given as follows: Clover seed, $15,606; grass seed, $3,498; sugar beet seed, $313; trees, bulbs and plants, $91,020; manure salt, $16,055.

BELGIUM PLANTS ARRIVING.

Confirming our letter of September 23, we are pleased to be able to advise you that shipments of Azaleas and other Belgium plants are now arriving in large volume. The steamers "Ryndam" and "Oosterdyk" which arrived on October 18, from Rotterdam, brought 458 packages for us and the steamer "Westerdyk" now in transit brings 338 packages more. Other Azalea shipments are also in transit and Holland shipments are also beginning to arrive in good volume.

Please give this information the widest circulation possible, to offset the many erroneous reports that have been published in recent weeks regarding Belgium shipments.

McHUTCHISON & Co.

New York.

CATALOGUES RECEIVED.

Harlan P. Kelsey, Salem, Mass.—Catalogue of Hardy American Plants.

Weeber & Don, New York City—Special Collections of Flowering Bulbs.

J. G. Harrison & Sons, Berlin, Md.—Illustrated Price List of Fruit and Ornamental Nursery Stock.

P. J. Berckmans Co., Inc., Augusta, Ga.—Illustrated Catalogue and Price List of General Nursery Stock.

W. A. Manda, Inc., South Orange, N. J.—Catalogue of Novelties and Specialties in Greenhouse and Garden Decorative Plants.

Fraser Nursery Co., Huntsville, Ala. —Annual Wholesale Price List, Fall 1915 and Spring 1916. For nurserymen and dealers only.

W. Atlee Burpee & Co., Philadelphia, Pa.—Illustrated List of Sweet Peas for 1916. Includes Fiery Cross, The President, Hilary Christie and other sensational novelties.

A. T. Boddington Co., New York—Florists List of Bulbs, Seeds, etc., for Forcing and Fall Planting, Autumn 1915. Finely illustrated and bears "The Seal of Quality."

A. T. Boddington Co., New York City—Summer and Autumn Garden Guide. A very attractive bulb catalogue bound in white covers, artistically decorated with hyacinths and irises in blue, green and gold.

HELP WANTED.

To My Fellow Florists:

Will not our fellow florists give a helping hand to a deserving fellow craftsman, who has met with an overwhelming calamity, whose work of a lifetime has been wiped out in a single night, and he left penniless?

Rose growers know Father Schoener as an indefatigable hybridizer, whose collection numbered species from every continent, and who has produced as high as 120,000 hybridized rose seeds in one season.

Attached letters explain themselves. Send your contributions to Mr. S. S. Pennock, President of the American Rose Society, No. 1618 Ludlow street, Philadelphia, Penna., who will acknowledge and forward same. May your response be prompt. Thank you.

Truly,

ROBERT PYLE.

West Grove, Pa.

Oct. 10, 1915.

My Dear Cousin:—

I know you will be shocked as I was when I learned today that fire originating in a neighboring house last night destroyed Father Schoener's church and his home. This, of course, means that many, if not all, of his seedlings have been destroyed, for they were largely planted in the churchyard, as well as his collection of briars. I tried to reach Father Schoener today, but evidently he overexerted himself during the fire, as he is ill in bed. I am going to Brooks on Tuesday and upon my return will advise you as to whether or not be saved anything, but I fear that this calamity has left Father Schoener penniless. Yours sincerely,

JESSE A. CURREY.

My Dear Mr. Pyle:—

I have to let you know the terrible news that my house, church and plants and roses burned last night, Oct. 9th. I am penniless. I do not know what to do for the present. I just had cut the last seedlings to send to you. Would there be no way to induce the people in my behalf? I ask this consideration to enable me to go on with my work. All I had is gone; a value of about $10,000 is lost. My sent me a check for $5; it is also burned. He was in the company with the Governor of Pennsylvania on his trip to the West. Could not some newspapers take up the matter to come to my rescue? I will be ever thankful to you for any kind of help in this terrible affliction.

Very respectfully yours,

(Signed) FATHER SCHOENER.

Brooks, Ore., Oct. 10, 1915.

NEWS NOTES.

West Grove, Pa.—Antoine Wintzer of Conard & Jones Co., has at last produced an absolutely pure white canna, so we are informed by the Philadelphia North American. The impressionable correspondent persists in dubbing Mr. Wintzer a "wizard" in spite of that gentleman's very sensible protest. When will people learn that to any really worthy worker in plant development the title of "wizard" is not only unwelcome but offensive?

Holyoke, Mass. — Arrangements for the third annual flower show under the auspices of the Holyoke and Northampton Florists' and Gardeners' Club, to be held in Windsor Hall, Nov. 3 and 4, have been made. Many exhibits by some of the finest flower growers in New England are promised, and a special feature will be an exhibit of orchids by W. A. Manda of South Orange, N. J. The arrangements committee consists of D. J. Gallivan, chairman; G. H. Sinclair, George Rackliffe and George Strugnell of this city, Edward Hennessey and William Downer of Northampton and James Whiting of Amherst.

Of Interest to Retail Florists

PENN THE FLORIST BRANCHES OUT.

Penn the Florist has leased the large store on the corner of Tremont street and Hamilton place, formerly occupied by Thomas F. Galvin and vacated by Galvin at the time of its re-

HENRY PENN.

modelling, on account of the exhorbitant advance in rent. It is one of the most valuable sites in Boston for a florist and under the management of Mr. Penn, who will run it in addition to his place on Bromfield street, will undoubtedly exercise a big influence

WILLIAM PENN.

on the retail centre of the flower trade. Mr. Penn is known all over the country as the most liberal and up-to-date advertiser in the retail flower trade. by means of which he has built up a

very large business in a few years. It
is understood that the owner has made
a very substantial concession on the
rental, which at its former figure was
practically prohibitive.

We take pleasure in presenting to
our readers portraits of Henry Penn,
the head of "Penn the Florist" and
his brother William Penn who is also
an important factor in the success
which the house has attained. Both
are Boston born boys and both started
their careers as newsboys. At the age
of 13 years Henry Penn supplemented
his paper business with flower selling.
By the time he was 20 he had saved
$300. This he invested in a tiny shop of his own
on Chapman place. With perseverance
and personality, carefulness and courtesy the smallest flower store in the
city grew rapidly. Everybody who
traded there came again. They liked
the Penn way of doing things. In five
years he took a store at 43 Bromfield
street. Three years later he enlarged
it and a year ago he had to take storage room in the Publicity Building
across the street. To Tremont street
was the next logical move.

He has been called "the Penn that
wrote service into flower selling." Liberal and clever advertising, courtesy,
skillfulness and excellent values for
moderate prices are the elements that
have brought him success.

NEWS ITEMS FROM EVERYWHERE

CHICAGO.

Frank Oechslin is preparing to erect a handsome dwelling. It will be near his greenhouses and face Jackson Boulevard.

M. Springer is opening a flower store in Lake Forest, Ill. Mr. Springer was formerly from Cheyenne, Wyo. and Waukegan, Ill.

Peter Dersa, formerly proprietor of the Jackson Flower Shop which he recently sold, has now opened a new store at 209 E. 26th street.

Local retailers are spending large sums of money on local advertising these days, a single insertion in the big dailies running well up into the hundreds.

John Poehlmann is convalescing from an attack of appendicitis. He may have to return to the hospital later for an operation. His many friends hope that this may not be necessary.

Chas. Erne with whom violets are a specialty, already offers Gov. Herrick, Princess of Wales and California. Gov. Herrick has remarkable keeping qualities but just now Princess of Wales brings the highest price.

According to those in charge of the Grand Floral Festival, everything is moving harmoniously, and a great success is expected to be scored. In addition to the $10,000 guarantee fund, several handsome special prizes are offered.

George Wienhoeber had a window decoration on National Apple Day that held a crowd constantly outside. A large high-handled basket decorated with yellow chrysanthemums was partly overturned and yellow apples had fallen on the fern covered window floor.

Only a trivial sum now stands between another large wholesaler and the agents of the new LeMoyne block. Wabash avenue has always been a favorite with the wholesale florist trade and while rent is high in the new building it seems likely to house a large proportion of the wholesalers.

The Columbia Flower Shop at 31st and Cottage Grove avenues, is one of the prettiest of the small shops in the city. Mrs. Albert Cole, the proprietor who is a native of Australia has now added four years' experience to her natural artistic ability and trade has developed accordingly. Albert Cole is the American Beauty salesman at E. C. Amling's wholesale house.

Miss Tuckfield of Melbourne, Australia who is visiting her cousin, Mrs. J. G. Hancock, has been much interested in visiting the wholesale flower market. In her city no frost of any account ever occurs and carnations, roses and other stock are grown in the open. Only tropical plants are under glass. It is the custom there in preparing flowers for shipment to dip the stems first in wax or paraffine and this will keep them for many days.

Philip Breitmeyer came from Detroit to Chicago Saturday, Oct. 16th to deliver in person the bridal flowers for a North Side wedding. The bridal bouquet was of the style known as the arm bouquet and was composed of vandas, white dendrobiums and cypripediums, tied with chiffon. The bouquet for the bridesmaid was also unusual, being entirely of Adiantum Farleyense and tied with green chiffon and narrow green ribbon. The gentlemen's boutonieres were of gardenias.

Splendid blooms of chrysanthemum Salamon Gold are now to be seen at Wietor Bros'. They are of a rich shade with large full round heads and are cut with stems five feet long. Mr. Wietor is growing 6,000 of them and thinks E. G. Hill's Salamon Gold a decided success. Alice Salamon so far is not doing well with Mr. Wietor. Marigold, another new yellow, sent out by Elmer D. Smith, is promising well. In carnations Mr. Wietor is cutting splendid blooms from 12,000 plants of Rosette, a deep pink of great size and substance.

The opening of the conservatory of J. Mangel, known as the Palmer House Florist, took place October 18, and adds something new to the downtown retail stores. It is between the store proper and the corridor of the Palmer House, and makes a fitting place for showing plants in an attractive and home-like manner as well as affording a place where choice plants will be protected from the heat of the store. The sides have benches for stock and are artistically designed. Under the glass dome, which gives the conservatory daylight, dozens of birds are flitting about adding an outdoor touch.

WASHINGTON, D. C.

Postal cards received from Mrs. J. A. Phillips, tell of the wonderful trip she is making in touring the west coast and visiting the fairs at San Francisco and San Diego.

Archibald F. Roberts, formerly employed at the store of George C. Shaffer, on Thursday of last week suffered the sad loss of his wife, Nellie E. Roberts, who died about one hour after having been stricken with paralysis. The sympathy of the entire trade is being conveyed to Mr. Roberts in his present bereavement.

Proposals will be received at the office of the Supervising Architect, Treasury Department, until November 3, for sodding and seeding, planting trees, shrubs, etc., on the grounds of the Federal Building, at Plymouth, Mass. Drawings and specifications may be had upon application to the custodian of the building or at the office in Washington.

BOSTON.

W. W. Edgar Co. have been successful in their suit against John L. Condon, formerly connected with the American Auxiliary Co., through Bion B. Libby as attorney, for the proceeds from the sale by Condon of a boiler belonging to the Edgar Co.

BUFFALO.

Ed Fancourt, of S. S. Pennock Meehan Co., dropped in on way back from the Exposition.

The Allen Flower Shop, formerly managed by Mrs. Blakeman has changed hands and has been taken over by Miss Emma Heintz.

Sangster, the Jefferson Florist, has redecorated the interior and exterior of his building and no finer shop is seen east of Main street.

Wm. F. Kasting left on Monday evening for Philadelphia to attend the National Flower Show Committee meeting and from there will go to Washington to attend a meeting on postal matters.

Jos. Streit, formerly with S. A. Anderson for a number of years, is about to leave Buffalo and will be associated in business with another local boy—Michael Bloy, of Detroit, Mich. Every success is wished for Mr. Streit by his Buffalo friends in his new undertaking.

Another new flower shop will be opened here by the growing firm of Galley Bro., of Gardenville, N. Y. The new store will locate at 161 E. Genesee street, at an early date. Extensive alterations, new fixtures, etc., are already under way and by all indications is to be one of the finest East Side shops.

A. J. Reichert & Son have closed the store on Jefferson street and are now located in a new building, 1227 Main street, Central Park district. The store is well adapted for a flower shop, having a spacious window and every convenience. New ice boxes, mirrors, counters and electrical fixtures make an attractive store in the growing section of the Central Park district.

SAN FRANCISCO.

Emile Serveau, who has long conducted a florist shop on Fillmore street, has taken his son, Alfred, into partnership.

Jeanette MacRorie, sister of Daniel MacRorie was the guest of honor at a dinner party given by John McLaren at "The Lodge" in Golden Gate Park a few evenings ago.

Plants and shrubs used in the landscape gardening at the Exposition will be sold to persons submitting the highest bids, according to an announcement by Exposition officials.

The success of the celebration of Columbus Day at the Exposition on October 12th, was largely due to Angelo J. Rossi, who acted as chairman of the arrangements committee.

The recent death of David Tisch in Oakland, Cal., was mourned by a wide circle of friends in the florist trade of this vicinity. He had been connected with the business practically all his life, coming to California many years ago from St. Louis, first locating in San Diego, and then taking charge of the nursery department of the H. M. Sanborn Co. in Oakland and Berkeley.

PHILADELPHIA.

A cheery letter was received on the 14th inst. from W. Atlee Burpee who is taking a well-earned rest in the high latitudes of Wernersville, Pa.

Samuel W. Sproul late with Stuart H. Miller has opened a new flower store at 60th and Locust street under the title of The Locust Flower Shop. He is reported as being a live wire and likely to do well.

August Muller of 65th and Elmwood avenue a noted grower of bedding and flowering plants has opened a retail store at 8th and Walnut street. It is newly and elegantly fitted up and decorated and makes a splendid appearance.

Abram L. Pennock left on October 20 for his winter home in Jupiter, Florida. He has been enjoying the cool breezes and fine atmosphere of Lansdowne and Ocean City the past six months, with the added enjoyment of association with family and friends, and departed spry as a cricket—a wonder for an eighty-nine-year old.

The appeal being sent out by Robert Pyle on behalf of Father Schoener, the famous rose hybridizer of Brooks, Oregon, should meet with a generous response from all interested in the advancement of horticulture. Samuel S. Pennock president of the American Rose Society is taking an active personal interest in the matter and is busy enlisting the sympathy of the trade in this worthy cause. Let others turn in and do their little share.

PITTSBURGH.

The Phipps School of Botany of the Phipps Conservatory, Schenley Park, is again in full swing under the regime of Miss L. F. Allabach of the Fifth Avenue High School.

The Botanical Section of the Academy of Science and Art held its opening session for the season of 1915-16, on Wednesday evening in the Herbarium of Carnegie Institute, President Neil McCallum, presiding. The brief business session included the annual election of officers.

The interesting exhibition of the Neglected Lot or Community Garden of the Civic Club was supplemented by an evening meeting when Garden Club prizes amounting to $25 were awarded. Stereopticon slides were shown of the gardens from the day work was begun, throughout the season, to the gathering of the crops. William Allen, superintendent of the Homewood Cemetery is chairman of the Community Garden Committee.

Both John W. Jones, foreman of the Phipps Conservatory and James Moore of the North Side or old Allegheny conservatory, are submerged in work preparatory to their respective Chrysanthemum Shows to open Oct. 31st. Mr. Moore has been having an influx of visitors to see his splendid specimen of Aristolochia. Likewise Mr. Jones' carpet beds nearby the conservatory have attracted unusual attention throughout the season.

The Zieger Company has opened a new store in the center of the East End shopping district in the Rowe Building, Highland avenue at Penn. The outside of the building has been greatly improved by placing boxes planted with evergreens on the two sides of the building on the second floor. The interior walls are fitted with lattice and covered with foliage decorations. In the center is a pergola with a pool and surrounded with a rockery of tufa stone. At the rear a portion is screened off for a work shop.

PROVIDENCE, R. I.

Ned Brooks has returned from a vacation at Cape Cod.

Thomas Curley of Harkness street, this city, is out around again after having recovered from an operation.

A number of citizens of Bristol have formed a Garden Club and are to affiliate with the Garden Club of America. A question box was started at a recent meeting and the pruning of roses, their protection, and the care of house plants were the leading topics.

The trade in and about Providence at the present time is regarded as the best that it has been for a long time. That there is a great deal of confidence in the future is indicated in the fact that there are nearly a dozen houses now in process of construction or planned ready for building. Joseph Koppleman, James Hay, William Hoffman of Pawtucket, Miss Eleanor E. Widener of Newport, Johnston Brothers, the Butler Hospital, Laurence Hay, Charles Hunt and Richard Higgins, are all adding new houses or enlarging.

NEW FLOWER STORES.

Cincinnati—Eck Bros., 1227 Vine street.

Toledo, O.—Lindley Floral Co., St. Clair street.

Southington, Conn.—R. C. Blatchley, Main street.

Chicago, Ill.—Wm. Lange, 2426 N. Halsted street.

Los Angeles, Cal.—J. W. Howell, 702 W. 7th street.

St. Joseph, Mo.—Rudolph Rau, Savannah avenue.

Yonkers, N. Y.—John Cullen, 36 South Broadway.

Pueblo, Col.—G. Fleischer, next to Majestic Theatre.

Denver, Col.—Speth Floral Co., 1201 E. Colfax avenue.

Atchison, Kan.—Groves Floral Co., Commercial street.

Columbus, O.—Evans Floral Co., Virginia Hotel lobby.

Baltimore, Md.—Frank Kocourek, 1834 Ashland avenue.

New York.—A. Rigo, East 68 street, near Madison avenue.

Wichita, Kan.—W. H. Culp, removed to 139 N. Main street.

Auburndale, Mass.—Wm. A. Riggs, Commonwealth avenue.

Uniontown, Pa.—The Rosary Company, Jerome O'Leary, Mgr.

Knoxville, Tenn.—A. H. Dailey, branch store on North Gay street.

Pawtucket, R. I.—Lapham Floral Co., Fanning building, Broad street.

Fairmont, W. Va.—Weber Flower Store, corner Madison and Main Sts.

Indianapolis, Ind.—A. Reynolds, 5 E. Ohio street, succeeding A. W. Brandt.

Newton, Mass.—Garden City Flower Shop, James L. Carney, proprietor, 301 Centre street.

Philadelphia.—S. W. Sproul, 60th and Locust streets. August Mullen, 8th and Walnut streets.

Houston, Texas.—Boyle & Pendarvis, 721 Main street. J. J. Boyle formerly conducted the Portland Floral Co., Portland, Me.

WHOLESALE FLOWER MARKETS — TRADE PRICES — Per 100 TO DEALERS ONLY

Roses	CINCINNATI Oct. 18		CHICAGO Oct. 18		BUFFALO Oct. 18		PITTSBURG Oct. 18	
Am. Beauty, Special	25.00	to 30.00	25.00	to 40.00	20.00	to 25.00	25.00	to 35.00
" " Fancy and Extra	20.00	to 25.00	15.00	to 25.00	15.00	to 20.00	18.00	to 20.50
" " No. 1	10.00	to 15.00	10.00	to 15.00	8.00	to 10.00	8.00	to 15.00
Russell, Hadley	4.00	to 8.00	6.00	to 16.00	6.00	to 8.00	4.00	to 10.00
Killarney, Richm'd, Hill'den, Ward	6.00	to 8.00	8.00	to 12.00	.....	to 7.00	6.00	to 10.00
" " " Ord.	3.00	to 5.00	4.00	to 6.00	3.00	to 4.00	.....	to 4.00
Arenburg, Radiance, Taft, Key, Ex.	6.00	to 8.00	.....	to	4.00	to 8.00	6.00	to 10.00
" " " Ord.	3.00	to 6.00	.....	to	5.00	to 6.00	.....	to 4.00
Ophelia, Mock, Sunburst, Extra	6.00	to 8.00	10.00	to 19.00	7.00	to 8.00	8.00	to 10.00
" " " Ordinary	3.00	to 5.00	5.00	to 6.00	5.00	to 6.00	.....	to 6.00
Carnations, Fancy	2.00	to 3.00	.....	to 4.00	4.00	to 2.50	3.00	to 4.00
" Ordinary	.....	to 1.50	2.50	to 3.00	2.50	to 0.50	2.00	to 3.00
Cattleyas	50.00	to 60.00	40.00	to 50.00	.....	to 50.00	40.00	to 50.00
Dendrobium formosum	.....	to	40.00	to 50.00	.....	to	30.00	to 50.00
Lilies, Longiflorum	10.00	to 12.50	12.00	to 15.00	10.00	to 12.00	.....	to 10.00
Rubrum	4.00	to 10.00	.....	to	3.00	to 4.00	.....	to .....
Lily of the Valley	4.00	to 5.00	3.00	to 5.00	3.00	to 4.00	3.00	to 5.00
Daisies	.....	to	.....	to	.....	to	.....	to 1.00
Violets	.50	to .75	.50	to 1.00	.....	to	.....	to .....
Snapdragon	.....	to	.....	to	7.00	to 4.00	.....	to .....
Chrysanthemums	8.00	to 20.00	15.00	to 30.00	8.00	to 30.00	10.00	to 25.00
Sweet Peas	.....	to	.....	to	.....	to	.....	to .....
Gardenias	.....	to	25.00	to 30.00	20.00	to 25.00	.....	to .....
Adiantum	.....	to 1.00	1.00	to 1.50	1.00	to 1.50	1.00	to 1.45
Smilax	.....	to 12.50	12.00	to 15.00	.....	to 15.00	12.50	to 12.50
Asparagus Plumosus, Strings (100)	25.00	to 50.00	40.00	to 50.00	40.00	to 60.00	35.00	to 50.00
" " & Spren. (100 bchs.)	.....	to 25.00	25.00	to 30.00	35.00	to 50.00	25.00	to 50.00

Flower Market Reports

BOSTON The summery weather which has prevailed without interruption for the past week, combined with the increasing influx of chrysanthemums has made a material change in the flower market situation. There is no longer any short supply in any line and some things, such as chrysanthemums and carnations, are beginning to accumulate ahead of the sales, and there are signs that roses are heading towards a similar predicament. The quality of the latter is really very fine and the large number carried by the retail stores in their show cases indicates a disposition on the part of the retailers to recognize and welcome the nice grade of goods which the rose growers are providing. Chrysanthemums, as a rule, are not of high quality. There are, of course, some exceptional lots coming in but the general supply does not seem to compare in foliage and finish of flower with the stock of previous years. As above remarked carnations are increasing rapidly in crop and the quality is also improving. The prices have taken a decided downward turn. Violets are being received in good sized quantity and the flowers are nice considering present conditions although not yet up to acceptable winter perfection. The downward tendency in quotations affects all lines, even lily of the valley experiencing a 25 per cent. drop from last week's prices. The retailers are all making a special effort in window adornment but most of the stores seem to be rather shy on customers this week, a condition for which the enjoyable outdoor conditions are no doubt largely to blame.

BUFFALO Trade continues on the upward course and every day seems to show some improvement. There is quite sufficient of everything coming in except carnations and these are having a decidedly heavy demand. Excellent chrysanthemums are coming in and clean up every day. Dahlias are still in good supply also cosmos, and these are taking well. Roses, lilies, orchids, etc., have all had a good demand.

CHICAGO There is very little increase in the amount of stock coming into this market. A few more chrysanthemums are cut than last week and possibly a few more long stemmed roses, but these do not help much for the demand is strongest for medium priced stock, and of that there is a decided scarcity. Carnations, for so early in the season, are extra fine large specimens, but their scarcity keeps the price well up. The last aster has probably been sold for this year and pompon chrysanthemums are hardly ready so there is nothing to be had in what is usually termed a cheap grade of flowers. The social events, always so welcome during chrysanthemum season, have not failed so far to use up the big Beauties. Lily of the valley is in good demand. Shipping trade is heavy to all points and telegraph orders are constantly coming. A good supply of green helps out greatly.

CINCINNATI The market is in a condition where enought stock is coming into the wholesale houses.

WHOLESALE FLOWER MARKETS — TRADE PRICES — Per 100 TO DEALERS ONLY

	BOSTON Oct. 21			ST. LOUIS Oct. 18			PHILA. Oct. 18		
Roses									
Am. Beauty, Special	12.00	to	25.00	25.00	to	35.00	25.00	to	30.00
" Fancy and Extra	8.00	to	10.00	15.00	to	20.00	15.00	to	20.00
" No. 1	3.00	to	5.00	5.00	to	10.00	8.00	to	12.00
Russell, Hadley	4.00	to	8.00	8.00	to	15.00	4.00	to	25.00
Killarney, Richmond, Hillingdon, Ward, Extra	4.00	to	6.00	8.00	to	10.00	4.00	to	8.00
" " " " Ordinary	1.00	to	3.00	4.00	to	6.00	2.00	to	3.00
Arenburg; Radiance, Taft, Key, Extra	4.00	to	8.00	......	to	......	4.00	to	8.00
" " " " Ordinary	1.00	to	3.00	......	to	......	2.00	to	4.00
Ophelia, Mock, Sunburst, Extra	4.00	to	6.00	8.00	to	10.00	5.00	to	10.00
" " Ordinary	1.00	to	3.00	4.00	to	6.00	3.00	to	4.00
Carnations, Fancy	1.50	to	2.00	2.00	to	3.00	3.00	to	4.00
" Ordinary	1.00	to	1.50	1.00	to	1.50	1.00	to	2.00
Cattleyas	20.00	to	30.00	35.00	to	50.00	25.00	to	50.00
Dendrobium formosum	......	to	25.00	......	to	......	......	to	50.00
Lilies, Longiflorum	8.00	to	10.00	8.00	to	12.00	12.00	to	15.00
" Rubrum	......	to	3.00	4.00	to	6.00	......	to	......
Lily of the Valley	2.00	to	4.00	3.00	to	4.00	3.00	to	5.00
Daisies	.50	to	1.00	.85	to	.50	1.00	to	2.00
Violets	.40	to	.50	.35	to	.50	......	to	......
Snapdragon	1.00	to	2.00	3.00	to	5.00	8.00	to	5.00
Chrysanthemums	6.00	to	20.00	12.00	to	25.00	8.00	to	25.00
Sweet Peas	......	to	1.00	.50	to	.75	......	to	......
Gardenias	15.00	to	25.00	......	to	......	......	to	25.00
Adiantum	......	to	1.00	1.00	to	1.25	1.00	to	1.00
Smilax	12.00	to	15.00	12.00	to	15.00	15.00	to	20.00
Asparagus Plumosus, Strings (100)	25.00	to	50.00	35.00	to	50.00	......	to	50.00
" & Sprea. (100 Bchs.)	25.00	to	35.00	20.00	to	35.00	35.00	to	50.00

Prices are reasonable. Shipping business is good. The cut of chrysanthemums is increasing and unless the call for them becomes greater they will begin to crowd. A good assortment in the various grades of the early varieties may be had. Roses are in a good supply and have a good market. Carnations, longiflorum lilies, and rubrum lilies have been having a pretty active market. Dahlias and cosmos both are good.

NEW YORK Increasing daily cuts, balmy weather and public indifference to flowers under prevailing conditions have brought about a much more sluggish market and falling off in values all along the list of staple flowers as compared with last week. Chrysanthemums are coming in heavily, some of them being of really exhibition quality and, as usual, some others mighty ragged and disruptable. Violets are also coming in more freely but inferior in quality. A few shipments of dahlias every day attest the summery character of the October weather which still persists. Cosmos, too, is plentiful from outdoor sources. Roses of splendid quality are arriving freely, as are carnations of much better grade than heretofore. Lily of the valley has sobered down somewhat from its recent soaring stunts, but nobody expects this flower to be very abundant or very cheap after the season gets well under way. Cattleya labiata has passed its high tide and the receipts are much lighter. Large quantities of oak foliage in orange and bronze tints are being displayed by the wholesale dealers in hardy greens, etc.

PHILADELPHIA There is no material change here since our last report. Business continues good at the advanced prices noted. Stocks remain on the short side and in some

(Continued on page 551)

Flower Market Reports

(Continued from page 540)

cases difficulty has been experienced in filling orders satisfactorily. However, crops are promising well and this situation may not last many days. A slight drop in quotations is imminent. They are considerably higher now all along the line than they were at this date one year ago.

PITTSBURGH — This week witnessed to any extent the first falling of the sear and yellow leaf. Owing to the exceptionally cool rainy summer and the light character of the autumn frosts, foliage until this time has seemed more like that of early July. Business is fair but there is a shortage of stock. There are still a few dahlias left, the fancy varieties being the finest ever seen in this section. Carnations are not in full crop, but coming in as well as to be expected so early in the season.

SAN FRANCISCO — Flowers have been more plentiful the past week and business was a little quieter than it had been for some time, with the result that stocks did not clean up so closely from day to day. Chrysanthemums are the principal feature. They are at their height and excellent, and the enormous quantities of them being used is felt in some of the other lines. At the same time roses are more plentiful and better; carnations show good quality, and violets are arriving in ample supply. There are plenty of most seasonable roses with the exception of Beauties and Cecile Bruner, more of which could be used if available. Maryland, Killarney and Richmond show good quality, but they do not seem to move as readily as Hadley, Ward, Ophelia, Russell and other newer varieties. Shipping is better than usual for this time of the year, this part of the business being helped greatly by the improved refrigerator car service. A good many dahlias and gladioli continue to arrive, but they have lost some of their popularity in face of the competition with chrysanthemums. There is no longer a cry of orchid shortage. Cattleya labiata and Mossiae are offered in abundance.

ST. LOUIS — Business has greatly improved and so has the stock. There has been no glut of any one flower, so we can say supply is equal to demand. Prices are a little stiff at present and especially on early chrysanthemums, but the trade wants them and pays the price. These are not as yet in an over supply and will not be for some time yet.

WASHINGTON — Local dealers generally report business as more favorable and at the wholesale houses the verdict is "good." The variable weather is not conducive to the production of good flowers and during the past ten days florists have often had to be content with what they could get. This has been particularly true of carnations which are not yet very plentiful. Lily of the valley is often hard to obtain for in this there is a real shortage. The shortage has caused an in-

crease in price and the best is now bringing $5 per hundred. The late coming of the chrysanthemums has caused a shortage of lilies. While the former are in bloom it is the practice of the growers of lilies to either discontinue or curtail their supply. The call continued much later this year than usual and the stocks were soon nearly exhausted. Calendulas made their appearance last week. The cattleya glut is over and those flowers that are being received meet with a more ready sale now that the social season has opened. Roses are more plentiful and in better quality. American Beauty roses show a marked improvement.

DURING RECESS.

On Friday evening, October 22, the R. and J. Farquhar Co. Nursery employees hold a social and dance at Memorial Hall, Dedham, Mass., from eight until twelve o'clock. The committee consists of Messrs. W. E. Gordon, R. Laurie, P. Fordom, R. G. Walsh, J. H. Scanlan, J. D. Cody, H. W. Steele and J. Traquair.

The Boston Florists' Bowling League scores on Thursday evening, Oct. 14, were as follows:

Flower Market,	1237	vs. Carbone,	1217
Flower Exchange,	1282	vs. Robinson,	1215
Zinn,	1205	vs. M. & M.	1106
Pansies,	1218	vs. Galvin,	1190

Neil Casey high man with 288.

STANDING TO DATE.

	Won	Lost
Flower Market	6	2
Galvin	6	2
Carbone	5	3
Flower Exchange	5	3
Pansies	4	4
Zinn	4	4
Robinson	1	7
M. & M.	1	7

BUSINESS TROUBLES.

New York City. — A petition in bankruptcy has been filed against Julius O. and J. Frederick Hanft, composing the firm of Hanft Brothers, florists, at 684 Madison avenue, by these creditors: New York Cut Flower Company, $2,009, and Joseph J. Levy, $447. The business is one of the oldest in the city, having been established in 1850, and the present partners succeeded to it in 1893. They catered to a society trade. Assets are estimated at $3,000,

NEW YORK QUOTATIONS PER 100. To Dealers Only

MISCELLANEOUS	Last Half of Week ending Oct. 16 1915	First Half of Week beginning Oct. 18 1915
Cattleyas	15.00 to 30.00	15.00 to 35.00
Dendrobium formosum	20.00 to 25.00	20.00 to 25.00
Lilies, Longiflorum	4.00 to 8.00	4.00 to 8.00
" Rubrum	1.00 to 4.00	1.00 to 3.00
Lily of the Valley	3.00 to 5.00	2.00 to 3.00
Daisies	...... to .50	...... to .50
Violets	.40 to .50	.35 to .50
Snapdragon	8.00 to 10.00	8.00 to 10.00
Chrysanthemums	4.00 to 20.00	4.00 to 25.00
Sweet Peas	...... to	...... to ......
Corn Flower	...... to .25	...... to ......
Gardenia	8.00 to 25.00	8.00 to 25.00
Adiantum	.50 to .75	.50 to .75
Smilax	8.00 to 10.00	8.00 to 10.00
Asparagus Plumosus, strings (per 100)	30.00 to 40.00	35.00 to 50.00
" & Spren. (100 bunches)	15.00 to 20.00	15.00 to 25.00

VISITORS' REGISTER.

Pittsburgh, Pa. — J. Smith, representing W. J. Boas, Phila.

Buffalo — E. J. Fancourt, representing S. S. Pennock-Meehan Co., Philadelphia.

New York — Joseph Koppelman, Providence, R. I.; L. J. Reuter, Westerly, R. I.

Cincinnati — J. N. Crismore, Chicago, Ill.; J. P. Keller, Lexington, Ky.; J. T. Nicks, Cleveland, Ohio; Mr. and Mrs. C. E. Ruch, Richmond, Ind.

Boston — Stephen Green, representing H. Bayersdorfer & Co., Phila., Pa.; Robert Shoch, representing M. Rice Co., Phila.; L. C. Vinson, on publicity work for the Cleveland Flower Show.

Philadelphia — John Walker and wife, Youngstown, O.; Arthur E. Holland, representing R. & J. Farquhar & Co., Boston, Mass.; George W. Smith, mgr. Cleveland Florists' Exchange, Cleveland, O.; Geo. Asmus, Chicago; P. Welch, Boston; John Young, New York, N. Y.; W. F. Kasting, Buffalo, N. Y.

Washington — Henry Eichholz, Waynesboro, Pa.; T. A. Bell, of Hamrick & Co., Phila.; C. W. Ward, Eureka, Cal.; P. Craig, Phila.; S. H. Bayersdorfer, Phila.; Joseph I. Adler, Chicago, Ill.; Charles E. Meehan, Phila.; Charles D. Ball, Holmesburg, Pa.; Joseph Goudy, representing H. A. Dreer, Phila.

Chicago — E. S. Thompson of the Central Seed & Bulb Co., Benton Harbor, Mich.; D. Commondrus of the Golden Rule Flower Department, St. Paul, Minn.; Martin Reukauf, representing H. Bayersdorfer & Co., Phila.; Geo. Pandell, Fort Wayne, Ind.; E. G. Hill Richmond, Ind.; C. P. Brunner, Springfield, O.; Walter Gray, Hamilton, O.; Fred Rupp, Lawrenceburg, Ind.; Frank Smith of Smith & Fetters, Cleveland, O.; J. J. Karins, representing H. A. Dreer, Phila.; Thomas Knight, New York City.

Buyer's Directory and Ready Reference Guide

Advertisements under this head, one cent a word.　Initials count as words.

Display advertisers in this issue are also listed under this classification without charge.　Reference to List of Advertisers will indicate the respective pages.

Buyers failing to find what they want in this list will confer a favor by writing us and we will try to put them in communication with reliable dealers.

ACCOUNTANT
R. Dysart, 40 State St., Boston.
For page see List of Advertisers.

ACHILLEA
"Pearl," Fine Seedlings, $3.00 per 1,000, cash. JAMES MOSS, Wholesale Grower, Johnsville, Pa.

ADIANTUM
The Storrs & Harrison Co., Painesville, Ohio.

APHINE
Aphine Mfg. Co., Madison, N. J.
For page see List of Advertisers.

APHIS PUNK
Nicotine Mfg. Co., St. Louis, Mo.
For page see List of Advertisers.

ASPARAGUS
The Storrs & Harrison Co., Painesville, Ohio.

Asparagus Sprengeri, fine 2¼-in., $2.50 per 100; $20.00 per 1000. Cash. M. F. BYXBEE, Norwalk, Conn.

AUCTION SALES
The MacNiff Horticultural Co., New York City.
Plants Sales by Auction.
For page see List of Advertisers.

Elliott Auction Co., New York City.
For page see List of Advertisers.

AZALEAS
P. Ouwerkerk, Hoboken, N. J.
For page see List of Advertisers.

BAY TREES
August Rolker & Sons, New York.
For page see List of Advertisers.

BEDDING PLANTS
A. N. Pierson, Inc., Cromwell, Conn.
For page see List of Advertisers.

R. Vincent, Jr. & Sons Co., White Marsh, Md.
For page see List of Advertisers.

BEGONIAS
Julius Roehrs Company, Rutherford, N. J.
For page see List of Advertisers.

Thomas Roland, Nahant, Mass.
For page see List of Advertisers.

The Storrs & Harrison Co., Painesville, Ohio.

	Per 100
BEGONIA LORRAINE, 2½ in.	$12.00
3 in.	20.00
4 in.	35.00
5 in.	50.00
BEGONIA CINCINNATI, 2½ in.	15.00
3 in.	25.00
3¼ in.	30.00
4½ in.	40.00

JULIUS ROEHRS CO., Rutherford, N. J.

BOILERS
Kroeschell Bros. Co., Chicago.
For page see List of Advertisers.

King Construction Co., North Tonawanda, N. Y.
"King Ideal" Boiler.
For page see List of Advertisers.

Lord & Burnham Co., New York City.
For page see List of Advertisers.

Hitchings & Co., New York City.

BOUGAINVILLEA
The Storrs & Harrison Co., Painesville, Ohio.

BOXES—CUT FLOWER FOLDING
Edwards Folding Box Co., Philadelphia.
For page see List of Advertisers.

Folding cut flower boxes, the best made. Write for list. HOLTON & HUNKEL CO., Milwaukee, Wis.

BOX TREES
BOX TREES—Standards, Pyramids and Bush. In various sizes. Price List on demand. JULIUS ROEHRS CO., Rutherford, N. J.

Breck-Robinson Nursery Co., Lexington, Mass.
For page see List of Advertisers.

BULBS AND TUBERS
Arthur T. Boddington Co., Inc., New York City.
For page see List of Advertisers.

J. M. Thorburn & Co., New York City. Wholesale Price List of High Class Bulbs. For page see List of Advertisers.

Ralph M. Ward & Co., New York City. Lily Bulbs.
For page see List of Advertisers.

John Lewis Childs, Flowerfield, L. I., N. Y.
For page see List of Advertisers.

August Rolker & Sons, New York City. Holland and Japan Bulbs.
For page see List of Advertisers.

R. & J. Farquhar & Co., Boston, Mass.
For page see List of Advertisers.

S. S. Skidelsky & Co., Philadelphia, Pa.
For page see List of Advertisers.

Chas. Schwake & Co., New York City. Horticultural Importers and Exporters. For page see List of Advertisers.

A. Henderson & Co., Chicago, Ill.
For page see List of Advertisers.

Burnett Bros., 98 Chambers St., New York.
For page see List of Advertisers.

Henry F. Michell Co., Philadelphia, Pa. Dutch Bulbs.
For page see List of Advertisers.

Joseph Breck & Sons Corp., Boston, Mass.
For page see List of Advertisers.

Raymond W. Swett, Saxonville, Mass. Darwin Tulips and Hyacinths.

Fottler, Fiske, Rawson Co., Boston, Mass.

C. KEUR & SONS, HILLEGOM, Holland. Bulbs of all descriptions. Write for prices. NEW YORK Branch, 8-10 Bridge St.

CANNAS
Canna Specialists.
Send for Canna book.
THE CONARD & JONES COMPANY, West Grove, Pa.

CARNATIONS
Wood Bros., Fishkill, N. Y.
For page see List of Advertisers.

F. R. Pierson, Tarrytown, N. Y. Carnation Matchless.
For page see List of Advertisers.

CARNATIONS—Continued
F. Dorner & Sons Co., Lafayette, Ind.
For page see List of Advertisers.

Jas. Vick's Sons, Rochester, N. Y. Field Grown Plants.
For page see List of Advertisers.

Littlefield & Wyman, North Abington, Mass. New Pink Carnation, Miss Theo. For page see List of Advertisers.

700 Pink Enchantress, 800 White Enchantress, 500 Mrs. Ward, $5.00 per 100, 500 Winsor, 250 Lawson, $4.50 per 100, 200 Queen, $4.00 per 100. Cash. CHAS. H. GREEN, Spencer, Mass.

CARNATION STAPLES
Split carnations quickly, easily and cheaply mended. Pillsbury's Carnation Staple, 1000 for 35c.; 3000 for $1.00 post paid. I. L. PILLSBURY, Galesburg, Ill.

Supreme Carnation Staples, for repairing split carnations, 35c. per 1000; 3000 for $1.00. F. W. WAITE, 85 Belmont Ave., Springfield, Mass.

CHRYSANTHEMUMS
Chas. H. Totty, Madison, N. J.
For page see List of Advertisers.

THE BEST 1915 NOVELTIES.
The Cream of 1914 Introductions.
The most popular Commercial and Exhibition kinds; also complete line of Pompons, Singles and Anemones. Trade list on application. ELMER D. SMITH & CO., Adrian, Mich.

COCOANUT FIBRE SOIL
20th Century Plant Food Co., Beverly, Mass.
For page see List of Advertisers.

DAHLIAS
Send for Wholesale List of whole clumps and separate stock; 40,000 clumps for sale. Northboro Dahlia and Gladiolus Gardens, J. L. MOORE, Prop, Northboro, Mass.

NEW PAEONY DAHLIA
John Wanamaker, Newest, Handsomest, Best. New color, new form and new habit of growth. Big stock of best cut-flower varieties. Send list of wants to PEACOCK DAHLIA FARMS, Berlin, N. J.

DECORATIVE PLANTS
Robert Craig Co., Philadelphia, Pa.
For page see List of Advertisers.

Woodrow & Marketos, New York City.
For page see List of Advertisers.

S. S. Skidelsky & Co., Philadelphia, Pa.
For page see List of Advertisers.

Bobbink & Atkins, Rutherford, N. J.
For page see List of Advertisers.

A. Leuthy & Co., Roslindale, Boston, Mass.
For page see List of Advertisers.

Araucarias, 7 in. pots, 3 to 5 tiers, $1.00 each; Cyclamen, 4 and 5 in. pots, 15c. and 25c. each; Primulas Obconica, 3 and 4 in. pots, 5c. and 8c. each; Begonias Chatelaine, 5 in. pans, 20c. each; Begonias Luminosa, 4 and 5 in. pots, 10c. and 15c. each; Asp. Sprengeri, 3 in. pots, $3.00 per 100; Asp. Plumosus, 3 in. pots, $4.00 per 100; Table Ferns, 2¼ in. pots, $3.00 per 100; Jerusalem Cherries, 4 in. pots, 6c. each; Jerusalem Cherries, from field, 5 in. pots, 10c. each; Var. Vincas, from field, $5.00 per 100. Write for prices on Holland Bulbs of all kinds. ROSENDALE NURSERY & GREENHOUSES, Schenectady, N. Y.

For List of Advertisers See Page 531

DRACENAS

The Storrs & Harrison Co., Painesville, Ohio.

EUONYMUS RADICANS VEGETUS

Euonymus Radicans Vegetus — Three-year-old potted plants for immediate delivery; also three-year field-grown plants, $20.00 per 100; $2.50 per doz. Illustrated booklet free for the asking. THE GARDEN NURSERIES, Narberth, Pa.

FERNS

H. H Barrows & Son, Whitman, Mass.
For page see List of Advertisers.

Robert Craig Co., Philadelphia, Pa.
For page see List of Advertisers.

McHutchison & Co., New York City.
Ferns in Flats.
For page see List of Advertisers.

A. M. Davenport, Watertown, Mass.
Boston and Whitman Ferns.
For page see List of Advertisers.

Roman J. Irwin, New York City.
Boston and Whitman Ferns.
For page see List of Advertisers.

The Storrs & Harrison Co., Painesville, Ohio.

ASPLENIUM NIDUS AVIS (Birds-nest fern).

Good strong healthy plants, 4 in. pots, $40.00 per 100; 5 in. pots, $75.00 per 100; 6 in. pots, $100.00 per 100. WM. K. HARRIS, 55th and Springfield Ave., W. Philadelphia. Pa.

FERTILIZERS

20th Century Plant Food Co., Beverly, Mass.
Cocoanut Fibre Soil.
For page see List of Advertisers.

Stumpp & Walter Co., New York City.
Scotch Soot.
For page see List of Advertisers.

Chicago Feed & Fertilizer Co., Chicago, Ill.
Magic Manures.
For page see List of Advertisers.

Pulverized Manure Co., Chicago, Ill.
Wizard Brand Cattle Manure.

FLORISTS' LETTERS

Boston Florist Letter Co., Boston, Mass.
For page see List of Advertisers.

FLORISTS' SUPPLIES

N. F. McCarthy & Co., Boston, Mass.
For page see List of Advertisers.

Reed & Keller, New York City.
For page see List of Advertisers.

S. S. Pennock-Meehan Co., Philadelphia, Pa.
For page see List of Advertisers.

H. Bayersdorfer & Co., Philadelphia, Pa.
For page see List of Advertisers.

Welch Bros. Co., Boston, Mass.
For page see List of Advertisers.

FLOWER POTS

W. H. Ernest, Washington, D. C.
For page see List of Advertisers.

A. H. Hews & Co., Inc., Cambridge, Mass.
For page see List of Advertisers.

Hilfinger Bros., Ft. Edward, N. Y.
For page see List of Advertisers.

FOLIAGE PLANTS

A. Leuthy & Co., Roslindale, Boston, Mass.
For page see List of Advertisers.

FREESIAS

Yokohama Nursery Co., Ltd., New York City.
Japan Grown Freesias.
For page see List of Advertisers.

FUNGINE

Aphine Mfg. Co., Madison, N. J.
For page see List of Advertisers.

GALAX

Michigan Cut Flower Co., Detroit, Mich.
For page see List of Advertisers.

GARDEN TOOLS

B. G. Pratt Co., New York City.

GERANIUMS

R. Vincent, Jr., & Sons Co.
White Marsh, Md.
For page see List of Advertisers.

Geraniums, rooted in Silica rock sand; show a better color and grow better. Let me have your order for Nutt, Ricard, Poitevine and La Favorite. $10.00 per 1000. Cash. JAMES MOSS, Johnsville, Pa.

GLASS

Sharp, Partridge & Co., Chicago.
For page see List of Advertisers.

Parshelsky Bros., Inc., Brooklyn, N. Y.
For page see List of Advertisers.

Royal Glass Works, New York City.
For page see List of Advertisers.

Greenhouse glass, lowest prices. JOHNSTON GLASS CO., Hartford City, Ind.

GLASS CUTTERS

Smith & Hemenway Co., New York City.
Red Devil Glass Cutter.
For page see List of Advertisers.

GLAZING POINTS

H. A. Dreer, Philadelphia, Pa.
Peerless Glazing Point.
For page see List of Advertisers.

GREENHOUSE BUILDING MATERIAL

King Construction Co., N. Tonawanda, N. Y.
For page see List of Advertisers.

Parshelsky Bros., Inc., Brooklyn, N. Y.
For page see List of Advertisers.

Lord & Burnham Co., New York City.
For page see List of Advertisers.

Metropolitan Material Co., Brooklyn, N. Y.

A. T. Stearns Lumber Co., Neponset, Boston.
Pecky Cypress.

GREENHOUSE CONSTRUCTION

King Construction Co., N. Tonawanda, N. Y.
For page see List of Advertisers.

Foley Greenhouse Mfg. Co., Chicago, Ill.
For page see List of Advertisers.

Metropolitan Material Co., Brooklyn, N. Y.

Lord & Burnham Co., New York City.
For page see List of Advertisers.

Hitchings & Co., New York City.

A. T. Stearns Lumber Co., Boston, Mass.

GUTTERS

King Construction Co., N. Tonawanda, N. Y.
King Channel Gutter.
For page see List of Advertisers.

Metropolitan Material Co., Brooklyn, N. Y.
Iron Gutters.

HAIL INSURANCE

Florists' Hail Asso. of America.
J. G Esler, Saddle River, N. J.
For page see List of Advertisers.

HARDY FERNS AND GREEN GOODS

Michigan Cut Flower Exchange, Detroit Mich.
For page see List of Advertisers.

Knud Nielsen, Evergreen, Ala.
Natural Green Sheet Moss, Fancy and Dagger Ferns and Huckleberry Foliage.
For page see List of Advertisers.

The Kervan Co., New York.
For page see List of Advertisers.

HARDY PERENNIALS

Bay State Nurseries, No. Abington, Mass.
For page see List of Advertisers.

P. Ouwerkerk, Hoboken, N. J.
For page see List of Advertisers.

Palisades Nurseries, Sparkill, N. Y.
For page see List of Advertisers.

HEATING APPARATUS

Kroeschell Bros. Co., Chicago.
For page see List of Advertisers.

Lord & Burnham Co., New York City.
For page see List of Advertisers.

HOT BED SASH

Parshelsky Bros., Inc., Brooklyn, N. Y.
For page see List of Advertisers.

Foley Greenhouse Construction Co., Chicago, Ill.
For page see List of Advertisers.

S. Jacobs & Sons, Brooklyn, N. Y.
For page see List of Advertisers.

Lord & Burnham Co., New York City.

A. T. Stearns Lumber Co., Neponset, Mass.
For page see List of Advertisers.

HOLLY

XMAS DECORATIONS — Selected Box Holly. Holly Wreaths a specialty in large and small quantities. Write your requirements. DELAWARE EVERGREEN CO. Milton, Delaware.

HOSE

H. A. Dreer, Philadelphia, Pa.
For page see List of Advertisers.

INSECTICIDES

Aphine Manufacturing Co., Madison, N. J.
Aphine and Fungine.
For page see List of Advertisers.

Nicotine Mfg. Co., St. Louis, Mo.
Aphis Punk and Nikoteen.
For page see List of Advertisers.

The Plantlife Co., New York City.
Plantlife Insecticide.
For page see List of Advertisers.

HYDRANGEAS

The Storrs & Harrison Co., Painesville, Ohio.

IRIS

John Lewis Childs, Inc., Flowerfield, L. I., N. Y.
For page see List of Advertisers.

IRRIGATION EQUIPMENT

Skinner Irrigation Co., Brookline, Mass.
For page see List of Advertisers.

LILIUM FORMOSUM

Yokohama Nursery Co., Ltd., New York City.
For page see List of Advertisers.

LILIUM MYRIOPHYLLUM

R. & J. Farquhar & Co., Boston, Mass.
For page see List of Advertisers.

LILY BULBS

Chas. Schwake & Co., New York City.
Horticultural Importers and Exporters.
For page see List of Advertisers.

R. M. Ward & Co., New York, N. Y.
Japanese Lily Bulbs of Superior Quality.
For page see List of Advertisers.

Corp. of Chas. F. Meyer, New York City.
Meyer's T. Brand Giganteums.
For page see List of Advertisers.

John Lewis Childs, Inc.,
Hardy Lilies.
Flowerfield, L. I., N. Y.
For page see List of Advertisers.

In writing to Advertisers kindly mention Horticulture

LILY OF THE VALLEY

Chas. Schwake & Co., Inc., New York City.
Hohmann's Famous Lily of the Valley Pips
For page see List of Advertisers.

McHutchison & Co., New York City.
For page see List of Advertisers.

Loechner & Co., New York City.
Lily of the Valley Pips.
For page see List of Advertisers.

Dudley Hartford, Bedford, Mass.
Berlin Valley Pips.

Lily of the Valley Pips, $5.00 per 1000;
Clumps, $8.00 per 100. Dahlia Clumps, $2.00
per 100. Write HENRY SCHAUMBERG,
Hammonton, N. J.

LIQUID PUTTY MACHINE

Metropolitan Material Co., Brooklyn, N. Y.
For page see List of Advertisers.

LOPEZIAS, ETC.

LOPEZIAS, 3-in., 3c. Stock Geranium,
$5.00 per 100. Coleus, assorted, $2.00.
Pansy Giants, $3.00 per 1000. Hardy seed-
lings, all kinds. Hibiscus Hardy, $6.00
per 100. Hollyhocks, $2.00 per 100. Cash,
please. S. P. VAN HEEST, Wortendyke,
N. J.

MASTICA

F. O. Pierce Co., New York City.
For page see List of Advertisers.

NATIONAL NURSERYMAN

National Nurseryman Publishing Co., Inc.,
Rochester, N. Y.
For page see List of Advertisers.

NIKOTEEN

Nicotine Mfg. Co., St. Louis, Mo.
For page see List of Advertisers.

NIKOTIANA

Aphine Mfg. Co., Madison, N. J.
For page see List of Advertisers.

NURSERY STOCK

P. Ouwerkerk, Weehawken Heights, N. J.
For page see List of Advertisers.

W. & T. Smith Co., Geneva, N. Y.
For page see List of Advertisers.

Bay State Nurseries, North Abington, Mass.
Hardy, Northern Grown Stock.
For page see List of Advertisers.

Bobbink & Atkins, Rutherford, N. J.
For page see List of Advertisers.

Framingham Nurseries, Framingham, Mass.
For page see List of Advertisers.

August Rolker & Sons, New York City.
For page see List of Advertisers.

NUT GROWING

The Nut-Grower, Waycross, Ga.

ORCHID FLOWERS

Jas. McManus, New York, N. Y.
For page see List of Advertisers.

ORCHID PLANTS

Julius Roehrs Co., Rutherford, N. J.
For page see List of Advertisers.

Lager & Hurrell, Summit, N. J.
For page see List of Advertisers.

PALMS, ETC.

Robert Craig Co., Philadelphia, Pa.
For page see List of Advertisers.

August Rolker & Sons, New York City.
For page see List of Advertisers.

A. Leuthy & Co., Roslindale, Boston, Mass.
For page see List of Advertisers.

PANSY PLANTS

PANSIES—The Big Giant Flowering
Kind—$3.00 per 1,000; $25.00 per 10,000. If
I could only show the nice plants, hundred
of testimonials and repeat orders, I would
be flooded with new business. Cash.
JAMES MOSS, Wholesale Grower, Johnsville, Pa.

PANSY SEED

Fottler, Fiske, Rawson Co., Boston, Mass.

PEONIES

Henry A. Dreer, Philadelphia, Pa.
Dreer's Special Offer or Hardy Paeonies.
For page see List of Advertisers.

Peonies. The world's greatest collection.
1200 sorts. Send for list. C. BETSCHER,
Canal Dover, O.

Rare and continental varieties. James
Kelway, Baroness Schroder, Eugenie Ver-
dier, Mlle. Rousseau. Mireille, Mme. Loise
Mere. $1.00 each. $10.00 doz.; Mons. M.
Cahuzac, $2.50 each, $25.00 doz.; Solange,
Tourangelle, Mignon, Primevere, Mme.
August Dessert, Rosa Bonheur—send for
list. D. W. C. RUFF, Buena Vista Gar-
dens, St. Paul, Minn.

PECKY CYPRESS BENCHES

A. T. Stearns Lumber Co., Boston, Mass.

PHLOX

Henry A. Dreer, Philadelphia, Pa.
For page see List of Advertisers.

PIPE AND FITTINGS

Kroeschell Bros. Co., Chicago.
For page see List of Advertisers.

King Construction Company,
N. Tonawanda, N. Y.
Shelf Brackets and Pipe Hangers.

PLANT AND BULB IMPORTS

Chas. Schwake & Co., New York City.
For page see List of Advertisers.

August Rolker & Sons, New York City.
For page see List of Advertisers.

PLANT TRELLISES AND STAKES

Seele's Tieless Plant Stakes and Trellises.—H. D. SEELE & SONS, Elkhart, Ind.

PLANT TUBS

H. A. Dreer, Philadelphia, Pa.
"Riverton Special."

RAFFIA

McHutchison & Co., New York, N. Y.
For page see List of Advertisers.

RHODODENDRONS

P. Ouwerkerk, Hoboken, N. J.
For page see List of Advertisers.

Framingham Nurseries, Framingham, Mass.
For page see List of Advertisers.

RIBBONS AND CHIFFONS

S. S. Pennock-Meehan Co., Philadelphia, Pa.

ROSES

Poehlmann Bros. Co., Morton Grove, Ill.
For page see List of Advertisers.

P. Ouwerkerk, Hoboken, N. J.
For page see List of Advertisers.

Robert Craig Co., Philadelphia, Pa.
For page see List of Advertisers.

W. & T. Smith Co., Geneva, N. Y.
American Grown Roses.
For page see List of Advertisers.

Bay State Nurseries, North Abington, Mass.
For page see List of Advertisers.

August Rolker & Sons, New York City.
For page see List of Advertisers.

ROSES—Continued

Framingham Nurseries, Framingham, Mass.
For page see List of Advertisers.

A. N. Pierson, Inc., Cromwell, Conn.
For page see List of Advertisers.

THE CONARD & JONES COMPANY,
Rose Specialists.
West Grove, Pa. Send for offers.

SCALECIDE

B. G. Pratt Co., New York City.

SEASONABLE PLANT STOCK

R. Vincent, Jr. & Sons Co., White Marsh,
Md.
For page see List of Advertisers.

SEED GROWERS

California Seed Growers' Association,
San Jose, Cal.
For page see List of Advertisers.

SEEDS

Carter's Tested Seeds,
Seeds with a Pedigree.
Boston, Mass. and London, England.
For page see List of Advertisers.

Kelway & Son,
Langport, Somerset, England.
Kelway's Celebrated English Strain Garden
Seeds.
For page see List of Advertisers.

Joseph Breck & Sons, Boston, Mass.
For page see List of Advertisers.

J. Bolgiano & Son, Baltimore, Md.
For page see List of Advertisers.

A. T. Boddington Co., Inc., New York City.
For page see List of Advertisers.

Chas. Schwake & Co., New York City.
For page see List of Advertisers.

Michell's Seed House, Philadelphia, Pa.
For page see List of Advertisers.

W. Atlee Burpee & Co., Philadelphia, Pa.
For page see List of Advertisers.

R. & J. Farquhar & Co., Boston, Mass.
For page see List of Advertisers.

J. M. Thorburn & Co., New York City.
For page see List of Advertisers.

S. Bryson Ayres Co., Independence, Mo.
Sweet Peas.
For page see List of Advertisers.

Loechner & Co., New York City.
For page see List of Advertisers.

Ant. C. Zvolanek, Lompoc, Cal.
Winter Flowering Sweet Pea Seed.
For page see List of Advertisers.

S. S. Skidelsky & Co., Philadelphia, Pa.
For page see List of Advertisers.

W. E. Marshall & Co., New York City.
Seeds, Plants and Bulbs.
For page see List of Advertisers.

August Rolker & Sons, New York City.
For page see List of Advertisers.

Burnett Bros., 98 Chambers St., New York.
For page see List of Advertisers.

Fottler, Fiske, Rawson Co., Boston, Mass.
Seeds for the Florist.

SKINNER IRRIGATION SYSTEM

Skinner Irrigation Co., Brookline, Mass.
For page see List of Advertisers.

SPHAGNUM MOSS

Live Sphagnum moss, orchid peat and
orchid baskets always on hand. LAGER
& HURRELL, Summit, N. J.

SPRAYING MATERIALS

B. G. Pratt Co., New York City.

STOVE PLANTS

Orchids—Largest stock in the country—
Stove plants and Crotons, finest collection.
JULIUS ROEHRS CO., Rutherford, N. J.

For List of Advertisers See Page 531

SWEET PEA SEED
Ant. C. Zvolanek, Lompoc, Calif.
Gold Medal of Honor Winter Orchid Sweet Peas.
For page see List of Advertisers.

S. Bryson Ayres Co.,
Sunnyslope, Independence, Mo.
For page see List of Advertisers.

VEGETABLE PLANTS
R. Vincent, Jr. & Sons Co.,
White Marsh, Md.
For page see List of Advertisers.

VENTILATING APPARATUS
The Advance Co., Richmond, Ind.
For page see List of Advertisers.

The John A. Evans Co., Richmond, Ind.
For page see List of Advertisers.

VERMICIDES
Aphine Mfg. Co., Madison, N. J.
For page see List of Advertisers.

WIRED TOOTHPICKS
W. J. Cowee, Berlin, N. Y.
For page see List of Advertisers.

WIREWORK
Reed & Keller, New York City.
For page see List of Advertisers.

WILLIAM E. HEILSCHER'S WIRE
WORKS, 266 Randolph St., Detroit, Mich.

WHOLESALE FLORISTS
Albany, N. Y.

Albany Cut Flower Exchange, Albany, N. Y.
For page see List of Advertisers.

Baltimore

The S. S. Pennock-Meehan Co., Franklin
and St. Paul Sts.
For page see List of Advertisers.

Boston

N. F. McCarthy & Co., 112 Arch St. and
31 Otis St.
For page see List of Advertisers.

Welch Bros. Co., 226 Devonshire St.
For page see List of Advertisers.

Patrick Welch, 262 Devonshire St., Boston,
Mass.
For page see List of Advertisers.

Brooklyn

Wm. H. Kuebler, 28 Willoughby St.
For page see List of Advertisers.

Buffalo, N. Y.

William F. Kasting Co., 383-87 Ellicott St.
For page see List of Advertisers.

Chicago

Poehlmann Bros. Co., Morton Grove, Ill.
For page see List of Advertisers.

Detroit

Michigan Cut Flower Exchange, 38 and 40
Broadway.
For page see List of Advertisers.

New York

H. E. Froment, 148 W. 28th St.
For page see List of Advertisers.

James McManus, 105 W. 28th St.
For page see List of Advertisers.

W. P. Sheridan, 133 W. 28th St.
For page see List of Advertisers.

P. J. Smith, 131 West 28th St., N. Y.
For page see List of Advertisers.

Moore, Hentz & Nash, 55 and 57 W. 26th St.

Charles Millang, 55 and 57 West 26th St.
For page see List of Advertisers.

W. P. Ford, New York
For page see List of Advertisers.

The S. S. Pennock-Meehan Co., 117 West
28th St.
For page see List of Advertisers.

WHOLESALE FLORISTS
New York—Continued

Traendly & Schenck, 436 6th Ave., between
26th and 27th Sts.
For page see List of Advertisers.

Badgley & Bishop, Inc., New York.
For page see List of Advertisers.

Woodrow & Marketos, 37 & 39 West 28th St.
For page see List of Advertisers.

Riedel & Meyer, Inc. 49 West 28th St.
New York City.
For page see List of Advertisers.

George C. Siebrecht, 109 W. 28th St.
For page see List of Advertisers.

John Young & Co., 53 West 28th St.
For page see List of Advertisers.

M. C. Ford, 121 West 28th St.
For page see List of Advertisers.

United Cut Flower Co., Inc., 111 W. 28th St.
For page see List of Advertisers.

Guttman & Reynor, Inc., 101 W. 28th St.,
New York.
For page see List of Advertisers.

Philadelphia

Leo. Niessen Co., 12th and Race Sts.
For page see List of Advertisers.

Edward Reid, 1619-21 Ranstead St.
For page see List of Advertisers.

The S. S. Pennock-Meehan Co., 1608-20
Ludlow St.
For page see List of Advertisers.

Philadelphia Wholesale Flower Exchange,
1625 Ranstead St., Philadelphia, Pa.
For page see List of Advertisers.

Richmond, Ind.

E. G. Hill Co.
For page see List of Advertisers.

Rochester, N. Y.

George B. Hart, 24 Stone St.
For page see List of Advertisers.

Washington

The S. S. Pennock-Meehan Co., 1216 H St.,
N. W.
For page see List of Advertisers.

New Offers In This Issue

CLEVELAND FLOWER SHOW NOTICE.
Cleveland, Ohio, November 10th to 14th.
For page see List of Advertisers.

FITTINGS FOR REPAIR WORK.
Advance Co. Richmond, Ind.
For page see List of Advertisers.

FRENCH HYDRANGEAS.
Henry F. Michell Co., Philadelphia, Pa.
For page see List of Advertisers.

GREENHOUSE CONSTRUCTION.
S. Jacobs & Sons, Brooklyn, N. Y.
For page see List of Advertisers.

PLANTS WANTED.
C. C. Trepel, New York City.
For page see List of Advertisers.

ROSE MRS. CHARLES RUSSELL.
S. S. Pennock-Meehan Co., Philadelphia, Pa.
For page see List of Advertisers.

STANDARD THERMOMETERS.
Standard Thermo Co., Boston, Mass.
For page see List of Advertisers.

WINTER FLOWERING SWEET PEAS.
Arthur T. Boddington Co. Inc.
New York City.
For page see List of Advertisers.

In writing to Advertisers kindly mention Horticulture

FREAKISH FACTS AND FACTLESS FREAKS.

Culled from the columns of our exchanges.

Among the flowers that will be shown at the Boston Chrysanthemum Show this year, I am told, will be some very beautiful specimens of that flower raised by John Dinan, gardener of the C. N. Winship estate, Wakefield. The seed from which these specimens grew were brought from Ireland several years ago by Mr. Dinan, when he left his position as gardener at the Blarney Castle conservatories.—*Boston Post.*

Some time ago there were stories printed in various publications to the effect that Massachusetts' famous old colony of Shakers had gone out of existence. The Mt. Lebanon colony of Shakers, however, prove themselves very much alive by the exhibit they made the past week at the Grange Fair up-State. The average yield of wheat in that part of Massachusetts is about 17 bushels to the acre; but the Shakers succeeded in producing 63 bushels. That's what Bay State soil can do when it gets proper treatment.—*Boston Post.*

When it was reported that Jameson (Mo.) boasted a cocklebur which towers 21 feet above the ground, people found it difficult to believe, despite the fact that they had been "shown" in any number of cases. And this lowly and despised plant was seldom given any attention except by those who were anxious to destroy it.

But people came to Jameson and were convinced—they saw the cocklebur growing on top of the rear end of the Jameson bank building. As the building is twenty feet high and the plant fully one foot in height, no one could complain of being deceived.

—*Saturday Blade, Chicago.*

A mushroom weighing more than 30 pounds and measuring 3½ feet in diameter was recently brought to Horticultural Hall for the Mycological Club exhibition. The mushroom was found in Beverly by Mrs. Alice Wool of Boston. It was like two great roses of cream fawn color, waxy white and full of irregular holes on the underside. A litter of boughs and pasteboard boxes had to be made for its transportation. Two men carried it to the station and placed it in a baggage car on a Boston-bound train. It could not be taken in the street cars, nor in a taxi, and an automobile had to be secured in order that it might reach the exhibition in perfect condition.

—*Boston Post.*

SCHOOL GARDENS.

(Continued from page 537)

pecting to use it in a talk to our society, but hoped at some future time to use it in the Parent-Teachers' Association work; however, I pass it along and hope it will help you in some way if you become interested in the work.

"A prize has been announced by the Home Yard and Garden Association, of Bridgeport, Conn. This prize will go to the person making the best development of a flower garden or porch. The small garden will have as good a chance as the large one, or even a porch development may win it, if the person competing has no place to plant but a porch."

The aim of the movement is to get everybody to plant something, however small the space may be. There is nothing so conducive of live interest as a prize for the reward of competition. While many persons will beautify their properties for the love of the beautiful, it usually takes more than that to beautify a town.

If I have been instrumental in inducing at least one person to undertake this work it will be well worth the effort of trying to comply with the president's wishes in sending you this talk.

Mr. Benjamin Hammond, of the S. A. F. and O. H., has for a long time been interested in School Gardens, and to those members who will undertake the spread of the work I would recommend consulting him.

MRS. ALBERT M. HERR.

NEWS NOTES.

Clinton, Mo.—The Clinton Greenhouses have been sold to Edgar Cornick.

Round Lake, N. Y.—Elmer Morris is about to engage in the florist business here.

Stratford, Ct.—Chauncey Mills has leased his range of greenhouses to John O'Neill.

Hackettstown, N. J. — Herrick & Ross have leased the Center street greenhouses.

Salem, O.—Harry E. Cooper, of West Grove, Pa., has purchased the Wm. Mundy property here and will devote the greenhouse to vegetable forcing.

New Haven, Conn.—M. B. Farquharson, for several years past associated with the Elm City Nursery Co. and the New Haven Nurseries Co., has purchased the floral shop at 123 Church street, conducted for twelve years by Alfred T. Ostermann.

Mrs. J. N. Champion, who has been ill for several months following an attack of double pneumonia early in the summer, is now slowly but surely regaining strength.

CLUB AND SOCIETY NOTES.

The October meeting of the Rhode Island Horticultural Society will be held in the Public Library, Providence, on Wednesday evening, October 20. William N. Craig, of Brookline, Mass., will speak on the "Hardy Herbaceous Garden, and the Planting of Bulbs." Business meeting at 7.45; lecture at

The annual chrysanthemum show under the auspices of the Silent Circle of King's Daughters, will be held on November 3, in Peace Dale, R. I., and the society is to make a determined effort to raise the standing of judging to conform to that set by the Chrysanthemum Society of America. The professional and amateur classes will be judged alike this year, the only change in the rules being that collections must include 20 or more plants. The raising of the standard is received with favor by the professional growers who believe it will be a boom to the business and the coming exhibit promises to be the largest and best in years.

S. A. G.

NEW CORPORATIONS.

La Crosse, Wis.—Hillview Greenhouses, capital stock, $15,000. Incorporators, Wm. G., Elizabeth and Emanuel Haehich.

Rahway, N. J.—C. E. Bauman, Inc., to engage in horticulture and gardening. Capital stock, $125,000. Incorporators, Camille E., John R. and Adolph H. Bauman.

Montgomery, Ala. — The Morning View Floral Company has changed its name to H. E. Mitting, Florist.

Obituary

William H. Maher

William H. Maher, a well-known
florist of Newport, died at his home
last Tuesday in that city following a
lingering illness. He was 38 years old.
Mr. Maher was a son of the late William H. Maher and he leaves three
sisters, Mrs. Michael A. McCormick,
Miss Mary T. Maher and Miss Lillian
E. Maher.

Mrs. Martha Ann Perry

Mrs. Martha Ann Perry, mother of
J. J. Perry, manager of the Baltimore
branch of the S. S. Pennock-Meehan
Company, passed away in Washington,
D. C., at the residence of her daughter,
Mrs. M. P. Gregory, on October 13.
Mrs. Perry, who was eighty-two years
of age, was recently stricken with
paralysis from which death resulted.
She was taken to Frederick, Md., for
interment.

PUBLICATIONS RECEIVED.

Our Little Boer Cousin, by Luna May
Innis, author of "Our Little Danish
Cousin." Illustrated by John Goss. This
is one more addition to the "Little
Cousin" series of books for young people, published by the Page Company,
Boston. It is a very interesting story,
instructively woven around historical
facts and there is plenty of life and
excitement in it to engross and captivate the boy readers. 140 pages and
six full-page illustrations, handsomely
printed and bound. Price 60 cents, net.

The Crimson Gondola, by Nathan
Gallizier. This is another of the Page
Company's sterling publications, first
impression September, 1915. It is a
romance of Venice and Constantinople
at the beginning of the thirteenth
century and the weird and nerve-stirring scenes so vividly pictured will
have a special fascination at the present time when the peoples and the
places which figure in its tales are
engaged in a furious death-grapple.
The story is replete with tragic incidents. Bulgars, Nubians, Greeks, Venetians, Armenians, all play their part
in this compelling tale of the strife of
factions which culminated in the
fourth crusade and the Latin conquest
of Constantinople—the most romantic
city in the world. 450 pages, with four
superb colored plates, bound in red and
gold, price $1.50, carriage paid.

*When writing to advertisers kindly
mention HORTICULTURE.*

GREENHOUSES BUILDING OR CONTEMPLATED.

Sandusky, O. — D. R. White, one house.

Handley, Tex. — R. C. Massie, house 28 x 72.

Lancaster, Pa. — Fred Ritchie, range of houses.

Birmingham, Mich. — Andrew Wilson, house 22 x 60.

Windsor, Ont. — Howe & Carter, house 14 x 50.

Monmouth, Ill. — Arling & Swanson, range of houses.

High Point, N. C. — High Point Floral Co., range of houses.

Beverly Farms, Mass. — R. S. Bradley, range of houses.

Canton, S. D. — Canton Floral Co., 5th street, one house.

Manchester, N. H. — O. R. Jacques, 268 Lowell street, one house.

Devils Lake, N. D. — P. J. Kersten, proprietor Devils Lake Greenhouses, additions.

Council Bluffs, Ia. — Henry Gerber Greenhouse Co., 7th avenue, near 30th street, range of houses.

Raleigh, N. C. — E. M. Hall, proprietor Raleigh Floral Co., Jones and Seawell avenues, additions and alterations.

MASSACHUSETTS AGRICULTURAL COLLEGE FALL SHOW.

The Department of Floriculture is making plans for its Annual Fall Flower Show which is to be held Monday and Tuesday, November 8 and 9. The entire first floor of the building, about 5200 square feet will be used for the show.

Last fall the Department received many favorable comments from men in the trade. This year it is planned to make the show a bigger, better and busier one. There will be exhibits of interest to the florist and gardener as well as to the general public. The Department wishes to extend to all a hearty invitation to attend the show.

There will be a large showing of chrysanthemums in named collections, in masses, in groups of foliage and flowering plants and in floral arrangements. Although the chrysanthemums will be dominant all other florists' flowers and plants will be freely used.

The competition in table decoration will be limited to the junior class, with fourteen entries. The seniors will have a competition in basket arrangement and there will be ten entries in this class. In addition there will be vase, plant basket and box arrangements, bouquets and corsages. There will be exhibits of pottery, baskets and various other types of containers, together with other accessories of the florist.

The Northampton and Holyoke Gardeners' and Florists' Club is to co-operate with the M. A. C. Florists' and Gardeners' Club for a joint meeting one evening of the Show, at which time some outside speaker will talk upon Floral Arrangements and Exhibits.

College Notes.

On Tuesday Paul Work, head of the Market Gardening Department at Cornell, visited the college.

On Saturday the classes in floriculture are to visit the Hartford flower stores and the A. N. Pierson houses at Cromwell.

A demonstration of apple packing under the new apple packing law was given at the Bay Road fruit farm, Amherst, last Thursday.

Tuesday was observed as Apple Day. The Pomology Department gave each student an apple and sent a basketful to each member of the Faculty.

One hundred new species have been added to the perennial collection during the past week. The work of planting has been done by the Junior class.

Stockbridge Hall was opened to classes this week. Stockbridge Hall is the new agricultural building and is now the largest building on the campus. The formal dedication of the building is to be on the evening of October 29.

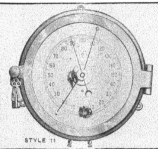

Vol. XXII
No. 18
OCT. 30
1915

HORTICULTURE

Display of Aquatic Plants at the San Francisco Exposition

By Henry A. Dreer, Philadelphia.

Published Every Saturday at 147 Summer Street, Boston, Mass.
Subscription, $1.00

LIST OF ADVERTISERS

**FOR BUYERS' DIRECTORY AND READY REFERENCE GUIDE
SEE PAGES 584, 585, 586, 587**

NOTES ON CULTURE OF FLORISTS' STOCK
CONDUCTED BY
John J. M. Farrell

Questions by our readers in line with any of the topics presented on this page will be cordially received and promptly answered by Mr. Farrell. Such communications should invariably be addressed to the office of HORTICULTURE.
"If vain our toil, we ought to blame the culture, not the soil."—*Pope.*

Carnations

Keep the surface of the soil for the present lightly cultivated, which will give the air and sun a chance to keep it sweet. Disbudding and removing the small side shoots on the flowering stem are important matters. Every one of the buds surrounding the main one, if allowed to remain, will draw nourishment from the plant which ought to go toward developing the flower. The carnation is not a warm house plant, and while you must keep it near the 50 degree point, in order to make the growing pay, the minute you get above that, go careful. A weakened carnation plant, caused by too much heat is hardly ever restored later in the season. Let the day temperature with sunshine run up to 65 to 70 degrees.

Cocos

Where we have a call for fern dishes there is nothing that will take place of Cocos Weddeliana for the center of these dishes. Be very careful about giving them water at the roots, as they will not stand a soaked condition all the time. Give careful ventilation and keep the atmosphere humid and warm by damping down two or three times a day. Never let the night temperature fall much below 65 degrees followed by a day temperature of from 75 to 80 degrees.

Ixias

Can be grown in 5, 6 or 7-inch pans, placing six, eight and ten bulbs respectively in each pan. They do well in a mixture of fibrous loam three parts, well rotted manure one part and a little sand. Crock the pans well. After planting them give a good soaking of water, and no more until they become tolerably dry again. These pans can be plunged in a frame where they will have some protection from very hard weather. The bulbs should be brought on slowly as they do not take

to hard forcing. Start them at 45 degrees and increase it until you have them standing about 55 degrees, night temperature, with a day heat of about 65 to 70.

Pot Roses for Easter

Do not forget to lift the roses intended for Easter. The best sizes to pot them in are 6, 7 or 8-inch pots. Where the roots are long or straggly prune them in somewhat. Do not fail to give proper drainage in each pot as when the spring comes they will require plenty of water. Firm the soil well among the roots. When potted give a good soaking of water. Do not prune them severely now, but cut them back a bit and just before starting them up you can head them back good. They can be given a cool pit for a couple of weeks before they are placed in a deep frame or cool shed. When placed in frames always plunge the pots so they will not break with hard freezing. During mild spells look them over for water, as they should never become too dry at the roots.

Shrubs for Spring Forcing

There is no better time for the lifting and potting of this stock for Easter forcing than now. Use pots just large enough to contain the roots. Give good drainage and good soil. After potting give a good watering and place anywhere handy to water. They will make some new roots between now and the time for very cold weather. When the winter sets in they can be placed in a cool shed or cellar until they are wanted for forcing.

Planting Violas, Daisies, Aubrieties, Myosotis, Etc.

It is time now to get all these planted in their winter quarters. Add some new soil and leaf mold to the frames, with enough of manure to make it rich and they will make better plants when needed. Give room enough and firm well around each plant. See that they have a good watering after they are all planted. Give plenty of air while the good weather lasts as this puts them in good condition to go through the winter.

Next week Azaleas; Cinerarias; Cyclamen; Orchids; Poinsettias; Starling Bulbs.

HORTICULTURE

VOL. XXII   **OCTOBER 30, 1915**   **NO. 18**

PUBLISHED WEEKLY BY

HORTICULTURE PUBLISHING CO.

147 Summer Street, Boston, Mass.

Telephone, Oxford 292.

WM. J. STEWART, Editor and Manager.

Entered as second-class matter December 8, 1914, at the Post Office at Boston, Mass., under the Act of Congress of March 3, 1879.

CONTENTS

Stand by the organizations

A most promising augury for the future was betokened in the close attention and cordial interest manifested at the Flower Exchange dinner in Boston last Saturday evening when President Farquhar of the Massachusetts Horticultural Society made his frank and timely appeal for a closer sympathy and co-operation between the commercial florists and that time-honored organization. The remarks by President Bartsch of the Gardeners' and Florists' Club plainly voiced the growing feeling of filial obligation also among the members of the club to the grand old mother society which for over three-quarters of a century has so staunchly championed the cause of horticulture in America. HORTICULTURE's attitude towards Club and Society organization is well known to its readers. From its first issue, when it established the first regular department of Club and Society news in the history of florists' trade papers, up to the present time, the news of these organizations in all sections of the country has been accorded priority each week, because we believed in them as valuable upbuilders of the art and welcomed the opportunity which was ours to foster and encourage them. That our zeal was not misplaced the columns of every issue of every trade journal now furnish abundant proof.

Go in and win

It was Huxley who said "The great end of life is not knowledge but action." The gardening and floral fraternity has always been rich in men of knowledge but these have not always been disposed to give their time and active support to those institutions without whose concrete force efficient action for the general welfare is practically impossible. Well-wishers of the craft will hail with hopeful gladness the "get together" spirit which is now so unmistakably extending throughout the horticultural community at large. The time seems not far distant when the gardener or florist unaffiliated with any organization of his fellow workers will be the exception. Not only among individuals is felt this impulse to link together for the common weal, but societies and institutions that hitherto have preferred to "flock by themselves" are also reaching out to one another in neighborly colleagueship. It is not to be expected that the horticultural millenium will at once dawn but that things are shaping themselves in the right direction for the prestige and influence of our profession cannot be questioned. And organization has been and must continue to be the best motive power.

Reporting the show

Exhibition time is now on and the papers which undertake to report the shows have their hands full. A word to the judges who make the awards and to the secretaries who report them may not be amiss here and now. Presumably the judges would like to have their verdicts recorded in such shape as to be read with interest and benefit and, also, no doubt, the secretaries who work so hard in copying and sending out these reports feel likewise. All should realize that a bare record of the names of winners in the various classes is of very limited interest to the majority of the readers of a paper such as HORTICULTURE. What they are anxious to know and will read with avidity is the names and qualities of the winning exhibits. It is not so much who grew and won 1st for an exhibit of white chrysanthemums or anything else as it is what variety he won with and against what variety or varieties and if this is all made clear in the judges' report it will in no way impair the advertising value of the triumph, but will accentuate it rather, for the note will be perused and memorized by many readers who would not otherwise take the trouble to scan it. Most secretaries instrusted with the duty of giving publicity to show awards do it according to the best light they have, at a most arduous and trying time. It is the duty first of the judges to give them the material, especially in the leading classes, on which they can draw to make their account of the competition and its results such as will be worth printing and disseminating and secretaries should not forget that it is a strenuous time in the office of a news journal when show reports are crowding in and putting the editor to his wits' end in the effort to give to all the attention they merit. So please help all you can by sending a clean, careful and instructive story about your show—one to which you can sign your name for publication and feel proud of it.

ROSE GROWING UNDER GLASS

CONDUCTED BY

Arthur C. Ruzicka

Questions by our readers in line with any of the topics presented on this page will be cordially received and promptly answered by Mr. Ruzicka. Such communications should invariably be addressed to the office of HORTICULTURE.

Ventilation

With the air outside becoming cold and colder it will be necessary to be very careful with the ventilators in the morning, for the days of summer are gone and it will not do to put air on several inches at a time. It will be necessary to add air very slowly as the houses go up. As the temperature at night will still run around 62, with air, more air can be put on at 64 in the morning, then more at 68 and then again at 72. Care should be taken not to apply too much air at the one time, so as not to chill the houses. On clear mornings the heat can be turned off at 66—that is the steam, for if hot water is used as well, the boilers had better be stopped sooner, for the water will stay warm for some time and the pipes will radiate heat for quite a while after the boilers are stopped off. On chilly, raw, cloudy days, it may be necessary to keep a pipe of steam in the houses all day, but care should be taken that the houses are not allowed to get too warm. 66 to 68 is all the heat that will be needed and if it is allowed to get warmer inside, the roses will be apt to become soft and will suffer, even if they do not get any mildew at the time. We find that the roses will keep clear of it if they are kept hardy all the time with plenty of air to keep the atmosphere in the houses sweet and clear. There may be times when a strong wind blows right in and we are tempted to close the vents a little, but this should not be done. In whole houses with ventilators on both sides of the ridge it will be well to have a weather vane to show which way the wind is blowing, and the air put on the opposite side. When all the air that can be put on the one side is not sufficient to keep the house cool then a little can be added on the other side, but with the wind blowing hard it will be best to apply only about half as much air on this side as on the other. There is little to gain by carrying a whole lot of air on wet foggy days. Apply only enough to insure a circulation through the houses and let it go at that, for the air inside on these days is drier and healthier than the moisture-laden air outside.

The Houses at Night

Any grower who is fortunate enough to have a real good night fireman should appreciate it and see that the man is paid what he is worth for if there are any very important men on the place the night man is one of these providing he does his work well and sleeps when he should sleep—that is in the day time. A good many growers will find that their roses will do much better if they are cared for properly at night. To have the houses going up and down is the worst that could happen. The houses should be gradually brought down to their night temperature and then they should be kept there and the heat should never vary more than two degrees. One degree is enough to indicate that the houses are going up or down and before they drop more the fault should be remedied. On a rose-growing range there should be little difficulty in keeping the houses where they should be and if there is a faulty heating system the sooner it is corrected the better. To eliminate all guess work the hot water boilers should be equipped with thermometers to register the heat of the water. Then there should be a good thermometer set up on a post on the north side of the place in an exposed position so that any change in the temperature outside will be recorded as soon as it occurs. Then, knowing the heat in the pipes whether it is steam or hot water and the number of pipes to the different houses, it should not be difficult to keep the regular temperature by watching the thermometer outside closely. A large private place growing everything in flowers, fruits and vegetables, which called for varied temperatures in the different departments was successfully heated from the same place and same battery of boilers by a night man who took care to study out the way to do it right. By knowing just how many turns of a valve or how many pipes are needed to a house to keep it where it should be when the thermometer outside registered a certain temperature it was a simple matter to speed up or slacken up the boilers if the temperature outside went up or down, and before the houses went either way the required heat was already there. The thermometer outside should be watched as much as the thermometer inside, for it is the temperature outside that drops or goes up before the houses change, taking it for granted of course that the heat is kept uniform. It is poor policy to open and close pipes, as then the house will go up and down. It is far better to regulate the heat in the pipes until of course they are not sufficient to carry the temperature, and then more must be added. Even this can be foreseen by the careful watchman who will know just how long the pipes going will keep the house up where it should be. Look after the houses well at night, for there is no use in worrying to death in the daytime, and then letting them run "every which way" at night.

NATIONAL FLOWER SHOW

The work of preparation for the Fourth National Flower Show, Philadelphia, March 25 to April 2, next, received a great impetus through the three-day visit in Philadelphia of the National Flower Show Committee, Monday, Tuesday and Wednesday, October 18, 19 and 20. With the exception of W. N. Rudd, Morgan Park, Ill., the whole of the committee, with President Patrick Welch of the S. A. F. and O. H., were present.

Early on Monday morning the members of the committee were greeted by Chairman George Asmus of Chicago, at the Bellevue-Stratford Hotel, and the sub-committee on schedule, Chairman Asmus, C. H. Totty, Thomas Roland, Adolph Farenwald and Secretary John Young, at once adjourned to Parlor 215, where the preparation of the Second Preliminary Schedule was at once proceeded with.

President S. S. Pennock, of the American Rose Society, was also present. Secretary Young presented a list of special prizes offered for various exhibits, and the disposition of them through the schedule occupied considerable time. In the section for private growers a class was added covering a group of flowering and foliage plants, arranged for effect, to occupy 25 sq. ft., the stock shown to be produced from 2500 sq. ft. of glass or less, the exhibitors to be members of the Florists' Club of Philadelphia. This class will be appreciated by private gardeners who are limited to a very small area of glass for their products. In the commercial section a class was added for a group of Crotons, arranged for effect, to cover 100 sq. ft., with prizes of $150 and $100. The premium list for the Carnation section was approved, and many other matters settled.

The sub-committee on schedule were again in session in the afternoon, and at this meeting there were present many of the chairmen of the local committees, and the gathering eventually merged into a meeting of the local executive committee, W. P. Craig, Arthur Niessen, secretary and treasurer of the local executive committee, Robert Craig, E. J. Fancourt, W. F. Therkildsen, Fred Cowperthwaite, Chas. Grakelow, S. S. Pennock, John P. Habermehl, Louis Burk, Wm. Kleinheinz, C. H. Fox, J. Otto Thilow and Franklin Barrett. All made reports for their respective committees, which showed the work was progressing in a most satisfactory manner. Mr. Therkildson, as chairman of the committee on publicity, presented samples of advertising "stickers" for use on stationery, packages, and in other ways, 250,000 of which had been ordered, and which could be obtained by anyone who could use them to advantage. He also displayed samples of large posters, and two sizes of card posters, all of which were approved by the committee and adopted. Mr. Therkildson's report was very interesting, and covered in detail the work and plans of his committee. In closing, he appealed to all who could do so

to furnish him with articles and photographs covering floricultural subjects, and adapted for use in his campaign of publicity. Mr. Thilow, for the Committee on Lectures, reported that his programme was practically complete; it provided for moving pictures each afternoon and illustrated lectures each evening. Mr. Grakelow, for the Committee on Special Features, outlined what his committee aimed to achieve, and some novel show features are now expected to evolve from the committee. Mr. Barrett, for the Committee on Aquariums, promised a very extensive line of exhibits in the Aquarium section.

On Tuesday morning there was a full meeting of the National Flower Show Committee, at the Bellevue-Stratford, there being present Chairman George Asmus, Secretary John Young, Treasurer W. F. Kasting, A. Farenwald, C. H. Totty, Thomas Roland, Wm. P. Craig, and Pres. Patrick Welch. Local Executive Secretary Arthur A. Niessen was also present. Secretary Young reported that the Guarantee Fund was practically complete, that space aggregating over $6,000 had been already reserved in the trade section, and that advertising contracts amounting to over $1,200 had been booked for the official Souvenir Programme. In all probability, he said, every available foot of space for trade exhibits would be sold. The committee voted that a call for 50 per cent. of the amounts subscribed to the Guarantee Fund be made on February 1 next. The recommendations of the various committees made at the meeting of the Local Executive Committee were considered, and appropriations made to cover the requirements of such committees. The Local Executive Committee was authorized to secure an office in a central location, and to employ the necessary clerical help for the committees. The price for trade tickets was fixed at 25c. each, not less than 25 tickets to be sold to anyone at this price. C. H. Totty, Madison, N. J., was appointed chairman of the Board of Jurors, and Wm. Graham, of Phil. adelphia, was appointed Manager of the Show.

In the afternoon the committee, with many of the chairmen of the local committees, visited Convention Hall and inspected it thoroughly. With the information now available as to the requirements of the competitive exhibits in point of space, it was obvious that more room would be required than was afforded by the present lay-out so it was decided to move the trade exhibits a little distance from the marked central area of the hall, to increase the room for the competitive exhibits. The secretary was instructed to notify any exhibitor who had made a reservation whose plans might be affected by the change, that the rearrangement was made necessary by the great number of competitive exhibits promised, and the elaborate scale on which many of

them are to be staged, all adding to the attractiveness of the exhibition. If found necessary, the secretary was authorized to issue a new plan.

Space was allotted for booths for the Pennsylvania Horticultural Society and the Garden Clubs of Philadelphia and vicinity, for the lecture room, and for the exhibits of aquaria.

On Tuesday evening the members of the National Flower Show Committee were guests of the Florists' Club of Philadelphia at a special meeting of the Club held in its rooms. President Burton of the Club surrendering the gavel to Chairman Asmus of the Flower Show Committee. The forthcoming Fourth National Flower Show was, of course, the whole subject of the program, and tremendous enthusiasm in the project was evoked. The spirit of optimism prevailed, and if there was a pessimist anywhere in the neighborhood he very discreetly kept away. It was a "get together" meeting, if ever there was one. Speeches came fast and thick, and applause was unspared. It was a meeting long to be remembered and spoke volumes for the success of the Show.

JOHN YOUNG, Sec'y.

R. C. KERR RESIGNS AS DIRECTOR.

Mr. Patrick Welch,
Pres. S. A. F.
Dear Mr. Welch,

Please accept my resignation as a director of the S. A. F., to become effective January 1, 1916, due to my election as vice-president of the S. A. F. at San Francisco, which office becomes effective at that time.

In resigning this office I want to express to you my gratefulness for being appointed on the Board of Directors of the S. A. F. I certainly have felt greatly honored. It has been the means of the southern florists coming in for recognition in this great organization. We have felt the need of this society for many years, but failed to develop enough interest in the South or to take sufficient interest in its affairs to deserve recognition in the past. If I could show you the many letters received from the florists through the South it would prove to you their appreciation also in this matter.

Yours for a large southern membership.   R. C. KERR.

A CORRECTION.

Editor HORTICULTURE:

I wish to correct an error I made in giving you the notice of the next F. T. D. meeting. Kindly insert it thus: "The meeting of The Florists' Telegraph Delivery will be held November 11 at 9 A. M., Hotel Hollenden, Cleveland. Ohio." instead of at the Hotel Statler as I gave you in a previous notice. If this has already been inserted in your columns, kindly make correction in your next issue and greatly oblige Yours very truly,

ALBERT POCHELON,
Secy. F. T. D.

THE FALL FLOWER SHOWS

CHICAGO GRAND FLORAL FESTIVAL.

All the plans for the Grand Floral Festival, to be held at the Coliseum, November 9-14, were fully discussed in a half-day meeting of the executive committee, held at the Morrison hotel, October 21, when A. Henderson, W. N. Rudd, W. J. Keimel, August Poehlmann, N. J. Wietor, E. F. Kurowski, Guy W. French, N. P. Miller, E. A. Kanst, Payne Jennings, Robert Brenton, J. H. Burdett, August Koch, James Morton and M. Barker were in attendance. The final premium list is in the hands of the printers and will be ready for mailing this week. Copies may be had on application to Secretary N. P. Miller, 179-183 North Wabash avenue, Chicago.

In addition to the handsome collection of cups donated by greenhouse construction concerns in the vicinity of Chicago a large number of other special prizes have been received, including the following:

E. C. Amling Co., The Armour Fertilizer Works, A. A. Arnold Paper Box Co., The W. W. Barnard Co., Bassett & Washburn, Brant & Noe Floral Co., Buchbinder Bros., J. A. Budlong, Chicago Feed & Fertilizer Co., Chicago Flower Growers' Assn., Darling Co., Erne & Klingel, Farmers' & Florists' Fertilizer Co., M. C. Gunterberg, A. Henderson & Co., Hoerber Bros., International Fertilizer Co., Kennicott Bros. Co., Kroeschell Bros. Co., Kyle & Foerster, Fred Lautenschlager, Miller & Musser, Nicotine Mfg. Co., Ernst Oechslin, Frank Oechslin, Everett R. Peacock Co., Poehlmann Bros. Co., Pulverized Manure Co., Pyfer & Olsem, A. L. Randall & Co., Sefton Mfg. Co., A. L. Vaughan & Co., Wietor Bros., Winterson's Seed Store, George N. Wright & Co., George Wittbold Co., Zech & Mann, all the foregoing from Chicago; Aphine Mfg. Co., Madison, N. J.; P. Bonvallet & Co., Wichart, Ill.; W. Atlee Burpee & Co., Philadelphia, Pa.; J. A. Evans Co., Richmond, Ind.; Benj. Hammond, Beacon, N. Y.; Ionia Pottery Co., Ionia, Mich.; W. J. Keimel, Elmhurst; P. R. Palethorpe & Co. Clarksville, Tenn.; M. Rice Co., Philadelphia, Pa.; W. N. Rudd, Morgan Park, Ill.; Chas. Schwake & Co., New York; S. S. Skidelsky & Co., Philadelphia, Pa.; J. D. Tompson Carnation Co., Joliet; Vaughan's Seed Store, Weil & Risch, Peter Reinberg, Chicago and New York.

M. BARKER,
Chairman Publicity Committee.

An item of unusual interest in connection with the Chicago Fall Flower Festival is the 25 silver cups being donated by the greenhouse manufacturers of Chicago. Instead of taking space in the Coliseum Annex, making trade exhibits of greenhouses and greenhouse appliances, the same as is usually done at the Annual Convention of the S. A. F., the greenhouse manufacturers of Chicago suggested that the space be sold to others and that a contribution of $500.00 be collected among the manufacturers and donated to the show to be used as prizes.

The following greenhouse manufacturers held a meeting Wednesday, October 13, at noon, at the Grand Pacific Hotel: Lord & Burnham Co., Foley Mfg. Co., Garland Mfg. Co., Ickes Braun Mill Co., A. Dietsch & Co. and John C. Moninger Co.

Prior to the meeting the manufacturers had luncheon. The following people were on hand to represent the various firms: P. J. Foley, Fred Sykes, Fred Dietsch, E. F. Kurowski, D. B. Dulmage and P. L. McKee.

It was the general opinion that this being the first Chicago show for some years, it was very necessary to make it a success and that the greenhouse manufacturers of this city ought to contribute to it on account of its being a local show and of direct interest to the Chicago firms. A subscription was taken and a fund of $500.00 was made up for the purchase of the cups. It is expected that the action of the

Grand Floral Festival

COLISEUM-NOV-9ᵗʰ-14ᵗʰ

greenhouse manufacturers in getting together in this way and making a bulk contribution will set a precedent for others of the allied trades and the future may bring more concerted action in this direction.

P. L. McKee was given authority to collect the funds, arrange for publicity and distribution of the prizes. The cups will be made shortly and it is expected that they will be exhibited in one of the large stores downtown prior to the opening of the show. When the show opens, the plan is to have the cups in a large glass case on exhibition. The names of all of the donors will be engraved on the cups as well as the name of the prize and a space left for the name of the winner. Winners of the prizes can have their names engraved on the cups without any charge.

More complete details as to prizes on which the various cups have been placed, kind of cups, values, etc., will be given later.

JOHN C. MONINGER CO.

CLEVELAND FLOWER SHOW.

Christening the chrysanthemum is the latest duty assumed by the President of the United States. During the present week President Wilson is to lay aside the job of successfully steering of the Ship of State long enough to gave a name to a new variety of chrysanthemum that will be exhibited for the first time at the Cleveland Flower Show.

Specimen blooms of the latest product of Elmer D. Smith & Co., Adrian, Mich., were sent to the White House the past week. A letter received by E. Prentiss Baldwin, chairman of the executive committee of the Cleveland Show states that the president will take pleasure in selecting a name for the flower. The announcement of the new variety will be made prior to the opening of the show. The flower is a rich golden color differing from the usual yellow varieties in that the color deepens at the centre of the blossom. Cleveland florists who have seen blooms say it is one of the most beautiful yet produced. Samples were received at the office of the Flower Show Committee in Cleveland the past week.

The local committees have completed the program for the week of the Show and provision is made for the entertainment of the delegates to the several organization meetings to be held in Cleveland during the Show. The complete program follows:

Outline of Meetings.

November 10.—Official opening of show to the public at 1 P. M.

November 11.—Meeting of Florists' Telegraph Delivery at 11 A. M. The Bowling Tournament will be held at the Erie Bowling Alleys; time to be announced next week. Visiting lady florists and wives of exhibitors to be given a "Pink Tea" with some novel entertainment features.

November 12.—Meeting of the American Rose Society. Meeting of Executive Committee of the American Carnation Society. In the evening a banquet to the visiting florists and exhibitors. Also on Friday the adjourned meeting of the Ohio Gladiolus Society.

November 13.—Saturday evening, a smoker for all visiting florists and exhibitors.

November 14.—Sunday; the show will close at 10 P. M.

Meetings of all societies will be held in the rooms of Cleveland Florists' Club at Hollenden Hotel. Schedule of time of meetings will be anounced next week.

Among the many additional classes in the prize list for the Cleveland

Flower Show is the following, received too late for printed schedule. Class 162A—150 lily of the valley, any greens allowed; flowers must be grown and arranged by exhibitor; prizes $12, $8, $5, by Chas. Schwake Co., New York. Cottage Gardens Co. have drawn honors by being the first to make entries in the big show.

The decorating committee met on Tuesday, Oct. 26 and Chairman F. C. W. Brown outlined the final plans for securing novel effects. The executive committee met on Wednesday with Chairman Baldwin, Mrs. L. Dean Holden, Mrs. A. S. Ingalls, General Chairman H. P. Knoble and Secretary F. A. Friedley present and plans were forwarded for making the tea garden a prominent social feature of the show.

MASSACHUSETTS HORTICULTURAL SOCIETY.

Grand Autumn Flower Show.

The last of the year's flower shows at Horticultural Hall will be held on Thursday, Friday, Saturday, and Sunday, November 4 to 7. While chrysanthemums will be the chief feature of this show there will be in addition large displays of foliage and flowering plants, evergreen trees and shrubs, orchids, carnations, and seasonable fruits and vegetables.

Other attractive features will be the artistic displays of chrysanthemums arranged for decorative effect showing the various ways the flowers can be used for home decoration. The collections of apples and pears especially will be on a large scale and will show the possibilities in the culture of fruit in New England. Prizes amounting to $2100.00, are offered at this exhibition which will be the largest show of the year.

The exhibition will open on Thursday, November 4, at 12 o'clock, continuing through Friday and Saturday from 10 a. m. to 10 p. m., and on Sunday, from 1 to 10 p. m. The Bostonia Orchestra will give concerts every afternoon and evening from 2 to 5 and from 7 to 10 o'clock.

WILLIAM P. RICH, Sec'y.

SAN FRANCISCO FALL FLOWER SHOW.

The Grand Fall Flower Show was opened in the Palace of Horticulture at the Panama-Pacific Exposition on October 21st, with about the finest showing of flowers ever assembled for exhibition purposes in this city. The opening day was "Horticulture Day" at the exposition. That special feature had been well advertised, which brought a large and enthusiastic attendance. The distribution of quantities of flower seeds, ferns, cut flowers, etc., donated by exhibitors, created quite a sensation. All available floor space is utilized for the display, and special features have been arranged for each day of the show, which will last a week. Seven bands have been engaged to furnish music every afternoon and evening in the various sections, with ten Spanish and eight Hawaiian singers, and Miss Pauline Turner, soprano, contributing songs. The show will be open until 10 o'clock each evening.

THE HORTICULTURAL SOCIETY OF NEW YORK.

The Fall Exhibition of this society will be held November 4th to 7th at the American Museum of Natural History, 77th street and Columbus avenue. A cordial invitation is extended to all to make exhibits at this, the largest fall exhibition in this city or its vicinity. Schedules will be sent upon application to the secretary, George V. Nash, New York Botanical Garden, Bronx Park, N. Y. City.

GEORGE V. NASH, Secretary.

COUNTRY FAIR FRUIT AND FLOWER SHOW.

The displays of vegetables, fruit and flowers, as departments of Chester I. Campbell's Country Fair at Mechanics' Hall, Boston, this week, formed a large and interesting section of the show on the main floor. The flower show was under the auspices of the Co-operative Flower Market and managed by Norris F. Comley. James Wheeler acted as judge.

W. H. Elliott was represented by a fine table of roses in vases and a collection of market chrysanthemum plants, E. F. Dwyer & Son made a brilliant showing of dahlias. Where they got them at this late date in such unblemished condition is a mystery. The carnation growers responded nobly, Patten & Co. showed large vases of ten leading varieties.

There were several dinner tables prettily decorated. One with centre of oncidiums and lily of the valley impressed us especially with its dainty elegance. One of yellow and white pompon chrysanthemum made a rich effect with croton foliage. Sweetheart roses and Bouvardia Humboldtii were very pretty in another. A very creditable collection of conifers in pots and tubs was shown by the Breck-Robinson Co. of Lexington.

The apple displays made the largest item. There were hundreds of boxes all carefully packed and showing all the qualities of perfect fruit. The Maine exhibit was in barrels. Vermont made a big showing as did New Hampshire, Massachusetts and Rhode Island, the latter winning first honors.

The array of vegetables by the Boston Market Gardeners' Association was very extensive and of high quality. Each variety was shown in a bushel box as packed for market. The Essex County Training School made a fine showing in this department.

In the flower section 1st prize for a table decoration was won by Henry R. Comley and 2d by Wax Bros. First prize for general display of cut flowers went to E. F. Dwyer.

A special prize has been offered Class 32, by John D. Rockefeller, Jr., for the most effectively arranged basket of cut chrysanthemums at the Tarrytown Horticultural Society's exhibition. Any foliage may be used. 1st, $10.00; 2nd, $6.00; 3rd, $4.00. Exhibit to be in place November 3rd at 1 P. M. Entries must reach the secretary, E. W. Neubrand, Tarrytown, N. Y., on or before October 30th.

Only Nine Days Until the Opening of the Cleveland Flower Show

The schedule of prizes for the Fifth Autumn Exhibition of the Westchester & Fairfield Horticultural Society has been issued. The show takes place on Friday and Saturday, Nov. 5 and 6, at the Armory, Stamford, Conn. The prizes are liberal and will no doubt bring out a fine display. Copies may be had on request to P. W. Popp, corresponding secretary, Mamaroneck, N. Y.

BOSTON FLOWER EXCHANGE.

Annual Meeting and Banquet.

On Saturday evening, October 23, this pleasant annual affair took place at Young's Hotel in the big banquet hall. As usual it took the form of a cheery reunion and joyous celebration of the continued prosperity of the institution as shown by the treasurer's balance sheet. This year it seemed to be even more than ever before a gathering of men with mind at ease, cheerily complacent and care free.

"Gladness in every face express'd,
'Their eyes before their tongues confess'd.
Friends to congratulate their friends made haste
And long inveterate foes saluted as they pass'd."

President Stickel presided with suave dignity, the amplification of nearly a quarter century of practice on the same job. J. K. M. L. Farquhar, president of the Massachusetts Horticultural Society, and Herman Bartsch, president of the Gardeners' and Florists' Club of Boston, were the guests of honor. Patrick Welch, president of the Society of American Florists had an invitation also, but being out of town was unable to be present, a telegram announcing his regret being read by the chairman.

The menu was of rare excellence and the hundred or more gentlemen present did full justice to it, occasional breaking out into chorus when the orchestra played some popular melody.

All through the speech making, from first to last the text and sentiment was "get together." Organization and co-operation between individuals and between associations, in flower shows and society work, received a splendid impetus and the results will be far-reaching. Mr. Farquhar started the ball with a vigorous and eloquent plea for a more hearty support for the Massachusetts Horticultural Society and this key-note was dominant to the end. W. H. Elliott expressed a message of cordial good will from the rival market of which he is president. Herman Bartsch was convincing and humorous as always. Wm. J. Stewart, editor of HORTICULTURE, William Nicholson, W. N. Craig, secretary of the Gardeners' and Florists' Club, Henry Robinson, Jr., Peter Fisher, J. Miller, A. Leuthy, W. Capstick, H. L. Cameron, A. S. Parker, John Walsh, Manager Thurston of the Market, M. A. Patten, J. T. Butterworth, all followed with words of wit or wisdom. Secretary Craig created a novel diversion by extolling woman suffrage and a vote on this proposition being called for he was rewarded with a count of two to one in favor. A surprise of the evening was a whirlwind speech on the superiority of the self-made man by Henry Robinson, Jr., 17 years old, which captured the house. The business meeting which followed the banquet was brief and harmonious.

The following named directors were unanimously chosen: W. C. Stickel, S. J. Goddard, L. W. Mann, A. Christensen, G. Cartwright, A. S. Parker, C. A. Paine, A. A. Pembroke and H. Bartsch.

The tables were gorgeous with the finest flower novelties of the season.

MASSACHUSETTS AGRICULTURAL COLLEGE NOTES.

A. E. Wilkins is working at The Flower Shop at Pittsfield. Mr. Wilkins graduated with the class of 1915.

During the past week the Committee on the College of the State Board of Agriculture inspected the greenhouses at M. A. C.

M. Headle, '13, of Springfield, who is about to open a new flower store in Springfield, was a visitor on the campus this week.

Miss G. M. White, who graduated from the college last year has now taken up work with Mrs. Merrill at the latter's flower shop in Brookline.

Last Wednesday, Prof. A. H. Nehrling gave a talk on his trip to the Panama-Pacific Exposition to The Florists' and Gardeners' Club of M. A. C.

Last Saturday the classes in Floriculture visited the Hartford flower stores. At each place visited they were very courteously received. At the Pierson range at Cromwell, where the afternoon was spent, Mr. Beers took the students on a tour of the range.

THE RHODODENDRON LACE BUG.

Rhododendrons are becoming such popular shrubs and so many improvements in varieties are being made that a little information on one of its worst insect enemies would not be amiss at this time. In view of the damage done by the Rhododendron Lace Bug in certain parts this summer, a few notes on their habits, control, etc., will probably be welcomed by many growers of this showy evergreen.

The Rhododendron Lace Bug, Leptobyrsa explanata (Heid.) is about one-eighth of an inch long. The body is oval in shape and shiny black, while its beautiful and delicate veined wings have the appearance of very fine lace with sharply defined brown spots near the middle.

The eggs are laid in late fall in the tissue of the leaf, for the most part along the mid-rib. The eggs hatch in May and the newly hatched young are whitish in color and spineless. The partially matured nymphs may be found on the under side of the leaves early in July. These latter are equipped with curious spines along the sides of the body.

The insect lives on the under side of the leaves where it sucks the sap. Their work causes a brown spotting of the leaves followed by more or less serious injury to the foliage. The adults may be found in July and August. The insect is a native form found abundantly on the Kalmias and Rhododendron maximum. It also attacks the cultivated Rhododendrons. The insect may be found all along the Atlantic seaboard. Boston, however, seems to be its northern limit.

Whale-oil soap solution applied at the rate of one pound to nine gallons of water to the underside of the foliage in May or June will serve to keep them down.

C. E. WILDON.

CLUBS AND SOCIETIES

MASSACHUSETTS HORTICULTURAL SOCIETY.

Annual Meeting.

The Annual Meeting of the Massachusetts Horticultural Society will be held at Horticultural Hall, Boston, at 12 o'clock, noon, on Saturday, November 13, 1915. The business of the meeting will consist in the election of a President, a Vice-President, four members of the Board of Trustees, and a Nominating Committee of five members. The voting will be by Australian Ballot and the polls will be open continuously between the hours of twelve, noon, and three in the afternoon.

The following proposed amendments to the By-Laws will be presented for the approval of the Society:

1. That the second paragraph of Section II of the By-Laws be amended so as to provide that the Trustees may appropriate a sum or sums amounting to more than $5000 for the purpose of prizes and gratuities, provided that there shall not be appropriated for the purpose of being expended in any one year, in addition to the income of special prize funds of the Society, a sum or sums exceeding the amount of the general income of the Society for the preceding year applicable for such purpose as shown by the report of the Treasurer.

2. That Clause 4 of Section IX of the By-Laws of the Society be and the same hereby is amended so as to provide that appropriations for prizes and gratuities may be made by the Trustees not more than three years in advance.

3. That Clause 7 of Section IX of the By-Laws of the Society be and the same hereby is amended so as to provide that exhibitions of flowers, plants, fruits and vegetables may be arranged for by the Trustees not more than three years in advance, and shall be announced at the annual meeting of the Society.

WILLIAM P. RICH, Secretary.

CHRYSANTHEMUM SOCIETY OF AMERICA.

Work of the Committees.

The examining committees have submitted reports in new varieties as follows:—

Exhibited at Philadelphia, Oct. 16, by G. A. Lotze, Glen Burnie, Md., No. 1, 1913, yellow, Jap., inc., Com. scale 90 points, Ex. scale 89 points.

Exhibited at New York, Oct. 16, by Chas H. Totty, Madison, N. J., Alice Day, white, Jap., inc. Com. scale 84 points.

Exhibited at Cincinnati, Oct. 16, by Elmer D. Smith, Adrian, Mich., Early Rose, rose pink, Jap., inc., Com. scale 87 points.

Exhibited at Philadelphia, Oct. 23, by Chas. H. Totty, Madison, N. J., Alice Day, white, Jap. inc., Com. scale 89 points.

Exhibited at Cincinnati, Oct. 23, by The E. G. Hill Co., Richmond, Ind., No. 45, yellow, Jap. inc., Com. scale 86 points. By Elmer D. Smith & Co., Adrian, Mich., October Queen, white Jap. reflexed, Com. scale 87 points; No.

Meetings Next Week

Monday, Nov. 1.

Bernardsville Horticultural Society, Bernardsville, N. J.
Elberon Horticultural Society, Elberon, N. J.
Houston Florist Club, Houston, Texas.
Montreal Gardeners' and Florists' Club, Montreal, Canada.
New Bedford Horticultural Society, New Bedford, Mass.
New Jersey Floricultural Society, Orange, N. J.
Washington Florist Club, Washington, D. C.

Tuesday, Nov. 2.

Lake Geneva Gardeners' and Foremen's Association, Lake Geneva, Wis.
Los Angeles County Horticultural Society, Los Angeles, Calif.
Paterson Floricultural Society, Paterson, N. J.
Philadelphia Florists' Club, Philadelphia, Pa.
Pittsburgh Florists' and Gardeners' Club, Pittsburgh, Pa.

Wednesday, Nov. 3.

Tuxedo Horticultural Society, Tuxedo Park, N. Y.

Thursday, Nov. 4.

Southampton Horticultural Society, Southampton, N. Y.

Friday, Nov. 5.

North Shore Horticultural Society, Manchester, Mass.
North Shore Horticultural Society, Lake Forest, Ill.
Pasadena Horticultural Society, Pasadena, Calif.
Yonkers Horticultural Society, Yonkers, N. Y.
People's Park Cottage Gardeners' Association, Paterson, N. J.

Saturday, Nov. 6.

Pacific Coast Horticultural Society, San Francisco, Calif.

111-1-13, yellow, Jap. inc., Com. scale 89 points.

Exhibited at Chicago, Oct. 23, by Elmer D. Smith & Co., Adrian, Mich., No. 111-1-13, yellow, Jap. inc., Com. scale 92 points; October Queen, white, Jap. reflexed, Com. scale 93 points.

C. W. JOHNSON, Sec'y.

NEW YORK AND NEW JERSEY ASSOCIATION OF PLANT GROWERS.

The annual fall inspection tours of the New York and New Jersey Association of Plant Growers have again been arranged for. The tour over Long Island takes place on Friday, October 29th. The party starts from the office of William H. Siebrecht, Jr., Queens Plaza Court Building, Long Island City, at 9 A. M. travelling in touring cars, furnished by the members, to visit the establishments in Long Island City, Woodside, Elmhurst, Middle Village, Flushing, Whitestone, Jamaica and Flatbush.

The trip through New Jersey will take place on Friday, November 5. Messrs. Zeller and Wagner are the committee which has the Long Island trip in charge and Messrs. Feisser and Schoelzel have charge of Jersey trip.

LANCASTER COUNTY FLORISTS' CLUB.

At one o'clock on Thursday afternoon, Oct. 21st, a number of the fraternity were dotted at various points of Center Square anxiously looking for a leader. Mr. Nagle who according to his official title should have led the party was busy at his new houses getting things into shape for a cold snap, and the President who was to have taken his place was lined up with a salesman from somewhere in the U. S. and so intent on buying a bill of goods that he could not get away. The consequence was the holding of an indignation meeting on the Square and arranging the visiting trip to suit ourselves.

The writer appointed himself a committee of one to meet the train which brought our guest of honor, Robert Pyle, of West Grove, Pa. Charles M. Weaver kindly volunteered the use of his car and we soon caught up to the main party, stopping first at The Wheatland Greenhouses where carnations are looking good and the best Chrysolora chrysanthemums were being cut that are shipped from this section. The next stop was at our own Thomas Frie's place where there is a continual interchange of stock and a use of space that is always a revelation to a stranger, we having gotten accustomed to seeing three times the quantity of stock turned out from this place that is usually produced from the same amount of glass.

President Barr met us at his greenhouses and did the honors for the rest of the afternoon. His place shows the usual variety grown by a retail man for his store trade, the most of it very good and carnations exceptionally good. Mr. Barr takes much pride in his nursery stock and deservedly so as he certainly has some very fine specimens.

At the writer's place the strangers were a bit surprised at the number of geraniums under way and more surprised at the beauty of Buddleia variabilis flocking round it like a bunch of butterflies, but there the simile ends for the florist is more like the busy bee, working hard to produce the money that the other fellow takes away from him in exchange for new houses, etc., as was witnessed at Rudolph Nagle's where two very fine houses are in the course of erection. He had some very good stock of Pelargonium Winter Cheer, a house of pompons just coming into good shape, several houses of early chrysanthemums that are cut and a few midseason ones coming on.

The next point was the establishment of H. D. Rohrer. Under the guidance of his two sons Harry K. and Abram we found the usual stock of carnations coming into shape and several houses of Bonnaffon chrysanthemums, a big house of Chrysalora, also lots of primulas, myosotis and sweet peas.

At Goldbach's we found the place planted up for a continuous store supply. Mrs. Goldbach devotes her time to the store in the city and I believe would sell this growing end of the business if she could get a buyer. In a little potting-bench discussion it was found that every one of the party would be willing to sell out if they could find a buyer; that is—every one excepting the baby of the crowd. Edward Beck, who is too new at the business to realize what he is up against. A little more experience and he will be with the majority. Siebold was next in line and here we found some thirty varieties of geraniums being grown for the wholesale trade and a bench of handsome begonia, with a few novelties that are being kept sub rosa until further developed. They also have just finished harvesting an immense crop of Salvia Zurich seed which will be put on the market with a germination test of 95 per cent. good.

The next was a round table at the Brunswick with President B. F. Barr, Treasurer Harry K. Rohrer, Ex-Officio Albert M. Herr, Guest of Honor Robert Pyle. T. J. Nolan and D. T. Connor who act as sort of connecting links between the outside world and the Club are too well known to need a title. This group was joined later by R. L. Mowbry, assistant treasurer of the Dingee Conard Co. The rest of the 23 who were on the visiting trip scattered to various points of interest until time for the regular Club meeting, which started at 7.30, with an attendance of some forty members

which was augmented during the next hour until seating capacity was exhausted. The Dahlia Show committee reported what they had accomplished at the Fair. The visiting committee reported that they had under consideration a trip to Reading providing that city had a flower show and if not Manheim would be the attraction for November.

Robert Pyle gave us a delightful travel talk and after the lecture he showed us some photographs made during the tour and well deserved the unanimous vote of thanks given him for the lecture. When we can get such men as Mr. Pyle to give us a talk and when he expresses his delight with the Club and its form of management we begin to swell up with pride—not the pride that goeth before a fall for ours is an ambitious pride, but if we want to be considered as having any wisdom I guess I'd better shut up for this time.

ALBERT M. HERR.

CLUB AND SOCIETY NOTES.

The Boston Retail Florists' Club held a special meeting at the Hotel Bellevue on Wednesday evening, October 20. Vice-President Henry R. Comley presided.

At the regular meeting of the Connecticut Horticultural Society, Oct. 22, the committee on the Chrysanthemum Show reported progress. The committee and members are heartily in favor of making the exhibition

free to the public of Hartford and vicinity, and if all is well the coming show will be one of the best ever given by the society.

ALFRED DIXON, Sec'y.

The November meeting of the Gardeners' and Florists' Club of Boston will be held on the fourth Tuesday in the month instead of the third Tuesday, the hall being otherwise engaged during that week.

NEWS NOTES.

Milwaukee, Wis.—The F. Schmeling Greenhouses on Blue Mound Road have been leased by Otto Wilke for five years.

Robinson, Ill.—Ernest T. Oldham has purchased land here and is moving his greenhouses from Palestine, Ill., to the new location.

Johnstown, Pa.—Harry W. Miltenberger has acquired the full ownership of the Mishler truck farm and greenhouses at Kring Station. The business will be conducted in future under the name of the Valley Produce Company. Mr. Miltenberger will reside at the plant, which already enjoys a large business. Mr. Mishler has purchased the Blough farm on Riverside.

Only Nine Days Until the Opening of the Cleveland Flower Show

SEED TRADE

AMERICAN SEED TRADE ASSOCIATION
Officers—President, J. M. Lupton,
Mattituck, L. I., N. Y.; First Vice-President, Kirby B. White, Detroit, Mich.;
Second Vice-President, F. W. Bolgiano,
Washington, D. C.; Secretary-Treasurer,
C. E. Kendel, Cleveland, O.; Assistant
Secretary, S. F. Willard, Jr., Cleveland,
O. Cincinnati, O., next meeting place.

Beaumont, Tex. — The Beaumont
Seed Company has moved into new
and enlarged quarters at 608 Pearl
street.

The value of imports of horticultural
material at the port of New York for
the week ending October 16, is given
as follows: Clover seed $2,618; grass
seed $6,232; sugar beet seed $216;
palm seed $867; trees, bulbs and
plants $10,239.

PUBLICATIONS RECEIVED.

A new issue of "Flower Talks by
Maurice Fuld," originally published in
1914, has been sent out, substantially
bound in attractive blue covers, for
1915.

Bulletin No. 1, of the American
Dahlia Society has been received. It
deals mainly with the details of the
first exhibition of the society held in
New York last month and the proceedings of the annual meeting. A
strong bid for membership accessions
is made and, we understand, responses
are many, from all sections.

We recently published some notes
on the book of Hybrid Orchids just
sent out by Sander & Sons, St. Albans,
England. We neglected to mention at
the time that we can supply copies of
this book at the publishers' price, $5.00,
postpaid. No one interested in orchids
and their production can get along
without this elaborate work. It has
no peer and is indispensable.

American Seed Trade Association—
Proceedings of the 33rd Annual Convention, held at The Palace of Horticulture, San Francisco, Cal., June 22-
23 and 24, 1915. A striking photograph of President Lester L. Morse is
used as a frontispiece in this very complete and interesting report by Secretary C. E. Kendel. Among the valuable papers presented at the Convention
and here given in full are the following: "The Value of Technical Training to a Seedsman," by Prof. H. E.
Van Norman, Davis, Cal.; "Report on
Postal Laws," by W. F. Therkildson,
Phila.; "Horticulture in the Hawaiian
Islands," by Prof. John N. Gilmore;
"Credits and Collections in the Seed
Business," by M. L. Germain; "Seed
Growing in the Northwest," by E. C.
Johnson; "Flower Seeds in California,"
by L. C. Routzahn.

CATALOGUES RECEIVED.

Mobile Nursery Co., Mobile, Ala.—
Price List for Season 1915-1916.
Trade List also inclosed.

Benj. Hammond, Beacon, N. Y.—
Slug-Shot Pamphlet. A catalogue of
the various indispensable remedies
against insects, fungus, etc., which
have made Hammond famous.

A GREAT ILLINOIS NURSERY.

A WINTER WINDOW-BOX
As filled by the D. Hill Nursery Co.

A revelation awaits one who has
never visited the D. Hill Nursery
Co.'s plant at Dundee, Ill. Lying as it
does in the beautiful Fox River Valley,
thirty-five miles northwest of Chicago,
it makes a delightful trip where
pleasure and profit can be combined.
One will find here the largest nurseries in this country, with every detail
carefully looked after by efficient men,
some of whom are graduates of our
highest schools of learning, and will

D. HILL,
President of the D. Hill Nursery Co.

get an idea of what can be done in developing a big business when scientific
knowledge goes hand in hand with
nature.

The firm consists of D. Hill, his
three sons A. H., G. W. and V. D. and
one daughter, all active. Their leading specialty is hardy evergreens and
a second is trees for reforestation.
The business was founded in a small
way, on a part of its present site, by
Wm. Hill, uncle of D. Hill, in 1855, but
was developed and brought to its high
state by the present firm. The nurseries include 500 acres, 400 of which
are devoted to stock and the rest to
general purposes.

Two large electric lighted service
sheds are used for receiving, sorting
and packing stock and another will be
built this winter. Glass-covered houses
are used for propagating fancy varieties, and for grafting, and cold slat
covered frames for most of the transplanted seed stock.

E. B. Stedman, assistant superintendent, who conducts visitors over
the place, is a graduate of the Forestry Department of Ann Arbor and
in reply to a question as to whether
he found the course of study of practical value, replied with enthusiasm,
that everything he had learned in the
University he had found of real value
in his work. Visitors drive under
long rows of European larch and beside native white pines and see the
great blocks of different kinds of evergreen and forest trees. An extra fine
lot of Scotch pine, grown from seed;
another of Black Hill spruce; Red
cedar from the Platte River Valley
were seen, and what remained of a
block of Norway spruce which at the
opening of the season contained one
million trees. There are many species
and varieties of juniper, from the low
creeping to the tall pyramidal forms,
and graceful native hemlocks and
blocks of many other evergreens. All
imported varieties are thoroughly
tested to prove their adaptability to
our climate before sending out.

A special feature is the window box
of hardy evergreens for winter use.
With the development of the outdoor
summer boxes, so popular in the down
town districts of Chicago, there has
followed a demand for something to
take their place in winter and the
boxes sent out by the D. Hill Nursery
Co. are graceful and artistic and do
not have the stilted effect so often
seen.

Mr. Hill has taken a large space at
the Grand Floral Festival and some
new features will be introduced which
will be a welcome addition to the nursery exhibits.

Of Interest to Retail Florists

Hanover, Pa.—Frank Cremer, the florist, has reopened his branch store in the Conrad Building, Baltimore street.

Portland, Ore.—The Swiss Floral Co. have leased the store and greenhouse range of the late Alfred C. F. Burkhardt.

Dallas, Tex.—David Hardie, president of the David Hardie Seed Co. has purchased E. H. R. Green's interest in the Green Floral Co.

Waterville, Me.—The florist store on Main street, run under the name of Mitchell & Co., has been taken over by George F. Terry and L. C. Sturtevant, a former Colby student, has been appointed as manager. The company is planning to continue the high class service which was furnished the public under the management of Mr. Mitchell.

NEW FLOWER STORES

Salem, N. J.—H. E. West.

Wissahickon, Pa. — Arthur Lush, 5231 Ridge avenue.

Fond du Lac, Wis.—W. H. Gooding, 106 S. Main street.

Salem, O.—Harry E. Cooper, succeeding Wm. Mundy.

Perry, Ia.—David Moore, Citizens Trust & Savings Bldg.

Kansas City, Mo.—Miss Edith Roberts, 11 East 11th street.

Burlington, Ia.—Burlington Floral Co., 514 Jefferson street.

Brooklyn, N. Y.—Claremont Florists, 48 Flatbush avenue.

Toronto, Ont.—Butland Flower store, Roncesvalles avenue.

Staten Island, N. Y.—Alex. S. George, 42 Richmond terrace.

Milwaukee, Wis.—Wm. Lubliner, removing to 222 Grand avenue.

Springfield, Mass. — Ahlquist & Johannes, successors to N. F. Higgins.

Memphis, Tenn.—The Rosery, 191 S. Main street, A. Haisch, proprietor.

St. Louis, Mo.—Foster, the Florist, removing to 6th street, opposite Barr Building.

New York, N. Y.—Bell Rosary Florists, 2654 Broadway. Peter Bounakas, 5th avenue and 23d street.

New York, N. Y.—Harold H. Burns, Madison avenue, between 52d and 53d streets. Wm. Kather, 754 Madison avenue.

NEW CORPORATIONS.

McKinney, Tex.—McKinney Floral Co., increasing its capital stock from $20,000 to $30,000.

Kankakee, Ill.—Schafer Floral Co., capital stock, $12,000. Incorporators, Chas., Peter and Clara Schafer.

Cedar Rapids, Ia.—Cedar Rapids Floral Co., capital stock, $25,000. Incorporators. J. S. and A. C. Bain, E. J. Birch and C. M. Hyde.

NEWS ITEMS FROM EVERYWHERE

CHICAGO.

D. D. P. Roy, the latest to enter the seed, bulb and plant business in Chicago, is now well established in his office at 168 N. Michigan avenue and getting his share of the fall business.

The Grand Floral Festival posters are now in the hands of the florists and the little posterettes are adorning business envelopes going out of the flower stores, wholesale and retail.

Mrs. H. A. Simpson is spending a couple of weeks with relatives at Rockford, Ill. During her absence the business is looked after by C. B. Le Mer, who has been right hand man here for a number of years.

Fred J. Wolfram is the proprietor of a new firm which opened a store known as The Warrington Flower Shop, in the Warrington Theatre Building in Oak Park, October 23. Mr. Wolfram was formerly with A. Lange.

A. Henderson reports the arrival of all kinds of bulbs to date and says no difficulty has been experienced in getting them. The market, however, is not very well supplied, owing to two causes, conservative importing and an unusually good demand.

The flower store at 23 S. Crawford avenue has been purchased by A. L. and H. E. Ackenbach and the name changed from The Clark to The Crawford Flower Shop. Mr. Ackenbach was formerly with A. Frauenfelder, and for four years manager of The Flower Shop at Racine, Wis.

R. R. Brenton, who has charge of the publicity end of the Floral Festival, secured good space in the large local papers this week, showing that the people are in a mood to respond to the idea of large, well-directed floral exhibits. There is no doubt but many miss this event when it fails to appear annually.

The advance orders from the South which always uses an extra amount of flowers for All Souls' and All Saints' days, the 28th and 29th of October, are reported by our large shipping houses to be very satisfactory. The usual number of telegraph orders at the last minute are also expected and seldom fail to arrive.

One of the large wholesale houses is offering a special prize to the one who can show the most attractive, original way of arranging flowers for personal adornment. This is a good move and it is to be hoped some good ideas will be brought out, for the new dances have made impossible the usual corsage, and the conventional bride's bouquet has been in "lo! these many years," while the fad of last year for the single flower is not much support to the average florist.

D. D. P. Roy, who has just returned from Lake Geneva, Wis., says the superintendents of the large estates there are taking a lively interest in the coming show. The usual local exhibition at Lake Geneva has been abandoned and all effort turned to the Chicago affair. Among the prominent exhibitors will be A. J. Smith, with J. J. Mitchell; Axel Johnson, with A. F. T. Junkin; Wm. Longland, with C. L. Hutchinson; Robt. Blackwood, with Mrs. A. C. Allerton, and Miles Barrett, with M. A. Ryerson.

Phil Schupp has signed a five-year lease for his firm, J. A. Budlong, for a space in the new LeMoyne building, covering 1,600 square feet of floor space. Should this not prove sufficient, space may be taken in the basement also. The Chicago Flower Growers' Association, which signed a lease two weeks ago, covering the same period, has the adjoining rooms and both firms will move into their new quarters the first week in November. This makes five, all doing a large business, to go into this new building.

PHILADELPHIA.

John Burton has been suffering for the past week with a severe attack of the grippe.

W. Atlee Burpee has returned from Wernersville and is reported as progressing favorably.

Alfred Campbell reports good success with disbudded outdoor chrysanthemums this season. In some cases they bring better prices than indoor stock. They are very hard and great keepers.

The annual Chrysanthemum Show will open Nov. 9th, and will last four days. This is one week later than usual; the reason evidently being to escape election day (Nov. 2) which has an effect on the box office. The prospects are for a good show, in all departments; but we hear of nothing sensational or out of the ordinary.

Felix X. Murphy, the popular Kensington florist is back to business again "firm on duty as a rock," after having successfully piloted the "Phillies" to a pennant—their first in about thirty years. Many people are under the impression that Pat Moran was the man, but this is a great mistake. There is always a power behind the throne.

The next meeting of the Florists' Club (Nov. 2) promises to be a lively one, the subject assigned being: "Is it good for the business at large to keep flower vendors off the street." William Graham has the affirmative and Robert Craig, Junior, the negative, so we may look for an able presentation on the question from both points of view.

Samuel S. Pennock reports that the appeal to help Rev. Geo. Schoener, of Brooks, Oregon, the great and unselfish amateur rosarian, published in our last week's issue has already borne good results. The first one was two dollars which came on Saturday (almost as soon as the paper) from a struggling lady florist in New England. That shows the right spirit. Every little helps. Those with greater means are contributing accordingly but much or little, the feeling heart is the great thing.

WASHINGTON, D. C.

Frank Good, who for some time has been manager for Fred H. Kramer, has relinquished that position and is said to have obtained employment in New York City.

Walter L. Hawley, of Gude Bros., spent several days last week with relatives in Brooklyn, N. Y. He also visited a number of the wholesale and retail establishments in the metropolis.

The store of Fred H. Kramer is being materially improved by the extension of his display window across the space formerly occupied by the entrance to the floors above. This will increase the length of the window by about eleven feet.

The next regular meeting of the Florists' Club is scheduled for Tuesday evening, November 2. It is the plan of the officers to extend an invitation to growers of roses, chrysanthemums and carnations to display vases of novelties at that time. Following the usual business meeting there will be an informal talk on plant production under existing conditions.

NEW YORK.

A new company to be known as Hanft Bros. has opened up a retail store on Madison Ave., near 62nd street.

John Miesem and John Donaldson made an official visit to C. W. Scott last Saturday and Sunday to inspect Mr. Scott's new and extensive estate at Montrose on the Hudson, near Fishkill.

Mr. Canning is wondering how to plan to get his 17ft.-wide trained chrysanthemum plants into the Museum Building this year. We understand that the specimens to be exhibited this year are even finer than those of last year.

A welcome visitor at Secretary John Young's this week was J. K. M. L. Farquhar of Boston, who signed up for a big block of space for the National Flower Show at Philadelphia. Mr. Young will be manager of the exhibition of the Horticultural Society of New York in the Museum of Natural History next week.

ST. LOUIS.

The Foster Floral Co. are also moving. Their new location is at 6th and Locust streets.

Mullanphy Floral Co. are moving this week to their new location a block away. They will have an attractive store, with all new fixtures, which show to a great advantage.

The county growers and friends of Oscar C. May extended their sympathy to him last week. Mr. May's mother died and the funeral took place October 24. Many beautiful floral emblems were sent by members of the trade.

PITTSBURGH.

The display of pitcher plants now in full bloom at the Phipps Conservatory is said to be the largest exhibition of this species in the country.

By virtue of a proclamation issued by Nathan C. Schaeffer, superintendent of public instruction in Pennsylvania, last Thursday was observed as the autumn Arbor Day of the Commonwealth, and marked the addition of many newly planted trees in this section. By legislative action enactment, the study of birds and their habits was added to the duties of Arbor Day, for "there is no song of birds in a treeless land."

On last Sunday the private conservatories of Henry J. Heinz, at "Greenlawn," were thrown open to the public, the occasion being Mr. Heinz's annual chrysanthemum show. About 2,000 chrysanthemums in bloom have been grown at the Heinz conservatories this year, and now make a magnificent and varied showing. Hundreds of people were present on this occasion and continue to come in from day to day.

Superintendent George W. Burke of the Bureau of Parks has announced that the annual chrysanthemum show at the Phipps Conservatory, Schenley Park, and West Park, will be postponed until November 7th. The exhibit will be open daily from 9 A. M. until 6 P. M. until November 21st, and John W. Jones and James Moore, the respective foremen, state that with a little cool weather this show should surpass all previous efforts.

SAN FRANCISCO.

A new florist shop will shortly be opened in Modesto, Cal., by Mrs. Frank Smith.

C. Kooyman has been busy for several days filling his orders for Holland bulbs. As part of his shipment was destroyed by fire en route he is having difficulty in making the supply go round.

The United Flower & Supply Co., which markets the chrysanthemums

VIEW IN THE NEW BRANCH STORE OF THE ZIEGER CO., PITTSBURGH, PA.

brought into this market by the Japanese growers, reports that this is the most satisfactory season they have ever had.

The Republic of Chili has called on the University of California to furnish men trained in horticulture and pathology, Edwardo Causasco, commercial delegate from the Chilean government, presenting the request in person.

The Panama-Pacific Commission of the State of New York has announced that on and after October 21st, proposals for the sale of the trees and plants in and around the New York State Building will be received, deliveries to be made after December 5th.

Only Nine Days Until the Opening of the Cleveland Flower Show

BUSINESS TROUBLES.

Baltimore, Md.—Former Collector of the Port William F. Stone was appointed in the United States Court on Oct. 21 receiver for the Franklin Davis Nursery Company, after the company had been adjudicated a bankrupt with its consent. Bond for $7,500 was given by the receiver, who will continue the business and act until a trustee is selected.

The petition to have the company adjudicated a bankrupt was filed by the following creditors: Samuel A. Burk and Joseph E. White, both employees of the company, $963.14 and $7,352.21, and estate of Rufus Woods, for rent $676.50. A petition for the appointment of a receiver was filed by the Western National Bank, to which the company owes about $30,000. It stated that among the assets of the company were orders aggregating $12,000 and others were coming in.

WHOLESALE FLOWER MARKETS — TRADE PRICES—Per 100 TO DEALERS ONLY

	CINCINNATI Oct. 25		CHICAGO Oct. 18		BUFFALO Oct. 25		PITTSBURG Oct. 18	
Roses								
Am. Beauty, Special	25.00 to	30.00	25.00 to	40.00	20.00 to	50.00	25.00 to	35.00
" " Fancy and Extra	20.00 to	25.00	15.00 to	25.00	15.00 to	20.00	18.00 to	20.50
" " No. 1	10.00 to	15.00	6.00 to	15.00	8.00 to	12.00	8.00 to	15.00
Russell, Hadley	4.00 to	8.00	6.00 to	25.00	8.00 to	12.00	4.00 to	10.00
Killarney, Richm'd, Hill'don, Ward	6.00 to	8.00	8.00 to	12.00	6.00 to	8.00	6.00 to	10.00
" " " Ord.	3.00 to	5.00	4.00 to	6.00	3.00 to	5.00	...... to	4.00
Arenburg, Radiance, Taft, Key, Ex.	6.00 to	8.00	...... to	.....	6.00 to	8.00	6.00 to	10.00
" " " " Ord.	3.00 to	5.00	...... to	.....	4.00 to	6.00	...... to	4.00
Ophelia, Mock, Sunburst, Extra	6.00 to	8.00	10.00 to	12.00	6.00 to	8.00	8.00 to	10.00
" " " Ordinary	3.00 to	5.00	5.00 to	6.00	3.00 to	4.00	...... to	6.00
Carnations, Fancy	3.00 to	4.00	...... to	4.00	2.50 to	3.00	...... to	4.00
" Ordinary	...... to	2.00	2.50 to	3.00	2.00 to	2.50	2.00 to	3.00
Cattleyas	...... to	50.00	40.00 to	50.00	40.00 to	60.00	40.00 to	60.00
Dendrobium formosum	...... to	.....	40.00 to	50.00	...... to	.....	30.00 to	50.00
Lilies, Longiflorum	8.00 to	10.00	12.00 to	15.00	10.00 to	12.00	...... to	10.00
" Rubrum	4.00 to	8.00	...... to	.....	3.00 to	4.00	...... to	.....
Lily of the Valley	4.00 to	5.00	3.00 to	5.00	...... to	4.00	3.00 to	5.00
Daisies	...... to	.....	...... to	.....	.75 to	1.00	...... to	1.00
Violets	.50 to	.75	.50 to	1.00	.60 to	.75	...... to	.....
Snapdragon	...... to	.....	...... to	.....	3.00 to	6.00	...... to	.....
Chrysanthemums	8.00 to	20.00	15.00 to	30.00	6.00 to	20.00	20.00 to	25.00
Sweet Peas	...... to	.....	...... to	.....	.75 to	1.00	...... to	.....
Gardenias	...... to	.....	25.00 to	30.00	...... to	.....	...... to	.....
Adiantum	...... to	1.00	1.00 to	1.25	1.00 to	1.25	1.00 to	1.25
Smilax	12.50 to	15.00	12.00 to	15.00	...... to	15.00	12.50 to	15.00
Asparagus Plumosus, Strings (100)	25.00 to	50.00	40.00 to	50.00	...... to	50.00	35.00 to	50.00
" & Spren. (100 bchs.)	...... to	35.00	25.00 to	30.00	25.00 to	35.00	25.00 to	50.00

Flower Market Reports

BOSTON This market is well supplied with flowers of every description. Although there has been one good frost this week cosmos from outside still comes in bright and smiling and the sunny warm days have pushed along all the indoor things in ever-increasing quantity, violets alone excepted. However, there are enough violets, too. Roses have taken a distinct drop. Carnations have been increasing in quantity as well as quality and prices are very modest. Chrysanthemums are plentiful, the low grade and medium constituting the main stock and no complaint being heard because of the absence of extraordinary specimens. Snapdragon begins to assert itself and there are some good spikes of white and pink already in evidence. Daisies, white and yellow, are also in adequate supply and will continue to be a regular staple from now on.

BUFFALO Trade continues good. There is ample supply to fill all orders. The only thing that has been short at times is good carnations and these at the present are coming in more plentifully. Chrysanthemums came in quite heavy and move satisfactorily, as do other standard items. Dahlias came in quite heavy last week, with quality not as good as a week previous. At time of writing—October 28—the market is filling up with roses and chrysanthemums, though the sales have been satisfactory.

CHICAGO The last week in October finds the market a little easier. Stock held back till the middle of the previous week and the general scarcity that had prevailed during the month in all lines seemed to give way as a few days of sunshine brought out the flowers. Carnations responded quickly but the demand also increased so the high prices that prevailed last week are still in effect. Splendid stock of American Beauty roses is being cut, especially in the long-stemmed ones. Chrysanthemums are moving steadily at good prices and there seems to be a larger proportion of what might be called a popular-sized large bloom, than of either an extremely large or under-sized one. Pompons are making themselves noticed now and will probably make the usual inroads on the carnation sales soon. Lily of the valley is in good demand and stock is fine. The demand for stock in general may be said to be a little less than earlier in the month owing possibly to the run of October weddings and debutante parties being over.

CINCINNATI The wholesale houses are becoming somewhat crowded with stock, the primary cause of which the heavy receipts of chrysanthemums and the cosmos and dahlias that may still be had. Blooms in the fancy grades of chrysanthemums have been rather scarce. Roses are continuing plentiful and since the heavy cut of chrysanthemums began to come in have not been selling as readily as before. Enough carnations and lilies may be had to take care of every request.

NEW YORK Business conditions are not as encouraging as they have been. The very warm weather has made all stock more plentiful and prices on most things have taken on a downward tendency. Roses of all varieties are much more in evidence and good stock is selling as low as $20 per 1000. Chrysanthemums are rapidly filling up the wholesale market, and bring but moderate prices except in the case of choice stock such as Marigold, which is by far the best yellow in the market and is selling for 60 cents a bloom. Violets are showing up more abundantly. Cattleyas are slacking off rapidly. Gardenias are in good demand. Dahlias and cosmos still linger but they find no welcome now.

PHILADELPHIA The general market conditions here have continued good, although not quite so brisk as they had been week before last. The expected increase in many crops materialized all right with a consequent recession in prices. This is especially noticeable in carnations, which are much more plentiful and the quality shows marked improvement. In the rose market the status quo holds a little firmer. This is especially true of American Beauty. It seems that the growers have begun pinching for Christmas and this reduces present yield and holds prices firm. It is too early yet for the pinching act in other roses, so figures quoted are a little easier. Russell and Jonkheer Mock are very fine just now. There is a lively market for the little rosebuds like Sweetheart, Cameo, Old Gold, Sweet Marie, George Elger and others of the polyantha group. These come in nicely for the debutante and the Hallowe'en girl and bring surprisingly good prices for what little one

(Continued on page 583)

WHOLESALE FLOWER MARKETS — TRADE PRICES—Per 100 TO DEALERS ONLY

	BOSTON Oct. 28		ST. LOUIS Oct. 25		PHILA. Oct. 25	
Roses						
Am. Beauty, Special	12.00 to	25.00	20.00 to	25.00	20.00 to	25.00
" " Fancy and Extra	8.00 to	10.00	10.00 to	15.00	15.00 to	18.00
" " No. 1	3.00 to	5.00	5.00 to	8.00	8.00 to	12.00
Russell, Hadley	4.00 to	8.00	5.00 to	20.00	4.00 to	12.00
Killarney, Richmond, Hillingdon, Ward, Extra	4.00 to	6.00	6.00 to	8.00	4.00 to	8.00
" " " " Ordinary	1.00 to	3.00	3.00 to	4.00	2.00 to	3.00
Arenburg; Radiance, Taft, Key, Extra	4.00 to	6.00	..... to		4.00 to	8.00
" " " " Ordinary	1.00 to	3.00	..... to		2.00 to	3.00
Ophelia, Mock, Sunburst, Extra	4.00 to	6.00	6.00 to	8.00	5.00 to	10.00
" " " Ordinary	1.00 to	3.00	2.00 to	4.00	2.00 to	4.00
Carnations, Fancy	1.50 to	2.00	2.00 to	3.00	2.00 to	3.00
Ordinary	1.00 to	1.50	.75 to	1.00	1.00 to	2.00
Cattleyas	20.00 to	40.00	35.00 to	50.00	25.00 to	50.00
Dendrobium formosum	..... to	25.00	..... to		..... to	50.00
Lilies; Longiflorum	8.00 to	10.00	12.00 to	15.00	8.00 to	12.00
Rubrum	..... to	3.00	4.00 to	6.00	.... to	
Lily of the Valley	2.00 to	4.00	3.00 to	4.00	2.00 to	4.00
Daisies	.50 to	1.00	.85 to	.50	1.00 to	2.00
Violets	.40 to	.50	.25 to	.50	.35 to	.50
Snapdragon	1.00 to	9.00	3.00 to	5.00	8.00 to	5.00
Chrysanthemums	4.00 to	16.00	4.00 to	25.00	5.00 to	25.00
Sweet Peas	..... to	1.00	.50 to	.75	.50 to	.75
Gardenias	20.00 to	25.00	..... to		15.00 to	25.00
Adiantum	..... to	1.00	1.00 to	1.25	..... to	1.03
Smilax	12.00 to	16.00	12.00 to	15.00	15.00 to	20.00
Asparagus Plumosus, Strings (100)	25.00 to	50.00	35.00 to	50.00	..... to	50.00
& Spren. (100 Bchs.)	25.00 to	35.00	20.00 to	35.00	25.00 to	50.00

Flower Market Reports

(Continued from page 581)

gets. Just think of four dollars for a thumb nail when you can get fine Killarueys big as a dollar for two. It sounds ridiculous, but there you are. Chrysolora is the leader among the big chrysanthemums, of which, by the way, there seem to be fewer big fellows than usual. Medium-sized flowers with rather short stems are the rule at present. Polly Rose is a conspicuous example, much smaller this year among all that have arrived so far. The experts say we are "over the lump" on the orchid question now, and that there will be no more cheap cattleyas. Fair to decent prices from now on. Gardenias for the moment seems to be about as scarce as hen's teeth. Maybe that is a blessing in disguise. It is never good to feed us too much on any one thing. Even beef and greens, kail and potatoes, can be overdone, and we fly to the lunch stand for hot milk on toast and a cup of tea. Bouvardia is becoming more conspicuous and we notice a little mignonette around.

PITTSBURGH The home-grown dahlias have had their day, although some splendid specimens are being distributed by the McCallum Company among their retail trade, being continuously ordered from New Jersey. To a certain extent these "Jersey Beauties" are affecting the sale of the home products of chrysanthemums, roses and lilies. There are now plenty of good roses and lilies, and chrysanthemums have commenced to come in more plentifully. While prices continue about as they have been, the increasing stock points to a reduction all around in a very short time.

SAN FRANCISCO Business was a little more brisk the past week than it was the week before, but the supply of flowers was even more plentiful, so the values remained about the same. Exposition festivities take a good many flowers, and dinners, weddings, and other social events furnish an outlet for many more, while the usual fall activity in counter trade is beginning to show at the downtown shops. The shipping trade is steadily increasing also. Although receipts of chrysanthemums are much heavier, the demand is sufficient to make them clean-up fairly well. Many of the finer specimens have been reserved for the last few days for exhibition purposes at the National Fall Flower Show, which has lowered the average of first-class stock in the market. Beauties are rather scarce and are clearing accordingly. Other roses are improving and getting more plentiful from day to day, and while buyers find it necessary to be in the market early to fill their wants to their liking, they have the advantage of selecting from stock of the first quality. Asters and gladioli have ceased to be a feature of the market. Dahlias continue plentiful and in good demand. Carnations are in somewhat better supply and enjoy a better call than for several weeks. Violets are in good supply. Flowering plants are rather scarce. An abundance of Holland bulbs have been placed on the market here the last few weeks.

ST. LOUIS The market has been unusually good. The chrysanthemum season is now in full force and the demand is fine, but other stock has to suffer, especially the roses and carnations, which are coming in heavy and prices have dropped. The store men say trade is fine in all lines, but they can't consume all the stock coming in. So we can look for cheap sales all week. Other flowers are having a fairly good demand and seem to hold up their end in price.

WASHINGTON Dahlias and cosmos practically demoralized the local market last week. This situation came as a great surprise, for it had been reported that there would be no glut of these. Chrysanthemums which had been bringing better prices than in previous years were victims of a very noticeable slump; carnations could not be moved because of an oversupply of the former. Lilies had been scarce and these promptly dropped 25 per cent, with plenty to be had. Lily of the valley is easily obtainable, whereas the previous week the filling of orders was doubtful. Roses alone have remained scarce, with just about enough good stock to fill all demands. Princess of Wales and Governor Herrick violets are now offered with long stems and fairly large heads, but the supply is not heavy. Yellow daisies are also to be had. Orchids are not overplentiful and these met with fair sale last week.

NEW YORK QUOTATIONS PER 100. To Dealers Only

MISCELLANEOUS	Last Half of Week ending Oct. 23 1915	First Half of Week beginning Oct. 25 1915
Cattleyas	20.00 to 30.00	40.00 to 50.00
Dendrobium formosum	25.00 to 35.00	35.00 to 50.00
Lilies, Longiflorum	4.00 to 8.00	8.00 to 5.00
Rubrum	1.00 to 3.00	1.00 to 3.00
Lily of the Valley	2.00 to 3.00	2.00 to 3.00
Daisies	.25 to .50	...... to .50
Violets	.40 to .50	.00 to .35
Snapdragon	2.00 to 3.00	2.00 to 3.00
Chrysanthemums	4.00 to 12.00	4.00 to 20.00
Sweet Peas	...... to	...... to ......
Corn Flower	...... to .25	...... to ......
Gardenias	20.00 to 25.00	15.00 to 35.00
Adiantum	.50 to .75	.50 to 1.00
Smilax	8.00 to 10.00	8.00 to 10.00
Asparagus Plumosus, strings (per 100)	30.00 to 40.00	35.00 to 50.00
& Spren. (100 bunches)	15.00 to 20.00	15.00 to 25.00

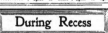

During Recess

The Farquhar Social.

On Friday evening, October 22, the Farquhar Nurseries employees gave their first annual social and dance, in Memorial Hall, Dedham, Mass. Over two hundred couples attended, Boston being represented by the employees of the firm, with their wives and friends. The stage was tastefully decorated with foliage and flowering plants by Robert Laurie and his assistants. Dancing commenced at 8 o'clock and was continued until 12 o'clock.

The Olympic Orchestra furnished the music. It was somewhat of a revelation to our city friends to find that the "hayseeds" could produce such accomplished musicians and entertainers. Through the generosity of John K. L. M. Farquhar the financial bugbear was removed.

Great credit is due to the various officers, President Robert Laurie, Treasurer P. Fordam, Secretary J. Traquair and committee, for the manner in which they labored to make the affair a success.

Boston Bowlers.

The Boston Florists' Bowling League scores for Thursday evening, October 21, were as recorded below. Our sporting readers should bear in mind that the bowling in Boston is done with "candle pins" and small balls, and the scores should be judged accordingly.

Carbone, 1220...vs...Robinson, 1210
Co-op. Market, 1353...vs...Flower Ex., 1218
Zinn, 1227...vs...Pansies, 1222
Galvin, 1263...vs...M. & M., 1207

Bresnahan high man with 307.

STANDING TO DATE.

	Won	Lost
Galvin	10	2
Co-op. Market	9	3
Carbone	7	5
Pansies	7	5
Zinn	6	6
Exchange	5	7
Robinson	3	9
M. & M.	1	11

Buyer's Directory and Ready Reference Guide

Advertisements under this head, one cent a word.   Initials count as words.

Display advertisers in this issue are also listed under this classification without charge. Reference to List of Advertisers will indicate the respective pages.

Buyers failing to find what they want in this list will confer a favor by writing us and we will try to put them in communication with reliable dealers.

ACCOUNTANT
R. Dysart, 40 State St., Boston.
For page see List of Advertisers.

ACHILLEA
"Pearl," Fine Seedlings, $3.00 per 1,000, each. JAMES MOSS, Wholesale Grower, Johnsville, Pa.

APHINE
Aphine Mfg. Co., Madison, N. J.
For page see List of Advertisers.

APHIS PUNK
Nicotine Mfg. Co., St. Louis, Mo.
For page see List of Advertisers.

ASPARAGUS
Asparagus Sprengeri, fine 2¼-in., $2.50 per 100; $20.00 per 1000. Cash. M. F. BYXBEE, Norwalk, Conn.

AUCTION SALES
The MacNiff Horticultural Co.,
New York City.
Plants Sales by Auction.
For page see List of Advertisers.

Elliott Auction Co., New York City.
For page see List of Advertisers.

AZALEAS
P. Ouwerkerk, Hoboken, N. J.
For page see List of Advertisers.

BAY TREES
August Rolker & Sons, New York.
For page see List of Advertisers.

BEDDING PLANTS
A. N. Pierson, Inc., Cromwell, Conn.
For page see List of Advertisers.

R. Vincent, Jr. & Sons Co.,
White Marsh, Md.
For page see List of Advertisers.

BEGONIAS
Thomas Roland, Nahant, Mass.
For page see List of Advertisers.

	Per 100
BEGONIA LORRAINE, 2½ in.	$12.00
3 in.	20.00
4 in.	36.00
5 in.	50.00
BEGONIA CINCINNATI, 2½ in.	15.00
3 in.	25.00
3½ in.	30.00
4½ in.	40.00
JULIUS ROEHRS CO., Rutherford, N. J.

BOILERS
Kroeschell Bros. Co., Chicago.
For page see List of Advertisers.

King Construction Co., North Tonawanda, N. Y.
"King Ideal" Boiler.
For page see List of Advertisers.

Lord & Burnham Co., New York City.

Hitchings & Co., New York City.
For page see List of Advertisers.

BOXES—CUT FLOWER FOLDING
Edwards Folding Box Co., Philadelphia.
For page see List of Advertisers.

Folding cut flower boxes, the best made. Write for list. HOLTON & HUNKEL CO., Milwaukee, Wis.

BOX TREES
BOX TREES—Standards, Pyramids and Bush. In various sizes. Price List on demand. JULIUS ROEHRS CO., Rutherford, N. J.

Breck-Robinson Nursery Co., Lexington, Mass.
For page see List of Advertisers.

BULBS AND TUBERS
Arthur T. Boddington Co., Inc., New York City.
For page see List of Advertisers.

J. M. Thorburn & Co., New York City Wholesale Price List of High Class Bulbs.
For page see List of Advertisers.

Ralph M. Ward & Co., New York City.
Lily Bulbs.
For page see List of Advertisers.

John Lewis Childs, Flowerfield, L. I., N. Y.
For page see List of Advertisers.

August Rolker & Sons, New York City.
Holland and Japan Bulbs.
For page see List of Advertisers.

R. & J. Farquhar & Co., Boston, Mass.
For page see List of Advertisers.

S. S. Skidelsky & Co., Philadelphia, Pa.
For page see List of Advertisers.

Chas. Schwake & Co., New York City.
Horticultural Importers and Exporters.
For page see List of Advertisers.

A. Henderson & Co., Chicago, Ill.
For page see List of Advertisers.

Burnett Bros, 98 Chambers St., New York.

Henry F. Michell Co., Philadelphia, Pa.
For page see List of Advertisers.

Joseph Breck & Sons Corp., Boston, Mass.
For page see List of Advertisers.

Fottler, Fiske, Rawson Co., Boston, Mass.
For page see List of Advertisers.

C. KEUR & SONS, HILLEGOM, Holland. Bulbs of all descriptions. Write for prices. NEW YORK Branch, 8-10 Bridge St.

CANNAS
Canna Specialists.
Send for Canna book.
THE CONARD & JONES COMPANY,
West Grove, Pa.

CARNATIONS.
Wood Bros., Fishkill, N. Y.
For page see List of Advertisers.

F. R. Pierson, Tarrytown, N. Y.
Carnation Matchless.
For page see List of Advertisers.

F. Dorner & Sons Co., Lafayette, Ind.
For page see List of Advertisers.

Jas. Vick's Sons, Rochester, N. Y.
Field Grown Plants.
For page see List of Advertisers.

Littlefield & Wyman, North Abington, Mass. New Pink Carnation, Miss Theo.
For page see List of Advertisers.

700 Pink Enchantress, 800 White Enchantress, 500 Mrs. Ward, $5.00 per 100. 500 Winsor, 250 Lawson, $4.50 per 100. 200 Queen, $4.00 per 100. Cash. CHAS. H. GREEN, Spencer, Mass.

CARNATION STAPLES
Split carnations quickly, easily and cheaply mended. Pillsbury's Carnation Staple, 1000 for 35c.; 3000 for $1.00 post paid. I. L. PILLSBURY, Galesburg, Ill.

Supreme Carnation Staples, for repairing split carnations. 35c. per 1000; 3000 for $1.00. F. W. WAITE, 85 Belmont Ave., Springfield, Mass.

CHRYSANTHEMUMS
Chas. H. Totty, Madison, N. J.
For page see List of Advertisers.

THE BEST 1915 NOVELTIES.
The Cream of 1914 Introductions.
The most popular Commercial and Exhibition kinds; also complete line of Pompons, Singles and Anemones. Trade list on application. ELMER D. SMITH & CO., Adrian, Mich.

COCOANUT FIBRE SOIL
20th Century Plant Food Co., Beverly, Mass.
For page see List of Advertisers.

DAHLIAS
Send for Wholesale List of whole clumps and separate stock; 40,000 clumps for sale. Northboro Dahlia and Gladiolus Gardens, J. L. MOORE, Prop, Northboro, Mass.

NEW PAEONY DAHLIA
John Wanamaker, Newest, Handsomest, Best. New color, new form and new habit of growth. Big stock of best cut-flower varieties. Send list of wants to PEACOCK DAHLIA FARMS, Berlin, N. J.

DECORATIVE PLANTS
Robert Craig Co., Philadelphia, Pa.
For page see List of Advertisers.

Woodrow & Marketos, New York City.
For page see List of Advertisers.

S. S. Skidelsky & Co., Philadelphia, Pa.
For page see List of Advertisers.

Bobbink & Atkins, Rutherford, N. J.
For page see List of Advertisers.

A. Leuthy & Co., Roslindale, Boston, Mass.
For page see List of Advertisers.

Araucarias, 7 in. pots, 3 to 5 tiers, $1.00 each; Cyclamen, 4 and 5 in. pots, 15c. and 25c. each; Primulas Obconica, 3 and 4 in. pots, 5c. and 8c. each; Begonias Chatelaine, 5 in. pans, 20c. each; Begonias Luminosa, 4 and 5 in. pots, 10c. and 15c. each; Asp. Sprengeri, 3 in. pots, $3.00 per 100; Asp. Plumosus, 3 in. pots, $4.00 per 100; Table Ferns, 2¼ in. pots, $3.00 per 100; Jerusalem Cherries, 4 in. pots, 6c. each; Jerusalem Cherries, from field, 5 in. pots, 10c. each; Var. Vincas, from field, $5.00 per 100. Write for prices on Holland Bulbs of all kinds. ROSENDALE NURSERY & GREENHOUSES, Schenectady, N. Y.

EUONYMUS RADICANS VEGETUS
Euonymus Radicans Vegetus — Three-year-old potted plants for immediate delivery; also three-year field-grown plants. $20.00 per 100; $2.50 per doz. Illustrated booklet free for the asking. THE GARDEN NURSERIES, Narberth, Pa.

FERNS
H. H. Barrows & Son, Whitman, Mass.
For page see List of Advertisers.

Robert Craig Co., Philadelphia, Pa.
For page see List of Advertisers.

McHutchison & Co., New York City.
Ferns in Flats.
For page see List of Advertisers.

For List of Advertisers See Page 563

LOPEZIAS, ETC.

LOPEZIAS, 3-in., 3c. Stock Geranium, $5.00 per 100. Coleus, assorted, $2.00. Pansy Giants, $3.00 per 1000. Hardy seedlings, all kinds. Hibiscus Hardy, $6.00 per 100. Hollyhocks, $2.00 per 100. Cash, please. S. P. VAN HEEST, Wortendyke, N. J.

MASTICA

F. O. Pierce Co., New York City.
For page see List of Advertisers.

NATIONAL NURSERYMAN

National Nurseryman Publishing Co., Inc., Rochester, N. Y.
For page see List of Advertisers.

NIKOTEEN

Nicotine Mfg. Co., St. Louis, Mo.
For page see List of Advertisers.

NIKOTIANA

Aphine Mfg. Co., Madison, N. J.
For page see List of Advertisers.

NURSERY STOCK

P. Ouwerkerk, Weehawken Heights, N. J.
For page see List of Advertisers.

W. & T. Smith Co., Geneva, N. Y.
For page see List of Advertisers.

Bay State Nurseries, North Abington, Mass. Hardy, Northern Grown Stock.
For page see List of Advertisers.

Bobbink & Atkins, Rutherford, N. J.
For page see List of Advertisers.

Framingham Nurseries, Framingham, Mass.
For page see List of Advertisers.

August Rolker & Sons, New York City.
For page see List of Advertisers.

NUT GROWING.

The Nut-Grower, Waycross, Ga.
For page see List of Advertisers.

ORCHID FLOWERS

Jas. McManus, New York, N. Y.
For page see List of Advertisers.

ORCHID PLANTS

Julius Roehrs Co., Rutherford, N. J.
For page see List of Advertisers.

Lager & Hurrell, Summit, N. J.

PALMS, ETC.

Robert Craig Co., Philadelphia, Pa.
For page see List of Advertisers.

August Rolker & Sons, New York City.
For page see List of Advertisers.

A. Leuthy & Co., Roslindale, Boston, Mass.
For page see List of Advertisers.

PANSY PLANTS

PANSIES—The Big Giant Flowering Kind—$3.00 per 1,000; $25.00 for 10,000. If I could only show the nice plants, hundred of testimonials and repeat orders, I would be flooded with new business. Cash. JAMES MOSS, Wholesale Grower, Johnsville, Pa.

PANSY SEED

Fottler, Fiske, Rawson Co., Boston, Mass.
For page see List of Advertisers.

PEONIES

Henry A. Dreer, Philadelphia, Pa. Dreer's Special Offer or Hardy Paeonies.

Peonies. The world's greatest collection 1200 sorts. Send for list. C. BETSCHER, Canal Dover, O.

Rare and continental varieties, James Kelway, Baroness Schroder, Eugenie Verdier, Mlle. Rousseau, Mireille, Mme. Loise Mere, $1.00 each, $10.00 doz.; Mons. M. Cabusac, $2.50 each, $25.00 doz.; Solange, Tourangelle, Mignon, Primevere, Mme. August Dessert, Rosa Bonheur—send for list. D. W. C. RUFF, Buena Vista Gardens, St. Paul, Minn.

PECKY CYPRESS BENCHES

A. T. Stearns Lumber Co., Boston, Mass.
For page see List of Advertisers.

PHLOX

Henry A. Dreer, Philadelphia, Pa.

PAPE AND FITTINGS

Kroeschell Bros. Co., Chicago.
For page see List of Advertisers.

King Construction Company, N. Tonawanda, N. Y. Shelf Brackets and Pipe Hangers.
For page see List of Advertisers.

PLANT AND BULB IMPORTS

Chas. Schwake & Co., New York City.
For page see List of Advertisers.

August Rolker & Sons, New York City.
For page see List of Advertisers.

PLANT TRELLISES AND STAKES

Seele's Tieless Plant Stakes and Trellises. H. D. SEELE & SONS, Elkhart, Ind.

PLANT TUBS

H. A. Dreer, Philadelphia, Pa. "Riverton Special."
For page see List of Advertisers.

PLANTS WANTED

C. C. Trepel, New York City.
For page see List of Advertisers.

RAFFIA

McHutchison & Co., New York, N. Y.
For page see List of Advertisers.

RHODODENDRONS

P. Ouwerkerk, Hoboken, N. J.
For page see List of Advertisers.

Framingham Nurseries, Framingham, Mass.
For page see List of Advertisers.

RIBBONS AND CHIFFONS

S. S. Pennock-Meehan Co., Philadelphia, Pa.
For page see List of Advertisers.

ROSES

Poehlmann Bros. Co., Morton Grove, Ill.
For page see List of Advertisers.

P. Ouwerkerk, Hoboken, N. J.
For page see List of Advertisers.

Robert Craig Co., Philadelphia, Pa.
For page see List of Advertisers.

W. & T. Smith Co., Geneva, N. Y. American Grown Roses.
For page see List of Advertisers.

Bay State Nurseries, North Abington, Mass.
For page see List of Advertisers.

August Rolker & Sons, New York City.
For page see List of Advertisers.

Framingham Nurseries, Framingham, Mass.
For page see List of Advertisers.

A. N. Pierson, Inc., Cromwell, Conn.
For page see List of Advertisers.

THE CONARD & JONES COMPANY. Rose Specialists. West Grove, Pa. Send for offers.

SCALECIDE

B. G. Pratt Co., New York City.
For page see List of Advertisers.

SEASONABLE PLANT STOCK

R. Vincent, Jr. & Sons Co., White Marsh, Md.
For page see List of Advertisers.

SEED GROWERS

California Seed Growers' Association. San Jose, Cal.
For page see List of Advertisers.

SEEDS

Carter's Tested Seeds. Seeds with a Pedigree. Boston, Mass., and London, England
For page see List of Advertisers.

SEEDS—Continued

Kelway & Son, Langport, Somerset, England. Kelway's Celebrated English Strain Garden Seeds.
For page see List of Advertisers.

Joseph Breck & Sons, Boston, Mass.
For page see List of Advertisers.

J. Bolgiano & Son, Baltimore, Md.
For page see List of Advertisers.

A. T. Boddington Co., Inc., New York City.
For page see List of Advertisers.

Chas. Schwake & Co., New York City
For page see List of Advertisers.

Michell's Seed House, Philadelphia, Pa.
For page see List of Advertisers.

W. Atlee Burpee & Co., Philadelphia, Pa.
For page see List of Advertisers.

R. & J. Farquhar & Co., Boston, Mass.
For page see List of Advertisers.

J. M. Thorburn & Co., New York City.
For page see List of Advertisers.

S. Bryson Ayres Co., Independence, Mo. Sweet Peas.
For page see List of Advertisers.

Loechner & Co., New York City.
For page see List of Advertisers.

Ant. C. Zvolanek, Lompoc, Cal. Winter Flowering Sweet Pea Seed.
For page see List of Advertisers.

S. S. Skidelsky & Co., Philadelphia, Pa.
For page see List of Advertisers.

W. E. Marshall & Co., New York City. Seeds, Plants and Bulbs.
For page see List of Advertisers.

August Rolker & Sons, New York City.
For page see List of Advertisers.

Burnett Bros., 98 Chambers St., New York.
For page see List of Advertisers.

Fottler, Fiske, Rawson Co., Boston, Mass. Seeds for the Florist.
For page see List of Advertisers.

SKINNER IRRIGATION SYSTEM

Skinner Irrigation Co., Brookline, Mass.
For page see List of Advertisers.

SPHAGNUM MOSS

Live Sphagnum moss, orchid peat and orchid baskets always on hand. LAGER & HURRELL, Summit, N. J.

SPRAYING MATERIALS

B. G. Pratt Co., New York City.
For page see List of Advertisers.

STANDARD THERMOMETERS

Standard Thermo Co., Boston, Mass.
For page see List of Advertisers.

STOVE PLANTS

Orchids—Largest stock in the country— Stove plants and Crotons, finest collection. JULIUS ROEHRS CO., Rutherford, N. J.

SWEET PEA SEED

Arthur T. Boddington Co., Inc., New York City. Winter Flowering Sweet Peas.
For page see List of Advertisers.

Ant. C. Zvolanek, Lompoc, Calif. Gold Medal of Honor Winter Orchid Sweet Peas.
For page see List of Advertisers.

S. Bryson Ayres Co., Sunnyslope, Independence, Mo.
For page see List of Advertisers.

VEGETABLE PLANTS

R. Vincent, Jr. & Sons Co., White Marsh, Md.
For page see List of Advertisers.

VENTILATING APPARATUS

The Advance Co., Richmond, Ind.
For page see List of Advertisers.

The John A. Evans Co., Richmond, Ind.
For page see List of Advertisers.

For List of Advertisers See Page 563

New Offers In This Issue

CLEVELAND FLOWER SHOW.
Cleveland, Ohio, Nov. 10th to 14th.
For page see List of Advertisers.

EASTER LILIES.
S. S. Pennock-Meehan Co., Philadelphia, Pa.
For page see List of Advertisers.

GLADIOLUS BULBS FOR FORCING.
Henry F. Michell Co., Philadelphia, Pa.
For page see List of Advertisers.

GLADIOLI FOR FORCING.
B. Hammond Tracy, Wenham, Mass.
For page see List of Advertisers.

HILL'S EVERGREENS.
The D. Hill Nursery Co., Dundee, Ill.
For page see List of Advertisers.

SCALECIDE.
B. G. Pratt Co., New York City.
For page see List of Advertisers.

WHOLESALE FLORIST.
B. S. Slinn, Jr., New York City.
For page see List of Advertisers.

In writing to Advertisers kindly mention Horticulture

Obituary

Mrs. Victor Dorval.

Mrs. Dorval, widow of Victor Dorval, died on Tuesday evening, October 26, at her home in Woodside, N. Y.

George H. Chase.

George H. Chase of Malden, Mass., a nurseryman with offices at 60 Summer street, that city, also in Rochester, N. Y., died suddenly on Thursday, Oct. 21, at his home in Malden from heart failure. His death occurred but a few moments after he had awakened from his customary after dinner nap. Mr. Chase, who was 71 years old, was born at Buckfield, Me., but had lived for the greater part of his life in Malden. He served for 10 years on the Malden street and water commission.

John White.

John White, one of the oldest florists in the country, died Sunday afternoon, October 17, at his home, 1263 Waverly place, Elizabeth, N. J., after a brief illness. He was ninety years of age. Born in Bedford, England, where he first studied horticulture, he came to this country when a young man and settled in Jersey City, where he established greenhouses and engaged in the florist business.

Mr. White was a frequent exhibitor at horticultural shows. Pansies were among his most prized specialties. He is survived by one son, John White, Jr.; one daughter, Mrs. D. A. Daland, and two grandchildren.

Henry Baldinger.

The funeral service for Henry Baldinger was held last Sunday at his home in Allentown, (the new eighteenth ward of Pittsburgh, Pa.) his death having taken place the previous Thursday as the result of a protracted attack of Bright's Disease. Mr. Baldinger, who was one of Pittsburgh's veteran commercial florists, was born on February 24, 1834, in Frieburg, Germany, where he became practically interested in floriculture when a mere lad. In 1850 he came to America, shortly after locating in Pittsburgh, where he has continued in business since. His wife died eight years ago. He is survived by three sons and two daughters, one of whom has for several years been a saleswoman for the Ludwig Floral Company. Julius W. Ludwig and Henry Muech of this firm, were among the pall bearers at the funeral of Mr. Baldinger.

Joseph F. Smith.

After an illness of several months, Joseph F. Smith, the florist, died at his home at 409 Washington street, Norwich, Conn., on Sunday evening, October 17, death resulting from a complication of diseases.

Joseph F. Smith was born in Gmund, Province of Wurtemburg, Germany, Dec. 6, 1838. He came to this country when 13 years of age and resided in Philadelphia, Pa., until he moved to Norwich in 1865 and engaged as a gardener for Joseph Ripley. In 1871 he started in business for himself at Norwich Town, which business he conducted up to the time of his death. He received his education in the public schools of his native town and at Philadelphia, Pa. In 1863 he married Katherine Spang of Philadelphia. He is survived by his wife, five sons and four daughters.

Enthusiastic and highly successful in the business which he had built up in Norwich Town, he not only possessed those qualities that led to success in his work, but he won esteem and high regard for what he was as a man. Always reliable, always helpful, smoothing many a troubled way, he won more than success. Not only in his own family will his loss be great, but also in that neighborhood from which so many who could ill be spared have passed on in the last few years. His last years of illness were made beautiful by the devotion of all in the home circle.

PERSONAL.

Christopher Schwab, who has been at the Wyndhurst greenhouses at Lenox, has taken a position in Arthur N. Cooley's greenhouses in Pittsfield, Mass.

Richard Vincent, Jr., of White Marsh, Md., will give a lecture before the Staten Island Garden Club at Rosebank, N. Y., on Friday afternoon, November 5.

Charles F. Kessler, salesman for his brother William, of 113 West 28th street, New York City, and Miss M Bente, were married at the bride's home, 327 W. 28th street, Saturday, Oct. 23d.

We learn with much regret that Mr. Fred Sander of St. Albans, England, has been ill but are glad to hear that he is now getting better. All the workmen in the Sander establishment, except a few elderly men, have gone to the front in the army and they have been replaced with girls.

John Carman has resigned his position as foreman at Bellefontaine, Lenox, Mass. under Mr. Jenkins, also the secretaryship of the Lenox Horticultural Society, and is going to Pittsburgh as superintendent of the estate of Col. J. M. Schoonmaker, Sewickley Heights.

At the last meeting of the Lenox Horticultural Society Lewis Barnet was elected secretary in Mr. Carman's place and Jesse Frampton assistant secretary.

SOLVING THE POTASH PROBLEM.

Several new methods of increasing the supply of American potash have recently been brought to the attention of the Bureau of Foreign and Domestic Commerce, of the Department of Commerce. One of the most promising of these efforts to find a substitute for German fertilizers is a patent taken out a few weeks ago by a Canadian for a method of using the potash in ordinary feldspar.

The process is a simple one, consisting of heating the feldspar with limestone and iron oxide at a temperature of about 2,200 degrees Fahrenheit, which produces a partly fused mass that is easily decomposed by a weak acid. From this product the potash salts can readily be extracted for further purification. The inventor has been in consultation with Dr. Norton, the expert who has been looking after the potash and dyestuff situations for the Bureau of Foreign and Domestic Commerce, and it seems very possible that a greatly simplified method of transforming feldspar into fertilizer will soon be available.

A practical try-out for another method of obtaining potash fertilizer will soon take place at a New Orleans distillery where molasses is used in large quantities. It is a fact that 106 tons of potash are wasted daily by the twenty-five or more distilleries in this country that subject molasses to processes of fermentation. The New Orleans company is planning to install the process of saving the potash in distillery waste recently brought to the attention of the public by the Bureau of Foreign and Domestic Commerce. It should be possible to make fertilizer from this otherwise worthless material at a price that will meet competition even after the war is over.

FREAKISH FACTS AND FACTLESS FREAKS.

Culled from he columns of our exchanges.

Janesville Wis., Oct. 25—Clarence Hammens, a dahlia fancier, discovered a bulb in his garden which has grown entirely through a large root of an elm tree some two inches in diameter, cutting it neatly in two as though with an axe.
—*Press-Telegram.*

After hearing a talk by William Gloeckner on "The Florist Business" at the weekly luncheon of the Rotary Club at the Ten Eyck today, more than one Rotarian decided that after all the only people in Albany who are making any money are the florists —*Albany Journal.*

A freak potato, presenting four interesting studies, was brought into the office of the Post last night by James F. Leavey of 10 Leon street, Somerville, who raised the potato with others at the Eagles Rest Cottage, North Weymouth. One view of the play of nature potato shows the outline and features of the human face; another pose strongly suggests the hippopotamus; a third, is a likeness to the mushroom, and a fourth position shows the spud resembling the monkey's head and face.—*Boston Post.*

Only Nine Days Until the Opening of the Cleveland Flower Show

Ames, Ia.—On Friday afternoon, November 5th, will take place the formal opening of the new greenhouse and Horticultural Laboratory building of the Iowa Agricultural Experiment Station. In the evening a banquet will be given under the auspices of the Students' Horticultural Club.

GREENHOUSES BUILDING OR CONTEMPLATED.

Pennsburg, Pa.—O. C. Trumbore. additions.

Berwyn, Md.—Henry Lavalle, addition 40 x 100.

Bowling Green, O.—J. S. Brigham. house 28 x 70.

Atchison, Kan.—Mangelsdorf Bros. Co., additions.

Cudahy, Wis.—Lakeside Rose Milk Farm, one house.

La Salle, Ill.—W. Moore, West 2d street, one house.

St. Clair, Mich.—Wm. Munt, Brown street, one house.

Davenport, Ia.—St. Ambrose College, conservatory.

La Grange, Ind.—C. M. Hissong. vegetable house 10 x 60.

Fairhaven, N. J.—Joseph Hayes. Church street, one house.

Rushville, Ind.—Glenn E. Moore. additions and alterations.

Fall River, Mass.—Charles Cyr, 184 Jones street, house 20 x 45.

Erie, Pa.—McCarthy & Klein, 724 W. 8th street, house 28 x 160.

Chicago, Ill.—John Vachout. 4518 N. Crawford avenue, one house.

Bucyrus, O.—F. J. Norton, West Charles street, additions and alterations.

Sandwich, Ill.—Sandwich Greenhouses, Mrs. Frances Spickerman. proprietor. one house.

Pittsfield, Mass. — Courtlandt F. Bishop, The Maples, conservatory 24 x 50, Hitchings & Co.

Louisville, Ky.—Fred Eisenmenger, 410 N. 44th street, one house. John W. Klein. owner of the property where Mrs. M. D. Reimers conducts her floral shop, 636 S. 4th street, is erecting a greenhouse in connection with the store.

DAMAGES AWARDED FOR INJURY BY GAS.

The suit of John Donaldson of Patchogue, N. Y., against the Newtown Gas Company for damages done to his greenhouse stock in his greenhouses at Elmhurst, L. I., has been settled. The Company paid Mr. Donaldson over $2,700 in settlement. William H. Siebrecht, Jr., of Long Island City, was Mr. Donaldson's attorney.

The settlement of this suit is of more than usual interest inasmuch as the gas main which caused the trouble was practically new, having been laid only two years prior to the damage and, furthermore, no one ever smelt gas in Mr. Donaldson's greenhouse. Nevertheless, the growth of his stock of Easter lilies was stunted and his callas destroyed. Experts who were called into the case pronounced illuminating gas as the cause of the injury to the plants and flowers and this was substantiated by certain experiments which Mr. Siebrecht caused to be conducted.

Shortly after this leakage Mr. Donaldson sold his property in Elmhurst and moved to Patchogue. His son, Alexander Donaldson, now conducts the florist business at his father's old place. The first winter that the son put through in the same house, there was another leak, or a continuation of the same leak, which resulted in another suit against the same Gas Company.

HORTICULTURE

New York Wholesale Cut Flower Protective Association
Luncheon at Hotel Breslin.

Published Every Saturday at 147 Summer Street, Boston, Mass.
Subscription, $1.00

LIST OF ADVERTISERS

FOR BUYERS' DIRECTORY AND READY REFERENCE GUIDE
SEE PAGES 616, 617, 618, 619

NOTES ON CULTURE OF FLORISTS' STOCK

CONDUCTED BY

John J. M. Farrell

Questions by our readers in line with any of the topics presented on this page will be cordially received and promptly answered by Mr. Farrell. Such communications should invariably be addressed to the office of HORTICULTURE.

"If vain our toil, we ought to blame the culture, not the soil."—*Pope.*

Azaleas

The best azaleas for early forcing, to be had in bloom easily by Christmas. are Simon Mardner, Apollo, Deutsche Perle, Pauline Mardner and Vervaeneana. Before the azaleas go into their pots a thorough soaking of the root balls is necessary. The inner core of the ball when once dried out, remains in that condition ever afterward, no matter how regularly and thoroughly the pots are watered. The failure of plants to do well may in nearly all instances be traced to dry roots. After being potted they should not be exposed to sunshine for eight or ten days, nor to frosty weather at any time although a very cool and airy place suits them. Those that are needed for Easter can be plunged in cold frames until later when you will have time to pot them up.

Cinerarias

Plants from seed that was sown from August 15 up to the first week in September and grown in flats, should now be ready for 3-inch pots. Use a soil composed of three parts of fibrous loam and two of leaf mold with a good sprinkling of sand for the first potting. Keep close for a few days until the roots take hold of the new soil, when they should be given a place near the glass in a house where the temperature runs near 40 degrees at night. For the second potting and others that are to follow leave out all leaf mold, but give them a rich compost of two-thirds fibrous loam to one-third of well-decayed cow manure with a dash of guano and soot. Fumigate often for the aphis. Never let them approach anything like a pot-bound condition before giving them a shift until flowering size is reached. Those that are intended for Christmas should be kept in a temperature of about 40 degrees to 45; anything higher will ruin your crops of flowers.

Cyclamen

Every good florist has lots on his mind at all times so it is very easy for him to overlook some of his plants. Cyclamens that you sowed the first half of September should be nicely above ground now. See that they are placed well up to the glass so as to keep them sturdy, and when they are large enough to handle shift into other flats. Here they can grow without being disturbed for another two months. Let them have a light compost for which one-half each of loam and leaf mold with plenty of sand will be suitable. Keep in a warm house at 55 to 60 degrees at night. Keep the surface soil frequently scratched. In transplanting these little cyclamens don't leave the little bulb on the surface, but put it just below. They will soon work their way to the top. Be careful in watering so as not to sour the compost.

Orchids

Watering should be done fairly early in the morning, so that the moisture dropped on foliage and benches will dry up before night. Syringing overhead should be gradually discontinued. When done at all, let it be on the mornings of clear days. Do not play the hose directly on the plants as this makes too heavy a stream. Always use a fine misty spray. A decreased water supply all around will be necessary now. It is always safe to underwater rather than overwater. This question of ventilation is not half considered. It is the rock on which many would-be orchid growers perish. Too many still persist in keeping orchids too hot and stuffy. Outside of the purely East Indian, tropical kinds, all like air in abundance. Cattleyas and Laelias above all enjoy plenty of fresh air. There are really but few days in the year when neither top nor bottom ventilators can be open. In the case of strong winds, enough will get between the laps of glass to satisfy them.

Poinsettias

These plants are not so easily kept in good condition when the late fall approaches. We have arrived at the critical time for poinsettias. Careful attention is required as to ventilation, firing, etc., and watering carefully from now on is of great importance. It cannot be good policy to apply water which is near the freezing point. Some plants may not be as particular in this respect as others, but poinsettias will not stand for sudden changes in temperature or for water much below the temperature of the house they are in. It is better to go over your pans, pots and benches often to prevent any from remaining too dry and on the other hand it will give a chance for any that are wet to dry out. Do not feed at all until the bracts are forming; then give it twice a week in moderately weak doses. Some soot with the manure helps to keep the leaves green.

Time to Start Bulbs

The time taken under ordinary condition for the different bulbs to form enough of roots to enable them to be forced with any kind of success are—Paper white narcissus, 6 to 8 weeks; Roman hyacinths, 8 to 10 weeks; Dutch hyacinths, 14 to 16 weeks; daffodils, jonquils and narcissus. 14 to 16 weeks; lilies such as Harrisii, longiflorum, gigantium, formosum, speciosum, etc., will take at least 16 to 18 weeks. Of course the time will vary either one way or the other according to the strength of the bulbs.

Next week—Ardisias; Callas; Crotons; French Bulbs; Rhododendrons; Storing Hydrangeas.

HORTICULTURE

VOL. XXII   NOVEMBER 6, 1915   NO. 19

PUBLISHED WEEKLY BY
HORTICULTURE PUBLISHING CO.
147 Summer Street, Boston, Mass.
Telephone, Oxford 292.
WM. J. STEWART, Editor and Manager.

SUBSCRIPTION RATES:
One Year, in advance, $1.00; To Foreign Countries, $2.00; To
Canada, $1.50.

ADVERTISING RATES:
Per inch, 30 inches to page................................... $1.00
Discounts on Contracts for consecutive insertions, as follows:
One month (4 times), 5 per cent.; three months (13 times), 10
per cent.; six months (26 times), 20 per cent.; one year (52 times),
30 per cent.
Page and half page space, special rates on application.

Entered as second-class matter December 8, 1914, at the Post Office
at Boston, Mass., under the Act of Congress of March 3, 1879.

CONTENTS   Page

Indulgent Jack Frost — Although most of the trees are bare, summer flowers still linger in the gardens in a large section of the country where usually gardens are desolated by the time November comes in. There are salvias, cannas, cosmos, ageratum, French marigolds, petunias, some roses and even dahlias, still in sufficient quantity to make the suburban plots look bright and to make quite a showing in the wholesale markets. We like to see them. They work no very great injury to the indoor flower trade and we shall have to face winter dreariness soon enough.

A thriving industry — While it is generally acknowledged that the flower business has made but little progress during the season of 1915, it appears from our observation and according to reports from various sources that the landscape gardening industry and the trade in hardy garden ornamental material have been enjoying a season of rare prosperity. Perhaps the enforced staying at home since the outbreak of the European war has conduced partly to this result and it is quite probable that the automobile, which has unquestionably had a reverse influence on the florist business, has given a new impetus to the laying out of suburban homes. No line of horticultural work holds out better promise for the ambitious young man than that of hardy ornamental gardening.

An ethical question — A notification has been received by all the wholesalers in New York to the effect that, at a joint session of the Association of Retail Florists and the Greek-American Florists' Association, it was the sense of the meeting that wholesale florists do not sell at retail and calling for an immediate statement of the wholesalers' position on the matter. No doubt the retailers know what they are doing. We hold no brief to speak for them or for the wholesalers or to proffer advice, both sides being presumably able to take care of their respective interests, yet, as unswerving advocates of organized co-operation we should much prefer to see questions of this character made the subject of friendly joint consideration between representative men of both interested parties. Knowing how averse the leading wholesale men in New York are to selling anything at retail we are at a loss to understand just why these wholesalers have alone been selected to receive a communication such as that referred to. The retail people may have some basis of complaint which does not appear on the surface but one naturally wonders, at this juncture, what their attitude is towards those large wholesale growers, for instance, who are openly competing for retail business while at the same time placing a considerable part of their product on the wholesale market. And, further, how can an organization of retail store keepers, none of whom are producers, consistently take such an issue with the legitimate wholesalers, if a combination of several of its own members is in the field as a competitor in the wholesale trade? We are heartily in accord with the proposition that wholesale dealers should keep strictly out of the retail business. But the rule of fairness demands that, in exchange for this protection, the retail dealer is in honor bound to extend to the wholesale dealer cordial support to the full extent of the latter's facilities for serving him. In this direction much more might be said as all those "close to the firing line" well know, but probably we have gone far enough for the present.

ROSE GROWING UNDER GLASS

CONDUCTED BY

Arthur C. Ruzicka

Questions by our readers in line with any of the topics presented on this page will be cordially received and promptly answered by Mr. Ruzicka. Such communications should invariably be addressed to the office of HORTICULTURE.

Watch the Feeding

With the weather staying warm it will be necessary to be very careful with the feeding, and see that it is applied at the proper time, and then withheld when it should be. As soon as a crop is well cut off the plants should be allowed to dry out just a trifle, being careful of course not to carry it too far. As soon as the plants are dry enough they can be watered well, being careful to make sure that the water penetrates through the soil, leaving no dry spots anywhere. To make this sure it may be necessary to water twice over the bench fronts where the plants will naturally be drier than anywhere else. Then if they are not showing any breaks to speak of they can be allowed to dry out fairly good again, after which they will break quite freely as a rule. As soon as the plants have quite a number of breaks all over they can be given a little liquid manure or bonemeal and as soon as the breaks lengthen out a little they should receive a light mulching if they need it. The surface of the benches will tell this. If the mulch that has been put on is pretty well gone and the soil in the benches lies exposed to the sun and air, it is time to apply more. If, however, there is plenty of rough material on the benches to keep the water from washing around when watering then it will not be necessary to apply any more manure, depending on the liquid to furnish all the necessary plant food, using plenty of bonemeal to go with it. However, it may not always be advisable to use too much liquid, especially if the plants show signs of getting soft. If this happens it will be well to run the houses a shade cooler, and keep the liquid away until the plants show signs of starving. This can be seen on the new growth which will become somewhat stunted in appearance.

The Coal Bins

With the warm sunny weather all along, growers are apt to neglect to order or have on hand sufficient coal. This is bad management for the warm weather will no doubt be followed by a severe cold snap, and coal will burn rapidly then. Keep the coal coming as fast as it is used so that in case of early snow there will be no heating problem to bother about. Considerable coal can be saved by keeping the boilers clean all the time. See to this as the boilers should be brushed every other night. There are no especial brushes required for this; a piece of old burlap on a stick will generally answer the purpose and nearly all the boilers built now can be cleaned while the fire is going full blast, as most of them are arranged to open one flue or part at a time.

Storing Manure

Manure for mulching which has to be kept outside in the weather will leach out a good deal, and this will mean loss. There is no way to prevent this except to have one of the sod heaps only three and a half feet high, and then keep the manure pile on top of this. Any liquid that may drain through the manure will be quickly absorbed by the sod in the heap and there will be little waste. Needless to say the heap should be covered with straw or hay or leaves or anything to keep it from freezing in the winter so that it will be ready to use at any time.

Soot

The prices that roses have been bringing the last few weeks will enable growers everywhere to indulge in little luxuries every now and then. Soot may be considered a luxury for commercial growers, but it will certainly put additional color into the roses if applied at the proper time. It can also be added to the liquid manure but we prefer to apply it directly to the benches, using only enough to slightly blacken the surface of the soil. After this a little more can be applied whenever it is needed. It is best applied when the buds are about to show color. It is quite strong and may damage the foliage somewhat if too much of it is applied all at once. Never apply it at the same time with bonemeal, or to benches that have been limed recently. The lime in the bonemeal or in the benches liberates a large portion of the ammonia in the soot all at once and this is waste, even if there is no harm done to the plants and flowers.

THE CLEVELAND FLOWER SHOW

The Cleveland Flower Show, more than ten days before the opening of the exposition at the Coliseum on November 10, finds itself with only two small spaces unsold. When it is considered that there is more than 65,000 square feet of space in the exposition building and that this area is to be filled with a representative display of horticulture and all that pertains to the trade one is able to gain an impression of the magnitude of the Cleveland Show.

Among the exhibitors to enter the lists since the last reports by the executive committee is Hubert V. Pearce, Detroit, steam heating engineer. There will be about sixty exhibits of appliances of the business in addition to the display of commercial and private growers, nurserymen and foreign exhibits.

One of the latest features secured is to come from the botanical garden, Washington, D. C. Superintendent Hess has promised to send examples of several of the rarest and most interesting plants from his collection and expects to personally accompany the shipment and attend the show throughout its progress.

The burden of bringing together these varied and representative exhibits for the most pretentious show ever held in the Middlewest has fallen upon the general committees although there has been heartiest co-operation on the part of all the local societies and clubs interested in flower culture.

H. P. KNOBLE
General Chairman Show Committee.

Following are the names of those behind the Cleveland Show:

General Committees.

H. P. Knoble, general chairman; M. A. Vinson, executive secretary.

Publicity—George Bate, chairman, H. B. Jones, T. J. Kirchner, F. Ritzenthaler, Chas. L. Gibson.

Trade Displays.—H. P. Merrick, chairman, R. F. Koch, Victor H. Morgan, E. B. George, Painesville, O.

Exhibition and Hall.—Frank A. Friedley, chairman, Herbert Bate, L. Utzinger, Carl Hagenberger, Mentor, O.

Entertainment.—G. W. Smith, chairman, S. N. Pentecost, F. C. Witthuhn, C. J. Graham, Robert Weeks.

Decorations.—F. C. W. Brown, chairman, G. B. Shearer, C. A. Meyers, Walter Priest, T. J. Kirchner.

Premiums.—Herbert Bate, chairman, J. Curnow, Akron, O., Frank A. Friedley.

Non-Commercial Displays.—Robert Weeks, chairman, George Jacques, J. Curnow, Akron, O.

Retail Displays.—C. E. Russell, chairman, Frank Ritzanthaler, C. M. Wagner.

Admissions.—Timothy Smith, chairman, A. B. Barber, W. A. Calhoon, Chas. F. Bastian, F. W. Griffin, W. A. Bramley, Albert Lingruen, F. R. Williams.

The revised program of the events of the Flower Show week announced by the Committee is as follows:

Wednesday, November 10th.—Registration of exhibitors and all out-of-town attendance of the trade will start at the Coliseum at 8 A. M. and will continue all day. It will be necessary for all visitors to register in order to receive the show badge that will admit them at the door, after the official opening, which takes place at 1 P. M. No special entertainment features scheduled for this day.

Thursday, November 11th.—Registration of visitors to continue, beginning at 9 A. M. at the Coliseum. Show opens to the public at 10 o'clock each morning. The meeting of the Florists' Telegraph Delivery will be held at 9 A. M., in the rooms of the Cleveland Florists' Club in the Hollenden. The annual meeting of the Chrysanthemum Society of America will be held in the Hollenden at 10.30

HERBERT BATE
Chairman Premium Committee and President Cleveland Florists' Club.

M. A. VINSON
Secretary to Committee.

TIMOTHY SMITH
Chairman Admission Committee.

G. W. SMITH
Chairman Entertainment Committee.

A. M. The Ladies' Bowling Tournament will begin at 10 A. M., in the Erie Bowling Alleys on Chestnut street near East 9th. The general tournament for the 5-men teams will start at 11 A. M. in the same alleys. At 3 P. M. the visiting ladies will be entertained at Hotel Statler by the members of the Ladies Florists' Club of Cleveland.

Friday, November 12th.—Registration of later arrivals will continue at the Coliseum beginning at 9 A. M. The American Rose Society will hold their fall meeting in the Hollenden at 10 A. M. The Ohio Gladiolus Society will hold an adjournment meeting for the election of officers in the Hollenden, at 11 A. M. The Executive Committee of the American Carnation Society will meet in the Hollenden at 2 P. M. At 8 P. M. the Cleveland Florists' Club will entertain all exhibitors and visitors at a banquet in the ball room of the Hollenden. All visitors are requested to register and receive their badges before 3 P. M. of the 12th so the entertainment committee will know the number of plates to provide for.

Saturday, November 13th.—A smoker will be given at Hotel Statler for the exhibitors and visiting florists at 8 P. M. There will be other entertainment features announced in the detailed program that will be handed to each visitor as he registers. A very large attendance is looked for.

An invitation has been extended through Mrs. John Vallance, president-elect of the Ladies' Society of American Florists, for the members of that Society to be guests of the show management during the time of the exhibition.

The exhibition of the American Rose Society at the Coliseum in Cleveland has apparently increased so as to make the approaching show one of very considerable size. There are two more special prizes offered, one by the Cleveland Cut Flower Company for $25 in Class $6, and the other by the Storrs & Harrison Co. for $25

CHRYSANTHEMUM TIGER (EXHIBITED AS 111-1-13)

At the solicitation of the management of the Cleveland Flower Show, President Wilson has kindly supplied the name for this new yellow. A seedling from Chrysolora, several shades darker than its parent. It is supremely fitted for the rank and file of growers, especially those who are unable to plant early, as its characteristics stamp it as a commercial of special merit. Fine incurved form producing flowers double to the center from September buds, sturdy semi-dwarf growth, with beautiful foliage and very rigid stem; height about 4 feet from June 1st plantings. Best bud September 5th. One of Elmer D. Smith's novelties.

in Class 87. The American Rose Society will hold a meeting on Thursday the 11th.

The Bowling Tournament.

The Bowling Tournament will be staged at Er.e Bowling Alleys, Thursday, November 11th, starting at 11 A. M., five-men teams bowling first. Individuals will follow and the roll off of five high men in the individual and high man on each team will compete for the H. P. Knoble prize, a life membership in the S. A. F.

Other prizes are as follows: High team, a silver cup, also five small cups donated by The J. M. Gasser Co.; second high team, $25.00, donated by the Cleveland Cut Flower Co.; high average man on each team, a special prize given by The Cleveland Florists' Exchange, $25.00 to be divided between them. High average game $5.00, offered by Cleveland Plant & Flower Co.

Total number of strikes, one man in three games, $5.00, offered by Herbert Bate. Total number of spares, one man in three games, $5.00, offered by Herbert Bate. Total number of splits, one man in three games, $5.00, offered by Cleveland Plant & Flower Co. Man making most strikes in succession, any one game, $5.00, offered by Frank A. Friedley.

In the Individuals: High average man, $10.00, offered by McCullum Co.; 2nd high average man, $9.00; 3rd, $8.00; 4th, $7.00; 5th, $6.00; 6th, $5.00; 7th, $4.00; 8th, $3.00; 9th, $2.00; 10th, $1.00.

After the regular tournament a special match game will be played between teams representing Buffalo and Rochester, N. Y., bowling for a silver cup, also five individual cups, to be given by F. C. W. Brown, of The J. M. Gasser Co.

The Ladies' Bowling Tournament will be staged at 10 A. M. on Thursday on the same alleys. A special list of individual prizes has been arranged. All visiting ladies are urged to take part in the tournament.

The money given in the Individuals from 2nd prize to 10th prize is contributed by the following: Chas. J. Graham, Fred C. Witthuhn, Stumpp & Walter Co., S. N. Pentecost, Brooklyn Floral Co., A. A. Hart, John Bleckschind, Smith & Felters, A. C. Fox, Carl Hagenburger, Jones & Russell Co. There will be twelve ladies' prizes (merchandise). C. J. GRAHAM, Chairman Bowling Tournament.

H. P. MERRICK   C. E. RUSSELL   ROBERT WEEKS   GEORGE BATE
Chairman Trade Display Committee.   Com-Chairman Retail Displays Committee.   Com-Chairman Non-Commercial Displays.   Chairman Publicity Committee.

THE FALL FLOWER SHOWS

SAN FRANCISCO FALL FLOWER SHOW.

The Grand National Fall Flower Show was brought to a very successful close on October 26 after running for six days. Members of the trade are agreed that it was the most elaborate and satisfactory show ever held in this city. The exhibits were excellent, the prizes strongly competed, and the attendance large, interest being stimulated by a large number of special events arranged in connection with the display. While all seasonable flowers were included in the prize list, chrysanthemums were the main feature. These exhibits were arranged to excellent advantage under the central dome of the Palace of Horticulture. The quality of the flowers was the subject of favorable comment both among members of the trade and the general public. It is certain finer specimens were never shown here before, and it is doubtful whether a better showing could have been produced in other sections of the country. The silver cup offered by the Chrysanthemum Society of America for the best ten blooms, one variety of chrysanthemums on long stems, was awarded to the Lynch Nursery of Menlo Park. The Hitchings & Co. prize for the best six vases chrysanthemums, six varieties, three blooms of each on long stems, went to T. Etow of San Mateo. The gold, silver and bronze medals offered by Wm. Wells and Chas. H. Totty for three blooms of the Earl Kitchener chrysanthemum, were awarded to the Lynch Nursery, Mrs. C. R. Waters of Menlo Park and Shibuya & Ishida of San Mateo, respectively. Percy Ellings of Menlo Park won the medal given by the National Association of Gardeners for the best six chrysanthemums of six varieties. The Elmer D. Smith prizes for the best six white, yellow and pink chrysanthemums went to the Lynch Nursery and the Hillsborough Nursery. Shibuya & Ishida were awarded the H. W. Buckbee prize for the best vase of twenty-five blooms chrysanthemum Mrs. W. H. Buckbee. Besides these special awards for chrysanthemums many other prizes were offered for chrysanthemums, roses, dahlias, begonias, orchids, etc. The large room at the entrance of the building was used for dahlias, begonias, annuals, etc., while the orchid display and some of the other exhibits were arranged in some of the side rooms. The gold medal for the best display of orchids in flower arranged for effect with other plants went to John A. Carbone of Berkeley.

Among the special features, Pelicano, Rossi & Co. were awarded the only prize for table decoration, competed for five successive days; also silver medal for the most artistic bridal bouquet; and first prize both for the best arranged hamper or basket and the most artistically arranged basket of cut flowers.

Other names which figure prominently as winners were E. James, H. Plath, H. J. Kessel, San Mateo Co.

Conservatories, Domoto Bros., Mrs. J. Roos, F. Agari, Mrs. R. E. Darbee, Geo. H. Young, Ferrari Bros., McLellan & Co., J. B. Smith, G. A. Pope, Bessie Boston Dahlia Co., Ruth C. Glendell, H. E. Bothin and John Vallance.

MORRIS COUNTY GARDENERS' AND FLORISTS' SOCIETY.

The 20th Annual Flower Show of this society was a complete success in every respect. The same committee, Wm. H. Duckham, Chas. H. Totty and Arthur Herrington have arranged every show since the shows started 20 years ago, so it is an old trick with them. The big groups put up by Robt. Tyson and John Downing, were the works of finished artists. The table decorations, which were just chrysanthemum flowers, were very attractive and drew crowds of the ladies. The vegetable exhibits were of the highest order and filled one large nail. We had two new carnations—Peace from Frank Dinda, Farmingdale, L. I., and Laura Weber from Chas Weber, Lynbrook, N. Y., the former a white, and the latter a pink. They showed up well, but the standard kinds were to the front. The best carnation in pink was Enchantress Supreme, and White Enchantress held its own, and more in white. Champion, shown by Wm. Duckham was easily the best in the reds. Princess Dagmar scored in crimson.

In red roses, Hoosier Beauty had it "all-over" everything. A vase of Lady Alice Stanley was considered by many the best in the show but Ophelia had so many admirers that it was hard to get near it. I mustn't forget Totty's vase of Gorgeous, not in competition: it was in a class by itself.

Duckham's table of orchids deserved special mention as did also Peter Duff's specimen plant of Lady Lydia. In Totty's new chrysanthemums No. 20 pink scored 89 points; Wm. Rigley single white, 90; Mrs. H. Gibson, 89.

There were 104 classes in the schedule and competition was lively all through. In the chrysanthemum bloom classes eight 1st were won by C. H. Totty, six by John Downing, five by Ernest Wild, four by James Fraser, three by Wm. Duckham and one each by George Fisher and Peter Duff who also was 1st on specimen plant. In the rose classes L. B. Coddington got five 1st, L. A. Noe three, C. H. Totty, Hamilton Farm and J. Wagner two each, and L. M. Noe one. Winnings in carnations were Ernest Wild four, Wm. Duckham, F. Brease and Hamilton Farm two each, J. G. Douglass, G. Ficher, Thos. Dorner and Springfield Floral Co. one each. Other awards were—Peter Duff for violets, Robert Tyson for plant group and for Lorraine begonias, Jas. Fraser for pot chrysanthemums, W. H. Duckham for orchids and J. K. Linaburg two 1st for greenhouse grapes. The entries in the classes for fruit and vegetables and farm produce were numerous and of high quality.   E. R.

CHICAGO GRAND FLORAL FESTIVAL.

The regular meeting of the executive committee was held at the Hotel Morrison, October 28, the members in attendance including A. Henderson, W. N. Rudd, W. J. Keimel, August Poehlmann, N. J. Wietor, Geo. Asmus, Guy W. French, E. F. Kurowski, N. P. Miller. Payne Jennings, Robert Brenton, H. B. Howard, K. Patterson, James Morton and M. Barker. Reports of the various sub-committees were presented, showing well matured plans for the big exhibition, to be held at the Coliseum, November 9-14. Widespread interest in the event is evident from the correspondence coming to the officials from all sections of the country, and the distribution of large quantities of posters and posterettes with liberal notices in the newspapers have awakened unusual enthusiasm locally. The competitive exhibits from leading growers will be well worth the attention of the trade in themselves and it is certain there will be a good array of new plants and flowers in the various sections. Many novel features are promised by the management, including elaborate floral dances and fashions. ancient and modern, in the use of flowers for personal adornment. Some contracts for trade space are still pending as this notice of the show goes to the press, the list of those closed being as follows with the value of space taken:

Chicago firms—W. W. Barnard Co., $111; Buchbinder Bros., $60; O. J. Friedman, $39.60; Ideal Lighting Co., $27; Kroeschell Bros. Co., $25; W. H. Kidwell & Son, $54; Frank Oechslin, $43.20; Poehlmann Bros. Co., $43.20; Raedlein Basket Co., $66; Schiller, the Florist, $66; Vaughan's Seed Store, $120; Ernst Wienhoeber Floral Co., $63; Geo. Wittbold Co., $54; C. C. Pollworth Co., Milwaukee, Wis., $43.20; A. N. Pierson, Inc., Cromwell, Conn., $72; Haeger Brick & Tile Co., Dundee, $55.80; D. Hill Nursery Co., Dundee, $96.

M. BARKER,
Chairman Publicity Com.

LENOX HORTICULTURAL SOCIETY

The fifteenth annual fall show was held in the Town Hall, Lenox, Mass., on October 26-27. Although the number of exhibitors were less than in the previous two or three years, the hall was well filled, all the exhibits being of the highest class and very tastefully arranged. In the centre was a large circular group of plants arranged for effect, shown by Giraud Foster, gard. E. Jenkins. One of the leading features was the magnificent group of orchids exhibited by A. N. Cooley, Pittsfield, orchid grower, Oliver Lines. Cut chrysanthemums were well shown, the winners in the leading classes being G. Foster, who won the Society's cup for the best vase of 10 blooms with the variety Mrs. G. L. Wigg, A. N. Cooley and Mrs. W. E. S. Griswold. A silver cup offered by W. H. Walker of Gt. Barrington, for the six best blooms in the show was won by A. N. Cooley. Roses and carnations were well shown, the winners in roses being

F. E. Lewis, Ridgefield, Conn., gard. W. Smith, C. Lanier and G. Foster. In carnations Mrs. W. Griswold and Mrs. R. Winthrop were winners in the leading classes. There was the usual keen competition in the vegetable classes, G. Foster winning the special prize offered by Mrs. W. E. S. Griswold for the best collection of 18 kinds, by the narrow margin of 1½ points, Carlos De Heredia, gard. Geo. H. Thompson, being placed second. In the class for 12 varieties one point separated the collection from Mrs. R. Winthrop, gard. S. Carlquist, and that from C. Lanier, gard. A. H. Wingett, in the latter's favor, this prize carried with it the silver cup offered by R. & J. Farquhar & Co. The prize offered by Peter Henderson & Co., for the best 10 varieties of potatoes was won by C. Lanier. There was a good show of fruit. Lord & Burnham's prize for 12 dishes of apples was awarded to A. Swift of Lee. W. M. Salisbury won the silver cup offered by Hitchings & Co. for the best two bunches of grapes in the show.

There was a good attendance on both days and a vote of thanks is due to all exhibitors and the committee of arrangements who helped to make the show a success.

J. FRAMPTON, Asst. Sec'y.

BOSTON FALL SHOW.

The annual fall exhibition of the Massachusetts Horticultural Society is being put in order in Horticultural Hall, Boston, as we go to press. We cannot tell anything about the awards until next week and some of the exhibits are at time of writing incomplete, but we have seen enough of the show as it is to unhesitatingly pronounce it one of the best, if not the very best, in the long series of Boston fall shows. This quality does not lie in the chrysanthemums—pot plants or flowers, or in any one other feature, but in the variety and finish of the exhibits individually and collectively and on the impressive arrangement as a whole.

The large exhibition hall space is flanked by four stupendous groups of flowering and foliage plants, two on the left and two on the right, banked high against the walls, from A. M. Davenport, Kameyama & Serada, R. & J. Farquhar & Co., and W. W. Edgar Company, respectively. Each group is unique in arrangement of colors and contour and we do not envy the job of the judges in deciding between at least two of them on 1st award.

The centre of the hall is devoted to the pot plants. There are no very prodigious trained specimens but there

is a fine showing of well-grown plants of moderate size, W. H. Elliott and A. M. Davenport being prominent contributors. Mr. Davenport is a new competitor in the heavy group classes and he has made a magnificent start. In addition to the afore-mentioned entries he has a fine group of Lorraine, Cincinnati and Mellor begonias and half a dozen superb plants of the Winter-flowering Begonia Mrs. Heal which illumine the scene with an unrivalled glory. Other groups in the large hall comprise one of choice flowering plants from Mrs. J. L. Gardner in which lancifolium lilies, bamboos and Jerusalem cherries make a beautiful combination; an extensive collection of conifers and broad-leaved evergreens in pots and tubs by Breck-Robinson Co., and another of like character from M. P. Haendler, of Old Town Nurseries.

There are two superb displays of orchids, long groups of elegant specimen plants in many genera from Wheeler & Co., of Waban, and F. J. Dolansky of Lynn, both commercial growers for cut flower purposes. No private estate could excell them. There are also two orchid specimen plants of rare merit. One is Laelio-Cattleya Moira (Mantini × Fabia) with a spike of three great blooms, from A. W. Preston, gard. John L. Smith. The other a specimen Cattleya Trianae from George W. Stewart. Two trained plants of Heavenly Blue Morning Glory from Mrs. C. G. Weld come in for much admiration, each nearly five feet in height and covered with big flowers and hundreds of buds. E. S. Webster showed Begonias Mrs. Heal and Optima, the latter a new one in the winter-flowering section with deep salmon flowers.

In the chrysanthemum cut flower section D. F. Roy, gard. for Col. Converse, presents an array of 71 gigantic blooms, never excelled in any previous show. W. D. Hathaway of New Bedford has an extensive display of dahlias in all classes, flowers as perfect as in the height of the season. Waban Rose Conservatories present mammoth vases of roses Hadley. Mrs. Moorfield Storey, Mrs. Bayard Thayer and Mrs. Russell. William Sim makes a display of pansy blooms such as he alone makes. They are close to perfection. W. W. Edgar Company exhibited two mammoth vases of chrysanthemums arranged with bronzy oak foliage, one being the variety Robert Halliday and the other Charles Razer. The retail florists are represented by ten decorated dinner tables, the taste shown being much ahead of that in any former competition here. The classes for small baskets and other

dainty floral receptacles drew out some very artistic arrangements by Wax Brothers, Penn the Florist and Mrs. Coran. Further details next week.

INTERNATIONAL FLOWER SHOW, NEW YORK.

April 5-12, 1916.

Five months might seem a long period to those of us who are not engaged in preparations for the next big flower show to be held in New York, although to the men who are working like beavers to make it certain that the 1916 show shall overshadow all previous shows, the time seems all too short. With monthly meetings, and a division of the general committee into sub-committees, the work of preparation is well advanced; but with the idea generally imbued among the workers that the next show must present new features, new ideas, and, above all, show progress from an expositional point of view, five months for further preparation is a period all too small.

The idea of the Rose Garden, so well carried out at the exhibition last spring, bids fair to become a most important feature of the next show, for the reason that the premiums offered are on a most liberal basis, and sufficiently attractive to ensure six or more exhibits in the class set apart for displays of this kind. Just think of it—six Rose Gardens!

The rock garden, a much cherished institution on the other side of the water, and an obect of curiosity to bany of our budding horticulturists, is to be featured strongly at the April show, and those who are able to compete for the $250 and $150 prizes offered would do well to get busy with their exhibits.

The charts showing the space available for trade exhibits are already well marked with reservations and proposed reservations of exhibitors, and any firms desirous of securing choice of locations should lose no time in communicating with the Secretary.

The committee is a little embarrassed just now over the problem of housing the number of large exhibits promised, and it seems quite probable that three floors of the big Grand Central Palace may have to be utilized for the exhibition instead of two as heretofore.

JOHN YOUNG, Sec'y.

Roslyn, Pa.—Edward Towill has reason to feel quite optimistic concerning a lot of very promising seedling roses —about a dozen in all—which he has in training. One is a very bright pink single, of Fireflame style.

Obituary

Harry Allen.

Harry Allen, son of Charles H. Allen, of Floral Park, Long Island, N. Y., died Saturday, October 30th, and was buried Tuesday, November 2d, on his twenty-sixth birthday.

Dennis Dwyer.

Dennis Dwyer, a member of the florist concern of Dwyer Brothers, of Brooklyn, N. Y., died at St. Anthony's Hospital, Woodhaven, on October 30. He was born in Brooklyn.

Edward G. Eggeling.

Edward G. Eggeling, a prominent florist of St. Louis, Mo., died on Saturday, Oct. 30, from throat trouble after a brief illness. Mr. Eggeling's store on Grand avenue was one of the oldest in the city, as it was started by his father right after the civil war. Mr. Eggeling was 43 years old and leaves a widow and one daughter. He was a member of the St. Louis Florist Club, which sent a floral offering to the funeral, on Monday, November 1.

Charles Thomas Lee.

Chas. T. Lee, florist, of South Brooklyn, N. Y., died on Thursday, Oct. 28. He was a resident of South Brooklyn for thirty-five years. He was born at Taunton, Mass., in 1839, and during the entire Civil War served as a member of the Seventh Regiment of Massachusetts. He enlisted as a private and for bravery in action was promoted until he was discharged a first lieutenant. He was wounded at the Battle of the Wilderness. He is survived by his wife, Emma Louise Marsh, and a son, Charles Reed Lee, who is also a florist.

Albert C. Huebner.

The sympathy of the trade goes out to a well beloved fellow craftsman, Paul Huebner, landscape gardener for the Reading R. R. system, in the loss of his son, Albert C. Huebner, who was killed in an automobile accident at Akron, Ohio, on Oct. 30th. The funeral took place from the family home in Philadelphia on November the 4th. Interment was at Northwood cemetery.

Mr. Huebner was 31 years of age and up to a few years ago held an important position in the Purchasing Department of the Rapid Transit Co. Since leaving that concern he has been connected with a big manufacturing concern with headquarters in Chicago. While not connected with the horticultural world in a business way he was well-known to many of us and much liked. The members of the Railroad Gardeners Association will remember him well as he took his father's place as host to them when they held their last convention in Philadelphia—the elder Huebner being at that time in the hospital.

George Economopoulas.

George Economopoulas passed away very suddenly on Wednesday, October 27, at the University Hospital in Chicago. Though but 37 years of age, he was a pioneer in the retail trade of the city, for he had been 24 years in the florist business. He came here

from Zaraphona, Greece, when a boy and sold flowers in the Union Depot. Later he had a small store on State street and still later the basement of the store, which he has occupied for the past ten years, on the corner of Adams and Wabash, and which is one of the best corners on the street. Mr. Economopoulas and Frank Williams, deceased, and Gus Pappas, of Des Moines, Ia., were partners under the name of The Alpha for many years. Four years ago Mr. Williams' share was purchased and The Alpha now owns the two stores at Chicago and Des Moines. The funeral was from the Orthodox Greek Church. La Salle and Oak streets, and the floral offerings were unusually fine. Mr. Economopoulas was not married, but has a mother and sister in Greece and a brother and a nephew in Chicago. Interment was at Elmwood and a special train carried out a large number of friends.

F. W. Timme.

Another of the pioneer florists of Chicago passed away on October 27 at his home, 4016 N. Tripp avenue. Frederick William Timme was born in Madgeburg, Germany, in 1843, and came to America when a boy of fourteen. He came to Chicago at the close of the civil war, in which he served. For three years he was private gardener for Allen Pinkerton and for fifteen years he held a similar position for Potter Palmer and for the last thirty years he has been in the florist business for himself, at the above address. where he was active till four years ago when his son took charge. He made a study of his work and put thought into it as well as labor. He had the distinction of being the first Chicagoan to grow carnations, bringing the stock here the year after they were brought over from France. Some of the older varieties were originated by Mr. Timme, and one called Lucia was recognized by the Horticultural Society of Chicago in 1892. He was also well known as the writer of frequent articles for the trade papers, under the title of Timme's Timely Teachings. He is survived by Mrs. Timme, who was Isabel Johnstone, of Crystal Lake, Wis.. one son, William Frederick, and one daughter, Mrs. Harry Blewitt, of Des Plaines. The funeral took place October 30 at Mee's Chapel and interment was at Crystal

Lake. Six brothers-in-law acted as pall bearers.

VISITORS REGISTER.

Washington—Joseph Goudy, representing H. A. Dreer, Philadelphia; Mr. and Mrs. Harold J. Patten, Tewksbury, Mass.

St. Louis: Martin Reukauf, representing H. Bayersdorfer & Co., Phila.; Thomas Knight, New York; J. J. Karins, representing H. A. Dreer, Phila.

Boston: A. E. Thatcher, Bar Harbor, Me.; George W. Hilliard, Exeter, N. H.; C. W. Hoitt, Nashua, N. H.; Chas. S. Strout, Biddeford, Me.; L. J. Reuter, Westerly, R. I.

Pittsburgh: Milton Alexander, New York; R. E. Blackshaw, Chicago; Isaac Bayersdorfer, of H. Bayersdorfer Co., Philadelphia; Julius Dilloff, New York; N. J. Hayman, Clarksbury, W. Va.

Philadelphia: D. Carmichael, representing J. M. McCullough's Sons, Cincinnati, O.; W. H. Vance, Wilmington, Del.; Richard Fowler, of J. Van Lindley Nursery Co., Greensboro, N. C.

Chicago: Gus Pappas, Des Moines, Ill.; Mrs. Edward Gullett, Lincoln, Ill.; S. J. Verhalen, Sherman, Tex.; D. W. Dunser, Battle Creek, Mich.; C. W. Scott, representing the Yokohama Nurseries, New York; H. Koster, Boskoop, Holland; A. Schultz, Hammond, Ind.; George Franks, Champaign, Ill.; Mrs. Gustave Ludwig, Pittsburgh, Pa.

TRANSPORTING A SPECIMEN PLANT

The problem of sending one of his big trained chrysanthemum plants from Ardsley, N. Y., to Cleveland, Ohio, for the Cleveland show, has been finally mastered by Mr. Canning. The plant, which is about 16 feet across will go on a platform car, under a movable greenhouse specially constructed for the purpose. On account of its width the plant will be tipped diagonally and an ingenious arrangement of rollers and shock absorbing bearings will keep the plant so nicely balanced that it is expected to make the journey without damage to a single bloom. The variety is Wells' Pink.

Its companion plant, a specimen of R. F. Felton, 17 feet in diameter, will be displayed at the Museum of Natural History in New York this week.

LONG ISLAND PLANT GROWERS

Twice in each year the New York and New Jersey Plant Growers participate in an inspection tour of the various establishments where greenhouse plants are grown for the New York florist trade, spending a day among the Long Island places and another day one week later with the New Jersey growers. The visit to Long Island took place last Friday, starting at Long Island City and finishing at Flatbush. The party comprised A. L. Miller, J. H. Fieser, Julius Roehrs, Harry Dreyer, George Scott, Alfred Zeller, John Birnie, H. C. Steinhoff, L. Schmutz, Jr., Harry Schmutz, W. H. Siebrecht, Jr., Henry Baumann, Paul Fischer, Chas. Koch, Jos. Baumann, H. A. Wagner, Jr., C. Madsen, K. Christensen, Anton Schultheis, Jr., Herman Schoelzel, T. B. De Forest and W. J. Stewart. The growers visited were A. Schultheis, College Point; Louis Dupuy, Dreyer Bros. and Keller Company, all of Whitestone; H. D. Darlington and Louis Enne, Flushing; John Miesem, Elmhurst; A. L. Miller, Jamaica; H. A. Wagner, John Scott, Louis Schmutz, Chas. Koch and Chas. Zeller & Son, all of Flatbush, Brooklyn. After a glimpse of these thirteen establishments—or rather, twelve, for Miesem grows only lilies—one is moved to marvel how or where this prodigious stock of Boston ferns, ericas, poinsettias, ardisias, cyclamen, primulas, genistas, pot chrysanthemums, azaleas, solanums, dracaenas, oranges, begonias, pandanuses, ficuses, and the long list of less abundant things is ever marketed. Even the visiting growers themselves were amazed at the stupendous aggregate of ericas and Boston ferns of all the popular forms that confronted them in this little trip around one limited section of the great metropolitan district. Azaleas have been coming in freely and there will doubtless be enough of them for both Christmas and Easter for most of the plants were received in good condition. Judging from the number of young ardisias coming on in several of the larger places there will be no scarcity of this favorite next year.

One of the prettiest sights was a house of Jerusalem cherries at Schultheis' place that fairly sparkled with the myriads of berries, and also we cannot pass without mention of one of several houses of chrysanthemums in 6-inch pots—the best the writer ever saw. Here and at Dupuy's, Keller's and Darlington's, are ericas—principally melanthera—that must number high in the hundreds of thousands, in all sizes from "fingerlings" up to 6-year-old giants 4 to 5 feet high, of which Keller shows a whole house. Darlington has exten-

sive ranges of frames filled with countless ericas and heated by subterranean boilers. Besides the extensive plant houses filled with the highest-class stock in the country, the Keller Company has quite an acreage of outside nursery. At Louis Dupuy's, Mr. Dupuy being absent at the funeral of Mrs. Dorval, Mrs. Dupuy did the honors. At Dreyer's it is ferns, ferns, ferns, and plenty of dwarf poinsettias and heavily fruited oranges, among other things. Louis Enne has an imposing range of houses, including a large new house just completed by Hitchings & Co., for sweet peas. Good taste is displayed in the planting of the entrance and driveway of Mr. Enne's place with lilacs, rambler roses and other fine hardy material.

A. L. Miller's establishment is a never-resting hive of activity. Men and wheelbarrows everywhere and the houses and grounds are the picture of neatness. There are four new houses of Lord & Burnham construction and heating. Mr. Miller is trying out the new Salvia Greggii in all conceivable ways as a future pot plant for the Christmas holidays. C. H. Wagner and John Scott have no end of ferns. There are veritable forests of them, and the "Home of Scottii" bids fair to hold its prestige for a long time yet. C. H. Wagner, Jr., is a shining light in the Wagner place, where cement walls and other improvements are being installed. Louis Schmutz has two places in Flatbush and both were visited. One is the old Meisner place and it is a pleasure to go through an establishment where artistic arrangement of the stock is so much in evidence. Zeller's is another place where one is impressed with the neatness and scrupulous care which count for so much. Young ferns and promiscuous plant stock are the specialties. At Chas. Koch's callas are a special crop and are blooming well already.

It was quite a privilege to see all these lucrative establishments in the short space of a late October day. Separated as they are, a trip of such extent would be impossible were it not for the now indispensable automobile, a luxury that is no burden to the prosperous Long Island grower. A sumptuous mid-day repast, presided over by that master of the art of masterful diplomacy, A. L. Miller, president of the association and frank and ingenuous friend to all who come, was enjoyed at Middle Village.

The Providence Journal for Sunday, October 24, devoted the greater part of an entire page to an illustrated story about George L. Stillman, the noted dahlia grower of Westerly, and his products. Mr. Stillman is looked upon by most of the dahlia specialists as invincible in the dahlia line.

The value of horticultural merchandize arriving at the Port of New York for the week ending October 23, is given as follows: Clover seed, $14,783; grass seed, $1,187; fertilizer, $665.

THE SEVEN BEST CARNATIONS.

Will you kindly publish in HORTICULTURE seven of the very best carnations grown for the market, in order according to value, including size, prolific growing, and value on the market?

Thanking you,   Very truly,
                                        M. B.
Long Island, N. Y.

WHITE.—1st, White Perfection. 2nd, Matchless will take its place after we get on to its little trick.

White Wonder with some people pays better than White Perfection.

LIGHT PINK.—1st, Enchantress Supreme or Gloriosa. 2nd, Alice looks good to me but have not had it long enough.

DARK PINK.—1st Winsor or Good Cheer. 2nd, Ward is very good every way except prolificacy; makes not enough flowers and splits sometimes.

SCARLET.—1st, Beacon. 2nd, Herald does well, but in winter Beacon is better.

CRIMSON.—1st, Harry Fenn. 2nd, Pocahontas.

VARIEGATED.—1st, Benora.

The above have so far always paid their board and mine when properly handled. They are my favorites; other growers have theirs.

                                        G. THOMMEN.
Billerica, Mass.

Our records would show the following varieties to be the best seven in the order named: Beacon; Enchantress Supreme; White Wonder; Benora; White Enchantress; Pink Delight; Gloriosa.

This refers only to the return per plant in dollars and cents as the matter of size, number of flowers produced, value in the market all contribute to this same end.

The variety Matchless has not been taken into consideration in making up this list nor has the old variety Enchantress. We question if the variety Enchantress would make a place, but Matchless might, depending on the locality where it is grown.

                                        L. J. REUTER.
Westerly, R. I.

Answering your inquiry, my experience has been that the following are the best paying carnations in the market: White Wonder, White Enchantress, Enchantress Supreme, Pink Delight, Mrs. C. W. Ward, Dorothy Gordon, Beacon.

                                        Yours,
                                        E. W. FENGAR.
Irvington, N. J.

Of Interest to Retail Florists

NEW FLOWER STORES.

Cleveland, O.—F. W. Griffin, 5711 Euclid avenue.

Gardenville, N. Y.—Galley Bros., Genesee street.

Pittston, Pa.—Andrew Velton, 16 Williams street.

Chicago, Ill.—Harry Rowe, 125 N. Wabash avenue.

Reading, Pa.—Rosedale Floral Co., 46 N. 9th street.

Salt Lake City, Utah.—Geo. Wray, State street and Broadway.

Sioux Falls, S. D.—Minnehaha Floral Co., 314 South Phillips avenue.

Huntington, N. Y.—Huntington Seed & Floral Co., 1050 Third avenue.

New York, N. Y.—Basket Flower Shop, succeeding E. M. Seixas Co.

Doylestown, Pa.—Oscar Snedeker, Randall Building, West Oakland avenue.

Hamilton, O.—Federle's Flower Shop, Jefferson Theatre Building, Miss Catherine Federle, proprietor.

Chambersburg, Pa.—Byer Bros., removing to new store opposite Cumberland Valley, R. R. Station.

DURING RECESS.

Boston Florists' Bowling League.

Team scores recorded for October 28 are as follows:

Galvin,	1347..vs..Flower Ex.	1238
M. & M.,	1288..vs..Robinson,	1252
Co-op. Market,	1258..vs..Pansies,	1230
Zinn,	1840..vs..Carbone,	1311

Vittello high man with 304.

Standing of the Teams.

	Won	Lost
Galvin	14	2
Co-op. Market	12	4
Zinn	9	7
Pansies	8	8
Carbone	8	8
Flower Exch.	5	11
M. & M.	4	12
Robinson	4	12

Fred Solari has been appointed a regular man on the Zinn team and Nell Casey on the Pansy team.

Several prizes have been received from friends and others will be welcome. It is hoped that those who are disposed to contribute will do so at once so that the complete schedule may be issued.

NEWS NOTES

Cleveland, O.—Wm. Q. Potter has purchased the Cleveland branch of the McCallum Company, of Pittsburgh, Pa.

Pawtucket, R. I.—John W. Seamans, proprietor of the Quality Flower Shop, 144 Main street, has been missing since Oct. 22. So far as is known, his business has been good, and his home life was happy with his wife and eight-year-old daughter. He was last seen in the Masonic Building, where he had placed some palms and foliage for stage decorations.

NEWS NOTES.

Hiddie Village, N. Y.—Joseph Klingenbeck has enlarged and improved his store at Metropolitan avenue and Bay Harbor road. A new front, with large plate glass windows, adds much to the appearance of the place.

Asheville, N. C.—A. C. Whitney has charge of the Idlewild Floral Company while David Lashley is recovering from injuries suffered in collapse of some building operations recently. It is stated that Mr. Lashley is not much improved. Mr. Whitney has had five years experience with the company.

NEWS ITEMS FROM EVERYWHERE

WASHINGTON.

Sealed proposals will be received at the office of the Supervising Architect, Treasury Building, Washington, D. C., until November 13, for planting trees, shrubs. etc., on the grounds of the Federal Building at Steelton, Pa. Drawings and specifications may be had on application to the custodian of the building or at the Washington office.

The Interstate Commerce Commission has ordered the Atchison, Topeka & Santa Fe and other railroads to apply the fourth class rate, with a minimum carload weight of 15,000 pounds, to all future shipments of sphagnum moss from City Point, Mather, Sparta, Tomah, and other points in the State of Wisconsin taking the same rates, to Oklahoma City, Okla., and has condemned the charge under the fifth class rating, with a minimum carload weight of 24,000 pounds as unreasonable. This action was taken on the complaint of the Barteldes Seed Company, of Lawrence, Kansas, and a traffic organization of Oklahoma City.

Nursery stock from Geneva, Dansville, and Brighton, N. Y.; North Abington, Mass., and Dresher, Pa., will hereafter take a rate of 37 cents per hundred pounds in carload lots, and 68 cents per hundred pounds in less than carload lots, to Lakeland, Minn. Wooden tree labels from Derry, N. H., will also take these rates. The L. L. May Company, of St. Paul, Minn., had filed a complaint with the Interstate Commerce Commission attacking the rates assessed by the railroads as being considerable higher than those applied to similar shipments to Stillwater, Minn. The Commission concurred and ordered the railroads to place the above quoted rates in effect on or before December 30, 1915.

One of the most successful chrysanthemum shows in the history of the Department of Agriculture has been in progress in the greenhouses at the north side of the grounds. An innovation this year is the lighting of the show after the hours usually observed for closing. Many of the exhibits are very noteworthy. Among the new varieties is Queen Mary white, and Mrs. William H. Walker sulphur yellow. It is said that this is better than either the Bob Pulling or Mrs. R. C. Pulling which were declared to be the best yellows at last year's show. James Wilson, white, shows fine form this year. William Saunders, bronze, is exceptionally good, and Amarantha is also worthy of mention.

A number of very excellent window displays were made last week for All Hallowe'en. At Gude Bros. store the window was banked with cornstalks and in the center yere placed very attractive baskets of flowers. At the store of George C. Shaffer pumpkins were hollowed out and filled with asters, small chrysanthemums and other flowers and laid on a moss covered floor. At the back of the window were standards of cornstalks and a rustic fence went across the entire width. One of the best of the windows was that of J. H. Small & Sons, where Old Mother Goose in appropriate costume and perched on a broom as if flying towards the skies was the central figure. Back and at the sides of this were palms, ferns, high standards of cornstalks, and vases of attractive looking chrysanthemums forming a sort of semi-circle within which had been heaped a large number of pumpkins.

BOSTON.

Ed Stout has severed his connection with the Boston Rose Company.

The Retail Florists' Club held its annual dinner at the Hotel Bellevue on Tuesday evening, November 2.

W. E. Turner, of Billerica, is helping toward the growing popularity of the pansy as a florists' cut flower by sending to market blooms of superb strain.

The Gorney brothers have bought out the Houghton interests in the Houghton-Gorney Company, retail florists on Tremont street. The old firm name will be retained.

J. A. Nelson, of Framingham, is in the hospital suffering from a very severe case of shingles. He has been ill two weeks and is getting along as well as could be expected with this vicious disease.

The Horticultural Club, of Boston, met at the Parker House, on Wednesday evening, November 3. An interesting discussion on the comparative advisability of fall and spring planting of trees, shrubs and hardy herbaceous plants was participated in by experts on the subject. Chrysanthemums from S. J. Goddard adorned the banquet table.

NEW YORK.

William Badgley, of the firm of Badgley & Bishop, was taken to the hospital on Sunday night to be operated on for appendicitis.

The funeral of Mrs. Victor S. Dorval at Woodside was largely attended by members of the florists and gardener fraternity on Friday, Oct. 29, among those from a distance being J. F. Huss of Hartford, Conn., a lifelong friend of Mr. and Mrs. Dorval. Many beautiful floral tributes were sent to the funeral.

The two veterans, John I. Raynor and John R. Weir, were overheard congratulating each other on having passed another birthday aniversary—Raynor on October 28 and Weir on October 29. These two have seen many changes and vicissitudes in the flower trade since their first skirmish as seller and buyer respectively.

Cincinnati—Last week the E. G. Hill Floral Co. gave a very successful chrysanthemum exhibition at the Lyric Theatre and in their store. L. H. Kyrk, after returning from his recent trip spoke in the highest terms of the appearance of the places of L. Frank & Sons, Portland, Ind., and Sam Bakon, Kalamazoo, Mich.

CHICAGO.

Earnest Farley is now with the Chicago Carnation Co.

Wm. J. Smyth spent the week end at his summer home in Antioch, Ill.

Chrysanthemum shows at the parks are now on and conservatories are open evenings.

Gus Pappas states that he will spend most of his time in Chicago hereafter and take charge of The Alpha.

Mrs. Russell rose has now started on its second season of being second in price to American Beauty only.

R. L. Nelson is the proprietor of a new retail store at 1528 E. 51st street. The firm is known as the Beach Flower Co.

Harry Rowe has taken a lease on the store at 123 N. Wabash avenue from Nov. 1st to May 1st and will open a retail store there.

The partitions are being put in the LeMoyne building and J. A. Budlong and the Chicago Flower Growers' Association expect to move in next week.

A. C. Kohlbrandt was hardly through receiving congratulations on being grandfather when the little one died and condolences were in order instead.

H. Koster, of Boskoop, Holland, was here on his way home from San Francisco, where he was sent by his government to inspect their part in the exposition.

Among the week's visitors was D. W. Dumser, who is settling his father's estate at Elgin, Ill. He is now with S. W. Coggan, at Battle Creek, and says that his firm will soon move into a new store at 5 E. Main street.

A beautiful five-piece silver service is seen this week at Poehlmann Bros. It is offered by this firm for the most tasteful arrangement of a basket of cut flowers, at the Grand Floral Festival. The basket of flowers is each year becoming more popular.

The news of the sudden death of Geo. Economopoulos early Wednesday morning came as a shock to the trade, very few of whom knew of his illness. He was about the market as usual on Monday. A little later on the same day came the news that F. W. Timme, one of Chicago's pioneer florists, passed away. A more complete notice of both will be found in the obituary columns.

The store operated by Mrs. and Geo. Lubliner, at 36 S. Wabash avenue, has been purchased by Schiller, the Florist. The transfer includes all the fixtures and the lease on the store for three years. Miss Bert Schiller will have charge and will be assisted by Chas. Zinns. This store will make a feature of floral gifts for all occasions, something new. The Schillers now have three stores, one on the west side, one on the north side and now the new Gift Shop in the loop.

PITTSBURGH.

George Hallam, the North Side florist, is seriously ill with pneumonia at his home in old Allegheny.

Julius W. Ludwig has just been elected a member of the Board of Directors of the Frosinn Singing Society.

Henry Meuschke, treasurer of the Ludwig Floral Company, has been appointed to take charge of the floral booth in connection with the bazaar to be held in December by the affiliated German societies.

Beginning with November 9th and ending on December 3rd, Norman Grubbs will conduct a number of exhibits and contests, principally corn and onions. Experts will be present from the Pennsylvania State College and award prizes for the quickest maturing and highest yielding products, and determine upon the varieties best adapted to this locality.

Among the commercial florists and private gardeners who will attend the Cleveland Flower Show next week are the following: W. Jarvis Smith, Joseph Koenig, Julius W. Ludwig, Gilbert Ludwig, E. C. Reineman, James Moore, E. C. Ludwig, DeForrest W. Ludwig, David Fraser, Aloysius Anthony Leach, Ernest R. Bolton, Ernest Guter, James Wiseman, Joseph Devlin, Henry B. Keiller, Fred Burki and William Usinger.

On last Tuesday evening a preliminary meeting was held in the office of the H. C. Frick greenhouse, to consider the advisability of organizing a club for all private gardeners and horticultural amateurs in Western Pennsylvania. About fifteen men were present and decided to call a meeting a little later in the East Liberty branch of Carnegie Library. Several financiers, owners of large estates and interested in the horticultural features thereof, have promised their co-operation and support.

ST. LOUIS

Mr. and Mrs. J. F. Ammann, of Edwardsville, celebrated their silver wedding on October 28. Many beautiful presents were sent by friends.

Miss Matilda Meinhardt, well known in the ladies' circle in the Society of

A VALENTINE HEART.

Used in a Window Scene at the Jones-Russell Co.'s Store, Cleveland, Ohio.

American Florists, surprised her many friends by her announcement of her engagement to Mr. William H. Boaz, a wealthy real estate man. Mr. Boaz is a widower with several children and has a beautiful home in Kirkwood.

The officers of the Florist Club, with the Spring Show Committee, and committees on the carnation meeting preparations, held a very interesting meeting October 28 at the home of Frank Windler. It was decided to call a special meeting of the club in order to place the regular meeting day one week later, as many of the members will be away attending flower shows at Cleveland and Chicago, so the next meeting will be held at the Missouri Botanical Garden, November 18. This will come right at the height of the Chrysanthemum Show at the garden, which opened this week to continue throughout the month. After the meeting the members sat down to a fine lunch, at which a great deal of talk on making interesting meetings was indulged in.

WHOLESALE FLOWER MARKETS — TRADE PRICES—Per 100
TO DEALERS ONLY

Roses	CINCINNATI Nov. 1		CHICAGO Nov. 1		BUFFALO Nov. 1		PITTSBURG Oct. 18	
Am. Beauty, Special	25.00	to 35.00	30.00	to 40.00	20.00	to 30.00	25.00	to 35.00
" " Fancy and Extra	20.00	to 25.00	20.00	to 25.00	12.00	to 20.00	18.00	to 20.00
" " No. 1	10.00	to 15.00	15.00	to 20.00	10.00	to 15.00	8.00	to 15.00
Russell, Hadley	4.00	to 8.00	5.00	to 15.00	8.00	to 15.00	8.00	to 10.00
Killarney, Richm'd, Hill'don, Ward	6.00	to 8.00	8.00	to 12.00	6.00	to 8.00	6.00	to 10.00
" " " " Ord.	3.00	to 5.00	3.00	to 5.00	3.00	to 5.00	...... to 4.00	
Arenburg, Radiance, Taft, Key, Ex.	6.00	to 8.00	8.00	to 10.00	6.00	to 8.00	6.00	to 10.00
" " " Ord.	3.00	to 5.00	5.00	to 5.00	4.00	to 6.00	...... to 4.00	
Ophelia, Mock, Sunburst, Extra	6.00	to 8.00	8.00	to 10.00	6.00	to 8.00	8.00	to 10.00
" " " Ordinary	3.00	to 5.00	3.00	to 5.00	3.00	to 4.00	...... to 6.00	
Carnations, Fancy	3.00	to 4.00	3.00	to 4.00	4.50	to 3.00	...... to 4.00	
Ordinary	......	to 2.00	2.50	to 3.00	2.00	to 2.50	2.00	to 3.00
Cattleyas	40.00	to 50.00	50.00	to 60.00	40.00	to 60.00	40.00	to 60.00
Dendrobium formosum	......	to	40.00	to 50.00	......	to	30.00	to 50.00
Lilies, Longiflorum	8.00	to 10.00	6.00	to 8.00	10.00	to 12.00	...... to 10.00	
Rubrum	4.00	to 8.00	......	to	3.00	to 4.00	...... to	
Lily of the Valley	3.00	to 4.00	4.00	to 6.00	......	to 4.00	3.00	to 5.00
Daisies	......	to	......	to .75	.75	to 1.00	...... to 1.00	
Violets	.50	to .75	.75	to 1.00	.50	to .75	...... to	
Snapdragon	......	to	4.00	to 5.00	3.00	to 6.00	...... to	
Chrysanthemums	8.00	to 30.00	10.00	to 35.00	6.00	to 20.00	10.00	to 25.00
Sweet Peas	......	to	1.00	to 2.00	.75	to 1.00	...... to	
Gardenias	......	to	25.00	to 30.00	......	to	...... to	
Adiantum	......	to	......	to 1.00	1.00	to 1.50	1.00	to 1.25
Smilax	12.50	to 15.00	12.00	to 16.00	......	to 12.50	15.00	to 15.00
Asparagus Plumosus, Strings (100)	25.00	to 50.00	40.00	to 50.00	......	to 50.00	35.00	to 50.00
" & Spren. (100 bchs.)	......	to 25.00	25.00	to 30.00	25.00	to 35.00	25.00	to 50.00

Flower Market Reports

BOSTON The market is tending downward as a result of the heavy influx of chrysanthemums which now begins to assume the proportions of an avalanche. Roses are feeling the stress and are in excess of requirements despite the optimistic assertion of a rising young salesman at the market that they are "scarce and kiting every minute." Carnations move slowly. Violets are not up to standard quality, the singles being particularly poor thus far. Calendulas and antirrhinums are in good supply now.

BUFFALO Quite a change in condition is noticed this week. Receipts are heavier all around and the demand has fallen off. The supply of everything has increased over 100 per cent. Chrysanthemums come in more plentifully, also carnations. Roses are a little overplentiful to hold up prices, though considerable business was had at the end of last week.

CHICAGO The increase in the amount of stock coming into this market, reported last week, still continues. Chrysanthemum season is at its height and the big flowers are coming in now in all colors. The rainy summer evidently has not affected most of the varieties for they are firm and come out of the boxes in splendid shape. Pompons are filling the counters. The early ones are late and the late ones are early, so they are here in great quantities now but will have a short season. Carnations are not so much in demand as before but stock is excellent and sales are fair. The supply of roses is also a little ahead of the demand which makes it easier for the retailer whose trade uses the cheaper grades of stock. The warm weather is not so favorable for violets. Sweet peas are coming in limited quantities. Long stemmed American Beauties are of splendid quality and the price keeps up accordingly. The supply of short and medium Beauties is not large. Potted chrysanthemums are offered at several of the wholesale houses.

CINCINNATI The market is pretty well supplied and is more than able to care for all present demands. Prices are not quite as high as they were. Chrysanthemums are in a very heavy supply. Roses are plentiful. The same is true of carnations and lilies. Dahlias and cosmos proved quite a factor in All Saints Day business and served to keep down the prices for this day. The first sweet peas came in last week. Many of the violet offerings are of the very highest quality.

NEW YORK The flower market is much more brilliant with stock this week than it is with customers and trade is very irregular. Chrysanthemums of all degrees are having their innings and are getting to that condition of abundance when a haggle is an indispensable part of every sale. Roses are coming in freely also and their movement is hampered for the time being by the overpowering presence of the chrysanthemums. Among the newer roses that stand out impressively as sure winners we must make mention of Stanley, which is a leading variety among Traendly & Schenck's daily receipts. It looks as though it might carry to California and back again in good order. Cattleyas are not over-plentiful and many of those seen are insignificant blooms. Violets do not come forward very fast and probably will not while the weather remains so warm. There is still more or less outdoor garden stock coming in, cosmos being especially good in this class. Lilies, carnations and lily of the valley are normal and call for no special mention at this time. Callas are beginning to appear here and there.

PHILADELPHIA What little change has taken place in the market during the past week may be summed up in a few words. Business demand remained about on an even keel but supplies with a few exceptions were much larger and so the general average of prices has declined. The increase in supplies is especially pronounced in chrysanthemums and carnations. Roses also come in more freely but not to such a degree. The most draggy on the rose list have been the Killarneys, both pinks and whites. Beauties and Russells go better and there is a good demand for Hoosier and Hadley among the reds. Another favorite red to be seen around is Leonard's thirty-three—whatever that is! Maybe some old variety that Leonard is keeping the real name of under his hat for the time being. Richmond seems to be down and out in this locality—not that the public don't like it, but that the growers refuse to grow anything that fails to show square-foot record the year 'round. The Polyantha class seem to be wonders when it comes to keeping qualities. We have seen some lots two and three weeks in the cooling rooms still fresh and

(Continued on page 615)

WHOLESALE FLOWER MARKETS — TRADE PRICES—Per 100 TO DEALERS ONLY

	BOSTON Nov. 4		ST. LOUIS Nov. 1		PHILA. Nov. 1	
Roses						
Am. Beauty, Special	12.00 to	25.00	20.00 to	25.00	20.00 to	25.00
" " Fancy and Extra	8.00 to	10.00	10.00 to	15.00	12.00 to	18.00
" " No. 1	3.00 to	5.00	5.00 to	8.00	6.00 to	10.00
Russell, Hadley	4.00 to	12.00	5.00 to	20.00	4.00 to	20.00
Killarney, Richmond, Hillingdon, Ward, Extra	4.00 to	6.00	6.00 to	8.00	4.00 to	8.00
" " " " Ordinary	1.00 to	3.00	3.00 to	4.00	2.00 to	3.00
Arenburg, Radiance, Taft, Key, Extra	4.00 to	6.00	...... to		4.00 to	8.00
" " " " Ordinary	1.00 to	3.00	...... to		2.00 to	3.00
Ophelia, Mock, Sunburst, Extra	4.00 to	8.00	6.00 to	8.00	5.00 to	10.00
" " " Ordinary	1.00 to	3.00	2.00 to	4.00	1.00 to	4.00
Carnations, Fancy	1.50 to	2.00	2.00 to	3.00	...... to	2.00
" Ordinary	1.00 to	1.50	.75 to	1.00	1.00 to	2.00
Cattleyas	20.00 to	40.00	35.00 to	50.00	25.00 to	40.00
Dendrobium formosum	...... to	25.00	...... to		25.00 to	50.00
Lilies, Longiflorum	4.00 to	8.00	12.00 to	15.00	6.00 to	10.00
" **Rubrum**	...... to	3.00	4.00 to	6.00	3.00 to	4.00
Lily of the Valley	2.00 to	4.00	3.00 to	4.00	2.00 to	4.00
Daisies	.50 to	1.00	.25 to	.50	.50 to	1.00
Violets	.40 to	.60	.25 to	.50	.25 to	.50
Snapdragon	1.00 to	3.00	3.00 to	5.00	8.00 to	5.00
Chrysanthemums	1.00 to	17.00	4.00 to	25.00	6.00 to	25.00
Sweet Peas	...... to	1.00	.50 to	.75	.50 to	.75
Gardenias	20.00 to	25.00	...... to		20.00 to	25.00
Adiantum	...... to	1.00	1.00 to	1.25	...... to	1.00
Smilax	12.00 to	16.00	12.00 to	15.00	15.00 to	20.00
Asparagus Plumosus, Strings (100)	25.00 to	50.00	35.00 to	50.00	...... to	50.00
" **& Spren.** (100 Bchs.)	25.00 to	35.00	20.00 to	35.00	15.00 to	50.00

Flower Market Reports
(Continued from page 613)

fragrant. Sweet Marie is especially notable in that connection. They say the ladies like a bunch of these for corsage wear as well as they do a bunch of cattleyas. Gardenias continue scarce. They say they dropped their buds in September, which accounts for the scarcity. We fancy there's another reason — too many grown in recent years and the result was "a lemon." Now the pendulum has swung to the other extreme. The best of the chrysanthemums now arriving are Razer, Enguehart, McNeice and Chieftain; a few good Bonnaffon also which is unusually early for that fine variety. There is an orange yellow one called Strafford that is in great vogue. It is only medium size but a great handler and keeper. Calendula and mignonette are among the new minor items that have made their advent; also a few cypripediums. Orchids generally are not so redundant as they were and better prices are being realized.

PITTSBURGH The bright sunny days are producing quantities of flowers of practically all kinds, the market value still remaining about the same for all. However, the legitimate trade is feeling the effect of the market gardeners, who are disposing of their chrysanthemums and other blooms at less than the wholesale prices. There are plenty of home-grown lilies and roses and fine fancy dahlias continue to come in from the New Jersey producers. Hallowe'en was never as generally and elaborately observed as this year, and consequently brought large compensation to the dispensers of Southern smilax, and artificial autumn leaves.

SAN FRANCISCO The continuation of summery weather is held responsible for the increased supplies of flowers which have been arriving the past week, also for the slight falling off in retail business. Everybody who can possibly do so is off for the exposition now that the close is drawing near and rain can be expected any day. The abundance of chrysanthemums overshadows everything else in the market and they have not been cleaning up so well the last few days as they did previously, although the quality is fully as good as earlier in the season, and new varieties continue to arrive. The only ground for complaint is the oversupply. Quantities are now being shipped and effort is being made to stimulate this demand in order to relieve the local market. Pompons are still offered freely, both cut and potted. As other potted plants are rather scarce, these are meeting with considerable popularity. Dahlias are holding out remarkably well, and for this late in the year show very good quality. There is no longer a cry of shortage of roses. with the exception possibly of Cecile Bruner, which has a big call both locally and for shipping. A good many violets are being shipped also. There are plenty orchids for all requirements, and the demand is fairly good. A few callas made their appear-

ance the past week, but the quantity was too limited for them to be much of a feature.

ST. LOUIS The commission men say the market was all that could be expected the last week, but are looking for a greatly increased supply this week owing to the very warm weather which is bringing out the stuff in big lots. The increased supply of chrysanthemums has caused the downfall of roses and carnations and the market is crowded up with these. Other flowers are all in plenty and trade is very light.

WASHINGTON The glut of chrysanthemums which now prevails has worked havoc with the flower market generally and all other stock is in over supply. There are fewer local roses coming in, but there are more than enough roses to fill all demands. Lily of the valley and longiflorum lilies are no longer reported as scarce. The warm weather has prevented a ready movement of single violets, which are now coming in fine shape,

as well as of the doubles which made their appearance last week. Sweet peas are again to be had and there is a small offering of yellow daisies. Orchids are no longer in oversupply and sold well during the week. Up to this time the frost has not been severe enough to clear the market of outdoor flowers and these are quite a factor in the day's business. Plenty of carnations are now to be had. American Beauty roses are selling better. Some very fine snapdragon was offered during the week.

BELGIAN ENTERPRISE.

McHutchison & Co. received from Belgium last week 458 packages of azaleas, etc., per steamers Ryndam and Oosterdyk. This week they received 666 packages more per S. S. Martensdyk and Rotterdam. This list excludes shipments of Holland origin. Considering the position of the Belgian growers, the difficulties of getting permits to ship—first from the British and then from the German authorities, the problem of getting transportation, etc., the Belgian growers certainly deserve great credit for their energy and resourcefulness.

Philadelphia—There are said to be twenty-two applicants for the position of landscape gardener for Fairmount Park to succeed the late Oglesby Paul. Most of them are high-class men and eminently fitted to fill the position. Consequently it will probably turn on a matter of either family or political influence or both, so that merit need not feel bad if it does not happen to have enough of these two important ingredients to land on top. Merit may perhaps not have been clever enough to choose its own grandfather.

Buyer's Directory and Ready Reference Guide

Advertisements under this head, one cent a word.   Initials count as words.

Display advertisers in this issue are also listed under this classification without charge. Reference to List of Advertisers will indicate the respective pages.

Buyers failing to find what they want in this list will confer a favor by writing us and we will try to put them in communication with reliable dealers.

ACCOUNTANT
R. Dysart, 40 State St., Boston.
For page see List of Advertisers.

APHINE
Aphine Mfg. Co., Madison, N. J.
For page see List of Advertisers.

APHIS PUNK
Nicotine Mfg. Co., St. Louis, Mo.
For page see List of Advertisers.

ASPARAGUS
Asparagus Sprengeri, fine 2¼-in., $2.50
per 100; $20.00 per 1000. Cash. M. F.
BYXBEE, Norwalk, Conn.

AUCTION SALES
The MacNiff Horticultural Co.,
New York City.
Plant and Bulb Sales by Auction.
For page see List of Advertisers.

Elliott Auction Co., New York City.
For page see List of Advertisers.

AZALEAS
P. Ouwerkerk, Hoboken, N. J.
For page see List of Advertisers.

BAY TREES
August Rolker & Sons, New York.
For page see List of Advertisers.

BEDDING PLANTS
A. N. Pierson, Inc., Cromwell, Conn.
For page see List of Advertisers.

R. Vincent, Jr. & Sons Co.,
White Marsh, Md.
For page see List of Advertisers.

BEGONIAS
Thomas Roland, Nahant, Mass.
For page see List of Advertisers.

		Per 100
BEGONIA LORRAINE,	2½ in......	$12.00
	3 in......	20.00
	4 in......	35.00
	5 in......	50.00
BEGONIA CINCINNATI,	2½ in......	15.00
	3 in......	25.00
	3½ in......	30.00
	4½ in......	40.00
JULIUS ROEHRS CO., Rutherford, N. J.		

BOILERS
Kroeschell Bros. Co., Chicago.
For page see List of Advertisers.

King Construction Co., North Tonawanda,
N. Y.
"King Ideal" Boiler.
For page see List of Advertisers.

Lord & Burnham Co., New York City.
For page see List of Advertisers.

Hitchings & Co., New York City.

BOXES—CUT FLOWER FOLDING
Edwards Folding Box Co., Philadelphia.
For page see List of Advertisers.

Folding cut flower boxes, the best made.
Write for list. HOLTON & HUNKEL CO.,
Milwaukee, Wis.

BOX TREES
BOX TREES—Standards, Pyramids and
Bush, in various sizes. Price List on de-
mand. JULIUS ROEHRS CO., Rutherford,
N. J.

Breck-Robinson Nursery Co., Lexington,
Mass.

BULBS AND TUBERS
Arthur T. Boddington Co., Inc.,
New York City.
For page see List of Advertisers.

J. M. Thorburn & Co., New York City
Wholesale Price List of High Class Bulbs.
For page see List of Advertisers.

Ralph M. Ward & Co., New York City.
Lily Bulbs.
For page see List of Advertisers.

John Lewis Childs, Flowerfield, L. I., N. Y.
For page see List of Advertisers.

August Rolker & Sons, New York City.
Holland and Japan Bulbs.
For page see List of Advertisers.

R. & J. Farquhar & Co., Boston, Mass.
For page see List of Advertisers.

S. S. Skidelsky & Co., Philadelphia, Pa.
For page see List of Advertisers.

Chas. Schwake & Co., New York City.
Horticultural Importers and Exporters.
For page see List of Advertisers.

A. Henderson & Co., Chicago, Ill.
For page see List of Advertisers.

Burnett Bros., 98 Chambers St., New York.

Henry F. Michell Co., Philadelphia, Pa.
For page see List of Advertisers.

Joseph Breck & Sons Corp., Boston, Mass.
For page see List of Advertisers.

Fottler, Fiske, Rawson Co., Boston, Mass.

C. KEUR & SONS, HILLEGOM, Holland.
Bulbs of all descriptions. Write for prices.
NEW YORK Branch. 8-10 Bridge St.

CANNAS
Canna Specialists.
Send for Canna book.
THE CONARD & JONES COMPANY,
West Grove, Pa.

CARNATIONS.
Wood Bros., Fishkill, N. Y.
For page see List of Advertisers.

F. R. Pierson, Tarrytown, N. Y.
Carnation Matchless.
For page see List of Advertisers.

F. Dorner & Sons Co., Lafayette, Ind.
For page see List of Advertisers.

Jas. Vick's Sons, Rochester, N. Y.
Field Grown Plants.
For page see List of Advertisers.

Littlefield & Wyman, North Abington, Mass.
New Pink Carnation, Miss Theo.
For page see List of Advertisers.

CARNATION STAPLES
Split carnations quickly, easily and
cheaply mended. Pillsbury's Carnation
Staple, 1000 for 35c.; 3000 for $1.00 post
paid. I. L. PILLSBURY, Galesburg, Ill.

Supreme Carnation Staples, for repairing
split carnations, 35c. per 1000; 3000 for
$1.00. F. W. WAITE, 85 Belmont Ave.,
Springfield, Mass.

CHRYSANTHEMUMS
Chas. H. Totty, Madison, N. J.
For page see List of Advertisers.

THE BEST 1915 NOVELTIES.
The Cream of 1914 Introductions.
The most popular Commercial and Exhibition kinds; also complete line of Pompons, Singles and Anemones. Trade list
on application. ELMER D. SMITH & CO.,
Adrian, Mich.

COCOANUT FIBRE SOIL
20th Century Plant Food Co., Beverly, Mass.
For page see List of Advertisers.

DAHLIAS
Send for Wholesale List of whole clumps
and separate stock; 40,000 clumps for sale.
Northboro Dahlia and Gladiolus Gardens,
J. L. MOORE, Prop, Northboro, Mass.

NEW PAEONY DAHLIA
John Wanamaker, Newest, Handsomest,
Best. New color, new form and new habit
of growth. Big stock of best cut-flower
varieties. Send list of wants to
PEACOCK DAHLIA FARMS, Berlin, N. J.

DECORATIVE PLANTS
Robert Craig Co., Philadelphia, Pa.
For page see List of Advertisers.

Woodrow & Marketos, New York City.
For page see List of Advertisers.

S. S. Skidelsky & Co., Philadelphia, Pa.
For page see List of Advertisers.

Bobbink & Atkins, Rutherford, N. J.
For page see List of Advertisers.

A. Leuthy & Co., Roslindale, Boston, Mass.
For page see List of Advertisers.

Araucarias, 7 in. pots, 3 to 5 tiers, $1.00
each; Cyclamen, 4 and 5 in. pots, 15c. and
25c. each; Primulas Obconica, 3 and 4 in.
pots, 5c. and 8c. each; Begonias Chatelaine,
5 in. pans, 20c. each; Begonias Luminosa,
4 and 5 in. pots, 10c. and 15c. each; Asp.
Sprengeri, 3 in. pots, $3.00 per 100; Asp.
Plumosus, 3 in. pots, $4.00 per 100; Table
Ferns, 2½ in. pots, $3.00 per 100; Jerusalem
Cherries, 4 in. pots, 6c. each; Jerusalem
Cherries, from field, 5 in. pots, 10c. each;
Var. Vincas, from field, $5.00 per 100. Write
for prices on Holland Bulbs of all kinds.
ROSENDALE NURSERY & GREEN-
HOUSES, Schenectady, N. Y.

FERNS
H. H Barrows & Son, Whitman, Mass.
For page see List of Advertisers.

Robert Craig Co., Philadelphia, Pa.
For page see List of Advertisers.

McHutchison & Co., New York City.
Ferns in Flats.
For page see List of Advertisers.

A. M. Davenport, Watertown, Mass.
Boston and Whitmani Ferns.
For page see List of Advertisers.

Roman J. Irwin, New York City.
Boston and Whitmani Ferns.
For page see List of Advertisers.

FERTILIZERS
20th Century Plant Food Co., Beverly, Mass.
Cocoanut Fibre Soil.
For page see List of Advertisers.

Stumpp & Walter Co., New York City.
Scotch Soot.
For page see List of Advertisers.

Chicago Feed & Fertilizer Co., Chicago, Ill.
Magic Manures.
For page see List of Advertisers.

Pulverized Manure Co., Chicago, Ill.
Wizard Brand Cattle Manure.

FLORISTS' LETTERS
Boston Florist Letter Co., Boston, Mass.
For page see List of Advertisers.

For List of Advertisers See Page 595

In writing to Advertisers kindly mention Horticulture

NURSERY STOCK

P. Ouwerkerk, Weehawken Heights, N. J.
For page see List of Advertisers.

W. & T. Smith Co., Geneva, N. Y.
For page see List of Advertisers

The D. Hill Nursery Co., Dundee, Ill.
Hill's Evergreens.
For page see List of Advertisers.

Bay State Nurseries, North Abington, Mass.
Hardy, Northern Grown Stock.
For page see List of Advertisers.

Bobbink & Atkins, Rutherford, N. J.
For page see List of Advertisers.

Framingham Nurseries, Framingham, Mass.
For page see List of Advertisers.

August Rolker & Sons, New York City.
For page see List of Advertisers.

NUT GROWING.

The Nut-Grower, Waycross, Ga.
For page see List of Advertisers.

ORCHID FLOWERS

Jas. McManus, New York, N. Y.
For page see List of Advertisers.

ORCHID PLANTS

Julius Roehrs Co., Rutherford, N. J.
For page see List of Advertisers.

Lager & Hurrell, Summit, N. J.
For page see List of Advertisers.

PALMS, ETC.

Robert Craig Co., Philadelphia, Pa.
For page see List of Advertisers.

August Rolker & Sons, New York City.
For page see List of Advertisers.

A. Leuthy & Co., Roslindale, Boston, Mass.
For page see List of Advertisers.

PANSY PLANTS

Pansy Plants, mixed varieties in bud and bloom, $15.00 per 1000. Cash. JAMES MOSS, Johnsville, Pa.

Pansy Plants for the benches, nice stocky plants, $5.00 per 1000, 5000 or more, $4.00 per 1000. Cash. JAMES MOSS, Johnsville, Pa.

PANSY SEED

Fottler, Fiske, Rawson Co., Boston, Mass.

PEONIES

Peonies. The world's greatest collection. 1200 sorts. Send for list. C. BETSCHER, Canal Dover, O.

PECKY CYPRESS BENCHES

A. T. Stearns Lumber Co., Boston, Mass.

PIPE AND FITTINGS

Kroeschell Bros. Co., Chicago.
For page see List of Advertisers.

King Construction Company, N. Tonawanda, N. Y.
Shelf Brackets and Pipe Hangers.
For page see List of Advertisers.

PLANT AND BULB IMPORTS

Chas. Schwake & Co., New York City.
For page see List of Advertisers.

August Rolker & Sons, New York City.
For page see List of Advertisers.

PLANT TRELLISES AND STAKES

Seele's Tieless Plant Stakes and Trellises. H. D. SEELE & SONS, Elkhart, Ind.

PLANT TUBS

H. A. Dreer, Philadelphia, Pa.
"Riverton Special."

PLANTS WANTED

C. C. Trepel, New York City.
For page see List of Advertisers.

RAFFIA

McHutchison & Co., New York, N. Y.
For page see List of Advertisers.

RHODODENDRONS

P. Ouwerkerk, Hoboken, N. J.
For page see List of Advertisers.

Framingham Nurseries, Framingham, Mass.
For page see List of Advertisers.

RIBBONS AND CHIFFONS

S. S. Pennock-Meehan Co., Philadelphia, Pa.
For page see List of Advertisers.

ROSES

Poehlmann Bros. Co., Morton Grove, Ill.
For page see List of Advertisers.

P. Ouwerkerk, Hoboken, N. J.
For page see List of Advertisers.

Robert Craig Co., Philadelphia, Pa.
For page see List of Advertisers.

W. & T. Smith Co., Geneva, N. Y.
American Grown Roses.
For page see List of Advertisers.

Bay State Nurseries, North Abington, Mass.
For page see List of Advertisers.

August Rolker & Sons, New York City.
For page see List of Advertisers.

Framingham Nurseries, Framingham, Mass.
For page see List of Advertisers.

A. N. Pierson, Inc., Cromwell, Conn.
For page see List of Advertisers.

THE CONARD & JONES COMPANY,
Rose Specialists.
West Grove, Pa. Send for offers.

SCALECIDE

B. G. Pratt Co., New York City.

SEASONABLE PLANT STOCK

R. Vincent, Jr. & Sons Co., White Marsh, Md.
For page see List of Advertisers.

SEED GROWERS

California Seed Growers' Association.
San Jose, Cal.
For page see List of Advertisers.

SEEDS

Carter's Tested Seeds.
Seeds with a Pedigree.
Boston, Mass., and London, England.
For page see List of Advertisers.

Kelway & Son,
Langport, Somerset, England.
Kelway's Celebrated English Strain Garden Seeds.
For page see List of Advertisers.

Joseph Breck & Sons, Boston, Mass.
For page see List of Advertisers.

J. Bolgiano & Son, Baltimore, Md.
For page see List of Advertisers.

A. T. Boddington Co., Inc., New York City.
For page see List of Advertisers.

Chas. Schwake & Co., New York City.
For page see List of Advertisers.

Michell's Seed House, Philadelphia, Pa.
For page see List of Advertisers.

W. Atlee Burpee & Co., Philadelphia, Pa.
For page see List of Advertisers.

R. & J. Farquhar & Co., Boston, Mass.
For page see List of Advertisers.

SEEDS—Continued

J. M. Thorburn & Co., New York City.
For page see List of Advertisers.

S. Bryson Ayres Co., Independence, Mo.
Sweet Peas.
For page see List of Advertisers.

Loechner & Co., New York City.
For page see List of Advertisers.

Ant. C. Zvolanek, Lompoc, Cal.
Winter Flowering Sweet Pea Seed.
For page see List of Advertisers.

S. S. Skidelsky & Co., Philadelphia, Pa.
For page see List of Advertisers.

W. E. Marshall & Co., New York City.
Seeds, Plants and Bulbs.
For page see List of Advertisers.

August Rolker & Sons, New York City.
For page see List of Advertisers.

Burnett Bros., 98 Chambers St., New York.
For page see List of Advertisers.

Fottler, Fiske, Rawson Co., Boston, Mass.
Seeds for the Florist.

SKINNER IRRIGATION SYSTEM

Skinner Irrigation Co., Brookline, Mass.
For page see List of Advertisers.

SPHAGNUM MOSS

Live Sphagnum moss, orchid peat and orchid baskets always on hand. LAGER & HURRELL, Summit, N. J.

SPRAYING MATERIALS

B. G. Pratt Co., New York City.

STANDARD THERMOMETERS

Standard Thermo Co., Boston, Mass.
For page see List of Advertisers.

STOVE PLANTS

Orchids—Largest stock in the country—Stove plants and Crotons, finest collection. JULIUS ROEHRS CO., Rutherford, N. J.

SWEET PEA SEED

Arthur T. Boddington Co., Inc.,
New York City.
Winter Flowering Sweet Peas.
For page see List of Advertisers.

Ant. C. Zvolanek, Lompoc, Calif.
Gold Medal of Honor Winter Orchid Sweet Peas.
For page see List of Advertisers.

S. Bryson Ayres Co.,
Sunnyslope, Independence, Mo.
For page see List of Advertisers.

VEGETABLE PLANTS

R. Vincent, Jr. & Sons Co.,
White Marsh, Md.
For page see List of Advertisers.

VENTILATING APPARATUS

The Advance Co., Richmond, Ind.
For page see List of Advertisers.

The John A. Evans Co., Richmond, Ind.
For page see List of Advertisers.

VERMICIDES

Aphine Mfg. Co., Madison, N. J.
For page see List of Advertisers.

VIOLETS

200 Princess of Wales Violet Plants, field grown, $5.00 per 100. Cash. CHAS. H. GREEN, Spencer, Mass.

WIRED TOOTHPICKS

W. J. Cowee, Berlin, N. Y.
For page see List of Advertisers

For List of Advertisers See Page 595

New Offers In This Issue

ANNOUNCEMENT OF INCORPORA-
TION.
   A. L. Young & Co., New York City.
For page see List of Advertisers.

ASPARAGUS PLUMOSUS NANUS
SEED.
W. H. Elliott, Brighton, Mass.
For page see List of Advertisers.

AZALEAS, PALMS, ARAUCARIAS.
Thomas Cogger, Melrose, Mass.
For page see List of Advertisers.

CATALOGUE OF VENTILATING AP-
PARATUS AND GREENHOUSE
FITTINGS.
Advance Co., Richmond, Ind.
For page see List of Advertisers.

FLOWERS BY TELEGRAPH.
Knoble Bros. Cleveland, Ohio.
For page see List of Advertisers.

HYACINTHS AND NARCISSUS.
F. R. Pierson, Tarrytown, N. Y.
For page see List of Advertisers.

LILIUM LONGIFLORUM FORMO-
SUM AND NARCISSUS BULBS.
Arthur T. Boddington Co. Inc. New York
City.
For page see List of Advertisers.

MEYER'S T. BRAND GIGANTEUMS.
Corp. of Chas. F. Meyer, New York City.
For page see List of Advertisers.

MICHELL'S FLOWER SEEDS.
Henry F. Michell Co., Philadelphia, Pa.
For page see List of Advertisers.

ROSE MRS. CHAS. RUSSELL.
S. S. Pennock-Meehan Co. Philadelphia, Pa.
For page see List of Advertisers.

SIM'S GOLD MEDAL PANSIES.
William Sim, Cliftondale, Mass.
For page see List of Advertisers.

THE HOME OF THE SCOTTII FERN.
John Scott, Brooklyn, N. Y.
For page see List of Advertisers.

WHOLESALE FLORIST.
J. K. Allen, 118 West 28th St., New York
City.
For page see List of Advertisers.

CLUBS AND SOCIETIES

FLORISTS' CLUB OF PHILADELPHIA.

The regular monthly meeting was held on Nov. 2nd. Exhibits consisted of a new rose from the Florex Gardens much after the style of Russell, but fuller; and five seedlings from Edward Towill showing quite some promise in the future progress of the Queen of Flowers.

The main entertainment of the evening was the debate: "Is it for the benefit of the business at large to keep flower vendors off the street?" For two hours the wit, wisdom and philosophy waxed and waned but there was not one dull moment and the crowded meeting was so primed that the chair had finally to call time on them. As one member expressed it to the writer after the meeting—it was as good as two hours at Keith's.

John Westcott, Robert Craig, Charles H. Grakelow, Harry S. Betz, Charles E. Meehan, Robert Kift, Alfred M. Campbell and Mr. Zeiger were the star orators of the occasion.

On the question finally being put to a vote the result was about eight to one in favor of removing the present restrictions against selling posies on the street and a petition will be sent to the authorities to that effect showing that that body was not properly informed some years ago as to the sentiment of the trade when it passed a restrictive ordinance on the subject.

The essay committee presented their program for February, March and April which was adopted as follows:

FEBRUARY:—"A Review of the newer Carnations: their value and promise: as shown by tests of the past season." Assigned to Robert T. Brown of the Cottage Gardens Co., New York.

Members are requested to bring to this meeting anything new or interesting, especially in Carnations—as this will be distinctly "Carnation night"—February being the month this flower shows the zenith of its splendor.

MARCH:—"The modern winter-flowering Sweet Pea—its origin and development to date." Assigned to Howard M. Earl, manager for W. Atlee Burpee & Co., pioneer developers of the Sweet Pea in America; and supplemented by Alban Harvey, of Brandywine Summit, one of the most successful commercial growers of the Sweet Pea in this locality—with remarks and exhibits of the most up-to-date varieties.

Exhibits are also requested from the Wideener conservatories, and all other growers who have anything interesting to show in the Sweet Pea.

APRIL:—"A symposium on the newer Roses: what they think of those they have tested during the past few seasons." Assigned to Stephen Mortensen, Edward Towill and Martin Samtman.

Richness and variety in the rose family (from a commercial cut flower standpoint) has made great progress recently. A dozen years ago we had about five varieties—now we have nearly thirty to choose from.

Samuel S. Pennock, president of the American Rose Society, is hereby authorized to request in the name of the club, a donation of twelve blooms each of the different standard varieties available from the different growers and to stage same for the information and delight of our members and their friends. Any other member of the club who may have something new or interesting is also requested to exhibit, so as to make this a gala night for "The Queen of Flowers."

Meetings Next Week

Monday, Nov. 8.

Cleveland Florists' Club, Hollenden Hotel, Cleveland, Ohio.
Gardeners' and Florists' Club of Baltimore, Florist Exchange Hall.
New York Florist Club, Grand Opera House, New York City.
Rochester Florists' Association, 96 Main St. East, Rochester, N. Y.

Tuesday, Nov. 9.

Florists' and Gardeners' of Holyoke and Northampton, Mass.
Newport Horticultural Society, Newport, R. I.

Wednesday, Nov. 10.

Cincinnati Florists' Society, Jabez Elliott Flower Market, Cincinnati, O.
Dutchess County Horticultural Society, Poughkeepsie, N. Y.
Lenox Horticultural Society, Lenox, Mass.
Morris County Florists' and Gardeners' Society, Madison, N. J.
Nassau County Horticultural Society, Pembroke Hall, Glen Cove, N. Y.

Thursday, Nov. 11.

Menlo Park Horticultural Society, Menlo Park, Calif.
New London Horticultural Society, Municipal Bldg., New London, Conn.

Friday, Nov. 12.

Connecticut Horticultural Society, County Bldg., Hartford, Conn.
Westchester and Fairfield Horticultural Society, Doran's Hall, Greenwich, Conn.

Saturday, Nov. 13.

Massachusetts Horticultural Society, Boston, Mass.

The program for the December and January meetings has already been reported in HORTICULTURE. Altogether the prospect for a lively winter in the pioneer Florists' Club of the country is good.

When you can get a man like John Westcott, who will be seventy-five if he lives to the 15th of next December, to get up and make a speech such as he did at this meeting almost on a minute's notice, you can bet there's a whole lot of life in the venerable organization yet. He surprised us all and covered himself with glory.

Liveliest and best attended meeting in many a long day and at no expense to the club for free eats or drinks; and the December meeting will be still better. Don't miss it.

The New Haven County Horticultural Society held a very interesting meeting last week. It was the summing up of the work at the annual exhibition in September. The president of the society, Herbert F. Clark, gave out hundreds of dollars in bank checks and hundreds of dollars in other valuable premiums to the fortunate exhibitors. In turn President Clark was presented with the Hitchings cup which he had won. This cup was presented by the secretary of the society, W. E. McIntosh, who took occasion to praise the president for the very fine blooms which he had grown.

NEW YORK WHOLESALE FLORISTS' PROTECTIVE ASSOCIATION.

The annual banquet of this association was held at the Hotel Breslin in New York on Thursday, October 28, and was a great success. To the committee in charge, A. H. Langjahr, P. J. Smith and Wm. P. Ford, great credit was accorded for the able manner in which all details were arranged. The banquet room was very tastefully decorated with autumn leaves and yellow chrysanthemums, and on the large table was a centre-piece of Hoosier Beauty roses. Each member wore a gardenia boutonnierre. A fine musical programme added to the enjoyment of the repast. Coffee and cigars being served, P. J. Smith introduced Walter F. Sheridan as master of ceremonies, who ably officiated, as might be expected of him. He first called upon Frank H. Traendly, president of the association, and to the great surprise of that gentleman, proceeded to pass sentence upon him for all the good he had done for the association during the eight years he had been at its head. After compelling his attention until everything in the way of nice things had been said of him, he presented him, on behalf of the association, with a beautiful gold clock and candelabra to match, as a token of the appreciation in which he was held by his fellow-members, and of his faithful service as their presiding officer.

Mr. Traendly, who for once in his life was taken completely unawares, upon recovering his composure, first assured himself that the clock was running on good time and was in good working order, then feelingly expressed his thanks, and those of Mrs. Traendly to use his best endeavors to still further advance the interests of the association, and to continue its efficiency. Each member present added a few words of appreciation to those of the toastmaster, and, it might be said, increased the discomfiture of the gentleman under sentence.

After these proceedings, a special meeting of the association was held, at which business coming properly before the association was disposed of. Much enthusiasm over the work of the organization was evinced, and many suggestions were made looking to a further extension of its scope. The impression prevailed that there could be no better organized body of business men today than that found in the Wholesale Florists' Protective Association, whose only aim is to improve, if possible, the wholesale market conditions in New York, and to advance and protect the interests of its members in every way. The secretary-manager, Ward W. Smith, was also warmly commended for the able manner in which he had fulfilled the duties of his office. At the close, announcement was made that Mr. Traendly had that day been appointed by President Welch a member of the Society of American Florists' Committee on National Credits and Collections Bureau.

SOCIETY OF AMERICAN FLORISTS AND ORNAMENTAL HORTICULTURISTS.

At a meeting of the National Flower Show Committee, held in Philadelphia, Pa., on Wednesday, October 20th, the following medals and certificates were awarded upon the report of the judges of the Trade Exhibition at the San Francisco Convention last August:

H. Bayersdorfer & Co., Philadelphia—Certificate of Merit for new and novel florists' baskets and supplies.

M. Rice Co., Philadelphia—Honorable Mention for display of florists' accessories and novelties.

S. S. Pennock-Meehan Co., Philadelphia—Certificate of Merit for novel ribbons and baskets.

A. L. Randall Co., Chicago—Highly commended for florists' supplies.

Domoto Bros., San Francisco, Cal.—Bronze Medal for new double Hydrangeas.

Bayersdorfer & Co., Philadelphia—Bronze Medal for new and novel ideas in baskets.

Richard Diener, Colma, Cal.—Cultural Certificate for Gladioli.

The Ferneries, San Francisco, Cal.—Certificate of Merit for collection of Ferns and Palms.

Henry J. Kessel, San Francisco, Cal.—Honorable Mention for Fern Californica.

Superior Nursery Co., Los Angeles, Cal.—Certificate of Merit for Ferns.

Swiss Floral Co., Portland, Ore.—Honorable Mention for Petunias.

Herbert & Fleishauer, McMinnville, Ore.—Cultural Certificate for Asters.

Mrs. F. J. Reidy, San Jose, Cal.—Cultural Certificate for Dahlias.

J. A. Peterson & Son, Cincinnati, O.—Requested to show Begonia Mrs. J. A. Peterson again, at National Flower Show, Philadelphia.

John A. Evans Co., Richmond, Ind.—Bronze Medal for new detachable pipe hangers.

Advance Co., Richmond, Ind.—Certificate of Merit for ventilating apparatus and greenhouse accessories.

JOHN YOUNG, Sec'y.
53 West 28th St., New York.

OYSTER BAY (N. Y.) HORTICULTURAL SOCIETY.

The regular monthly meeting of the Oyster Bay, N. Y., Horticultural Society was held on Wednesday, October 27. The meeting room was a Flower Show in itself. The judges Messrs. Bell, Robertson and Gibson reported as follows: Chrysanthemums, s o c i e t y's prize, Jos. Robinson; celery, society's prize, Lewis Donelle; cauliflower, society's prize, Frank Petroccia; collection dahlias, Jos. Robinson, cultural certificate; roses, Ophelia, Wm. Ford, honorable mention; single chrysanthemums, Jas. Duthie, certificate of merit; Frank Kyle, honorable mention; J. Sorosick, thanks of society; Cosmos, J. Sorosick, thanks of society; dahlias, J. Sorosick, thanks of society; phlox, J. Sorosick, honorable mention; figs, A. Tanoski, thanks of society.

Exhibits for next meeting will be 50 violets, 12 roses, one variety, 3 heads lettuce.

A. R. KENNEDY, Sec'y.

MASSACHUSETTS AWARDS AT SAN FRANCISCO.

Following is the full list of the second (and final) seasonal awards to Massachusetts exhibitors in horticulture:

Forbes & Keith, New Bedford, collection of dahlias, grand prize; Francis A. Butts, dahlias, silver medal; seedling dahlias, silver medal.

R. & J. Farquhar & Co., Boston, collection of dahlias, medal of honor.

George H. Walker, Dighton, collection of dahlias, gold medal.

William Sim, Cliftondale, gladiolus America, gold medal.

B. Hammond Tracy, Wenham, collection of gladioli, gold medal.

Edward F. Dwyer & Sons, Lynn, collection of dahlias, silver medal.

Bay State Nurseries, North Abington, collection of hardy perennials, silver medal.

Cherry Hill Nurseries, West Newbury, herbaceous perennials, silver medal.

New England Nurseries, Bedford, herbaceous perennials, silver medal; asters, silver medal; Michaelmas daisies, silver medal.

GREENHOUSES BUILDING OR CONTEMPLATED.

Ogden, Utah.—State Industrial School, one house.

Westfield, N. Y.—Jas. H. Dann & Son, additions.

Mars, Pa.—E. C. Ludwig Co., bulb forcing house, 16 x 200.

San Francisco, Cal.—John Olson, 17th street, one house.

Trenton, N. J.—E. H. Frenking, Ingham avenue, one house.

Toledo, O.—Geo. Bayer & Son, two violet houses, each 25x130.

Old Bridge, N. J.—C. O. Wahrendorf, Brunswick Gardens, two houses.

Warren, Pa.—Daniel Offerle & Son, one house, near entrance to Oakland Cemetery.

Bar Harbor, Me.—R. Hall McCormich, Eden street and Central avenue, house, 19x50.

The Cincinnati Florists Society's regular meeting will be held at J. A. Peterson's place in Westwood on Monday, November 8th, at 4 P. M. Mr. Peterson expects to show lantern slides of his trip to California this summer.

MASSACHUSETTS AGRICULTURAL COLLEGE.

The Department of Floriculture is busily engaged making the final plans and arrangements for its Autumn Flower Show and Exhibition of Floral Arrangements. It has been decided to open the show on Sunday, November 7, from 2 until 10 P. M., in order that more people from the surrounding cities may have an opportunity to visit the show. The show will continue through Monday and Tuesday, November 8 and 9, being open from 10 A. M. to 10 P. M.

From the present indications it begins to look as if it would be necessary to use part of the second floor of the building in order to accommodate the various exhibits. Several of the florists in this section have offered to exhibit, for they fully understand the opportunity for advertising which this show with its free admission offers. Also several other members of the trade have signified their intention to send in exhibits of new varieties and other specialties, for they realize that the florists of this section are much interested in the show. A few of the private gardeners around the state are also intending to send something of interest. This is a show for everybody and space will be provided for anyone who wishes to send in anything of interest.

At the request of the Northampton and Holyoke Gardeners' and Florists' Club special classes, open only to their members, have been arranged. Much interest is being shown by the students in floriculture who are anticipating the competitions provided for them. Mr. Butler, of Northampton, will be on hand to give suggestions to the students in floral arrangement.

The chrysanthemums in the college greenhouses are coming along nicely and include some very fine blooms, so that a wealth of these flowers will be available. There will be a large exhibit of named varieties of the different types which should prove of interest to the growers. Chrysanthemums will be freely used in baskets, large vases, and as pot plants. Besides these and various floral arrangements the department will also have groups of house plants, Christmas plants, foliage plants, etc. There will be two large groups composed of foliage and flowering plants. There will be collections of books for amateur gardeners, of various types of ornamental containers for the home and other things of interest to the general public.

Once again the department wishes to invite one and all, and sincerely hopes that it may have an opportunity to welcome many of the florists and gardeners.

Notes.

Last Friday the formal dedication of Stockbridge Hall took place. Among the prominent speakers were W. H. Bowker, of Concord; W. Wheeler, Secretary of the State Board of Agriculture, and President K. L. Butterfield.

The floriculture department is placing exhibits in several classes at the Northampton and Holyoke Florists' and Gardeners' Club show in Holyoke this week.   A. S. T.

PATENTS GRANTED.

1,158,209. Plant Spraying Machine. Lewis Albert Hart, Binghamton, N. Y., assignor to Bateman Manufacturing Company, Grenloch, N. J., a corporation of New Jersey.

The side posts of Mr. Kropp's houses are all flat bars of guaranteed wrought iron which will greatly outlast steel.
Notice the way the pipe cross-tie is in turn tied to an intermediate purlin.

Two Pipe Framers, at Columbus, Ohio

FOR H. W. Kropp, we built three Ridge & Furrow houses 28x 190 feet and one 28x109 feet.
Mr. Kropp had some old time, narrow, wooden houses, which in their day had been money makers for his fathers. But they would not produce the kind of stock demanded to-day.

It was a case of build modern houses, or go out of the business. Of course growers don't go out of business. They keep getting into more and more business. It's the way the growers have of growing.

Hill and Dupre carry on their business under the name of the Indianola Floral Company. Their flower shop, in the heart of Columbus, is an attractive as it is prosperous looking.
In their two houses 28x190 feet and 12x81 feet, they grow a lot of their potted stock; carnations and ferns.
More and more, the shop owners are also owning their greenhouses.
It means just that much more profit for the shop owners.

One of the supply houses of the Indianola Floral Company. You get just a peek at the gable of the other house.

Lord & Burnham Co.

SALES OFFICES:

NEW YORK	BOSTON	PHILADELPHIA	CHICAGO	ROCHESTER	CLEVELAND
42nd Street Bldg.	Tremont Bldg.	Franklin Bank Bldg.	Rookery Bldg.	Granite Bldg.	Swetland Bldg.

TORONTO, CANADA, Royal Bank Bldg.
MONTREAL, CANADA, Transportation Bldg.　　　　FACTORIES : Irvington, N. Y.　Des Plaines, Ill.
　　　　　　　　　　　　　　　　　　　　　　　　　　　　　　St. Catharines, Canada.

FLOWER
SHOW
NUMBER

HORTICULTURE

Chrysanthemum Bob Pulling
One of the Best Novelties of the Year 1915

LIST OF ADVERTISERS

FOR BUYERS' DIRECTORY AND READY REFERENCE GUIDE
SEE PAGES 648, 649, 650, 651

NOTES ON CULTURE OF FLORISTS' STOCK
CONDUCTED BY

John J. M. Farrell

Questions by our readers in line with any of the topics presents on this page will be cordially received and promptly answered by Mr. Farrell. Such communications should invariably be addressed to the office of HORTICULTURE.
"If vain our toil, we ought to blame the culture, not the soil."—*Pope.*

Ardisias

These popular holiday plants should be kept from 50 to 55 degrees at night. If kept too warm and overhumid they will make a premature growth of foliage which is not wanted at this time. Turn the plants around frequently so that the sun may reach them on all sides. To develop the coloring of their berries, they require a sunny house and abundant ventilation. Give them plenty of room between so that the berries will have a chance to color up. It is important to look carefully to watering because when allowed to become too dry or too wet at the roots the plants will soon show permanent injury.

Callas

These plants when grown in pots soon exhaust the soil and should have some liquid manure once or twice a week. Those growing in beds or benches will not need feeding as yet but with the coming of spring when the beds are full of roots mulching and feeding must be resorted to. Fumigate with regularity for fly and thrips for these are difficult pests to eradicate when they have secured a firm foothold. Give a temperature of not less than 60 degrees at night. Dampen down the walks two or three times a day, especially when the temperature goes up with the sun-heat, for callas delight in a moist growing atmosphere. Those that are growing in pots soon dry out now so give them plenty of moisture at the roots.

Crotons

There is no excuse to have crotons overrun with mealy bug, thrips and red spider. Use the hose on them with proper force once or twice a week. To keep them symmetrical they should be turned around frequently. To develop their coloring they should have as much sunlight as they can possibly stand. Some varieties can not bear as much sun as others, which peculiarity can easily be noted and such plants given a little shade. Crotons like lots of heat so see that the temperature does not fall below 65 degrees at night with 10 to 15 degrees more with sunshine. If the plants are very much potbound their color can be intensified and the plants otherwise benefited by giving them some liquid manure about once a week. Plants that have grown too lanky or that are out of shape can be propagated by mossing now as well as at any other time of the year.

French Bulbs

Roman hyacinths and Paper White narcissus for early cutting must now be placed in heat to have them come in time for a trade not far off now. If the boxes are still in outside frames, in sheds or under the benches of a cool greenhouse, they must now be brought forward and the bulbs be gradually inured to a higher temperature, letting them have 45 degrees for four or five days, when real forcing may begin. But assuming that the boxes and pots were brought into greenhouses directly from outdoor trenches, that an abundance of roots were present at the time, and that these greenhouses, although styled cool could not be kept much below 50 degrees, the growth of the bulbs will have advanced to such an extent that the flower buds will by this time be plainly showing. If this be so actual forcing may be said to have already begun, and in the case of Roman hyacinths, a gradual rise to 65 degrees will bring out the blooms in about fifteen days.

Rhododendrons

Rhododendrons for the past two seasons have sold well especially at Easter. When received they can be placed in soil in some root house or cool pit and the roots kept moderately moist, wetting them as you did the azaleas. When being potted they want a very porous soil, such as two parts of fibrous loam, one part of leaf mold and about half this quantity of sand. Keep them in a cool place, anywhere just above freezing. By February bring them into a cool house where they can be started up slowly. Be sure when ordering that you get the varieties that are suitable for forcing and that they are well set with buds. In February they can be brought into a temperature of about 45 degrees at night which can be increased to about 62 degrees at night. At this stage they like a moist atmosphere and should be freely syringed, but must be removed to a more airy and a cooler house when their flowers begin to open.

Storing Hydrangeas

By this time hydrangeas should be well ripened up. Take off any dead leaves and store the plants in some place that is kept near the freezing point but not below it, say a cool shed or pit at 35 to 40 degrees, but no higher. Give them a look over now and again so they will not become dust dry. They will have plenty of time if brought in about the middle of January, as Easter is the 23rd of April.

Next Week:—Cattleyas; Violets; Pot Evergreens for Winter; Primulas; Sowing Fern Spores; Storing Cannas, Dahlias, etc.

HORTICULTURE

VOL. XXII   NOVEMBER 13, 1915   NO. 20

PUBLISHED WEEKLY BY

HORTICULTURE PUBLISHING CO.

147 Summer Street, Boston, Mass.

Telephone, Oxford 292.

WM. J. STEWART, Editor and Manager.

ADVERTISING RATES:

Per inch, 30 inches to page........................... $1.00
Discounts on Contracts for consecutive insertions, as follows;
   One month (4 times), 5 per cent.; three months (13 times), 10
per cent.; six months (26 times), 20 per cent.; one year (52 times),
30 per cent.
   Page and half page space, special rates on application.

Entered as second-class matter December 8, 1914, at the Post Office
at Boston, Mass., under the Act of Congress of March 3, 1879.

CONTENTS   Page

The
street vendor
championed

As recorded in our news columns last
week the Florists' Club of Philadelphia,
at its recent meeting, seriously tackled
the old vexed question of the street
flower vendor and after a full debate
from all view points decided by an overwhelming vote
that the street man provides the only practical outlet
for the surplus stock of the grower and wholesaler under
present conditions. The result will be a petition on behalf of the club to the city authorities asking that the
ordinance restricting flower selling on the public streets
be rescinded. With this recognition the despised street
"fakir" is advanced to the position of street "vendor."
We shall watch with much interest the outcome of this

emphatic action by the oldest florists' club in the country. It requires some courage to take such a stand, but
of what use is a club without courage?

The
new "drive"

Clubs and societies, like business firms,
must keep moving ahead with the trend
of the times or otherwise they will lose
ground and drop behind. That the
Massachusetts Horticultural Society, the oldest organization of its kind in this country in uninterrupted activity, appears to be fully alert to the opportunities and
demands of the hour is well demonstrated in the progressive character of the measures that are being adopted to ensure the highest efficiency in all its departments.
The great exhibition which has just closed was in many
respects a distinct advance over its predecessors in its
appeal to the public interest and plans are now being
perfected which it is believed will still further enhance
the scope and prestige of all the Boston exhibitions of
the future. The value of the chief special prizes will
be increased and schedules for the important shows will
be issued three years in advance. Innovations equally
radical in character are contemplated in connection with
meetings for discussion.

Good
seed on
fertile ground

Speaking of exhibitions, the record of
attendance at the show of the Horticultural Society of New York last
week, as given in our account of that
event, on another page, inspires con-
fidence in the dependability of the New York public as
patrons of floral exhibitions, if such were lacking. A
turnout of over 20,000 people an hour for a period of
four hours on a Sunday afternoon, certainly means
much in inspiration and encouragement for all who
take an active part in these efforts to engage the attention and excite the interest of the multitude of city
dwellers in the products of the florist and gardener.
True, it was a "free" show and, furthermore, quite a
percentage of the people there might have visited the
Museum even had there been no flower show at the time,
but the fact that all these took occasion to inspect and
admire in detail all these triumphs of horticultural art
counts for much in educating these people up to the
standpoint where they will be prepared to willingly
pay to see a flower show. Good seed has been sown in
fertile ground and there can be no question as to the
fruit.

Unrequited
service

The Rhode Island Horticultural Society
has sent out a circular letter to its members and friends calling attention to the
important part the society has played in
the development of horticultural and allied interests in
the State, and appealing for donations to ensure the carrying out of the excellent program provided for the
balance of the year. Providence, where the headquarters
of the society is located, is reputed to be, per capita,
one of the wealthiest, if not the wealthiest city on the
American continent and there should be no grudge or
reluctance on the part of the people of that city to provide generously for this organization which has served
them so faithfully and well with free lectures, free exhibitions and all the good influences which such a society
exerts on a community. The Rhode Island Society was
organized in 1845 and incorporated in 1854, so its good
work covers the period of seventy years. Its meetings and
exhibitions are frequently referred to in the horticultural literature of sixty years ago and it appears to have
been doing its duty without intermission ever since.
Horticultural societies merit better consideration from
people of means than seems to be their lot in most cases.
There are other places besides Rhode Island where the
same dilemma exists.

ROSE GROWING UNDER GLASS

CONDUCTED BY

Arthur C. Ruzicka

Questions by our readers in line with any of the topics presented on this page will be cordially received and promptly answered by Mr. Ruzicka. Such communications should invariably be addressed to the office of HORTICULTURE.

Mildew on Outdoor Roses

Mr. Arthur Ruzicka,

Dear Sir: Can you give me some formula to be used for mildew other than sulphur flowers. on outdoor growing roses? I would like to overcome mildew on outdoor roses and up to the present time have not been successful.

What would you advise? Can you give me information as to where I could procure new German roses?

Would like to know of some German rosarians in Germany.

Thanking you, I am, gratefully,

M. H. S., Walla Walla, Wash.

Mildew on outdoor roses is much more difficult to control than in the greenhouses, for outside you have no control of heat or cold, dry or wet, so that it may be almost impossible to keep your roses free from mildew. Spraying three times a week with Fungine will do a good deal to prevent the disease, and all mildew will be killed instantly on coming into contact with the spray. Grape Dust is also used, but is objected to at times because the leaves must be dusted with it. Sulphur mixed with a little lime can also be used, but this too will be objectionable because of the dust on leaves. Fungine will not mark the foliage, will cleanse it if anything. In spraying white roses in full bloom, be careful not to let the spray hit the flowers very much, as it is liable to discolor these.

I have never been on the Pacific-Northwest coast, so perhaps some rose growers either in your state or in California could help you more than I can. As for names of German firms in Germany, I am sorry to say I know none, and doubt very much that you could get into communication with any firms over there at present, because of the war. There are some good firms advertising in HORTICULTURE, who make a specialty of rose growing, and who have acres and acres of acclimated stock, in all the leading varieties, and I would advise you to look over these firms' catalogues or write to them, and I am sure that you will get better satisfaction than importing from a foreign country. Perhaps some one connected with the German Embassy or Consulate in this country could furnish you names of these firms, or some of HORTICULTURE's readers may know of German firms who make a specialty of growing roses.

Blackspot on Roses

Mr. Arthur Ruzicka,

Dear Sir: Will you kindly explain to me why you recommend ammoniacal copper solution for blackspot on roses, at the same time recommending Fungine?

I have used the latter for several seasons with excellent results. A short time ago I took over a place, which had a large stock of the older insecticides in the potting room, and the only fungicide was the copper solution. I invariably spray roses each week with Fungine, but at this place could not order until the other fungicide had been used up. I sprayed a couple of weeks ago with the copper, using the prescribed dose and all the young growths were scalded. It was a dull day and what surprised me was the fact that a batch of Alternanthera Jewel and nana compacta that were on a shelf on one side of the house that did not come in contact with the spraying were literally scalded. Can it be that the ammonia fumes in the compound were too strong or what? I mixed in a wooden pail as I always do Fungine.

I shall never use the copper solution again but shall stick to Fungine. It is the best fungicide I know and I would not be without it.

Yours truly,

W. R. F., New York.

Speaking from personal experience, we have not had a serious case of spot for a long time, and we have had little occasion to use either copper carbonate or Fungine for the disease mentioned, and as we are interested in roses commercially, we have not been spraying regularly, in order to keep operating expenses as low as possible. I do not remember recommending a prepared solution of the ammoniacal copper carbonate such as you mention, having always preferred to use home-made mixture whenever we had occasion to use same. From your letter I would be of the opinion that the mixture was old, and possibly badly settled to the bottom of the container. If this was the case, the amount of ammonia poured off would be out of proportion with the other materials in the mixture, and the chances are it would be too strong. You mention spraying on a cloudy day: this, I think is a mistake when using the copper mixture for a spray. I would much prefer a clear day, when the houses can be aired freely, so there will be little danger from the fumes. Of course with nicotine solutions it is different, and these should be used on cloudy days when there is little air on the houses in order that full benefit of the spray may be obtained. Fungine is a very good article, and has been advertised freely, and I think I am right in assuming that all progressive growers should be familiar with it. I would recommend a number of patented articles that are real good to have around the greenhouses, but there would be growers who would fail to get the desired results even with the most minute directions, and the outcome would be that I would be accused of accepting pay for doing so. That is why I recommend mixtures that are home-made as far as possible, and if the grower does not get the results expected, his failure can usually be traced to his own mistake. This is also true of using prepared articles, but they can always be blamed for not being mixed right or something, but when the grower mixes his own he can find no fault with the mixture as he made it himself.

THE FALL FLOWER SHOWS

Boston

We were able to give a fairly descriptive summary in our last issue of the situation on the opening day of the annual Autumn Exhibition of the Massachusetts Horticultural Society. The prizes had not then been awarded, however, and these with the new exhibits in the following days and other items of interest furnish material for a few further notes this week.

A significant fact which many will readily note is the rapid advancement of the commercial florists in the competitive classes as compared with the situation a few years ago when the plant groups and specimens and orchid collections were mostly contributed by the private gardeners. A glance over the list of awards which follows will be sufficient to show the drift of present development. It is gratifying to be able to state that the attendance was just double that of last year.

List of Awards.

Foliage and Flowering Plants—Group, covering three hundred square feet: 1st, A. M. Davenport; 2d, W. W. Edgar Co.; group covering one hundred and fifty square feet (for private gardeners only): 1st, Mrs. J. L. Gardner. Orchids—plants and flowers: 1st, F. J. Dolansky; 2d, Wheeler & Co.; six plants, 1st, F. J. Dolansky; specimen, 1st, F. J. Dolansky; 2d, Miss Cornelia Warren. Evergreen trees and shrubs in tubs or pots: 1st, Breck, Robinson Co.; 2d, Old Town Nurseries. Chrysanthemums — Group of plants 200 square feet: 1st, Mrs. J. L. Gardner; 2d, A. M. Davenport; six trained specimens: 1st, Jason S. Bailey; specimen plant, white: 1st, Galen L. Stone; 2d, Mrs. C. G. Weld; yellow, 1st, Mrs. C. G. Weld; 2d, Mrs. C. G. Weld; pink, 1st, A. M. Davenport; 2d, Jason S. Bailey; twenty-five plants, commercial specimens, 1st, W. H. Elliott; 2d, A. M. Davenport; twelve single-flowering sorts, 1st, Mrs. Lester Leland; twelve blooms, Japanese, 1st, Harry E. Converse; twelve Japanese Incurved, 1st, Harry E. Converse; twelve Reflexed, 1st, Harry E. Converse; twelve sprays Anemone, 1st, Frank P. Putnam; twelve vases Pompons, 1st, Frank P. Putnam; collection of sprays of single chrysanthemums, Frank P. Putnam; best Chrysanthemum plant on exhibition, Galen L. Stone, Garza, silver medal; twenty-five blooms of twenty-five distinct varieties, 1st, Harry E. Converse; vases of ten blooms on long stems, pink, 1st, Mrs. Lester Leland with Chieftain; 2d, F. J. Dolansky with Chieftain; red, 1st, W. S. Russell with F. T. Quittenton; white, 1st, James Nicol with Beatrice May; 2d, F. J. Dolansky with Wm. Turner; yellow, 1st, Mrs. Lester Leland with Mrs. Wm. Duckham; 2d, W. S. Russell with Col. D. Appleton; any other color, 1st, F. J. Dolansky with Polly Salis; Henry A. Gane Memorial Prize for the best vase of blooms of the Mrs. Jerome Jones or the Yellow Mrs. Jerome Jones: 1st, James Nicol. Begonias—Gloire de Lorraine, or any of its varieties, six plants: 1st, Mrs. C. G. Weld; 2d, Galen L. Stone; any other winter-flowering variety, six plants: 1st, A. M. Davenport with Mellor. Table decoration (for private gardeners only): 1st, Duncan Finlayson; 2d, Wm. Thatcher. Artistic display of cut flowers to cover 100 sq. ft.: 1st, Penn, the Florist. Mantel decoration: 1st, Wax Bros.; 2d, Penn, the Florist. Carnations—Six vases, 50 each: 1st, A. A. Pembroke; 2d, C. S. Strout; 100 mixed: 1st, A. A. Pembroke; 2d, M. A. Patten Co.; 50 mixed: 1st, James Wheeler; 25 mixed (for private gardeners only): 1st, William C. Rust; 2d, Charles D. Sias. Table decoration: (Thursday) 1st, F. J. Dolansky; 2d, Mrs. Christine Finlayson. (Friday) 1st, Boston Cut Flower Co.; 2d, Henry R. Comley. (Saturday) 1st, Henry R. Com-

ley; 2d, F. J. Dolansky. Collection of vegetables exhibited by seedsmen: 1st, Thomas J. Grey Co., silver medal.

SPECIALS AND GRATUITIES

The Appleton Silver Medal—R. & J. Farquhar & Co., group of decorative plants. Silver Medals—William C. Winter, Davallia Mooreana; Waban Rose Conservatories, new rose Mrs. Bayard Thayer; R. & J. Farquhar & Co., artistic display of plants and flowers. First Class Certificates of Merit—Littlefield & Wyman, Carnation Theo; Edwin S. Webster, new winter-flowering Begonia, Optima; A. W. Preston, Hybrid Cattleya Moira; Ernest B. Dane, Hybrid Cattleya Moira. Honorable Mention—Mrs. C. G. Weld, Ipomoea (Morning Glory), Heavenly Blue; F. E. Palmer, arrangement of window plants; George Detlefsen, new Heliotrope, Elsie; Gen. S. M. Weld, 3 plants Dracaena indivisa var. Parei excelsa; George Detlefsen, new Anemone-flowered chrysanthemum, Waverly Star.

THE SPECIMEN CHRYSANTHEMUMS AT BOSTON FALL SHOW.
Part of Farquhar Plant Group in Background.

Vote of Thanks—F. J. Dolansky, Cattleya labiata varieties. Cash Gratuities—Edwin S. Webster, Begonia Mrs. Heal; Mrs. Lester Leland, chrysanthemums; W. A. Riggs, chrysanthemums; James Wheeler, carnations; S. J. Goddard, carnations; Peter Fisher, carnations; A. A. Pembroke, carnations; Miss Cornelia Warren, group of plants; Kameyama & Serada, group of plants and flowers; A. Leuthy & Co., display of palms; W. W. Edgar Co., display of palms; S. R. Cowey, seedling Pompoo chrysanthemums; W. D. Hathaway, dahlias; Edward Winkler, carnation Morning Glow; Waban Rose Conservatories, vases of roses; George F. Stewart, Cattleya Trianae; Kidder Bros., violets; William Sim, pansies; Belcher's Flower Shop, table decoration.

The annual chrysanthemum show of the Montreal Gardeners' and Florists' Club was held on November 1. J. Keene of the Mt. Bruno Floral Company made a splendid display of chrysanthemums, roses and carnations which won a special certificate of merit. A. C. Wilshire with single flowered chrysanthemums, John Walsh with cattleyas and W. H. Whiting with promiscuous plants were among the prominent contributors.

New York

The Horticultural Society of New York has good reason to feel elated over the success of its Fall Show which was held at the American Museum of Natural History on November 4 to 7 inclusive. There were many notable displays by commercial growers and private gardeners of high repute and the public appeared to take an unusual interest in it all. On Sunday, the last day, the attendance reached 88,593 between the hours of 1 and 5 P. M., making the stupendous total of 194,024 visitors during the four days.

The sensational trained chrysanthemum plants for which John Canning, supt. for Adolph Lewisohn has become famous were again the central feature of the spacious foyer of the Museum. The varieties were R. F. Felton, Lady Lydia and Greystone. The Felton plant reached the unprecedented spread of 17 ft. and, in addition to the 1st prizes won by the trio, this plant got the $100 sweepstakes cup for the best plant shown. The honors in the other chrysanthemum plant classes were all with Samuel Untermyer.

The cut flower classes for commercial growers were cleaned up by Charles H. Totty and Scott Bros. In the non-commercials, Adolph Lewisohn captured four 1sts, Mrs. F. A. Constable, gard. Jas. Stuart, four; Edwin Jenkins one, Mrs. Payne Whitney, gard. L. R. Forbes, one; A. Iselin, Jr., gard. Jos. Tiernan one, and Frederick Sturgis, gard. Thos. Bell, one. Arthur N. Cooley, gard. E. W. Edwards; D. E. Oppenheimer, gard. Alex Macdonald, and Mrs. Pauline Boettger, gard. Rudolph Heidkamp, were close 2nds in second classes. For dinner table decoration of chrysanthemum flowers only, open to all, the winners were A. Lewisohn 1st, Mrs. Payne Whitney 2nd. Mrs. P. Boettger 3rd.

The rose entries were excellent. Chas. H. Totty won the silver medal for best new variety not in commerce. The other commercial classes were monopolized by F. R. Pierson Co. and L. A. Noe. J. B. Duke, gard. A. A. Macdonald, S. Untermyer, H. C. Sturgis, gard. Henry Kulberg, were the high liners in the non-commercial classes.

In carnations Cottage Gardens won 1st and the silver medal sweepstakes, and Springfield Floral Co. 2nd, J. A. Macdonald, gard. R. Hughes winning four 1st and Mrs. Payne Whitney and H. C. Sturgis one each in non-commercial. A. Lewisohn on begonias, F. R. Pierson Co. on Nephrolepis display and Mrs. P. Boettger on specimen Bostoniensis and Mrs. F. A. Constable in all the palm and ciborium classes followed by Mrs. Boettger as 2nd, was the story of the foliage and decorative plant section. Lager & Hurrell won all the commercial orchid prizes including the silver medal for Cattleya Olivia. The non-commercial orchid exhibitors were George Schlegel and Clement Moore and the collections from these two famous establishments were superb, as usual. A specimen of Brasso-Cattleya Maronæ superba by Clement Moore won the sweepstakes silver medal as the best orchid shown.

The list of special prizes when same are given with discretion by the judges and not merely used to indulge the promiscuous exhibitors, will often give a more intelligent idea of the intrinsic merits of a flower show than a perusal of the awards in the scheduled classes. In this exhibition the following special awards were made:

Bobbink & Atkins, collection of chrysanthemums, special mention; Mrs. F. A. Constable, for specimen of Adiantum Crowianum, cash, for two specimen palms, cash, for collection of Nerines, silver medal; Mrs. H. Darlington, gard. P. W. Popp, for display of dahlias, cash; J. B. Duke, general display from Duke's Farm, gold medal and cash; H. Gaut, vase of bronze seedling chrysanthemum, No. 19, certificate, vase apricot seedling chrysanthemum, special mention; Adolph Lewisohn, for two bush chrysanthemum plants, cash; Jas. A. Macdonald, for carnation seedlings, special mention; J. A. Manda, for specimen Cattleya lablata, silver medal; W. A. Manda, for collection of ferns and foliage plants, silver medal, for collection dahlias, special mention; A. L. Miller, for Salvia Greggii, special mention, for Otaheite oranges, certificate of merit; Clement Moore, for vase of Eucharis amazonica, certificate of merit; A. N. Pierson, Inc., for display of new roses, carnations and chrysanthemums, silver medal; Mrs. W. H. Pullan, for plate of pears, special mention; Julius Roehrs Co., for collection of chrysanthemums, special mention; John Scheepers & Co., Inc., collection of lilacs, spiraeas, etc., in flower, silver medal; Max Schling, artistic designs, certificate; G. T. Schuneman, three vases sweet peas, special mention; Scott Bros., for chrysanthemum White Dotty, certificate of merit; Chas. H. Totty, new roses, silver medal, collection of chrysanthemums.

special mention; Wm. Tricker, for winter-flowering begonias, certificate of merit, for Nymphaea Panama Pacific, certificate of merit; R. Vincent, Jr., & Sons Co., for display of hardy chrysanthemums, special mention; Chas. Webber, for new carnation Laura Webber, special mention; Robt. Wilson, for new fern, bronze medal.

The judges were: Walter Angus, Chapinville, Ct.; John B. Urquhart, Lands End, Newport, R. I.; Alex. Michie, Memorial Cemetery, Cold Spring Harbor, N. Y.; Robert Walker, Bridgeport, Ct.; Jas. Ballantine, Ridgefield, Ct.; Geo. H. Thompson, Lenox, Mass.

The management of the show was in the able hands of John Young.

American Institute.

The American Institute Chrysanthemum Show opened on Wednesday, November 3, continuing for three days, and was in all respects fully equal to any of its predecessors. The chrysanthemum blooms were very fine as were the roses, orchids and carnations. Max Schling made a sensational display of decorative flower work which attracted much attention from visitors and a display was also made by G. E. M. Stumpp showing artistic arrangements in baskets, vases, etc., that was at once interesting and educational. In the very lengthy list of prize winners we find frequent mention of the names of Chas. H. Totty, Scott Bros., Wm. Vert, gard. to Howard Gould; Ernest Robinson, gard. to Mrs. M. F. Plant; Robt. Jones, gard. to Percy Chubb; Fred. Hitchman, gard. to R. Pulitzer; W. F. Gordon, gard. to S. Untermyer; Geo. R. Kuhn, gard. to H. T. Borden; L. G. Forbes, gard. to Mrs. Payne Whitney; Jas. Bill, gard. to C. K. G. Billings; R. E. Jones, H. Gaut, gard. to H. L. Pratt; Peter Duff, gard. to Mrs. J. C. Brown; Robt. Petrie, gard. to D. T. Millspaugh; Jas. MacDonald, gard. to Mrs. J. H. Ottley; Richard Thomas, gard. to H. F. Guggenheim; Lager & Hurrell, L. A. Noe, A. N. Pierson, Inc.; Wm. Cameron, gard. to Thos. N. McCarter, and many others. Many special gratuities were awarded, including the following honors:

George T. Schuneman, Rockville Centre,

I, I.; Exhibit of Spencer Orchid Flowering Sweet Peas, Diploma; G. E. M. Stumpp; An artistic display of Floral Decorations, Diploma; Max Schling, 22 W. 59th street; Display of Floral Decorations, Diploma; Robert Jones; Best Collection of Chrysanthemum varieties, Silver Medal; Peter Duff; Best specimen Chrysanthemum plant, Silver Medal; Ernest Robinson, best vase of Chrysanthemums, Medal of Superiority.

Chicago

As we go to press the Grand Floral Festival is fast getting into shape and though the hour of the formal opening has scarcely arrived, there are troops of visitors coming through the doors. The Coliseum building, the home of so many floral shows, never looked more beautiful, with its festoons of wild smilax draping the roof to the very top, through which myriads of electric lights look down upon the most artistic arrangement of cut flowers ever shown in this building. The chrysanthemums are queen of the day as was expected and the tall vases are filled with blooms reaching to a height of twelve feet. Much of the floor space is taken by the allied trades as well as by growers and retailers who responded more generously than in many of the past events. Much interest centers round the vases containing 100 large chrysanthemums arranged for effect. the cash prizes being an interesting item. Exhibitors from the east and from the west have added their part to the good showing made by the local trade. The formal opening is expected to be honored by the presence of Mayor Thompson and the many special features which include an orchestra, fancy dancing, and young ladies dressed in evening gowns to demonstrate how flowers may best be worn. all have stimulated an interest in the show and there is every indication now that it will be a grand success.

One of the first awards was for (Class 16) display of chrysanthemums arranged for effect. Geo. Wienhoeber captured first prize of $200 for this entry with a very elaborate collection arranged in vases covered with dark velvet which gave a very pleasing and striking effect.

A CHRYSANTHEMUM DISPLAY AT PHIPP'S CONSERVATORY, SCHENLEY PARK, PITTSBURGH, PA.

Cleveland

With a large number of trade exhibits and a record breaking attendance of florists from all parts of the country, the Cleveland Flower Show opened auspiciously on Wednesday, Nov. 11. Prominent growers in attendance were of a single mind in pronouncing the show a success from every standpoint and without qualification many of them said it is the best show they ever attended.

The Chrysanthemum Society of America staged a display estimated at more than 100,000 blooms. Special interest centered in the contest of Ohio private growers for the James W. Corrigan cup, valued at $500, and is the largest of more than $10,000 worth of cups and medals offered for exhibits on the part of private growers. It was won by H. S. Firestone of Akron.

The special $250 cup was easily won by Adolph Lewisohn, Ardsley, N. Y., whose mammoth plants fifteen feet in diameter and bearing more than 1,200 blossoms, arrived at the show in fine condition under personal escort of John Canning, superintendent of the Lewisohn estate. Mr. Canning also exhibited in several other classes.

The individual exhibits number more than 2,000. This includes commercial exhibits, garden accessories, literature, etc. There is a floor space of 65,000 square feet in the Coliseum and every available inch is covered, leaving only adequate aisle space. The retailers' section is complete with a variety of examples of table decorations and other practical suggestions for the use of flowers about the home, and in connection with society events.

The tea garden, a feature in charge of the Women's Committee of the show, proved a popular attraction from the moment the show opened. To avoid overcrowding it was found necessary to charge a small admission for entrance and even with this restriction the capacity of the garden has been taxed throughout the afternoon and evening. At intervals examples of society dancing and vocal selections are given from the stage and refreshments are served at all times. Visiting florists commented favorably upon this feature and it is indicated that no flower show of the future will be complete without a tea garden.

The local florists who have worked earnestly for many months to make the show of interest to the trade, are gratified with the large attendance of florists present on the opening day. It was stated by many that considering there is no convention, the show has attracted a remarkable attendance of trade people. No show held west of New York and Philadelphia has had a similar attendance and many others will arrive tomorrow and on succeeding days of the exhibition.

E. G. Hill, Richmond, Ind., was a big winner, capturing the C. S. A. silver cup with a display of Turners, the sweepstakes prize for the best twelve blooms with a staging of Odessa, and figured in several other winnings, including the prize for best fifty blooms, in variety.

Frank Allan, Grosse Point, Mich., also won in several classes. He captured the sweepstakes for best eighteen blooms with a showing of Turners and the special vase of fifteen blooms, three varieties.

Philadelphia

This annual event took place the past week, opening on Tuesday and closing on Friday. A very creditable display was furnished in all departments. Three of the biggest exhibitors of former shows were missing this year, the Widener and Hunter conservatories being absent on account of the recent demise of the owners and the Newbold display from some change of policy in the management of that estate. The chrysanthemum was of course the main feature and we have never seen finer flowers in the cut bloom section. The pot plants were also very creditable.

A magnificent display of orchids was staged by Louis Burk, consisting of eighty-four distinct species all beautifully arranged and accurately labeled. He was awarded four firsts and a crowning compliment in the shape of the Society's gold medal as an additional appreciation.

Two fine groups of foliage and flowering plants put up by Dodds and Robertson added greatly to the general effect in the main hall. The first honors went deservedly to Mr. Dodds, whose staging and arrangement was not only in the finest taste, but the rich and varied specimens were unusually abundant for the limited space allowed.

The front of the stage was occupied by a fine collection of foliage plants and ferns from the Dreer nurseries at Riverton. The Robert Craig Co. staged a small but select collection of crotons, dracenas and cyclamens which showed excellent finish and culture.

The outer and inner vestibules and the lower hall were occupied by the trade displays of the nurserymen and seedsmen—Adolph Muller, Thomas Meehan & Sons, and Harry S. Betz showing excellent displays of evergreens. Thos. Long showed here his big specimen ferns including the famous Davallia with a spread of some ten feet or so and running four feet in height.

The Michell display was unique this year being an enclosed square of hardy chrysanthemums in pots mixed with boxwood specimens—a walk all round, and in the center an elevated acorn, which opened and shut by clock work, showing pot of hyacinths inside—the whole brightly illuminated by electric bulbs. Surrounding this, lower down, were plants and bulbs of a seasonable nature—all very attractive in arrangement.

The Dreer seed store display consisted mainly of pottery and sundries very well arranged. H. Waterer also had a small display of bulbs and sundries and the greenhouse men. Lord & Burnham, Hitchings, and King, were out in force with sash and frame samples and pictures and order books.

Tarrytown

The seventeenth annual flower show of the Tarrytown Horticultural Society was held in Music Hall, Tarrytown, N. Y., Nov. 3d to 5th inclusive. The hall was completely filled with exhibits of the finest decorative plants and cut blooms, notably among which was a fine display of palms, foliage and flowering plants, exhibited by William B. Thompson, supt. R. M. Johnston. This exhibit was awarded the Untermyer silver cup for the most meritorious exhibit.

The principal exhibitors were Finley J. Shepard. supt. Chas. R. Russell; Joseph Eastman, gard. Robert Angus; Emil Berolzheimer, gard. Wm. Jamieson; Mrs. F. E. Lewis, supt. James Ballantyne; William B. Thompson; Adolph Lewisohn, gard. John Canning; Mrs. S. Hermann, gard. Abel Weeks; David L. Luke, gard. John Elliott; Mrs. S. Neustadt, gard. David Gordon; Hugh Hill, gard. Robert Grieve; Mrs. I. N. Seligman, supt. M. MacPherson; Richard Delafield and Paul M. Warburg. Notably among the exhibits was a fine display of ferns and baskets of Ophelia, Francis Scott Key, Sunburst, Mrs. Aaron Ward, Mignon and Hoosier Beauty roses, exhibited by F. R. Pierson Company; also a fine collection of pompon and other chrysanthemums, exhibited by Scott Bros., Elmsford, N. Y. These two displays were for exhibition only, the exhibits for competition being entirely from private estates.

The Society's silver medal was awarded to Finley J. Shepard in Class 1, for seedling Croton Roxbury. Certificate of merit was awarded to Mrs. A. McEwen for an exhibit of standard seedling single chrysanthemums; also certificate of merit to Jacob Ruppert for six standard chrysanthemums, Miss Cornelia A. Ruppert. Cultural certificate was awarded to Finley J. Shepard for Phoenix Roebelenii, and to John C. Scheepers for specimen lilac in flower. There were two exhibits from the local schools that attracted considerable attention—one from the Washington Irving High School, Tarrytown, and the other from Elmsford. Honorable mention was awarded to Mrs. Rockwell Kent for a vase of cosmos.

Special cups and cash prizes were awarded in forty-three out of one hundred and one classes, the donors being F. R. Pierson, J. F. Detmer, J. D. Archbold. Mrs. F. Herrmann, I. T. Bush, W. F. McCord, Chas. Vanderbilt, Hugh Hill, D. G. Reid, Mrs. W. C. Osborn, Wm. Rockefeller, W. B. Thompson, Pierson U-Bar Co., Mrs. H. Darlington, H. Graves, Jr., Chas. Mallory, Mrs. F. E. Lewis, Mrs. H. Ollesheimer, John Scheepers, Dr. C. C. Brace, Burnett Bros., W. E. Marshall & Co., Peter Henderson & Co., John Wilk, Stumpp & Walter Co., S. Untermyer, Mrs. Stuyvesant Fish, R. B. Dula, Mrs. H. F. Osborn, A. Lewisohn, Lord & Burnham Co., R. Langle, Mrs. I. N. Seligman, F. M. Warburg, Jas. Speyer and Mrs. J. B. Trevor.

Chrysanthemums, orchids, plants vegetables and fruit were staged on the first day. On the second day were roses, carnations, centre pieces, etc.

The judges for the first day were John T. Burns, New Canaan, Conn.,

Ewen Mackenzie and N. Butterbach, New Rochelle, N. Y.; second day, W. R. Waite, Rumson, N. J.; James Macmahon, Tuxedo Park, N. Y., Herbert H. Fletcher, Millbrook, N. Y.; third day, Joseph Bradley, Dobbs Ferry, N. Y., Joseph Mooney, Hastings, N. Y., and John Featherstone, North Tarrytown, N. Y.

MT. KISCO.

The 13th annual show of the N. W. County Horticultural and Agricultural Society of Mount Kisco, N. Y., was held in Civic Hall, Mt. Kisco, Oct. 29, 30 and 31st, and was in all respects equal to any show of former years, both in quality and quantity. Competition was very keen in chrysanthemums, roses and carnations. The Society's Special Cup brought out some magnificent blooms of chrysanthemums, there being three very close competitors in this class. A summary of the chief events follows:

Chrysanthemums—12 blooms, 6 varieties, 1st, E. Meyer, Jr., gard. Chas. Ruthven; 2d, Mrs. Neustadt, gard. A. Rose; 3d, David Gordon. Collection singles, 1st, Mrs. Meyer; 2d, M. J. O'Brien; 3d, Mrs. Taylor, gard. Alex. Thomson. Chrysanthemum plants— 8 6-inch pots, E. Meyer. Largest chrysanthemum bloom in show, E. Bayer.
Roses—12 pink, 1st, E. S. Bayer; 2d, Mrs Taylor. 12 red, 1st, E. S. Bayer; 2d, Mrs. Taylor. 12 white, 1st, E. S. Bayer; 2d, Mrs. Neustadt.
Carnations—12 red, 1st, E. S. Bayer; 2d, Mrs. Taylor. 12 white, 1st, E. S. Bayer; Mrs. Taylor. 12 light pink, 1st, E. S. Bayer; 2d, H. A. Spavins. 12 dark pink, H. A. Spavins.
Ornamental plants—Collection 8 ft. circle, H. A. Spavins. Begonia Lorraine, 1st, John Magee; 2d, John Magee, gard. Jas. Aitcheson.
Orchids—Collection, H. A. Spavins.
Dinner Table Decoration—1st, E. S. Bayer; Chas. Scott, asst. gard.; 2d. Mrs. Taylor; 3d, H. A. Spavins.
Apples—12 varieties, 1st, A. W. Butler. Supt. John Holl; 2d, Mrs. Taylor; 3d, Chas. Brown, gard. E. Pilz.
Vegetables—15 varieties, 1st, Mrs. Taylor; 2d, E. Meyer; 3d, Wm. Sloane; 2d, Cullum. 12 varieties, 1st, Wm. Sloane; 2d, Mrs. Taylor; 3d, E. Meyer, 8 varieties, J. H. Hammond, gard. John Connolly.
Collection Farm Produce—1st, A. W. Butler; 2d, Mrs. Taylor; 3d, J. H. Hammond.

The judges were Adam Paterson, Saugatuck, Ct., A. T. Brill, Pawling, N. Y., and Wm. Jamieson, Tarrytown, N. Y.

BUFFALO.

Local papers advertised the annual city flower shows beginning on Sunday and holding over for two weeks. Sunday last, the opening day, saw throngs of visitors, especially at South Park, where Supt. Elbers reigns. Mr. Elbers was more than pleased to see such a flow of flower lovers. At times it was so congested that exits wereof opened for the people to get outside.

Mr. Elbers has a fine show. Pompons and specimen plants are not extensively grown this season but these were found at the Humboldt conservatories where Supt. Chas. Keitsch has supervision. There are not as many single blooms grown here as at South Park. Palm and cactus houses in both parks were also well patronized.

TEXAS FLOWER SHOW.

Reports from Houston assure us that everything is in readiness for the flower show, and reports from over the state indicate that the attendance is going to be very heavy. The fact that special rates will be made on all railroads is going to prove very beneficial to the florists, and the nearer the date for the show arrives the greater the list, of exhibitors grows and something very unusual will now have to happen to prevent our having a big show in every respect.

It is indeed very gratifying to note the excellent interest shown by florists and supply houses out of the state and from the way reservations for space are being asked for the trade displays will be worth any one's visit to Houston to see. Reports are pouring in from all parts of the state from florists who will make exhibits. The show will open with an automobile parade with beautiful girls bedecked with chrysanthemums. Two hundred florists from within the state and fifty florists from without the state are expected to attend. The Auditorium will be packed to its capacity with exhibits and headliner features for drawing crowds, living models displaying gowns and showing the uses of flowers, such as shoulder sprays, corsages of various types, etc. The ankle bouquet will be featured and a bridal party using bridal bouquets will be made a feature. One hundred per cent. better show and attendance than last year is assured.

SAN FRANCISCO.

At the National Fall Flower Show held at San Francisco, in the exposition grounds, on October 21 to 26, gold medals were awarded as follows: Lynch Nursery Co. for 12 chrysanthemums, 12 varieties; Shibuya & Ishida for 100 chrysanthemums, 10 varieties; John A. Carbone for display of orchids; San Mateo County Conservatories for group of stove and greenhouse plants; E. James for collection crotons; H. Plath for collection of ferns; E. James for collection of Nephrolepis; Pelicano-Rossi & Co. for table decoration. Also numerous silver and bronze medals.

NEW BEDFORD, MASS.

The New Bedford Horticultural Society held a chrysanthemum show on Tuesday and Wednesday of this week, in point of quality the very best in its history. The Free Public Library where the exhibition was staged proved much too small for the exhibits. The two rival estates—that of Col. H. E. Converse, represented by supt. D. F. Roy, president of the Society, and that of Galen L. Stone, represented by supt. A. E. Griffin and assistant George Holliday, put up some wonderful blooms and in the contest for the T. J. Grey & Co. cup ran neck and neck, Mr. Roy winning out. Mr. Griffin captured the Converse cup and the Benson cup and Mr. Roy the Standard cup. Other prominent prize winners were H. S. Walsh, Post & Gray, Peckham Floral Co., J. V. Pierce. H. A. John and James Garthly.

NOTES.

The Maine State Florists' Society held its first chrysanthemum show at Bangor, Maine, last week. Among the exhibitors were J. W. Minot & Co., Portland; C. S. Strout, Biddeford; Mount Desert Nurseries, Bar Harbor; P. M. Olm, Bath; E. Saunders, Lewiston; P. Burr, Freeport; Miss A. M. Clark, Ellsworth; A. J. Loder, Bangor, and the horticultural department, University of Maine.

The Menlo Park (Cal.) Horticultural Society held its fall show at Menlo Park, Cal., on the last three days of October. As that is in one of the important nursery districts of the Bay section, considerable interest was given to the event, both by professionals and amateurs, and in some lines, especially chrysanthemums, the exhibits were about as good as those shown the week before at the Exposition. In fact, most of the mum growers, and several in other lines, who exhibited at the Exposition also participated in the Menlo Park show. In mums, provision was made for both private gardeners and commercial growers, as well as a free-for-all class; and the entries included a good showing of dahlias, roses, carnations, flowering plants, etc. D. Bassett, P. Ellings, J. M. Daley, G. Nunn and D. W. Dale were in charge of the show.

CLUBS AND SOCIETIES

NEW YORK FLORISTS' CLUB.

A regular meeting of the New York Florists' Club was held in the club's rooms, Grand Opera House Building, November 8.

A. L. Miller, for the Flower Show Committee, reported progress. F. R. Pierson, chairman of the general committee, also made a brief report and handed in a check for $297.44 as the balance coming to the club on the settlement of the affairs of last spring's show.

Resolutions on the death of Edwin Lonsdale were read and adopted, as also were resolutions on the death of Lawrence W. Kervan. The death of Edw. Walz, a member, was announced, and A. J. Manda, J. A. Shaw and Geo. Hildenbrand were appointed a committee to prepare resolutions of sympathy with the deceased's family. F. W. Wagenföhr, Philip F. Kessler and John Donaldson were appointed a committee to prepare resolutions on the death of Mrs. Victor Dorval. A. M. Henshaw, for the transportation committee, made a final report on the preparations made for the party going to the Cleveland Flower Show.

The committee on nominations presented the names of the following as candidates for election to office at the December meeting:

For president—Harry A. Bunyard, Henry Weston and Philip F. Kessler; vice-president—Chas. Knight, Alex. E. Hogg and G. E. M. Stumpp; secretary —John Young and J. Harrison Dick; Treasurer—Wm. C. Rickards, Jr., and Roman J. Irwin; trustees—Joseph S. Fenrich, Chas. Schenck, Ed. Sceery, W. R. Pierson, Robt. G. Wilson and Max Schling. Mr. Bunyard declined his nomination for president, as also did Mr. Dick for the secretaryship.

There was an animated and rather harmonious discussion on "The Chrysanthemum Situation," in which Messrs. A. J. Guttman, W. H. Long, J. T. Scott, A. Herrington, G. E. M. Stumpp, H. A. Barnard of England, and others took part. Taken from the different standpoints of grower, wholesaler and retailer, it was agreed that while the chrysanthemum was at times "a bit of a nuisance," the trade could not get along without it, and the public liked it. A good word, however, was put in for the singles and pompons, which seemed to gain in popularity each year. Some complaint was made of shipments by some growers of varieties which did not appear to keep, wilting badly when in the hands of consumers, and causing loss and annoyance to the retailers handling them.

It being "Chrysanthemum Night," there were several exhibits staged for the attention of the committee on awards, as well as exhibits of other flowers. The following is the list with the awards:

By Philip F. Kessler, Chrysanthemum Julia Lagravere, grown by W. W. Matthews, Great Neck, N. Y., vote of thanks; Pompon Western Beauty, by the same grower, vote of thanks;

Meetings Next Week

Monday, Nov. 15.
Detroit Florists' Club, Bemb Floral Hall, Detroit, Mich.
Houston Florists' Club, Chamber of Commerce Rooms, Houston, Tex.

Tuesday, Nov. 16.
Gardeners' and Florists' of Ontario, St. George's Hall, Toronto, Can.
Lake Geneva Gardeners' and Foremen's Association, Horticultural Hall, Lake Geneva, Wis.
Minnesota State Florists' Association, Minneapolis, Minn.
Pennsylvania Horticultural Society, Horticulutral Hall, Philadelphia, Pa.

Wednesday, Nov. 17.
Rhode Island Horticultural Society, Public Library, Providence, R. I.

Thursday, Nov. 18.
Essex County Florists' Club, Kreuger Auditorium, Newark, N. J.
New Orleans Horticultural Society, Association of Commerce Bldg., New Orleans, La.
North Westchester County Horticultural Society, Mt. Kisco, N. Y.
Tacoma Florists' Association, Maccabee Hall, Tacoma, Wash.

Friday, Nov. 19,
North Shore Horticultural Society, Manchester, Mass.

Single W. E. Buckingham, grown by Chas. Smith & Sons, Woodside, cultural certificate. By Scott Bros., Elmsford, N. Y., Pompon White Dotty, 91 points, certificate of merit. By James Bell, Oyster Bay. N. Y., single cactusflower chrysanthemum seedling, certificate of merit. By Wm. Tricker, Arlington, N. J., New Hardy Chrysanthemum Arlington, certificate of merit. By Frank Dinda, Farmingdale, N. Y., white Anemone Seedling, certificate of merit; collection of Anemone seedlings and vase of Glenview, vote of thanks. By Florex Gardens, North Wales, Pa., Rose Prima Donna, award of merit. By Charles Weber, Lynbrook, N. Y., Carnation Laura Weber, vote of thanks.

NEW LONDON HORTICULTURAL SOCIETY.

This society held its annual Chrysanthemum Show at the Court House, New London, Conn., on the 3rd and 4th inst. The society congratulates itself on the success it obtained. Fruit was scarce compared to last year's display but the quality was a trifle better. Vegetables and flowers were better than last year and much keener competition. E. Robinson, foreman of the Branford Farm Greenhouses, staged grapes, roses and cattleyas. The leading varieties of chrysanthemums were, Mrs. H. J. Jones, Bob Pulling, Odessa, Nerissa, Meudon, F. S. Vallis. Wm. Turner, Mrs. Gilbert Drabble, F. T. Quittenton, Mrs. H. Stevens, Glenview, etc.   H. E. L.

PITTSBURGH GARDENERS' AND FLORISTS' CLUB.

The gathering of members for the meeting November 2d in the Fort Pitt Hotel was the largest of the season. It was Chrysanthemum Night, which always is very popular. Wm. Falconer, having sent a note that he would be unable to attend the meeting on account of a celebration of his birthday being in progress at his house, congratulations and good wishes were 'phoned him from the club. It developed that about ten members were expecting to attend the Cleveland Flower Show and arrangements were made looking toward their going in a body.

H. A. Dreer, of Philadelphia, made a large display of the late outdoor flowering chrysanthemums, both pompon and aster-flowering varieties. The blooms were in good order for so late in the season, and were very interesting and a vote of thanks was tendered the exhibitor. The exhibit of the large greenhouse-grown chrysanthemums was very fine, and shown by many exhibitors, although curiously enough the displays were all by private gardeners and the Bureau of Parks, except in one instance.

As has been the case for the last few years the largest blooms shown were those of Wm. Turner and Gilbert Drabble. Wells' Late Pink brought out favorable comment. The single C. L. Hutchinson was thought better than Garza, and singles Roupel Beauty, Dorothy Dunn and Betsy Presbrey were very fine. A potted plant of a yellow sport of Anna was shown. The exhibits of chrysanthemums were of such a high order of merit that the club did not attempt to designate shades of excellence in their awards of certificates, but awarded cultural certificates to the following:

Herman Rapp, gard. with D. T. Watson, Leetsdale. Pa.; M. Curran, gard. with Mrs. Horne, Sewickley, Pa.; A. A. Leech, gard. with H. J. Heinz, Pittsburgh; H. B. Keilfor, gard. with A. Peacock, Pittsburgh; Bureau of Parks, Northside; Bureau of Parks, Schenley; T. Tyler, gard. for C. D. Armstrong, Pittsburgh.

H. P. JOSLIN, Sec'y.

NORTH SHORE HORTICULTURAL SOCIETY.

The North Shore Horticultural Society held its annual meeting and election of officers at Manchester, Mass., on Friday evening, Nov. 5. The

various annual reports were read and accepted, the officers elected for the ensuing year are as follows: President, Mrs. W. Scott Fitz; vice-president, Eric H. Wetterlow; treasurer, John Jaffray; clerk, Leon W. Carter; librarian, P. A. Gilmore; executive committee, A. E. Parsons, Wm. Till, Herbert Shaw, James Salter, Axel Magnuson.

A vote of thanks was extended to Ernest Townsend for display of chrysanthemums, including a nice lot of seedlings, also to Mr. Warner for collection of pansies.

The treasurer turned over to the society the title deeds to the land recently purchased near the R. R. station by the society, and where it hopes soon to erect a Horticultural Hall. Contrary to reports recently circulated there is no building committee appointed as yet. The sale of Lee's Hall, where the society had its headquarters for many years necessitated their moving to new quarters. The next meeting will be held in Lane's Hall, School street, Nov. 19th, at 7.30 P. M.

WILLIAM TILL.

AMERICAN DAHLIA SOCIETY.

A meeting of the Executive Board of the American Dahlia Society was held at the office of Secretary Joseph J. Lane, 11 West 32nd St., N. Y. City. Those present were as follows:

Richard Vincent, Jr., president, White Marsh, Md.; Frank R. Austin, treasurer, Tuckerton, N. J.; George L. Stillman, Westerly, R. I.; Hugo Kind, Hammonton, N. J.; John Merritt, Farmingdale, N. Y.; L. K. Peacock, Berlin, N. J.; Geo. W. Kerr, Doylestown, Pa.; James Kirby, Huntington, N. Y.; James Duthie, Oyster Bay, N. Y.; J. Harrison Dick, N. Y. City; Joseph J. Lane, N. Y. City.

The subject of nomenclature was discussed at great length and a letter read by Prof. Hall, Chairman of the Nomenclature Committee. Among other suggestions put forth were the registering of new varieties and the publication of 4,500 names of Dahlias and types, the appointment of local committees, like the Chrysanthemum Society, etc. Mr. Vincent suggested that a life membership be offered for a stipulated sum. The subject was laid on the table until next meeting.

A committee was appointed to solicit terms and places to hold our show in 1916 and get the best offers to bring up at the April meeting. This comprised Geo. W. Kerr, F. R. Austin, Frank R. Stillman, James Duthie and Richard Vincent. Mr. Peacock suggested that a leaflet be gotten up about the Dahlia Society and his suggestion was accepted. Mr. Peacock agreed to pay for 10,000 of these leaflets and mail them out with his catalogue.

A Publication Committee was appointed by the President, comprising Messrs. Kerr, Dick and Peacock, it being understood that the Secretary was to act as editor of the bulletin. The Secretary argued for the establishment of a sinking fund to tide the Society over any expenses that might be incurred during this first year in the form of investments, such as the printing of reports of the Nomenclature Committee, etc. Mr. Peacock started the fund with a contribution. This was followed by one from Messrs. Austin, Vincent, Kirby, Duthie, Stillman, Merritt and Kind.

JOSEPH J. LANE, Sec'y.

CHRYSANTHEMUM SOCIETY OF AMERICA.

Work of Committees.

The examining committees have submitted reports in new varieties as follows:

Exhibited at New York, Oct. 30, by Chas. H. Totty, Madison, N. J., No. 16, bronze, single, com. scale, 86 points; single white No. 20, white, single, com. scale, 90 points; Mrs. J. Gibson, light pink, Jap. ref., ex. scale, 89 points; Wm. Rigby, sp. of Mrs. G. Drabble, light yellow, Jap., ex. scale, 90 points; Seedling No. 1, yellow, Jap. inc., ex. scale, 88 points; Seedling No. 1, yellow, Jap. inc., ex. scale, 88 points. By Elmer D. Smith & Co., Adrian, Mich., Josephine Foley, white, Jap. inc., com. scale, 87 points. By Elmsford Nursery, Elmsford, N. Y., White Dotty, sp. of Lil Dotty, white, pompon, ex. scale, 95 points.

Exhibited at Boston, Mass., Oct. 30, by Elmer D. Smith, Adrian, Mich., Josephine Foley, white, Jap. inc., com. scale, 90 points, ex. scale, 87 points.

Exhibited at Chicago, Oct. 30, by Elmer D. Smith & Co., Adrian, Mich., Josephine Foley, white, Jap. inc., com. scale, 89 points.

Exhibited at Cincinnati, Oct. 30, by Elmer D. Smith & Co., Adrian, Mich., Josephine Foley, white, Jap. inc., com. scale, 90 points.

Exhibited at Philadelphia, Oct. 30, by Elmer D. Smith & Co., Adrian, Mich., Josephine Foley, white, Jap. inc., com. scale, 89 points; ex. scale, 90 points.

C. W. JOHNSON, Sec'y.

FLORISTS' CLUB OF WASHINGTON

The monthly meeting of the Florists' Club of Washington, D. C., was held November 2. There were quite a number of exhibits and the evening was made pleasant with a discussion as to the qualities of the flowers on view. The largest individual exhibit was that of Richard Vincent, Jr., of White Marsh, Md., who sent some seventy-five varieties of hardy pompon chrysanthemums. The several vases of Ophelia shown by David J. Grilbortzer, of Alexandria, Va. and the display of the new rose, Mrs. Moorfield Storey, by Otto Bauer for the S. S. Pennock-Meehan Company, attracted considerable attention.

What was considered to be the handsomest snapdragon be had at the present time was exhibited by John Gutman, of Congress Heights.

Seed Trade

Americus, Ga.—A new seed store has been opened here by the Planters Seed Company, W. C. Gardner, Mgr.

Los Angeles, Cal.—F. J. Poor and L. D. Rising have opened a seed store at 116-118 East 7th street under the name of the Western Seed Company.

The value of imports of horticultural material at the Port of New York for week ending October 30, is given as follows: Fertilizer, $3,205; manure salt, $5,427; clover seed, $765; grass seed, $5,116; trees, bulbs and plants, $12,186.

Minneapolis, Minn.—Northrup, King & Co. have purchased eight acres of land on Central avenue, between 14th and 18th avenues N. E., on which they plan to erect buildings next spring. The general offices will continue for a year or two at First street and Hennepin avenue.

CATALOGUES RECEIVED.

Wilbur A. Christy, Warren, Ohio—Price List of Mapleshade Gladioli.

M. Rice Co., Philadelphia, Pa.—Portfolio of Florists' Supplies and "Helpful Hints for Christmas."

Raymond W. Swett, Saxonville, Mass.—Price List of Riverbank Gardens Gladioli and Dahlias for 1915-1916.

P. A. H. Mathiji, Steenbergen, Holland—Trade Catalogue of Vegetable, Flower and Farm Seeds. A very complete price list.

Of Interest to Retail Florists

NEW FLOWER STORES.

Walden, N. Y.—Fred W. Zeitfuss.

Galt, Ont. — Fred Wells, N. Water street.

Rock Island, Ill.—Joseph R. Ruckis, 4th avenue.

Logan, Pa.—Jacob Wilhelm, 4943 N. Broad street.

Chicago, Ill.—Mrs. J. R. Foster, 4736 S. State street.

Glendale, Cal.—Kelly & McElroy, 422 S. Grand Blvd.

Reading, Pa.—Rosedale Floral Co., 46 N. 9th street.

Springfield, Mass.—Marshall Headle, Worthington street.

Milton, Mass.—M. F. Gray, 61 Adams street, Milton Village.

Waterville, Me.—Geo. F. Terry, succeeding Mitchell & Co.

Guthrie, Okla. — Mrs. Paul Bethel, 1310 W. Cleveland street.

Richmond Hill, N. Y.—Cross Flower Shop, 310 Lefferts avenue.

Pueblo, Col. — Majestic Flower Palace, G. Fleischer, proprietor.

Seattle, Wash. — L. W. McCoy, removing to Second avenue and Marion street.

Baltimore, Md. — Old Town Floral Co., removing to 2301 East Fayette street.

Houston, Tex.—Cotney Floral Company. H. C. Blecker, Washington street.

Elizabeth, N. J.—Union Square Floral Shop, removing to 807 Elizabeth avenue.

New York, N. Y.—Cunio's, 5th ave., near 59th street. Pitol & Constant, 66th street and Columbus avenue.

NEWS NOTES.

Kokomo, Ind.—Leroy Shauman, 600 West Walnut street, has leased the Aaron Deardoff Greenhouses.

New Haven, Ct.—M. B. Farquharson has purchased the flower store of Alfred T. Osterman, 123 Church street.

Providence, R. I.—Samuel Risnick, an employe of Joseph Koppelman of this city, was operated last Monday for appendicitis at a private hospital. He is reported as improving.

Brattleboro, Vt. — The management of the flower shop of Carl S. Hopkins has been transferred by the owner to Royal W. Smith, Mr. Hopkins' son-in-law, who took over the management Nov. 1.

New Hampton, Ia.—The greenhouses of F. R. Robinson were badly damaged by fire on Friday morning, October 22. The heating apparatus was put out of commission and much stock was destroyed.

Bristol, R. I.—Damage estimated at several hundred dollars resulted from a fire in the early morning of Nov. 3 in the greenhouses of Le Baron Bradford. The fire is said to have started from an oil stove and the sides of the house were burned through before the blaze was discovered. Mr. Bradford and others did good work with garden hose and the flames were under control when the firemen reached the scene.

CLUB AND SOCIETY NOTES.

A joint flower show will be held by the State Florists' Society of Minnesota, the Minneapolis Florists' Club and St. Paul Florists' Club on December 3 and 4, at the West Hotel.

The Montreal Gardeners' and Florists' Club will hold its annual banquet early in December. The next business meeting will take place on December 6, when election of officers will be in order.

A Florists' Club has been organized at Evansville, Ind., at the greenhouses of Niednagel & Sons. About twenty charter members were recorded. Officers were elected as follows: President, Wm. Halbrooks; Vice-President, Karl Zeidler; Secretary, E. L. Fenton; Treasurer, Emil Niednagel.

The State Florists' Association of Indiana had a field day at Richmond on Tuesday, Nov. 2, visiting the establishments of E. G. Hill Co., Chas. Knopf Floral Co., G. R. Gause, F. H. Lemon, Edw. Ruch, Fulle Bros., John A. Evans Co. and The Advance Co. The next meeting will be held at Fort Wayne on December 7.

The monthly meeting of the New Jersey Floricultural Society was held in Orange, N. J., on Monday, Nov. 1st. A talk on Tree Surgery and Entomology was given by F. A. Cutter, of Orange, which was enjoyed by the members. Max Schneider, gard. to Peter Hauck, Jr., received points in the following order: Begonia metallica 80, violets 60, carnations 70, chrysanthemums 70. Emil Panuska received 85 points for a fine specimen plant of Celosia Pride of Castle Gould. A vote of thanks was extended to Mr. Cutter.

The Cincinnati Florists' Society met at J. A. Peterson's place on Monday afternoon. Before the meeting J. A. Peterson and his sons showed the members through the greenhouses. There we saw a wonderful lot of Begonias, Mrs. J. A. Peterson, Mellor, and Glory of Cincinnati as well as cyclamen and other Peterson specialties. After luncheon Mrs. Peterson and Clarence Peterson exhibited pictures that were taken in the west when Mr. and Mrs. Peterson went to San Francisco last summer. The hosts were tendered a hearty vote of thanks for their generous hospitality.

Frank Dunlop, son of J. H. Dunlop, Toronto, Ont., will take the course in Floriculture at Cornell this season.

BUSINESS TROUBLES.

New York — Hanft Bros., florists, have filed schedules showing liabilities of $17,536 and assets of $1,828, consisting of accounts, $1,500; fixtures, $200; horse and wagon, $65; stock, $50, and cash, $13.

NEWS ITEMS FROM EVERYWHERE

NEW YORK.

The Brooklyn Wholesale Cut Flower Market has been opened at 408 Fulton street.

Clarence Slinn, the wholesale florist, has moved to a new and more commodious store at 123 West 28th street.

Riedel & Myer report business as starting in well for a new firm and see a good outlook for the coming winter's trade.

Guttman & Raynor express much confidence in the future of the new rose, Prima Donna, which they are especially featuring.

The MacNiff Horticultural Co. are working night and day to try to keep up with the volume of business that is coming in, and find it impossible to take care of it all properly. The sales they are having this fall are unquestionably the largest that have ever been conducted in this country, and nursery stock from Holland combined with local consignments.

At a meeting of the International Flower Show Committee, held in New York on Monday, November 8, Arthur Herrington, Madison, N. J., was appointed manager of the show to be held in the Grand Central Palace, New York, next April. At the meeting, also, details concerning the show were discussed, and the work of preparation seen to be well advanced.

SAN FRANCISCO.

D. Lichtenstein and Herbert Blumenthal, partners in the Terminal Florist establishment on the Embarcadero near the ferry, have separated, Mr. Lichtenstein continuing the business.

The Cottage Gardens Nurseries at Eureka is getting in a big shipment of European stock at present. The new house is ready for the new arrivals, and a large reservoir is under construction to hold water for irrigation.

M. Ebel, of Sacramento, is visiting the local trade at present. He is getting a fine lot of chrysanthemums from the Lynch Nursery Company, from the same lots that took a lot of first prizes at the San Francisco and Menlo Park shows, which he says are creating a sensation in Sacramento.

PHILADELPHIA.

H. A. Dreer, Inc., have been officially notified that a gold medal was awarded to them for their aquatic exhibit at San Francisco, an illustration of which was given in HORTICULTURE for October 30.

The business of H. Bayersdorfer & Co., has again overtaxed the facilities of the big establishment on Arch street and an adjoining four-story building on 12th street has been acquired. The new floors will be devoted to the basket manufacturing department which has within the last few years been growing tremendously.

BOSTON.

W. Joseph Karp succeeds Ed. Stout as salesman for the Boston Rose Co.

J. K. M. L. Farquhar goes to St. Louis next week, where he is to deliver a lecture at the Missouri Botanical Garden.

N. F. McCarthy & Co. are happy over the winning of three 1st prizes in the rose classes at the Holyoke and Northampton exhibition last week.

Waverly Star is the name of a very large and perfectly formed Anemone chrysanthemum exhibited at the show by George Detlefsen of Watertown.

John J. Cassidy, retail florist, and an appointee to the Sinking Fund Commissioners by Mayor Curley, is a candidate for election to the City Council.

The Co-operative Flower Market stockholders' annual meeting was held on Saturday evening, October 30, at Hurlburt's Hotel. Perry Green and Carl Strieferd were elected directors. The treasurer's statement showed an excellent financial condition.

CHICAGO.

Mrs. Frank Oechslin is again very ill.

Fifteen florists from St. Louis and vicinity arrived Tuesday to visit the flower show. Most of them are going on to Cleveland and will return to Chicago.

A visit to Sam'l Pearse's place on Higgins avenue, will be a delight to lovers of the big flower, for they are in their prime this week. The collection includes all colors and curves and the tables in the large service shed gave one the impression that a chrysanthemum show was in progress.

The J. C. Moninger Co. are exhibiting a miniature greenhouse at the Cleveland Flower Show. It is a complete model of an iron frame greenhouse true to a scale of ¼. It occupies a space of 8x12 ft. and is under the personal charge of Mr. Kurowski, vice-president of the firm. This firm is so busy that the steel department is working nights to fill orders.

WASHINGTON, D. C.

The silver loving cup offered to the florist making the best exhibit of flowers at the Maryland State Fair, recently held in Laurel, Md., was again awarded to Gude Bros. Company, who exhibited a large collection of roses, chrysanthemums and dahlias.

Michael J. McCabe, of Anacostia, D. C., successfully defended himself in the case brought against him by the Merchants' Transfer and Storage Company, which alleged that it had delivered in error to him a consignment of bulbs from abroad intended for another party. They sued to recover the value of the bulbs, the duty thereon, and other expenses amounting to $166.90. A jury brought in a verdict for the florist but the plaintiff has since filed a motion for a new trial.

ST. LOUIS

Quite a good-size delegation of local florists left here Monday night, November 8, for a trip to Chicago and Cleveland to visit the flower shows. They visit Chicago on Tuesday, and the rest of the week will be spent in Cleveland.

The annual meeting of the State Horticultural Society will be held in St. Louis at the Planters Hotel the latter part of December. At this meeting an effort will be made to organize a state florists' association such as the Illinois State Florists' Association.

The special meeting of the Florist Club held on November 4 at Windler's wholesale house was attended by twenty-five members and they decided to change the regular meeting day from November 11 to November 18. This meeting to be held at Shaw's Garden.

The 26th annual banquet given by the Missouri Botanical Garden to florists, nurserymen and gardeners will be held at the Leiderkranz Club, Friday night, November 19. Covers will be laid for about four hundred and talks will be made by prominent speakers.

NOTES.

Woburn, Mass. — An old Colonial home, dating from 1775, was destroyed in a $10,000 fire on Nov. 9, that also burned a barn and carriage shed. J. W. Howard, the Somerville florist, is owner of the property.

Bristol, R. I. — The Bristol Garden Club held an interesting meeting Nov. 3 at the home of Mrs. S. S. Drury. The cultivation of bulbs was the subject of discussion. The following officers were elected. Honorary President, Mrs. E. S. Babbitt; President, George M. Millard: treasurer, Miss S. V. G. Peck; secretary, Miss M. R. Drury.

Pawtucket, R. I. — Kissing his wife and baby before going to a lodge meeting John W. Seamans, a prominent florist, has been missing since October 22. Chief of Police Hill says Seamans was a model husband and he believes the missing man would return home if he was alive. Seamans, according to Chief Hill, is thirty, height five feet, seven inches, weight 180 pounds, black hair, dark brown eyes, rosy cheeks.

North Andover, Mass.—The Osgood Hill greenhouses, where the fifth annual chrysanthemum show was open to public inspection on Sunday, were the scene of a gathering of gardeners from Lawrence, Haverhill, Andover and Methuen on Monday, Nov. 9, who were the guests of George Westland, the gardener in charge of the estate. The magnificent array of blooms was greatly admired by the visiting experts who paid glowing tribute to the skill of Mr. Westland in floriculture. Luncheon was afforded the visitors by Mr. and Mrs. Nathaniel Stevens.

During Recess

Boston Florists' Bowling Club.

Galvin	1337	vs.	Carbone	1254
Flower Market	1330	"	M. & M.	1216
Flower Ex	1267	"	Pansies	1232
Robinson	1214	"	Zinn	1185

STANDING AS TO POINTS:

	Won	Lost		Won	Lost
Galvin	17	3	Carbone	9	11
Flower M'k't	16	4	Flower Ex.	8	12
Zinn	11	9	Robinson	6	14
Pansies	9	11	M. & M.	4	16

New York Florists' Bowling Club.

At the opening meeting of the N. Y. Florists' Bowling Club the following officers were elected for the coming season: J. Miesem, pres.; H. C. Riedel, sec'y; P. Jacobson, treas.; J. Fenrich, cap't.

SCORES.

J.Miesem	178 155 160	P.J'c'bs'n	140 157 145
J.Fenrich	140 147 147	A.Kakuda	160 145 150
C.W.Scott	148 164 144	W.P.Ford	137 134 159
H.C.R'del	 181	A.J.G'tm'n	... 131 156

H. C. RIEDEL, Sec'y.

Members of the Pacific Coast Horticultural Society of San Francisco and the Ladies' Auxiliary enjoyed a very pleasant evening at Red Men's Hall on the evening of October 28, at which the Ladies' Auxiliary were hosts. A good crowd of the men attended, both from this city and across the bay. Part of the evening was taken up with a whist contest, at which Mrs. Rose won the prize, and later the younger or more active members of the party danced until well into the night. An enjoyable musical program was also given during the evening.

PERSONAL.

Harry A. Barnard, representative of Stuart Low & Co., England, sails for home on the St. Louis, on Saturday, November 13.

E. M. Miller of Miller & Sons, Toronto, Ont., met with an accident on October 31 while out shooting, his shotgun being accidentally discharged and injuring his right arm so badly that amputation was necessary.

Joseph Rosenthal, who for the past two years has been foreman at the Reuter greenhouses at Westerly, R. I., has gone to Cornell University, Ithaca, N. Y., where he will take a course in

DIRECTORS OF THE CHICAGO FLOWER GROWERS' ASSOCIATION.

Names of board of directors of the Chicago Flower Growers' Association, shown in the accompanying picture, reading from left to right, are Jos Schoos, Anton Then, R. Ellsworth, C. McCauley, Paul Klingsporn, Fred Schramm, Ed. Meuret, Geo. Weiland. F. Stielow. The association was incorporated in 1911 at 176 N. Michigan avenue, and in the main, the stock handled by them is of their own growing. They are all men who have made good in the business, hence the success of the association. F. Stielow and A. Then are pioneer growers of Chicago. Jas. Schoos, of Evanston, is

floriculture, upon the conclusion of which he will accept a position as instructor of floriculture and superintendent of grounds at the Baron De Hirsh school at Woodbine, N. J.

FOR BETTER COLLECTIONS.

The wholesale florists of St. Louis have sent out the following circular letter to the retail trade:

To Our Patrons:

Owing to the unsatisfactory credit system now in vogue by the wholesale florists of St. Louis, it has become neces-

a well-known carnation specialist and has introduced new varieties; Chas. McCauley came here from Washington, D. C., to be superintendent of a large place at Lake Geneva, Wis.; Geo. We'land succeeded his father in a business started many years ago at Evanston; Ed. Meuret, president of the association, is a carnation specialist at Park Ridge; R. Ellsworth, a rose grower at Downer's Grove, and Paul Klingsporn, manager, came here from Philadelphia and to his efforts largely is due the success of the past two years and the removal into a more desirable location.

sary to make some changes for the betterment of both the wholesaler and the legitimate retailer.

In the future all statements rendered on the first of the month must be paid on or before the 15th of the month. (There are no exceptions to this rule.) In all cases where accounts are not settled on or before that date, goods purchased the next day and thereafter will be sent C. O. D. until the account is put in good standing.

Thanking you for your patronage in the past and hoping that you will continue to favor us, we are,

Respectfully,

Geo. H. Angermueller, H. G. Berning, C. A. Kuehn, Wm. C. Smith Whol. Flo. Co., Windler Whol. Flo. Co.

Flower Market Reports

BOSTON We have seldom seen the wholesale flower market in so unpromising and hopeless condition as at this time, and the worst feature of it is that prospects do not favor any immediate improvement, but on the contrary, the bottom does not seem to be reached yet, and we may see it much worse before it is any better. Chrysanthemums, lilies and carnations are congested beyond description. Roses are probably just as badly accumulated but the surplus is tucked away in the storage boxes and consequently does not tell its predicament as openly as do those things which must stand around in vases in full view. Orchids, lily of the valley, violets and, indeed, every other flower common to the trade at this season are in supply far beyond the needs of the dull market now prevailing. Naturally, there are no fixed values at such a time.

BUFFALO Business quiet. Receipts heavy on most lines and especially on roses of which there is an enormous supply and the demand weak. Chrysanthemums are plentiful enough though at the end of last week they cleaned up well. Turner, Bonnaffon, Dr. Enguehard, Adelia, Ivory, Josephine, Maud Dean and Brutus are all of exceptional good quality. Violets moving only fair, plenty of carnations and lily of the valley. Lilies about equal the demand. Beauties scarce and price holding firm.

CHICAGO Flower Show week and chrysanthemum season at its height, give the market a gala appearance. All other flowers are temporarily in the background. Business is fairly good and all kinds of stock are moving, though there are days when the market could take care of more orders for the warm, bright sunshine is bringing the flowers along at a rapid rate. There are a great many chrysanthemum plants coming into the market all this week, nearly all the large houses keeping a good supply or taking orders from sample plants. Carnations are rather ahead of demand. Roses of all kinds are to be had in any quantity and American Beauties are in good supply and of excellent quality.

CINCINNATI The market is somewhat overloaded with stock, while the demand is not all it might be. The daily cut of chrysanthemums is more than able to care for all demands upon it. Both Pompons and the Anemone varieties are in a large supply. The rose cut, too, is very large and excellent. Carnations and lilies are each plentiful.

NEW YORK This market is more than supplied with every possible line of cut flowers. The heavy crop that comes naturally at this particular date in which chrysanthemums take the lead, of course, is aggravated by the continued series of warm, sunny days which pushes everything along at a rapid rate but which awakens one compensating possibility — that when the wintry blasts do come, there will be "something doing" for every good flower that strikes the market. At present, nothing is scarce and the retail people get their stock at their own price and in quantity as they choose to take it. They all report trade as exasperatingly slow.

PHILADELPHIA General conditions have remained fairly good. On the whole there is not very much to complain of. Roses continue plentiful and in fine shape, American Beauty, Russell and Hadley being leaders. There is also an extra fine showing in Shawyer at present and we have never seen Ophelia to better advantage. The Killarneys are fine but too many, which hits the returns and raises a storm. The producer sits at home and smokes his pipe and waits for his check. When it isn't big enough—wow! look out! Does he blame the market? No, siree. There are cutthroats and scoundrels around and he hies him to the city and starts in to raise cain. O yes, there are still a few such left. They don't keep track of the market by frequent visits to the city but instead froth at the mouth when things are not up to their exaggerated anticipations. Carnations are about as satisfactory as could be expected. The best demand is for the higher grades. The vast majority are medium flowers however, and so plentiful as to be rather draggy. The chrysanthemum is of course right in the flush of her splendor as the Queen of Autumn. Roman Gold is a remarkable favorite—not so big but fine form and color and a great keeper. But the par excellence is still Bonnaffon. Probably more good points to the square inch than any other variety of its color. It sells well no matter how big the flower. In

(Continued on page 647)

WHOLESALE FLOWER MARKETS — TRADE PRICES—Per 100 TO DEALERS ONLY

Roses	BOSTON Nov. 11		ST. LOUIS Nov. 8		PHILA. N. v. 8	
Am. Beauty, Special	12.00 to	25.00	20.00 to	25.00	20.00 to	25.00
" " Fancy and Extra	8.00 to	10.00	10.00 to	15.00	12.00 to	8.00
" " No. 1	3.00 to	5.00	5.00 to	8.00	8.00 to	10.00
Russell, Hadley	4.00 to	8.00	5.00 to	10.00	4.00 to	20.00
Killarney, Richmond, Hillingdon, Ward, Extra	4.00 to	5.00	2.00 to	6.00	4.00 to	8.00
" " " " Ordinary	1.00 to	3.00	1.00 to	2.00	2.00 to	3.00
Arenburg, Radiance, Taft, Key, Extra	4.00 to	6.00	..... to	.....	4.00 to	8.00
" " " " Ordinary	1.00 to	3.00	..... to	.....	2.00 to	3.00
Ophelia, Mock, Sunburst, Extra	4.00 to	8.00	5.00 to	6.00	4.00 to	8.00
" " " Ordinary	1.00 to	3.00	2.00 to	4.00	2.00 to	3.00
Carnations, Fancy	1.50 to	2.00	1.00 to	2.00	..... to	2.00
" Ordinary	.50 to	1.50	.50 to	.75	..... to	1.00
Cattleyas	20.00 to	40.00	..... to	50.00	60.00 to	75.00
Dendrobium formosum	..... to	25.00	..... to	.....	40.00 to	50.00
Lilies, Longiflorum	3.00 to	5.00	10.00 to	12.50	6.00 to	10.00
" Rubrum	..... to	3.00	4.00 to	6.00	3.00 to	6.00
Lily of the Valley	2.00 to	4.00	3.00 to	4.00	2.00 to	4.00
Daisies	.50 to	1.00	.85 to	.50	.50 to	.75
Violets	.40 to	.60	.25 to	.35	.25 to	.50
Snapdragon	1.00 to	3.00	4.00 to	6.00	3.00 to	5.00
Chrysanthemums	1.00 to	12.00	3.00 to	25.00	5.00 to	25.00
Sweet Peas	..... to	1.00	.50 to	1.00	.50 to	.75
Gardenias	20.00 to	25.00	..... to	.....	30.00 to	40.00
Adiantum	..... to	1.00	1.00 to	1.25	..... to	1.00
Smilax	12.00 to	16.00	10.00 to	12.50	15.00 to	20.00
Asparagus Plumosus, Strings (100)	25.00 to	50.00	25.00 to	50.00	..... to	50.00
" & Spren. (100 Bchs.)	25.00 to	35.00	20.00 to	35.00	35.00 to	50.00

Flower Market Reports

(Continued from page 645)

holiday market, and many of the pompons the best sellers are the indoor grown. These are better as to color, form and finish than the outdoor and always get the preference. No other ills worthy of mention in Pennsylvania for the time being. Massachusetts has annexed a citizen of East Providence, this state, and made him governor, but never mind, we take that as a compliment.

PITTSBURGH   The wonderfully beautiful weather that has made the present autumn distinctive, is proving detrimental to the wholesale florists and these retail firms as well. All flowers in season are plentiful and of the best. Last Saturday the football game happily made big inroads on the chrysanthemum growers and dispensers.

SAN FRANCISCO   The trade has been hoping for a good rain, which would stimulate trade and clear a lot of unseasonable stuff out of the way, but only a little shower has fallen so far. There is quite a lot of small outdoor stock coming in every day—stocks, cosmos. etc., even a few zinnias, and most of it finds a market. It looks as if this week would finish the gladioli and dahlias, after a long season. The market is fairly glutted with chrysanthemums, and the finest kind of stock goes begging. A great many growers and dealers are making heavy shipments east nearly every day, but fail to clean up the offerings, and the Chinese chrysanthemums are a drug on the market. Pompons are extensively used. Cooler weather has helped the violets, which are about at their prime; even the shipping varieties seem to be reaching the east in fine shape and shipments have increased rapidly this week. With them also are shipped many Cecile Brunner roses, of which there is a fine large crop, but not any too much for requirements. Carnations are showing up well now, but receive little attention. Roses are good and most varieties fairly plentiful, but the daily arrivals are pretty well taken up by the local trade. Of Killarneys. only the white variety now finds much favor. Russell is very popular and Ophelia is as big a seller as ever. In flowering plants, the supply of cyclamen is gradually increasing, and potted chrysanthemums are also quite popular. There will be a large supply of

cyclamen, from all indications, on the plants now blooming are exceptionally fine. Orchids are offered freely and rather less attention is given to gardenias.

ST. LOUIS   All of the past week the market has been in an overcrowded condition and prices have dropped considerably. The weather has been too good for good business. Chrysanthemums are at their height now and nearly all varieties are coming into this market in big lots. Roses and carnations have hardly any fixed value. Violets have been ruined by the warm spell and have little demand. Some extra fancy Spencer peas are now coming in and they sell well. Fine lily of the valley and lilies are in good supply and demand.

WASHINGTON   The market continues overstocked, with chrysanthemums predominating. Good chrysanthemums are selling well. There is, however, a surplus of cheap stock and much of this must be thrown away. The weather continues too warm for violets and the sale on these is de-

cidedly draggy. Sweet peas meet with as plentiful as they have been, while there are more lilies and lily of the valley than during the previous week. Some exceptionally fine roses are now being offered. Dahlias have passed off the market for this season. The retailers say that business is up to, if not in advance of standard, and present indications are that a very busy season is ahead.

Buyer's Directory and Ready Reference Guide

Advertisements under this head, one cent a word.   Initials count as words.

Display advertisers in this issue are also listed under this classification without charge. Reference to List of Advertisers will indicate the respective pages.

Buyers failing to find what they want in this list will confer a favor by writing us and we will try to put them in communication with reliable dealers.

ACCOUNTANT
R. Dysart, 40 State St., Boston.
For page see List of Advertisers.

APHINE
Aphine Mfg. Co., Madison, N. J.
For page see List of Advertisers.

APHIS PUNK
Nicotine Mfg. Co., St. Louis, Mo.
For page see List of Advertisers.

ARAUCARIAS
Thomas Cogger, Melrose, Mass.
For page see List of Advertisers.

ASPARAGUS
Asparagus Sprengeri, fine 2¼-in., $2.50 per 100; $20.00 per 1000. Cash. M. F. BYXBEE, Norwalk, Conn.

W. H. Elliott, Brighton, Mass.
Asparagus Plumosus Nanus Seed.

AUCTION SALES
The MacNiff Horticultural Co.,
New York City.
Plant and Bulb Sales by Auction.
For page see List of Advertisers.

Elliott Auction Co., New York City.
For page see List of Advertisers.

AZALEAS
P. Ouwerkerk, Hoboken, N. J.
For page see List of Advertisers.

Thomas Cogger, Melrose, Mass.
For page see List of Advertisers.

BAY TREES
August Rolker & Sons, New York.
For page see List of Advertisers.

BEDDING PLANTS
A. N. Pierson, Inc., Cromwell, Conn.
For page see List of Advertisers.

R. Vincent, Jr. & Sons Co.,
White Marsh, Md.
For page see List of Advertisers.

BEGONIAS
Thomas Roland, Nahant, Mass.

		Per 100
BEGONIA LORRAINE,	2½ in.	$12.00
	3 in.	20.00
	4 in.	35.00
	5 in.	50.00
BEGONIA CINCINNATI,	2½ in.	15.00
	3 in.	25.00
	3½ in.	30.00
	4½ in.	40.00

JULIUS ROEHRS CO., Rutherford, N. J.

BOILERS
Kroeschell Bros. Co., Chicago.
For page see List of Advertisers.

King Construction Co., North Tonawanda, N. Y.
"King Ideal" Boiler.
For page see List of Advertisers.

Lord & Burnham Co., New York City.

Hitchings & Co., New York City.
For page see List of Advertisers.

BOXES—CUT FLOWER FOLDING
Edwards Folding Box Co., Philadelphia.
For page see List of Advertisers.

Folding cut flower boxes, the best made. Write for list. HOLTON & HUNKEL CO., Milwaukee, Wis.

BOX TREES
BOX TREES—Standards, Pyramids and Bush, in various sizes. Price List on demand. JULIUS ROEHRS CO., Rutherford, N. J.

BULBS AND TUBERS
Arthur T. Boddington Co., Inc.,
New York City.
For page see List of Advertisers.

J. M. Thorburn & Co., New York City
Wholesale Price List of High Class Bulbs.
For page see List of Advertisers.

Ralph M. Ward & Co., New York City.
Lily Bulbs.
For page see List of Advertisers.

John Lewis Childs, Flowerfield, L. I., N. Y.
For page see List of Advertisers.

August Rolker & Sons, New York City.
Holland and Japan Bulbs.
For page see List of Advertisers.

R. & J. Farquhar & Co., Boston, Mass.
For page see List of Advertisers.

F. R. Pierson, Tarrytown, N. Y.
Hyacinths and Narcissus.
For page see List of Advertisers.

S. S. Skidelsky & Co., Philadelphia, Pa.
For page see List of Advertisers.

Chas. Schwake & Co., New York City.
Horticultural Importers and Exporters.
For page see List of Advertisers.

A. Henderson & Co., Chicago, Ill.
For page see List of Advertisers.

Burnett Bros., 98 Chambers St., New York.
For page see List of Advertisers.

Henry F. Michell Co., Philadelphia, Pa.
For page see List of Advertisers.

Joseph Breck & Sons Corp., Boston, Mass.
For page see List of Advertisers.

Fottler, Fiske, Rawson Co., Boston, Mass.
For page see List of Advertisers.

C. KEUR & SONS, HILLEGOM, Holland.
Bulbs of all descriptions. Write for prices.
NEW YORK Branch, 8-10 Bridge St.

CANNAS
Canna Specialists.
Send for Canna book.
THE CONARD & JONES COMPANY,
West Grove, Pa.

CARNATIONS
Wood Bros., Fishkill, N. Y.
For page see List of Advertisers.

F. R. Pierson, Tarrytown, N. Y.
Carnation Specialists.
For page see List of Advertisers.

F. Dorner & Sons Co., Lafayette, Ind.
For page see List of Advertisers.

Jas. Vick's Sons, Rochester, N. Y.
Field Grown Plants.
For page see List of Advertisers.

Littlefield & Wyman, North Abington, Mass.
New Pink Carnation, Miss Theo.
For page see List of Advertisers.

CARNATION STAPLES
Split carnations quickly, easily and cheaply mended. Pillsbury's Carnation Staple, 1000 for 35c.; 3000 for $1.00 post paid. I. L. PILLSBURY, Galesburg, Ill.

Supreme Carnation Staples, for repairing split carnations, 35c. per 1000; 3000 for $1.00. F. W. WAITE, 85 Belmont Ave., Springfield, Mass.

CHRYSANTHEMUMS
Chas. H. Totty, Madison, N. J.
For page see List of Advertisers.

THE BEST 1915 NOVELTIES.
The Cream of 1914 Introductions.
The most popular Commercial and Exhibition kinds; also complete line of Pompons, Singles and Anemones. Trade list on application. ELMER D. SMITH & CO., Adrian, Mich.

COCOANUT FIBRE SOIL
20th Century Plant Food Co., Beverly, Mass
For page see List of Advertisers.

DAHLIAS
Send for Wholesale List of whole clumps and separate stock; 40,000 clumps for sale. Northboro Dahlia and Gladiolus Gardens. J. L. MOORE, Prop, Northboro, Mass.

NEW PAEONY DAHLIA
John Wanamaker, Newest, Handsomest, Best. New color, new form and new habit of growth. Big stock of best cut-flower varieties. Send list of wants to PEACOCK DAHLIA FARMS, Berlin, N. J.

DECORATIVE PLANTS
Robert Craig Co., Philadelphia, Pa.
For page see List of Advertisers.

Woodrow & Marketos, New York City.
For page see List of Advertisers.

S. S. Skidelsky & Co., Philadelphia, Pa.
For page see List of Advertisers.

Bobbink & Atkins, Rutherford, N. J.
For page see List of Advertisers.

A. Leuthy & Co., Roslindale, Boston, Mass.
For page see List of Advertisers.

FERNS
John Scott, Brooklyn, N. Y.
The Home of the Scottii Fern.
For page see List of Advertisers.

H. H. Barrows & Son, Whitman, Mass.
For page see List of Advertisers.

Robert Craig Co., Philadelphia, Pa.
For page see List of Advertisers.

McHutchison & Co., New York City.
Ferns in Flats.
For page see List of Advertisers.

A. M. Davenport, Watertown, Mass.
Boston and Whitmani Ferns.
For page see List of Advertisers.

Roman J. Irwin, New York City.
Boston and Whitmani Ferns.
For page see List of Advertisers.

FERTILIZERS
20th Century Plant Food Co., Beverly, Mass.
Cocoanut Fibre Soil.

Stumpp & Walter Co., New York City.
Scotch Soot.
For page see List of Advertisers.

Chicago Feed & Fertilizer Co., Chicago, Ill.
Magic Manures.

Pulverized Manure Co., Chicago, Ill.
Wizard Brand Cattle Manure.
For page see List of Advertisers.

FLORISTS' LETTERS
Boston Florist Letter Co., Boston, Mass.
For page see List of Advertisers.

For List of Advertisers See Page 627

NURSERY STOCK—Continued
The D. Hill Nursery Co., Dundee, Ill.
Hill's Evergreens.
For page see List of Advertisers.

Bay State Nurseries, North Abington, Mass.
Hardy, Northern Grown Stock.
For page see List of Advertisers.

Bobbink & Atkins, Rutherford, N. J.
For page see List of Advertisers.

Framingham Nurseries, Framingham, Mass.
For page see List of Advertisers.

August Rolker & Sons, New York City.
For page see List of Advertisers.

NUT GROWING.
The Nut-Grower, Waycross, Ga.

ORCHID FLOWERS
Jas. McManus, New York, N. Y.
For page see List of Advertisers.

ORCHID PLANTS
Julius Roehrs Co., Rutherford, N. J.
For page see List of Advertisers.

Lager & Hurrell, Summit, N. J.

PALMS, ETC.
Robert Craig Co., Philadelphia, Pa.
For page see List of Advertisers.

August Rolker & Sons, New York City.
For page see List of Advertisers.

A. Leuthy & Co., Roslindale, Boston, Mass.
For page see List of Advertisers.

Thomas Cogger, Melrose, Mass.
For page see List of Advertisers.

PANSY PLANTS
William Sim, Cliftondale, Mass.
Sim's Gold Medal Pansies.
For page see List of Advertisers.

Pansy Plants, mixed varieties in bud
and bloom, $15.00 per 1000. Cash. JAMES
MOSS, Johnsville, Pa.

Pansy Plants for the benches, nice stocky
plants, $5.00 per 1000, 5000 or more, $4.00
per 1000. Cash. JAMES MOSS, Johnsville,
Pa.

PANSY SEED
Fottler, Fiske, Rawson Co., Boston, Mass.
For page see List of Advertisers.

PEONIES
Peonies. The world's greatest collection.
1200 sorts. Send for list. C. BETSCHER,
Canal Dover, O.

PECKY CYPRESS BENCHES
A. T. Stearns Lumber Co., Boston, Mass.
For page see List of Advertisers.

PIPE AND FITTINGS
Kroeschell Bros. Co., Chicago.
For page see List of Advertisers.

King Construction Company,
N. Tonawanda, N. Y.
Shelf Brackets and Pipe Hangers.
For page see List of Advertisers.

PLANT AND BULB IMPORTS
Chas. Schwake & Co., New York City.
For page see List of Advertisers.

August Rolker & Sons, New York City.
For page see List of Advertisers.

PLANT TRELLISES AND STAKES
Seele's Tieless Plant Stakes and Trellises. H. D. SEELE & SONS, Elkhart, Ind.

PLANT TUBS
H. A. Dreer, Philadelphia, Pa.
"Riverton Special."
For page see List of Advertisers.

PLANTS WANTED
C. C. Trepel, New York City.
For page see List of Advertisers.

RAFFIA
McHutchison, & Co., New York, N. Y.
For page see List of Advertisers.

RHODODENDRONS
P. Ouwerkerk, Hoboken, N. J.
For page see List of Advertisers.

Framingham Nurseries, Framingham, Mass.
For page see List of Advertisers.

RIBBONS AND CHIFFONS
S. S. Pennock-Meehan Co., Philadelphia, Pa.
For page see List of Advertisers.

ROSES
Poehlmann Bros. Co., Morton Grove, Ill.
For page see List of Advertisers.

P. Ouwerkerk, Hoboken, N. J.
For page see List of Advertisers.

Robert Craig Co., Philadelphia, Pa.
For page see List of Advertisers.

W. & T. Smith Co., Geneva, N. Y.
American Grown Roses.
For page see List of Advertisers.

Bay State Nurseries, North Abington, Mass.
For page see List of Advertisers.

August Rolker & Sons, New York City.
For page see List of Advertisers.

Framingham Nurseries, Framingham, Mass.
For page see List of Advertisers.

A. N. Pierson, Inc., Cromwell, Conn.
For page see List of Advertisers.

THE CONARD & JONES COMPANY,
Rose Specialists.
West Grove, Pa. Send for offers.

SCALECIDE
B. G. Pratt Co., New York City.
For page see List of Advertisers.

SEASONABLE PLANT STOCK
R. Vincent, Jr. & Sons Co., White Marsh
Md.
For page see List of Advertisers.

SEED GROWERS
California Seed Growers' Association,
San Jose, Cal.
For page see List of Advertisers.

SEEDS
Carter's Tested Seeds,
Seeds with a Pedigree.
Boston, Mass., and London, England.
For page see List of Advertisers.

Kelway & Son,
Langport, Somerset, England.
Kelway's Celebrated English Strain Garden
Seeds.
For page see List of Advertisers.

Joseph Breck & Sons, Boston, Mass.
For page see List of Advertisers.

J. Bolgiano & Son, Baltimore, Md.
For page see List of Advertisers.

A. T. Boddington Co., Inc., New York City.
For page see List of Advertisers.

Chas. Schwake & Co., New York City.
For page see List of Advertisers.

Michell's Seed House, Philadelphia, Pa.
For page see List of Advertisers.

W. Atlee Burpee & Co., Philadelphia, Pa
For page see List of Advertisers.

R. & J. Farquhar & Co., Boston, Mass.
For page see List of Advertisers.

SEEDS—Continued
J. M. Thorburn & Co., New York City.
For page see List of Advertisers.

S. Bryson Ayres Co., Independence, Mo.
Sweet Peas.
For page see List of Advertisers.

Loechner & Co., New York City.
For page see List of Advertisers.

Ant. C. Zvolanek, Lompoc, Cal.
Winter Flowering Sweet Pea Seed.
For page see List of Advertisers.

S. S. Skidelsky & Co., Philadelphia, Pa.
For page see List of Advertisers.

W. E. Marshall & Co., New York City.
Seeds, Plants and Bulbs.
For page see List of Advertisers.

August Rolker & Sons, New York City.
For page see List of Advertisers.

Barnett Bros., 98 Chambers St., New York.
For page see List of Advertisers.

Fottler, Fiske, Rawson Co., Boston, Mass.
Seeds for the Florist.
For page see List of Advertisers.

SKINNER IRRIGATION SYSTEM
Skinner Irrigation Co., Brookline, Mass.
For page see List of Advertisers.

SPHAGNUM MOSS
Live Sphagnum moss, orchid peat and
orchid baskets always on hand. LAGER
& HURRELL, Summit, N. J.

SPRAYING MATERIALS
B. G. Pratt Co., New York City.
For page see List of Advertisers.

STANDARD THERMOMETERS
Standard Thermo Co., Boston, Mass.
For page see List of Advertisers.

STOVE PLANTS
Orchids—Largest stock in the country—
Stove plants and Crotons, finest collection.
JULIUS ROEHRS CO., Rutherford, N. J.

SWEET PEA SEED
Arthur T. Boddington Co., Inc.,
New York City.
Winter Flowering Sweet Peas.
For page see List of Advertisers.

Ant. C. Zvolanek, Lompoc, Calif.
Gold Medal of Honor Winter Orchid Sweet
Peas.
For page see List of Advertisers.

S. Bryson Ayres Co.,
Sunnyslope, Independence, Mo.
For page see List of Advertisers.

VEGETABLE PLANTS
R. Vincent, Jr. & Sons Co.,
White Marsh, Md.
For page see List of Advertisers.

VENTILATING APPARATUS
The Advance Co., Richmond, Ind.
For page see List of Advertisers.

The John A. Evans Co., Richmond, Ind.
For page see List of Advertisers.

VERMICIDES
Aphine Mfg. Co., Madison, N. J.
For page see List of Advertisers.

WIRED TOOTHPICKS
W. J. Cowee, Berlin, N. Y.
For page see List of Advertisers.

WIREWORK
Reed & Keller, New York City.
For page see List of Advertisers.

WILLIAM E. HEILSCHER'S WIRE
WORKS, 264 Randolph St., Detroit, Mich.

For List of Advertisers See Page 627

MASSACHUSETTS AGRICULTURAL COLLEGE.

"The best show that the department ever gave," was the general comment on the flower show held at the
college this week. The show was
opened Sunday noon by ex-President
Taft, who in company with President
Butterfield made an inspection of the
whole show. The exhibits were the
result of the co-operation of the Northampton and Holyoke Florists' and Gardeners' Club and of the students in
floriculture.

The Northampton and Holyoke Florists and Gardeners are especially to
be complimented on their exhibit of
carnation, Butler & Uhlman, R. S.
Carey, Keyes, Sinclair and G. Strugnell being the contributors. An extraordinary exhibit was that of some
foliage plants by W. P. Downer of
Smith College. The student decorative
was also of excellent calibre.

In the senior flower basket competition, first was awarded E. J. Cadarelli,
of Boston, for a basket of Major Bonnaffons arranged with oak foliage and
tied with yellow chiffon. C. E. Wildon,
of Melrose Highlands, 2nd, for a basket of Mary Colliday and Irene Craigg
chrysanthemums, the handle tied with
pink chiffon. S. W. Hall of Saxonville
3rd for an arrangement of Mrs. Russell roses and blue ribbon. R. L. Chis-
holm, of Melrose Highlands, received
honorable mention for a basket of
Major Bonnaffons and barberries.

Campbell received 1st for a table
arrangement of Peter Pan chrysanthemums. E. S. Duffill, Melrose Highlands, 2nd with yellow pompons and
oak leaves. J. T. Dizer, East Weymouth, 3rd for a table of Hadley and
White Killarney roses. M. R. Lawrence, Falmouth, received honorable
mention for a table of small yellow
chrysanthemums. A shower bouquet
of gardenias and valley and a basket
of marguerites by Mr. Butler, Northampton, together with a bouquet of
Aaron Ward roses made by Prof.
Nehrling were the center of much favorable comment.

The rooms were all decorated with
southern smilax and oak branches.
Among the potted plants, those especially worthy of mention were a standard chrysanthemum exhibited by Geo.
Strugnell, Holyoke, and some cypripediums exhibited by Mr. Sinclair,
Holyoke.

NEW CORPORATIONS.

Portland, Ore.—Epperson Nursery
Company, capital stock, $2,000. Incor-
porators, C. A. Epperson, James G.
Kelly and E. Langley.

East Cleveland, Ohio—The Friedley
Company, $10,000; floral business. A.
A. Smith, Frank A. Friedley, H. W.
Lower, R. L. Toben and B. Fennell.

The Corn Show of the Rhode Island
State Corn Growers' Association will
be held in the Elysium Hall, Weybosset street, Providence, on December 2
and 3. Copies of the premium list may
be obtained from John J. Dunn, Secretary, State Board of Agriculture, Providence, R. I.

In writing to Advertisers kindly mention Horticulture

VISITORS REGISTER.

Washington.—F. W. Taylor, Denver, Colo.

Westerly, R. I.—P. G. Rigby, S. S. Pennock-Meehan Co., New York.

Cincinnati: I. Rosnosky, Phila., Pa.; Bob Newcomb, representing W. W. Barnard & Co., Chicago, Ill.; J. T. Herdegen, Aurora, Ind.

Boston: William Bassett, sec'y Michigan Horticultural Society; W. C. Langbridge, Cambridge, N. Y.; George D. Hollister, Park Dept., Hartford, Conn.

Chicago: A. C. Reicher, Michigan City, Ind.; Chas. C. Case, Prairie du Chine, Wis.; C. E. Pinney, representing The Kentucky Tobacco Products Co., Inc., Louisville, Ky.; J. S. Wilson, Des Moines, Ia.; and many others arriving hourly for the show.

Pittsburgh: Martin Reukauf, representing H. Bayersdoffer Co., Phila.; Julius Dillhoff, Schloss Bros., New York; S. T. Fletcher, Peters & Reed Pottery Co., Zanesville, Ohio; S. S. Pennock, Pennock-Meehan Co., Phila.; T. T. Fryer, The Tajima Co., New York.

Philadelphia: W. C. Langbridge, of Jerome B. Rice & Co., Cambridge, N. Y.; Parker Thayer Barnes, Ass't Zoologist, Department of Agriculture, Harrisburg, Pa.; C. B. Coe, of D. M. Ferry & Co., Detroit, Mich.; H. D. Rohrer, Lancaster, Pa.; Chas. L. Seybold and Thos. Phillips, Wilkesbarre, Pa.

RESOLUTIONS ON THE DEATH OF LAWRENCE W. KERVAN.

Adopted by the N. Y. Florists' Club.

Lawrence W. Kervan, our brother, has joined the innumerable throng. Those of us who knew him best loved him the most. His was a noble character, genuine, unselfish, generous, true as steel. He was a friend worth while. Full of hope and good cheer, he always looked on the bright side of life, and his companionship was an inspiration. Notwithstanding his 72 years of labor and vicissitude, he had the heart and enthusiasm of youth. Such men are needed here. It is not easy to become reconciled to such bereavement as his family suffered when he passed away. Patient and resigned, in much physical suffering, he taught us all the lesson of brave submission to the inevitable, and the faith in immortality. He was not afraid to die; to him there was no sting to death. The grave has lost its victory. It was but crossing, with suspended breath, a little strip of sea to find

"His loved ones on the other shore,
More beautiful, more precious than before."

Mr. Kervan was born in New York City. He was a veteran of the Grand Army of the Republic, and in the Gallery of the National Museum at Washington his portrait will ever remain a monument to his loyalty and love of country. He built up the most successful business in evergreens in the world—this also a monument to his unfailing business integrity. He was never heard to speak ill of any man. He was respected by every man who knew him. His name is honored and unsullied, a blessed heritage to his family.

Be it resolved that these resolutions be spread upon the minutes of the club, and that a copy be sent to his bereaved ones.

(Signed)   PERCY RIGBY,
            SOL. HAUFLING,
            J. AUSTIN SHAW.

Obituary

Henry Hess.

Henry Hess, a retired florist of Cockeysville, Md., died on Friday, October 29. His age was 73 years.

Mrs. C. R. Dane.

Mrs. Dane, wife of Chas. R. Dane, florist of Roxbury, Mass., died on Sunday, October 31. The Flower Exchange sent a floral tribute to the funeral.

Patrick E. Dolan.

Patrick E. Dolan died Saturday afternoon at his home in Hartford, Conn., after an illness of four months from leakage of the heart. Mr. Dolan was a landscape gardener and florist. He was born in Athlone, County Westmeath, Ireland, February 4, 1849. He came to this country in 1866, and for ten years lived in New York. In 1876 he took up his residence in Hartford and became well-known in his business.

UNIVERSITY OF ILLINOIS.

The Floricultural Club of the University gave a reception on Saturday night to the members of the faculty. This affair was well represented and was a great success.

Professor White, of Cornell, visited the University on Monday, November 8. After a brief visit, he left for Ames, Iowa, where he expects to visit the University. Although the visit was only a short one, we certainly were glad to have Professor White with us.

Over 3,500 people attended the Fourth Annual Chrysanthemum Show, which was held in the Floricultural Greenhouses on Sunday afternoon, November 7th. A large number of people who were not able to see the show on Sunday, on account of the crowd, came out the following day. Two houses 30x110 feet were devoted almost entirely to chrysanthemums. One of these was used to stage 2,000 seedling plants of anemones, pompons and singles. Nearly all of these plants are products of the Floricultural Division. Besides the small-flowered types, there were at least 800 plants of the commercial varieties. The masses of color, however, were not so great or varied as in the case of the other plants and, therefore, more of the attention was centered in the small-flowered type. This show has become a popular event with the university and town people.

A NEW "RED DEVIL" GLASS CUTTER.

The "Red Devil" Tool people, Smith & Hemenway Co., Inc., of New York, have added a new glass cutter to their large line of 40 styles of cutters, known as No. 3. This new cutter is of the magazine type, having three extra steel cutting wheels in an air-tight chamber in the removable handle behind the head, in addition to a wheel in the head. In all it has four wheels. A new wheel can be instantly put into place by removing a piece of wire in the head. This cutter is fitted with genuine hand-honed cutting wheels, used for stripping plate, sheet or cathedral and rough glass. It has a scientifically shaped handle with a small end and a large finger rest which will not tire the hand. It is handsomely finished, having a polished head and a red enameled handle. This cutter retails for only twenty-five cents and is a high grade tool, despite its price.

GREENHOUSES BUILDING OR CONTEMPLATED.

Eugene, Ore. — F. B. Chase, two houses.

Sandusky, O.—L. E. Wagner, range of houses.

Rydal, Pa.—J. H. Sheble, Jr., L. & B. conservatory.

West Annapolis, Md. — R. Kaiser, house 53½ x 100.

Atlantic City, N. J.—P. J. Mooney, L. & B. house, 20 x 60.

Portsmouth, Va. — Hubert Bulb Co., L. & B. house, 28 x 100.

Coshocton, O.—Andy Kiefer, 15th street, vegetable house.

Aberdeen, S. D.—Siebrecht Flower Shop, conservatory 20 x 80.

Hillside, N. J.—Mrs. C. M. Hutchinson, two houses each 28 x 96.

Attica, N. Y.—A. J. Pauly, four houses, each 28 x 100, in the spring.

Nashville, Tenn. — Leslie Littell, house 26 x 48, near National Cemetery.

Chicago, Ill. — Fred Greager, 6952 Cottage Grove avenue, Foley house, 24 x 200.

Houston, Tex.—Board of Park Commissioners, one house in Wright Flower Garden.

Bridgeton, N. J.— Seabrook Farms, L. & B. house 60 x 300. Oberlin Smith, L. & B. conservatory.

FLOWER
SHOW
NUMBER

HORTICULTURE

General View of the Chicago Grand Floral Festival

Published Every Saturday at 147 Summer Street, Boston, Mass.
Subscription, $1.00

LIST OF ADVERTISERS

FOR BUYERS' DIRECTORY AND READY REFERENCE GUIDE
SEE PAGES 680, 681, 682, 683

NOTES ON CULTURE OF FLORISTS' STOCK

CONDUCTED BY

John J. M. Farrell

Questions by our readers in line with any of the topics presented on this page will be cordially received and promptly answered by Mr. Farrell. Such communications should invariably be addressed to the office of HORTICULTURE.
"If vain our toil, we ought to blame the culture, not the soil."—*Pope.*

Cattleyas

All such varieties as C. Dowiana, C. Eldorado, C. Harrisoniae, C. Loddigesii, C. marginata and C. Bowringeana, as they pass out of flower will need new feeding material. Where the compost is in good condition it is not necessary to repot them—a top-dressing will suffice, but where the compost is sour it is better to repot them. Every subject should be carefully looked over and when the material looks dry give the whole mass a thorough soaking. Watering should be done early enough in the day from now on so as to get the atmosphere dry before closing up time or night. During the winter months water must not be applied indiscriminately or a good deal of damage will follow. Give ventilation on all good days.

Violets

Keep a temperature from 40 to 45 degrees at night, with 10 degrees warmer when possible during the day. Syringe occasionally on bright days for red spider. At all times give all the air that outside conditions and weather will permit, at the same time putting a little heat on in order to keep the air dry. Don't start and water the whole bench when there are only a few places dry. It is a good plan every morning to examine the beds in order to find the dry spots. To keep them too wet is as bad as keeping them too dry; we must guard against these two extremes and if we expect to keep our plants in a healthy growing and flowering .condition the soil should be kept as evenly moist as possible all the time. It will soon be the days of dark and gloomy weather, which means more fire heat. Fumigating each week will keep the plants clean of fly; but should not be given too heavy.

Evergreens in Pots for Winter Use

Now is the proper time to get a good lot of these potted up and they can be set under cover outside for some time, which will help to keep the foliage in better color and give the plants time to make some roots before they are sold. Every year there is more demand for evergreens in pots or tubs. On the approach of winter the florists of all large cities are called upon to have something to break the bareness of the entrances to hotels, stores and dwellings. These should be available in all sizes. When plants are wanted for inside or where freezing will be very slight, Euonymus japonica and its varieties will make excellent plants to break the monotony of so many conifers. Make an assortment of the many varieties of, retinosporas, arbor vitaes, junipers, yews, spruces, etc. Where you want trailing ever-greens, Euonymus radicans and English ivy can be used to good effect.

Primulas

Give the primulas room to spread out. From now on a temperature near 50 degrees at night will suit them well. Keep them as near the glass as possible. Four, five and six-inch pot plants and make-up pans, fancy dishes, and baskets arranged for Christmas sales, should by this time be almost full grown. Plants that are wanted for late winter flowering should have their last shift now. Five-inch makes a very good size, but where exceptionally large and fine plants are required a six-inch pot can be used. A suitable soil can be prepared by intermixing equal parts friable loam, leaf mold, and cow manure, and enough of sand to keep it open. With proper protection from frosts there is no better place for these plants than a cold frame until late in December.

Lily of the Valley for Christmas

A period of four weeks—rather a little over from the day the pips are planted in the pots—until they are ready to sell. Take five-inch and six-inch pots (or half pots will do), fill them full of pips, spacing the pips properly, having the neck even with the rim of the pot, allowing the three-quarter-inch long pips to project above. It is too early yet to force freshly imported stock. If not on hand, order some cold storage pips now from any supply house advertising in HORTICULTURE. Perhaps the main thing is to be able to maintain about 85 degrees for bottom heat with a few degrees less on top. If at all well-grown a six-inch pot of lily of the valley with several dozens of flowers and trimmed with red water-proof crepe paper always sells well at Christmas. When the flowers are beginning to open, give more air and be very careful about watering so as not to let any rest on the bells. Gradually inure to the light and air to harden them up.

Storing Cannas, Dahlias, Etc.

Most of the cannas and dahlias are lifted by this time and placed in the shed. Before they are put away for the winter see that they are correctly labeled. Cannas will do fine in a violet house under the benches or some place as cool. Dahlia roots will require a dry place in some shed that does not fall below 45 degrees in the coldest weather. Gladioli will do in the same place. Gloxinias and tuberous-rooted begonias should be gradually dried off and packed in dry sand in a temperature of about 50 degrees.

Next Week—Begonia de Lorraine; Christmas Cultural Suggestions; Cyclamens; Poinsettias; Sowing Fern Spores.

HORTICULTURE

VOL. XXII   **NOVEMBER 20, 1915**   **NO. 21**

PUBLISHED WEEKLY BY
HORTICULTURE PUBLISHING CO.
147 Summer Street, Boston, Mass.
Telephone, Oxford 292.
WM. J. STEWART, Editor and Manager.

ADVERTISING RATES:

Per inch, 30 inches to page.................................... $1.00
Discounts on Contracts for consecutive insertions, as follows:
   One month (4 times), 5 per cent.; three months (13 times), 10
per cent.; six months (26 times), 20 per cent.; one year (52 times),
30 per cent.
   Page and half page space, special rates on application.

Entered as second-class matter December 8, 1914, at the Post Office
at Boston, Mass., under the Act of Congress of March 3, 1879.

CONTENTS   Page

Horticulture,   Our task with the fall exhibitions
in the ascendant   for 1915 is now almost finished. We
have done our best to give publicity
and due credit to all, in the limited
space at our disposal from week to week. Of necessity,
considerable detail matter has been cut out from the
voluminous mass reaching us from so many sources,
but it has been our earnest endeavor to retain
as much as possible of whatever has had educational
value or interest for the greatest number of our readers.
Each exhibition described has its individual features of
superiority or distinction. There is something to be
learned from all. It does not detract from our estimate of the achievements of other cities that we have
given so much more space to the show in Cleveland.

We could discern in this affair phases and potential
possibilities different from and of wider significance than
in the case of any other of the 1915 exhibitions and
we feel that results as recorded are certain to have a
distinct effect on future efforts of a similar character.
One direct outcome of the Cleveland success is the movement already started to vivify and establish as an active
working force the hitherto somewhat nebular organization known as the Ohio Horticultural Society. The
right spirit seems to have been thoroughly aroused in
the right place and in the right way and that is always
good news.

Factors   That was an almost invincible motto
that make   which the Cleveland flower show pro-
for success   moters adopted as their shibboleth in
their big undertaking. All such affairs
mean hard work—harder than is ever adequately understood or appreciated by those not directly
involved—but it is all to little purpose unless there is
complete harmony and hearty cooperation within and
without. The Cleveland workers not only adopted this
but lived up to it from start to finish; and that had
much to do with the great success which they achieved.
It was a shining example of efficient team work, despite
the fact that it was a new experience to many and that
the facilities and accessories available in halls accustomed to be used for flower shows had to be extem-
porized, and the result presents an object lesson for us
all. The day of deficits in public floral exhibitions is
gone forever if all interests, private and commercial, will
unite and work on some lines of "get together" and
"pull together," coupled with intelligent initiative and
aggressive modern publicity promotion methods. That
the interest in flowers in the time to come will be vastly
increased in the community where such successful dem-
onstrations of the florists' art are given, no one can
question, and thus the ultimate purpose of the Cleveland enterprise was worthily accomplished.

The status of the   The annual conventions of the So-
trade exhibition   ciety of American Florists and, recently, the National flower shows
conducted by that body, have been
highly esteemed for the unique advantages they have
provided for the craft from places widely separated to
meet together for mutual social intercourse and for
trade purposes. The events of the past week, however,
prove that this latter distinction does not necessarily belong exclusively to the national conventions but that it
is possible for a locally managed affair to consummate
a very potent attraction on similar lines. The fact of
the remoteness of the national society's meeting place
this year undoubtedly had some influence in making
possible the unprecedented trade gathering under local
auspices which was witnessed at Cleveland last week.
The magnitude of the trade exhibition thus brought
together and space paid for, the attendance of our six
hundred trade and professional visitors from far and
near and the expressed satisfaction with the amount
of business transacted by the trade exhibitors—all this
in the absence of any discussions, elections or other organization proceedings, affords food for thought. This
event, so successfully carried out should, and doubtless
will, be regarded as sufficiently important for consideration by the executive body of the S. A. F. as to the
particular part played by the trade exhibit as an influential factor in the popularity of the annual conventions
and the attendance thereat. Cleveland's exploit certainly has opened up a new and far-reaching vista of
possibilities.

ROSE GROWING UNDER GLASS

CONDUCTED BY

Arthur C Ruzicka

Questions by our readers in line with any of the topics presented on this page will be cordially received and promptly answered by Mr. Ruzicka. Such communications should invariably be addressed to the office of HORTICULTURE.

Blind Wood on Shawyers

We have never experienced any trouble with Shawyer going blind in the winter, and so far this variety has done wonderfully well with us. We do find, however, that if the plants are growing very freely, and are not given sufficient plant food, here and there will be a shoot that will seem to lose its bud while it is very small, and thus appear blind. We go over these few and take the top off with the first leaf, and the growth that will start nearly always produces a good bud. This can also be done with the shorter blind wood which is natural on a rose plant. We find that nearly always the top eye and leaf will go to one side. the other eyes and leaves forming the straight stalk. If the top is taken out the growth will nearly always bring a bud. We find that Shawyer likes to be planted late, say after the first of July, and then kept going. It will stand much more drying out than the Killarneys and nothing better could happen to a bench or house of Shawyers just when they have finished a crop than a good drying out. This will make them break much better and stronger, and as soon as they start good, liquid manure, bonemeal or what. ever is available should be applied in liberal doses. This will push them right along, and there will be very little blind wood. Weak, mildewed stock we find is generally the result of too much water, not enough air and feed. When the plants are growing real good it is almost impossible to overfeed them. Growers requiring long stems will find this an ideal rose, as we find it will cut mostly specials and extras, only a few No. ones and no No. twos at all. In cutting, cut all bottom breaks away down to two eyes above the bench, as it is almost impossible to cut them back far enough. They will break much stronger if cut away back.

The Thanksgiving Crop

In the long run it does not pay to run the houses warmer around the holidays to increase the cut of roses. unless there is a very heavy crop on the plants so that nearly all the wood is in bud. When it happens this way, then an increase of two to four degrees will not prove harmful and will help open up a good many flowers that would otherwise come late. It should never be done only under the circumstances just mentioned, for if there is not a very heavy crop the wood that is just coming on will become soft and will show the effects of the warm nights for quite a while. Keeping the plants well watered when a crop is on will also help push the buds along: in fact plants with a big crop just beginning to show color should never be allowed to become at all dry. This of course does not apply to plants with a bud here and there, but to Killarneys, etc., say when there are ten or more buds on each all to be cut in a week or ten days. With the warm weather that we have had all along the chrysanthemums should be out of the way pretty well and prices for roses should come up. Roses should never be held back for a long time and then dumped on the market on the day before Thanksgiving. The buyers know a pickled rose the minute they lay their eyes on it and the grower who will hold up his stock for shipment before a holiday will fool no one but himself. The grower shipping in a good grade of stock of standard quality, well graded and always of a uniform cut, will come out far better than anyone who will send in pickled stock every now and then in hopes of realizing a cent or two more during the holiday rush. The former will have buyers waiting to take their stock as soon as it reaches the market, and the latter's stock will as a rule lie and wait for a chance buyer to come along. Ship only fresh cut stock and win credit not only for yourself but for the Flower Business as a whole.

Last Chance to Clean Up

Winter will soon be here and the ground covered with snow. It will not be possible to do much cleaning up so no opportunity should be lost to burn up the remaining few heaps of brush and so on, and leave the grounds clean for the winter. It is surprising what a large number of insects, mice, etc., will make their home in a heap of brush all winter, ready to come out in the spring and attack the garden or anything which we would like to grow. Do not burn the leaves. We have yet to find a place where the soil in the garden or fields contained all the necessary humus, and leaves will give us a good deal of it, if only they are taken care of. As a rule the maple leaves, and others coming from ornamental trees will fall when they are still yellow and not dried up altogether, and if they are plowed under, or added to the manure, they will decay very rapidly and enrich the soil considerably. Where stock is kept, these leaves can be used to good advantage as bedding and will then work into the manure very nicely. Where the manure is to be used for mulching later we would not use too many, but for field work it is impossible to have too much leaves in the manure. Many people are of the opinion that brush will not burn on a wet morning, but this is not true. A little dry straw or hay to start the fire, and any brush will burn up well except perhaps apple tree branches. Even these will quickly disappear if they are cut up a little.

THE CLEVELAND SHOW

THE PRIZE AWARDS.

We herewith present a summarized report on the prize awards at the Cleveland Flower Show, followed by some special notes, supplementing the general account of the show which we gave last week.

Lack of space prevents our giving the complete list of awards in detail.

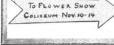

To Flower Show Coliseum Nov. 10-14

The classes from No. 2 to 21 inclusive were Chrysanthemum Society specials. In these classes three 1sts were won by the Dale Estate, Brampton, Ont., four by W. W. Vert, Fort Washington, N. Y., two by E. G. Hill Co., Richmond, Ind., and one each by A. N. Pierson, Cromwell, Conn., Lamborn Floral Co., Alliance, O., L. K. Duckham, Madison, N. J., Mt. Greenwood Cemetery asso., Morgan Park, Ill., and H. S. Firestone, Akron, O. The Cleveland Cut Flower Co. captured all the chrysanthemum plant prizes from No. 22 to 35. In the vases of 100 and 50 blooms E. G. Hill Co. led, but the entries by C. Merkel & Son, Mentor, O., J. M. Gasser Co., W. W. Vert and C. H. Totty were all grand also. In the twelve "color classes" E. G. Hill Co. had sweepstakes with five 1sts, Dale Estate four, Frank Allan, Grosse Pt., Mich., A. N. Pierson and C. H. Totty one each. In the nine classes of special varieties E. G. Hill had the sweepstakes with four 1sts, Lamborn Floral Co., two, C. H. Totty, The Friedley Co. and Elmer D. Smith, Adrian, Mich., one each. In the remaining 17 classes for chrysanthemums, including pompons and singles, C. H. Totty won five 1sts, Mt. Greenwood three, W. W. Vert, Frank Allan, Dale Estate, A. N. Pierson, C. Merkel & Son, E. G. Hill Co. and The Friedley Co. one each, and the 2nd and 3rd prizes were variously divided among the foregoing principally. J. M. Gasser Co. got a certificate of merit for single white chrysanthemums.

In the non-commercial chrysanthemum section there were some superb entries. Winners of 1st were Robert Weeks, Akron, O., eleven, L. K. Duckham three, C. W. Sieberling, gard. G. Gerwind, H. S. Firestone and Frank Allan two each, F. E. Drury, gard. R. F. Nuermann. Cleveland. C. V. Easton, Buffalo, one each. H. S. Firestone won a silver cup with a superb set of 36 blooms in 6 varieties.

The rose classes from No. 81 to 117 in-clusive were vigorously competed for. Waban Rose Conservatories, Natick, Mass., took the prize for best variety not yet in commerce with Mrs. Bayard Thayer. For the prettiest vase of roses J. H. Dunlop, Toronto, took 1st and certificate of merit; C. H. Frey Co., Lincoln, Neb., certificate of merit for Hadley; P. H. Olinger, New Castle, Ind., honorable mention for seedling 300. For the best vase arrangement of 100 yellow roses the J. M. Gasser Co. won 1st with a lovely combination of Mrs. Aaron Ward with crotons and Polygonum aureum. For the best 100 dark red roses A. N. Pierson won with Hadley, 1st for 50 blooms, "any other color" went to the new Prima Donna shown by Guttman & Raynor for The Florex Gardens. North Wales, Pa. In the regular color and special variety classes, ten 1sts went to J. M. Gasser Co., three each to F. R. Pierson and Lamborn Floral Co., two each to A. N. Pierson, Holton & Hunkel, Milwaukee, Wis., C. H. Totty, Rolf Zetlitz, Lima, O., and one each to E. G. Hill Co., S. J. Reuter & Son, Westerly, R. I., Anna Dean Farm, Barberton, O., and Cleveland Cut Flower Co.

In the carnation color classes, 100 blooms, Cottage Gardens Co. won 1st in white with Matchless, light pink with Cottage Maid, dark pink with Mrs. C. W. Ward; E. G. Hill Co., 1st in red with Champion; J. M. Gasser Co., 1st in flesh pink with Pink Delight; 150 blooms white won by E. G. Hill Co. with Matchless; 50 blooms flesh pink, J. D. Thompson Carnation Co., 1st with Superb; dark pink, Cleveland Cut Flower Co. do. with Mrs. C. W. Ward; red, E. G. Hill Co. with Beacon; crimson, E. G. Hill Co. with Pocahontas; yellow, Baur & Steinkamp with Yellow Prince; any other color, Littlefield & Wyman with seedling 4SA, a beautiful shell pink with petals white tipped. Cottage Gardens Co. got a silver medal for Crystal White and A. N. Pierson 1st for introduction of 1914-15 with Good Cheer. Other awards of 1st in carnation classes were Mrs. Price McKinney, gard. G. J. Lawton, six; E. G.

Hill Co., four; Cottage Gardens Co. and J. M. Gasser Co., three each; J. D. Thompson Carnation Co., Cleveland Cut Flower Co. and Anna Dean Farm, two each; H. S. Firestone, gard. Wm. Fisher, one. Guttman & Raynor secured a certificate of merit for Laura Webber.

While not so strong in large palms and foliage plants as is the case with exhibitions in eastern cities, still there was a good showing of this material, Boston ferns being especially notable in size and number.

Hart Bros., Robert Weeks, Mrs. Price McKinney and F. R. Pierson all showed mammoth Boston ferns, Hart Bros. winning 1st in three classes. Winners in other fern classes were The Friedley Co., Robert Weeks, Mrs. L. Dean Holden, Bretenahl, O., and J. L. Severance, Woodside Farms, West Park, O., won 1st on group of foliage plants with a beautiful collection, also on a superb collection of crotons and on pandanus. Other 1st prizes in foliage classes went to Mrs. McKinney, J. L. Severance and H. S. Firestone.

Julius Roehrs Co. won the orchid plant group prize with a beautiful collection, all neatly labeled. On cut orchids the Dale Estate was 1st with a very fine display. Other notable 1st prize winnings were L. Westerberg, Warrensville, O., pansies; Gasser Co., sweet peas; Friedley Co., lily of the valley; John Scheepers Co., spiraeas; Wm. Sim, Cliftondale, Mass., pansies (silver medal); W. G. Mather, begonias (gold medal); F. E. Drury, cyclamen (certificate of merit); E. A. Coon, Rhinebeck, N. Y., and C. Hagenburger, Cleveland, violets; C. Merkel & Son, cyclamen; J. M. Gasser Co., antirrhinums and calendulas; Friedley Co. and Julius Roehrs Co., lily of the valley; Friedley Co., giganteum lilies; Julius Roehrs Co., Lorraine begonias; Wilson Floral Co., Cleveland; C. Merkel & Son; A. Lewisohn, Mrs. Price McKinney and H. S. Firestone, begonias; W. G. Mather, primulas; Nug-itroc Garden, gold medal, and C. A. Otis, certificate of merit for lily of the valley.

On the afternoon of the closing day the judges awarded the following prizes:

For the vase of roses remaining in best condition through the five days of the show, Rolf Zelitz, Lima, Ohio; variety, Mrs. Charles Russell. For the best vase of carnations under same conditions, Cottage Gardens, Queens, N. Y.; variety, Cottage Queen. For the best vase of chrysanthemums under same conditions, Frank Allan, Grosse Point, Mich.; variety, William Turner. J. M. Gasser Co. got the Molinger cup for the largest number of entries.

LIST OF TRADE EXHIBITORS.

The trade displays were arranged in booths which extended completely around the four sides of the Coliseum. All reported a satisfactory business. The list was as follows:

H. Bayersdorfer & Co., Philadelphia, Pa., represented by Martin Reukauf, Stephen Greene and I. Bayersdorfer, a rich exhibit of florists' supplies; Robert Craig Co., Philadelphia, represented by W. P. and Robert Craig, Jr., very high class crotons, dracaenas, etc.; Henry A. Dreer, Inc., Philadelphia, represented by J. J. Karins, ferns and plants; R. & J. Farquhar & Co., Boston, represented by Frank Murray, choice plants; Hitchings & Co., Elizabeth, N. J., photos and diagrams of greenhouse structures; Roman J. Irwin, New York, sample plants and bulbs; Kroeschell Bros. Co., Chicago, Ill., office, represented by Fred Lautenschlager; Lord & Burnham Company, New York, Victor Morgan representa-

PARTIAL VIEW IN THE COLISEUM, CLEVELAND.

CHRYSANTHEMUM VASES.
By E. G. Hill Co. and R. Vincent Jr. & Sons Co.

tive, photos and plans of greenhouses; H. F. Michell Co., Philadelphia, represented by I. Rosnosky, specialties; S. S. Pennock-Meehan Co., Philadelphia, represented by R. Greenlaw, ribbons; A. N. Pierson, Inc., Cromwell, Ct., plants and novelties; F. R. Pierson Co., Tarrytown, N. Y., ferns and roses; Reed & Keller, New York; Julius Roehrs Co., Rutherford, N. J., choice plants, J. Muller in charge; Skinner Irrigation Co., Troy, O.; Stumpp & Walter Co., New York, Mr. McCook in charge, a large and comprehensive display; Chas. H. Totty, Madison, N. J., chrysanthemums and roses; B. Hammond Tracy, Wenham, Mass.; Vaughan's Seed Store, Chicago, Ill., bulbs and plants; Wertheimer Bros., New York; McCallum Co., Pittsburgh, Pa., boxwood; A. A. Arnold Paper Box Co., Chicago; John Bader Company, Pittsburgh, palms and ferns; Morris Cohen & Co., New York; Florists' Exchange, New York; Florists' Telegraph Delivery, suggestive booth with telegraph operator, etc.; Hammond's Paint & Slug Shot Works, Beacon, N. Y., in charge of C. H. Hudson; Kentucky Tobacco Product Co., Louisville, Ky.; Lion & Co., New York; C. Merkle & Son, Mentor, O., fine nursery stock; John C. Moninger Co., Chicago, model steel greenhouse, ⅛ size; Jos. G. Neidinger, Philadelphia; H. V. Pearce, Detroit, Mich., steam traps; Peters & Reed Pottery Co., S. Zanesville, O.; A. L. Randall Co., Chicago, big vases of roses, etc.; Chas. W. Reep, N. Olmsted, O., garden art vases; M. Rice Company, Philadelphia, represented by Mr. Farney, florists' supplies; Richmond Cedar Works, Richmond, Va., represented by Mr. Parrish, plant tubs; Russin & Hanfling, New York; John Scheepers & Co., New York, bulbs; J. L. Schiller, Toledo, O.; Schloss Bros., New York; Sherwood Pottery Co., New Brighton, Pa.; Storrs & Harrison Co., Painesville, O., a beautiful arrangement of plant groups; The Tajimi Co., New York, Japanese baskets; Mentor Nurseries, rhododen-

drons, conifers, etc.; Bird Lovers' Asso., Geo. H. Bowman Co., Eagle Wire Works, Geo. M. Edmondson, Fowler Mfg. Co., Frank Gompf, Grasselli Chemical Co., Leopold Furniture Co., National Pure Water Co., The Naumann Co., and Sixth City Wire Works, all of Cleveland, O.

THE BANQUET.

The banquet given to the visiting florists and gardeners on Friday evening, November 12, was a very enjoyable occasion. The spacious banquet hall of the Hollenden Hotel was well filled with ladies and gentlemen representing all sections of the country and all departments of the business. The tables were prettily decorated with dainty handle baskets of pompon chrysanthemums and roses in the centre and large blooms, with greenery, on the cloth. A "cabaret" entertainment with music and singing provided abundant annimation and fun until the hour had arrived for some brief speaking.

George W. Smith, chairman of the entertainment committee, introduced Frank Williams, of the Cleveland Cut Flower Co., as toastmaster, who stated that up to the previous evening the receipts had fully covered all the expenses of the show and attributed the success of the enterprise to the harmony and hard work which had prevailed among all concerned from the highest to the humblest. He read congratulatory telegrams from Patrick Welch, president of the S. A. F., and from Alex. Henderson, on behalf of the Chicago Floral Festival. He then called upon the following named gentlemen, each of whom responded entertainingly: Herbert Bate, president of the Cleveland Florists' Club; William Kleinheinz, president of the Chrysanthemum Society of America; Jos. Hill, president of the American Carnation Society; S. P. Baldwin, chairman of the flower show executive committee; R. Vincent, Jr., president of the American Dahlia Society; W. F. Gude, Washington representative of the S. A. F.; Irwin Bertermann, president of the Florists' Telegraph Delivery; A. Pochelon, secretary of the F. T. D.; J. F. Ammann, a judge; Wm. Nicholson, a judge; F. R. Pierson; E. G. Hill; H. P. Knoble, chairman of the Florists' Club executive committee. This pleasant occasion closed with the singing of "America."

COMMENTS BY A DOWN-EASTER.

The management of the Cleveland Flower Show was given unstinted praise at the banquet and elsewhere generally by the visitors for the splendid enterprise shown and results attained in the publicity campaign. Most striking and unique in this line was the series of arrows pointing out the way to the exhibition hall. These were of wood, painted green and lettered in white. In connection with a heavy mass of mountain leurel that could be seen from afar, these arrows were attached to the electric light poles on the streets leading from the railroad station and other principal points and converging at the Coliseum. No one, however strange to the city, had occasion at any time to inquire the way.

The special table decorations and

THE CANNING PLANT.
Eleven Months Old, 1200 Blooms. Dimensions: 15 ft. Diameter, 6 ft. High at Center.

feature retail florists' displays were placed on Saturday. A large space was enclosed for them, with latticed arbor entrances on four sides. There were daintily decorated tables bearing the names of numerous Cleveland florists, too numerous for individual mention here. Knoble Bros.' arrangement with central fountain, Smith & Fetters' Co.'s lovely bridal work, and several artistic arrangements by the Gasser Company were among them. This extensive retailers' department was a show in itself and the space was at all times uncomfortably crowded with admiring throngs of ladies.

One of the notable speeches at the banquet on Friday evening was that of E. G. Hill who although always eloquent and clever, quite outdid himself on this occasion. He asserted that no show in America or Europe had equalled this one and in eulogizing Pernet-Ducher and others who had spent their life in developing new and improved roses and other plants, took occasion to vigorously lampoon the vain-glorious and empty pretentions of Luther Burbank as compared with what these great, yet modest and unassuming, men had accomplished for the noblest profession open to mankind.

The Coliseum is not an ideal hall for the display of flowers. Low studded, without galleries or alcoves, or auxiliary rooms, with its vast floor space of 65,000 feet unbroken except by the main entrance, this structure offers little opportunity for impressive effects, vistas, or other striking decorative possibilities. But such as it was, the management had taken full advantage of, and after the unavoidable confusion of the opening day it presented a very bright and attractive appearance.

E. G. Hill said in his banquet speech that he never before had so many ribbons and cups to carry home and the decisions of the judges met his unqualified approval! He and C. H. Totty were large factors in the big bloom section. The pompons and singles were only second to the large blooms as a factor and, as Mr. Vincent declared, if they were not there it would have left a great vacancy.

On Saturday, the following telegram was sent, which tells its own story:
Mr. John D. Rockefeller,
　Pocantico, Hills, N. Y.
　Entertaining sixty thousand school children, mothers and teachers this fine bright morning at Cleveland Flower Show as your guests. Thursday forty-one thousand. Yesterday forty-five thousand. Largest party in history and an honor to giver of it. No accidents. Show big success. We thank you.
　　　　Cleveland Flower Show.
　　　　S. Prentiss Baldwin.

Over 100,000 school children were privileged to see the show on the forenoons of Thursday, Friday and Saturday. In a continuous file, two and four abreast, they came, and for hours each day the touching scene continued. It will be long remembered as one of the most impressive features of Cleveland's big horticultural event.

The Tea Garden as an adjunct to any large flower show, first given prominence in New York, seems to have quickly established itself in the approval of the "society" people. The experience in Cleveland was similar to that in New York and the Tea Garden must hereafter have its place in all well-regulated exhibitions.

There were many massive plant and flower groups, not for competiton by the Nag-ir-roc Garden, Wickliffe. The letters of this mystic word reversed, read "Corrigan"; the name of one of Cleveland's philanthropists and donor of the coveted Corrigan Cup. E. A. Bause is superintendent and Fred. Altknecht gardener in charge.

The official handbook and program was made doubly valuable by the introduction of original practical contributions on horticultural subjects from a popular standpoint, including both house and garden plant topics. Descriptive lists of unusual flowers worth growing were particularly praiseworthy.

The new rose shown for a name by C. H. Totty and christened "Cleveland" is a good deep pink but it needs the prime quality of fragrance. Gorgeous, also shown by Totty, captivated all with its delicious fragrance and shell-pink petals deeping to peach pink in the heart of the flower.

All expenses were covered by the receipts up to Friday noon and the receipts from that time until Sunday night were "velvet," thus assuring the return of all guarantee subscriptions with a substantial dividend and a proportionate rebate to trade exhibitors on space purchased.

The attendance on Friday evening reached its high tide. Five fire wardens were posted in various parts of the hall and at one time the chief was about to order the doors closed against any more admissions. The foyer was completely blocked with the crowds seeking entrance.

The "Smoker" on Friday night at the Moose Club was enjoyed by a large number of the male visitors and local people. A cabaret entertainment and "Dutch lunch" were the conspicuous features in the program.

The stipulation that in nearly 100 classes in the premium list a special prize of $5 in gold would be given to the section man or actual grower of the stock, taking first prize undoubtedly stimulated competition.

The vases, etc., were, as a rule, freshened up with new flowers as they became untidy and altogether the show was much more attractive at the closing of the fifth day than it usually the case.

A large crowd was continually seen at the booths where the Women's Florist Club of Cleveland offered flowers for sale. The receipts from this quarter must have been considerable.

The Richmond Cedar Works supplied the cedar bark which was used to decorate the columns in the Coliseum and the electric light poles on the streets leading to the show.

The blue badge of the local committees was in evidence continually. Posted like sentinels in every part of the exhibition hall the boys were everlastingly "on their job."

The registration of visitors was acceptably conducted under the amiable direction of George W. Smith. There were 643 registered visitors recorded, representing 551 firms.

A heavy non-competitive exhibitor was W. G. Mather, president of the Ohio Horticultural Society. George Jacques is superintendent of the estate.

Canada showed up well in the many chrysanthemum exhibits by the Dale Company and splendid long-stemmed roses by J. H. Dunlop.

Cyclamen must be rapidly growing in popularity in the middle west judging from the very large number of exhibits staged.

The music was excellent and the change of performers each day was a well-considered and potent attraction.

A. J. Loveless, of Lenox, Mass., showed a handsome yellow sport of Thanksgiving Queen, a noble flower.

Cleveland will probably be a candidate for the National Flower Show following that at Philadelphia.

There was an excellent and well-arranged display of hot-house grapes by O. C. Barber, of Barberton, O.

Craig's croton exhibit was a gem, or rather a cluster of gems. Smith & Fetters purchased it.

Wm. Tricker had a beautiful aquatic display in a rock-rimmed pool with spray fountain.

Carnation Belle Washburn, exhibited by Bassett & Washburn, strikes us as a fine thing.

AMERICAN ROSE SOCIETY.

At the Cleveland Flower Show the following five roses were entered as undisseminated varieties, and the score of points recorded as follows:

Tipperary: Size, 6; color, 14, stem, 13; form, 13; substance, 8; Foliage, 13; Fragrance, 2; distinctiveness, 5; total, 74 points.

Gorgeous: Size, 9; color, 16; stem, 12; form, 13; substance, 8; foliage, 13; Fragrance, 4; distinctiveness, 8; total, 83 points.

Red Radiance: Size, 8; color, 17; stem, 12; form, 12; substance, 7; foliage, 14; fragrance, 3; distinctiveness, 8; total, 81 points.

Mrs. W. R. Hearst: Size, 9; color, 18; stem, 13; form, 13; substance, 8; foliage, 14; fragrance, 4; distinctiveness, 8; total, 87 points.

Mrs. Bayard Thayer: Size, 9; color, 18; stem, 15; form, 14; substance, 9; foliage, 13; fragrance, 4; distinctiveness, 8; total, 90 points.

The judges were Emil Buettner and John H. Dunlop.

A silver medal will be awarded to Mrs. Bayard Thayer and Mrs. W. R. Hearst. A certificate of merit to Gorgeous and Red Radiance.

　　　　BENJAMIN HAMMOND, Sec.

West Grove, Pa.—For their superb exhibits of roses, plants and shrubbery, the Conard & Jones Co. have received official notification that they have been given the gold medal (highest award) at both the Panama-Pacific and Panama-California Expositions, at San Francisco and San Diego.

THE FALL FLOWER SHOWS

Chicago

Another flower show has become history and already those whose hard work and untiring energy for many weeks past made this one of the best exhibits ever held in the great Coliseum, are laying plans for another year and a still better show. The attendance was not so large as the affair deserved, but this is due in part to the fact that the time of the show was co-incident with that of the chrysanthemum shows in each of the larger Chicago parks and they are each year drawing larger crowds. The special new features of this show were the giving of more space to the cut flower exhibits and the more artistic setting of the same; the bringing of the musicians to a large stage on the main floor, the barefoot dancing and, to some, most important of all, demonstrating how to wear cut flowers, which seems almost to have become a lost art.

The retailers in general did not take the opportunity to advertise their business and to educate the public in the use of flowers, but those who did received a most gratifying amount of publicity and the prizes awarded were the smallest part of the results. Booths were attractively arranged and maintained in perfect condition each day and thousands stopped and admired the tables and other features. The retailers exhibiting were A. Lange, J. Mangel, Geo. Wienhoeber, J. Simpson, E. Wienhoeber, O. J. Friedman, Geo. Wittbold Co., Schiller the Florist and W. H. Kidwell & Co.

The largest prizes offered were for chrysanthemums, flowers arranged for effect. 1st prize, $200; 2nd, $150; 3rd, $100. 1st was awarded to Geo. Wienhoeber. The display consisted of an assortment of large chrysanthemums arranged in one large and four smaller vases of rectangular design, covered with green velvet and placed on a green rug, the tallest in the center and the others the corners. There were no ribbons or other accessories. 2nd was won by O. J. Friedman and 3rd by J. Mangel. The arrangement of the large chrysanthemums in each entry was above the ordinary in artistic skill and no part of the show attracted more attention. Each booth deserves special mention. They were full of suggestion for the arrangement of flowers in the home and the public lingered longest in front of the booths.

Groups and tables of plants for commercial purposes were shown by A. H. Schneider of Oak Park; A. N. Pierson, Inc., Cromwell, Conn.; C. C. Pollworth, Milwaukee, Wis.; Poehlmann Bros. Co. of Morton Grove; Ernest Rober, of Wilmette; Vaughan's Seed Store, of Western Springs; Frank Oechslin and Geo. Wittbold, of Chicago. Lincoln Park also had a large and finely arranged bed of palms and decorative plants.

The space taken by the private gardeners was especially attractive, four large beds of potted chrysanthemums and one of crotons making that part a delightful riot of color relieved by the large specimen ferns. A new exhibitor appeared this year, J. E. Tilt, of Chicago, gard. Wm. Allen. All the private gardeners entered into the work with enthusiasm and their displays did much toward making the whole a success.

The young ladies demonstrating the use of flowers for personal adornment were in evening dress and arm bouquets, ankle bouquets, how to wear flowers in the hair and how to carry flower-bedecked swagger sticks and parasols, all served greatly to interest the public and a very high-class orchestra added its full share each day.

A beautiful sight which met the eye as the visitor entered the room was the large glass case containing the dozens of silver cups and the 20-inch silver punch bowl, all of which were given by the Chicago Greenhouse Manufacturers.

The visitors register contained 250 names of out of town visitors, and it is fair to presume that a large number failed to register.

List of Awards.

In the chrysanthemum classes for 50 blooms of specially named varieties, there were many notable entries. First prize were awarded as follows: three to E. G. Hill Co., three to Poehlmann Bros. Co. and one each to Fritz Bahr, Bassett & Washburn, F. R. Lemon Co., Mt. Greenwood Cemetery Association and Vaughan's Seed Store. A. Lange won first in the vases of singles and pompons, and Elmer D. Smith & Co. in collection of named varieties. Other exhibitors of prominence in this section were Kroeger & Keenan and Wietor Bros. On chrysanthemum display the contributors were Geo. Wienhoeber, O. J. Friedman, John Mangel, Schiller the Florist and Geo. Wittbold, to whom prizes were awarded in order as given.

In the rose classes for one hundred blooms each, there was splendid competition, the winners of first prizes being Cudahy Floral Co., one; Poehlmann Bros. Co., three; Peter Reinberg, three; Bassett & Washburn, two; Geo. Weinhoeber, one. Poehlmann's Hadley was the winner in red, Bassett & Washburn's Shawyer in any other color except red. In the Vases of fifty, Poehlmann Bros.' Francis Scott Key won in the "any other color" class. Other awards in this section were Poehlmann Bros. Co., three; Reinberg, three; Bassett & Washburn, two; A. Lange, two; Gullett & Sons, C. Cutler and George Weinhoeber, one each. Poehlmann's Lady Stanley won in the class for twelve any new Variety, and E. G. Hill's Tipperary for twenty-five any Variety not in commerce.

Carnations also made a grand showing in the classes for Vases of one hundred each. Bassett & Washburn's Matchless won in white, Weitor's Enchantress in pink, Reinberg's Rose Pink Enchantress in light pink, Poehlmann's Mrs. C. W. Ward in medium pink, Weitor Bros.' Rosette in dark pink. Weitor's Champion in red and a seedling from Mt. Greenwood Cemetery Association in "any other color." In the classes for Vases for fifty, J. D. Thompson Carnation Co. and Bassett & Washburn had three 1sts each; W. C. Manke, Weitor Bros., Poehlmann Bros. and V. Bezdek, one each. Poehlmann Bros.' White Perfection won as "any other white" and their Akehurst as best introduction of 1915. Weitor Bros. won 1st with Bonfire as best introduction in red, and with Alice as "any other pink" and best introduction in its color of 1915. J. D. Thompson Carnation Co. won with Conquest as Variety not otherwise provided for, and Princess Dagmar as the best crim-

son. In the classes for twenty blooms, several novelties came to notice, including Comet, Ellen Washburn and some seedlings by Anton Then, one of which took the sweepstakes, and seedlings by Mt. Greenwood Cemetery Association.

In the classes for specimen chrysanthemum plants, Iowa State College took four prizes, Vaughan's Seed Store four, and Poehlmann Bros. one.

In the display of orchids, Poehlmann was first and for orchid cut blooms, Chas. W. McKellar.

For ferns and foliage plants, Poehlmann Bros. took five 1st prizes in the different classes, Schiller the Florist two, Geo. Weinhoeber two, Wittbold the Florist, F. Oechslin, Gustav Bendal, H. N. Bruns, Vaughan's Seed Store and Merriam Park Floral Company, one each.

Other interesting awards were: Basket of plants, 1st, Geo. Weinhoeber; 2d, Schiller. Display of carnations, 1st, John Mangel; 2d, A. Lange. Basket of chrysanthemums, Geo. Weinhoeber. Fern dish, 1st, Schiller; 2d, Geo. Weinhoeber. Wedding outfit, 1st, John Mangel; 2d, E. Weinhoeber. Basket of flowers, 1st, A. Lange, and honorable mention for O. J. Friedman, John Mangel and Geo. Weinhoeber on account of the uniformity of merit in all. Vase of Major Bonnaffon arranged for effect, Geo. Wittbold. Basket of Russell roses, A. Lange. Violets, O. J. Friedman. Lily of the Valley, H. N. Bruns, Poehlmann Bros. and August Jurgens, respectively. Lilies, Weiland & Risch and Poehlmann Bros. Co. Bouvardia, Fritz Bahr.

New chrysanthemums scored as follows: 6 white, E. G. Hill Co. No. 1000, comm. score 85, exhibition 86; 6 yellow, E. G. Hill Co., Illinois, comm. score 87, exhibition 85; 6 pink, Elmer D. Smith & Co., Cameo, comm. score, 90; 6 sprays pompons, Mt. Greenwood Cemetery Association, comm. score, 89; 6 sprays singles, Mt. Greenwood Cemetery Association, comm. score, 87; sweepstakes, Elmer D. Smith & Co., Cameo, comm. score, 90.

The following additional awards were made on Sunday: Most attractive display by retailer in booth, O. J. Friedman; Most artistic Dresden bouquet with collarette, Schiller the Florist; Most artistic corsage bouquet, 1st A. Lange, 2d Schiller the Florist; fifty White Killarney arranged for effect, A. Lange.

Allied Trades.

The Foley Greenhouse Mfg. Co. made the only exhibit in its line. They showed a full-sized greenhouse, of iron frame with curved eaves.

Perhaps the most novel of the large exhibits was that of the D. Hill Nursery Co., who used a large central space in the form of a Japanese garden, with rock, water, bridge, etc. This gave opportunity to show their evergreen trees.

Other exhibitors in this department were the following: Kroeschell Bros. Co., the Kroeschell boilers, one of which was on the floor; Raedlein Basket Co., baskets; Buchbinder Bros., refrigerators; Haeger Brick & Tile Co., Dundee, Ill., flower pots; Ideal Lighting Co., Davenport, Ia., self-watering window boxes; W. W. Barnard Co., seed packeting machine in operation; Vaughan's Seed Store, seeds, bulbs, etc.

Tuxedo, N. Y.

The Tuxedo Horticultural Society's Annual Fall Show was held in the Tuxedo Club House on November 5th, 6th and 7th, 1915, and proved to be the finest ever held in Tuxedo. Great credit is due to Manager Fred Bentley, for the splendid manner in which

he planned the floor. The exhibits were up to the usual high standard and the entries were larger than in former years. The groups were again the main feature of the show. Chrysanthemums, roses and carnations were very good. The trade exhibits were as follows:

Collection of single and pompon chrysanthemums and roses, A. N. Pierson, Inc., Cromwell, Conn. Collection of single and hardy chrysanthemums, Scott Bros., Elmsford, N. Y. Fern "John Wanamaker," C. A. Peterson, Tarrytown, N. Y. Collection of Japanese and pompom chrysanthemums, Elmer D. Smith, Adrian, Mich.

There was a very interesting and attractive exhibit of seedling anemone chrysanthemums from Carl D. Schaeffer, superintendent of the Richard Mortimer estate. Mr. Schaeffer has worked hard to improve the anemone type, and by the quality of his exhibit, his efforts have not been in vain. The judges awarded them a certificate of merit.

H. M. Tilford, gard. Joseph Tansey won in the 18 bloom class with the following chrysanthemums:

R. C. Pulling, Mrs. Wm. Tricker, Mrs. J. P. Mitchell, Rose Pockett, Mrs. G. Drabble, Pockett's Crimson, Kewanee, Ernest Wild, Mrs. Bogg, Wm. Kleinheinz, Mrs. W. H. Walker, F. S. Vallis, Kate Ainsley, A. Griswold, Earl Kitchener, Elberon, Mrs. Surrey, Nakota.

Mrs. J. Murray Mitchell, gard. Thos. Wilson won in the 12 bloom class, with the following:

Lady Hopetown, R. C. Pulling, Rose Pockett, Calumet, Elberon, Mrs. J. P. Mitchell, Jas. Fraser, Odessa, F. S. Vallis, H. E. Converse, Alganoc, Naressia.

David Wagstaff, gard. Thos Lyons won in the six bloom class with:

Jas. Fraser, Wm. Turner, Elberon, Mendon, Mrs. Bogg, Mrs. G. Drabble.

Mr. Wagstaff's "Mrs. G. Drabble" won the prize for the largest bloom in the show.

The visitors were Messrs. R. Spears and E. Jenkins, Lenox, Mass.; J. Muller from Julius Roehrs, Rutherford, N. J.; L. Don and J. Morrison from Weeber & Don, N. Y.; J. Wilk; P. Fay from Peter Henderson & Co.; Joseph A. Manda, W. Orange, N. J.; C. Ebel, Madison, N. J.; Mr. Storey of the Metropolitan Material Co.; T. Beers from A. N. Pierson, Inc.; Wm. Scott of Scott Bros.; C. A. Peterson, Tarrytown.

The judges were A. Herrington, Madison, N. J.; Thos. Page, Great Barrington, Mass., and Alex. MacKenzie, Highland Falls, N. Y.

Julius Roehrs Co., special for group of plants: 1st, H. M. Tilford, gard. Joseph Tansey; 2nd, Geo. F. Baker, gard. James MacMachon. Scott Bros., special for group of chrysanthemums: 1st, G. G. Mason, gard. D. MacGregor; 2nd, H. M. Tilford.

Henry A. Dreer specials for group of ferns: 1st, A. Monell, gard. C. Davidson; 2nd, Geo. F. Baker; three specimens ferns: 1st, David Wagstaff, gard. Thos. Lyons; 2nd, A. Monell; one specimen fern: 1st, A. Monell; 2nd, H. M. Tilford.

Winners in the other classes, of which there were many, covering chrysanthemums—pot and cut, roses, carnations, fruit, vegetables, decorations, centerpieces, etc., included H. M. Tilford, G. G. Mason, G. F. Baker, Mrs. J. Murray Mitchell; gard. Thos. Wilson, D. Wagstaff, Mrs. A. S. Car-

hart, gard. C. Costecki, R. Mortimer, C. B. Alexander, gard. Wm. Hastings, A. Monell, A. Seton, gard. P. Cassidy, Mrs. S. Spencer, gard. Emile Barth, W. M. V. Hoffman, J. I. Blair, gard. D. S. Miller, Neil MacMillan, H. H. Rogers, R. Delafield, Arden Farms Dairy Company and Alex. Roy.

Special prizes other than those already mentioned were contributed by Weeber & Don, John Scheepers & Co., C. H. Totty (gold, silver and bronze medals), A. N. Pierson, Inc., Harry A. Bunyard and Bon Arbor Chemical Co.

STAMFORD, CONN.

The 5th annual fall show of the Westchester and Fairfield Horticultural Society was held at Stamford, Ct., Nov. 5-6. The exhibition throughout was of exceptional merit. The schedule was composed of 118 classes and the entries were numerous and the competition very keen. The judges were Samuel J. Trepess, of Glen Cove, Howard Nichols, of Yonkers, Samuel Redstone, of Philadelphia, and Wm. Turner, of Oceanic, N. J. The exhibition was well attended and was a financial success as well as a display of rare beauty and a credit to the enterprising and progressive element in this vicinity. There was a very fine display of decorative work, dinner tables, floral baskets and centerpieces being numerous and varied, and each a credit to the exhibitor. The trained chrysanthemum bush plants were fine, and in form and quality equalled those exhibited elsewhere. Several groups of flowering and foliage plants and cut chrysanthemum flowers arranged for effect, added attractiveness to the show. The vegetables were of exceptional merit.

The most meritorious exhibit was staged by A. Ailns, gard. for J. B. Cobb, and was awarded a special prize. Lilacs and spiraea were featured. The largest bloom was Ewen McKenzie's Wm. Turner. The prize for display of outdoor blooms was won by J. P. Sorensen, Essex Fels, N. J. The winning table decoration was by Thos. Aitchison. The chief honors for bush plants went to W. J. Sealey, gard. for Chas. Mallory. Other winners were Mrs. L. P. Childs, W. H. Maginnis, Mrs. Wheeler, gard. John Orr, W. W. Heroy, gard. A. Wynne, M. I. Borg, gard. Owen A. Hunwick, G. D. Barron, gard. Jas. Linane, A. G. Smith, gard. Carl Hankenson.

Among the many other successful chrysanthemum exhibitors were Mrs. W. G. Nichols, gard. G. D. Sullivan, J. B. Cobb, Wm. Ziegler, gard. A. Bieschke, Miss G. Iselin, Robert Grunnert, Mrs. Nathan Strauss, gard. Thos. Aitchison, Mrs. J. H. Flegler, gard. Wm. Whitton, John I. Downey, gard. Thos. Ryan, W. W. Heroy, Mrs. Henry Darlington, Mrs. F. A. Constable, gard. Jas. Stuart and A. G. Smith. In the pompom classes honors were divided by W. J. Sealey, Thos. Bell and Joseph Tiernan, gard. for Adrian Iselin, Jr. Among the carnation classes, the most successful were W. W. Heroy, J. B. Cobb. Mrs. N. Strauss, W. H. Maginnes, Henry Holberg and E. C. Benedict. The same names serve as a list of principal winners in the rose classes

with premier honors going to W. H. Maginnis and Anton Peterson. The winners of the vegetable classes are all enumerated among the above exhibitors. On orchids, palm and foliage plants, the honors were divided by A. Bieschke, A. Ailns, E. C. Benedict, Mrs. J. H. Flagler, Mrs. Oliver Hoyt, gard. Jas. Foster and Robert Grunnert. The manager of the show was Henry Wild, Riverside, Conn.

P. W. POPP, Cor. Sec.

NEWARK, N. J.

There was a chrysanthemum show moderate in extent but very high in quality at the Bamberger department store on Thursday, November 11. First prizes were won in the chrysanthemum classes by Guttman & Raynor, Jacob Hauck, Irvington Greenhouses, W. S. Miller, Chas. H. Totty, H. Hornecker, Davis & Davis, Elizabeth Nursery Co., George Penek and Hausmann Bros. Phillips Bros. got a silver cup for the best retail exhibit and 1st prizes for table decoration and mantel decoration. The silver cup for best growers' group was won by H. Hornecker as well as 1st for handle basket. Begerow was awarded first for wedding decoration, John Crosley won first for bouquet, William Tricker a special for water lilies, H. Hornecker first for group of foliage plants and Boston fern, F. N. Eskesen for group of ferns, Guttman & Raynor for roses and violets, Irvington Greenhouses a special for carnations. John Pfeiffer and Chas. Weber also won 1st in carnation classes. Other prize winning exhibitors were A. Linserman, E. Jacoby, Rasbach & Son, J. Wagner and E. C. Strobell & Co.

SEED TRADE NOTES.

Chicago, Ill.—A Chicago agency of Carter's Tested Seeds has been established with A. L. Berry & Co., 230 South La Salle street, J. Fisher in charge.

The Board of Directors of the Merchants' Club of Baltimore. City, at a meeting held on Nov. 9th, 1915, elected as a member Charles J. Bolgiano of the seed firm of J. Bolgiano & Son....

The value of imports of horticultural material at the Port of New York for the week ending Nov. 6, is as follows: Nitrate of soda, $341,297; manure salt, $3,085; fertilizer, $930; clover seed, $23,639; grass seed, $1,737; trees, bulbs and plants, $182,239.

Of Interest to Retail Florists

NEW FLOWER STORES.

Oswego, N. Y.—E. Kendig, 126 West 2d street.

Montreal, Que.—McKenna's, Ltd., St. John street.

Battle Creek, Mich. — J. S. Krebs, Ward block.

Chicago, Ill. — J. H. McNeilly, 1431 E. 63d street.

Fair Haven, Ct. — David Rees, 355 Grand avenue.

Galveston, Tex.—Mrs. W. H. Bryant, 2917 Avenue Q.

Schenectady, N. Y.—Otto H. Selke, 723 State street.

Boyertown, Pa. — O. C. Trumbore, Reading avenue.

Laramie, Wyo.—Overlands Gardens Co., Grand avenue.

Waterbury, Ct. — Albert S. Nodine, 134 S. Main street.

Uniontown, Pa.—W. R. Barton, 44 Morgantown street.

Melrose, Mass. — Houghton-Kravath Co., 445 Main street.

Oelwein, Ia.—Kemble Floral Co., 201-205 S. Frederick street.

Milwaukee, Wis. — Lubliner Floral Co., 225 Grand avenue.

Nashville, Tenn. — L. H. Haury & Sons, 625 Church street.

Philadelphia, Pa. — Ideal Flower Shop, 52d and Arch streets.

Fort Wayne, Ind.—Fort Wayne Flower Shop, 828 Calhoun street.

Minot, N. D.—The Rosery, Flatiron Bldg., Geo. E. Valker, proprietor.

Doylestown, Pa. — Oscar Snedeker, Randall Bldg., West Oakland avenue.

Des Moines, Ia. — Kirkwood Flower Shop, Walnut street, next to Kirkwood Hotel.

Phoenix, Ariz.—Howard J. Brazee, 115 North 1st avenue, successor to Morton Flower Shop.

NEWS NOTES.

Raleigh, N. C.—J. L. O'Quinn is now located at 119 West Martin street, to which place he moved following the big fire of Nov. 6, which completely destroyed his former place of business. Mr. O'Quinn's stock and fixtures were destroyed by water and by the falling in of the walls of the building in which he was located.

Philadelphia — Chas. H. Grakelow opened his new flower store at Broad and Cumberland streets on the 19th inst. The property is 125 feet deep and 25 feet front and has a fine conservatory in the rear. The front store has been fitted up in the best modern style with all the latest devices to attract trade. We understand that Mr. Grakelow has spent over fifteen thousand dollars on this stride forward from his old store at 15th and Cumberland. So it looks as if the fakir whom Mr. Grakelow pretends to stand in such fear of would have to get a hustle on him. Very few of the fakirs have any fifteen thousand yet to spread out with.   G. C. W.

THE STREET FAKIR IN PHILADEL-
PHIA.

Editor of HORTICULTURE:

Your editorial in issue of November
13th, calling attention to the overwhelming vote of the Florists' Club of
Philadelphia, that the street man provides the only practical outlet for the
surplus stock of the grower and wholesaler under present conditions, is misleading. In the cut flower business as
in any other industry self interest is
the dominating force in every large
community. The growers and the commission men outnumber the retail florists three to one, which is about the
percentage of the representation found
in the Florists' Clubs. At the meeting
referred to, about one-third of the
membership, or some 75 members, a
very good attendance as meetings go,
were present. Not over twelve retailers were in evidence and when a vote
was called after the discussion, it was
this small representation against the
growers and wholesale men who made
up the balance of the assembly. Of
course, the vote was almost unanimous
in favor of the street vendor because
of the self-interest which so closely
identifies his business with theirs. The
fact that vending of any kind is for-
bidden by law on any of the principal
business streets on which it would pay
the fakir to operate, and that if by any
legal process the way could be opened,
it would also permit all street men in
other lines, does not concern these
gentlemen. They have flowers to sell.
They want a broader market and like
the man in the crowd they push ahead
not caring whose toes they tread on.
This question of the fakir will never
down. It was a live issue twenty-five
years ago. Today should the street
men have to retire it would in some
localities prove disastrous. causing
great financial loss. Many successful
retail men have risen from the ranks
of the street men. So that storekeep-
ing with all its attending expense
must have been found more profitable.

So, Mr. Editor, this action while it
may seem to have been the almost
unanimous opinion of all the interests
of the trade, was but the expression of
the men who grow and those who
handle the flowers for them, prompted
by their self interests in striving for
a larger market, whether it interfered
with the regular channels being of
little or no concern to them.

Philadelphia.   ROBERT KIFT.

NEWS ITEMS FROM EVERYWHERE

CLEVELAND.

Frank Friedley has purchased the greenhouse property of the James Eadie Company and the Friedley Co. will run them for plant growing for the Cleveland market.

All the local flower stores made especial efforts to have their show windows artistic and noticeable during the continuance of the show. To mention one and not all would be unfair, for all were creditable.

The writer took occasion to visit the beautiful Gasser home on Saturday, November 13, and found Mrs. Gasser in the garden gathering flowers, having an armful of rudbeckias, verbenas, marigolds and other garden flowers as bright and perfect as in August. Truly a most unusual autumn. Cosmos was seen in abundance in many of the suburban gardens.

ROCHESTER, N. Y.

A host of trade friends will be pleased to learn that George B. Hart, Rochester's high-pressure wholesale florist, was chosen supervisor by a big majority in the recent election.

The active spirits here, encouraged by the success achieved in the floral department of the recent Industrial Fair, and further stirred by Cleveland's exploit, are already laying plans for next year and expect to completely fill with exhibits the large building in which they occupied only a part of the space this year. The Rochester Horse Show at this Exposition is admittedly the most notable annual event of its kind in the country and the flower show was rated as second only to the horse show in the successful features of the 1915 event.

SAN FRANCISCO.

The appropriate name of "Alaska" has been given by F. Burns, of San Rafael, to a new white dahlia which he recently originated.

Angelo J. Rossi acted as marshal of the parade of farewell to the Liberty Bell, on November 11, as he did on the occasion of its arrival.

Joseph's, the Grant avenue store, will celebrate the first aniversary of its opening on Nov. 16. The business has made good progress from the start.

T. A. Monroe, formerly of Golden Gate Park and lately manager of the nursery for the Exposition, will have charge of the sale of the stock to be disposed of from the grounds after the closing.

Pawtucket, R. I. — M. J. Leach & Sons have purchased the stock and fixtures of the Quality Flower Shop, 144 Main street, and will continue the business. No tidings as yet have been received of John W. Seamans, the former proprietor, who disappeared several weeks ago.

WASHINGTON, D. C.

Mrs. Nettie Supper is now with George C. Shaffer, having severed her connection with Gude Bros. Co.

Donald Malcolm, who for several years has been employed at the store of Gude Bros. Co., has been appointed a sanitary inspector in the health department of the District of Columbia.

An examination is to be held in Alexandria, Va., on Dec. 8, by the Civil Service Commission to secure eligibles for the position of assistant superintendent of plant introduction field station.

William F. Gude and Adolphus Gude were the Washingtonians who attended the flower show in Cleveland, Ohio, last week. They took with them a choice collection of roses from their houses.

On Thursday, Fred B. Kramer announced that, with the view of encouraging children in the study of plant life, he would offer for Friday and Saturday a Pteris Mayii in a four-inch pot and four tulip bulbs for ten cents. This offer was for children and young people only but the streets were well filled with adults carrying home the plants. His large display window was cleared out and four employees put to work repotting the ferns and a heavy business was done.

A committee of retail florists, accompanied by Attorney Burton T. Doyle, last week called on Major Raymond Pullman, superintendent of police, and took up with him the subject of street vendors. The florists told of how these men were a menace to legitimate trade and asked that some action be taken to discourage them. It was suggested that they be subjected to some sort of a license. They were informed that the action desired was not within the province of the police department, but Major Pullman promised to take the matter up with the District Commissioners.

Gude Bros. Co., are extremely gratified at the results obtained from their annual chrysanthemum show held during the week at their store. The attendance was both large and appreciative. The entire first floor for a distance back of nearly 130 feet was a mass of color. The store was illuminated with red, white and blue electric lights and the salesroom was lined on either side by masses of palms, ferns and autumn blossoms and spruce trees. Here and there were stands on which rested vases, covered with birch bark, containing specimen William Turner chrysanthemums. The plate glass mirrors were outlined with spruce and vines entwined in which were yellow pompons. In the long work-room were vases of roses, carnations, and chrysanthemums. On the mezzanine floor had been placed a Victrola, which played during the store hours, and another smaller machine which contained a record imitating the song of the mocking bird. To this latter was added the songs of a half dozen canaries in cages.

NEW YORK.

Colin Campbell has just received a heavy shipment of dracœna canes.

Frank H. Traendly has been quite seriously ill for the past two weeks with a cold which came very close to being a case of pneumonia.

Charles H. Totty sustained a severe injury to the thumb of his right hand, on the trip to Cleveland. The heavy door of the dining car slammed on it as he was passing through jamming it so badly as to necessitate the removal of part of the bone.

PERSONAL.

Frederick J. Brady and Ethel M. Horan, daughter of the late James Horan and sister of Stephen Horan, florist, Bridgeport, Ct., were married Wednesday morning, November 10th.

The marriage of Miss M. Meinhardt and Wm. M. Boaz took place Wednesday November 11th at the home of the bride, 7637 Florisant avenue, St. Louis. The happy couple left the same night for an extended honeymoon journey through the south and west and will return December 15th to be at home to their friends at their home in Kirkwood, Mo.

Newport, R. I.—Robert Hunnick, one of Newport's noted gardeners, and Miss Clara Langford, sister of Samuel Langford, another well-known gardener, were married on the evening of October 28 in the rectory of Emmanuel church, in the presence of relatives and a few immediate friends. After the ceremony the bridal party motored to the home of the groom on Slocum street, where a bridal supper was served and a number of handsome gifts were shown. This will be the future home of Mr. and Mrs. Hunnick.

MASSACHUSETTS AGRICULTURAL COLLEGE, NOTES.

Last Tuesday the classes in Floriculture visited the greenhouses at Smith college. Mr. Downer showed the students around explaining many interesting things. Of especial interest were the aquatic and the cactus house. In the cactus house, besides various species of cereus, opuntia, agave, eucalyptus, etc., there was a very large specimen of the night blooming cereus which Mr. Downer explained had fifty flowers at one time last summer. On Wednesday evening Mr. Thurston spoke before the Landscape Art Club on annuals and perennials.

Boston—Visitors in Cleveland from this section last week included William Nicholson, W. R. Nicholson, E. Allan Peirce, Sydney Littlefield, Wm. J. Stewart, Eber Holmes, A. J. Loveless, Mr. and Mrs. B. Hammond Tracy and Frank Murray.

During Recess

THE BOWLING TOURNAMENT AT CLEVELAND.

Team Bowling.

Prize, $25.00 cash offered by Cleveland Cut Flower Co., won by Buffalo.

Buffalo vs. Rochester Special—Prizes, one large cup and five small cups offered by J. M. Gasser Company, won by Rochester.

Detroit versus Cleveland—High man on each team to divide $20.00, offered by Cleveland Florists' Exchange; Detroit high man, J. Stock, 477; Cleveland high man, H. P. Knoble, 516.

Highest number of strikes, $5.00 to team or individual, offered by Herbert Bate; Ben Hart, Cleveland; Sandiford, Buffalo; tied 16 each.

Highest number of spares, $5.00 to team or individual, offered by Herbert Bate; Weeks, Cleveland; Rahaley, Detroit; Scott, Buffalo; tied 17 each.

Highest single game, $5.00 to team or individual, offered by Cleveland Plant & Flower Co.; Weeks, 222.

Highest number of splits in three games, $5.00 to team or individual, offered by Cleveland Plant & Flower Co.; Hart, Buffalo; Salter, Rochester; McClure, Buffalo; tied three times.

Highest number pins in three games, $5.00 to team or individual; W. Glenn, Rochester, 559.

Individual.

1st, $10.00, Ben Hart, 554; 2nd, $9.00, Pautke, 552; 3rd, $8.00, Joe Kolisky, 548; 4th, $7.00, Weeks, 544; 5th, $6.00, Graham, 508; 6th, $5.00, Balliff, 467; 7th, $4.00, Rowlands, 466; 8th, smoking stand, Critchell, 463; 9th, card case and chips, Hampden, 423 10th, glass vase, Taylor, 389.

Cash for the above individual prizes and for the alleys was contributed by C. J. Graham, Brookline Floral Co., McCallum Co., Carl Hagenburger, Stumpp & Walter Co., A. A. Hart. F. W. Griffin, Fred Whittuhn, S. N. Pentecost, C. M. Wagner, Smith & Fetters Co., John Murkel, Storrs & Harrison Co., and John Kirchner.

High man on each team and five high men, individual, in three games, total pins to count, life membership in S. A. F. & O. H. for the winner, value $25.00, offered by H. P. Knoble, won by C. J. Graham, Cleveland.

Ladies' Bowling Prizes.

1st, electric lamp, J. M. Gasser Co. donor, won by Mrs. F. A. Friedley; 2nd, ladies' hand bag, Mr. Vinson donor, won by Mrs. A. Pochelon; 3rd, thermos bottle, Cleveland Cut Flower Co. donor, won by Mrs. J. Henninger; 4th, rock crystal bowl, A. Graham & Son donor, won by Mrs. C. A. Myers; 5th, set of vases, Smith & Fetters donor, won by Mrs. H. P. Knoble; 6th, cut glass rose bowl, Lord & Burnham donor, won by Mrs. C. J. Graham; 7th, ladies' scarf, Robert Weeks donor, won by Miss Ida Meikel; 8th, silk umbrella, Cleveland Plant & Flower Co. donor, won by Mrs. Naumann; 9th, mohg. vases, Cleveland Florists' Exchange donor, won by Mrs. W. C. Priest; 10th, cut glass compote, F. J. Ritsenthaler donor, won by Mrs. S. H. Berthold; 11th, purse, Naumann & Son donor, won by Miss Pearl B. Fulmer; 12th, silver creamer and sugar, Albrecht donor, won by Miss Eleise D. R. Swenton; booby prize, box candy, Peter Nichols donor, won by Mrs. Stahelin.

C. J. GRAHAM,
Chairman Bowling.

Boston Florists' Bowling Club.

Scores and standing, November 11:

	Scores	Won	Lost
Coop. Market	1358	20	4
Zinn	1287	11	15
Flower Exchange	1210	9	15
M. & M.	1292	7	17
Robinson	1275	6	18
Galvin	1369	21	3
Carbone	1341	13	11
Pansies	1184	9	15

New York Florists' Bowling Club

Scores on Nov. 11.

W. P. Ford	147	157	158
P. Jacobson	142	161	146
C. W. Scott	144	161	145
J. Miesem	175	147	182
A. Kakuda	163	140	153
H. C. Riedel	132	190	143

BUSINESS TROUBLES.

Easton, Pa. — A. B. Kleinhans has left Easton and the receiver appointed has among his assets 3000 chrysanthemums which must be grown on for market.

The Lady Florists' Home Circle, of St. Louis, held its regular monthly gathering at Mrs. Geo. B. Windler's home and spent a highly enjoyable afternoon. Mrs. Fred Bruenig will entertain the members next month.

Obituary

John Kapp.

John Kapp, an old and retired florist, aged 71 years, was burned to death last week at his home in Oxford, Ohio. He was the father of Mrs. W. S. Wells of St. Louis.

William C. Young.

William C. Young, former member of the C. Young & Sons Co., St. Louis, died on Thursday, November 11th, at his home, 5553 Waterman avenue. The cause of his death was heart failure following a long spell of sickness. Mr. Young was 59 years old, born in Toronto, Canada, in 1856. He leaves a wife, daughter and two sons to mourn his loss. Mr. Young was a valued member of the St. Louis Florist Club and was its presiding officer in 1908 and 1909 and his loss will be keenly felt by the members. His brothers are Harry, Charles and James Young, and Mrs. William Ellison and Mrs. Dr. Helwig, his sisters. John and Thomas Young of New York are his cousins. The funeral took place on Saturday, Nov. 13, from his late home in charge of the masonic order. The home was filled with large and beautiful floral pieces sent by friends and members of the trade. The Florist Club sent its usual wreath.

CLUB AND SOCIETY NOTES.

The Reading (Pa.) Retail Florists' Society held a meeting on November 4. J. Stanley Giles presided.

The St. Louis Retail Florists' Society held a regular monthly meeting on Monday, November 15. The special features were reports of the Cleveland Flower Show, which some of the members had attended.

Richard M. Saltonstall was elected president at the annual meeting of the Massachusetts Horticultural Society at Horticultural Hall, Boston, last Saturday. Other officers chosen were Walter Hunnewell, vice-president; George E. Barnard, William C. Endicott, Arthur F. Estabrook and John K. M. L. Farquhar, trustees for three years.

WHOLESALE FLOWER MARKETS — TRADE PRICES—Per 100 TO DEALERS ONLY

	CINCINNATI Nov. 15		CHICAGO Nov. 15		BUFFALO Nov. 15		PITTSBURG Oct. 28	
Roses								
Am. Beauty, Special	40.00	to 45.00	25.00 to 35.00		30.00 to 35.00		30.00 to 35.00	
" " Fancy and Extra	25.00	to 35.00	20.00 to 25.00		11.00 to 25.00		20.00 to 25.00	
" " No. 1	15.00	to 20.00	10.00 to 20.00		8.00 to 12.00		10.00 to 12.50	
Russell, Hadley	8.00	to 12.00	5.00 to 25.00		8.00 to 12.00		6.00 to 12.00	
Killarney, Richm'd, Hill'don, Ward	8.00	to 15.00	8.00 to 10.00		6.00 to 8.00		6.00 to 12.00	
" " Ord.	4.00	to 6.00	3.00 to 5.00		3.00 to 5.00		.... to 4.00
Arenburg, Radiance, Taft, Key, Ex.	8.00	to 10.00	6.00 to 10.00		6.00 to 8.00		6.00 to 12.00	
" " Ord.	4.00	to 6.00	3.00 to 5.00		4.00 to 6.00		.... to 4.00
Ophelia, M ck, Sunburst, Extra	8.00	to 10.00	8.00 to 10.00		6.00 to 8.00		6.00 to 12.00	
" " " Ordinary	4.00	to 6.00	3.00 to 5.00		3.00 to 5.00		.... to 4.00
Carnations, Fancy	3.00	to 4.00	.... to 3.00		2.50 to 3.00		.... to 4.00
" Ordinary	....	to 2.50	1.00 to 2.00		2.00 to 2.50		.... to 2.00
Cattleyas	50.00	to 65.00	35.00 to 50.00		40.00 to 60.00		35.00 to 50.00	
Dendrobium formosum	....	to 35.00	50.00		.... to 25.00		.... to 30.00
Lilies, Longiflorum	10.00	to 12.50	8.00 to 10.00		.... to 12.00		8.00 to 8.00
" Rubrum	4.00	to 8.00	4.00 to 5.00		3.00 to 4.00		.... to ....
Lily of the Valley	4.00	to 6.00	3.00 to 4.00		.... to 4.00		3.00 to 4.00
Daisies	....	to	.... to		.75 to 1.00		.75 to 1.50
Violets	.75	to 1.00	.50 to .75		.50 to .60		.50 to 1.00
Snapdragon	....	to 4.00	4.00 to 5.00		3.00 to 6.00		4.00 to 6.00
Chrysanthemums	10.00	to 35.00	10.00 to 25.00		5.00 to 25.00		8.00 to 30.00
Sweet Peas	.75	to 1.00	.50 to 1.50		.75 to 1.00		.... to 1.50
Gardenias	....	to	20.00 to 25.00		.... to		.... to ....
Adiantum	....	to 1.00	1.00 to 1.25		1.00 to 1.25		1.00 to 1.25
Smilax	12.50	to 15.00	10.00 to 15.00		.... to 12.50		12.50 to 15.00
Asparagus Plumosus, Strings (100)	25.00	to 50.00	40.00 to 50.00		.... to 50.00		.... to 50.00
" & Spren. (100 bchs.)	25.00	to 35.00	25.00 to 30.00		25.00 to 35.00		35.00 to 50.00

Flower Market Reports

BOSTON More seasonable weather and the approach of the Thanksgiving holiday already begin to make their impress on the flower market. At present moment the upward trend is felt more than it is seen but it is in the air and it makes everybody feel better. American Beauty roses have stiffened up about 25 per cent. and carnations have made a similar advance. Violets have jumped to double their price of last week and will undoubtedly go higher within a day or two. Football games favor the violet as well as the crimson chrysanthemums, such as Harvard, Mrs. G. W. Childs and Cullingfodil. Lily of the valley sells up to the limit and there are not too many orchids. Chrysanthemums as a general proposition are still very draggy and sell cheap. Roses of the standard run are also low but are booked for a good advance very soon.

BUFFALO There is too much stock in the market considering the small amount of business. Everything along the line practically has to be forced on the buyers. Roses and carnations come in abundance and prices are all cut up. It was impossible to hold up prices under such conditions. Chrysanthemums have been coming in quantity, pompons accumulating to some extent. Lilies, violets and other stock are moving very slowly. Cold weather with snow flurries have now set in and this will check the supply.

CHICAGO Business moved along in a very satisfactory way the past week and the middle of November shows the half month footings are of good proportions. The first fall of snow occurred on the night of the 15th when a cold wave swept over Chicago and the ground was well covered in the morning. The effect of the flower show on the market was good. Previous to its opening a sort of reaction had come from the brisk opening of the fall business but sales were lively when the attention of the public centered on the big exhibition at the Coliseum. Stock has been coming very fast and the drop in temperature and cloudy sky are acting as a desirable check just now. Chrysanthemum season is on the down side, the heaviest cuts having been made by most growers. There is plenty of good stock of all kinds and an abundance of green.

CINCINNATI The market is far from being what it might be. Receipts are very heavy and are not cleaning up at all. Low prices naturally result. The demand from out of town is pretty good. Roses continue in heavy supply. Among the offerings are some very fine American Beauties, Killarney and White Killarney, Taft, Sunburst and Hoosier Beauty. Carnations are not having a very good market. Chrysanthemums are very plentiful. The cut of lilies and callas is more than adequate. Violets, orchids and lily of the valley are all in a good supply.

NEW YORK The wholesale stores are heavily overcrowded with chrysanthemums. They run very fine as to quality, better in size, finish and uniformity than ever before, we should say. But they are away beyond any demand sufficient to clear the storerooms of the enormous accumulation which becomes a daily increasing problem for the wholesale dealer. Roses are also seen in large numbers and they, together with the violets are the principal stock of the street vendors. A favorite combination with these curbstone dealers just now is violets and Mrs. Aaron Ward rosebuds, the contrasting colors making a pleasing impression and indicating that the street fakir is not devoid of color discrimination. While the roses and violets, as well as other standard flowers, are all badly stagnated, it is nevertheless quite likely that if the chrysanthemums were out of the way the market would have little trouble in assimilating the stock and we should not be surprised to see the really good chrysanthemums come to an abrupt ending before long, especially if the weather continues as mild and stimulating as it has been thus far. Thanksgiving Day is a week distant at present writing and many things can happen in the meantime. One of the really good selling things of humble antecedents is the calendula. These are eagerly sought by the first-class stores at the price of the best carnations. Referring again to the chrysanthemums, it is to be noted that the proportion of pompons in the wholesale markets is much larger than in past seasons and the varieties are well selected as to color and form. There is already some stevia being brought in.

PHILADELPHIA General conditions have acting as a little draggy and prices generally in favor of the buyer. But as we write today (Nov. 17) things have improved and there is a little more life and a promise of lively demand for Thanksgiving week. American Beauty roses are very plentiful and very fine quality; but of course they are not bringing the prices they should. The same applies to the whole list of roses. If we were to specify leaders the Russell and ophelia would certainly head the list. Carnations have been too plentiful but have slackened off a little in the past few days and are now in more normal shape. The golden flower is queening the autumn in true regal style, happy and glorious, the bright particular stars in her galaxy at present being the Chadwicks, the Eatons and the Bonnaffons—not forgetting our good old standby among the pinks, Dr. Enguehard. Orchids are scarce. The best cattleya we notice at present is

(Continued on page 679)

WHOLESALE FLOWER MARKETS — TRADE PRICES—Per 100 TO DEALERS ONLY

	BOSTON Nov. 18		ST. LOUIS Nov. 15		PHILA. Nov. 15	
Roses						
Am. Beauty, Special	20.00	to 35.00	20.00	to 25.00	25.00	to 35.00
" Fancy and Extra	12.00	to 20.00	10.00	to 15.00	12.00	to 18.00
" No. 1	3.00	to 5.00	5.00	to 8.00	6.00	to 10.00
Russell, Hadley	4.00	to 10.00	5.00	to 10.00	4.00	to 15.00
Killarney, Richmond, Hillingdon, Ward, Extra	4.00	to 5.00	2.00	to 6.00	4.00	to 6.00
" " Ordinary	1.00	to 3.00	1.00	to 2.00	2.00	to 3.00
Arenburg Radiance, Taft, Key, Extra	4.00	to 6.00		to	4.00	to 10.00
" " Ordinary	1.00	to 3.00		to	2.00	to 3.00
Ophelia, Mock, Sunburst, Extra	4.00	to 8.00	5.00	to 6.00	4.00	to 8.00
" " Ordinary	1.00	to 3.00	2.00	to 4.00	2.00	to 3.00
Carnations, Fancy	1.50	to 2.50	1.00	to 2.00	2.00	to 3.00
" Ordinary	1.00	to 1.50	.50	to .75	1.00	to 2.00
Cattleyas	20.00	to 50.00		to 35.00		to 75.00
Dendrobium formosum		to 25.00		to		to 50.00
Lilies, Longiflorum	3.00	to 6.00	10.00	to 12.50	6.00	to 8.00
" Rubrum		to 3.00	4.00	to 6.00	3.00	to 6.00
Lily of the Valley	2.00	to 4.00	3.00	to 4.00	4.00	to 6.00
Daisies	.50	to 1.00	.25	to .50	.50	to .75
Violets	.50	to 1.00	.15	to .35	.35	to .50
Snapdragon	1.00	to 3.00	4.00	to 8.00	8.00	to
Chrysanthemums	1.00	to 15.00	5.00	to 15.00	10.00	to 20.00
Gardenias		to 1.00	.50	to 1.00	.50	to 1.00
Adiantum		to 1.00	1.00	to 1.85		to 1.00
Smilax	12.00	to 16.00	10.00	to 12.50	15.00	to 20.00
Asparagus Plumosus, Strings (100)	25.00	to 50.00	35.00	to 50.00		to 50.00
" & Spren. (100 Bchs.)	25.00	to 50.00	20.00	to	15.00	to 50.00

Flower Market Reports
(Continued from page 677)

Percivaliana. Cypripediums are to be seen but the supply is limited so far. Violets are becoming more of a feature and pretty good prices are being asked for them, Thanksgiving and Rugby anticipations having a very tonic effect.

The wholesale market ST. LOUIS has been greatly overstocked. All other stock has to suffer while chrysanthemums last. All of the late varieties are now coming in and the demand for them has been good all the week. Carnations and roses were so many last week that a considerable amount went to waste. Prices are low in all the grades. Fancy stock is the only kind that has any demand. Violets, lily of the valley, sweet peas and lilies have had quite a nice demand at normal prices.

The market is SAN FRANCISCO stronger. Rain and several frosty mornings have killed the less hardy stuff in private gardens and stimulating the demand for cut stock. Chrysanthemums are still quite abundant. The call for roses has been especially heavy this week and practically everything is bought up most of the time before the day is fairly started. Beauties are still a little

NEW YORK QUOTATIONS PER 100.   To Dealers Only

MISCELLANEOUS	Last Half of Week ending Nov. 13 1915			First Half of Week beginning Nov. 15 1915		
Cattleyas	20.00	to	40.00	25.00	to	50.00
Dendrobium formosum	25.00	to	35.00	25.00	to	35.00
Lilies, Longiflorum	4.00	to	5.00	4.00	to	5.00
Rubrum	1.00	to	3.00	1.00	to	3.00
Lily of the Valley	2.00	to	3.00	2.00	to	3.00
Daisies	.25	to	.50	.25	to	.75
Violets	.20	to	.35	.20	to	.50
Snapdragon	2.00	to	3.00	2.00	to	3.00
Chrysanthemums	4.00	to	35.00	4.00	to	35.00
Sweet Peas	......	to	.50	......	to	.50
Corn Flower	......	to	.25	......	to	.25
Gardenias	20.00	to	35.00	25.00	to	35.00
Adiantum	.50	to	1.00	.50	to	1.00
Smilax	8.00	to	10.00	8.00	to	10.00
Asparagus Plumosus, strings (per 100)	30.00	to	40.00	35.00	to	50.00
& Spren. (100 bunches)	15.00	to	20.00	15.00	to	25.00

scarce and Cecile Bruner is far short of requirements. Violet shipments are larger than ever, the rain having benefited the stock. There is a good supply of carnations. Lily of the valley has been a little scarce, but the supply is about normal again. Other lilies are not much of a factor, only a little cold storage stock being offered. Orchids are doing very well, both as to supply and demand.

Chrysanthemums WASHINGTON continue to be the leading factor in the day's business. Roses are not bringing what they should, despite the fact that the supply has decreased somewhat and those received are of good grade. Carnations also sell low. Cattleyas are quite scarce and lily of the valley is very plentiful. The cooler weather has brought violets into better shape but their movement continues slow. William Turner is the leading chrysanthemum at this time. Bonnaffon in the yellows is selling well. There are far more whites than can be moved to advantage. Pompons sell but moderately, either potted or cut. American Beauty roses are very good. Mrs. W. R. Hearst, the dark

pink sport of My Maryland, was seen last week in prime condition.

VISITORS' REGISTER.

St. Louis: Abe Newland, Pittsburgh, Pa.

Rochester, N. Y.: C. B. Knickman, representing McHutchison & Co., New York; Wm. J. Stewart, Boston.

Washington, D. C.—Sidney Bayersdorfer, Phila. Pa.; Walter Mott, representing Benjamin Hammond, Beacon, N. Y.; and J. A. Petersen, Cincinnati, Ohio.

Cincinnati: Charles Falkenstein, representing the Basket Novelty Co., New York, N. Y.; Mr. Romer, Scarborough, New York; Mrs. Karl Heiser, Hamilton, Ohio; Warren Huckleberry, North Vernon, Ind.

Buyer's Directory and Ready Reference Guide

Advertisements under this head, one cent a word.   Initials count as words.

Display advertisers in this issue are also listed under this classification without charge. Reference to List of Advertisers will indicate the respective pages.

Buyers failing to find what they want in this list will confer a favor by writing us and we will try to put them in communication with reliable dealers.

ACCOUNTANT
R. Dysart, 40 State St., Boston.
For page see List of Advertisers.

APHINE
Aphine Mfg. Co., Madison, N. J.
For page see List of Advertisers.

APHIS PUNK
Nicotine Mfg. Co., St. Louis, Mo.
For page see List of Advertisers.

ARAUCARIAS
Thomas Cogger, Melrose, Mass.

AUCTION SALES
The MacNiff Horticultural Co.,
New York City.
Plant and Bulb Sales by Auction.
For page see List of Advertisers.

Elliott Auction Co., New York City.
For page see List of Advertisers.

AZALEAS
P. Ouwerkerk, Hoboken, N. J.
For page see List of Advertisers.

Thomas Cogger, Melrose, Mass.

BAY TREES
August Rolker & Sons, New York.
For page see List of Advertisers.

BEDDING PLANTS
A. N. Pierson, Inc., Cromwell, Conn.
For page see List of Advertisers.

R. Vincent, Jr. & Sons Co.,
White Marsh, Md.
For page see List of Advertisers.

BEGONIAS
		Per 100
BEGONIA LORRAINE,	2½ in	$12.00
	3 in	20.00
	4 in	35.00
	5 in	50.00
BEGONIA CINCINNATI,	2½ in	15.00
	3 in	25.00
	3½ in	30.00
	4½ in	40.00
JULIUS ROEHRS CO., Rutherford, N. J.

BOILERS
Kroeschell Bros. Co., Chicago.
For page see List of Advertisers.

King Construction Co., North Tonawanda, N. Y.
"King Ideal" Boiler.
For page see List of Advertisers.

Lord & Burnham Co., New York City.
For page see List of Advertisers.

Hitchings & Co., New York City.

BOXES—CUT FLOWER FOLDING
Edwards Folding Box Co., Philadelphia.
For page see List of Advertisers.

Folding cut flower boxes, the best made.
Write for list. HOLTON & HUNKEL CO.,
Milwaukee, Wis.

BOX TREES
BOX TREES—Standards, Pyramids and Bush. In various sizes. Price List on demand. JULIUS ROEHRS CO., Rutherford, N. J.

BOXWOOD
Breck-Robinson Nursery Co., Lexington, Mass.
For page see List of Advertisers.

BOXWOOD SPRAYS
Pittsburgh Cut Flower Co., Pittsburgh, Pa.
For page see List of Advertisers.

BULBS AND TUBERS
Arthur T. Boddington Co., Inc.,
New York City.
For page see List of Advertisers.

J. M. Thorburn & Co., New York City
Wholesale Price List of High Class Bulbs.
For page see List of Advertisers.

Ralph M. Ward & Co., New York City.
Lily Bulbs.
For page see List of Advertisers.

John Lewis Childs, Flowerfield, L. I., N. Y.
Gladioli.
For page see List of Advertisers.

August Rolker & Sons, New York City.
Holland and Japan Bulbs.
For page see List of Advertisers.

R. & J. Farquhar & Co., Boston, Mass.
For page see List of Advertisers.

F. R. Pierson, Tarrytown, N. Y.
Hyacinths and Narcissus.
For page see List of Advertisers.

S. S. Skidelsky & Co., Philadelphia, Pa.
For page see List of Advertisers.

Chas. Schwake & Co., New York City.
Horticultural Importers and Exporters.
For page see List of Advertisers.

A. Henderson & Co., Chicago, Ill.
For page see List of Advertisers.

Burnett Bros., 98 Chambers St., New York.
For page see List of Advertisers.

Henry F. Michell Co., Philadelphia, Pa.
For page see List of Advertisers.

Joseph Breck & Sons Corp., Boston, Mass.
For page see List of Advertisers.

Fottler, Fiske, Rawson Co., Boston, Mass.

C. KEUR & SONS, HILLEGOM, Holland.
Bulbs of all descriptions. Write for prices.
NEW YORK Branch, 8-10 Bridge St.

CANNAS
Newest list of the newest Cannas just out. Complete assortment of the finest sorts, at remarkable rates.
Send for list today.
THE CONARD & JONES CO.
West Grove, Pa.

CARNATIONS
Wood Bros., Fishkill, N. Y.
For page see List of Advertisers.

F. Dorner & Sons Co., Lafayette, Ind.
For page see List of Advertisers.

Jas. Vick's Sons, Rochester, N. Y.
Field Grown Plants.
For page see List of Advertisers.

Littlefield & Wyman, North Abington, Mass.
New Pink Carnation, Miss Theo.
For page see List of Advertisers.

CARNATION STAPLES
Split carnations quickly, easily and cheaply mended. Pillsbury's Carnation Staple, 1000 for 35c.; 3000 for $1.00 post paid. I. L. PILLSBURY, Galesburg, Ill.

Supreme Carnation Staples, for repairing split carnations, 35c. per 1000; 3000 for $1.00. F. W. WAITE, 85 Belmont Ave., Springfield, Mass.

CHRYSANTHEMUMS
Chas. H. Totty, Madison, N. J.
For page see List of Advertisers.

THE BEST 1915 NOVELTIES.
The Cream of 1914 Introductions.
The most popular Commercial and Exhibition kinds; also complete line of Pompons, Singles and Anemones. Trade list on application. ELMER D. SMITH & CO., Adrian, Mich.

DAHLIAS
Send for Wholesale List of whole clumps and separate stock; 40,000 clumps for sale.
Northboro Dahlia and Gladiolus Gardens, J. L. MOORE, Prop, Northboro, Mass.

NEW PAEONY DAHLIA
John Wanamaker, Newest, Handsomest, Best. New color, new form and new habit of growth. Big stock of best cut-flower varieties. Send list of wants to
PEACOCK DAHLIA FARMS, Berlin, N. J.

DECORATIVE PLANTS
Robert Craig Co., Philadelphia, Pa.
For page see List of Advertisers.

Woodrow & Marketos, New York City.
For page see List of Advertisers.

S. S. Skidelsky & Co., Philadelphia, Pa.
For page see List of Advertisers.

Bobbink & Atkins, Rutherford, N. J.
For page see List of Advertisers.

A. Leuthy & Co., Roslindale, Boston, Mass.
For page see List of Advertisers.

Thomas Roland, Nahant, Mass.
High Grade Plants for Retail Florists.
For page see List of Advertisers.

Frank Oechslin, Chicago, Ill.
Decorative and Blooming Plants.

FERNS
John Scott, Brooklyn, N. Y.
The Home of the Scottii Fern.
For page see List of Advertisers.

H. H Barrows & Son, Whitman, Mass.
For page see List of Advertisers.

Robert Craig Co., Philadelphia, Pa.
For page see List of Advertisers.

McHutchison & Co., New York City.
Ferns in Flats.
For page see List of Advertisers.

A. M. Davenport, Watertown, Mass.
Boston and Whitmani Ferns.
For page see List of Advertisers.

Roman J. Irwin, New York City.
Boston and Whitmani Ferns.
For page see List of Advertisers.

FERTILIZERS
Stumpp & Walter Co., New York City.
Scotch Soot.
For page see List of Advertisers.

Chicago Feed & Fertilizer Co., Chicago, Ill.
Magic Manures.

Pulverized Manure Co., Chicago, Ill.
Wizard Brand Cattle Manure.

FLORISTS' LETTERS
Boston Florist Letter Co., Boston, Mass.
For page see List of Advertisers.

For List of Advertisers See Page 659

FLORISTS' SUPPLIES

N. F. McCarthy & Co., Boston, Mass.
For page see List of Advertisers.

Reed & Keller, New York City.
For page see List of Advertisers.

S. S. Pennock-Meehan Co., Philadelphia, Pa.
For page see List of Advertisers.

H. Bayersdorfer & Co., Philadelphia, Pa.
For page see List of Advertisers.

Welch Bros. Co., Boston, Mass.
For page see List of Advertisers.

FLOWER POTS

W. H. Ernest, Washington, D. C.
For page see List of Advertisers.

A. H. Hews & Co., Inc., Cambridge, Mass.
For page see List of Advertisers.

Hilfinger Bros., Ft. Edward, N. Y.
For page see List of Advertisers.

FOLIAGE PLANTS

A. Leuthy & Co., Roslindale, Boston, Mass.
For page see List of Advertisers.

FORGET-ME-NOTS

Myosotis palustris, True Forget-Me-Not.
Two clumps in Carton sent by Parcel Post
on receipt or price, 25 cents. CHATEMUC
NURSERIES, Barrytown, Dutchess County,
New York.

FUNGINE

Aphine Mfg. Co., Madison, N. J.
For page see List of Advertisers.

GALAX

Michigan Cut Flower Co., Detroit, Mich.
For page see List of Advertisers.

GARDEN TOOLS

B. G. Pratt Co., New York City.

GERANIUMS

R. Vincent, Jr., & Sons Co.
White Marsh, Md.
For page see List of Advertisers.

Geraniums Madame Salleroi, rooted cut-
tings, $1.00 per 100, $9.00 per 1,000. PAS-
COAG GREENHOUSES, Wm. Doel, Prop.,
Pascoag, R. I.

Geraniums, mixed varieties out of 2¼
inch pots. Am booking orders for December delivery at $20.00 per 1000. Cash.
JAMES MOSS, Johnsville, Pa.

GLASS

Sharp, Partridge & Co., Chicago.
For page see List of Advertisers.

Parshelsky Bros., Inc., Brooklyn, N. Y.
For page see List of Advertisers.

Royal Glass Works, New York City.
For page see List of Advertisers.

Greenhouse glass, lowest prices. JOHN-
STON GLASS CO., Hartford City, Ind.

GLASS CUTTERS

Smith & Hemenway Co., New York City.
Red Devil Glass Cutter.
For page see List of Advertisers.

GLAZING POINTS

H. A. Dreer, Philadelphia, Pa.
Peerless Glazing Point.
For page see List of Advertisers.

GREENHOUSE BUILDING MATERIAL

King Construction Co., N. Tonawanda, N. Y.
For page see List of Advertisers.

Parshelsky Bros., Inc., Brooklyn, N. Y.
For page see List of Advertisers.

GREENHOUSE BUILDING MATERIAL— Continued

Lord & Burnham Co., New York City.
For page see List of Advertisers.

Metropolitan Material Co., Brooklyn, N. Y.

A. T. Stearns Lumber Co., Neponset,
Boston.
Pecky Cypress.

GREENHOUSE CONSTRUCTION

King Construction Co., N. Tonawanda, N. Y.
For page see List of Advertisers.

Foley Greenhouse Mfg. Co., Chicago, Ill.
For page see List of Advertisers.

Lord & Burnham Co., New York City.
For page see List of Advertisers.

Metropolitan Material Co., Brooklyn, N. Y.

Hitchings & Co., New York City.

A. T. Stearns Lumber Co., Boston, Mass.

American Greenhouse Mfg. Co., Chicago, Ill.

John C. Moninger Co., Chicago, Ill.

GUTTERS

King Construction Co., N. Tonawanda, N. Y.
King Channel Gutter.
For page see List of Advertisers.

Metropolitan Material Co., Brooklyn, N. Y.
Iron Gutters.

HAIL INSURANCE

Florists' Hail Asso. of America.
J. G Esler, Saddle River, N. J.
For page see List of Advertisers.

HARDY FERNS AND GREEN GOODS

Michigan Cut Flower Exchange, Detroit,
Mich.
For page see List of Advertisers.

Knud Nielsen, Evergreen, Ala.
Natural Green Sheet Moss, Fancy and Dag-
ger Ferns and Huckleberry Foliage.
For page see List of Advertisers.

The Kervan Co., New York.
For page see List of Advertisers.

HARDY PERENNIALS

Bay State Nurseries, No. Abington, Mass.
For page see List of Advertisers.

P. Ouwerkerk, Hoboken, N. J.
For page see List of Advertisers.

Palisades Nurseries, Sparkill, N. Y.
For page see List of Advertisers.

HEATING APPARATUS

Kroeschell Bros. Co., Chicago.
For page see List of Advertisers.

Lord & Burnham Co., New York City.
For page see List of Advertisers.

HOLLYHOCKS

Hollyhocks in separate colors and mixed,
fine large plants, $6.00 per 100, smaller
plants, $4.00 per 100. Cash. JAMES MOSS,
Johnsville, Pa.

HOT BED SASH

Parshelsky Bros., Inc., Brooklyn, N. Y.
For page see List of Advertisers.

Foley Greenhouse Construction Co.,
Chicago, Ill.
For page see List of Advertisers.

S. Jacobs & Sons, Brooklyn, N. Y.
For page see List of Advertisers.

Lord & Burnham Co., New York City.
For page see List of Advertisers.

A. T. Stearns Lumber Co., Neponset, Mass

HOLLY

XMAS DECORATIONS — Selected Box
Holly. Holly Wreaths a specialty in large
and small quantities. Write your requirements. DELAWARE EVERGREEN CO.,
Milton, Delaware.

HOSE

H. A. Dreer, Philadelphia, Pa.
For page see List of Advertisers.

HYACINTHS

5000 Hyacinths—No. 1, No. 2 and Miniatures in La Innocence, Gertrude, Grand
Maitre, King of Blues, Jaynes: No. 1, $22.00
per 1000; No. 2, $20.00 per 1000; Miniatures,
$14.00 per 1000, 3 in. Sprengeri, 3c. Mum
stock plants, 15 varieties, 50c. per doz.;
$3.00 per 100, or will exchange any of these
for Vincas Var., Geraniums, Ferns or
what have you? ROSENDALE GREEN-
HOUSES AND NURSERIES, Schenectady,
New York.

INSECTICIDES

Aphine Manufacturing Co., Madison, N. J.
Aphine and Fungine.
For page see List of Advertisers.

Nicotine Mfg. Co., St. Louis, Mo.
Aphis Punk and Nikoteen.
For page see List of Advertisers.

The Plantlife Co., New York City.
Plantlife Insecticide.
For page see List of Advertisers.

IRRIGATION EQUIPMENT

Skinner Irrigation Co., Brookline, Mass.
For page see List of Advertisers.

LILIUM MYRIOPHYLLUM

R. & J. Farquhar & Co., Boston, Mass.
For page see List of Advertisers.

LILY BULBS

Chas. Schwake & Co., Inc., New York City.
Horticultural importers and exporters
For page see List of Advertisers.

R. M. Ward & Co., New York, N. Y.
Japanese Lily Bulbs of Superior Quality.
For page see List of Advertisers.

Corp. of Chas. F. Meyer, New York City.
Meyer's T. Brand Giganteums.
For page see List of Advertisers.

Arthur T. Boddington Co., Inc., New York
City.
Lilium Longiflorum Formosum.
For page see List of Advertisers.

LILY OF THE VALLEY

Chas. Schwake & Co., Inc., New York City.
Hohmann's Famous Lily of the Valley Pips
For page see List of Advertisers.

McHutchison & Co., New York City.
For page see List of Advertisers.

Loechner & Co., New York City.
Lily of the Valley Pips.
For page see List of Advertisers.

MASTICA

F. O. Pierce Co., New York City.
For page see List of Advertisers.

NATIONAL NURSERYMAN

National Nurseryman Publishing Co., Inc.,
Rochester, N. Y.
For page see List of Advertisers.

NIKOTEEN

Nicotine Mfg. Co., St. Louis, Mo.
For page see List of Advertisers.

NIKOTIANA

Aphine Mfg. Co., Madison, N. J.
For page see List of Advertisers.

NURSERY STOCK

P. Ouwerkerk, Weehawken Heights, N. J.
For page see List of Advertisers.

W. & T. Smith Co., Geneva, N. Y.
For page see List of Advertisers.

In writing to Advertisers kindly mention Horticulture

NURSERY STOCK—Continued
The D. Hill Nursery Co., Dundee, Ill.
Hill's Evergreens.
For page see List of Advertisers.

Bay State Nurseries, North Abington, Mass.
Hardy, Northern Grown Stock.
For page see List of Advertisers.

Bobbink & Atkins, Rutherford, N. J.
For page see List of Advertisers.

Framingham Nurseries, Framingham, Mass.
For page see List of Advertisers.

August Rolker & Sons, New York City.
For page see List of Advertisers.

NUT GROWING.
The Nut-Grower, Waycross, Ga.

ORCHID FLOWERS
Jas. McManus, New York, N. Y.
For page see List of Advertisers.

ORCHID PLANTS
Julius Roehrs Co., Rutherford, N. J.
For page see List of Advertisers.

Lager & Hurrell, Summit, N. J.
For page see List of Advertisers.

PALMS, ETC.
Robert Craig Co., Philadelphia, Pa.
For page see List of Advertisers.

August Rolker & Sons, New York City.
For page see List of Advertisers.

A. Leuthy & Co., Roslindale, Boston, Mass.
For page see List of Advertisers.

Thomas Cogger, Melrose, Mass.

PANSY PLANTS
William Sim, Cliftondale, Mass.
Sim's Gold Medal Pansies.
For page see List of Advertisers.

Pansy Plants, mixed varieties in bud
and bloom, $15.00 per 1000. Cash. JAMES
MOSS, Johnsville, Pa.

Pansy Plants for the benches, nice stocky
plants, $3.00 per 1000, 5000 or more, $4.00
per 1000. Cash. JAMES MOSS, Johnsville,
Pa.

PANSY SEED
Fottler, Fiske, Rawson Co., Boston, Mass.

PEONIES
Peonies. The world's greatest collection.
1200 sorts. Send for list. C. BETSCHER,
Canal Dover, O.

PECKY CYPRESS BENCHES
A. T. Stearns Lumber Co., Boston, Mass.

PIPE AND FITTINGS
Kroeschell Bros. Co., Chicago.
For page see List of Advertisers.

King Construction Company,
N. Tonawanda, N. Y.
Shelf Brackets and Pipe Hangers.
For page see List of Advertisers.

PLANT AND BULB IMPORTS
Chas. Schwake & Co., New York City.
For page see List of Advertisers.

August Rolker & Sons, New York City.
For page see List of Advertisers.

PLANT TRELLISES AND STAKES
Seele's Tieless Plant Stakes and Trellises. H. D. SEELE & SONS, Elkhart, Ind.

PLANT TUBS
H. A. Dreer, Philadelphia, Pa.
"Riverton Special."

PLANTS WANTED
C. C. Trepel, New York City.
For page see List of Advertisers.

RAFFIA
McHutchison & Co., New York, N. Y.
For page see List of Advertisers.

RHODODENDRONS
P. Ouwerkerk, Hoboken, N. J.
For page see List of Advertisers.

Framingham Nurseries, Framingham, Mass.
For page see List of Advertisers.

RIBBONS AND CHIFFONS
S. S. Pennock-Meehan Co., Philadelphia, Pa.
For page see List of Advertisers.

ROSES
Poehlmann Bros. Co., Morton Grove, Ill.
For page see List of Advertisers.

P. Ouwerkerk, Hoboken, N. J.
For page see List of Advertisers.

Robert Craig Co., Philadelphia, Pa.
For page see List of Advertisers.

W. & T. Smith Co., Geneva, N. Y.
American Grown Roses.
For page see List of Advertisers.

Bay State Nurseries, North Abington, Mass.
For page see List of Advertisers.

August Rolker & Sons, New York City.
For page see List of Advertisers.

Framingham Nurseries, Framingham, Mass.
For page see List of Advertisers.

A. N. Pierson, Inc., Cromwell, Conn.
For page see List of Advertisers.

THE CONARD & JONES COMPANY.
Rose Specialists.
West Grove, Pa. Send for offers.

SCALECIDE
B. G. Pratt Co., New York City.

SEASONABLE PLANT STOCK
R. Vincent, Jr. & Sons Co., White Marsh
Md.
For page see List of Advertisers.

SEED GROWERS
California Seed Growers' Association,
San Jose, Cal.
For page see List of Advertisers.

SEEDS
Carter's Tested Seeds,
Seeds with a Pedigree.
Boston, Mass., and London, England.
For page see List of Advertisers.

Kelway & Son,
Langport, Somerset, England.
Kelway's Celebrated English Strain Garden
Seeds.
For page see List of Advertisers.

Joseph Breck & Sons, Boston, Mass.
For page see List of Advertisers.

J. Bolgiano & Son, Baltimore, Md.
For page see List of Advertisers.

A. T. Boddington Co., Inc., New York City.
For page see List of Advertisers.

Chas. Schwake & Co., New York City
For page see List of Advertisers.

Michell's Seed House, Philadelphia, Pa.
For page see List of Advertisers.

W. Atlee Burpee & Co., Philadelphia, Pa
For page see List of Advertisers.

R. & J. Farquhar & Co., Boston, Mass.
For page see List of Advertisers.

J. M. Thorburn & Co., New York City
For page see List of Advertisers.

S. Bryson Ayres Co., Independence, Mo.
Sweet Peas.
For page see List of Advertisers

Loechner & Co, New York City.
For page see List of Advertisers

Ant. C. Zvolanek, Lompoc, Cal.
Winter Flowering Sweet Pea Seed
For page see List of Advertisers.

SEEDS—Continued
S. S. Skidelsky & Co., Philadelphia, Pa.
For page see List of Advertisers.

W. E. Marshall & Co., New York City.
Seeds, Plants and Bulbs.
For page see List of Advertisers.

August Rolker & Sons, New York City.
For page see List of Advertisers.

Burnett Bros., 98 Chambers St., New York
For page see List of Advertisers.

Fottler, Fiske, Rawson Co., Boston, Mass.
Seeds for the Florist.

SKINNER IRRIGATION SYSTEM
Skinner Irrigation Co., Brookline, Mass.
For page see List of Advertisers.

SPHAGNUM MOSS
Live Sphagnum moss, orchid peat and
orchid baskets always on hand. LAGER
& HURRELL, Summit, N. J.

SPRAYING MATERIALS
B. G. Pratt Co., New York City.

STANDARD THERMOMETERS
Standard Thermo Co., Boston, Mass.
For page see List of Advertisers.

STOVE PLANTS
Orchids—Largest stock in the country—
Stove plants and Crotons, finest collection.
JULIUS ROEHRS CO., Rutherford, N. J.

SWEET PEA SEED
Arthur T. Boddington Co., Inc.,
New York City.
Winter Flowering Sweet Peas.
For page see List of Advertisers.

Ant. C. Zvolanek, Lompoc, Calif.
Gold Medal of Honor Winter Orchid Sweet
Peas.
For page see List of Advertisers.

S. Bryson Ayres Co.,
Sunnyslope, Independence, Mo.
For page see List of Advertisers

VEGETABLE PLANTS
R. Vincent, Jr. & Sons Co.,
White Marsh, Md.
For page see List of Advertisers.

VENTILATING APPARATUS
The Advance Co., Richmond, Ind.
For page see List of Advertisers.

The John A. Evans Co., Richmond, Ind.
For page see List of Advertisers.

VERMICIDES
Aphine Mfg. Co., Madison, N. J.
For page see List of Advertisers.

WIRED TOOTHPICKS
W. J. Cowee, Berlin, N. Y.
For page see List of Advertisers.

WIREWORK
Reed & Keller, New York City.
For page see List of Advertisers.

WILLIAM E. HEILSCHER'S WIRE
WORKS, 204 Randolph St., Detroit, Mich.

WHOLESALE FLORISTS
Albany, N. Y.

Albany Cut Flower Exchange, Albany, N. Y.
For page see List of Advertisers.

Baltimore

The S. S. Pennock-Meehan Co., Franklin
and St. Paul Sts.
For page see List of Advertisers.

Boston

N. F. McCarthy & Co., 112 Arch St. and
31 Otis St
For page see List of Advertisers.

Welch Bros. Co., 226 Devonshire St.
For page see List of Advertisers.

Patrick Welch, 262 Devonshire St., Boston,
Mass.
For page see List of Advertisers.

For List of Advertisers See Page 659

CLUBS AND SOCIETIES

CHRYSANTHEMUM SOCIETY OF AMERICA.

The annual meeting was held at the Hotel Hollenden, Cleveland, O., on November 11, 1915. President Kleinheinz presiding.

Officers were elected as follows: President, Wm. Kleinheinz, Ogontz, Pa.; vice-president, Wm. Vert, Port Washington, L. I., N. Y.; secretary, Chas. W. Johnson, 2134 W. 110th street, Chicago; treasurer, John N. May, Summit, N. J. Philadelphia was chosen for the 1916 meeting.

The annual address of President Kleinheinz follows.

Fellow Members of the Chrysanthemum Society of America:

It gives me great pleasure to welcome you in the City of Cleveland, at this, the 25th annual meeting of this society, which was organized in Buffalo, in 1890, during the convention of the Society of American Florists. The officers then elected were as follows: President, John Thorp; vice-president, Wm. K. Harris; treasurer, John Lane; secretary Edwin Lonsdale. All these gentlemen (I regret) have passed away; but this society is indebted to them forever for organizing and promoting the good of the Chrysanthemum Society of America, which has become, during its existence, a necessity to the " 'Mum" growers, and everyone interested in chrysanthemums should do his best to increase the membership, and thus make this society one of the strongest in America. Everyone should feel it his duty to help. This would prove the most suitable memorial to its founders and promoters, and would express our sentiments and appreciation to them forever.

I intended to arrange (if possible) to make this 25th convention an exceptionally fine chrysanthemum show; but as our financial standing does not justify any extra expenses, I feel that the Ohio Horticultural Society, the Cleveland Florists' Club and the Garden Club of Cleveland have relieved us of a great consideration by extending their kind invitation for our exhibition for 1915 just at the proper time. This excellent exhibition proves that the gentlemen from Cleveland have fulfilled their promise given in Indianapolis last year to the fullest extent.

Our secretary reported to me some time ago that he solicited several new members during and after the show of 1914 in Indianapolis. I hope and shall expect that through this exhibition in Cleveland our membership will be considerably enlarged.

Every year the cry is coming up· "The demand for chrysanthemums is waning." With this I cannot agree. All gardening in America, in my opinion, is still in its infancy and everyone knows that range after range of greenhouses for commercial or private purposes are erected every year. In every private place and in every little garden you find chrysanthemums. Under glass the large flowering varieties as well as the pompons

Meetings Next Week

Monday, Nov. 22.
Florists' and Gardeners' Club of Rhode Island, Swartz Hall, Providence, R. I.
Gardeners' and Florists' Club of Baltimore, Florist Exchange Hall, Baltimore, Md.

Tuesday, Nov. 23.
Gardeners' and Florists' Club of Boston, Horticultural Hall, Boston, Mass.
Newport Horticultural Society, Newport, R. I.
Tarrytown Horticultural Society, Tarrytown, N. Y.

Wednesday, Nov. 24.
Oyster Bay Horticultural Society, Oyster Bay, N. Y.

Friday, Nov. 26.
Connecticut Horticultural Society, County Bldg., Hartford, Conn.
Monmouth County Horticultural Society, Red Bank, N. J.
Pasadena Horticultural Society, Pasadena, Calif.

Saturday, Nov. 27.
Dobbs Ferry Gardener's Association, Dobbs Ferry, N. Y.

and singles are grown; outdoors the hardy varieties are installed and used for decorative purposes very extensively and are considered the most beautiful flowers for late season. As a border plant or mixed with herbaceous, it is the only flower that beautifies the gardens late in the year.

The commercial men are able to give figures on the demands for chrysanthemums and the records show that the sale of plants is increased yearly by thousands, and as long as this keeps up there is no danger of "Mums" becoming unpopular. And why should they become unpopular? The progress we are making you can see yourself by looking over the exhibits. The large flowering type is increased yearly in size; the pompons and singles are superior to the varieties of the past.

In closing, I wish to express my thanks to the trade and to the press for the many courtesies extended for the welfare of the society; and to our competent secretary, Chas. W. Johnson, who places his time and efforts at our disposal whenever needed. I also wish to express my highest appreciation to all those who so liberally offered prizes, enabling us to form such a complete schedule.

Report of Secretary Chas. W. Johnson.

Mr. President and members of the Chrysanthemum Society of America, your Secretary submits his report for the past year as follows:

He is pleased to report continued progress. The numbers of seedlings submitted to the examining committees as you may see by the review of their work in the Society's Annual Report shows an increase over the preceding year and for many years past. Some of the varieties which received a certificate have upheld the committee's judgment and have gained the favor of the growers. The reports of the examining committees were sent to the trade papers each week as they were received and a final summary of the season's work was published. The trade press very generously printed these and other notices sent to them from time to time for which we owe to them our vote of thanks.

While our membership has not increased as much as your officers would like, yet we have made considerable gain for the year. Some of the members delinquent with dues, after repeated requests for payment, have been dropped from the roll. Our Society has gained greater publicity during the past year.

At the invitation of Mr. G. A. Dennison, Chief of Horticulture, Panama Pacific International Exposition, San Francisco, for the Chrysanthemum Society to have a part in a seasonal exhibition of Chrysanthemums at the Exposition in San Francisco, your secretary presented the matter to the members of the executive committee who unanimously voted that our Society take part in the event and offer a C. S. A. Silver Cup for the ten blooms of Chrysanthemums one variety. Consequently your secretary wrote to the Pacific Horticultural Society asking them to join us, which they consented to do with the result that a very fine exhibition was held, especially so in cut blooms of Chrysanthemums.

Your secretary appreciates the kindness of the following firms and individuals in offering the special prizes at San Francisco and at this exhibition here in Cleveland:

Hitchings & Co., New York; Lord & Burnham Co., New York; Elmer D. Smith & Co., Adrian, Mich.; The E. G. Hill Co., Richmond, Ind.; A. N. Pierson, Inc., Cromwell, Conn.; Chas. H. Totty, Madison, N. J.; Vaughan's Seed Store, Chicago, Ill.; H. F. Michell Co., Philadelphia; H. W. Buckbee, Rockford, Ill.; Henry A. Dreer, Philadelphia; Wm. Wells & Son, Merstham, England; H. E. Converse, Esq., Marion, Mass.; President Wm. Kleinheinz, Ogontz, Pa.; National Association of Gardeners, Society of American Florists and Ornamental Horticulturists.

Through the kindness of these our special premium list for this year is larger than it has been before.

The routine work of the secretary's office consisting of sending out the statements to the members, recording the varieties disseminated, getting out the report of the Thirteenth Annual Meeting and the solicitation of the Special premiums was attended to in due season.

The secretary wishes to acknowledge the kindness of Mr. Elmer D. Smith in furnishing him with a complete list of varieties disseminated in 1914 which was a great help in making up the annual report.

A detailed report of all money received and paid over to the Treasurer accompanies this.

NATIONAL ASSOCIATION OF GARDENERS.

The annual convention of the National Association of Gardeners, will take place this year in Boston on December 9 and 10.

The first session will convene in Horticultural Hall, on Thursday afternoon, December 9 at two o'clock. A number of papers will be submitted by gardeners prominent in the profession which should provoke a good discussion. Among the subjects will be "Is Gardening a Profession?" "The Gardener's Place in the Public Service." "The Management of a Private Country Estate, as viewed by a College Graduate." "The Young Gardeners' Opportunity in this Country." "Is Co-operation Between Garden Clubs and Gardeners' Societies Desirable?" President Everitt has appointed W. N. Craig, Duncan Finlayson and W. J. Kennedy a Committee on Convention Arrangements and they promise that the meetings will be made interesting, entertaining and instructive to all who attend. An invitation is extended to all gardeners to attend the Boston convention so that they may familiarise themselves with the scope of the work the national association has undertaken.

Owing to the small number of articles received in the Essay Contest, which closed on October 1, the winners of which were to be announced at the convention in December, the Essay Committee.—(William H. Waite, W. N. Craig, Edwin Jenkins, Arthur Smith and Theodore Wirth).—has decided to reopen and continue the contest so that gardeners may participate in it during the winter months, when they have more time than any other season of the year to devote to the writing of essays. The contest will close on February 1 and the winners will be announced at the association's meeting during the National Flower Show in Philadelphia, in March, 1916.

There are four classes as follows:

Class 1—Prize $35, gold. Subject: Horticulture as a Profession, from the Standpoint of a Gardener.

Class 2—Prize $25, gold. Subject: The Proper Grouping and Culture of Trees, Shrubs, Perennials and Annual Bedding Plants in the Ornamentation of Private Grounds.

Class 3—Prize $20, gold. Subject: Preparation of Ground for and General Treatment of Hardy Herbaceous Perennials. Naming a list of species (limited to one hundred) providing a succession of flowers throughout the entire season.

Class 4—Prize $20, gold. Subject: How to Secure a Year's Vegetable Supply with the Aid of Cold Frames or Hotbeds (but no Greenhouses), including Soil Preparation.

The essay contest is open to professional gardeners who are engaged in the capacity of superintendents, head gardeners or assistant gardeners. Contestants will address William H. Waite, Chairman Essay Committee, National Association of Gardeners, P. O. Box 290, Madison, N. J., for further particulars.

WESTCHESTER AND FAIRFIELD HORTICULTURAL SOCIETY.

There was a large attendance at the monthly meeting of this society on Friday evening, Nov. 12th, at Greenwich, Ct. Among the principal features was the exceptionally fine display of carnations. First prize was awarded to Wm. Graham, second to Robert Allen. In the non-competitive exhibits, Ewen McKenzie received a cultural certificate for chrysanthemums Odessa and Wm. Turner. A. Wynne was highly commended for seedling carnations, W. J. Sealey for pompon chrysanthemums, and votes of thanks were accorded to P. W. Popp for lily of the valley, Robert Grunnert for chrysanthemums, Wm. Whitton for antirrhinums, Louis Wittman for cosmos, Carl Hankensen for roses. John Andrew was highly commended for celeriac Giant Prague.

It was voted to change the meeting place from present location to the Isaac Hubbard Hall, in Greenwich, the change to take place in January, 1916. A rising vote of thanks was accorded all those who helped to make the 5th annual flower show such a grand success. A communication from the Nassau County Horticultural Society asking the W. & F. Society to co-operate in establishing an interchange of courtesies between local societies, was endorsed. Election of officers will take place at the next meeting, Dec. 10.

P. W. POPP, Cor. Sec.

GARDENERS' & FLORISTS' CLUB OF BOSTON.

The next meeting of the club will be held on Tuesday evening, Nov. 23, the halls of the Massachusetts Horticultural Society being rented on the regular date, Nov. 16th. An expert from the Pilgrim Publicity Association of Boston will lecture on "Advertising, the light that serves and saves," illustrated with stereopticon views. Nomination of officers for 1916 will be made at this meeting. M. C. Ebel, Madison, N. J., will be present and speak on the coming convention of the National Association of Gardeners to be held in Boston on Dec. 9 and 10. There will be interesting exhibits of late chrysanthemums and other seasonable flowers. A cordial invitation is extended to non-members to be present and enjoy the lecture.

W. N. CRAIG, Sec.

OHIO GLADIOLUS SOCIETY.

An adjourned meeting of the Ohio Gladiolus Society was held in the assembly room of the Hollenden Hotel, Cleveland, on Nov. 11. Officers were elected as follows: President, C. B. Gates, Mentor, O.; vice-president, Joseph Coleman, Lexington, O.; secretary-treasurer, Wilbur A. Christie, Warren, O. Friday and Saturday, Aug. 12 and 13, 1916, were the dates selected for the next exhibition.

There was an executive committee meeting of the American Carnation Society on Friday evening, November 12, at the Hollenden Hotel, Cleveland. It was decided to signalize the meeting at St. Louis next January by the issue of a number of jubilee silver medals in honor of the occasion, which will be the 25th anniversary of the society's birth.

**GREENHOUSES BUILDING OR
CONTEMPLATED.**

Niles Center, Ill.—F. Stielow, additions.

Camden, N. J.—Emil Lelache, violet
house.

Mineral Point, Wis.—L. C. Stair, one
house.

Warren, O.—A. M. Campbell, house
25 x 100.

Mellenville, N. Y.—G. J. Anderson,
enlarging.

Riverton, N. J. — E. S. Woodward,
one house.

Jamestown, N. Y. — Gustav Wick-
strom, enlarging.

Columbus, O.—H. J. Woolman, Camp
Chase, one house.

Rumson, N. J.—John Achelis, Rumson road, one house.

Chester, Pa. — Wm. Williams, additions and alterations.

Natick, Mass.—Stanley I. Coley, Oakland street, one house.

Great Falls, Mont.—Carl Gallin, 1209
7th avenue, one house.

Vincennes, Ind. — Paul C. Schultz,
Main street, one house.

Woodstock, Ill. — E. A. Rogers, S.
Madison street, one house.

Murray Hill, N. J.—L. B. Coddington,
two rose houses next spring.

Mt. Pleasant, Mich.—John Zimmer,
proprietor Mt. Pleasant Greenhouses,
additions.

NEWS NOTES.

New Hampton, Ia. — The Robinson
Greenhouses suffered a loss of $3,000
by fire last week; no insurance.

Springfield, Mass.—E. B. Beals has
sold his greenhouse property in Eastern avenue. The purchaser will probably remove the greenhouses and
erect an apartment block on the site.

Madison, N. J.—Fire, said to have
been due to faulty insulation, caused
quite a damage to the Noe homestead
on Noe avenue, on November 14. It
was put out, however, before it got
beyond control. Water is said to have
done considerable injury to furniture
and decorations.

The show windows are changed every day. Never are they crowded; always is there a choice, tasty suggestion in floral possibilities.

To get an interior that does justice to this charming shop, was out of the question.
It was a good deal like "not being able to see the woods because of the trees."

Getting Both Ends of the String
Or the Schroeter—Stahelin Method

IF you happen to be fortunate enough to know Mr. A. J. Stahelin of Detroit, you can best admire the quiet, thorough-going way he has with him.

Every once in a while, he does something that makes some of his fellow growers sit up and take notice. One of them was, building a house on wheels.

The next was building a big Lord & Burnham Iron Framer, 72x400 feet, for sweet peas.

Then came the opening of a flower shop—unique and charming in every particular.

Here it is, you will find Mr. Schroeter giving vent to

his hustling progressiveness; while Mr. Stahelin looks more particularly after the producing end.

In one of his many pilgrimages for ideas I had the pleasure of spending a day with him among the Kennett Square growers near Philadelphia. Later, I was most delightfully entertained at his home when visiting his greenhouses.

Both times, I was impressed with the fact of his being very much like the description of a straight line: "The shortest distance between two points"; which dominating trait, doubtless had a lot to do with his buying one of our finest type of houses.

This iron frame house is 72 feet wide and 400 feet long. When the photo was taken last winter, the house was filled with sweet peas.

Lord & Burnham Co.

SALES OFFICES:

NEW YORK	BOSTON	PHILADELPHIA	CHICAGO	ROCHESTER	CLEVELAND
42nd Street Bldg.	Tremont Bldg.	Franklin Bank Bldg.	Rookery Bldg.	Granite bldg.	Swetland Bldg.

TORONTO, CANADA, Royal Bank Bldg.   MONTREAL, Transportation Bldg.

FACTORIES: Irvington, N. Y.   Des Plaines, Ill.   St. Catharines, Canada

Vol. XXII
No. 22
NOV. 27
1915

HORTICULTURE

Aquatic Pool and Fountain

William Tricker's Exhibit at the Cleveland Flower Show.

Published Every Saturday at 147 Summer Street, Boston, Mass.
Subscription, $1.00

LIST OF ADVERTISERS

FOR BUYERS' DIRECTORY AND READY REFERENCE GUIDE
SEE PAGES 712, 713, 714, 715

NOTES ON CULTURE OF FLORISTS' STOCK
CONDUCTED BY

John J. M. Farrell

Questions by our readers in line with any of the topics presented on this page will be cordially received and promptly answered by Mr. Farrell. Such communications should invariably be addressed to the office of HORTICULTURE.
"If vain our toil, we ought to blame the culture, not the soil."—*Pope.*

Begonia Gloire de Lorraine

To have exceptionally fine stock of Begonia Lorraine for next year propagating should be started now. There is no doubt as to the superiority of early-propagated stock. When selecting material, take well matured leaves of a spotless green from the most vigorous plants. Trim away the stubby end of the leaf stalk, about half an inch below the leaf and insert in the sand until the base of the leaf is in close contact with the surface and see that they are well firmed in the sand. Exclude sunshine and give them frequent sprinklings and they should root in about eight or nine weeks. Every day they should have fresh air admitted. It is a good plan to have them covered with sashes while you are ventilating the house to ward off draughts or excessive changes in the temperature.

Christmas Trade Suggestions

To be well prepared for a run of good business is very often all-sufficient to assure its coming. Good stock, plenty of it, rich in variety and temptingly displayed never fails to attract custom. This fact should not be overlooked by those new in the retail florist business. Have a good supply of holly, mistletoe, laurel, lycopodium and boxwood and wreaths for use in decorations. The filling of pans, baskets and other receptacles with plants other than bulbous stock or poinsettias should be done now or as soon as possible. See that the plants are well watered or thoroughly dipped before being made up. The buds of lilies should be well forward now. You will have to do some figuring during the next ten days in moving around those lilies so as to time them to a nicety. The most advanced ones should be removed to cooler quarters while those that are backward should be given some high forcing unless too far behind.

Cyclamen

Cyclamen will not last long in fine condition, nor prove of so great a value for living room or house adornment, if they had to be grown and flowered in great heat in order to make them Christmas plants. They can be grown to perfection in a night temperature of about 50 degrees. Perfect foliage is the proper setting to their flowers and without the former the latter, if ever so abundant, fails to arouse admiration. Plants which have a number of buds well-developed but not quite out should be put into about 55 to 58 degrees at night, as near the glass as possible and in full sun. Cyclamen should be frequently examined and if not entirely free of insects should receive a good sponging especially on the under side of the leaves. From this out see that they do not suffer for water at the roots.

Poinsettias

Those that are coming along not so fast can be held at from 60 to 65 degrees at night. By this time most poinsettias should be well advanced and if so a temperature of about 55 degrees will be sufficient to hold them in good condition. No plant more quickly resents neglect than a finely developed poinsettia. Failure with poinsettias can usually be traced to insufficient heat. Grown in a low temperature, the leaves will turn yellow and drop. The best poinsettia bracts with their stems leafless lose the greater part of their value. Keep your pans and pots from drying out too much by giving water when necessary. The loss of foliage is often caused by the exhaustion of the soil. If they have had some liquid manure occasionally up to now, it will help them materially. It is not safe to abruptly bring about a great change in temperature of poinsettias, but they can be gradually lowered until they are standing 55 degrees at night and 10 to 15 degrees more with sun heat.

Sowing Fern Spores

Those who are sowing spores should bear in mind that the most desirable commercial varieties will take from 10 to 12 months before they are fit to sell in pot. To have success in growing ferns from spores it is necessary to have the compost sterilized. A great deal of what is known as damping off has its origin in a minute fungus. Where you do not have a better means the soil can be baked in the furnace or soaked with boiling water. Fill the pans about one-third with crocks, larger ones in the bottom and those on the top finely broken and over this place a layer of moss, then fill to within an inch and a half of the top with the sterilized compost. This compost should consist of loam, leaf mold, peat and sand in equal parts. The surface soil in the pan should be pressed down and made as smooth as possible. A good soaking of water should be given and allowed to drain off before sowing the spores. Don't cover the spores with soil but place over the pan a close-fitting pan of glass and place where they can have 65 degrees.

Propagating Vincas

Large clumps of vincas, say in 5 or 6-inch pots can be broken up into pieces large enough for a three-inch pot. Give them a compost of fibrous loam three parts and well rotted manure one part. Leaf mold add one part will also be good. Keep shaded for a little while. Give them a temperature of not less than 60 degrees at night.

Next Week:—Christmas Greens; Azaleas for Christmas; Decorative Stock; Getting Ready for Christmas; Lorraine Begonias; Soil for Small Seeds.

HORTICULTURE

VOL. XXII   NOVEMBER 27, 1915   NO. 22

PUBLISHED WEEKLY BY
HORTICULTURE PUBLISHING CO.
147 Summer Street, Boston, Mass.
Telephone, Oxford 292.
WM. J. STEWART, Editor and Manager.

Entered as second-class matter December 8, 1914, at the Post Office
at Boston, Mass., under the Act of Congress of March 3, 1879.

CONTENTS

Origin of the Boston fern	The subject of the origin of the so-called "Boston fern" recently opened up by HORTICULTURE in questioning some of the evidence gathered for the records of the Brooklyn Botanic Garden, has been taken up in the columns of one of our contemporaries. So far as we know there is no proof that

the Boston fern was the first "variation from type," if indeed, any authentic type has ever been located. At the time of the agitation twenty years ago which resulted in the general adoption of the name "Bostoniensis" for the graceful form of Nephrolepis exaltata generally grown about Boston for many years previous, we obtained permission to examine the specimens in the herbarium of the late Asa Gray at Harvard Botanic Garden. Very many variant forms—arching, stiff, wide, narrow, etc., gathered from various sources, were there found simply under the name of Nephrolepis exaltata. The inference we drew at that time was that the "Boston variety" was but one of the many forms in which this widely distributed fern had been found in nature and we have seen no reason since to change our opinion. As to which one of the various forms collected was the original "type" and which are the "sports", perhaps something reliable may yet be uncovered but "I hae my doots."

Commercial unpreparedness	We learn from the Consular and Trade Reports issued by the Department of Commerce that American glass manufacturers, who have hith-

erto felt the necessity of depending upon foreign clays, will be able hereafter to assert their independence of foreign material, as a result of experiments that have been conducted in the Pittsburgh laboratory of the U. S. Bureau of Standards, where it has now been proven that American clays are superior to German plastic clays for the preparation of glass refractories. The opinion of those in charge of the experiments is that from now on no foreign clays will be needed in this branch of manufacture and the benefit to American industry will be consequently very great. We are further advised that Americans have at last succeeded in solving the secret of an extremely fine quality of steel, for a supply of which our manufacturers have been forced hitherto to depend on the Krupp works in Europe. It has been truly said that "Hunger is the teacher of the arts and the bestower of invention" and this proverb holds particularly true now in many lines of industry, more or less deranged by the gigantic convulsion which has overwhelmed their accustomed foreign sources of supply. It is hardly becoming that so many of our industrial activities are thus almost prostrated from unpreparedness, our "captains of industry" having waited until forced by hunger before they would bestir themselves to look about for and bring to the front our home resources. We have in mind also the potash problem, an attempt at solution of which has been actually forced upon us, and which, we doubt not, will yet be successful, should the present famine continue.

Looking ahead	As is well known, plant products came very near sharing the fate of the potash and the clay and there was much jubilation among

the plant and flower trade when it was learned that azaleas and other floricultural products would be received from Europe this fall as usual and that our growers would not be compelled to devise ways and means for supplying the Christmas and Easter demand with the products of home industry exclusively. Yet, it is not at all certain that it would not have been a "blessing in disguise" had the threatened famine become a fact and our commercial horticulturists obliged to sharpen up their inventive wits accordingly. We should like to see the question of the possibilities of successful competition with foreign-grown plants and bulbs given a real test. Why not incorporate in the advance schedules of our big public exhibitions a set of substantial prizes for home-grown plants, and flowers from home-grown bulbs of varieties not hitherto produced commercially in this couuntry? The Massachusetts Horticultural Society, we understand, has in contemplation a plan for issuing its prize schedules two or three years in advance and it is probable that the promoters of important shows elsewhere will yet find it desirable to adopt similar methods in order to keep up with the advancing standards of quality. A period of three years for preparation and an adequate prize in sight should be a sufficient inducement to systematic effort, and in the hands of a competent advertising expert would prove a most effective publicity asset for any large flower show. President Welch brought this timely subject before the Society of American Florists in a very practical manner in his address before that body at San Francisco last August and we hope that the committee appointed as a result of the Society's approval will act promptly and decisively. The active cooperation of the Bureau of Plant Industry with this committee should not be difficult to secure. There will never be a more propitious time than the present for making a beginning.

ROSE GROWING UNDER GLASS

CONDUCTED BY

Arthur C. Ruzicka

Questions by our readers in line with any of the topics presented on this page will be cordially received and promptly answered by Mr. Ruzicka. Such communications should invariably be addressed to the office of HORTICULTURE.

Fungine. Gladioli Among Roses

Mr. Arthur Ruzicka:

Dear Sir:—Will you kindly give me the formula for making Fungine? I notice that you always recommend a grower to make his own fungicides. The only objection I have in the use of this article is the filthy mess it makes on the benches, glass and woodwork with which it comes in contact; otherwise it is a fairly good article.

Also please inform me if I can grow a few gladiolus bulbs among the rose bushes.

Yours truly,   A. M.

New York.

From the way the inquiry is written it would seem that you do not like Fungine as well as you might, and I cannot see why you should want to mix it at home. It is a patented article, and the price for which it sells is by no means prohibitive, and it is therefore within reach of all. The formula is unknown to me, and I would not make a business of telling it to everyone if it was, as it is the property of The Aphine Manufacturing Co. As for the mess you say you object to, I would suggest that you let a trained rose grower apply the Fungine next time, and I am sure he can do so without messing up the benches, glass and woodwork. To do so he should have an "Auto-Spray" or some other good sprayer that will take a fine nozzle, thus making it very simple to control the spray. We have used Fungine in private conservatories without getting any of it on any glass or woodwork, and if we did, we never found any filthy mess such as you mention. Regarding the gladiolus among rose plants, I would not advise you to plant them there, for they will not amount to much. If you are at all familiar with the culture of the gladiolus you will know that they require conditions quite different from the rose, needing a much warmer and damper atmosphere right up to the time the buds begin to show. Roses too, do best when they are alone, and with us there is never any room among the plants for anything, as they take up all the soil room with their roots, and all the head room with their growth. If you are not particular as to the quality of gladioli you will cut, you could make a few narrow boxes about eight inches deep and plant your bulbs in these, setting them in the walks wherever you may have room. By using good bulbs you may be successful enough to get a cut of fair quality spikes.

Early Propagation

If there are any houses that are doing at all poorly, it will be best to figure on getting these planted early in the season, and towards that end it will be advisable to start propagating early, and a batch of cuttings can be put in at once. If no propagating house is on the place, one of the cross-houses can generally be fixed up to answer the purpose very nicely. In doing this, one should make sure that the heat can be controlled, as otherwise success is not likely to be the result. As a rule there is far too much heat in the cross-houses and to cover up all the pipes would be quite an expense. As these are generally in a trench through the center of the house, with a walk over it, a layer of newspaper can be put down on this and a three-inch coat of ashes applied over this. The ashes can be kept from getting under the benches by putting a narrow board against the bench supports, thus keeping the ashes over the trench only. If plenty of paper is put under the ashes there will be little trouble from the ashes sifting through the cracks into the trench underneath, and when the house is no longer needed for propagating the ashes can be taken away and the heat allowed to come through again. We like the temperature in the sand as near 66 as possible, with a top temperature of 50. The low temperature in the house is necessary to keep the cuttings from making top growth, until after they are rooted. It can then be gradually raised to 58 or 60 until the cuttings are potted. Do not use old or dirty sand. To test sand, rub a little of it between the hands and, on stopping, if they are at all dirty the sand is not clean. It can be washed if no other is available, but should not be used unless it is absolutely necessary. A medium grain sand does best with us and it must be finely screened to take out even the smallest gravel. The benches should be well cleaned and whitewashed before the sand is put in. Where slate can be had for a bottom, or tile, so much the better. Where it is impossible to have either, then a layer of bricks can be put on the bottom of the ordinary wooden bench and the sand put on these. Needless to say the sides of the benches should be closed in order to make the heat go through into the sand. Doors should be provided to let out some heat should the temperature in the sand run up too high. The glass will need a coat of shading, and for this we find it best to use a little green paint mixed into a good deal of kerosene with a little touch of drier added. This will give ideal shade.

Selection of Wood

It will pay to take only real good, clean wood and with live thorns. Wood that has brown or dead thorns on it will not root as easily as wood with live thorns, as the former is much harder, and will not only take longer to root but will require much better care. With Beauties we prefer to make only two-eye cuttings, but with teas we like to make three eye cuttings if we have plenty of wood. Also as many heel cuttings as we can get. There are a large number of small eyes at the bottom of a heel cutting and these come up later in bottom shoots. The more of these of course the better. As soon as a bunch of wood is cut sprinkle it well to keep it from wilting. It is best not to put it into a tub of water as water-soaked wood will not root nearly as well. However, it must not be allowed to wilt, for if it does it will be worthless. The same is true of cuttings. The place to make these would be in the rose cellar where it is cool and not too dry. These cuttings should be kept sprinkled all the time yet not submerged in water for any length of time. As soon as a lot of cuttings is made they should be put into sand at once and well firmed by laying a lath across the bench and striking it gently with a hammer or a brick.

NEPHROLEPIS EXALTATA BOSTONIENSIS

CONCERNING NEPHROLEPIS BOSTONIENSIS.

Editor HORTICULTURE:

Dear Sir—Your comment in HORTICULTURE for October 16th, regarding my Boston fern note in a Brooklyn Botanic Garden Leaflet is welcome, as you suggest it might be, although I question the force of your correction.

It is welcome because I hope it may bring out further facts bearing on the question which may throw light on the dark parts in the antecedents of bostoniensis. I have spent a considerable number of days and dollars during the last year visiting growers of bostoniensis or its varieties about New York, Boston, and Philadelphia, besides corresponding with those further west, all in search of accurate information about these ferns. I have not, however, yet reached the point where I am inhospitable to additional facts even though they may contradict matters which I now believe settled. At the present time I have assembled at the Brooklyn Garden nearly sixty-five distinct forms of Nephrolepis of which probably forty are named American varieties. These latter with two exceptions, I have obtained directly from their original producers, having taken this procedure in the interests of accuracy. Of Piersoni and Anna Foster (or Fosteriana, Fosterae, or Fosteri as it is variously known) I have as yet only uncertain specimens. Barrowsi I have not at all as yet but hope to get it next year from England. Or can you tell me of some American grower who has authentic material of the Foster plant or of Barrowsi?

I question the force of your correction because I do not believe there is any real difference in our information. It is true in a sense that Becker did not originally discover bostoniensis. He sold, by his own statement, 50,000 or more plants of it as "davallioides" until G. W. Oliver convinced him that it was not davallioides, when it was then sent to England (Kew) for identification, where it was "discovered" and named as bostoniensis, if this expression may be permitted. But was not the material sent Becker material and is there any real misstatement in saying that bostoniensis was discovered in the Becker establishment? Had the new form been recognized and described in the literature before Becker obtained it? I ask these questions in the same good part in which I judge your note to have been conceived. My information was derived from two independent sources both presumably reliable and I hope my statement may stand investigation.

The collection at the Brooklyn Botanic Garden deserves further mention. The Garden has given it space not only because the variations are of considerable scientific interest but because it is within the function of the garden to further horticultural knowledge. Besides the present collection mainly of American forms, it is intended to obtain next year all the English forms and to grow these to determine their value. If the tests show any to be superior to those now grown here the results will be published for the benefit of American growers. In the meantime the garden will welcome any help which American florists can render. From the scientific standpoint all variations, whether of horticultural value or not, are of interest and the garden will be glad to receive any additional kinds. At the same time it will reciprocate as far as possible by supplying small plants or runners of varieties now in stock which it is permitted to send out. A number of growers have already sent in new unnamed forms on the understanding that these will not be allowed to go out. As it happens a number of exchanges have already been made or arranged but the distribution of plants by the garden is somewhat limited owing to the small space at present available.

Yours truly,
R. C. BENEDICT.
Brooklyn Botanic Garden.

VARIETIES OF NEPHROLEPIS.

At the Brooklyn Botanic Garden there has been assembled a collection of between sixty and seventy varieties of Nephrolepis; over fifty of which are named, as shown in the lists given below. The catalogs of English growers offer about forty additional varieties which the Garden expects to purchase within a few months.

In addition to maintaining this collection for the purpose of scientific study, the Garden desires to make it of value to American growers of Nephrolepis, and makes, herewith, the following offer. Small plants or runners of any of the plants named will be furnished to growers interested in trying them out, as fast as a limited supply of stock plants will allow. Requests for information regarding any of the varieties listed below will be answered by the writer of this note as completely as available data will permit. Furthermore, the Garden is having reprinted the writer's article on Nephrolepis prepared for Bailey's Cyclopaedia of American Horticulture, and will be glad to send a copy of this reprint to any grower on request. This contains a general discussion of Nephrolepis, with descriptions of all the varieties about which information was obtainable.

In return, growers are asked to send in any new form which they may produce, and also any old forms, such for example as Barrowsi, which has not yet been obtainable in the United States although listed in English catalogs. In connection with the Cyclopaedia article, the writer will welcome and greatly appreciate notification of any mistakes or omissions, or other information pertinent to the subject.

List 1. Varieties of N. exaltata of authenticated identification (two or three exceptions noted), the stock plants having been obtained from their original source:

N. exaltata (from Porto Rico).
bostoniensis (Becker).
Piersoni (?), elegantissima, elegantissima "improved," elegantissima compacta, superbissima, muscosa, viridissima, "dwarf Boston"; Whitmani, Whitmani compacta, magnifica, gracillima (?); Amerpohli; Clarki, Smithi; Craigi, robusta, Wanamakeri; Scotti; Wagner, falcata; Anna Foster (?); Elmsfordi; Harrisi, Millsi; Roosevelti, Teddy, Jr.;
Scholzeli (typical two-pinnate), Scholzeli (3-pinnate, erect lvd.), Scholzeli (3-pinnate, spreading); Giatrasi, New York; todeoides (?).

List 2. Varieties of other species N. exaltata; identification not yet verified:

N. cordifolia, tuberosa plumosa, pectinata, Duffii, rivularis, new species (?), biserrata (davallioides?), biserrata furcans, hirsutula, hirsutula tripinnatifida, Wittboldi, floccigera, acuminata, philippinensis, superba (or Westoni).

Besides these, other forms to the number of ten or fifteen are being grown at the Garden. Some of them are possibly of no commercial value, but others are of value and are likely to be introduced eventually. The latter have been sent to the Garden with the understanding that they will not be allowed to go out.

R. C. BENEDICT.
Brooklyn Botanic Garden.

ODE TO THE DAHLIA.

By a Dahlia Lover.

Written in honor of the first Exhibition of the American Dahlia Society, held in the American Museum of Natural History, Sept. 24, 25 and 26, 1915.

Queen of the waning summer time, I greet thee,
It is indeed a joy sublime, to meet thee!
Wonderful robes, with colors bright enfold thee,
Crimson and pink and dark as night: they hold me!

Centuries old, and yet, with youth eternal,
And heart of gold, and character supernal,
Down from the everlasting hills to meet us,
With open arms, and smiling face to great us.

Why do we love thee, we of these later days,
We who are fascinated, as we gaze?
Surely some memory dear and sweet enthralls us!
Helpful and strong, thy silent voice, it calls us.

Back to our mother's garden, memories call,
And, as we journey, loving thoughts grow fonder,
This was her flower, she loved it best of all;
We feel her, see her, love her, as we ponder.

So, Summer Queen, and autumn queen, we greet thee;
Thou art the flower to memory most dear.
Our mother's flower—proud are we all to meet thee;
Proud of thy triumph, manifested here:

And so with mother's name we link thee ever,
Mother and dahlia, through all the years gone by;
And naught in all the years to come can sever,
What beauty, love and memories supply.

CLUBS AND SOCIETIES

GARDENERS' AND FLORISTS' CLUB OF BOSTON.

The November meeting of this Club on Tuesday evening, was very well attended. The main business was an address by George B. Gallup, president of the Pilgrim Publicity Association of Boston, on 'Advertising—the Light that Serves and Saves." The speaker presented his subject in such an attractive manner that it deeply impressed all who heard it. He emphasized the duty of the horticulturist to do their part to improve the esthetic environment of the places where people live and contribute by such support to the advancement of civilization and culture which is so distinctively characteristic of the present epoch of unprecedented scientific revelation. He told of the plans under way for the proposed Model City of the World which is to commemorate the landing of the Pilgrims at Plymouth, on the anniversary of that event five years hence and made a strong presentation of the part that the florist and landscape gardener is expected to take in this great project for which the initial expenditure will exceed twenty million dollars. The florists' great mission is to help bring about a fuller popular appreciation of the beauties of nature and to inculcate by effort and example the ambition for more beautiful cities and happier homes and to help increase the joy and honor of living, through the message of the goods in which they deal. The eloquent presentation of this timely subject was received with a spirited demonstration of approval.

W. J. Kennedy as chairman of the legislative committee read a list of the various bills to be presented before the legislature during the coming session, having a direct interest for the trade. One of these is in the interest of the birds and bees as affected by the poison-spraying of the trees. One provides for the utilization of forest land for cultivation. One provides the sum of $5000, towards the instruction of boys and girls in gardening. Another contemplates the taking of a State census of everybody connected with any branch of agriculture or horticulture. Still another proposes that the Mass. Agricultural College be equipped to test seeds for all who wish, and one other provides for a special experiment station to investigate diseases of vegetables.

Communications were read from John Young, secretary of the S. A. F., asking for count and voucher to show the Club's eligibility to have a representative on the S. A. F. executive board, and from R. Vincent, Jr., concerning the newly organized American Dahlia Society.

Nomination of officers followed and the following were named without any competing candidates: James Methuen for president; W. J. Patterson for vice-president; Peter Fisher for treasurer, and W. N. Craig for secretary. Nine names were nominated for the executive committee. A re-election

Meetings Next Week

Wednesday, Dec. 1.
Tuxedo Horticultural Society, Tuxedo Park, N. Y.

Thursday, Dec. 2.
Southampton Horticultural Society, Southampton, N. Y.

Friday, Dec. 3.
North Shore Horticultural Society, Manchester, Mass.
North Shore Horticultural Society, Lake Forest, Ill.
Pasadena Horticultural Society, Pasadena, Calif.
Yonkers Horticultural Society, Yonkers, N. Y.
People's Park Cottage Gardeners' Association, Paterson, N. J.

Saturday, Dec. 4.
Pacific Coast Horticultural Society,

as president was offered to Herman Bartsch but he declined the honor. Six new members were admitted.

M. C. Ebel, secretary of the National Association of Gardeners made an interesting address on the history and purposes of the Association and the approaching convention in Boston. W. N. Craig, Duncan Finlayson and W. J. Kennedy were appointed to act with a similar number from the executive committee of the Horticultural Interests of Boston to provide a suitable welcome and entertainment for the visitors on the occasion of the convention, Dec. 9, 10 and 11.

On the exhibition table were groups of Christmas plants from W. W. Edgar Co., Carnation Miss Theo from Littlefield & Wyman, vase of Bouvardia Humboldti corymbiflora and specimen plants of Solanum capsicas-

trum. Montreal variety, from Faulkner Farm. Splendid blooms of chrysanthemums Wm. Turner, Col. Appleton, Wells' Late Pink, Wm. Duckham and Mrs. Kelley from Alex McKay, a lovely pale pink seedling rose of delicious fragrance from C. E. Holbrow and a showy plant of Begonia Ensign from the same exhibitor, this being the first time it has been shown in this country.

LANCASTER COUNTY FLORISTS' CLUB.

The visitors to Manheim on November 18 numbered an even half dozen—a small but select party. At Phares Hostetter's we saw callas by the ten thousand and sweet peas, all in excellent shape. At Phares Hostetter's sweet peas, mignonette, carnations, etc., uniformly good. At E. P. Hostetter's, the giant place of the county, Asparagus Sprengerii and plumosus are a big money making proposition and one house of plumosus is laden with seed. A house of yellow dasies three years old was in full bloom and an evidence of what can be done by careful culture. Carnations, of which there are tons of thousands, were in fine form and especially those that had been planted in all summer. A house of Matchless, 400 feet long, planted from two-inch pots in June, were equal to those shown by the originators in the New York show the year previous to its introduction.

7.30 P. M., President Barr rapped the meeting to order. The Dahlia Show committee reported. The Visiting committee reported arrangements for a trip to Lititz next month. A short talk on Chrysanthemums and on the psychology of plant growing was made by B. F. Barr. Harry K. Rohrer gave a list of varieties for early, midseason and late that they had found valuable. Rudolph Nagle gave his experience

POMPONS AND SINGLES
At the Cleveland Flower Show.

with the early varieties and Chas. Tucker gave some of his experience as an amateur grower.

For our show next fall it was decided to send out a list of varieties suitable for exhibition purposes and let every member check up which he would volunteer to grow so as to get a good variety and not too much duplication. This line of action is made necessary by the fact that there are only a few members who grow chrysanthemums and yet all want a part in the preparation for this show.

F. Spihner exhibited a fine vase of Roman Gold, H. D. Rohrer single blooms of Wm. Turner, Dolly Dimple and Nakota and B. F. Barr staged Wm. Turner, America, Harvard, Thanksgiving Queen, Patti and Rosette, all first flowers.

For the December meeting there will be an oyster supper and a general social time in the Brennman building with prizes for the bowling, billiards and pool and a doctor to look after the man who eats the most oysters, "Dutch treat," $1.25 per head. We hope to have some of our out-of-town friends with us for this occasion.

ALBERT M. HERR.

CHRYSANTHEMUM SOCIETY OF AMERICA.

Work of Committee.

The examining committees of the C. S. A. have submitted reports on new varieties as follows:

New York, Nov. 6th, submitted by Henry Gaut, Glen Cove. Seedling No. 60, amber bronze, single, scored as follows: color 37, form 16, substance 16, stem and foliage 15, total 84. Seedling No. 75, pink, shading to white center, single: color 39, form 19, substance 18, stem and foliage 18, total 94. Seedling No. 19, bronze, single, color 38, form 17, substance 15, stem and foliage 17, total 87. Seedling No. 53, terra cotta, bronze, single: color 38, form 18, substance 17, stem and foliage 16, total 89. Seedling No. 74, bronze, single: color 35, form 16, substance 18, stem and foliage 17, total 86.

Philadelphia, Nov. 6th, submitted by G. A. Lotze, Glen Burnie, Md. Seedling No. 6, white inc. Jap.: com. scale, color 15, form 10, fullness 9, stem 13, foliage 12, substance 14, size 8, total 81. Seedling No. 7, white, Japanese: Ex. scale, color 14, stem 4, foliage 4, fullness 12, form 13, depth 13, size 25, total 85.

Cleveland, Nov. 11th. Submitted by the E. C. Hill Co., Richmond, Ind. Autocrat, white inc.: Com. scale, color 18, form 13, fullness 8, stem 14, foliage 13, substance 14, size 9, total 89. Seedling No. 69, yellow, inc.: Com. scale, color 18, form 13, fullness 9, stem 14, foliage 13, substance 13, size 7, total 87. Submitted by A. N. Pierson, Inc., Cromwell, Conn., seedling No. 23, bronze terra cotta, Jap.: Com. scale, color 18, form 12, fullness 8, stem 13, foliage 15, substance 13, size 7, total 86. Submitted by Chas. S. Totty, Madison, N. J., Autocrat, white, inc.: Com. scale, color 18, form 13, fullness 8, stem 14, foliage 13, substance 14, size 9, total 89; Ex. scale, color 14, stem 4, foliage 4, fullness 14, form 13, depth 13, size 26, total 87. Submitted by Fred Pautke, Grosse Point, Mich., seedling No. 15, yellow anemone: color 38, form 16, stem and foliage 17, fullness 18, total 89. Seedling No. 2, bronze, pompon: color 30,

form 18, stem and foliage 17, fullness 18, total 83. Seedling No. 65, bronze, pompon: color 35, form 15, stem and foliage 18, fullness 15, total 83. Seedling No. 7, pink, pompon: color 30, form 17, stem and foliage 17, fullness 17, total 81. Seedling No. 26, pink, pompon: color 34, form 18, stem and foliage 15, fullness 18, total 85. Submitted by Carl Becherer, Dixmont, Pa., seedling No. 20, A. yellow, single, color 25, form 15, substance 15, stem and foliage 15, total 70. Seedling No. 26, L. bronze, inc., Com. scale, color 16, form 13, fullness 9, stem 14, foliage 14, substance 13, size 6, total 84. Seedling No. 216, A. bronze, reflexed. Com. scale, color 10, form 13, fullness 7, stem 14, foliage 15, substance 13, size 6, total 78. Seedling No. 234, D. bronze, reflexed, Com. scale, color 15, form 10, fullness 9, stem 14, foliage 13, substance 12, size 6, total 79. Submitted by Elmer D. Smith & Co., Adrian, Mich. Ogontz, light yellow, inc., Ex. scale, color 13, stem 4, foliage 4, fullness 13, form 13, depth 13, size 27, total 87. Josephine Foley, white, inc., Com. scale, color 18, form 13, fullness 8, stem 14, foliage 14, substance 13, size 7, total 87. Nordi, white, pompon, color 35, form 16, stem and foliage 16, fullness 6, total 83. Little Gein, pink, pompon, color 37, form 19, stem and foliage 16, fullness 19, total 91.

Philadelphia, Nov. 12th, submitted by Wm. Kleinheinz for Elmer D. Smith & Co. Ogontz, yellow, with light yellow reverse, Com. scale. color 18, form 14, fullness 9, stem 14, foliage 13, substance 13, size 9, total 90. Ex. scale. color 13, stem and foliage 9, fullness 14, form 14, depth 12, size 27, total 89. New York, Nov. 13th, submitted by Henry Gaut, Glen Cove, L. I., N. Y. Seedling No. 30, bronze, single, color 36, form 17, substance 18, stem and foliage 17, total 88. Seedling No. 7, light bronze, single, color 30, form 15, stem and foliage 17, substance 16, total 78. Seedling No. 50, yellow single. Com. scale, color 35, form 17, stem and foliage 17, substance 17, total 86. Seedling No. 32, Indian Red, single, Com. scale, color 38, form 18, stem and foliage 18, substance 18, total 92. CHAS. W. JOHNSON, Sec'y.

GROUP OF CROTONS.
By Robert Craig Co., at the Cleveland Flower Show.

PARK INSTITUTE OF NEW ENGLAND.

A meeting of the Park Institute of New England was held in the City Hall, Lowell, Mass., November 18th. There were thirty Park Superintendents and Park Commissioners present and it proved to be one of the most interesting meetings that have been held. The speakers were Chairman John Dillon, of the Boston Park Commission, who spoke along the lines of the uses of parks and playgrounds; James McCaffrey, Supt. of Recreations, Providence, R. I., on "The Laying Out and Equipment of Playgrounds," after which there was a discuss on by those present and Mr. James B. Shea, who read a very interesting paper on "Greater Uses of Our Parks and Playgrounds."

The meeting was followel by a visit to Fort Hill Park, Shedd Playgrounds, the South Common, and the Casino, where the Board of Trade was conducting an exhibition of "Things Made in Lowell." At six o'clock all assembled at the hotel and partook of a fine dinner provided by the Board of Trade. Following dinner G. A. Parker, of Hartford, Conn., Dean of the Park Superintendents, gave a talk which was greatly appreciated.

ST. LOUIS FLORIST CLUB.

The St. Louis Florist Club held a very interesting meeting November 18 at the Missouri Botanical Garden. When President Bourdet called the meeting to order eighty-five members were present. The Spring Flower Show committees read their report advising a spring show but not before the spring of 1917, as the Carnation Society Meeting in January, 1916, would take the edge off a show of this kind. The Carnation Society committee reported through its general chairman, J. F. Ammann. J. F. Ammann, F. Fillmore and E. W. Guy were appointed to draw up resolutions on the deaths of W. C. Young and E. G. Eggeling. Adolph Janeicke and J. F. Ammann gave glowing reports of the Chicago and Cleveland Flower shows also other members who visited the shows. The sum of $100 was subscribed to the National Convention Committee. After adournment the members visited the big conservatory in the Garden. Secretary Beneke announced that the next meeting would be held in the regular meeting hall Thursday, December 9th.

CLUB AND SOCIETY NOTES.

The Southampton (N. Y.) Horticultural Society held its regular meeting on Nov. 18th. J. Johnson, superintendent of the G. Warrington Curtis estate, read an interesting and instructing essay on that all-important subject, "Lime;" he dealt with it in a detailed and comprehensive manner. There was an animated discussion, where points of the utmost importance were brought to light. The next meeting will be held on Dec. 2, in Odd Fellows Hall.

S. R. CHANDLER.

The Horticultural Society of Western Pennsylvania has been organized to meet semi-monthly in the East Liberty Branch of Carnegie Library, Pittsburgh. The officers are as follows: David Fraser, president; William Allen, vice-president; Thomas E. Tyler, secretary, and William Thompson, treasurer. With the addition of William Thompson, Sr., they also form a committee to draft by-laws at a meeting in the near future. While the society has been founded principally by private gardeners, all interested in horticulture are invited to become members. A feature of the work will be the giving of autumn and spring flower shows.

The Medford (Mass.) Horticultural Society is planning a course of practical lectures on horticultural subjects during the winter months. Already two have been given. F. E. Palmer of Brookline gave a talk on house plants, in October, which has been the means of solving many problems for the window gardener. On Nov. 18 Eric Wetterlow of the North Shore Horticultural Society gave a very instructive address on "The Children's Gardens of Manchester, Mass.," telling how they had aroused the interest of the town officials in their behalf.

The society feels very much indebted to these gentlemen for the information and entertainment imparted. GEO. F. STEWART.

The Exhibitions

HARTFORD.

The Chrysanthemum Show of the Connecticut Horticultural Society held at the old City Hall, Hartford, on Friday, Nov. 12th, was a gratifying success. The hallway and stairway were adorned with palms and chrysanthemums and a very attractive exhibit of anemone-flowered seedlings. The south side of the lobby was beautifully decorated by the Park Department. The private gardeners and growers brought the best they had and the show was the best ever given by the society. It is conservatively estimated that some 10,000 visitors viewed the exhibition. No premiums were offered but certificates were given to John F. Huss for specimen chrysanthemum plants; Alfred Cebelius, for specimen chrysanthemum plant and for Ophelia, Mrs. Aaron Ward, Mrs. Charles Russell, Hadley and Radiance roses; Fred Boss for cut blooms and pot plants; A. N. Pierson, Inc., for palms and for cut roses; Geo. H. Hale, gard. for W. E. Sessions of Bristol, for seedlings of anemone flowered chrysanthemums; Warren S. Mason, supt. of the A. A. Pope estate, Farmington, and Elmer D. Smith & Co., Adrian, Mich., for general displays. The staging was under the direction of G. H. Hollister, supt. of Keney Park. Edward A. Brassill, manager for W. W. Hunt & Co., was chairman of the committee in charge of the exhibition.

ALFRED DIXON, Sec'y.

PROVIDENCE, R. I.

The November exhibition of the Rhode Island Horticultural Society was held in the Narragansett Hotel on the 11th and 12th inst. There were more than 40 exhibitors and more than 300 exhibits. In addition to the prizes many gratuities for special exhibits were given. First prize winners were as follows: Roses—Burke & Bruns, Warwick Greenhouses. Carnations—Fred. Hoffman, Warwick Greenhouses. Maplehurst Greenhouses. R. J. Taylor, John Marshall. Violets — Warwick Greenhouses. Chrysanthemum cut blooms—Fred. Hoffman, Jess Tartaglia, Warwick Greenhouses. Albert Holscher, Johnston Bros. Pot plants—Rhode Island Hospital. Palms—Wm. Appleton. Floral art—Johnston Bros.,

William Appleton. James Dillon, berried shrubs; Hope Greenhouses, begonias, E. J. Bevin, seedling chrysanthemums and MacNair, ferns, were among the exhibitors recognized with a gratuity.

The exhibition committee is composed of Eugene A. Appleton, Joshua Vose, Pontiac; Arthur Sellew, Cornelius Hartstra, Dr. H. W. Heaton, and the president and secretary ex-officio.

VISITORS REGISTER.

St. Louis, Mo.—Rudolph J. Mohr, Chicago; J. K, M. L. Farquhar, Boston.

Boston—A. E. Thatcher, Bar Harbor, Me.; M. C. Ebel, Madison, N. J.; T. A. Havemeyer, New York.

Pittsburgh: C. F. Schermerhorn, representing H. F. Michell Company, Phila.; J. L. Pennock Bros., Phila.

Washington, D. C.—J. Canning, Ardsley, N. Y.; C. VanGuihaven, Hillegom, Holland; J. A. Peterson, Cincinnati, O.; Mr. and Mrs. Thomas Knight, New York; Robert Shoob, representing Rice Co., Phila.

Philadelphia—W. H. Weatherby, of Livingston Seed Co., Columbus, Ohio; T. Malbrane, Johnstown, Pa.; Charles L. Seybold, Supt. of Parks, Wilkesbarre, Pa.; Chas. Sim; Rosemont, Pa.; Walter Mott, representing Benj. Hammond, Beacon, N. Y.; Frank Perkins, representing Holmes Seed Co., Harrisburg, Pa.

Chicago: Frank Sylvester, of J. M. Fox & Son, Milwaukee, Wis.; Martin Reukauf, rep. H. Bayersdorfer & Co., Phila.; Mr. and Mrs. Frank Davis, Davenport, Iowa; Milton Alexander, New York; W. P. Craig, Philadelphia, Pa.; Martin Edlefsen, Milwaukee, Wis.; Julius Dilloff, representing Schloss Bros., New York.

ARDISIA.

Ardisias may be propagated in two ways—by seeds and by cuttings. Seeds may be sown at any time, for it is continually flowering and fruiting and the berries last a long time. If it is desirable to grow them on for eighteen months, which gives an excellent size plant for Christmas sale, the seeds should be planted in the spring. As soon as large enough they are pricked out into small pots and shifted as necessary.

Better plants, however, are grown from cuttings, because the plant will branch nearer the base and so give a more shapely specimen and, moreover, a saleable plant can be gotten in a shorter time. A plant is usually not saleable after three years of age and such are the ones generally used for stock. Plants may be obtained from these by girdling the tops and wrapping moss around the wound. In about six weeks the moss will be well filled with roots and the layers may then be severed from the stocks and potted up. Place them in a propagating frame until they have taken hold of the soil well.

The old stock will now answer fine for taking cuttings from. Place them in a close, warm atmosphere at 65 degrees and they will readily break. The half matured young shoots that will result make the best of cuttings. Place the cuttings in a bench with both a bottom heat and air temperature of 70 degrees. In about a month they will have rooted, when they should be potted up and shifted as necessary. The best soil is one of loam, peat and sand in equal parts. For later shifts, one-fourth part of decomposed manure may be added to good advantage.

When the plants begin flowering, give them more air and stop syringing until after the fruits have set. For the best development, they should always be kept near the glass. In the summer, it is well to shade the house on sunny days with cheese cloth or slat shutters. When the berries are well developed—about the first of October—they should be given plenty of sunshine, and they will also do with less heat, say 50 to 55 degrees. To help the berries and leaves to a color, soot water may be applied occasionally. Never allow the plants to become pot-bound, for unsightly, "leggy" plants are liable to result. Occasionally turn the plants to get a symmetrical form. In propagating from seeds, use care in selecting the plants from which the seeds are to be taken. There is some variation in size and productiveness of fruit, and only the most productive and best colored plants should be selected.

There is also a white-berried variety—A. japonica—but this is not as popular a pot plant.

C. E. WILDON.

Amherst, Mass.

AN AQUATIC POOL.

Our cover illustration shows one of the prettiest exhibits made at the Cleveland Flower Show, and certainly one which attracted much attention and admiration from the visiting public. Mr. Tricker says that the same beautiful scene can be reproduced at any time during the winter. Such a feature would be a prime addition to any park or private conservatory or sun parlor. The cut nymphæa flowers travel well and keep a long time, as was well demonstrated at Cleveland. The most of those exhibited were shipped from New Jersey on Monday, Nov. 8, some of the blooms having been cut on Friday previous and all were still good on Friday the 12th.

BRITISH HORTICULTURE.
New Chrysanthemums.

At a meeting of the Floral Committee of the National Chrysanthemum Society on Oct. 25th, a batch of novelties was exhibited for awards. These were made as follows: Bertha Fairs, a single, Mensa type, golden fawn florets suffused with ruby red; Norman Davis, Framfield, Sussex, first class certificate. Champagne, red crimson, early flowering, classed with Source d'Or, Wells & Co., Merstham, Surrey, card of commendation. Charlotte E. Soer, large flowered Jap, canary yellow, shaded at the tips with bronze, first class certificate; Sir Edward Letchworth, large incurved Jap, broad deep pink florets, silvery reverse, Martin Silsbury, Shanklin, Isle of Wight, first class certificate. Master A. Ewen, golden bronze single, W. Newton, Potters Bar, card of commendation. Miranda, terra cotta, single sport from Portia, Cragg, Harrison & Cragg, Heston, Middlesex, first class certificate. Mrs. Harold Phillips, mauve pink single, Godfrey & Son, Exmouth, Devon, card of commendation. Norman Pearson, chestnut crimson, single, Mensa type, G. Mileham, Leatherhead, Surrey, first class certificate. Phyllis Cooper, golden yellow single, P. Ladds, Swanley, Kent, first class certificate. Tom Wren, pure white single, Thos. Stevenson, Addiestone, Surrey, card of commendation.

The Society is holding a show at the Royal Horticultural Society's Hall, on the 11th and 12th of Nov., instead of at the Crystal Palace—now used for naval purposes—as in former years.

W. H. ADSETT.

MILDEW ON OUTDOOR ROSES.

To the Editor of HORTICULTURE:

Dear Sir:—The request of Mr. M. H. S., Walla Walla, Wash., for a formula to overcome mildew on outdoor roses impels me to send you the recipe for a remedy that I use with unfailing success.

Liner of sulphur .... ¼ oz.
Fel's Naptha soap or Ivory soap. ½ oz.
Water .... 1 gallon

Dissolve the liner of sulphur in cold water and the soap by the aid of leah; when thoroughly dissolved mix. The plants must be sprayed early in the morning to prevent scalding—never late in the day. I am convinced that more mildew is developed on roses by wetting the foliage late in the day than from any other cause. I never have mildew on my roses unless we have much rain at night and always spray with the above mixture as soon as possible after a rainy night. In sections where mildew is prevalent I would suggest spraying before it appears. Roses should always be watered early in the morning.

Yours very truly,
ROBERT HUEY.

Philadelphia, Nov. 13, 1915.

SOME CHOICE GARDEN SUBJECTS.

GORDONIA ALTAMAHA. Flowers are still opening on this beautiful southern tree. They first appear in September and open in succession for fully six weeks. Gordonia is related to the Camellia, and the pure white flowers which vary from three to three and a half inches in diameter, although more cup-shaped, resemble single Camellia flowers. This small tree was discovered in 1765 near Fort Barrington on the Altamaha River; it has entirely disappeared, however, as a wild plant, and it has only been preserved by the specimens cultivated chiefly in the neighborhood of Philadelphia where it was sent by its discoverers. In these sheltered positions the plants are doing well here and have not suffered at all in recent severe winters. This Gordonia, however, grows more rapidly and to a larger size in the middle states and there are many good specimens in Pennsylvania gardens.

ABELIA GRANDIFLORA resembles in shape the flowers of some of the Honeysuckles; they are white faintly tinged with rose color, and their delicate beauty is set off by the small, dark green and lustrous leaves. Abelia grandiflora is a slender shrub with arching stems from three to four feet high and is thought to be a hybrid between two Chinese species. Until the introduction by the Arboretum of some of the species of this genus from western China it was believed to be the hardiest of the Abelias. In the Arboretum it suffers in severe winters but in sheltered positions it flowers well every year and the flowers continue to open during nearly two months. This Abelia has become an exceedingly popular plant in the gardens of the southern states and is cultivated with more or less success as far north as New York.

(W. A. Manda regards Abelia runestris as the hardiest species, this being entirely reliable at South Orange, N. J.—Ed.)

THE CHINESE BUDDLEIAS. Buddleia Davidii or, to use its more common name, B. variabilis. Has one-sided, pointed, many-flowered clusters which curve downward from arching stems and are thickly covered with small, blue-purple, fragrant flowers. In some of the forms of this plant are found perhaps the most beautiful of all summer and autumn flowering shrubs, and although only recently brought to the United States and Europe by Wilson they are already largely planted in this country where they have received the name of Summer Lilacs. Here at the north Buddleia Davidii is not perfectly hardy, and the stems are killed to the ground by cold, but new stems spring up and as the flower-clusters are produced at the ends of branches of the year this severe pruning improves the flowers. Few plants in their season are better suited to supply cut flowers, and for this purpose as well as for garden decoration this Buddleia in its various forms has proved one of the most useful shrubs of recent discovery.—Arnold Arboretum Bulletin.

SEED TRADE

AMERICAN SEED TRADE ASSOCIATION
Officers—President, J. M. Lupton, Mattituck, L. I., N. Y.; First Vice-President, Kirby B. White, Detroit, Mich.; Second Vice-President, F. W. Bolgiano, Washington, D. C.; Secretary-Treasurer, C. E. Kendel, Cleveland, O.; Assistant Secretary, S. F. Willard, Jr., Cleveland, O. Cincinnati, O., next meeting place.

Beans Kiting

The very great scarcity of certain standard seed stocks is just now beginning to be realized by the trade. The shortage of beans has no doubt been more or less understood but when we hear of certain wax-pod varieties selling at $14 and $15 per bushel, it is something of a shock even to those who had some fair idea of how scarce the wax-varieties were. Even the green-pod sorts, excepting possibly the Black Valentines, have reached new high levels in price, and what is more, there are no indications that any stocks are being held in reserve for higher figures. The scarcity is unqualifiedly genuine.

Vine Seed Shortages

Vine seeds, squashes, cucumbers, musk and watermelons are short, as previously indicated in these columns, but a very large number of items have been returned as crop failures, where it was expected that some small percentages at least would be delivered. It is stated that summer crook-neck squash is a practical failure this year and whatever seed is for sale must be of last year's growth. Fortunately this does not detract from the value of the seed, however, as it might with certain other items. Several varieties of musk and watermelons are reported practical failures and some cucumbers are also extremely short although the standard popular varieties will be procurable at 20 or 25 per cent. advance over last year's prices.

The Sweet Corn Situation

We had supposed that by this date the situation on sweet corn seed would have been cleared up but inquiry develops the fact that nearly all varieties are more or less short, while some of the later sorts will prove decidedly so. It is learned that one or two very sharp frosts within the past six weeks have probably damaged the vitality of a large percentage of the late varieties, and when the seed is dried it may be practically worthless for seed purposes. Until the corn is cured and

suitable for testing as to vitality, it will be impossible to state how serious this feature will be. Country Gentleman is said to be especially short, and several of the larger dealers will not quote it at the present time at any figure. Stowell's Evergreen is offered rather sparingly.

Canners' Convention.

We assume that those seedsmen and seed growers who usually attend the canners' conventions have secured reservations at the hotels for the period of the next canners' convention which is to be held in Louisville, Ky. As we understand it, this convention opens the second week in February. We recently were informed that nearly all of the hotels, in fact, all the leading ones—are booked to capacity and late comers will have to be content with quarters in rooming houses.

Notes.

Nashville, Tenn.—A retail seed store has been opened in Market square by the Cumberland Seed Co.

Chicago—The retail seed stores now have a change almost as great as going into another business.

With the cold wave the bulbs and shrubbery drop out of sight and holiday attractions are filling the counters.

Wichita, Kan.—The Marlow Seed Co., 119 West Douglas avenue, are building an addition to their present quarters.

The value of horticultural imports at the Port of New York for the week ending Nov. 13 is given as follows: Clover seed, $31,915; grass seed, $31,572; sugar beet seed, $35,778; trees, bulbs and plants, $87,314.

Our readers are all more or less interested in the condition of Mr. W. Atlee Burpee; we are sorry to report that the latest information is that he is no better, and those near him are said to be deeply worried, but they have not abandoned hope of his ultimate recovery. Like his many friends we earnestly hope that he may be spared for many years of usefulness yet.

San Francisco—The Bay Counties Seed Company is a new concern recently organized here to engage in the seed, bulb and plant business. John H. W. Field is head of the firm, and associated with him is Milton Tonini, who was formerly connected with C. C. Morse & Co. Tonini will have charge of the business. Quarters have been secured at 404 Market street, where a comprehensive stock has been assembled. It is understood that the new concern contemplates working gradually into the cut-flower business.

CATALOGUES RECEIVED.

Pittsburgh Cut Flower Co., Pittsburgh, Pa.—Christmas Flowers and Supplies for Florists. A handsome illustrated catalogue of holiday supplies, moss and green goods, including boxwood sprays as a leading specialty.

John Lewis Childs, Flowerfield, N. Y.—Trade Catalogue of Gladioli and

other Summer Flowering Bulbs and Plants. Illustrated with portraits of gladiolus novelties.

Eltweed Pomeroy, Donna, Texas.—Fifth Annual Price List and Information Book for 1915-1916. Many interesting illustrations of Amaryllises.

Frederick Roemer, Quedlinburg, Germany—Illustrated Price List of Novelties in Flower Seeds for 1916.

Atlantic Nursery Co., Berlin, Md.—Fall-Spring Trade Price List, 1915-1916, Nursery stock.

M. Herb, Naples, Italy—1916 List of Flower and Vegetable Seed Novelties, Illustrated.

NEW CORPORATIONS.

Omaha, Neb.—Nebraska Seed Co., increasing capital stock from $50,000 to $150,000.

Circleville, O.—Marion Bros. Co., to deal in horticultural supplies, capital stock, $30,000.

Alexandria, Va.—Potomac Gardens, capital stock, $50,000. Incorporators, R. B. Washington, L. B. Duffy, et al.

Portsmouth, Va.—Hubert Bulb Company, capital $50,000. Vernon A. Brooks, pres.; W. J. Gullie, sec.; both of Portsmouth, Va.

Boston.—Henry M. Robinson & Co., Inc. Henry M. Robinson, Charles A. Robinson, Joseph Margolis; flowers and plants; $150,000.

Sioux City, Ia.—Glassacres Gardens & Nursery Co., capital stock, $20,000. Incorporators, J. L. and A. F. Hanchetti and J. Kroonemeyer.

Chicago, Ill.—Farmers' Mutual Seed Association, capital stock, $60,000. Incorporators, A. A. Berry, John F. Summers, A. F. Galloway and J. F. Sinn.

Alvin, Tex.—Fred L. Webster, well known as a grower, has located permanently in Alvin, where he will grow a general line of plants and flowers.

Of Interest to Retail Florists

NEW FLOWER STORES.

Austin, Tex.—Novelty Floral Co., 913 Congress avenue.

Winston-Salem, N. C.—William Morgenroth, Hinshaw building.

Baltimore, Md. — Parkway Flower Shop, 35 East North avenue.

Logan, U.—Cache Valley Floral Co., succeeding Marvold Floral Co.

Pittsfield, Mass.—F. I. Drake & Co., New American House building.

St. Louis, Mo.—Kohr & Breidenbach, 39th street & Shaw avenue.

Pittsburgh, Pa. — Liberty Flower Shop, Joseph Feinberg, proprietor, 946 Liberty avenue.

Philadelphia, Pa. — Ideal Flower Shop, 52d street, above Market, Miss A. Walker, proprietor.

Chicago, Ill.—Nicholas Korson, 29 West Washington street; Simpson's, 432 North Parkside avenue.

Farmington, U.—W. T. Gray, Broadway and State street; E. Lambourne, Main and Second streets, south.

DURING RECESS.

Boston Florists' Bowling Club.

Scores and Standing Nov. 19.

Galvin .... 1324 vs. Flower M'k't... 1319
Carbone ...... 1301 vs. M. & M........ 1262
Zinn .... 1323 vs. Flower Ex..... 1238
Pansies ...... 1254 vs. Robinson 1240

..Standing as to Points.

	Won	Lost
Galvin	24	4
Flower Market	21	7
Zinn	15	13
Carbone	17	11
Pansies	11	17
Flower Exchange	9	19
Robinson	8	20
M. & M.	7	21

NEWS NOTES.

Austin, Tex.—Fred H. Hall has been made a member of the Hyde Park Floral Co.

Fargo, N. D.—The Smedley Company opened their newly refurnished salesroom at 69 Broadway last week.

Claremont, N. H.—The Claremont Floral Shop, which was in charge of Mrs. Allen, has discontinued business.

Boston—A priest in Waltham has joined the chorus against the waste of money for flowers at funerals. He is said to have emphatically scored this so-called useless expenditure and declared strongly that the money might better be spent for other things.

St. Louis—The 26th annual banquet given to florists, gardeners and nurserymen by the Missouri Botanical Garden took pace at Liederkranz Club Hall, Friday night, Nov. 19. Some 250 were present, including about 25 members of the Florist Club. The feature of the evening was the illustrated lecture on Bulb Culture in Holland, by J. K. M. L. Farquhar of Boston, which will long be remembered by those present. Dr. G. T. Moore was toastmaster.

BUSINESS TROUBLES.

Chicago, Ill.—Manusos Bros., florists, Van Buren and State streets, are in the hands of a receiver.

NEWS ITEMS FROM EVERYWHERE

CHICAGO.

W. W. Barnard, who was taken violently ill with ptomaine poisoning a week ago, is now at the Presbyterian Hospital, where he is reported as improving slowly.

The failure of Manusos Bros., who have operated a flower store at S. State and Van Buren streets for some years, leaves several of the wholesalers in the lurch. Considerable talk on the inefficiency of the present bankrupt laws is heard in the market.

The Chicago Flower Growers' Association is rapidly getting settled in its new quarters and with the rush of Thanksgiving trade it takes a general to keep all moving smoothly. But Paul Klingsporn never misses an order and this firm's shipping trade is rapidly increasing.

J. A. Budlong is getting settled in the new Le Moyne Bldg. as fast as possible considering this firm is one of the oldest and heaviest shipping houses in Chicago. Phil Schupp will have a fine light office when completed and the packing room is especially convenient. opening as it does on Lake street.

Handsome folders are being distributed among the patrons of Schiller the Florist, announcing the opening of their new loop store known as the Gift Shop. The new store located at 36 S. Wabash avenue, has been rearranged in an attractive and artistic manner and passersby can now look at two particularly neat retail flower stores in one block, for the Gift Shop and Geo. Wienhoeber's are opposite, and competition in novel window displays is keen.

The last of the chrysanthemum plants are being used up for Thanksgiving trade. The season has not been a prolonged one, the plants seemingly all coming into bloom at the same time and finishing up the same way. The price has accordingly averaged the growers less this year than in a

longer season but they will have the benches for other stock. For high class stock cyclamen is the chief offering for the week, salmon shades leading because they hold color better than others. The standard Glory of Wansbek (salmon) is still grown in quantity and is hard to beat, though some of similar color are offered with larger flowers. The novel orchid-flowering types are greatly in demand for the most expensive offerings, though they do not make so large a plant nor produce so many blossoms but their graceful form and delicate coloring make them very popular for high-class stock. The rococo strains are not so well liked in this market. The begonias are the companion plants of the cyclamen and the windows are displaying many of them. Cincinnati having a decided lead over Gloire d'Lorraine. For cheaper plants Primula obconica are used. A few poinsettias are showing brilliant color but the bracts are not so well developed as they will be later.

WASHINGTON, D. C.

Mrs. George W. Hess, wife of the superintendent of the United States Botanical Gardens, has been seriously ill for the past two weeks suffering from an attack of congestion of the lungs.

The British Foreign Office has granted permits for the movement from Rotterdam of 56 pounds of alyssum seed for H. A. Dreer, Inc., Phila., and 300,000 lily of the valley roots for Walter P. Stokes. Moorestown, N. J. A number of other Philadelphia and New York concerns have filed applications to secure permits to remove horticultural goods which were bought and paid for prior to March 1, which are still in Rotterdam. According to Fred H. Kramer and William F. Gude, both large importers of foreign horticultural products, no trouble is being experienced, other than the usual delays incident to slow transpor-

tation and increased freight rates, in obtaining the regular supplies of such goods. Many of them have received a majority of their consignments from both Belgium and Holland in fine condition. Both of the florists named have been getting in stock right along. Although the present season's business is being taken care of as above stated some little concern is present as to what will happen next year. Salesmen representing foreign growers now in the United States intimate that there will be a great shortage of production if the war continues as the armies are making the labor question a very serious one. One concern offered an order for 150,000 paper white narcissi agreed to furnish about one-third of that amount stating that it was impossible to get enough workmen to take care of all of the business that would be offered.

Cattleya bulbs which have already flowered and produced leaves are admissible as imports free of duty as bulbs for propagating purposes, according to a decision of the United States Court of Customs Appeals. An importation consigned to Maltus & Ware, reported by the appraiser of customs at New York to be orchid plants, was assessed at 25 per cent. ad valorem as orchids. The importers protested that the goods were not orchids, but that they were mature mother bulbs, imported exclusively for propagating purposes. This protest was overruled by the Board of United States General Appraisers and the case carried to the Court of Customs Appeals. It was shown by the evidence that while strictly speaking the merchandise in question was not what is botanically known as "bulbs" yet the method of propagating was such as to bring it commercially within that meaning. The court did not decide whether cattleya bulbs which have not yet flowered are entitled to free entry under the proviso to paragraph 210.

PITTSBURGH.

William M. Turner, florist of Wilkinsburg, is having a two weeks' hunting trip in Cameron County.

Richard Harris, superintendent of Mrs. Martha J. Armstrong's estate, has been serving on a ten days' jury service.

George L. Huscroft, the Steubenville, Ohio, retailer, has the sympathy of his many friends hereabouts in the death of his father.

F. M. Smith, formerly an attache of Hennone's, Beaver Falls, Pa., is an addition to the sales force of the G. P. Weaklin Co., East End.

Miss Laura Beckert, formerly in the sales department of the A. W. Smith Company entered the employ of Randolph & McClements last Monday.

J. Gerry Curtis, who has charge of and has been living on the George Westinghouse estate, "Solitude," Homewood, is again around after a four weeks' attack of pneumonia in the West Penn Hospital.

During the absence of the Alexander R. Peacocks in New York this year, Henry B. Keller, head gardener at their estate, is selling cut blooms, and pot plants, both wholesale and retail.

Mr. and Mrs. Julius W. Ludwig celebraied their joint birthday anniversary last Sunday with a family reunion at their home on Merritt street, North Side. Mrs. Ludwig was 57, and Mr. Ludwig 61 years of age.

The Chamber of Commerce of the North Side has just appointed E. C. Ludwig the chairman of a committee to further the advancement of the first municipal Christmas tree to be placed in City Hall Park.

Thomas E. Tyler has been supervising the planting of twenty thousand bulbs on the grounds of Charles D. Armstrong, although, as usual, devoting his direct personal attention to the large range of orchid houses.

The Gardeners' Club of Allegheny County was entertained on Nov. 19th at the Pittsburgh Golf Club by Mr. and Mrs. Finley Hall Lloyd. The annual meeting was held on Friday, Nov. 19, at the home of Mr. and Mrs. W. L. Mellon.

H. C. Frick, who closed the conservatory on his Homeward estate, last spring, has decided to reopen it. David Fraser, who has been in charge for the past nineteen years, will continue the supervision of the flowers and bedding stock for the Frick Park, of Homestead.

J. F. Zimmerman, who has an independent landscape and floral business on the old Carr estate. Point Breeze, has erected a 12 by 4 addition to his greenhouse. Mr. Zimmerman continues in charge of these grounds, where he was the head gardener years before the death of the owner.

Frank Wagner is anticipating the addition of a flower shop to his plant in Aspinwall. Mr. Wagner recently purchased the Aspinwall holdings of the John Bader Company of which he has for sometime been the manager. There are eight complete houses, where the sales and decorative work are now carried on.

Christmas stock is coming on freely from Belgium, although in most cases most disappointing in condition. One firm a few days ago lost 75 per cent. of a large consignment of azaleas, supposedly attributable to excessive heat on board ship. Others have lost in smaller quantities, although it seems all are covered by insurance in Lloyd's agency.

PHILADELPHIA.

George Anderson is able to be wheeled around his greenhouses now and can talk a little better. Improving slowly.

Who might brother Kift be feinting at when he breaks into HORTICULTURE's boxing ring when he has a boxing ring of his own. And didn't he say all that at the meeting? A thing is never settled until it's settled right, especially if it's settled by a minority by underhand work. In a democracy the few should not get benefits at the expense of the many. Such a thing is inartistic, unethical and immoral. In its final analysis its effect is to burst the eighth commandment. What did we fight and bleed and die for in 1776? "Give us liberty or give us death."

SAN FRANCISCO NOTES.

The United Flower & Supply Company, which markets the chrysanthemums grown by the Japanese in this vicinity, reports heavy damage from the frosts of last week which practically winds up the season for them.

Elaborate preparations have been made by the Menlo Park Horticultural Society for its annual banquet this Friday evening, at which John Daly will act as toastmaster. A feature of the meeting will be the awarding of prizes to members who have made the best exhibits during the year.

WHOLESALE FLOWER MARKETS — TRADE PRICES—Per 100 TO DEALERS ONLY

	CINCINNATI Nov. 22		CHICAGO Nov. 15		BUFFALO Nov. 22		PITTSBURG Oct. 18	
Roses								
Am. Beauty, Special	35.00	to 40.00	25.00	to 35.00	30.00	to 40.00	30.00	to 35.00
" " Fancy and Extra	20.00	to 30.00	20.00	to 25.00	20.00	to 25.00	20.00	to 25.00
" " No. 1	10.00	to 15.00	10.00	to 20.00	10.00	to 15.00	10.00	to 18.50
Russell, Hadley	4.00	to 10.00	5.00	to 25.00	8.00	to 12.00	6.00	to 12.00
Killarney, Richm'd, Hill'don, Ward	6.00	to 8.00	8.00	to 10.00	5.00	to 6.00	6.00	to 12.00
" " " " " Ord.	3.00	to 5.00	5.00	to 6.00	3.00	to 4.00	......	to 4.00
Arenburg, Radiance, Taft, Key, Ex.	6.00	to 8.00	8.00	to 10.00	......	to 10.00	6.00	to 12.00
" " " " " Ord.	3.00	to 5.00	5.00	to 5.00	6.00	to 8.00	......	to 4.00
Ophelia, Mock, Sunburst, Extra	6.00	to 8.00	8.00	to 10.00	6.00	to 8.00	6.00	to 12.00
" " " " Ordinary	3.00	to 5.00	3.00	to 5.00	3.00	to 6.00	......	to 4.00
Carnations, Fancy	......	to 4.00	4.00	to 3.00	2.00	to 3.00	......	to 3.00
" Ordinary	......	to 6.00	1.00	to 2.00	1.50	to 2.00	......	to 2.00
Cattleyas	40.00	to 50.00	35.00	to 50.00	50.00	to 60.00	35.00	to 50.00
Dendrobium formosum	......	to	35.00	to 50.00	......	to	25.00	to 50.00
Lilies, Longiflorum	10.00	to 12.50	8.00	to 10.00	8.00	to 12.00	6.00	to 8.00
" Rubrum	4.00	to 8.00	4.00	to 5.00	4.00	to 5.00	......	to ......
Lily of the Valley	......	to 4.00	3.00	to 4.00	3.00	to 4.00	3.00	to 4.00
Daisies	......	to	......	to	.50	to 1.00	.75	to 1.50
Violets	.75	to 1.00	.50	to .75	.60	to .75	.50	to 1.00
Snapdragon	......	to	4.00	to 5.00	4.00	to 6.00	4.00	to 8.00
Chrysanthemums	8.00	to 30.00	10.00	to 25.00	6.00	to 20.00	8.00	to 30.00
Sweet Peas	.75	to 1.00	.50	to 1.50	.75	to 1.00	......	to 2.50
Gardenias	......	to	25.00	to 25.00	20.00	to 25.00	......	to ......
Adiantum	......	to 1.00	1.00	to 1.25	1.00	to 1.25	1.00	to 1.25
Smilax	12.50	to 15.00	12.00	to 15.00	12.00	to 15.00	12.50	to 15.00
Asparagus Plumosus, Strings (100)	25.00	to 50.00	40.00	to 50.00	40.00	to 60.00	......	to 50.00
" & Spren. (100 bchs.)	......	to 25.00	25.00	to 30.00	25.00	to 50.00	35.00	to 50.00

Flower Market Reports

BOSTON We are writing this report on the day before Thanksgiving a n d can only judge by appearances as to the final outcome of the trade for the holiday. But one certainty is that the chrysanthemums — general run — are badly "up against it" and are sure to be sacrificed in quantities. This does not include the pompons, however, as the finer varieties in this class are selling splendidly. If it were not for the depressing accumulation of unsold chrysanthemums that encumber the wholesale markets we think there would be a fine clean-up. Carnations are holding over badly but only because of the chrysanthemums, and even of these the bright red ones are enjoying a satisfactory call. Roses as a general proposition are moving all right. Violets show some accumulation but at the moderate figure asked they should clean up pretty well. All other market staples are in normal condition of supply and demand, except cattleyas which are very few but are not in sufficient demand to warrant any phenomenal values. All of a sudden, stevia is received in quantity. Lilies are quite abundant.

BUFFALO The change for colder weather has helped conditions somewhat although the market has seen plenty of stock the past week. Roses are shortened up and sales are better. Carnations have been very plentiful and prices low. Chrysanthemums are in good supply especially pompons and these have had fair sales. Violets have had no special demand and lily of the valley had no life. Lilies are of only ordinary quality. Beauties have a better demand than week previous.

CHICAGO Following t h e flower show, local sales were reported by most wholesalers as very good and the week of Thanksgiving opens with orders for that holiday coming in. Local florists are placing orders more freely than usual, not caring to take a chance on getting stock at the last hour, but the shipping trade seems likely to be of the telegraph or last minute kind, for, up to Monday evening, books generally showed few orders. Stock is of fine quality and the display of the late chrysanthemums seen in all the large stores shows that flower still in large supply. The Eatons are especially good. Pompons are all cut and this week will close them out. American Beauties are in fair supply the stock of long ones running much less than in the medium lengths. Roses are not exceeding the demand for them and good sized cuts come in each day. Sweet peas are good. the Spencers comprising nearly all of the stock. Lilies, violets, lily of the valley and gardenias are all in good supply and of fine quality. The ilex berries are seen in many of the stores.

NEW YORK Nothing new to be reported in this market —which means that the oversupply of flowers and undersupply of business which has characterized the situation for the past several weeks continues unchanged. A good Thanksgiving Day trade is looked for, but what it will bring forth in the way of better encouragement is not yet apparent at this writing; that it can clean up the product in sight is too much to hope for. Chrysanthemums are everywhere, with no staid prices on any variety or class. Roses are moving somewhat better. Carnations are plentiful. There are practically no cattleyas and gardenias are very few. Lily of the valley is nicely balanced and American Beauty roses are doing very well. Lilies are very slow and violets are floundering at the very bottom of the list. The football games have had no appreciable influence on either chrysanthemums or violets.

PHILADELPHIA Since our last on November 17th to the present minute November 22nd, there is a continuing stimulus in the business situation and no one can complain either from the producing or consuming standpoint. The commission men are working their end most assiduously and are withheld from advancing prices only by the fear that they may go too far. On the other hand they are worried for fear that they may not be asking enough. For instance, they think they have done well to get a dollar for cattleyas but inside of an hour comes a telephone from—from—well never mind—that they are getting a dollar and a quarter. So it's "fierce" if you are too high and it's equally fierce if you are too low. You are between the trenches and the iron works unless you can strike the happy medium. However, everything is going well and while prices on the whole are moderate we feel sure of a good Thanksgiving week. HORTICULTURE ought to be a daily instead of a weekly. Who can tell what a week will bring forth?

PITTSBURGH Flowers of practically all kinds are now in abundance, as the rapidly increasing number of street-boy venders bears evidence. There are lots of carnations and roses of all kinds, American Beauties have not been moving along as rapidly as could be desired. Other varieties, however, have been going splendidly at moderate prices. Just what effect the present splendid crispy cold snap will have, remains to be seen, although both wholesalers and retailers are optimistic. Society work is "picking up," as it were, and funeral work. from the civic point of view, is all too plentiful. Outside of a holiday, last Saturday saw the best business in a long time,

(Continued on page 712)

OPHELIA

As the weather gets cooler, what wonderfully beautiful coloring Ophelia takes on—a favorite with everyone. In quantity with us and of the choicest quality.

Special	$12.00 per 100
Fancy	10.00 " "
Extra	8.00 " "
First	5.00 " "
Second	3.00 " "

A few extra long specials at $15.00 per 100.

VALLEY

Special	$4.00 per 100
Extra	2.00 " "

S. S. PENNOCK-MEEHAN CO.

The Wholesale Florists of Philadelphia

PHILADELPHIA	NEW YORK	BALTIMORE	WASHINGTON
1608-1620 Ludlow St.	117 W. 28th St.	Franklin and St. Paul Sts.	1216 H St., N. W.

WHOLESALE FLOWER MARKETS — TRADE PRICES—Per 100 TO DEALERS ONLY

	BOSTON Nov. 24			ST. LOUIS Nov. 22			PHILA. Nov. 20		
Roses									
Am. Beauty, Special	30.00	to	50.00	40.00	to	50.00	30.00	to	35.00
" " Fancy and Extra	15.00	to	20.00	25.00	to	30.00	20.00	to	25.00
" " No. 1	5.00	to	10.00	10.00	to	15.00	10.00	to	15.00
Russell, Hadley	4.00	to	15.00	8.00	to	10.00	5.00	to	25.00
Killarney, Richmond, Hillingdon, Ward, Extra	4.00	to	6.00	8.00	to	10.00	6.00	to	10.00
" " " Ordinary	1.00	to	3.00	4.00	to	6.00	3.00	to	5.00
Atenburg; Radiance, Taft, Key, Extra	4.00	to	6.00	......	to	......	6.00	to	10.00
" " " Ordinary	2.00	to	3.00	......	to	......	3.00	to	5.00
Ophelia, Mock, Sunburst, Extra	4.00	to	8.00	8.00	to	10.00	6.00	to	12.00
" " " Ordinary	1.00	to	3.00	4.00	to	6.00	3.00	to	5.00
Carnations, Fancy	1.50	to	7.50	4.00	to	5.00	3.00	to	4.00
" Ordinary	1.00	to	1.50	2.00	to	3.00	2.00	to	3.00
Cattleyas	50.00	to	60.00	......	to	50.00	......	to	75.00
Dendrobium formosum	......	to	25.00	......	to	......	......	to	50.00
Lilies, Longiflorum	4.00	to	6.00	12.00	to	15.00	8.00	to	10.00
" Rubrum	......	to	3.00	6.00	to	8.00	4.00	to	6.00
Lily of the Valley	3.00	to	4.00	3.00	to	4.00	2.00	to	4.00
Daisies	.50	to	1.00	.25	to	.50	.50	to	1.00
Violets	.40	to	.60	.75	to	.30	.50	to	1.00
Snapdragon	3.00	to	8.00	3.00	to	4.00	3.00	to	6.00
Chrysanthemums	1.00	to	10.00	5.00	to	25.00	6.00	to	25.00
Sweet Peas	1.00	to	1.00	.50	to	1.00	.50	to	1.50
Gardenias	10.00	to	25.00	......	to	......	30.00	to	35.00
Adiantum	......	to	1.00	1.00	to	1.25	......	to	1.00
Smilax	12.00	to	16.00	10.00	to	15.00	15.00	to	20.00
Asparagus Plumosus, Strings (100)	25.00	to	50.00	35.00	to	50.00	......	to	50.00
" & Spren. (100 Bchs.)	25.00	to	35.00	20.00	to	35.00	......	to	50.00

Flower Market Reports

(Continued from page 700)

everything seemingly undergoing a general stimulation.

SAN FRANCISCO Trade has been about all that could be expected during the past week. Cut flowers moved fairly well considering the approach of the Thanksgiving festivities, which like other similar occasions usually has a depressing effect upon the sale of flowers just before and after the holiday. Regarding the stock offered on the market, the principal feature is the great reduction in the supply of chrysanthemums as the result of two sharp frosts last week. In some of the growing sections the entire late crop, even to the buds, was caught, but other growers were more fortunate and will be able to bring in a good many more blooms. There are plenty magnificent greenhouse varieties for show purposes and select trade, but the reduced supply of outdoor stock has stiffened up values somewhat. From all reports this has been a very satisfactory season for chrysanthemums. The average quality has been excellent, the supply large, the demand good and prices fairly firm. Chinese pompons are still appearing in considerable quantity and maintain their popularity well. A fine cut of roses is now appearing, the quality showing improvement from day to day. All varieties are in ample supply with the exception of Cecile Brunner, more of which could be used nicely. Carnations are well up to standard now. The supply of violets finds an easy outlet. The local demand takes large quantities and an active shipping movement cleans up the surplus closely. The demand for lily of the valley has kept the supply down and there has been no surplus. The market is well supplied with orchids and gardenias are a little more plentiful.

ST. LOUIS The market opened brisk the last week and stock of all kinds moved lively for a while. Chrysanthemums are at their height and the market has been glutted with them all week. Prices have not been high on medium quality but fancy stock has brought good figures. Roses, too, have been so plentiful that they went begging at almost any price, quality, though, of the best. Carnations are too many also and often big lots went to waste. Thanksgiving week is looked upon as a busy one and flowers other than chrysanthemums will have a look

in this week; so look for a better report next time.

WASHINGTON Business last week showed a general improvement in all lines. Severe frosts have finally killed off the outdoor stock but the market is still flooded with small chrysanthemums of very good quality which tend to keep down the prices of roses and carnations to or below normal for this time of the year. Good roses are still selling at below $5 per hundred. Carnations are bringing from $1 to $3. Chrysanthemums are to be had at almost any price the buyer wishes to pay for them. Cattleyas are very scarce and the price has gone to $7.50 per dozen. Gardenias are to be had but in too small quantities to warrant a quotation.

New York—Wm. Hanft is ill at the Presbyterian Hospital in this city.

A. Herrington has been appointed manager of the exhibition arrangement at the Grand Central Palace for next spring's flower show.

Buyer's Directory and Ready Reference Guide

Advertisements under this head, one cent a word.   Initials count as words.

Display advertisers in this issue are also listed under this classification without charge. Reference to List of Advertisers will indicate the respective pages.

Buyers failing to find what they want in this list will confer a favor by writing us and we will try to put them in communication with reliable dealers.

For List of Advertisers See Page 691

In writing to Advertisers kindly mention Horticulture

NURSERY STOCK—Continued
Framingham Nurseries, Framingham, Mass.
For page see List of Advertisers.

August Rolker & Sons, New York City.
For page see List of Advertisers.

NUT GROWING.
The Nut-Grower, Waycross, Ga.
For page see List of Advertisers.

ORCHID FLOWERS
Jas. McManus, New York, N. Y.
For page see List of Advertisers.

ORCHID PLANTS
Julius Roehrs Co., Rutherford, N. J.
For page see List of Advertisers.

Lager & Hurrell, Summit, N. J.

PALMS, ETC.
Robert Craig Co., Philadelphia, Pa.
For page see List of Advertisers.

August Rolker & Sons, New York City.
For page see List of Advertisers.

A. Leuthy & Co., Roslindale, Boston, Mass.
For page see List of Advertisers.

PANSY PLANTS
William Sim, Cliftondale, Mass.
Sim's Gold Medal Pansies.

Pansy Plants, mixed varieties in bud
and bloom, $15.00 per 1000. Cash. JAMES
MOSS, Johnsville, Pa.

Pansy Plants for the benches, nice stocky
plants, $5.00 per 1000, 5000 or more, $4.00
per 1000. Cash. JAMES MOSS, Johnsville,
Pa.

PANSY SEED
Fottler, Fiske, Rawson Co., Boston, Mass.
For page see List of Advertisers.

PEONIES
Peonies. The world's greatest collection.
1200 sorts. Send for list. C. BETSCHER,
Canal Dover, O.

PECKY CYPRESS BENCHES
A. T. Stearns Lumber Co., Boston, Mass.
For page see List of Advertisers.

PIPE AND FITTINGS
Kroeschell Bros. Co., Chicago.
For page see List of Advertisers.

King Construction Company,
N. Tonawanda, N. Y.
Shelf Brackets and Pipe Hangers.
For page see List of Advertisers.

PLANT AND BULB IMPORTS
Chas. Schwake & Co., New York City.
For page see List of Advertisers.

August Rolker & Sons, New York City.
For page see List of Advertisers.

PLANT TRELLISES AND STAKES
Seele's Tieless Plant Stakes and Trellises. H. D. SEELE & SONS, Elkhart, Ind.

PLANT TUBS
H. A. Dreer, Philadelphia, Pa.
"Riverton Special."
For page see List of Advertisers.

PLANTS WANTED
C. C. Trepel, New York City.
For page see List of Advertisers.

RAFFIA
McHutchison & Co., New York, N. Y.
For page see List of Advertisers.

RHODODENDRONS
P. Ouwerkerk, Hoboken, N. J.
For page see List of Advertisers.

Framingham Nurseries, Framingham, Mass.
For page see List of Advertisers.

RIBBONS AND CHIFFONS
S. S. Pennock-Meehan Co., Philadelphia, Pa.
For page see List of Advertisers.

ROSES
Poehlmann Bros. Co., Morton Grove, Ill.
For page see List of Advertisers.

P. Ouwerkerk, Hoboken, N. J.
For page see List of Advertisers.

Robert Craig Co., Philadelphia, Pa.
For page see List of Advertisers.

W. & T. Smith Co., Geneva, N. Y.
American Grown Roses.
For page see List of Advertisers.

Bay State Nurseries, North Abington, Mass.
For page see List of Advertisers.

August Rolker & Sons, New York City.
For page see List of Advertisers.

Framingham Nurseries, Framingham, Mass
For page see List of Advertisers.

A. N. Pierson, Inc., Cromwell, Conn.
For page see List of Advertisers.

THE CONARD & JONES COMPANY.
Rose Specialists.
West Grove, Pa. Send for offers.

E. G. Hill Co., Richmond, Ind.
E. G. Hill's Quality Stock.

SCALECIDE
B. G. Pratt Co., New York City.
For page see List of Advertisers.

SEASONABLE PLANT STOCK
R. Vincent, Jr. & Sons Co., White Marsh
Md.
For page see List of Advertisers.

SEED GROWERS
California Seed Growers' Association.
San Jose, Cal.
For page see List of Advertisers.

SEEDS
Carter's Tested Seeds,
Seeds with a Pedigree.
Boston, Mass., and London, England
For page see List of Advertisers.

Kelway & Son,
Langport, Somerset, England.
Kelway's Celebrated English Strain Garden
Seeds.
For page see List of Advertisers.

S. D. Woodruff & Sons, New York City.
Garden Seed.
For page see List of Advertisers.

Joseph Breck & Sons, Boston, Mass
For page see List of Advertisers.

J. Bolgiano & Son, Baltimore, Md.
For page see List of Advertisers.

A. T. Boddington Co., Inc., New York City
For page see List of Advertisers.

Chas. Schwake & Co., New York City
For page see List of Advertisers.

Michell's Seed House, Philadelphia, Pa.
For page see List of Advertisers.

W. Atlee Burpee & Co., Philadelphia, Pa
For page see List of Advertisers.

R. & J. Farquhar & Co., Boston, Mass.
For page see List of Advertisers.

J. M. Thorburn & Co., New York City
For page see List of Advertisers.

Loechner & Co., New York City.
For page see List of Advertisers.

Ant. C. Zvolanek, Lompoc, Cal.
Winter Flowering Sweet Pea Seed
For page see List of Advertisers.

S. S. Skidelsky & Co., Philadelphia, Pa
For page see List of Advertisers.

W. E. Marshall & Co., New York City.
Seeds, Plants and Bulbs.
For page see List of Advertisers.

August Rolker & Sons, New York City.
For page see List of Advertisers.

SEEDS—Continued
Burnett Bros., 98 Chambers St., New York.
For page see List of Advertisers.

Fottler, Fiske, Rawson Co., Boston, Mass.
Seeds for the Florist.
For page see List of Advertisers.

SKINNER IRRIGATION SYSTEM
Skinner Irrigation Co., Brookline, Mass.
For page see List of Advertisers.

SPHAGNUM MOSS
Live Sphagnum moss, orchid peat and
orchid baskets always on hand. LAGER
& HURRELL, Summit, N. J.

SPRAYING MATERIALS
B. G. Pratt Co., New York City.
For page see List of Advertisers.

STANDARD THERMOMETERS
Standard Thermo Co., Boston, Mass.
For page see List of Advertisers.

STOVE PLANTS
Orchids—Largest stock in the country—
stove plants and Crotons, finest collection.
JULIUS ROEHRS CO., Rutherford, N. J.

SWEET PEA SEED
Arthur T. Boddington Co., Inc.,
New York City.
Winter Flowering Sweet Peas.
For page see List of Advertisers.

Ant. C. Zvolanek, Lompoc, Calif
Gold Medal of Honor Winter Orchid Sweet
Peas.
For page see List of Advertisers.

VEGETABLE PLANTS
R. Vincent, Jr. & Sons Co.,
White Marsh, Md.
For page see List of Advertisers.

VENTILATING APPARATUS
The Advance Co., Richmond, Ind.
For page see List of Advertisers.

The John A. Evans Co., Richmond, Ind.
For page see List of Advertisers.

VERMICIDES
Aphine Mfg. Co., Madison, N. J.
For page see List of Advertisers.

WIRED TOOTHPICKS
W. J. Cowee, Berlin, N. Y.
For page see List of Advertisers.

WIREWORK
Reed & Keller, New York City.
For page see List of Advertisers.

WILLIAM E. HEILSCHER'S WIRE
WORKS, 264 Randolph St., Detroit, Mich.

WHOLESALE FLORISTS
Albany, N. Y.

Albany Cut Flower Exchange, Albany, N. Y.
For page see List of Advertisers.

Baltimore

The S. S. Pennock-Meehan Co., Franklin
and St. Paul Sts.
For page see List of Advertisers.

Boston

N. F. McCarthy & Co., 112 Arch St. and
31 Otis St
For page see List of Advertisers.

Welch Bros. Co., 226 Devonshire St.
For page see List of Advertisers.

Patrick Welch, 262 Devonshire St., Boston,
Mass.
For page see List of Advertisers.

Brooklyn

Wm. H. Kuebler, 28 Willoughby St.
For page see List of Advertisers.

Buffalo, N. Y.

William F. Kasting Co., 383-87 Ellicott St.
For page see List of Advertisers.

For List of Advertisers See Page 691

New Offers In This Issue

LILY OF THE VALLEY, COLD
STORAGE.
Arthur T. Boddington Co., Inc.,
New York City.
For page see List of Advertisers.

LILY OF THE VALLEY, COLD
STORAGE.
Fottler, Fiske, Rawson Co., Boston, Mass.
For page see List of Advertisers.

ROSES, CARNATIONS, CHRYSAN-
THEMUMS AND LILY OF THE
VALLEY.
J. A. Budlong, Chicago, Ill.
For page see List of Advertisers.

ROSE OPHELIA.
S. S. Pennock-Meehan Co., Philadelphia, Pa.
For page see List of Advertisers.

VEGETABLE FORCING ROOTS.
Warren Shinn, Woodbury, N. J.
For page see List of Advertisers.

WATER LILIES
Wm. Tricker, Arlington, N. J.
For page see List of Advertisers.

WANTS, FOR SALE, Etc.

SITUATIONS WANTED

NURSERY SITUATION WANTED—As
foreman on ornamental nursery, thorough
knowledge of all ornamentals, their care,
propagation and landscape uses—life experience—references. M. B., care HORTI-
CULTURE.

FOR SALE

FOR SALE—Fresh from factory, new,
10 x 12, 16 x 18, 16 x 24, double thick. A
and B qualities. Market dropped. Now is
the time to buy and save money.
PARSHELSKY BROS., INC., 215-217
Havemeyer St., Brooklyn, N. Y.

GREENHOUSE FOR SALE.
One 17 ft. x 180 ft. greenhouse with
piping, tanks and steam pumps, all in
good condition. Will sell as a whole or in
part. Price $300.00. Apply to W. D. HALL,
105 Pine Street, Walpole, Mass.

MISCELLANEOUS

SECOND-HAND BOOKS WANTED—Any
set of agriculture. Horticulture preferred.
Give description and price. T. LAUPHIT,
912 W. Green St., Urbana, Illinois.

In writing to Advertisers kindly mention Horticulture

A PROSPEROUS CLEVELAND ESTABLISHMENT

During the time of the Cleveland Flower Show, a good many of the visitors took occasion to visit the extensive greenhouses of the Gasser Company at Rocky River. This is the largest range of glass in the Cleveland section, covering approximately ten acres, we were told. Much space is devoted to roses where practically all the present commercial favorites, with the exception of American Béauty, are grown, and grown well. Mrs. Shawyer is here very fine. A pale sport from Melody is so nearly identical with the old Perle des Jardins that it cannot be told apart. Of carnations there are 35,000 grown and all the favorite sorts are grown in a vast range of ridge and furrow construction. Just at present, chrysanthemums hold the centre of interest. The best liked include the three Chadwicks—Supreme, White and Yellow; Chieftain and Bonnaffon, and there are lots of pompons among which Western Beauty, a lovely deep pink, Golden Quinola, White Helen Newberry, Baby and Mrs. Frank Beu (Frank Wilcox) are particularly liked. Adiantum California, Dreer's specialty, is doing magnificently here and with its splendid fronds 2 feet in length bids fair to supplant all the other varieties of A. cuneatum. There is no end of other material grown here for the requirements of the Cleveland flower trade. Callas, poinsettias, Euphorbia jacquinaeflora, cypripediums, lily of the valley, stevia, mignonette, calendulas, sweet peas, antirrhinums, freesia, gardenias—these are only a portion of the promiscuous stock which finds a place in this up-to-date place, which is under the efficient management of F. C. Bartels. An interesting feature is the heating outfit, which is supplied from three gas wells right on the place. These wells have a capacity of 15,000,-000 feet of gas per day. The pressure at the wells is 98 pounds to the square foot and this is reduced by various devices to a pressure of but 16 oz. to the square foot before the gas reaches the boilers. Even with the big cost of installation this is a very economical heating arrangement as compared with the cost of coal, which in Cleveland is far below what growers in most sections of the country have to pay. But it has its disadvantages, the greatest of which is the uncertainty of the duration of the supply, as the wells may run out at any time.

PERSONAL

We had the pleasure of meeting again an old-time celebrity at the Cleveland Flower Show—A. T. Simmons, of Geneva, O. With Hallock, Son & Thorpe, and later under his own name at Geneva, Mr. Simmons "did things" which meant much for the florist of those days and even of the present time. S. A. Nutt geranium, unbeaten in its class today, was raised by him and he has to his credit such carnations as Portia, Tidal Wave, Silver Spray and Ferdinand Mangold—surely a record to be proud of. The years have dealt very kindly with Mr. Simmons; he has changed but little with the passing of time.

AT IT AGAIN.

The New York Sun prints a communication from H. G. Walters, who signs himself President Plant Research Institute, Langhorne, Pa., who states it to be his "intellectual duty in advancing human knowledge to be ahead of the average," and adds "Hence on a peach tree at this writing I have grafts of cedar, lilac, blackberry and five varieties of roses all on one peach tree. I also have two varieties of rambler roses grafted to a privet hedge."

We had just begun to wonder how long our old friend "the Wizard" would allow this new wonder-worker to usurp the stage when, lo, in the columns of the daily newspaper the following appears:

Santa Rosa, Cal.—The manufacture of linseed oil may be revolutionized by a new production of Luther Burbank, the plant wizard. He has grown a new white flax with seeds twice the ordinary size and more productive.

Now, will you be good.

OBITUARY.

John Sharkey.

John Sharkey, a teamster employed by George F. Johnson, florist, Elmwood avenue, Providence, R. I., was killed almost instantly Thursday afternoon, Nov. 18, when a horse attached to the wagon he was driving became unmanageable. His companion, John J. Brophy, was removed to the Rhode Island Hospital. Both were employees of Johnson.

Robert Aull.

Robert Aull, former Park Commissioner of St. Louis and well-known throughout the country in park work circles, died on Saturday, November 20th, at St. Luke's Hospital, St. Louis. Mr. Aull was 62 years of age and leaves a wife, son and daughter. Col. Bob as he was familiarly known was a great lover of flowers.

Carl Waldecker.

A visit to Germany some time ago proved fatal to Carl Waldecker, of Braintree, Mass., according to a message received by his brother, Herman, announcing his death from wounds received while doing foraging work on the Russian frontier. The Waldecker brothers were engaged in plant growing and bulb forcing. Last June Carl went to Holland on business, and, while across, visited his mother in Germany. While there, as a German subject, he was pressed into service for the war, and wounded September 27, according to the message.

Augustus E. Scott.

Augustus Elwin Scott, lawyer and instructor, eminent for his botanical researches, died in Lexington, Mass., on November 19, aged 77 years. Mr. Scott organized the Lexington Field and Garden Club, for village improvement, the first organization of its kind in Massachusetts. He was also an authority on the flora of eastern Massachusetts and the higher altitudes, having made the growths on the Appalachian and White Mountains the subject of special study. He contributed many essays to "Appalachia" on horticultural subjects.

He was a member of the Lexington Board of Park Commissioners, and worked for parks and playgrounds for the younger people. Last spring he gave to the town a plot of more than 30 acres as 'ne site for a park.

PUBLICATIO RECEIVED.

Landscape Gardening as Applied to Home Decoration. By Samuel T. Maynard, formerly Professor of Botany and Horticulture at the Massachusetts Agricultural College. This is the second edition of this charming and useful book, originally dedicated "to the thousands of home-makers who are trying to beautify their homes" and which now comes to us after the lapse of fifteen years in a new dress, greatly enlarged and improved in keeping with the advancement which has been made in the numbers and character of the garden material available and the knowledge of their culture.

For the vast majority of garden lovers, unable to employ professional landscape gardening assistance, this book is especially a treasury of information and encouragement in which all the operations contributing to a well-planned, intelligently planted and properly cared-for garden, large or small, are explained in a thoroughly practical manner, in addition to much valuable advice as to location of buildings, architecture, walks and drives, country roads and roadside improvement, schoolyards and parks, etc. The book contains 396 pages and many fine plates. It is published by John Wiley & Sons, Inc., New York and London. Price $1.50 net. Copies can be supplied from the office of HORTICULTURE.

The issue of The Garden, London, for October 23, is devoted especially to the Rose. There are some very interesting articles and beautiful illustrations, including one of the popular Hadley. In the notes accompanying the latter the writer has curiously failed to state that Hadley is an American production and the drift of the lines is such that the uninformed reader would be apt to infer that it was a foreign variety which had been popularized as a forcing rose in America. This we are sure was not intended. A beautiful colored plate of the new crimson single rose Princess Mary is given with this issue of The Garden.

We have received a circular from the Russian-American Chamber of Commerce in Moscow, giving a brief idea of the purposes of the organization which is primarily to promote trade and establish close business relations between Russia and America. The special problem at the present time is to re-establish the exchange of commodities which has been hindered by the European war.

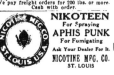

GREENHOUSES BUILDING OR CONTEMPLATED.

Barnard, N. Y.—Chas. Lee, propagating house.

Baltimore, Md.—E. W. Heinbuck, house 25x100.

Point Breeze, Pa.—J. F. Zimmerman, house 12x41.

Louisville, Ky.—James Guthrie, Slate Run road, alterations.

Sayville, N. Y.—Jacob Becvar, Lakeland avenue, one house.

Arlington Heights, Ill.—Paul Schramm, house 28x152.

Bay City, Mich.—Boehringer Bros., two houses, next spring.

New Albany, Ky.—J. D. Bettman, three houses each 28x150.

Lancaster, Pa.—Benjamin Avenue Nursery Co., house 30x100.

Fayetteville, N. Y.—F. W. Siefker, High Bridge road, one house.

Altoona, Pa.—W. H. Brouse, Orchard Crossing, additions and alterations.

NEWS NOTES

East Milford, N. H.—Woodman Bros. are placing a Kroeschell boiler in their new house.

Shindle, Me.—F. W. Knepp's greenhouse was partially destroyed by fire November 16; loss $500; no insurance.

Augusta, Me.—Hon. Geo. E. Macomber is having a new rose and perennial garden constructed on his estate 75x150 feet.

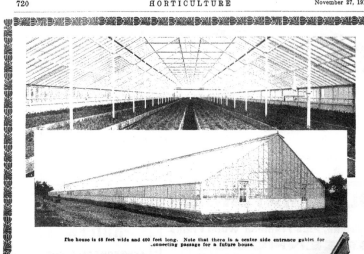

Vol. XXII
No. 23
DEC. 4
1915

HORTICULTURE

Dendrobium Falconeri

LIST OF ADVERTISERS

FOR BUYERS' DIRECTORY AND READY REFERENCE GUIDE
SEE PAGES 744, 745, 746, 747

NOTES ON CULTURE OF FLORISTS' STOCK

CONDUCTED BY

John J. M. Farrell

Questions by our readers in line with any of the topics presente on this page will be cordially received and promptly answered by Mr. Farrell. Such communications should invariably be addressed to the office of HORTICULTURE.
"If vain our toil, we ought to blame the culture, not the soil."—*Pope.*

Christmas Greens

A few words on this will not go amiss now. Practically everyone in the retail business handles Christmas greens, and with most of us it pays as well as anything we do around the holidays. We will want all such kinds as holly, fresh cut boxwood, laurel wreathing, lycopodium, moss, mistletoe, etc. A deep coldframe can't be beaten for storing greens. Spread some heavy paper or burlap over the bottom to keep the greens clean; the made-up wreaths can be piled up here, also the loose holly and most of the other stock if the weather isn't too severe. Sprinkle lightly, place heavy paper over the top of all followed by the sashes and such protection on the outside as will be necessary to keep out frost.

Azaleas for Christmas

Azaleas left over from last Christmas will come in good now. There is very little difficulty in having such varities as Deutsche Perle, Hexe, Mme. Petrick or Verveaneana in flower for the holidays. It should be borne in mind that for the last ten days before Christman it would be a great advantage to the keeping qualities of the flower if they were kept down to a temperature from 50 to 55 degrees at night with a rise of ten degree during the day and a good amount of fresh air circulating. If these plants do not show color by this date they should be kept in a temperature of 70 degrees at night and sprayed with lukewarm water two or three times a day. Also give them the sunniest bench you have. Azaleas that are now showing the first flowers open can be kept about 60 to 55.

Getting Ready for Christmas

The weather isn't going to get any warmer. There are very few of us who will always do things ahead of time. We should have our holiday plant display on hand and properly staged at least several days before Christmas. Study the advertising pages of HORTICULTURE carefully, mark up your needs and place your order in time. Too often is the ordering of plants for the holiday trade put off too late to either get satisfactory stock or receive it in time. Get ready; advertise; make people come to see your display; and have it ready at least 10 days before the 25th.

Lorraine Begonias

Most sensitive to sudden changes of temperature are begonias of all kinds, those of the Gloire de Lorraine type in particular. They should be as near 60 degrees as possible. Where large specimen plants are grown— say in 6 to 8-inch pots—they should have plenty of room. Raise them up close to the glass on inverted pots and far enough apart to have every one fully exposed to light. Give them air on all possible occasions, but cold currents should not blow over the plants. Avoid dryness at the roots or any excess in the way of watering. Lorraine begonias are very sensitive to any sudden changes of temperature. Never let them dry out, for if this happens—as it frequently does—their beauty will be of brief duration. Any pans or baskets that are to be filled can be done now before the burly-burly of the Christmas trade is with us. The atmosphere should now be kept rather dry for Lorraine begonias.

Soil for Small Seeds

All soil for small seeds is better for being sterilized as it kills fungus spores or mycelium, insects, weeds, etc. With steam heat it can be done by letting the steam into perforated pipes covered with the soil to the depth of 5 to 6 inches. The temperature for the best results should not be lower than 180 degrees and 212 degrees would be better. This should be maintained for an hour or more. The soil should be covered with canvas, so as to retain the steam as long as possible. Where you have not steam use boiling water, or baking soil will be the next best.

Next Week:—Propagation and Care of Carnations; Palms; Pelargoniums; Sweet Peas; Double Sweet Alyssum.

Dendrobium Falconeri

(See cover illustration.)

I was in the office of HORTICULTURE one morning recently, when Friend Stewart showed me some photographs taken by M. J. Pope the well-known orchid grower to Mrs. Tuttle, Naugatuck, Conn. Among them was one of Dendrobium Falconeri, a magnificent specimen, exceedingly well flowered, one such as is not often seen. It carried me back in memory some fifty years when I first saw this lovely variety. It was a plant sent to Messrs. Low, then at Clapton, from Sir William Marriott Baronet, Down House, Blandford. This plant was carefully packed in a box standing upright and as soon as the cover was removed there it stood in all its glory and I have never seen a Dendrobium more beautiful, the bright crimson purplish tips making a striking contrast to the base of the flower. Falconeri Gigantea has perhaps finer and more substantial looking flowers, but misses the graceful charm of the original type. I have seen perhaps as many Dendrobiums as most people, but none have made so lasting an impression on my mind as good old Falconeri.

Mr. Pope seems to have got the knack of flowering it well. From what I have seen and from what my old friend Boxall who collected thousands, told me, it seems to want keeping very cold during the resting season, and then to be put into sharp heat, when it will flower well; otherwise it goes into growth.

H a Barnard

HORTICULTURE

VOL. XXII **DECEMBER 4, 1915** **NO. 23**

PUBLISHED WEEKLY BY

HORTICULTURE PUBLISHING CO.

147 Summer Street, Boston, Mass.

Telephone, Oxford 292.
WM. J. STEWART, Editor and Manager.

SUBSCRIPTION RATES:
One Year, in advance, $1.00; To Foreign Countries, $2.00; To Canada, $1.50.

ADVERTISING RATES:

Per inch, 30 inches to page.....................$1.00
Discounts on Contracts for consecutive insertions, as follows:
One month (4 times), 5 per cent.; three months (13 times), 10 per cent.; six months (26 times), 20 per cent.; one year (52 times), 30 per cent.
Page and half page space, special rates on application.

Entered as second-class matter December 8, 1914, at the Post Office at Boston, Mass., under the Act of Congress of March 3, 1879.

CONTENTS

Welcome guests

When the time arrives for our next issue to go to press the National Association of Gardeners will be in session in Boston. The gardeners have always held a preferred position in the esteem of the trade and the public of Bos-ton and we take this opportunity to tell them that they will find nothing lacking in the fervency of this regard when they gather here. The greater their numbers the better the Boston fraternity, commercial or otherwise, will be pleased. It is not the time of the year when gardening art, outside of glass houses, has much to present, but hearts do not change with the seasons and whatever the weather may be, we are safe in promising that it will in no wise affect the warmth of Boston's welcome.

Opportunity knocks again

We are now at the threshold of the busiest season of the year for a large proportion of those who read and support HORTICULTURE. It has been a long, and often discouraging period for many since opportunity stopped knocking at the door and the outlook became misty and ominous. But now we are glad to note that a spirit of optimism seems to have been awakened and a willingness to look upon the bright side only, and we all know that this factor of confidence more than half wins the battle. So we start upon the winter campaign with hopeful anticipations and this fact is, in itself, its own best justification. For the man who will now come out into the open and, by liberal yet judicious advertising, let the world know who he is and what he has to offer, there never has been a more promising chance for rapid progress in business than the present situation brings. As a starter let everyone take hold in serious earnest to make the coming Christmas a record breaker in amount and quality of business and a fitting "curtain raiser" for the unprecedented season of prosperity which we sincerely hope is to follow.

In Memoriam

W. Atlee Burpee has gone and a chill has fallen upon the heart of horticulture—not alone in America but far abroad wherever horticulture is known and loved. The news of the passing away of this truly great man will bring deep sorrow and a profound sense of irreparable loss to hundreds—yes, thousands—who, like the writer, will feel grievously the taking away, in the prime of life, of a friend dearly loved and whom the world could so illy spare. With all his magnificent genius, his phenomenal success as a business man, his widely diversified interests, his fine mentality and everything that made him a captain of captains in industrial life, yet that which we shall remember longest and dwell upon with most affectionate memory will be his considerate, generous spirit, his kindly impulses and philanthropy which knew no limits of time, place or condition. His greatest happiness seemed to come from doing something to make others happy. Wherever Burpee went there was sunshine. In contemplating a personality so rare, a life so full of nobility, the lines of Robert Louis Stevenson seem aptly impressive.

"He is not dead—this friend—not dead.
But in the paths we mortals tread,
Got some few trifling steps ahead,
And nearer to the end,
So that you, too, once past the bend
Shall meet again as face to face this friend
You fancy dead.

* * * * "The while
You travel forward mile and mile
He loiters with a backward smile
Till you can overtake,
And strains his eyes to search this wake,
Or, whistling as he sees you thro' the brake,
Waits on a stile."

ROSE GROWING UNDER GLASS

CONDUCTED BY

Arthur C. Ruzicka

Questions by our readers in line with any of the topics presented on this page will be cordially received and promptly answered by Mr. Ruzicka. Such communications should invariably be addressed to the office of HORTICULTURE.

Disbudding.

With the season well advanced now and the roses growing well, it will be necessary to go over the benches at least once a week and take away all the side shoots that may start on the longer grades of roses. We find that Ophelia especially needs attention in this respect and if this work is not attended to when it should be a good deal of energy and strength will go into these side shoots that should be going into the bud proper. While doing this work it is a good idea to keep an eye open for signs of spot or spider and pick the leaves that are affected with the former and burn them. Plants where spider is found should be marked, and then when syringing give these an extra good dose. While disbudding it is also well to look for all the poor buds, if there are any, and take these out, giving the side shoots a chance to come on. As a rule these will come good.

Weeds Under the Benches

It is not always that weeds will start under the benches, but should some seed have dropped under from the hay that was put into the benches before they were filled last summer and started a crop of weeds sticking out into the walks, get after these at once and remove them. They are nearly always a breeding place for red spider, and although we are not sure that these will crawl from the weeds onto the roses we would rather not trust them. It does not take very long to remove these weeds and the houses are much better off for it. The same may be said of weeds in the benches. These should be pulled out as soon as they appear for they too are only a breeding place for insects.

Whitewashing the Bench Sides

If there is a house or two on the place which is shaded or which is rather old and dark it can be made much lighter and more cheerful by wetting down the sides of the benches and applying a good coat of hot whitewash. This will have a surprising effect on the light and the roses will surely be benefited thereby. Of course this alone will not grow the roses but it will be a great help during the dark months of the winter. If applied real hot to a wet surface the work can be done quickly and it will not rub off so easily.

The Supply of Pots.

With the propagating season close at hand it would be well to go over the pot supply and make sure that there is enough of all the different sizes on hand. It will be best not to use two-inch pots for the first potting unless there is a lot of them on hand and it looks bad to see them idle. We find them a little too small, for no sooner are the young roses rooted than they have to be repotted and this means a good deal of work. With the cost of labor ever increasing, saving on the work will cut quite a figure in a year's run of business. It will take a while for the pots to arrive when they come by freight and the sooner they are ordered the better.

The Novelties.

There will be several new roses to come out in the coming spring and any grower interested will do well to look them up now and see just what they are doing. In order to tell, it is best to see them growing, as notes can then be made under what conditions they do best. If these are the same as can be given on your own place then the variety will no doubt be a success. With the market prices for novelties double those paid for the older varieties the new roses are well worth looking up.

SOME NEPHROLEPIS HISTORY.

Mr. R. C. Benedict,
    Brooklyn Botanic Garden.

Dear Sir:—What I write you, I can scarcely call information, yet it may help you. When the old Horticultural Building in Boston, Mass., was erected at corner of Tremont and Bromfield streets, the main floor contained two stores, one occupied by Mr. Washburn as a fruit and confectionary store, with a nice restaurant in rear, the other by Mr. Washburn as a seed store.

In course of time Mr. Lucius Foster had, first, a window privilege and later had a large part or whole as a florists' store. Mr. Foster had greenhouses at Dorchester. I understood his wife was named Anna, and the fern, named Anna Foster, was a sport in the greenhouses of Mr. Foster. I doubt if the fern can now be traced, as Mr. Foster died years ago.

On page 692 of November 27, HORTICULTURE, is a fern advertisement of H. H. Barrows & Son of Whitman, Mass. The form Barrowsii, I first saw at their place, and I think I understood Mr. Barrows that it sported with him from Bostoniensis.

The Boston form I first saw at North Easton at the greenhouses of the late Frederick L. Ames, and I always supposed that form of it had originated on their premises.

As most of these "suppositions" date back over forty years (I have been in business over fifty-five years) they are somewhat misty.

Respectfully,
FRANK BUFFINTON.
Fall River, Mass.

Referring to the set of sixty-five or more varieties of Nephrolepis exaltata already collected and identified at the Brooklyn Botanic Garden as stated by R. C. Benedict in our last week's issue, we mention N. Mentori, shown by C. Hagenburger at the Cleveland Flower Show as another new one to be added to the long list. This struck us as a very pretty variety, the fronds long and slender, with sub-divided pinnae.

CHINESE COTONEASTERS.

Several of the Chinese Cotoneasters in the collection of Chinese plants will be objects of much beauty for several weeks, for many of them retain their fruit until winter and their leaves are only now beginning to take on their brilliant autumn colors. The most beautiful of them perhaps now is the red-fruited *Cotoneaster Dielsiana*. *C. divaricata*, another red-fruited species, will be more beautiful in ten days' time when the leaves will be bright scarlet. *C. horizontalis* and its variety *perpusilla* with their dark green leaves and small bright red fruits, will not lose their autumn beauty much before Christmas. These two plants with their prostrate stems spreading into broad, compact mats are well suited for the rock garden or to train against low walls.—*Arnold Arboretum Bulletin.*

W. ATLEE BURPEE

In Fordhook, his beautiful home, near Doylestown, Pa., at 6.45 Friday evening, November 26, Washington Atlee Burpee, one of America's most famous seedsmen and horticulturists, died at the age of 57 years of an illness baffling in its complications. He became ill several months ago, and went to Wernersville, Pa., to recuperate. His condition grew worse, and he went to Philadelphia, occupying a suite at the Ritz-Carlton. Recently he was taken to his country home, and there the engineers on the Reading Railway avoided bell-ringing and whistle-blowing that they might not disturb him.

At his bedside when he died were his wife, two of his sons, David and W. Atlee, Jr.; his sister, Mrs. A. B. Scott, and her husband, and Dr. Frank B. Swartzlander, his lifelong friend and physician.

W. Atlee Burpee was born at Sheffield, N. B., April 5, 1858, but was predestined to be a Philadelphian, his father having married the daughter of his instructor in medicine, Dr. Washington L. Atlee of Philadelphia, under promise that within five years he would move to that city. He was also predestined to be a physician, but objected to that part of the program, and at the age of 18 opened in connection with G. S. Benson, Jr., a little store at 223 Church street, dealing chiefly in seeds, fancy pigeons, poultry and dogs. Another partner was taken into the firm the following year, but the combination proved unsuccessful, and two years later he embarked under the firm name of W. Atlee Burpee & Co., for himself. The growth of the concern

was steady until now it is the largest mail order seed house in the world. Immense seed farms are located at Doylestown, Pa., Swedesboro, N. J., and in the Lompoc Valley, California. The headquarters of the firm in Philadelphia are located one on North Fifth street and the other on York avenue.

While a Canadian by birth, Mr. Burpee was a thorough American by preference, although he always maintained a deep interest in matters connected with the natives of the Dominion who resided in his city. He was a lifelong director of the Canadian Society

of Philadelphia, and was elected to the presidency several times.

Mr. Burpee's unprecedented success brought him in touch with many other interests, and he was a director of the Market Street National Bank, the Northern Trust Company and the Colgate Company. He was a director of the Wholesale Seedsmen's League, ex-president of the American Seed Trade Association, ex-president of the National Sweet Pea Society of America and vice-president of the National Sweet Pea Society of Great Britain. He was a member of the Trades League of Philadelphia and the Philadelphia Board of Trade and a trustee of the Howard Hospital and Sanitarium Association of Philadelphia and of the National Farm School. He was also a life member of the Royal Horticultural Society of Great Britain and the Society Nationale Horticulture de France.

Mr. Burpee married Miss Blanche Simons in 1892. and they have three children — David, Washington Atlee, Jr., and Stuart Alexander Burpee.

He is credited with having done a great deal of charitable work among families in Doylestown and neighboring towns. Several years ago he gave to Doylestown a splendidly equipped playground, known as the Blanche Burpee Playgrounds.

Our estimate of Mr. Burpee personally and the heartfelt tributes to his memory by others who knew him well will be found on the editorial page and in the columns herewith. More than six hundred people attended the funeral at Doylestown on Monday, including many representatives of the

W. ATLEE BURPEE.

seed and horticultural interests of Philadelphia, New York, Washington and other cities. The establishment of W. Atlee Burpee & Co. in Philadelphia, was closed for the day, and the 200 employees attended the funeral in a body. There was also a large representation of members of the Poor Richard Club of Philadelphia, whom Mr. Burpee had hospitably entertained so often at "Fordhook."

The casket reposed in the drawing room of the Burpee residence at Fordhook, surrounded by a great wealth of floral tributes. A simple but impressive funeral service was conducted by the Rev. M. A. Brownson, pastor of the Tenth Presbyterian Church, Philadelphia, in which church Mr. Burpee has been an elder for many years. Mrs. Margaret Mitchell, a niece of Mrs. Burpee, sang "Lead, Kindly Light." The Rev. Mr. Brownson paid a touching tribute to the loyalty of Mr. Burpee in his friendships and to his warmhearted generosity and kindliness. Pall-bearers were ex-Governor Edwin S. Stuart, John Gribbel, president of the Union League; Samuel Y. Heebner, ex-Judge Harman Yerkes, William E. Helme, Henry M. Warren, Percy B. Bromfield and William F. Fell. Interment was made in Doylestown cemetery.

FROM GEORGE C. WATSON.
Philadelphia.

When we survey the field of achievement of the American seed trade during the past fifty years many prominent figures stand out. James Vick, Peter Henderson, B. K. Bliss, John Lewis Childs, Wm. Henry Maule, D. M. Ferry, Albert Dickinson, Jerome B. Rice, John Farquhar and J. C. Vaughan are among the many who have made history and headed the forward movement. But the most striking figure of them all has been W. Atlee Burpee, who started in 1878—37 years ago—and has just passed away at the early age of 57 years.

To get a clear idea of what Mr. Burpee stood for we must first get the right idea of what a true seedsman stands for. The seedsman does business on a confidential basis. You can't tell from looking at him. The first principle of a true seedsman is a high sense of honor. Mr. Burpee had that in a remarkable degree. No dishonorable dollar ever went into his pocket. The second principle is a deep love of truth. No man ever heard Mr. Burpee depart one hair's breadth from the absolute truth about anything he had to offer—and that is saying a lot when you get enthusiastic about some of your pet novelties. In addition to a high sense of honor and a deep love of truth there is this further supreme requirement to enforce the latter: unsubduable courage in its defence. Business was a courageous man to that final supreme test. He never put a fake on the market himself, and he would even fight a friend who did, no matter how innocently the friend might do so.

Gentlemen, that man was a man among men. A big man. A strong man. A wise man. An honest man. A hale man. A jolly man. A witty man. A loving man. A prince. One of the most unique and wonderful characters it has been my fortune to know during my thirty-two years' sojourn in this country on my way around the world.

His friends and the universe have suffered an irreparable loss in his sudden taking away. But let us thank the Lord that He vouchsafed to give us a Burpee even for a limited time.

"Sound, sound the clarion, fill the fife!
To all the sensual world proclaim,
One crowded hour of glorious life
Is worth an age without a name."

That's from good old Sir Walter, and it fits Burpee.

We have seen many remarkable popular outpourings to a popular hero, both at home and abroad—from royalty down and from theocracy up, but never have we seen so ardent a flowing out of the human heart to a real man as we saw at Fordhook today, Nov. 29, 1915.

For miles around the roads were lined with auto wagons, buggies, ox-carts; East, West, North and South—as far as the eye could reach. They had been paying their respects for hours before we got there on the 1.02 P. M. train, from the Reading Terminal. From Fordhook siding, at the bottom of the Burpee lawn, we watched a sea of heads (from that one train) half-a-mile-long-and-seven-deep, trudging up to pay their last respects to the great departed.

To count the thousands that made their last bow of respect to Burpee is impossible, not only that but the kind of people who came. Every one there was a prince in the business—from Maine to California—he came to do homage to his king—king not by heredity but by achievement. And not only in our own line of industry but in all walks of life. Merchants, manufacturers, farmers, florists, lawyers, clergymen, statesmen, suffragettes — every phase and form of human feeling was represented.

The worthy successors of the great Burpee business—while they have sustained (with us all) a great and stunning loss, have the inspiration of this wonderful tribute to their honored chief and founder:—to gird up their loins and do all that is in them to carry the Burpee flag to even bigger heights. From stepping stones of our dead selves to higher things. That's the slogan.

FROM W. C. LANGBRIDGE,
Cambridge, N. Y.

"Death loves a shining mark," and this is exemplified in the passing of W. Atlee Burpee. For many years he has stood in the front rank among living representatives of the seed trade, not alone of this country but of the world. Few men have filled so large a space in their chosen line of business, and his strong forceful character has left an impress on the seed trade of this country that will endure for generations to come.

Mr. Burpee was an honor to the seed business, a force for square upright dealing, a living protest against shams and fakes. While as an advertiser he always emphasized the name of Burpee, he was in the broadest sense a public benefactor, not only to those in his own line of business but to horticulture in general. It can be said without fear of contradiction that during the last quarter of a century,

Mr. Burpee has introduced more new types of vegetables of sterling merit, which have become standard varieties, than any other house in all America.

One feature of the Burpee establishment has always been commented on —the intense loyalty of every employee from the highest to the lowest. Every one seemed to be proud of his connection with the house of Burpee; eager to serve the "chief;" eager to do anything to spare him. There is a cause, a reason for this devotion—it was the thoughtful kindliness of the man. For many years it has been Mr. Burpee's custom to look after his employees' welfare and comfort, and any who became ill while in his employ received his salary during the period of his illness, or at least for a considerable time, and in addition, often received the best medical attention free. These are a few of the reasons for the quite unique loyalty of his employees.

It is not the purpose of the writer to act as biographer for Mr. Burpee, but knowing him for many years we regard it as a privilege to bear brief testimony to the qualities of heart and brain of this true nobleman. With a considerable part of the allotted three score years and ten still unused, and just where the twilight mingles with the day, he has passed to the great beyond.

"Take him all in all, we shall not look upon his like again."

FROM MR. BURPEE'S FIRST EMPLOYEE.
Harrisburg, Pa.

The half can never be told. The men closest to Mr. Burpee are the ones that knew of the many good deeds he did. Many a blessing has he showered on the poor and needy that no one but those directly interested knew anything about. He was always thoughtful about his employees, their welfare, their homes, and their habits. The writer recalls an incident that happened many years ago, when an employee did Mr. Burpee a great injury, but instead of retaliating he said "well, let him go and I hope he may yet see the error of his ways." He was not the man to hold a grudge,—far from it. The writer, an old employee, always looked upon Mr. Burpee as a brother and I have every reason to believe he felt this same brotherly affection for me, being the first employee of the great house of Burpee. It is not only a pleasure to look back and think of the happy days spent with this house but the constant companionship with Mr. Burpee made it more so. When I say that I believe I have lost in the death of Mr. Burpee the best friend I ever had, I "say but little." Last spring Mr. Burpee stopped in my city and spent the evening at my home. Needless to say the conversation ran back to the old days of '78 and '9. I can see his countenance now, radiant, when many old things were brought up. He seemed to like to look back. Speaking of the first edition of Burpee's Farm Annual which was mailed from his old residence, 1332 Arch street, he said: "We had a lot of fun that night."

God in all his goodness cannot fail to crown him for the many good works he has accomplished on this earth.

THE EXHIBITIONS

HOUSTON FLOWER SHOW.

Houston's fall flower show was a notable success and amply repaid the workers who gave their time and effort to the cause. The influence of such a well-ordered and creditable exhibition cannot be other than educational and elevating to the community and, eventually, conducive to the prosperity of commercial floriculture in the section of the country where it was held. As our illustrations indicate some wise and enterprising publicity was set in motion with a view to focusing public attention on the affair. The picture showing the ladies who participated in the opening ceremonies sufficiently indicates that the public interest was effectively corralled. The bridal flower array as seen in the illustration could not fail to captivate in any city and was an innovation of more than passing merit. Among the prize winners were R. C. Kerr, who was the live wire behind the enterprise and who won a whole string of premiums for artistic floral work; H. W. Kuhlmann, who also won many honors, and Mrs. M. A. Hanson. Many out-of-town displays were made, not for competition, which helped very materially towards the general effectiveness of the display. It is proposed that this fall exhibition be made an annual event.

NATIONAL FLOWER SHOW.

Philadelphia, March 25 to April 2, 1916

When the National Flower Show Committee took a lease of Convention Hall, the building in which the National Flower Show is to be held, they had some misgivings as to whether the Show could occupy the tremendous amount of floor space presented. Subsequent preparations, however, have shown that instead of being too big, the hall is really too small; consequently, the floor plan as originally arranged has had to be altered to accommodate the pressure already felt upon the space. The space set apart for the trade exhibits has been minimized, and every available inch has been relegated to the area required for the competitive exhibits. It is not too soon to state that the exhibition will fill the building completely. The National Flower Show Committee ad-

Partial View Houston Flower Show. Display of Park Floral Co., Denver, in foreground.

vance the idea of "Show first," therefore other interests must give way. Those who have already taken space in the trade section have acted wisely, for even at this early date the space available for trade displays is nearly all reserved, and it is only a matter of a few weeks before all the space will be taken up. Among those who have contracted for space are the following:

H. F. Michell Co. Phila.; Henry A. Dreer, Inc. Phila.; A. N. Pierson Inc. Cromwell, Conn.; Joseph Heacock Co. Inc. Wyncote, Pa.; Arthur Cowee, Berlin, N. Y.; Bon Arbor Chemical Co., Paterson, N. J.; J. L. Dillon, Bloomsburg, Pa.; Coldwell Lawn Mower Co. Newburgh, N. Y.; Thomas Meehan & Sons, Germantown, Pa.; Alphano Humus Co., New York-Phila.; Cloche Co. New York; F. R. Pierson, Tarrytown, N. Y.; Lord & Burnham Co., New York-Phila.; George L. Stillman, Westerly, R. I.; Spencer Henter Co., Scranton, Pa.; Richmond Cedar Works, Richmond, Va.; Hitchings & Co. Elizabeth, N. J.; W. Atlee Burpee & Co. Phila.; Metropolitan Material Co., Brooklyn, N. Y.; Galloway Terra Cotta Co. Phila.; Benjamin Hammond, Beacon, N. Y.; S. S. Skidelsky & Co., Phila.; The Pfaltzgraff Pottery Co., York, Pa.; Gude Bros. Co., Washington, D. C.; Robert Craig Co. Phila.; Conard & Jones Co., West Grove, Pa.; S. S. Pennock-Meehan Co. Phila.; Julius Roehrs Co., Rutherford, N. J.; R. & J. Farquhar & Co.,

Boston; W. K. Harris, Phila.; Bobbink & Atkins, Rutherford, N. J.; John A. Evans Co. Richmond, Ind.; Vaughan's Seed Store, Chicago-New York; Knight & Struck Co., New York; The Florists' Exchange, New York; B. Hammond Tracy, Wenham, Mass.; Kirke Chemical Co., Brooklyn, N. Y.; Andorra Nurseries, Phila.; Charles Grakelow, Phila.; S. P. Townsend & Co., Orange, N. J.; J. A. Peterson & Sons, Cincinnati, O.; M. Rice & Co., Phila.; John Kuhn, Phila.; H. Bayersdorfer & Co. Phila.; Harry S. Betz, Phila.; Jos. Neidinger & Co., Phila.; Chas. Henry Fox, Phila.; Voltax Paint & Var, Co., Phila.; The Garland Co., Cleveland, O.

The Schedule Committee has just completed the Second Preliminary Schedule, and the same will be mailed to those interested in a few days. The prizes offered approximate a grand total of $20,000, eclipsing the schedules of all preceding National Flower Shows.

The bid for feature exhibits is well exemplified in the offer of $600 for Rose Gardens, with a prospect of the prizes being increased to $1000 in this class. JOHN YOUNG, Sec'y. 53 West 28th street, New York.

NEW YORK INTERNATIONAL FLOWER SHOW

In recognition of the public interest attaching to New York's big flower show, April 5 to 12, 1916, the Park Department of the City of New York, through Commissioner Cabot Ward, has communicated to Secretary John Young, its intention of staging an exhibit at the forthcoming show which shall at least equal the magnificent display made at last spring's show. An exhibit of this character is greatly appreciated by the management, because it reflects in great measure the interest taken in floriculture by our civic government whose efforts to promote the love of flowers and plants among its citizens need no exploitation. It goes without saying that Park Super-

Exhibits of Bridal Flowers at Houston Flower Show.

intendent J. H. Beatty will seek to eclipse his former staging by making the "people's exhibit" one of the most noteworthy in the exhibition. Space in the trade section is being taken up readily, and this department of the show bids fair to be larger than in former years. The following have made reservation for space:

Max Schling, New York; Julius Roehrs Co., Rutherford, N. J.; Bon Arbor Chemical Co., Paterson, N. J.; Woodrow & Marketos, New York; George L. Stillman, Westerly, R. I.; John Scheepers, Inc.. New York; Alphano Humus Co., New York; Arthur Cowee, Berlin, N. Y.; Wm. T. Leary, New Rochelle, N. Y.; A. T. Bunyard, New York; J. M. Thorburn & Co., New York; Aphine Mfg. Co., Paterson, N. J.; Bobbink & Atkins, Rutherford, N. J.; C. E. M. Stumpp, New York; H. A. Bunyard Co., New York; S. P. Townsend & Co., Orange, N. J.; F. R. Pierson, Tarrytown, N. Y.; C. H. Totty, Madison, N. J.; B. Hammond Tracy, Wenham, Mass.; Stumpp & Walter Co., New York; A. N. Pierson, Inc., Cromwell, Conn.; J. J. Stringham, New York; W. E. Marshall Co., New York; Reed & Keller, New York; Miller & Doing, Brooklyn; Knight & Struck Co., New York; Coldwell Lawn Mower Co., Newburgh, N. Y.; Reade Mfg. Co., Jersey City; V. & R. Industries, New York; Sharonware Work Shop, New York; Metropolitan Material Co., Brooklyn; A. Kotmiller, New York; Scott Bros.. Elins-

ford, N. Y.; Doubleday Page Co.. New York; Japanese Floral Perfume Co., New York; The Cloche Co., New York; E. C. Brown Co.. Rochester, N. Y.; H. Langelere, New York; A. L. Miller, Brooklyn; A. J. Jerome Craft Shop, New York.

The committee is considering the classes as set forth in the preliminary schedule, and will shortly prepare the final schedule. The preliminary schedule should convey the idea that the management is making a feature of displays. The rose garden display will be most notable in the classes looking to the artistic end of the show.

Considerable interest also attaches to the rock garden class. During the fall planting season, growers intending to compete in this class were busy over the problem of what to grow, and it is safe to say that we shall see many plants strange to American flower shows.

What was perhaps the most interesting feature of the last show—the table decoration class for hotels only —will be given similar prominence in the forthcoming show. Judging from the interest taken in this class, the stagings will be much more magnifi-

cent in their appointments than at the last show.

It is to be pointed out that the class calling for "new Holland plants" is not to be interpreted literally. The meaning is that the plants to be offered in this class are to be what are known as New Holland plants, such as tree ferns and the flora of Australasia. Why this term should continue to be customary is beyond comprehension. Australia, as a name, needs little explanation nowadays.

JOHN YOUNG, Sec'y.

MILDEW ON OUTDOOR ROSES.

We reprint the following communication which appeared in our issue of last week with some typographical inaccuracies which made it unintelligible.

To the Editor of HORTICULTURE:

Dear Sir:—The request of M. H. S., Walla Walla, Wash., for a formula to overcome mildew on outdoor roses impels me to send you the recipe for a remedy that I use with unfailing success.

Liver of sulphur................ ¼ oz.
Fel's Naptha soap or Ivory soap.. ½ oz.
Water .... 1 gallon

Dissolve the liver of sulphur in cold water and the soap by the aid of heat; when thoroughly dissolved mix. The plants must be sprayed early in the morning to prevent scalding—never late in the day. I am convinced that more mildew is developed on roses by wetting the foliage late in the day than from any other cause. I never have mildew on my roses unless we have much rain at night and always spray with the above mixture as soon as possible after a rainy night. In sections where mildew is prevalent I would suggest spraying before it appears. Roses should always be watered early in the morning.

Yours very truly,
ROBERT HUEY.
Philadelphia, Nov. 13. 1915.

Group of Ladies Who Took Part in the Auto Parade Proceeding the Opening of the Houston Flower Show.

CLUBS AND SOCIETIES

SOCIETY OF AMERICAN FLORISTS AND ORNAMENTAL HORTICULTURISTS.

The following committees have been appointed by President Welch in accordance with resolutions passed at the San Francisco Convention:

On amendment to by-laws providing for selection of convention city two years in advance—Theodore Wirth, chairman, Minneapolis, Minn.; W. A. Manda, South Orange, N. J.; John F. Huss, Hartford, Conn.

On Publicity — Irwin Bertermann, chairman, Indianapolis, Ind.; J. C. Vaughan, Chicago, Ill.; Ed. P. Tracey, Albany, N. Y.; Henry Penn, Boston, Mass.; Ralph M. Ward, New York.

On Development of American Products—H. P. Knoble, chairman, Cleveland, O.; C. W. Ward, Eureka, Cal.; E. H. Wilson, Jamaica Plain, Mass.

On National Credit and Collections Bureau—F. H. Traendly, chairman, New York, N. Y.; W. F. Kasting, Buffalo, N. Y.; S. S. Pennock, Philadelphia, Pa.; N. A. Benson, Denver, Colo.; Fred'k A. Danker, Albany, N. Y.; Geo. W. Smith, Cleveland, O.; Thos. Roland, Nahant, Mass.; F. L. Atkins, Rutherford, N. J.; Hans Plath, San Francisco, Cal.

———

Public notice is hereby given that the Conard & Jones Co., West Grove, Pa., offers for registration the Cannas mentioned below. Any person objecting to the use of the proposed names or registration is requested to communicate with the secretary at once. Failing to receive objection to the registration, the same will be made three weeks from this date.

Canna Lafayette—In some respects it resembles the famous "Meteor" but the flowers are a more intense scarlet. The heads of bloom are carried erect above the healthy, green foliage; producing a brilliant effect in mass planting.

Canna Windmar — This canna is rather dwarf in habit; the flowers are medium in size, fine rounded petals; color, clear distinct orange, broadly margined with canary-yellow. An early and free bloomer, self cleaning, erect trusses carried well above the foliage, which is a marine shade of green. Parentage, Buttercup × seedling.

JOHN YOUNG, Sec'y.

FLORISTS' CLUB OF PHILADELPHIA.

The next meeting of The Florists' Club of Philadelphia will be held on Tuesday evening, December 7th. At this meeting there will be a debate, as follows:

"Is it wise for the producer to depend entirely on the enterprise of the retailer for marketing his products." Affirmative assigned to Chas. H. Grakelow; negative assigned to W. Frank Therkildson.

There will also be several new roses

Meetings Next Week

Monday, Dec. 6.

Bernardsville Horticultural Society, Bernardsville, N. J.
Elberon Horticultural Society, Houston Florist Club, Houston, Texas.
Montreal Gardeners' and Florists' Club, Montreal, Canada.
New Bedford Horticultural Society, New Bedford, Mass.
New Jersey Floricultural Society, Orange, N. J.
Washington Florist Club, Washington, D. C.

Tuesday, Dec. 7.

Lake Geneva Gardeners' and Foremen's Association, Lake Geneva, Wis.
Los Angeles County Horticultural Society, Los Angeles, Calif.
Paterson Floricultural Society, Paterson, N. J.
Philadelphia Florists' Club, Philadelphia, Pa.
Pittsburgh Florists' and Gardeners' Club, Pittsburgh, Pa.
State Florists' Association of Indiana, Anthony Hotel, Fort Wayne, Ind.

Wednesday, Dec. 8.

Cincinnati Florists' Society, Jabez Elliott Flower Market, Cincinnati, O.
Dutchess County Horticultural Society, Poughkeepsie, N. Y.
Lenox County Florists' and Gardeners' Society, Madison, N. J.
Nassau County Horticultural Society, Pembroke Hall, Glen Cove, N. Y.

Thursday, Dec. 9.

National Association of Gardeners' Convention, Horticultural Hall, Boston, Mass.

Friday, Dec. 10.

Connecticut Horticultural Society, County Bldg., Hartford, Conn.
Westchester and Fairfield Horticultural Society, Doran's Hall, Greenwich, Conn.

Saturday, Dec. 11.

Massachusetts Horticultural Society, Boston, Mass.

on exhibition. E. J. Fancourt of Pennock Meehan Company, is chairman of the Novelties Committee.

DAVID RUST, Sec'y.

THE GARDENERS' CONVENTION.

Everything is in readiness for the annual convention of the National Association of Gardeners which will be held in Boston next week, December 9th and 10th.

The committee on arrangements—W. N. Craig, Duncan Finlayson and William J. Kennedy—announces that the convention will be opened in Horticultural Hall promptly at two o'clock on Thursday. That day will be devoted to the disposing of the business before the convention. Friday will be given up to visiting points of horticultural interest in and around Boston. The Copley Square Hotel has been selected as the headquarters of the association.

A joint committee of the horticultural interests of Boston and the Gardeners' and Florists' Club of Boston, is planning to make the visit of the gardeners to their city a memorable one.

TWO IMPORTANT FORESTRY MEETINGS.

On Thursday, December 9th, 1915, at two o'clock, the Massachusetts Forestry Association will hold its annual meeting at 3 Joy street, Boston. Dr. H. T. Fernald, State Nursery Inspector, will talk about "The White Pine Blister Rust" and tell of its discovery in Massachusetts. Mr. Lewis R. Speare, will discuss "The Advantages of Shade Tree Planting on State Highways" and the plans of beautifying the Circuit. The cost of growing a crop of white pine will be given in figures from actual experience by Elliott R. B. Allardice, superintendent of the Wachusetts Department of the Metropolitan Water and Sewerage Board. Opportunity will be given for questions and discussion.

The American Forestry Association is to honor Boston with its annual meeting on January 17 and 18. Speakers of national prominence will be on the program, and all of the forestry interests of New England will take part. This is a get together meeting of conservationists of the entire country and many states are expected to be represented. All meetings will be held at the Copley-Plaza. Seats at the banquet which will be given on the evening of January 17th should be ordered in advance. These may be engaged through the Massachusetts Forestry Association. All meetings will be open to the public.

ST. LOUIS SOCIETY MEETINGS.

The officers of the St. Louis Florist Club met at the home of W. C. Smith on Monday night, November 29, to perfect plans for the next club meeting. An interesting program was mapped out and the officers were nicely entertained by Mr. and Mrs. Smith.

The St. Louis Florist Club will meet in Odd Fellows Hall, Thursday afternoon, December 9, at 2 o'clock, when one hundred members are expected to be present.

The Growers' Association meeting was held on Wednesday, December 1, at the Eleven Mile House.

The Lady Florists' Home Circle will meet at the home of Mrs. F. W. Bruening on Wednesday afternoon, December 8.

The Retail Florists' Association meet on Monday night, December 20, at The Mission Inn Garden. Secretary Weber says that quite a few new applications are pending.

CLUB AND SOCIETY NOTES.

The Florists' and Gardeners' Club, Dayton, Ohio, voted to hold a flower show during the Industrial Exhibition.

which will be held in the Delco building, January 14-22, 1916. The committee of arrangements consists of J. W. Rodgers, W. G. Matthews, C. O. Siebenthaler and Horace M. Frank.

At the regular monthly meeting of the Oyster Bay Horticultural Society, held in Fireman's Hall, Oyster Bay, N. Y., on Nov. 24th, the exhibition tables were well filled and prominent among the exhibits was Mr. Robinson's collection of vegetables of which there were twenty-nine varieties. The judges, Messrs. Milburn, Gale and Hothersall reported as follows: Lettuce, Jos. Robinson, Society's first; violets, Prince of Wales, Geo. Wilson, Society's prize; seedling chrysanthemum, J. Bell, certificate of merit; collection of vegetables, J. Robinson, cultural exhibit.

Jas. Bell gave an interesting talk on his new type of chrysanthemum to be known as the cactus type. A lecture on Hickory Bark Beetles, etc., was given by Mr. J. J. De Vyver. Prizes for next meeting are for 1 primula, 1 schizanthus, 12 mushrooms.

     A. R. KENNEDY, Sec'y.

The Rhode Island Horticultural Society received $179 in response to its appeal for funds according to reports submitted at the regular meeting held

Wednesday evening at Providence. Of this amount, $100 was from the Ladies' Auxiliary and the balance from well-wishing friends and the Society was gratified with the results. At the business session a committee, composed of President H. H. York, Eugene A. Appleton and Thomas Hope, was appointed to confer with a committee of three from the Ladies' Auxiliary on a plan of co-operation and work in the interest of the Society for the coming year. Secretary Thomas read an editorial in a recent issue of HORTICULTURE concerning the career and work of the Rhode Island Society and it was received with much satisfaction by the members.

Professor J. Franklin Collins read a number of articles from Government bulletins and State agricultural stations, making special reference to bulletin 277 issued by the N. J. agricultural station which deals with the growing of roses in greenhouses. S. A. G.

TO THE

ADVERTISING

TRADE

HORTICULTURE is a business-getting medium for those firms who make use of its advertising columns. This paper is read every week by men representing enough buying power to make the investment of a few dollars in telling them what you have to sell, a wise business proposition. The position of its subscribers in the industry and the quality of its reading matter make HORTICULTURE an unexcelled publicity medium

--------FOR--------

They All Read It

--------AND--------

They Read It All

☞ *Next Week's Issue will be the Eleventh Anniversary and Holiday Trade Number. Order space now and we shall take good care of your interests.*

SEED TRADE

AMERICAN SEED TRADE ASSOCIATION
Officers—President, J. M. Lupton, Mattituck, L. I., N. Y.; First Vice-President, Kirby B. White, Detroit, Mich.; Second Vice-President, F. W. Bolgiano, Washington, D. C.; Secretary-Treasurer, C. E. Kendel, Cleveland, O.; Assistant Secretary, S. F. Willard, Jr., Cleveland, O. Cincinnati, O., next meeting place.

Resolutions on the Death of W. Atlee Burpee.

The following resolutions on the death of the late W. Atlee Burpee were adopted at a meeting of seedsmen and others held at the Hotel Sherman, Chicago, on November 29.

WHEREAS, The death of W. Atlee Burpee, of Philadelphia, Pa., has taken from us one of our most earnest coworkers in the cause of horticulture and one whose high standard of business ethics has aided materially in advancing the trade to a higher plane, we, the undersigned, representing the Chicago Seed Trade, the Horticultural Society of Chicago and the Chicago Florists' Club, desire to place on record our high appreciation of his life work and it is therefore

RESOLVED, That we consider the services of W. Atlee Burpee in his chosen field, particularly his work in sweet peas, and garden flowers and vegetables generally, worthy of the greatest prominence in the annals of American horticulture, and it is further

RESOLVED, That we extend to his family and business associates our heartfelt sympathy in the great loss they have sustained. It is further

RESOLVED, That signed copies of these resolutions be forwarded to his family and business associates.

Signed
Chas. Dickinson, The Albert Dickinson Co.
J. C. Vaughan, Vaughan's Seed Store.
Arnold Ringier, The W. W. Barnard Co.
Simeon F. Leonard, Leonard Seed Co.
O. L. Coulter, C. C. Morse & Co.
Chas. Hollenbach, For Peter Hollenbach.
W. N. Rudd, Pres. Hort. Society of Chicago.
W. J. Keimel, Pres. Chicago Florists' Club.

Lily of the Valley Pips Arriving

On the steamship "Hellig Olav" arriving Nov. 17, there were 360 cases of valley pips for Loechner & Co., New York, and S. S. "Oscar II," which arrived Nov. 29, 72 cases valley pips for Loechner & Co., New York, and 13 cases for R. & J. Farquhar & Co., Boston. As far as we can find out, these are the first valley pips arriving from the other side, of this year's crop.

By S. S. "Orduna" from Liverpool, arriving on Nov. 29, Loechner & Co. received also twenty bags of Spencer sweet peas, which were shipped from Wellington, New Zealand, on Aug. 13, 1915.

Notes.

New York, N. Y.—On or about January 1, 1916 after extensive alterations are completed A. T. Boddington Co., Inc., will move to their new and more convenient quarters at 128 Chambers street.

The Bureau of Foreign and Domestic Commerce is in receipt of a letter from a firm in Cuba stating that a fertilizer is being manufactured in that country, and they desire to find a market for it in the United States. It is composed of the following substances: Nitrogen, ammonia, phosphoric acid and phosphate. Address may be obtained from the Bureau of Foreign and Domestic Commerce in Washington, or any of its branch offices.

Value of horticultural material imported at New York for the week ending November 20 is given as follows: Fertilizer, $973; clover seed, $29,061; grass seed, $12,516; trees and plants, $66,154.

MINNESOTA STATE HORTICULTURAL SOCIETY.

The forty-ninth annual meeting of the Minnesota State Horticultural Society will be held in the West Hotel, Minneapolis, on Tuesday, Wednesday, Thursday, Friday, December 7, 8, 9, 10.

The Minnesota Garden Flower Society, the Plant Breeders' Auxiliary, the Woman's Auxiliary, the Minnesota State Florists' Society and the Gardeners' Associations of St. Paul and Minneapolis meet at same time and place and will have some part on the program.

The program is a lengthy one and full of snap. The Minnesota State Florists' Society will meet on Tuesday evening, 8.00 o'clock, Wm. D. Desmond, president, in the chair. The program includes "Bulbs," by Max Kaiser, florist, Merriam Park, and "Greenhouses and Their Appurtenances," Wm. Keeling, florist, with Holm & Olson, St. Paul. Two new floral productions of the year, including the cherry pink rose, "Champ Weiland," will be exhibited during the week.

FLORISTS AND GARDENERS OF RHODE ISLAND.

The last meeting of the Florists' & Gardeners' Club of Rhode Island elected James Dillon, president; Wm. Steele, vice-president; James Hockey, treasurer; Cornelius Hartstra, Owen McManmon and John Marshall, executive committee; Wm. E. Chappell, secretary.

The officers will be installed at the first meeting of the new year which occurs on the fourth Monday of January.

The large attendance and spirit of good fellowship was one of the features of the meeting. At the regular December meeting the Club will take up the matter of the annual banquet.

S. A. G.

Midlothian, Va.—The packing shed of J. B. Watkins & Bro., nurserymen of Midlothian, was destroyed by fire entailing a loss of nearly $800. The cause of the fire is unknown. It was discovered shortly after workmen had left the shed for the day and it was rapidly consumed. All of the tools and materials for packing were destroyed.

Of Interest to Retail Florists

NEW FLOWER STORES.

Chicago, Ill.—Weiss Bros., 541 East 47th street.

New London, Ct.—George E. Fisher, State street.

New Haven, Ct.—David Rees, 355 Grand avenue.

Austin, Tex.—Novelty Floral Co., Congress avenue.

Raleigh, N. C.—J. L. O'Quinn, 119 West Martin street.

Joliet, Ill.—Heaton Nichols, Adam Arcade, Ottawa street.

New York, N. Y.—John P. Gilbanks, Standard Arcade, Broadway.

Cleveland, O.—Crane's, 1132 Euclid avenue, Frank J. Schoen, Mgr.

Wheeling, W. Va.—Virginia Flower Shop, McClure Hotel building.

Cambridge, Mass.—E. H. Alger & Son, 706 Massachusetts avenue.

Kansas City, Mo.—Hattie Jewell, removing to 11th and Walnut streets.

Salem, O.—Wm. Mundy, removing to E. Main street and Lincoln avenue.

Somerville, Mass.—McGarry, Florist, Hurst's Theatre building, Broadway.

Beaver Falls, Pa.—Hennon Floral store, removing to store south of the Grand Confectionery Shop.

Modesto, Cal.—The Floral Shop, Mrs. Frank Smith, proprietor, 926 Tenth street.

Milwaukee, Wis.—Edlefsen-Leidiger Co., removing to Milwaukee street December 1.

New York, N. Y.—M. A. Battista, 17 East 59th street. Mrs. A. Shumann, 336 Bleecker street.

THE "SPIRITUAL BOUQUET."

A subscriber in Connecticut asks for information regarding a "spiritual bouquet" which has been mentioned of late in the newspapers as having been sent as a funeral token and for which inquiry has been made by customers. We are unable to enlighten our correspondent concerning the make-up of this latest thing in funeral offerings and would thank any of our readers who can supply the information.

NEWS NOTES.

Gloversville, N. Y.—The floral business of the late E. J. Denham will be continued by Mrs. Denham and her daughter, Mrs. D. L. Bradt.

Kingston, Pa.—Albert Carr, of the firm of Carr Bros., florists, Maple avenue, was struck by an automobile November 19, and his collar bone broken.

NEWS ITEMS FROM EVERYWHERE

CHICAGO.

Beginning Dec. 1, all the wholesale stores are displaying the $2.00 per 1000 price on ferns.

The Kedzie Floral Co., 3403 W. Madison street, has sold out to J. Feeran, who has left the undertaking business to become a florist.

John Michaelson calls attention to the fact that violets are not so popular this year for some reason and that whenever this flower is not meeting with favor, sweet peas of dark color share the same fate.

Mrs. J. Simpson who has successfully conducted a retail flower store at 3656 Ogden avenue, has now opened a second one at 432 N. Parkside avenue. Mrs. Simpson has as active partner C. B. Lemer, one of the rising young men in the business.

The flower show accounts are not all in yet but the management states that the guarantee fund will have to be called in. The show is generally regarded as one of the best ever held in Chicago and the light attendance due largely to the unusually excellent shows given in the park conservatories at the same time.

The American Greenhouse Co. was awarded the Albert F. Amling contract for a new range of houses, to consist of about 225,000 square feet of glass, to be erected by May 1, at Maywood, Ill. The range will be up-to-date in every particular. P. H. McKee, president of the newly organized American Greenhouse Co., won the contract. The work goes forward at once.

The first cuts of Helen Frick chrysanthemum are coming now. It is a splendid late variety and comes in pink and in white. It is regarded by the Chicago Flower Growers' Association as the best late chrysanthemum and their stock of it is certainly fine. Mrs. Francis King gladioli are coming also this week, a supply of which will be kept on hand constantly all winter.

Frank Oechslin had a car load of azaleas arrive, badly frozen. After reporting their condition to the shipper and to the railway company he took the stock to the greenhouses where he will hold plants till damage is adjusted. The ends of the refrigerator car had been left open and the temperature dropped below freezing.

The J. C. Moninger Co., is doing some splendid work in spite of the winter weather. A large conservatory with a one-piece forty-foot truss is being built for Joseph Leiter, at Georgetown, Ill. A rush order, which shows the rapidity with which this firm can execute work with its large force of trained men, is being filled for H. J. Borowski of Roslindale, Mass. It consists of their newest steel-frame house 40 by 150 feet and shipping began immediately the order was placed.

Boston—The bowling teams start on the second lap of the series this week. There was no bowling last Thursday on account of its being the Thanksgiving holiday.

PITTSBURGH.

The E. C. Ludwig Company has just completed a commodious office on their plant at Mars, Pa.

The Ludwig Floral Co. will add four new greenhouses to their range at Castle Shannon, Pa. A new stoker system has just been completed.

Miss Emma B. Maxwell, of 812 Wood street, Wilkinsburg, has just added a handsome new auto truck to her equipment—the second within the year.

Gilbert Ludwig has been added to the finance committee in charge of the Municipal Christmas tree to be "planted" this year in City Hall Park, North Side.

George E. Hallam, who has been confined to his home with pneumonia for the past six weeks, was able last Monday to come down to business for a short time. During his absence Mrs. Hallam has supervised the floral work.

The following have contributed to the flower booth of the German-Austrian Red Cross bazaar in Exposition Hall: William F. Kasting, Buffalo, N. Y.; Mr. Lempke of W. W. Barnard Company, Chicago; John Bader Company; F. C. Hinkel and brothers, and John Schweiger of West View; Harmony Nurseries, Evans City, Pa.; Joseph Thomas, Greensburg; P. S. Randolph & Sons, Verona, Pa.; I. Shelby Crall, Monongahela, Pa.; Pittsburgh Cut Flower Co., McCallum Co., Ludwig Floral Co., Sasonwald Nurseries, and C. Philipp, all of Pittsburgh. Henry Meuschke is chairman of the committee in charge of this booth.

This season's debutantes' affairs have been the inspiration for some of the most artistic floral combinations ever used in this section. For one of these the centerpiece on the tea table was a massive silver tray and basket, the latter filled with assorted oncidiums, laelias, cypripediums, cattleyas and dendrobiums in combination with Hamburgh grapes. On each end were silver vases of white lilacs, the first of the season. On the floor flanking the mantle of the ball room where the receiving party stood, were tall, gold urns each filled with seventy-five Golden Wedding chrysanthemums. Tokay grapes in combination with oncidiums in a Roman gold basket were used on the tea table for the debut of another young lady. Even the garage and canopied walk were transformed into veritable bowers of flowers for the purpose of serving. One hundred and sixty-two gift bouquets added their beauty and fragrance to the scene. Silver-pink snapdragon and Mrs. Russell roses in pink willow baskets dominated the decorations for the coming out of one other young lady.

NEW YORK.

S. Lecakes, wholesale florist, has leased a store at 106 West 28th street.

J. J. Coan has resigned as manager of the Growers' Cut Flower Co., and will embark in the wholesale cut flower business on his own account.

WASHINGTON, D. C.

Harry McCabe has returned after an eleven weeks' stay in Detroit, Mich., to again take up his work in his father's greenhouses in Anacostia.

In commenting upon the Maryland Week Flower Show held recently in Baltimore, F. Gude, George Field, and S. S. Pennock, who were the judges, declare this to have been one of the finest exhibitions of flowers that they have visited. They speak well of the manner in which the show was managed and of the many courtesies shown them.

Because the order resulted in many persons failing to get mail matter that means much to them during the holidays, the Postmaster General has announced the suspension of the order treating as unmailable matter having adhesive stickers on the same side as the stamp. The suspension will, however, remain in force only during the month of December.

Miss Marie Lott, who for the past three years or more has been employed by M. J. McCabe, of Anacostia, was married on Tuesday of last week at the home of her employers to W. C. Fry, of Miami, Fla. The McCabe home was extensively decorated for the occasion for Miss Lott is a great favorite among her friends. Mr. and Mrs. Fry later took the boat for Jacksonville. They will hereafter reside in Miami.

Superintendent George W. Hess, of the Botanic Gardens, is making a special show this week of poinsettias, of which there are now nearly a thousand in full bloom. It had not been expected that these would come into flower until about Christmas, but the hot weather caused them to fairly jump into maturity. The cuttings were put in last February, then planted out in beds until August. The plants have reached an average height of about five feet and are very fine.

SAN FRANCISCO.

Extensive alterations have just been completed in the shipping room of Joseph's flower shop on Grant avenue. They report business for Thanksgiving week double that of last year.

The Francis Floral Co., which specializes on novelty pottery and baskets, reports very good success with a special line of Dutch baskets filled with the different varieties of small pompons for the Thanksgiving trade.

E. W. McLellan, of the E. W. McLellan Co., has the sympathy of the trade on account of the untimely death of his brother, Wm. S. McLellan, who was stabbed to death on his place in San Mateo County, Nov. 19, by a fanatic, accused of starting fires on the McLellan ranch.

Kansas City, Mo.—Sam Murray reports a record Thanksgiving week for business. He had one of the best floral jobs ever given out in Kansas City, the opening of the new Hotel Muehlebach.

VISITORS' REGISTER.

Washington, D. C.—C. W. Ward, Eureka, Cal.; Palmer Gordon, Ashland, Va.

Pittsburgh—C. B. Knickman, rep. McHutchison & Company, N. Y.; Mr. Lempke, of W. W. Barnard Co., Chicago.

San Francisco—Mr. Currier, bulb grower of Santa Cruz, Cal., accompanied by Mrs. Currier; J. W. Koning, representing the Holland bulb house of Baartman & Koning; C. W. Howard, of Howard & Smith, Los Angeles, Cal., and wife.

Boston—C. E. Wildon, Amherst, Mass.; George B. Hart, Rochester, N. Y.; Eugene Schaettel, of Vilmorin & Co., Paris, France; A. E Thatcher Bar Harbor, Me.; Leonard Barron, Garden City, N. Y.; Walter R. Siebrecht, New York; L. J. Reuter, Westerly, R. I.

Cincinnati—Frank Farney, of M. Rice & Co., Phila.; J. C. Sisley, representing The McCallum Co., Pittsburgh; Wm. Geilach, Jr., Piqua, O.; Jos. Hill, Richmond, Ind.; G. A. Beckman, Middletown, Ohio; Fred P. Collyer, Falmouth, Ind.; W. J. Cox, representing The Sefton Co., Chicago; Sam Seligman, New York; Miss Lampert, Xenia, O.; J. T. Heidegen, Aurora, Ind.

Chicago—E. R. Sackett, Fostoria, Ohio; Mr. and Mrs. W. C. Johnson, Memphis, Tenn.; W. K. Palmer, Jr., Champaign, Ill.; A. H. Burger, Elgin, Ill.; George A. Kaup, Urbana, Ill.; A. Owens, Gary, Ind.; M. D. Bullock and son Otis, Elkhart, Ind.; C. B. Knickman, of McHutchison & Co., New York; W. De Ruyter, Noordwyk, Holland; Robt. Groves, Adams, Mass.; Mrs. Lord of Mrs. Lord's Flower Shop, Topeka, Kansas.

Cincinnati—Alex. Ostendarp of the Cincinnati Cut Flower Exchange who was on the sick list for a time last week is now at his work and hustling to make up for the time he lost.

Harry Sunderhaus of C. E. Critchell's accidently shot himself in the thumb last week.

Jim Allen, after successfully passing a civil service examination and heading the list of eligibles with a grade of 98.1 per cent., was recently re-appo'nted to his position in the Park Department.

Obituary

Mrs. Emma Critchell.

Mrs. Emma Critchell, wife of C. E. Critchell, died on Monday morning, November 29, at her home in Cincinnati, O. She had been ill but a few days and her demise was unexpected and a shock to her many friends who mourn her death and give their sympathy to her husband C. E. Critchell and son C. E. Critchell, Jr. who sur-

MRS. EMMA CRITCHELL.

vive her. Mrs. Critchell was 42 years of age. She was a life member and former president of the Ladies' Society of American Florists. She was a charming lady who made friends everywhere she went and her death is a great loss to her family and the community.

Otto Stumpp.

Otto Stumpp, a well known New York seedsman, died at his home in West Hoboken. N. J., on Monday, November 15. He was born in Gonningen, Germany, on March 9, 1846, and came to this country in 1865. He worked in various seed houses, but for the last 32 years he has been associated with Peter Henderson & Co. at 88 Gansevoort street. He is survived by his widow, one daughter and two sons, Otto J., who has been in business with his father and who will continue the business at Gansevoort street, the connection with Peter Henderson & Co. having been discontinued on Septem.. ber 20th of this year, and George G.. Stumpp, of Stumpp & Walter Co., New York.

EXCLUDING FLOWERS AT FUNERALS.

Editor HORTICULTURE:

In HORTICULTURE of Nov. 27 is an article about a priest in Waltham condemning the use of flowers at funerals. Is it not about time that the trade start in to protest or do something against all this ignorant argument? In this city we got last winter the "knockout" from the City Hall, besides the school, graduations, the money to go to the "poor" and the florists lost about two thousand dollars in business and "the poor" got about twenty dollars. Nothing was said about it, with the exception of the comment in HORTICULTURE at the time. Now comes this priest. I would say that the florist business is just as important and necessary as the church, and certainly gives as many a living. Now the florists do not interfere with the church, so if we all mind our own business there won't be any hard times or feelings. Yours very truly,

JOHN C. LINDBLOM.

279 Mass. Ave.,
Providence, R. I.

Detroit—General business in the flower stores has increased in a gratifying manner for the past two months, owing to an unusual number of debutante affairs and promises to so continue all through December. Breitmeyer reports an advance of about 150 per cent. over last year for the same period.

WHOLESALE FLOWER MARKETS — TRADE PRICES—Per 100 TO DEALERS ONLY

	CINCINNATI Nov. 29		CHICAGO Nov. 29		BUFFALO Nov. 29		PITTSBURG Nov. 30	
Roses								
Am. Beauty, Special	35.00	to 40.00	40.00	to 50.00	35.00	to 40.00	30.00	to 40.00
" " Fancy and Extra	20.00	to 30.00	25.00	to 35.00	20.00	to 30.00	20.00	to 25.00
" " No. 1	10.00	to 15.00	10.00	to 20.00	12.00	to 15.00	12.50	to 15.00
Russell, Hadley	4.00	to 20.00	4.00	to 25.00	10.00	to 18.00	6.00	to 18.00
Killarney, Richm'd, Hill'don, Ward	6.00	to 8.00	8.00	to 10.00	7.00	to 8.00	8.00	to 10.00
" " " Ord.	3.00	to 5.00	5.00	to 6.00	4.00	to 6.00	......	to 6.00
Arenburg, Radiance, Taft, Key, Ex.	6.00	to 8.00	8.00	to 10.00	8.00	to 10.00	8.00	to 18.00
" " " Ord.	3.00	to 5.00	3.00	to 6.00	3.00	to 6.00	......	to 6.00
Ophelia, Mock, Sunburst, Extra	6.00	to 8.00	8.00	to 15.00	8.00	to 12.00	8.00	to 12.00
" " " Ordinary	3.00	to 5.00	3.00	to 6.00	4.00	to 6.00	......	to 6.00
Carnations, Fancy	3.00	to 4.00	2.00	to 4.00	......	to 3.00	2.00	to 3.00
" Ordinary	......	to 2.00	1.00	to 2.00	1.50	to 2.00	......	to 2.00
Cattleyas	40.00	to 50.00	60.00	to 75.00	50.00	to 60.00	50.00	to 75.00
Dendrobium formosum	......	to	50.00	to 60.00	...	to	......	to 40.00
Lilies, Longiflorum	......	to 12.50	8.00	to 10.00	10.00	to 12.50	10.00	to 12.00
" Rubrum	4.00	to 8.00	3.00	to 6.00	......	to 6.00	4.00	to ......
Callas	10.00	to 15.00	......	to	8.00	to 10.00	......	to ......
Lily of the Valley	......	to 4.00	3.00	to 4.00	3.00	to 4.00	2.00	to 5.00
Daisies	......	to	......	to 1.50	......	to	.75	to 1.50
Violets	.75	to 1.00	.75	to 1.00	.60	to .75	.50	to 1.00
Mignonette	......	to	4.00	to 8.00	3.00	to 4.00	......	to ......
Snapdragon	......	to	4.00	to 6.00	2.00	to 3.00	2.00	to 6.00
Narcissus, Paper-White	3.00	to 4.00	......	to	......	to	......	to ......
" Trumpet	......	to	......	to	......	to	......	to ......
Hyacinths, Roman	......	to	......	to	......	to	......	to ......
Freesia	......	to	......	to	......	to	......	to ......
Calendulas	......	to	......	to	......	to	......	to ......
Stevia	2.00	to 4.00	1.50	to 2.00	1.00	to 1.25	......	to ......
Sweet Peas	.75	to 1.00	1.00	to 1.50	1.00	to 1.25	......	to 1.00
Gardenias	......	to	30.00	to 60.00	......	to	......	to ......
Adiantum	......	to 1.00	1.00	to 1.25	......	to 1.25	1.00	to 1.25
Smilax	12.50	to 15.00	10.00	to 18.00	......	to 15.00	12.50	to 15.00
Asparagus Plumosus, Strings (100)	25.00	to 50.00	40.00	to 50.00	40.00	to 60.00	35.00	to 50.00
" " & Spren. (100 bchs.)	......	to 25.00	25.00	to 30.00	20.00	to 30.00	35.00	to 50.00

Flower Market Reports

BOSTON The market is in unsatisfactory shape since Thanksgiving and it is very liable to so continue until Christmas. This reaction is an annual occurrence between the two holidays and it is aggravated this year by the unusual persistence of the late chrysanthemums which, judging from appearances will stay with us all through December. Carnations are badly overstocked and many go to loss for lack of a customer. Just how far the chrysanthemum is responsible for this is not apparent but appreciation for the carnation is not what it should be this fall. Roses are lower in price than they were last week but they are of good quality and clean up quite well. Beauties move rather slowly at reduced figures.

BUFFALO The weather was ideal for Thanksgiving week and the trade were satisfied with and thankful for the extra business done. From Monday to Saturday the merchants were busy. Chrysanthemums were the leading sales and a good supply was had at prices within reach of all. Pompons were in good supply, as well as everything else, except roses, which were a trifle off, and those held firm in price. Carnations were in good supply. Beauties were equal to the demand, also all other stock. Violets had no special call and on Thursday, as usual, an oversupply.

CHICAGO Thanksgiving week brought general satisfaction to the wholesalers. It is estimated that at least double the number of chrysanthemums were offered this year that were on the market last year and the quantity of pompons that appeared were a great surprise. It seemed as if every grower had underestimated his supply or had been keeping his stock to try for the top price on Thanksgiving week, with the result that prices could not remain as previously quoted. The supply of all kinds of stock, excepting roses, was so great that to move it concessions were made and a large amount was disposed of and the returns aggregated a good sum. The greatest disappointment was felt by the carnation growers whose stock had to compete with the quantity of pompons and only the very highest grade brought full prices, while the great bulk of medium sold very low. Roses continue scarce, most growers being off crop and the weather conditions if favorable will assure a big crop for Christmas. Orchids and gardenias are decidedly scarce and the same may be said of longiflorum lilies. American Beauties are hardly equal to demand. It looks now as if there would be chrysanthemums in the market till Christmas. Sweet peas are in fair supply and usually sell readily.

CINCINNATI Thanksgiving business was very good. Some stock was left over, but this was mostly stock that was soft or bruised when it came in or it would have had a buyer. Prices were moderate. At the beginning of this week colder weather set in and the supply gave indications of short-

ening. Roses and carnations are not as plentiful as they were but still are enough. Lilies are plentiful. Chrysanthemums are now on the decline and the daily receipts include only limited quantities of late blooms. These, however, are of good quality.

NEW YORK Expectations for Thanksgiving Day business did not quite materialize. There was a large surplus of flowers of all descriptions and the market was unable to clean it up. Since then the situation has not improved and at present writing has a stale and unprofitable look which neither growers, wholesalers or retail

dealers relish. There are lots of roses from stately American Beauties down to microscopic Mignons they are sold in large quantities to one or the other class of dealers but prices are decidedly down and the buyers dominate the situation. Carnations move slowly. Orchids are still scarce. Chrysanthemums still hold the trenches and will not be dislodged as early as was hoped. Lilies very plentiful. Paper White narcissi are coming forward freely. Of gardenias there are very few. Lily of the valley normal. Violets too abundant for the demand but excellent in quality.

(Continued on page 743)

WHOLESALE FLOWER MARKETS — TRADE PRICES—Per 100 TO DEALERS ONLY

	BOSTON Dec. 2		ST. LOUIS Nov. 22		PHILA. Nov. 22	
Roses						
Am. Beauty, Special	20.00 to 25.00	40.00 to 50.00	30.00 to 35.00
" Fancy and Extra	12.00 to 15.00	25.00 to 30.00	20.00 to 25.00
" " No. 1	5.00 to 10.00	10.00 to 15.00	10.00 to 15.00
Russell, Hadley	4.00 to 12.00	8.00 to 10.00	5.00 to 25.00
Killarney, Richmond, Hillingdon, Ward, Extra	3.00 to 6.00	8.00 to 10.00	6.00 to 10.00
" " Ordinary	1.00 to 2.00	4.00 to 6.00	3.00 to 5.00
Arenburg, Radiance, Taft, Key, Extra	3.00 to 6.00	..... to	6.00 to 10.00
" " " Ordinary	1.00 to 2.00	..... to	3.00 to 5.00
Ophelia, Mock, Sunburst, Extra	4.00 to 8.00	8.00 to 10.00	6.00 to 12.00
" " " Ordinary	1.00 to 3.00	4.00 to 6.00	3.00 to 5.00
Carnations, Fancy	1.50 to 2.00	4.00 to 5.00	3.00 to 4.00
" Ordinary	1.00 to 1.50	2.00 to 3.00	2.00 to 3.00
Cattleyas	50.00 to 60.00	..... to 60.00	..... to 75.00
Dendrobium formosum	..... to 40.00	..... to	..... to 50.00
Lilies, Longiflorum	4.00 to 6.00	12.00 to 15.00	8.00 to 10.00
" Rubrum	..... to 3.00	6.00 to 8.00	4.00 to 6.00
Callas	6.00 to 8.00	..... to	8.00 to 10.00
Lily of the Valley	2.00 to 4.00	3.00 to 4.00	2.00 to 4.00
Daisies	.50 to 1.00	.75 to .50	.50 to 1.00
Violets	.40 to .75	.15 to .50	.50 to 1.00
Mignonette	2.00 to 3.00	..... to	..... to 10.00
Snapdragon	1.00 to 3.00	3.00 to 4.00	3.00 to 6.00
Narcissus, Paper-White	1.50 to 2.00	..... to	..... to 10.00
" Trumpet	..... to	..... to	..... to .....
Hyacinths, Roman	..... to	..... to	..... to 10.00
Freesia	..... to	..... to	..... to .....
Calendulas	1.00 to 2.00	..... to	..... to 10.00
Stevia	..... to 2.00	..... to	..... to .....
Sweet Peas	..... to 1.00	.50 to 1.50	.50 to 1.50
Gardenias	25.00 to 35.00	..... to	30.00 to 35.00
Adiantum	..... to 1.00	1.00 to 1.25	..... to 1.00
Smilax	12.00 to 10.00	10.00 to 15.00	15.00 to 20.00
Asparagus Plumosus, Strings (100)	25.00 to 50.00	35.00 to 60.00	..... to 50.00
" & Spren. (100 Bchs.)	25.00 to 35.00	20.00 to 35.00	..... to 50.00

H. E. FROMENT

Wholesale Commission Florist
Choice Cut Flowers'

New Address, 148 West 28th St., NEW YORK
Telephones: 2200, 2201, Madison Square.

Moore, Hentz & Nash

Wholesale Commission Florists

55 and 57 West 26th Street
Telephone No. 756
Madison Square   **New York**

—WM. P. FORD—

Wholesale Florist

107 W. 28th Street, NEW YORK
Telephone 5335, Farragut.
Call and inspect the Best Establishment
in the Wholesale Flower District.

GEO. C. SIEBRECHT

WHOLESALE FLORIST
109 WEST 28th ST
CONSIGNMENTS SOLICITED
PHONE { 608 } MADISON SQ., **NEW YORK**
{ 699 }

JOHN YOUNG & CO.

WHOLESALE FLORISTS

53 WEST 28th STREET   NEW YORK CITY
Consignments Solicited
Phone 7362 Madison Square

THE KERVAN COMPANY

Ferns, Mosses, Wild Smilax, Galax,
Leucothoe, Palmetto, Cycas, both fresh
cut and prepared.
Laurel, Hemlock, all Decorative Evergreens.
Tel { 1293 } Mad. Sq. **119 W. 28 St., New York**
{ 3893 }

WILLIAM H. KUEBLER

Brooklyn's Foremost and Best
WHOLESALE COMMISSION HOUSE
A First Class Market for all CUT FLOWERS
28 Willoughby St.,   Brooklyn, N. Y.

M. C. FORD

121 West 28th St.,   NEW YORK

FINE ROSES, FANCY CARNATIONS

A Full Line of ALL CUT FLOWERS.
Telephone, 3870 or 3871 Madison Square.

GEORGE B. HART

WHOLESALE FLORIST

24 Stone St., Rochester, N. Y.

Regular Shipments Wanted of

Pansies and Violets

I have a good market for them.

B. S. SLINN, JR.

55 and 57 West 26th St. **NEW YORK**

NEW YORK QUOTATIONS PER 100.   To Dealers Only

ROSES AND CARNATIONS		Last Half of Week ending Nov. 27 1915		First Half of Week beginning Nov. 29 1915	
American Beauty, Special		25.00	to 35.00	20.00	to 25.00
" " Fancy and Extra		15.00	to 20.00	12.00	to 15.00
" " No. 1		8.00	to 8.00	5.00	to 8.00
Russell, Hadley		8.00	to 8.00	2.00	to 8.00
Killarney, Richmond, Hillingdon, Ward, Extra		8.00	to 5.00	2.00	to 5.00
Aronburg, Radiance, Taft, Key, Extra	Ordinary	.50	to 2.00	.50	to 2.00
" " " " Ordinary		2.00	to 6.00	2.00	to 6.00
Ophelia, Mock, Sunburst, Extra		.50	to 6.00	.50	to 6.00
" " " Ordinary		3.00	to 6.00	2.00	to 6.00
Carnations, Fancy		.50	to 2.00	.50	to 2.00
" Ordinary		...	to 2.00	1.00	to 2.00
		.75	to 1.00	.75	to 1.00

Flower Market Reports

(Continued from page 741)

In the words of a **PITTSBURGH** prominent wholesale florist, "the 'mum game is over" and conditions have settled down to the regular lines of stock. Business, undoubtedly, is good and the retailers are delighted over the receipts of Thanksgiving. Several firms pronounced it their "best Thanksgiving," while others more conservatively put it as "the best in several years." One—a North Side firm—was open throughout two consecutive days and nights, the holiday itself, included. The street venders appear a day or two each week. It is generally conceded that they serve a good purpose in educating and developing the masset into flower buyers, who in the years to come may often turn to the more pretentious shops. Undoubtedly, they are a blessing to the grower, whose inferior stock otherwise would go to the bow-wows, figuratively speaking.

General satisfaction is expressed among **SAN FRANCISCO** the local florists over the outcome of Thanksgiving business. On account of attendance at the Exposition maintaining such a high level as the date for final closing draws near, some little uneasiness was felt by different members of the trade early in the week regarding the outlook for holiday business, but they were agreeably surprised, the week's sales running substantially ahead of last year's. Stock was plentiful, but nothing to speak of was left over. Poinsettias were featured quite prominently. Some very nice cut stock arrived from the south, and it cleaned up readily. Some potted plants were in evidence, also, but most of the local growers are holding back their poinsettias for the Christmas trade. Cyclamen, begonias, azaleas and primulas were in good demand. Chrysanthemums are getting lighter from day to day and no heavy supplies are expected from now on. Pompons are still plentiful and sell well, both potted and cut. The cool, damp weather has brought violets into better shape and their movement is all that can be desired. Some excellent carnations were brought in for Thanksgiving, everything cleaning up at fair prices, while the finest blooms sold at a high figure. Though the rose offerings are more satisfactory than for some time both in quality and quan-

tity, more fine stock could have been used, especially American beauties and Cecile Bruners. Killarney is going strong. Lily of the valley is plentiful and in good demand. The supply of orchids about equals the demand, and the gardenia situation is about the same. Special basket arrangements are popular here. Some California holly appears on the market, but it is not nearly so plentiful as it was a year ago at this time.

Thanksgiving business **ST. LOUIS** was as good as any of the previous years. Some even say it was better. Flowers were enough for all and the commission houses cleaned out early of the best grades of stock at satisfactory prices.

(Continued on page 740)

There are some new and interesting offers in the Buyers' Directory this week. Look them over. Pages 744-45-46-47.

Buyer's Directory and Ready Reference Guide

Advertisements under this head, one cent a word.   Initials count as words.

Display advertisers in this issue are also listed under this classification without charge. Reference to List of Advertisers will indicate the respective pages.

Buyers failing to find what they want in this list will confer a favor by writing us and we will try to put them in communication with reliable dealers.

ACCOUNTANT
R. Dysart, 40 State St., Boston.
For page see List of Advertisers.

APHINE
Aphine Mfg. Co., Madison, N. J.
For page see List of Advertisers.

APHIS PUNK
Nicotine Mfg. Co., St. Louis, Mo.
For page see List of Advertisers.

ASPARAGUS
Asparagus Plumosus, Thumb pot plants, sure to please, $1.50 per 100. B. C. BLAKE, R. D. 4, Springfield, Ohio.

. AUCTION SALES
The MacNiff Horticultural Co., New York City.
Plant and Bulb Sales by Auction.
For page see List of Advertisers.

Elliott Auction Co., New York City.
For page see List of Advertisers.

AZALEAS
P. Ouwerkerk, Hoboken, N. J.
For page see List of Advertisers.

BAY TREES
August Rolker & Sons, New York.
For page see List of Advertisers.

BEDDING PLANTS
A. N. Pierson, Inc., Cromwell, Conn.
For page see List of Advertisers.

R. Vincent, Jr. & Sons Co., White Marsh, Md.
For page see List of Advertisers.

BEGONIAS

	Per 100
BEGONIA LORRAINE, 2½ in	$12.00
3 in	20.00
4 in	36.00
5 in	50.00
BEGONIA CINCINNATI, 2½ in	15.00
3 in	25.00
3½ in	30.00
4½ in	40.00

JULIUS ROEHRS CO., Rutherford, N. J.

BOILERS
Kroeschell Bros. Co., Chicago.
For page see List of Advertisers.

King Construction Co., North Tonawanda, N. Y.
"King Ideal" Boiler.
For page see List of Advertisers.

Lord & Burnham Co., New York City.
For page see List of Advertisers.

Hitchings & Co., New York City.

BOXES—CUT FLOWER FOLDING
Edwards Folding Box Co., Philadelphia.
For page see List of Advertisers.

Folding cut flower boxes, the best made. Write for list. HOLTON & HUNKEL CO., Milwaukee. Wis.

BOX TREES
BOX TREES—Standards, Pyramids and Bush. In various sizes. Price List on demand. JULIUS ROEHRS CO., Rutherford, N. J.

BOXWOOD
Breck-Robinson Nursery Co., Lexington, Mass.

BOXWOOD SPRAYS
Pittsburgh Cut Flower Co., Pittsburgh, Pa.
For page see List of Advertisers.

BULBS AND TUBERS
Arthur T. Boddington Co., Inc., New York City.
For page see List of Advertisers.

J. M. Thorburn & Co., New York City.
Wholesale Price List of High Class Bulbs.
For page see List of Advertisers.

Ralph M. Ward & Co., New York City.
Lily Bulbs.
For page see List of Advertisers.

John Lewis Childs, Flowerfield, L. I., N. Y.
Gladioli.
For page see List of Advertisers.

August Rolker & Sons, New York City.
Holland and Japan Bulbs.
For page see List of Advertisers.

R. & J. Farquhar & Co., Boston, Mass.
For page see List of Advertisers.

F. R. Pierson, Tarrytown, N. Y.
Hyacinths and Narcissus.
For page see List of Advertisers.

S. S. Skidelsky & Co., Philadelphia, Pa.
For page see List of Advertisers.

Chas. Schwake & Co., New York City.
Horticultural Importers and Exporters.
For page see List of Advertisers.

A. Henderson & Co., Chicago, Ill.
For page see List of Advertisers.

Burnett Bros., 98 Chambers St., New York.
For page see List of Advertisers.

Henry F. Michell Co., Philadelphia, Pa.
For page see List of Advertisers.

Joseph Breck & Sons Corp., Boston, Mass.
For page see List of Advertisers.

Fottler, Fiske, Rawson Co., Boston, Mass.

C. KEUR & SONS, HILLEGOM, Holland.
Bulbs of all descriptions. Write for prices. NEW YORK Branch, 8-10 Bridge St.

Bulbs—150,000 Late Shipment HYACINTHS, TULIPS, NARCISSUS. Prices Low. Stock the Best. Send for List or Phone Melrose 761-W. THOMAS COGGER, 229 Laurel St., Melrose, Mass.

CANNAS
Newest list of the newest Cannas just out. Complete assortment of the finest sorts, at remarkable rates.
Send for list today.
THE CONARD & JONES CO. West Grove, Pa.

CARNATIONS
Wood Bros., Fishkill, N. Y.
For page see List of Advertisers.

F. Dorner & Sons Co., Lafayette, Ind.
For page see List of Advertisers.

Jas. Vick's Sons, Rochester, N. Y.
Field Grown Plants.

Littlefield & Wyman, North Abington, Mass.
New Pink Carnation, Miss Theo.
For page see List of Advertisers.

CARNATION STAPLES
Split carnations quickly, easily and cheaply mended. Pillsbury's Carnation Staple. 1000 for 35c.; 3000 for $1.00 post paid. I. L. PILLSBURY, Galesburg Ill.

Supreme Carnation Staples, for repairing split carnations. 35c. per 1000; 30c0 for $1.00. F. W. WAITE, 85 Belmont Ave., Springfield. Mass.

CHRYSANTHEMUMS
Chas. H. Totty, Madison, N. J.
For page see List of Advertisers.

COLEUS
Christmas Gem Coleus, 3c. B. C. BLAKE, R. D. 4, Springfield, Ohio.

Coleus, Golden Bedder, Verschaffeltii, Queen Victoria, Firebrand and all leading varieties, including the Pink and Yellow Trailing Queen, clean, strong, well rooted cuttings, 50c. per 100, $4.00 per 1000. Cash with order, and satisfaction guaranteed. Send for list. Largest grower of coleus in the U. S. A. NAHLIK, 261-75 Lawrence St., Flushing, N. Y.

DAHLIAS
Send for Wholesale List of whole clumps and separate stock; 40,000 clumps for sale. Northboro Dahlia and Gladiolus Gardens. J. L. MOORE, Prop, Northboro, Mass.

NEW PAEONY DAHLIA
John Wanamaker. Newest, Handsomest, Best. New color, new form and new habit of growth. Big stock of best cut-flower varieties. Send list of wants to PEACOCK DAHLIA FARMS, Berlin, N. J.

DECORATIVE PLANTS
Robert Craig Co., Philadelphia, Pa.
For page see List of Advertisers.

Woodrow & Marketos, New York City.
For page see List of Advertisers.

S. S. Skidelsky & Co., Philadelphia, Pa.
For page see List of Advertisers.

Bobbink & Atkins, Rutherford, N. J.
For page see List of Advertisers.

A. Leuthy & Co., Roslindale, Boston, Mass.
For page see List of Advertisers.

Thomas Roland, Nahant, Mass.
High Grade Plants for Retail Florists.
For page see List of Advertisers.

DRACENAS
Dracaena Indivisa, 4-in. pot plants, 6c. B. C. BLAKE, R. D. 4, Springfield, Ohio.

FERNS
Henry A. Dreer, Philadelphia, Pa.
Dreer's Fine Ferns.
For page see List of Advertisers.

John Scott, Brooklyn, N. Y.
The Home of the Scottii Fern.
For page see List of Advertisers.

H. H. Barrows & Son, Whitman, Mass.
For page see List of Advertisers.

Robert Craig Co., Philadelphia, Pa.
For page see List of Advertisers.

McHutchison & Co., New York City.
Ferns in Flats.
For page see List of Advertisers.

A. M. Davenport, Watertown, Mass.
Boston and Whitmani Ferns.
For page see List of Advertisers.

Roman J. Irwin, New York City.
Boston and Whitmani Ferns.
For page see List of Advertisers.

Ferns, 2-in., Boston, Whitmani, Roosevelt, Elegantissima, Compacta and Teddy Jr. B. C. BLAKE, R. D. 4, Springfield, Ohio.

FERTILIZERS
Stumpp & Walter Co., New York City.
Scotch Soot.
For page see List of Advertisers.

Pulverized Manure Co., Chicago, Ill.
Wizard Brand Cattle Manure.

For List of Advertisers See Page 723

FLORISTS' LETTERS
Boston Florist Letter Co., Boston, Mass.
For page see List of Advertisers.

FLORISTS' SUPPLIES
N. F. McCarthy & Co., Boston, Mass.
For page see List of Advertisers.

Reed & Keller, New York City.
For page see List of Advertisers.

S. S. Pennock-Meehan Co., Philadelphia, Pa.
For page see List of Advertisers.

H. Bayersdorfer & Co., Philadelphia, Pa.
For page see List of Advertisers.

Welch Bros. Co., Boston, Mass.
For page see List of Advertisers.

FLOWER POTS
W. H. Ernest, Washington, D. C.
For page see List of Advertisers.

A. H. Hews & Co., Inc., Cambridge, Mass.
For page see List of Advertisers.

Hilfinger Bros., Ft. Edward, N. Y.
For page see List of Advertisers.

FOLIAGE PLANTS
A. Leuthy & Co., Roslindale, Boston, Mass.
For page see List of Advertisers.

FORGET-ME-NOTS
Myosotis palustris, True Forget-Me-Not.
Two clumps in Carton sent by Parcel Post
on receipt of price, 25 cents. SHATEMUC
NURSERIES, Barrytown, Dutchess County,
New York.

FUNGINE
Aphine Mfg. Co., Madison, N. J.
For page see List of Advertisers.

GALAX
Michigan Cut Flower Co., Detroit, Mich.
For page see List of Advertisers.

GARDEN TOOLS
B. G. Pratt Co., New York City.

GERANIUMS
R. Vincent, Jr., & Sons Co.
White Marsh, Md.
For page see List of Advertisers.

Geraniums, mixed varieties out of 1½
inch pots. Am booking orders for December delivery at $20.00 per 1000. Cash.
JAMES MOSS, Johnsville, Pa.

Geraniums—Ricard, Doyle, Nutt, Poitevine and Chevalier, from 2½-inch pots, immediate or later delivery, $20.00 per 1000.
Rooted Cuttings, $15.00 per 1000. Cash
with order. WM. F. KOENIG, 566 Hamilton Ave., West New York, N. J.

Rooted cuttings of the new Geranium
Margaret Walsh are now for sale at $5.00
per 100; out of 2½-inch pots, $9.00 per 100.
A limited quantity only offered now for
sale. Cash must accompany each order.
JOHN WALSH, Franklin St., Melrose H'l'ds,
Mass.

GLADIOLI
John Lewis Childs, Flowerfield, L. I., N. Y.
For page see List of Advertisers.

Gladioli America, $6.00; Augusta, $6.00;
Halley, $7.00; Princeps, $7.00; Mrs. F. King,
$8.00; all first size bulbs. Booking orders
for Spring Delivery. THOMAS COGGER,
229 Laurel St., Melrose, Mass.

GLASS
Sharp, Partridge & Co., Chicago.
For page see List of Advertisers.

Parshelsky Bros., Inc., Brooklyn, N. Y.
For page see List of Advertisers.

Royal Glass Works, New York City.
For page see List of Advertisers.

Greenhouse glass, lowest prices. JOHN-
STON GLASS CO., Hartford City, Ind.

GLASS CUTTERS
Smith & Hemenway Co., New York City.
Red Devil Glass Cutter.
For page see List of Advertisers.

GLAZING POINTS
H. A. Dreer, Philadelphia, Pa.
Peerless Glazing Point.
For page see List of Advertisers.

GREENHOUSE BUILDING MATERIAL
King Construction Co., N. Tonawanda, N. Y.

Parshelsky Bros., Inc., Brooklyn, N. Y.
For page see List of Advertisers.

Lord & Burnham Co., New York City.
For page see List of Advertisers.

A. T. Stearns Lumber Co., Neponset,
Boston.
Pecky Cypress.

GREENHOUSE CONSTRUCTION
King Construction Co., N. Tonawanda, N. Y.
For page see List of Advertisers.

Foley Greenhouse Mfg. Co., Chicago, Ill.
For page see List of Advertisers.

Lord & Burnham Co., New York City.
For page see List of Advertisers.

Hitchings & Co., New York City.

A. T. Stearns Lumber Co., Boston, Mass.

S. Jacobs & Sons, Brooklyn, N. Y.

GUTTERS
King Construction Co., N. Tonawanda, N. Y.
King Channel Gutter.
For page see List of Advertisers.

HAIL INSURANCE
Florists' Hail Asso. of America.
J. G. Esler, Saddle River, N. J.
For page see List of Advertisers.

HARDY FERNS AND GREEN GOODS
Michigan Cut Flower Exchange, Detroit,
Mich.
For page see List of Advertisers.

Knud Nielsen, Evergreen, Ala.
Natural Green Sheet Moss, Fancy and Dag-
ger Ferns and Huckleberry Foliage.
For page see List of Advertisers.

The Kervan Co., New York.
For page see List of Advertisers.

HARDY PERENNIALS
Bay State Nurseries, No. Abington, Mass.
For page see List of Advertisers.

P. Ouwerkerk, Hoboken, N. J.
For page see List of Advertisers.

Palisades Nurseries, Sparkill, N. Y.
For page see List of Advertisers.

HEATING APPARATUS
Kroeschell Bros. Co., Chicago.
For page see List of Advertisers.

Lord & Burnham Co., New York City.
For page see List of Advertisers.

HOLLYHOCKS
Hollyhocks in separate colors and mixed,
fine large plants, $6.00 per 100, smaller
plants, $4.00 per 100. Cash. JAMES MOSS,
Johnsville, Pa.

HOT BED SASH
Parshelsky Bros., Inc., Brooklyn, N. Y.
For page see List of Advertisers.

Foley Greenhouse Construction Co.,
Chicago, Ill.
For page see List of Advertisers.

S. Jacobs & Sons, Brooklyn, N. Y.

Lord & Burnham Co., New York City.
For page see List of Advertisers.

A. T. Stearns Lumber Co., Neponset, Mass

HOSE
H. A. Dreer, Philadelphia, Pa.
For page see List of Advertisers.

HYACINTHS
6000 Hyacinths—No. 1, No. 2 and Miniatures in La Innocence, Gertrude Grand
Maître, King of Blues, Jaynes: No. 1, $22.00
per 1000; No. 2, $20.00 per 1000; Miniatures,
$14.00 per 1000. 3 in. Sprengeri, 3c. Mum
stock plants, 15 varieties, 50c. per doz.;
$3.00 per 100, or will exchange any of these
for Vincus Var., Geraniums, Ferns or
what have you? ROSENDALE GREEN-
HOUSES AND NURSERIES, Schenectady,
New York.

INSECTICIDES
Aphine Manufacturing Co., Madison, N. J.
Aphine and Fungine.
For page see List of Advertisers.

Nicotine Mfg. Co., St. Louis, Mo.
Aphis Punk and Nikoteen.
For page see List of Advertisers.

The Plantlife Co., New York City.
Plantlife Insecticides.
For page see List of Advertisers.

IRRIGATION EQUIPMENT
Skinner Irrigation Co., Brookline, Mass.
For page see List of Advertisers.

LILIUM MYRIOPHYLLUM
R. & J. Farquhar & Co., Boston, Mass.
For page see List of Advertisers.

LILY BULBS
Chas. Schwake & Co., New York City.
Horticultural Importers and Exporters
For page see List of Advertisers.

R. M. Ward & Co., New York, N. Y.
Japanese Lily Bulbs of Superior Quality.
For page see List of Advertisers.

Corp. of Chas. F. Meyer, New York City.
Meyer's T. Brand Giganteums.
For page see List of Advertisers.

Arthur T. Boddington Co., Inc., New York
City.
Lilium Longiflorum Formosum.
For page see List of Advertisers.

LILY OF THE VALLEY
Chas. Schwake & Co., Inc., New York City
Hohmann's Famous Lily of the Valley Pips
For page see List of Advertisers.

McHutchison & Co., New York City.
For page see List of Advertisers.

Loechner & Co., New York City.
Lily of the Valley Pips.
For page see List of Advertisers.

McHutchison & Co., New York City.
Berlin Valley Pips.
For page see List of Advertisers.

Arthur T. Boddington Co., Inc.,
New York City.
Cold Storage.
For page see List of Advertisers.

Fottler, Fiske, Rawson Co., Boston, Mass.
Cold Storage.

MASTICA
F. O. Pierce Co., New York City.
For page see List of Advertisers.

NATIONAL NURSERYMAN
National Nurseryman Publishing Co., Inc.,
Rochester, N. Y.
For page see List of Advertisers.

NIKOTEEN
Nicotine Mfg. Co., St. Louis, Mo.
For page see List of Advertisers.

NIKOTIANA
Aphine Mfg. Co., Madison, N. J.
For page see List of Advertisers.

NURSERY STOCK
P. Ouwerkerk, Weehawken Heights, N. J.
For page see List of Advertisers.

W. & T. Smith Co., Geneva, N. Y.
For page see List of Advertisers.

The D. Hill Nursery Co., Dundee, Ill.
Hill's Evergreens.
For page see List of Advertisers.

In writing to Advertisers kindly mention Horticulture

For List of Advertisers See Page 723

WHOLESALE FLORISTS
Buffalo, N. Y.

William F. Kasting Co., 383-87 Ellicott St.
For page see List of Advertisers.

Chicago

Poehlmann Bros. Co., Morton Grove, Ill.
For page see List of Advertisers.

Chicago Flower Growers' Association,
182 N. Wabash Ave., Chicago, Ill.
For page see List of Advertisers.

J. A.; Budlong, 184 North Wabash Ave.,
Chicago, Ill.
For page see List of Advertisers.

Detroit

Michigan Cut Flower Exchange, 204-266
Randolph St.
For page see List of Advertisers.

New York

H. E. Froment, 148 W. 28th St.
For page see List of Advertisers.

James McManus, 105 W. 28th St.
For page see List of Advertisers.

W. F. Sheridan, 133 W. 28th St.
For page see List of Advertisers.

P. J. Smith, 131 West 28th St., N. Y.
For page see List of Advertisers.

Moore, Hentz & Nash, 55 and 57 W. 26th St.
For page see List of Advertisers.

Charles Millang, 55 and 57 West 26th St.
For page see List of Advertisers.

W. P. Ford, New York
For page see List of Advertisers.

J. K. Allen, 118 West 28th St., New York
City.
For page see List of Advertisers.

The S. S. Pennock-Meehan Co., 117 West
28th St.
For page see List of Advertisers.

Traendly & Schenck, 436 6th Ave., between
26th and 27th Sts.
For page see List of Advertisers.

Badgley & Bishop, Inc., New York.
For page see List of Advertisers.

Woodrow & Marketos, 37 & 39 West 28th St.
For page see List of Advertisers.

Riedel & Meyer, Inc., 49 West 28th St.,
New York City.
For page see List of Advertisers.

George C. Siebrecht, 109 W. 28th St.
For page see List of Advertisers.

John Young & Co., 53 West 28th St.
For page see List of Advertisers.

M. C. Ford, 121 West 28th St.
For page see List of Advertisers.

B. S. Slinn, Jr., New York City.
For page see List of Advertisers.

United Cut Flower Co., Inc., 111 W. 28th St.
For page see List of Advertisers.

Guttman & Raynor, Inc., 101 W. 28th St.,
New York.
For page see List of Advertisers.

Leo, Niessen Co., 12th and Race Sts.
For page see List of Advertisers.

Philadelphia

Edward Reid, 1619-21 Ranstead St.
For page see List of Advertisers

The S. S. Pennock-Meehan Co., 1608-20
Ludlow St.
For page see List of Advertisers

Philadelphia Wholesale Flower Exchange,
1625 Ranstead St., Philadelphia, Pa.
For page see List of Advertisers.

Richmond, Ind.

E. G. Hill Co.
For page see List of Advertisers.

Rochester, N. Y.

George B. Hart, 24 Stone St.
For page see List of Advertisers.

Washington

The S. S. Pennock-Meehan Co., 1216 H St.,
N. W.
For page see List of Advertisers.

New Offers In This Issue

**ARAUCARIAS, FERNS AND KEN-
TIAS.**
James Vick's Sons, Rochester, N. Y.
For page see List of Advertisers.

CHRISTMAS PLANTS.
A. M. Davenport, Watertown, Mass.
For page see List of Advertisers.

CHRYSANTHEMUMS.
Elmer D. Smith & Co., Adrian, Mich.
For page see List of Advertisers.

CYPRIPEDIUMS.
S. S. Pennock-Meehan Co., Philadelphia, Pa.
For page see List of Advertisers.

DOUBLE PETUNIAS.
R. Vincent, Jr. & Sons Co.,
White Marsh, Md.
For page see List of Advertisers.

FLOWERS BY TELEGRAPH.
Henry R. Comley, 6 Park St., Boston, Mass.
For page see List of Advertisers.

FLOWERS BY TELEGRAPH.
I. L. Pillsbury, Galesburg, Ill.
For page see List of Advertisers.

FLOWERS BY TELEGRAPH.
Rochester Floral Co., Rochester, Minn.
For page see List of Advertisers.

**GLADIOLUS, COLVILLEI AND
NANUS.**
Arthur T. Boddington Co., Inc.,
New York City.
For page see List of Advertisers.

GREENHOUSE FITTINGS.
Advance Co., Richmond, Ind.
For page see List of Advertisers.

GREENHOUSE CONSTRUCTION.
Metropolitan Material Co., Brooklyn, N. Y.
For page see List of Advertisers.

KENILWORTH GIANT PANSY SEED
Chas. Frost, Kenilworth, N. J.
For page see List of Advertisers.

LILY OF THE VALLEY PIPS.
J. M. Thorburn & Co., New York City.
For page see List of Advertisers.

WHOLESALE FLORIST.
J. A. Budlong, 184 Wabash Ave., Chicago, Ill.
For page see List of Advertisers.

**YOUNG ROSES—OWN ROOT AND
GRAFTED.**
Montrose Greenhouses, Montrose, Mass.
For page see List of Advertisers.

WANTS, FOR SALE, Etc.

SITUATIONS WANTED

NURSERY SITUATION WANTED—As
foreman on ornamental nursery, thorough
knowledge of all ornamentals, their care,
propagation and landscape uses—life experience—references. M. B., care HORTI-
CULTURE.

FOR SALE

FOR SALE—Fresh from factory, new:
10 x 12, 16 x 18, 16 x 24, double thick. A
and B qualities. Market dropped. Now is
the time to buy and save money.
PARSHELSKY BROS., INC., 215-217
Havemeyer St., Brooklyn, N. Y.

MISCELLANEOUS

SECOND-HAND BOOKS WANTED—Any
set of agriculture. Horticulture preferred.
Give description and price. T. LAUPIIIT,
912 W. Green St., Urbana, Illinois.

In writing to Advertisers kindly mention Horticulture

FOR A

"Bigger, Better, Busier"

SEASON

The Special Fall Trade and Christmas Number of Horticulture will be issued under date of December 11. The paper will go to press on Thursday, December 9. Copy for Advertisements in this

Annual Trade Publicity Promoter

should reach us as many days in advance as possible so that every care and attention in setting-up, approving and placing may be exercised.

This issue will be made as attractive to the buying trade, as serviceable to the selling trade and as creditable to the publishers as any of its predecessors and as much better as zeal and experience can make it.

If you have plants, flowers, florists' supplies and horticultural requisites of any kind to offer to the leading trade buyers, here is your opportunity to "get there."

TRY IT!

British Horticulture

Chrysanthemum Show.

Judging from the recent annual show of the National Chrysanthemum Society the "Autumn Queen" still has many loyal supporters, whilst the attention given to it by British raisers shows no signs of diminution. The exhibition proved in every way successful, and the trade, despite the fact that they have been handicapped by the shortage of labor, made some meritorious displays. The new varieties recently certificated, particulars of which I recently forwarded, found many admirers. British raisers seem determined to reach a still higher standard amongst the exhibition blooms, whilst some of the newcomers will doubtless be found very useful for market work. Keen interest was taken in a fine new golden bronze bloom, Edith Cavell, shown by Wells & Co., who have introduced in recent years many present day popular varieties. Some excellent effects were produced by the bold groups arranged by the leading specialists. There was a bank of varied hues at one end of the hall, containing 150 Japanese varieties, ranging from the neat pompons to the massive show blooms. Commercial growers were attracted by a new variety, Market Bronze, raised by Norman Davis. It has been raised from Bronze Soleil d'Octobre and December Gold, and has the combined good qualities of its parents.

W.H. Adsett.

NEW CORPORATIONS.

Evansville, Ind.—McCoy Nut Nurseries, capital stock, $30,000. Incorporators, Robert L. McCoy, Geo. Durkee and P. E. Tichenor.

Pittsburgh, Pa.—Keystone State Nurseries, to grow, buy and sell nursery stock wholesale and retail. Incorporators, J. M., F. R. and D. G. George.

Rhinelander, Wis.—Rhinelander Nursery Co., capital stock, $10,000. Incorporators, D. F. Recker, A. E. Weesner, J. O. Moen, D. R. Hanford, C. P. Crosby and J. Weisman.

PERSONAL.

Sheridan H. Hall, florist, of Salem, Mass., and Miss Irene Cutting, were married Nov. 26th.

Alfred Warner, formerly of Chicago, is now associated with Honaker, the Florist, Lexington, Ky.

Mt. Clemens, Mich. — Fred Breitmeyer has a promising pink sport from Ophelia rose.

Flower Market Reports

(Continued from page 741)

WASHINGTON The Thanksgiving Day business this year was above normal. All classes of stock sold well and in some of the lines the retailers and wholesalers alike experienced a general clean-up. There was a heavy run on lily of the valley which replaced orchids, now a great scarcity. Violets sold well and American Beauties were in good demand. There are still large quantities of extra fine chrysanthemums including Bonnaffon, William Turner, Dr. Enguehard, the Chadwicks and Eatons. Carnations are improving in quality and quantity and are selling fairly well. There are few gardenias yet to be had. Poinsettia made its appearance during the week. Sweet peas are to be had in limited quantities but are very good. There are not enough of the smaller and medium grade roses to go around and prices on roses have generally advanced as usual at this time of the year.

THE CEDAR OF LEBANON.

The Cedar of Lebanon (*Cedrus Libani*) in the Arboretum shows the importance of careful selection of the seeds from which to raise trees for any particular climate. One of the fir trees of Asia Minor, *Abies cilicica*, has been growing for many years in New England where it has proved to be one of the best of all conifers of its class to cultivate here as an ornamental tree. With this fir the Cedar or Lebanon grows in Asia Minor on the Anti-Taurus, far north of the Lebanon range in Palestine and in a much colder climate. As the Palestine cedar is not hardy here in New England the Arboretum had seeds of this tree collected on the Anti-Tarus with the view of attempting to introduce a hardy race of cedars into New England. The seeds were sown here in the spring of 1902 and a large number of plants were raised. They all proved perfectly hardy, not one having suffered from drought or cold. Some, however, have been lost in attempts at transplanting, for no other tree here has proved so difficult to move. The average height of all these young cedars in the Arboretum is now about

13 feet. The tallest is 21 feet high and there is another specimen 20 feet high. It is doubtful if any other conifer can be grown in New England from seed to the height of 21 feet in 13 years.— *Arnold Arboretum Bulletin.*

PREVENTING DEATH OF CLEMATIS PLANTS.

The sudden dying of clematis plants, especially wherever the large-flowered kinds are grown extensively in America and Europe, has been noted for many years, and the cause and methods for prevention of this disease have recently been reported in the Journal of Agricultural Research of the United States Department of Agriculture, by W. O. Gloyer of the New York Agricultural Experiment Station at Geneva, N. Y. This investigator found that the primary cause of the dying of these plants is a fungus known as Ascochyta clematidina. Experiments have shown that the transferring of this fungus to healthy plants causes them to take the disease.

The disease shows itself differently on various species. On hybrids grown in the field it is a stem-rot, while at the greenhouse where cuttings are propagated it is a leaf-spot as well as a stem-rot. On the clematis paniculata the disease takes both forms.

The following methods for controlling this fungus are recommended: There is less disease when the hybrids are supported while growing than when they are permitted to trail on the ground. In the case of the clematis paniculata, however, the selling price of this variety does not warrant incurring the expense of supports. The authority in this case advises transplanting the plants from beds to the open field after the first year and placing them far enough apart to prevent wilting, which is always a condition favorable to the disease. The following spray applied lightly controls the disease on clematis paniculata growing in the beds and on cuttings in the greenhouse: One pound of laundry soap and 6 pounds of sulphur to 15 gallons of water. The disease can be controlled on the hybrids in the forcing frames or in the greenhouse by the use of sprays. In all cases it is best to remove the diseased leaves and dead vines before spraying. It is particularly important to clear out such leaves and vines, especially if the plant is wintering outdoors, as the fungus is able to survive cold weather. This indicates also that the same beds should not be used for clematis during successive years.

The retail purchaser of clematis can prevent the dying of plants by taking proper simple precautions. The plants should be placed in good soil, well drained and on a sunny exposure. As soon as the new shoots have formed the old vine tissue should be carefully cut away close to the new shoots, removing all traces of the brown, discolored wood in which the fungus is to be found. Proper ventilation is obtained by training the plants to a strong trellis.

EXCHANGE PROFESSORSHIP IN LANDSCAPE GARDENING.

The Massachusetts Agricultural College and the University of Illinois have arranged an exchange professorship in Landscape Gardening for the present year. Professor R. R. Root, head of the department in Illinois, will come to Massachusetts for two weeks in December to give a special course of lectures in Landscape Gardening. During the same time Professor F. A. Waugh, head of the department at the Massachusetts Agricultural College, will go to Illinois and deliver a course of lectures and exercises before Professor Root's students.

This is a somewhat novel departure in college teaching, but has in it the promise of success. It will, of course, be a distinct advantage to the students in both institutions to get in touch with another teacher and to secure a new point of view. It is expected to arouse considerable interest in the course by this method. The Massachusetts Agricultural College and the University of Illinois have two of the largest and strongest departments of Landscape Gardening in America, and both are endeavoring to turn out practical men well equipped for the profession. In the past much of the teaching in this field has been of the strictly amateur variety. While the amateur point of view is highly important in gardening and should be constantly encouraged, it is equally important that a few institutions should give thoroughgoing professional courses not only in agriculture, horticulture, floriculture, forestry, etc., but in the highly specialized field of Landscape Gardening.

MASSACHUSETTS AGRICULTURAL COLLEGE NOTES.

The landscape gardening class made a trip recently to several of the estates in town for the purpose of studying planting and formal garden layouts. Among the places visited were the Carruth estate and Prof. Clark's estate.

The junior pomology students have been getting much practical work in pruning in renovating Prof. Todd's orchard at Amherst College.

The students in floriculture are building a cement cold frame thirty feet long. The cost of the entire frame is $45.00.

GREENHOUSES BUILDING OR CONTEMPLATED.

Bridgeport, Ct.—W. B. Leigh, Park avenue, additions.

Vincennes, Ind.—Paul C. Schulze, Main street, one house.

Seymour, Ct.—Thomas J. Kelleher, Maple street, one house.

Pittsfield, Mass.—Drake & Engleman, one house in spring.

Maywood, Ill.—Albert F. Amling Co., nine houses, each 44x950, American Greenhouse Mfg. Co. construction.

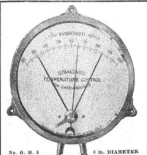

F. B. Abrams House at Blue Point, N. Y.

The greenhouse and work room are both iron frame. One is 63 x 100. The other 60 x 100.

The whole, that fuel around this house in the winter are certainly fierce. That's why we used lattice rafters to stiffen the gables.

BEFORE I tell you about our friend Abrams and his houses, let me first tell you of some good fruits of ours out at Kirkwood, Missouri, 20 miles from St. Louis. I was out there the first week, in November, at the extent of an 8,000 miles trip that the firm hustled me out to make angh a number of the numerous growers in the West that we have built for in the past year.

Th man I wanted to see at Kirkwood was W. J. Piled. Th genial citizen who accommodatingly drov me over in his car was amazed whi he got to Pilcher's place to find su an ...e plant, and to learn that he had "sen way to Old ; for his big iron frame house 72 x 200 feet. whi ... we put up for him last year. Turning to me, he said, "Why, I had no idea Pher had a layout like this. Wy . it dip seems two or three years ago whe he started wth his first little shack."

"What has all this to do with Abrams?" you ask.

Just this much—Both men have developed their business in a surprisingly short time to the conclusion that every cent our iron frame houses cost was a mighty good invest-

ment. Pilcher is sending to the St. Louis market some of the finest roses grown in that section and everybody on the 25th Street Market at New York knows the high quality and dependableness of Mr. Abrams' Carnations, which he is growing so successfully in his 63 x 400 "Foster."

About the first iron frame power house and work room we put up was for Thomas Roland at Revere, Mass. When Mr. Abrams came to build, he saw the advantage of its construction and we erected one for him, 49 x 100 feet.

The boilers are placed on the same level as the greenhouse floor and the heating system is vacuum.

We do not say that either Mr. Pilcher or Mr. Abrams would not be the prominent growers they now are if they hadn't built our iron frames; but it is a conspicuous fact that when they began sending their cut from these houses, they began to be talked about in the market. If you have the least doubt whether it pays to build a Lord & Burnham house, let us send you (entirely at our expense), to some who own them. See the houses; and talk with their owners. It's one of the surest ways we know of to sell you one of our houses.

HORTICULTURE

View in Flower Store of Samuel Murray, Kansas City, Mo.

CHRISTMAS NUMBER

LIST OF ADVERTISERS

FOR BUYERS' DIRECTORY AND READY REFERENCE GUIDE
SEE PAGES 796, 797, 798, 799

NOTES ON CULTURE OF FLORISTS' STOCK

CONDUCTED BY

John J. M. Farrell

Questions by our readers in line with any of the topics presented on this page will be cordially received and promptly answered by Mr. Farrell. Such communications should invariably be addressed to the office of HORTICULTURE.
"If vain our toil, we ought to blame the culture, not the soil."—*Pope.*

Carnations

The second tier of wire and string supports will now be needed so the stems will grow straight and some of the taller ones will also soon need the third support. It can be put on just as easily now as later and will not be in the way. Look after the disbudding from now on. Not only will it enlarge the bloom, but it will also help to stiffen the stems. If disbudding is ever needed it is at this season. One great mistake which inexperienced growers often make is to close the ventilators tight in the evening after a bright day, thinking to corral a lot of heat in a house. It is better to run a little more heat and have a crack of air on all night. Plenty of fresh air is the best preventive of disease. It makes no difference whether the temperature is abnormally high or low, fresh air will aid the plants to bear the unnatural conditions.

Care of Palms

Most palms should have plenty of light during the winter, only keeping enough shade so they will not scorch. Do not neglect syringing, and, once a month, give them a good sponging. All palms like a short winter season of rest. This can be brought about by lower temperature and drier atmosphere with less water at the roots. At all seasons of the year they should have as much air as possible according to outside weather conditions.

Pelargoniums

Those that were struck in September will require now or before long a 4-inch pot. Use a compost of fibrous loam three parts and well rotted manure one part somewhat roughly broken up and give plenty of drainage. Give them uniform ventilation whenever possible. These plants like a dry atmosphere. When they have filled their pots with roots they can be given a shift. Fumigate with tobacco smoke regularly once a week. Have the temperature run anywhere from 45 to 50 degrees at night with usual rise during the day. Be very careful and do not apply water until the soil is quite dry.

Propagation of Carnations

Having decided to begin propagating your carnations and having overhauled and whitewashed the bench, filling in the sand is the next step. The whitewash should be thoroughly dried before any sand is put on. Fill in to a depth of about three inches or a little over before it is packed down. It is well to screen all propagating sand to make sure there is no trash of any kind or lumps of clay in it. When packed down it should be two and one-half inches deep. When inserting the cuttings always begin at the back of the bench and work towards you, and when one row is full draw another line to the right of it and one and one-half to two inches away, and begin inserting from the back again. When you have inserted the last cutting then place the label directly in front of it as though it were a cutting. On this label should be written plainly the name of the variety in full and the date they were inserted.

Sweet Peas

Great care is necessary to avoid a too dry or too moist atmosphere. An excess of fire heat and aridity will bring red spider, while opposite conditions with irregular ventilation will just as surely cause an attack of mildew. Give uniform minimum temperature of about 50 degrees. There are no days so cold but some ventilation can be given. On bright days the thermometer can run up to 60 degrees before air is given, and, with free ventilation a shade maximum of 70 degrees is all right. At this season it is safer to underfeed rather than the opposite. Avoid the use of forcing stimulants. Safer foods are cow or sheep manure, applied either in liquid form or as a top-dressing, which can be lightly forked in. The plants are unable to assimilate anything like the same amount of plant food now as two months hence. Tying must be regularly attended to for once any stems become bent the flowers are unsalable.

Double Sweet Alyssum

Stock plants lifted early in the Autumn, and potted should be given a position at about 55 degrees at night. These will later on make fine material for cuttings. They can be propagated in a cool propagating bed.

Next Week:—Asparagus plumosus; Calanthes; Decorative Ferns; Manure for Crops; Propagation.

HORTICULTURE

VOL. XXII   **DECEMBER 11, 1915**   **NO. 24**

PUBLISHED WEEKLY BY

HORTICULTURE PUBLISHING CO.

147 Summer Street, Boston, Mass.

Telephone, Oxford 292.
WM. J. STEWART, Editor and Manager.

SUBSCRIPTION RATES:
One Year, in advance, $1.00; To Foreign Countries, $2.00; To
Canada, $1.50.

ADVERTISING RATES:

Per inch, 30 inches to page............................... $1.00
Discounts on Contracts for consecutive insertions, as follows:
   One month (4 times), 5 per cent.; three months (13 times), 10
per cent.; six months (26 times), 20 per cent.; one year (52 times),
30 per cent.
   Page and half page space, special rates on application.

Entered as second-class matter December 8, 1914, at the Post Office
at Boston, Mass., under the Act of Congress of March 3, 1879.

CONTENTS

Good Wishes

According to custom, HORTICULTURE herewith presents its eleventh Annual Greeting to the trade in whose interest it works, with cordial good wishes for a successful and joyous Christmas, and increased prosperity for the New Year which is soon to open. Considering the world-wide disturbed condition of horticultural trade, the year that has passed since we last wished our readers a merry Christmas has not been an altogether bad one, and the commercial enterprises with which we are in touch have, as a rule, weathered the storms in a manner creditable to the stability of the horticultural industries and full of promise for a brilliant future. The signs are certainly auspicious for a greatly improved business this season, as anyone whose work brings him close to the active and farseeing men who set the pace for the different departments of commercial horticulture must already have convincingly learned. We hope the realization will not fall short but far exceed the promise which now appears so bright in contrast with the somewhat gloomy outlook of one year ago.

One province of the flower show

Commendable activity is observed in the office of the Secretary of the S. A. F. in the preparatory work for the Fourth National Flower Show at Philadelphia as indicated in the prospectus of special prizes appearing in this issue. We are particularly pleased to note the special effort made by the American Carnation Society to bring out exhibits which shall demonstrate the popular uses to which the divine flower may be put. This is one very essential province of the flower show, that it may accomplish its object as an educator of the people of the crowded town in the knowledge of and appreciation for Nature's products, to proclaim the gospel of beauty and to arrouse a universal desire to brighten life by the possession of these gems of the florists' art. In the years to come the flower show is destined to fill a very prominent part in the great uplift work in which the gardener and florist and Nature work hand in hand and no means should be neglected which may encourage the use of flowers in the home, for personal adornment, as tributes of affection between friends and as an approved accompaniment for all occasions, public or private, which draw people together. HORTICULTURE has from the first considered this one of its chief duties to the art and to the craft, to make our flower shows recognized exponents not only of advanced cultural skill but of good taste and appropriateness in the arrangement and use of the material we exhibit.

Still Improving

Anybody who had been thinking that the limit of development in certain classes of florists' flowers, such as the roses, carnations and chrysanthemums, had been reached, and who took opportunity to attend a few of the fall flower shows, must have found there sufficient evidence to the contrary to modify his previous conclusions. At the exhibitions and in other places that have come under our notice we have seen enough to convince us in regard to these three specialties that among the novelties now ready or soon to be put out there are varieties that in one or more respects will show a material advance over the older sorts. In the development of the forcing rose we think we can see a greater evolution going on than in any of the other florists' flowers. Without specifying varieties, we can discern distinct advances in the qualities of fragrance, form, persistence and uniformity of bloom and the welcome extended by the public to the diminutive flowered classes shows a gratifying tendency to break away somewhat from the the monotonous preference for bigness which prevailed in times past. The same is equally true in regard to the chrysanthemum, as evinced in the rapidly growing appreciation of the smaller flowered types and this popularity is being handsomely stimulated in the way of pompons and singles of purer colors, better formed flowers and improved habit of growth for cutting. In the carnation, the most welcome advance appears to be on a line imperatively needed if the carnation is to retain its place in the flower market—that of inherent good keeping quality after being cut. If the hybridists can do this and, retaining all the other good points characteristic of the modern carnation, restore this grand old trait which had so much to do with the popularity of the pioneer sorts, the building of more carnation houses can go on without fear of over-production.

Grevillea robusta

The Grevillea is a valuable decorative plant because of its graceful, grayish foliage. The plant is a native of Australia and in nature attains a height of 150 feet It is used in California and Florida as a shade tree. Some species make useful timber trees. It is a very rapid grower and will stand a considerable amount of drouth. It will also stand some frost.

In the north, it is used in window boxes, baskets, and other receptacles and is a good conservatory plant. For decorative purposes, the plant is seldom used over five feet in height. After it attains this height the lower leaves begin to drop off and the plant begins to become ragged looking.

The Grevillea is propagated mostly by seed sown late in winter or in spring (March). As soon as they are large enough to handle, the young plants should be transplanted into small pots and shifted as they grow. When they reach the three-inch size, plunge them to the rims in a frame until they are ready for the five-inch pots. The plants will stand much hard usage and neglect and will not need to be shaded. They require frequent repotting as they are rapid growers. A cool temperature is best for them—say 50 degrees. It does not pay to carry the old stock over from year to year and fresh stock should be propagated every year. The one-year-old plants make the best specimens, but rapidly deteriorate in decorative value after that.

There are two varieties of G. robusta—pyramidalis and Fosteri. The latter has silvery foliage with red instead of yellow flowers and it is also a stronger grower. G. Banksii and G. glabrata are used to some extent in Europe, but in this country G. robusta is practically the only one grown.   C. E. WILDON.
Amherst, Mass.

A Christmas Story With a Moral

For generations, national, state and local agencies upheld by the pro rata contribution from every one of us, have been working hard to increase production in horticulture. Production increases of course; how about distribution?

What's the use of production without distribution? We don't seem to move much on the distribution proposition.

For instance: (This is the story) We called on one of our best growers one day and suggested that in view of the fact that he had one of the finest lots of well-grown stock, well finished and just right for the market, he ought to advertise it. He looked at us with that super-wise air, and said, George, we don't have to advertise. Good goods sell themselves!

Good goods sell themselves? My lord! More people have fallen by the wayside on that fallacy than anything else I can think of. Good goods do not sell themselves. If you have the good goods haven't you got to tell people about it? There are very many ways to do this. You can send men out on the road; you can exhibit; you can use many different ways—the cost of same being all a charge on distribution.

The late Godfrey Aschmann once told me: (This is the moral) that he could go anywhere around this old city and buy first-class well-grown stuff from growers who did not advertise, for twenty-five cents and sell it for a dollar. Did that show that good goods sold themselves? No sir. It showed that the good advertiser was the fellow that sold the goods and reaped the lion's share of the profit, and it's not only people like Aschmann but every big house. They advertise, spend their good money and get the trade. When they see a bargain they are quite justified in picking it up because they have the outlet which the non-advertiser hasn't.

The science and practice of distribution is the big thing for the trade to get busy on at this minute. Production without its corollary is no good. And don't forget that the cost of distribution may be as great if not much greater than the cost of production. What a thing costs to produce has nothing to do with the cost of marketing it.

You can't divorce the two propositions, production and distribution. Advertising is just as much one of the legitimate costs of production as food and clothes for the kid until it is able to earn its own living.

If you have a good thing you must tell them about it —and to buy a thousand tongues you must remember that the laborer is worthy of his hire.

Some sermon! Wishing you all a Merry Xmas.

G. C. Watson

ROSE GROWING UNDER GLASS

CONDUCTED BY

Arthur Ruzicka

Questions by our readers in line with any of the topics presented on this page will be cordially received and promptly answered by Mr. Ruzicka. Such communications should invariably be addressed to the office of HORTICULTURE.

Lining the Boxes

With the first fall of snow here and there, and the thermometer standing around 22 in the morning, boxes will need to have more paper in them when shipping to the market. Make sure to get the paper into the corners well, as it is there where the cold will work in as a rule. It will be a good idea to order some heavy wrapping paper so that the boxes can be wrapped on the outside when severe weather comes along. Paper is not very expensive, and roses are worth quite a little money and will be worth more as the holidays come around. When packing it is well to lift the roses out of the jars so as to shake off a good deal of the water which would stick to the stems. This water would soak the paper lining. Cold will penetrate the wet paper very easily.

Soil for the Season's Potting

If this has not been put under cover or covered up as yet it should be done at once for it may not be long before the ground will freeze up, and even if it did thaw out again the work will not be as easy or as pleasant to do later. Straw, leaves, cornstalks, any of these can be used but the best will be coarse horse manure. This will keep the soil much cleaner, and it is much warmer than straw or leaves alone. The same is true of sand. If there is a sand pit on the place cover up a part of it so that you can get to the sand even in the most severe weather. If a storage house is to be had so much the better but it must be right near the greenhouses so that the extra handling of the soil and sand would not be too expensive.

The Xmas Rush

The prospect for good business is much better this year than it has been for several years past. With the holidays only a fortnight away it is high time to see that everything is ready and orders placed for greens so that there will be no confusion when all the customers will want to get their flowers at the one time. Growers who do not bother doing any retail work will miss a good deal of fun and some money, as often many roses can be sold to much better advantage to the home trade than they could be in the wholesale market and the selling cost is not very large—practically nothing in most places. A little good advertising in the local papers will help wonderfully in developing this trade. In doing this do not adopt the bargain counter kind of advertising. Flowers are one of God's greatest gifts to man and they should be treated as something sacred. Then, too, there are so many ads. in the papers that are never read only when people happen to be in the market for certain articles. Have your ad. written neatly and well. Speak of the quality of the flowers, the joy they bring, rather than the price. Make your ad. an oasis on the desert of advertising, for then the eye will be at-tracted to it at once and the ad. will be read through before the readers realize that it is an advertisement. It is different when advertising to the trade as it is best then to say what you have to sell and the price. But with retail trade it is different, and the grower or retailer who realizes this will get most out of his investment and not an expense and a well advertised name and business is one of the greatest assets any one can have. Needless to say the goods must be there to back up the ads. and so must the service, as these win the confidence of the readers and customers.

Damage by Thrips

Mr. Arthur Ruzicka:

Dear Sir—Am a most interested reader of your notes on rose growing in HORTICULTURE, and as I see you answer questions of readers, am venturing a request for information. I have some apparently good bushes of outdoor roses, white ones, variety unknown, that seem to wish to bear pretty good blooms, but the buds never materialize perfectly. They always have a brown, chewed up sort of look when they come out. It is evidently not an insect; a neighbor thinks it is a blight. Now is that a good enough description to mean anything to you, and if so can you give me any hints as to what to do? I have come into possession of a lot of rather old, neglected bushes and want to see if I can make anything good out of them. Might it be best to simply cut down these no-account bushes and start new good ones, or shall I give them a chance?

Tryon, N. C.   C. M. B.

The trouble with your buds is caused by thrips, very small insects that delight in attacking the best roses that grow. As near as I can tell there are several species, some of which are so small as to be invisible without the aid of a microscope. To rid the buds and plants of these, spray with Aphine every day early in the morning until the rose buds show signs of improvement. Then spray three times a week. It will also be of advantage to spray and keep the plants well sprayed with brown sugar dissolved in water, with a little paris green added to it. The amount of the poison should not be very large, as it is very apt to burn some of the leaves. About one-half a teaspoonful to a gallon of water will be plenty. This spray should be applied after every rain or right after watering in the morning, as water will wash this off and the object is to keep the spray there all the time so that the thrips will eat it, and of course if they do so once they will not do so again. We prefer the brown sugar to the white granulated for the former has an odor which the latter lacks. In using Aphine it is well to direct the spray right on the buds as it is a contact poison and must touch the insects it is to kill. Do all spraying early in the morning before the sun gets hot and make sure that the soil is plenty wet enough around the roots of the plants. Regarding the old rose bushes you mention I would certainly give them a chance for there are some nice varieties in these old collections at times. To insure an abundance of roses, I would recommend planting plenty of new ones besides, so that there will be no disappointment.

VALUABLE SHRUBS FOR THE AUTUMN GARDEN

FROM THE ARNOLD ARBORETUM BULLETIN.

Evonymus Bungeanus, which has been an inhabitant of the Arboretum for thirty years, deserves more general cultivation than it has yet received in this country. It is a small tree or treelike shrub with slender rather pendulous branches and narrow, pointed, pale green leaves, which turn yellow or yellow and red, but the great beauty of this plant is in the rose-colored fruit which every year is produced in great quantities and remains on the branches for several weeks after the leaves have fallen, making this native of northern China a desirable plant for the autumn garden.

Evonymus lanceifolius. This shrub, which is one of Wilson's introductions from western China, promises to become a valuable garden plant in this climate. On the mountains of western China it grows as a large bush or occasionally as a tree, and is sometimes fifty feet high with a tall trunk nearly a foot in diameter. In the Arboretum it is perfectly hardy and is now a bush from three to four feet tall and broad, covered with bright scarlet fruit and leaves which partly turn to shades of orange and red. In the size and brilliancy of the fruit few of the plants of this group equal this Chinese species.

Evonymus yedoensis. After the leaves have fallen from this Japanese plant in the Evonymus Group, the large rose-colored fruits which cover the naked branches make it one of the conspicuous plants in the Arboretum.

Evonymus semipersistens. There is a large specimen of this little known Chinese plant in the collection. Fruit of this Evonymus has no ornamental value for it is small and hidden by the foliage, and its value is found in the persistence of the leaves which remain perfectly green and do not fall until December. This is one of the handsomest of the shrubs in the Arboretum which retain their foliage, without change in color until the beginning of winter. Such plants are valuable in the autumn garden to contrast with plants of brilliant autumn coloring. Another valuable plant for this purpose is

Magnolia glauca, the Sweet Bay of the Atlantic and Gulf Coast regions from Massachusetts to Texas, with bright shining leaves which are silvery white on the lower surface and will not become discolored or fall until December. Attention has often been called in these Bulletins to the value of this tree in New England gardens. Few deciduous-leaved trees have more beautiful and more persistent foliage; the cup-shaped creamy white flowers continue to open during at least two months of early summer and fill the air with their abundant fragrance, and the fruit, like that of all the Magnolias, is interesting and handsome when the bright red seeds hang from it on slender threads.

Ligustrum vulgare. This is the European Privet and another plant which retains its dark green leaves well into the winter. During the last twenty or thirty years much attention has been paid by botanists and gardeners to the Privets of Eastern Asia where many species have been discovered. None of these, however, are as valuable in this climate as the European species, which is perhaps the handsomest here of all black-fruited shrubs. The bright shining fruit is borne in compact clusters which are on the ends of the branches and stand up well above the dark green lustrous leaves; they remain on the plants during the early winter months and after the leaves have fallen. During the first half of the nineteenth century this Privet was a common garden plant in the northern United States where it was much used in hedges; and it is now sparingly naturalized in the northern and middle states. There are several forms of this Privet in cultivation, including one yellow fruit (var. *chlorocarpum*) which can now be seen covered with fruit in the Shrub Collection. The variety *foliolosum* is also growing here; this has rather narrower leaves and larger fruits than the common form and at this season of the year is one of the handsomest plants in the Arboretum.

Myrica carolinensis. This is the common Wax Myrtle of the northern United States and one of the plants which holds its dark green shining leaves very late in the autumn without change of color. The plants are covered with their small gray fruits, unlike in color those of any other plant hardy in this climate. Naturally the Wax Myrtle grows on sterile sandy soil and, spreading into wide masses, makes attractive thousands of acres of barren fields during several months of the year. The Wax Myrtle takes kindly to cultivation; in good soil it grows rapidly and forms a tall round-headed shrub, and it can be used with advantage to cover soil so poor that few plants can be kept alive in it. From the waxy substance which covers the seeds of this shrub and that of the arborescent *Myrica cerifera* of the southern coast early settlers in America made wax candles which are still occasionally produced in some parts of Cape Cod where *Myrica carolinensis* grows in immense quantities.

Lonicera Maackii, var. podocarpa. Of the plants in the Arboretum conspicuous for the beauty of their fruit in autumn none perhaps is more beautiful than this Honeysuckle which was introduced by Wilson from central China. It is a large, vigorous and hardy shrub with wide-spreading branches and open habit. The flowers are larger than this of most Honeysuckles and are white and in one form white slightly tinged with rose color. The period of the greatest beauty of this plant, however, is late October, when it is still covered with bright green leaves and the large scarlet lustrous fruits are only just ripe. The type of this species, *Lonicera Maackii*, is a native of eastern Siberia and is an old inhabitant of the Arboretum. It is a narrow shrub with stems more erect than those of the form from central China. The flowers are pure white, and more beautiful than those of the Chinese plant, but the fruit

NEW HERBACEOUS SPIRAEAS IN MT. DESERT NURSERIES, BAR HARBOR, ME.

which is now ripe is smaller, and the leaves have already fallen.

Ribes fasciculatum, var. chinense. This Chinese Currant is interesting because it is the only species here with fruit which does not ripen until late in the autumn. The beauty of the scarlet fruit is increased, too, at this time by the color of the leaves which turn to bright shades of orange and scarlet.

Evonymus radicans, var. vegetus. Attention is again called to this form of a well known plant from Japan, fruit pale yellow or nearly white, and as it ripens the bright orange color of the seeds is displayed. This northern variety is the best for general cultivation in this climate as it appears to be hardier than more southern forms; the leaves are broader and it flowers and fruits much more freely; indeed it is the only form which produces much fruit in the Arboretum and the fruit adds greatly to the beauty of the plants. Like the other vigorous growing varieties it may be grown against a wall to which it clings firmly or as a broad, round-headed bush. There is a form of this Evonymus with leaves hardly a quarter of an inch long and known both as var. *minimus* and as var. *kewensis* which appears to be still little known in the United States. It is a good plant for the rock garden and for the margins of garden walks. The form from western China discovered by Wilson, var. *acutus*, has narrower pointed leaves distinctly veined below. Here in the Arboretum the plants of this form lie flat on the ground and show no tendency to rise and form a bush. They have proved perfectly hardy but have not flowered yet. If this form retains in cultivation the prostrate stems of its present state it may prove an excellent subject for covering the ground under trees and shrubs.

Asiatic Crabapples. Many of these small trees and shrubs have been well covered with fruit this year. When the whole group is considered few plants are more valuable for garden decoration in this climate if attention is paid to keeping them free from the scale insects which are destructive to all plants of the Apple tribe. All the Asiatic Crabs are perfectly hardy; they grow quickly in good soil, and many of them begin to flower and produce fruit when only a few years old. No plants are more beautiful at the end of May when they are covered with their countless pink and white flowers; and on some of them the fruit is showy and long persistent. A few of the conspicuous plants are *Malus ringo* with yellow fruit, interesting as the plant from which the Apple cultivated in China has been derived, and the only Apple cultivated in Japan until recent years; *Malus floribunda* and the hybrid raised in the Arboretum from that species, *Malus Arnoldiana*, with yellow fruits; *Malus zumi* and *M. Sargentii* from Japan with bright scarlet fruit; the latter is the only Apple which is shrubby in habit. Interesting, too, is the form of the Japanese *Malus toringo* from northern China with small fruits yellow on some plants and red on others. These are only a few of the plants in this large collection which at this time deserve careful study.

CATTLEYAS FOR CUT FLOWERS

It is a well established fact that the trade for orchid bloom has not suffered to the same extent as that of many other classes of flowers at the hands of the price-cutting competitor; for the greater part of the year the demand for first-class Cattleya blooms is in excess of the supply. (Hardly holds true in the U. S. now, Ed.) Certain it is that there are periods when returns are lower than usual, as, for instance, at the height of the flowering season of Cattleya Mossiæ, but, as a rule, this state of things does not last for long, and when once the back of this crop is broken there is a rise to the normal and more satisfactory prices.

The cause of this fall is, no doubt, the great quantity of flowers of this particular species that find their way into the markets, mainly due to the large importations of collected pieces which have reached these shores during recent years, often to be sold at very low figures, thus causing a glut of flowers in their season. But even then it is a question whether the crop is not remunerative. It is seldom that a lower figure than 6s. ($1.50) per dozen is reached even on a chance sale, and although cases have been known where returns have been lower than this they can only be reckoned as rare exceptions.

Anyone contemplating taking up this interesting and attractive branch of the trade would do well to pay very careful attention to the stocking of the houses, for by this means only can the desired result be brought about. No haphazard buying of plants must be tolerated, but each purchase be made in accordance with a fixed plan of getting together such a stock of plants, both species and hybrids, as will maintain a regular and even supply of flowers throughout the year. This is one of the chief items towards establishing and holding a successful market and shop trade; the grower should, by careful selection, build up his stock in accordance with this idea.

Although it is upon species that we must rely for the bulk of flowers, yet judicious selections of quantities of hybrids should be introduced with a view to filling in the otherwise inevitable blank periods between the respective flowering seasons. Such hybrids may be picked up very reasonably now, as owing to the great advance made by hybridists during recent years many of the old-time good things are of little more value than ordinary Lælia and Cattleya species. Strong and healthy pieces only should be purchased, whether established or freshly imported, and it is advisable to invest as much as possible in imported stuff, for there is always the chance of getting one or two really good things, which, if well disposed of, might pay for the whole consignment or a large part thereof.

To a large extent the sale for Orchid bloom is a bespoke trade, and, speaking generally, there is room for a better supply during the autumn and winter months. It is at these periods and during early spring that prices rule higher than otherwise. A good stock of Cattleya Gaskelliana, labiata, Trianæ, and any hybrids flowering about the same time, should be grown. As regards prices realized for individual species, Cattleya Warscewiczii (C. gigas of the trade) takes the lead, although this good point is handicapped by its shyness of flowering. The variety Sanderiana is more free in this respect than the type. One great mistake made with this species by many amateurs is the use of too heavy shading material during the growing and flowering periods. When the growths are well advanced only sufficient shade to prevent actual scorching of the foliage should be applied, and all means employed to obtain that hard and leathery texture of both pseudo-bulbs and leaves as is seen on newly imported plants. This condition can only be brought about by thorough ripening with a maximum of air and light. Therefore, this species should be allotted either a separate house or a complete portion of one. Other plants, less adapted to withstanding such extremes, can then receive their requisite treatment. I make no pretence at giving any very explicit instructions as to growing Cattleyas, but I would like, *en passant*, to record an opinion that many a man, otherwise a first-class grower, is far too lavish with his shading and watering pot. In justification of this statement I would call attention to the weak and sappy nature of a large proportion of the plants offered for sale in our orchid auction rooms.

Many Lælio-Cattleyas, apart from their usefulness as inter-season flowering plants, are strongly recommended on account of their floriferous nature, as, for instance, many Lælia purpurata hybrids, of which callisoglossa and Canhamiana are well-known examples. It is advisable to avoid any large quantities of species or hybrids of other colors than mauve, pink, or white with colored lips, for which there is always a sure demand at one price or another, whereas yellow and similar shades are more often than not a chance value pure and simple. Cattleya Dowiana and C. aurea might, perhaps, be classed as an exception to this rule, as they generally sell on sight, but it is questionable whether there would ever be that sure demand for this gorgeous member of the aristocracy of the floral world as exists for those of mauve tints.—*A. R. M., The Orchid World, London.*

SOCIETY of AMERICAN FLORISTS

Fourth National Flower Show, Philadelphia, March 25 to April 2, 1916.

With a view to adding to the attraction of some of the display classes, the schedule committee last week decided to increase the prizes in the class covering Rose Gardens to $1,000, offering $500 as first, $300 as second, and $200 as third prizes. The prizes in the class for display of rose plants to cover 200 sq. ft. of space, have been increased from $125 and $75 to $200 and $100.

Special Prizes.

The second preliminary schedule has just been mailed. It comprises 44 pages, and the prizes offered approximate $20,000. It is the largest schedule ever put out for a flower show in America. Many of the prizes offered by outside interests appear in the new edition. Quite a number of classes are underwritten by Henry A. Dreer, Inc., Philadelphia, Henry F. Michell Co., Phila., Hosea Waterer, Phila., W. Atlee Burpee & Co., Phila., and Zandberger Bros., Valkenburg, Holland. Other donors of special prizes noted are Philip Breitmeyer, Detroit; Harry Balsley, Detroit; H. G. Berning, St. Louis; Hugh B. Barclay, Marion, Pa.; Emil Buettner, Park Ridge, Ill.; John Cook, Baltimore; Eugene Dailledouze, Brooklyn, N. Y.; J. H. Dunlop, Toronto; W. H. Elliott, Brighton, Mass.; A. Farenwald, Roslyn, Pa.; Gude Bros. Co, Washington, D. C.; Geo. B. Hart, Rochester, N. Y.; Hess & Swoboda, Omaha, Neb.; Benj. Hammond, Beacon, N. Y.; A. H. Hews Co., Cambridge, Mass.; Wm. F. Kasting, Buffalo, N. Y.; Leo Niessen Co., Phila.; Michigan Cut Flower Exchange, Detroit; J. A. Peterson & Sons, Cincinnati; S. S. Pennock-Meehan Co., Phila.; A. N. Pierson, Inc.. Cromwell, Conn.; M. Rice Company, Phila.; Max Schling, New York; U. S. Cut Flower Co., Elmira, N. Y.; Mrs. Chas. Wheeler, Bryn Mawr, Pa.; Anton C. Zvolanek, Lompoc, Cal. Other special prizes have been received and will find places in the final schedule.

Rose Rules.

Exhibitors of roses in both commercial and private classes are reminded that under a new rule of the American Rose Society, all roses with more than two growths (one pinch) will be disqualified, excepting in the classes calling for displays, and for 100 or more blooms in a vase, when two pinches will be allowed. The rose section as prepared by the American Rose Society, contains an unusually liberal list of premiums, which aggregate considerably over $4000. Almost all the variety of roses used commercially as cut flowers are classed, and new varieties are provided for; while Perpetuals, Teas, Wichuraianas and Polyanthas, and their hybrids, grown in pots and tubs, are amply provided for.

Carnation Classes.

There is a liberal schedule prepared by the American Carnation Society covering carnations. The prizes for display covering 150 sq. ft. are $200, $150 and $100. Prizes of $50, $35 and $15 are offered for vase of carnations, not to exceed 300 blooms, one or more varieties, greens and ribbons allowed. The retail classes in the carnation section are somewhat novel. In the class for table decorations, $50 will be awarded to each table scoring not less than 90 points, $40 to each table scoring not less than 80 points, and $30 to each table scoring not less than 70 points. Another class covers basket arrangements, and the same idea prevails as to awards; $25 will be awarded to each arrangement scoring not less than 90 points, $20 to each arrangement scoring not less than 80 points, and $15 to each arrangement scoring not less than 70 points. But only six entries will be accepted in either of these classes. Immediately following the judging, the secretary will remove the entry cards from all the exhibits in these classes, and only the regulation display cards as prescribed by the management will be permitted on the displays. The reason for this ruling is obvious to retailers. The carnation display will really form the "Jubilee Exhibition" of the American Carnation Society, celebrating the society's 25th anniversary, and in commemoration of it the society offers its special Silver Jubilee Medal for award to each winner of one or more first premiums in the vase classes.

Sweet Peas, Etc.

The American Sweet Pea Society includes a schedule covering standard winter orchid-flowering varieties and 1915 novelties. Notable in this section are the classes covering the Burpee prizes for the largest display of Winter or Summer-flowering, or both, and the Zvolanek prizes for the best and largest collection of Winter-flowering Grandiflora and Orchid Sweet Peas, all correctly named, varieties introduced prior to 1916. Liberal prizes are offered for retailers' exhibits.

The American Gladiolus Society aims for a display of forced blooms at this show, and has prepared a section of the schedule calling for about $300 in prizes.

In the plant sections very little change has been made, the provisions made therein having been considered ample.

Copies of the Second Preliminary Schedule may be had on application to John Young, Secretary, 53 W. 28th Street, New York.

NEW YORK INTERNATIONAL FLOWER SHOW.
April 5 to 12, 1916.

What will be something of an innovation at Flower Shows will be the class added to the Premium Schedule for the forthcoming show in the Grand Central Palace, New York, covering a window box, of wood, to contain flowering plants of a nature to last through summer, outdoors. The first prize, $25, is offered by Miss Georgie Wayne Day, of New York. Louis Sherry, the well-known restaurateur, has offered, through A. L. Miller, a $100 cup, to be awarded in the discretion of the committee. The Hotel Astor, also through Mr. Miller, offers a $50 cup. Emile W. Savoy, of Secaucus, N. J., offers $25 sweepstakes for the best specimen Bougainvillea, open class.

There is still a good supply of copies of the Preliminary Schedule on hand. Any one interested, not in possession of a copy, should make application for one to John Young, Secretary, 53 W. 28th street, New York.

FRIEDLEY'S LILIES.

Winning 1st Prize at the Cleveland Show.

CLUBS AND SOCIETIES

NATIONAL ASSOCIATION OF GARDENERS.

A bright sunshiny day following a spell of bleak wintry weather greeted the members of the National Association of Gardeners on the opening of their annual Convention at Boston, Mass., on Thursday, December 9. The opening session at Horticultural Hall convened at 2 P. M. and when the meeting was called to order by Mr. Farquhar he had a good sized and enthusiastic audience before him, including a liberal representation from points more or less distant.

The meeting was opened with a cordial welcoming address by President J. K. M. L. Farquhar of the Massachusetts Horticultural Society, telling of the work and aims of this time-honored organization and its dependence upon the gardener as the advance guard of the art of horticulture. He then introduced His Honor Mayor Curley of Boston, who spoke enthusiastically and eloquently of Boston's Park System and told of his observations on his recent trip to the Pacific Coast, where, at San Diego, San Francisco, Portland and Chicago, he learned that all the splendid public reservations of those cities had been laid out by a Boston firm, the Olmsted Brothers. He invited the visitors to enjoy a visit through the Boston Park System on Friday, and aroused much enthusiasm when he told of the plans for the proposed horticultural building and winter garden in the Fenway. John H. Dillon, chairman of the Boston Park Commission, ably seconded the Mayor's graceful welcome and paid a nice tribute to the position and influence of the gardening fraternity.

Mr. Farquhar then turned over the meeting to President J. W. Everitt of the Association, who made a brief address, thanking the previous speakers for their generous welcome and told of the objects of the Association of which he had the honor to be chief officer, an association which is still young but which has great opportunities for future usefulness and proposes to benefit the profession in all that it undertakes. Sec. M. C. Ebel followed with a report of the business and standing of the Association.

Election of officers followed the reading of the treasurer's report. W. N. Craig, of Brookline, Mass., was nominated for president and there being no other nominee Mr. Craig was unanimously elected. M. C. Ebel was also re-elected secretary by a unanimous vote. Full detailed report of the remaining proceedings and the auto ride through the park system and to several of the leading private gardens and the Farquhar nurseries in Dedham on Friday will appear in our next issue.

There were a number of interesting exhibits, including the following: A. H. Hews & Co., Cambridge, Mass., Flower Pots; John Scheepers & Co., New York, Lily bulbs, Astilbes and Ferns; Littlefield & Wyman, North Abington.

Meetings Next Week

Monday, Dec. 13.

Cleveland Florists' Club, Hollenden Hotel, Cleveland, Ohio.
Gardeners' and Florists' Club of Baltimore, Florist Exchange Hall.
New York Florist Club, Grand Opera House, New York City.
Rochester Florists' Association, 45 Main St. East, Rochester, N. Y.

Tuesday, Dec. 14.

Florists' and Gardeners' of Holyoke and Northampton, Mass.
Newport Horticultural Society, Newport, R. I.

Wednesday, Dec. 15.

Rhode Island Horticultural Society, Public Library, Providence, R. I.

Thursday, Dec. 16.

Essex County Florists' Club, Kreuger Auditorium, Newark, N. J.
New Orleans Horticultural Society, Association of Commerce Bldg., New Orleans, La.
North Westchester County Horticultural Society, Mt. Kisco, N. Y.
Tacoma Florists' Association, Maccabee Hall, Tacoma, Wash.

Friday, Dec. 17.

North Shore Horticultural Society, Manchester, Mass.

WILLIAM N. CRAIG.
President-elect National Association of Gardeners.

Mass., Carnation Miss Theo; Peter Fisher, Ellis, Mass., Carnation Alice; Ed. Winkler, Wakefield, Mass., Carnation Morning Glow; W. C. Rust, Antirrhinum Weld Pink; Duncan Finlayson, Calanthes; Wm. Downs, Begonias Winter Cheer, Optima, Aureana, Cincinnati and Lorraine.

The Cincinnati Florists' Society's regular December meeting will be held on Monday evening, December 13th, at Hotel Gibson.

MASSACHUSETTS HORTICULTURAL SOCIETY.

A meeting of the Board of Trustees of the Massachusetts Horticultural Society was held on Saturday, December 4. The special committee on the award of the George Robert White Medal of Honor for the year 1915 reported the name of Ernest Henry Wilson. The committee stated that Mr. Wilson was worthy of this award, for no one in recent years had done more for the advancement of horticulture than he, for he had introduced to cultivation a greater number of desirable garden plants than had ever before been accomplished by any one man. It was voted, with acclamation, to award the George Robert White Medal of Honor for the year 1915 to Ernest Henry Wilson.

The following standing committees of the Society for the ensuing year were appointed:

Finance.—Walter Hunnewell, chairman; Arthur F. Estabrook, Stephen M. Weld.

Membership. — R. M. Saltonstall, chairman; Thomas Allen, Thomas Roland.

Prizes and Exhibitions. — James Wheeler, chairman; John K. M. L. Farquhar, Duncan Finlayson, T. D. Hatfield, A. H. Wingett.

Plants and Flowers.—William Anderson, chairman; Arthur H. Fewkes, S. J. Goddard, Donald McKenzie, William Sim.

Fruits.—Edward B. Wilder, chairman; William Downs, Ralph W. Rees.

Vegetables.—John L. Smith, chairman; Henry M. Howard, William O. Rust.

Gardens.—Richard M. Saltonstall, chairman; David R. Craig, Jackson T. Dawson, William Nicholson, Charles Sander.

Library.—Charles S. Sargent, chairman; Ernest B. Dane, Nathan'l T. Kidder.

Lectures.—Wilfrid Wheeler, chairman; John K. M. L. Farquhar, F. C. Sears, Fred A. Wilson.

Children's Gardens. — Henry S. Adams, chairman; Wm. N. Craig, Dr. Harris Kennedy, Mrs. W. Rodman Peabody, Miss Margaret A. Rand.

WM. P. RICH, Sec.

Horticultural Hall, Boston.

GARDENERS' AND FLORISTS' CLUB OF BOSTON.

The following nominations of officers were made at the club meeting held on November 23, to be voted on December 21: President, James Methven; vice-president, W. J. Patterson; treasurer; Peter Fisher; secretary, W. N. Craig; executive committee, H. H. Bartsch, Peter M. Miller, W. J. Kennedy, Geo. W. Butterworth, W. H. Judd, W. C. Rust, A. K. Rogers, L. G. Van Leeuwen. The usual monthly circular will be issued on or about December 17, as a reminder to members of this important meeting.

H. H. BARTSCH, Pres.
W. N. CRAIG, Sec.

AMERICAN ROSE SOCIETY.

There will be a meeting of the executive committee of the American Rose Society on Monday, December 13, at the office of Traendly & Schenck, 436 Sixth avenue, New York City, at 2 P. M.

We have received notice of the following special premiums for the rose exhibition at the coming Philadelphia show:

Special Premiums.

Leo Niessen, Philadelphia, Pa., for 50 blooms of any new rose not in commerce, $25.00. Hess & Swoboda, Omaha, Neb., Vase of 25 Ophelia or Russell, $10.00. Benjamin Hammond, Beacon, N. Y., for the prettiest vase of roses, to be decided by vote of the ladies, $10.00. William H. Elliott, Brighton, Mass., cash prize, $25.00. M. Rice & Co., Philadelphia, Pa., cash prize, $10.00. H. G. Berning, 1402 Pine street, St. Louis, Mo., cash prize, $25.00. Gude Bros., Washington, D. C., cash prize $25.00. Jos. Heacock, Wyncote, Pa., trophy of $50.00. Florex Gardens, North Wales, Pa., gold medal, value $25.00. A. H. Hews & Co., Cambridge, Mass., cash prize $10.00. Geo. Burton, Chestnut Hill, Philadelphia, Pa., cash prize $25.00. Stephen Mortensen, Southampton, Pa., cash prize $25.00.

Specials for Rose Garden—Philip Breitmeyer, Detroit, Mich., 1st prize, $200.00. 2rd Prize—J. H. Dunlop, Richmond Hill, Ontario, $25.00; Adolph Farenwald, Roslyn, Pa., $25.00; United States Cut Flower Co., Elmira, N. Y., $25.00; Emil Buettner, Park Ridge, Ill., $25.00; Michigan Cut Flower Co., Detroit, Mich., $25.00; Eugene Dailledouze, Brooklyn, N. Y., $25.00; Thomas Roland, Nahant, Mass., $25.00.

3d Prize—A. N. Pierson, Inc., Cromwell, Conn., $75.00.

It is expected that these prizes for the Rose Garden may be increased, while several of the prizes so far received are left with the committee for designation as to their particular use.

Application is made for the registration of the new roses—William R. Hearst and Little Sunshine, by A. N. Pierson, Inc., Cromwell, Conn.

There has been received advice of a shipment of 24 varieties of Holland roses and 12 each of two other varieties, from Messrs. Kallen & Lunnemann, Boskoop, Holland, for the test garden at Cornell, Ithaca, N. Y.

The affiliated Rose Society of Syracuse, with 266 members, have renewed their annual membership with the American Rose Society.

BENJAMIN HAMMOND, Sec.
Beacon, N. Y.

AMERICAN SWEET PEA SOCIETY.

The executive committee and other interested members of the American Sweet Pea Society held a meeting at

EXHIBITION BOOTH OF STORRS & HARRISON CO., AT THE CLEVELAND FLOWER SHOW.

the Hotel Belmont, New York City, on December 4, and it was considered the best meeting in the society's history. Among those present were President William Gray, Newport, R. I.; Lester Morse, San Francisco, Cal.; George W. Kerr, Doylestown, Pa.; A. T. Boddington, W. A. Sperling, J. Harrison Dick and Secretary H. A. Bunyard, all of New York City. Exhibitions are planned for Bar Harbor, Me.; San Francisco, New York and Philadelphia during 1916.

NEW JERSEY FLORICULTURAL SOCIETY.

A regular monthly meeting of this society was held in Orange, N. J., on Monday, Dec. 6. Election of officers took place as follows: Henry Halbig, re-elected president; Max Schneider, vice-president; Edward A. Manda, treasurer; Geo. W. Strange, secretary; Wm. Jorden (chairman), Andrew Nichols, Gustave Christensen, Charles W. Ashmead and Rev. L. H. Lighthipe, arbitration committee.

The monthly competition for the year 1915 resulted as follows: Max Schneider, carnations, 668 points; foliage or flowering plant, 707; cut flowers, 720; violets, 500. Emil Panuska, foliage or flowering plant, 740. Joseph A. Manda exhibited a fine variety of Cattleya Empress Frederick.

GEORGE W. STRANGE, Sec.

FLORISTS' CLUB OF PHILADELPHIA.

A well attended meeting of this club was held on Dec. 7th to listen to a spirited debate between Charles H. Grakelow and W. Frank Therkildson on "Is it wise for the producer to depend entirely on the retailer in marketing his products." Some excellent points were brought out on both sides, all of them of educative value, especially to the younger element. In addition to this much wit and merriment prevailed and a very enjoyable evening was spent and the members could hardly believe their eyes when the clock showed quarter of eleven at the wind-up. In addition to the debate a lively discussion took place on how to get more members, and the outcome of that was the suspension of the entrance fee for three months so that we can have a whirlwind campaign for a thousand new members by next Easter.

The Cornwalls Orchard Farm exhibited a new variegated carnation. Wieland & Risch of Chicago sent a fine vase of their new rose Champ Wieland. S. J. Reuter & Son of Westerly, R. I., exhibited their new light yellow rose Mrs. H. T. Hillas and Chas. H. Totty sent Gorgeous, a light pink rose of fine form. Both the latter were staged by the Pennock-Meehan Co. The Zieger Co. staged some remarkable white and pink double bouvardia with stems 18 inches long. Florex Gardens made an excellent exhibit of rose Prima Donna (Mme. P. Euler.)

CLUB AND SOCIETY NOTES.

E. W. Breed, of Clinton, for the past four years president of the Worcester County (Mass.) Horticultural Society, declined re-election to that office Wednesday evening at the annual meeting of that society. The logical candidate for that office is the senior vice-president, Arthur J. Marble.

Walter R. Siebrecht, of New York City, was a guest of the Horticultural Club of Boston at its December meeting. The banquet table was resplendent with carnations from S. J. Goddard including some superb Dorner seedlings and a vase of Mignonette Farquhar's Universal, also grown by Mr. Goddard.

EXHIBIT OF WILCOX & SONS AT THE HOUSTON SHOW.

FLORISTS AS ADVERTISERS AND BOOKKEEPERS

(By A. F. Koehle, Sherman, Texas.)

We are all more or less loose in handling our advertising and bookkeeping but we should not be. What is the use of growing a splendid lot of stock unless one has a means in view of letting the trade, be it wholesale or retail, know what he has? What is the use of selling if one hasn't a system of book-keeping to keep proper record of the sales, not only to know where you stand financially, but for future reference to know what quantity to grow the coming year; thereby eliminating that awful pest of both retailer and wholesaler — gluts—and then find you have to run to some department store to unload it? A preventive for these gluts, which also means a preventive of antagonism among brother florists, can be sifted down and controlled by the two means in this subject:

1st. Advertise judiciously and insistently. There are poor ways of advertising as well as good ones, and best results can not be obtained without careful study. Select a medium which you know reaches the most desirable customers, make your ad. brief and to the point and above all make your opening display interesting and attractive. Put yourself in the public's place. How many ads. do you read that are not started with some catchy phrase? Unless one is looking for that certain line of stock there are very few people who pick up a paper to find out who is selling flowers the cheapest or what the most seasonable flower is. It is up to us to catch their eye and make them see "who is who" in the flower and plant line. Last Valentine's Day I decided to use a slide in all the picture shows in town. One can obtain these slides at the office of our daily paper. Being well acquainted with the advertising manager of this paper, he asked me why I didn't use his paper for an ad. I told him I thought the shows would reach more people. His only reply was "Then why do the picture shows in this town use one whole sheet of my paper to advertise their shows, if your theory works out? I told him those visiting the shows mighty near had to read the ads. when thrown on the screen, while they would never look at them in a paper. He replied that if my ad. was overlooked it was my fault and not the paper's, and I guess be was about right. However, we have found the following: Picture show good, leading papers better and direct advertising best. The last named we have worked down to a very fine point. We have tried some of the various folders that are now on the market but find our own letters pay

best and we attribute the enormous growth of our business to this means.

In sending out circular communications for any special day, we prepare these letters—one to be addressed to the married men, one to the single men and one to the ladies who entertain. Each letter is carefully filled in with typewriter, signed with pen and mailed under two cent postage. Of course we endeavor at all times to make these letters attractive and brief. For our mailing list locally, we use the City Directory, carefully marked by someone who is well acquainted in the city. In fact, we have as many as three different clerks check over this list, all of whom are well acquainted in the city, so as to get a very complete list of those persons most likely to purchase flowers. We also use these same letters for our out-of-town customers, using lists of names furnished, us by, our, local agents in the different towns.

Now as to our out-of-town advertising. All ads. of this kind should of course be keyed, and all inquiries received carefully recorded and followed up. For keeping record of the number of inquiries and of sales through our different advertising mediums, we use a monthly card for each paper. When an inquiry is received, the name is recorded on a 3x5 card, marked at the top with the numbers from 1 to 31 and a clip placed on the number corresponding to the date on which the inquiry should be followed up. When a sale is made it is duly recorded on this card, and the card then placed in "Sold File" for future reference and for future advertising. Repeat orders are where our profits come. The first order frequently is not of sufficient importance to reimburse us for what it cost to secure, but a satisfied customer is the very best advertisement, and we endeavor at all times to please, for we know if we "sell satisfaction our goods will sell themselves." Advertising is worth little if we don't back it up with A1 quality, the best of service and the most pleasing courtesy. One might think it takes considerable capital and time to carry on this line of direct advertising but such is not the case. If you are not fortunate enough to have the use of a typewriter or any of the machines now on the market for this purpose, all you need is pen, ink, raper, envelopes and stamps. There is a druggist in our city, and by the way one of the leading ones, who follows this method of advertising by the following means. Between the days, he has in mind to use his letters, all his spare time (and we all have much of it) he writes his letters with pen

(bear in mind he has a typewriter and multigraph too) but prefers a personally penned letter signed by himself, and he advises me it brings big returns. Another very important item to bear in mind is to select some slogan suggestive of your business or special line if you have one, and use it always. You will find it will not be long until it is a by-word with all your customers as well as new customers. We use one in our local advertising, and we contract with the leading paper here for a number of local ads. to run the whole year through and scattered it over various parts of the paper. All we used in these locals was our slogan—"When you think of Flowers think of us" and unless you have tried it you have no idea how much attention it attracts. It will pay any one to try it. In conclusion on this part of my subject I would say Advertise, and advertise lots, but do it judiciously and carefully.

2nd. Book-keeping—so much can be said about this and so many of us florists need to be hammered and pounded so hard on this point, I scarcely know where to begin. It embraces so much of our line that most of us think it does not require any book-keeping, in which we are very badly mistaken. Most of us can tell any time about how much we owe or how much is due to come in, but how many can go to their books and tell which line of stock paid best for the past year? I don't mean guess at it, but in actual figures. While our floral department is not kept separate on our books, it is kept in such a way that at any time we can see just where this department stands. For the general book-keeping of the Company we keep an account for everything—for instance all improvements are charged to a separate account, likewise the following items—interest, implements, live stock, growing, purchase, and so on. Every individual thing has an account of its own on our books; then when a sale of these various things is made, it is credited to that account, so that any time we wish we can see just how that department stands, how much we have in it and what we are getting from it. Of course most florists do not need so large a system as ours, but we would suggest something like this for even the smallest general sales account, cut flowers, advertising, purchasing, flower store account, greenhouse account, improvement, plant purchases, delivery account, live stock or auto account, supplies, etc. Whatever item is a factor in the conduct of the business ought to be on your books, that you may refer to it at any time, and be able to tell how deep you are into it and put on the check valve if getting an overload. It would be hard for me to state just what one should keep, and each one should be able to tell which are the more important items to keep, but above all—start right now even if on only a part of the items, and you will like it so well at the end of the year that I am sure you will have a perfect bookkeeping system thereafter; and without much extra expense or trouble. Each year you will be able to see where you can improve on it and make it clearer and easier to keep. There are lots of ways and forms on which to keep these records, but to most of us these need considerable explanation to keep properly, and the busy florist hasn't the time to take a course in such things. I believe it is best to work out a system of one's own and by his own experience he will gradually improve on it, until he has a plain, neat, compact system, that will be a pride to himself as well as a pleasure to all whom he may have any occasion to show or tell it to. The most satisfactory system of bookkeeping is the double entry system, which, as its name implies, requires two entries for each transaction. This may sound like too much work to do, but by it one can always tell if all items have been posted in the proper amounts. There are only two fundamental rules to be followed to carry out this system, and they are, "all items, cash, flowers, merchandise, or whatsoever we may 'take in' go on the credit side of the proper account, and all items paid out or sent out, go on the debit side of the proper account." The other rule is based on the same principle and is "for every debit there must be a corresponding credit, and conversely for every credit there must be a corresponding debit." For in-

stance—we will send to our flower store a dozen American Beauty roses; we debit our Flower Store Account 1 doz. A. B. roses $3.00, we credit our Greenhouse Sales Account by 1 doz. A. B. roses to F. Store $3.00. Our Flower Store sells these to Mrs. John Doe for $5.00, so we credit Flower Store Sales Account by $5.00 and charge Mrs. John Doe's account 1 doz. A. B. roses $5.00. Later Mrs. John Doe sends us a check, so we credit her account $5.00 and charge Cash Account $5.00.

Thus by charging the proper or selected accounts with the items properly belonging thereon, and crediting these accounts with all items belonging thereon, one is able to determine if it is profitable to run an uptown flower store, or to hire delivery men, or to know out of which flowers profits are made, etc.

In conclusion of these subjects, would say the moral of all this talk is "Don't hide your light under a bushel," but let it shine by careful, judicious advertising and reflect upon the pages of a perfect bookkeeping system.

PHILIPPINE ORCHIDS AT SAN FRANCISCO.

The collection of orchids in charge of W. E. Eglintgon, representing the Philippine Islands, has been awarded the grand prize, the highest award, by the superior jury of the Panama-Pacific International Exposition. We are advised that about ten million people have passed through the orchid house where many plants were in flower all the time from April till August. This collection is to be sold after the fair is over.

KEEP GOING.

By Ella Wheeler Wilcox.

Is the goal distant, and troubled the road,
  And the way long,
And heavy the load?
  Then gird up your courage and say, "I
    am strong,"
      And keep going!

Is the work weary and endless the grind,
  And petty the pay?
Then brace up your mind,
  And say, "Something better is coming
  my way,"—
    And keep doing!

Is the drink bitter life pours in your cup—
  Is the taste gall?
Then smile and look up,
  And say, "God is with me whatever be-
  fall"—
    And keep trusting!

Is the heart heavy with hope long deferred,
  And with prayers that seem vain?
Keep saying the word;
  And that which you strive for you yet
  shall attain—
    Keep praying!

FLOWERS VERSUS WAR.

We call attention to the plans of the Massachusetts Horticultural Society for the year ahead. Why not stop gasping war thoughts and political spasms long enough to face the really big things of life? A war is a very little thing, considered in the gigantic scheme of creation and evolution. This is a very old world; and there are very much older worlds out and about, concerning which we know little. Wars hit here and there, bury civilizations, raise new hopes, set puppets on thrones, topple them over, grind out new governments, destroy joys, torture generations — and pass down into the caverns of history, where they are forgotten. And all this time, all through the little groppings of self-esteeming man, trees, plants, blooms, fruits—all Nature's bounty pours itself out in the lap of time. Mankind works hard and long to exalt himself and make a show; but he never comes to the height of a violet at the edge of a wood. So when a society talks about plants and flowers for a year's interest there come focussed before eyes that see, something bigger than a war in Europe or a political campaign at our doorstep. —*Boston Record.*

NEW CORPORATIONS.

West Park, O.—Riverside Greenhouse Co. Capital stock, $35,000. Incorporator, Peter Barthelman.

Melrose, Mass. — Houghton-Kravath Co., florists, capital stock, $2,000. Incorporators, F. H. Houghton, Samuel Kravath and C. D. Houghton.

Boston, Mass.—Fisher, Florist, Inc. Capital stock, $5,000. Incorporators, Geo. E. Fisher, Nathan M. Silverman and E. Silverman.

BUSINESS TROUBLES.

Hoosick Falls, Mass.—R. Marshall & Co., florists; assets, $1,500; liabilities, $4,151.

Our correspondent in Houston, Texas, inadvertently omitted mention of W. W. Coles' exhibit at the flower show in that city. Mr. Coles made a very creditable display. He made a magnificent showing of carnations, roses and chrysanthemums and contributed greatly to the success of the show.

WHEN A DEBTOR OFFERS LESS THAN 100 PER CENT.

I feel like emphasizing in this article the importance of a fight which the National Credit Men's Association is making to induce creditors to act a little more stiff-backed in considering offers of settlement from embarrassed debtors. The association contends that a constant series of bad frauds are being perpetrated by alleged bankrupts or financially embarrassed business people, right under the noses of their creditors, merely because the latter are too ready to accept almost any offer that is made.

In writing on the subject the association says:—

When a business man becomes financially embarrassed, and offers a certain percentage in settlement, if a creditor holds back and begins to show signs of wanting to know a little about the case, the reply is apt to be to the effect that he is the only creditor who hasn't come in, that he is showing a very uncooperative spirit, or else there is a hint that he is holding out for a preferential payment. The idea clearly is to stampede the creditor into an acceptance of the offer through sharp criticism to the effect that he is playing the part of an obstructionist. To such tactics most creditors are weak-kneed enough to capitulate.

The association cites a case where a debtor, as late as last January, gave his creditors a statement of assets and liabilities which showed ownership of two pieces of valuable real estate. A few months later, this man sent out notices to his creditors that he was financially embarrassed and offered a certain percentage in compromise. He accompanied it with a statement of assets and liabilities, but the former this time contained no real estate. One of the creditors wanted to know where it had gone, but the other creditors cried him down because he was threatening a fight which would tie the thing up, eat up the funds, and delay settlement. He persisted for a little, but was finally overborne, and the mystery of the missing real estate was never solved. Very likely it had been manipulated in some way which would not have stood the test of an investigation—if only some one had been man enough to make it. Had it been recovered, the percentage of settlement would have been about doubled, but the creditors believed the bird in the hand to be worth the two in the bush.

If a few more creditors would be slower to accept the first offer of settlement made them by embarrassed debtors, bankruptcy and insolvent business frauds would probably be reduced one-half in a very short while. Debtors have grown astonishingly bold, so confident are they that creditors will gladly and gratefully take whatever is offered them and ask no questions.

Let me cite a few cases from my own experience, and from the records, to show how this works:—

A retail hardware dealer became embarrassed and called a meeting of his creditors. His assets were about $6,000 and his liabilities over $12,000. The assets had to be scaled down because book accounts were a part of them. The hardware dealer offered 35 per cent. in full, payable in cash. Practically all the creditors favored taking it, after the manner of creditors. One fairly large creditor held off and the bankrupt began to talk about going into bankruptcy, and the expense and the fees of that, and so on, until the other creditors actually began to get indignant at the obstructionist, as they considered him. He persisted, however, and to make a long story short, the investigation that ensued unearthed the fact that the hardware dealer owned a share in a prosperous hotel business, which, of course by oversight he had neglected to list among his assets. The percentage of settlement was finally 55 per cent. instead of 35.

In another case a wholesale grocer offered his creditors 50 per cent. professing that in order to offer even that, he had had to borrow from his wife. It would have gone through with a rush had not two of the creditors been a little suspicious. They insisted on being shown and finally the wholesale grocer was compelled to admit that he, or somebody for him—the thinnest kind of a subterfuge had been used—held a block of stock in a chain of retail stores. When these were added to his assets the man proved to be solvent and he promptly arranged to pay in full. Two creditors out of about forty were all that had the courage of their convictions here. The rest were so afraid something would happen to reduce the 50 per cent. they had been offered, that they were very impatient with the two who stood out.

In a third case, one creditor out of quite a number insisted that the item of "stock on hand" which a debtor had included in a statement on which he based an offer of 40 per cent., was suspiciously small. He presented reasons for his opinion, but the other creditors were practically all anxious to accept the 40 per cent. and get out. As in the other cases, they looked on the one man who held out as an enemy. The one man persisted, however, and finally made the debtor disgorge $4,000 of goods which he had "sold" to another man.

There are quite a number of such cases, but cases which don't happen in this way are of course much more numerous. I heard a bankruptcy lawyer not long ago offer to lay a wager that he could induce the creditors of any insolvent debtor to accept settlement of around 50 per cent. merely by writing one letter. Perhaps it was exaggerated, but not necessarily a great deal. In most cases I have no doubt it could easily be done.

The creditor when offered a percentage settlement by a debtor, should not be too quick to accept. It is remarkable how many such offers are increased merely by creditors holding off. It will be a service not only to one's self, but to the whole cause of commercial honesty, if a creditor will insist on being shown before he accepts any offer of less than 100 per cent.

Obituary

James Hynes.

James Hynes, 50 years, for the past 15 years florist and gardener for the Houghton estate, North Adams, Mass., died December 1st, after a long illness. He leaves a widow and nine children.

Edward F. Skahan.

Edward F. Skahan, market gardener, died at his home in Belmont, Mass., Dec. 1st. He was 50 years of age. A widow and eight children survive him.

Mrs. Gertrude Brinton.

Mrs. Gertrude Brinton, wife of Maurice J. Brinton, a leading florist of Christiana, Pa., died on December 4. Death was the result of a complication of diseases and after an illness extending over several months. She was the daughter of the late Henry Rakestraw, Chester county, and a graduate of the West Chester Normal School, a member of the Friends' Church and a woman who will be deeply missed in her community, having been active in any matter pertaining to the welfare of her home town. A devoted wife, a loving mother and a woman who was of incalculable help to her husband in his business, the florists of Lancaster County all extend their sympathy to Mr. Brinton and his two children, Grace and Maurice, Jr. She is also survived by her mother, Mrs. Jennie Rakestraw and two married sisters. The funeral services were held Monday, Dec. 6th, with a profusion of the flowers she loved so well.　　　　　A. M. H.

W. ATLEE BURPEE.

(Died at Fordhook Farms, Nov. 26.)

How fittingly this man's life closes,
　That like blown petals on the grass
In this sere time of summer's roses
　He, too, should pass!

Light be the churchyard loam above him
　And sweet the Spring that he shall know!
There shall God's blossoms lean to love him,
　Who loved them so.
　　—Tom Daly in Phila. Ledger, Nov. 27, 1915.

PUBLICATIONS RECEIVED.

The Garden Blue Book. A Manual of the Perennial Garden. By Leicester B. Holland. This new publication by Doubleday, Page & Co., has the merit of originality to a degree seldom met with in these days when of the making of garden books there is no end. The body of the work consists of text descriptions of a selection of 169 of the most desirable and varied herbaceous border plants suited to our northern U. S. conditions. Each right-hand page is devoted to a full description accompanied by a half-tone picture of one species, giving botanical and common name, place of origin and season of flowering, etc., together with a number which refers back to an elaborate color chart which is bound into the first part of the book which shows approximately the tint or tints of each flower described. The charts also show in ingenious and convenient tabulated form the exact time and duration of blooming, the exposure—sunny, half shade or shade—which each subject should have, the height in feet and the soil conditions most conducive to success with each. Each left hand page opposite the descriptive notes and cultural directions contains a table with blank spaces for notes on the behavior of the plant each month in the year for a series of years, climatic conditions and other pertinent observations, also a blank table for similar notes on any other species or variety grown but not listed in this manual. A careful filling in of these blanks for a period of several years would constitute a most valuable record such as but few have ever attempted to keep but which, with the convenience here provided, will no doubt hereafter become a useful occupation and pastime for many garden lovers.

The descriptive lists are arranged alphabetically without regard to consanguinity or other relationship between the subjects described, all these latter facts being fully covered and instantly ascertained by reference to the charts. In the case of chrysanthemums, irises, paeonies, phloxes and some other subjects, copious lists of garden varieties are included in the text. The introductory chapters are interesting and instructive, covering practical advice on garden designing, planting and arrangement, in detail, with plans and figures for reference. The book contains 425 pages and in binding and other mechanical features is handsome and very appropriate as a timely holiday gift which in the hands of an interested recipient will prove a wellspring of pleasure and inspiration for every day, the season through. Price $3.50 net. Copies may be obtained from Doubleday, Page & Co., New York or the office of HORTICULTURE, Boston.

·St. Louis—The five wholesale houses have formed a combination and hold meetings twice a month. They met last week at Smith's. Each house has put up $100 forfeit to live up to the rules of the association for one year.

SEED TRADE

Imports This Week.

The manifest of the S. S. Frederick
VIII from Copenhagen, Denmark,
show 695 cases of lily of the valley
for Loechner & Co., N. Y., 50 do. for
Julius Roehrs Co., Rutherford, N. J.,
280 cases for Canada, through American Express, and 8 cases of lilacs for
Loechner & Co. From Rotterdam via
S. S. Osterdyck, there came for J. T.
Noll & Co., Newark, N. J. 25 cases of
seed; for Stumpp & Walter Co., one
do.; for The Darrow Co., 3 packages
do.; for A. T. Boddington Co., 1 case
bulbs; MacNiff Horticultural Co., 28
do.; McHutchison & Co., 66 cases
trees; John Scheepers & Co., one case
bulbs; R. F. Lang, 77 cases roots (lily
of the valley?); H. Langelier, 90 cases
bulbs; B. C. Kuyper & Co., 56 cases
trees and 52 cases roots (lily of the
valley?); Maltus & Ware, 73 do., and
15 packages of seed.

A Simple Device for Counting Seeds.

In preparing tests of seed germination a great deal of rather monotonous work is required in counting the
seeds. The device to be described was
worked out to obviate part of this
labor, and has proved very efficient
in our seed laboratory. In the hope
that it will save valuable time for
other workers in this field the following description is presented:

The seed counter is made from a
piece of brass or copper tubing 20 cm.
in length and about .5 cm. in diameter.
This is bent in the middle at an angle
of 45° and then on one side filed almost paper thin for a distance of 8
cm. At intervals of .7 cm. on this
flattened side 10 holes of suitable diameter are punched with a needle and
hammer. One end of the tube on the
side nearest the holes is sealed with
solder or sealing wax, and the other
end is connected by .5 cm. rubber
pressure tubing to a small Richards
air pump.

The seeds to be counted are placed
in a flat tray and the pump started.
The suction through the fine openings
holds the seeds in lots of 10 to the
tube, which are removed by a flick of
the finger. In case more than one
seed adheres to a hole the extra ones
can be quickly removed by tapping the
tube, or with the finger. It will be
found advisable to have tubes made
up with various sizes of holes, one for
small seeds such as tobacco, with
openings as small as can be made with
a No. 7 needle; one with medium-sized
holes of .5 mm., which are best adapted to seeds of the size of radish,
clover, etc., and one with holes of 1
mm. in diameter. Seeds with a very
rough exterior such as beet seed do
not lend themselves well to this method of counting as the surface is too
uneven to be held by the suction.
Large seeds—beans, peas and corn for
instance—are too heavy to be held by
the suction produced by the small
Richards pump, but there is no doubt
that with a stronger suction such as
that produced by a vacuum cleaner

Pressure Tubing to Suction Pump.

this method could be used in counting these heavier seeds.

ORTON L. CLARK.
Mass. Agri. Exp. Station,
Amherst, Mass.

Round Spinach Seed—Restrictions on Shipment Modified.

Gentlemen: As the result of the representations made by the State Department at Washington, the Dutch government has expressed a willingness to permit the exportation of a certain quality of round spinach seed on which, as is well known, an embargo had been placed. To obtain the actual permits of exportation, it will be necessary for the Dutch growers to apply to the Dutch Minister of Agriculture.

The above information will be of interest to your readers.

CURTIS NYE SMITH.

Notes

The value of imports of horticultural merchandise at the port of New York, from November 22 to November 30, inclusive, is given as follows: Manure salt, $9,261; nitrate of soda, $290,258; fertilizer, $22,669; clover seed, $56,284; sugar beet seed, $17,678; grass seed, $17,478; trees and plants, $81,547.

New York, N. Y.—At the annual meeting of the Wholesale Seedmen's League, held November 30, F. W. Bruggerhof, of J. M. Thorburn & Co., was re-elected president for the 17th year. The other officers elected were L. W. Bowen, of D. M. Ferry & Co., Detroit, vice-president; B. Landreth, Bristol, Pa., secretary and treasurer.

We learn from a letter just received from Paris that Mr. Louis Vilmorin of the firm of Vilmorin, Andrieux & Co., has been called, as a private soldier, to the trenches, where he spends twelve days out of each month. Although deprived of all toilet luxuries, unable to undress while there or get hot meals he seems to take it philosophically and does not complain of these hard lines in the soldier's lot. Thirteen of the staff of the Vilmorin house out of several hundred who are at the front have won the war cross.

Mr. Eugene Schaettel of Vilmorin, Andrieux & Co., who has been on a business trip in this country for several weeks received news on Monday of this week that his mother, 84 years of age, had died on November 19, at her home in Saarunion, Alsace. She had been in failing health for some time and the bereavement is a keen one for Mr. Schaettel because the war restrictions have made it impossible for him to see her, or to hear from her except rarely, since the war began. Mr. Schaettel sails from New York for home on the S. S. Lafayette, Saturday, December 11.

German papers comment upon the fact that flowers from Italy via Switzerland are still coming into Germany in quantity and protest is made against this on the ground that the money paid for these flowers will eventually be converted into "silver bullets" against the Germans. It is urged that instead of this importing business an effort be made to use up lily of the valley pips and other products of German origin which now cannot be exported to England, Russia and other countries which formerly were large consumers.

Sluis & Groot of Enkhuizen, Holland, write us as follows:

We herewith beg to advise you of a change in our firm that has taken place the 16th inst., for we have decided to transform our seed-growing establishment, which is existing already since about half a century under the name of Sluis & Groot, into a limited company under the name of Sluis & Groot's Zandtleelt & Zaadhandel. The direction of our business remains in the same competent hands, which have also the same capital at their disposal and will use all efforts to maintain the high standing of our firm.

SLUIS & GROOT'S
ZAADTEELT & ZAADHANDEL

ESTATE OF W. ATLEE BURPEE.

Doylestown, Pa., Nov. 30.—By the will of W. Atlee Burpee, the widely known horticulturist and seedman, who died at Fordhook Farm last Friday, an estate of from $500,000 to $700,000 was disposed of. The figures given are approximate.

The will, executed on May 27, 1913, names as executors the testator's wife, Mrs. Blanche Simons Burpee; his brother-in-law, Alexander Buchanan Scott; ex-Judge Harman Yerkes, of Doylestown, and David Burpee, his oldest son.

It is plainly the intention of Mr. Burpee, as expressed in the will, that the seed business he established and conducted so successfully should be continued by his sons, David Burpee and W. Atlee Burpee, Jr. One-half interest in the business is left to the sons, one-third to Mrs. Burpee, one-sixth to the testator's sister, Mrs. Sarah Coburn Burpee Scott, and, until the estate is settled by the executors, one-sixth of the profits from the business is to go to Howard M. Earl, who has been Mr. Burpee's business manager for many years.

The Burpee property at 9th and York streets, Philadelphia, containing the seed establishment, is given to David Burpee and W. Atlee Burpee, Jr. Fordhook Farm, Doylestown, and Floradale, in the Lompoc Valley, California, are bequeathed to David Burpee. Sunnybrook Farm, near Swedesboro, N. J., goes to W. Atlee Burpee, Jr. But Mrs. Burpee retains a one-third life right in all these properties in lieu of dower. Mrs. Burpee is bequeathed all the personal effects and household articles of her husband and $5,000 immediately. Her one-third interest in the seed business must remain invested there unless she should remarry, when it may be withdrawn if she so desires.

Other bequests to relatives are as follows: Belinda Beatrice Kennedy, a cousin of Mrs. Burpee, $10,000 in trust; Helen Burpee, L. Kate Burpee and Charles L. Atlee, cousins, $5,000 each. Full power to will the principal sums is given in these bequests.—Phila. Public Ledger.

Of Interest to Retail Florists

NEW FLOWER STORES.

Sandwich, Ill.—Mrs. F. Spickerman.

Hartford, Ct.—Old Floral Place, Asylum and Ann streets.

New York, N. Y.—J. J. Coan, wholesale, 115 West 28th street.

New London, Conn. — J. Henry Schaeffer, Lyric Hall Bldg.

Philadelphia, Pa.—Richard Umphried, 1307 N. Broad street, succeeding Charles Fox.

Rochester, N. Y.—Bohnke Bros., Monroe avenue. Harry Brush, North Clinton avenue.

Des Moines, Ia.—Lozier, the Florist, 521 E. Locust street. C. W. Crum, Kirkwood Hotel.

Brooklyn, N. Y.—Edward Dressel, removing from 403 Bedford avenue to 214 Broadway.

Portland, Ore.—F. W. Geiger, 430 Washington street. Chappell's Flower Shop, 347 Morrison street.

Fall River, Mass.—Mrs. Sarah Lambert will continue the florist business of her late husband, John Lambert, at 72 Jepson street.

CONDEMNING FLOWERS AT FUNERALS.

Editor HORTICULTURE:

Dear Sir—I wonder if that Waltham priest who is said to be condemning the use of flowers at funerals could not use his breath to better advantage against the liquor evil that causes many funerals and more loss financially, physically and morally a thousand times than all the flowers used—not wasted—at funerals.

Yours respectfully
EDWARD F. DWYER.

East Lynn, Mass.

Watch the Buyers' Directory these days for information as to good plants, seeds, supplies, etc., and where they can be purchased to best advantage.

Pittsburgh, Pa.

Ludwig Floral Co.

502 Federal St.

FLOWERS

NEWS ITEMS FROM EVERYWHERE

WASHINGTON.

Dr. J. N. Rose, associate in botany, of the National Museum, and his assistant, Paul G. Russell, have just returned from an extensive botanical exploration trip in Brazil and Argentine Republic.

Examination for laboratory aid in seed testing in the bureau of plant industry, which positions carry a salary of from $600 to $720 per annum, will be held in this city on January 5, by the Civil Service Commission.

The judges of the Mt. Rainier Times beauty contest have made award to Miss Frances Kingsbury, a member of the salesforce at the store of F. H. Kramer. In addition to having been selected as the most beautiful girl whose picture was submitted, Miss Kingsbury has been given a handsome gold watch. Miss Kingsbury is a resident of Laurel, Md.

At a meeting of the Takoma Park Citizens' Association held last week it was decided that an effort will be made to secure the appointment of a supervisor to train the school children of the District of Columbia in home garden work. The retail florists of Washington some time ago went on record as favoring the home garden work to the end that eventually there will be "a rose in every garden."

Congressman Albert Johnson, of Washington, has introduced a bill in the House of Representatives providing, "That the centigrade scale of temperature measurement shall be standard in United States Government publications, the use of the Fahrenheit scale being discontinued, at the option of heads of departments or other independent branches of the Government, either immediately upon the signing of this bill or at any time before January 1, 1920, except as provided in Section 3."

The event of the week was the electrical parade held in connection with Electrical Prosperity Week celebration in which automobiles of J. H. Small & Sons and Gude Bros. Company were entered but not in competition. The Gude Bros. car was one of the most unique in the parade. A platform, 20 feet in length, was built on a low truck. Three arches, decorated with white roses and illuminated with a large number of miniature electric lights, were built up from the platform. In the space behind the chauffeur's seat, placed 12 feet apart, were two telegraph poles between which silver wires were strung. These were decorated with tinsel and on them fell the rays from two arc lights, the tinsel and light giving one the impression of messages going over the 24 wires. Beneath the wires was an illuminated sign visible from both sides of the street which read "Flowers by Telegraph Everywhere," while bunched around the two poles was a number of boxes of flowers ready for delivery. The body of the truck and the front was covered with yellow chrysanthemums. At the front of the machine was a large number of flying doves. Between the seats wherein sat the chauffeur and footman dressed in white mohair coats and white hats was a standard supporting a double sign, electrically illuminated, of blue glass with silver lettering, having the firm's name and address and in the center its seal with the word "Progressiveness."

CINCINNATI.

Max Rudolph, Gus. Adrian and Roy Rudolph were in Richmond, Ind., and New Castle, Ind., on Monday of this week. P. J. Olinger went up to his greenhouses at New Castle on Tuesday to get a line on his prospective Christmas supply.

Floral offerings and tokens of sympathy at Mrs. C. E. Critchell's funeral last Wednesday were many and very beautiful. Without a doubt they were the largest and finest assortment ever seen at a funeral in this city. The casket was enshrouded in a magnificent blanket of violets, lily of the valley and orchids.

SAN FRANCISCO.

A new florist shop has been opened on 12th street near Broadway, in Oakland, Cal., by A. J. Rossi, who was formerly with Seulberger's in that city.

John R. Wolf, superintendent of Sperry Park in Vallejo, Cal., is preparing a large hillside acreage for planting. The MacRorie-McLaren Co. is to supply 800 trees.

At their meeting on Dec. 1, the Ladies' Auxiliary of the Pacific Coast Horticultural Society made arrangements for a social and entertainment to be held on the first Tuesday in January.

W. A. Hoffinghof has just returned from Vallejo, Cal., where he went to present plans to the mayor and council for the beautification of a ten-acre tract at the entrance to the town, which the city has purchased for park purposes.

The MacRorie-McLaren Co. expect to begin the planting of about 25,000 pine and cypress trees in San Mateo County as soon as weather conditions permit. The order, which is one of the largest orders for trees ever placed in this section, came from an eastern capitalist who is interested in a forestry project down the peninsula.

It has been decided to hold another Sweet Pea Show in San Francisco during the early part of June next year, under the auspices of the American Sweet Pea Society. Already considerable interest is being shown. C. C. Morse & Co. have offered a 1st prize of $15, a 2nd of $10 and a 3rd of $5 for twelve vases of sweet peas from their "Grand Prize" collection. Two prizes are offered by W. Atlee Burpee & Co. for single vases of their new sweet pea, Fiery Cross, and they also offer prizes for Spencer sweet peas amounting to $25. Other firms have promised their support, and the committee hopes to have a complete schedule ready for distribution within the next few weeks. In the meantime, growers are urged to begin planting with a view to participating in the Spring show.

NEW YORK.

Wm. A. Hanft in convalescent and we are glad to say has now left the hospital.

The trustees of the Growers' Cut Flower Co., will hold their annual meeting middle of January.

E. J. Van Reyper succeeds J. J. Coan as manager of the Growers' Cut Flower Co. at their 28th street store.

There was a meeting of the directors of the Flower Market in Queens Plaza Building, on Saturday afternoon, December 4.

The Wholesale Florists' Protective League held its annual meeting at the Hotel Breslin on Friday afternoon, December 2.

The New York and New Jersey Plant Growers' Association held its annual meeting at the McAlpin on Tuesday, Dec. 7.

Gardenias are beginning to show up once more. George C. Siebrecht sets a pan of them in his window as a special temptation.

The annual ball of the Joseph Trepel Employees will be held at Arion Hall, Brooklyn, N. Y., on January 16, 1916. Tickets 50c.

Wm. J. Elliott is still confined to his bed with the injuries received by being run down by an automobile while crossing the avenue near his home.

The front of the MacNiff Horticultural Company's building in Vesey street is resplendent in green and Christmas red, very tastily and effectively done.

Hoosier Beauty, as grown by L. B. Coddington and marketed by H. E. Froment, is one of the finest dark red roses ever seen in this city. It brings the price all right.

Frank H. Traendly is again able to come in to business from his home in

Brooklyn. No man in the city trade is more actively in the foreground or could be more noticeably missed.

Woodrow & Marketos had a good job out of the Ford peace vessel which sailed from New York on Dec. 4. Eighty-six staterooms were lavishly decorated with palms, cyclamen, begonias, poinsettias, etc.

"The House of Ferns" is the title of a new wholesale place at 41 West 28th street. Their only specialty for the present is Florida-grown Asparagus

Chrysanthemum Alexander Guttman.

plumosus, which is shipped here by fast express from the farms in Florida.

An unusual number of fine imported hollies, with perfect foliage and heavily loaded with berries are to be seen in this market this season. Our native holly looks very inferior when compared with these attractive little trees.

The real thing in Dendrobium formosum giganteum is a regal flower. We were attracted by a dish of them

in Walter R. Seibrecht's window and they were truly giganteums in size. This flower still holds its own as a bridal specialty.

Phil. F. Kessler is receiving a very beautiful single pink chrysanthemum which finds a very rapid sale under the name of "pink daisy." There are two or three rows of petals and the color is in the class with the pyrethrums as to clearness of tint.

One gets some faint idea of the enormous dimensions of the trade in florists' decorative greens by a look-in at Kervan's establishment at this season of the year. It is one of the busiest spots in the wholesale district and the new building they have recently added was much needed.

Guttman & Raynor are exploiting a new early flowering chrysanthemum, originated by Frank Dinda of Farmingdale, N. Y., and named Alexander Guttman. Its character is well shown in the cut which appears herewith. Its color is lavender pink and it does not shed the bloom when one or two petals are pulled out. The foliage is not too large and it can be planted quite close. By taking a bud about August 1st a nice exhibition bloom may be had by middle of September. The parents are Beatrice May × a 3-year pink seedling. It was awarded a certificate of merit by the New York Florists' Club.

D. C. Arnold & Co., who conduct a wholesale cut flower market at West 28th street under the management of H. Weiss, have a modern range of carnation houses at Babylon, N. Y., consisting of three Lord & Burnham houses, each 50x300 and one 60x300. Their pet novelty at the present time is Mrs. Arnold, a light pink sport from Mrs. C. W. Ward, which has attained instant popularity with the trade here because of its good keeping character and its exceptional color, which is a little deeper than that of Enchantress but with a rare salmon glow and a suggestion of orange when seen on the plant in the sunlight.

CHICAGO.

The E. C. Amling Co. had some of the best Mrs. Russell roses last week that the season has produced. Five hundred were sold in one order for $115.

The tiny rose George Elgar is seen in the wholesale houses and is quickly picked up. It is the smallest rose grown in this vicinity and a bunch of 25 is no larger than a bunch of violets. They are used in corsages.

Mrs. Frances Rubel, who was financially interested in the Fleischman Floral Co., passed away Dec. 5, at her home at 4337 Grand Boulevard. A great many flowers were used at the funeral which took place Dec. 7, one order alone calling for over twenty thousand violets.

The opening of a department of Christmas decorations in one of Chicago's largest stores, has caused quite a ripple in florists' circles. All of the leading State street stores have handled this class of goods but not on so large a scale as this one which employs fifty or more clerks, and has a buying power which makes it possible to retail below the florists' wholesale prices. The development of the trade in artificial flowers and plants and in all kinds of decorative substitutes for cut flowers, has been noted year after year and its effect in limiting the sale of cut flowers has become an acknowledged fact.

Chas. W. Ward, who has 160 acres

in one of the valleys of California near Eureka, was a Chicago visitor this week, and expressed himself as pleased with the outlook for growing there azaleas, rhododendrons and other plants, heretofore imported from Europe. The trial so far is satisfactory. In the lower parts of the valley citrus fruits are grown and higher up the English walnut, pecan and other nut-bearing trees are planted. Mr. Ward believes in the future of California as a producer of the stock which florists have not grown here and is backing up his ideas by going into the business there where one of the advantages is the unlimited supply of water. His place is known as the Cottage Gardens Nurseries.

NEWS NOTES.

Albion, Mich.—F. E. Hubert has purchased the greenhouses of Carl Jacobs.

Wilmington, Mass.—Wm. M. Wylie has purchased the greenhouses of Dr. M. E. Brande on West street.

Hillside, N. J.—One of the Elizabeth Nursery Company's greenhouses was badly damaged by fire Nov. 27th. It is thought the fire was of incendiary origin.

New Castle, Pa.—W. H. Weinschenk's boiler house and greenhouse were destroyed by fire Nov. 30th. The loss will amount to about $1200. Besides the buildings, a large amount of onion sets were destroyed.

PHILADELPHIA.

Mr. and Mrs. Alexander B. Scott of Sharon Hill will leave for the Pacific Coast on Saturday, the 11th inst., for rest and change of scene. Mrs. Scott, who is a sister of the late W. Atlee Burpee, has devoted herself, with other members of the family, to soothing the fevered hours of the departed with true sisterly devotion. It is not a thing to talk about—being too sacred for that.

H. Bayersdorfer & Co. are now doing the largest business in the history of their house. Mr. Bayersdorfer's visit to Japan last summer was very fruitful as is shown in the vast quantity and wide variety of the Japanese manufactured goods they are handling. The Japanese have quickly learned the manufacture of baskets, jardinieres and other things heretofore imported from Germany and even Porto Rico matting of perfect weave. These with the goods being made in their own factory give Bayersdorfer & Co. an immense advantage and the demand from all parts of the country is such that 25 or 30 more employees were necessarily been added. Mr. Berkowitz says that the Japs are making a strong bid to control this line of work and it looks as if they would entirely supersede the European manufacturers.

Watch the Buyers' Directory these days for information as to good plants, seeds, supplies, etc., and where they can be purchased to best advantage.

SOME NEW ROSES.

Respecting the new American Rose Hadley, nothing I have written is derogatory to it. Having grown it in the open from original imported plants, I have been able to estimate its worth, and for this reason was rather surprised that it gained an A. M. on the samples shown, presumably from run-out buds. As exhibited, the flowers were far from representing it at its best, and the same may be said of Hoosier Beauty, shown by Stuart Low & Co. at the same time. Both varieties are really fine and I would couple with them Crimson Beauty also. All, however, have their off color turns. Get them in true form, and especially from home budded stock, I imagine this American trio will be something to conjure with, especially Crimson Beauty, which is very quick, and has a very long bud.—

W. A. T. in Hort. Trade Journal, London.

Mr. Harry A. Barnard, of Stuart Low & Co., has just returned from his usual business trip through U. S. A., bringing back with him a number of blooms of a fine new light pink Rose named Mrs. Bayard Thayer, raised by A. Montgomery, of the Waban Rose Conservatories, Natick, Mass. Unfortunately, most of the flowers failed to last out the fortnight of travel, otherwise it was intended to exhibit them at the R. H. S. Meeting. Mr. Barnard did, however, bring along a couple of blooms, and we feel safe in hazarding that Mrs. Bayard Thayer is an important rose. It appears to have the build and growth of Mrs. Chas. Russell, another of the Waban Rose Conservatories' seedlings, and these characteristics coupled with its strong perfume, should make it a serious rival to Mme. A. Chatenay.—

Hort. Trade Journal, London.

Hadley and Hoosier Beauty are both standards in the commercial cut flower market this year, up in the front with Russell and Beauty. There is no Crimson Beauty so far as I have seen; maybe that one will make good later. Mrs. Bayard Thayer is well liked in the American flower market, where Mme. Chatenay has practically been outclassed and forgotten.   G. C. W.

VISITORS' REGISTER.

San Francisco: M. Simmers, Fresno, Cal.; Geo. C. Roeding, Fresno; Mrs. Lena McCoy, Seattle, Wash.

St. Louis—H. C. Neubrand, representing A. N. Pierson Co., Cromwell, Conn.; A. L. Vaughan, Chicago; Frank J. Farney, representing M. Rice Co., Philadelphia.

Chicago—Paul Beyer, South Bend, Ind.; Chas. P. Mueller, Wichita, Kas.; R. D. Whorton, of the Huron Greenhouses, Huron, South Dakota; Chas. W. Ward, Eureka, Cal..

Philadelphia—Robert Pyle, Conard & Jones Co., West Grove, Pa.; W. H. Vance, Wilmington, Del.; Walter A. Stewart, Stecher Lith. Co., Rochester, N. Y.; L. J. Reuter, Westerly, R. I.; Wm. Feast, Baltimore, Md.; Will Rehder, Wilmington, N. C.

New York—Lester Morse, San Francisco, Cal.; L. J. Reuter, Westerly, R. I.; Wm. Gray, Newport, R. I.; Geo. W. Kerr, Doylestown, Pa.; T. Murray, Tuxedo, N. Y.; Eugene Schaettel, Paris, France; E. F. Coe, New Haven, Conn.; W. J. Newton, Norfolk, Va.

Washington, D. C. — Joseph J. Goudy, representing H. A. Dreer, Sidney H. Bayersdorfer, representing H. Bayersdorfer & Co., I. Rosnosky, of H. F. Michell Co., and James F. Smith, all of Philadelphia, Pa.; Will Rehder, Wilmington, N. C.; Winfried Roelker, New York; G. L. Freeman, Fall River, Mass.

Boston — John Canning, Ardsley, N. Y.; Prof. A. H. Nehrling, Amherst, Mass.; Robert Greenlaw, representing S. S. Pennock-Meehan Co., Phila.; Wm. Kleinheinz, Ogontz, Pa.; J. W. Everitt, Glen Cove, N. Y.; M. C. Ebel, Madison,

N. J.; Jas. Stuart, Mamaroneck, N. Y.; J. F. Huss, Hartford, Ct.; J. S. Hay, representing H. A. Dreer, Inc., Phila.; P. W. Popp, Mamaroneck, N. Y.; Fred Carter, Newport; Jas. Aitchison, Mt. Kisco; Peter Murray, Plymouth, Mass.; Herbert Clark, Manchester, Mass.; W. A. Sperling, representing Stumpp & Walter Co., New York; Vernon T. Sherwood, Charlestown, N. H.; Jas. MacMachan, Tuxedo, N. Y.; Arthur Smith, Reading, Pa.; Eric Wetterlow, Manchester, Mass.; John Scheepers, New York; D. F. Roy, Marion, Mass.; Joseph Manda, West Orange, N. J.; W. F. Leary, New Rochelle, N. Y.; Wm. Angus, Buzzards Bay, Mass.; A. J. Newell, Hopedale, Mass.; George Barker, Swampscott, Mass.; Jas. Marlborough, Topsfield, Mass.; John Allcock, East Burke, Vt.

FLOWER MARKET REPORTS

BOSTON Trade at present writing is quite dull although for a few days past there was a fair demand. The inactivity naturally reflects on the wholesale market rates although not so much as would be the case if there were heavier receipts. Receipts have fallen off very noticeably and to this fact is due the comparative stability of prices on many staples. Roses hold their own in good fashion but American Beauties have been forced down somewhat and figures on the better grades are below those prevalent last week. Carnations have actually advanced, the cause for this being probably the gradual shrinking of the chrysanthemum supply. However, there will be a considerable number of the latter coming in until after Christmas, judging from appearances. Violets are difficult to find and are selling at a sharp advance. This does not include the Hudson River doubles which are difficult to move and bring scarcely more than half the price of singles. Stevia and paper white narcissi hang fire. Pansies sell well at excellent prices. The little George Elgar roses and others of that class are seen in considerable numbers. There is some call for them but for the present there are about all the market will take.

BUFFALO The receipts were heavy on chrysanthemums the past week, which has had a tendency to weaken the sales of carnations and other stock though the near ending is soon looked for. Roses are not overplentiful and have had good sales. Beauties are fine with only normal demand. There are some good violets and plenty of lily of the valley on which the demand was light, however. Lilies are in normal supply. There has been a heavy supply of pompon chrysanthemums on which the demand is gradually falling away. Holly, laurel, pine and other decorative material are gradually growing in demand.

CHICAGO Comparative quiet exists in the market following a good Thanksgiving week and preparations for an active holiday trade are general among the wholesalers and retailers. At this time much depends upon the amount of sunshine during the next ten days. Growers report quantities of buds in sight but without bright weather they will not open in time for the florists' best season of the year. So far December has been cloudy. There are plenty of blooming plants in all the Christmas varieties advanced far enough so their condition is assured.

The condition of American Beauties remains unsatisfactory, with stock scarce and of rather poor quality. Mrs. Russell is showing more deviation in color than at any previous time since its introduction here and just what is the cause has not been agreed upon by the growers. Carnations are selling better now that pompons are leaving. Chrysanthemums are nearly gone. A few only of the late varieties will be in market till Christmas.

CINCINNATI The local market is cleaning up pretty well but this is due to a small general supply rather than to active demand. If the demand for stock were as brisk as it might be there would be a shortage. Shipping business is very good. Roses, while not as plentiful as they were, still are in supply sufficient for present needs. Pink roses and American Beauties, relatively speaking, are not as plentiful as the white ones. The carnation cut has shortened greatly. Lilies are having a good market now that the chrysanthemums are not as plentiful as they were. Callas, too, sell more readily. Double violets are fairly plentiful. Lily of the valley, orchids and sweet peas come in regularly and meet with an active market. Narcissus

(Continued on page 790)

Flower Market Reports

(*Continued from page 788*)

receipts are rather limited as yet. Stevia receipts are so heavy that it is impossible to clean up on all each day.

NEW YORK — This market has seen many market fluctuations during the past week, some of which are hard to understand. Violets have taken an abrupt upward turn and have about doubled in price, the singles, of which a good many come from the vicinity of Boston, enjoying the best sale. The situation looks as though the violet growers were beginning to hold back on their picking in anticipation of a holiday advance. If that is so they have a fine chance to lose out as has been repeatedly demonstrated in past years. Chrysanthemums still linger and they are really good. All the Chadwicks, Goldmine, Harvard and the perennial Bonnaffon are the chief varieties now in the large flowered section but there are lots of pompons, anemones and late singles, all of which classes are being grown more and more and of better quality than ever before. There are some beautiful sunny bronzes among the pompons which sell at sight. The quality of roses is excellent everywhere. Ophelia, Sunburst, Hoosier Beauty and Aaron Ward are seen in rich array and Hoosier Beauty and Prima Donna are bringing almost or quite the price of American Beauty. The latter had advanced steadily for some days but on Tuesday of this week seemed to strike the doldroms and fall back to the old fall figure of $3.00 a dozen for the best—and the "best" were well worthy to be so considered. Very many of the tiny rose buds of Mignon type are seen this fall and they appear to find a good market. Cattleyas are now becoming more plentiful but the majority of the blooms one sees are under sized and do not impress one as being worth the prices asked. Lily of the valley has maintained an advanced price for some time and it looks as if the standard winter value on this indispensable flower would be higher by fifty per cent. than it has been in any recent year. About carnations there is little to be said. They are not much in the public eye just at present although there are some fine flowers being sent in. Growers will be chary about letting many of their red ones get out of their sight and very soon we may expect to see these go aeroplaning. Pansies are having much popular favor and are classed among the things that every well conducted store must have. The sweet peas are now asserting themselves, some of the stock being well up to exhibition quality. Gardenias are again to be had in limited number. Among the newer—or rather, in old things revived, are the bouvardias, of which generous quantities in several colors, both double and singles are shown on long stems and well filled trusses. Reverting to the chrysanthemums once more we should not fail to mention Frank Dinda's anemone flowered Emma which is in our opinion the best in its class on the market.

PHILADELPHIA — We had a very steady market here for the past week and stock generally has cleaned up pretty well. Towards the end of last week carnations shortened up a good deal and the tone of the market for these has improved very considerably. The orchid situation, on the other hand, experienced a great change as several new sources of supply came in crop and prices are now very much easier. American Beauty roses were never finer. The supply is good. The demand is good. On the whole prices have firmed up a little notwithstanding the excellent crops which are larger than for years at this period. (Martin Santman, Senator Heacock and other apostles of the supply and demand theory please take notice.) All other red roses are selling well but at rather lower figures. The double white Killarney is now in her glory and getting better every day; the most wonderful

(*Continued on page 703*)

WHOLESALE FLOWER MARKETS — TRADE PRICES—Per 100 TO DEALERS ONLY

Roses	CINCINNATI Dec. 6		CHICAGO Dec. 6		BUFFALO Dec. 6		PITTSBURG Dec. 6	
Am. Beauty, Special	40.00	45.00	50.00	75.00	35.00	40.00	30.00	40.00
" " Fancy and Extra	25.00	35.00	30.00	40.00	20.00	30.00	20.00	25.00
" " No. 1	10.00	20.00	15.00	25.00	12.00	15.00	10.00	15.00
Russell, Hadley	8.00	15.00	4.00	25.00	10.00	12.00	8.00	12.00
Killarney, Richm'd, Hill'don, Ward	7.00	10.00	8.00	10.00	7.00	8.00	8.00	10.00
" " " Ord.	4.00	6.00	3.00	5.00	3.00	6.00	4.00	6.00
Arenburg, Radiance, Taft, Key, Ex.	7.00	10.00	8.00	10.00	8.00	10.00	8.00	12.00
" " " Ord.	4.00	6.00	3.00	5.00	3.00	6.00		6.00
Ophelia, Mock, Sunburst, Extra	7.00	10.00	8.00	12.00	8.00	12.00	8.00	15.00
" " " Ordinary	4.00	6.00	3.00	5.00	4.00	6.00		6.00
Carnations, Fancy	3.00	4.00	2.00	3.00	3.00			4.00
" Ordinary		3.00	1.00	2.00	1.50	2.00	2.00	3.00
Cattleyas	60.00	75.00	60.00	75.00	50.00	60.00	40.00	75.00
Dendrobium formosum			50.00	60.00			35.00	60.00
Lilies, Longiflorum	10.00	12.50	6.00	10.00	10.00	12.50	10.00	12.00
Rubrum	4.00	8.00	5.00	6.00		4.00		
Callas	10.00	15.00		10.00	8.00	10.00	8.00	12.00
Lily of the Valley		4.00	3.00	4.00	3.00	4.00	3.00	4.00
Daisies		2.00				.75	.75	1.00
Violets	.75	1.00	.75	1.00	.60	.75	.50	1.00
Mignonette		2.00		3.00	3.00	4.00	3.00	4.00
Snapdragon		2.00	4.00	6.00	2.00	4.00	4.00	6.00
Narcissus, Paper-White	3.00	4.00	2.00	3.00			3.00	4.00
Trumpet		2.00						
Hyacinths, Roman		2.00		2.00		2.00		
Freesia		2.00		2.00			3.00	4.00
Calendulas		2.00		2.00				
Stevia	2.00	4.00	1.00	1.50	1.00	1.25	1.00	2.00
Sweet Peas	.75	1.00	1.50	2.00	1.00	1.25	1.00	2.00
Gardenias			40.00	50.00				2.00
Adiantum		1.00	1.00	1.00	1.00	1.25	1.00	1.25
Smilax	12.50	15.00	10.00	12.00		15.00	12.50	15.00
Asparagus Plumosus, Strings (100)	25.00	50.00	40.00	50.00	40.00	60.00	30.00	50.00
& Spren. (100 bchs).	25.00	35.00	25.00	50.00	30.00	50.00	30.00	50.00

Flower Market Reports

(Continued from page 700)

pure white rose the world has ever seen; reigns alone and has the market all to herself; brooks no rival to her throne. We all bow to her and your humble scribe must try to make her glorious by his pen, and incidentally he would cast a ray or two of the dazzle towards Casper Pennock of Lansdowne. The chrysanthemum crop is nearly over; some yellow and a sprinkling of pink but mostly Jeanie Nonin.

Business has SAN FRANCISCO been a little quiet comparatively, the past week, which came as a natural sequence after the heavy Thanksgiving rush, accentuated by the all-absorbing interest in the Exposition as the date for the final closing drew near. It seemed everyone who could possibly do so, rushed to the grounds for a last look at the greatest spectacle of its kind the world has ever known. The spirit of unrest pervaded the entire city, and many lines of regular business suffered a temporary slump. As to the market an unusual condition has confronted the florists the last month in that outdoor summer stock has held on so late. The present storm will probably put a stop to the abundant supplies of summer flowers, but up until this time the shops have been full of such offerings. During the exposition the large number of decorations furnished an outlet for great quantities of this small outdoor stock, but now that the fair is closed, the florists are glad to see the supply vanish, as it will make toward

(Continued on page 795)

WHOLESALE FLOWER MARKETS — TRADE PRICES—Per 100 TO DEALERS ONLY

Roses	BOSTON Dec. 9		ST. LOUIS Dec. 6		PHILA. Dec. 6	
Am. Beauty, Special....................	40.00 to	50.00	40.00 to	50.00	30.00 to	35.00
"　"　Fancy and Extra..........	12.00 to	15.00	25.00 to	30.00	20.00 to	25.00
"　"　No. 1....................	5.00 to	10.00	10.00 to	15.00	5.00 to	15.00
Russell, Hadley....................	4.00 to	10.00	8.00 to	10.00	4.00 to	25.00
Killarney, Richmond, Hillingdon, Ward, Extra......	3.00 to	6.00	8.00 to	10.00	6.00 to	10.00
"　"　"　Ordinary....	1.00 to	3.00	4.00 to	6.00	3.00 to	5.00
Arenburg Radiance, Taft, Key, Extra...........	3.00 to	6.00	...... to		6.00 to	10.00
"　"　"　Ordinary..........	2.00 to	3.00	...... to		3.00 to	5.00
Ophelia, Mock, Sunburst, Extra..............	4.00 to	8.00	8.00 to	10.00	6.00 to	12.00
"　"　"　Ordinary............	2.00 to	4.00	4.00 to	6.00	3.00 to	5.00
Carnations, Fancy....................	3.00 to	4.00	4.00 to	5.00	3.00 to	4.00
"　Ordinary....................	1.00 to	2.00	2.00 to	2.00	2.00 to	3.00
Cattleyas....................	50.00 to	60.00	...... to		50.00 to	75.00
Dendrobium formosum....................	...... to		40.00 to		...... to	50.00
Lilies, Longiflorum....................	1.00 to	10.00	12.00 to	15.00	8.00 to	10.00
"　Rubrum....................	...... to	3.00	6.00 to	8.00	4.00 to	6.00
Callas....................	8.00 to	12.00	...... to		10.00 to	12.50
Lily of the Valley....................	2.00 to	4.00	3.00 to	4.00	2.00 to	4.00
Daisies....................	.50 to	1.00	.25 to	.50	.75 to	1.50
Violets....................	.50 to	1.00	.25 to	.50	.25 to	1.00
Mignonette....................	2.00 to	3.00	...... to		2.00 to	5.00
Snapdragon....................	2.00 to	4.00	3.00 to	4.00	3.00 to	8.00
Narcissus, Paper-White....................	1.50 to	2.00	...... to		...... to	3.00
"　Trumpet....................	...... to		...... to		...... to	
Hyacinths, Roman....................	...... to		...... to		...... to	
Freesia....................	...... to		...... to		...... to	
Calendulas....................	2.00 to	3.00	...... to		2.00 to	3.00
Stevia....................	...... to	2.00	...... to		.50 to	.75
Sweet Peas....................	...... to	1.00	.50 to	1.50	.50 to	1.00
Gardenias....................	25.00 to	35.00	...... to		15.00 to	35.00
Adiantum....................	...... to	1.00	1.00 to	1.25	...... to	1.00
Smilax....................	12.00 to	16.00	16.00 to	20.00	15.00 to	20.00
Asparagus Plumosus, Strings (100)............	25.00 to	50.00	35.00 to	50.00	...... to	50.00
"　& Spren. (100 Bchs.)............	15.00 to	35.00	35.00 to	50.00	35.00 to	50.00

Flower Market Reports

(Continued from page 703)

a better demand for roses and other more seasonable offerings. The rain is damaging the outdoor chrysanthemums also, which will no doubt strengthen the market on other varieties of seasonables still further. Violets, on the other hand, will benefit by the rain. They are in good supply and an active shipping demand cleans up the daily arrivals closely. Carnations have weakened a little owing to heavy arrivals and only fair demand. From all reports flowers will be in fine shape for Christmas. Roses are improving steadily with a splendid cut in view for the holidays. The same is true of poinsettias. Some fine specimens are being offered now, but most of the growers are holding their crop. Gardenias promise well. In potted stock, cyclamen holds a strong position, and begonias are getting more plentiful, as well as azaleas and primulas.

Prime Thanksgiving

ST. LOUIS stock of all kinds has been scarce and a rise in prices has occurred all along the line. Cold and clear weather assures a good quality of stock and a good supply for the holidays. There is a scarcity of roses in all varieties and prices have advanced. There are more Killarneys than others. Beauties are very scarce but the local grown are just beginning to come in on crop. Carnations are also somewhat scarce. Sweet peas and violets are not enough for the demand. Lily of the valley, paper white narcissi and lilies have a large demand but with no advance in prices. Chrysanthemums are over for this season.

The flower market

WASHINGTON is in fine shape with prices advancing normally. Roses show something of a shortage in the lower grades. Carnations and roses both clean up well each day. While chrysanthemums are still very plentiful not nearly as many are going to waste and sales are good. There is almost a glut of double violets which sell low. Single violets of local production are exceptionally good and are bringing a little better price. Orchids are more plentiful but still clean up quickly and there are not enough to go around. Gardenias are to be had in larger quantities. Sweet peas are coming in better shape and sell fairly well. Easter and Rubrum lilies are very plentiful. Lily of the valley is in good demand.

Buyer's Directory and Ready Reference Guide

Advertisements under this head, one cent a word.   Initials count as words.

Display advertisers in this issue are also listed under this classification without charge. Reference to List of Advertisers will indicate the respective pages.

Buyers failing to find what they want in this list will confer a favor by writing us and we will try to put them in communication with reliable dealers.

ACCOUNTANT
R. Dysart, 40 State St., Boston.
For page see List of Advertisers.

APHINE
Aphine Mfg. Co., Madison, N. J.
For page see List of Advertisers.

APHIS PUNK
Nicotine Mfg. Co., St. Louis, Mo.
For page see List of Advertisers.

ASPARAGUS
Asparagus Plumosus, Thumb pot plants,
sure to please, $1.50 per 100. B. C. BLAKE,
R. D. 4, Springfield, Ohio.

500 Plumosus, 2½ in. for $10.00; 300
Sprengerii, 4 in., for $16.00.   RONEY
BROS., West Grove, Pa.

AUCTION SALES
The MacNiff Horticultural Co.,
New York City.
Plant and Bulb Sales by Auction.
For page see ·List of Advertisers.

Elliott Auction Co., New York City.
For page see List of Advertisers.

AZALEAS
P. Ouwerkerk, Hoboken, N. J.
For page see List of Advertisers.

BAY TREES
August Rolker & Sons, New York.
For page see List of Advertisers.

BEDDING PLANTS
A. N. Pierson, Inc., Cromwell, Conn.
For page see List of Advertisers.

R. Vincent, Jr. & Sons Co.,
White Marsh, Md.
For page see List of Advertisers.

BEGONIAS
BEGONIA LORRAINE,		Per 100
	2½ in.	$12.90
	3 in.	20.00
	4 in.	35.00
	5 in.	50.00
BEGONIA CINCINNATI,	2½ in.	15.00
	3 in.	25.00
	3½ in.	30.00
	4½ in.	40.00

JULIUS ROEHRS CO., Rutherford, N. J.

BOILERS
Kroeschell Bros. Co., Chicago.
For page see List of Advertisers.

King Construction Co., North Tonawanda,
N. Y.
"King Ideal" Boiler.
For page see List of Advertisers.

Hitchings & Co., New York City.
For page see List of Advertisers.

Lord & Burnham Co., New York City.

BOXES—CUT FLOWER FOLDING
Edwards Folding Box Co. Philadelphia.
For page see List of Advertisers.

Folding cut flower boxes, the best made.
Write for list. HOLTON & HUNKEL CO.,
Milwaukee, Wis.

BOX TREES
BOX TREES—Standards, Pyramids and
Bush. In various sizes. Price List on de-
mand. JULIUS ROEHRS CO., Rutherford,
N. J.

BOXWOOD
Breck-Robinson Nursery Co., Lexington,
Mass.

BULBS AND TUBERS
Arthur T. Beddington Co., Inc.,
New York City.
For page see List of Advertisers.

J. M. Thorburn & Co., New York City
Wholesale Price List of High Class Bulbs.
For page see List of Advertisers.

Ralph M. Ward & Co., New York City.
Lily Bulbs.
For page see List of Advertisers.

John Lewis Childs, Flowerfield, L. I., N. Y.
Gladioli.
For page see List of Advertisers.

August Rolker & Sons, New York City.
Holland and Japan Bulbs.
For page see List of Advertisers.

R. & J. Farquhar & Co., Boston, Mass.
For page see List of Advertisers.

F. R. Pierson, Tarrytown, N. Y.
Hyacinths and Narcissus.

Chas. Schwake & Co., New York City.
Horticultural Importers and Exporters.
For page see List of Advertisers.

A. Henderson & Co., Chicago, Ill.
For page see List of Advertisers.

Burnett Bros., 98 Chambers St., New York.
For page see List of Advertisers.

Henry F. Michell Co., Philadelphia, Pa.
For page see List of Advertisers.

Joseph Breck & Sons Corp., Boston, Mass.
For page see List of Advertisers.

Fottler, Fiske, Rawson Co., Boston, Mass.
For page see List of Advertisers.

C. KEUR & SONS, HILLEGOM, Holland.
Bulbs of all descriptions. Write for prices.
NEW YORK Branch, 8-10 Bridge St.

Bulbs—150,000 Late Shipment
HYACINTHS, TULIPS, NARCISSUS.
Prices Low. Stock the Best.
Send for List or Phone Melrose 761-W.
THOMAS COGGER,
229 Laurel St., Melrose, Mass.

CANNAS
Newest list of the newest Cannas just
out. Complete assortment of the finest
sorts, at remarkable rates.
Send for list today.
THE CONARD & JONES CO.
West Grove, Pa.

CARNATIONS
Wood Bros., Fishkill, N. Y.
For page see List of Advertisers.

F. Dorner & Sons Co., Lafayette, Ind.
For page see List of Advertisers.

Littlefield & Wyman, North Abington, Mass.
New Pink Carnation, Miss Theo.
For page see List of Advertisers.

CARNATION STAPLES
Split carnations quickly, easily and
cheaply mended. Pillsbury's Carnation
Staple. 1000 for 35c.; 3000 for $1.00 post
paid. I. L. PILLSBURY, Galesburg, Ill.

Supreme Carnation Staples, for repairing
split carnations. 35c. per 1000; 3000 for
$1.00. F. W. WAITE, 85 Belmont Ave.,
Springfield, Mass.

CHRISTMAS PLANTS
A. M. Davenport, Watertown, Mass.
For page see List of Advertisers.

Elmer D. Smith & Co., Adrian, Mich.
For page see List of Advertisers.

CHRYSANTHEMUMS
Chas. H. Totty, Madison, N. J.
For page see List of Advertisers.

COLEUS
Christmas Gem Coleus, 3c. B. C. BLAKE,
R. D. 4, Springfield, Ohio.

Coleus, Golden Bedder, Verschaffeltii,
Queen Victoria, Firebrand and all leading
varieties, including the Pink and Yellow
Trailing Queen, clean, strong, well rooted
cuttings, 60c. per 100, $4.00 per 1000. Cash
with order, and satisfaction guaranteed.
Send for list. Largest grower of coleus in
the U. S. A. NAHLIK, 261-75 Lawrence St.,
Flushing, N. Y.

DAHLIAS
Send for Wholesale List of whole clumps
and separate stock; 40,000 clumps for sale.
Northboro Dahlia and Gladiolus Gardens.
J. L. MOORE, Prop, Northboro, Mass.

NEW PAEONY DAHLIA
John Wanamaker. Newest, Handsomest.
Best. New color; new form and new habit
of growth. Big stock of best cut-flower
varieties. Send list of wants to
PEACOCK DAHLIA FARMS, Berlin, N. J.

DECORATIVE PLANTS
Robert Craig Co., Philadelphia, Pa.
For page see List of Advertisers.

Woodrow & Marketos, New York City.
For page see List of Advertisers.

S. S. Skidelsky & Co., Philadelphia, Pa.
For page see List of Advertisers.

Bobbink & Atkins, Rutherford, N. J.
For page see List of Advertisers.

A. Leuthy & Co., Roslindale, Boston, Mass.
For page see List of Advertisers.

Thomas Roland, Nahant, Mass.
High-Grade Plants for Retail Florists.
For page see List of Advertisers.

DRACENAS
Dracena Indivisa, 4-in. pot plants, 6c.
B. C. BLAKE, R. D. 4, Springfield, Ohio.

FERNS
Henry A. Dreer, Philadelphia, Pa.
Dreer's Fine Ferns.
For page see List of Advertisers.

John Scott, Brooklyn, N. Y.
The Home of the Scottii Fern.
For page see List of Advertisers.

H. H. Barrows & Son, Whitman, Mass.
For page see List of Advertisers.

Robert Craig Co., Philadelphia, Pa.
For page see List of Advertisers.

McHutchison & Co., New York City.
Ferns in Flats.
For page see List of Advertisers.

A. M. Davenport, Watertown, Mass.
Boston and Whitmani Ferns.
For page see List of Advertisers.

Roman J. Irwin, New York City.
Boston and Whitmani Ferns.
For page see List of Advertisers.

Ferns, 2-in., Boston, Whitmani, Roosevelt, Elegantissima, Compacta and Teddy Jr.
B. C. BLAKE, R. D. 4, Springfield, Ohio.

FERTILIZERS
Stumpp & Walter Co., New York City.
Scotch Soot.
For page see List of Advertisers.

Pulverized Manure Co., Chicago, Ill.
Wizard Brand Cattle Manure.
For page see List of Advertisers.

FLORISTS' LETTERS
Boston Florist Letter Co., Boston, Mass.
For page see List of Advertisers.

FLORISTS' SUPPLIES
N. F. McCarthy & Co., Boston, Mass.
For page see List of Advertisers.

For List of Advertisers See Page 723

FLORISTS' SUPPLIES—Continued

Reed & Keller, New York City.
For page see List of Advertisers.

S. S. Pennock-Meehan Co., Philadelphia, Pa.
For page see List of Advertisers.

H. Bayersdorfer & Co., Philadelphia, Pa.
For page see List of Advertisers.

Welch Bros. Co., Boston, Mass.
For page see List of Advertisers.

FLOWER POTS

W. H. Ernest, Washington, D. C.
For page see List of Advertisers.

A. H. Hews & Co., Inc., Cambridge, Mass.
For page see List of Advertisers.

Hilfinger Bros., Ft. Edward, N. Y.
For page see List of Advertisers.

FOLIAGE PLANTS

A. Leuthy & Co., Roslindale, Boston, Mass.
For page see List of Advertisers.

FORGET-ME-NOTS

Myosotis palustris. True Forget-Me-Not. Two clumps in Carton sent by Parcel Post on receipt of price, 25 cents. SHATEMUC NURSERIES, Barrytown, Dutchess County, New York.

FUNGINE

Aphine Mfg. Co., Madison, N. J.
For page see List of Advertisers.

GALAX

Michigan Cut Flower Co., Detroit, Mich
For page see List of Advertisers.

GARDEN TOOLS

B. G. Pratt Co., New York City.
For page see List of Advertisers.

GERANIUMS

R. Vincent, Jr., & Sons Co.
White Marsh, Md.
For page see List of Advertisers.

Geraniums, mixed varieties out of 2¼ inch pots. Am booking orders for December delivery at $20.00 per 1000. Cash. JAMES MOSS, Johnsville, Pa.

Geraniums—Ricard, Doyle, Nutt, Poitevine and Chevalier, from 2¼-inch pots, immediate or later delivery, $20.00 per 1000. Rooted Cuttings, $15.00 per 1000. Cash with order. WM. F. KOENIG, 566 Hamilton Ave., West New York, N. J.

Rooted cuttings of the new Geranium Margaret Walsh are now for sale at $5.00 per 100; out of 2½-inch pots, $9.00 per 100. A limited quantity only offered now for sale. Cash must accompany each order. JOHN WALSH, Franklin St., Melrose H'l'ds, Mass.

GLADIOLI

John Lewis Childs, Flowerfield, L. I., N. Y.
For page see List of Advertisers.

Gladioli America, $6.00; Augusta, $6.00; Halley, $7.00; Princeps, $7.00; Mrs. F. King, $8.00; all first size bulbs. Booking orders for Spring Delivery. THOMAS COGGER, 229 Laurel St., Melrose, Mass.

ATTENTION, MR. FLORIST!

300,000 Gladioli must be sold at once, ready for shipment now. America, 1¾ in. up, $8 per 1000; 1½ in., $7 per 1000. Halley, 1½ to 2½ in., $7 per 1000. Baron Hulot, blue, 1½ in., $7 per 1000. Brenchleyensis, 1½ in., $7 per 1000. Augusta, 1½ in., $8 per 1000. Lilly Lehman, pure white, $10 per 1000. Pink Beauty, $7.50 per 1000.

50,000 Monbretia, $5 per 1000. Every florist ought to buy this bulb, as it is hardy, the best flower for cut and decorative purpose; flowers from July until the frost kills it.

10,000 single Begonias in 6 colors, $11 per 1000; 3,000 Dielytra (Bleeding Heart), $30 per 1000; 4,000 Lilium Rubrum and Album, Dutch grown, $20 per 1000. Ask our special price on large quantities. Credit until May 1st, when satisfactory references. Our new catalogue for bulbs will be out shortly; do you want one? Speak quick and write us today. VAN TIL HARTMAN, Hillegom, Holland, care of P. C. Kuyper & Co., 10-12 Broadway, New York.

GLASS

Sharp, Partridge & Co., Chicago.
For page see List of Advertisers.

Parshelsky Bros., Inc., Brooklyn, N. Y.
For page see List of Advertisers.

Royal Glass Works, New York City.
For page see List of Advertisers.

Greenhouse glass, lowest prices. JOHNSTON GLASS CO., Hartford City, Ind.

GLASS CUTTERS

Smith & Hemenway Co., New York City.
Red Devil Glass Cutter.
For page see List of Advertisers.

GLAZING POINTS

H. A. Dreer, Philadelphia, Pa.
Peerless Glazing Point.
For page see List of Advertisers.

GOLD FISH

Gold fish, aquarium plants, snails, castles, globes, aquarium, fish goods, nets, etc., wholesale. FRANKLIN BARRETT, Breeder, 4815 D St., Olney, Philadelphia, Pa. Large breeding pairs for sale. Send for price list.

GREENHOUSE BUILDING MATERIAL

King Construction Co., N. Tonawanda, N. Y.
For page see List of Advertisers.

Parshelsky Bros., Inc., Brooklyn, N. Y.
For page see List of Advertisers.

A. T. Stearns Lumber Co., Neponset, Boston.
Pecky Cypress.
For page see List of Advertisers.

Lord & Burnham Co., New York City.

GREENHOUSE CONSTRUCTION

King Construction Co., N. Tonawanda, N. Y.
For page see List of Advertisers.

Foley Greenhouse Mfg. Co., Chicago, Ill.
For page see List of Advertisers

Hitchings & Co., New York City.
For page see List of Advertisers.

Metropolitan Material Co., Brooklyn, N. Y.
For page see List of Advertisers.

A. T. Stearns Lumber Co., Boston, Mass.
For page see List of Advertisers.

Lord & Burnham Co., New York City.

GUTTERS

King Construction Co., N. Tonawanda, N. Y.
King Channel Gutter.
For page see List of Advertisers.

HAIL INSURANCE

Florists' Hail Asso. of America.
J. G Esler, Saddle River, N. J.
For page see List of Advertisers.

HARDY FERNS AND GREEN GOODS

Michigan Cut Flower Exchange, Detroit. Mich.
For page see List of Advertisers.

Knud Nielsen, Evergreen, Ala.
Natural Green Sheet Moss, Fancy and Dagger Ferns and Huckleberry Foliage.
For page see List of Advertisers.

The Kervan Co., New York.
For page see List of Advertisers.

HARDY PERENNIALS

Bay State Nurseries, No. Abington, Mass.
For page see List of Advertisers.

P. Ouwerkerk, Hoboken, N. J.
For page see List of Advertisers.

Palisades Nurseries, Sparkill, N. Y.
For page see List of Advertisers.

HEATING APPARATUS

Kroeschell Bros. Co., Chicago.
For page see List of Advertisers.

Lord & Burnham Co., New York City.

HOLLYHOCKS

Hollyhocks in separate colors and mixed, fine large plants, $6.00 per 100, smaller plants, $4.00 per 100. Cash. JAMES MOSS, Johnsville, Pa.

HOT BED SASH.

Parshelsky Bros., Inc., Brooklyn, N. Y.
For page see List of Advertisers.

A. T. Stearns Lumber Co., Neponset, Mass.
For page see List of Advertisers.

HOT BED SASH—Continued

Foley Greenhouse Construction Co., Chicago, Ill.
For page see List of Advertisers.

Lord & Burnham Co., New York City.

HOSE

H. A. Dreer, Philadelphia, Pa.
For page see List of Advertisers.

HYACINTHS.

5000 Hyacinths—No. 1, No. 2 and Miniatures in La Innocence, Gertrude Grand Maitre, King of Blues, Jaynes: No. 1, $32.00 per 1000; No. 2, $20.00 per 1000; Miniatures, $14.00 per 1000. 3 in. Sprengeri, 3c. Mum stock plants, 15 varieties, 50c. per doz.; $3.00 per 100, or will exchange any of these for Vincas Var., Geraniums, Ferns or what have you? ROSENDALE GREENHOUSES AND NURSERIES, Schenectady, New York.

INSECTICIDES

Aphine Manufacturing Co., Madison, N. J.
Aphine and Fungine.
For page see List of Advertisers.

Nicotine Mfg. Co., St. Louis, Mo.
Aphis Punk and Nikoteen.
For page see List of Advertisers.

The Plantlife Co., New York City.
Plantlife Insecticide.
For page see List of Advertisers.

IRRIGATION EQUIPMENT

Skinner Irrigation Co., Brookline, Mass.
For page see List of Advertisers.

LILIUM MYRIOPHYLLUM

R. & J. Farquhar & Co., Boston, Mass.

LILY BULBS

Chas. Schwake & Co., New York City.
Horticultural Importers and Exporters.
For page see List of Advertisers.

R. M. Ward & Co., New York, N. Y.
Japanese Lily Bulbs of Superior Quality.
For page see List of Advertisers.

Corp. of Chas. F. Meyer, New York City.
Meyer's T. Brand Giganteums.
For page see List of Advertisers

Arthur T. Boddington Co., Inc., New York City.
Lilium Longiflorum Formosum.
For page see List of Advertisers.

LILY OF THE VALLEY

Chas. Schwake & Co., Inc., New York City.
Hobmann's Famous Lily of the Valley Pips.
For page see List of Advertisers.

Loechner & Co., New York City.
Lily of the Valley Pips.
For page see List of Advertisers.

J. M. Thorburn & Co., New York City.
For page see List of Advertisers.

McHutchison & Co., New York City.
Berlin Valley Pips.
For page see List of Advertisers.

Arthur T. Boddington Co., Inc., New York City.
Cold Storage.
For page see List of Advertisers.

MASTICA

F. O. Pierce Co., New York City.
For page see List of Advertisers.

NATIONAL NURSERYMAN

National Nurseryman Publishing Co., Inc., Rochester, N. Y.
For page see List of Advertisers.

NIKOTEEN

Nicotine Mfg. Co., St. Louis, Mo.
For page see List of Advertisers

NIKOTIANA

Aphine Mfg. Co., Madison, N. J.
For page see List of Advertisers.

NURSERY STOCK

P. Ouwerkerk, Weehawken Heights, N. J.
For page see List of Advertisers

W. & T. Smith Co., Geneva, N. Y.
For page see List of Advertisers

The D. Hill Nursery Co., Dundee, Ill.
Hill's Evergreens.
For page see List of Advertisers.

NURSERY STOCK—Continued
Bay State Nurseries, North Abington, Mass.
Hardy, Northern Grown Stock.
For page see List of Advertisers.

Bobbink & Atkins, Rutherford, N. J.
For page see List of Advertisers.

Framingham Nurseries, Framingham, Mass.
For page see List of Advertisers.

August Rolker & Sons, New York City.
For page see List of Advertisers.

NUT GROWING.
The Nut-Grower, Waycross, Ga.

ORCHID FLOWERS
Jas. McManus, New York, N. Y.
For page see List of Advertisers.

ORCHID PLANTS
Julius Roehrs Co., Rutherford, N. J.
For page see List of Advertisers.

Lager & Hurrell, Summit, N. J.

PALMS, ETC.
Robert Craig Co., Philadelphia, Pa.
For page see List of Advertisers.

August Rolker & Sons, New York City.
For page see List of Advertisers.

A. Leuthy & Co., Roslindale, Boston, Mass.
For page see List of Advertisers.

PANSY PLANTS
Pansy Plants, mixed varieties in bud
and bloom, $15.00 per 1000. Cash. JAMES
MOSS, Johnsville, Pa.

Pansy Plants for the benches, nice stocky
plants, $5.00 per 1000, 5000 or more, $4.00
per 1000. Cash. JAMES MOSS, Johnsville,
Pa.

PANSY SEED
Chas. Frost, Kenilworth, N. J.
Kenilworth Giant.
For page see List of Advertisers.

PEONIES
Peonies. The world's greatest collection.
1200 sorts. Send for list. C. BETSCHER,
Canal Dover, O.

PECKY CYPRESS BENCHES
A. T. Stearns Lumber Co., Boston, Mass.
For page see List of Advertisers.

PIPE AND FITTINGS
Kroeschell Bros. Co., Chicago.
For page see List of Advertisers.

King Construction Company,
N. Tonawanda, N. Y.
Shelf Brackets and Pipe Hangers.
For page see List of Advertisers.

PLANT AND BULB IMPORTS
Chas. Schwake & Co., New York City.
For page see List of Advertisers.

August Rolker & Sons, New York City.
For page see List of Advertisers.

PLANT TRELLISES AND STAKES
Seele's Tieless Plant Stakes and Trellises. H. D. SEELE & SONS, Elkhart, Ind.

PLANT TUBS
H. A. Dreer, Philadelphia, Pa.
"Riverton Special."
For page see List of Advertisers.

PLANTS WANTED
C. C. Trepel, New York City.
For page see List of Advertisers.

RAFFIA
McHutchison & Co., New York, N. Y.
For page see List of Advertisers.

RHODODENDRONS
P. Ouwerkerk, Hoboken, N. J.
For page see List of Advertisers.

Framingham Nurseries, Framingham, Mass.
For page see List of Advertisers.

RIBBONS AND CHIFFONS
S. S. Pennock-Meehan Co., Philadelphia, Pa.
For page see List of Advertisers.

ROSES
Poehlmann Bros. Co., Morton Grove, Ill.
For page see List of Advertisers.

P. Ouwerkerk, Hoboken, N. J.
For page see List of Advertisers.

Robert Craig Co., Philadelphia, Pa.
For page see List of Advertisers.

W. & T. Smith Co., Geneva, N. Y.
American Grown Roses.
For page see List of Advertisers.

Bay State Nurseries, North Abington, Mass.
For page see List of Advertisers.

August Rolker & Sons, New York City.
For page see List of Advertisers.

Montrose Greenhouses, Montrose, Mass.
Young Roses—Own Root and Grafted.
For page see List of Advertisers.

Framingham Nurseries, Framingham, Mass.
For page see List of Advertisers.

A. N. Pierson, Inc., Cromwell, Conn.
For page see List of Advertisers.

THE CONARD & JONES COMPANY,
Rose Specialists
West Grove, Pa. Send for offers.

SCALECIDE
B. G. Pratt Co., New York City.
For page see List of Advertisers.

SEASONABLE PLANT STOCK
R. Vincent, Jr. & Sons Co., White Marsh
Md.
For page see List of Advertisers.

SEED GROWERS
California Seed Growers' Association.
San Jose, Cal.
For page see List of Advertisers.

SEEDS
Carter's Tested Seeds,
Seeds with a Pedigree.
Boston, Mass., and London, England.
For page see List of Advertisers.

Keiway & Son,
Langport, Somerset, England.
Kelway's Celebrated English Strain Garden
Seeds.

S. D. Woodruff & Sons, New York City.
Garden Seed.
For page see List of Advertisers.

Joseph Breck & Sons, Boston, Mass.
For page see List of Advertisers.

J. Bolgiano & Son, Baltimore, Md.
For page see List of Advertisers.

A. T. Boddington Co., Inc., New York City.
For page see List of Advertisers.

Chas. Schwake & Co., New York City.
For page see List of Advertisers.

Michell's Seed House, Philadelphia, Pa.
For page see List of Advertisers.

W. Atlee Burpee & Co., Philadelphia, Pa.
For page see List of Advertisers.

R. & J. Farquhar & Co., Boston, Mass.
For page see List of Advertisers.

J. M. Thorburn & Co., New York City
For page see List of Advertisers.

Loechner & Co., New York City.
For page see List of Advertisers.

Ant. C. Zvolanek, Lompoc, Cal.
Winter Flowering Sweet Pea Seed.
For page see List of Advertisers.

S. S. Skidelsky & Co., Philadelphia, Pa
For page see List of Advertisers.

W. E. Marshall & Co., New York City.
Seeds, Plants and Bulbs.
For page see List of Advertisers.

August Rolker & Sons, New York City.
For page see List of Advertisers.

SEEDS—Continued
Burnett Bros., 98 Chambers St., New York.
For page see List of Advertisers.

Fottler, Fiske, Rawson Co., Boston, Mass.
Seeds for the Florist.
For page see List of Advertisers.

SKINNER IRRIGATION SYSTEM
Skinner Irrigation Co., Brookline, Mass.
For page see List of Advertisers.

SPHAGNUM MOSS
Live Sphagnum moss, orchid peat and
orchid baskets always on hand. LAGER
& HURRELL, Summit, N. J.

SPRAYING MATERIALS
B. G. Pratt Co., New York City.
For page see List of Advertisers.

STANDARD THERMOMETERS
Standard Thermo Co., Boston, Mass.
For page see List of Advertisers.

STOVE PLANTS
Orchids—Largest stock in the country—
Stove plants and Crotons, finest collection.
JULIUS ROEHRS CO., Rutherford, N. J.

SWEET PEA SEED
Arthur T. Boddington Co., Inc.,
New York City.
Winter Flowering Sweet Peas.
For page see List of Advertisers.

Ant. C. Zvolanek, Lompoc, Calif.
Gold Medal of Honor Winter Orchid Sweet
Peas.
For page see List of Advertisers.

VEGETABLE PLANTS
R. Vincent, Jr. & Sons Co.,
White Marsh, Md.
For page see List of Advertisers.

Forcing Tomatoes, Comet, 2½ in., 2c.
RONEY BROS., West Grove, Pa.

VENTILATING APPARATUS
The Advance Co., Richmond, Ind.
For page see List of Advertisers.

The John A. Evans Co., Richmond, Ind.
For page see List of Advertisers.

VERMICIDES
Aphine Mfg. Co., Madison, N. J.
For page see List of Advertisers.

WATER LILIES
Wm. Tricker, Arlington, N. J.
For page see List of Advertisers.

WIRED TOOTHPICKS
W. J. Cowee, Berlin, N. Y.
For page see List of Advertisers.

WIREWORK
Reed & Keller, New York City.
For page see List of Advertisers.

WILLIAM E. HEILSCHER'S WIRE
WORKS. 264 Randolph St., Detroit, Mich.

WHOLESALE FLORISTS
Albany, N. Y.

Albany Cut Flower Exchange, Albany, N. Y.
For page see List of Advertisers.

Baltimore

The S. S. Pennock-Meehan Co., Franklin
and St. Paul Sts.
For page see List of Advertisers.

Boston

N. F. McCarthy & Co., 112 Arch St. and
31 Otis St.
For page see List of Advertisers.

Welch Bros. Co., 226 Devonshire St.
For page see List of Advertisers.

Patrick Welch, 262 Devonshire St., Boston,
Mass.
For page see List of Advertisers.

Brooklyn

Wm. H. Kuebler, 28 Willoughby St.
For page see List of Advertisers.

For List of Advertisers See Page 723

WHOLESALE FLORISTS
Buffalo, N. Y.

William F. Kasting Co., 383-87 Ellicott St.
For page see List of Advertisers.

Chicago

Poehlmann Bros. Co., Morton Grove, Ill.
For page see List of Advertisers.

Chicago Flower Growers' Association,
182 N. Wabash Ave., Chicago, Ill.
For page see List of Advertisers.

J. A., Budlong, 184 North Wabash Ave.,
Chicago, Ill.
For page see List of Advertisers.

Detroit

Michigan Cut Flower Exchange, 264-266
Randolph St.
For page see List of Advertisers.

New York

H. E. Froment, 148 W. 28th St.
For page see List of Advertisers.

James McManus, 105 W. 28th St.
For page see List of Advertisers.

W. F. Sheridan, 133 W. 28th St.
For page see List of Advertisers.

P. J. Smith, 131 West 28th St., N. Y.
For page see List of Advertisers.

Moore, Hentz & Nash, 55 and 57 W. 26th St.
For page see List of Advertisers.

Charles Millang, 55 and 57 West 26th St.
For page see List of Advertisers.

W. P. Ford, New York
For page see List of Advertisers.

J. K. Allen, 118 West 28th St., New York
City.
For page see List of Advertisers.

The S. S. Pennock-Meehan Co., 117 West
28th St.
For page see List of Advertisers.

Traendly & Schenck, 436 6th Ave., between
26th and 27th Sts.
For page see List of Advertisers.

Badgley & Bishop, Inc., New York.
For page see List of Advertisers.

Woodrow & Marketos, 37 & 39 West 28th St.
For page see List of Advertisers.

Riedel & Meyer, Inc., 49 West 28th St.,
New York City.
For page see List of Advertisers.

George C. Siebrecht, 109 W. 28th St.
For page see List of Advertisers.

John Young & Co., 53 West 28th St.
For page see List of Advertisers.

M. C Ford, 121 West 28th St.
For page see List of Advertisers.

R. S. Slinn, Jr., New York City.
For page see List of Advertisers.

United Cut Flower Co., Inc., 111 W. 28th St.
For page see List of Advertisers.

Guttman & Raynor, Inc., 101 W. 28th St.,
New York.
For page see List of Advertisers.

Leo. Niessen Co., 12th and Race Sts.
For page see List of Advertisers.

Philadelphia

Edward Reid, 1619-21 Ranstead St.
For page see List of Advertisers.

The S. S. Pennock-Meehan Co., 1608-20
Ludlow St.
For page see List of Advertisers.

Philadelphia Wholesale Flower Exchange,
1615 Ranstead St., Philadelphia, Pa.
For page see List of Advertisers.

Richmond, Ind.

E. G. Hill Co.
For page see List of Advertisers.

Rochester, N. Y.

George B. Hart, 24 Stone St.
For page see List of Advertisers.

Washington

The S. S. Pennock-Meehan Co., 1216 H St.,
N. W.
For page see List of Advertisers.

NEW OFFERS IN THIS ISSUE

**AMERICAN BEAUTY ROSES—CUT
FLOWERS, ETC.**
Patrick Welch, Boston, Mass.
For page see List of Advertisers.

BURPEE'S SEEDS GROW.
W. Atlee Burpee & Co., Philadelphia, Pa.
For page see List of Advertisers.

**CARNATIONS, ROSES, CHRYSAN.
THEMUMS.**
Guttman & Raynor, New York City.
For page see List of Advertisers.

CHOICE CHRISTMAS OFFERINGS.
Julius Roehrs Co., Rutherford, N. J.
For page see List of Advertisers.

**CHOICE FLOWERS FOR THE HOLI-
DAYS.**
Traendly & Schenck, New York City.
For page see List of Advertisers.

**CHRISTMAS AND NEW YEAR
FLOWERS BY TELEGRAPH**
Penn, The Telegraph Florist, Boston, Mass.
For page see List of Advertisers.

**CHRISTMAS AND NEW YEARS
FLOWERS BY TELEGRAPH.**
Samuel Murray, Kansas City, Mo.
For page see List of Advertisers.

CHRISTMAS DECORATIVE PLANTS.
Anton Schultheis, College Point, N. Y.
For page see List of Advertisers.

**CHRISTMAS FLOWERS, PLANTS
AND GREENS.**
N. F. McCarthy & Co., Boston, Mass.
For page see List of Advertisers.

CHRISTMAS GREENS.
Henry F. Michell Co., Philadelphia, Pa.
For page see List of Advertisers.

**CHRISTMAS GREENS—HOLLY
WREATHS.**
S. S. Pennock-Meehan Co., Philadelphia, Pa.
For page see List of Advertisers.

CHRISTMAS GREETING.
D. C. Arnold & Co., Inc, New York City.
For page see List of Advertisers.

CHRISTMAS PLANTS.
William W. Edgar Co., Waverley, Mass.
For page see List of Advertisers.

CHRISTMAS PLANTS.
Shepard's Garden Carnation Co., Lowell,
Mass.
For page see List of Advertisers.

CHRISTMAS PLANT STOCK.
Frank Oechslin, Chicago, Ill.
For page see List of Advertisers.

CUT FLOWERS FOR CHRISTMAS.
Berger Bros., Philadelphia, Pa.
For page see List of Advertisers.

CUT FLOWERS FOR CHRISTMAS.
H. E. Froment, New York City.
For page see List of Advertisers.

EVERYTHING IN SEASON.
Zech & Mann, Chicago, Ill.
For page see List of Advertisers.

EXCELLENT XMAS PLANT STOCK.
W. A. Riggs, Auburndale, Mass.
For page see List of Advertisers.

EXTRA FINE STOCK OF JUNIPERS.
Mt. Desert Nurseries, Bar Harbor, Me.
For page see List of Advertisers.

FERNS.
F. R. Pierson Co., Tarrytown, N. Y.
For page see List of Advertisers.

**FLOWERING AND FOLIAGE
PLANTS.**
A. L. Miller, Jamaica, N. Y.
For page see List of Advertisers.

FLOWERS BY TELEGRAPH.
Julius A. Zinn, Boston, Mass.
For page see List of Advertisers.

FLOWERS BY TELEGRAPH.
Thomas F. Galvin, Inc., Boston and New
York.
For page see List of Advertisers.

FLOWERS BY TELEGRAPH.
Ludwig Floral Co., Pittsburg, Pa.
For page see List of Advertisers.

FLOWERS BY TELEGRAPH.
Wm. H. Long, New York City.
For page see List of Advertisers.

FLOWER SEEDS FOR THE FLORIST
Fottler, Fiske, Rawson Co., Boston, Mass.
For page see List of Advertisers.

FUCHSIAS.
R. Vincent, Jr. & Sons Co., White Marsh,
Md.
For page see List of Advertisers.

**GARDENIAS, ORCHIDS, LILY OF
THE VALLEY, CARNATIONS.**
George C. Siebrecht, New York City.
For page see List of Advertisers.

GLADIOLUS FOR FORCING.
Arthur T. Boddington Co., Inc., New York
City.
For page see List of Advertisers.

GREENHOUSE CONSTRUCTION.
J. C. Moninger Co., Chicago, Ill.
For page see List of Advertisers.

**HAMMOND'S SLUG SHOT—GRAPE
DUST AND FUNGICIDE.**
Benjamin Hammond, Beacon, N. Y.
For page see List of Advertisers.

**HEADQUARTERS FOR LILIES,
CHRYSANTHEMUMS AND
FREESIAS.**
Philip F. Kessler, New York City.
For page see List of Advertisers.

HIGH CLASS ROSES.
J. J. Coan, New York City.
For page see List of Advertisers.

HOLIDAY GREETINGS.
Badgley & Bishop, Inc., New York City.
For page see List of Advertisers.

KEYSTONE SNAPDRAGON.
S. S. Skidelsky & Co., Philadelphia, Pa.
For page see List of Advertisers.

LILY BULBS.
Yokohoma Nursery Co., New York City.
For page see List of Advertisers.

ONE MILLION CYCAS LEAVES.
Henry M. Robinson & Co., Boston, Mass.
For page see List of Advertisers.

PLANT POTS AND PEDESTALS.
Jones, McDuffee & Stratton Co., Boston,
Mass.
For page see List of Advertisers.

RED CHRISTMAS GOODS.
H. Bayersdorfer & Co., Philadelphia, Pa.
For page see List of Advertisers.

SEASONABLE SEEDS.
R. & J. Farquhar & Co., Boston, Mass.
For page see List of Advertisers.

**SPECIMEN IMPORTED HOLLY
TREES.**
The MacNiff Horticultural Co., New
York City.
For page see List of Advertisers.

**SUPERIOR RETARDED LILY OF
THE VALLEY.**
Stumpp & Walter Co., New York City.
For page see List of Advertisers.

VINCA VARIEGATA.
James Vick's Sons, Rochester, N. Y.
For page see List of Advertisers.

WHOLESALE FLORISTS.
D. C. Arnold & Co., Inc., 112 West 28th St.,
New York City.
For page see List of Advertisers.

WHOLESALE FLORISTS.
Henry M. Robinson Co., New York City.
For page see List of Advertisers.

WHOLESALE FLORISTS.
Gunther Bros., New York City.
For page see List of Advertisers.

WHOLESALE FLORISTS.
W. R. Siebrecht, 111 West 28th St., New
York City.

FREAKISH FACTS AND FACTLESS FREAKS.

Pleasant Lake, Mass., Dec. 7—While snowflakes were falling here yesterday, a bunch of mayflowers was picked in the woods near this village. Old residents declare that this is the result of a few mild days about a week ago, and indicates an exceedingly severe winter, followed by a late spring.—*Boston Traveler.*

Apples growing on birch trees may be a possibility in the opinion of "Johnny" Martin of Canton, who is experimenting along that line. He claims that on his estate twigs of apple trees continued to live for three years after being grafted to birch trees. He expects to make additional experiments this spring, and if successful is thinking of calling the result of his labor "the birch apple."

—*Boston Traveler.*

Don't, fair reader, turn up your nose and exclaim that a seed is a seed. So is an egg an egg. Somebody even proved that "pigs is pigs." Compared to some of the seeds Mr. Burpee raises, gold is a cheap and insignifi-

cent commodity. It is only worth around $250 a pound.

A particular flower seed commands $1000 a pound. "But we don't deal in it by the pound, only by the ounce or the dozen of seeds," remarked this erstwhile physician, who turning from healing sick humanity to perfecting flowers and vegetables.

If you can develop a fine new variety of sweet-peas, for instance, it will bring you more than Kipling gets for one of his poems, and, measured by the poet's recent output, I think it worth considerably more.

—*Philadelphia Ledger.*

"What is their little game anyway?" That is what people asked us at the time the Luther Burbank Society was sending out its knighted guff and asking people to join the immortals by becoming a "life member." We did not know what the game was, but it is being developed now. All capital stock in this Burbank Society has been assessed one dollar per share! There are liabilities of $73,023.58! Among the "assets" is the item of $287,500 as "value of the exclusive right to use the name of Luther Burbank and to distribute his horticultural productions." The "little game" seems to have been the same as that of the shell-game man—a run for your dollar. You had the run after the society of Burbank and then you give up your dollar! What a farce the whole thing was. How they did play on the vanity of hundreds of men and women who ought to have known better. The Burbank Society! A seat in it has proved just about as satisfactory as a seat on a bunch of dried burdocks!

—*Rural New Yorker.*

That there are meat eating plants is generally known, but that there are also plants that cough—not figuratively, but in the true literal sense of the word—will be surprising to most readers. Indeed, to the researches of the French botanist we owe the description of a plant growing in certain tropical regions which obviously "coughs" like a human being. The plant externally is in many respects related to our common bean. It is very sensitive, and shows a strange dislike of every kind of dust. No sooner do a few grains of dust settle on its leaves and thereby irritate the air chambers of the sheath scale, which represents the organs of breathing, than these organs fill with a kind of gas, swell up and then explosively reject the gas, whereby the dust is expelled. But this explosion produces a sound that has a striking resemblance to the cough of a child that has caught a cold. The stranger who, in the midst of the wilderness, hears the sound involuntarily looks about for some man or animal, and discovering, of course, nowhere a living being that might have coughed, will be seized with the uncanny feeling of the presence of some spook.—*Exchange.*

The U. S. Court of Customs Appeals has decided against the appeal of George Quirk and others from the assessment of duty on budding and

pruning knives, which they claimed should be admitted free as "agricultural implements," and proclaims that such knives "with folding blades and spring backs" are dutiable at ad valorem rate under paragraph 128 of the tariff act of October 3, 1913.

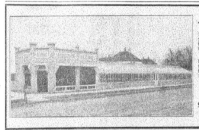

GREENHOUSES BUILDING OR CONTEMPLATED.

Sandwich, Ill.—Mrs. F. Spickerman.

Los Angeles, Cal.—Fred Hills, house, 30x100.

Philadelphia, Pa.—Mrs. Jas. Shelly, Llanerch, three houses.

Worcester, Mass.—Wm. E. Norcross, May street, one house.

Brunswick, Maine.—Thomas Pegler, Jordan avenue, addition.

New Haven, Ct.—City of New Haven, East Rock Farm, addition.

Methuen, Mass. — Ernest Russell, Merrimack street, one house.

Altoona, Pa.—W. H. Brouse, Orchard Crossing, additions and alterations.

Lowell, Mass.—Amy W. Andrew, 1522 Varnum avenue, conservatory, 20x50.

Westchester, Bronx, N. Y.—John Mesker. 1253 Fort Schuyler road, one house.

Rochester, N. Y.—Hugo Teute, two houses, each 40x150. Walter Tickner, Lexington avenue, house, 18x75.

MASSACHUSETTS AGRICULTURAL COLLEGE NOTES.

Mr. H. W. Collingwood, editor of the New York Ruralist, spoke before the Stockbridge Club Tuesday evening.

Last week the junior classes in floriculture visited the Sinclair range at Smith's Ferry, while the senior classes visited the Mt. Holyoke College greenhouses on Tuesday.

Prof. R. R. Root, of the University of Illinois, took up his work in the landscape department here on last Monday.

Joseph Crawford of New York will be manager of the new flower store of J. Henry Schaeffer at New London, Conn.

Curved Eave Show House at Louis Dupuy's, Whitestone, L. I.

Some Interesting Show House Showings

WHEN you think of the hundreds and thousands of dollars that are continually being spent to show goods to the best advantage in all other lines; what a tremendous opportunity it suggests for Show Houses in the plant and flower business.

We might mention off hand, half a dozen such houses that we have built in and around the New York section; every one of which you doubtless know about.

Among the number, however, there are two which are conspicuous for their success.

One is the Plant Show House of Louis Dupuy at Whitestone, L. I.

The other, the Flower Shop at Forest Hills, L. I.

Knowing as you do, that Mr. Dupuy sells the bulk of his plants to the leading New York Florists, you will wonder what particular advantages a Show House would be to him.

If you have ever gone into a big department store and had the exasperating experience of chasing from one floor to another, and from one counter at one end of the building, to the other you know full well the welcome advantage it would be if you could leisurely walk through a light, attractive room of moderate size, where everything you wanted, was right handy by.

With this in mind, Mr. Dupuy shrewdly overcame the necessity of his customers going from house to house, through his big range; by concentrating his plants for sale, in a fine, curved eave Show House we designed and built for him.

Not only will Mr. Dupuy tell you of its saving in time; but that it has greatly increased his sales.

Can't we build you one of these business builders? You know we go anywhere for business, or to talk business.

Forest Hills Flower Shop with Glimpse of the Show House.

Hitchings and Company

NEW YORK	BOSTON	PHILADELPHIA
1170 Broadway	49 Federal Street	40 S. 15th Street

General Offices and Factory: Elizabeth, N. J.

Vol. XXII
No. 25
DEC. 18
1915

HORTICULTURE

Vanda Sanderiana

Published Every Saturday at 147 Summer Street, Boston, Mass.
Subscription, $1.00

LIST OF ADVERTISERS

FOR BUYERS' DIRECTORY AND READY REFERENCE GUIDE
SEE PAGES 828, 829, 830, 831

NOTES ON CULTURE OF FLORISTS' STOCK
CONDUCTED BY

John J. M. Farrell

Questions by our readers in line with any of the topics presented on this page will be cordially received and promptly answered by Mr. Farrell. Such communications should invariably be addressed to the office of HORTICULTURE.
"If vain our toil, we ought to blame the culture, not the soil."—*Pope.*

Asparagus plumosus

From now on there is nothing better than a good rich mulch put on from time to time. After the New Year they can have plenty of liquid manure. Asparagus plumosus is a greedy feeder, and additional nourishment in some form must be given. From this out it is always well to let the surface of the soil become fairly dry before giving water. When doing it, however, give them a good soaking. Keep the house moist, as when this is wanting luxuriant growth is impossible. See that the young leading growths are kept nicely wound around the strings. Give the surface a frequent stirring to keep the soil open and sweet. About 65 degrees at night, in the coolest weather, and a deep and richly manured compost are the essentials to successful asparagus culture.

Calanthes

. When the blooms begin to open, calanthes should be kept as near the glass as possible and in a night temperature of from 60 to 65 degrees. During the day, if the sun shines, 70 or 75, but if the day is dark 65 to 70 will be about right. .When the flowers are half expanded they can be removed to the cooler end of the warm house where their long sprays of bloom will keep in perfection for some weeks. Don't apply too much water when the plants are in flower—only enough to keep the soil from drying out too much. This is a good orchid for the commercial growers, excellent for cut flower purposes and having fine lasting qualities. Calanthe Veitchii and C. vestita are good sorts. After flowering they should be rested in about the same degree of heat as they were grown in for a period of from eight to ten weeks during which time water should be withheld gradually.

Decorative Ferns

From now and up to the middle of February all ferns generally used by the florist will stand full sun. For ferns that require a medium temperature, 55 to 60 degrees will do, while those that require stove heat should be given from 60 to 65 degrees at night. Handle the ventilation so as to give them a proper amount of fresh air without chilling draughts. Ferns always like a certain amount of atmospheric moisture through the house, but extremes either way should not be allowed. As a rule from this out wait until they show a slight dryness at the root and then give them enough water so it will run through the bottom of the pot. Go over them often and give a cleaning of old foliage, etc.

Manure for Crops

On the amount of plant food we have in all composts for crops growing inside, will depend success or failure. Florists all agree in giving a good grade of well-decayed barnyard manure first place among fertilizers for general use, but all experience the same difficulty in procuring it in a condition sufficiently decomposed for immediate use. They must therefore lay in fresh manure which at this time of the year is not hard to obtain. Pile it up and give it time to decay. Forked over once or twice during the progress of decomposition it will be in proper condition for use next spring. Horse manure, if not stirred up frequently, burns quickly and is then of little value. Refuse or spent brewers' hops does not heat so quickly and needs no forking.

Propagation

It is much more satisfactory to take cuttings now and pot them along. Plants so treated will later on produce plenty of cuttings, Coleus, alternanthera, achyranthes, verbenas, petunias, salvias, heliotropes, fuchsias, German ivy etc., will all root in a short time. Lobelias, ageratums and petunias should be propagated now, and of course geraniums can hardly be overdone. For alternantheras, it is better to use flats about 2 to 3 inches in depth, using either sandy soil or a layer of soil in the bottom with sand on top. Insert cuttings of about $2\frac{1}{4}$ inches in length and they can remain in these flats all winter in a temperature about 65 degrees at night.

Secure Plenty of Flats

In two or three weeks we shall have need for a lot of flats to sow seed and to prick stock into. See that they are put in good order. Do not leave this job until later on but get busy now and prepare enough of them.

Next Week:—Cinerarias; Cyclamens; Stock Chrysanthemums; Lilies for Easter; Violets; Verbenas.

HORTICULTURE

VOL. XXII   DECEMBER 18, 1915   NO. 25

PUBLISHED WEEKLY BY
HORTICULTURE PUBLISHING CO.
147 Summer Street, Boston, Mass.
Telephone, Oxford 292.
WM. J. STEWART, Editor and Manager.

Entered as second-class matter December 8, 1914, at the Post Office
at Boston, Mass., under the Act of Congress of March 3, 1879.

CONTENTS   Page

**A
well-judged
tribute**

The award of the George Robert White
medal of honor for 1915 to E. H. Wilson
of the Arnold Arboretum is a well-judged
recognition of the achievements and the
devotion of a man whose services for horticulture, great as they appear to us now, will, after the
lapse of a few years, appear vastly greater than is yet
apparent. HORTICULTURE congratulates Mr. Wilson on
the honor so worthily won and also the Massachusetts
Horticultural Society on having been the medium entrusted with the bestowal of such a tribute.

**All interests
covered**

The New York Florists' Club sets a
good example of impartiality in the selection of its officers for the coming
year. The president is a grower, the
vice-president a retail florist, secretary a wholesale flower dealer, treasurer a seedsman, trustees for two years
one wholesaler, one retailer and one growing retailer.

The Gardeners' and Florists' Club of Boston at its election last month was equally unbiased in choosing its
officers. While, of course, ability to fill the position assigned to him should be the foremost consideration in
selecting a man for any office, yet a fair recognition of
all the interests represented in the membership is always a wise course in the bestowal of honors as well as
in the general policies and activities of any organization.

**Calling
a halt**

While on the topic of the New York Florists'
Club we desire to throw one more bouquet in
approval of its very praiseworthy action, as
recorded in our reading columns, of refusing
official recognition to a rose under a name other than
that under which it had heretofore been known and
sold. The New York Club is all the more worthy of
special commendation because the course of action adopted affected most directly, for the moment, one of its own
highly esteemed members, of whom it must be said that
he explained that he had brought the rose in question
to the meeting not for the purpose of being scored but
for exhibit only, to give the members an opportunity
of seeing it. The culpability appears to lie with the grower in California who re-named the variety. We are glad
to see this Club take so exemplary a stand on a growing
abuse that has been too long condoned.

**The
gardeners
awakening**

The meeting of gardeners in Boston last
week brought together some of the leading
and progressive spirits and was characterized by a confident and optimistic tone
which promises well for the future advancement of their profession in the character and attainments of those who follow it as their life work and
in the position accorded to it by the public among the
honorable callings in which men are employed. Whether
it be an individual, an association or an avocation, before a high position in the respect of the people can be
attained, self-respect and a steadfast effort to develop
a worthiness of the coveted recognition is an essential
requirement. That commendable progress is being made
in this direction ample evidence was given in the Boston
meeting and the new incentive there created will spread
its influence far and wide. The young gardener of today
in love with his work and fired with honest purpose and
noble aim should find abundant encouragement in the
sentiment and spirit of this meeting at Boston and the
quality of the men who participated.

**Work
ahead**

One prerequisite for improvement in anything
or anybody is a clear realization of the existing defects or short comings which make improvement desirable. As all plants have their
insect and fungous enemies so also are there maladies
ready at all times to prey upon and hinder the growth
of any occupation in which well-meaning men may be
engaged. If it should appear that any practices have
been taking root which affect the relations between gardener and employer or between gardeners and the trade
and which might react unfavorably upon the profession
as a whole and retard its progress toward the pinnacle
of world-wide honor in the great field of industry, this
Association now has the opportunity and the where-
withal to search out and eradicate it, however deep-root-
ed they may find it to be. The names of the gentlemen
who have been selected as standard bearers for the Association for the coming year are an assuring guarantee
that the activities of the organization will be conducted
upon lines which make for the true welfare and advancement of the gardening fraternity. Much is expected of
such men and we feel sure that much will be forthcoming.

ROSE GROWING UNDER GLASS

CONDUCTED BY

Arthur C. Ruzicka

Questions by our readers in line with any of the topics presented on this page will be cordially received and promptly answered by Mr. Ruzicka. Such communications should invariably be addressed to the office of HORTICULTURE.

Feeding During December.

We are now going through the shortest days in the year, and unless the plants are growing very freely, the amount of feed given them will have to be somewhat the plants all that they will take. If bonemeal is limited, until the New Year, when it will be safe to give the plants all that they will take, and if they are growing good—there will hardly be a limit. If bonemeal is to be used and the plants are in need of a little food, then apply it now, for they are sure to get a large portion of it. We would not use much of this after the first of February. We prefer sheep manure, tankage, or other manures that may be available, not forgetting liquid manure. If the plants are not dried out properly the soil can nearly always be found to be acid or may contain large numbers of earthworms. These can be killed and the soil sweetened by an application of fresh hydrated or air-slacked lime. These are the only two limes we would use in the rose houses. This dose of lime can also take the place of plant food as it will decompose a good deal of matter in the soil, thus making available plant food that would otherwise lie inert.

Syringing.

As often as the weather will permit the plants should receive a good syringing so that there will be no spider anywhere to start breeding as soon as the warmer and brighter days of the spring come. They are a long way off as yet but most places are clean in the fall but are allowed to breed spider during the winter months and these come out in such large numbers in the spring that it is almost impossible to keep them down. Syringe early in the morning and shake the plants as soon as you are through so that they will have every possible chance to dry off before the night comes on. Do not neglect dusting plenty of air-slacked lime under the plants, especially in the Beauty houses. If not too cold, it is also advisable to carry a little air until about nine at night, unless the houses are not very tight and get plenty of air as it is. The thing to avoid is a damp, stale atmosphere, as this will soften the plants so that they will be almost sure to get a dose of mildew. It will also have a good deal to do in turning the flowers pale. Syringe as rapidly as possible, being careful not to throw too much water on the benches.

Tying.

It will be necessary to go over the plants quite often and see that there are no buds up against the glass where they will freeze into the ice that forms on cold mornings. Growers with wide houses with high sides will not have to worry about this but all the growers have not the up-to-date houses built but recently. All varieties, save the Beauty, will not mind going untied for a while, but the latter will not bud if allowed to lay around at all. Keep after the tying as much as possible, especially in the Beauty houses. We have seen a case of a grower's failing to grow Beauties successfully merely because they were not tied up properly all the time. Some of the long shoots will have to be bent down, and

in doing this be careful to keep the growth on the same side of all three wires as it is rather unhandy to have them mixed up. Keep the tops all the same distance above the top wire as this will insure a square deal to all the tops and give them all a chance to get some sun and set, for Beauties that will not set are not very profitable. In tying teas to stakes be careful not to bunch them up too much, as they are bound to lose some of their leaves this way and are much harder to syringe.

Blackspot

Mr. Arthur Ruzicka.

Dear Sir:—Mr. George C. Thomas, Jr., in his "The Practical Book of Outdoor Rose Growing," second edition, suggests a new remedy for black spot in the shape of a formaldehyde solution. He credits the "American Florist" issue of June 14, 1914, and the National Rose Society of England with the recommendations of this remedy.

Have you ever tried this remedy or know of any one who has, and what has been the results obtained? This remedy has no doubt been tried out the past season by some rose growers, and it certainly would be very interesting to me, and perhaps others as well, to get some report on its use in this country.

Black spot is, of all the diseases and enemies of the rose, the worst that I have had to contend with in out-door rose growing. We can control mildew by spraying and dusting with the usual recommended remedies, but black spot strips our roses of foliage, blights the bloom and refuses to respond to sprayings. If the formaldehyde solution has any virtue, the rose-growing public ought to know it, for there is nothing so discouraging as a disease of this kind and the laborious and tedious task of picking off diseased foliage, recommended by the writers, and its constant repetition acts only as a check, and a mild one at that, and dampens one's ardor for roses.

Yours truly, J. N. P.

Washington, Pa.

I am very sorry to say that I have never tried the treatment mentioned and I do not know of any gardener who has. Our outdoor rose growing has been limited, I regret to say, to only such varieties of roses that do not contract blackspot so easily and should any of these get it we have never gone to any trouble to cure it outside of a spraying or two of some good fungicide which we thought best to use. We are interested in cut roses commercially you see, so we cannot spend more on a plant than about a fourth of what we get from it. With private gardeners it is different as the roses are wanted regardless of cost. The only real cure for spot we have ever been able to find satisfactory is to grow the plants out of it. In other words, try to keep the plants growing all the time. This can only be done by being very careful to prepare a good soil when they are planted. The soil should be well drained if it is inclined to be wet and the plants should be watered only in the early morning when dry weather sets in. In watering it is best to water thoroughly, so that the water goes a good ways down. We also find it helps to mulch the plants as soon as hot weather comes around as this keeps the soil cool around the roots and the plants do not suffer so badly. It may be that some of HORTICULTURE's readers may have tried the remedy recommended in the book you mention, and if they have I am sure they will be glad to write of their experience.

NATIONAL ASSOCIATION OF GARDENERS

Our notes published last week gave an account of the opening session of this Association, then holding its annual meeting in Boston. We are pleased to add to that the statement by the treasurer, James Stuart, that the Association has today in bank the sum of $1,289. Encouraging reports were made by several committees, including that on meritorious exhibits which was as follows:

Report of Exhibition Committee.

Certificate of Culture for a well-grown specimen Begonia Glory of Cincinnati, exhibited by W. Downs, Chestnut Hill, Mass.

Special mention for two specimens Begonias Lorraine, and Certificate of Culture for fine display of Calanthes by D. Finlayson, Brookline, Mass.

Vote of thanks to W. W. Edgar Company for display of palms.

Certificate of Culture for vase of well-grown Carnation Alice Coombs, and Certificates of Merit for vases of Carnations Commonwealth, Grace, and Seedling No. 360, by A. Roper, Tewksbury, Mass.

Honorable mention for a vase of Carnation Morning Glow, by Edward Winkler, Wakefield, Mass.

Certificate of Merit for a vase of Carnation Miss Theo. exhibited by Littlefield & Wyman, North Abington, Mass.

Certificate of Merit for a vase of Rose Mrs. Bayard Thayer, by A. Montgomery, Waban Rose Conservatories, Natick.

Certificate of Merit for three plants of winter-flowering Begonias, consisting of Winter Cheer, Aureana and Optima, by William Downs, Chestnut Hill, Mass.

Certificate of Culture for vase of well-grown Carnation Alice, by Peter Fisher, Ellis, Mass.

Certificate of Merit for vase of pink Snapdragon Weld Pink, and special mention for Plumbago coccinea, by W. C. Rust, Brookline, Mass.

Special mention for a fine collection of Lilium bulbs, by John Scheepers & Co., Inc., New York, and vote of thanks to same for display of Nephrolepis and Spiraeas.

Vote of thanks to A. H. Hews & Co., Cambridge, Mass., for a display of pottery.

Judges—Wm. Kleinheinz, John F. Huss and P. W. Popp.

A resolution was unanimously adopted commending Adolph Lewisohn and his superintendent, John Canning, for their able and unselfish services in the promotion of the interests of the chrysanthemum in the New York and Cleveland exhibitions. Messrs. W. N. Craig, Duncan Finlayson and M. C. Ebel were constituted a committee to draw up a resolution to be sent to Mrs. Francis King in appreciation of her kind and influential words in the gardeners' behalf in her book, "The Well Considered Garden." An amendment to the Constitution was unanimously adopted providing for the suspension of members more than one year in arrears on payment of dues.

As recorded in our account of last week, W. N. Craig, of Brookline, Mass., was unanimously elected president for the coming year. Other officers selected, all by a unanimous vote, were: ·Vice-president, Theodore Wirth. Minneapolis, Minn.; secretary, M. C. Ebel, Madison, N. J.; treasurer, James Stuart, Mamaroneck, N. J.; trustees, Peter Duff, Orange, N. J.; Wm. Duckham, Madison, N. J.; Wm. Turner, Oceanic, N. J.; Wm. Kleinheinz, Ogontz, Pa.; J. F. Huss, Hartford, Conn. Interesting papers were read (the authors not being present) on "Is Gardening a Profession?" submitted by W. W. Ohlweiler, St. Louis, Mo.; "The Management of Country Estates, from the Viewpoint of the·College Graduate," by Morell Smith, superintendent of the Ralph Pulitzer Estate; "The Young Gardener's Opportunity in This Country," by Henry Gibson, of New York. The first and third of these papers elicited plenty of spirited and often amusing debate. The fourth and last paper was by William Gray, of Newport, R. I., on "Is Co-operation Between Garden Clubs and Gardeners' Societies Desirable?"

A vote of thanks was recorded for the authors of all the papers.

The Dinner.

At 6 p. m. the meeting adjourned and the members repaired to the banquet hall below, where an excellent dinner was served under the auspices of the Gardeners' and Florists' Club and Allied Horticultural Interests of Boston, and the rest of the evening was spent in speechmaking and pleasant companionship. During the banquet a clever young lady entertained the guests with singing and dancing. W. N. Craig, president-elect of the Association and secretary of the Gardeners' and Florists' Club presided. The list of speakers was a long one, ·and included President J. K. M. L. Farquhar of the Massachusetts Horticultural Society, who voiced the pleasure of that organization in having the gardening fraternity its guests, Patrick Welch, president of the Society of American Florists, John H. Dillon, chairman of the Boston Park Commission, Wm. Kleinheinz of Ogontz, Pa., Peter Fisher, S. J. Goddard, P. W. Popp, J. W. Everitt, retiring president. Prof. A. H. Nehrling of Amherst Agri. College, Secretary M. C. Ebel, James McMachan of Tuxedo, N. Y., M. H. Norton, Jos. A. Manda, President H. H. Bartsch of the Gardeners' and Florists' Club of Boston, Wm. J. Stewart, editor of Horticulture, Robert Cameron of Harvard Botanic Garden, W. P. Rich, sec'y Massachusetts Horticultural Society, Wm. Nicholson, James Methven, J. F. Huss of Hartford, Conn., James Wheeler, Duncan Finlayson, Wm. Downs, W. J. Kennedy and A. P. Calder, the silvertongued orator of the Boston florist fraternity. The speeches were all optimistic in tone and emphasized the golden opportunities for the gardening profession in this country and the

service which a well conducted organization could render in developing a high standard of efficiency among its members. On the part of the visitors there was much praise for Boston's part in making the convention a marked success and on the part of the local speakers a welcome gratulation and expression of good wishes for the future of the Association. The tables were profusely decorated with plants and flowers. A rising vote of thanks was extended to the committee in charge for the efficient manner in which they had attended to their work.

Friday's Outing.

The program for Friday included an automobile ride through the park system of Boston, Metropolitan Park Reservations, Arnold Arboretum and the estates of Prof. C. S. Sargent, E. D. Brandegee, E. S. Webster and Larz Anderson, refreshments being served at the latter place. The trip culminated at the nurseries of R. & J. Farquhar & Co., at Dedham, where the extensive greenhouses and nursery buildings with their contents were certainly an eye-opener to the majority of the visitors who had no idea of the tremendous development of this establishment within the past two years. An elaborate spread was served in the big packing shed. The autos for the trip were generously supplied by the Boston Park Department.

ST. LOUIS FLORIST CLUB.

The Florist Club met for the last time this year, December 9, in Odd Fellows' building, at 2 o'clock P. M., with half the membership in attendance. The usual opening proceedings were disposed of quickly when the chair called up all committees for final reports. The trustees reported that the February meeting would be held in the evening and the ladies would be invited. Mr. Ohlweiler, chairman of the Spring Flower Show Committee, read a lengthy report in which he named all sub-committees with President Bourdet as chairman of the Executive Committee and manager of the show. Chairman Ammann, of the Carnation Society Committee, made a brief report and suggested that a guarantee fund of $500 be raised to defray the expenses, which was quickly subscribed by the members of the club. Frank Fillmore reported for the Resolution Committee on the deaths of E. G. Eggeling and W. C. Young, and the report was accepted by a rising vote. H. C. Irish, vice-president of the Missouri State Horticultural Society, read a program for the meeting of the society to be held January 12, 13 and 14 at the Planters' Hotel, and named the thirteenth as Florists' Day, when several prominent florists would read papers. The question box formed a pleasing feature and several long discussions made things interesting to the members.

The New Year's meeting will take place Thursday afternoon, January 13.

CLUBS AND SOCIETIES

NEW YORK FLORISTS' CLUB.

The meeting on Monday evening, December 13, was attended by about 75 members—a very creditable representation considering the wild storm which was raging, and gave memorable significance to the ill-omened 13th. The big business of the evening was the election of officers for the year 1916. There were no contests except on vice-president and trustees, all the other officers being elected by unanimous vote. The successful candidates are as follows: President, Henry Weston; vice-president, George E. M. Stumpp; secretary, John Young; treasurer, Wm. C. Rickards; trustees, Chas. Schenck, Robt. G. Wilson, Max Schling. All these gentlemen made brief addresses except Messrs. Schling and Wilson, who were absent. Quite a discussion took place regarding the exhibit of the rose re-named "Prima Donna" and this matter was given careful consideration by many of the leading members; it was decided that the New York Florists' Club could not and would not countenance the award of certificates or officially recognize plants and flowers which were given improper names. After the exhibitor had affixed the proper name of the variety Madam Paul Euler the exhibit was accorded a vote of thanks.

A. L. Miller introduced the subject of the coming National Flower Show in Philadelphia which he considered was recognized as the great coming event by all florists from Maine to California and suggested that the Club request of the National Flower Show Committee, that a day be set aside to be known as "New York Day" and that a committee be appointed to make arrangements for a party of five or six hundred to go to Philadelphia in a special train on New York Day. The motion of Mr. Miller was warmly seconded by Chas. H. Totty and the consensus of opinion was that the members of the Club should make it a point to join the party and make the attendance at the National Flower Show on "New York Day" a record breaker. A. L. Miller, Frank H. Traendly, Joseph Manda, Wm. Duckham and C. H. Totty were appointed a committee to make the necessary arrangements.

Resolutions were presented on the death of Edward Wale and Mrs. Victor Dorval. A committee was appointed to draw up resolutions on the death of the late W. Atlee Burpee, the committee being E. C. Vick, W. A. Sperling, W. C. Rickards, Jr., J. B. Deamud, H. A. Bunyard.

Richard Vincent, Jr., addressed the meeting in the interest of the American Dahlia Society. In the absence of Chairman F. R. Pierson, of the general Flower Show Committee, A. L. Miller and Frank H. Traendly reported for the coming Spring Show. Their report was very rosy, showing the

Meetings Next Week

Monday, Dec. 20.

Detroit Florists' Club, Bemb Floral Hall, Detroit, Mich.
Houston Florists' Club, Chamber of Commerce Rooms, Houston, Tex.

Tuesday, Dec. 21.

Gardeners' and Florists' Club of Boston, Horticultural Hall, Boston, Mass.
Gardeners' and Florists' of Ontario, St. George's Hall, Toronto, Can.
Lake Geneva Gardeners' and Foremen's Association, Horticultural Hall, Lake Geneva, Wis.
Minnesota State Florists' Association, Minneapolis, Minn.
Pennsylvania Horticultural Society, Horticultural Hall, Philadelphia, Pa.

Wednesday, Dec. 22.

Oyster Bay Horticultural Society, Oyster Bay, N. Y.

Friday, Dec. 24.

Connecticut Horticultural Society, County Bldg., Hartford, Conn.
Monmouth County Horticultural Society, Red Bank, N. J.
Pasadena Horticultural Society, Pasadena, Calif.

Saturday, Dec. 25.

Dobbs Ferry Gardeners' Association, Dobbs Ferry, N. Y.

HENRY WESTON,
President-Elect New York Florists' Club.

work well under way and in a satisfactory condition.

The exhibits were Rose Mme. Paul Euler, by Guttman & Raynor; Carnation Gorgeous, by B. Willig; Chrysanthemums Mistletoe and Mrs. E. D. Godfrey, grown by Charles Smith & Son, and exhibited by Phil. F. Kessler. Cultural commendation was awarded on the chrysanthemums and vote of thanks on the others.

NASSAU CO. HORTICULTURAL SOCIETY.

The regular monthly meeting of the Nassau Co. Horticultural Society was held in Pembroke Hall, Glen Cove, N. Y., Dec. 8. The following awards were made: Begonia Gloire de Lorraine—1st to Frederick Hitchman; 25 carnations—1st, Robert Jones. Mr. Jones also exhibited a splendid vase of chrysanthemum Odessa for which he was awarded a cultural certificate. This being the annual meeting, Treasurer Ernest Brown read his financial report, showing that the Society is in a first class condition financially. Mr. Brown received a very hearty vote of thanks for his efficiency.

The election of officers now being in order President Westlake, after thanking his fellow members for their harmonious co-operation during his term of office, appointed James Duthie as chairman to conduct the election. The following officers were elected: President, James McDonald; vice-president, Joseph Adler; treasurer, Ernest Brown; secretary, Harry Jones; corresponding secretary, James McCarthy; trustee, Ernest Westlake; executive committee, Robert Jones, John Johnstone, Arthur Cook, James Gladstone, August Fournier, Walter McKinley and Thomas Twigg. The newly elected officers were installed by Mr. Duthie and Mr. McDonald then took the chair and conducted the remainder of the meeting.

It was decided to hold our annual dinner on January 25, and a committee composed of Messrs. Ernest Brown, Joseph Adler and James Duthie was appointed by President McDonald to make full arrangements.

JAMES McCARTHY, Cor. Sec'y.

PITTSBURGH FLORISTS' AND GARDENERS' CLUB.

The meeting of the club December 7th in the Fort Pitt Hotel was well attended. The main topic for discussion was the late Cleveland Flower Show. There had been a good attendance from Pittsburgh and every one was delighted. The introducer and grower of the Mrs. M. R. Morgan, yellow sport from Timothy Eaton chrysanthemum, which took the third prize at the show, was present, and we all agreed with him that it was a fine commercial chrysanthemum. Some were so enthusiastic over the Cleveland Flower Show that they raised the question of Why cannot Pittsburgh do likewise? and the main obstacle seemed to be the lack of a hall centrally located, but the leaven of a flower show seemed to be working, and who can tell what may happen yet?

There were exhibits of pink Astilbe Japonica in pots by Carl Becherer, of poinsettias by Pasquale Fabbozzi, gardener for J. C. Trees, the latter also showing Roman hyacinths in pots. Poinsettias were also shown by the Phipps Conservatories. To all three exhibitors cultural certificates were awarded. It was thought the pink astilbes would make fine Christmas plants.

Our President read an extract from a noted scientist on the origin of kissing. What has started our President on this investigation we cannot imagine, and we are awaiting further developments with great interest.

At the January meeting the election of officers for 1916 will take place.

H. P. JOSLIN, Secretary.

WESTERN PENNSYLVANIA HORTI-CULTURAL SOCIETY.

The semi-monthly session of this society in Pittsburgh last Wednesday evening, was characterized by a fine display of poinsettias, cyclamen, Lorraine begonias and ardisias, by the various gardeners. The original intention was to have had a talk on "Christmas Decorations," by one of the local florists, but owing to the rush attendant upon the approaching holiday season in commercial circles, this was, unfortunately, precluded. The first regular session of the new society was held on the first inst., when sixteen new associate members were reported by the vice-president. Superintendent William Allen of the Homewood Cemetery. All are members of the Garden Club of Allegheny County and joined at the annual meeting of the same, when Mr. Allen made a representative visit in the interest of his organization.

Thomas Edward Tyler, who has charge of the orchid houses of Charles D. Armstrong, had an exhibition of Cypripediums in variety, including several fine types of Sanderæ, to which he devotes an entire house. There was also a display of late chrysanthemums (single and pompons) by Mr. Huyler, chrysanthemum grower for the Phipps Conservatory. Mr. Huyler stated that his experience was that the single varieties were usually pinched too late in the season, thereby precluding the desirable long stems. The next session of the society on January fifth, will be devoted to a discussion on the advisability of giving the first annual Chrysanthemum Show

CLEVELAND FLORISTS' CLUB.

At the last meeting of the Cleveland Florists' Club it was decided to have a banquet and jollification in celebration of the November Show, which was a success from practically every angle. The premiums are all paid with a very few exceptions, there being some delay in a few cases, which will soon be straightened out. The club voted to go after the National Flower Show for 1918, and President H. Bate appointed the following committee: H. P. Knoble, chairman; Chas. Russell, Timothy Smith, F. C. W. Brown, Geo. Bate and F. A. Friedley.

CLUB AND SOCIETY NOTES.

J. Stanley Giles, president; Harry C. Huesman, vice-president, and Fulmer H. Lauck, secretary and treasurer, were re-elected to serve for the ensuing year at a meeting of the Reading (Pa.) Florists' Association, held in Moore's Hall, Dec. 2. There was a discussion on the Carnation. A social hour followed the meeting.

The 49th annual meeting of the Minneapolis Horticultural Society was

PHIPPS CONSERVATORIES, SCHENLEY PARK, PITTSBURGH.

It has been our privilege and pleasure, from time to time, to regale our readers with descriptions of the periodical public floral exhibitions that have been given in the Phipps Conservatories, together with occasional interior views of these great winter gardens which mean so much for Pittsburgh horticulture. No doubt the gen-

in session last week with a large attendence and great enthusiasm. The program was carried out and everything was at high tide with weather delightful and a splendid exhibit of fruit and vegetables. The membership is now over 3,400 and an effort is being made to win it up to 4,000. It is now the largest in America if not in the world.

A very few members attended the monthly meeting of the Lenox Horticultural Society on December 9th. A request from the Nassau Horticultural Society that this society co-operate in their plan for membership transfer for members changing place of residence was unanimously agreed to. Mr. Loveless gave a very interesting talk on his visit to the Cleveland show. The next meeting will be held on January 12th.

The New London Horticultural Society at its annual meeting elected officers as follows: President, Donald Miller; first vice president, Gustav Neumann; second vice president, E. Robinson; secretary, Stanley Jordan; financial secretary, William J. Morgan; treasurer, Simon L. Ewald; librarian, Herbert Lickman; executive committee, Alfred Flowers. John Maloney, Thomas Leydon, Edward A. Smith, W. J. Schoonman, Miss Harriet Allen, Mrs. Joseph Beebe, Mrs. C. W. Nichols.

The Southampton, N. Y., Horticultural Society held its regular fortnightly meeting on Dec. 2nd. The talk of the evening was on "Sweet Peas Under Glass," when W. McCleod, superintendent for Mrs. Horace Russell, gave a very interesting, cultural address. Mr. McCleod has proved to be a very skillful cultivator of these beautiful winter flowers. The next meeting will be held on Dec. 16th at 8 P. M. in Odd Fellows Hall, Southampton.

eral exterior view accompanying these notes will be particularly interesting, now that the question of great public conservatories in park reservations is coming so strongly to the front. A place of resort, full of tropical luxuriance in the dreary months of winter, constitutes an unrivalled attraction and delight for all classes of people.

The members of the Norwood (Pa.) Horticultural Society held their annual election of officers December 6. Dr. John A. Borneman was chosen president; John S. High, vice-president; L. Deppen, treasurer. William L. Edward, a florist of Norwood, delivered an address on the "Care of Home Plants During Winter." It was decided that in the future, instead of having the regular flower show in September, the Society would hold a show early in September of each year for early fall flowers, to be followed in October by a show especially for chrysanthemums and dahlias, the idea being to promote the growth of the latter.

The annual meeting of the Connecticut Horticultural society was held at the county building, Friday evening. George H. Hollister, superintendent of Keney park, was elected president, and was welcomed to his new position by the retiring president Warren S. Mason, with congratulations and good wishes. The other officers elected were: First vice-president, Frank Roulier; second vice-president, Fred Boss; third vice-president, O. F. Gritzmacher; treasurer, W. W. Hunt; secretary, Alfred Dixon; librarian, William T. Hall; botanist, J. Vidbourne; pomologist, C. H. Sierman.

An unusually fine exhibit of poinsettias was shown by Alfred Cebelius. It was awarded a first-class certificate. The judges were Alexander Cumming, Jr., Frank Roulier, and A. Righeszi. John F. Huss gave an interesting account of the meeting of the National Gardeners' Association in Boston, and introduced William Kleinheinz, of Ogontz, Penn.; Joseph Manda, of West Orange, N. J., and P. W. Popp, of Mamaroneck, N. Y. All three gave interesting talks.

PITTSBURGH NOTES.

Mrs. Gustave Ludwig has returned from a two months' visit in Chicago with her daughter, Mrs. Victor Bergman.

Earl Tipton has severed his connection with the A. W. Smith Company to enter the employ of Penn, the Florist, in Boston, Mass.

Frank Crooks, who has charge of the James H. Park greenhouses and grounds, has the sympathy of many friends in the serious illness of Mrs. Crooks, who has been a patient in the West Penn Hospital for the past six weeks.

Eleven hundred and fifty dollars was realized from the flower stand at the Austria-German Red Cross benefit held in Exposition Hall last week. The committee in charge included Henry Mueschke, chairman; C. Phillipps, Julius W. Ludwig and Gilbert Ludwig.

Preparatory to remodeling the grounds of "Greystone," the Michael C. Benedum estate, Berthold C. Frosch and his foreman, Joseph Irwin, supervised the transplanting of four trees from the Westinghouse estate. "Solitude," last week. They were fifty feet high, two being pin oaks between twenty-five and thirty years old, and two birches about fifteen years of age. At the same time a red and three Norway maples were removed from the Westinghouse grounds to those of Grant McCargo in Woodland Road. They also were of uniform size, twenty feet high, of six-inch calibre and ten feet "spread."

Debutante entertaining continues to tax the skill and ingenuity of the society florists. Simple elegance in the form of clusters of exquisite blooms and hundreds of gift bouquets and baskets add their charm to these magnificent affairs and the ballrooms call into requisition the most elaborate decorations. At one of these 2500 Mrs. Russell roses were used, entwined in a white lattice over the orchestral stage, beyond which was a boxwood hedge bordering an Italian garden and ocean scene, and on the tables in white willow baskets. Another ballroom was transformed into a charming Chinese garden hedged with boxwood and Easter lilies. On each side was a bronze vase six feet high filled with 100 yellow chrysanthemums; 150 Mandarin orange plants, each with from twelve to eighteen oranges, formed the table centerpiece.

CALIFORNIA NOTES.

A new shop was opened recently at 1125 Oak street, Oakland, Cal., by P. W. Coger.

A new florist shop has just been opened in Fresno, Cal., by Miss Pearson. It is known as the Rose Maur and is nicely fitted up.

The December meeting of the Pacific Coast Horticultural Society was postponed a week on account of the closing of the exposition falling on the regular date. A large attendance is expected this Saturday, as officers will be elected for the ensuing year, and other matters of interest are scheduled.

K. & M. Hannon, of San Francisco, have made arrangements for improved quarters. The building in which they are located at 1438 Polk street is to be replaced early next year with a

ANGRÆCUM EBURNEUM.

This noble hothouse orchid, a native of Madagascar, is also known as A. superbum. The plant shown in our illustration was grown and flowered by M. J. Pope, whose cultural skill is conclusively demonstrated in the splendid specimen here portrayed. Angræcum eburneum is one of the parents, with A. sesquipedale, of A. Veitchii, one of the two Angræcum hybrids thus far recorded.

The Angræcums are true air plants and need no soil at the roots, but simply sphagnum moss frequently renewed. A warm moist place is essential to their well-being in winter. They have no pseudo-bulbs, hence must never be allowed to become dry.

modern structure, and they have secured quarters in the new building. They will probably have to move to a temporary location immediately after the holidays.

RESTRICTIONS ON FUNERAL FLOWERS.

The article, "Flowers at Funerals," by John C. Lindblom, in December 4th issue, is well and timely taken, but there are two sides to every question and I have no doubt that whether priest or prelate raises the question of flowers at funerals, it is not with any feeling of animosity against the florist or his business. It is a never failing fact that the habit of giving flowers at funerals to an alarming extent, not alone among the wealthy but the poorer classes, who very often can poorly bear such expense and often are not able to pay for them when they get them. Another question along these lines on funeral occasions is that unscrupulous florists get in the habit of charging about 200% more for flowers used in funeral designs than for any other purpose, taking into consideration that it takes an artist to arrange a design, and it might be well, all things considered, not to stir up a hornet's nest without first viewing all the circumstances surrounding the case.

Yours for justice,
Roanoke, Va.　　　PATRICK FOY.

OBITUARY.

Frank H. Timmerhof.

Frank H. Timmerhof, for six years cashier for the A. L. Randall Co., Chicago, passed away on Sunday, Dec. 12th, at his home at 2725 N. Ballou street, after a short illness. Mr. Timmerhof was a young man and had been married but a few months.

Lorenze Krodel, Sr.

Lorenze Krodel, a veteran florist of Pittsburgh, Pa., died suddenly on Sunday morning, December 5. Mr. Krodel was aged sixty-two years, nine months and fifteen days. He is survived by his widow, Elizabeth Schmitt Krodel, and a son, Lorenze Krodel, Jr., who is connected with the L. W. Scott Company, seed dealers.

VANDA SANDERIANA.

The beautiful illustration of this famous Philippine orchid which adorns our cover page this week, calls for no other description than to say that it is from a photograph sent to Horticulture by Sander & Sons, of the specimen Vanda Sanderiana which was awarded a silver Lindley Medal at the Royal Horticultural meeting in London on the 28th of last September. The variety was exceptionally fine and the plant carried 42 expanded flowers and a spike in bud.

BOSTON FLORIST BOWLERS.

We see in the accompanying group picture the members of the Boston Florists' Bowling League, whose scores we have been publishing weekly. In the centre of the second row from the top, directly under the light, with arms crossed, is the president of the league, Seymour Grose, who is also captain of the Carbone team. Meetings for practice and competition are held at the Arch Street Alleys every Thursday evening and much interest is manifested by the active young men connected with the flower markets and the wholesale and retail establishments. They bowl "candle pins" and small balls only. Owing to the busy holiday demands no bowling will be done until December 30.

Visitors' Register

San Francisco: Frank Smith, Merced, Cal.

Cleveland, O.: Frank Farney, representing M. Rice Co., Phila.

Philadelphia: Frank B. Rine, Lewisburg, Pa.; Mr. Hayman, Clarksburg, W. Va.

Washington, D. C.—Frederick C. Solari, of Solari Archie Co., Boston, Mass.; Thomas Cahill, Des Moines, Iowa; Julius Dilloff, New York; William P. Craig, Philadelphia; Charles M. Waring, York, Pa.

Boston: Mr. Meehan of the Posey Shop, Springfield, Mass.; N. F. Higgins, Springfield, Mass.; E. J. Harmon, Portland, Maine; J. O. Elwell, Kennebunk, Maine; Stephen Green, representing H. Bayersdorfer & Co., Philadelphia.

Pittsburgh: Isaac Bayersdorfer and Martin Reukauf, representing H. Bayersdorfer & Co., Phila.; E. J. Fancourt, of Pennock-Meehan Company, Phila.; C. J. Watson, for Leo Niessen Co., Phila.; Eber Holmes, for W. A. Manda, Inc., South Orange, N. J.

Cincinnati: Mrs. B. A. Durham, Ashland, Ky.; Mr. Bradford, of Bradford Flower Store, Springfield, Ohio; H. V. Thomas, Augusta, Ky.; C. P. Brumier, Springfield, Ohio; Joseph Hill, Richmond, Ind.; Mrs. M. Frisch, Dayton, O.; H. C. Neubrand, rep. A. N. Pierson, Cromwell, Conn.; Walter Gray, Wm. Sodder, Karl Weiser and Miss Fedeck, of Hamilton.

Chicago: A. C. Reicher, Michigan City, Ind.; F. Farney, rep. Rice & Co., Phila.; Fred Heinl, Terre Haute, Ind.; Geo. L. Freeman, Fall River, Mass.; Saml. Seligman, New York; A. M. Augspurger, Peoria, Ill.; C. Watson, rep. Leo Niessen Co., Phila., Pa.; Theo. Meyer, Waukegan, Ill.; A. Schutz, Hammond, Ind.; H. Rudolph, Manitowoc, Wis.; Mrs. Roy Wilcox, Council Bluffs, Iowa; Mrs. M. E. Irby, Memphis, Tenn.

NEW YORK.

Thorley has leased the store 36 W. 46th street for a holiday annex.

E. Allan Peirce of Waltham, Mass., arrived last Tuesday evening after an 18-hour trip from Boston, being snowed-in two miles from Stamford, Conn.

There are rumors of several houses caving in through the weight of last Monday's snow which was wet and sticky and did not slide off as is usually the case.

J. J. Coan has got nicely settled down to business in his new wholesale flower store at 115 W. 28th street, where for the first week he worked at great disadvantage on account of delay in telephone and light installation.

During Recess

Boston Florists' Bowling Club.

Scores and standing December 9:

Flower Ex...	1279	vs. Robinson	1203
Zinn	1313	vs. M. & M.......	1255
Pansies	1346	vs. Galvin	1329
Carbone	1295	vs. Flower Mkt..	1281

Standing as to Points:

	Won	Lost
Galvin	30	6
Flower Market	26	10
Carbone	22	14
Zinn	18	18
Pansies	17	19
Flower Exchange	13	23
Robinson	10	26
M. & M.	8	28

N. Y. Florists' Bowling Club.

Following are the scores recorded at the game of the New York bowlers on Thursday evening, December 9:

Siebrecht	139	157	145
Jacobson	154	187	177
Ford	164	156	134
Miesem	201	189	172
Irwin	178	178	106
Riedel	110	121	149
Scott	146	157	160

H. C. RIEDEL, Sec'y.

Streator, Ill.—The Hill Floral Co. has been purchased by the former manager, Fred R. Thornton, who will conduct business under the name of the Thornton Floral Co.

SEED TRADE

American Seed Trade Association.

A cordial invitation has been extended to the members of the American Seed Trade Association, in behalf of the Association of Official Seed Analysts, through Secretary John P. Helyar, to attend the Program Session of the annual meeting to be held at Columbus, O., December 28th, 1915, in Townshend Hall.

The program follows:

1. Variations Observed in Germination and Purity Tests — C. P. Smith, Maryland.

2. Variations in Germination and Purity Tests—O. A. Stevens, N. Dakota.

3. Temperature Conditions for the Germination of Certain Flower Seeds —G. T. Harrington, Washington, D. C.

4. The Germination of Blue Grass Seed—J. R. Fryer, Calgary, Alta.

5. Hard Seed Investigations—H. D. Hughes, Iowa.

6. The Effect of Incubation at Cool Temperatures Upon the Subsequent Germination of Hard Clover Seed— G. T. Harrington, Washington, D. C.

7. Notes on Seed Germination—W. L. Goss, Washington, D. C.

8. Some Results of a Critical Study of Alternating Temperatures—G. T. Harrington, Washington, D. C.

9. An Improved Seed Mixer—E. D. Eddy, Ottawa.

10. The Development of Analytical Methods in European Seed Laboratories—A. L. Stone, Wisconsin.

11. The West Virginia Law—H. E. Williams, Com. Agr., West Virginia.

12. Distinguishing Characteristics of the Seeds of Sudan and Johnson Grass—W. L. Goss and F. H. Hillman, Washington, D. C.

13. Imported Low-Grade Crimson Clover and Orchard Grass Seed — E. Brown and F. H. Hillman, Washington, D. C.

15. A Study of Oat Impurities in Iowa—L. H. Pammel, Iowa.

Notes.

Muskogee, Okla. — The Oklahoma Seed Company have moved into larger quarters at 112 N. Main street.

Columbia, Mo.—Thomas Berry, formerly with the Archias Seed & Floral Company, has purchased a half interest in the Wheat Floral Co.

Raleigh, N. C.—All seed dealers must promptly renew their licenses, according to notices being sent out by the Commissioner of Agriculture of this state. Those not complying may be barred from the state or suffer the penalties of the law. The new licenses go into effect on January 1, 1916, and running for a year will cost $25.

Senator Gronna, of North Dakota, filed on December 7, 1915, a bill (S. 578) "To Prohibit the Interstate Shipment of Impure Seeds."

This is identically the same bill filed by Mr. Gonna in the 62d Congress (February 5, 1913), S. 8382, and in the 63d Congress, S. 480, the former being unacted upon, the latter unfavorably reported by the Senate Committee on Agriculture and Forestry.

The present bill is thoroughly unwise, impracticable, and would, if enacted, wholly prohibit the shipment in interstate commerce of certain seeds. It applies to all field, vegetable and flower seeds, arbitrarily defining adulterations which no expert can detect, and making all seeds unfit for sale which are under 90 per cent. germination.

The following letter which is being sent to all members of the American Seed Trade Association should have a direct interest for many of our readers:

My dear Sir:—

As you are perhaps aware, Representative Anderson has introduced House Bill H. R. 636, which purposes to subject seeds, plants, etc., to the same rate of postage as other merchandise.

You know it was by considerable effort we were able to keep seed at the old rate, 2 oz. for 1c. up to and including 8 oz. It would be a mistake to let this bill slip through at this time after so much effort. I will depend on you to use every means in your power to prevent this from becoming a law.

Please furnish me carbon copies of the letters you will write to the Senators and Representatives so as to prevent duplication. It is also well to have these copies on file.

You can readily understand that the matter of having to zone over 4 oz. is going to add very considerable burden. Please let me hear from you at your earliest convenience.   Sincerely yours,
        W. F. THERKILDSON, chairman,
        Postal Laws Committee A. S. T. A.

CATALOGUES RECEIVED.

Clark W. Brown, Ashland, Mass.— 1916 Catalogue and Price List of Gladiolus Bulbs.

Geo. S. Woodruff, Independence, Ia. —Wholesale Price List of Gladiolus Bulbs, 1915-1916.

West Hill Nurseries, Fredonia, N. Y.—63d Semi-Annual Wholesale Price List of Grape Vines, Small Fruits, etc.

North Eastern Forestry Company, Cheshire, Conn.—Price List for 1916 of High Grade Tree Seeds and Young Trees.

Henry F. Michell Co., Philadelphia, Pa.—Order Sheet for December, 1915. Illustrates and describes Verbenas, Antirrhinum, Sweet Peas and other desirable strains of Florists' Flowers.

REPORT OF THE SECRETARY OF AGRICULTURE.

In his annual report for the fiscal year ending June 30, 1915, which has just been issued, David F. Houston, Secretary of Agriculture, indicates a number of important measures necessary for the betterment of agriculture, both on the production and marketing sides, and for the conservation of the resources of the Nation. It is a very interesting document for any one occupied with the problems of farming, marketing and distribution, meat supply, national forests, etc. For the horticulturist the section concerning the potash supply will be found interesting.

MASSACHUSETTS AGRICULTURAL COLLEGE NOTES.

The series of trips to neighboring greenhouses being made by the junior classes in floriculture has been completed this week by visits to Butler & Uhlman's houses in Northampton and the Montgomery and several other ranges in Holyoke.

Practically all the students in floriculture have gotten places for the Christmas holidays in either retail stores or greenhouses. The department gratefully appreciates the interest shown by the commercial men to get some practical work.

Professor R. R. Root of the University of Illinois, addressed the floriculture club on "Color Combinations in Formal Garden Work."

The junior classes in pomology are pruning in the Owen orchard this week.

NEW CORPORATIONS.

Makanda, Ill.—Illinois Seed & Nursery Company, capital stock, $10,000. Incorporators, J. H., A. L. and H. J. Bradley.

Cincinnati, O.—The William Murphy Co., by Mrs. Laura F. Murphy, Miss Alice Murphy, Miss Laura Murphy, W. Pray Murphy and Miss Clare Murphy. Capital, $10,000.

Of Interest to Retail Florists

NEW FLOWER STORES.

Galena, Kan.—C. M. Weintz.
Syracuse, N. Y.—Robert Bard.
Omaha, Neb.—Parker Floral Co., 411 S. 16th street.
Los Angeles, Cal. — Paul Howard, 1521 W. 7th street.
Birmingham, Ala. — T. G. Owen & Son, Second avenue.
Greensburg, Ind. — Bartsch Floral Co., Red Men's building.
Wheeling, W. Va.—Virginia Flower Shop, 1212 Market street.
New Orleans, La.—Henry Scheuermann, 108 Baronne street.
New York, N. Y.—Wm. B. Nugent, Lexington avenue, between 73d and 74th streets.
Schenectady, N. Y. — The Flower Shop, Walter Lockrow, proprietor, Baker building.
New York, N. Y.—John F. Schnaufer, removing from Dale avenue to 969 West 180th street, Bronx.
Chicago, Ill. — Sullivan Bros., 92d street and Commercial avenue. Victor Young, 1239 N. Clark street.
Cleveland, Ohio—Von Floral Co. has opened two branches—The Heights Floral Co., Cedar and E. 105th street, and The Euclid Floral Co., at Euclid and Lake Front. The Christine Floral Co. has opened a new branch store at 1940 E. 6th street.

Secretary Pochelon has sent the following communication to all members of the F. T. D.:

At the meeting of The Florists' Telegraph Delivery held at Cleveland, O., it was decided by officers and members present that on bills not paid within thirty-five days from member to member the discount of 20 per cent. shall be forfeited. This would help to do away with a lot of unpleasant feeling and also would help us find out people who are negligent in paying their bills. If we wish to have any further success in the F. T. D. we must have prompt paying members on our list.

The responsibility of the F. T. D. through this act becomes a much greater value than it has been heretofore, so please do not let bills to F. T. D. members hang fire but settle them as quickly as possible.

When you make out your statement on January 1, send the secretary a list of all bills overdue and owed you by members of F. T. D. These bills will have to be settled immediately, and members refusing to do so will lose the 20 per cent. and their names are liable to be taken off our list.

The tone of this letter may seem harsh but it is the only way to uphold the prestige of The F. T. D.

NEWS ITEMS FROM EVERYWHERE

BOSTON.

Henry Marshall has opened a new flower store at Davis Sq., Somerville, Mass.

J. Frank Edgar, prominent grower at Waverley, has been elected to the Board of Aldermen of Waltham, Mass.

On account of the Christmas rush all games of the Bowling Association have been postponed until the 30th of this month.

Frank Leavitt has severed his connection with the Montrose Greenhouses and his place has been filled temporarily by George Mullen.

The double range of small houses built on the side-hill system and all heated by a single Kroeschell boiler was one of the features which especially interested the visiting gardeners at the Farquhar Nurseries last Friday. These houses are models of economy and convenience for the purpose of plant growing and well worth a close study by anyone wishing to accomplish the most at the least cost.

Penn's palatial new flower store at corner of Tremont St. and Hamilton Place opens its doors to the public on Saturday, December 18. This place is heralded as the most modern and artistic floral establishment in New England, if not in the United States. The exterior glows with golden trimmings and the interior is as elaborate as mirrors, carving, sculpture and fountains can make it.

The selling section is tiled like all the rest in soft buff-colored stone, and the walls are of Caen stone colored blocks. The show windows are so fashioned as to make the interior of the store elliptical at the front with the door in the centre, over which there is a white marble clock. The windows themselves are inclosed at the top with a green lattice work. Both the front and back of the show windows are of all glass construction, which practically makes the whole shop open—a veritable crystal palace.

On either side of the store is a refrigerating system of new type, which is strictly hygienic in that it neither uses ice nor ammonia. This sort of refrigerator has never been used in a florist shop before, although generally adopted by the newer hospitals.

At the back the visitor will see the crowning feature, the fountain court. There, in the centre of the tiled floor, spurts a wonderful Italian fountain by a Boston sculptor. The court is surrounded by eight marble pillars topped with an ornamental frieze. Above is an iron and leaded glass ceiling which will light the court day and night. C. J. S.

CHICAGO.

Victor Young, who lately went into business with Fred Ronsley, on Dearborn street, now has a store of his own at 1239 N. Clark street.

Mrs. M. E. Irby, of Memphis, Tenn., was taken ill while in Chicago making her selections of holiday stock and was obliged to return home.

The new store opened by Mrs. J. Simpson in Austin, two weeks ago, is getting well established and a fair amount of trade is coming its way.

Traveling salesmen took Chicago customers by storm last week, each trying to make his yearly sales as large as possible in the few days left.

The wholesale houses report the once a year customers who want to place large orders at lowest prices are all writing for holiday stock. "Nothing doing."

One of the attractive holiday window displays is that of the Atlas Floral Co., with Herbert Stone in charge. The overhead is a canopy of green coated with white calcimine and sprinkled with mica and hung with the finest possible threads of tinsel. A background of ribbon-trimmed araucaria gave color, and the floor space in front held the usual cut flowers of the season.

That it is to be another plant Christ-

mas is predicted, and the way orders are coming in is in favor of the plant side of the question. Aside from calls for carnations, which have been reported scarce, orders are slow on cut flowers, while the largest plant houses report practically all stock booked by December 10th.

Allie Zech, of Zech & Mann, 30 E. Randolph street, on December 13, had quite possibly a narrow escape from injury if not death and did not know it till the next morning. Remembering something he had left in the rear of the store, Mr. Zech went in and turned on the light, passing the side of the office on his way. A bent form was seen to dart out, but supposing it to be a messenger boy after flowers from the barrel, he thought no more of it after the first start and left without entering the office. The next morning it was found the cash drawer had been robbed of about ten dollars, but the safe had not been touched.

PHILADELPHIA.

Frank Alderberger, the well known and popular Wayne florist has been ill for a week or more. At last accounts he was improving a little.

Holly is not quite so well berried this year as for the past few years—taking it all around. Even the best Delaware brand, which leads the list always, is a little under the average.

WASHINGTON.

Florists have been warned to be on the lookout for a man giving the name of Fred R. Forth who is wanted in this city for giving one of their number a worthless check in payment of an order, the man collecting the balance in cash. His description is as follows: Between 5 ft. 7 and 5ft. 9 in. in height; age 35 to 40; weight 150 to 160 lbs.; well built, smooth face, dark complexion and hair, neatly dressed in sort of gray or brown Balmacaan overcoat and dark colored soft hat. The check passed upon the florist who notified the police was drawn on the Security Savings and Commercial Bank of this city.

J. H. Small & Sons, as usual, furnished the decorations for the annual banquet of the Gridiron Club last Saturday evening. The decorations were handsome and in part very unique. The feature was the "forest" for as the guests entered the banquet hall they passed down a lane bordered by growing cedars and spruce trees. The walls were lined with American Beauty roses, chrysanthemums and poinsettias. The enormous gridiron, emblazoned with electric lights, was decorated with American Beauty roses on either side. Vases of flowers were on each of the tables. The small ball room, in which the reception was held, was decorated with palms and flowering plants, together with standards of American Beauty roses. Wall pockets also contained chrysanthemums and roses.

In appreciation of his efforts in making the convention of the G. A. R. last September, the brilliant success that it turned out to be, 100 members of the Citizens' Committee met in the New Willard Hotel and presented William F. Gude, chairman of the committee, a handsome mahogany chest containing thirteen dozen pieces of equally handsome silver flatware. The presentation speech was made by Simon Wolf who said, "We are fortunate in having found in William F. Gude such a representative as has stamped the city of Washington as the leading center of hospitality and good cheer." Mr. Gude thanked those present in a few well chosen words and later held a reception during which he was congratulated by all upon the good work he had done.

WHOLESALE FLOWER MARKETS — TRADE PRICES—Per 100 TO DEALERS ONLY

Roses	BOSTON Dec. 16			ST. LOUIS Dec. 13			PHILA. Dec. 13		
Am. Beauty, Special	20.00	to	20.00	40.00	to	60.00	30.00	to	35.00
" " Fancy and Extra	12.00	to	15.00	25.00	to	30.00	20.00	to	25.00
" " No. 1	5.00	to	10.00	10.00	to	15.00	8.00	to	15.00
Russell, Hadley	4.00	to	10.00	10.00	to	15.00	4.00	to	20.00
Killarney, Richmond, Hillegdon, Ward, Extra	4.00	to	6.00	3.00	to	10.00	8.00	to	12.00
" " Ordinary	2.00	to	3.00	5.00	to	6.00	3.00	to	6.00
Arenburg: Radiance, Taft, Key, Extra	4.00	to	8.00	....	to	....	8.00	to	12.00
" " Ordinary	2.00	to	4.00	....	to	....	3.00	to	6.00
Ophelia, Mock, Sunburst, Extra	5.00	to	10.00	8.00	to	10.00	8.00	to	12.00
" " Ordinary	2.00	to	4.00	5.00	to	6.00	3.00	to	6.00
Carnations, Fancy	3.00	to	4.00	4.00	to	6.00	4.00	to	5.00
" Ordinary	1.50	to	2.00	2.00	to	3.00	2.00	to	3.00
Cattleyas	50.00	to	60.00	50.00	to	60.00	40.00	to	60.00
Dendrobium formosum	....	to	40.00	....	to	....	35.00	to	50.00
Lilies, Longiflorum	8.00	to	10.00	12.00	to	15.00	8.00	to	12.00
" Rubrum	....	to	6.00	6.00	to	8.00	4.00	to	6.00
Callas	10.00	to	18.00	1.00	to	12.00	10.00	to	12.50
Lily of the Valley	2.00	to	4.00	3.00	to	4.00	2.00	to	4.00
Daisies	.50	to	2.00	.75	to	.50	1.00	to	2.00
Violets	.75	to	1.75	.50	to	.75	.25	to	1.00
Mignonette	2.00	to	4.00	3.00	to	4.00	2.00	to	5.00
Snapdragon	2.00	to	4.00	4.00	to	5.00	4.00	to	12.50
Narcissus, Paper-White	2.00	to	2.50	3.00	to	4.00	3.00	to	4.00
" Trumpet	....	to	....	....	to	....	....	to	....
Hyacinths, Roman	....	to	....	3.00	to	4.00	....	to	....
Freesia	....	to	....	....	to	....	....	to	....
Calendulas	2.00	to	3.00	3.00	to	4.00	2.00	to	4.00
Stevia	1.00	to	2.00	1.00	to	1.50	1.00	to	2.00
Sweet Peas	.75	to	2.00	1.00	to	2.00	.75	to	2.00
Gardenias	25.00	to	....	....	to	....	25.00	to	40.00
Adiantum	....	to	1.00	1.00	to	1.25	....	to	1.00
Smilax	12.00	to	16.00	12.00	to	15.00	15.00	to	20.00
Asparagus Plumosus, Strings (100)	25.00	to	50.00	35.00	to	50.00	....	to	....
" & Spren. (100 Bchs.)	25.00	to	35.00	35.00	to	35.00	25.00	to	50.00

Flower Market Reports

BOSTON   Market conditions are responsive to the sharp wintry weather which has prevailed for the past week. Chrysanthemums are rapidly closing out and the receipts of other materials are small and, as a consequence, prices have stiffened up all along the line, although there is really very little business coming in and not much is expected now until the holiday rush opens up. The table of price quotations furnishes information for those familiar with market ways as to the price situation at present.

BUFFALO   Wintry weather and the market unchanged from the week previous. Chrysanthemums have practically ended and this tends to throw the demand toward other stock, especially carnations, which have been too plentiful to hold up prices, but Saturday last saw the clean-up of the week and at this writing, Dec. 13, the day's receipts of carnations moved promptly and have stiffened in price. Roses are coming in long grades. Lilies are fine and there is also some fine stevia, mignonette, sweet peas, and lily of the valley, the latter too plentiful with demand very light. Decorative material is selling well—in fact better than for years previous. This should be a good week for the merchants and they are in readiness for a little hustle.

CHICAGO   In the Chicago market all is being made in readiness for the florists' busiest season and most of those in the trade are looking for one of the best years in their experience. There are many letters of inquiry but the positive orders are, as in the past two years, coming late. Each year the orders come later. The quantity of stock is generally conceded to be sufficient in roses and shy in carnations with the possible sunshine an important factor. Trade the past week has been good from the wholesalers' standpoint and rather quiet from the retailers', which means that shipping trade has been brisk. Chrysanthemums of the latest varieties are still here, but they show the end of the season is near. The pink shades seem to be the best this week but growers expect white ones also for the last. All kinds of roses, with few exceptions, are being cut heavily and there is every indication of a good crop. Orchids are scarce and the American Beauty supply is still very limited. Holly is fine and well berried.

CINCINNATI   A fortnight before Christmas shows the market to be in a rather tight condition. Supplies are not very large but are able to take care of a moderately active demand. If promises for Christmas come here we are due to have a good supply of cut flowers for that day, otherwise we will run decidedly short. Roses and carnations are not very plentiful. Enough lilies are coming in to take care of the call for them. Up to this time the narcissus cut has not been very large. Stevia is plentiful. Callas, lily of the valley, violets and orchids

are all in a pretty fair supply. Sweet peas are not very plentiful. Baby primrose and forget-me-not may be had, also poinsettias, which promise to be plenty. Some good late chrysanthemums are still offered.

CLEVELAND   The local market is cleaning up every day with not half enough stock to take care of the orders. Carnations have been very scarce for the past week. Roses have cleaned up every day. Violets and American Beauties have been very

fine. Chrysanthemums are over for this season. Callas and lilies have a good demand. Narcissi and sweet peas are very scarce and not enough for the demand. Lily of the valley is very fine. From all reports flowers will be very scarce for Christmas.

NEW YORK   The wild storm of last Monday upset business conditions in every direction. Demand there was not, hence the almost entire suspension of the supply did not affect the

(Continued on page 817)

WHOLESALE FLOWER MARKETS — TRADE PRICES—Per 100
TO DEALERS ONLY

Roses	CINCINNATI Dec. 13		CHICAGO Dec. 13		BUFFALO Dec. 13		PITTSBURG Dec. 6	
Am. Beauty, Special	90.00 to 100.00	50.00 to 75.00	35.00 to 40.00	30.00 to 40.00
" " Fancy and Extra	50.00 to 75.00	30.00 to 40.00	20.00 to 30.00	20.00 to 25.00
" " No. 1	35.00 to 40.00	15.00 to 25.00	12.00 to 15.00	10.00 to 15.00
Russell, Hadley	15.00 to 25.00	4.00 to 25.00	10.00 to 12.00	8.00 to 18.00
Killarney, Richm'd, Hill'don, Ward	10.00 to 15.00	8.00 to 10.00	8.00 to 10.00	8.00 to 10.00
" " Ord.	5.00 to 8.00	3.00 to 6.00	4.00 to 6.00	6.00
Arenburg, Radiance, Taft, Key, Ex.	10.00 to 15.00	8.00 to 10.00	8.00 to 10.00	8.00 to 12.00
" " Ord.	4.00 to 8.00	5.00 to 5.00	5.00 to 6.00	to 6.00
Ophelia, Mock, Sunburst, Extra	10.00 to 15.00	8.00 to 10.00	8.00 to 10.00	8.00 to 15.00
" " Ordinary	4.00 to 8.00	3.00 to 5.00	4.00 to 6.00	6.00
Carnations, Fancy	8.00 to 10.00	4.00 to 5.00	3.00 to 3.50	to 4.00
" Ordinary	to 6.00	3.00 to 4.00	2.00 to 3.00	2.00 to 3.00
Cattleyas	to 100.00	60.00 to 75.00	75.00 to 100.00	40.00 to 75.00
Dendrobium formosum	to	50.00 to 60.00	to	35.00 to 50.00
Lilies, Longiflorum	12.50 to 15.00	8.00 to 10.00	10.00 to 12.00	10.00 to 12.00
" Rubrum	5.00 to 12.50	5.00 to 6.00	4.00 to 5.00	to
Callas	12.50 to 15.00	to	8.00 to 12.00	8.00 to 12.00
Lily of the Valley	to	3.00 to 4.00	3.00 to 4.00	3.00 to 4.00
Daisies	to	to	1.00 to 2.00	.75 to 1.00
Violets	1.50 to 2.00	.75 to 1.00	.75 to 1.0	.50 to 1.00
Mignonette	to	3.00 to 6.00	3.00 to 5.00	3.00 to 4.00
Snapdragon	to	4.00 to 6.00	4.00 to 10.00	4.00 to 6.00
Narcissus, Paper-White	3.00 to 4.00	3.00 to 3.00	3.00 to 3.00	3.00 to 4.00
" Trumpet	to	to	to	to
Hyacinths, Roman	to	to	to	3.00 to 4.00
Freesia	to	to	to	to
Calendulas	to	to	3.00 to 4.00	2.00 to 4.00
Stevia	to	3.00	to	1.00 to 1.50
Sweet Peas	1.00 to 1.50	1.00 to 1.50	.75 to 1.50	1.00 to 2.00
Gardenias	to	40.00 to 50.00	50.00 to 30.00	to
Adiantum	to	to	1.00 to 1.25	1.00 to 1.85
Smilax	12.50 to 15.00	to 12.00	to 15.00	12.50 to 15.00
Asparagus Plumosus, Strings (100)	25.00 to 50.00	40.00 to 50.00	to 60.00	30.00 to 50.00
" " & Spren. (100 bchs.)	25.00 to 50.00	50.00 to 50.00	15.00 to 50.00	30.00 to 50.00

Flower Market Reports
(Continued from page 825)

market situation. Shipments due on Tuesday morning did not arrive, as a rule, until Wednesday morning and much of the stock was in badly damaged condition when received at the wholesale markets. Things are gradually righting themselves and considerable satisfaction is felt that this outbreak of winter's worst temper came at a time comparatively inactive and hopes are entertained for a reaction to moderate and kindly conditions for the Christmas holiday trade now about to open. The outlook is for a fair supply of all seasonable things and in most excellent quality.

Carnations were the feature last week. They took quite a jump on account of the shortened supply caused by the dark, cool weather. Loud and long were the protests from the buyers, while the harrassed salesmen on the other hand smiled with satisfaction—glad that the tables had at last turned. In the rose market Mrs. Russell is the bright particular star — magnificent stock, much of it bringing forty and fifty dollars a hundred. Hadley and other reds are rather on the short side. Chrysanthemums are about over. What few Nonius there are coming in are quickly picked up by the local buyers. so that there are none for outside shipping. Calenthe Veitchi is the latest addition to the orchid show. Cattleyas. vandas and cypripediums are plentiful and good. Demand rather sluggish. Prospects for Christmas week are very good, some big orders having been already booked and more coming in every mail. The market is rising right now (Wednesday, Dec. 15th). They

(Continued on page 837)

Buyer's Directory and Ready Reference Guide

Advertisements under this head, one cent a word.   Initials count as words.

Display advertisers in this issue are also listed under this classification without charge. Reference to List of Advertisers will indicate the respective pages.

Buyers failing to find what they want in this list will confer a favor by writing us and we will try to put them in communication with reliable dealers.

ACCOUNTANT
R. Dysart, 40 State St., Boston.
For page see List of Advertisers.

APHINE
Aphine Mfg. Co., Madison, N. J.
For page see List of Advertisers.

APHIS PUNK
Nicotine Mfg. Co., St. Louis, Mo.
For page see List of Advertisers.

ASPARAGUS
Asparagus Plumosus, Thumb pot plants, sure to please. $1.50 per 100. B. C. BLAKE, R. D. 4, Springfield, Ohio.

500 Plumosus, 2½ in. for $10.00; 300 Sprengerii, 4 in., for $16.00. RONEY BROS., West Grove, Pa.

AUCTION SALES
The MacNiff Horticultural Co., New York City.
Plant and Bulb Sales by Auction.
For page see List of Advertisers.

Elliott Auction Co., New York City.
For page see List of Advertisers.

AZALEAS
P. Ouwerkerk, Hoboken, N. J.
For page see List of Advertisers.

BAY TREES
August Rolker & Sons, New York.
For page see List of Advertisers.

BEDDING PLANTS
A. N. Pierson, Inc., Cromwell, Conn.
For page see List of Advertisers.

R. Vincent, Jr. & Sons Co., White Marsh, Md.
For page see List of Advertisers.

BEGONIAS
		Per 100
BEGONIA LORRAINE,	2½ in......	$12.00
	3 in......	20.00
	4 in......	35.00
	5 in......	50.00
BEGONIA CINCINNATI,	2½ in......	15.00
	3 in......	25.80
	3½ in......	30.00
	4½ in......	40.00
JULIUS ROEHRS CO., Rutherford, N. J.		

BOILERS
Kroeschell Bros. Co., Chicago.
For page see List of Advertisers.

King Construction Co., North Tonawanda, N. Y.
"King Ideal" Boiler.
For page see List of Advertisers.

Hitchings & Co., New York City.

Lord & Burnham Co., New York City.
For page see List of Advertisers.

BOXES—CUT FLOWER FOLDING
Edwards Folding Box Co., Philadelphia.
For page see List of Advertisers.

Folding cut flower boxes, the best made. Write for list. HOLTON & HUNKEL CO., Milwaukee, Wis.

BOX TREES
BOX TREES—Standards, Pyramids and Bush. In various sizes. Price List on demand. JULIUS ROEHRS CO., Rutherford, N. J.

BULBS AND TUBERS
Arthur T. Boddington Co., Inc., New York City.
For page see List of Advertisers.

J. M. Thorburn & Co., New York City
Wholesale Price List of High Class Bulbs.
For page see List of Advertisers.

Ralph M. Ward & Co., New York City.
Lily Bulbs.
For page see List of Advertisers.

John Lewis Childs, Flowerfield, L. I., N. Y.
Gladioli.
For page see List of Advertisers.

August Rolker & Sons, New York City.
Holland and Japan Bulbs.
For page see List of Advertisers.

R. & J. Farquhar & Co., Boston, Mass.
For page see List of Advertisers.

Chas. Schwake & Co., New York City.
Horticultural Importers and Exporters.
For page see List of Advertisers.

A. Henderson & Co., Chicago, Ill.
For page see List of Advertisers.

Burnett Bros., 98 Chambers St., New York.
For page see List of Advertisers.

Henry F. Michell Co., Philadelphia, Pa.
For page see List of Advertisers.

Joseph Breck & Sons Corp., Boston, Mass.
For page see List of Advertisers.

Fottler, Fiske, Rawson Co., Boston, Mass.

C. KEUR & SONS, HILLEGOM, Holland.
Bulbs of all descriptions. Write for prices.
NEW YORK Branch, 8-10 Bridge St.

CANNAS
Newest list of the newest Cannas just out. Complete assortment of the finest sorts, at remarkable rates.
Send for list today.
THE CONARD & JONES CO.
West Grove, Pa.

CARNATIONS.
Wood Bros., Fishkill, N. Y.
For page see List of Advertisers.

F. Dorner & Sons Co., Lafayette, Ind.
For page see List of Advertisers.

Littlefield & Wyman, North Abington, Mass.
New Pink Carnation, Miss Theo.
For page see List of Advertisers.

CARNATION STAPLES
Split carnations quickly, easily and cheaply mended. Pillsbury's Carnation Staple. 1000 for 35c.; 3000 for $1.00 post paid. I. L. PILLSBURY, Galesburg Ill.

Supreme Carnation Staples, for repairing split carnations. 35c. per 1000; 3000 for $1.00. F. W. WAITE, 85 Belmont Ave., Springfield, Mass.

CHRISTMAS GREENS
Henry F. Michell Co., Philadelphia, Pa.
For page see List of Advertisers.

CHRISTMAS PLANTS
A. M. Davenport, Watertown, Mass.
For page see List of Advertisers.

Elmer D. Smith & Co., Adrian, Mich.
For page see List of Advertisers.

Shepard's Garden Carnation Co., Lowell, Mass.

CHRISTMAS PLANTS—Continued
Frank Oechslin, Chicago, Ill.

William W. Edgar Co., Waverley, Mass.

W. A. Riggs, Auburndale, Mass.
Excellent Xmas Plant Stock.
For page see List of Advertisers.

CHRYSANTHEMUMS
Chas. H. Totty, Madison, N. J.
For page see List of Advertisers.

COLEUS
Christmas Gem Coleus, 3c. B. C. BLAKE, R. D. 4, Springfield, Ohio.

Coleus, Golden Bedder, Verschaffeltii, Queen Victoria. Firebrand and all leading varieties, including the Pink and Yellow Trailing Queen, clean, strong, well rooted cuttings, 60c. per 100, $4.00 per 1000. Cash with order, and satisfaction guaranteed. Send for list. Largest grower of coleus in the U. S. A. NAHLIK, 261-75 Lawrence St., Flushing, N. Y.

DAHLIAS
Send for Wholesale List of whole clumps and separate stock; 40,000 clumps for sale. Northboro Dahlia and Gladiolus Gardens, J. L. MOORE, Prop, Northboro, Mass.

NEW PAEONY DAHLIA
John Wanamaker. Newest, Handsomest, Best. New color, new form and new habit of growth. Big stock of best cut-flower varieties. Send list of wants to PEACOCK DAHLIA FARMS, Berlin, N. J.

DECORATIVE PLANTS
Robert Craig Co., Philadelphia, Pa.
For page see List of Advertisers.

Woodrow & Marketos, New York City.
For page see List of Advertisers.

S. S. Skidelsky & Co., Philadelphia, Pa.
For page see List of Advertisers.

Bobbink & Atkins, Rutherford, N. J.
For page see List of Advertisers.

A. Leuthy & Co., Roslindale, Boston, Mass.
For page see List of Advertisers.

Thomas Roland, Nahant, Mass.
High Grade Plants for Retail Florists.
For page see List of Advertisers.

Anton Schultheis, College Point, N. Y.
Christmas Decorative Plants.

A. L. Miller, Jamaica, N. Y.
Flowering and Foliage Plants.

DRACENAS
Dracsena Indivisa, 4-in. pot plants, 6c. B. C. BLAKE, R. D. 4, Springfield, Ohio.

FERNS
Henry A. Dreer, Philadelphia, Pa.
Dreer's Fine Ferns.
For page see List of Advertisers.

F. R. Pierson Co., Tarrytown, N. Y.
For page see List of Advertisers.

John Scott, Brooklyn, N. Y.
The Home of the Scottii Fern.
For page see List of Advertisers.

H. H. Barrows & Son, Whitman, Mass.
For page see List of Advertisers.

Robert Craig Co., Philadelphia, Pa.
For page see List of Advertisers.

McHutchison & Co., New York City.
Ferns in Flats.
For page see List of Advertisers.

For List of Advertisers See Page 807

FERNS—Continued

A. M. Davenport, Watertown, Mass.
Boston and Whitmani Ferns.
For page see List of Advertisers.

Roman J. Irwin, New York City.
Boston and Whitmani Ferns.
For page see List of Advertisers.

Ferns, 2-in., Boston, Whitmani, Roosevelt, Elegantissima, Compacta and Teddy Jr.
B. C. BLAKE, R. D. 4, Springfield, Ohio.

FERTILIZERS

Stumpp & Walter Co., New York City.
Scotch Soot.
For page see List of Advertisers.

Pulverized Manure Co., Chicago, Ill.
Wizard Brand Cattle Manure.

FLORISTS' LETTERS

Boston Florist Letter Co., Boston, Mass.
For page see List of Advertisers.

FLORISTS' SUPPLIES

N. F. McCarthy & Co., Boston, Mass.
For page see List of Advertisers.

Reed & Keller, New York City.
For page see List of Advertisers.

8. S. Pennock-Meehan Co., Philadelphia, Pa.
For page see List of Advertisers.

H. Bayersdorfer & Co., Philadelphia, Pa.
For page see List of Advertisers.

Welch Bros. Co., Boston, Mass.
For page see List of Advertisers.

FLOWER POTS

W. H. Ernest, Washington, D. C.
For page see List of Advertisers.

A. H. Hews & Co., Inc., Cambridge, Mass.
For page see List of Advertisers.

Hilfinger Bros., Ft. Edward, N. Y.

FOLIAGE PLANTS

A. Leuthy & Co., Roslindale, Boston, Mass.
For page see List of Advertisers.

FUCHSIAS

R. Vincent, Jr. & Sons Co., White Marsh, Md.
For page see List of Advertisers.

FUNGINE

Aphine Mfg. Co., Madison, N. J.
For page see List of Advertisers.

GALAX

Michigan Cut Flower Co., Detroit, Mich.
For page see List of Advertisers.

GARDEN TOOLS

B. G. Pratt Co., New York City.

GERANIUMS

R. Vincent, Jr., & Sons Co.
White Marsh, Md.
For page see List of Advertisers.

Geraniums—Ricard, Doyle, Nutt, Poitevine and Chevalier, from 2¼-inch pots, immediate or later delivery, $20.00 per 1000. Rooted Cuttings, $15.00 per 1000. Cash with order. WM. F. KOENIG, 566 Hamilton Ave., West New York, N. J.

Rooted cuttings of the new Geranium Margaret Walsh are now for sale at $5.00 per 100; out of 2½-inch pots, $9.00 per 100. A limited quantity only offered now for sale. Cash must accompany each order. JOHN WALSH, Franklin St., Melrose H'l'ds, Mass.

Geraniums, S. A. Nutt. Grant, well rooted top cuttings, $10.00 per 1,000. Cash. ROSS BROS., Dubois, Pa.

Geraniums—rooted in Silica rock sand. Show a better color and grow better. Let me have your order for Nutt. Ricard, Poitevine and La Favorite. $12.50 per 1000. Cash. JAMES MOSS, Johnsville, Pa.

GLADIOLI

Arthur T. Boddington Co., Inc., New York City.
Gladiolus for Forcing.
For page see List of Advertisers.

John Lewis Childs, Flowerfield, L. I., N. Y.
For page see List of Advertisers.

Gladioli America, $6.00; Augusta, $6.00; Halley, $7.00; Princeps, $7.00; Mrs. F. King, $8.00; all first size bulbs. Booking orders for Spring Delivery. THOMAS COGGER, 229 Laurel St., Melrose, Mass.

GLASS

Sharp, Partridge & Co., Chicago.
For page see List of Advertisers.

Parshelsky Bros., Inc., Brooklyn, N. Y.
For page see List of Advertisers.

Royal Glass Works, New York City.
For page see List of Advertisers.

Greenhouse glass, lowest prices. JOHNSTON GLASS CO., Hartford City, Ind.

GLASS CUTTERS

Smith & Hemenway Co., New York City.
Red Devil Glass Cutter.
For page see List of Advertisers.

GLAZING POINTS

H. A. Dreer, Philadelphia, Pa.
Peerless Glazing Point.
For page see List of Advertisers.

GREENHOUSE BUILDING MATERIAL

King Construction Co., N. Tonawanda, N. Y.
For page see List of Advertisers.

Parshelsky Bros., Inc., Brooklyn, N. Y.
For page see List of Advertisers.

A. T. Stearns Lumber Co., Neponset, Boston.
Pecky Cypress.

Lord & Burnham Co., New York City.
For page see List of Advertisers.

GREENHOUSE CONSTRUCTION

King Construction Co., N. Tonawanda, N. Y.
For page see List of Advertisers.

Foley Greenhouse Mfg. Co., Chicago, Ill.
For page see List of Advertisers.

Hitchings & Co., New York City

Metropolitan Material Co., Brooklyn, N. Y.

A. T. Stearns Lumber Co., Boston, Mass.

Lord & Burnham Co., New York City.
For page see List of Advertisers.

J. C. Moninger Co., Chicago, Ill.

GUTTERS

King Construction Co., N. Tonawanda, N. Y.
King Channel Gutter.
For page see List of Advertisers.

HAIL INSURANCE

Florists' Hail Asso. of America.
J. G. Esler, Saddle River, N. J.
For page see List of Advertisers.

HARDY FERNS AND GREEN GOODS

Michigan Cut Flower Exchange, Detroit, Mich.
For page see List of Advertisers.

The Kervan Co., New York.
For page see List of Advertisers.

HARDY PERENNIALS

Bay State Nurseries, No. Abington, Mass.
For page see List of Advertisers.

P. Ouwerkerk, Hoboken, N. J.
For page see List of Advertisers.

Palisades Nurseries, Sparkill, N. Y.
For page see List of Advertisers.

HEATING APPARATUS

Kroeschell Bros. Co., Chicago.
For page see List of Advertisers.

Lord & Burnham Co., New York City.
For page see List of Advertisers.

HOLLYHOCKS

Hollyhocks in separate colors and mixed, fine large plants, $5.00 per 100, smaller plants, $4.00 per 100. Cash. JAMES MOSS, Johnsville, Pa.

HOT BED SASH.

Parshelsky Bros., Inc., Brooklyn, N. Y.
For page see List of Advertisers.

A. T. Stearns Lumber Co., Neponset, Mass.

Foley Greenhouse Construction Co., Chicago, Ill.
For page see List of Advertisers.

Lord & Burnham Co., New York City.
For page see List of Advertisers.

Standard hotbed sash, 1¾ in. thick, with crossbar, 80c. each; lots of 25 and over, 75c. each. Blind tenons; white leaded in joints. The life of a sash depends on this construction. We GUARANTEE our sash to be satisfactory or refund your money. Glass, 6 x 8, 8 x 10, 10 x 12, or 10 x 14, $1.50 per box of 50 sq. ft. C. N. ROBINSON & BRO., Dept. 29, Baltimore, Md.

HOSE

H. A. Dreer, Philadelphia, Pa.
For page see List of Advertisers.

HYACINTHS

5000 Hyacinths—No. 1, No. 2 and Miniatures in La innocence. Gertrude Grand Maitre, King of Blues, Jaypes: No. 1, $32.00 per 1000; No. 2, $20.00 per 1000; Miniatures, $14.00 per 1000, 3 in. Sprengeri, 3c. Mum stock plants, 15 varieties, 50c. per doz.; $3.00 per 100, or will exchange any of these for Vincas Var., Geraniums, Ferns or what have you? ROSENDALE GREENHOUSE and NURSERIES, Schenectady, New York.

INSECTICIDES

Benjamin Hammond, Beacon, N. Y.
Hammond's Slug Shot—Grape Dust and Fungicide.
For page see List of Advertisers.

Aphine Manufacturing Co., Madison, N. J.
Aphine and Fungine.
For page see List of Advertisers.

Nicotine Mfg. Co., St. Louis, Mo.
Aphis Punk and Nikoteen.
For page see List of Advertisers.

IRRIGATION EQUIPMENT

Skinner Irrigation Co., Brookline, Mass.
For page see List of Advertisers.

LILIUM MYRIOPHYLLUM

R. & J. Farquhar & Co., Boston, Mass.
For page see List of Advertisers.

LILY BULBS

Chas. Schwake & Co., New York City.
Horticultural Importers and Exporters.
For page see List of Advertisers.

R. M. Ward & Co., New York, N. Y.
Japanese Lily Bulbs of Superior Quality.
For page see List of Advertisers.

Corp. of Chas. F. Meyer, New York City.
Meyer's T. Brand Giganteums.
For page see List of Advertisers.

Arthur T. Boddington Co., Inc., New York City.
Lilium Longiflorum Formosum.
For page see List of Advertisers.

Yokohoma Nursery Co., New York City.

LILY OF THE VALLEY

Chas. Schwake & Co., Inc., New York City.
Hohmann's Famous Lily of the Valley Pips.
For page see List of Advertisers.

Loechner & Co., New York City.
Lily of the Valley Pips.
For page see List of Advertisers.

J. M. Thorburn & Co., New York City.
For page see List of Advertisers.

McHutchison & Co., New York City.
Berlin Valley Pips.
For page see List of Advertisers.

Arthur T. Boddington Co., Inc., New York City.
Cold Storage.
For page see List of Advertisers.

Stumpp & Walter Co., New York City.
Superior Retarded Lily of the Valley.

MASTICA

F. O. Pierce Co., New York City.
For page see List of Advertisers.

In writing to Advertisers kindly mention Horticulture

NATIONAL NURSERYMAN
National Nurseryman Publishing Co., Inc.,
Rochester, N. Y.
For page see List of Advertisers.

NIKOTEEN
Nicotine Mfg. Co., St. Louis, Mo.
For page see List of Advertisers.

NIKOTIANA
Aphine Mfg. Co., Madison, N. J.
For page see List of Advertisers.

NURSERY STOCK
P. Ouwerkerk, Weehawken Heights, N. J.
For page see List of Advertisers.

W. & T. Smith Co., Geneva, N. Y.
For page see List of Advertisers.

The D. Hill Nursery Co., Dundee, Ill.
Hill's Evergreens.
For page see List of Advertisers.

Bay State Nurseries, North Abington, Mass.
Hardy, Northern Grown Stock.
For page see List of Advertisers.

Bobbink & Atkins, Rutherford, N. J.
For page see List of Advertisers.

August Rolker & Sons, New York City.
For page see List of Advertisers.

NUT GROWING.
The Nut-Grower, Waycross, Ga.
For page see List of Advertisers.

ORCHID FLOWERS
Jas. McManus, New York, N. Y.
For page see List of Advertisers.

ORCHID PLANTS
Julius Roehrs Co., Rutherford, N. J.
For page see List of Advertisers.

Lager & Hurrell, Summit, N. J.
For page see List of Advertisers.

PALMS, ETC.
Robert Craig Co., Philadelphia, Pa.
For page see List of Advertisers.

August Rolker & Sons, New York City.
For page see List of Advertisers.

A. Leuthy & Co., Roslindale, Boston, Mass.
For page see List of Advertisers.

PANSY PLANTS
Pansy Plants, mixed varieties in bud
and bloom, $3.00 per 1000. Cash. JAMES
MOSS, Johnsville, Pa.

Pansy Plants for the benches, nice stocky
plants, $3.00 per 1000. 5000 or more, $4.00
per 1000. Cash. JAMES MOSS, Johnsville,
Pa.

Pansies, the big giant flowering kind,
$3.00 per 1000; in bud and bloom, $5.00 and
$15.00 per 1000. Cash. If I could only
show the nice plants, hundreds of testimonials and repeat orders I would be
flooded with new business. JAMES MOSS,
Johnsville, Pa.

PANSY SEED
Chas. Frost, Kenilworth, N. J.
Kenilworth Giant.
For page see List of Advertisers.

PEONIES
Peonies. The world's greatest collection.
1200 sorts. Send for list. C. BETSCHER,
Canal Dover, O.

PECKY CYPRESS BENCHES
A. T. Stearns Lumber Co., Boston, Mass.

PIPE AND FITTINGS
Kroeschell Bros. Co., Chicago.
For page see List of Advertisers.

King Construction Company,
N. Tonawanda, N. Y.
Shelf Brackets and Pipe Hangers.
For page see List of Advertisers.

PLANT AND BULB IMPORTS
Chas. Schwake & Co., New York City.
For page see List of Advertisers.

August Rolker & Sons, New York City.
For page see List of Advertisers.

PLANT TRELLISES AND STAKES
Seele's Tieless Plant Stakes and Trellises. H. D. SEELE & SONS, Elkhart, Ind.

PLANT TUBS
H. A. Dreer, Philadelphia, Pa.
"Riverton Special."

PLANTS WANTED
C. C. Trepel, New York City.
For page see List of Advertisers.

RAFFIA
McHutchison & Co., New York, N. Y.
For page see List of Advertisers.

RHODODENDRONS
P. Ouwerkerk, Hoboken, N. J.
For page see List of Advertisers.

RIBBONS AND CHIFFONS
S. S. Pennock-Meehan Co., Philadelphia, Pa.
For page see List of Advertisers.

ROSES
Poehlmann Bros. Co., Morton Grove, Ill.
For page see List of Advertisers.

P. Ouwerkerk, Hoboken, N. J.
For page see List of Advertisers.

Robert Craig Co., Philadelphia, Pa.
For page see List of Advertisers.

W. & T. Smith Co., Geneva, N. Y.
American Grown Roses.
For page see List of Advertisers.

Bay State Nurseries, North Abington, Mass.
For page see List of Advertisers.

August Rolker & Sons, New York City.
For page see List of Advertisers.

Montrose Greenhouses, Montrose, Mass.
Young Roses—Own Root and Grafted.
For page see List of Advertisers.

A. N. Pierson, Inc., Cromwell, Conn.
For page see List of Advertisers.

THE CONARD & JONES COMPANY.
Rose Specialists
West Grove, Pa. Send for offers.

SCALECIDE
B. G. Pratt Co., New York City.

SEASONABLE PLANT STOCK
R. Vincent, Jr. & Sons Co., White Marsh
Md.
For page see List of Advertisers.

SEED GROWERS
California Seed Growers' Association,
San Jose, Cal.
For page see List of Advertisers.

SEEDS
Carter's Tested Seeds,
Seeds with a Pedigree.
Boston, Mass., and London, England.
For page see List of Advertisers.

Kelway & Son,
Langport, Somerset, England.
Kelway's Celebrated English Strain Garden
Seeds.
For page see List of Advertisers.

S. D. Woodruff & Sons, New York City.
Garden Seed.
For page see List of Advertisers.

Joseph Breck & Sons, Boston, Mass.
For page see List of Advertisers.

J. Bolgiano & Son, Baltimore, Md.
For page see List of Advertisers.

A. T. Boddington Co., Inc., New York City.
For page see List of Advertisers.

Chas. Schwake & Co., New York City.
For page see List of Advertisers.

Michell's Seed House, Philadelphia, Pa.
For page see List of Advertisers.

W. Atlee Burpee & Co., Philadelphia, Pa.
For page see List of Advertisers.

R. & J. Farquhar & Co., Boston, Mass.
For page see List of Advertisers.

SEEDS—Continued
J. M. Thorburn & Co., New York City.
For page see List of Advertisers.

Loechner & Co., New York City.
For page see List of Advertisers.

Ant. C. Zvolanek, Lompoc, Cal.
Winter Flowering Sweet Pea Seed.
For page see List of Advertisers.

S. S. Skidelsky & Co., Philadelphia, Pa.
For page see List of Advertisers.

W. E. Marshall & Co., New York City.
Seeds, Plants and Bulbs.
For page see List of Advertisers.

August Rolker & Sons, New York City.
For page see List of Advertisers.

Burnett Bros., 98 Chambers St., New York.
For page see List of Advertisers.

Fottler, Fiske, Rawson Co., Boston, Mass.
Seeds for the Florist.

SKINNER IRRIGATION SYSTEM
Skinner Irrigation Co., Brookline, Mass.
For page see List of Advertisers.

SNAPDRAGON
S. S. Skidelsky & Co., Philadelphia, Pa.
For page see List of Advertisers.

SPHAGNUM MOSS
Live Sphagnum moss, orchid peat and
orchid baskets always on hand. LAGER
& HURRELL, Summit, N. J.

SPRAYING MATERIALS
B. G. Pratt Co., New York City.

STANDARD THERMOMETERS
Standard Thermo Co., Boston, Mass.
For page see List of Advertisers.

STOVE PLANTS
Orchids—Largest stock in the country—
Stove plants and Crotons, finest collection.
JULIUS ROEHRS CO., Rutherford, N. J.

SWEET PEA SEED
Arthur T. Boddington Co., Inc.,
New York City.
Winter Flowering Sweet Peas.
For page see List of Advertisers.

Ant. C. Zvolanek, Lompoc, Calif.
Gold Medal of Honor Winter Orchid Sweet
Peas.
For page see List of Advertisers.

VEGETABLE PLANTS
R. Vincent, Jr. & Sons Co.,
White Marsh, Md.
For page see List of Advertisers.

Forcing Tomatoes, Comet. 2½ in., 2c.
RONEY BROS., West Grove, Pa.

VENTILATING APPARATUS
The Advance Co., Richmond, Ind.
For page see List of Advertisers.

The John A. Evans Co., Richmond, Ind.
For page see List of Advertisers.

VERMICIDES
Aphine Mfg. Co., Madison, N. J.
For page see List of Advertisers.

VINCA VARIEGATA
James Vick's Sons, Rochester, N. Y.
For page see List of Advertisers.

WATER LILIES
Wm. Tricker, Arlington, N. J.

WIRED TOOTHPICKS
W. J. Cowee, Berlin, N. Y.
For page see List of Advertisers.

WIREWORK
Reed & Keller, New York City.
For page see List of Advertisers.

WILLIAM E. HEILSCHER'S WIRE
WORKS, 264 Randolph St., Detroit, Mich.

For List of Advertisers See Page 807

New Offers In This Issue

CHRISTMAS BEAUTIES.
S. S. Pennock-Meehan Co., Philadelphia, Pa.
For page see List of Advertisers.

FLOWERS BY TELEGRAPH.
Alexander McConnell, 611 Fifth Ave., New
York City.
For page see List of Advertisers.

HOT BED SASH.
King Construction Co., N. Tonawanda, N. Y.
For page see List of Advertisers.

**LILIUM GIGANTEUM AND OTHER
BULBS.**
Joseph Breck & Sons Corp., Boston, Mass.
For page see List of Advertisers.

WHOLESALE FLORISTS.
Gunther Bros., 110 West 28th St., New
York City.
For page see List of Advertisers.

In writing to Advertisers kindly mention Horticulture

Flower Market Reports

(Continued from page 827)

are getting eight for good carnations today and some orders they can't fill at any price. Looks lively for Christmas week.

PITTSBURGH Owing to the combination of several weeks of cloudy weather and the pinching of plants for the Christmas trade, stock has been exceptionally "shy" since Thanksgiving. Society work is at "concert pitch," figuratively speaking and funeral work continues plentiful, so that the demands are really far in excess of the supply, the latter being considerably reinforced from the outside. While prices hold up well, there is nothing really extravagant. From an all-round point of view, the approaching holiday business will far exceed that of last year, when business conditions were marked by the quintessence of depression.

SAN FRANCISCO The downtown retailers enjoyed a better counter trade the past week than for some time, as large crowds of holiday shoppers are now visiting the large stores daily. The florists make quite a feature of novel and attractive window displays, and these are strong drawing cards for drop-in business. The trade anticipates a banner Christmas business and is preparing accordingly. Indications are toward plenty of stock with high average quality. Shipping business is a little above normal for this time of the year. Violets are the big feature, but a good many chrysanthemums, roses and greens are being sent out also. Locally the demand for chrysanthemums has dropped off decidedly, probably because the late offerings are off-quality for the most part. Bonnaffon is very scarce and good Nonin is hard to find. Pompons are still fairly plentiful, and continue to sell well. The rose situation has been improving for several weeks, until there is enough medium stock to fill all requirements. As there are not enough really good roses to supply the demand, the finest offerings clean up early in the day. More Cecile Brunner could be used, and Beauties are being held back for the holidays. A splendid crop of gardenias is coming on, and the demand is all that can be desired. The same is true of cattleyas. Paper white narcissi made their appearance at Thanksgiving time in limited quantity and are now being offered quite freely. Freesias are quite plentiful also and hyacinths are more in evidence. Plenty of poinsettias, primulas and begonias are in sight for the Christmas trade. California holly appears everywhere and a strong demand is reported. Lots of greens are being shipped.

ST. LOUIS Trade has been fair. The wholesale market shows a decided shortage, especially so in carnations, and prices are now doubled up. Roses are going to be in abundance as our local growers are all coming on crop, also shipments from outside show roses will be plentiful. Extra fine cut poinsettias are coming in. Other stock generally will be in plenty at usual prices.

WASHINGTON There is a heavy demand for stock of all varieties and a noticeable decrease in the supply. Flowers have been blooming in this locality since last August and it is but natural that there should be a shortening up. Carnations have jumped to from $3 to $6 and hardly enough to fill the orders. Roses are in excellent shape and bring up to $15. American Beauty roses are also of fine quality and sell well at from $3 to $5 per dozen. The call for lily of the valley has been very good and gardenias which are increasing in quantity are selling well. The holiday sale of blooming plants has already begun. Azaleas, poinsettias, Cincinnati begonias and cyclamen are as good as have ever been seen in this locality. The days have been generally dark and cloudy, although perhaps not sufficiently so to have an adverse effect on floral production. The stock offered is A1.

Elizabethtown, Pa.—E. H. Zercher has purchased the I. W. Hoffman greenhouses on South Market street, and will carry on the business in the future. Mr. Zercher will conduct the business in addition to his extensive greenhouse business at Mt. Joy.

10,000
KING HOT BED SASH

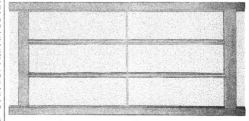

Size 3 ft. wide and 6 ft. long 1⅜ in. thick.
Made of strictly clear sun dried

CALIFORNIA REDWOOD

Three rows 10 inch glass wide. Blind mortise and tenons. ⅜ inch galvanized steel center rod.
Made the best we know how.

Prices of Sash Only — Unpainted

Lots of 12 Sash . . .95 each   Lots of 48 Sash . . .85 each
Lots of 24 Sash . . .90 each   Lots of 96 Sash . . .80 each

Prices of Glass, Paint, Putty and Zinc Glazing Nails

Enough for 12 Sash . . $17.00   Enough for 48 Sash . . $60.00
Enough for 24 Sash . . 32.00   Enough for 96 Sash . . 115.00

The glass is double thick B. quality. The paint — enough for two coats — and the putty are made of the pure raw materials only.
Ready for delivery now. All orders filled in rotation.

Terms: Cash with order.

KING CONSTRUCTION CO., King's Road, N. Tonawanda, N. Y.

NEWS NOTES.

Grosse Isle, Mich.—James Bremer has purchased the greenhouses of David Beyers.

Webster, Mass.—Olson & Co. succeed F. C. Riebe in the wholesale flower and plant trade in this place.

Columbia City, Ind.—Chas. S. Adair has purchased the North Side Greenhouses, formerly owned by Elmer Cox.

Dallas, Tex. — The Lang Floral & Nursery Company have purchased the greenhouses and the store on Elm street of the Brown-Dawson Company.

THE POTASH SUPPLY.

From the Report of the Secretary of Agriculture.

The potash situation continues very serious and a grave condition confronts the American farmer. There is practically no potash in this country for fertilizer use, and present indications are that the supply for this purpose will not be increased materially during the coming year. The investigations of the department and of the Geological Survey have shown the possibility of producing from American sources an ample quantity of potassium salts for domestic consumption. During the year no new sources have been discovered, but the conditions surrounding the development of known sources have been clarified considerably. There are four possible domestic sources of potash: The giant kelp of the Pacific coast from Lower California to Alaska; the alunite deposits, mainly in the mountains of Utah; the feldspathic rocks of the eastern part of the United States; and the mud of Searles Lake, in California.

Undoubtedly a large supply of potash salts could be obtained from the giant kelp. The kelp beds have been surveyed and a report, accompanied by maps showing in detail their extent and location, has been issued. Harvesting is accomplished easily, as the kelp grows in open water and barges fitted with moving attachments can be used.

For utilizing the kelp several methods are feasible. It may be dried and ground. In this condition it contains all the salts originally present, which are mainly potassium chlorid and sodium chlorid. This material has ideal mechanical proprieties for use in mixed fertilizers. When the potassium chlorid is desired it is necessary to separate the juice from the organic material and then to remove the sodium chlorid. The latter can be done readily by recrystallization; but the separation of the juice from the organic material is more difficult, for the reason that the kelp is nonfibrous and in attempts to effect separation by filtration the filters become clogged and unworkable. The problems yet to be worked out commercially are the best methods of drying the wet kelp and of effecting the ready and efficient separation of the plant juices from the organic material. Investigation of these questions has proceeded far enough to indicate that their solution should not be very difficult.

But the development of a supply of potash from the kelp beds is still remote. There are several reasons for this. No one knows how long the European war may last or how soon potash from the former usual sources may be available. The American fertilizer companies heretofore have depended largely on the mining of phosphate rock and the manufacture of sulphuric acid for superphosphates. In these lines they are deeply interested financially. There is, furthermore, an element of doubt as to the control of the kelp beds. Just what jurisdiction the Federal Government has over them does not appear, and the Pacific Coast States have not legislated concerning those lying opposite their shores. It is unlikely, even in the event of an early peace, that there immediately will be a great supply of potash salts. It is a question how long it would take

the former agencies to resume their usual operations. The experts of the department are of the opinion that under normal conditions, if the Panama Canal is utilized, potash from the kelp beds of the Pacific coast can be sold in the east under free competition.

Next to the kelp the massive alunites present the best possibilities as a source of potash. This material is decomposed by roasting, with the evo-

lution of oxids of sulphur, and a residue consisting of alumina and potassium sulphate remains. From this residue the potassium salt can be obtained readily by leaching and evaporation. The process is simple. The fumes liberated could be used to manufacture sulphuric acid; but this commodity would be in little demand in the locality and some method of disposal or utilization would have to be devised. Alumina resulting as a by-product would be suitable for the manufacture of metallic aluminum; but this metal is produced by one concern which controls sufficient bauxite deposits for its purposes and is not interested in other sources of alumina.

Work has been done along the line of producing potash from feldspar. This is commercially feasible if a salable by-product can be secured at the same time. The suggestion has been made by the Bureau of Soils that cement is a possible product from the feldspar treated to render the potash soluble. But the difficulty of marketing this cement in competition with thoroughly standardized products would be a great deterring factor.

The development of Searles Lake as a source of potash presents a number of unsolved technical problems. In addition, the question of title to the property is so involved that considerable time will elapse before it can be settled. In the meantime nothing can be done.

It is a matter of distinct regret that responsible business concerns have not made more earnest efforts to provide potash for agricultural purposes. Only recently, although the need of potash has been felt for a year, two companies have begun to develop a supply from alumite, but unfortunately it will be some months before any considerable quantity from this source can be placed upon the market.

PATENTS GRANTED.

1,162,126. Plant and Tree Digger. John C. Bates, Lake City, Fla.

1,162,175. Flower Holder. Rollin C. Lewis, Stamford, Conn.

1,162,902. Roller Cultivator. Henry Edward Colleys, Hammond, Ind.

1,162,944. Process of Making Phosphate Fertilizers. Spencer B. Newberry and Harvey N. Barret, Baybridge, Ohio.

1,163,130. Process of Manufacturing Fertilizers. James H. Connor, Sharpsburg, Pa.

1,163,238. Lawn Trimmer. August Huberty, Canton, Ohio.

Indiana, Pa.—The Indiana Floral company has purchased the flower store of W. S. Smathers on Philadelphia street and it is understood the latter store will be closed.

GREENHOUSES BUILDING OR CONTEMPLATED.

Galesburg, Ill.—I. L. Pillsbury, three houses.

Hoopeston, Ill.—E. A. Raasch, two houses.

Omaha, Neb.—Hess & Swoboda, additions.

Providence, R. I.—Swanson Bros., one house.

Midland, Mich.—W. E. Thayer, rose house 20 x 118.

Wichita, Kan.—Chas. P. Mueller, two houses each 30 x 150.

Wakefield, Mich.—James Corelli, additions and alterations.

Hartford, Conn.—S. Bordinat, Oakland avenue, one house.

Bay City, Mich.—Rudolph Strohner, 1600 Campeau avenue, one house.

North Milwaukee, Wis.—A. Reinhardt, two houses each 27 x 126.

New Providence, N. J.—L. B. Coddington, four rose houses, each 61 x 500.

NEWS NOTES.

Paterson, N. J.—Ed. Sceery, florist and park commissioner, is confined to his home, very ill.

Tarrytown, N. Y.—F. R. Pierson is suffering from a very severe cold and cannot leave his room.

Newburyport, Mass.—The greenhouses of E. W. Pearson were badly damaged and many plants ruined in the storm of last Monday night.

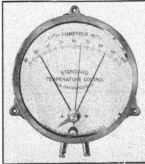

You see what a thoroughly practical attractive side interior it makes. Certainly it's light enough.

Of Interest to Gardeners

WHEN the first curved eave houses were constructed, it was at once evident to us that altho the placing of the gutter at the sill, and substituting welf vents for continuous side ventilating sash, produced an exceedingly attractive house, it was also evident that practicalness was being somewhat sacrificed to attractiveness. It was, however, what owners and many of the gardeners demanded.

There were, on the other hand, some gardeners who put their foot down hard and declared they must have some kind of side sash so they could have ample top of bench ventilation. Some liked the idea of having every third light made a separate vent sash. Altho this was a decided improvement in results over the wall vents, still, in the opinion of some, it rather detracted from the attractiveness of the house.

In some cases we put a neat angle iron at the bottom of the eave curves, and hinged the sash directly to it. This made a good fix, from a construction standpoint.

Still it had certain drawbacks, as the angle, while being large enough for the purpose, was not big enough to overcome the effect of an architecturally meaningless strip.

So the logical thing was to return to our ornamentally moulded gutter and place it at the eave. This gave a cornice effect, which as used in our old straight roof houses, was so heartily endorsed by architects. The little shade which this gutter may cast is more than overbalanced by the advantage of the ventilation. The sides are also higher, giving much the same head room as in the more expensive curvilinear house. Those who have this modified curved eave construction speak in high terms of it.

If you would like photographs of these subjects shown along with other general exterior views, we will be glad to send you a set to show to your employer.

The greater height at the side overcomes that somewhat squatty effect, so commented on with the old house.

Just another proof of its light, pleasing interior effect. Note the ample head room there is on the side benches.

Lord & Burnham Co.

SALES OFFICES:

NEW YORK   BOSTON   PHILADELPHIA   CHICAGO   ROCHESTER   CLEVELAND
42nd Street Bldg.   Tr-mont Bldg.   Franklin Bank Bldg.   Rookery Bldg.   Granite Bldg.   Swetland Bldg.

TORONTO, CANADA, Royal Bank Bldg.   MONTREAL, Transportation Bldg.

FACTORIES: Irvington, N. Y.   Des Plaines, Ill.   St. Catharines, Ontario

Vol. XXII
No. 26
DEC. 25
1915

HORTICULTURE

Victoria Regia Tank
At West Park, Pittsburgh, Pa.

Published Every Saturday at 147 Summer Street, Boston, Mass.
Subscription, $1.00

LIST OF ADVERTISERS

**FOR BUYERS' DIRECTORY AND READY REFERENCE GUIDE
SEE PAGES 860, 861, 862, 863**

NOTES ON CULTURE OF FLORISTS' STOCK
CONDUCTED BY
John J. M. Farrell

Questions by our readers in line with any of the topics presented on this page will be cordially received and promptly answered by Mr. Farrell. Such communications should invariably be addressed to the office of HORTICULTURE.
"If vain our toil, we ought to blame the culture, not the soil."—*Pope.*

Cinerarias

Give the plants a cool house and keep the green fly away. A cineraria must have plenty of water, but if you notice traces of yellow in the leaves let up a little. When the plant once starts to get buds, transplanting or shifting will do it but little good, if you wish it to grow longer before flowering. Rather apply light doses of liquid cow manure instead. This is the time for the cinerarias to grow and while there may be nothing very beautiful about their coarse leaves, they are necessary to give the flower heads their proper setting; they belong to it and in order to have them the plants must have sufficient room to develop nicely. From early January up to Easter, as a plant for the show house they are hard to beat, and they will always be grown by the florist for that purpose. Do not keep them in too high a temperature. When given 40 to 48 they will grow into fine sturdy stock that will bear flowers profusely.

Cyclamens

The young plants for next winter should have every encouragement. If elevated on shelves or in a house kept at 53 degrees at night they will be all right. When ready for their first potting, use a compost of three parts loam and one-half part each of well decayed dried manure and leaf-mold with some sand added. Continue to give the potted plants the same temperature as when in flats. So long as they remain in flats go over them once a week and scratch over the surface soil. Avoid a close atmosphere, however, as this will cause the plants to become leggy. Cyclamens which are not wanted until spring must be kept in a cool, airy house, with a night temperature of from 42 to 45 degrees. On through the winter there is a constant call for these plants at all retail places, and to get plants along, 8 to 10 degrees more of heat is advisable. On all good days give ventilation even if only a very little. Watch the pots so they do not dry out.

Chrysanthemum Stock Plants

Too often we see these in pots and boxes on the walks or even below the benches, exposed to drip and every unfavorable condition. Cuttings taken from such plants cannot be expected to give flowers at all equal to those grown well up to the light in a cool house. There are all kinds of ways for wintering stock. Where the climate is not too severe it can be planted in coldframes, held practically dormant for several months, and when opened in early spring the plants will soon give a grand crop of strong cuttings, better than those to be had in any other way. Good flowers always will sell. The best method for the average commercial grower who may need to start propagating early with special varieties is to plant in benches in a cool house. A violet temperature of 40 degrees at night will answer admirably. Let us all try to treat our stock plants better than we have in years past. I am quite sure it will pay in the end.

Lilies for Easter

We must now look to our Easter lilies, but there is no hurry as yet as Easter is very late—April 23—and it will be more of a case of holding them back than forcing them. If the buds show plainly by the 10th or 15th of March they will be all right. Longiflorums should be through the soil now. In the case of multiflorums a temperature of 55 degrees at night will suffice, while Formosas will do nicely at 50 degrees as a minimum. Giganteum is the lily par excellence for the pot plants. Bulbs of this arrive later than other varieties. It likes heat from the start and if given 55 degrees at night after potting, and 60 to 65 degrees once growth is started, it is almost sure to do well. If these lilies are just showing their growth above the soil they will be all right in an average minimum 60 degrees. Of course it is to force or retard a certain number which always come earlier or later than the main batch.

Violets

At this season the violets will not need frequent watering but sometimes the surface soil may seem damp and that below be rather dry. Violets like to have their roots cool and moist and anything like dryness will injure them and make them an easier prey for red spider if they chance to be near the heating pipes. To hold singles down to 40 degrees at night has not been possible sometimes. On the other hand, the doubles in midwinter should be kept at 42 to 45 degrees at night or they will not open well. A few degrees higher will speedily excite the plants and cause an increased crop of leaves which we do not want. Look out for green fly or it will speedily cause lots of trouble. Violets will not stand heavy fumigation. Avoid, therefore, the use of tobacco stems and any of the nicotine extracts. The nicotine papers are perfectly safe. Change the air of the house even if it is for only a short time, as they like fresh air at all times.

Verbenas

While some of us keep stock plants lifted in the fall to take cuttings from, plants raised from seed can be depended on to furnish the best flowering. To have good sized plants by next spring seed should be sown now. Give them a mixture of soil, leaf mold and sand in equal parts. Place in a temperature of 60 degrees until they come up, when they should have from 50 to 55 degrees. When large enough prick off.

Clematis Jackmani

Mr. John J. M. Farrell,
 Dear Sir: Please tell me in your valuable paper the best way to get a stock of Clematis Jackmani. It seems as if I cannot get seed to come true.
 Yours truly,
 Chillicothe, Mo.   R. L. I.

In answer to the inquirer I would say that they can be readily increased either by cuttings, grafting or layering. The best time to take cuttings is about the middle of June. Taking the young wood leaving three or four joints. These can be placed in a gentle bottom heat in a greenhouse or make a hot bed with horse manure, letting it stand a week until the violent heat passes off. By keeping them shaded and moist in either case they will root. They can be potted off when well rooted and given shade until they take hold of the soil. By the grafting method you can get some roots of Clematis legustrifolia, C. paniculata or C. viticella to use for stock to graft on. This grafting can be done anytime from January up to the end of March. The best mode is whip grafting. Make a scion, leaving one eye to the piece, and tie on to the stock. The roots of stock can be potted up during the fall and brought into heat about four or five weeks before they are wanted. These pots can be plunged in sand in a warm propagating frame in a temperature of 65 to 70 degrees. Keep close and moist for four or five weeks when they should be gradually inured to the air. When they become hardened they can be grown on in a cool house. Clematis Jackmani can also be increased by layering or pegging down the vines in the ground during the fall and leaving them there until the next fall when they can be removed with roots and planted where desired. Where these layers enter the soil they are better to be cut half through which stops the flow of sap, thereby encouraging the formation of roots more quickly.

Poinsettias Wilting

Editor HORTICULTURE,

Dear Sir: I would like to get information from your Mr. Farrell as to the best method of keeping the blooms of poinsettias from wilting after they are cut from the plant.   Yours truly,

Roanoke, Va.   P. F.

In answer to P. F., I would say that the stems should be placed about half an inch in boiling water just as soon as possible after they are cut. Bring the boiling water into the house where you cut them so you will lose no time in sealing the ends. They should remain from 30 to 40 seconds in the boiling water in order to seal them well. After the ends are treated they should be placed in water well up the stems. We use a tub. They should remain in the water from 8 to 10 hours. This will put them in good condition for shipping or any other use. We have used this method with success so can recommend it.

Next Week:—Compost for Winter; Orchids; Starting Freesias; Sweet Peas; Winter Protection; Placing Seed Order.

A Substitute for Potassium Cyanide

A good substitute for potassium cyanide is something that all florists who practice hydrocyanic acid gas fumigation would welcome. The present war has caused a scarcity in many products which Germany has always supplied, but there are few things that have affected those who pursue the various branches of agriculture more than the scarcity of the potassium fertilizers and chemicals. Potassium cyanide is no exception to the rule. However, a good substitute for potassium cyanide is sodium cyanide.

At present, sodium cyanide is much cheaper than the potassium cyanide and can be used in the same way for gas fumigation. But, certain prerequisites are necessary, if one is to use this substitute. First, only $\frac{3}{4}$ as much sodium cyanide as potassium cyanide is used. Second, a different grade of sodium cyanide must be used. The same strength sodium cyanide as potassium cyanide used would ruin the plants, for much free hydrochloric acid (H Cl) would be given off.

One of the most common impurities is sodium chloride and its action would result in the freeing of the hydrochloric acid as can be seen by the equation:— $H^2SO^4 + 2\ Na\ Cl = Na^2SO^4 + 2\ H\ Cl$. We must, then, use a grade of sodium cyanide which is much purer, in proportion, than the potassium cyanide. It must be 128% pure. The ordinary potassium cyanide that is used is about 98% pure. Such a grade contains 40% cyanogen. However, a grade of sodium cyanide containing but 40% cyanogen would ruin your plants as shown by the preceding formula. We, therefore, use 128% to 130% pure sodium cyanide which contains as much as 52% cyanogen and for this reason only three-quarters as much is needed. Don't buy the ordinary druggists' sodium cyanide, for they carry only the impure grades. Roessler & Hasslacher Chemical Company, N. Y. can supply the pure grade and doubtless there are other chemical companies from which it can be purchased.

In using either sodium or potassium cyanide for gas fumigation, use in lump form only. This will offer some resistance to decomposition by the acid and so will give a slower and better distribution of the gas and, most important, will give you more time to leave the house. Cloth bags for holding the chemical are needless. Using lumps one-half the size of an egg, the operation is quite simplified. The acid is poured in the pans, beforehand, and when everything is ready you simply pass through the house and drop the cyanide into each container. Do not use glass containers as much heat is generated and it is liable to break a glass dish. Use earthen ware or granite containers.

The proportions of chemicals and the directions are as follows: Two parts (fluid measure) of water are placed in the container and into this is carefully poured and stirred one and one-half parts (fluid measure) of sulfuric acid 98% pure. When everything is ready, drop in one part by weight of cyanide.

The amounts of cyanide to use in a house vary with the plants, the insects and the cubic feet of space. For white fly on tender plants, you may use .075 grams cyanide per cubic foot of space, while for hardier plants you may use stronger doses. Always remember, however, that you use only three-quarters as much sodium cyanide as you use potassium cyanide. By calculating the amount of cubic feet of space and multiplying by the strength to be used you get the total quantity of cyanide necessary for the house in grams. To get the equivalent in ounces divide by 28.35.

Always exercise the greatest care in using this fumigant as it is a deadly poisonous gas. Always air the house out thoroughly for at least one-half an hour before entering after you have fumigated.

If you are in doubt as to how much you should use, try a weak dose first and, if this does not accomplish results, try a stronger dose next time. Always be careful of using the stronger doses until you know your plants will stand it.

C. E. Wilson.

Amherst, Mass.

ROSE GROWING UNDER GLASS

CONDUCTED BY

Arthur C. Ruzicka

Questions by our readers in line with any of the topics presented on this page will be cordially received and promptly answered by Mr. Ruzicka. Such communications should invariably be addressed to the office of HORTICULTURE.

Work After Christmas.

With Christmas over we settle down to the regular work once more. Any mistakes made during the rush will be charged to experience and they should never occur again another year. The new year will soon be here now, but there will not be as much buying as there was for Christmas, although flowers will be in demand as much as ever. The work that will confront us after the holidays will be propagation. Many places have already started, and have several thousand plants in pots now. On large places this is well, for there are so many plants to be grown that it is necessary to start in real early. On a small place with the houses doing well it will be best to wait until the first of February for then it will not be necessary to tear out plants so soon and so many of them.

Marking Poor Plants

Even in the best houses there will be plants that are not doing as well as they should or they may bear flowers that are off in color. All these should be marked and no wood taken from them. Take all wood from strong healthy plants, for like produces like and the poor plants resulting after years of growing can generally be traced to selection of poor wood from poor plants. If time permits it would be well to go over the houses and find the plants that produce the most flowers and then take as much wood from these as you can get. There is such a thing as "blood" in plants. We have a good demonstration here of two benches of Killarneys. These plants are several years old and had been neglected a good deal in years past and the plants they came from were of a questionable quality. These will not respond to treatment as some healthy plants next to them will; they will not give the quality or quantity, and will not be nearly as profitable as the plants with plenty of energy—those that have been bred up, not down. The simplest way of marking the plants that are tied to stakes is with a piece of cardboard tied to the top of the stake.

Making Cuttings.

Select proper wood, which should not be too old and have nice red thorns or live thorns at least. The knife should be sharp enough to shave as a good edge is absolutely necessary for a smooth cut, free from bruise. With Teas we prefer three eyes to a cutting where we have plenty of wood. When propagating Beauties, or Teas with the wood scarce, two-eye cuttings are made. Beauties should never be made with three eyes as the plants will not thrive nearly as well as those grown from two-eyed cuttings. Do not leave too much leaf to a cutting. Generally the first two leaflets will suffice, but should these be small it will be well to leave half of the next two. The idea is to leave enough leaf for the cutting to breathe properly, but at the same time not so much as to make it hard work for it to keep the leaf alive. With too much leaf, the propagating bench will be crowded and blackspot is likely to set in, which strips the leaves off terribly and traces of it can be found months later when the plants are already in the benches. Make a slanting cut quite close to the eye, slanting away from it. Care should be taken not to cut too close as that would weaken the eye and the cutting might not root, or else produce a poor plant. Do not put in any cuttings with diseased leaves. These will only make trouble, and are likely to spread the disease to the leaves that were healthy when put into the sand. As soon as some wood is cut, sprinkle it well but do not put it into a tub of water for any length of time. This was the custom years ago, but we find the cuttings made from wood that is not water-soaked root much better and are less likely to rot if the heat in the sand happens to run up a little higher than it should be. Keep the cuttings well sprinkled, for if they should wilt they will be worthless. Do not keep them out of the sand very long for if they are allowed to lie around for any length of time, they are bound to wilt, and even though it may not be noticeable they will not root well then. The sand should be all packed and ready for them, with proper bottom heat. Never put cuttings in first and then turn on the heat, have everything read for them, so that they will start callousing at once. A good watering will be necessary every morning if the sand is well drained. An occasional sprinkling may be necessary if the weather is clear and cold but see that the cuttings do not have any water on the leaves at night. This will start blackspot quicker than anything else.

HORTICULTURE

VOL. XXII   DECEMBER 25, 1915   NO. 26

PUBLISHED WEEKLY BY
HORTICULTURE PUBLISHING CO.
147 Summer Street, Boston, Mass.
Telephone, Oxford 292.
WM. J. STEWART, Editor and Manager.

Entered as second-class matter December 8, 1914, at the Post Office
at Boston, Mass., under the Act of Congress of March 3, 1879.

CONTENTS   Page

Optimism   So far as we have been privileged to learn,
a genuine revival of prosperity is now
confidently looked for by the entire florist
trade of the country, who find cheering promise and
assurance in the volume and quality of the advance holiday business. We realize that there will be no time to
spare for the reading of this week's trade papers until
Christmas has passed into history and its results, for
better or for worse, all known beyond any speculation,
consequently, expectations and forecasts have no useful
place in these lines. All we can say is that we most
eagerly hope that the optimism which is unmistakably
evident on all sides at the time of this writing may prove
to have been fully justified.

A golden   We are pleased to see that the landscape
opportunity   gardening classes for this season, conducted by the Gardeners' and Florists'
Club of Boston, are nicely filled up with
young men desirous of perfecting themselves in this very
important branch of horticultural art. Earlier in the
season the success of the course seemed somewhat in
doubt. Its abandonment, on account of waning interest,
would be a great pity and far from creditable to the
aspirations of the large proportion of young gardeners
which goes to make up the nearly five hundred members
of the Boston club. In opportunity for honors and
emolument, landscape gardening in America stands today far ahead of all other branches of horticulture, and
there need be no fear of overcrowding.

Seems im-   It was stated by one of the speakers at
probable   the recent convention of gardeners in
Boston that the rather small attendance
of members from places outside of the
immediate environments of Boston was due to the failure to incorporate more recreation, such as bowling, etc.,
in the regular program. This does not seem a valid explanation. There are a number of other reasons that
might be offered, as being more likely and at the same
time more to the credit of the gentlemen who make up
the membership of the association. That any gardener
worthy of the name would absent himself from a gathering of his fellows in such a centre of progressive horticulture as Boston is acknowledged to be, for no other
reason than that no bowling had been promised, seems
quite preposterous and we should be sorry to have to
believe it true.

To enlist   Comment has been heard in gardener
all interests circles upon the comparatively greater
prominence of the commerical floricul-
tural element in the leading flower
shows, of late. The fact that the trade firms are thus
in the ascendant is used as an incentive to spur the
private gardeners on to a greater interest and activity
in this direction. While we have never found ourselves
quite in sympathy with any movement tending to array
the private gardening people against the commercial
section, yet there can be no harm but much good to come
from an amicable emulation between these two classes
on the exhibition tables and if a further segregation of
the prizes offered in the schedules will help to strengthen
any exhibition, let this be done. It was not so long ago
that frequent complaints were being made by the trade
people that it was unfair to expect them to compete
against private exhibitors with unlimited time and
money at their disposal, but now the situation appears
to be reversed, as it is the private gardener who asks
protection in the majority of cases. We believe that the
best interests of horticulture might be better served by
giving as far as possible, distinct departments to each
of the two classes of exhibitors than by simply duplicat-
ing the premiums as has been done in some instances
recently. The private gardener has exceptional facilities for acquiring and testing out new things. In fact,
quite a few of our finest commercial plant and cut flower
favorites had their first exploitation in the country at
the hands of some clever private gardener. A bigger
inducement to activity by the private gardeners in this
particular sphere would be vastly more useful as a rule
than, for instance, offering them a set of premiums for
established commercial varieties of roses and carnations
which are sure to be well taken care of by the trade exhibitors. The opportunities in floriculture are still ex-
haustless. Improvement and demonstration on new
lines are essentials which should never be lost sight of
in our exhibition promotion and in this direction there
is room enough for all—private gardeners especially.

CHRISTMAS GLORY AT RUTHER-FORD.

It is conceded that the holiday plant growers have had the most remarkable demand ever experienced for their products this fall. Christmas orders began to come in long ahead of the time and have continued with increasing momentum until "sold out" has been the unavoidable reply in many cases. We visited the Julius Roehrs Company's place at Rutherford, N. J., one week previous to the holiday, and found it a veritable hive of industry and hustle, packing and shipping, with no more orders accepted on most of the Christmas specialties and some of them even oversold. One who has not visited such a place under similar circumstances cannot realize the stupendous proportions of the business done at such a time—plants by thousands standing like forests, in their wrappings in the spacious packing shed, and actually acres of begonias, cyclamens, camellias and azaleas in the houses awaiting their turn to be wheeled out and prepared for shipment by a swarm of busy workers.

There is no finer sight anywhere at this time than the three large houses filled with camellias—plants two to five feet high in pots and resplendent with bloom. We would not have missed seeing it for anything. Many of these camellias were made up into groups of four or five in one pan in combination with nice little clumps of Asparagus plumosus, and the arrangement was very pleasing to look at. There were azaleas in gorgeous billows of color, house after house of them. For quantity Begonia Gloire de Lorraine took the lead, there being no less than thirteen houses filled with them in many sizes—pots and suspended baskets. Most impressive of all was Begonia Mrs. Peterson. There were two houses filled with this beautiful novelty which we believe is destined to take the leading place among recent plant introductions. Its ample inflorescence of sparkling pink against the lustrous dark foliage needs but to be seen to make a sensation.

There are many other things in this big establishment that arrest the attention of the plant lover in passing through, about which we shall have a word to say later on.

The Holyoke & Northampton (Mass.) Florists' & Gardeners' Club held its annual meeting Tuesday evening, Dec. 14th, at the greenhouses of G. H. Sinclair, Holyoke. Mr. Sinclair took occasion at the same time to christen the Belle Skinner cup which he won at the recent flower show with an exhibit of chrysanthemums. Officers were elected as follows: President, Aubrey Butler, Northampton; Vice-president, Geo. Strugnell, of the Bonnie Brae greenhouses; Secretary and Treasurer, James Whiting, Amherst; Executive Committee, William Downer, Prof. E. J. Canning and Edward Hennessey, all of Northampton. After the business of the meeting had been transacted, there was an enjoyable social time, refreshments being served and music furnished by an orchestra; also songs by Norman Dash. The January meeting of the club will be held with George Rackliffe.

BRASSAVOLA NODOSA.

This is one of the prettiest of the twenty species of this genus. It has also been known as B. grandiflora and B. subulifolia. The photograph was taken by M. J. Pope in the orchid houses under his charge at Naugatuck, Conn. The Brassavolas are natives of tropical America, the one here pictured being found in Southern Mexico and Jamaica. They are closely related to the Lælias and require the same treatment. They need plenty of sun to mature the young growths, and, when resting, a somewhat drier atmosphere than during growth. They do best suspended on blocks, near the glass. Flowers pale green and white.

NEWS NOTES.

San Francisco — Announcement has been made that the Exposition's $1,000 cash prize for the best rose entered in the international rose contest went to Dickson & Son of Belfast, Ireland, for a rich yellow creation.

Newton, Mass.—A. W. Wilson, proprietor of the Flower Shop, 406 Center street, has newly fitted up and adorned his store, which is now the most attractive of its kind in this section. Fixtures and furniture are of quartered oak, and the floor of mosaic marble.

Hackettstown, N. J.—Herrick & Roos have recently purchased the Harte greenhouse establishment, and will grow flowers for the New York wholesale trade. Mr. Roos was for many years with Siebrecht, of New Rochelle, and later with J. H. Small & Sons, of New York City.

Rahway, N. J.—Trial of the suit of Wilbur N. Bauman, florist, of Rahway, against George R. Sloane, of Newark for $500 which the plaintiff alleged had been illegally collected by the defendant by representing that he was executing an order of the court, resulted in a victory for Sloane in District Court, when Judge David awarded the defendant a judgment of $362.73.

Sloane was arrested last week on a warrant sworn out by Bauman, charging him with fraud. Last April 1, Sloane was deputized by Oliver Conlin, sergeant-at-arms of the District Court, to execute a judgment of about $150 granted against Bauman in favor of Hitchings & Company and was placed in the store for four days until the amount was collected. In the present suit, Bauman contended that Sloane remained at the store until November 11, under the pretense that he was acting by authority of the court, and that he collected $500. Sloane contended that Bauman had employed him to remain at the store at a salary of $2.50 a day and had given him a bill of sale for the business as security for his wages. Sloane set up a counter claim for wages and was awarded the sum mentioned.

Wm. R. Beverly, one of the oldest residents and a former florist of Rockland, Mass., celebrated his 83d birthday December 17th.

Obituary

Christian Muno.

Christian Muno, of 108 Ridge Ave., Chicago, passed away Dec. 20th, at his home after years of illness. About twenty years ago he built a range of houses and specialized in carnations, but soon gave it up and rented the houses, as his health would not permit work of that kind.

Leonard G. Townsend.

Leonard G. Townsend, head of the Townsend Floral Co., doing business at 4248 Olive street, St. Louis, Mo., for the past sixteen years died at St. John's Hospital, December 12, after a short illness. Mr. Townsend was born in 1861, in Ohio and so far as known had no relatives. Miss A. Histon who was with him in business will continue same with her brother.

Alfred C. Smith.

Alfred C. Smith, a well-known gardener of Westerly, R. I., who had charge of a number of summer estates at Watch Hill, died suddenly from heart disease at the Central Theater, Pawcatuck, on Wednesday evening, Dec. 15. He and Mrs. Smith had been seated in the theatre only a few minutes when he was taken ill and died shortly afterwards. Mr. Smith, who was 52 years of age, is survived by his wife, mother and one brother, Albert Smith, of Westerly.

Henry Blume.

Henry Blume, well known in the New York flower market for many years, and for the past two years in the employ of P. J. Smith, 131 West 28th street, died suddenly at his home, Flatbush avenue, Brooklyn, from hardening of the intestines, on Monday morning, Dec. 20, aged 42 years. Previous to his employment with P. J. Smith, Mr. Blume had been 13 years with Frank Lichtenhand at the Grand Central Station, later with Metz at 117th street and 3rd avenue, having started in the flower business as a boy with Le Moult on the Bowery. Mr. Blume was universally liked by all who came in contact with him. He was a quiet, industrious man of the strictest integrity, and no one was ever heard to say an ill word regarding him. Much sorrow was expressed at the place where he was employed when the news of his death was received. He had been at work as usual up to closing time on Saturday evening.

Norfolk, Va. — The Art Floral Company, recently formed with a capital of $15,000, has opened at the City Market, Monticello and Tazewell streets. The large plate glass front, sides and roof, add very materially to the handsome appearance of the store. The officers of the corporation are Lyons H. Williams, president; F. W. Herrgen, vice-president, and H. R. Weller, secretary and treasurer. Messrs. Williams and Weller are officers of the Williams Seed Company, while Mr. Herrgen is well-known to the trade, having been associated with a retail florist here for many years.

PHLOX SYLPHIDE.

Of the many good white herbaceous phloxes now on the market it is probable that, all things considered, none are superior to the variety Sylphide. While many of the new varieties have the unfortunate draw back of being constitutionally weak and in the course of a few years drop out, Sylphide is one of those which retains its vigor and given even ordinary cultivation is always satisfactory. It is a pure white and the individual flowers and truss are large. It is nominally a strong free grower, devoid of any disease, but if occasionally replanted and given good cultivation it grows into a magnificent plant as fine as anything in the whole herbaceous garden. The photograph from which our illustration was made, was taken at the grounds of the Mt. Desert Nurseries, Bar Harbor, Me.

FREE LECTURES ON HORTICULTURE.

The Massachusetts Horticultural Society announces its annual winter course of lectures on horticultural subjects to be given at Horticultural Hall at 2 o'clock on Saturday afternoons during January, February and March. These lectures are free to all and the programe is as follows: January 8. Flowers and Gardens of Japan. Illustrated. By E. H. Wilson, Jamaica Plain.

January 15. Vegetables for Home and Exhibition. By Edwin Jenkins, Lenox.

January 22. Annual Meeting, Mass. Fruit Growers' Association, January 21 and 22. Addresses on Fruit Growing, forenoon and afternoon.

January 29. The Missouri Botanical Garden. Illustrated. By Dr. George T. Moore, St. Louis, Mo.

February 5. Alfalfa Culture in New England. By Prof. S. C. Damon, Kingston, R. I.

February 12. The Development of Fruits for Special Conditions. By Prof. W. T. Macoun, Ottawa, Canada.

February 19. Some History of the Grape in the United States. Illustrated. By George C. Husmann, Washington, D. C.

February 26. Garden Writings in America. By Leonard Baron, Garden City, N. Y.

March 4. Practical Demonstration of the Methods used in the Propagation of Plants. By Theophilus D. Hatfield, Wellesley.

March 11. Taming the Wild Blueberry. Illustrated. By Frederick V. Coville, Washington, D. C.

March 18. No Lecture on this date. Spring Flower Show.

March 25. Sweet Pea Diseases and their Control. Illustrated. By Prof. J. J. Taubenhaus, Newark, Del. The John Lewis Russell Lecture.

WM. P. RICH, Sec.,
Horticultural Hall, Boston.

CLUB AND SOCIETY NOTES.

The next officers' meeting of the St. Louis Florist Club will take place January 6 at the home of Vice-president Wells, at 8 o'clock.

The December session of the Botanical Society of Western Pennsylvania was held as usual in the Herbarium of Carnegie Institute, President John Bright presiding. He also spoke at some length on the collections made during his last summer vacation at Ohio Pyle. Illustrating this were some fine specimens of marshallia, which has recently come from the Southern mountains. The plant, which flowers in July, has blossoms of an unusual and exquisite shade between a pink and lavender, and has just come into commercial use for bedding purposes.

CLUBS AND SOCIETIES

AMERICAN SWEET PEA SOCIETY.

At the executive committee meeting held at the Hotel Belmont, New York, on Saturday, December 4, 1915, the following resolution on the death of W. Atlee Burpee was adopted:

The Executive Committee of the American Sweet Pea Society, held in New York City, Dec. 4th, 1915, speaking for its members, desires to express in this feeble manner its sense of immeasurable loss sustained by the passing away of its most devoted charter member, W. Atlee Burpee. The Society has lost its best friend and the flower we all love so well has lost its most ardent lover.

Wherever the Sweet Pea is grown, it will always be known as an emblem of pure devotion to the memory of our devoted friend.

RESOLVED, That a copy of these minutes be sent to the bereaved family, spread upon the minutes and a copy be sent to the Trade Press.

Signed: William Gray, President; W. C. Kerr, Vice-President; Lester L. Morse; A. N. Kirby; A. J. Sperling; J. Harrison Dick; Arthur T. Boddington, Treasurer; Harry A. Bunyard, Secretary.

J. Harrison Dick was elected to the executive Committee, to fill the vacancy occurring through the death of Mr. Burpee.

Lester L. Morse was authorized to hold an exhibition in San Francisco, 1917, under the auspices of the American Sweet Pea Society with full power to act. Frank G. Cuthbertson was appointed assistant secretary to act at the exhibition.

President Gray appointed the following as a general committee on exhibitions: W. C. Kerr, William H. Duckham, J. Harrison Dick, A. N. Kirby, W. A. Sperling. A letter was read from the Bar Harbor Horticultural Society stating they were preparing the schedule for the summer exhibition of 1916. It was resolved, in view of the fact that the Bar Harbor exhibition must be held three weeks later than any date in which New York and vicinity growers could possibly exhibit, that the society hold an exhibition and convention in New York City contingent upon a sufficient sum for premiums being assured and a suitable hall for the exhibition be secured and that the matter should be at the discretion of the exhibition committee. Several members present volunteered premiums should the committee decide upon an exhibition.

It was voted that the Society issue a Year Book, to be known as the "Sweet Pea Oracle" to be sent to the members free, and to others for 25c., also that any firm desiring a quantity of these bulletins, should be supplied with same at cost. J. Harrison Dick, chairman; W. A. Sperling, and Harry A. Bunyard were appointed to take the matter in hand at once.

It was resolved that Horticultural Societies may become associate members on the payment of $10.00 annual dues. Such societies will have the privilege of receiving and awarding one each of the American Sweet Pea Society's medals, namely: One silver and one bronze at their local exhibitions; will also have the privilege of sending one delegate with power to vote at the annual conventions. The

Meetings Next Week

Monday, Dec. 27.

Florists' and Gardeners' Club of Rhode Island, Swartz Hall, Providence, R. I.

Gardeners' and Florists' Club of Baltimore, Florist Exchange Hall, Baltimore, Md.

Tuesday, Dec. 28.

Newport Horticultural Society, Newport, R. I.

Tarrytown Horticultural Society, Tarrytown, N. Y.

secretary was instructed to notify all horticultural societies to this effect.
HARRY A. BUNYARD, Sec'y.

NATIONAL ASSOCIATION OF GARDENERS.

Report of Committee on Final Resolutions.

RESOLVED, That a hearty vote of thanks and appreciation from the members of the National Association of Gardeners be tendered to His Honor Mayor James M. Curley, of Boston, Capt. John H. Dillon, chairman of the Park Commission of Boston, J. K. M. L. Farquhar, president Massachusetts Horticultural Society, and Patrick Welch, president Society of American Florists, for the cordial welcome extended to those attending the annual convention held in that city December 9 and 10.

To the Massachusetts Horticultural Society which so generously provided the facilities within its building for holding the convention.

To the Gardeners' and Florists' Club and the Horticultural Interests of Boston, for the excellent repast and entertainment tendered the members.

To the Park Department and Superintendent James B. Shea, for the automobile trip through the parks of Boston, the Arnold Arboretum and private estates.

To R. & J. Farquhar & Company for the excellent luncheon served to the automobile party at their Dedham nurseries.

To our local committee on arrangements, W. N. Craig, Duncan Finlayson and William J. Kennedy, which so ably arranged the affairs of the convention.
ARTHUR SMITH,
JOHN CANNING,
F. W. POPP,
Committee on Final Resolutions.

AMERICAN CARNATION SOCIETY.

In making up the forms for printing the premium schedule the printers inadvertently dropped class 6 in section A. This class calls for a vase of 100 blooms any red or scarlet, to include all varieties generally included in those colors. Same prizes as other classes in section A. A special notice will be sent to all members about January 1.   A. F. J. BAUR, Sec'y.

AMERICAN ROSE SOCIETY.

The executive committee of the American Rose Society held a meeting in New York on December 13. It was reported that the Rose Garden premium for the National Flower Show in Philadelphia, March 25 to April 2, had been raised so that the first prize would be $500 in cash; second prize $400 cash, and third prize $300 cash.

Michell Seed House offers a gold medal for the best vase of 25 blooms of American Beauty roses; a gold medal for the best vase of 25 blooms Mrs. Charles Russell; a gold medal for the best vase of 25 blooms of red roses. Other special prizes have been received from August Doemling, Lansdowne, Pa., $25; Conard & Jones Company, West Grove, Pa., $25; Charles H. Totty, Madison, N. J., $25; S. S. Skidelsky & Co., Phila., Pa., $10.; S. J. Reuter & Son, Westerly, R. I., $25.; Lord & Burnham Company, New York City, $25.; Harry O. May, Summit, N. J., $25.; Pulverized Manure Company, Chicago, $25.; Kroeschell Bros. Company, Chicago, $25., and Dingee & Conard Co., West Grove, Pa., $25.

These prizes are all at the disposition of the American Rose Society to place where they will be most useful.

The secretary was directed to notify all affiliated societies that beginning January, 1916, they will be required to pay 25c. to each member instead of 10c. as heretofore. The reason for this action is that the furnishing of medals and annuals as now proposed makes it an impracticable arrangement when based upon 10c. for the American Rose Society to carry out.

The committee appointed at the last annual meeting to report upon the standardization of stems of various cut flowers for commercial sale reported progress. The committee was composed of Messrs. S. S. Pennock, Phila., Pa.; Patrick Welch, Boston, Mass.; Frank H. Traendly, New York City.

The arranging of suitable lengths of stem was brought up by Ex-President Elliott and from time to time has been requested by commercial florists in various parts of the country. A matter was referred to the executive committee asking if something could not be done in regard to preventing the renaming of roses different from the name under which they were first disseminated. Action was referred to the committee to be presented at the coming annual meeting.

There are 114 members of the American Rose Society who stand in good and regular form with the Society of American Florists and Ornamental Horticulturists, and this entitles the president of the American Rose Society who is S. S. Pennock of Philadelphia, Pa., to membership on the Board of Directors of the S. A. F. for the year 1916.

The following roses were registered and publication of the same directed according to the rules and regulations of the A. R. S.:

Mrs. Wm. R. Hearst—A sport from

My Maryland with the same productive habit of growth and freedom of flowering. In color, a clear, dark pink, a shade resembling Bridesmaid, and a decided improvement on the parent.

Red Radiance—A sport from Radiance. Similar in habit and growth, but a clear, even shade of red in color and of equal merit to its parent as a forcing and garden rose.

Little Sunshine — Seedling from Rosa multiflora nana × Soleil d'Or. Color, creamy yellow varying to deep golden yellow occasionally flecked or splashed with crimson. Double flowers one and one-half to two inches in diameter, carried in large panicles throughout the season. Habit, dwarf, spreading and vigorous similar to Multiflora nana. Very hardy and valuable for garden planting, but of special value for pot culture.

These are submitted for registration by A. N. Pierson, Inc., Cromwell, Conn.
BENJAMIN HAMMOND, Sec'y.
Beacon, N. Y., December 20, 1915.

LANCASTER COUNTY FLORISTS' CLUB.

December 16 is getting pretty close to Christmas and most florists are pretty busy around Christmas time, but notwithstanding all this we had a representative crowd on our visiting trip to Lititz, a pretty little burgh of Lancaster County noted from Minnesota to Texas and Maine to California for its "pretzels" and incidentally to see our compatriots Mr. Spinner who has a very neat little place devoted principally to vegetables and from which he makes quite as much as the average florist specialist would from the same amount of glass, the houses being used early for chrysanthemums, and C. F. Loeffler who has the past summer added two King houses and now has a good sized plant complete in every particular and a general assortment of cut flower stock, delphiniums, calendulas, snapdragons, alyssum, sweet peas and carnations, with chrysanthemums all out of the way excepting a few Nonin which he says he will not plant next season, it being a nuisance on account of its lateness. His new houses were unfortunately delayed in the finishing and the carnations have suffered considerably, but are now starting to produce.

A stop was made to see Enos Kohr's model place. Mr. Kohr has the business insight to keep everything right up to the top notch of productiveness, utilizing all available space and recognizing cleanliness as next to godliness. He has some 45,000 paper white narnissi coming in and his carnations, of which he has house after house, are exceptionally uniform in quality; in fact, most of Lancaster County carnations are a little higher up in quality than just "good" this season. Mr. Kohr likes White Perfection better than Matchless and has a very fine bench of Alice of which he thinks considerable and with good reason. Bench after bench of Mrs. C. W. Ward were a sight worth the whole trip.

Some thirty-two were present in the evening for the "Oyster Feed" among whom as guests were D. T. Connor of the Lord & Burnham Co.; T. J. Nolan of the King Construction Co. and Ed who from a few remarks that he made before leaving, will be a booster for

ward J. McCallum from Pittsburgh the club. A short meeting was held before the "feed" and H. A. Schroyer was nominated for president; E. J. Weaver for vice-president; Harry K. Rohrer for treasurer and Frank Kohr for secretary. Lemon Landis our secretary since organization insisting on being relieved from his job.

The committee on supper, Frank Kohr, David Rose and John Shreiner, certainly gave us full value for the money expended but they forgot one important thing at a florists' banquet and that was the decorations which might have been a little more elaborate than what they gave us.

After supper bowling teams were organized under the leadership of Messrs Connor and Nolan and some heavy scores were made. Mr. Connor winning the first prize, a very handsome umbrella, Willis B. Girvin the second and Frank Kohr, the booby

JAMES METHVEN
President-Elect of the Gardeners' and Florists' Club of Boston.

prize called by courtesy the third. In duck pins David Rose won first and A. Rohrer the low prize.

The singing and playing of Alponzo Petrs was a feature of the evening and billiards and pool and several hotly contested card games kept every one busy until 11.30 when we broke up a jolly party feeling all the better ready for work during the coming year under a new president.
ALBERT M. HERR.

AMERICAN ASSOCIATION OF NURSERYMEN.

The forty-first annual convention of the American Association of Nurserymen, will be held in Milwaukee, Wis., June 28-30, next. Hotel Wisconsin has been chosen as convention headquarters. T. J. Ferguson, of Wauwatosa, Wis., is the local representative of the Association in the matter of arrangements, entertainment, etc. Questions regarding membership, etc., may be sent to Secretary John Hall, 204 Granite Building, Rochester, N. Y., who will promptly respond. It is the hope of the executive committee that every

nurseryman in the country, actively engaged in the business, but not yet identified with the Association, will take the necessary steps to become one.

PACIFIC COAST HORTICULTURAL SOCIETY.

The regular monthly meeting of the Pacific Coast Horticultural Society on the evening of Dec. 11, was followed by a very enjoyable smoker. The nomination of officers for the ensuing year was one of the principal matters of business and the results were as follows: Eric James for president, Thomas Fenton for vice-president, W. A. Hofinghoff, incumbent, secretary; J. A. Axtell for treasurer, D. Raymond and F. Poss for ushers, and John McLaren for trustee. A long list of names were proposed for the exhibit committee. The evening exhibits made a very creditable showing. A vase of late varieties of carnations by N. Patterson of San Mateo took 92 points; a display of Cibotium Schiedel by F. Pelicano was rated at 95 points, and Nephrolepis Superior by H. Plath took 90 points. The exhibit committee announced the prize winners having the highest scores on exhibits for the year as H. Plath, first, 980 points; F. Pelicano, second, 762 points; MacRorie-McLaren Co., third, 444 points. Splendid entertainment was provided by Jas. Keegan and his committee for the latter part of the evening.

GARDENERS' AND FLORISTS' CLUB OF BOSTON.

The December meeting, held on Tuesday evening, Dec. 21, was pretty well attended, considering the nearness of the date to Christmas. Election of officers was the principal business. The result was as follows: President, James Methven of Readville; vice-president, W. J. Patterson of Wollaston; secretary, W. N. Craig, Brookline; treasurer, Peter Fisher, Ellis; executive committee, Peter Miller, W. J. Kennedy, Herman Bartsch, W. C. Rust and Andrew Rogers.

Secretary Craig read a paper on the prospects in this country for the young gardener, and a very interesting and vigorous discussion followed.

The landscape class of the club meets at Horticultural Hall every Monday evening at 7 o'clock, and interested visitors are always welcome.

WESTCHESTER AND FAIRFIELD HORTICULTURAL SOCIETY.

The annual meeting of this society was held on December 10 and officers for 1916 were elected as follows: president, W. J. Sealey; vice-president, Owen A. Hunwick; treasurer, Robt. Williamson; secretary, J. B. McArdle; corresponding secretary, P. W. Popp. The attendance was the smallest on record owing no doubt to the severity of the weather, and the gloom cast over the members due to the death of our beloved friend and associate member, Hon. John M. Brown, Mayor of Stamford, Conn. He was one of nature's noblemen whose charming personality and cheerful presence will be greatly missed at all of our gatherings. A committee was appointed to draw up suitable resolution of sympathy to be presented to the bereaved family and a copy of same to be spread on the records of the society.

The treasurer's report showed the society to be in a very flourishing condition financially, the membership constantly increasing. Our society was well represented at the convention of the N. A. G. at Boston, December 9 and 10. The Boston horticultural interests entertained the members in a royal manner and the 1915 convention will long remain a pleasant memory. The fall show committee rendered their final report and was discharged with thanks.

The next meeting will be held January 14, 1916. Best wishes to all for a Merry Christmas and a Bright and Prosperous New Year.

P. W. Popp, Cor. Sec'y.

SOCIETY OF AMERICAN FLORISTS AND ORNAMENTAL HORTICULTURISTS.

Second preliminary schedule, National Flower Show, Philadelphia, March 25 to April 2, 1916—Errata, Page 8. Cornflower "Dreer's Blue Annual" should read: "Dreer's Double Blue Annual." Group of flowering and foliage plants, Hugh B. Barclay prize. "Exhibitor to be a member of the Florists' Club of Philadelphia," should read: "Exhibitor to be a member of The Pennsylvania Horticultural Society."

Department of Plant Registration

Public notice is hereby given that, as no objection has been filed, the following registrations become complete: Cannas Lafayette and Wyoming, by Conard & Jones Co., West Grove, Pa.

John Young, Sec'y.

The Minnesota Florists' Association united with the Minnesota Horticultural Society in its annual meeting and exhibition last week. Exhibits in the floral department were quite profuse. Among the contributors from Chicago were Bassett & Washburn, who sent their carnation Belle Washburn, and J. D. Thompson Carnation Co., who showed carnations Aviator and Superb.

SEED TRADE

AMERICAN SEED TRADE ASSOCIATION

Officers—President, J. M. Lupton, Mattituck, L. I., N. Y.; First Vice-President, Kirby B. White, Detroit, Mich.; Second Vice-President, F. W. Bolgiano, Washington, D. C.; Secretary-Treasurer, C. E. Kendel, Cleveland, O.; Assistant Secretary, S. F. Willard, Jr., Cleveland, O. Cincinnati, O., next meeting place.

"Honest Dealers."

There is one seed seller in the United States who deals honestly and openly with his customers on the Question of guaranteed seed. That is Henry Field, of Iowa. Field sells seed corn, for example, subject to the buyer's own test and approval and, if it isn't satisfactory, it can be returned at his expense and with money refunded. He doesn't promise a full stand in the field. Nobody could honestly do that. But he does promise that he will send seed corn which has shown a germination test of 94 per cent. or better and that if it doesn't show a high test for the buyer the latter can fire it back. And Field makes good on his promise, too.

I don't mean to suggest that our southwestern folks should buy their seed corn from Henry Field. Most of his corn is grown too far north of us to be a good yielder under our climatic conditions.

I do wish, though, that some of our southwestern seed dealers would take a leaf out of Henry Field's book and sell us seed that is recommended in the same sort of way. If they did we might get a lot better stands from some of the seed which we buy. Nowadays the only guarantee we get is something like this:

"We give no warrantee, expressed or implied, as to description, purity, productiveness or any other matter of any seeds, plants or bulbs we send out, and we will not be in any way responsible for the crops grown thereon."

How many folks have bought seeds under some name and succeeded in raising something entirely different? How many have bought some fine new variety of oats and found the seed mixed with wild oats, wild rye, quack grass, slender wheat grass and Johnson grass? How many have paid high prices for seed that wouldn't grow no matter what you did to it? Then when you kicked about it the seed house laughed a "guaranty" about like the one I have quoted above and showed you where you should have been glad of the chance to buy seed from them at all.

—Oklahoma Farmer-Stockman.

Brother Carl Williams, editor of the Oklahoma Farmer-Stockman, Oklahoma City, Okla., seems to have an idea that a farmer would make a better seedsman than a seedsman. He seems to fail to realize that the seedsman evolutes from the farmer, the gardener, the forester, the florist; and becomes in time the expert result of all of them. If Carl refuses to take a look at Darwin, then he should stop sending his wooly western paper so far east as Philadelphia. G. C. Watson.

White Clover Seed.

White clover seed is still going up. The latest cable advices (received from Europe on the 16th inst.) indicated an advance of two inside of a week. Those who have been prophesying seventy-five by spring may not be so far off after all. It looks pretty serious.

Notes.

Atlanta, Ga.—H. G. Hastings Company are distributing this season 600,-000 of their attractive annual catalog, which has just been issued to their customers throughout the southern states.

Chicago—Onion set shipping is now beginning in earnest. J. C. Leonard of the Leonard Seed Co., says that it appears now that shrinkage will be considerable and the cost of hand picking will be high. This is quite an item and has a direct influence on the market price of onions later. The bean situation does not improve and a very serious shortage on all sorts has developed. Though some portions of the country seem to have escaped, in general the crop has been very small. Sales have been reported at $12.00 per bu. on Giant Stringless in quantity and $14.00 and $15.00 on Wardwell's wax bean.

CATALOGUES RECEIVED.

Sluis & Groot, Enkhuizen, Holland—Advance Price List of Vegetable, Flower and Agricultural Seeds. Date, November, 1915.

Mathews Garden Craft Manufacturing Company, Cleveland, O.—A 48 page pictorial album with decorated cover, size 10 x 13, has been sent out by this company as catalogue and price list of their garden furniture specialties. The pages devoted to Japanese garden work are daintily illustrated in colors. There are 200 handsome illustrations.

NEWS ITEMS FROM EVERYWHERE

NEW YORK.

Charles Thorley has been using an extra store at 36 West 46th street for his holiday overflow.

P. J. Smith's 13-year-old-daughter has been quite seriously ill with tonsilitis for the past week.

Mrs. Ritta Rankin, proprietor of the "House of Ferns," is suffering from a severe attack of the grip.

J. J. Coan added a department of Christmas trees and holly temporarily to his wholesale flower business this week.

Reed & Keller report an extraordinary holiday demand for the various florists' supplies in which they specialize.

J. K. Allen, who was laid up at his home, is able to be out again, having made his first appearance at his place of business this week.

A. Rynveld, of Rynveld Bros., Lisse, Holland, sailed from New York on Wednesday, December 15. He expects to return in March, and will have a permanent office in New York at 44 Whitehall street.

Frank H. Traendly is now able to come to business for a portion of every day, and customers and others who visit the Traendly & Schenck establishment are all overjoyed to find him at his post once more.

Chas. Schwake returned on Saturday night from his Western trip, having been absent from his office since the time of the Cleveland show. He reports very enthusiastic business expectations all through the West.

G. Van der Mey, of Van der Mey & Sons, bulb dealers of Lisse, and Johann Harduyzer, nurseryman, of Boskoop, Holland, arrived from Holland last Saturday on the S. S. Noordam. Their headquarters will be with Maltus & Ware.

That the carnation Matchless is living quite up to its name no one could question after seeing the quality in which this superb white is being received by Jos. A. Millang at the New York Cut Flower Co.'s place, from Cottage Gardens. It is a "top-notcher."

Phil. F. Kessler is still receiving elegant flowers of the late blooming Chrysanthemum Misletoe. The flowers of this variety are very large, incurved, white, with a faint luminous flush in the depths of the blossom. Foliage and stem leave nothing to be desired.

Charles Millang went very heavily into imported holly trees for Christmas this year and made a great success of it, disposing of many hundreds of trees. They were very handsome specimens, all loaded with scarlet fruit and some of them having variegated foliage.

The leading flower stores are going heavily into zinc-lined baskets and jardinieres of ornamental plants in various combinations for the holiday trade. Alex. McConnell utilized the large basement of his store for this class of work and kept many hands busy putting up exquisite combinations of poinsettias, cyclamen, ericas, crotons and other appropriate things. Brilliant red Christmas ribbon is quite generally used on these combination gifts, but the old custom of using crepe paper and an excessive decoration of ribbon bows seems to have gone into disuse.

WASHINGTON.

A bill has been introduced into the House of Representatives by Congressman George S. Graham, of Pennsylvania, providing for an appropriation of $50,000 to be expended in the erection of a monument to the late William R. Smith, to perpetuate the memory of the "father of horticulture." The bill, H. R. 6419, has been referred to the Library Committee of the House of Representatives.

A bill introduced by Congressman Charles H. Dillon, of South Dakota, establishes for various commodities the following net weights per bushel: 14 pounds, blue grass seed, orchard grass seed, red top; 28 pounds, top onion sets; 30 pounds, broom corn seed; 32 pounds, bottom onion sets; 22 pounds, timothy seed; 40 pounds, apple seeds; 44 pounds, hemp seed; 45 pounds, herds grass; 46 pounds, castor beans; 50 pounds, Hungarian grass seed, millet, rape seed, sorghum seed; 60 pounds, alfalfa seed, clover seed. Fraud is punishable by fines of not more than $500, by imprisonment for not more than three months, or both, in the discretion of the court.

J. H. Small & Sons furnished the decorations for the Wilson-Galt wedding. Cattleyas and American Beauty and Lady Stanley roses were used in profusion and the corsage bouquet worn by the bride was of orchids. The salon and dining room had been thrown into one room and a large bower erected in the bay window of the latter. Ferns and American Beauty roses and many choice orchids were used. The general decorations of the dining room were carried out in pink and green. At one end was a bank of ferns and clusters of pink roses, while on the buffets and tables were pots of growing roses and ferns. Cattleyas ornamented the wedding cake. Aside from the wedding decorations there was little business for the local stores. To say that the simplicity of the affair was a disappointment from the standpoint of the retail stores is putting it mildly.

PITTSBURGH.

Edward L. McGrath, manager of the Blind Floral Company, has a holiday display of exceptionally fine poinsettias grown at the greenhouses at West View.

During the past week Gilbert Ludwig of the Ludwig Floral Company, Federal Street, North Side, has been confined to the house with a cold, which seriously threatens to develop into pneumonia.

On last Sunday evening a "Ford" ran into a truck belonging to William M. Turner, the Penn Avenue (Wilkinsburg) florist, more or less injuring the five occupants and completely demolishing the aggressive "peace" (?) car.

At the Russian ball given last Friday evening at the Pittsburgh Club by Mrs. Horne, the stage on each side had a large urn of old bronze holding two hundred poinsettias. Maidenhair ferns in baskets of gold tied with the colors of the czar were used for the table centerpieces. At a dinner dance given Monday evening at the same club the table was decorated with mounds of poinsettia separated by tall silver shafts of white lilies.

CHICAGO.

A. F. Longren, is home for the holidays and says the supply business is all right. He will start out again in two weeks.

Schiller's Gift Shop was filled with every kind of offering that a florist could supply. The window was trimmed overhead with drooping branches of red foliage and masses of gray southern moss and mistletoe.

Many of the down-town retailers have taken extra pains to beautify their stores. Special attention has been given to the overhead effects and the results are good. All employed red as the predominating color.

J. Mangel, found his new conservatory indispensable for holding his blooming plants and showing them to good advantage. A line of pottery for holding small plants, etc., is having a good run.

Eastern growers are trying to sell their American Beauties this year before shipping them into this market. The experiences of last year, when thirty thousand were dropped down here proved a lesson not to be risked again.

The Alpha had its entire windows, which are the largest of the down-town flower stores, all done in red and green. Gus Pappas, proprietor of the store since his partner's death, went to the other store at Des Moines, Ia., Monday and will return Christmas day.

At the Chicago Flower Growers' Association all are busy filling the early orders and the books show a long list to be filled later in the week. Some especially fine cut poinsettias were seen here. They were four feet long and the bracts very large and of extremely brilliant color. Another lot will follow these, both sent by one of their growers who enjoys the reputation of being an expert.

At Poehlman Bros.' southern shipments are under way and the orders are fully up to a normal year. The quartette of red roses which are playing such an important part in the

holiday sales are Hadley, Hoosier Beauty, Richmond and Milady. Speaking of their respective merits, Mr. Freese regards Milady as having the best shipping qualities and the first two as excelling in richness of color. Mrs. Russell at this house is exceptionally good; not a trace of blue in its color and the size and shape of the flower being all that could be desired in a rose.

The lily of the valley situation is reviewed by Phil Schupp, manager for J. A. Budlong, about as follows: The number of pips now in this locality nowhere near approaches the quantity used in a normal season, though a few who had forethought to lay in a good supply have their stock assured. Should the war in Europe terminate before warm weather comes again, shipments could be safely made which would take care of next year, but the acreage is small in Germany compared to that of other years, and even with best of shipping facilities stock will be scarce. The Budlong lily of the valley this week measures 15 inches and the bells are of large size.

BOSTON.

Edward Stout, formerly salesman for the Boston Rose Co., is now first assistant to Wm. Penn, buyer for Penn the Florist.

Friends of Mrs. Fisher of Worcester are glad to see her once more around the market early in the morning as before after her late illness.

George Libbey of Lynn, who has recently sold out his florist business in Lynn and retired, has gone to spend the winter and spring with his son in New Haven, Conn.

One of the most attractively dressed and illuminated florist's windows ever seen in Boston is that of Thomas F. Galvin this week. A splendid electrical display in many colors adds to the external attractiveness of the building at night.

The Boston Herald of Sunday, Dec. 19th, devotes considerable space to a picture and accompanying story about Harry Brinkgrieve, who, although blind for the past three years, is able

to conduct his greenhouse at Hyde Park successfully, and who has made a good record with his chrysanthemums this season. Lettuce and early tomatoes will follow the chrysanthemums in his greenhouse.

Penn, the Florist, opened his new store at 124 Tremont street on Saturday, Dec. 18th, with a superb display of plants, flowers and floral work. A large advertisement in the Boston morning papers invited the public to come and attend the opening. The advertisement stated that there were no cards for this opening, no selective lists or special invitations, but that friends, customers and the public alike were bidden welcome, and the people responded in large numbers.

VISITORS' REGISTER.

Boston.—G. X. Amrhyn, New Haven, Ct.

New York.—L. W. Wheeler, Gilroy, Cal.; A. Farenwald, Roslyn, Pa.

Cincinnati: Ed. Fancourt, of S. S. Pennock-Meehan Co., Phila.; Miss Fannie White, Lexington, Ky.

Chicago: B. H. Klus, Anderson, Ind.; Geo. Pandell, Fort Wayne, Ind.; H. Kusik, Kansas City, Mo.; W. J. Fosgate, Santa Clara, Cal.

Philadelphia: James Brown Coatesville, Pa.; Enos B. Engle, Harrisburg, Pa.; P. Joseph Lynch, New Castle, Indiana; Frank B. Rine, Lewisburg, Pa.

Washington, D. C.: Ralph M. Ward, New York, N. Y.; Wallace R. Pierson, Cromwell, Conn.; S. S. Skidelsky, Philadelphia, Pa.; E. L. Darnell of Cleveland, Ohio.

South Orange, N. J.—W. A. Manda has just received what he believes to be the biggest shipment of herbaceous plants ever received from Japan. These are the result of a two-years' collecting tour, and it is possible some new and specially valuable things may be included in the shipment. Laelias and cypripediums are now blooming handsomely in the greenhouses, and Polypodium Mandaianum still holds its place as a leading favorite, both for use as a plant and as cut fronds.

WHOLESALE FLOWER MARKETS — TRADE PRICES—Per 100 TO DEALERS ONLY

Roses	BOSTON Dec. 23		ST. LOUIS Dec. 23		PHILA. Dec. 23	
Am. Beauty, Special	60.00 to	75.00	40.00 to	60.00	30.00 to	35.00
" " Fancy and Extra	40.00 to	50.00	25.00 to	30.00	20.00 to	25.00
" " No. 1	6.00 to	25.00	10.00 to	15.00	8.00 to	15.00
Russell, Hadley	8.00 to	20.00	10.00 to	15.00	4.00 to	20.00
Killarney, Richmond, Hillingdon, Ward, Extra	6.00 to	15.00	3.00 to	10.00	8.00 to	10.00
" " Ordinary	4.00 to	6.00	5.00 to	6.00	3.00 to	6.00
Arenburg; Radiance, Taft, Key, Extra	6.00 to	15.00	...... to	......	8.00 to	10.00
" " Ordinary	4.00 to	6.00	...... to	......	3.00 to	6.00
Ophelia, Mock, Sunburst, Extra	5.00 to	12.00	8.00 to	10.00	8.00 to	12.00
" " Ordinary	4.00 to	5.00	5.00 to	6.00	3.00 to	6.00
Carnations, Fancy	4.00 to	10.00	4.00 to	6.00	4.00 to	6.00
" Ordinary	2.00 to	4.00	2.00 to	3.00	2.00 to	3.00
Cattleyas	50.00 to	60.00	50.00 to	60.00	40.00 to	60.00
Dendrobium formosum	...... to	6.00	6.00 to	8.00	4.00 to	6.00
Lilies, Longiflorum	...... to	40.00	...... to	......	35.00 to	......
Rubrum	8.00 to	12.00	12.00 to	15.00	8.00 to	12.00
Callas	10.00 to	18.00	10.00 to	18.00	10.00 to	12.50
Lily of the Valley	2.00 to	4.00	3.00 to	4.00	2.00 to	4.00
Daisies	1.00 to	2.00	.25 to	.50	1.00 to	2.00
Violets	.75 to	1.50	.50 to	.75	.25 to	1.25
Mignonette	2.00 to	6.00	3.00 to	4.00	2.00 to	5.00
Snapdragon	2.00 to	4.00	4.00 to	5.00	4.00 to	12.50
Narcissus, Paper-White	2.00 to	2.50	3.00 to	4.00	3.00 to	4.00
Trumpet	...... to	......	...... to	......	...... to	......
Hyacinths, Roman	...... to	......	3.00 to	4.00	...... to	......
Freesia	...... to	6.00	...... to	......	...... to	......
Calendulas	2.00 to	4.00	3.00 to	4.00	2.00 to	4.00
Stevia	.75 to	1.00	1.00 to	1.50	1.00 to	2.00
Sweet Peas	1.00 to	1.50	1.00 to	2.00	.75 to	2.00
Gardenias	25.00 to	35.00	...... to	......	15.00 to	40.00
Adiantum	1.00 to	1.50	1.00 to	1.25	...... to	......
Smilax	10.00 to	16.00	12.00 to	15.00	15.00 to	20.00
Asparagus Plumosus, Strings (100)	25.00 to	50.00	35.00 to	50.00	...... to	50.00
" & Spren. (100 Bchs.)	25.00 to	35.00	20.00 to	35.00	25.00 to	50.00

Flower Market Reports

BOSTON The dark weather of the last two weeks has made an apparent great scarcity of certain flowers in the market. Good carnations have been almost impossible to obtain and red ones are being held at unheard-of prices. Unfortunately the quality is not there in a large proportion of the carnations offered. Pickling is decidedly in evidence. Roses are more plentiful and outside of red are selling at a medium figure. American Beauties are rather unsecure from present outlook. Sweet peas of the Spencer variety are in brisk demand at a good figure and Blanch Ferry and White varieties of the grandiflora type sell well. Lilies, callas, marguerites, calendulas, etc., also sell rapidly. In the plant line there has been a brisk trade and dealers are generally sold out. The market on azaleas is especially good. Cyclamen have been all cleaned up and are in great demand.

CHICAGO At this writing, long distance shipments are clearing the market for the heavier trade which is expected later in the week. All kinds of roses are in good supply as predicted, and there is every indication that there will be enough to fill all orders. The shortage is in carnations, particularly red ones. When it was asserted by some of the large growers weeks ago, that carnations would be scarce for the holidays, few were inclined to take it seriously, but those who had accepted orders at a low price are now unable to fill them. The plants are off crop, and buds are not far enough advanced to create any hope even should the sun shine all of each day, or as one grower put it, "24 hours of each day." American Beauties are fine, the supply being mostly of the long-stemmed ones. Mrs. Russell is distinctly of two types, the good ones and the bad, the latter being decidedly off color. The very last cuts of chrysanthemums are now in and no one regrets that the season is over. The last ones are not equal to those of mid-season, but fair. Lily of the valley is bringing good prices.

CINCINNATI Supply has been rather short, but roses are getting more plentiful as the holidays approach and there will undoubtedly be a fair cut for Christmas. American Beauties which up to this time have moved out rather slowly are now meeting with a good call. Carnations are very scarce. Poinsettia receipts are very heavy and very good. The supply of lily of the valley, double violets and orchids is equal to the demand, while single violets and sweet peas may be had in large quantities. Narcissus receipts continue rather light. Lilies are plentiful and very good. Up to this time the demand for boxwood has been exceptionally heavy.

BUFFALO Business has been gradually growing heavier each day. Last week was quite a busy one for those handling decorative greens and the sales so far have exceeded any previous year. There was also a good supply of cut material in roses, lilies, carnations, chrysanthemums and other stock and things cleaned up fair at end of week, excepting long Beauties, lily of the valley and white roses. Every indication points toward a heavy holiday business as a slight hustle has already begun at this writing (Tuesday).

NEW YORK This market has been going through a rare experience during the past week. The demand for cut flowers in the retail stores has been slack, as is the case usually preceding the Christmas onslaught, yet prices have stiffened up to a limit seldom reached and the wholesale places have been cleaning up very well, everything considered. Much doubt is expressed by wise observers as to the outcome when the holiday trade develops its capacity. That more or less stock—especially carnations and violets—is being held back for the final windup by some growers, seems very probable. Many of the carnations seen in previous to the holiday have shown a very suspicious drowsiness after being exposed to the air for a brief time. So few violets have been in evidence that the whereabouts of the crop is quite a mystery. We hope that the disheartening experience of other years will not be repeated—an avalanche of violets on the last day and the back of the market broken.

(Continued on page 859)

WHOLESALE FLOWER MARKETS — TRADE PRICES—Per 100 TO DEALERS ONLY

	CINCINNATI Dec. 13		CHICAGO Dec. 13		BUFFALO Dec. 20		PITTSBURG Dec. 20	
Roses								
Am. Beauty, Special	50.00 to 100.00		50.00 to 75.00	60.00 to 75.00		...... to 75.00	
" " Fancy and Extra	50.00 to 75.00		30.00 to 40.00	50.00 to 60.00		...... to 60.00	
" " No. 1	25.00 to 40.00		15.00 to 25.00	30.00 to 50.00		30.00 to 50.00	
Russell, Hadley	15.00 to 25.00		4.00 to 25.00	25.00 to 35.00		10.00 to 35.00	
Killarney, Rich'm'd, Hillf'dco, Ward	10.00 to 15.00		8.00 to 10.00	10.00 to 15.00		10.00 to 15.00	
" " " " Ord.	5.00 to 8.00		3.00 to 5.00	6.00 to 8.00		6.00 to 8.00	
Arenburg, Radiance, Taft, Key, Ex.	10.00 to 15.00		8.00 to 10.00	12.00 to 15.00		...... to	
" " " " Ord.	4.00 to 8.00		3.00 to 5.00	6.00 to 8.00		...... to	
Ophelia, Mock, Sunburst, Extra	10.00 to 15.00		8.00 to 10.00	10.00 to 15.00		15.00 to 30.00	
" " Ordinary	4.00 to 8.00		3.00 to 5.00	5.00 to 6.00		8.00 to 12.00	
Carnations, Fancy	8.00 to 10.00		4.00 to 5.00	8.00 to 10.00		8.00 to 10.00	
Ordinary	...... to		3.00 to 4.00	4.00 to 6.00		...... to 6.00	
Cattleyas	...... to 100.00		60.00 to 75.00	60.00 to 75.00		75.00 to 80.00	
Dendrobium formosum	...... to		50.00 to 60.00	...... to 50.00		...... to	
Lilies, Longiflorum	12.50 to 15.00		8.00 to 10.00	10.00 to 12.00		12.00 to 15.00	
" Rubrum	5.00 to 12.50		5.00 to 6.00	...... to 6.00		...... to	
Callas	12.50 to 15.00		...... to	10.00 to 12.00		...... to	
Lily of the Valley	...... to		3.00 to 4.00	4.00 to 6.00		4.00 to 5.00	
Daisies	...... to		...... to	1.00 to		3.00 to 4.00	
Violets	1.50 to 2.00		.75 to 1.00	1.00 to 1.50		1.50 to 2.00	
Mignonette	...... to		3.00 to 6.00	3.00 to 4.00		4.00 to 8.00	
Snapdragon	...... to		4.00 to 6.00	4.00 to 8.00		...... to	
Narcissus, Paper-White	3.00 to 4.00		2.00 to 3.00	2.00 to 3.00		...... to 4.00	
" Trumpet	...... to		...... to	...... to		...... to	
Hyacinths, Roman	...... to		...... to	...... to		3.00 to 4.00	
Freesia	...... to		...... to	...... to		...... to	
Calendula	...... to		...... to	...... to		1.00 to 4.00	
Stevia	2.00 to 3.00		...... to	1.00 to 1.00		1.00 to 2.00	
Sweet Peas	1.00 to 1.50		1.00 to 1.50	...... to 1.00		1.50 to 2.00	
Gardenias	...... to		40.00 to 50.00	...... to 50.00		...... to	
Adiantum	...... to 1.00		...... to 1.00	...... to 1.00		...... to 1.25	
Smilax	12.50 to 15.00		...... to 10.00	15.00 to 15.00		15.00 to 15.00	
Asparagus Plumosus, Strings (100)	25.00 to 50.00		40.00 to 50.00	50.00 to 50.00		50.00 to 50.00	
& Spren. (100 bchs.)	25.00 to 50.00		25.00 to 50.00	30.00 to 30.00		35.00 to 50.00	

Flower Market Reports

(Continued from page 857)

Roses have been doing well. They appear to be in good crop everywhere, quality very good and the signs of pickling not so apparent as in the case of the carnations. There are relatively more of the long stem grades than the short, while the demand is mostly the reverse. We look to see an abundance, if not an excess, of roses and heavy sales at moderate prices. Poinsettias in cut state are among the most despised things at Christmas time usually, and this year is no exception. They are hardly worth growing for cut-flower purposes. Of lily of the valley there is an abundance. Longiflorum lilies are holding out at a good price but many of the lots seen are of low grade quality. All white flowers naturally suffer at Christmas. Red is in the saddle, but whether it be roses, carnations, poinsettias or anything else be such as will hold up in good fresh condition after delivery to the consumer. Anything else, nowadays, will only make trouble for the dealer and obloquy for the cut flower trade. As for the plant trade the most of the story is told when we say that all the growers were sold out clean long before the demand ceased. The stock is very fine as a rule with the exception of the small poinsettias grown for pan use. Of these there is a greater amount of inferior material on the market than we have ever seen before. Cyclamens are very fine; so are azaleas. Foliage plants, such as crotons and dracaenas, are brilliantly colored, and the fruited plants such as solanums, ardisias and oranges are uniformly excellent. Erica melanthera, also several of the ventricosa sorts, are also very well done.

PITTSBURGH　The past week's ideal weather augurs well for the florists, whose only troubles now seem to be scarcity of stock to supply the demand, which increases as the days go on. Roses are fairly plentiful, including special American Beauties, but carnations are so scarce that the wholesalers do not even care to quote prices. Of these flowers, it is estimated that the various retailers are able to fill about only twenty per cent of the calls. Holly is not coming in the quantities required, the quality being "hof and hof," some about perfect and other again most inferior.

SAN FRANCISCO　Preparations for Christmas are demanding principal attention all along the line now. Some fine windows have already made their appearance. Stock has cleaned up very closely all week, and in some instances more flowers could have been used to advantage. It is believed the growers are holding back for the Christmas trade and that there will be a much better showing than present offerings would indicate. A heavy rain the first of the week about finished the chrysanthemums and this was followed by a few cold days, which acted as a set-back to roses and some other seasonables. Good stock is bringing high prices. On the other hand violets are even more plentiful and the demand continues excellent. There is little to be said about carnations, the offerings being light, quality poor and demand only fair. The supply of roses

has hardly equalled the demand for several days, so the arrivals have been readily absorbed. Hadley, Ophelia, Aaron Ward, Sunburst and Russell show fine quality, and American Beauty is all that can be desired. Flowering plants are showing up well, and a

good demand is reported. Holly appears everywhere.

ST. LOUIS　The Christmas market all depends upon the weather. With clear weather from now on there should be

(Continued on page 863)

NEW YORK QUOTATIONS PER 100.　To Dealers Only

MISCELLANEOUS	Last Half of Week ending Dec. 18 1915		First Half of Week beginning Dec. 20 1915	
Cattleyas	40.00	to 60.00	40.00	to 60.00
Dendrobium formosum	25.00	to 30.00	25.00	to 50.00
Lilies, Longiflorum	8.00	to 10.00	8.00	to 10.00
Rubrum	5.00	to 6.00	5.00	to 6.00
Callas	6.00	to 8.00	6.00	to 10.00
Lily of the Valley	2.00	to 3.00	2.00	to 4.00
Daisies	.50	to 1.00	1.00	to 8.00
Violets	.75	to 1.25	.75	to 1.50
Mignonette	2.00	to 4.00	2.00	to 4.00
Snapdragon	2.00	to 3.00	2.00	to 3.00
Narcissus, Paper-White	1.00	to 2.00	1.00	to 2.00
Trumpet		to	......	to ......
Hyacinths, Roman		to	......	to ......
Fresia		to	......	to ......
Calendulas	1.00	to 2.00	1.00	to 2.00
Stevia		to 1.00	......	to 1.50
Sweet Peas	1.00	to 1.50	1.00	to 1.50
Gardenias	20.00	to 35.00	25.00	to 35.00
Adiantum	.50	to 1.00	.50	to 1.00
Smilax	8.00	to 10.00	8.00	to 10.00
Asparagus Plumosus, strngs (per 100)	30.00	to 40.00	35.00	to 50.00
& Spren (100 bunches)	15.00	to 20.00	15.00	to 25.00

Buyer's Directory and Ready Reference Guide

Advertisements under this head, one cent a word. Initials count as words.

Display advertisers in this issue are also listed under this classification without charge. Reference to List of Advertisers will indicate the respective pages.

Buyers failing to find what they want in this list will confer a favor by writing us and we will try to put them in communication with reliable dealers.

ACCOUNTANT
R. Dysart, 40 State St., Boston.
For page see List of Advertisers.

APHINE
Aphine Mfg. Co., Madison, N. J.
For page see List of Advertisers.

APHIS PUNK
Nicotine Mfg. Co., St. Louis, Mo.
For page see List of Advertisers.

ASPARAGUS
Asparagus Plumosus, Thumb pot plants, sure to please, $1.50 per 100. B. C. BLAKE, R. D. 4, Springfield, Ohio.

AUCTION SALES
The MacNiff Horticultural Co., New York City.
Plant and Bulb Sales by Auction.
For page see List of Advertisers.

AZALEAS
P. Ouwerkerk, Hoboken, N. J.
For page see List of Advertisers.

BAY TREES
August Rolker & Sons, New York.
For page see List of Advertisers.

BEDDING PLANTS
A. N. Pierson, Inc., Cromwell, Conn.
For page see List of Advertisers.

R. Vincent, Jr. & Sons Co.,
White Marsh, Md.
For page see List of Advertisers.

BEGONIAS

		Per 100
BEGONIA LORRAINE,	2½ in.	$12.00
	3 in.	20.00
	4 in.	35.00
	5 in.	50.00
BEGONIA CINCINNATI,	2½ in.	15.00
	3 in.	25.00
	3½ in.	30.00
	4½ in.	40.00
JULIUS ROEHRS CO., Rutherford, N. J.		

BOILERS
Kroeschell Bros. Co., Chicago.
For page see List of Advertisers.

King Construction Co., North Tonawanda, N. Y.
"King Ideal" Boiler.
For page see List of Advertisers.

Hitchings & Co., New York City.
For page see List of Advertisers.

Lord & Burnham Co., New York City.

BOXES—CUT FLOWER FOLDING
Edwards Folding Box Co., Philadelphia.
For page see List of Advertisers.

Folding cut flower boxes, the best made.
Write for list. HOLTON & HUNKEL CO., Milwaukee, Wis.

BOX TREES
BOX TREES—Standards, Pyramids and Bush. In various sizes. Price List on demand. JULIUS ROEHRS CO., Rutherford, N. J.

BULBS AND TUBERS
Arthur T. Boddington Co., Inc.,
New York City.
For page see List of Advertisers.

BULBS AND TUBERS—Continued
J. M. Thorburn & Co., New York City.
Wholesale Price List of High Class Bulbs.
For page see List of Advertisers.

Ralph M. Ward & Co., New York City.
Lily Bulbs.
For page see List of Advertisers.

John Lewis Childs, Flowerfield, L. I., N. Y.
Gladioli.
For page see List of Advertisers.

August Rolker & Sons, New York City.
Holland and Japan Bulbs.
For page see List of Advertisers.

R. & J. Farquhar & Co., Boston, Mass.
For page see List of Advertisers.

Chas. Schwake & Co., New York City.
Horticultural Importers and Exporters.
For page see List of Advertisers.

A. Henderson & Co., Chicago, Ill.
For page see List of Advertisers.

Burnett Bros., 98 Chambers St., New York.

Henry F. Michell Co., Philadelphia, Pa.
For page see List of Advertisers.

Joseph Breck & Sons Corp., Boston, Mass.
For page see List of Advertisers.

Fottler, Fiske, Rawson Co., Boston, Mass.
For page see List of Advertisers.

C. KEUR & SONS, HILLEGOM, Holland.
Bulbs of all descriptions. Write for prices.
NEW YORK Branch, 8-10 Bridge St.

CANNAS
Newest list of the newest Cannas just out. Complete assortment of the finest sorts, at remarkable rates.
Send for list today.
THE CONARD & JONES CO.
West Grove, Pa.

CARNATIONS
Wood Bros., Fishkill, N. Y.
For page see List of Advertisers.

F. Dorner & Sons Co., Lafayette, Ind.
For page see List of Advertisers.

Littlefield & Wyman, North Abington, Mass.
New Pink Carnation, Miss Theo.
For page see List of Advertisers.

CARNATION STAPLES
Split carnations quickly, easily and cheaply mended. Pillsbury's Carnation Staple, 1000 for 35c.; 3000 for $1.00 post paid. I. L. PILLSBURY, Galesburg, Ill.

Supreme Carnation Staples, for repairing split carnations, 35c. per 1000; 3000 for $1.00. F. W. WAITE, 85 Belmont Ave., Springfield, Mass.

CHRISTMAS PLANTS
A. M. Davenport, Watertown, Mass.
For page see List of Advertisers.

Frank Oechslin, Chicago, Ill.

W. A. Riggs, Auburndale, Mass.
Excellent Xmas Plant Stock.

CHRYSANTHEMUMS
Chas. H. Totty, Madison, N. J.
For page see List of Advertisers.

COLEUS
Christmas Gem Coleus, 3c. B. C. BLAKE, R. D. 4, Springfield, Ohio.

Coleus, Golden Bedder, Verschaffeltii, Queen Victoria, Firebrand and all leading varieties, including the Pink and Yellow Trailing Queen, clean, strong, well rooted cuttings, 50c. per 100, $4.00 per 1000. Cash with order, and satisfaction guaranteed. Send for list. Largest grower of coleus in the U. S. A. NAHLIK, 261-75 Lawrence St., Flushing, N. Y.

DAHLIAS
Send for Wholesale List of whole clumps and separate stock; 40,000 clumps for sale. Northboro Dahlia and Gladiolus Gardens. J. L. MOORE, Prop, Northboro, Mass.

NEW PAEONY DAHLIA
John Wanamaker, Newest, Handsomest, Best. New color, new form and new habit of growth. Big stock of best cut-flower varieties. Send list of wants to PEACOCK DAHLIA FARMS, Berlin, N. J.

DECORATIVE PLANTS
Robert Craig Co., Philadelphia, Pa.
For page see List of Advertisers.

Woodrow & Marketos, New York City.
For page see List of Advertisers.

S. S. Skidelsky & Co., Philadelphia, Pa.
For page see List of Advertisers.

Bobbink & Atkins, Rutherford, N. J.
For page see List of Advertisers.

A. Leuthy & Co., Roslindale, Boston, Mass.
For page see List of Advertisers.

Thomas Roland, Nahant, Mass.
High Grade Plants for Retail Florists.
For page see List of Advertisers.

DRACENAS
Dracaena Indivisa, 4-in. pot plants, 6c.
B. C. BLAKE, R. D. 4, Springfield, Ohio.

FERNS
Henry A. Dreer, Philadelphia, Pa.
Dreer's Fine Ferns.

John Scott, Brooklyn, N. Y.
The Home of the Scottii Fern.
For page see List of Advertisers.

H. H. Barrows & Son, Whitman, Mass.
For page see List of Advertisers.

Robert Craig Co., Philadelphia, Pa.
For page see List of Advertisers.

F. R. Pierson Co., Tarrytown, N. Y.

A. M. Davenport, Watertown, Mass.
Boston and Whitmani Ferns.
For page see List of Advertisers.

Roman J. Irwin, New York City.
Boston and Whitmani Ferns.
For page see List of Advertisers.

Ferns, 2-in., Boston, Whitmani, Roosevelt, Elegantissima, Compacta and Teddy Jr. B. C. BLAKE, R. D. 4, Springfield, Ohio.

FERTILIZERS
Stumpp & Walter Co., New York City.
Scotch Soot.
For page see List of Advertisers.

Pulverized Manure Co., Chicago, Ill.
Wizard Brand Cattle Manure.
For page see List of Advertisers.

For List of Advertisers See Page 839

In writing to Advertisers kindly mention Horticulture

NURSERY STOCK
P. Ouwerkerk, Weehawken Heights, N. J.
For page see List of Advertisers.

W. & T. Smith Co., Geneva, N. Y.
For page see List of Advertisers.

The D. Hill Nursery Co., Dundee, Ill.
Hill's Evergreens.
For page see List of Advertisers.

Bay State Nurseries, North Abington, Mass.
Hardy, Northern Grown Stock.
For page see List of Advertisers.

Bobbink & Atkins, Rutherford, N. J.
For page see List of Advertisers.

August Rolker & Sons, New York City.
For page see List of Advertisers.

NUT GROWING.
The Nut-Grower, Waycross, Ga.
For page see List of Advertisers.

ORCHID FLOWERS
Jas. McManus, New York, N. Y.
For page see List of Advertisers.

ORCHID PLANTS
Julius Roehrs Co., Rutherford, N. J.
For page see List of Advertisers.

Lager & Hurrell, Summit, N. J.

PALMS, ETC.
Robert Craig Co., Philadelphia, Pa.
For page see List of Advertisers.

August Rolker & Sons, New York City.
For page see List of Advertisers.

A. Leuthy & Co., Roslindale, Boston, Mass.
For page see List of Advertisers.

PANSY PLANTS
Pansies, the big giant flowering kind,
$3.00 per 1000; in bud and bloom, $5.00 and
$15.00 per 1000. Cash. If I could only
show the nice plants, hundreds of testimonials and repeat orders I would be
flooded with new business. JAMES MOSS,
Johnsville, Pa.

PANSY SEED
Chas. Frost, Kenilworth, N. J.
Kenilworth Giant.
For page see List of Advertisers.

PEONIES
Peonies. The world's greatest collection.
1200 sorts. Send for list. C. BETSCHER,
Canal Dover, O.

PECKY CYPRESS BENCHES
A. T. Stearns Lumber Co., Boston, Mass.
For page see List of Advertisers.

PIPE AND FITTINGS
Kroeschell Bros. Co., Chicago.
For page see List of Advertisers.

King Construction Company,
N. Tonawanda, N. Y.
Shelf Brackets and Pipe Hangers.
For page see List of Advertisers.

PLANT AND BULB IMPORTS
Chas. Schwake & Co., New York City.
For page see List of Advertisers.

August Rolker & Sons, New York City.
For page see List of Advertisers.

PLANT TRELLISES AND STAKES
Seele's Tieless Plant Stakes and Trellises. H. D. SEELE & SONS, Elkhart, Ind.

PLANT TUBS
H. A. Dreer, Philadelphia, Pa.
"Riverton Special."
For page see List of Advertisers.

PLANTS WANTED
C. C. Trepel, New York City.
For page see List of Advertisers.

RAFFIA
McHutchison & Co., New York, N. Y.
For page see List of Advertisers.

RHODODENDRONS
P. Ouwerkerk, Hoboken, N. J.
For page see List of Advertisers.

RIBBONS AND CHIFFONS
S. S. Pennock-Meehan Co., Philadelphia, Pa.
For page see List of Advertisers.

ROSES
Poehlmann Bros. Co., Morton Grove, Ill.
For page see List of Advertisers.

P. Ouwerkerk, Hoboken, N. J.
For page see List of Advertisers.

Robert Craig Co., Philadelphia, Pa.
For page see List of Advertisers.

W. & T. Smith Co., Geneva, N. Y.
American Grown Roses.
For page see List of Advertisers.

Bay State Nurseries, North Abington, Mass.
For page see List of Advertisers.

August Rolker & Sons, New York City.
For page see List of Advertisers.

A. N. Pierson, Inc., Cromwell, Conn.
For page see List of Advertisers.

THE CONARD & JONES COMPANY.
Rose Specialists
West Grove, Pa. Send for offers.

SCALECIDE
B. G. Pratt Co., New York City.

SEASONABLE PLANT STOCK
R. Vincent, Jr. & Sons Co., White Marsh
Md.
For page see List of Advertisers.

SEED GROWERS
California Seed Growers' Association.
San Jose, Cal.
For page see List of Advertisers.

SEEDS
Carter's Tested Seeds,
Seeds with a Pedigree.
Boston, Mass., and London, England.
For page see List of Advertisers.

Kelway & Son,
Langport, Somerset, England.
Kelway's Celebrated English Strain Garden
Seeds.
For page see List of Advertisers.

S. D. Woodruff & Sons, New York City.
Garden Seed.
For page see List of Advertisers.

Joseph Breck & Sons, Boston, Mass.
For page see List of Advertisers.

J. Bolgiano & Son, Baltimore, Md.
For page see List of Advertisers.

A. T. Boddington Co., Inc., New York City.
For page see List of Advertisers.

Chas. Schwake & Co., New York City.
For page see List of Advertisers.

Michell's Seed House, Philadelphia, Pa.
For page see List of Advertisers.

W. Atlee Burpee & Co., Philadelphia, Pa
For page see List of Advertisers.

R. & J. Farquhar & Co., Boston, Mass.
For page see List of Advertisers.

J. M. Thorburn & Co., New York City.
For page see List of Advertisers.

Loechner & Co., New York City.
For page see List of Advertisers.

Ant. C. Zvolanek, Lompoc, Cal.
Winter Flowering Sweet Pea Seed.
For page see List of Advertisers.

S. S. Skidelsky & Co., Philadelphia, Pa.
For page see List of Advertisers.

W. E. Marshall & Co., New York City.
Seeds, Plants and Bulbs.
For page see List of Advertisers.

August Rolker & Sons, New York City.
For page see List of Advertisers.

Barnett Bros., 98 Chambers St., New York
For page see List of Advertisers.

Fottler, Fiske, Rawson Co., Boston, Mass
Seeds for the Florist.
For page see List of Advertisers.

SKINNER IRRIGATION SYSTEM
Skinner Irrigation Co., Brookline, Mass.
For page see List of Advertisers.

SNAPDRAGON
S. S. Skidelsky & Co., Philadelphia, Pa.
For page see List of Advertisers.

SPHAGNUM MOSS
Live Sphagnum moss, orchid peat and
orchid baskets always on hand. LAGER
& HURRELL, Summit, N. J.

SPRAYING MATERIALS
B. G. Pratt Co., New York City.

STANDARD THERMOMETERS
Standard Thermo Co., Boston, Mass.
For page see List of Advertisers.

STOVE PLANTS
Orchids—Largest stock in the country—
Stove plants and Crotons, finest collection.
JULIUS ROEHRS CO., Rutherford, N. J.

SWEET PEA SEED
Arthur T. Boddington Co., Inc.,
New York City.
Winter Flowering Sweet Peas.

Ant. C. Zvolanek, Lompoc, Calif.
Gold Medal of Honor Winter Orchid Sweet
Peas.
For page see List of Advertisers.

VEGETABLE PLANTS
R. Vincent, Jr. & Sons Co.,
White Marsh, Md.
For page see List of Advertisers.

VENTILATING APPARATUS
The Advance Co., Richmond, Ind.
For page see List of Advertisers.

The John A. Evans Co., Richmond, Ind.
For page see List of Advertisers.

VERMICIDES
Aphine Mfg. Co., Madison, N. J.
For page see List of Advertisers.

VINCA VARIEGATA
James Vick's Sons, Rochester, N. Y.
For page see List of Advertisers.

WIRED TOOTHPICKS
W. J. Cowee, Berlin, N. Y.
For page see List of Advertisers.

WIREWORK
Reed & Keller, New York City.
For page see List of Advertisers.

WILLIAM E. HEILSCHER'S WIRE
WORKS, 264 Randolph St., Detroit, Mich.

WHOLESALE FLORISTS
Albany, N. Y.

Albany Cut Flower Exchange, Albany, N. Y.
For page see List of Advertisers.

Baltimore

The S. S. Pennock-Meehan Co., Franklin
and St. Paul Sts.
For page see List of Advertisers.

Boston

N. F. McCarthy & Co., 112 Arch St. and
31 Otis St.
For page see List of Advertisers.

Welch Bros. Co., 226 Devonshire St.
For page see List of Advertisers.

Patrick Welch, 262 Devonshire St., Boston,
Mass.
For page see List of Advertisers.

Brooklyn

Wm. H. Kuebler, 28 Willoughby St.
For page see List of Advertisers.

Buffalo, N. Y.

William F. Kasting Co., 383-87 Ellicott St.
For page see List of Advertisers.

For List of Advertisers See Page 839

New Offers In This Issue

COLD STORAGE LILY OF THE VALLEY.
Dietrich Heydemann, New York City.
For page see List of Advertisers.

FORCING GLADIOLI.
A. Henderson & Co., Chicago, Ill.
For page see List of Advertisers.

LILY BULBS.
Yokohama Nursery Co., New York City.
For page see List of Advertisers.

LILY OF THE VALLEY PIPS.
Loechner & Co., New York City.
For page see List of Advertisers.

NEW CROP ASPARAGUS PLUMO-SUS NANUS SEED.
R. & J. Farquhar & Co., Boston, Mass.
For page see List of Advertisers.

NEW CROP FLOWER SEEDS.
H. F. Michell Co., Philadelphia, Pa.
For page see List of Advertisers.

NEW ROSE MRS. BAYARD THAYER.
Waban Rose Conservatories, Natick, Mass.
For page see List of Advertisers.

SEEDS—ONION SETS.
Leonard Seed Co., Chicago, Ill.

STANDARD GREENHOUSE STOCK.
Julius Roehrs Co., Rutherford, N. J.
For page see List of Advertisers.

SURPLUS BULBS.
Hogewoning & Sons, New York City.
For page see List of Advertisers.

RETARDED LILY OF THE VALLEY
Stumpp & Walter Co., New York City.
For page see List of Advertisers.

ROSES AND CARNATIONS OF UN-RIVALED QUALITY.
Joseph A. Millang, New York City.
For page see List of Advertisers.

WANTS, FOR SALE, Etc.

HELP WANTED

WANTED

A man with experience in propagating and caring for trees and shrubs, at Mount Auburn Cemetery, Cambridge, Mass.

WANTED—First class assistant in large flower store in Middle West. Address with record and references, M. M., care HORTICULTURE.

WANTED—Stumpp & Walter Company require one or two young men, that have had a few years' experience in Flower Seed Department. STUMPP & WALTER CO., 30 Barclay Street, New York.

SITUATIONS WANTED

Who wants an experienced correspondent, sales or office manager—Nursery line? Steady, sober, honest, live wire. B. C., care HORTICULTURE.

FOR SALE

FOR SALE—Fresh from factory, new; 10 x 12, 16 x 18, 16 x 24, double thick. A and B qualities. Market dropped. Now is the time to buy and save money. PARSHELSKY BROS., INC., 215-217 Havemeyer St., Brooklyn, N. Y.

FOR SALE—Greenhouses and residence; paying retail business; amount of business shown and reason for selling; 65 miles from Boston. Address R., care of HORTICULTURE.

Flower Market Reports

(Continued from page 850)

abundance of roses. The prices are high this year, roses bringing all the way from $6 to $35 per 100. Carnations are scarce and high. All shippers are away off crop. Stock should be enough to supply the demand. Last year at this time all kinds of stock was in plenty, but it is just the reverse this year. All expect a big Christmas business.

WASHINGTON   It is generally believed that the business done during the holidays will exceed that of previous years by no small margin. In this city flowers have replaced to quite an extent jewelry and other more expensive luxuries as Christmas and New Year's gifts. Early in the week it was predicted that there would be a shortage of carnations and that orchids, Richmond roses, lily of the valley and gardenias would not be obtainable in sufficient quantities to meet all demands. Only those of the retailers who placed orders for these flowers in advance are guaranteed against disappointment. The usual Christmas prices prevail, but considering the supply and demand and the extra fine quality of the stock, quotations are not excessive. Advance orders for plants indicate a very satisfactory business in these.

BOILER RATINGS AND CAPACITIES

To the Editor of Horticulture:

I wish to call your attention to a very common error which works to the detriment of boiler users (greenhouse men), and of well meaning and honest boiler manufacturers and salesmen. The fallacy I refer to is this; "A square foot of radiation is a square foot of radiation wherever it is." No statement could be more incorrect in its obvious meaning.

Most boilers are rated for utmost capacities under best conditions, i. e., with chimneys of proper height and area, good coal, frequent firing, etc. Many boilers are rated for capacities entirely beyond them under any conditions.

Greenhouse boiler manufacturers only, rate their boilers in lineal feet of pipe for greenhouse heating (generally 3½ and 2-inch pipe).

Any boiler will take care of a greater amount of radiation in a dwelling house than in a greenhouse, and a salesman who attempts to sell a boiler for greenhouse service on its dwelling house rating either does not understand what he is doing, or is trying to deceive.

I am sending to you herewith a paper written for a purpose other than greenhouse heating, but it may be of interest to greenhouse people.

Yours very truly,
FRED J. ELDER.

"Conditions Under Which a Boiler Should Fulfill Its Ratings."

A Talk by F. J. Elder, Mgr. Boston Office, Lord & Burnham Company. Given at the Burnham Boiler Get-Together Convention, April 23-24, 1914.

It has become a custom to rate heating boilers in square feet of cast iron radiation of standard height (38 in.) and two columns wide, to specify that the radiation be proportioned to heat the building to 70 degrees, and that the boiler be connected to a flue of sufficient area to provide volume and sufficient height to produce the required velocity or intensity of draft.

Ratings are also based on a standard of two pounds pressure for steam boilers, and a temperature of 180 degrees F. in radiating surfaces for water boilers. It is also called to the catalog reader's attention that he must include in his total radiation figure all exposed pipe surface of mains, risers, connections, etc., plus 25 per cent., and it is explained that pipe surface is approximately 25 per cent more efficient for heat transmission than standard cast iron radiation. It is further stated that 25 per cent. should be added to the total amount of direct-indirect radiation, and 50 per cent. to the amount of indirect radiation, that proper allowance be made for the absorption of heat by fire pot coils, and that greenhouses, factories, garages, storage buildings, etc., which are heated to low temperatures, will condense more steam per square foot, or require more heat units per square foot of radiation than in living rooms heated to 70 degrees.

Radiation now means any one of three things. It means first to the fitter and the buyer of a boiler a quantity of radiating or transmitting surface, a number of cast iron radiating units or radiators. Radiation particularly means the heat projected in rays, or straight lines from a heated surface, that is, radiant heat. Radiation is now considered in its broader sense, that is, as including the whole transmission of heat from a heating unit. It covers the radiant heat that projected in rays, the transmission by convexion, or rising in fluid masses, or through flues, and the transmission by conduction, or heating by contact with the hot surface.

Air can be heated only by conduction, that is, by direct contact with hot surfaces, or substances. Pure dry air cannot be heated by radiant heat. Rays of heat pass through air unless intercepted by particles of dust or vapor. These, and other substances and surfaces which may intercept the rays, will in turn heat the quiet surrounding air by conduction. This property possessed by air is called diathermacy. The same property is possessed by glass through which sun rays pass without warming the glass. Hot surfaces are surrounded by films or fluid masses of hot air, which cling to the surfaces, and it is evident that an easy circulation or passage of air over the surfaces by convexion currents is desirable in order to constantly remove the film of heat, and for this reason extended surface radiation, such as pin and corrugated or ridged radiators, are not as efficient in quiet air as the more common types. The fluid masses of heat cannot be disengaged from the rough surfaces without swifter currents of air than are possible by convexion only, as with direct radiation. Extended surface radiators are, however, most satisfactory in indirect heating where air velocities are greater.

Radiators are rated or measured according to the number of square feet of surface with which air may come in contact. The efficiency of a radiator or its coefficient of transmission is the number of heat units transmitted per hour through one square foot of emitting surface for each degree of difference in temperature of the radiating surface and that of the air surrounding. Efficiency depends on the form, shape, and condition. As explained above, extended surface radiators would have a low efficiency in quiet air. Single column radiators give off more heat per square foot than two column radiators, because there is an easier circulation of air around the single column radiators, and the heat film, as it has been called, is more easily disengaged from the radiator's surfaces. With three, four and five column radiation, efficiency is correspondingly lower because the heating is pocketed or trapped, and because every column interferes more or less with the radiant heat from every other column.

Efficiency of radiators depends also on their height. A low radiator is more efficient than a high one. Air is drawn to the bottom of a radiator or induced by convexion currents to rise beside and against the radiator's hot surfaces, and it is obvious that the higher a current of air rises against or the longer it passes over a heated surface, the higher its temperature becomes, and its ability to absorb heat decreases at the same rate. Low radiators give off more heat foot by foot than high ones. The efficiency of a radiator is affected by its location or position; a radiator should not be too close to a wall, or otherwise pocketed so as to prevent a free circulation of air around it. Radiators, whether of cast iron or in the form of pipe coils, are much reduced in efficiency when placed high on walls, or hung from ceilings. It is about as hard to get warm air to circulate below the level of the heating device as it is to get hot water to do so inside of radiators and piping.

The efficiency of horizontal pipe surface is greater than that of any other form of radiator, and pipe coils placed flat, or side by side in horizontal runs, as in greenhouse practice, have the highest possible efficiency. Different authorities have given coefficients of transmission ranging from 1.4 to 1.8 for cast iron radiators of common type, and efficiencies of 2.2 to 3+ for horizontal pipe.

To determine the amount of heat given off by a steam radiator in a specified time, it is only necessary to weigh the water condensed in that time and to multiply the quantity in pounds by 965, which is the number of thermal units given up by the condensation of one pound of steam at zero gauge pressure or transforming one pound of steam at 212 degrees to water the same temperature. The product will be the number of heat units, or quantity of heat given off by the radiator in the time named.

From the foregoing, it is obvious that very little or very much heat may be emitted from a square foot of radiation, and that this all depends briefly on the form, shape, character, position and location of the radiator. It also depends even more on the temperature of the air surrounding.

In greenhouse and garage heating and in other such special cases where the temperatures required are below 70 degrees, it should be remembered that each square foot must emit in B. T. U.'s the product of its coefficient of transmission times the difference between the temperature of the radiating surface and that of the air surrounding it.

The lower the temperature required, the greater will be the difference, the higher the product, and the greater the heat transmission.

In looking through a boiler catalog recently, I noticed that greenhouse boiler ratings were given for various temperatures and for the various quantities of greenhouse glass surface, and the following are the ratings of a particular boiler as set forth in that catalog:—

Size Grate	Lin. ft.		4"
	Outside Diam.		Pipe
24 x 24	1200		

Sq. ft. Glass.				
40-45	45-50	50-55	55-60	60-65
5600	4800	4150	3600	3150

In greenhouse heating the water temperature is assumed to be 150 degrees, and the coefficient of transmission 2. In the table the same boiler with the same pipe is rated to heat different amounts of glass to temperatures ranging from 40 to 45 degrees up to 60 to 65 degrees. Or, in other words, the same boiler is rated to produce or transmit through 1200 ft. of 4" outside diameter greenhouse pipe 252,000 B. T. U. to a house requiring a temperature of 40 to 45 degrees, or 204,000 B. T. U. to a greenhouse requiring 60 to 65 degrees. A very accommodating boiler indeed.

The amounts of pipe catalogued are correct for the temperatures named, but as has been stated, the same amount of radiation or piping may give off different quantities of heat and the boiler, or generator of units of heat, must be large enough for the number of units required, and not large enough for the quantity of piping or radiation merely.

In regard to the chimney, the flue should never be oblong if it is possible to avoid such a shape. It should be square at least, and a round flue is best of all. The effective area of the square is the same as that of a circle inscribed in the square. The flue should be smooth, and absolutely tight, and the area should be ample to carry away the products of combustion, which are noxious gases. The height of the chimney must be sufficient to produce intensity of draft. Both volume of air and intensity of draft are required for complete combustion. Neither one is sufficient without the other. Many boilers are condemned when the only thing wrong is the chimney, and the trouble is not always apparent. When combustible is completely burned, there must be a hot fire and an ample supply of oxygen. The resultant gas is carbon dioxide (CO_2) and nothing remains but ash. When coal is incompletely burned because of lack of oxygen, it is converted into carbon monoxide (CO), and nothing remains but ash, the same as if complete combustion had taken place. In such cases much of the real value of the fuel goes up the chimney unconsumed, and is lost.

Insufficient air, a low degree of heat in the furnace, and poor mixing of air and fuel, are responsible for enormous wastes. One cannot determine merely by looking at a fire whether or not there is sufficient air or sufficient draft, and one cannot decide from the ashes afterward whether or not combustion has been complete or incomplete.

The catalog may be filled with instructions and directions, it may mention precautions and don'ts ad libitum, but much of the success or failure is due to the quality of the fuel used and the quality of the handling or method of feeding that the boiler receives.

The fireman is responsible to a large degree for the satisfaction or dissatisfaction given. A good quality of fuel

should be used; a proper amount should be fed; the fire should neither be too deep nor too thin, and sufficient air should be admitted under the grates.

In view of all the factors that make for success or failure, many of them too, over which the designer has no control, it is only ordinary common sense that the boiler should be well able for its work, and should have from 33⅓% to 50% surplus capacity after making all allowances strictly in accordance with catalog directions for figuring radiation.

This will not cover a multitude of sins, but it will help.

GREENHOUSES BUILDING OR CONTEMPLATED.

Lowell, Mass.—Amy W. Andrew, one house.

Youngstown, O.—E. J. Richards, one house.

Redford, Mich.—A. J. Stahelin, Foley house 72 x 400.

Boonville, Mo.—E. C. Stammerjohn, house 30 x 110.

Belle Vernon, Pa.—H. E. Abraham, house 20 x 100.

Smithsburg, Md.—Earl O. Blickenstaff, one house.

Rockland, Mass.—C. A. Berry, Main street, one house.

North Easton, Mass.—Clarence Galligan, house 32 x 76.

Franklinville, N. Y.—J. A. Godfrey, plant house 21 x 84.

Clayton, Mo.—A. and H. Werner, addition in the spring.

Johnsville, Pa. — James Moss, 5 houses each 15 x 150.

Houlton, Me.—H. F. Chadwick, Hillside Floral Co., additions.

Hartford, Ct.—James F. Horan, 27 S. Whitney street, one house.

Tyrone, Pa.—W. H. Brouse & Son, range of houses in spring.

New Carlisle, O. — Chas. Taynor, Lord & Burnham house 17 x 75.

Providence, R. I.—J. E. Koppelman has bought a range of six semi-iron greenhouses at Eden Park and will re-erect them at his place in Riverside.

Lightning Source UK Ltd.
Milton Keynes UK
UKHW020232070119
334855UK00012B/2143/P